The Concise Oxford Dictionary of

Opera

John Warrack is a former University Lecturer in Music, and Fellow of St Hugh's College, at Oxford. He studied at the Royal College of Music, and played in various opera orchestras before turning to research and criticism. He was Music Critic of the *Sunday Telegraph*, then director of the Leeds Musical Festival. His books include *Carl Maria von Weber*, *Tchaikovsky*, and the Cambridge Opera Handbook on *Die Meistersinger*. He is on the boards of *Opera* and the *Cambridge Opera Journal*, and has translated operas from German, Italian, and Russian. Oxford conferred the Degree of D.Litt. on him in 1989.

Ewan West read music at Exeter College, Oxford. After further study in Vienna on an Austrian Government Scholarship, he returned to Oxford for postgraduate work, with a dissertation on Schubert and German song. He was Lecturer in the History of Music at Worcester College from 1986 to 1994, Junior Research Fellow of Mansfield College from 1988 to 1992, and Director of Studies and Lecturer in Music at Somerville College, Oxford from 1989 to 1994. He has published articles and essays on many aspects of eighteenth and nineteenth century music, particularly that of the German and Central European traditions.

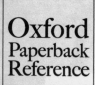

**Oxford
Paperback
Reference**

The most authoritative and up-to-date reference books for both students and the general reader

The Concise
Oxford Dictionary of

Opera

THIRD EDITION

JOHN WARRACK *and* EWAN WEST

Oxford   New York

OXFORD UNIVERSITY PRESS

1996

Oxford University Press, Walton Street, Oxford OX2 6DP

Oxford New York
Athens Auckland Bangkok Bombay
Calcutta Cape Town Dar es Salaam Delhi
Florence Hong Kong Istanbul Karachi
Kuala Lumpur Madras Madrid Melbourne
Mexico City Nairobi Paris Singapore
Taipei Tokyo Toronto
and associated companies in
Berlin Ibadan

Oxford is a trade mark of Oxford University Press

First edition (prepared by Harold Rosenthal and John Warrack) 1964
Second edition (Rosenthal and Warrack) 1979
Third edition 1996

British Library Cataloguing in Publication Data
Data available

Library of Congress Cataloging in Publication Data
Data available
ISBN 0–19–280028–0

10 9 8 7 6 5 4 3 2 1

Typeset in Swift Light by Selwood Systems
Printed in Great Britain by
Mackays of Chatham
Chatham, Kent

Contents

Preface

Since the appearance of the first edition of *The Concise Oxford Dictionary of Opera* in 1964, much has changed in the world which it sought to chart. Not least, new composers and artists have emerged, new opera-houses have been opened, and new works have been staged. However, the changes which have come about in the operatic world go far beyond this natural process of rejuvenation.

First and foremost, perhaps as important as any new composition, have been the rediscovery and representation of masterpieces from earlier centuries, sometimes as fully staged performances, more frequently by means of recordings. Underpinning this phenomenon has been an ever-burgeoning mass of critical scholarship, dealing not only with the works themselves but also with their relationship to other arts as well as to social, literary, and theatrical history generally. Advances in recording techniques have given new life to the voices of the past, while at the same time ensuring that those of the present are preserved for posterity in greater profusion and across a wider repertory. Finally, composers have increasingly sought to redefine the boundaries of the genre itself, for example by taking it in the direction of musical theatre, or by drawing consciously upon non-Western dramatic forms for inspiration. Above all, opera has now achieved a far wider breadth of appeal than at any point in its history, from musicological research and the application of critical disciplines of varying degrees of value to the staging and relaying of spectacular mass events. The publication of many more operatic reference books is itself a reflection of this growth of interest.

Some of these changes were already apparent in 1979, when an enlarged second edition of *The Concise Oxford Dictionary of Opera* was issued. However, it was not until the publication of the much larger *Oxford Dictionary of Opera* in 1992 that any real possibility for full-scale reassessment and expansion of the book was provided. Now, over thirty years since *The Concise Oxford Dictionary of Opera* first appeared, a further opportunity for revision presents itself.

In preparing this third edition, we have been very conscious of the existence of its larger stable-mate. Consequently, rather than merely updating the second edition, we have drawn upon *The Oxford Dictionary of Opera* as our primary text. The coexistence of these two works has allowed us to differentiate not only by length, but by character too. While the two dictionaries follow the same essential format, in *The Concise Oxford Dictionary of Opera* we have, in addition to some inevitable contraction, dropped a number of the secondary features of the larger book (such as bibliographies, worklists, lists of works dealing with mythological characters or treating particular literary works) in order not to have to truncate unduly entries more relevant to the current repertory of the opera-house and those who perform in it.

The question of what to include or exclude faces the authors of every reference book, though it is particularly acute for a work which claims conciseness rather than completeness. We are well aware, particularly where artists are concerned, that other authors would doubtless make a different selection. Our primary concern has been to strike a balance between chronicling the current repertory and its executants and painting something of its colourful and many-faceted history, in a manner which is intended to be helpful both to the reader new to opera, and to the seasoned opera-goer or student in search of information in a handy format.

The book is, we hope, self-explanatory, though there are some points towards which the reader's attention is particularly drawn.

Within the text, cross-references are indicated by asterisks: these indicate an entry relevant to the one being consulted and which contains significant further information or comment, but do not automatically occur every time there is mention of someone or something with a separate entry in the book.

In an era of renewed European upheaval, place-names and nationalities present their customary difficulties. We follow general English usage in writing Munich, Warsaw, Florence, etc., not München, Warszawa, Firenze; and when a town or city has changed its name, we try to give this according to how it was widely known at the time. Thus it becomes possible to be born in St Petersburg, study in Petrograd, work in Leningrad, and die in St Petersburg, all without moving. However, it is not possible to be born in Pressburg, study in Poszony, and retire in Bratislava, since these are the German, Hungarian, and Slovak names of what is now the Slovak capital. As far as nationality is concerned, we have tried to identify artists by the nationality they claim, but it is often difficult to know how local this should be. If we have offended, it is not through any wish to make political points.

For dates, we retain the Old Style English dates before the adoption of the Gregorian calendar in 1752, as far as possible, but calendar changes are complex and potentially misleading (for instance, as to which year saw a work's première when the New Year is not 1 January). Russian dates, and those of other countries that maintained the Julian calendar into modern times, are given in New Style. Dates of operas, unless otherwise explained, are of the first stage production; we have normally given the date of composition only when it significantly predates that of first performance, or in the case of unperformed works.

Opera titles are usually given in their original language, and in the form reflecting widest usage at the time of production. We have not, however, used Cyrillic, Greek, or other non-Roman alphabets, though we do give foreign accents; and in general reference we follow conventional English usage with titles such as *The Bartered Bride*, and sometimes use familiar abbreviations, e.g. *Die Meistersinger*. Works are, with rare exceptions, described simply as 'opera', rather than by a more specific designation such as 'opera buffa', or 'italienisches Singspiel', since it is often impossible to establish what the original should be: even so immediately popular a work as *Figaro* was described by these and several other titles in the original librettos, score, playbill, and Mozart's catalogue of his works. Voice categories are given (sop, ten, etc.) after roles, though here, too, there is sometimes inconsistency of description; we do not include them for early operas where no definition was given by the composer and where often the range does not correspond closely with any modern category. Under composers, we give surname and then the first name or names in conventional use; we do not usually list alternative names or spellings, maiden names, or Russian patronymics. In performer entries, the seasons and appearances are only some of the most notable. We use the conventional 'created' to mean 'first singer of'.

We continue to owe an enormous debt to that army of friends, acquaintances, scholars, and correspondents who troubled to provide us with information and practical help for *The Oxford Dictionary of Opera*, as well as those who have contributed specifically to this edition of *The Concise Oxford Dictionary of Opera*. We should like to thank particularly Karina Asenova, William S. Ashbrook, Corinne Auger, Rosamund Bartlett, Lucy Beckett, Jack Belsom, Victor Borovsky, Peter Branscombe, Jonas Bruveris, Julian Budden, Bojan Bujić, Janet Caldwell, Tim Carter, Martin Dreyer, June Emerson, Anthony Ernst, Rómulo Ramírez Esteva, Pablo Fernandez, Per Fosser, Angel Fumagalli, Elena Komarova, S. Kortes, George

Leotsakos, Antonia Malloy, Arda Mandikian, the Earl of Mexborough, Rodney Milnes, Maia Museridze, Małgorzata Nawrocka, Alena Nemčová, Ágnes Nyilassy, Matilda Onofrei-Voiculet, Richard Osborne, Mare Põldmäe, Caroline Rae, Patrick J. Smith, David Trendell, John Tyrrell, Richard Vendome, Jaak Viller, and Chris Walton. We also remain indebted to our two research assistants on *The Oxford Dictionary of Opera*, Gwen Hughes and Theresa Lister, whose past labours continue to bear fruit, while at the Oxford University Press, Pam Coote, Angus Phillips, and Rowena Anketell provided their characteristically benevolent and informed assistance.

During the preparation of this edition of *The Concise Oxford Dictionary of Opera* we were extremely fortunate to have the services of David Cummings, not least to give generous and expert guidance on present-day artists and repertory and to supply us with the material for many new entries. It is also gratifying to be able to report that the transatlantic special relationship is alive and not just well, but positively thriving, through the person of John M. Gehl of New Orleans. His encyclopedic knowledge of opera, particularly concerning developments in the USA, has once again been laid enthusiastically at our door. Without his indefatigable correspondence our task would have been infinitely more difficult, not to mention considerably less enjoyable.

Oxford–London–Rievaulx   JOHN WARRACK
September 1995   EWAN WEST

Key to Vocal Compasses

 c''' to c''''

 c'' to b''

 c' to b'

c to b

C to B

C, to B,

Abbreviations

Voice ranges

alt	alto	mez	mezzo-soprano
con	contralto	mez cas	mezzo-soprano castrato
con cas	contralto castrato	sop	soprano
counter-ten	counter-tenor	sop cas	soprano castrato
bar	baritone	ten	tenor
bs	bass	treb	treble
bs-bar	bass-baritone	nar	narrator

Opera-Houses, Conservatories, Companies, and Venues

Barcelona	L	Teatro Liceo
Berlin	D	Deutsche Oper
	H	Hofoper (Court Opera, i.e. Königliche Oper)
	K	Komische Oper
	S	Staatsoper
	Sch.	Schauspielhaus
	SO	Städtische Oper
	V	Volksoper
Bologna	C	Teatro Comunale
Brussels	M	Théâtre Royale de la Monnaie
Buenos Aires	C	Teatro Colón
Dresden	H	Hofoper (Court Opera)
	S	Staatsoper (Semperoper)
Florence	P	Teatro alla Pergola
	C	Teatro Comunale
Genoa	CF	Teatro Carlo Felice
Glyndebourne	Gly.	Glyndebourne
Hamburg	S	Staatsoper (Stadttheater)
Hanover	H	Hofoper (Court Opera)
Leningrad		See St Petersburg
London	BNOC	British National Opera Company
	C	Coliseum
	CG	Covent Garden
	COG	Chelsea Opera Group
	CR	Carl Rosa Opera Company
	DL	Drury Lane
	ENO	English National Opera
	GSM	Guildhall School of Music (pre-1935)
	GSMD	Guildhall School of Music and Drama (post-1935)
	H	Haymarket 1705–14 : Queen's Theatre
		1714–1837 : King's Theatre
		1837– : see Her Majesty's
	HM	Her (His) Majesty's
	J	St James's Theatre
	L	Lyceum (English Opera House)
	QEH	Queen Elizabeth Hall
	QH	Queen's Hall

London (cont.)	RAH	Royal Albert Hall
	RAM	Royal Academy of Music
	RCM	Royal College of Music
	RFH	Royal Festival Hall
	SW	Sadler's Wells Theatre
	TCM	Trinity College of Music
Manchester	RMCM	Royal Manchester College of Music
	RNCM	Royal Northern College of Music
Milan	S	Teatro alla Scala
	L	Teatro Lirico
	N	Teatro Nuovo
	PS	Piccola Scala
	RD	Teatro Regio Ducal
	V	Teatro dal Verme
Moscow	B	Bolshoy Teatr
	Z	Zimin Teatr
Munich	N	Hof- und Nationaltheater
	P	Prinzregententheater
	S	Staatsoper
Naples	B	Teatro San Bartolomeo
	C	Teatro San Carlo
	†N	Teatro Nuovo
New York	AM	Academy of Music
	CC	City Center
	CO	City Opera
	M or Met.	Metropolitan Opera House
	P	Palmo's Opera House
Paris	B	Opéra Bastille
	BP	Bouffes-Parisiens
	C	Théâtre du Châtelet
	CE	Théâtre des Champs-Elysées
	CI	Comédie-Italienne
	FP	Fantaisies-Parisiennes
	I	Théâtre Italien
	L	Théâtre Lyrique
	O	Opéra (Académie Royale de Musique)
	OC	Opéra Comique
	SB	Théâtre Sarah Bernhardt
Philadelphia	AM	Academy of Music
Prague	C	Czech Theatre
	N	Národní Divadlo (National Theatre)
	P	Prozatimní Divadlo (Provisional Theatre)
Rome	Ad.	Teatro Adriano
	Ap.	Teatro Apollo
	Arg.	Teatro Argentina
	C	Teatro Costanzi
	R	Teatro Reale dell'Opera
		(after 1946 Teatro dell'Opera)
St Petersburg	B	Bolshoy Teatr
	K	Kirov Teatr (when Leningrad)
	M	Maryinsky Teatr
Turin	R	Teatro Regio
	V	Teatro Vittorio Emanuele

Venice	B	Teatro San Benedetto
	C	Teatro San Cassiano
	F	Teatro La Fenice
	GG	Teatro San Giovanni Grisostomo
	GP	Teatro Santi Giovanni e Paolo
	L	Teatro Santa Lucia
	S	Teatro San Samuele
Vienna	B	Burgtheater
	H	Hofoper
	J	Theater in der Josephstadt
	K	Kärntnerthortheater (Theater nächst dem Kärntnerthor)
	L	Theater in der Leopoldstadt
	S	Staatsoper
	V	Volksoper
	W	Theater auf der Wieden (an der Wien)

Nationalities and Languages

Belg.	Belgian	Hung.	Hungarian
Brit.	British	It.	Italian
Bulg.	Bulgarian	Lat.	Latin
Cz.	Czech	Nor.	Norwegian
Dan.	Danish	Pol.	Polish
Dut.	Dutch	Port.	Portuguese
Eng.	English	Rom.	Romanian
Finn.	Finnish	Russ.	Russian
Flem.	Flemish	Span.	Spanish
Fr.	French	Srb-Cr.	Serbo-Croatian
Ger.	German	Swed.	Swedish
Gr.	Greek		

Miscellaneous

abr.	abridged	dir.	director/directed
ad.	adapted	E	Eastern/East
anon.	anonymous	ed(s).	edited/editor(s)
arr.	arranged	edn.	edition
Assoc.	Association	F	French franc
bapt.	baptized	facs.	facsimile
BBC	British Broadcasting Corporation	Fest.	Festival
cap.	capacity	GDR	German Democratic Republic
Carn.	Carnival	gns.	guineas
CBS	Columbia Broadcasting System	H	Hall
cent(s).	century/centuries	incl.	including/inclusive
Co.	Company	introd.	introduction/introduced
Coll.	College	jun.	junior
collab.	collaborated	L	Italian lire
comp.	composed	lit.	literally
compl.	compiled	LPO	London Philharmonic Orchestra
cond.	conductor/conducted	LSO	London Symphony Orchestra
Cons.	Conservatory/Conservatoire	m	metres
dim.	diminutive	MS	manuscript

N	Northern	recit.	recitative
Nat.	National	rev.	revised/revived
NBC	National Broadcasting Corporation	RAI	Radio Italiana
		RPO	Royal Philharmonic Orchestra
n.d.	no date	S	San, Santa, Santo, or Santi (e.g. S Carlos T)
net.	network (e.g. net. TV)		
nr	near	S	Southern/South
NSW	New South Wales	sen.	senior
NYPO	New York Philharmonic Orchestra	Sig.	Signor
		SO	State Opera (also Staatsoper)
O	Opera, Opéra, Oper	Soc.	Society
OC	Opera Company	St	Saint
OED	*Oxford English Dictionary*	St.	Street
OH	Opera-House	T	Theatre (also for e.g. Teatro, Teatr, Theater, etc.)
Orch.	Orchestra		
orig.	originally	TH	Town Hall
OT	Opera Theatre	trans.	translated
OUOC	Oxford University Opera Club	TV	television
perf.	performance	U	University
pf.	pianoforte	UK	United Kingdom
prem(s).	première(s)	US	United States of America
prod.	producer/produced	USAF	United States Air Force
pseud.	pseudonym	unfin.	unfinished
post.	posthumous(ly)	unprod.	unproduced
pt	part (e.g. pt2)	vol.	volume
pub.	published	W	Western/West
q.v.	*quod vide* (which see)	WNO	Welsh National Opera
R	(in bibliographies) reprinted	*	see marked entry for further information
(R)	has made operatic gramophone record		

A

Abbado, Claudio (*b* Milan, 26 June 1933). Italian conductor. Studied Milan, Vienna with Swarowsky. Won Koussevitsky and Mitropoulos competitions (1958 and 1963). Milan, S, 1961, music dir. 1971–86; London, CG, 1968; New York, M, 1968. Salzburg since 1965, including first visit by a British symphony orch. (LSO) in 1973. Vienna, S, music dir. 1986–91. Although recognized as an especially fine conductor of Verdi, and Italian opera generally, Abbado's intelligent musicianship encompasses a wide stylistic range. He has conducted much contemporary opera, including works by Nono and Manzoni, with whose *Atomtod* he made his Salzburg début in 1965, and has conducted distinguished revivals in Vienna, including *Khovanshchina* (with Stravinsky's ending) and Schubert's *Fierrabras*. Artistic dir., Salzburg Fest. from 1994 (*Boris Godunov* there same year). (R)

Abbatini, Antonio Maria (*b* Città di Castello, 26 Jan. 1595; *d* Città di Castello, ?1679). Italian composer and scholar. His first stage work, *Dal male il bene* (1654), written in collaboration with Marazzoli, was a seminal work in the history of opera buffa.

Abbott, Emma (*b* Chicago, 9 Dec. 1850; *d* Salt Lake City, 5 Jan. 1891). US soprano. Studied New York with Achille Errani and in Europe with Wartel, Sangiovanni, and Delle Sedie. Début London, CG, 1876 (Marie, *La fille du régiment*) and New York 1877 (same role). Married Eugene Wetherell 1875; together promoted Emma Abbott English Grand OC. Introduced 'specialities', such as popular ballads, into operas in which she appeared.

Abencérages, Les, ou L'étendard de Grenade. Opera in 3 acts by Cherubini; text by V. J. Étienne de Jouy, after J. P. Florian's novel *Gonzalve de Cordove* (1791). Prem. Paris, O, 6 Apr. 1813, in the presence of Napoleon.

The plot tells of the disputed triumphs of Almansor, the last of the Moorish Abenceragi warriors, and his final overthrow at Granada in 1492.

Abigaille. Nabucco's supposed daughter (sop) in Verdi's *Nabucco*.

abonnement (Fr.: 'subscription'). The term used in German and French opera-houses for the various subscription series, the financial mainstay of the season. The subscribers are known in Germany as *Abonnenten*, in France as *abonnées*, in Italy as *abbonati*.

Ábrányi, Emil (*b* Budapest, 22 Sept. 1882; *d* Budapest, 11 Feb. 1970). Hungarian composer, son of Emil (1851–1920), a poet, librettist, and translator of many librettos into Hungarian, including *Tristan* and *Carmen*. Emil jun. composed a number of operas, some to his father's texts. His works include *Monna Vanna* (1907), *Paolo és Francesca* (1912), *Don Quijote* (1917), and an opera on Bach, *A Tamás-templom karnagya* (1947). Music dir. Cologne 1904–6, Hanover 1907–11, Budapest from 1911 in various theatres.

Abreise, Die (The Departure). Opera in 1 act by D'Albert; text by Ferdinand von Sporck, after August von Steigentesch's drama. Prem. Frankfurt 28 Oct. 1898.

A simple story about the efforts of Trott (ten) to persuade a suspicious Gilfen (bar) to depart on a much-delayed journey, thus leaving Luise (sop), Gilfen's neglected wife, free to receive his advances. Gilfen pretends to leave, but soon returns to discover that his fears were well grounded and that Trott is already wooing his wife. Eventually, it is Trott who is sent off, his attentions having served to renew Gilfen's devotion to Luise.

'Abscheulicher!'. Leonore's (sop) aria in Act I of Beethoven's *Fidelio*, in which she first rages against her husband Florestan's imprisoner Don Pizarro, and then prays for a rescue.

Abu Hassan. Opera in 1 act by Weber; text by Franz Carl Hiemer, after a tale in the *1,001 Nights* (added by Antoine Galland to the original collection; pub. 1712). Prem. Munich 4 June 1811.

Abu Hassan (ten) and his devoted wife Fatime (sop) are being pursued for debt by the money-lender Omar (bs). Their ruse of attempting to obtain funeral money for each other's faked death from the Caliph and his wife Zobaide (both spoken roles) is eventually exposed, but they are forgiven. Omar, who has been pressing his attentions on Fatime, is imprisoned for his bad behaviour.

Abul Hassan. In full, Abul Hassan Ali Ebn Bekar (bar), the eponymous Barber of Bagdad in Cornelius's opera.

'Ach, ich fühl's'. Pamina's (sop) aria in Act II of Mozart's *Die Zauberflöte*, lamenting Tamino's apparent indifference.

Ackermann, Otto (*b* Bucharest, 18 Oct. 1909; *d* Wabern, 9 Mar. 1960). Swiss conductor. Studied Bucharest and Berlin. When 15 conducted Royal Romanian O on tour. Düsseldorf 1928–32; Brno 1932–5; Berne 1935–47. Guest at leading Italian operahouses, Vienna, Paris, Brussels, Barcelona, 1946–53. Music dir. Cologne 1955–8; Zurich 1958–60. A fine Mozart conductor, also good in operetta. (R)

Ackté (orig. Achté), **Aïno** (*b* Helsinki, 23 Apr. 1876; *d* Nummela, 8 Aug. 1944). Finnish soprano. Daughter of Lorenz Nikolai Achté, baritone and conductor, and Emmy Achté (Strömer), soprano. Studied with her mother and then Duvernoy in Paris. Début Paris, O, 1897 (Marguerite); Paris until 1904; New York, M, 1903–5; London, CG, 1907. First British Salome, 1910. Had a voice of purity and power, and an excellent dramatic instinct and stage presence. Dir. of Finnish Nat. O 1938–9. Wrote libretto for Merikanto's *Juha* and published two vols. of autobiography in 1925 and 1935. (R) Her sister **Irma Tervani** (1887–1936) was for many years leading mezzo-soprano in Dresden. (R)

act (Fr., *acte*; Ger., *Aufzug*; It., *atto*). After the model of spoken drama, the formal subdivision of an opera (indicated as such by the composer), often further subdivided into scenes or tableaux.

Adalgisa. A Druid priestess, Norma's rival (sop), in Bellini's *Norma*.

Adam, Adolphe (*b* Paris, 24 July 1803; *d* Paris, 3 May 1856). French composer. Studied with Reicha and Boieldieu, who encouraged him in the direction of opera composition. His fluency as a composer of opéra-comique hindered his success with larger forms; but as he said himself, 'my only aim is to write music which is transparent, easy to understand, and amusing to the public'. He had some early successes, despite political difficulties that drove him briefly to London. Following his return to Paris in 1832, he triumphed with *Le chalet* (1834), and there followed a long list of works that won easy acceptance for the qualities Adam had said he sought. His most important opera is *Le postillon de Lonjumeau* (1836), a lively, entertaining piece that offers a brilliant part to the central character but is also written with a vivid sense of situation. He also achieved a wide success with *Si j'étais roi* (1852). In 1847, having been banned from the Opéra-Comique by the new director, Basset, he opened what was then Paris's third operahouse, the Opéra-National, but was bankrupted when it had to close in 1848. He was able to return to the Opéra-Comique in 1850.

Adam, Theo (*b* Dresden, 1 Aug. 1926). German bass-baritone. Sang in Dresden Kreuzchor, then studied with Dietrich. Début Dresden 1949 (Hermit, *Freischütz*). Bayreuth since 1952; Berlin, S, since 1953. New York, M, 1969–72. Sang his first Wotan in 1963, and has performed the role in many leading European opera-houses (incl. Bayreuth) and at the New York, M. Has also sung with success as Don Giovanni, Pizarro, Boris, and Wozzeck, and has produced opera in Berlin. A fine, powerful artist, with a well-placed voice and a warm, striking stage presence. (R)

Adami, Giuseppe (*b* Verona, 4 Nov. 1878; *d* Milan, 12 Oct. 1946). Italian playwright, librettist, and film writer. A successful light playwright, he met Puccini through Ricordi and wrote for him first *La rondine* (1917), then *Il tabarro* (1918) and (with Simoni) *Turandot* (1926). Also wrote librettos for Vittadini and for Zandonai, among others. Published his correspondence with Puccini and also wrote a sympathetic biography of the composer.

Adams, Donald (*b* Bristol, 20 Dec. 1928). English bass. Studied Bristol Cathedral School; principal, D'Oyly Carte Co. 1953–69. Co-founder, touring co. G&S for All, 1983. US début, Chicago, 1983 (Mikado). London, CG, from 1983; ENO and WNO from 1985 (Baron Ochs, 1990). Guest at Gly., S Francisco, Amsterdam. Roles include Bottom, Dikoy, Bartolo (Mozart and Rossini). Noted for his clear diction and ebullient personality. (R)

Adams, John (*b* Worcester, MA, 15 Feb. 1947). US composer and conductor. One of the most prominent living composers of opera, he employs a highly characteristic minimalist style which depends for its effect upon strict systems of rhythmic repetition and continuous modulation. Despite their superficial complexity, Adams's scores have proved widely accessible, aided perhaps by his choice of contemporary subject-matter to which a modern audience can easily relate.

Nixon in China (1987) deals with the visit of the US President (the first by a Western leader) in 1972, while *The Death of Klinghoffer* (1991) was inspired by the murder of an elderly American tourist during the hijack of the cruise-liner *Achille Lauro* in 1985. The latter is virtually staged oratorio, with dancer doubles for the main characters, while the score makes important use of electronic music. Adams's collaboration with Peter *Sellars in *Klinghoffer* and *Nixon* was fundamental: both work towards opera as a new dramatic view of the present world as also in *I was Looking at the Ceiling and then I saw the Sky* (1995).

added number. An aria or other number inserted in the text of an opera, usually for a special occasion with a distinguished guest singer. The practice was widespread in the 18th cent. and survived well into the 19th cent. Mozart, for example, wrote several numbers for insertion into other composers' works, such as the quartet 'Dite almeno' (K479) for insertion in Francesco Bianchi's *La villanella rapita* (1783). Some singers would arrive with a favourite number in their luggage, hence the term *aria di baule* (suitcase aria). In the Lesson Scene in Act II of Rossini's *Barbiere*, the original 'Contro un cor' was often dislodged by the visiting prima donna in favour of a piece the better to flatter her talents. Many different arias, including some prophetically produced from the future, have been here laid under contribution. Melba would have a piano wheeled on to the stage and turn the scene into a ballad concert, ending with 'Home, Sweet Home'. The same song was used by Joan Sutherland in the Ball Scene of *Die Fledermaus*, an occasion appropriate, if not originally intended, for all manner of added numbers.

'Addio del passato'. Violetta's (sop) aria in Act III of Verdi's *La traviata*. After reading Germont's letter, she bids farewell to her happy past with Alfredo.

'Addio fiorito asil'. Pinkerton's (ten) aria in Act III of Puccini's *Madama Butterfly*, bidding farewell to the home where he has lived with Butterfly.

'Addio senza rancor'. Mimì's (sop) aria bidding farewell to Rodolfo in Act III of Puccini's *La bohème*.

Adelaide. City in South Australia. The first opera staged was *La muette de Portici* in 1840, followed by an Italian season in 1865 by the Bianchi Co., one of the touring companies upon which Adelaide was long dependent. There was also a local Intimate Opera Group. Performances were normally given in the Tivoli T, opened in 1913, reopened as Her Majesty's in 1962, and renovated in 1979: now known as the Opera T (cap. 1,009). In 1970 foundations were laid for a new Fest. T on the south bank of Torrens Lake. The project was oversubscribed within a week, and the theatre (cap. 1,978) opened in 1973. The Festival Centre includes a smaller theatre (cap. 635), opened 1974, together with an experimental open-air amphitheatre, The Space (cap. 380). The New Opera South Australia, formed in 1974, pursued an adventurous policy under the musical direction of Myer Fredman (resigned 1979). The company is now the State Opera of South Australia, and has contributed some notable productions to the Adelaide Festival.

Adele. Eisenstein's maid (sop) in Johann Strauss's *Die Fledermaus*.

Adelson e Salvini. Opera in 3 acts by Bellini; text by Andrea Leone Tottola. Prem. Naples, T del Conservatorio di S Sebastiano, between 11 and 15 Feb. 1825.

17th-cent. Ireland. Nelly (sop), fiancée of Lord Adelson (bs), is also being courted by the Italian painter Salvini (ten) who, when his advances are rejected, attempts suicide. He is then persuaded by Struley (bs), Adelson's sworn enemy, to help in a plot to abduct Nelly, but their plans are thwarted and he wrongly thinks that she has been killed. Tried for his part in the conspiracy, Salvini comes to realize that he no longer loves Nelly; she marries Adelson, while he turns his affections to his pupil Fanny.

'Adieu, notre petite table'. Manon's (sop) aria in Act II of Massenet's *Manon*, bidding farewell to the little table in the room she has shared with Des Grieux.

Adina. A wealthy landowner (sop) in Donizetti's *L'elisir d'amore*.

Adler, Kurt Herbert (*b* Vienna, 2 Apr. 1905; *d* S Francisco, 9 Feb. 1988). Austrian, later US, conductor and manager. Studied Vienna. Worked with Reinhardt; one of Toscanini's assistants, Salzburg 1936. Emigrated to US 1938. Chorus-master and assistant cond., Chicago 1938–42 and S Francisco 1943. Later also assistant to dir., S Francisco O Association, Gaetano Merola; succeeded him 1956, as artistic dir. Lengthened season, greatly enlarged the repertory, and enterprisingly developed the range and importance of the company. (R)

Adler, Peter Herman (*b* Jablonec, 2 Dec. 1899; *d* Ridgefield, CT, 2 Oct. 1990). Czech, later US, conductor. Studied Prague with Zemlinsky. After appointments at Brno, Bremen, Kiev, and Prague, emigrated to US 1939. Helped Fritz Busch to launch New OC, New York 1941. Dir. NBC TV O 1949–59, and did much to establish TV opera in the US, commissioning Martinů's *The Marriage* and Menotti's *Amahl and the Night Visitors* and *Maria Golovin*; cond. latter Brussels World Fair 1958. Founded Nat. Educational TV O (NET), giving first US *House of the Dead*, 1969, and commissioning Henze's *La cubana*. New York, M, 1972–3.

Admeto, rè di Tessaglia. Opera in 3 acts by Handel; text adapted from Ortensio Mauro's *Alceste* (1679), after Aureli, *Antigona delusa da Alceste* (1660). Prem. London, H, 31 Jan. 1727.

The libretto is a much elaborated treatment of the classical myth of Admetus (con cas), King of Thessaly, saved from death by the love of his devoted wife Alcestis (sop). Told by Apollo (bs) that the ailing Admetus will live only if a friend dies in his place, Alcestis commits suicide. Eventually rescued from the Underworld by Hercules (bs), she returns to claim her husband Admetus, who has in the meantime been subject to the attentions of his former betrothed Antigona (sop).

Adolar. The Count of Nevers (ten), lover of Euryanthe, in Weber's *Euryanthe*.

Adriana Lecouvreur. Opera in 4 acts by Cilea; text by Arturo Colautti, from the drama *Adrienne Lecouvreur* (1849) by Scribe and Legouvé. Prem. Milan, L, 6 Nov. 1902.

The opera tells of the famous actress Adriana (Adrienne) Lecouvreur (1692–1730) (sop), of the Comédie-Française, rival of Princess de Bouillon (mez) for the love of Maurizio, Count of Saxony (ten). She dies from inhaling the scent of a bunch of poisoned violets sent by the Princess. Michonnet (bar), the stage-manager of the theatre, is also in love with Adriana.

Adriano. Steffano Colonna's son (mez) in Wagner's *Rienzi*.

Aegisth. Aegistheus (ten), lover of Klytemnästra, in Strauss's *Elektra* (1909).

Aeneas. The Trojan hero (bar) of Purcell's *Dido and Aeneas* (?1680s or earlier) and as Énée (ten) of Berlioz's *Les Troyens* (comp. 1856–8).

Aennchen. Agathe's cousin (sop) in Weber's *Der Freischütz*.

Africaine, L'. Opera in 5 acts by Meyerbeer; text by Scribe. Prem. Paris, O, 28 Apr. 1865.

The opera tells how Vasco da Gama (ten) sails to find a new land beyond Africa, and is wrecked on the African coast. He returns to Portugal with two captives, Nélusko (bar) and Sélika (sop) ('l'Africaine' of the title). Though she falls in love with Vasco, on a subsequent expedition to India—and after many vicissitudes—she nobly sacrifices her life in order that he may marry his former beloved, Inès (sop).

Agache, Alexandru (*b* Cluj, 16 Aug. 1955). Romanian baritone. Studied Cluj. Sang throughout Eastern Europe, 1979–86; roles included Luna, Malatesta, Nabucco. Début in Western Europe at Livorno Fest., 1986 (Don Giovanni). Berlin, S, 1987 (Mozart's Almaviva); London, CG, from 1988 (Renato, Boccanegra, Amonasro). Milan, S, 1989 (Belcore). Admired for his strong and sympathetic portrayals of the major Verdi roles.

Agathe. The daughter (sop) of Kuno, the Prince's head forester, and lover of Max in Weber's *Der Freischütz*.

Agazzari, Agostino (*b* Siena, ?1579/81; *d* Siena, Dec. 1641/Jan. 1642). Italian composer and writer on music.

His *Eumelio* (1606), composed in only 15 days for a Jesuit seminary, is one of the earliest operas to survive and presents an instructive tale combining Christian and mythological themes. Owing much in its musical style to the example of Peri, Caccini, and Cavalieri, it was one of the earliest operas written for Rome, initiating a tradition which flourished until the mid-17th cent.

Shortly after *Eumelio*, Agazzari published his important treatise *Del sonare sopra'l basso*, in which the ideals of the earliest opera composers regarding the continuo are cogently summarized and discussed.

Agnesi-Pinottini, Maria Theresa (*b* Milan, 17 Oct. 1720; *d* Milan, 19 Jan. 1795). Italian composer, harpsichordist, singer, and librettist. One of the first female opera composers, her most important work was *Ciro in Armenia* (1753), for which she provided her own libretto.

Agnes von Hohenstaufen. Opera in 3 acts by Spontini; text by Ernst Raupach. Prem. Berlin 12 June 1829 (Act I had already been given on 28 May 1827).

Set in Mainz in 1194, the plot tells of the love of Agnes (sop), daughter of the Countess Irmengard (sop), for Henry of Brunswick (ten), son of the rebel Duke of Saxony, and describes the political intrigues by the Emperor Henry VI of Hohenstaufen (bs) and the French King (disguised as the Duke of Burgundy) (bar), to prevent Agnes and Henry of Brunswick marrying.

Agricola, Johann Friedrich (*b* Dobitschen, 4 Jan. 1720; *d* Berlin, 2 Dec. 1774). German composer, conductor, organist, and musicographer. Studied Leipzig with Bach and Berlin with Quantz. Appointed to the Berlin court by Frederick the Great in 1751. Though his several stage works rarely rise above the conventional, he made a lasting contribution to operatic history through his writings. These include a glossed translation of Tosi's *Opinioni*, recognized today as one of the most important documents for a study of contemporary vocal performing practice.

Agrippina. Opera in three acts by Handel; text by Vincenzo Grimani. Prem. Venice, GG, 26 Dec. 1709.

The plot revolves around the efforts of Agrippina (sop), wife of the Roman Emperor Claudio (bs), to ensure that her son by a previous marriage, Nero (sop cas), ascends the throne. When Ottone (con) saves Claudio's life, he is promised the succession: however, by exploiting the two men's love for Poppea (sop), Agrippina is finally able to achieve her aims.

Ägyptische Helena, Die (The Egyptian Helen). Opera in 2 acts by Richard Strauss; text by Hugo von Hofmannsthal, after various classical legends. Prem. Dresden 6 June 1928.

Divining that Menelas (ten) is on the point of murdering his adulterous wife Helena (sop), the sorceress Aithra (sop) causes the ship in which they are sailing to be wrecked. To them both she gives a potion of lotus juice: for Helena, it erases her memory of past events; for Menelas, it persuades him of Aithra's claim that Helena has spent the past ten years in an enchanted sleep, and that the Helena whom Paris stole away to Troy was only a phantom.

Transported by Aithra to the Atlas mountains, they at first enjoy new-found conjugal love, but Helena soon realizes that the lotus juice has not really obliterated Menelas's desire for vengeance. When desert warriors gallop in, they are captivated by Helena's beauty, none more so than their chieftain, Altair (bar). Menelas's jealousy is reawakened, particularly by the attentions of Altair's son Da-ud (ten), whom he contrives to kill during an ensuing hunt. However, when Helena gives him Aithra's antidote to the lotus juice, he eventually comes to accept her for what she is and renounces thoughts of revenge.

'Ah! Belinda'. Dido's (sop) aria in Act I of Purcell's *Dido and Aeneas*, in which she confesses her anguish over her love for Aeneas.

'Ah! fors' è lui'. Violetta's (sop) aria in Act I of Verdi's *La traviata*, in which she asks herself if she is really falling in love (then rejecting the idea in 'Sempre libera').

'Ah, fuggi il traditor'. Donna Elvira's (sop) aria in Act I of Mozart's *Don Giovanni*, in which she urges Zerlina to flee from Giovanni's advances.

'Ah, fuyez, douce image'. Des Grieux's (ten) outburst in Saint-Sulpice in Act III of Massenet's *Manon*, when he tries in vain to drive the image of Manon from his mind.

'Ah! non credea mirarti'. Amina's (sop) sleep-walking aria in Act III of Bellini's *La sonnambula*, which leads to the final cabaletta, 'Ah! non giunge!', as she awakens and sees her beloved Elvino beside her.

'Ah sì, ben mio'. Manrico's (ten) aria to his beloved Leonora, consoling her as they shelter in a fortress in Act III of Verdi's *Il trovatore*.

'Ah taci, ingiusto core'. The trio at the beginning of Act II of Mozart's *Don Giovanni*, in which Don Giovanni (bar) pretends to woo Donna Elvira (sop), while Leporello (bar) mocks the situation.

Aida. Opera in 4 acts by Verdi; text by Ghislanzoni from the French prose of Camille du Locle (1868), plot by August Mariette Bey. Prem. Cairo OH, 24 Dec. 1871.

Aida was not, as is often supposed, written for the opening of the Suez Canal (1869), nor commissioned by the Khedive of Egypt to open the new Cairo OH the same year; Mariette did suggest his story to the Khedive to celebrate the opening of the Canal, but the synopsis did not reach Verdi until 1870.

Egypt, in the age of the Pharaohs. Radamès (ten), captain of the Egyptian guards, is in love with Aida (sop), the Ethiopian slave girl of Princess Amneris (mez), daughter of the King of Egypt (bs). He does not know that she is in fact the daughter of Amonasro (bar), King of Ethiopia, nor that Amneris also loves him herself. Chosen to lead the Egyptian army against the Ethiopian invaders, he is acclaimed by the people and in a ceremony in the temple Ramfis the High Priest (bs) consecrates his armour.

By falsely claiming that Radamès has been killed in battle, Amneris provokes Aida into admitting her love for him. A grand triumphal scene ensues as the victorious Egyptian army returns, with Radamès at its head. As his reward, he asks that the Ethiopian prisoners be released. All are freed except Aida and Amonasro, who has acknowledged her as his daughter without disclosing his regal status.

On the banks of the Nile, Amonasro urges Aida to obtain from Radamès details of the Egyptian army's proposed route on its next attack against her people. Though, after much persuasion, she agrees, she cannot bring herself to betray her lover and when Radamès appears, proposes instead that he should elope with her and Amonasro to Ethiopia, where they can reign in wedded bliss. When Amneris and Ramfis suddenly appear and thwart this plan, Radamès gives himself up in order that Aida and her father may escape.

In vain Amneris urges Radamès to exonerate himself, but he remains silent when accused of treason. Sentenced to be entombed alive, as the stones close above his head he laments that he will never see Aida

again. But she appears, having hidden herself in the tomb so as to die with him. In the temple above, Amneris prays that his soul may rest in peace.

Aiglon, L' (The Eaglet). Opera in 5 acts by Honegger (Acts II–IV) and Ibert (Acts I & V); text by Henri Cain after Edmond Rostand's drama (1900). Prem. Monte Carlo 11 Mar. 1937.

The opera portrays the delusory fantasies of Napoleon's son the Duke of Reichstadt (sop) who, though held captive by the Austrian Prince Metternich (bar), remains loyal to the French cause.

'Ai nostri monti'. The duet for Manrico (ten) and Azucena (mez) in Act IV of Verdi's *Il trovatore*, in which they console one another with memories of their homeland.

Ainsley, John Mark (*b* Crewe, 9 July 1963). English tenor. Studied Oxford U and with Rolfe Johnson. Sang in concert from 1984; opera début at Innsbruck (Scarlatti's *Gli equivoci nel sembiante*). Monteverdi's Eurimaco (*Ulisse*) with ENO, 1989; Orfeo with New London Consort, 1992. Admired for the sense of style with which he sings such Mozart roles as Idamante (WNO, 1991), Ferrando, and Ottavio (Gly. 1992, 1994). (R)

'Air des bijoux'. See JEWEL SONG.

Aix-en-Provence. City in Bouches-du-Rhône, France. At the annual summer festival founded 1948, now the most important in France, opera is mostly staged in the open-air theatre of the Archbishop's palace (cap. 1,639, rebuilt 1975 and 1985). The festival's repertory was at first largely classical, with emphasis on Mozart: after a decline in standards in the 1960s, the repertory was extended under Bernard Lefort, 1973–80, to include more Romantic and modern works and standards recovered; his interest in English singers led to early appearances by Masterson, Langridge, and Robert Lloyd. Under Louis Erlo (from 1982), tradition has been preserved but extended with an interest in period instruments, in the lesser-known Mozart, and the exploration of Campra (born in Aix) and Rameau. English conductors have included Mackerras and Gardiner.

Ajo nell'imbarazzo, L' (The Embarrassed Tutor). Opera in 2 acts by Donizetti; text by Jacopo Ferretti, based on Giovanni Giraud's comedy (1807). Prem. Rome, T Valle, 4 Feb. 1824.

The Marchese Giulio (bar) wants his sons Enrico (ten) and Pipetto (bs) to be brought up in total ignorance of women until the age of 25. However, Enrico has already married Gilda (sop), and they have a son, while Pipetto has fallen for the old house-keeper Leonarda (mez). With the help of their tutor, Don Gregorio (bs), and through Gilda's wiles, Enrico and Pipetto eventually make their father come to his senses and all ends happily.

Aladdin. (1) Fairy opera in 3 acts by Bishop; text by G. Soane, based on the oriental tale *Aladdin and his Wonderful Lamp*. Prem. London, DL, 29 Apr. 1826.

(2) Opera by Atterberg. Prem. Stockholm 18 Mar. 1941.

'A la faveur de cette nuit obscure'. The trio in Act II of Rossini's *Le comte Ory*, in which the Count (ten), disguised as Sœur Colette, is deceived in the darkness into making advances to the page Isolier (mez), whom he mistakes for the Countess (sop).

Alagna, Roberto (b Clichy-sur-Bois, 7 June 1963). French tenor of Sicilian parentage. Studied Paris. Sang Alfredo with Gly. Touring O, 1988. Milan, S, 1990; London, CG, from 1992 (Rodolfo and Romeo). Guest in Paris, Vienna, Berlin, and New York (Rodolfo, 1996); roles include Don Carlos, Duke of Mantua, Edgardo, and Faust. He is valued for the elegant phrasing which he brings to the French and Italian repertory. (R)

Alaimo, Simone (b Villabate, Palermo, 3 Feb. 1950). Italian bass-baritone. Studied Palermo and Milan. Début Pavia 1977 (Don Pasquale). Brings a keen sense of comic timing to such Rossini *buffo* roles as Mustafà (Chicago and London, CG), Dandini, Alidoro, and Don Basilio. Also admired in such serious roles as Rossini's Mahomet (S Franciso, 1988), Donizetti's Henry VIII, Torquato Tasso, and Nottingham. (R)

Albanese, Licia (b Bari, 22 July 1913). Italian, later US, soprano. Studied with Baldassare-Tedeschi. Début Milan, L, 1934 (Butterfly); London, CG, 1937 (Liù and Nannetta); New York, M, 1940–66. Broadcast and recorded Mimì and Violetta with Toscanini. A singer of great feeling. (R)

Albani, (Dame) **Emma** (b Chambly, nr. Mon-treal, 1 Nov. 1847; d London, 3 Apr. 1930). Canadian soprano. Studied Paris with Duprez, Milan with Lamperti. Début Messina 1870 (Amina). London, CG, 1872–96; New York, M, 1891–2; also Paris, Germany, Australia, etc. She was a famous Elsa and Elisabeth (one of the few English-speakers to sing these roles in German), and her repertory encompassed Gilda, Lucia, Violetta, Valentine, and Isolde. A beautiful woman, she possessed a rich voice that lasted unimpaired until her retirement in 1911. (R)

Albéniz, Isaac (b Camprodón, 29 May 1860; d Cambô-les-Bains, 18 May 1909). Spanish composer. Though known principally as a pianist-composer, his pioneering work for Spanish music included the composition of operas and zarzuelas. In 1891 he signed a contract with the banker Francis Burdett Money-Coutts to set the latter's librettos, but the only successful work to result was *Pepita Jiménez* (1896). The ambitious trilogy *King Arthur* (comprising *Merlin*, *Lancelot*, and *Guenevere*) remained unfinished. Of his zarzuelas, *San Antonio de la Florida* (1894) had some success.

Alberich. The Nibelung (bs-bar) of the title of Wagner's *Der Ring des Nibelungen*, whose renunciation of love and theft of the Rhinegold helps to precipitate the events of the whole cycle.

Albert, Eugen d' (b Glasgow, 10 Apr. 1864; d Riga, 3 Mar. 1932). German pianist and composer. Largely self-taught, though he was much encouraged and influenced by Liszt. His first real success came with his fourth opera, *Die Abreise* (1898), a light, cheerful romantic comedy with a direct, tuneful idiom barely touched by the musical tensions of the day. He capped this with his best-known opera, *Tiefland* (1903), a work of distinct power which owes something to verismo but also appeals to a nostalgia for the 'clean' world of the mountains in contrast with the corrupt life of the 'lowlands' of the title. *Flauto solo* (1905), a light opera about Frederick the Great, was briefly popular; and he had a certain success with another work in highly charged verismo manner, *Die toten Augen* (1916).

Albert Herring. Opera in 3 acts by Britten; text by Eric Crozier, after Maupassant's story *Le rosier de Madame Husson* (1888). Prem. Gly. 20 June 1947, cond. Britten.

The plot turns on the attempt of a small Suffolk town to elect a May Queen, and, in default of one of sufficient virtue being found, the choice of Albert Herring (ten) as May King: he dismays the community by spending his prize money on a debauch, which nevertheless serves to liberate him from his domineering mother. The Suffolk types include the formidable Lady Billows (sop).

Albery, Tim (*b* Harpenden, 4 June 1952). English director. Opera début with *The Turn of the Screw* (Batignano Fest. 1983). *The Midsummer Marriage* (O North, 1985) was followed by *Les Troyens*, seen throughout the regions and at London, CG. Bregenz Fest. 1990 (*La Wally*); London: ENO, *Béatrice et Bénédict* (1990), *Peter Grimes* (1991), *Lohengrin* (1993); CG, *Chérubin* (1994). His work is noted for its striking images and strong sense of musical values.

Albrecht, Gerd (*b* Essen, 19 July 1935). German conductor. Studied Hamburg. Stuttgart O, 1958–61; Mainz 1961–3; Lübeck 1963–6; Kassel 1966–72. Directed prem. of Fortner's *Elisabeth Tudor* at Berlin, D (1972); chief cond. 1972–9. London, CG, 1986 (*Fliegender Holländer*); Munich, S, 1978 and 1986, prems. of Reimann's *Lear* and *Troades*. Music dir., Hamburg O, 1988 (*Ring* cycle 1993). He brings clear textures and buoyant rhythms to the modern repertory; also distinguished in Czech music. (R)

Alceste. Opera in 3 acts by Gluck; text by Calzabigi, after the tragedy by Euripides (438 BC). Prem. Vienna, B, 26 Dec. 1767. French version rev. by Gluck, with text by du Roullet, prem. Paris, O, 23 Apr. 1776.

There are many differences between the Viennese and Parisian operas: the synopsis below is of the French revision, the version in which *Alceste* became established in the operatic repertory.

A few years after the Trojan war. The people of Thessaly call on the gods to cure their king, Admète (ten), who is dangerously ill. His wife Alceste (sop) offers sacrifices to Apollo. As the High Priest (bar) invokes the god in his temple, the earth shakes and an oracle is heard declaring that Admète will die unless someone is sacrificed in his place. Alceste is torn between love for her children and her husband but finally offers herself.

Admète, now recovered, much to the joy of the people, is told that a stranger has promised to sacrifice her life for his. He discovers from his wife that it is she, and vows to die with her. The people implore her to change her mind, but she resolves to keep her promise to the gods.

When Hercule (bs) learns Alceste's fate, he determines to save her. Alceste reaches the entrance to Hades but, since she must wait till night before she can enter, is driven back. She is joined by Admète, who refuses to be separated from her in death. However, only one of the couple may enter Hades; Alceste and Admète vow to die for each other. Hercule then appears and, pointing to the couple as a model of conjugal love, declares that they shall both live.

Alcina. Opera in 3 acts by Handel; text adapted from A. Fanzaglia's *Alcina* (1728), after Ariosto's *Orlando furioso* (1516). Prem. London, CG, 16 Apr. 1735.

The plot turns on the attempts of Bradamante (con) to rescue her beloved, Ruggiero (con cas), from an enchanted island where he is held captive by the sorceress Alcina (sop), who has fallen in love with him. After many tribulations, in which Bradamante is ably assisted by her guardian, Melisso (bs), Alcina's spell is finally broken and the lovers are reunited.

Alda (orig. Davies), **Frances** (*b* Christchurch, 31 May 1879; *d* Venice, 18 Sept. 1952). New Zealand soprano. Studied Paris with Marchesi. Début Paris, OC, 1904 (*Manon*). Appearances at Brussels, M; London, CG; and Milan, S. Here she met Toscanini, who became her lifelong friend, and Gatti-Casazza, whom she later married. New York, M, 1908–29. Created female leads in operas by Damrosch, Victor Herbert, and Henry Hadley. Famed for her volatile temperament, professional quarrels, and lawsuits. (R)

Aldeburgh. Town in Suffolk, England. In 1948 Benjamin Britten, Eric Crozier, and Peter Pears founded a festival of music and the other arts. Britten's own music and taste were at the centre of the programmes, which rapidly won a reputation for high standards and enterprise (and the capacity to draw the greatest artists), together with a holiday atmosphere. Performances were originally given in the Jubilee Hall (cap. 300), with Britten's church parables in Orford Church (cap. 475). In 1967 the disused Maltings building at Snape was adapted as an auditorium, but burnt down on the first night of the 1969 fest. It was rebuilt for use the following summer (cap. 840). Prems. given by the festival include Britten's *Let's Make an Opera!* (1949), *Noyes Fludde* (1958), *A Midsummer Night's Dream* (1960), three *church parables (1964, 1966, 1968), and *Death in Venice* (1973), Berkeley's *A Dinner Engagement* (1954), Williamson's *English Eccentrics* (1964), Walton's *The Bear* (1967), Birtwistle's *Punch and Judy* (1968), Crosse's *The Grace of Todd* (1969), Gardner's *The Visitors* (1973), and Musgrave's *The Voice of Ariadne* (1974). With Britten's death in 1976 the fest. lost its importance as an operatic centre.

Alden, David (*b* New York, 16 Sept. 1949). US producer. Scottish O 1979; O North; London, ENO, from 1984; New York, M (*Fidelio*, 1980); New Israeli O (*Faust*, 1994); Netherlands O. Other productions include *Calisto*, *Rigoletto*, *Masked Ball*, *Boccanegra*, *Don Carlos*, *Werther*, *Mazeppa*, *Rake's Progress*, *Mahagonny*, *Ariodante*. Works regularly with the designer David Fielding: their unconventional productions are typically provocative and intense. His twin brother Christopher is also an opera producer.

Aleko. Opera in 1 act by Rakhmaninov; text by Vladimir Nemirovich-Danchenko, after Pushkin's poem *The Gypsies* (1824). Prem. Moscow, B, 9 May 1893.

Aleko (bs) has abandoned his settled life to wander with a group of gypsies. He falls in love with a gypsy girl, Zemfira (sop), but when she tires of him and plans to run off with a young gypsy (ten), he kills her. As punishment, he is exiled from the gypsy community and abandoned.

Aler, John (*b* Baltimore, 4 Oct. 1949). US tenor. Studied New York with O. Brown, Tanglewood with Malas. Début Juilliard American O Center, 1977 (Ernesto). Brussels, M, 1979; Gly. 1979; New York, CO, 1981; London, CG, 1986; also Milan, S; Lyons; etc. Roles incl. Ferrando, Don Ottavio, Tamino, Ory, Nemorino, Percy (*Anna Bolena*), Iopas (*Troyens*). A musicianly singer of poise and elegance. (R)

Alessandro. Opera in 3 acts by Handel; text by P. A. Rolli, after Ortensio Mauro's *La superbia d'Alessandro* (1690). Prem. London, H, 5 May 1726.

Though the plot is largely fictional, it takes as its main subject the historical figure of Alexander the Great (356–23 BC). Against the backdrop of his Indian campaign (*c.*327 BC) a complicated web of love and intrigue is spun, involving Alessandro (con cas), the slave girl Rossane (sop), and the Scythian princess Lisaura (sop), who is eventually given in marriage to the Indian king, Tassile (con cas).

Alessandro Stradella. Opera in 3 acts by Flotow; text by 'W. Friedrich' (Friedrich Wilhelm Riese) after a French *comédie mêlée de chants* by P. A. A. Pittaud de Forges and P. Duport. Prem. Hamburg, 30 Dec. 1844.

Set in Venice and Rome *c.*1670, the opera tells of episodes in the life of the composer Stradella. Learning that his beloved Leonore (sop) is to be forced to marry her evil ward Bassi (bs), Stradella (ten) takes advantage of carnival revelry to abduct her to safety. Bassi hires the assassins Malvolino (bs) and Barbarino (ten) to pursue them and, claiming to be pilgrims, they infiltrate the couple's wedding celebrations. However, so moved are they by Stradella's singing that they cannot carry out their task; when Bassi appears, he too experiences the same emotions. Confessing their treachery to Stradella, he and his henchmen are forgiven.

Alexander, John (*b* Meridian, MS, 21 Oct. 1923; *d* Meridian, MS, 8 Dec. 1990). US tenor. Studied Cincinnati with Weede. Début Cincinnati 1952 (Gounod's Faust). New York, CO, 1957; New York, M, from 1961; S Francisco from 1967; Vienna, S, 1968; London, CG, 1970. A highly versatile singer, whose repertory included Idomeneo, Ferrando, Elvino, Edgardo, Pollione, Alfredo, Rodolfo, Pinkerton, Hoffmann, Julien (*Louise*), Walther, Lohengrin, and Bacchus. (R)

Alexander, Roberta (*b* Lynchburg, VA, 3 Mar. 1949). US soprano. Studied U of Michigan and Den Haag. First major role Pamina, with Netherlands O, 1979. US début, Houston 1980. S Fe 1981 (Daphne); New York, M, 1983 (Zerlina); London, CG, 1984 (Mimì); Gly. 1989 (Jenůfa). Also admired for her strongly projected portrayals of Gershwin's Bess, Donna Elvira, and Barber's Cleopatra. (R)

Alfano, Franco (*b* Posillipo, 8 Mar. 1875; *d* Sanremo, 27 Oct. 1954). Italian composer. His first operatic success came with *Risurrezione* (1904): rapidly taken up, and a favourite work of Mary Garden's, this shows him moving away from the verismo tradition. He revealed a weightier and more personal vein with *L'ombra di Don Giovanni* (1914), which he developed, especially under the influence of

Debussy, in his most important stage work, *La leggenda di Sakùntala* (1921). Accused over *Madonna Imperia* (1927) of having Frenchified Italian opera, he attempted a reconciliation with his origins in subsequent works, though these mark a continued decline from *Sakùntala* and only *Cyrano di Bergerac* (1936) has found any substantial following.

Though some of these operas have retained a hold on the Italian repertory, it is for his completion of Puccini's *Turandot* that he is best remembered. He had once planned an opera on the subject himself, and was chosen for the task by Toscanini, who conducted the opera's prem. without Alfano's ending, adding it at the next performance. Enough was left in the sketches for Alfano to work them up into an acceptable shape; and though a break in style has been observed, no major attempt has been made, despite some revision, to improve upon Alfano's work.

Alfio. A teamster (bar), husband of Lola and rival of Turiddu, in Mascagni's *Cavalleria rusticana*.

Alfonso. 1. Don Alfonso (bs), the cynical philosopher who proposes the wager that produces the plot of Mozart's *Così fan tutte*.
2. Alfonso d'Este (bar), Duke of Ferrara, in Donizetti's *Lucrezia Borgia*.
3. Alfonso XI (bar), King of Castile, in Donizetti's *La favorite*.

Alfonso und Estrella. Opera in 3 acts by Schubert; text by Franz von Schober. Comp. 1821–2; prem. Weimar 24 June 1854.

Alfonso (ten), son of the deposed King Froila (bar), meets and falls in love with Estrella (sop), daughter of Froila's usurper, Mauregato (bar). When Adolfo (bs), Mauregato's general, is refused Estrella's hand in marriage, he plots against the throne. The situation is saved by Alfonso, who is welcomed as the rightful heir. Adolfo is put in prison but King Froila forgives everyone else's misdemeanours, and Alfonso marries Estrella.

Alfred. Rosalinde's lover (ten) in Johann Strauss's *Die Fledermaus*.

Alfredo. The younger Germont (ten), Violetta's lover, in Verdi's *La traviata*.

Algarotti, Francesco (*b* Venice, 11 Dec. 1712; *d* Pisa, 3 May 1764). Italian poet and writer on music. His importance to opera

rests chiefly on his *Saggio sopra l'opera in musica* (Essay on Opera) (1755). One of the classic documents of opera, this argues for a unified art form, with all the elements at the service of a poetic idea.

Alice. 1. Ford's wife (sop) in Verdi's *Falstaff*.
2. Robert's foster-sister (sop) in Meyerbeer's *Robert le diable*.

Allen, Thomas (*b* Seaham Harbour, 10 Sept. 1944). English baritone. Studied London with Hervey Alan. Début WNO 1969 (Rossini's Figaro), then regularly WNO. London, CG, from 1972; Gly. from 1973. Milan, S, 1976. London, ENO. Also New York, M, 1981; Vienna; Munich; etc. Repertory includes Don Giovanni, Almaviva (Mozart), Valentin, Posa, Pelléas, Billy Budd, Doktor Faust (Busoni). Sang Ulisse in the Henze/Monteverdi *Il ritorno d'Ulisse* at Salzburg (1985) and his first Beckmesser at London, CG (1993). Created Valerio in Musgrave's *Voice of Ariadne*. Musically and dramatically intelligent, with a virile, mellifluous voice, and assured stage presence. (R)

Almaviva. The Count who, as a tenor, woos and wins Rosina in Rossini's *Il barbiere di Siviglia*, and, as a baritone, has to be taught a lesson for his infidelity to her as his Countess in Mozart's *Le nozze di Figaro*.

Almeida Theatre. Theatre in London where the enterprising choice and staging of opera grew into a fest. by 1982 with the prem. of Jean-Jacques Dunki's *Prokrustes*. This was followed by Thomson's *Four Saints in Three Acts* (1983), Robert Ashley's *Perfect Lives (Private Parts)* (1984), Claude Vivier's *Kopernikus* (1985), Wolfgang Rihm's *Jakob Lenz* (1987), Michael Finnissy's *The Undivine Comedy* (1988), John Casken's *Golem* (1989), Smirnov's *The Lamentations of Thel* (1989), Cage's *Europeras 3 and 4* (1990), Gerald Barry's *The Intelligence Park* (1990), and Adès's *Powder Her Face* (1995).

Almira. Opera in 3 acts by Handel; text by Friedrich Christian Feustking, after Pancieri's *Almira* (1691). Prem. Hamburg 8 Jan. 1705.

According to her father's will, Almira (sop) is to become Queen of Castile, but must marry into the family of her ward, Consalvo, Prince of Segovia (bs). Though she is intended for his son, Osman (ten), her real love is for her secretary, Fernando (ten). After many entanglements, it transpires that Fernando is actually Consalvo's long-lost youngest son Floralbo, believed drowned in a shipwreck. By marrying her lover, Almira is thus able still to fulfil her father's wishes.

Altani, Ippolit (*b* S Ukraine, 27 May 1846; *d* Moscow, 17 Feb. 1919). Russian conductor. Studied St Petersburg with Zaremba and A. Rubinstein. Chorus-master Kiev 1868–9, then cond. to 1882; conducted there first provincial performance of a Tchaikovsky opera (*Oprichnik*, 1874). Chief cond. Moscow, B, 1882–1906, including prems. of Tchaikovsky's *Mazeppa* (1884) and Rakhmaninov's *Aleko* (1893), and first Moscow performances of works including *Boris* (1888), *Queen of Spades* (1891), *Yolanta* (1893), and *Snow Maiden* (1893). Tchaikovsky had some lessons from him before conducting the prem. of *Cherevichki*.

Altmeyer, Jeannine (*b* La Habra, CA, 2 May 1948). US soprano. Studied S Barbara and Salzburg Mozarteum. Début New York, M, 1971 (Heavenly Voice, *Don Carlos*). Salzburg 1973 and London, CG, 1975 (Freia). Bayreuth 1976 and 1986 (Sieglinde and Isolde). Also valued for her fully committed performances as Brünnhilde, Salome, and Leonore (Milan, S, 1990). (R)

alto (It.: 'high'). A term for certain voices. The female alto is usually known as a *contralto. The male alto is usually a bass voice singing *falsetto. It is also one of the categories of the *castrato voice. The range is about from f to a″. See COUNTER-TENOR.

Alva, Luigi (*b* Lima, 10 Apr. 1927). Peruvian tenor. Studied Lima with Morales, and Milan with Ghirardini. Début Lima 1949 (in the zarzuela *Luisa Fernanda*). Sang Paolino (*Il matrimonio segreto*) at the opening night of Milan, PS, in Dec. 1955; Edinburgh 1957; Début London, CG, 1960 (Rossini's Almaviva), subsequently Fenton and Ferrando; New York, M, 1964–76. Retired 1989. Sang extensively in Europe; especially admired in Mozart and Rossini. (R)

Alvaro. Don Alvaro (ten), a Peruvian of Inca blood, in Verdi's *La forza del destino*.

Alvary, Max (orig. Maximilian Achenbach) (*b* Düsseldorf, 3 May 1856; *d* Gross-Tabarz, 7 Nov. 1898). German tenor. Studied Frankfurt with Stockhausen, Milan with Lamperti. Début Weimar 1879 (Alessandro Stradella).

Weimar till 1885; New York, M, 1885–9 (début as Don José opposite Lilli Lehmann, also making her US début). First US Loge, Siegfried, and Adolar. Bayreuth 1891 (Tristan and Tannhäuser); sang in the first CG *Ring* under Mahler, 1892, which began with *Siegfried* so that Alvary could make his début in his favourite role. Retired 1897.

Alyabyev, Alexander (*b* Tobolsk, 15 Aug. 1787; *d* Moscow, 6 Mar. 1851). Russian composer. Fought as a hussar against Napoleon in 1812; then studied music in St Petersburg, leaving the Army in 1823. His comic opera *Lunnaya noch* (The Moonlit Night) appeared in this year; and he then also wrote the song 'Solovey' ('The Nightingale'), which became very popular and was often used by Patti, Viardot, and Sembrich for the Lesson Scene in Act II of Rossini's *Il barbiere di Siviglia*. He was banished from Moscow in 1828 partly for alleged murder, partly perhaps for his Decembrist associations; he returned at the end of the 1830s, after travels in the East and South of Russia. His knowledge of folk music, systematically acquired in exile, and his understanding of oriental and Caucasian subjects were significant in the development of Russian opera in the years immediately preceding Glinka. His later works included *Burya* (The Tempest, *c*.1835) and *Rybak i rusalka* (The Fisherman and the Water Nymph, comp. 1841–3).

Alzira. Opera in a prologue and 2 acts by Verdi; text by Cammarano, after Voltaire's tragedy *Alzire, ou Les Américains* (1730). Prem. Naples, C, 12 Aug. 1845.

Peru, *c*.1550. Zamoro (ten), chief of the Incas, betrothed to Alzira (sop), is presumed dead after being taken prisoner by Gusmano (bar), the son of the Governor of Peru. Gusmano takes over as Governor and Alzira is forced to marry him. Zamoro has been captured in battle but is released when Alzira's wedding is announced. On the day of the ceremony, he returns and stabs Gusmano, who pardons Zamoro and returns Alzira to him as he dies.

Amadis. Opera in a prologue and 5 acts by Lully; text by Quinault, based on a Spanish chivalric romance by Garcí Ordonez de Montalvo. Prem. Paris, O, 18 Jan. 1684.

Amadis (ten) is in love with the Princess Oriane (sop); she, however, believes him to be unfaithful, and has anyway been promised by her father to another man. To win

Oriane's hand and her trust, Amadis embarks upon a chivalric quest in the course of which he has to rescue their respective confidants, Florestan (bar) and Corisande (sop), from the clutches of the sorcerer knight Arcalaus (bar) and his sister Arcabonne (sop). After many vicissitudes, all ends happily and Amadis is united with his beloved.

Amahl and the Night Visitors. Opera in 1 act by Menotti; text by composer, after Bosch's painting *The Adoration of the Magi*. Prem. NBC TV, 24 Dec. 1951 (the first opera written for TV); stage prem., Bloomington, Indiana U, 21 Feb. 1952.

Amahl (boy sop), a little crippled boy, and his mother (sop) receive the Magi, Kaspar (ten), Melchior (bar), and Balthazar (bs), who are journeying to pay homage to the infant Christ. As they sleep, Amahl's mother tries to steal some of their riches; though apprehended by the page (bs), she is forgiven by Melchior. When the kings prepare to depart, Amahl offers them his crutch as a further gift for the Christ child. His generosity is rewarded by the miraculous healing of his crippled leg; he joins the Magi on their quest.

Amalia. An orphan (sop), niece of Count Moor, in Verdi's *I masnadieri*.

Amato, Pasquale (*b* Naples, 21 Mar. 1878; *d* Jackson Heights, NY, 12 Aug. 1942). Italian baritone. Début Naples 1900 (Germont). London, CG, 1904, with Naples, C, but despite success never returned. New York, M, 1908–21, where he created Jack Rance, Cyrano de Bergerac (Damrosch), and Napoléon (*Madame Sans-Gêne*). Successes in Italy, Germany, and Odessa, 1902–13. An excellent singer, with a resonant voice and a wide range of dramatic expression. (R)

Amelia. 1. Boccanegra's daughter Maria, brought up as Amelia Grimaldi (sop), in Verdi's *Simon Boccanegra*.
2. The wife (sop) of Anckarstroem (Renato) and lover of Gustavus III (Riccardo) in Verdi's *Un ballo in maschera*.
3. The heroine (sop) of Menotti's *Amelia Goes to the Ball*.
4. The heroine (sop) of Donizetti's *Il Duce d'Alba*.

Amfortas. The Keeper of the Grail (bar) in Wagner's *Parsifal*, the son of Titurel.

Amico Fritz, L' (Friend Fritz). Opera in 3 acts by Mascagni; text by P. Suardon (N. Daspuro), after Erckmann-Chatrian's novel (1864). Prem. Rome, C, 31 Oct. 1891.

A light pastoral comedy about the confirmed bachelor Fritz (ten), a rich landowner; Rabbi David (bar), the consummate matchmaker; and Suzel (sop), the charming daughter of one of Fritz's tenants, with whom Fritz eventually falls in love.

Amina. An orphan (sop), adopted daughter of the mill-owner Teresa, the sleepwalker in Bellini's *La sonnambula*.

Aminta. The wife (sop) of Henry Morosus in R. Strauss's *Die schweigsame Frau*.

Amirov, Fikret (*b* Gyanja (Kirovabad), 22 Nov. 1922; *d* Baku, 20 Feb. 1984). Azerbaijani composer. Studied Baku with Zeydman and Hadjibekov. After war service, resumed studies and graduated with his first opera *Ulduz* (1948). His most important work, a pioneering one for Azerbaijani opera, is *Sevil* (1953), which incorporates local folk music into a number opera.

Amneris. The King of Egypt's daughter (mez) and Aida's rival for Radamès in Verdi's *Aida*.

Amonasro. The King of Ethiopia (bar), Aida's father, in Verdi's *Aida*.

Amore dei tre re, L' (The Love of the Three Kings). Opera in 3 acts by Montemezzi; text by Benelli, after his verse tragedy (1910). Prem. Milan, S, 10 Apr. 1913.

Fiora (sop) has been forced for political reasons to marry Manfredo (bar), son of King Archibaldo (bs). While Manfredo is absent on a campaign, the old king murders his daughter-in-law for refusing to reveal the name of her lover Avito (ten). He poisons her lips, hoping Avito will come to see her body. Avito dies from kissing the poison, as does Manfredo, who cannot live without his wife.

'Amour, viens aider ma faiblesse'. Dalila's (mez) aria in Act II of Saint-Saëns's *Samson et Dalila*, in which she invokes the power of love to fetter Samson.

Amphion. Opera in 1 act by Honegger; text by Paul Valéry. Prem. Paris, O, 23 June 1931.

Apollon (bar) gives his lyre to Amphion (ten), a favourite of the gods. The music Amphion plays is so powerful that stones form themselves into shapes of their own accord; the event is cited as the birth of architecture. Amphion builds a temple to Apollon and the city of Thebes, but is prevented from appreciating his achievements: he is led away by a veiled woman, who also casts away his lyre.

Amsterdam. Capital of The Netherlands. The first opera performed was *Le fatiche d'Ercole per Deianira* by P. A. Ziani on 31 Dec. 1680. Together with the pastoral play with music *De triomfeerende Min* by Hacquart (1678), it was given in a specially built theatre on the Leidse Gracht. When this burnt down in 1770, performances were given in the Stadsschouwburg (burnt down 1772), in the Operahuis (where a German-Jewish company played in 1784), and in the T Français (where a French company, having previously performed in an inn, was established 1788–1855). Some of these performances were in Dutch. In 1882 Angelo Neumann's Wagner company gave *The Ring* in the Paleis voor Volksvlijt; and in 1883 the successful Wagner-Vereniging was founded: it gave many performances of operas by composers other than Wagner. There was also a resident Italian company, 1897–1942.

During the German occupation the Municipal O Enterprise was formed (1941), and from this developed in 1946 the Stichting de Nederlandse O, which gave performances in Dutch in the Stadsschouwburg. The first company with that name had been founded in 1886, and eventually gave 200 performances a year not only in Amsterdam but in N Holland, Rotterdam, Utrecht, and Hilversum. In 1964 it was reorganized as the Nederlandse Operastichting under Maurice Huismann (also administrator of the Brussels M), performing in other Dutch cities regularly. An opera studio was established in the 1974–5 season, to encourage young audiences and to give chamber opera in schools. After many delays and difficulties, the Muziektheater (cap. 1,594) opened in 1986 with a programme including Otto Ketting's *Ithaka*. The Nederlandse O was formed and rapidly developed an enterprising policy. The VARA broadcasting network has run an adventurous opera-in-concert series.

'Am stillen Herd'. Walther's (ten) song in Act I of Wagner's *Die Meistersinger von Nürnberg*, telling the Mastersingers where and from whom he learnt to sing.

Anckarstroem. A secretary (bar) in the service of King Gustavus III in the 'Swedish' version of Verdi's *Un *ballo in maschera*.

Anders, Peter (*b* Essen, 1 July 1908; *d* Hamburg, 10 Sept. 1954). German tenor. Studied Berlin with Grenzebach, later with Mysz-Gmeiner. Début Berlin 1931, in Max Reinhardt's prod. of *La belle Hélène*. Berlin, SO, 1936–49 in the lighter lyric roles; especially successful as a Mozart singer. Hamburg 1950 (Walther and Verdi's Otello). British début 1950, Edinburgh Fest., Bacchus (*Ariadne*) under Beecham, with whom he also sang Walther at London, CG. An intelligent and musical singer. (R)

Anderson, June (*b* Boston, 30 Dec. 1952). US soprano. Studied New York with Leonard. Début New York, CC, 1978 (Queen of the Night). Successes in US; Rome 1982; Munich 1983; New York, M, 1989 (Gilda); Milan, S, and Paris, O, 1985; London, CG, 1986 (as Semiramide (concert)). Roles incl. Donna Elvira, Desdemona (Rossini), Rosina, Semiramide, Amina, Lucia, Norma, Gilda, Isabella (*Robert le diable*). (R)

Anderson, Marian (*b* Philadelphia, 17 Feb. 1897; *d* Portland, OR, 8 Apr. 1993). US contralto. Studied New York with Boghetti. Most of career a concert artist; operatic début as first Black singer at New York, M, 1955 (Ulrica). (R)

André, Johann (*b* Offenbach, 28 Mar. 1741; *d* Offenbach, 18 June 1799). German composer and publisher. Translated opéras-comiques by Philidor and others into German and wrote over 20 Singspiels. In 1775 he was commissioned by Goethe to set his text *Erwin und Elmire*; he later set another of Goethe's Singspiels, *Claudine von Villa Bella* (1778). Though his compositions have generally not stood the test of time, they were influential in their day, particularly through their introduction of exotic elements into the Singspiel genre. His most significant Singspiels were *Belmonte und Constanze* (1781: a setting of the Bretzner libretto used by Mozart in *Die Entführung aus dem Serail*) and *Der Barbier von Bagdad* (1783).

André, Martin (*b* West Wickham, 10 Dec. 1960). English conductor. Studied Menuhin School and RCM. Cond. own edition of Purcell's *King Arthur* at Cambridge, 1982. WNO from 1982 (*Aida, Jenůfa, Ernani*). Vancouver 1986 (*From the House of the Dead, Cunning Little*

Vixen); Seattle O, 1987 (*Carmen*). London, ENO from 1990 (prem. of Buller's *Bakxai*, 1992). Cond. of English Touring O 1993. Gives well-integrated performances in a wide repertory.

Andrea Chénier. Opera in 4 acts by Giordano; text by Illica. Prem. Milan, S, 28 Mar. 1896.

France, the time of the Revolution. Charles Gérard (bar), one of the Countess de Coigny (mez)'s servants, is helping with preparations for a ball. Though secretly enamoured of her daughter, the beautiful Madeleine de Coigny (sop), he rails against the privileges of the aristocracy. Among the guests is the poet Andrea Chénier (ten) who, when pressed to demonstrate his art, responds with an improvisatory outburst denouncing the evil of the *ancien régime*. Gérard strengthens Chénier's case by leading in a group of beggars.

The Café Hottot in Paris, after the Revolution has started. Suspected of being a Counter-revolutionary, Chénier is being shadowed by the government spy, Incredibile (ten). His friend Roucher (bs) advises him to flee Paris, but Chénier will not leave until he has identified the authoress of anonymous letters he has received. Madeleine arrives, and at first Chénier does not recognize her; soon though, he discovers that she is the mystery woman. Swearing love for each other, the couple plan to abscond, but are apprehended by Gérard, now a prominent Revolutionary leader. The two men engage in combat, and only when Gérard has been wounded does he recognize his opponent as Chénier.

The Revolutionary Tribunal. Gérard learns that Chénier has been arrested; though reluctant to indict him, desire for Madeleine eventually overcomes his resistance. When she comes in search of Chénier, Gérard declares his feelings; after initial repulsion, she offers her love in return for Chénier's freedom. However, despite Gérard's efforts, the Tribunal finds Chénier guilty and passes the death sentence.

The courtyard of St Lazare prison. Awaiting his execution, Chénier reads his last poem to Roucher. Gérard appears with Madeleine, and by bribing the gaoler, she is allowed to take the place of a condemned female prisoner. United in love, Madeleine and Chénier face their end with fortitude.

Andreozzi, Gaetano (*b* Aversa, 22 May 1755; *d* Paris, 21 or 24 Dec. 1826). Italian composer. Studied in Naples, though also received instruction from his uncle Nicolò Jommelli (hence his nickname 'Jommellino'). Highly regarded in his day, he wrote *c.*40 operatic works, mainly opere serie in the conventional Metastasian mould: most interesting, because of their subject-matter, are *Giovanna d'Arco* (1789) and *Amleto* (1792). In 1786 Andreozzi married the famous soprano **Anna de Santi** (*c.*1772–1802); later he was to renounce composition in favour of a second career as a singing-teacher.

'Andrò ramingo e solo'. The quartet in Act III of Mozart's *Idomeneo*, in which Idamante (sop) announces his wish to leave and seek death; Ilia (sop) declares she will follow him, while Idomeneo (ten) curses Neptune and Elettra (sop) asks herself when she will be avenged.

Anelli, Angelo (pseud. Nicolò Liprandi, Marco Landi) (*b* Desenzano, 1 Nov. 1761; *d* Pavia, 9 Apr. 1820). Italian librettist. Attached to Milan, S, 1793–1817. A highly practical man of the theatre, with a particular gift for comedy, he wrote the texts for *L'italiana in Algeri* (set by Rossini in 1813) and *Ser Marcantonio* (the basis of the text for Donizetti's *Don Pasquale*). The many other composers for whom he wrote include Cimarosa, Coccia, Dussek, Gazzaniga, Guglielmi, Martín y Soler, Mayr, Paer, Pacini, Pavesi, and Zingarelli.

Anfossi, Pasquale (*b* Taggia, 5 Apr. 1727; *d* Rome, ?Feb. 1797). Italian composer. He produced at least 60 operas, of which five, including *Il trionfo della costanza* (1782), were written for London. In his opere serie he demonstrated a fondness for heroic themes, often setting Metastasian librettos, including *La clemenza di Tito* (1769/1772) and *Lucio Silla* (1774). His comic operas—beginning with his first major success, *L'incognita perseguitata* (1773)—won him more lasting fame and he is generally regarded as one of the most skilled exponents of 18th-cent. opera buffa. Though *La finta giardiniera* (1774) is overshadowed by Mozart's more famous setting, *La vera costanza* (1776) is a worthy companion to Haydn, while *L'avaro* (1775) and *Il curioso indiscreto* (1777) proved particularly popular, not least for their catchy melodies.

Angel, Marie (*b* Pinnaroo, 3 June 1953). Australian soprano. London début 1980 with O

Factory Zurich (Galatea). Member of the O Factory London 1982–92, as Denise (*Knot Garden*), Pretty Polly (*Punch and Judy*), Calisto, Poppea, Donna Anna, Fiordiligi. Sang Queen Tyre in *Akhnaten* at Houston and New York, CO (1984). Created Oracle of the Dead in *The Mask of Orpheus* (London, ENO, 1986) and Morgan le Fay in *Gawain* (London, CG, 1991). Particularly valued in the modern repertory.

Angélique. Opera in 1 act by Ibert; text by Nino (pseud. of Michel Veber). Prem. Paris, T Bériza, 28 Jan. 1927.

Boniface (bar), the owner of a Paris china shop, is persuaded by his friend Charlot (bar) that the only way to rid himself of his shrewish wife Angélique (sop) is to put her up for sale. She is eventually bought by the Devil (ten), but soon returned, for even he cannot put up with her.

Angelo. Opera in 4 acts by Cui; text by Victor Burenin, based on Victor Hugo's *Angelo, tyran de Padoue* (1835). Prem. St Petersburg, M, 13 Feb. 1876.

Padua, 1549. Caterina (sop) and Thisbe (mez), wife and mistress of Angelo (bs) respectively, both really love Ezzelino da Romano (ten), otherwise Rodolfo. Homodei, an Inquisition spy, also loves Caterina. He jealously arranges a meeting between her and Rodolfo, meaning to betray her to Angelo. But Thisbe, discovering that Caterina had once saved her mother's life, sacrifices herself for her former rival, and is killed. Rodolfo then discovers that he has misinterpreted a selfless act.

Aniara. Opera in 2 acts by Blomdahl; text by Erik Lindegren, after Harry Martinson's epic poem (1956). Prem. Stockholm 31 May 1959.

The space craft Aniara, carrying refugees from an earth devastated by atomic war, is knocked off course and its passengers forced to spend the rest of their lives travelling towards a distant constellation. Some of them reveal insight into their condition and that of the world, including Mimaroben (bsbar), operator of the computer which controls Aniara; the commander Chefone (bar); the Blind Poetess (sop); the lesbian Daisy Dodd (sop); and the comedian Sandon (ten).

Anna Bolena. Opera in 2 acts by Donizetti; text by Romani. Prem. Milan, T Carcano, 26 Dec. 1830.

Loosely based on the well-known historical events, the plot tells how King Henry VIII

(bs), in love with Jane Seymour (mez), wants to dispose of his wife Anne Boleyn (sop). He tries to accuse her of treason and recalls Percy, Earl of Northumberland (ten), to give evidence against her. Percy, however, professes his continuing love for Anne, as does her page Smeaton (mez). Having come upon Anne alone with Percy, the King believes her guilty of adultery although Smeaton protests Anne's innocence; Henry has all three arrested.

Jane visits Anne in prison to persuade her to confess and so save her life. Although Anne refuses, she forgives Jane for supplanting her in the King's favour. When it emerges that Anne and Percy do in fact love each other, they are both condemned to death, as is Rochefort (bs), Anne's brother. The two men are offered pardons, which they refuse since Anne must still die. As she awaits her execution in the Tower of London, Anne loses her senses and imagines it is the day of her wedding to the King. As Anne and her three accomplices are led to the scaffold, a cannon and bells are heard acclaiming the new Queen.

Anne Trulove. The daughter (sop) of Trulove, lover of Tom Rakewell, in Stravinsky's *The Rake's Progress*.

Anselmi, Giuseppe (*b* Nicolosi, nr. Catania, 6 Oct. 1876; *d* Zoagli, 27 May 1929). Italian tenor. Studied violin and composition, then joined an operetta company touring Italy and the Near East. Heard by Giulio Ricordi, who suggested that he study with Mancinelli. Début Athens 1896 (Turiddu). Italian début 1901. London, CG, 1901, and occasionally until 1909. Much admired in Buenos Aires; also appeared regularly in Warsaw, St Petersburg, and Madrid. Left his heart to Madrid's theatrical museum, where it is preserved. One of the foremost exponents of bel canto, with a beautiful voice and finished style. (R)

Ansermet, Ernest (*b* Vevey, 11 Nov. 1883; *d* Geneva, 20 Feb. 1969). Swiss conductor. Studied Lausanne, becoming professor of mathematics. Then studied composition with Bloch, and had advice from Nikisch. Début 1911. Conducted prems. of *The Soldier's Tale* (1918), *Rape of Lucretia* (1946), and Martin's *Der Sturm* (1956). His opera performances, especially of *Pelléas*, *Boris*, *Magic Flute* in Hamburg, Geneva, and elsewhere in his latter years, were widely admired for the clarity and judgement that marked all his music-making. Wrote several books and essays on music and philosophy. (R)

antefatto (It.: 'antecedent fact'). The device for explaining to an audience background facts or previous events which they must know in order to understand the plot from the start; it may be contained in a narration, as with *Il trovatore*, or printed in a prefatory paragraph to a libretto, as with some by Piave and Romani.

Antheil, George (*b* Trenton, NJ, 8 July 1900; *d* New York, 12 Feb. 1959). US composer and pianist. Studied with Sternberg and Bloch. Assistant music dir., Berlin Stadttheater, 1928–9. His first opera, *Transatlantic* (1930), caused a stir on its first production: it concerns a corrupt presidential campaign, and includes prominent jazz elements. Among his later works were *Helen Retires* (1934) and the Jonson-inspired *Volpone* (1953).

Antonacci, Anna Caterina (*b* Ferrara, 5 Apr. 1961). Italian soprano. Studied Bologna Cons. Début Arezzo 1986 (Rosina). She is best known for her sensitive portrayals of Rossini's dramatic heroines: Semiramide at Catania; Ninetta (Philadelphia), Dorliska, and the title-role in *Ermione*, in the first British perf. of the opera (London, concert, 1994; also Gly. 1995). London, CG, 1994 (Elcia, *Mosè in Egitto*). (R)

Antonia. The consumptive singer (sop), one of Hoffmann's lovers, in Offenbach's *Les contes d'Hoffmann*.

Antonio. The gardener (bs), Barbarina's father and Susanna's uncle, in Mozart's *Le nozze di Figaro*.

Antony and Cleopatra. Opera in 3 acts by Samuel Barber; text by Franco Zeffirelli, based on Shakespeare's drama (1606–7). Prem. New York, M, 16 Sept. 1966 (commissioned for opening of new theatre).

The opera tells of the love between Antony (bs-bar), ruler of the eastern portion of the Roman Empire, and Cleopatra (sop), Queen of Egypt. Despite conflict between their two nations, and Antony's marriage to Octavia (sop), daughter of another member of the ruling triumvirate, the couple are united in death. Antony kills himself when he believes Cleopatra to be dead and, poisoned by the bite of an asp smuggled to her past guards, she also dies.

Antwerp (Fr., Anvers; Dut., Antwerpen). City in Antwerpen, Belgium. Home of the Royal Flemish O, founded 1893 by the bass Hendrik Fontaine as the Vlaamse O (Flemish O). Performances were originally given in the Royal Dutch T, but since 1907 the Opera has had its own theatre (cap. 1,050), and the title Royal was granted to it in 1920. The company is subsidized by state, city, and province. All operas are sung in Flemish, and over 300 artists are employed each season. During the 1960s several important foreign works had their Belgian prems. there, e.g. *A Midsummer Night's Dream* (1962), *Capriccio* (1964), and *The Nose* (1965). Performances of *The Ring* are a regular feature. The large repertory also includes works by Flemish composers, e.g. Blockx and August de Boeck. Now known as the Vlaamsoper.

The Antwerp Chamber O, founded 1959, amalgamated with the Dutch Chamber O in 1971 to form the Flemish Chamber O, with its headquarters in the Ring T.

Anvil Chorus. The chorus of gypsies 'Chi del gitano' in Act II of Verdi's *Il trovatore*, swinging their hammers in time to the music as they work at their forging.

Apollo et Hyacinthus, seu Hyacinthi Metamorphosis. Opera in 1 act by Mozart; text by Rufinus Widl. Prem. Salzburg 13 May 1767.

The plot, a revised version of the story in Ovid's *Metamorphoses*, concerns the love of Zephyrus (boy alt) for Melia (treb) and his jealousy of Apollo (boy alt). Apollo slays Hyacinthus (treb), turning him into a flower, has Zephyrus borne away by the winds, and himself weds Melia.

The work, comprising a prologue and nine numbers, is not strictly an opera, but an intermezzo to Widl's drama *Clementia Croesi*.

Apostolescu, Nicu (*b* Brăila, 31 July 1896). Romanian tenor, formerly baritone. Studied Bucharest with Popovici. Début Cluj, 1921 (Amonasro); début as tenor, 1923 (Radamès), while continuing to sing Scarpia, Rigoletto, etc. Bucharest 1926–44, where he was the first Romanian Parsifal, Tristan, Tannhäuser, Walther, and Otello (Verdi). Italy 1928–30. A fine singing actor. (R)

appaltatore (It.: 'contractor'). A theatrical agent, sometimes also impresario.

Appia, Adolphe (*b* Geneva, 1 Sept. 1862; *d*

Nyon, 29 Feb. 1928). Swiss designer. Studied Geneva, Leipzig, and Dresden; also spent much time examining contemporary theatrical practice, especially at Bayreuth. His pioneering designs for Wagner are based on three-dimensional forms, sometimes stylized or abstract, intended as an extension of the music so as to express it visually, and with the singing actor giving them life. He also interested himself in lighting as part of the scenery in its own right. His intention was to realize the works' inner action, 'to enable the audience to see things the way the heroes of the drama typically see them': thus, Isolde should be surrounded not with 'the mild summer's night' but 'the terrible space that separates her from Tristan'. He designed *Tristan* for Milan, S (1923), *Rheingold* and *Walküre* for Basle (1924–5). Cosima Wagner, though interested, rejected his designs on the grounds that Wagner himself had already said all there was to be said on the subject; but Appia's influence on the ideas of Wieland and Wolfgang Wagner was crucial.

Arabella. Opera in 3 acts by Richard Strauss; text by Hofmannsthal. Prem. Dresden, S, 1 July 1933.

Vienna, Carnival 1860. Graf Waldner (bs) has amassed large gambling debts, so hopes to find a rich husband for his daughter Arabella (sop). She, however, has spurned all her many suitors to date, among them the ardent Matteo (ten), secretly loved by Arabella's younger sister Zdenka (sop). Because Waldner cannot afford to have two débutante daughters, Zdenka has been brought up as a boy; thus unable to declare her feelings openly, she has to write to Matteo pretending to be Arabella. When Waldner contacts several friends for financial help, the nephew of one of them, Mandryka (bar) is captivated by a portrait of Arabella enclosed with the letter. He comes to seek her hand, and his gift of money soon earns him Waldner's approval.

At the Fiakerball, Arabella meets Mandryka and realizes that he is the interesting stranger she has seen outside their hotel; she abandons her other suitors, to Matteo's despair. However, Zdenka gives Matteo a note, purportedly from Arabella, containing the key to her room. Mandryka overhears, and suspects Arabella's behaviour; for revenge, he flirts with the *Fiakermilli, much to Waldner's consternation.

After his assignation, Matteo descends to the hall of the hotel and is astonished to see Arabella entering. In the middle of their misunderstanding, Arabella's parents and Mandryka arrive; the situation seems to confirm their worst suspicions. Zdenka then appears, declaring her love for Matteo and her intention of throwing herself into the Danube; it emerges that it was she who made, and kept, the assignation. Matteo seems happy to transfer his attentions to the younger sister. Arabella offers Mandryka a glass of water, following an old folk custom symbolizing a bride's purity, and the couple embrace.

Aragall, Giacomo (*b* Barcelona, 6 June 1939). Spanish tenor. Studied Barcelona with Puig, Milan with Badiali. Début Venice, F, 1963 (Gaston, *Jérusalem*). Milan, S, from 1963; Vienna, S, and London, CG, 1966; New York, M, 1968; Naples, C, 1972; also Chicago, Edinburgh, S Francisco, Berlin, etc. Roles incl. Don Carlos, Duke of Mantua, Rodolfo, Pinkerton, Werther, and Faust and Roméo (Gounod). (R)

Araia, Francesco (*b* Naples, 25 June 1709; *d* ?Bologna, before 1770). Italian composer. After writing several operas for Italian cities, he was appointed to the St Petersburg court by the Empress Anne. He began with a new version of his *La forza dell'amore e dell'odio* in 1736. After a return to Italy to form a new troupe, he staged for the Empress Elizabeth operas including *Tsefal i Prokris* (Cephalus and Procris, 1755), the first opera sung in Russian. His work thereafter became less popular, and he withdrew to Italy.

Araiza, Francisco (*b* Mexico City, 4 Oct. 1950). Mexican tenor. Studied Mexico City with Iruna Gonzalez. Début Mexico City 1973 (Rodolfo). Munich, Bayreuth 1978; Paris, O, 1981; Salzburg 1983; London, CG, 1983 (Ernesto, *Don Pasquale*); New York, M, 1984; also Brussels, Aix, Vienna, S Francisco, etc. Roles incl. Belmonte, Ferrando, Tamino, Idreno (*Semiramide*), Steersman, Des Grieux (Massenet). In recent years he has turned to some heavier roles: Lohengrin (Zurich 1990) and Walther (New York, M, 1993). (R)

Archer, Neill (*b* Northampton, 31 Aug. 1961). English tenor. Studied Brevard Music Center, N Carolina. Début Kent O 1987 (Tamino). Sang Conti's Don Quixote at Buxton (1987) and appeared with WNO as Ottavio, Scottish

O as Ferrando. London, C and CG, 1990 (Tamino and Jacquino). His Pelléas for WNO (under Boulez, 1992) was admired for its vocal style and dramatic poise. (R)

Arditi, Luigi (*b* Crescentino, 22 July 1822; *d* Hove, 1 May 1903). Italian composer and conductor. Conducted in Milan, then in Havana, US, and Russia, before settling in London. Conducted London, HM, 1858–67 and CG, 1869. Also conducted for many touring companies, including those organized by Mapleson with Patti, as well as continuing to make many appearances on the Continent. Conducted first London performances of many operas. Composed several operas, though he is best remembered for the song 'Il bacio', which Patti used to sing in the Lesson Scene of *Il barbiere di Siviglia*.

'Ardon gl'incensi'. The beginning of the Larghetto section of Lucia's (sop) Mad Scene in Act III of Donizetti's *Lucia di Lammermoor*, in which she imagines her wedding to Edgardo.

Arensky, Anton (*b* Novgorod, 12 July 1861; *d* Terioki, 25 Feb. 1906). Russian composer and conductor. Studied St Petersburg, including with Rimsky-Korsakov. Moving to Moscow, he taught Rakhmaninov, Skryabin, and Glière, and made friends with Tchaikovsky and Taneyev. His greatest operatic success was with *Son na Volge* (A Dream on the Volga, 1891), on a text passed on to him by Tchaikovsky on abandoning *The Voyevoda*. His later operas, including *Raphael* (1894) and *Nal i Damayanti* (1904) were less successful. His style, elegant and lyrical if somewhat lacking in personality, owes much to Tchaikovsky's manner.

Argenta, Nancy (*b* Nelson, British Columbia, 17 Jan. 1957). Canadian soprano. Studied U of West. Ontario and with Vera Rozsa. Début 1983 (*Hippolyte et Aricie*). Lyons 1985 (Susanna); London 1988 (Poppea). Handel roles include Asteria (*Tamerlano*), Rossanne (*Floridante*, Toronto 1990). Also valued for the purity and agility of her voice in Purcell's *King Arthur* and *Fairy Queen* (Aix 1990). (R)

Argentina. For all its present richness, the operatic life of Argentina did not develop until the last third of the 19th cent. The country was then dependent on Italian singers visiting Buenos Aires. As in most countries, the first national operas treated local subjects (Inca stories and, to a lesser degree, popular tales of pampas life) in an Italianate style; later works drew upon folk melodies and national musical characteristics. The first important Argentinian opera was *La gata blanca* (1877) by Francisco Hargreaves (1849–1900), a work in buffo vein that proved very influential. Arturo Berutti (1862–1938) won a popular success with his *Pampa* (1897, after the gaucho drama *Juan Moreira* by Juan José Podestá); his other works include *Yupanki* (1899), the very successful *Khryse* (1902), *Horrida nox* (1908), and *Los héroes* (1909), each in some way making use of indigenous Argentinian subjects and colouring. Ettore Panizza's *Aurora* (1908; libretto by Illica) sought to reconcile folklore with a verismo manner. Other operas showing a strong European influence were by Constantino Gaito (1879–1945) (11 operas, including *Shaffras* (1910), *Caio Petronio* (1919), *Flor de Nieve* (1922), and *Ollantay* (1926)), and E. García Mansilla (a Rimsky-Korsakov pupil whose *Ivan* was produced in St Petersburg).

The first work which really sought to make fully operatic use of Argentinian musical characteristics was *Huemac* (1916), by Pascual de Rogatis (1880–1980), though it retains a European tinge. The first local opera in Spanish was by Felipe Boero (1884–1958), his *Tucumán*, which won the first local opera competition in 1918. Many Argentinian operas now began to appear, including Felipe Boero's *Raquela* (1923), set on a pampas ranch, and his *El matrero* (1929), also set in the countryside and, for its effective use of local tunes and dances, regarded as one of the most important Argentinian operas. Other significant works were written by Alfredo Schiuma (1885–1963) (*Amy Robsart* (1920), *Tabaré* (1925)), Gilardo Gilardi (1889–1963) (*Ilse* (1923), *La leyenda del Urutaú* (1934)), Raúl Espoile (1888–1958) (*La ciudad roja* (1936)), and Arnaldo D'Esposito (1907–45) (*Lin-Candel* (1941)). These works use local subjects and music drawn either from Inca scales and rhythms or from folk-song and dance. Parallel with this development went a movement that kept strong links with European opera: important works were written by Carlos López Buchardo (1881–1948) (*El sueno del Alma* (1914)), Athos Palma (1891–1951) (*Nazdah* (1924)), Rafael Peacan del Sar (1884–?) (*Chrysanthème* (1927): a Puccinian work based on Pierre Loti and set in Japan),

J. B. Massa (1885–1938) (*La Magdalena* (1929)), Panizza (*Bizancio* (1939)), and Juan José Castro (1895–1968) (*Proserpina y el extranjero* (1951)), a Verdi prize opera transferring classical legend to South America). The most important post-war opera composer has been Alberto *Ginastera. His pupil Antonio Tauriello (*b* 1931) has conducted at the Colón and in the USA; his operas include *Les guerres picrocholines* (after Rabelais, comp. 1971).

Outside Buenos Aires, the country has been largely dependent on touring opera, with few prems. Exceptions are Massa's *L'evaso* (1922) at Rosario and Enrique Casella's *Corimayo* (1926) and *Chasca* (1939) at Tucumán. Occasional seasons have been given at Rosario, Tucumán, Mendoza, S Fe, Córdoba, and Bahía Blanca, by companies based on Buenos Aires. At the T Argentino of La Plata, the capital of the province of Buenos Aires, there have been regular seasons. See also BUENOS AIRES, COLÓN.

Argento, Dominick (*b* York, PA, 27 Oct. 1927). US composer. Studied Baltimore with Nabokov and Cowell; Rochester with Hovhaness and Hanson, also acting as opera coach; Italy with Dallapiccola. Music director, Hilltop O, Baltimore, also forming Center OC, Minnesota, for which he wrote the opening work, *The Masque of Angels* (1964), and *Postcard from Morocco* (1971): later works include *The Voyage of Edgar Allan Poe* (1976) and *The Aspern Papers* (1988). Opera has been at the centre of his interests, and his works show a wide range of taste and techniques, as well as a sympathetic understanding of the voice.

Århus. City in Jutland, Denmark. Founded in 1947 at the Musikhuset (cap. 1,477), Den Jyske Opera (Jutland Opera) is Denmark's second largest company, and tours widely. A new concert-house, in which opera is given, opened in 1982 with Nielsen's *Maskarade*. A complete *Ring* was given there in 1987. Århus Sommeropera opened in the Helsingore T (cap. 300) in 1989.

aria (It.: 'air', from Gr. and Lat., *aer*, a term which came to mean a scheme or model, i.e. a melody which could be repeated with different words). The elaborated song-form of opera (and oratorio) for solo voice (occasionally two voices) with instrumental accompaniment. Its nature has changed substantially, with its high point of formality *c*.1680–1780 and then growing looser.

In the earliest operas, moments of heightened expression or deepened contemplation were emphasized by the use of a more melismatic style: the subsequent imposition of a regular formal structure resulted in the aria, the first great examples of which occur in Monteverdi's *Orfeo*. During the first half of the 17th cent. the stylistic division between the music used for narrative and reflective text widened further in Roman and Venetian opera, gradually settling into the categories of *recitative and aria, although such rigid definitions were not widely accepted until much later.

Following the reforms of the libretto initiated by *Zeno and his contemporaries, and even more so *Metastasio, composers concentrated increasingly on the aria, maintaining the recitative as a narrative link between stylized outpourings of feeling. Most of the arias were of the *da capo variety and so uniform was the treatment of emotions that arias could be transposed from one opera to another, even from one composer's work to that of another. In part, the supremacy of the da capo aria was a response to the pre-eminence of the solo singer whose virtuosity had increasingly come to dominate opera.

In time, the unvarying alternation of aria and recitative became a suffocating convention, and from the 1750s onwards a gradual reform of opera seria took place. Instead of recitative–aria chains, composers began to prefer longer sequences in which aria was replaced by *arioso, and freely mixed with recitative, ensemble, and choral writing. The most important reform of the mid-18th cent. came with Gluck, who found his inspiration in French opera, characterized from its beginnings by a more refined style of melodic writing in which florid virtuosity was of less importance. Some of Gluck's reforms are apparent in Mozart, whose arias display a variety and flexibility without parallel in the 18th cent.

After 1800 the growth of strong national traditions lent the solo vocal passages in opera a richness and diversity that prevents easy description. However, two main concerns may be identified: the expression of emotion, and the display of vocal technique, demonstrated above all in 19th-cent. Italian opera. The main movement throughout the 19th cent. was not towards a development of the aria as an individual form, but in favour of its subsumption into a more genuinely dramatic framework, where solo vocal music of all kinds merged with ensemble and choral writing. This breakdown of formal divisions reached its apotheosis, and most cogent expression as a principle of operatic writing, in Wagner. Subsequently, the rise of the neo-classical movement in the 20th cent. has rekindled an interest in the more or less formal aria as capable of playing a functional role in modern opera.

Ariadne auf Naxos (Ariadne on Naxos). Opera in 1 act, later with a scenic prelude, by Richard Strauss; text by Hofmannsthal. Originally intended to follow Molière's comédie-ballet, *Le bourgeois gentilhomme* (1670), for which Strauss had written incidental music: in this form, prem. Stuttgart 25 Oct. 1912, cond. Strauss. Second version prem. Vienna, H, 4 Oct. 1916.

The work's first form was impracticable, requiring both a theatrical and an operatic company for the same evening. The second, operatic, version substitutes for Molière's play a prologue in which word is sent from the 'bourgeois gentilhomme', who has engaged an opera company and a *commedia dell'arte* troupe, that their entertainments must take place simultaneously so as to be over in time for a fireworks display.

Prologue: Vienna, a rich house. The Composer (sop), troubled about his art, is consoled first by the old Music Master (bar), then by Zerbinetta (sop), leader of a group of players, and lastly by his faith in music.

Opera: on her island, the comedians try to comfort the desolate Ariadne (sop). She sings of her longing for the kingdom of death, though Zerbinetta tries to convert her to a less serious philosophy. When the youthful Bacchus (ten) arrives, Ariadne greets him as Death. Singing of their new-found love, they embrace passionately, to Zerbinetta's delighted approval.

Ariane et Barbe-bleue (Ariadne and Bluebeard). Opera in 3 acts by Dukas; text adapted from Maeterlinck's drama (1901), written with Dukas in mind. Prem. Paris, OC, 10 May 1907.

Barbe-Bleue (bs) has just married his sixth wife Ariane (mez). The villagers fear she will disappear mysteriously, as her predecessors have done. Ariane resolves to discover their fate: she finds them hidden in a vault in the castle and releases them. The villagers attack Barbe-bleue, bind him up, and offer him to

his wives, so that they may take their revenge. They, however, seem to bear no grudges and choose to tend his wounds and remain in the castle, while Ariane takes her leave.

Arianna in Creta (Ariadne in Crete). Opera in 3 acts by Handel; text after Pariati's text *Arianna e Teseo* (1715) set by Leo (1721 and 1729) and Porpora (1727). Prem. London, H, 26 Jan. 1734.

The plot is loosely based on the myth of Theseus (mez cas) and his journey to Crete where, with the help of Ariadne (sop), daughter of King Minos (bs), he slays the Minotaur. A complicated subplot involves Carilda (con), in love with Theseus, but herself courted by both his friend Alcestes (mez cas) and the Cretan general Tauris (mez).

ariette (Fr.). In 18th-cent. French opera a short vocal number, lively in character, with orchestral accompaniment. Later took on the more general meaning of 'song': used in this sense in the generic term *comédie mêlée d'ariettes.

Ariodant. Opera in 3 acts by Méhul; text by F. B. Hoffman, after Ariosto's poem *Orlando furioso* (1516). Prem. Paris, OC, 11 Oct. 1799.

The plot (which has some anticipations of Weber's *Euryanthe*) turns on the attempts of Othon (ten) to compromise Ina (sop) so as to force her to abandon her lover Ariodant (ten) and marry him; these are eventually frustrated.

Ariodante. Opera in 3 acts by Handel; text ad. from A. Salvi's *Ginevra, principessa di Scozia* (1708), after Ariosto's poem *Orlando furioso* (1516). Prem. London, CG, 8 Jan. 1735.

The plot turns on the attempts of Polinesso (con), Duke of Albany, to win the hand of Ginevra (sop), daughter of the King of Scotland and betrothed of the vassal prince Ariodante (mez cas). Though Polinesso manages to trick Ginevra's confidante Dalinda (sop) into aiding his evil task, his plans are eventually frustrated and he is killed in a duel with Ariodante's brother Lurcanio (ten). All ends happily, with Ariodante and Ginevra united.

arioso (sometimes also **recitativo arioso**; It.: 'like an aria'). A musical style and manner of setting text falling between that of *recitative and *aria, which, lacking the essentially declamatory nature of the former and the regular phrase structure and organization of the latter, is characterized by an expressive melodic line and frequent melismatic word-setting.

Ariosti, Attilio (*b* Bologna, 5 Nov. 1666; *d* London, 1729). Italian composer. Having worked in both Italy and Austria, he came to England in 1716 and, together with Handel, was one of the founders of the Royal Academy of Music. Of his various works for the stage, *Coriolano* (1723) and *Vespasiano* (1724) enjoyed the greatest popularity in their day.

Arkel. The old blind King of Allemonde (bs) in Debussy's *Pelléas et Mélisande*.

Arkhipova, Irina (*b* Moscow, 2 Dec. 1925). Russian mezzo-soprano. Studied Moscow with Savransky, then joined the Sverdlovsk O as soloist (1954–6). Moscow, B, 1956 (Carmen); then Eboli, Amneris, Azucena, and the classic Russian mezzo roles, as well as the first performances of many new works there. In the 1960s began to sing widely in Europe. Montreal 1967, with Moscow B; S Francisco 1972; London, CG, 1975. Possesses a rich, dramatic voice, and an imposing stage presence. (R)

Arlecchino (Harlequin). Opera in 1 act by Busoni; text by composer. Prem. in the same bill as his *Turandot*, Zurich 11 May 1917, cond. Busoni.

Set in Bergamo in the 18th cent., the opera presents four facets of Harlequin's character: 'Harlequin as Rogue', 'Harlequin as Soldier', 'Harlequin as Husband', and 'Harlequin as Conqueror'. In addition to Arlecchino (spoken), several familiar *commedia dell'arte* figures appear, including Columbine (sop), Doctor Bombasto (bs), the tailor Matteo del Sarto (bs-bar), and Leandro (ten).

Arlesiana, L' (The Girl from Arles). Opera in 3 acts (originally 4) by Cilea; text by Leopoldo Marenco, after Daudet's drama (1872). Prem. Milan, L, 27 Nov. 1897, with Ricci, De Paz, Caruso, cond. Zuccari. 3-act version, same theatre, 22 Oct. 1898.

Federico (ten), son of Rosa Mamai (sop), is in love with a girl from Arles, but discovers she is the mistress of Metifio (bar), a mule-driver; his family arrange that he marry his foster-sister, Vivetta (sop) instead. Unable to reconcile himself to this fate, Federico kills himself on the eve of the wedding.

Arline. Count Arnheim's daughter (sop) in Balfe's *The Bohemian Girl*.

Armed Men. In Mozart's *Magic Flute*, two armed men (*Zwei Gerharnischter*) (ten and bs) lead Tamino and Pamina to the ordeals they must undergo.

Arme Heinrich, Der (Poor Heinrich). Opera in 3 acts by Pfitzner; text by James Grun, after a medieval legend. Prem. Mainz 2 Apr. 1895.

The knight Heinrich (ten) is struck ill in punishment for his arrogance towards God; he will recover only if a virgin sacrifices herself for him. As Dietrich (bar), a faithful servant, and his wife Hilde (sop) fear, their daughter Agnes (sop) offers herself. At the moment of her sacrifice, Heinrich suddenly finds his strength and is in time to snatch away the sacrificial knife.

Armide. Opera in 5 acts by Gluck; text by Quinault, after Tasso's poem *Gerusalemme liberata* (1575). Prem. Paris, O, 23 Sept. 1777.

The sorceress Armide (sop), Princess of Damascus, has vanquished the crusader knights, but failed to captivate the valiant Renaud (ten) with her charms. Intent on killing him, she carries him away to her enchanted realm, where her uncle, the magician Hidraot (bar), King of Damascus, puts him into a magic sleep. Armide uses her powers to cause Renaud to fall in love with her and to forget his obligations as a crusader. Two fellow knights come after him and by using a diamond shield manage to break Armide's spell and bring Renaud to his senses. When he resumes his worthy quest, Armide falls into a fury and, destroying her realm, sets out again with vengeance in her heart.

Also opera by Lully (1686).

Arminio. Opera in 3 acts by Handel; text adapted from A. Salvi's *Arminio* (1703). Prem. London, CG, 12 Jan. 1737.

Set against the background of the Roman war with the German tribes AD 15–16, the opera tells the story of the rebel chieftain Arminius (con cas) and his freedom from imprisonment by the Roman general Varo (ten) through the devotion of his wife Thusnelda (sop) and sister Ramise (con).

Armstrong, Richard (*b* Leicester, 7 Jan. 1943). Studied Cambridge. Répétiteur, London, CG, 1966–8. Début WNO as assistant; music dir. WNO 1973–86, where successes included a Janáček cycle, *Midsummer Marriage*, *The Ring*, also Verdi's *Otello* with Peter Stein. WNO subsequently, incl. tours to New York, Milan, and Japan. CG from 1982; London ENO and Geneva 1990; also Netherlands O; Berlin, K; Monte Carlo; Frankfurt O (principal guest conductor, 1986). Scottish O from 1993. Repertory incl. *Fidelio*, *Dutchman*, *Boccanegra*, *Salome*. (R)

Armstrong, Karan (*b* Horne, MT, 14 Dec. 1941). US soprano. Studied S Barbara with Lotte Lehmann. Début S Francisco 1966 (Elvira, *Italiana in Algeri*). New York, CO, 1975–8 (roles incl. Minnie, Tosca, Queen of Shemakha). European début Strasburg 1974 (Micaela); Bayreuth 1979 (Elsa). London, CG, from 1981 (Lulu, Sieglinde, Gutrune). Sang in the prems. of von Einem's *Jesu Hochzeit* (Vienna, S, 1980), Sinopoli's *Lou Salomé* (Munich, S, 1981) and Berio's *Un re in ascolto* (Salzburg 1984). A strong dramatic presence in modern repertory. (R)

Arne, Thomas Augustine (*b* London, 12 Mar. 1710; *d* London, 5 Mar. 1778). English composer. Active at both London, DL and CG, his works included masques such as *Alfred* (1740)—the original home of 'Rule Britannia'—and the opera *Artaxerxes* (1762). This English opera 'after the Italian manner' enjoyed continuing popularity into the 19th cent., as did the pasticcio *Love in a Village* (1762). One of the few English-born composers to succeed in London in an era dominated by Italians; his music has an easy charm which found many admirers.

Arnold. Arnold Melcthal (ten), lover of Mathilde in Rossini's *Guillaume Tell*.

Arnold, Samuel (*b* London, 10 Aug. 1740; *d* London, 22 Oct. 1802). English composer, organist, conductor, and editor. His pasticcio *The Maid of the Mill* (based on Richardson's *Pamela*) was performed to enormous acclaim at Covent Garden in 1765, launching him on a spectacular career as a theatrical composer. He produced over 100 stage works, about half of which were pasticcios, burlettas, and ballets: most were for the Marylebone Gardens, which he leased 1769–76, or for the Little T Royal in the Haymarket, where he was composer from 1777. Among the most successful were *Tom Jones* (1769) and *The Servant Mistress* (1770). His son **Samuel James**

Arnold (1774–1852) was a librettist and theatrical impresario.

Arnoldson, Sigrid (*b* Stockholm, 20 Mar. 1861; *d* Stockholm, 7 Feb. 1943). Swedish soprano. Studied with her father, the tenor Oscar Arnoldson (1830–81), Paris with Strakosch and Marchesi, and Berlin with Artôt. Début Prague 1885 (Rosina). Moscow 1886; London, DL, 1887, and CG from 1888; New York, M, 1893. Charlotte in first US and British *Werther*, 1894. Her voice covered three octaves. Retired 1916. (R)

Arnould, Sophie (*b* Paris, 13 Feb. 1740; *d* Paris, 18 Oct. 1802). French soprano. Studied Paris with Marie Fel. Début Paris, O, 1757, and sang there for 20 years. Created title-role of Gluck's *Iphigénie en Aulide* and was the first Eurydice in the French version of his *Orfeo*. Also highly successful in the works of Rameau (notably in *Castor et Pollux*), Francœur (creating the title-role in *Aline*), and Monsigny. She was an impassioned actress (the only one in France of whom Garrick spoke with enthusiasm) and possessed a good voice, but her laxness led to a vocal decline before she was 40. She retired in 1788 with a state pension of 2,000 livres. Lively and intelligent, she numbered Voltaire, Rousseau, and Beaumarchais among her intellectual circle in Paris. Piérné's *Sophie Arnould* (1927) is based on events in her life. Her portrait by Greuze is in the Wallace Collection, London.

Aroldo. See STIFFELIO.

Aron. Aaron (ten), Moses' brother in Schoenberg's *Moses und Aron*.

Arrieu, Claude (*b* Paris, 30 Nov. 1903; *d* Paris, 7 Mar. 1990). French composer. Studied Paris with Dukas. Her stage works include the early experimental *Noé* (comp. 1934), a number of works in more traditional language such as *Cadet Roussel* (1939) and *Cymbeline* (comp. 1963), some lighter works and works for radio and for children.

Arroyo, Martina (*b* New York, 2 Feb. 1936). US soprano. Studied New York with Gurewich. Début New York, M, 1959 (Voice from Heaven, *Don Carlos*). Zurich 1963–8; then regular appearances all over Europe. She returned to New York to sing principal roles in 1965. London, CG, from 1968. Her repertory includes Reiza, Norma, and the Verdi dramatic soprano roles. (R)

Arsace. Semiramide's son (mez) in Rossini's *Semiramide*.

Artaserse. Metastasio's libretto has had over 100 settings including those by Gluck (1741) and J. C. Bach (1760).

The plot concerns repeated attempts by Artabano to gain the throne. He first of all kills King Serse and then attempts to poison Artaserse, the king's son. Arbace, Artabano's son, thwarts these efforts, since he is true to the crown. Loyalties are further confused by Arbace's love for Mandane, King Serse's daughter, and Artaserse's love for Semira, Artabano's daughter. The couples are eventually united and Artabano exiled.

Artôt, Désirée (*b* Paris, 21 July 1835; *d* Berlin, 3 Apr. 1907). Belgian mezzo-soprano, later soprano. Studied Paris with Viardot. Engaged for Paris, O, on Meyerbeer's suggestion; début 1858 (Fidès). Italy and Germany as mezzo, then sang as soprano, including in London concerts, 1859–60: HM 1863 as Marie (*La fille du régiment*), Violetta, and Adalgisa; CG 1864–6. Russia 1868, where she was briefly engaged to Tchaikovsky; in 1869 she married the Spanish baritone **Mariano Padilla y Ramos** (1842–1906). They toured together in Europe and Russia. Their daughter, the soprano **Lola Artôt de Padilla** (1876–1933) created Vreli (*A Village Romeo and Juliet*), Berlin, K, 1907 and was a member of the Berlin, H, 1909–27.

Arts Florissants, Les. See CHRISTIE, WILLIAM.

Arturo. Lord Arthur Talbot (ten), a Cavalier betrothed to Elvira, in Bellini's *I Puritani*.

Arundell, Dennis (*b* London, 22 July 1898; *d* London, 10 Dec. 1988). English actor, producer, author, and composer. Studied Cambridge with Rootham and Stanford. Prem. Rootham's *The Two Sisters* 1922, and other Cambridge performances incl. the first staged *Semele* (1925), and *The Fairy Queen* (1931). Prods. at London, SW, incl. *Shvanda* (own trans., 1948), first English *Káťa Kabanová* (1951), and *Flying Dutchman* (1958). Collaborated with Beecham on *Bohemian Girl* at London, CG (1951) and prem. of *Irmelin*, in Oxford (1953). Also worked in Helsinki and in Australia. His two operas are *Ghost of Abel* and *A Midsummer Night's Dream*.

Arvidson. Mlle Arvidson (mez), the fortuneteller in the 'Swedish' version of Verdi's *Un *ballo in maschera*.

Ascanio in Alba. Opera in 2 acts by Mozart; text by G. Parini, perhaps after Count Claudio Stampa. Prem. Milan, RD, 17 Oct. 1771.

In an Arcadian landscape near Rome, Venus (sop) tells her grandson Ascanio (sop cas) that he is to rule part of her nation in her place and is to marry Silvia (sop), a wise nymph. He is to go in search of Silvia, but in disguise so as to test her true feelings for him.

Ascanio and Silvia meet and fall in love. However, she puts herself under the protection of Aceste (ten), a priest of Venus, to await the arrival of her destined groom. Venus, convinced of the nymph's virtue, reveals Ascanio's real identity to Silvia. The couple are delighted and everyone sings Venus's praises.

Aschenbach. Gustav Aschenbach (ten), the writer in Britten's *Death in Venice*.

Assassinio nella cattedrale (Murder in the Cathedral). Opera in 2 parts, with an intermezzo, by Pizzetti; text by the composer, after A. Castelli's translation of T. S. Eliot's dramatic poem (1935). Prem. Milan, S, 1 Mar. 1958.

The plot is based on the historical events leading to the assassination in Canterbury Cathedral of Thomas à Becket (bs), Archbishop of Canterbury, by four knights in the service of Henry II.

'Assisa al piè d'un salice'. See WILLOW SONG.

Astarita, Gennaro (*b* ?Naples, *c*.1745–9; *d* ?, after 1803). Italian composer. Though noted in his own country as a composer of mainly opere buffe, including *Il marito indolente* (1778), Astarita played an important role in the development of opera in Russia, which he first visited in 1781. In 1784 he became dir. of the orch. of the Petrovsky T in Moscow, moving to St Petersburg in 1786. In 1794, at the request of the director of the Imperial Theatres in St Petersburg, Prince Nicolay Yusupov, Astarita recruited an Italian troupe, which he directed until 1799.

Astuzie femminili, Le (Feminine Wiles). Opera in 2 acts by Cimarosa; text by Giovanni Palomba. Prem. Naples, Teatro di Fiorentini, 16 Aug. 1794.

According to the terms of her father's will, Bellina (sop) will receive a large dowry if she marries a rich old family friend, Don Gian-paolo Lasagna (bs). Her tutor Dr Romualdo (bs), himself the unwelcome object of attentions from Leonora (mez), Bellina's governess, also wants to marry the young girl. Bellina herself, however, is in love with the young Filandro (ten); they run off together and, returning disguised as hussars, are successful in their ruse to get married. Lasagna eventually marries Bellina's friend Ersilia (sop).

Atalanta. Opera in 3 acts by Handel; text anon., after B. Valeriani's *La caccia in Etolia*. Prem. London, CG, 12 May 1736 on the occasion of the marriage of Frederick, Prince of Wales (son of George II), to Princess Augusta of Saxe-Gotha.

This *pièce d'occasion* tells of the love of Atalanta (sop), the princess huntress-nymph, for the king shepherd, Meleager (sop cas). The opera ends with Mercury (bs) bringing Jupiter's greeting to the newly-weds, i.e. Prince Frederick and Princess Augusta.

Atanasov, Georgy (*b* Plovdiv, 18 May 1882; *d* Fasano, 17 Nov. 1931). Bulgarian composer and conductor. Studied privately, in Bucharest, and (1901–3) in Pesaro with Mascagni. He worked as a bandmaster, and conducted the first opera performances in Bulgaria. Known as The Maestro, he is regarded as the founder of Bulgarian opera. In his operas, still highly esteemed in Bulgaria, he sought to confer technical maturity on the emergent local art by absorbing Italian influences and later, less successfully, those of Wagner and Strauss. His most important works include *Borislav* (1911), *Zapustyalata vodenitsa* (The Abandoned Mill, 1923), and *Altsec* (1930); he also composed the first Bulgarian operetta, *Moralisti* (1916), and five children's operettas.

Athanaël. The coenobite monk (bar) who tries to save and then falls in love with Thaïs in Massenet's *Thaïs*.

Atherton, David (*b* Blackpool, 3 Jan. 1944). English conductor. Studied Cambridge and London O Centre. Début Cambridge 1966 (*Ariadne auf Naxos*). London, CG, from 1968 (*La traviata*)—the youngest conductor ever to appear there—Henze's *We Come to the River* (prem., 1976), *Les Huguenots*. Prem. of *Punch and Judy* (Aldeburgh 1968). Toronto 1990 (*Wozzeck*); London, C, 1991 (*Peter Grimes*). Conducts modern works with outstanding precision and control. (R)

Atlantide, L'. Opera in 4 acts by Tomasi; text by F. Didelot, after Pierre Benoit's novel (1920). Prem. Mulhouse 26 Feb. 1954.

Antinea (mimed role), a maenad, rules the land of Atlantis. She lures two officers of the French Foreign Legion, a Lieutenant (ten) and Captain (bs), to her domain, and they fall in love with her. One she kills with a silver hammer, the other dies in the desert pursuing a phantom that is her double.

Atlantov, Vladimir (*b* Leningrad, 19 Feb. 1939). Russian tenor. Studied Leningrad with Bolotin. Début as soloist Leningrad, K, 1963. Student artist, Milan, S, 1963–5. Moscow, B, since 1967. Guest appearances Milan, Vienna, Wiesbaden, New York, etc., as Hermann, Lensky, Don José, and Italian roles. Considered the outstanding tenore robusto of his day. (R)

Attaque du moulin, L' (The Attack on the Mill). Opera in 4 acts by Bruneau; text by Louis Gallet, after the story in Zola's *Soirées de Médan* (1880). Prem. Paris, OC, 23 Nov. 1893.

The miller Merlier's (bar) daughter, Françoise (sop), is betrothed to a young Flemish peasant, Dominique (ten); but their celebrations are interrupted by a recruiting party, causing Françoise's foster-mother, Marcelline (mez), to denounce all war. Though Dominique is not in fact called up, when the mill is attacked he is seized by the Germans and condemned to be shot. When he escapes, the German captain demands Merlier's life in his stead; in order to save Dominique for his daughter, Merlier sacrifices himself.

At the Boar's Head. Opera in 1 act by Holst; text by the composer, after Shakespeare's dramas *Henry IV*, pt 1 and pt 2 (1597–8), with two Shakespeare sonnets. Prem. Manchester, O House, 3 Apr. 1925.

The plot is closely derived from the Falstaff episodes in Shakespeare's Henry plays. Falstaff (bs) arrives at The Boar's Head, where Bardolph (bar) and Pistol (bar) are drinking, after his bungled highway robbery: Poins (bs) and Prince Hal (ten) reveal that they have tricked him. News comes of civil war. Hal and Poins disguise themselves so as to observe Falstaff's pursuit of Doll Tearsheet (sop). A distant march is heard, and Bardolph brings Hal a summons to Westminster. Hal and Poins set off; Pistol quarrels with Doll, and is thrown out. Bardolph announces that a dozen captains are searching for Falstaff;

they set off for the wars together, leaving the women in tears until Bardolph slyly returns to say Falstaff wants to see Doll once more.

Attila. Opera in prologue and 3 acts by Verdi; text by Solera, after Zacharias Werner's drama *Attila, König der Hunnen* (1808). Prem. Venice, F, 17 Mar. 1846.

Italy, AD 454. Attila's army has ransacked the town of Aquileia. Odabella (sop) is among the prisoners; her father was killed by Attila (bs) and she swears to avenge his death. Ezio (bar), a Roman general, arrives and suggests that they divide Italy between them. Attila rejects the offer, calling Ezio a traitor.

Odabella is delighted by the arrival of her lover Foresto (ten), whom she believed dead, but has to convince him that she is loyal to her country. She discloses a plan to murder Attila. He is troubled by dreams and resolves to attack Rome. Foresto and Ezio plan to over-throw Attila, who is given poison; but Oda-bella (determined that he shall die by her hand alone) prevents him from drinking it. The grateful Attila promises to marry Oda-bella and prepares to resume the attack on Rome.

As the wedding celebrations begin, Ezio and Foresto plot to ambush the Huns. Foresto once again accuses Odabella of treason: Attila arrives to find her with his enemies. He realizes he has been betrayed and Odabella stabs him.

Auber, Daniel-François-Esprit (*b* Caen, 29 Jan. 1782; *d* Paris, 12–13 May 1871). French composer. Studied with Ladurner, then with Cherubini, who had been impressed by his *L'erreur d'un moment* (1805). Nevertheless, further success in opera eluded him until through Cherubini he re-established himself, at first with *La bergère châtelaine* (1820) and *Emma* (1821). In 1823 he began his long and fruitful collaboration with *Scribe, and after a brief flirtation with an Italianate style (as in *Leicester* (1823) and *La neige* (1823)), found himself with *Léocadie* (1824). He then gave his career as a master of opéra-comique, in succession to Boieldieu and Isouard, a sure foundation with *Le maçon* (1825). There fol-lowed a long series of highly successful works in which to his appreciation of the wit of Rossini was added his own Gallic lightness of touch. Of the works of this period and in this vein, the most enduring has been *Fra Diavolo* (1830): it epitomizes his lighter style with its mixture of sentimentality and wit,

expressed in graceful melodies deftly accompanied. Among his later most popular and enduring successes in opéra-comique were also *Le cheval de bronze* (1835) and *Le domino noir* (1837).

Auber's career took a new turn with *La muette de Portici* (1828). Commissioned for the Opéra, it was the most significant of the works which inaugurated the era of French *Grand Opera. Its essential ingredients included a substantial group of important leading roles, powerful and functional choruses, increased reliance on the orches-tra, the inclusion of ballet, and not least music written with an awareness of the vivid and imposing scenic effects provided by *Cicéri and *Daguerre. The work was influ-ential on Meyerbeer and Halévy, but also (especially in *Lohengrin*) on Wagner, who wrote an enthusiastic article praising the work's swiftness and urgency of action. Later, in 1830, a performance in Brussels was to spark off the revolt of the Belgians against the Dutch. Other successful works in this vein include *Gustave III* (1833) and *Lestocq* (1834).

After about 1840 Auber's lighter style (Wagner now compared him to a barber who lathers but does not shave) developed into a more lyrical manner, marked with a limited increase in harmonic range, as in *Haydée* (1847) and *Le premier jour de bonheur* (1868). He was also a distinguished director of the Paris Cons., 1842–70. Shy and diminutive of stature, he was characterized by Rossini as 'piccolo musico, ma grande musicista' ('a small musician, but a great maker of music').

Auden, W(ystan) **H**(ugh) (*b* York, 21 Feb. 1907; *d* Vienna, 29 Sept. 1973). English, later US, poet. He wrote librettos for Britten's *Paul Bunyan* (1941) and, with Chester Kallman, Stravinsky's *The Rake's Progress* (1951), Henze's *Elegy for Young Lovers* (1961) and *The Bassarids* (1966), and Nabokov's *Love's Labour's Lost* (1973). Also with Kallman translated *Don Giovanni* and *Die Zauberflöte*.

Audran, Edmond (*b* Lyons, 12 Apr. 1840; *d* Tierceville, 17 Aug. 1901). French composer. Studied Paris with Duprato. Success with an early operetta, *Le grand mogol* (1877) brought an invitation from the Paris, BP, that led to a string of light, tuneful works of which the most popular was *La mascotte* (1880). He never equalled this success despite a considerable development and expansion of his style, especially in *La poupée* (1896).

'Au fond du temple saint'. The duet between Nadir (ten) and Zurga (bar) in Act I of Bizet's *Les pêcheurs de perles*, in which they recall the beautiful Leïla they both once loved.

Aufstieg und Fall der Stadt Mahagonny (Rise and Fall of the City of Mahagonny). Opera in 3 acts by Weill; text by Brecht. Prem. Leipzig 9 Mar. 1930 (prem. as a Songspiel, Baden-Baden, 1927).

Mahagonny is the city of material pleasure. Jenny (sop) and her colleagues move in, followed by Jim Mahoney (ten) and his lumberjack friends on the spend; there develops a love affair between the two, based upon hard cash as well as affection. A hurricane threatens the city, but is miraculously deflected. Act II illustrates Gluttony, Love, Fighting, and Drinking, all carried on to excess and without restraint. Jim cannot pay for his drinks; tried according to Mahagonny's scale of values, he is sentenced to two days for indirect murder, four years for 'education, by means of money', and, for not paying his whisky bill, death.

Auftrittslied (Ger.: 'entry song'). The aria in a Singspiel in which a character introduces himself to the audience, either directly or by addressing another character, e.g. Papageno's 'Der Vogelfänger bin ich ja' in Mozart's *Die Zauberflöte*.

Augér, Arleen (*b* South Gate, CA, 13 Sept. 1939; *d* Leusden, 10 June 1993). US soprano. Studied Los Angeles with Frey, Chicago with Errolle. Début Vienna, S, 1967 (Queen of the Night). Vienna until 1974; New York, CO, 1968–9; Milan, S, from 1975; New York, M, 1978; also Moscow, B; Bayreuth; Salzburg; Munich; Frankfurt; Cologne; Aix; etc. A musical singer with a sweet-toned, flexible voice. Roles incl. Ilia, Servilia, Marzelline, Countess (Mozart), Poppea. (R)

Austin, Frederic (*b* London, 30 Mar. 1872; *d* London, 10 Apr. 1952). English baritone. Studied with Charles Lunn. Début London, CG, 1908 (Gunther, in the English *Ring* under Richter). Principal baritone, Beecham Co. Peachum in his own new version of *The Beggar's Opera*, London, Lyric Hammersmith, 1920. Artistic dir., London, BNOC, 1924. Pupils include Constance Shacklock. (R)

His son **Richard** (1903–88) conducted with the London CR and at SW. (R)

Austin, Sumner (*b* London, 24 Sept. 1888; *d* Oxford, 9 July 1981). English baritone. London, CR, 1919, then sang with O'Mara OC. Old Vic OC in 1920s. London, SW, until 1940. Especially distinguished in Mozart. Produced several operas at SW, including *Falstaff*, *Walküre*, *Don Carlos*, and *The Wreckers*; also *Tannhäuser* and *Wozzeck* at London, CG, in the 1950s.

Austral, Florence (*b* Melbourne, 26 Apr. 1894; *d* Newcastle, NSW, 15 May 1968). Australian soprano. Studied Melbourne Cons. and New York with Sibella. Début London, BNOC, 1922 (Brünnhilde); also Aida and Isolde, and Brünnhilde during international seasons 1924, 1929, and 1933. Guest artist London, SW, 1937–9. A generous and musical singer, who, like Leider, sang Wagner using the principles of bel canto. (R)

Australia. The first operas were in the late 18th cent., especially in Sydney. An early performance was of *Cenerentola* by the Dramatic Co. (in which the only trained singer was Vincent Wallace's sister Wallace Bushelle). Other seasons followed. In 1845 Count Carandini, a political refugee from Italy, founded a company with his wife as prima donna and gave successful performances of *Der Freischütz*, *Fra Diavolo*, and some Italian operas. The first operas written in Australia were *Merry Freaks in Troublous Times* (comp. 1843) and *Don John of Austria* (Sydney 1847) by Isaac *Nathan (1790–1864). The Anna Bishop OC gave seasons in New South Wales 1850–60. Among companies active during these years were the Lyster Grand OC, an American group that gave English-language performances until 1880; local singers were increasingly employed in their seasons. Other companies included the Montague Turner (1881–4) and Martin Simonson: the latter toured 1866 and 1886–7 with works including *Belisario* and *Roberto Devereux*, and with some Italian singers. Other groups followed in the 1890s. The first Wagner performances were under the auspices of George Musgrove. J. C. Williamson staged opera in 1893, and a season of Italian opera by the J. C. Williamson Co. followed in 1901, when Musgrove also toured with more German opera (including parts of *The Ring*); each singer used his own language. Other touring companies included the Quinlan and Gonzales. An early nationalist composer was Alfred *Hill (1870–1960).

In 1911 Nellie Melba, who had long wanted to take a company to her native land, joined Williamson in a tour with singers including John McCormack, Eleonora de Cisneros, and Rosina Buckman in a catholic repertory. The Quinlan OC toured in 1912 with Beecham among its conductors; their success led to a return in 1913 with a repertory including the first Australian *Meistersinger*. An Italian company toured in 1916; in 1921 Williamson formed a company of local artists. In 1924 the Melba–Williamson Co. was back with Toti dal Monte and Dino Borgioli; and their last season was in 1928. Melba helped to organize a further season in 1928 with a similar company strengthened by Arangi-Lombardi, Merli, and John Brownlee. New standards of presentation were set in 1932 by the Imperial Grand OC, including Lina Pagliughi and Primo Montanari.

After the Second World War, further seasons were given by the Nevin Trust. Then in 1952 the two leading groups, the Nat. Theatre OC of Melbourne and the New South Wales Nat. O of Sydney, pooled their resources as a first step towards a national opera; each received a grant of £A5,000. Singers included Elizabeth Fretwell, Marie Collier, and Ronald Dowd. When rivalries developed, each company continued separately until the formation of the Elizabethan Trust in 1954. In 1955 Warwick Braithwaite became director of the Sydney company, resigning in mid-season because of managerial interference. With the arrival of Hugh Hunt, director of the Elizabethan Trust, a new company was formed, the Australian O. Also in 1955, the NSW State Government launched a design competition for a new Sydney opera-house, won by Jørn Utzon. In July 1956 the Trust launched its first season at Adelaide with a Mozart season, followed by a tour until February 1957. In December 1957 Karl Rankl became music director, launching his first season in July

1958, but resigned in 1961. In 1965 Joan Sutherland toured with her own Sutherland–Williamson company. The Trust was renamed the Australian OC in 1969, with Carlo Felice Cillario as music director. He was succeeded by Edward Downes 1972–6, then Richard Bonynge. The early 1970s saw a rapid expansion in operatic activity all over the country. The new opera-house in Sydney, the first in the country specially built for opera, opened in 1973 with Prokofiev's *War and Peace*.

Composers who have worked to develop an Australian style in opera include Richard Meale (b 1932) with *Voss* (1985) and *Mer de Glace* (1991). Among many of foreign origin active in the country have been the Germans Felix Werder (b 1922) with *The Affair* (1974) and George Dreyfus (b 1928), and Larry Sitsky (b 1934 of Russian parents) with *Lenz* (1974), *Fiery Tales* (1976), and *The Golem* (1993). A younger generation includes Anne Boyd (b 1946) with *The Little Mermaid* (1985).

See also ADELAIDE, MELBOURNE, SYDNEY.

Austria. The history of Austrian opera is not readily separable from that of Germany; for though Austria, or Austria-Hungary, was a political entity long before Germany, the two traditions merge, overlap, and frequently coincide. Nevertheless, certain traditions and composers claim a more specifically Austrian identity. Viennese operetta as a distinctive genre finds expression in the work of *Suppé, *Millöcker, *Heuberger, but especially the Johann *Strauss family, later Oscar Straus, *Lehár, and Fall. *Schoenberg and *Berg (with Anton Webern) constitute the so-called Second Viennese School, more palpably Viennese than their predecessors Mozart, Haydn, and Beethoven.

See also SALZBURG, VIENNA. See further GERMANY.

'Avant de quitter ces lieux'. Valentin's (bar) aria in Act II of Gounod's *Faust*, calling upon God to protect his sister Marguerite as he prepares to leave for the wars.

B

Baba the Turk. A bearded lady from a circus (mez) in Stravinsky's *The Rake's Progress*.

Baccaloni, Salvatore (*b* Rome, 14 Apr. 1900; *d* New York, 31 Dec. 1969). Italian bass. Treble, Sistine Chapel. Studied Rome with Kaschmann. Début Rome, Ad., 1922 (Dr Bartolo, *Barbiere*). Milan, S, 1926, where after three seasons in normal bass repertory, he specialized in buffo roles. London, CG, 1928–9. Gly. 1936–9, Leporello, Dr Bartolo, Osmin, Alfonso, and Pasquale (his greatest role). US début, Chicago 1930; New York, M, 1940–62. Appeared in every major opera-house, and was considered by many the greatest buffo since Lablache. After his retirement from opera, appeared in comedy films. (R)

Bach, Johann Christian (*b* Leipzig, 5 Sept. 1735; *d* London, 1 Jan. 1782). German composer. Youngest son of Johann Sebastian and Anna Magdalena Bach. After study with his brother Carl Philipp Emmanuel, in 1754 he travelled to Italy, producing his first opera, *Artaserse*, in 1760. Further successes led to an invitation to come to London, where he became composer at the H. *Orione*, performed in Feb. 1763 before George III, was enthusiastically received, as was *Zanaida* (1763), leading to an appointment as music master to the Queen: he was now one of the most active figures in London's musical life. Bach's subsequent stage works had mixed fortunes. However, an invitation to compose for the Mannheim court resulted in his two most consummately fashioned works, *Temistocle* (1772) and *Lucio Silla* (1775). His last London opera, *La clemenza di Scipione* (1778), also fared well, though following the rise in popularity of opera buffa, his star began to wane and he died relatively forgotten.

His cosmopolitan education, with its combination of German and Italian influences, perhaps explains why Bach developed such a distinctive style in an era of great uniformity. One of his most important influences was on Mozart, whom he met in both London and Paris and with whose early works he shares several obvious points of stylistic similarity.

His brother **Johann Christoph** (1732–95) also wrote some successful dramatic works to texts by Herder and others. Their brother **Wilhelm Friedemann** (1710–84) is the subject of an opera by Graener (1931). Their father **Johann Sebastian** (1685–1750) is the subject of an opera by Emil Ábrányi (1947).

Bacquier, Gabriel (*b* Béziers, 17 May 1924). French baritone. Studied Paris. Début Nice 1950 (Landowski's *Le fou*, with José Beckmans's Compagnie Lyrique Française). Brussels, M, 1953–6; Paris, OC, 1956, O since 1958. Gly. 1962 as Almaviva (Mozart); London, CG, 1964 (Ford, Malatesta, Scarpia, etc.). New York, M, 1964. Aix Fest. as Don Giovanni, Falstaff (Verdi). An elegant and stylish artist. (R)

Bahr-Mildenburg, Anna (*b* Vienna, 29 Nov. 1872; *d* Vienna, 27 Jan. 1947). Austrian soprano. Studied Vienna with Papier, Hamburg with Pollini. Début Hamburg 1895 (Brünnhilde), cond. Mahler, whose protégée and mistress she became. Endowed with a magnificent voice and physique, she was musical, impassioned, and a superb actress. Soon became leading Wagner soprano. Bayreuth 1897 (Kundry); also 1909–14. London, CG, 1906 (Isolde, Elisabeth), and first London Klytemnästra 1910. Vienna 1898–1916. Darmstadt 1915–16 as actress. Vienna 1919–20. After retirement taught, but sang final Klytemnästra, Augsburg 1930. (R)

Bailey, Norman (*b* Birmingham, 23 Mar. 1933). English baritone. Studied Vienna with Vogel, Patzak, and Witt. Début Vienna 1959 (Tobias Mill, *Cambiale di matrimonio*). Linz 1960–3; Wuppertal 1963–4; Düsseldorf 1964–7. London, SW, from 1967 (début Manchester as Mozart's Almaviva), then London as Sachs in the memorable prod. of *Die Meistersinger* under Goodall 1968. London, C (Wotan, Gunther, Pizarro, Kutuzov, Gremin). Has appeared in the Wagner repertory at London, CG, and Bayreuth. Milan, S, 1967; New York, M, 1976. Sang Oroveso (*Norma*) for O North, 1993. His Sachs, wise, human and benevolent, and his Wotan, both magisterial and moving, displayed an inherent musicality and feeling for the text. (R)

Baker, (Dame) **Janet** (*b* Hatfield, 21 Aug. 1933). English mezzo-soprano. Studied London with Helene Isepp. Début OUOC

1956 (Róza, *The Secret*). 1959 Eduige in *Rod-elinda* with Handel OC, first of a number of Handel roles. Sang regularly with EOG 1961–76, Dido, Lucretia, Nancy, Kate (*Owen Wingrave*). Dorabella, Octavian, the Composer, and Dido (Berlioz) for Scottish O. From 1966 at London, CG, incl. Dido, Cressida, Idamante; Gly. 1965–82, incl. Penelope (*Ulisse*), Diana (*Calisto*), Orfeo (Gluck). Her repertory included Vitellia, Giulio Cesare, Maria Stuarda, and Charlotte. Her highly individual and beautiful voice, warmth, commitment, and wide dramatic range made her one of the outstanding artists of the day. Retired from opera 1982 and from all public performance 1989. (R)

Balanchivadze, Meliton (*b* Banodzha, 24 Dec. 1862; *d* Kutaisi, 21 Nov. 1937). Georgian composer and singer. Studied privately, and from 1880 sang in the chorus at the Tbilisi O, then studying St Petersburg with Rimsky-Korsakov. Part of his opera *Tamar tsbiery* (Tamara: The False Tamar, 1897) was given in concert there; though not produced till Tbilisi, 1926, this is regarded as a founding work of Georgian opera. His elder son Georg became a distinguished choreographer as George Balanchine; his younger son **Andrey Balanchivadze** (*b* St Petersburg, 1 June 1906) is a composer and conductor who studied in Kutaisi with Ippolitov-Ivanov and has been very active in his country's musical life. His operas include *Mziya* (1950).

Balfe, Michael (*b* Dublin, 15 May 1808; *d* Rowney Abbey, 20 Oct. 1870). Irish composer, singer, and violinist. Studied Wexford, and London with Charles Horn. Début as violinist in London, 1823, as baritone in Norwich in an adaptation of *Der Freischütz* (Caspar). After further study in Italy with Galli, went to Paris and with Rossini's encouragement sang at the I (Figaro in *Barbiere*). He was principal baritone in Palermo, 1829–30, producing his first opera there. Back in London in 1835, he began his career as a composer of English operas with the very successful *The Siege of Rochelle* at DL, following it with the almost equally successful *The Maid of Artois* (1836) for Malibran. He also sang Papageno in the first performance in English of *The Magic Flute*. Back in Paris by 1841, having failed in an attempt to establish English opera at the *Lyceum (Këolanthé, 1841), he continued his career there, returning to England for the greatest success of his 29 operas, *The Bohemian

Girl* (1843). From 1857 to 1863 he was closely associated with the Pyne-Harrison project for an English national opera: his own chief success was *The Rose of Castille* (1857). He continued to travel, making two successful visits to Russia, before turning gentleman farmer and retiring to an estate in Hertfordshire. His melodies are often graceful and charming, and his gift for a memorable tune led him to place much importance on ballads in his operas, but he was little interested in characterization and had less flair for dramatic development. However, he did write, in *Catherine Grey* (1837), one of the first English Romantic operas without spoken dialogue.

ballabile (It.: 'suitable for dancing'). A term used to describe sung dances in 19th-cent. Italian opera. Examples include the song and dance of the witches in Act III of Verdi's *Macbeth* and the opening chorus to Act II of *Ernani*.

ballad opera. A popular form of English entertainment flourishing in the mid-18th cent., in which spoken dialogue alternated with musical numbers, usually fitting new words to old ballads, folk tunes, or (particularly in its later stages) melodies by different composers. The first and most famous example was Gay/Pepusch *The *Beggar's Opera* (1728), characteristic in its satire of contemporary politicians and of the excesses of Italian opera and its prima donnas.

ballet de cour (Fr.: 'court ballet'). A popular French court entertainment of the 16th and 17th cent., comprising a sumptuous mélange of ballet, music, and drama whose development paralleled that of the English *masque. The earliest work with surviving music is *Circé, ou le balet comique de la royne* (1581). Later, in the mid-17th cent., at the hands of Isaac de Benserade, the genre underwent a significant revival and became an important influence on nascent French opera.

Balling, Michael (*b* Heidingsfeld, 28 Aug. 1866; *d* Darmstadt, 1 Sept. 1925). German conductor. Studied Würzburg. Violist in Mainz, Schwerin, then Bayreuth, where he was assistant cond. 1896; cond. *Parsifal*, *Tristan*, and *The Ring*, 1904–25, and was one of Siegfried Wagner's right-hand men. Cond. *The Ring* in English for the Denhof OC, Edinburgh 1910, and *Orfeo* with Brema in London.

Founded a school of music in Nelson, New Zealand, 1892. Succeeded Richter as cond. of Hallé, 1912. From 1919 music dir. in Darmstadt. From 1912 editor of Breitkopf und Härtel Wagner Edition.

Ballo in maschera, Un (A Masked Ball). Opera in 3 acts by Verdi; text by Somma, based on Scribe's text for Auber's *Gustave III, ou Le bal masqué*, in turn based on an historical event. Prem. Rome, Ap., 17 Feb. 1859.

Stockholm, 1789. King Gustavus III (ten) is warned of a plot against his life by his faithful secretary Captain Anckarstroem (bar), with whose wife, Amelia (sop) he is secretly in love. When the renowned fortune-teller Mlle Arvidson (con) is denounced for sorcery, the King decides to visit her in disguise, to test her powers for himself.

Among those who consult her is Amelia. She has come for advice on how to overcome her illicit passion and is told to gather a herb at midnight at the foot of the public gallows. In front of his courtiers, the King then asks Mlle Arvidson to tell his fortune: she warns that he is shortly to die, at the hand of the first person to shake his hand. Since this turns out to be Anckarstroem, the King pours scorn on her prophecies.

As Amelia is collecting her herbs, she is surprised by the King and they confess their love. Anckarstroem arrives to warn of imminent ambush, but though the King makes his escape, he and Amelia are captured. Only then does Anckarstroem discover that the King's veiled companion is his wife and, mockingly taunted by the conspirators, he is filled with anger.

Convinced of Amelia's adultery, Anckarstroem resolves to kill her, but eventually relents until she has seen her son for one last time. He now turns his bitterness against the King and, when the conspirators reappear, Amelia is forced to draw lots to decide who shall kill him: Anckarstroem's name emerges.

At a masked ball, the remorseful King announces to Amelia his intention of sending her and Anckarstroem on a foreign mission. But it is too late: Anckarstroem steps between them and shoots him. As he dies, the King pardons his enemies.

When Verdi first submitted his libretto to the San Carlo Theatre, Naples, the censor protested that the assassination of a king could not be shown on the stage, and demanded that Verdi adapt his music to a new libretto. Verdi refused, and left Naples. A Rome impresario offered to produce an altered version of the work; and so the locale was changed from 18th-cent. Stockholm to 17th-cent. Boston. Another version used at the Paris prem. (1861) set the story in Naples. The names of the leading characters are thus (in the order of setting, Stockholm, Boston, Naples): Gustavus III, Riccardo (Count of Warwick), Riccardo (Duke of Olivares); Anckarstroem, Renato, Renato; Count Ribbing, Samuele, Armando; Count Horn, Tomaso, Angri; Mlle Arvidson, Ulrica, Ulrica. The 'Stockholm' version has now established itself over the formerly popular 'Boston' version.

Baltsa, Agnes (*b* Levkas, 19 Nov. 1944). Greek mezzo-soprano. Studied Athens, Munich, and Frankfurt. Début Frankfurt 1968 (Cherubino). Frankfurt 1968–72; Berlin, D, from 1972. London, CG, from 1976 (Dorabella, Carmen, Octavian, etc.). Houston 1971 (Carmen). Vienna since 1976, Salzburg since 1977, New York, M, from 1979. Roles include Orfeo (Gluck), Sesto, Dalila, Azucena, Dido (Berlioz), Herodias, the Composer, Rosina, Eboli. (R)

Bampton, Rose (*b* Cleveland, OH, 28 Nov. 1908). US soprano, orig. contralto. Studied Philadelphia with Connell and Queena Mario. Début Chautauqua 1928 (Siebel). New York, M, 1932–50, début as Laura (*Gioconda*). Soprano début there 1937 (Leonora, *Il trovatore*). Acclaimed as Donna Anna and Alceste, and in the 1940s in several Wagner roles, including Kundry and Sieglinde. London, CG, 1937 (Amneris). A fine musician, with a rounded, velvety voice. (R)

Bánk bán. Opera in 3 acts by Erkel; text by Béni Egressy, after József Katona's tragedy (1815). Prem. Budapest 9 Mar. 1861.

The fortress of Visegrád in Hungary, 1213. Otto (ten), brother of Queen Gertrud (mez), pays court to Melinda (sop), the wife of Bánk bán, Palatine of Hungary. When he learns of this, Bánk bán (ten) joins the cause of the rebelling natives. Having gone to seek an explanation from the Queen, Bánk bán kills her in self-defence after she threatens him with a dagger. On the King's return from the Crusades, the rebellion is quashed; Bánk bán confesses his crime, and the King challenges him to a duel. However, at that moment Tiborc (bar), Bánk bán's friend, enters bearing the body of Melinda, who drowned during a rescue attempt. Distraught, Bánk bán stabs himself.

Banti, Brigida Giorgi. See GIORGI-BANTI, BRIGIDA.

Bantock, (Sir) **Granville** (*b* London, 7 Aug. 1868; *d* London, 16 Oct. 1946). English composer. His only mature opera is *The Seal-Woman* (1924), which owes much to Wagnerian example. It also makes use of some genuine Hebridean tunes collected by Marjorie Kennedy-Fraser, who took part in the first performance as an old crone spinning in the corner.

Baranović, Krešimir (*b* Šibenik, 25 July 1894; *d* Belgrade, 17 Sept. 1975). Croatian conductor and composer. Studied Zagreb with Kaiser, Vienna 1912–14. Music dir. at the Operas of Zagreb 1915–25, Belgrade 1927–9, Bratislava 1945–6. At Zagreb introduced wide new repertory, especially of Russian and Yugoslav opera, and gave first local *Ring*. Prof. Belgrade Cons. 1946. His operas are *Striženo-košeno* (Shaven and Shorn, 1932), praised for its witty situations and skilful use of folk music, and another comedy, *Nevjesta od Cetingrada* (The Bride of Cetingrad, comp. 1942, prem. 1951). (R)

Barbaia, Domenico (*b* Milan, ?1778; *d* Posillipo, 19 Oct. 1841). Italian impresario. Began his career as a waiter, inventing *barbaiata*, coffee or chocolate with a head of whipped cream; then ran the gambling tables at Milan, S, 1806. Director Naples, C and N, and other royal opera-houses (1809–40, with interruptions). His productions included Spontini's *La vestale*, with his mistress Isabella *Colbran. Brought Rossini to Naples 1815 on a six-year contract to compose two operas a year. Though Colbran soon left him for Rossini, relations remained friendly. When the C burnt down in Feb. 1816, he promptly rebuilt it and reopened Jan. 1817. Also obtained the concession of the Vienna, K and W (1821–8). Here he organized brilliant seasons, introducing to Vienna Rossini and other Italian composers including Bellini and Mercadante, and commissioning *Euryanthe* from Weber. Also controlled the Scala and Cannobbiana in Milan (1826–32). A man of sharp instincts and artistic flair, he was quick to spot the talents of Rossini, Bellini, Donizetti, Mercadante, Pacini, and others, and to find effective outlets for their talents; and his practical encouragement served to set them and other composers of the day on their careers. By introducing *La vestale* and Gluck's *Iphigénie en Aulide* to Naples, he began the Italian tradition of opera seria with orchestral recitative, as in Mayr's *Medea in Corinto* (1813) and Rossini's *Elisabetta, regina d'Inghilterra* (1815). He appears as the impresario Bolbaya in Auber's *La sirène* (1844).

Barbarina. The gardener Antonio's daughter (sop) in Mozart's *Le nozze di Figaro*.

Barber, Samuel (*b* West Chester, PA, 9 Mar. 1910; *d* New York, 23 Jan. 1981). US composer. The success of his first mature opera, *Vanessa* (1958), couched in a skilful late-Romantic style, was a prime factor in him being chosen to write the new opera by a US composer that was felt essential for the opening of the new New York, M, in 1966. However, the similar but less effectively handled idiom of *Antony and Cleopatra* (1966) proved unsuitable for the inauguration of a major new house, and even in its own terms was a failure. It was revived in 1974 and has had some success in more recent revivals, notably at Chicago. (R)

Barbier, Jules (*b* Paris, 8 Mar. 1825; *d* Paris, 16 Jan. 1901). French librettist. Collaborated with Michel *Carré on numerous librettos, providing composers with texts which derived from many authors, including Goethe, Dante, and Shakespeare, but which formed the subjects into a conventionalized, often sentimentalized, version of the original that was highly effective in the terms of most contemporary French opera. Their librettos include those for Gounod's *Faust*, *Polyeucte*, *Philémon et Baucis*, and *Roméo et Juliette*; Meyerbeer's *Dinorah*; Thomas's *Mignon*, *Françoise de Rimini*, and *Hamlet*; and Offenbach's *Les contes d'Hoffmann*. Their lighter side is shown in their text for Massé's *Les noces de Jeannette*.

Barbiere di Siviglia, Il (orig. *Almaviva, ossia L'inutile precauzione*) (The Barber of Seville; orig. Almaviva, or The Useless Precaution). Opera in 2 acts by Rossini; text by Sterbini, after *Beaumarchais's comedy (1775). Prem. Rome, Arg., 20 Feb. 1816, cond. Rossini.

In a square in Seville, Count Almaviva (ten), masquerading as Lindoro, a poor student, woos Rosina (mez), the ward of old Doctor Bartolo (bs). The barber and general factotum, Figaro (bar), promises to help Almaviva in his courtship. Rosina, whom Bartolo himself intends to marry, has meanwhile taken notice of her suitor and drops him a note from her balcony asking his name.

When Bartolo reveals his mistrust of Count Almaviva to the singing-teacher Don Basilio (bs), he is advised that the spreading of false rumour would be the best way to cause his demise. Unnoticed by them, Figaro assists in Almaviva's amorous plans by acting as a go-between with Rosina.

Pretending to be a drunken soldier (with a forged billeting order), Almaviva gains access to Bartolo's house and to Rosina. Basilio and Bartolo are rightly suspicious of the 'soldier' and try, unsuccessfully, to have him removed. When the police eventually arrive there is uproar and Almaviva is almost arrested until he manages to exert some authority.

To effect entry a second time, Almaviva disguises himself as the music teacher, Don Alonso, standing in for Basilio, who he says is ill. Having gained Bartolo's trust, 'Don Alonso' gives Rosina her music lesson; while shaving Bartolo, Figaro manages to steal a key which will enable the lovers to escape from the house at night.

When Basilio arrives, Almaviva bribes him to support his story, but in vain. Bartolo, realizing some scheme is afoot, sends Almaviva and Figaro on their way and, anxious to hasten his marriage to Rosina, despatches Basilio to fetch a notary. He then manages to convince her that Lindoro does not really love her. Upset, she reveals her plans to elope with the student and now agrees to marry Bartolo.

However, when Lindoro returns and reveals his true identity to Rosina, the couple are reconciled. They reaffirm their love but are unable to escape because the ladder on to the balcony has been removed. When Basilio arrives with the notary he is further bribed by Figaro to witness the marriage of Rosina and Almaviva and by the time Bartolo reappears, the ceremony is over. After initial anger, he accepts the marriage, not least since the Count makes good the dowry he would otherwise have received from Rosina.

The first performance in Rome was one of the greatest fiascos in the history of opera. As Paisiello's opera (see below) enjoyed great popularity, the opera was originally entitled *Almaviva, ossia L'inutile precauzione*; the title *Il barbiere di Siviglia* was first used at Bologna in 1816. The overture had already been used by Rossini for *Aurelio in Palmira* (1813) and *Elisabetta, regina d'Inghilterra* (1815).

Barbiere di Siviglia, ossia La precauzione inutile, Il. Opera in 4 acts by Paisiello; text by G. Petrosellini, after Beaumarchais's comedy (1775). Prem. St Petersburg 26 Sept. 1782.

Barbieri, Fedora (*b* Trieste, 4 June 1920). Italian mezzo-soprano. Studied Trieste with Toffolo and Giulia Tess. Début Florence 1940 (Fidalma, *Il matrimonio segreto*). After appearances at all leading Italian opera-houses, sang at Buenos Aires, C, 1947. London, CG, 1950, with Milan, S Co., as Quickly; 1957–8 Azucena, Amneris, Eboli. New York, M, 1950–4, 1956–7, 1967–8, making début on opening night of Bing's régime as Eboli. Among over 100 roles, much admired as Orfeo and Carmen. (R)

Barbieri-Nini, Marianna (*b* Florence, 18 Feb. 1818; *d* Florence, 27 Nov. 1887). Italian soprano. Teachers included L. Barbieri, Pasta, and Vaccai. After a disastrous Milan, S, début in *Belisario* (1840), and several other unfortunate appearances in which her ugliness distracted attention from her vocal gifts, she finally made a successful appearance at Florence, 1840–1, as Lucrezia Borgia–wearing a mask. One of the finest dramatic sopranos of her day. Created the leading roles in Verdi's *I due Foscari*, *Il corsaro*, and *Macbeth*. Retired 1856. Married the pianist L. Hackensöllner, who published her memoirs, *Le memorie di una cantatrice*.

Barbier von Bagdad, Der (The Barber of Baghdad). Opera in 2 acts by Cornelius; text by the composer, after *The Tale of the Tailor*, from the *1,001 Nights*. Prem. Weimar 15 Dec. 1858, cond. Liszt.

The plot turns on the efforts of Nureddin (ten), abetted by the barber Abul Hassan Ali Ebn Bekar (bar), to contrive a meeting with Margiana (sop), the Caliph's daughter. Despite Nureddin's imprisonment and near-suffocation in a chest, all is eventually resolved and the blessing of the Caliph is obtained.

The work was initially a failure owing to local intrigues against Liszt, whose departure from Weimar this occasioned; after Mottl's revision and revival (Karlsruhe 1884) it became more popular.

Barbirolli, (Sir)**John** (*b* London, 2 Dec. 1899; *d* London, 29 July 1970). English conductor of Italian parentage. Studied London, TCM and RAM. Began career as cellist. Formed

string orch. 1924; cond. for London, BNOC
1926–8. London: CG, 1928–33, 1951–4; SW,
1934; CG, 1937 (*Tosca* and *Turandot*). Then
appointed cond. of New York Philharmonic-
Symphony Orch. Vienna, S, 1946–7. Cond.
new prod. of *Orfeo* with Ferrier 1953, *Tristan*
with Sylvia Fisher's first Isolde. Rome 1969,
Aida. Though the centre of his career was as
a concert conductor, notably with the Hallé
Orchestra from 1943, he had a deep understanding of the Italian operatic tradition and
a sensitive feeling for the voice. (R)

barcarolle. The French, in international
use, for the Italian *barcaruola* or *barcarola*, a
boat-song, especially of the Venetian gondoliers. The rhythm, ostensibly imitating the
motion of a gondola or other small boat, is a
gentle 6/8 with alternating strong and weak
beats. It has been used in opera by Hérold in
Zampa, Auber in *Fra Diavolo* and *La muette de
Portici*, Donizetti in *Marino Faliero*, Verdi in *Un
ballo in maschera*, and, most famously, Offenbach in *Les contes d'Hoffmann*.

Barcelona. City in Cataluña (Catalunya),
Spain. (Names in Catalan are given in
brackets.) Opera was first given at the T de la
Santa Cruz (Creu), opened in 1708 with the
prem. of Caldara's *Il più bel nome*. The first
opera by a Catalan composer was *Antigona*
(1760) by José Durán (?–?after 1791). In 1838
the rival T Montesión (T Mont-Sion) opened,
and the Santa Cruz changed its name to the
T Principal. In 1834 opera was given at the T
Nuevo (T Nou). The Gran T Liceo (Gran T del
Liceu) (cap. 3,500) opened in 1847. Rivalry
between the Principal and the Liceu tended
to be between conservative and progressive.
The Liceu burnt down in 1861: 1,000 shares
were issued to raise funds to rebuild, and the
shareholders' descendants owned the
theatre with the right to individual seat
occupation. The rebuilt house (cap. 2,700)
opened on 20 Apr. 1862; by its charter it had
to give at least one Spanish opera a year. The
first opera in Catalan, *A la voreta del mar* (On
the Seashore, 1881) by Juan Goula (1843–
1917), was premiered there. The theatre
closed with the Civil War in 1939 and did
not reopen until 1942. Financial and other
problems in the late 1970s led to reor-
ganization and improvement. Seasons were
given from Nov. until Mar., and included
visits from French, German, Italian, and even
Russian companies. Singers who were born
and began their careers here include Victoria

de los Angeles, Montserrat Caballé, José Carreras, and Giacomo Aragall. The Liceu burnt
down again 31 Jan. 1994. Summer performances in the T Grec have included a
Catalan *El mikado* (Sullivan) in 1986. Opera is
also given in the nearby town of Sabadell at
the T de la Faràndula.

Barenboim, Daniel (*b* Buenos Aires, 15 Nov.
1942). Argentinian, later Israeli, conductor
and pianist. Studied conducting Salzburg
and Rome. Initially a successful pianist
(début Buenos Aires, aged 7); conducting
début Israel 1962. Edinburgh 1973 (*Don
Giovanni*); Bayreuth 1981 (*Tristan*), 1988 (*Ring*);
Paris 1986. Appointed music dir. new O Bastille 1987; dismissed amid much publicity
over the size of his salary 1989, before the
opera-house opened. Berlin, D, 1992 (*Parsifal*);
music dir. from 1993. Has developed a spacious conducting style in emulation of his
early mentor, Furtwängler. Repertory incl.
Figaro, Così. (R)

Barham, Edmund (*b* Beckenham, 22 Mar.
1950). English tenor. Studied London and
made his earliest appearances in Germany
(Wuppertal and Munich). London, C, from
1985 (Jeník, Cavaradossi, Alfredo, Vakula
(Rimsky-Korsakov's *Christmas Eve*)). Also
admired for his strong portrayals of Enzo
Grimaldi (O North), Don José (Bregenz
Festival) and Manrico (Victoria State O). (R)

baritone (Gr., *barytonos*: 'heavy-tone'). The
middle category of the natural male voice.
Several subdivisions exist within opera-
houses: the commonest in general use
(though seldom by composers in scores) are
given below, with examples of roles. These
divisions often overlap, and do not correspond from country to country. In general,
distinction is more by character than by tessitura, especially in France: thus the
examples of the roles give a more useful indication of the different voices' quality than
any attempted technical definition.

French: bariton (Escamillo); bariton-
Martin (Pelléas). In early music (Lully to
Rameau), basse-taille.

German: Spielbariton (Don Giovanni); Heldenbariton (Orestes in *Iphigénie en Tauride*);
hoher Bariton (Hans Heiling); Kav-
alierbariton (the Count in *Capriccio*). There is
also the Bass-Bariton (Wotan, Sachs).

The Italian baritono (Dandini) is not generally subdivided, though professionals may

speak of baritono brillante and baritono cantante.

Barlow, Stephen (*b* Seven Kings, 30 June 1954). English conductor. Studied London, GSMD, and cond. Gly. Touring O and Fest. 1979–85: *Arabella*, *Così fan tutte*, *Rosenkavalier*, Knussen double bill. Opera 80 from inception; music dir. 1987. Scottish O, 1983. London, C (*Entführung*, *Carmen*); CG 1989 (*Turandot*). S Francisco 1990 (*Capriccio*). Australian début 1991 (*Zauberflöte*) at Melbourne.

Barnaba. The Inquisition spy (bar) in Ponchielli's *La Gioconda*.

Barnett, John (*b* Bedford, 1 or 15 July 1802; *d* Cheltenham, 16 Apr. 1890). English composer and singer of Prussian and Hungarian extraction (his father, Joseph Beer, was possibly a cousin of Meyerbeer). He appeared as a treble at the London Lyceum, 1813–18. He then studied with William Horsley and Charles Horn. From 1826 he wrote incidental music for farces and other pieces. He became music dir. of the Olympic T in 1832, but when Samuel Arnold reopened the Lyceum as the English OH in 1834, he began to write operas for it. His 'Romantic Grand Opera' *The Mountain Sylph* (1834) replaced dialogue with recitative, and is continuously composed in freer forms than were known in England at the time. It ran for 100 nights, and long remained popular. Influenced by Weber, especially by *Der Freischütz* and *Oberon*, it is in turn the immediate object of the satire of Sullivan's *Iolanthe*. Having quarrelled with Arnold, Barnett transferred to DL for *Fair Rosamond* (1837) and *Farinelli* (1839), which returned to ballad opera in style. After abortive attempts to form a permanent English OH at St James's T (1838) and the Prince's T (1840), he moved to Cheltenham as a singing-teacher, and wrote no more operas. His daughters **Rosamund** and **Clara** became singers; of his brothers, **Joseph** was a singing-teacher and father of J. F. Barnett and **Zarah** wrote texts for some of his operas.

Barraud, Henry (*b* Bordeaux, 23 Apr. 1900). French composer. Studied Paris, including with Dukas, but was expelled from the Conservatoire for avant-garde work. A scrupulous attention to novel ideas, coupled with a religious attitude, shows in his operas, which have won admiration in France: they include *La farce de maître Pathelin* (1948), *Numance* (1955), and *Tête d'or* (1985). He was

from 1948 to 1965 an innovatory head of music in Radiodiffusion Française.

Barry, Gerald (*b* Clarecastle, 28 Apr. 1952). Irish composer. Studied in Cork; later Cologne with Stockhausen and Vienna with Cerha. His shorter dramatic works, including *Unkrautgarten* (1980) own much to music theatre, while his two full-length operas draw consciously from earlier traditions. *The Intelligence Park* (1990) and *The Triumph of Beauty and Deceit* (1993) make explicit reference to 18th-cent. style and gesture; parts of the former have appeared as independent pieces in the concert-hall.

Barsova, Valeriya (*b* Astrakhan, 13 June 1892; *d* Sochi, 13 Dec. 1967). Russian soprano. Studied Moscow with Mazetti. Début Moscow, Z, 1917. Sang in Petrograd, then at Moscow, B, 1920–48, also at Stanislavsky O Studio and Nemirovich-Danchenko Moscow Arts T Studio, 1920–4. Her most famous roles included Lyudmila, Queen of Shemakha, Snow Maiden, Gilda, Violetta, Butterfly, Lakmé, Manon. After 1929 toured widely in the West. Had a light, expressive voice and a brilliant coloratura technique. In 1939 initiated operatic performances under professional guidance for workers in collectives and on the Volga-Don Canal. (R)

Barstow, Josephine (*b* Sheffield, 27 Sept. 1940). English soprano. Studied London with Eva Turner and Andrew Field. Joined O for All 1964: début as Mimì. London, SW, 1967–8 (Cherubino, Gluck's Euridice); WNO from 1968. London, CG, from 1969, creating Denise in *The Knot Garden* and Gayle in *The Ice Break*. SW, later ENO, from 1972: Natasha in first English *War and Peace*, Jeanne in *The Devils of Loudun*, and Autonoe in *The Bassarids*; also acclaimed as Emilia Marty, Octavian, Salome, Violetta, Lady Macbeth of Mtsensk, and Gloriana (O North and London, CG, 1993). Aix-en-Provence, Geneva, Berlin, Salzburg, and Moscow. An outstanding singing actress with a highly individual voice. (R)

Bartered Bride, The (Cz.: *Prodaná nevěsta*; lit. 'The Sold Bride'). Opera in 3 acts by Smetana; text by Sabina. Prem. Prague, P, 30 May 1866, cond. Smetana.

A Bohemian village, 19th cent. Mařenka (sop) loves Jeník (ten), but her parents have decided she must marry a man she has never seen, the son of Tobias Micha, as arranged by the marriage broker Kecal (bs). This unknown proves to be Vašek (ten), a stuttering simpleton whom Mařenka persuades to have nothing to do with her. Meanwhile Jeník eventually succumbs to Kecal's attempts to buy him off, though he insists that Mařenka only be allowed to marry Micha's eldest son. When a travelling circus arrives, Vašek falls for the dancer Esmeralda, but when Jeník appears, the bitter Mařenka decides she will after all marry Vašek—until it is revealed that Jeník has outwitted Kecal and the others, since he is himself Micha's son by a previous marriage and so can both marry Mařenka and keep the money.

Smetana made five versions of the opera: No. 1 (virtually operetta): 2 acts, overture and 20 numbers, 2 perfs.; No. 2: 2 acts, omitting a duet and adding a ballet, 27 Oct. 1866, 13 perfs.; No. 3: 2 acts, alterations incl. new Beer Chorus and Polka, 29 Jan. 1869, 4 perfs.; No. 4: 3 acts, alterations incl. new Furiant and Skočna, 1 Jan. 1869, 9 perfs.; No. 5: 3 acts, with recitatives in place of spoken dialogue and minor alterations, 25 Sept. 1870. After initial failure, this became Smetana's most popular opera.

Bartók, Béla (*b* Nagyszentmiklós, 25 Mar. 1881; *d* New York, 26 Sept. 1945). Hungarian composer. His large output includes only one opera, *Duke Bluebeard's Castle* (1918). Influenced on the one hand by Debussy (*Pelléas*) together with Poe and the French Romantics, on the other by Schoenberg and Freud, the opera is an original and powerful piece of music drama, adapting the old Bluebeard legend as a Symbolist handling of the theme of man's essential loneliness and woman's fatal inability to penetrate it.

Bartoletti, Bruno (*b* Sesto Fiorentino, 10 June 1926). Italian conductor. Début Florence 1953 (*Rigoletto*). Music dir., Rome O, 1965–73. Cond. prem. of Ginastera's *Don Rodrigo*, Buenos Aires, 1964. Principal cond. Chicago, Lyric T, from 1965 (first *Gambler* in US, 1991). Artistic dir., Maggio Musicale, 1986–91. (R)

Bartoli, Cecilia (*b* Rome, 4 June 1966). Italian mezzo-soprano. Sang the Shepherd in *Tosca*, Rome, aged 9, and sang in memorial concert for Callas, Paris O, aged 19. Her first recording was as Rosina, and it is with Rossini's heroines that she has been particularly associated: Rome; Milan, S; Lyons; Zurich; Cologne; Hamburg; etc. A singer with a robust chest voice, a strong, ringing high soprano range, and a brilliant technique, together with an attractive stage presence and a lively sense of characterization. (R)

Bartolo. See DOCTOR BARTOLO.

Basilio. See DON BASILIO.

bass (It., *basso*: 'low'). The lowest category of male voice. Many subdivisions exist within opera-houses: the commonest in general use (though seldom by composers in scores) are given below, with examples of roles. These divisions often overlap, and do not correspond exactly from country to country. In general, distinction is more by character than by tessitura, especially in France: thus, the examples of the roles give a more useful indication of the different voices' quality than any attempted technical definition.

French: basse-bouffe (Jupiter); basse de caractère (Gounod's Méphistophélès); basse chantante or basse noble (Brogni). In early music (Lully to Rameau), basse-contre.

German: tiefer Bass (Sarastro); Bass-buffo or komischer Bass (Osmin); hoher Bass (Kaspar).

Italian: basso profondo (Ramfis); basso comico or basso buffo (Don Bartolo, Don Basilio); basso cantante (Padre Guardiano).

Slavonic basses are able to achieve great depth, sometimes reaching G'.

Bassarids, The. Opera, with intermezzo, in 1 act by Henze; text by W. H. Auden and Chester Kallman, after Euripides' *The Bacchae*. Prem. Salzburg 6 Aug. 1966, in a German trans. by Maria Basse-Sporleder.

When the god Dionysus (ten) comes to Thebes, his followers, the Bassarids, go to Mount Cytheron to celebrate. The new king, Pentheus (bar), has outlawed the cult of Semele, mother of Dionysus, and orders the arrest of all those on Mount Cytheron. Brought before him, they include his mother Agave (mez), her sister Autonoe (sop) and the disguised Dionysus. Unmasked, Dionysus is tortured by Pentheus, though an earthquake eventually allows him to escape back to the mountain. In the following intermezzo, a parody of 18th-cent. French courtly entertainments, Pentheus' subconscious fantasies are drawn out by Dionysus, who persuades him to dress as a woman in order to observe the revels on Mount Cytheron. Once there, he is denounced as a spy and torn to pieces by the Bassarids, including his mother Agave, who does not recognize him. When it gradually dawns on her what she has done, she bitterly rebukes Dionysus. The god commands that Thebes be burnt, and he and Semele receive the people's worship.

bass-baritone. See BARITONE.

basse chantante. See BASS.

basse-taille. See BARITONE.

Bassl **Manna, Carolina** (*b* Naples, 10 Jan. 1781; *d* Cremona, 12 Dec. 1862). Italian contralto. One of the outstanding singers of her day (Stendhal considered her 'the only singer whose genius approaches that of Mme Pasta'), she used her powerful vocal and dramatic resources to particular effect in the Rossini contralto repertory. She created leading roles in Meyerbeer's *Semiramide riconosciuta*, *Margherita d'Anjou*, and *L'esule di Granata*; Rossini's *Bianca e Faliero*; and works by Pacini and Mercadante. Retired 1828, but continued to sing in concerts. Her brother **Nicola Bassi** (1767–1825), considered by Stendhal to be the best buffo bass of the day, sang in Paris and Milan.

Bastianini, Ettore (*b* Siena, 24 Sept. 1922; *d* Sirmione, 25 Jan. 1967). Italian baritone. Début (as bass) Ravenna 1945 (Colline). Second début Bologna 1951 (Germont). New York, M, 1953–60, 1964–6. London, CG, 1962. Milan, Salzburg, etc. Sang Prince Andrey in first stage performance outside Russia of *War and Peace*, Florence 1953. Greatly admired as a Verdi baritone, he possessed a voice dark enough in timbre to enable him to sing Eugene Onegin. (R)

Bastien und Bastienne. Opera in 1 act by Mozart; text by F. W. Weiskern, J. Müller, and J. A. Schachtner, after M. J. B. and C. S. Favart and H. de Guerville's comedy *Les amours de Bastien et Bastienne* (1753), a parody of Rousseau's *Le devin du village* (1752). Probably prem. Vienna, in Anton Mesmer's garden theatre, Sept. 1768.

France, 18th cent. Bastienne (sop), a shepherdess, complains to Colas (bs), the village magician, that Bastien (ten) no longer loves her. He answers that Bastien has been distracted by the attentions of a grand lady. Colas tells Bastienne to hide and then informs Bastien that Bastienne has left him. At Bastien's request, Colas reads a spell and Bastienne appears. The couple are reconciled and thank Colas.

Bastin, Jules (*b* Pont, 18 Mar. 1933). Belgian bass. Studied Brussels Cons. Début Brussels, M, 1960 (Charon, *Orfeo*). New York, M; Chicago; Milan, S; London, CG, 1974 (Ochs). Paris, C, 1979 (Banker in first complete *Lulu*). Roles incl. Bartolo (Mozart and Rossini), Osmin, Varlaam, Grand Inquisitor. (R)

Battaglia di Legnano, La. Opera in 3 acts by Verdi; text by S. Cammarano, after Joseph Méry's drama *La battaille de Toulouse* (1828). Prem. Rome, Arg., 27 Jan. 1849.

Milan and Como, 1176. Lombard soldiers gather to form an army against the German invaders. Rolando (bar) is overjoyed to find his old friend Arrigo (ten), whom he thought dead. Lida (sop), Rolando's wife (who was once betrothed to Arrigo) spurns the attention of Marcovaldo (bar), a German prisoner released by Rolando though he declares his love for her. Rolando and Arrigo arrive. When they are alone together, Arrigo reproaches Lida for her faithlessness.

Rolando and Arrigo go to Como to ask the people to join their army. The city has already signed a pact with Barbarossa (bs), the German leader, and Arrigo accuses them of treachery. Barbarossa appears and a furious dispute ensues.

Members of the Lombard League swear to drive out the enemy. Marcovaldo shows Rolando a note Lida sent to his friend in which she declares her love for Arrigo. Lida visits Arrigo to say they must part but is surprised there by Rolando. He disowns her and denies Arrigo the honour of fighting for his country. Arrigo has to jump from a window to join the army.

The Lombards win their battle, but Arrigo is mortally wounded. When Arrigo swears to Rolando that he and Lida have not betrayed him, the two friends are reconciled and Arrigo dies a hero.

'Batti, batti, O bel Masetto'. Zerlina's (sop) aria in Act I of Mozart's *Don Giovanni*, in which she invites her lover's wrath and regains his heart.

Battistini, Mattia (*b* Contigliano, 27 Feb. 1856; *d* Colle Buccaro, 7 Nov. 1928). Italian baritone. Studied Rome with Cotogni and Persichini. Début Rome, Arg., 1878 (Alfonso, *Favorita*). Visited S America 1881, but thereafter would never cross the Atlantic. London, CG, 1883 (Riccardo, *Puritani*), with little success; DL 1887. Returned to London 1905, by when he had established himself as 'il rè dei baritoni'. Possessed a voice of exceptional range (Massenet rewrote Werther for him), reaching a', and was also masterly in florid music. In his repertory of 82 roles, he preferred noble or regal characters: his friendship with Verdi was affected by his refusal to sing Falstaff (humour was in any case not his strong point), but he was outstanding as Renato, Posa, Amonasro, and Iago. However, he was at his most characteristic in the earlier Verdi, and in Bellini and Donizetti. Other famous roles included Don Giovanni, Valentin, Wolfram, and Onegin. Sang all over Europe, including Russia and Poland. The master of a technique that included a superb messa di voce, he continued to sing into his 70s. (R)

Battle, Kathleen (*b* Portsmouth, OH, 13 Aug. 1948). US soprano. Studied Cincinnati. Début New York, CO, 1976 (Susanna). New York, M, 1977–93; Gly. 1979; Paris, O, 1984; London, CG, 1985; also Salzburg, Chicago, and major European opera-houses. Roles incl. Blonde, Susanna, Zerlina, Despina, Pamina, Norina, Adina, Sophie (Massenet and Strauss), Zdenka, Zerbinetta. Possesses a radiant, burnished tone and a lively temperament. (R)

Baturin, Alexander (*b* Oshmyany, 17 June 1904). Belorussian baritone. Studied Leningrad with Isachenko, Rome with Battistini. Stage début Moscow, B (Miller, Dargomyzhsky's *Rusalka*). Moscow, B, until 1958. An acclaimed William Tell, Prince Igor, Ruslan, Pimen, Dosifey, Tomsky, Escamillo. At Moscow Cons. from 1948, his students incl. Vedernikov and Ghiaurov. (R)

Baylis, Lilian (*b* London, 9 May 1874; *d* London, 25 Nov. 1937). English musician and manager. Daughter of Newton Baylis, a singer, and Liebe Cons, singer and pianist. Her aunt, Emma Cons, became lessee of the Royal Victorian Coffee Music-Hall, known as the *Old Vic, and invited her to manage it, which she did from 1898 to her death. She laid the foundations of a national English opera company, and, with Ninette de Valois, of a ballet company. Reopened *Sadler's Wells, 1931 as the north London equivalent of the Old Vic.

Bayreuth. Town in Franconia, Germany. Opera had been performed in Bayreuth by various travelling companies since the late

17th cent., mostly in the magnificent Markgräfliches Opernhaus (constructed 1745–8 by Joseph Saint-Pierre and decorated by Carlo and Giuseppe Galli-Bibiena). It was through its association with Wagner that the town came to universal prominence, however. He had intended to build the festival theatre to stage his works in Munich under the patronage of Ludwig II, and plans were drawn up by Gottfried Semper. When intrigues forced the abandonment of this plan, the Bayreuth authorities in 1871 provided land for the theatre and a home ('Wahnfried'). The theatre foundation stone was laid 22 May 1872, when Wagner conducted Beethoven's Ninth Symphony in the existing opera-house with many of Germany's leading musicians (among them Richter as timpanist).

The Festspielhaus (cap. 1,925), originally planned as temporary, is mostly of wood and brick, with an auditorium resembling a classical amphitheatre. It has superb acoustics, largely due to the innovation of a hooded orchestra pit, and no aisles or pillars. It opened 13 Aug. 1876 with *Das Rheingold*, launching the first complete *Ring* cycle. The event, the most important in musical Europe, drew to the audience Liszt, Grieg, Bruckner, Mahler, Tchaikovsky, Saint-Saëns, Nietzsche, Kaiser Wilhelm I, and Ludwig II. The first season lost over £12,000 and there were no more until 1882, when *Parsifal* was premiered. Directors have all been members of Wagner's family: his wife Cosima 1883–1908, son Siegfried 1908–1930, daughter-in-law Winifred 1931–44, grandsons Wieland and Wolfgang 1951–66, Wolfgang from 1966. Under Cosima, the production style religiously perpetuated Wagner's own, though there was some cautious evolution under Siegfried. Winifred appointed Heinz Tietjen as artistic director. Bayreuth suffered from its associations with Hitler's patronage, but reopened after war closure in 1951. The greatest revolution in staging then came with Wieland and Wolfgang, who abandoned the strongly traditional productions in favour of simplified sets and costumes, with particular emphasis on lighting, so as to detach the works from particular associations and stress their universality. Since Wieland's death in 1966, the festival has encouraged experiment and reinterpretation (as with Patrice Chéreau's *Ring* under Pierre Boulez for the 1976 centenary), which with all its risks is seen as an essential Wagnerian tradition.

Bazin, François (*b* Marseilles, 4 Sept. 1816; *d* Paris, 2 July 1878). French composer. Studied Paris with Berton and Halévy. In 1846 he began a long line of stage works in popular style with *Le trompette de Monsieur le Prince*, having his greatest success with *Maître Pathelin* in 1856; his most ambitious large-scale work was *Le voyage en Chine* (1865). An entrenched conservative, he refused to accept Massenet into his class in the Cons., only to find his career being eclipsed by the younger man.

Bear, The. Opera in 1 act by Walton; text by Paul Dehn, after Chekhov's play (1888). Prem. Aldeburgh, 3 June 1967.

The widow Popova (mez) is urged in vain by her servant Luka (bs) to end her period of mourning. Confronted by Smirnov (bar), a creditor of her late husband, so violent a quarrel ensues that he challenges her to a duel. But neither can go through with it, for they have fallen in love.

Beatrice di Tenda. Opera in 2 acts by Bellini; text by Felice Romani. Prem. Venice, F, 16 Mar. 1833.

The castle of Binasco, near Milan, 1418. Beatrice (sop), married to Filippo Visconti, Duke of Milan (bar), is in love with Orombello (ten). Orombello is loved in vain by Agnese (mez), with whom the Duke, having tired of Beatrice, is himself in love. Agnese betrays the lovers to the Duke and, although she later pleads with him to spare Beatrice's life, the Duke refuses, as Beatrice's followers have risen in revolt against him.

Béatrice et Bénédict. Opera in 2 acts by Berlioz; text by the composer, after Shakespeare's comedy *Much Ado About Nothing* (1598–9). Prem. Baden-Baden, 9 Aug. 1862.

Messina, 1700. While Hero (sop) looks forward to seeing her love Claudio (bar) on his return from the wars, his friend Bénédict (ten) is greeted more sardonically by Béatrice (sop). Gradually the love beneath their banter is disclosed, and they agree to marry, as do Hero and Claudio. Berlioz introduces the character of Somarone (bs), a Kapellmeister whose dull fugue is a satire on pedantry in general and probably Cherubini in particular.

Beaumarchais, Pierre Augustin Caron de (*b* Paris, 24 Jan. 1732; *d* Paris, 19 May 1799). French playwright and amateur musician. His fame rests upon the first two plays of the

Figaro trilogy, *Le barbier de Séville* (1775) and *La folle journée, ou Le mariage de Figaro* (1778), from which were derived the librettos used by Rossini (1816) and Mozart (1786) respectively. As a librettist Beaumarchais is known chiefly for *Tarare*, a 5-act opera with music by Salieri (it had been declined by Gluck) (1787).

Bechi, Gino (*b* Florence, 16 Oct. 1913; *d* Florence, 2 Feb. 1993). Italian baritone. Studied Florence with Frazzi and Di Giorgi. Début Empoli 1936 (Germont). Rome 1937–52; Milan, S, 1939–44, 1946–53; London, CG, 1950, DL, 1958. Leading baritone of his day in Italy; at his peak celebrated as Nabucco, Amonasro, Iago (Verdi), Gérard (*Chénier*), Hamlet. Retired 1965. (R)

Beckmesser. Sixtus Beckmesser (bs), the town clerk in Wagner's *Die Meistersinger von Nürnberg*.

Bedford, Steuart (*b* London, 31 July 1939). English conductor. Studied London, RAM (*Poppea* 1969). Début London, SW, 1965 (*Beggar's Opera*); cond. first stage *Owen Wingrave* (London, CG, 1973). Cond. prem. of *Death in Venice* (Aldeburgh 1973) then London, CG, and New York, M. Joint artistic dir. English Music T Co. 1975 (Oliver's *Tom Jones* 1976). Cond. first British *Paul Bunyan*; O North; WNO; ENO. (R)

Beecham, (Sir) **Thomas** (*b* St Helens, 29 Apr. 1879; *d* London, 8 Mar. 1961). English conductor. Son of Sir Joseph, an industrialist and musical amateur whose wealth greatly helped his early career. Studied composition with Charles Wood and Moszkowski; self-taught as conductor. Toured with small opera company 1902–4. In 1910 launched his first season at London, CG, opening with the first English *Elektra* and operas by two other English composers he championed, Delius (*A Village Romeo and Juliet*) and Smyth (*The Wreckers*). Also introduced, surviving difficulties with the censor, *Salome*, later *Feuersnot*, *Ariadne*, and *Rosenkavalier*. Responsible for the Russian opera seasons at London, DL, 1913–14. Formed the Beecham OC 1915. Became lessee of CG 1919, forced into liquidation 1920. Returned to CG 1932, remaining as music and artistic director, and financier, until 1939; his own performances including several of *The Ring*. Also Cologne, Munich, Hamburg, and Berlin, then at New York, M, 1941–4. Conducted little opera after the war, notable exceptions being *Ariadne*

(Edinburgh 1950), *Meistersinger* and *The Bohemian Girl* (CG 1951), the prem. of Delius's *Irmelin* (Oxford 1953), Grétry's *Zémire et Azor* (Bath 1955), and some broadcasts. His last opera conducting was at Buenos Aires, C, 1958.

Beecham's contribution to English opera was inestimable, and in a sense tragic. He spent his fortune, as well as his talent, on heroic enterprises in days when England was unreceptive to his ideals; and at CG he was unable to achieve all of which he was capable. In part this was due to a seigneurial disregard for practicalities; but his genius burned no less brightly in the opera-house than on the concert platform, and his achievements contributed more than some superlative performances to the development of opera in England. (R)

Beeson, Jack (*b* Muncie, IN, 15 July 1921). US composer. Studied Eastman School, and with Bartók. His operas, such as *Lizzie Borden* (1965), make use of a tuneful folk-influenced idiom in setting US folk or legendary subjects.

Beethoven, Ludwig van (*b* Bonn, 15 or 16 Dec. 1770; *d* Vienna, 26 Mar. 1827). German composer. Beethoven's reputation as an operatic composer rests upon his only completed work *Fidelio*, but his interest in dramatic music was much wider. He composed incidental music to several stage plays, including Goethe's *Egmont* (1810), and made numerous other operatic attempts, some of which have survived as fragments. The many revisions of *Fidelio* are, however, proof of his fundamental difficulties with the genre and no subsequent operatic plans ever came to fruition.

It was around 1804 that Beethoven began work on an adaptation by Sonnleithner of Bouilly's *Léonore* libretto (first set by Gaveaux, 1798), and later used by Paer (1804) and Mayr (1805). Cast in three acts, and with the overture Leonore No. 2, the opera was first performed in 1805. It was so poorly received that it was immediately revised and given in slightly altered 2-act version, with the overture Leonore No. 3, the following year. But this attempt was also unsuccessful, and only after a third, more extensive revision in 1814, made with the assistance of Treitschke, was Beethoven even moderately satisfied with his opera, by now known as *Fidelio*.

Beethoven's model in *Fidelio* was that of French *rescue opera, then in vogue in

Vienna. Here he found a style with which he could identify, with an emotional integrity lacking in contemporary French and Italian opera. *Leonore* was clearly fashioned after the model of Cherubini, though like Mozart, Beethoven also brought to opera his skills as a symphonist: the canonic quartet, Leonore's aria 'Abscheulicher!', and the finales display an unmatched complexity of musical organization and depth of expression. The supreme achievement of *Fidelio* lies in the skill with which characters in a popular, almost stereotyped plot are imbued with humane feelings and passions, and an appropriate musical language: the opera's expression of faith in liberty and loathing of tyranny makes it a monument both to Beethoven's artistic vision, as well as more generally to the triumph of good over evil. In this context it is not surprising that *Fidelio* was chosen to open many opera-houses after the Second World War, including the rebuilt Vienna S (5 Nov. 1955).

Beggar's Opera, The. Ballad opera in 3 acts arranged, adapted, and partly composed by Pepusch; text by John Gay. Prem. London, Lincoln's Inn Fields T, 29 Jan. 1728.

The Beggar (spoken), in the prologue, presents the work as his own creation. The highwayman Macheath (ten) has married Polly Peachum (sop). Her father (bs) is so irate at this that he informs against Macheath, who has been receiving stolen goods.

Macheath is arrested and sent to Newgate Prison, but the gaoler's daughter, Lucy (sop), who is in love with him, helps him escape. Macheath has promised to marry Lucy, and when she discovers he is already married to Polly, great rivalry ensues.

After further accusations by more women, Macheath finds himself back in Newgate under Lockit's (bar) care. However, the Beggar intervenes to secure release for Macheath, because 'an opera must end happily'.

Begnis, Giuseppe de and **Giuseppe Ronzi de**. See DE BEGNIS, GIUSEPPE.

Behrens, Hildegard (*b* Varel, 9 Feb. 1937). German soprano. Studied Freiburg with Leuwen. Début Freiburg 1971 (Countess, *Figaro*). Frankfurt 1974; Salzburg 1977; New York, M, from 1975; Bayreuth from 1983. Début London, CG, 1976 (Leonore, *Fidelio*). An intelligent, committed artist who combines lyrical singing with striking dramatic intensity. Her wide repertory includes Fiordiligi, Agathe, Rusalka, Isolde, Brünnhilde, Marie (*Wozzeck*), Salome, Elektra (New York, M, 1992). (R)

'Bei Männern'. The duet in Act I of Mozart's *Die Zauberflöte* in which Pamina (sop) and Papageno (bar) sing of the joys and power of love.

bel canto (It.: 'beautiful song', 'beautiful singing'). The traditional Italian art of singing in which beautiful tone, fine legato phrasing, and impeccable technique are emphasized, though not at the total expense of dramatic expression, as some of its greatest exponents, above all Callas, have demonstrated.

Belcore. The sergeant (bar) in Donizetti's *L'elisir d'amore*.

Belfagor. Opera in 2 acts with prologue and epilogue by Respighi; text by Claudio Guastalla, after Marselli's comedy (1920). Prem. Milan, S, 26 Apr. 1923.

A Tuscan village. Candida (sop), daughter of the apothecary Mirocleto (bs), is coerced into marrying Ipsilonne (bar). Ipsilonne is, in fact, a devil, Belfagor, who has come to earth to see if it is true that marriage leads to man's downfall. When Candida's beloved Baldo (ten) returns, he refuses to believe the wedding was not of her own will. In answer to Candida's prayers, the church bells ring of their own accord to indicate her innocence.

Belfiore. The Cavaliere di Belfiore (bar), posing as Stanislao, King of Poland, in Verdi's *Un giorno di regno*.

Belgium. Under the Spanish domination of the 17th cent., French taste, especially for ballet, ruled the theatre. In Brussels in 1682 the Académie de Musique was opened, and the first opera theatre, the T de la Monnaie, followed there in 1700. Few Belgian composers emerged at first in a tradition dominated by the French; opéra-comique was established with the occupation of Maréchal Saxe in 1746. The first opera by a Belgian was Pierre van *Maldere's Le déguisement pastoral (1759). Other Belgian operas were written by the Austrian director of the Monnaie, Ignaz Vitzthumb. In Liège, Jean-Noël Hamal (1709–78) wrote some 'opéras burless' in Walloon, first *Li voedge di Chaudfontaine* (1757). Also from Liège came the greatest Belgian opera composer, Grétry. In the 19th cent. an inter-

national repertory began to be heard in the principal Belgian cities, as well as works by Belgian composers (e.g. Jean-Englebert Pauwels, 1795–1839, and Charles Borremans, 1769–1827). One of the first Belgian composers of opéra-comique was Albert Grisar, though the scholar-composers François-Joseph Fétis (1784–1871) and François-Auguste Gevaert (1828–1908) had opéras-comiques produced in Paris. In 1830 a famous performance of Auber's *La muette de Portici* set in motion the revolution that led to Belgian independence. A taste for Grand Opera developed, and respected works were written by Franck and Blockx. The influential Paul Gilson (1865–1942) wrote *Prinses Sonenschijn* (1903) in Flemish, but drew on an international musical language that included use of Leitmotiv. Jan Van der Eeden (1842–1913) was influenced by verismo. Eugène Samuel-Holeman (1863–1944) was an Impressionist.

See also ANTWERP, BRUSSELS.

Belinda. Dido's lady-in-waiting (sop) in Purcell's *Dido and Aeneas*.

Belisario. Opera seria in 3 acts by Donizetti; text by Cammarano after Jean-François Marmontel's drama *Bélisaire* (1776). Prem. Venice, F, 4 Feb. 1836.

Byzantium, 6th cent. Belisario (bar), general in the Emperor Justinian's (bs) army, returns in triumph to Constantinople after defeating the Bulgarians. His wife Antonina (sop) believes him guilty of their son's murder, and denounces him on forged evidence. He is blinded and led into exile by his daughter Irene (mez). They overhear a freed captive Alamiro (ten) and Ottarino (bs) planning revenge for this on Byzantium; but Alamiro recognizes Belisario, and Irene Alamiro as her long-lost brother. Belisario is fatally wounded in the defence of Byzantium.

'Bella figlia dell'amore'. The quartet in Act III of Verdi's *Rigoletto*, in which the Duke (ten) woos Maddalena (mez) while Rigoletto (bar) comforts the anguished Gilda (sop) with promises of retribution.

Belle Hélène, La (Fair Helen). Operetta in 3 acts by Offenbach; text by Meilhac and Halévy. Prem. Paris, Variétés, 17 Dec. 1864.

Sparta and Nauplia, before the Trojan war. Vénus has decreed that Paris (ten), in the guise of a shepherd, shall win the most beautiful woman in the world in a competition: this is undoubtedly Ménélas's wife Hélène (sop). When Paris is victorious, the High Priest Calchas (bs), at Hélène's request, arranges for Ménélas (ten) to be dispatched in order that she and Paris may dine alone.

Hélène resists Paris's love but he returns later, in what she imagines to be a dream. Ménélas arrives unexpectedly to find them kissing and packs Paris off.

Vénus, upset at Ménélas's behaviour, causes a spate of adultery in Sparta. In an effort to restore peace, Ménélas summons the High Priest of Venus from Cythera (Paris in disguise), who promises that Vénus will forgive Ménélas if he permits Hélène to return with him to Cythera to make a sacrifice. The couple embark on their voyage.

'Belle nuit, ô nuit d'amour'. The *bar-carolle in Act II of Offenbach's *Les contes d'Hoffmann*, sung by Giulietta (sop) and Nick-lausse (mez) in a palace overlooking the Grand Canal in Venice, asking the night to favour their love.

Bellezza, Vincenzo (*b* Bitonto, 17 Feb. 1888; *d* Rome, 8 Feb. 1964). Italian conductor. Studied Naples with Martucci. Début Naples, C, 1908 (*Aida*). Toured Italy; Buenos Aires, C; New York, M, 1926–35; London, CG, 1926–30, conducting Shalyapin's London début (*Mefistofele*), Melba's Farewell, the first English *Turandot*, and the London débuts of Ponselle and Gigli; CG again 1935–6. Rome and other Italian theatres 1935–64. London, Stoll T, 1957; DL, 1958. A highly professional, effective conductor, with a reliable ability to control and deliver a successful performance. (R)

Bellincioni, Gemma (*b* Como, 18 Aug. 1864; *d* Naples, 23–4 Apr. 1950). Italian soprano. Daughter of the buffo bass Cesare Bellincioni, with whom she studied. Début Naples 1879 (Dell'Orefice's *Il segreto della duchessa*). Considered an outstanding Violetta by Verdi, who said 'she gave new life to the old sinner' but nevertheless rejected her for Desdemona and Alice ('intelligent but too sentimental'). The verismo repertory provided her greatest successes, of which the most momentous was the creation of Santuzza (to the Turiddu of her husband Roberto *Stagno). She was the first Italian Salome, much admired by Strauss. Her gifts lay in strength of personality and characterization rather than in the quality of her voice. (R)

Bellini, Vincenzo (*b* Catania, 3 Nov. 1801; *d* Puteaux, 23 Sept. 1835). Italian composer. Studied with his father; Naples with Zingarelli. The success of his student opera *Adelson e Salvini* (1825) led to a commission for the Naples C, *Bianca e Fernando* (1826). This in turn brought a commission from Barbaia for Milan, where he at once made his name with *Il pirata* (1827), finding also in Luigi *Romani a loyal and sympathetic librettist.

Already the essential elements of his style were formed. From Zingarelli he had learnt to give primacy to the elegant melody which came naturally to him; from his admiration for Rossini came his graceful coloratura and a feeling for orchestral drama; the grave, tender sentiment in much of the music was wholly individual. All these qualities appealed to audiences, responding to a new element of Romantic feeling in the music, no less than to singers, from whom Bellini demanded not merely beautiful singing but expressive vocal artistry. The art of *bel canto, with which he was above all composers to be associated, meant for him the expression of character and feeling through the singer's intelligent and sensitive phrasing, shading, and inflection of the melody.

His next two works, *La straniera* (1829) and *Zaira* (1829), met with rather less success than *Il pirata*, but *I Capuleti e i Montecchi* (1830) triumphed; and with *La sonnambula* (1831) and *Norma* (1831) his gifts reached full maturity. While the former is a tenderly elegiac rustic idyll, *Norma* is a lyric drama reaching in its last act tragic grandeur. It shows his melodic mastery at its greatest, as in the famous 'Casta diva': not only does the melody develop from small phrases into a long, expressive span, but the device of introducing it at first simply on flute puts on the singer the full responsibility of giving the melody human life and expressiveness. It is not surprising that these qualities, especially the ease and length of his melodies, should have been admired by Verdi; a less likely admirer was Wagner.

Norma was followed by the less successful *Beatrice di Tenda* (1833), over which Bellini quarrelled with Romani. Carlo Pepoli was the less expert librettist for his last work, *I Puritani* (1835), in which the melodic elegance is unaffected but cannot really engage fully with the drama. It was nevertheless a popular success. But Bellini was now drained in health and exhausted; and while in Paris, hoping to conclude various operatic plans, he fell ill and died, alone, in a house in the suburbs. At his requiem mass in the Invalides his shroud was held at each corner by Cherubini, Carafa, Paer, and Rossini. Reinterred in Catania, 1876.

Bell Song. The name generally given to the soprano aria 'Où va la jeune Hindoue?' sung by Lakmé (sop) in Act II of Delibes's *Lakmé*.

Belmonte. A Spanish nobleman (ten), lover of Constanze, in Mozart's *Die Entführung aus dem Serail*.

'Bel raggio lusinghier'. Semiramide's (sop) aria in Act I of Rossini's *Semiramide*, in which she rejoices that a ray of love will shine into her heart now that Arsace has returned.

Beňačková, Gabriela (*b* Bratislava, 25 Mar. 1944). Czech soprano. Studied Zilina with Kresáková, Bratislava with Blaho. Prague 1970 (Natasha). Prague until 1980; London, CG, 1979; Munich 1981; Cologne 1983; Vienna, S, 1985; New York, M, 1991; also S Francisco, Salzburg, etc. An expressive performer with a rich, sweet tone. Roles incl. Leonore, Verdi's Desdemona, Jenůfa, Vixen, Natasha. (R)

Benda, Jiří (*b* Staré Benátky, *bapt.* 30 June 1722; *d* Köstritz, 6 Nov. 1795). Czech composer. Kapellmeister at Gotha, he produced a number of successful stage works, including the Singspiels *Der Dorfjahrmarkt* (1775) and *Romeo und Julie* (1776): these were some of the first with serious plots and represent a great advance over Hiller and Weisse. He is best remembered as the composer of spoken 'duodramas', beginning with *Ariadne auf Naxos* (1775) and *Medea* (1775). Their unique style of melodrama was an inspiration to many, including Mozart, who declared 'I like those two works so much that I carry them about with me'.

Bendl, Karel (*b* Prague, 16 Apr. 1839; *d* Prague, 20 Sept. 1897). Czech composer. A noted choral conductor, including of the Hlahol Choral Society (where he succeeded Smetana), his first opera, *Lejla* (1868), was in the manner of French Grand Opera, and made a considerable impression. In 1874 he joined the Prague, P, as second conductor; but his *Starý ženich* (The Old Bridegroom, comp. 1871–4, prem. 1882) proved too similar in manner to *The Bartered Bride*, and was withheld by the composer until after

Smetana's death. After a period abroad, he settled again in Prague and wrote another opera, *Černohorci* (The Montenegrins, 1881), on Grand Opera scale; a comedy in the Smetana manner, *Karel Šréta* (1883), that in its treatment of the life of the Czech painter also owes something to Berlioz's *Benvenuto Cellini*; and an attempt at verismo, *Gina* (1884). His works reveal great theatrical skill and versatility, if not a strong central personality; he was, nevertheless, one of the most important composers to emerge in Smetana's immediate wake.

Benedetti, Michele (*b* Loreto, 17 Oct. 1778; *d* ?). Italian bass. Italy and Amsterdam 1805–9; 1811 sang in first Italian *La vestale* in Naples, where he continued to work for 25 years. Created numerous roles in Rossini operas, including *Otello*, *Armida*, *Ermione*, *La donna del lago*, and *Mosè in Egitto* (to which the composer added Moses' Prayer in the last act for him). Also created roles in works by Pacini, Mercadante, and Bellini. London 1822. He was at his best as strong, imposing characters and was much admired as Mosè by Stendhal.

Benedict, (Sir) **Julius** (*b* Stuttgart, 27 Nov. 1804; *d* London, 5 June 1885). German, later English, composer, conductor, teacher, pianist, and writer. Studied Weimar with Hummel, then Dresden as Weber's first pupil. In 1823 Weber took him to Vienna, where he became conductor at the K. Two years later he went to Naples as conductor of the SC and Fondo theatres. Here his *Giacinta ed Ernesto* (1827) was found too German for Italian taste. In 1834 he moved to Paris, where he met Malibran: at her suggestion he visited London, where he was to remain until his death. He was at the L 1836–7, DL 1838–48, HM from 1852. At DL, as well as producing English Romantic operas including *The Bohemian Girl* and *Maritana*, he introduced operas of his own. His greatest success, however, was at CG with *The Lily of Killarney* (1862). In the concert-hall, he was closely associated with Jenny Lind both as pianist and conductor. His music reflects the influence of Weber, and is skilfully written with a good appreciation of the voice; but in unpropitious conditions his operas were no more successful than those of his contemporaries.

benefit. In the 18th and 19th cents. these were special performances, generally at the end of the season, the proceeds of which went to a certain composer, singer, or impresario. In more modern times the term has come to mean any performance with a generally charitable aim.

Benelli, Ugo (b Genoa, 20 Jan. 1935). Italian tenor. Début Milan, PS, 1960; Milan, S; Rome, R; etc. Wexford 1966 (Fra Diavolo); Gly. from 1967 (Nemorino, Narciso (*Turco in Italia*), Mozart's Don Basilio). London, CG, 1974 (Ernesto). Particularly admired in comic roles (Rossini's Almaviva, Lindoro, Ramiro). (R)

Bennett, Richard Rodney (b Broadstairs, 29 Mar. 1936). English composer. Studied London, RAM, with Lennox Berkeley and Howard Ferguson. His excellent craftsmanship and fluent capacity for providing music for different situations are shown in his operas, which include *The Ledge* (1961), *The Mines of Sulphur* (1965) and *Victory* (1970). These qualities are also at the service of a quick sense of immediate dramatic effect, though the range of characterization is comparatively narrow and the more serious works, especially, tend not to engage dramatically with the issues the texts propose.

Bennett has also interested himself in music theatre and in concert works in quasi-dramatic forms, as in his series of pieces entitled *Commedia* and *Scena*.

Benvenuto Cellini. Opera in 2 acts by Berlioz; text by Léon de Wailly and August Barbier, after the autobiography of Benvenuto Cellini (1558–66) (pub. 1728). Prem. Paris, O, 10 Sept. 1838.

Set in Rome in 1532, the opera is based on events in the life of Benvenuto Cellini. Teresa (sop), daughter of the Papal Treasurer Balducci (bs), plans to elope with Cellini (ten), disguised as a friar, during the Roman Carnival, but their plan is overheard by Fieramosca (bar), a sculptor also in love with Teresa. In the confusion of the Carnival, with Fieramosca also disguised as a friar, a fight develops in which Cellini kills Pompeo (bar). Ascanio (mez), Cellini's apprentice, brings Teresa to Cellini's studio and Cardinal Salviati (bs) arrives to demand by midnight a statue he has commissioned if Cellini is not to be handed over to the law for abduction and murder. Despite a strike organized by Fieramosca, Cellini, having thrown into the crucible every piece of precious metal he

possesses, succeeds in casting his Perseus and thus earning a pardon.

Berbié, Jane (b Villefranche-de-Lauragais, 6 May 1931). French mezzo-soprano. Studied Toulouse. Début Toulouse 1954 (Nicklausse). Milan, S, 1958, 1971; Paris, O, from 1959, B, 1990–1; Gly. 1967, 1969; London, CG, 1971–2. A singer of great character, whose repertory includes Rosina, Dorabella, Zerlina, Marcellina, Orsini (*Lucrezia Borgia*), Ascanio (*Cellini*), Concepción. (R)

Berendey. The Tsar (ten) in Rimsky-Korsakov's *The Snow Maiden*.

Berg, Alban (b Vienna, 9 Feb. 1885; d Vienna, 24 Dec. 1935). Austrian composer. Studied with Schoenberg, 1904–10, who deeply influenced him and to whom *Lulu* is dedicated. The 1914 Vienna prem. of Büchner's *Woyzeck* profoundly affected Berg, and his army experiences confirmed his sense of identification with the humble, downtrodden soldier. In his opera *Wozzeck*, he was also encouraged to find succinct musical forms to express the play's sequence of short, pregnant scenes, so that each act, and within that each scene, has its own self-contained form. Thus, Act I consists of five character-pieces, Act II is a five-movement symphony, and Act III a group of five inventions on ostinati. Berg also extended control over aspects of the work's production, relating lighting and other features to the motivic design. However, he was always insistent that his fugues, passacaglias, sonata movements, and so on should go unnoticed in appreciation of the compassionate musical drama which they strengthen and serve. The musical language is based on an extended diatonic idiom, and is at no time dodecaphonic. Nevertheless, the opera's prem., in 1925, was made the occasion for veiled political attacks on Schoenbergian aesthetics and in particular on the conductor Erich Kleiber for his championship of Berg. The work in fact triumphed, and has retained a firm hold on the international repertory.

By contrast, *Lulu*, based on Wedekind's *Erdgeist* and *Die Büchse der Pandora*, draws on serial techniques and is organized in a dense network of formal relationships expressing the differing contacts between the characters; it also makes use of shorter, self-contained traditional forms such as arietta, canzonetta, etc. There is further a significant use of doubling of roles, with Lulu's victims at the beginning being identified with her clients as she sinks to becoming a prostitute and is herself eventually murdered. The rise to power of the Nazis prevented the hoped-for prem., and Berg died without quite completing the full score: given in its unfinished form in 1937, it was later completed by Cerha, in which version it was premiered in 1979. Musically, *Lulu* rises to greater heights than *Wozzeck*, though the latter's more easily shared compassion for an underdog, rather than for a more grotesque group of characters destroyed by raw feminine sexuality, has given it much wider popular currency.

Bergamo. Town in Lombardy, Italy. Opera was first given when the T Riccardi opened 24 Aug. 1791 with Piccinni's *Didone*; burnt down 1797; reopened 1799. In the early 19th cent. many famous singers appeared, including the locally born Rubini and Donzelli, and great attention was given to the works of Mayr; later Rossini was more popular. Rebuilt 1897, and renamed, after Bergamo's most famous composer, the T Donizetti (cap. 2,000). Toscanini conducted the opening *Lucia di Lammermoor*, but withdrew in dissatisfaction with standards and public. In 1937 it was given a subsidiary title, T della Novità, producing each season new works by Ghedini, Barilli, Napoli, Tosatti, Malipiero, Viozzi, Ferrari, Zanon, Sanzogno, etc., and reviving many Donizetti works. The audience is considered the most difficult to please in Italy, after that of Parma.

Berganza, Teresa (*b* Madrid, 16 Mar. 1934). Spanish mezzo-soprano. Studied Madrid with Lola Rodriguez Aragon. Début Aix-en-Provence 1957 (Dorabella). Milan, S, from 1957; Gly. 1958–9 (Cherubino and Cenerentola); London, CG, 1960 (Rosina) and 1963; New York, M, from 1967; Paris, O, and Edinburgh 1977. Repertory also includes Dido (Purcell), Octavian, Zerlina, and Carmen. A rich-voiced and sensitive singer, excellent in florid music and with a fresh stage presence. (R)

Berger, Erna (*b* Cossebaude, 19 Oct. 1900; *d* Essen, 14 June 1990). German soprano. Studied Dresden with Hirzel. Début Dresden 1925 (First Boy, *Zauberflöte*). Dresden until 1928. Bayreuth 1929–33; Berlin, SO, 1929 and 1932; Berlin, S, from 1934; Salzburg 1932 (Blonde) and 1953–4; New York, M, 1949–51; London, CG, 1934–47. Retired 1955.

Famous for her Constanze, Queen of the Night, Gilda, and Sophie. Her voice retained its youthfulness throughout a long career. Taught Rita Streich. (R)

Berghaus, Ruth (*b* Dresden, 2 July 1927). German producer. Berliner Ensemble from 1964, dir. 1971–7. Dir. Berlin, S, 1977–9. Frankfurt from 1980; also Munich, Mannheim, Vienna, Brussels, WNO, etc. Her style, essentially alienating, symbolic, and satirical, has been admired for its stimulating qualities, and criticized for sterility, forced effects, and trivialization of great works. She has had much influence on the subsequent generation of producers. Repertory incl. *Idomeneo*, *Don Giovanni*, *Zauberflöte*, *Fierrabras*, *Tristan*, *The Ring*, *Lulu*. Prod. her husband Paul *Dessau's *Lukullus*, and the posthumous prem. of his *Leonce und Lena*, 1979.

Bergman, Ingmar (*b* Uppsala, 14 July 1918). Swedish producer and film director. Early experience in opera included work at Stockholm, Royal O, 1940–2. Most of his career has been spent in film and drama, but his production for television in Swedish of *The Magic Flute* (1975) captivated a large audience with its mixture of fantasy, realism, and warm treatment of the characters. Wrote text for, and prod., Daniel Börtz's *Backanterna* (1991).

Bergonzi, Carlo (*b* Polisene, 13 July 1924). Italian tenor. Studied Parma with Grandini. Début Lecce 1948 (Rossini's Figaro). Sang as baritone for two years, then after further study made second début Bari 1951 (Chénier). Milan, S, from 1953; London, CG, from 1962 (Manrico, Radamès, Cavaradossi); Chicago 1955; New York, M, 1956–83. A repertory of more than 40 roles included Canio, Don José, Edgardo, and Rodolfo. His beautiful voice and musical refinement were particularly memorable in Verdi. (R)

Berio, Luciano (*b* Oneglia, 24 Oct. 1925). Italian composer. Berio's theatre music began with mime pieces, including *Mimusique No. 2* (1955) and *Allez Hop* (1959), his first collaboration with Calvino. His interest in the sounds of languages led to *Passaggio* (1963), for Milan, PS, which includes multilingual speaking groups in the auditorium: Berio ingeniously made the predicted audience protests material for their improvisation. *Laborintus II* (1965) was an open-ended drama, performable either on stage or in concert, using texts by Dante and others as phonetic material to create a labyrinth of meanings for the listener to explore. It draws on jazz, madrigal style, taped sounds, and traditional instruments in an intricate amalgam of styles. Berio's first full-length theatre work, premiered in 1970, was *Opera* (here meaning 'Works'). A more traditional music drama, this interweaves three different commentaries on human attitudes towards death (the Orpheus legend, a terminal hospital ward, and the *Titanic* disaster), and makes use of imaginative techniques that call into question the relationship between the theatre and music-making, between the music-makers and the audience. Resuming his collaboration with Calvino, Berio wrote *La vera storia* (1982), partly influenced by Verdi's *Il trovatore* and denouncing political oppression, and his major work for the theatre, *Un re in ascolto* (1984). Here, the different levels of reality revolve around the dying Prospero rehearsing his new musical version of *The Tempest* in an extravagant production. This includes the preparation of a musical play drawn from Gotter's Singspiel *Die Geisterinsel* (1791), and a score of great virtuosity contains some vocal writing that suggests Berio's acknowledgement of enduring Italian skills. His long preoccupation both with death and with the nature of theatrical reality, which to some extent places him in the Italian tradition of Pirandello, finds expression here in the final abandonment of Prospero to the extinction of both human and theatrical illusion.

Berkeley, (Sir) **Lennox** (*b* Oxford, 12 May 1903; *d* London, 26 Dec. 1989). English composer. He took music up seriously after leaving Oxford in 1926, and studied with Nadia Boulanger for six years. He did not write an opera until 1954, when he produced the full-scale 3-act *Nelson* for London, SW. This was not a success, in part due to a lengthy plot with some contrived situations. Berkeley found a happier vein of invention with a 1-act comedy, *A Dinner Engagement* (1954), in which his graceful invention and wry humour are well displayed. His interest in opera led him to return twice more to the medium of 1-act opera, with the mild but well-crafted *Ruth* (1956) and a more sharply written piece, *Castaway* (1967): another opera, *Faldon Park*, was unfinished at his

death. His son **Michael Berkeley** (*b* London, 29 May 1948) has written the successful opera *Baa Baa Black Sheep*, on Kipling's *The Jungle Book* (O North 1994).

Berlin. City in Prussia, Germany; capital of united Germany 1871–1945; capital of German Democratic Republic 1945–90; capital of united Germany again 3 Oct. 1990. The first operas were Italian, given in 1688 during the reign of Frederick I. The first opera-house, the Hofoper (or Lindenoper), opened Dec. 1742 under Frederick the Great with *Cleopatra e Cesare* by Carl *Graun, director until his death in 1759. Opera developed chiefly at the Nationaltheater under B. A. Weber from 1795. The first German opera was Johann *Reichardt's *Brenno* (1798). The Hofoper and the Nationaltheater merged in 1814 as the Königliches Schauspiel, with August Iffland as director. The influential Count Brühl was director from 1815; he wanted C. M. von *Weber as music director, but was overruled and *Spontini held the position 1820–42. However, the first opera at the Neues Schauspielhaus, Weber's *Der Freischütz* (1821) proved a national triumph, unifying national sentiment in favour of German opera and, together with the fame of Spontini's work, giving Berlin a dominant role in a still divided Germany. The Königstädter-T opened 1824, becoming the Wallnertheater 1851; here Italian opera was given, including with Sontag and Pasta. Meyerbeer succeeded Spontini 1842, with Nicolai as a conductor. The Königliches Schauspiel burnt down 1843, reopening 1844. Opera was also given at Kroll's 'Etablissement' (1843), especially Lortzing, and at the Friedrich-Wilhelm-Städtisches-T (from 1883 Deutsches T), directed by Lortzing 1850–1. The Victoria-T gave Italian opera with singers including Artôt and Patti. Berlin continued to increase its standing as a major centre of opera, especially German: high standards were achieved under Weingartner (1891–8) and Strauss (1898–1918).

In 1919 Max von Schillings took over the Königliche O, renamed the Staatsoper Unter den Linden. He was succeeded by Heinz Tietjen (1925–43), with as music directors Blech (1918–23, 1926–37) sharing with Kleiber (1923–34), Furtwängler (1933–4), Krauss (1935–6), and from 1936 to 1943 Heger, Schüler, Egk, Karajan, and Elmendorff. Under Kleiber prems. were given of *Wozzeck* (1925) and works by Busoni, Janáček,

Richard Strauss, Stravinsky, and Krenek. This adventurous policy was restrained by the Nazis. The theatre was bombed in the war, and activities were resumed under Ernst Legal at the Admiralspalast on 8 Sept. 1946 with Gluck's *Orfeo*. On 4 Sept. 1955 the Oper Unter den Linden (cap. 1,354) reopened with *Meistersinger* under Konwitschny.

In 1896 Kaiser Wilhelm II planned a new opera-house, and Kroll's T in the Königsplatz was bought. The war prevented its opening, which took place in 1924. Until May 1926, while the Oper unter den Linden was being rebuilt, the company played at the Kroll Oper (officially renamed Oper am Platz der Republik), alternating from summer 1927 with the Kroll's independent company under Klemperer with Legal as director. Under this joint direction, and when the Linden company returned home, the Kroll became the leading experimental opera theatre in Europe, with a repertory concentrating on enterprising productions and novel works, including by Hindemith (prem. of *Neues vom Tage*), Krenek, Milhaud, Schoenberg (*Erwartung*), Weill, Stravinsky, and Janáček (*From the House of the Dead*); conductors included Zemlinsky and Fritz Zweig. The theatre closed in 1931, and became the home of the Reichstag in 1933.

The Städtische Oper (originally the Deutsches Opernhaus on the Bismarckstrasse, sometimes known as the Charlottenburg Opera) opened Nov. 1912 (cap. 2,100). It reached a high standard 1925–34 with Walter (1925–9) and Stiedry (1929–33) as conductors, Tietjen, Singer, and Ebert as directors. Singers included Ivogün, Lehmann, Reinhardt, Nemeth, Onegin, and Kipnis. Bombed 1943; company moved to Admiralspalast; reopened 1945 in the T des Westens (cap. 1,529), former home of the Volksoper, with Bohnen as director. He was succeeded by Tietjen 1948, and Carl Ebert 1955–61. The rebuilt house on the Bismarckstrasse opened 1961 with *Don Giovanni*, reverting to the name Deutsche Oper (cap. 1,885). Maazel was music director 1965–71. Götz Friedrich has been director since 1981.

The Komische Oper, formerly the Metropol T, opened 1947 (cap. 1,208) and under Walter *Felsenstein became one of the most discussed opera-houses in Europe, with some famous opera productions, emphasizing an integrated ensemble and dramatic realism, that made brilliant use of the excellent rehearsal conditions. Felsenstein was responsible for

29 productions; he was succeeded by his disciple Joachim Herz, in turn by Harry Kupfer in 1981.

Berlioz, Hector (*b* La Côte-Saint-André, 11 Dec. 1803; *d* Paris, 8 Mar. 1869). French composer. Almost all Berlioz's music was dramatic in conception, whether ostensibly a symphony (*Symphonie fantastique*, *Harold en Italie*) or one of his hybrids—the dramatic symphony *Roméo et Juliette*, the monodrama *Lélio*, and the *légende dramatique*, *La damnation de Faust*. He completed five operas, and considered other projects throughout his life, including a treatment of *Othello*.

The early *Estelle et Némorin* is lost; and what survives of *Les Francs-juges* (included in other works) indicates his well-known admiration for Weber. He was drawn to his first complete surviving opera by the idea of setting episodes from the life of Benvenuto Cellini, whose autobiography he probably first read in 1831. Greatly attracted to a fellow-artist of heroic and Romantic individuality, he also sensed a kinship with Cellini's struggles to assert himself in the face of academicism and intrigue and to produce against all the odds a masterpiece. The project of a 2-act opéra-comique was turned down by the Opéra-Comique, and Berlioz cast the work instead for the Opéra. *Benvenuto Cellini* (1838) is an uneven opera, but the brilliance and warmth of the music in general far outweigh its weaker patches.

Faced with public neglect in the field of opera after its failure, Berlioz found himself cut off from the medium into which his talents should naturally have flowed; thus, when he made an opera out of Virgil, he took less account of practical considerations of performance in France. *Les Troyens*, composed 1856–8, is an epic on the largest scale, and triumphs over normal operatic considerations. It embraces the spectacular and the lyrical, and combines startling originalities with a classical grandeur that looks back past Spontini to Gluck. Traces of the conventions of French Grand Opera may readily be found, but these are absorbed into a grandeur of vision that dwarfs the genre. Though the work is constructed in a sequence of episodes, making no use of *Leitmotiv, there is the connecting theme of the divine command that the Trojans (with their *reminiscence motive of the Trojan March) shall found their new city of Rome; and this lends dramatic impetus and cohesion to all the skilfully contrasted scenes.

It was as a rest after the exertions of *Les Troyens*, so Berlioz said, that the comedy *Béatrice et Bénédict* (1862) was written, as well as in tribute to Shakespeare. It includes some infelicities (the leaden parody of academicism in Somarone's repeated fugue), but there is in the musical handling of the separate numbers a tenderness and an ironic wit worthy of Shakespeare's own, justifying Berlioz's description of the opera as a 'caprice written with the point of a needle'. Its German successes, before the production of the second part of *Les Troyens* (the Carthage acts) in 1863, gave Berlioz false hopes of a good reception for the greater work.

In 1847 Berlioz was invited by Jullien to become music director at London DL, as part of an ill-fated attempt to found an English national opera.

Bernstein, Leonard (*b* Lawrence, MA, 25 Aug. 1918; *d* New York, 14 Oct. 1990). US conductor, composer, and pianist. Studied Harvard, including with Piston, and Curtis Institute with Reiner. Also studied with Koussevitsky, whose assistant he became; at Tanglewood, he conducted the US prem. of *Peter Grimes*. He also conducted the prem. of his own *Trouble in Tahiti* at Brandeis U in 1952; other important operatic conducting appearances included Visconti's productions of *Medea* and *La sonnambula* at Milan, S, in 1954 and 1955, and *Falstaff* at New York, M, 1964, Vienna 1966.

Bernstein's music for the theatre ranged wide, including ballet, musical, and opera. His 1-act *Trouble in Tahiti* won respect for its serious theme, and later was given a sequel *A Quiet Place* (1983). But his lively, irreverent score for *Candide* (1956) indicated that his real talent lay in the musical; and this was conclusively demonstrated with *West Side Story* (1957). Its fundamentally serious theme—a modern version of the *Romeo and Juliet* story—was expressed in music that drew on jazz, Latin American music, and Broadway idioms, skilfully and wittily handled, mixing them with a more sentimental popular manner. Its enormous popularity did much to loosen distinctions between opera and Broadway musical, not least since dance scenes were an essential ingredient of the work. (R)

Berry, Walter (*b* Vienna, 8 Apr. 1929). Aus-

trian bass-baritone. Studied Vienna with Gallos. Début Vienna, S, 1950. Sang small roles, then 1953 Masetto, and later Figaro (Mozart), Leporello, Guglielmo, Wozzeck, Barak, Ochs, and the Italian repertory. Salzburg since 1952; Berlin, SO, from 1961; New York, M, 1966–78 (including Wotan); London, CG, from 1976; S Francisco 1985 (Alberich). Roles also include Pizarro, Escamillo, and Telramund. (R)

Bersa, Blagoje (*b* Dubrovnik, 21 Dec. 1873; *d* Zagreb, 1 Jan. 1934). Croatian composer. A leading figure in Croatian music 1900–20, he gave a new lead to opera especially with *Oganj* (1911). Written in post-Wagnerian style, this is set in a factory and makes advanced use of music to represent machinery and its role in workers' lives. He also wrote *Jelka* (1901) on Italian models, and a comedy, *Postolar od Delfta* (The Cobbler of Delft, 1914). His many pupils benefited from his new ideas, especially the enlarged awareness of German and Russian music. His brother **Vladimir** (1864–1927) wrote *Cvijeta* (1898) and *Andrija Čubranović* (1900). A third brother, **Josip**, sometimes acted as their librettist.

Bertini, Gary (*b* Brichevo (Moldova), 1 May 1927). Israeli conductor of Moldovian birth. Studied at the Milan and Paris Cons. Scottish O, 1971 (Rossini and Mozart); Paris, O, 1975 (*Ariane et Barbe-bleu*). Cond. prems. of Tal's *Asmedai* (Hamburg 1971), *Masad 967* (Jerusalem 1973), *Die Versuchung* (Munich 1977). Dir. Frankfurt O 1987–91. Music dir. New Israeli O 1994, opening new house at Tel Aviv with *Boris Godunov*. (R)

Berton, Henri-Montan (*b* Paris, 17 Sept. 1767; *d* Paris, 22 Apr. 1844). French composer. His most famous work, *Les rigueurs du cloître* (1790) is a pioneering example of *rescue opera, while *Le délire* (1799) and *Montano et Stéphanie* (1799) show a feeling for chromatic harmony and make enterprising use of motive; the latter, in particular, remained popular during the early 19th cent. Its success was only overtaken by *Aline, reine de Golconde* (1803), which even reached America; it is one of his many operas to give marked extra emphasis to the orchestra, and to allow the chorus a more functional part in the drama. He was music dir. of Paris I, 1807–9, then chorus-master at the Opéra. The failure of the new operas in more grandiose vein which he wrote after *Françoise de Foix* (1809) increasingly embittered him.

Berton, Pierre-Montan (*b* Maubert-Fontaines, 7 Jan. 1727; *d* Paris, 14 May 1780). French tenor, conductor, and composer; father of above. Held various posts at the Paris, O: cond. (1755), manager (1767), dir. (1770), and dir.-general (1775–8), where he was responsible for helping to introduce the works of both Gluck and Piccinni. His arrangements of Rameau and Lully also earned him widespread popularity.

Bertoni, Ferdinand (*b* Salò, 15 Aug. 1752; *d* Desenzano, 1 Dec. 1813). Italian composer. Also active as a church musician, he came to prominence as an opera composer with *Le pescatrici* (1751) and *Quinto Fabio* (1778). The success of the latter led to engagements at the London, H (1778–83), for which he wrote several works, including *Il convito* (1782). Unremarkable by the standards of the day, Bertoni's operas had a 'grace and facility' (Burney) which won them many admirers.

Bertram. The father of Robert (bs), in reality the Devil, in Meyerbeer's *Robert le Diable*.

Berwald, Franz (*b* Stockholm, 23 July 1796; *d* Stockholm, 3 Apr. 1868). Swedish composer. Studied with his father Christian Berwald (1740–1825) and Dupuy, violinist of the Hovkapellet, which he then joined. He began composing seriously in 1817, beginning with an opera *Gustav Wasa* in 1827. In Berlin 1829 he considered other opera subjects, but his first completed stage works were two operettas. Three operas followed, including *Eine ländliche Verlobung in Schweden* (A Swedish Country Wedding, 1847: dedicated to Jenny Lind, who sang the first performance of excerpts), and his best-known opera, *Drottningen av Golconda* (The Queen of Golconda, comp. 1864–5).

Bess. Crown's girl (sop), but lover of Porgy, in Gershwin's *Porgy and Bess*.

'Bess, you is my woman now'. The love duet between Porgy (bar) and Bess (sop) in Act II of Gershwin's *Porgy and Bess*.

Besuch der alten Dame, Der (The Visit of the Old Lady). Opera in 3 acts by Gottfried von Einem; text by Friedrich Dürrenmatt, after his drama of the same name. Prem. Vienna, S, 23 May 1971.

The once impoverished Claire Zachanassian (mez), originally known as Klari Wäscher, now one of the richest women in the world, returns to her home town of Güllen. She meets Alfred Ill (bar), her former lover and father of her illegitimate child, and offers the town a huge sum if he is killed. This eventually happens; the cause of his death is declared to be heart failure. Claire claims the body and gives the mayor the cheque she promised. The people of Güllen express their happiness and satisfaction that justice has been done.

Bevignani, Enrico (*b* Naples, 29 Sept. 1841; *d* Naples, 29 Aug. 1903). Italian conductor and composer. Studied Naples with Albanese and Lillo. Had an early success with *Caterina Blum* (Naples 1863). Engaged by Mapleson 1864 as répétiteur for London, HM, then cond. London, CG, 1869–87 and 1890–6: cond. first London *Aida* (1876), *Gioconda* (1883), *Amico Fritz* (1892), and *Pagliacci* (1893), and Patti's CG Farewell (1895). Much admired for his skill in accompanying singers, though Shaw had hard words for him. Moscow and St Petersburg 1871–83, receiving the Order of St Stanislas. Cond. first Bolshoy *Onegin*, 1881; Tchaikovsky declared that he owed its success mostly to Bevignani. Berlin and Vienna, 1898; New York, M, 1894–1900.

Bianca e Fernando. Opera in 2 acts by Bellini; text by Gilardoni after Carlo Roti's drama *Bianca e Fernando alla tomba di Carlo IV, Duca di Agrigento* (1820). Prem. Naples, C, 30 May 1826.

The opera tells how Fernando (ten), the son of the usurped Duke of Agrigento, overcomes Filippo (bs), the usurper, first by pretending to support him and then by rescuing his father and preventing the marriage of his sister Bianca (sop) to Filippo.

Bellini completely revised the music for the second version, retaining only two original pieces. Orig. version prod. as *Bianca e Gernando* as the Naples censorship forbade references to the royal name Ferdinando.

Bianchi, Francesco (*b* Cremona, *c*.1752; *d* London, 27 Nov. 1810). Italian composer. One of the most productive and highly regarded opera-composers of his day, he wrote over 50 works, many characterized by a well-judged mixture of comic and serious elements. The thinly veiled social critique of *Il disertore francese* (1784), as well as its bourgeois costumes, caused an outcry on its first performance and earned it rapid notoriety: the highly popular *La villanella rapita* (1783), taken up enthusiastically throughout Europe, was a more conventional opera buffa. From 1794 Bianchi was active at London, H; 1798–1800 he was director of opera at Crow Street T, Dublin.

Bibiena. See GALLI-BIBIENA.

Bignens, Max (b Zurich, 9 June 1912). Swiss designer. Studied Zurich, Munich, Florence, and Paris. Resident designer Berne 1939–45, Basle 1945–51 and 1956–61, Munich 1951–6 and 1963–5, Darmstadt 1961–3, Cologne 1965. Has also designed in many other European opera-houses.

Billy Budd. Opera in 4 acts by Britten; text by E. M. Forster and Eric Crozier, after Melville's unfinished story (1891). Prem. London, CG, 1 Dec. 1951, cond. Britten.

The opera, which has no female roles, is set on a man-o'-war, HMS *Indomitable*, in Napoleonic times. The ship is short of crew and Billy Budd (bar) is press-ganged into service from a merchant ship. His natural goodness and affability arouse the resentment of the master-at-arms, John Claggart (bs), who persecutes Billy and tries to bribe him into leading a mutiny.

Claggart accuses Billy of treachery to Captain Vere (ten), for whom Billy has great respect. When summoned to Vere's cabin, Billy, instead of getting the promotion he expects, is accused of mutiny; unable to defend himself because of his stammer, he becomes so frustrated that he lashes out, killing Claggart. The court of officers decides Billy must hang. As he is about to die, Billy shouts 'Starry Vere, God bless you!', and the cry is echoed by the crew. The opera is told as a memory of distant events by the aged Vere, haunted by the belief that he could have saved Billy.

Bing, (Sir) **Rudolf** (b Vienna, 9 Jan. 1902). Austrian, later British, manager. Studied Vienna. Manager of Viennese concert agency 1923. Worked Darmstadt, and Berlin under Carl Ebert, who brought him to Gly., 1934. Manager, Gly., 1936–46. Helped found Edinburgh Fest.; dir. 1947–9. Manager New York, M, 1950–72. Played silent role of Sir Edgar in New York, C, prem. of Henze's *The Young Lord*, 1973.

Binički, Stanislav (b Jasika, 27 July 1872; d Belgrade, 15 Feb. 1942). Serbian composer. Studied Belgrade, Munich with Rheinberger. First music dir., Belgrade Nat. T 1920–4. His music includes an opera, *Na uranku* (Dawn, 1903), a pioneering Serbian national opera

in the manner of verismo making ingenious use of contrasting musical styles to depict the struggle between Turks and Serbs.

Birmingham. City in Warwickshire, England. The city was long dependent on occasional and touring performances. Raybould's *The Sumida River* (1916) was followed by the prem. of Messager's *Monsieur Beaucaire* (1919) and then a series of productions at the Repertory T from 1920 under Sir Barry Jackson that included the prem. of Smyth's *Fête galante* (1923). Local amateur companies have contributed, e.g. the Barfield OC with some lesser-known 19th-cent. works and a novelty, Margaret More's *The Mermaid* (1951), and the Midland Music Makers with some enterprising productions including *William Tell*, *Prince Igor*, *Les Troyens*, *Ivan the Terrible*, *The Jacobin*, and the British prem. of *Die Feen*.

The Barber Institute, part of Birmingham U, has also staged some important productions, including revivals of Handel and the British prem. of Rameau's *Hippolyte et Aricie* (1965). English Touring O and Birmingham Music T have combined forces at the Canon Hill Arts Centre. The City of Birmingham Touring O commissioned *Ghanashyam* (A Broken Branch, 1989) from Ravi Shankar and has given a reduced, two-evening version of Wagner's *Ring* (1990).

Birtwistle, (Sir) **Harrison** (b Accrington, 15 July 1934). English composer. Studied Manchester, with Richard Hall; then at London RAM. Together with Peter Maxwell Davies, he founded the Pierrot Players so as to give performances of works with some element of *music theatre. The group was reorganized as The Fires of London in 1970.

Though almost all Birtwistle's music is theatrical, he distinguishes between traditional opera and his own stage works, which owe at least as much to Greek theatre. *Punch and Judy* (1968), 'a tragical comedy or a comical tragedy', tells the old puppet-show story making use of costumed instrumentalists and a 'choregos' to introduce the plot and initiate some of the action. In *Down by the Greenwood Side* (1969), 'a dramatic pastoral', the choregos has become the traditional figure of Father Christmas, and the work combines a mummers' play with a ballad, dividing singers and a speaker into two groups; again, the action is ritualized and includes some horrifying child murders in its representation of seasonal death and rebirth. *Bow Down* (1977), described simply as 'music theatre', once more uses ballads to tell of the murder of a fair sister by her dark sister; and it repeats from earlier works the use of several versions of the same ballad not in linear narrative but so as to reflect several aspects of the story.

Much in these pieces points towards *The Mask of Orpheus* (1986). This 'lyrical tragedy' uses a large orchestra, which carries the drama forward as much as the singing does. There is again no linear narrative, rather the juxtaposition of contrasting accounts of the same dramatic moment so as to further the exploration of the Orpheus myth. Use is made of electronic music (in six interludes), and of music constructed in Birtwistle's favourite blocks of sounds. Use of masks and of puppets again serves to ritualize immediate emotion on to the eternal.

Birtwistle followed this large-scale work with *Yan Tan Tethera* (1986), adapted from a TV commission. The favourite ritual framework now concerns a folk-story, and use is made of the incantatory effect of the ancient sheep-counting method of the title. This is used to outline the conflict of good and evil, with the shepherd representatives of these absolutes never confronting one another but staring out at the audience.

Gawain (1991) marks a departure from Birtwistle's preference for material taken directly from folklore. His treatment of the 14th-cent. romance *Sir Gawain and the Green Knight* provides recognizably human characters; and the moral problem posed by the hero's compromise of chivalric honour, accepting magic protection in order to outwit his challenger, shows a more realistic approach to the problems of human nature dealt with in earlier works, even though there is still a large ritualistic element. His most recent opera, *The Second Mrs Kong* (Gly. 1994) combines a return to the Orpheus legend with Hollywood myth-making.

Birtwistle has also written dramatic works for performance in schools, *Music for Sheep*, *The Mark of the Goat*, and *Visions of Francesco Petrarca*, which also make use of the dramatic method of presenting different aspects of identical action. Even his purely instrumental works may incorporate a dramatic element involving players moving or perhaps opposing one another in conflict.

Bishop, (Sir) **Henry** (*b* London, 18 Nov. 1786;

d London, 30 Apr. 1855). English composer and conductor. His first opera, *The Circassian Bride* (1809), was lost when the score was burnt in the fire that destroyed *Drury Lane the day after the first performance; but its success led to other works. Music dir. London, CG, 1810–24. Moving to DL, he produced among many other works *Aladdin* (1826), in an attempt to rival Weber's *Oberon* at CG. He later became music dir. at Vauxhall. Most of his works consist of numbers interpolated into a spoken play; in many cases 'operas' credited to him include only a few numbers, or even a single number. Even *Aladdin*, his most substantial work, includes spoken dialogue. He used his song 'Home, Sweet Home' in many forms as a theme song in *Clari*.

Bizet, Georges (*b* Paris, 25 Oct. 1838; *d* Bougival, 3 June 1875). French composer. Studied Paris with Gounod. His earliest operas are in the first period of composition which he later disavowed, too harshly in the cases of *Le docteur Miracle* (1857) and *Don Procopio* (comp. 1859); these take Italian example (especially Rossini and Donizetti) and contain some charming music already showing a witty sense of the stage. With the unfinished *Ivan IV* (comp. *c.*1862–5) the model is French Grand Opera, the result awkward and most successful in the less grandiose moments.

Bizet's first important opera was *Les pêcheurs de perles* (The Pearl Fishers, 1863), where the influences are still more diverse, but are more expertly absorbed; there is a lyrical impulse that is recognizably Bizet's own, and some ambitious (occasionally over-ambitious) harmonic adventures, but the characters are alive, and the drama compelling. These gains are consolidated in *La jolie fille de Perth* (The Fair Maid of Perth, 1867), which triumphs over a lame libretto and makes of the situations a genuine drama, with some excellent individual arias and ensembles. The surviving fragments of *La coupe du roi de Thulé* suggest that ambition was growing, especially in the handling of motive.

Bizet completed his father-in-law F. Halévy's *Noé*, unpromisingly; and then a brief but intense concentration on opéra-comique, with *Calendal*, *Clarissa Harlowe*, and *Grisélidis* (none of them completed), led to *Djamileh* (1872). The characterization is stronger than anything in the earlier works, and the sense of the exotic stimulates some of his most original harmony and exquisite orchestral passages. With it he attains full maturity; though even this could not have led listeners to expect *Carmen* (1875). Here his gifts are most completely realized. It was not achieved easily, and the score went through many revisions before reaching its present state. The subject suited him ideally, with its exotic setting and violent passions; its opportunity for striking, tuneful arias that fit easily into the drama (and advance it) and for brilliant orchestral colour; and its brilliant use of motive, of which he was now a master. It was notoriously a failure at first, and Bizet did not live to see it triumph. After his death, Ernest Guiraud composed recitatives so as to turn it into a Grand Opera; though they remain in use in some opera-houses, they are regrettable for their betrayal of Bizet's original opéra-comique, not least since historically the work stands at the head of the whole genre. *Carmen* was admired by a wide variety of musicians, influencing Tchaikovsky (whose favourite opera it was) in *The Queen of Spades*, and giving Nietzsche a stick with which to belabour Wagner with a demand for 'Mediterranean' values; and it has with good reason never lost its hold on audiences.

Bjoner, Ingrid (*b* Kråkstad, 8 Nov. 1927). Norwegian soprano. Studied Oslo with Boellemose, Frankfurt with Lohmann. Début Oslo 1957 (Donna Anna). Bayreuth 1960; Munich from 1961 (Dyer's Wife there, 1988); New York, M, 1961–7; London, CG, 1967; also Paris, O; Milan, S; Salzburg; Berlin, SO. Roles incl. Leonore, Senta (at Oslo, 1989), Isolde, Brünnhilde, Tosca, Elektra, Ariadne. (R)

Björling, Jussi (*b* Stora Tuna, 5 Feb. 1911; *d* Stockholm, 9 Sept. 1960). Swedish tenor. Studied with his father, the tenor David Björling, and Stockholm with Forsell and Hislop. First appearance Royal Swedish O, July 1930 (Lamplighter, *Manon Lescaut*); official début there August 1930 (Don Ottavio). Sang at Stockholm O regularly until 1938, then intermittently until his death. Vienna 1936; Chicago 1937; London, CG, 1939, 1960; New York, M, 1938–60 (except during the war). A great lyric tenor of his generation, memorable in the Verdi and Puccini repertory, but also as Faust (Gounod); his voice was radiant, even, and resonant, and was used with refinement and musicianship. (R)

Bjornson, Maria (*b* Paris, 1949). British

designer of Norwegian-Romanian origin. Studied London with Koltai. Glasgow Citizen's T 1970–2, working on 13 productions in 18 months. London from 1972: CG, ENO regularly; also WNO, Scottish O, Sydney O, Japan, etc. A dedicated and highly sought-after artist, whose large repertory contains *The Ring*, *Queen of Spades*, *Carmen*, a Janáček cycle for WNO/Scottish O, *Toussaint* (prem.), and *The Phantom of the Opera*. Her very individual style, allied to a sharp eye for detail, incorporates elements of mythology, fairy-tale, and symbolic distortion; its tone encompasses the romantic, the spectacular, the harsh, and the oblique; her costumes similarly range from elaborate fullness to deceptive simplicity.

Blacher, Boris (*b* Newchang, China, 19 Jan. 1903; *d* Berlin, 30 Jan. 1975). German composer. His inventiveness and intelligence were applied particularly to the problems of theatre music. He wrote ballets and dance dramas, and works defined as dramatic notturno (*Die Nachtschwalbe*, 1947) and ballet-opera (*Preussisches Märchen*, 1952); also such operas as *Fürstin Tarakanowa* (1941), *Romeo und Julia* (1947), *Die Flut* (1947), and *Rosamunde Floris* (1960). Even in these, there is often a reconsideration of the conventions of opera to create, and explore sensitively, novel dramatic conditions, which in some cases anticipate the increased interest in music theatre. His *Abstrakte Oper No. 1* (1953) substitutes for narrative some considerations of fundamental human emotions and their consequences. Librettist, with von *Einem, of the latter's *Dantons Tod* and *Der Prozess*.

Blachut, Beno (*b* Ostrava-Vítkovice, 14 June 1913; *d* Prague, 10 Jan. 1985). Czech tenor. Studied Prague with Kadeřábek. Début Olomouc 1939 (Jeník). Prague, N, from 1941, his Dalibor in 1945 establishing him as the leading Czech tenor of his day. Distinguished in the Czech repertory, he was also successful as Florestan, Don José, Otello, Hermann, and Walther. Holland 1959; Edinburgh 1964; also Venice, F; Moscow, B; Berlin, K; etc. He made skilful use of his expressive voice, and was a fine actor. (R)

Blake, Rockwell (*b* Plattsburgh, NY, 10 Jan. 1951). US tenor. Studied Plattsburgh. Début New York, CO, 1979 (Ory). New York, M, from 1981; Boston 1982; Aix from 1983; also Chicago, Lisbon, and Italy, where he is highly regarded. A fine bel canto singer of great virtuosity; roles incl. Don Ottavio, Almaviva, Lindoro, Rinaldo (*Armida*), Osiride (*Mosè*), Rodrigo (*Donna del Lago*), Arturo, Tonio (*Fille du régiment*), Rossini's Otello. (R)

Blangini, Felice (*b* Turin, 18 Nov. 1781; *d* Paris, 18 Dec. 1841). Italian tenor and composer. A chorister at Turin Cathedral, he went to Paris in 1799 where, with the support of such influential patrons as Napoleon's sister Princess Borghese, he soon became one of the most sought-after singing-teachers in Europe. Though it was his shorter vocal pieces that brought him greatest recognition as a composer, he also produced about 30 stage works—mostly opéras-comiques—of which the most successful was *Encore un tour de Caliphe* (1805).

bleat. Vocal device whereby a single note is quickly reiterated with varied pressure of the breath. Also known as Goat's Trill (Fr., *chévrotement*; Ger., *Bockstriller*; It., *trillo caprino*; Span., *trino de cabra*).

Blech, Leo (*b* Aachen, 21 Apr. 1871; *d* Berlin, 24 Aug. 1958). German conductor and composer. Studied Berlin with Bargiel and Rudorff, then Humperdinck. Aachen 1893–9; Prague, Deutsches T, 1899–1906; Berlin, H, 1906–23 (music dir. from 1913). Toured US 1923. Berlin, Deutsches Opernhaus (later SO), 1923 and 1926–37. As a Jew, he was prevented from returning to Berlin after conducting in Riga in 1937. Riga 1937–41, then Stockholm 1941–7. Returned to Berlin, SO, 1949. A fine Wagner and Verdi conductor, with a wide knowledge and understanding of opera. His own operas include *Das war ich* (Dresden 1902), *Alpenkönig und Menschenfeind* (Dresden 1903), and the most successful, *Versiegelt* (Hamburg 1908). (R)

Blegen, Judith (*b* Missoula, MT, 27 Apr. 1941). US soprano. Studied at Curtis Institute and sang at Spoleto Fest. 1963. Nuremberg O 1965–8 (début as Olympia). Salzburg 1967 (Papagena); Vienna, S, 1968 (Rosina); New York, M, from 1970. London 1975 (Despina). Most successful in such lighter roles as Sophie (Paris, O, 1977). (R)

Bliss, (Sir) Arthur (*b* London, 2 Aug. 1891; *d* London, 27 Mar. 1975). English composer and conductor. The dramatic nature of Bliss's music was first revealed in his ballet and film scores, one of which was a version of *The Beggar's Opera*: he did not turn to opera until

The Olympians in 1949. Though he had an imaginative subject for a Romantic opera, and provided some fine music especially in Act II, the work did not make its expected impact.

Blitzstein, Marc (*b* Philadelphia, 2 Mar. 1905; *d* Fort-de-France, Martinique, 22 Jan. 1964). US composer. Studied principally with Boulanger and Schoenberg. He abandoned his early experimental style under the influence of Hanns Eisler, and in the late 1930s began developing a more populist operatic style as reflection of his theories of the artist as social activist. His first significant work in this new manner was *The Cradle Will Rock* (1937), produced by Orson Welles and John Houseman, in improvised circumstances after its stage prem. was blocked by officials. Here he brought into his style a feeling for US vernacular music, including blues, jazz, Broadway, and other popular musical manners, in his wish to engage a broad audience in his social message. Other operas of the period include *No for an Answer* (1941), on the plight of immigrants. *Regina* (1949), a version of Lillian Hellman's *The Little Foxes*, marked a return from the musical towards more traditional opera (or perhaps a modern Singspiel), though *Reuben, Reuben* (1955) resumed his Broadway manner. He had his greatest success with a version of Brecht's *Die Dreigroschenoper* (1954). His versatility in moving between different genres, without losing his distinctive musical personality, in some ways anticipates more recent developments in music theatre.

Bloch, Ernest (*b* Geneva, 24 July 1880; *d* Portland, OR, 15 July 1959). Swiss, later US, composer. His only opera is *Macbeth* (1910). Written in a style that owes something to *Pelléas et Mélisande* and to Dukas, it has been highly praised for its intelligent and dramatic handling of the subject.

Blochwitz, Hans Peter (*b* Garmisch, 28 Sept. 1949). German tenor. Studied Frankfurt and Mainz. Début Frankfurt 1984 (Lensky). Outstanding in Mozart, e.g. at London, CG, 1989 (Fernando) and New York, M, 1990 (Don Ottavio). Other roles incl. Lucio Silla, Belmonte, and Nero (*Poppea*). (R)

Blockx, Jan (*b* Antwerp, 25 Jan. 1851; *d* Kapellenbos, 26 May 1912). Belgian composer. The most gifted Belgian composer of his day, he wrote seven operas which did much to establish a native operatic tradition. Of them, *Herbergprinses* (The Princess of the Inn, 1896) was the most significant and successful. This work, *De Bruid der Zee* (The Bride of the Sea, 1901), and *Baldie* (1908) constitute a trilogy of works on Flemish national life. Blockx's operas reveal his Romantic tendencies and his feeling for native folklore.

Blodek, Vilém (*b* Prague, 3 Oct. 1834; *d* Prague, 1 May 1874). Czech composer. An influential flautist and teacher, of his several operas the most important is *V studni* (In the Well, 1867). Blodek's knowledge of *The Bartered Bride*, and his use of that work's librettist, show in this amiable 1-act village comedy, which in the 19th cent. came close to rivalling its popularity.

Blomdahl, Karl-Birger (*b* Växjö, 19 Oct. 1916; *d* Kungsängen, 14 June 1968). Swedish composer. His most important opera, and his best-known work, is *Aniara* (1959). Its novel techniques, which include a pioneering use of electronic music, aroused much interest when it first appeared, as did its wide-ranging eclecticism of style. The work also impressed international audiences for its exploration of serious issues, using a group of people in a doomed spaceship both as setting and metaphor.

Blonde. Constanze's maid (sop), sometimes known as Blondchen, in Mozart's *Die Entführung aus dem Serail*.

Blow, John (*b* Newark, *bapt.* 23 Feb. 1649; *d* London, 1 Oct. 1708). English composer. *Venus and Adonis* (1683), his only work for the stage, was composed as part of his duties as court composer to Charles II. Described by him as a 'masque for the entertainment of the King', it is in effect a miniature opera in a prologue and three acts and stands as an important predecessor to Purcell's *Dido and Aeneas*.

Bluebeard's Castle. See DUKE BLUEBEARD'S CASTLE.

Boatswain's Mate, The. Opera in 1 act by Ethel Smyth; text by the composer, after W. W. Jacobs's story. Prem. London, Shaftesbury T, 28 Jan. 1916.

Harry Benn (ten), a former boatswain, hopes to persuade the landlady of The Beehive, Mrs Waters (sop), to marry him. He arranges that his friend Travers (bs) will pretend to attack Mrs Waters in order that Harry can rescue her. When Travers enters the house, the landlady is not frightened in the least; she takes up a gun, and locks him in a cupboard. A series of incidents then leads her to abandon Harry and marry Travers instead.

bocca chiusa (It.: 'closed mouth'; Fr., *bouche fermée*; Ger., *Brummstimmen*). Singing without words and with closed mouth, i.e. humming. The most famous uses of bocca chiusa in opera occur with the Humming Chorus in Act II of *Madama Butterfly* and in the last act of *Rigoletto*.

Bockelmann, Rudolf (*b* Bodenteich, 2 Apr. 1892; *d* Dresden, 10 Oct. 1958). German bass-baritone. Studied Celle, and Leipzig with Lassner and Scheidemantel. Début Leipzig 1921 (Herald, *Lohengrin*). Hamburg 1926–32; Berlin, S, 1932–45. Bayreuth 1928–42. London, CG, 1929–30, 1934–8. Chicago 1930–2. One of the finest singers of Sachs and Wotan of his generation, with a warm voice and an elegant sense of phrasing. His Nazi sympathies prevented him from resuming a full career after 1945. (R)

Bockstriller. See BLEAT.

Bodanzky, Artur (*b* Vienna, 16 Dec. 1877; *d* New York, 23 Nov. 1939). Austrian conductor. Studied Vienna, later with Zemlinsky. Début České Budějovice 1900. Vienna 1903–4 as Mahler's assistant; Berlin, Prague, Mannheim. Cond. first stage *Parsifal* in England, London, CG, 1914. New York, M, 1915–39. A conductor of wide range and professionalism, he was known above all for his Wagner; however, he was as notorious for the cuts he made in Wagner as he was for the versions he prepared, with unsuitable additions, of operas including *Oberon*, *Freischütz*, *The Magic Flute*, and *Fidelio*. (R)

Bogianckino, Massimo (*b* Rome, 10 Nov. 1922). Italian pianist, musicologist, and administrator. Studied Rome with Rossi, Casella, and Mortari. After a short career as a pianist, taught in Pittsburgh and Pesaro. Artistic dir. Accademia Filarmonica, Rome, 1960–3; Rome, O, 1963–8; Spoleto 1968–71; Florence, C, 1975–81; Paris, O, 1982–5; Florence, C, from 1991.

Bohème, La (Bohemian Life). Opera in 4 acts by Puccini; text by Giacosa and Illica, after Henri Murger's novel *Scènes de la vie de Bohème* (serially, 1847–9). Prem. Turin, R, 1 Feb. 1896.

The Latin Quarter of Paris, *c.*1830. On

Christmas Eve, Marcello (bar), a painter, and Rodolfo (ten), a poet, are joined in their garret by the philosopher Colline (bs) and the musician Schaunard (bar), who brings food. When the landlord Benoit (bs) arrives, his tenants ply him with drink and he leaves without his rent. Rodolfo tells his friends he will join them in the café when he has finished the article he is writing. He hears a knock at the door: it is his neighbour Mimì (sop), who asks for a light for her candle. Gradually a mutual attraction becomes apparent and they express their new-found love.

The crowds gather at the Café Momus. Mimì, wearing a new bonnet Rodolfo has just bought her, is introduced to his friends. Musetta (sop) appears with her elderly admirer Alcindoro (bs). Seeing her ex-lover Marcello, she attracts his attention and leaves with him.

A few weeks later, Mimì is seeking Marcello; she and Rodolfo have quarrelled and she asks Marcello to advise them. She overhears Rodolfo saying that he can no longer live with Mimì; he also knows she is dying from consumption. The couple agree to part when spring comes.

Back in the garret, Rodolfo and Marcello contemplate the women they have left. Spirits rise when Colline and Schaunard enter, but shortly Musetta arrives to say that Mimì has left her rich protector and is dangerously ill. She wants to spend her last hours with Rodolfo. She is brought in and Marcello is sent to pawn Musetta's earrings for medicine. While Rodolfo is covering the window, his friends notice that Mimì has died. He thinks she is asleep but realizing the truth, throws himself sobbing over her body.

The story is also the subject of an opera in 4 acts by Leoncavallo; text by composer, after Murger. Prem. Venice, F, 6 May 1897. Leoncavallo's opera keeps more strictly to the events and in most ways to the characters and spirit of the novel.

Bohemian Girl, The. Opera in 3 acts by Balfe; text by Alfred Bunn, after the ballet-pantomime *The Gypsy* by Saint-Georges (1839), based in turn on Cervantes's novel *La gitanilla* (1614). Prem. London, DL, 27 Nov. 1843.

The opera tells of a Polish aristocrat, Thaddeus (ten), who is in political exile, and Arline (sop), daughter of Count Arnheim (bs); she was kidnapped and brought up by gypsies. Her father recognizes her and is so overjoyed at her discovery that he permits her marriage to Thaddeus.

Böhm, Karl (*b* Graz, 28 Aug. 1894; *d* Salzburg, 14 Aug. 1981). Austrian conductor. Studied first law, then music in Graz, and Vienna with Mandyczewski and Adler. Répétiteur Graz 1917, second cond. 1918, first cond. 1919. Début 1917 (*Trompeter von Säckingen*). Recommended by Karl Muck to Walter, who engaged him Munich 1921. Music dir. Darmstadt, 1927–31; Hamburg 1931–3; Dresden 1934–42, conducting prems. of *Schweigsame Frau* (1935) and *Daphne* (1938). Music dir. Vienna, S, 1943–5, and of rebuilt house in 1954–6; resigned after criticism of his long absences abroad. Regularly Salzburg 1938–80; Bayreuth 1962–71. London, CG, 1936, 1954, 1977, 1979; Buenos Aires, C, 1950–3; New York, M, 1957–78. With Krauss, he was the leading Strauss conductor of his day, and also outstanding in Mozart and Berg: his clarity and sense of proportion served both composers well, but were also admirably effective in the whole range of the Austro-German tradition, which lay closest to his heart. That heart was only worn on his sleeve near the end of his career; earlier, his greatest performances seemed to represent the mellowing of vast experience and ruthless professionalism into a wise maturity. (R)

Böhme, Kurt (*b* Dresden, 5 May 1908; *d* Munich, 20 Dec. 1989). German bass. Studied Dresden Cons.; member of Dresden, S, 1930–50 (first *Schweigsame Frau*; Sutermeister's *Romeo und Julia*, *Die Zauberinsel*). London, CG, 1936, 1956–60 as Hunding, Ochs (his most successful role), Hagen. New York, M, 1954–7; Bayreuth; Milan, S; Salzburg; etc. (R)

Boieldieu, (François-)Adrien (*b* Rouen, 16 Dec. 1775; *d* Jarcy, 8 Oct. 1834). French composer. He came early to know the operas of Grétry, Méhul, Le Sueur, and especially Dalayrac, and wrote his own first opera in 1793. Moving to Paris, he quickly established himself as a successful composer of opéras-comiques, in which melodic grace and fluency, together with simple but elegant harmony, won him a wide following. His subjects ranged wider than his essential style, though he was capable of responding to the stimulus both of extremes of emotional tension, as in *Béniowski* (1800), and of exotic settings, as in *Le calife de Bagdad* (1800). The popularity of the latter is said to have irritated Cherubini, who then gave the modest Boieldieu some further technical instruction.

Other successes followed, especially with *Ma tante Aurore* (1803) and *Aline, reine de Golconde* (1804), before Boieldieu left to become court composer in St Petersburg. Here he wrote about an opera a year, also greatly improving operatic standards, before returning to Paris and new triumphs with *Jean de Paris* in 1812. The assurance, vigour, and charm of this work confirmed Boieldieu's wider reputation, with several German versions being produced in the same year and in 1815 Boieldieu was appointed court composer.

A deepening of style, and developing awareness of Romantic influences, show in his next work, *Le petit chaperon rouge* (1818), but for seven years thereafter he wrote little. It was in part the stimulus of Rossini's influence on the French musical scene that led him to return to it in 1825 with his masterpiece, *La dame blanche*. This is a richer and subtler work than anything he had composed, one of the most important French Romantic operas of the decade, skilfully exploiting the atmosphere of mystery and suspense and showing a new freedom of construction. As Wagner found, these virtues are sustained in his next work, *Les deux nuits* (1829), whose chorus 'La belle nuit' was (Berlioz pointed out) a source for the *Lohengrin* bridal march. In both works, the traditions of earlier Romantic opera are turned to new expressive effect, especially by means of an individual vein of chromatic harmony and skilful orchestration. With them, Boieldieu reaches the peak of his achievement. His health, affected by his Russian years, then deteriorated into tuberculosis, and the 1830 Revolution removed him from his official positions.

'Bois épais'. Amadis's (ten) aria in Act II of Lully's *Amadis*, in which he declares that the sombre woods can never be as dark as his despair, since he will never again see his lover Oriane.

Boito, Arrigo (orig. Enrico) (*b* Padua, 24 Feb. 1842; *d* Milan, 10 June 1918). Italian composer, librettist (sometimes as 'Tobia Gorrio'), and critic. Son of an Italian painter and a Polish countess; studied Milan with Mazzucato, and there formed a lifelong friendship with Faccio. Together they went to Paris, where Boito first met Verdi, began to consider Faust and Nero as operatic subjects, and wrote the libretto for Faccio's *Amleto* (1865). Back in Milan, he associated himself with the artistic reform movement known as the Scapigliatura, and served under Garibaldi. In 1868 *Mefistofele* was performed at Milan, S; it failed, partly through its length and the inadequacy of the performance (to which Boito's own conducting contributed). Depressed, Boito turned to writing librettos for other composers and to translating operas (incl. *Der Freischütz*, *Rienzi*, and *Ruslan and Lyudmila*). A revised version of *Mefistofele* was successful in 1875; further revisions were made and performed in 1876 and 1881.

The revision of *Simon Boccanegra* for revival in 1881 pleased the hitherto hostile Verdi, and led to work on *Otello* and hence to the friendship that Boito regarded as the most important event of his life. After *Falstaff* had followed, he began work on *King Lear* and even wrote part of the opening scene. Verdi had meanwhile urged Boito to continue his own musical career with *Nerone*; but he never completed it, and it was eventually posthumously performed in a version edited by Toscanini and Vincenzo Tommasini.

Boito's intelligence and skill as a librettist have been widely praised. He served many composers excellently, and furnished Verdi with the brilliant (though by no means flawless) text for *Otello* and the incomparable one for *Falstaff*: the occasional misjudgements in the tragedy, such as the distortion of the character of Iago, are absent from the comedy, in which Boito's verbal brilliance (he took delight in complex rhyme and arcane vocabulary) are supreme. His texts for his own two operas are ambitious, too much so for his own musical powers and his creative resolve, and the many revisions and procrastinations reveal his difficulty in realizing his lifelong vision of the conflicting attractions of virtue and evil: his greatest fascination was always for the figure of magnificent evil. His own music is capable of grandeur, but it is a quality he has difficulty in sustaining, and the idiom frequently degenerates into mechanical gestures. As a critic, he was a keen but discriminating Wagnerian, latterly unenthusiastic, and a champion of Meyerbeer and Verdi. His most celebrated non-Verdian libretto was for Ponchielli's *La Gioconda*.

Bologna. City in Emilia-Romagna, Italy. The first opera given was Girolamo Giacobbi's *Andromeda* at the T Pubblico in 1610; burnt down 1623. Opera was then given at the T Formigliari (1636–1802) and the T Malvezzi (1653–1745), and opera buffa at the T Marsigli (1710–1825). When the T Malvezzi burnt down in 1745, the T Comunale was designed by Antonio Galli-Bibiena and opened in 1763 with Gluck directing his *Trionfo di Clelia*. Under Angelo Mariani, 1859–72, Martucci, and Toscanini, it championed Wagner, giving the Italian prems. of *Lohengrin* (1871), *Tannhäuser* (1872), *Fliegender Holländer* (1877), and *Tristan* (1888), and also of Verdi's *Don Carlos* (1867). It has continued to sustain an adventurous policy and maintain high standards.

Bolshoy Theatre. See MOSCOW.

Bolton, Ivor (*b* ?, 17 May 1958). English conductor. After study at Cambridge and London, RCM, at Gly. from 1982 (*La bohème*, *The Rake's Progress*, *Die Zauberflöte*; *Orfeo* at the Fest.); dir Touring O from 1992. Dir., English Touring O, 1990–3: *Lucia*, *Così fan tutte*. London, ENO 1992 (*Xerxes*); Bologna 1993 (*Poppea*); CG 1995 (*Arianna*).

Bonci, Alessandro (*b* Cesena, 10 Feb. 1870; *d* Viserba, 9 Aug. 1940). Italian tenor. Studied Pesaro with Pedrotti, Paris with Delle Sedie. Début Parma 1896 (Fenton). Milan, S, 1897; London, CG, 1900; New York, M, 1907–10; Chicago 1919–21; Rome; St Petersburg; Berlin; Madrid. Retired 1925. With his agile, exceptionally beautiful voice and fine phrasing, a great rival of Caruso; repertory incl. Paolino (*Matrimonio segreto*), Arturo, Alfredo, Faust (Gounod), Rodolfo. (R)

Bondeville, Emmanuel (*b* Rouen, 29 Oct. 1898; *d* Paris, 26 Nov. 1987). French composer. Dir. Paris, OC (1948–51) and O (1951–9). His shrewd sense of the theatre, his elegant vocal writing, and his intelligent appreciation of the operatic possibilities in works by authors as distinguished and contrasted as Molière, Flaubert, and Shakespeare, have won his operas much appreciation in France. His most important include *L'école des maris* (1935), *Madame Bovary* (1951), and *Antoine et Cléopâtre* (1974).

Bonney, Barbara (*b* Montclair, NJ, 14 Apr. 1956). US soprano. After study in Salzburg, début at Darmstadt 1979 (Anna, *Lustige*

Witwe). London, CG, 1984 (Sophie, *Rosenkavalier*); Milan, S, 1989 (Pamina). Her attractive stage presence lends credibility to such roles as Cherubino, Susanna, Gilda, and Manon. (R)

Bonno, Giuseppe (*b* Vienna, 29 Jan. 1711; *d* Vienna, 15 Apr. 1788). Austrian composer of Italian origin. Active at the Viennese court from 1736, he composed about 30 operas, in a style much influenced by his study in Italy and by the models of Fux and Caldara. Most of his works set librettos by Metastasio: especially significant are *Il re pastore* (1751) and *Il sogno di Scipione* (1763). Though his music was soon eclipsed by a younger generation, Bonno occupied an important place in Viennese operatic history; his occasional rudimentary use of opera buffa techniques in the framework of opera seria is noteworthy.

Bononcini, Giovanni (*b* Modena, 18 July 1670; *d* Vienna, 9 July 1747). Italian composer. After leaving Italy, where his first operas were produced, he joined the Viennese court in 1697 and with such works as *Endimione* (1699) and *Etearco* (1707) achieved fame throughout Europe. In 1719 he was engaged for the newly founded Royal Academy of Music in London, joining Handel and Amadei in a valiant attempt to establish Italian opera. Although Bononcini was initially the most popular of the trio, he was soon eclipsed by Handel, against whom his works today appear lacking in dramatic involvement and depth. They are, however, balanced by a gentler, pastoral mood and by a lighter melodic style, perhaps reflecting more accurately the general taste in opera in the early 18th cent.

It was at the first performance of Bononcini's final London opera, *Astianatte* (1727), that the two celebrated prima donnas Cuzzoni and Bordoni engaged in their infamous on-stage brawl.

Bontempi, Giovanni (*b* Perugia, 21 Feb. 1625; *d* Brufa, 1 July 1705). Italian composer, singer, and writer on music. He is remembered above all for *Il Paride* (1662), one of the first Italian operas staged in C Germany, and for *Dafne* (1671), one of the first German operas to survive in full score. These follow the general model of Mazzocchi; *Paride*, described by Bontempi as an 'erotopegno musicale' (pledge of love), was given to celebrate the marriage of the Princess of Saxony and is one of the most lavish of all Baroque operas.

Bonynge, Richard (*b* Epping, NSW, 29 Sept. 1930). Australian conductor. Début Vancouver 1963 (Gounod's *Faust*). Coached his wife Joan *Sutherland in leading bel canto roles and has conducted her in most leading opera-houses. Music dir. Vancouver O 1974–8, Australian O 1975–86. A specialist in the bel canto repertory, particularly Bellini, Donizetti; has also conducted Handel, Verdi, Massenet, Gounod. (R)

Bordeaux. City in Gironde, France. Opera was first given in 1688, and French singers began making regular appearances soon after. Francœur's *Pirame et Tisbé* was staged 1729. Mme Dujardin built an opera-house for her company in the Jardin Municipal; burnt down 1756. In 1752 there was founded an Académie Royale de Musique, with a company including ten soloists. The Grand T Municipal, one of the finest opera-houses in France, opened 1780 (cap. 1,158); damaged in the Revolution, restored 1799. The theatre increased its reputation in the 19th cent., with a number of prems. and visits from Parisian companies. It was rebuilt 1919, 1938, and 1977 (cap. 1,205), and in the 1930s strengthened its international reputation with a repertory of new works and with distinguished guest artists. Vanni Marcoux was director 1948–51, Roger Lalande 1954–70, developing an attention to enterprising productions and giving many prems. and French prems. of foreign works. He was succeeded by Gérard Boireau, who concentrated more on a 19th-cent. repertory, while continuing to attract international artists. The Mai Musical de Bordeaux, founded 1950, has taken more interest in novelties.

Bordoni, Faustina (*b* Venice, 1700; *d* Venice, 4 Nov. 1781). Italian soprano (though Quantz describes her as mez). Début Venice 1716 (Pollarolo's *Ariodante*). Known as 'the New Siren', she soon became famous throughout Italy and in Munich and Vienna (1725–6). In 1726 Handel brought her to London, where she was admired for her exquisite singing and acting, and her beauty, intelligence, and courtesy. She was involved in an on- stage brawl with her rival *Cuzzoni during a performance of Bononcini's *Astianatte* in 1727. She created several Handel roles, e.g. Alcestis (*Admeto*) and Elmira (*Siroe*). In 1730 she married *Hasse; they were described by Met-

astasio as 'a truly exquisite couple'. From 1731 he worked at the Dresden court with her as prima donna where she remained unchallenged until her retirement in 1751, except perhaps by Mingotti. One of the greatest singers of her time, she possessed a strong, agile voice, superb breath control, excellent diction, and an expressive dramatic talent well suited to contrasting roles. A fine portrait of her by Rosalba Carriera hangs in the Ca' Rezzonico, Venice. Subject of an opera, *Faustina Hasse*, by Louis Schubert (1879).

Borgatti, Giuseppe (*b* Cento, 17 Mar. 1871; *d* Reno, Lago Maggiore, 18 Oct. 1950). Italian tenor. Studied Bologna with Busi. Début Castelfranco Veneto 1892 (Faust). Created Andrea Chénier at short notice, Milan, S, 1896; thereafter sang with success in Italy, Spain, and Buenos Aires as Cavaradossi, Don José, Canio, Puccini's Des Grieux, etc. In 1899 sang Siegfried at Milan, S, under Toscanini, deeply impressing Richter. Italy's finest Heldentenor, he became particularly identified with the Wagner roles to which his virile, resonant voice, fine physique, and dramatic insight brought a heroic quality. Forced by blindness to retire in 1914. Taught Heddle Nash.

Borgioli, Dino (*b* Florence, 15 Feb. 1891; *d* Florence, 12 Sept. 1960). Italian tenor. Studied Florence with E. Giacchetti. Début Milan, V, 1917 (*La favorita*). Milan, S, from 1918, and subsequently most of the major opera-houses, as Rodolfo, Des Grieux (Puccini), Arturo. London, CG, 1925–39 (Edgardo, Rossini's Almaviva, Duke of Mantua, Don Ramiro), and Gly. 1937–9 (Don Ottavio, Ernesto), at both of which he was very popular. New York, M, 1934–5. Artistic director of New London OC at Cambridge T 1949. One of the best light lyric tenors of his day, with a clear, free voice and elegant phrasing. (R)

Bori, Lucrezia (*b* Valencia, 24 Dec. 1887; *d* New York, 14 May 1960). Spanish soprano. Studied Milan with Vidal. Début Rome, Ad., 1908 (Micaëla). Paris, C, 1910 (Manon); first Italian Octavian, Milan, S, 1911. New York, M, 1912–36, except 1915–20 when she withdrew with throat trouble. Also sang in Buenos Aires, C, and Monte Carlo. Her delicate, transparent tone and natural expressiveness particularly suited vulnerable heroines such as Mélisande, Mimì, Butterfly, and Violetta, though she was also a successful Norina. Created The Duchess of Towers in Deems Taylor's *Peter Ibbetson*. (R)

Boris. Boris Grigorievich (ten), nephew of Dikoj and lover of Káťa in Janáček's *Káťa Kabanová*. See also below.

Boris Godunov. Opera in 4 acts, with a prologue, by Musorgsky; text by the composer, after Pushkin's drama *The Comedy of the Distress of the Muscovite State, of Tsar Boris, and of Grishka Otrepiev* (1825) and Karamzin's *History of the Russian Empire* (1829). Orig. version comp. 1868–9, rejected by St Petersburg O 1870. Three scenes of the composer's revision (1871) prod. St Petersburg, charity perf., 17 Feb. 1873, with Petrov (as Varlaam), Komisarzhevsky, Platonova; whole opera (with further minor revisions) 8 Feb. 1874. Withdrawn after 25 performances, revived after composer's death in Rimsky-Korsakov's first rev. edn., St Petersburg 10 Dec. 1896. Rimsky-Korsakov's second version (1906–8), prod. Paris, O, 19 May 1908. Orig. version first performed abroad London, DL, 30 Sept. 1935, with Stear. This has seven scenes—four from Pushkin, two devised by Musorgsky from indications in the play, one developed from two separate scenes in it. Other versions by Meligailis (Riga 1924) and Shostakovich (Leningrad 4 Nov. 1959).

Russia and Poland, 1598–1605. Scene 1: Boris (bs) has murdered the young Dmitry, heir to the throne, and is pretending to decline the crown himself. His agents incite the crowd to persuade him to 'relent'. Scene 2: Though plagued by guilt, Boris goes to be crowned. Scene 3: In his cell the old monk Pimen (bs) is concluding a history of Russia; with him is the novice Grigory (ten), who resolves to avenge Dmitry. Scene 4: Grigory, who claims to be Dmitry, with two other friars Varlaam (bs) and Missail (ten), reaches an inn on the Lithuanian border. Grigory is identified but escapes the pursuing soldiers. Scene 5: To Boris in his rooms, word is brought by his councillor Shuisky (ten) of the pretender in Lithuania. To reassure him of the death of Dmitry, Shuisky recounts the murder, which throws the guilt-racked Tsar into a state of hallucination. Scene 6: Outside St Basil's Cathedral in Moscow the people begin to believe in the right of the false Dmitry. A simpleton (ten), robbed of a kopek, asks Boris to repeat his murder on the robbers; Boris prevents his arrest, and asks for prayer, but the simpleton refuses and falls to mending his shoes with a song for poor Russia. Scene 7: In the Council Hall an edict against the pretender is being read when Boris breaks in, distraught, and collapses dead.

In his second version Musorgsky made considerable additions and alterations, and arranged the scenes as follows:

Prologue: Scenes 1 and 2. Act I: Scenes 3 and 4. Act II: Scene 5. Act III (recast): Scene 1—Dmitry's lover, Marina (mez), sits in her father's Polish castle dreaming of when she will rule Russia, and Rangoni (bs) pleads the Catholic cause; Scene 2—Marina joins Dmitry in the gardens, and she persuades him not to give up his ambitions. Act IV: Scene 7, and an extra scene in the Kromy Forest, in which the people are in revolt against Boris; the pretender passes *en route* for Moscow, leaving the simpleton singing sadly for Russia as in the now discarded Scene 6. The order of these last two scenes is frequently reversed in order to allow the protagonist the final curtain; the counter-argument holds the protagonist to be, in fact, the Russian people. A revival at London, CG, 1958, with Christoff, used all these scenes, as did that at New York, M, in 1953. Both reverted to the original orchestration.

Borkh, Inge (*b* Mannheim, 26 May 1917). Swiss soprano. After beginning her career as an actress, studied Milan with Muratti and at Mozarteum, Salzburg. Début Lucerne 1941. Sang in Switzerland until 1951, when her sensational Magda Sorel in Basle led to engagements in Vienna, Berlin, and London. S Francisco 1953 (Elektra), and 1955 (Lady Macbeth); New York, M, 1958; London, CG, 1959 and 1967 (Salome and Dyer's Wife); also Salzburg; Milan, S; and Bayreuth. An intense and intelligent dramatic singer. She returned to acting in 1977. (R)

Borodin, Alexander (*b* St Petersburg, 12 Nov. 1833; *d* St Petersburg, 27 Feb. 1887). Russian composer. Studied music privately while a child and at the Medico-Surgical Academy, continuing to benefit from advice and guidance, including from Musorgsky, while pursuing his career as a chemist. Only one of his operatic projects was completed, a pastiche *The Bogatyrs* (1867). Material from sketches for *The Tsar's Bride* was used in other works; his Act IV of the collective project *Mlada* (1892) includes material from his unfinished masterpiece, *Prince Igor*. This was, after 18 years of work, left unfinished and mostly unscored, in part through Borodin's self-imposed difficulties in trying to prepare his own libretto. The opera was eventually prepared for publication by Rimsky-Korsakov and Glazunov. Despite their labours, its magnificent music remains expressed in a series of tableaux rather than in an evolving drama.

Borodina, Olga (*b* Minsk, 29 July 1963). Russian mezzo-soprano. Studied Leningrad; member of Kirov O from 1987. Appearances in the West from 1992: Paris, O (Marina); London, CG (Dalila, Marguerite (*Damnation de Faust*), Cenerentola). Admired for the strong dramatic commitment she brings to Musorgsky's Marina (New York, M, 1992) and Marfa. (R)

Boronat, Olimpia (*b* Genoa, 1867; *d* Warsaw, 1934). Italian soprano, of Spanish descent. Studied Milan with Leoni. Début Genoa or Naples, *c*.1885. Appearances in Spain, Portugal, and S America. St Petersburg, Imperial O, 1890–3, leaving to marry a Polish aristocrat. Resumed her career in Russia and Poland 1901–14, returning to Italy 1909. Opened a singing school in Warsaw, where she gave her last concert in 1922. Her voice was of an exceptional clarity and beauty, and her coloratura singing celebrated in the roles of Rosina, Elvira, and Violetta. (R)

Boston. City in Massachusetts, USA. The first opera given was Arne's *Love in a Village* in July 1769 (concert, owing to a 1750 ban on stage performances). The first staged work was a ballad opera, *The Farmer*, in July 1794. Opera in English was the rule until the 1820s, when touring companies began visiting. The Boston T opened 1854 and remained the city's opera-house for half a century. In 1855 Mario and Grisi appeared, and in 1860 Patti sang her first Rosina. The Mapleson Co. began visiting in 1878, and Grau's French Co. in 1879. During the 1880s and 1890s the Boston Ideal OC, the Theodore Thomas American Co., and the Castle Square Co. all gave seasons.

In Nov. 1909 the Boston OC, for which the Boston OH was built, began its short but spectacular career (516 perfs. of 51 operas) with *La Gioconda* (with Nordica). Under Henry Russell the company gave five seasons with Bori, Garden, Destinn, Leblanc, Dalmorès, Mur-

atore, and Marcoux; Weingartner made his US début in 1912 (*Tristan*). After a disastrous visit to Paris in 1914, it went bankrupt. The Boston Grand Opera Co. gave two seasons 1915–16 with many of Russell's singers. Nine seasons were organized by the Boston O Association, which brought the Chicago O each spring; and the New York, M, gave annual seasons 1934–86. Local companies, performing at Boston OH (demolished 1958), included the Fleck Grand O, the Boston Civic O, and the Boston Grand O.

In 1946 Boris Goldovsky founded the New England OT (which gave the US prem. of a shortened *Les Troyens*, 1955). In 1958 the Boston O Group (OC of Boston, 1965) was established under Sarah Caldwell: the company has given the US prems. of *Moses und Aron* (1966), *Benvenuto Cellini* (1975), and *The Ice Break* (1979). It has been based at the old Savoy T, now OH (cap. 2,605), since 1978.

Bottom. The weaver (bs-bar), one of the 'rude mechanicals' and Tytania's illusory love, in Britten's *A Midsummer Night's Dream*.

Bottone, Bonaventura (*b* London, 19 Sept. 1950). English tenor. Studied at London, RAM, and toured with Phoenix O from 1975. Gly. Fest. and Tour 1976; Wexford 1977; London, ENO, as David, Duke of Mantua, Alfredo, Nanki-Poo (*Mikado*). Scottish O (Loge). US début: Houston O 1987 (Pedrillo). London, CG, 1987. Particularly successful in the lighter lyric repertory.

bouche fermée. See BOCCA CHIUSA.

Bouffons, Guerre des. See GUERRE DES BOUFFONS.

Bouffes-Parisiens. Theatrical enterprise in Paris, opened 5 May 1855 by Offenbach at the Salle Marigny, when refused by other managements, with an entertainment including *Les deux aveugles*. He succeeded partly through the proximity of the Exposition Universelle; when this closed, he moved to a larger theatre (cap. 820), which he named Bouffes-Parisiens d'Hiver (later Bouffes-Parisiens), opening 29 Dec. 1855 with *Ba-ta-clan*. The home of light opera in general including works by Bizet, Lecocq, Chabrier, Audran, Messager, and Serpette.

Boughton, Rutland (*b* Aylesbury, 23 Jan. 1878; *d* London, 24 Jan. 1960). English composer. Self-taught. His attempt to establish an English school of Wagnerian music drama, drawing on Celtic and especially Arthurian myth, was pursued with remarkable single-mindedness; and although his small-scale (and partly amateur) 'Bayreuth' based on a commune at Glastonbury did not, after many efforts, establish itself permanently, he won wide popularity with *The Immortal Hour* (1914). This had 216 consecutive performances at one revival. His music is lightly tuneful and fluently written.

Boulevard Solitude. Opera in 7 scenes by Henze; text by the composer and Grete Weil, after Walter Jockisch's play based on Abbé Prévost's novel *L'histoire du chevalier des Grieux et de Manon Lescaut* (1731). Prem. Hanover, Landestheater, 17 Feb. 1952.

In this modern setting of the Manon Lescaut story, Des Grieux (ten) becomes a drug addict and Manon (sop) ends up wrongly accused of murder.

Boulez, Pierre (*b* Montbrison, 25 Mar. 1925). French composer and conductor. Studied Paris with Messiaen and Leibowitz. Has composed some incidental music, including *Orestie* (1955), *Mon Faust* (1962) and *Ainsi parla Zarathoustra* (1974), but has never been attracted to opera: indeed his controversial utterances on the subject include a proposal that all opera-houses should be blown up. This has not prevented him from giving distinguished performances in them. Conducted *Wozzeck* (Paris, O, 1963), and first complete *Lulu* (Paris, O, 1979). Engaged by Wieland Wagner in 1966 to conduct *Parsifal* at Bayreuth and *Wozzeck* in Frankfurt. In 1976 conducted Chéreau's centenary production of *The Ring* at Bayreuth. WNO 1992 (*Pélléas*). (R)

Bowman, James (*b* Oxford, 6 Nov. 1941). English counter-tenor. Studied London with De Rentz and Manén. Début Aldeburgh, EOG, 1967, Oberon (Britten). London, EOG, from 1967; London, SW, and Gly. 1970; London, CG, 1972; Sydney 1978; Paris, OC, 1979, C, 1982; also Aix, S Fe, Dallas, Verona, Buxton, etc. An attractive, lively, and musical performer, distinguished in the second generation of counter-tenors after *Deller. Roles incl. Endymion, Tamerlano, Xerxes, Polinesso, Giulio Cesare, Astron (*The Ice Break*); created Priest (Davies's *Taverner*), Apollo (*Death in Venice*). (R)

Braithwaite, Nicholas (*b* London, 26 Aug. 1939). English conductor. Son of below.

Studied London with Miles, Vienna with Swarowsky, and Bayreuth. Début WNO 1966 (*Don Pasquale*). London, SW, 1970, resident cond. 1971–2, associate principal cond. 1972–4; associate principal cond. London ENO 1970–4; CG 1973; music dir. Gly. Touring O 1977–80. Repertory incl. Wagner, Verdi, Puccini, Bizet; also first British *Devils of Loudun*. (R)

Braithwaite, Warwick (*b* Dunedin, 9 Jan. 1898; *d* London, 18 Jan. 1971). New Zealand conductor. Father of above. Studied London, RAM. O'Mara OC 1919; Vic-Wells (later SW) Co. 1932–40, when he was responsible, with Lawrance Collingwood, for many important productions. London, CG, 1950–3; Artistic dir. Australian Nat. O 1954–5; music dir. WNO 1956–60; London, SW, 1960–8. Repertory incl. *Fidelio*, *Don Carlos*, *Meistersinger*, *May Night*, *Mefistofele*, *Fledermaus*. (R)

Brandenburgers in Bohemia, The (Cz., *Braniboři v Čechách*). Opera in 3 acts by Smetana; text by Karel Sabina. Prem. Prague 5 Jan. 1866.

The opera tells of the fate of the three daughters of Volfram Obramovic (bs), Mayor of Prague, during an attack on their native Bohemia by the Brandenburgers. Tausendmark (bar), a Brandenburg spy, attempts to keep them under his control but they are eventually released thanks to the effort of Junoš (ten), a burgher of Prague, and Jíra (ten), the Bohemians' 'beggar king'.

Brangäne. Isolde's attendant (mez) in Wagner's *Tristan und Isolde*.

Brannigan, Owen (*b* Annitsford, 10 Mar. 1908; *d* Newcastle upon Tyne, 9 May 1973). English bass. Studied London, GSMD. Début Newcastle with SW Co. 1943 (Sarastro). London, SW, 1944–9 and 1952–8. Created Swallow (*Peter Grimes*), Collatinus, Noye, and Bottom for Britten; also roles by Malcolm Williamson and John Gardner. Gly. from 1947; London, CG, from 1948. Repertory included Leporello, Don Alfonso, Don Pasquale, and Dikoj. One of the best English buffo singers, with a large, ripe voice and a warm stage presence. (R)

Branzell, Karin (*b* Stockholm, 24 Sept. 1891; *d* Altadena, CA, 15 Dec. 1974). Swedish mezzo-soprano. Studied Stockholm with Hofer, New York with Rosati. Début Stockholm 1912 (Prince Sarvilaka, D'Albert's *Izeyl*).

Stockholm until 1918; Berlin, S, 1918–33; New York, M, 1924–44, 1951; Bayreuth 1930–1; London, CG, 1935–8. An admired Orfeo (Gluck), Fricka, Erda, Azucena, Amneris, Klytemnästra, Kostelnička. (R)

Braun, Victor (*b* Windsor, Ont., 4 Aug. 1935). Canadian baritone. Studied Toronto, singing with Canadian O Co. from 1961 (début as Escamillo). Frankfurt O 1963; Munich, S, 1968; London, CG, from 1969: Searle's Hamlet, Onegin, Mozart's Almaviva. First successful in such lyric roles as Jupiter (*Liebe der Danae*, S Fe 1982), Wolfram, Mandryka. Dramatic repertory from 1986, incl. Hans Sachs, Wozzeck (Chicago 1988), Pizarro. (R)

Braunfels, Walter (*b* Frankfurt, 19 Dec. 1882; *d* Cologne, 19 Mar. 1954). German composer. His operas show a strong theatrical instinct, and are cast in a late-Romantic, post-Wagnerian style that does not exclude a lightness of touch (he acquired an admiration for Berlioz from Mottl) and a feeling for the grotesque. His greatest popular success was with *Die Vögel* (1920).

Brautwahl, Die (The Marital Lottery). Opera in 3 acts by Busoni; text by the composer, after E. T. A. Hoffmann's story. Prem. Hamburg, S, 13 Apr. 1912.

Fantasy world in Berlin, *c.*1920. A young artist, Edmund Lehsen (ten), falls in love with Albertine (sop), daughter of the 'Kommissionsrat' Voswinkel (bs). She is already promised to Thusmann, but when he reports having seen her dancing at an inn, Voswinkel assumes his interest has waned. However, when an old Jew, Manasse (ten), asks for Albertine's hand for his nephew, Thusmann (bs), renews his promise of marriage. Voswinkel summons all the suitors; the one who chooses the correct one of three caskets shall win Albertine. Lehsen selects a casket containing a letter promising bliss and, eventually united with Albertine, he heads for Rome, where artistic fame awaits him.

Bravo, Il. Opera in 3 acts by Mercadante; text by Rossi and M. M. Marcello, based on Fenimore Cooper's novel, and on A. Bourgeois's play *La vénitienne*. Prem. Milan, S, 9 Mar. 1839.

Venice, 18th cent. Foscari (bs), a Venetian nobleman, loves Violetta (sop), and has her guardian murdered. Her mother, Teodora (sop), regrets having abandoned her daughter and pays the government assassin, the Bravo (ten), to abduct Violetta. After the reunion of mother and daughter the Bravo discloses that he is Violetta's father. The government has ordered him to kill Teodora since she has offended them; Teodora seizes the dagger from the Bravo and stabs herself. A messenger then arrives with news which releases the Bravo from his dreadful occupation. Violetta is able to depart with Pisani (ten), who has returned to Venice from exile in order to arrange their elopement.

break. See REGISTER.

Brecht, Bertolt (*b* Augsburg, 10 Feb. 1898; *d* Berlin, 15 Aug. 1956). German dramatist. With Elisabeth Hauptmann, he wrote the version of *The Beggar's Opera* known as *Die *Dreigroschenoper* (1928) for Kurt Weill, and often with other female collaborators, the texts for *Happy End* (1929), *Mahagonny* (1930), *Der Jasager* (1930), and some of Wagner-Régeny's *Persische Episode* (*Der Darmwäscher*) (1940–50), with Caspar *Neher. *The Trial of Lucullus* by Sessions (1947) and Dessau (1951) are based on his works, as is Cezar's *Galileo Galilei* (1964).

breeches part. See TRAVESTI.

Bregenz. City in Vorarlberg, Austria. A summer open-air festival opened 1946, with opera added 1956 in the specially built lakeside theatre (cap. 4,400) with floating stage. International artists take part in large-scale productions. 18th- and 19th-cent. works are staged in the Festspielhaus (cap. 1,800) and T am Kornmarkt (cap. 633). Opera has also been given at nearby Hohenems Castle.

Brendel, Wolfgang (*b* Munich, 20 Oct. 1947). German baritone. Studied Wiesbaden; début Kaiserslautern 1969 (Guglielmo). Munich, S, from 1971 (Papageno, Don Giovanni, Germont, Renato). New York, M, 1975 (Mozart's Almaviva); London, CG, 1985 (Luna). His voice is essentially lyrical in quality, but he possesses the power for dramatic roles: admired also as Wolfram (Bayreuth 1985) and Amfortas (Milan, S, 1991). (R)

Bretan, Nicolae (*b* Năsăud, 25 Mar. 1887; *d* Cluj, 1 Dec. 1968). Romanian composer, baritone, conductor, and critic. Studied Cluj with Farkas, Vienna with Geiringer, Budapest with Siklós and Sik. Principal baritone Bratislava 1913–14, 1916–17; baritone and prod. Oradea 1914–16; baritone, prod., cond., and dir. variously Cluj 1917–48 at both Romanian and Hungarian operas. One of the pioneers of Romanian opera, he reflects his cosmopolitan training in his musical style, and his gifts as a singer in his excellent vocal writing. His most substantial opera, *Horia* (1937), shows some influence of Wagner, but he is better known in his native country (despite a ban on his music when he refused to join the Communist Party) for his other, 1-act operas, which include *Luceafârul* (1921), *Golem Lásadása* (1924), and *Arald* (1942, prem. 1982).

Bretzner, Christoph Friedrich (*b* Leipzig, 10 Dec. 1748; *d* Leipzig, 31 Aug. 1807). German librettist and dramatist. The most successful and frequently set German author of the late 18th cent., his *Belmont und Constanze* (first set by André in 1781) formed the basis of the libretto for Mozart's *Die Entführung aus dem Serail* (1782).

Bréval, Lucienne (*b* Männedorf, 4 Nov. 1869; *d* Neuilly-sur-Seine, 15 Aug. 1935). Swiss, then French, soprano. Studied Paris with Wartot. Début Paris, O, 1892 (Selika). New York, M, 1901–2; London, CG, 1899, 1901, 1906. Created Grisélidis and Ariane (Massenet), Lady Macbeth (Bloch), Pénélope (Fauré), and Monna Vanna (Février). One of the great French singers of her time, celebrated as Brünnhilde and in the grand classical roles of Rameau and Gluck. (R)

Brian, Havergal (*b* Dresden, Staffs., 29 Jan. 1876; *d* Shoreham, 28 Nov. 1972). British composer. Mainly self-taught, he never enjoyed any popular success and most of his large output remains unpublished and unperformed. The subject-matter of his seven operas reveals his catholic tastes: the most important works are *The Tigers* (comp. 1917–19), *Turandot: Prinzessin von China* (1949–51), and *Faust* (1954–6). Only *Agamemnon* (comp. 1957, prem. 1971) has ever been staged, and here the influence of Strauss is strikingly apparent. *The Tigers* was successfully performed by BBC forces under Lionel Friend in 1983.

Bridesmaids' Chorus. The chorus in Act II of Weber's *Der Freischütz*, in which the village girls bring a wreath to Agathe and prepare her for her wedding.

brindisi (It. *far brindisi*: 'to give a toast', from Span. *brindis*: 'toast', from German *Ich bring*

dir's: 'I bring it to you'; cf. Juan Corominas, *Breve diccionario etimológico de la langua castellana*). A drinking or toasting song, with choral refrain. A famous example is Alfredo and Violetta's 'Libiamo' in Verdi's *Traviata*.

British Broadcasting Corporation. Opera entered British broadcasting on 6 Jan. 1923, when the London station 2LO relayed a BNOC performance of *Hänsel und Gretel* from CG. Further BNOC broadcasts included *Figaro*, *Walküre*, and *Siegfried*. In Oct. 1923 the first studio opera was given, *Roméo et Juliette*. As well as broadcasts from CG and other theatres in the 1920s, the BBC gave an ambitious series of studio performances under Percy Pitt 1926–30, including *Roi d'Ys*, *Pelléas*, and *Louise*. The Labour government subsidized CG through the BBC 1929–31, and many broadcasts were given. Studio opera ceased until 1937, when a Music Productions Unit was formed with Stanford Robinson as music director. At London, QH, the first performances in England were given of operas including *Wozzeck*, *The Lady Macbeth of Mtsensk*, *Cardillac* and *Mathis der Maler*, 1934–9. The war interrupted further progress, which was resumed in 1945 especially with the impetus given to music broadcasting first by the Third Programme, then the Music Programme. By now opera was established as an essential part of national and international broadcasting. The Promenade Concerts, held under BBC auspices every summer in the RAH, include visiting semi-staged performances from Gly. and CG.

Britten, Benjamin (Lord Britten of Aldeburgh) (*b* Lowestoft, 22 Nov. 1913; *d* Aldeburgh, 4 Dec. 1976). English composer, conductor, and pianist. Studied with Frank Bridge, and at London, RCM with John Ireland. His early opera *Paul Bunyan* (1941) was originally withdrawn; on its revival in 1976, the work proved to have a deftness of touch and flair for the stage that gave some precedent to the achievement of *Peter Grimes*. Nevertheless, the appearance of *Grimes* in 1945 was a sensation at the time and has long been seen as a historical turning-point. With it English opera seemed to come of age, and Britten was established as an opera composer of the first rank. Though rooted in tradition, the work is individual not only in its virtuosity and dramatic instinct, but in such characteristics as a crucial use of bitonality to indicate the divided nature of the hero and his separation from the Borough. There is little doubt that this, and other of Britten's operatic themes, related to problems of acceptance by society of homosexuality: he was to show in his art an acute sympathy for the victims of intolerance and a painful sensibility towards the abuse of innocence. The opera also consolidated the position of the composer's companion Peter *Pears as an operatic artist of the first importance: Pears was to have roles in every one of Britten's operas, and his artistry lent a particular hue to Britten's writing for the tenor voice.

Largely owing to the uneconomic conditions of large-scale opera, Britten now turned to chamber opera, forming the *English Opera Group for the presentation of such works. The Rape of Lucretia (1946) shows his mastery of limited means to expressive ends, especially in his handling of the 12-piece orchestra. From this tragedy, he turned to a version of a comic Maupassant story, resituated in Suffolk, for Albert Herring (1947). There is again a brilliant use of the small orchestra to point up and lend some depth to the work, though the satire of what are village types rather than characters prevents it from taking its place among the great operatic comedies. For his next two works, Britten turned to unusual forms: Gay's Beggar's Opera was cleverly recomposed; and Let's Make an Opera (1949) is in the first part a play rehearsing a cast of children and grown-ups for participation in the second, the opera The Little Sweep. Two years later he gave further proof of his versatility with a free realization of Dido and Aeneas: he was a profound admirer of Purcell, to whom he consciously owed much in his setting of English.

1951 saw the appearance of Billy Budd, Britten's first full-scale opera since Peter Grimes. As in the earlier work, there is a radical use of bitonality to embody the subject, the separation of the handsome and innocent sailor from his fellows and his destruction at the hands of evil and inaction. Its successor Gloriana (1953) was also large in scale. Written for the Coronation of Queen Elizabeth II, it excited hostility chiefly for the libretto: this naturally drew a non-musical public's attention more than the music, whose quality has been impressively revealed in revivals.

Returning to chamber opera, Britten produced in The Turn of the Screw (1954) a work whose taut thematic integration is a reflection of the intense, painful story of two children possessed by ghosts: the technique includes the use of one principal theme which 'turns' in orchestral interludes as a metaphor of the tightening cruelty of the story. By contrast, Noyes Fludde (1958) represents Britten's freshest and most delightful vein, setting a miracle play in church and drawing on amateurs and children as well as professionals with enchanting skill and understanding. The presence of the dark and the light in his experience found new balance in one of the few Shakespeare operas worthy to stand near Verdi, A Midsummer Night's Dream (1960). Aided by a skilfully arranged libretto, Britten penetrated into the heart of the play and into the mysterious world of sleep, central to the drama but given musical articulation, which had become another of his fascinations.

He now followed up some of the techniques in Noyes Fludde, as well as his experience of Japanese Noh plays, with three church parables: Curlew River (1964), The Burning Fiery Furnace (1966), and The Prodigal Son (1968). Designed to be performed in church, and taking some of their ritual nature and their dramatic and instrumental techniques from Noh, they are nevertheless individual works that absorb the Japanese influence into a form that is at least as strongly rooted in early English religious music drama. Curlew River, which uses a Japanese story, is not only the most oriental but also technically the strictest and most successful of the three; having mastered the disciplines he set himself, Britten felt able to use them more freely. The common framework is a dramatic fiction of performance by a group of monks who arrive to plainchant (providing musical material for the work) and withdraw to it after their performance.

A new set of problems was presented when Britten was commissioned by the BBC to write a TV opera. The theme of Owen Wingrave (1971) reflected Britten's own pacifism, and though dramatically it is assertion rather than argument, the work is expertly written and turns the limitations of TV to advantage in its use of special techniques such as cross-fading between characters in different places for a duet. Britten's last opera, Death in Venice (1973), is in the sparer style of his final phase. It draws on ballet sequences (especially for a boy dancer) and concentrates on major roles for the central figure of Aschenbach and the figure who, in various guises, draws him away from his Apollonian stance towards a Dionysian homosexual temptation and destruction.

Britten also made an edition (1951) of Holst's *The Wandering Scholar* with Imogen Holst, his long-time assistant at Aldeburgh. As a conductor, he largely confined himself to his own works in the opera-house; but especially at the Aldeburgh Festival and on tour, he directed brilliant performances of works in the English Opera Group's repertory. (R)

Brno (Ger., Brünn). City in Moravia, Czech Republic. Opera was given from the 1730s by Italian companies, including those of A. and P. Mingotti, in the T in der Taffern (opened 1732 on the site of the present Reduta T). Operas included Luchini's *Vincislao* (1739) on the subject of King Václav II. In 1767 Jan Tuček's Singspiel *Zamilovaný ponocný* (The Lovelorn Nightwatchman) was given in Czech; the first opera sung in Czech was Méhul's *Joseph* (in 1839), followed by Škroup's *Dráteník* (in 1840) and the Brno composer František Kott's *Žižkův dub* (1841). The theatre burnt down in 1785. In 1786 the Nationaltheater (Redoutensaale) opened (cap. *c*.1,200); it burnt down in 1870 and was later restored as the Reduta (cap. 414) (now used for operetta). Traditions for long reflected the proximity of Vienna. However, the Czech Provisional T opened in 1884 (cap. 771), and was enlarged as the Národní Divadlo (National T) in 1894 (cap. 1,000); but standards were erratic. The German Stadttheater opened in 1882; this was the first theatre with electric light in Central Europe (cap. 1,195, later 572) (now the Mahen T). Standards were particularly high between the wars under František Neumann and after the war under František Jílek. Opera is now given in the Janáček OH, opened in 1965 (cap. 1,317), the largest in the Czech Republic. The repertory has been notable for its enterprise, especially with contemporary works; it gave the prems. of all Janáček's operas except *Mr Brouček*. There is an opera studio, the Miloš Wasserbauer Chamber O, built in 1957 by the Janáček Academy.

Brook, Peter (*b* London, 21 Mar. 1925). English producer of Russian-Jewish origin. Studied Oxford. Director of productions, London, CG, 1947–50. Though many of his productions were admired, notably *Figaro* and *The Olympians* (1949), he had to contend

with many problems, including differences with *Rankl, and his intention to give the producer a more inventive role in opera was frustrated. He resigned after opposition to his methods came to a head with his production of *Salome* with décor by Dali (1949). His last conventional opera production was of *Eugene Onegin* at New York, M, in 1957. From the season 1981–2 he has toured widely with his own company in much-truncated versions of *Carmen* (*La tragédie de Carmen*) and *Pelléas et Mélisande*.

Brooks, Patricia (*b* New York, 7 Nov. 1937; *d* Mt. Kisco, NY, 22 Jan. 1993). US soprano. After study at the Manhattan School sang with New York, CO, 1960–77; created Abigail Williams in *The Crucible*, 1961. Her dramatic gifts were admired as the Queen of Shemakha (London, CG, 1969) and as Lulu (S Fe 1974). Other roles incl. Gilda, Mélisande, Violetta. (R)

Broomhill. The house of the 19th-cent. financier Sir David Salomons, near Tunbridge Wells, which has a theatre (cap. *c*300), with fine acoustics, where small-scale opera is given in short summer seasons. Productions have included *Ariadne auf Naxos* (Jonathan Miller), *A Midsummer Night's Dream*, and *Il Trittico* (Simon Callow). One new opera a year is commissioned, and there is an international opera course for young singers.

Brouček, The Excursions of Mr. See EXCURSIONS OF MR BROUČEK, THE.

Brouwenstijn, Gré (*b* Den Helder, 26 Aug. 1915). Dutch soprano. Studied Amsterdam with Stroomenbergh. Début Amsterdam 1940 (one of the Three Ladies, *Die Zauberflöte*). Netherlands O, from 1946, début as Tosca. London, CG, 1951–64 in Verdi; Bayreuth 1954–6; Vienna from 1956; Gly. from 1959 (Leonore); Chicago 1959 (Jenůfa); also at Buenos Aires, Stuttgart, and Paris. Retired 1971. A musical and intelligent singer with a firm, warm tone. (R)

Brownlee, John (*b* Geelong, 7 Jan. 1901; *d* New York, 10 Jan. 1969). Australian baritone. Studied Melbourne, then Paris with Dinh Gilly. Début Paris 1926 (in *Lakmé*). Brought by Melba to London, CG, where he sang Marcello at her final appearance there in 1926. Paris, O, 1927–36 as principal baritone. CG, 1930 (Golaud). Gly. from 1935 (one of its first members) as Don Alfonso, Don Giovanni,

Almaviva (Mozart). New York, M, 1937–57, début Rigoletto. Distinguished in the French repertory and Mozart, with a well-schooled rather than outstanding voice. (R)

Bruch, Max (*b* Cologne, 6 Jan. 1838; *d* Friedenau, 2 Oct. 1920). German composer. Studied Bonn, later Cologne with Hiller and Reinecke.

His first opera was a setting of Goethe's *Scherz, List und Rache* (1858) in three scenes with 16 musical numbers. He followed this with *Loreley* (1863), his most important opera, which contains some fine and characteristic music, especially in the choral writing; this also marks his third opera, *Hermione* (1872).

Brummstimmen. See BOCCA CHIUSA.

Bruneau, Alfred (*b* Paris, 3 Mar. 1857; *d* Paris, 15 June 1934). French composer and critic. Studied Paris with Massenet. His early, and to conservative listeners sensational, *Le rêve* (1891) was based on Zola, whose influence on Italian literary verismo Bruneau to some extent reflects. He was to follow Zola, who wrote many of his librettos, in a number of ideas, and his *Messidor* (1897) suffered from the public opposition to Zola during the Dreyfus case. However, *L'ouragan* (1901) triumphed, as did *L'enfant roi* (1905), a lighter work despite its serious theme on the importance of children to marriage. Zola died in 1902, mourned by Bruneau in *Lazare* (comp. 1902). Though not fundamentally influenced by Wagner, he benefited French opera by his appreciation of Wagner's strength, without relinquishing the individually French manner he had in part acquired from his teacher Massenet. His music serves its texts faithfully and seriously, despite a certain intrusive crudity in its realism.

Brünn. See BRNO.

Brünnhilde. A Valkyrie (sop), Wotan's favourite daughter, in Wagner's *Die Walküre*, *Siegfried*, and *Götterdämmerung*.

Brünnhilde's Immolation. The name generally given to the final scene of Wagner's *Götterdämmerung*, in which Brünnhilde (sop) bids farewell to life and rides on her horse *Grane into the flames.

Bruscantini, Sesto (*b* Porto Civitanova, 10 Dec. 1919). Italian baritone. Studied Rome with Ricci. Début Civitanova 1946 (Colline).

Milan, S, from 1949. Gly. from 1951 in Mozart, Rossini, and Verdi. Chicago from 1961, and other major opera-houses, including London, CG; Paris; and Sydney. A thoroughly accomplished singer, whose enormous repertory encompasses lyric, dramatic, and buffo roles: in later years he sang character roles. (R)

Bruson, Renato (*b* Este, 13 Jan. 1936). Italian baritone. Studied Padua with Ceriati. Début Spoleto 1961 (Di Luna). Milan, S, 1972 in *Linda di Chamounix*. New York, M, from 1968; Edinburgh, 1972; London, CG, from 1976; Florence 1980; Orange 1984, etc. A distinguished Verdi and Donizetti singer, especially in dramatic and noble parts, he was a notable Falstaff at Los Angeles (1982), then at CG. (R)

Brussels (Fr., Bruxelles; Dut., Brussel). Capital of Belgium. The O du Quai du Foin opened in 1682, with a repertory that centred on works by Lully; this reopened in 1700 (cap. 1,200) on the site of the old Mint as the T sur la Monnaie (1763 Grand T et O de la Monnaie), with P. A. Fiocco (*c.*1650–1714) as director. French opera dominated the repertory until 1746. With the occupation by the French after the Battle of Fontenoy, Maréchal Saxe imported Favart and the Paris, OC, who remained until 1749; the theatre was then run by a succession of directors, with French taste still prevailing. The French occupation of 1794–1814 freed the theatres and saw Belgian as well as French works. In 1815, under the Anglo-Dutch occupation, the Monnaie's title became Flemish (Schouwburg op de Munte). A new, enlarged theatre was opened in 1819, and the repertory and reputation increased. At a performance of *La muette de Portici* on 24 Aug. 1830, the call to arms in the duet 'Amour sacré de la patrie' inspired the audience to initiate forthwith the revolt that overthrew the Dutch. In 1832 gaslight was introduced; in 1855 the theatre burnt down. It was reopened in 1856 (cap. 1,170), introducing a repertory that closely mirrored Parisian taste. The fame of the theatre became international, and attracted important prems. (Massenet's *Hérodiade* (1881), Chabrier's *Gwendoline* (1886)), new and great singers (Patti, Alboni, Albani, Faure, Calvé; Melba's 1887 début as Gilda), and the transfer of the original Bayreuth *Ring* (1883). The arrival in 1900 of Maurice Kufferath, an enthusiastic Wagnerian, at once improved dramatic standards and brought in a stronger German influence. After the war, under Corneil de Thoran, the theatre further widened its repertory to include a number of prems. (Prokofiev's *The Gambler*, 1929) and welcomed great singers of the day (Shalyapin, Caruso, Destinn). After 1945 the Wagner influence returned; and the régime of Maurice Huisman, director from 1959, turned the emphasis on visiting foreign companies. In 1981 Gerard Mortier thoroughly, and controversially, reorganized the theatre, emphasizing music drama rather than stars and concentrating on intensive rehearsal; he left in 1991. There has been a famous Mozart series and Janáček series, and an emphasis on new works (Hans Zender's *Stephen Climax* (1990), John Adams's *The Death of Klinghoffer* (1991)). There have also been prems. of works by Belgian composers (Philippe Boesmans's *La passion de Gilles* (1983) and *Reigen* (1993); André Laporte's *Das Schloss* (1986)).

Operetta has been given in many theatres, including the T Royal du Parc (opened 1782), the Château des Fleurs (opened 1847), the Bouffes-Belges (opened 1858), and the Alcazar (opened 1867), especially the Alhambra (opened 1846 as T du Cirque); but the principal home of opéra-comique has been the T Royal des Galeries (later Fantaisies-Parisiennes) (opened 1847), and enterprising productions have been given at the Palais des Beaux-Arts from 1936.

Brydon, Roderick (*b* Edinburgh, ? 1939). Scottish conductor. Studied with Celibidache in Siena. Début London, SW, 1964 (*Attila*). Scottish O 1965–70: *Butterfly*; *Pelléas*; *Egisto*; operas by Mozart. Music dir. Lucerne O 1984–7; Berne O 1988–90: *Capriccio*, *Peter Grimes*. London, CG, 1984 (*Midsummer Night's Dream*). Los Angeles 1990 (*Idomeneo*); Aldeburgh 1992 (*Rake's Progress*).

Bucharest (Rom., Bucureşti). Capital of Romania. Opera was first given by Francesco's Italian company in 1787. The Theatrum Vlahicum Bucharestini opened in 1814, used by visiting companies. Johann Gerger's Viennese company came from Transylvania, a German-dominated area with a Mozart tradition, to play in Princess Ralu's theatre 'At the Red Fountain' in 1818, with a repertory of Rossini and Mozart (*Idomeneo*). Eduard Kriebig's company followed in 1823, the Fourreaux Co. in 1831–2, Theodor Müller's in 1833 on its way home from Russia; artists of the latter remained to work in a theatre built by Momolo, including Ion Wachmann (1807–63), who had directed the company in Timişoara, 1831–3, and continued in the capital until 1835. The repertory included French and Italian works, Mozart, and Wachmann's own *Braconierul* (The Poacher, 1833); 60 performances were given in 1833–4. Application for an Italian theatre in 1833 led eventually to the opening of the Teatrul Naţional in 1852 (dir. Wachmann 1852–8); the company alternated with an Italian one under Basilio Sansoni that had had a state subsidy since 1843.

A new departure came with the appointment to the T Naţional in 1877 of George Stephănescu (1843–1925), who in the face of many difficulties kept opera active: he founded O Română (1885–6), the Compania Lirică Română (1892–3), and the Societatea Lirică Română (1902–4). Romanian artists were still lower paid than Italians, leading to the closure of the Romanian company and the emigration of its best artists. Stephănescu gave 31 performances between 1889 and 1891; from 1897 to 1901 another company occupied the theatre. At the T Naţional between 1901 and 1910 Italian seasons were given which, though uneven, included Tetrazzini, Litvinne, Battistini, and Ruffo. French and German seasons were also given. During wartime German occupation, the Dessau O visited, and local activity included a Student O that gave 63 performances in 1914–15, a company under Stefănescu-Cerna at the Blanduzia Garden (1915), the formation of the Gabrilescu Co. and another at the Leon Popescu T (1915) and of another under Jean Atanasia (1916). In 1919 the Asociaţia Lirică Română Opera was formed under the composer Ion Nonna Otescu (1888–1940); it opened with *Aida* at the T Naţional, and as well as encouraging local artists drew famous singers (Slezak) and conductors (Weingartner, Nedbal). In 1921 this success led to the opera being made a state institution, O Română, and housed at the Lyric T, where the season opened with *Lohengrin* under Enescu; his successors included George Georgescu (1922–7) and Jonel Perlea (1929–30). In 1924 11 singers resigned in protest against the government's restrictive attitude, and in 1930 the company had to move to an unsuitable building and halve salaries. Nevertheless, new Romanian operas were staged. Earthquake in 1940 and bombing in 1944 wrecked the old theatre.

The new O Română theatre (cap. 610) opened in 1953. In 1989 work began on a huge arts complex to include an opera-house (cap. over 3,000).

Operetta, first given at the T Momolo in 1850 and very popular, was neglected between the wars when two revue companies dominated the stage, but is again well established in its own T de Stat de Operetă.

Buckley, Richard (b New York, 1 Sept. 1953). US conductor. Studied Aspen and Salzburg. Associate cond., Seattle O 1974–7. Chicago; Houston O; New York, CO. First US staging *The King Goes Forth to France* (S Fe 1986); *Hoffmann* in Los Angeles; *Il viaggio a Reims* at St Louis. London, CG, 1992 (*Elisir d'amore*). (R)

Budapest. Capital of Hungary (uniting in 1872 the cities of Buda and Pest). Regular opera performances were given in German from 1787, when the Castle T opened, some also in Hungarian from 1793, the year of the first national opera, Chudy's *Pikkó Herceg* (Prince Pikkó). Most important foreign operas were performed soon after their local prems. A large German City T opened in 1812; this burnt down in 1847. The Pestí Magyar Színház (Pest Hungarian T) opened on 22 Aug. 1837; the first opera to be staged was *Il barbiere di Siviglia* on 29 Aug. This remained the country's most important musical theatre until 1884: the directors were Ferenc *Erkel (1838–74), Hans *Richter (1871–5), and Sándor Erkel (1875–84). The repertory was at first largely Italian, with Hungarian translations gradually supervening, and this helped to encourage the development of national opera. From the 1840s Erkel's operas joined the repertory, and the theatre was quick to stage important foreign works as they appeared (with the major exception of Wagner's, resisted by Erkel but encouraged by Richter). It was a mature company of international standard that moved into the Operaház (cap. 1,310), opened on 27 Sept. 1884 with acts of *Lohengrin* and *Bánk bán*. All performances (even by guest artists) were in Hungarian until the turn of the century. Performances were also given at Buda Castle.

Mahler introduced much German opera (1888–91); Nikisch (1893–5) added more Italian, French, and Hungarian works. After a slack period (1900–12), the company was revivified under Miklós Bánffy: despite the war and its aftermath, operatic life was re-established on a healthy basis, and, despite opposition, the works of Bartók and Kodály entered the repertory. With Miklós Radnai as intendant (until 1935) and Sergio Failoni conducting (1928–48), many other contemporary works followed. Damaged in the war, the theatre reopened as the Magyar Allami Operaház (Hungarian State O) (cap. 1,343) on 15 Mar. 1945, and the repertory began to include more Russian works; the company was also much enlarged. Important conductors have included Ferenc Fricsay (1945–9), Otto *Klemperer (1947–50), and János Ferencsik (1931–84). The theatre closed for renovation in 1980–4, when the company moved to the Erkel T. Before the Second World War performances were also given in the open air on Margaret Island; today they are sometimes given in the courtyard of the Budapest Hilton. Chamber opera is also given on the stage of the Odry Theatre School. The company also toured (1948–53) as Gördülő Opera (Rolling Opera), visiting towns and industrial centres in a special train.

The city's second theatre opened in 1911 as the Népopera (People's O) (cap. 2,450). In 1917 it became the Városi Színház (Civic T), and from 1925 was privately owned, giving both opera and operetta. It reopened as a filial of the OH in 1951, as the Erkel T. Operetta has also been given at the Pesti Népszínház (opened 1875), the Budai Népszínház (1861–4 and 1867–70), the Kisfaludy Színház (opened 1897), and especially the Király Színház (T Royal, opened 1903).

Buenos Aires. Capital of Argentina. At the beginning of the 19th cent. Buenos Aires had one small and simply constructed theatre, the Coliseo (1804, renamed the T Argentino in 1838). The first operatic performances here were selections from Italian opera organized by Juan Picazzarri in 1813. From various visiting singers a regular company was formed, and gave the first complete opera, *Il barbiere di Siviglia*, in 1825. Visiting French companies came from 1831. The T de la Victoria opened in 1838. From 1848 there were many performances of Bellini, Donizetti, Mercadante, and Verdi, by leading Italian singers. Two French companies were also formed in 1852 and 1854, both of which gave an almost exclusively French repertory; these two groups, though very different in quality, managed to win an increasingly loyal public. By 1854 30 new productions were given in the city; and two years later zarzuelas were added to the repertory.

These successes led to the demand for a new and improved theatre; and the first T *Colón (cap. 2,500, with a special women's gallery) was duly opened on 25 Apr. 1857 with *La traviata*. This became the centre of the country's operatic life. The smaller T de la Opera was opened on 25 May 1872 with *Il trovatore*; it was demolished in 1935. From 1868 the Colón was directed by the powerful and influential Angelo Ferrari; though he ran a basically Italian repertory that included early performances of works by Verdi, Ferrari also saw to it that the Colón reflected the general European operatic scene of the day, and even gave a number of prems. of works by Marotta, Agostini, Cavalieri, and Torrens Boqué. In 1881 a visiting French company under Maurice Grau gave a season that included *Carmen*. At the same time the T de la Opera was widening its repertory to include more Italian works; both houses were by now of sufficient repute to attract the finest Italian singers of the day. The T de la Victoria had meanwhile not ceased activity, and was responsible for the prem. of the first opera by an Argentinian composer, Francisco Hargreaves's *La gata blanca* (1877). At the T Politeama, local prems. were given, including *Le Villi* (1886), *Der fliegende Holländer* and *Roméo et Juliette* (1887), *Lakmé* (1888), and *Otello* (1888, a few days ahead of the Colón); one of the stars of the season was Patti.

After the Colón was closed in 1889, the rebuilt T de la Opera became the city's operatic centre in a busy period. There were regular visits from major Italian singers and conductors (Campanini, 1889 and from 1893; Mascheroni from 1894; Mugnone from 1898; Toscanini in 1901, 1903–4, and 1906), and the repertory was broadened to include more German and French and even Argentinian works, though little pre-19th-cent. opera was given.

On 25 May 1908 a performance of *Aída* opened the new T Colón (cap. 2,487, with standing room for 1,000). In 1935 the administration passed into municipal hands. The long domination of Italian opera finally began to give way to a truly international repertory that included French, German, Russian, English, Czech, and Polish, as well as Argentinian and Spanish works, and later pre-Classical opera and Mozart. The first complete *Ring* was given in 1922 under Wein-gartner (with Lotte Lehmann). Moreover, the rapid expansion of the Colón's activities and its emergence as one of the world's great opera-houses were reflected in the busy life of the capital: at the T Coliseo, Mascagni conducted the prem. of his *Isabeau* (1911), *Parsifal* was given as early as 1913, and new Argentinian works were staged; new operas were also given at the T Politeama and a more limited and sporadic repertory at the T Avenida, T Odéon, and other smaller theatres. Buenos Aires remains the richest operatic city of the continent, and one capable of challenging the greatest European and North American cities in the excellence and diversity of its operatic life.

See also ARGENTINA, COLÓN.

buffo (It.: 'buffoon, comedian': possibly derived from the Lat. *bufo* = toad, from the inflated gloves used for exchanging comic blows on the stage). In the theatre a *buffone* is a comic actor; in opera, a *buffo* is a singer of comic roles, hence *basso buffo*. *Opera buffa is a term for comic opera.

Buffonistenstreit. See GUERRE DES BOUFFONS.

Bühne (Ger.: 'stage or theatre'). The term is also used in the plural for a theatre, e.g. Städtische Bühnen = Civic T.

Bullant, Antoine (*b* ?nr. Amiens, ?*c*.1750; *d* St Petersburg, 25 June 1821). French composer and bassoonist. A member of the court orchestra of Empress Catherine II, he composed some five comic operas for St Petersburg and Moscow of which *Sbitenshchik* (The Sbiten Seller, 1784) enjoyed greatest popularity.

Bülow, Hans von (*b* Dresden, 8 Jan. 1830; *d* Cairo, 12 Feb. 1894). German conductor and pianist. Studied Dresden with Wieck and Eberwein; then studied law in Leipzig, also music with Hauptmann. In Berlin, wrote for *Die Abendpost*, defending Liszt and Wagner. The first *Lohengrin* in Weimar (1850) so overwhelmed him that he went to Zurich to seek out Wagner, who helped him to find some conducting experience. Studied the piano with Liszt, who also admired his talent, and whose daughter Cosima he married in 1857. Conductor Munich, N, from 1865, conducting prems. of *Tristan* (1865) and *Meistersinger* (1868), of which he also made vocal scores. When Cosima left him for Wagner in 1869, he abandoned Munich and toured

Europe. Hanover, H, 1878; music dir. Meiningen 1880. A brilliant pianist and one of the great virtuoso conductors of the day, he was also a man of difficult temperament. But he behaved nobly over Cosima's desertion, and sent her a consoling message on Wagner's death; and his forceful personality exercised a strong influence on musicians of his time, including the young Richard Strauss. His compositions do not include an opera, though he had considered one on the Tristan legend.

Bumbry, Grace (*b* St Louis, MO, 4 Jan. 1937). US mezzo-soprano. Studied S Barbara with Lotte Lehmann. Début Paris, O, 1960 (Amneris). Bayreuth 1961 (Venus; the first Black artist to appear there); London, CG, from 1963; Salzburg from 1964; New York, M, from 1965; Paris, B, 1990 (at its inauguration). Roles include Eboli, Azucena, Fricka; from 1970 has also sung soprano parts, e.g. Tosca, Salome, Lady Macbeth. Sang Cassandre in *Les Troyens* at the opening of Paris, B (1990) and has recently assumed such character parts as Baba the Turk in *The Rake's Progress*. Has a warm, vibrant voice and a powerful personality. (R)

Bungert, August (*b* Mülheim, 14 Mar. 1845; *d* Leutesdorf, 26 Oct. 1915). German composer. In 1889 he formed a friendship with the Queen of Romania, who as 'Carmen Sylva' wrote poems for him to set and also used her influence to found in 1911 the *Bungert-Bund*, with a magazine *Der Bund*, for the advancement of his music. His first opera was a comedy, *Die Studenten von Salamanca* (1884). However, he is best known for his Wagnerian tetralogies (one incomplete) on Homeric subjects—comprising *Kirke* (1898), *Nausikaa* (1901), *Odysseus' Heimkehr* (1896), and *Odysseus' Tod* (1903)—for the performance of which he hoped to build a Western 'Bayreuth' at Bad Godesberg on the Rhine.

Buona figliuola, La (The Good Girl). Properly *La Cecchina, ossia La buona figliuola*. Opera in 3 acts by Piccinni; text by Goldoni, after Samuel Richardson's novel *Pamela, or Virtue Rewarded* (1740). Prem. Rome, T delle Dame, 6 Feb. 1760.

The opera tells of the love and eventual marriage of Cecchina (sop) and the Marquis Conchiglia (ten). The Marquis's sister opposes the match, since Cecchina is apparently of low birth, and tries to spread malicious rumours about the girl. However,

when it emerges that Cecchina is the long-lost daughter of a German baron, she is quite happy for the marriage to proceed.

Burchuladze, Paata (*b* Tblisi, 12 Feb. 1951). Georgian bass. Studied Tblisi; début there 1975 as Méphistophélès. London, CG, from 1984 as Ramfis, Khan Konchak (*Prince Igor* 1990), Boris, Inquisitor (*Fiery Angel*). His commanding stage presence also makes him effective as Basilio (New York, M, 1989), Banquo (Milan, S), Commendatore (*Don Giovanni* at Salzburg). (R)

Burgess, Sally (*b* Durban, 9 Oct. 1953). English mezzo-soprano. Studied London with Alan and Studholm. Début as soprano London, ENO, 1977 (Bertha, *Euryanthe*). Sang soprano roles until 1980; further study with Salaman and Veasey. London, CG, and Gly., 1983; O North, from 1986. Roles include Orfeo, Amneris, Dido (Berlioz), Charlotte, Carmen, Octavian, Nefertiti (*Akhnaten*), Julie La Verne (*Showboat*). A highly attractive performer with a fresh voice and a strong stage presence. (R)

Burgstaller, Alois (*b* Holzkirchen, 21 Sept. 1871; *d* Gmund, 19 Apr. 1945). German tenor. Studied Frankfurt with Bellwidt, and Bayreuth with Kniese. Début Bayreuth 1894. Bayreuth 1894–1902 (Siegfried (his greatest role), Siegmund, Parsifal, Erik). London, CG, 1906. New York, M, 1903–9. First US Parsifal; subsequently banned from Bayreuth for infringing copyright. (R)

Burian, Karel (also known as Carl Burrian) (*b* Rousinov, 12 Jan. 1870; *d* Senomaty, 25 Sept. 1924). Czech tenor. Studied with Wallerstein. Début Brno 1891 (Jeník). Hamburg 1898–1902; Dresden from 1902 (creating Herod, 1905); London, CG, 1904–14; New York, M, 1906–13; Bayreuth 1908. Sang mainly Wagner roles (Tristan, Parsifal, Tannhäuser, etc.). Linguistically gifted, he possessed a powerful voice, and an impressive stage presence. Arnold Bax wrote of his 'horrifying Herod, slobbering with lust and apparently almost decomposing before our eyes'. (R) His brother **Emil** (1876–1926) was a leading baritone at Prague, N, 1906–26, and sang regularly in Germany.

Burian, Emil František (*b* Plzeň, 11 Apr. 1904; *d* Prague, 9 Aug. 1959). Nephew of above. Czech composer, stage director, and writer. Studied Prague with Foerster. He was then already working in Prague avant-garde theatre and music, later also in Brno and Olomouc and elsewhere in various roles (including as jazz band leader). In 1933 he founded the experimental theatre D34 (for *divadlo*, or theatre, of 1934), mounting many avant-garde productions that anticipate so-called 'director's theatre' (e.g. a Brecht–Weill *Dreigroschenoper*, D35) and place him as one of the most important directors of the century. He returned after the war (which he spent in a concentration camp) in 1945 to reopen it (as D46) and to work as a director in Prague and Brno. His busy theatrical and public life included the composition of a number of operas. His earlier works are cast in a post-Romantic style, which he discarded in favour of an attachment to folk and cabaret music, jazz, and speech rhythms in a manner strongly influenced by Stravinsky and especially Janáček. He experimented with transferring essentially musical rhythms into spoken dialogue; and his work in the theatre, including the musical theatre, involved functional use of lighting and film. Janáček's manner shows particularly in his most important opera, *Maryša* (1940). Also operettas and other stage works and films.

Burkhard, Paul (*b* Zurich, 21 Dec. 1911; *d* Zell, 6 Sept. 1977). Swiss composer and conductor. Cond. Berne Stadttheater (1932–4) and Zurich Schauspielhaus (1939–45). Popular for his operettas, including *Casanova in der Schweiz* (1942) and *Das schwarze Recht* (1939, rev. as *Feuerwerk* 1950).

Burkhard, Willy (*b* Évilard-sur-Bienne, 17 Apr. 1900; *d* Zurich, 18 June 1955). Swiss composer. Best known for his sacred choral music, he achieved considerable success with his only opera, *Die schwarze Spinne* (1949).

Burning Fiery Furnace, The. Church parable by Britten; text by William Plomer. Prem. Orford Church, Suffolk, 9 June 1966.

Based closely on the biblical narrative in Daniel 3, the work is set in Babylon in the 6th cent. BC. Three young Israelite captives are appointed by Nebuchadnezzar (ten) to rule over three provinces. At a feast, they arouse the wrath of the Astrologer (bar) by refusing to eat with the courtiers, since their faith will not permit this. They also refuse to worship the Babylonian god Merodak. Nebuchadnezzar commands that a furnace be lit; the three are thrown into it but are saved by an angel. When Nebuchadnezzar sees the result of their faith he himself becomes a convert.

Burrowes, Norma (*b* Bangor, Co. Down, 24 Apr. 1944). Irish soprano. Studied London with Flora Nielsen, and later with Bruce-Lockhart. Début Gly. Touring O 1970 (Zerlina). London: CG from 1970 (Fiakermilli, Woodbird, Despina); ENO from 1971. Salzburg 1971–3 (Blonde); Gly. 1975 (Vixen); Aix 1977; Paris 1976–80. An attractive singer with a clear, appealing voice, whose early retirement was much regretted. (R)

Burrows, Stuart (*b* Pontypridd, 7 Feb. 1933). Welsh tenor. Studied Trinity Coll., Carmarthen. Début WNO 1963 (Ismaele, *Nabucco*). London, CG, from 1967; S Francisco, 1967; New York, M, 1971–82. Guest appearances Vienna, Paris, etc. Repertory includes Elvino, Ernesto, Lensky, Alfredo; also the Mozart roles, of which, with his fine coloratura and beauty of tone, he has been an excellent exponent (e.g. Titus at London, CG (1989)). (R)

Bury, John (*b* Aberystwyth, 27 Jan. 1925). English designer. Studied London. After working with Joan Littlewood and Peter Hall, contributed a number of highly effective sets for opera. With Hall as producer, he designed *Moses and Aaron*, *The Magic Flute*, and *Tristan* for London, CG; *Calisto*, *Ulisse*, *Don Giovanni*, and *Figaro* for Gly. His designs for Monteverdi and Cavalli in particular succeeded in catching a Baroque spirit, including the use of modern stage apparatus to suggest Baroque ingenuity.

Busch, Fritz (*b* Siegen, 13 Mar. 1890; *d* London, 15 Sept. 1951). German conductor. Studied locally, then Cologne with Steinbach. Cond. Deutsches T, Riga, 1909. Music dir. Aachen 1909 and, after war service, 1918; Stuttgart 1918, giving Hindemith prems. and broadening the repertory. Music dir. Dresden 1922–33, building a fine ensemble and giving prems. of Strauss's *Intermezzo* (1924) and *Ägyptische Helena* (1928), Busoni's *Doktor Faust* (1925), Weill's *Protagonist* (1926), and Hindemith's *Cardillac* (1926). Always worked closely with designers including Appia and Kokoschka; from 1932 also collaborated with Carl *Ebert. Though not Jewish, resisted Nazism and left Germany 1933. Bayreuth 1924 (*Meistersinger*); Buenos Aires 1933–6, 1941–5. With Ebert, established Gly. 1934–9,

1950–1. New York, M, 1945–9; many European appearances. A fine representative of the best German opera-house traditions, he brought to Mozart, in particular, a care and sensitivity (extending to his work with his singers and players) that gave Gly. some of its classic years and bequeathed a legacy of treasured recordings. (R)

Bush, Alan (b London, 22 Dec. 1900). English composer. Studied London, RAM with Corder and Matthay, later also with Ireland, Moiseiwitsch, and Schnabel. The intellectual rigour of his idiom, which is fundamental tonal, was increasingly used to simplify his music, not least in the interests of the broadly popular approach associated with his belief in Communism. This has also dictated the choice of subjects for his operas, which had more of a following in Communist countries, especially the GDR, than in the UK. Nevertheless, the quality of mind shown in his music has won him many admirers among those who cannot share his sometimes simplistic operatic portrayals. His most important works include *The Press Gang* (1947), *Wat Tyler* (1953), and *Men of Blackmoor* (1956).

Busoni, Ferruccio (b Empoli, 1 Apr. 1866; d Berlin, 27 July 1924). German-Italian composer and pianist. Studied with his parents. In his operas, he consciously sought to portray inner psychological states and scenic atmosphere and meaning, rather than the outward and visible action. He argued his position carefully in various writings, influential for their shrewd and pioneering intellectual reasoning. *Die Brautwahl* (1912) reveals his ability to create atmosphere, in this case the fantastic and sinister. Nevertheless, he also sought a light touch (as in *Arlecchino* (1917)) and a sharp use of irony (as in *Turandot* (1917)): his Italian heritage gave him an instinct for the stage that also shows in his excellent vocal writing. His masterpiece *Doktor Faust* (1925) is a work of great power that confronts, among much else, the nature of the creative quest. It is further characteristic of Busoni in its highly unusual construction, and in its capacity to draw on the long range of European music from Renaissance polyphony to extreme chromaticism. He wrote the libretto for Schoeck's *Das Wandbild*.

Büsser, Henri (b Toulouse, 16 Jan. 1872; d Paris, 30 Dec. 1973). French composer and conductor. Studied Paris with Franck, Widor, and Guiraud, also benefiting from Gounod's advice. Prix de Rome 1893. Cond. T du Château d'Eau 1900; Paris, OC, 1902 (incl. early perfs. of *Pelléas*); Paris, O, 1905–38. Made versions of *Les Indes galantes* (1952) and *Oberon* (1954), the latter including orchestrations of Weber's piano works. Also revived Bizet's *Ivan IV* (Bordeaux 1951). Continued to conduct at Paris, O and OC, in the 1950s. His most successful operas, traditional in language, are *Colomba* (1921) and *Le carrosse du Saint-Sacrement* (1948). (R)

Bussotti, Sylvano (b Florence, 1 Oct. 1931). Italian composer. Studied Florence Cons. with Lupi and Dallapiccola and privately 1949–56. His distinctive avant-garde approach was influenced by membership of Gruppo 70 and contact with Boulez and Cage. Artistic dir. of Venice, F, 1975. His stage works range from music theatre to genuine opera and are characterized by a general fascination with themes of sexual decadence and political protest: typical are the 'operina monodanza' *Syron-Sadun-settimino* (1974), the 'dramma lirico' *Nottetempo* (1976), and the opera *Lorenzaccio* (1972). His most notorious work is *La passion selon Sade* (1969), a macabre pyschological study. Also *L'ispirazione* (1988) and *Fedra* (1988).

Buxton. Town in Derbyshire, England. The OH (built 1903) was restored in 1979 (cap. 980) for the opening of the festival, which has concentrated on reviving neglected works, generally in connection with a specific theme. Outstanding productions have included the British prems. of Kodály's *Spinning Room* (1982), Vivaldi's *Griselda* (1983), and Donizetti's *Il Pigmalione* (1987), also *Béatrice et Bénédict* (1980), and *Médée* (with Rosalind Plowright, 1984).

C

Caballé, Montserrat (*b* Barcelona, 12 Apr. 1933). Spanish soprano. Studied Barcelona with Eugenia Kemmeny and Annovazzi. Début Basle 1956 (First Lady). Basle 1956–9; Milan, S, 1960 (Flowermaiden) and from 1969 in major roles; New York, Carnegie H, 1965 (Lucrezia Borgia (from which dates her international fame)); New York, M, 1965; Gly. 1965 (Mozart's Countess and R. Strauss's Marschallin); London, CG, from 1972. Her wide repertory includes much Bellini and Donizetti, Verdi, and Rossini; also the roles of Manon Lescaut, Mimì, Tosca, Tatyana, Adriana Lecouvreur, Salome, Isolde. Physically strong and musically sensitive, she is, with her limpid tone, impeccable *messa di voce*, and vocal versatility, a consummate singer. (R)

Caccini, Francesca (*b* Florence, 18 Sept. 1587; *d* ?Florence, after 1637). Italian singer, composer, and teacher, daughter of Giulio *Caccini. Her *La liberazione di Ruggiero dall'isola d'Alcina* (1625), written for the visit of Prince Władisław Zygmunt of Poland to the Tuscan court, was one of the earliest operas not to have a mythological plot, and the first known opera by a female composer. Its subsequent performance in Cracow was of seminal importance for the development of opera in Poland.

Caccini, Giulio (*b* Rome or ?nr. Tivoli, 8 October 1551; *d* Florence, 10 Dec. 1618). Italian singer, lutenist, harpist, composer, and teacher. He was active at the Medici court from around 1564, and contributed to the music for the famous intermedi to Bargagli's *La pellegrina* (1589): he was also a prominent member of the Bardi *camerata.

An early and influential exponent of *stile rappresentativo, in 1600 he made settings of librettos by Chiabrera (*Il rapimento di Cefalo*) and Rinuccini (*Euridice*). Peri, who used the latter text for his own *Euridice* opera (also 1600), acknowledged that some of the music had been provided by Caccini; though the score of Caccini's version appeared in 1600, and was the first opera to be published, it was not performed until 1602. Later, Caccini was to claim priority over Peri as the 'inventor' of the operatic style.

Caccini's greatest monument is the collection of monodic pieces, *Le nuove musiche* (1602), whose very title expresses the mood of inventiveness characteristic of Florentine musicians at this time. Its preface is a cogent summary of their objectives; by drawing on his comprehensive understanding of vocal technique, Caccini produced music of considerable flexibility and eloquence. Such was its popularity that a second collection was published in 1614.

Caccini's family was closely involved with his musical activities. Both of his wives, Lucia and Margherita, were singers, as were his two daughters, **Settimia** (1591–1638), who married the Mantuan composer Alessandro Ghivizzani (*c*.1572–*c*.1632) and created the role of Venus in Monteverdi's *Arianna* in Mantua (1608), and Francesca *Caccini.

Cachemaille, Gilles (*b* Orbe, 25 Nov. 1951). Swiss baritone. Studied Lausanne Cons. and appeared in concert from 1978. Début in first staged *Boréades* (Lyons 1982). His well-schooled voice and fine comic timing are much admired in Mozart (e.g. Guglielmo at Lausanne; Leporello at Houston, Hamburg, and Vienna S; Giovanni at Gly. 1994). (R)

Caddy, Ian (*b* Southampton, 1 Mar. 1947). English bass-baritone. Studied London, RAM (President's Prize 1970) and later with O. Kraus. Debut Gly. Touring O 1973 (Schaunard, *La bohème*). Kent O 1976. London, ENO from 1976, CG 1982–5. Also Houston; Nantes; O North; Scottish O; Wexford; WNO; etc. Repertory includes Count (*Capriccio* and *Figaro*), Falke (*Fledermaus*), Hunding (*Walküre*), Pooh-Bah (*Mikado*), but best-known for stylish performances in baroque roles, esp. at English Bach Festival (Purcell's Aeneas, Rameau's Pollux). A versatile singer with a resonant voice and a strong dramatic presence. (R)

cadenza (It.: 'cadence'). An elaborate flourish ornamenting a cadence at any point in an aria. Before the 19th cent., these were usually improvised by the singer, but from Rossini onwards, composers began to write out their preferred versions.

Cadman, Charles Wakefield (*b* Johnstown,

PA, 24 Dec. 1881; *d* Los Angeles, 30 Dec. 1946). US composer and pianist. Studied with Oehmler and Kunitz. His lifelong interest in American Indian music was reflected in a number of operas, of which by far the most successful was *Shanewis* (1918). In them, he draws upon Indian folk legend and incorporates Indian music into his own late-Romantic idiom.

Cagnoni, Antonio (*b* Godiasco, 8 Feb. 1828; *d* Bergamo, 30 Apr. 1896). Italian composer. While still a student, he composed the highly successful, somewhat Donizettian *Don Bucefalo* (1847). In 1856 he became maestro di cappella at Vigevano, then in 1863 director of the Istituto Musicale at Novara, and in 1886 maestro di cappella at Bergamo. *Michele Perrin* (1864) shows an awareness of Wagner, but the less successful *Claudia* (1866) reverts to a simpler manner. He had greater success with *Papà Martin* (1871) and especially with his last performed work, *Francesca da Rimini* (1878), which shows a quite advanced use of *Leitmotiv.

Calaf. A Tartar prince (ten) in Puccini's *Turandot*.

Caldara, Antonio (*b* Venice, *c.*1670; *d* Vienna, 28 Dec. 1736). Italian composer. After holding positions in Italy, in 1716 he was appointed to the court of Charles VI in Vienna as deputy to Fux. His talents were admirably suited to the Habsburg tradition of grandiose musical entertainment, and with such heroic operas as *Mitridate* (1728), *Demetrio* (1731), and *La clemenza di Tito* (1734) he found much favour. About 80 operas survive: in general, they share some similarity with those of his near-contemporaries Vivaldi and Alessandro Scarlatti, and follow the mainstream tradition of early-18th-cent. opera seria.

Caldwell, Sarah (*b* Maryville, TN, 6 Mar. 1924). US producer and conductor. Studied Boston, while still a student producing Vaughan Williams's *Riders to the Sea*. Founded Boston OC 1957, dir. since. Produced first US original version *Boris Godunov*, and first US *Trojans* (nine scenes), *Intolleranza 1960*, *Moses and Aaron*, and *War and Peace*. New York, CO, 1973. Has conducted most of her Boston productions, which have shown an inventive and intelligent view of opera as music theatre. First woman cond. at New York, M, 1976 (*Traviata*).

Calife de Bagdad, Le. Opera in 1 act by Boieldieu; text by Saint-Just, after an oriental tale. Prem. Paris, OC, 16 Sept. 1800.

Bagdad. The Calif Harun al Rashid (ten), wandering Bagdad disguised, rescues Zobeide (sop) from robbers. In the house of her mother Lemaide (sop) he is in turn suspected of being a robber, but privately identifies himself to the Cadi (bs) and police. Lemaide's nephew Messun (bar) appears to announce the approach of a bridal procession. All is cleared up, and the Calif claims the delighted Zobeide as the bride.

Calisto, La. Opera in 3 acts by Cavalli; text by Giovanni Faustini, after Ovid's *Metamorphoses*, ii. 401–507. Prem. Venice, T San Apollinare, 28 Nov. 1651.

Destiny informs Nature and Eternity that Jove has decreed that Calisto, daughter of Lycaon, King of Pelasgia, should be added to the stars as one of the immortals. Jove descends to an earth laid waste, accompanied by Mercury, to help restore nature, only to discover that Calisto has become a nymph of Diana. Calisto rejects Jove's advances, so he disguises himself as Diana and tries to seduce her. Endymion, in love with the real Diana, is taken captive by Pan and his shepherds, but eventually united with his beloved. Meanwhile Calisto, who has been changed into a little bear by Juno, is taken to Mount Olympus by Jove, now restored to his normal godhood; there she will shine eternally as Ursa Minor.

Callas, Maria (orig. Mary Kalogeropoulou) (*b* New York, 2 Dec. 1923; *d* Paris, 16 Sept. 1977). US, later Greek, soprano. Studied Athens with Hidalgo. Début Athens O, 1941 (Tosca). Verona Arena 1947 (La Gioconda); then throughout Italy as Turandot, Isolde, Brünnhilde, etc., but also in the coloratura repertory, e.g. Elvira (*Puritani*), evincing a Lilli-Lehmann-like versatility. Eventually deciding to concentrate on bel canto roles, she sang in (and was responsible for) revivals of many works by Bellini, Donizetti, Rossini, and Cherubini. Milan, S, 1950–8 and 1960–2; London, CG, 1952–3, 1957–9, 1964–5; Chicago 1954–6; New York, M, 1956–8, 1965; also Dallas, Vienna, Berlin, Edinburgh. A striking woman, she possessed both personal magnetism and true artistry, and was compelling in her dramatic intensity and emotional commitment. Especially memorable as Norma, Medea, and Tosca, she also brought a touching pathos and vulnerability to Violetta and Lucia. Her voice was of unique timbre, combining power with brilliance, flexibility, and a rich variety of colours. However, like Malibran (an artist with whom she bears comparison), she had a constant struggle with its imperfections, and in 1965 she withdrew from public appearances. She made a last concert tour 1973–4 with her former colleague Di Stefano. She was one of the century's greatest singing actresses, and an artist who touched every role she sang with her genius. (R)

Calvé, Emma (b Decazeville, 15 Aug. 1858; d Millau, 6 Jan. 1942). French soprano. Studied Paris with Puget, Marchesi, and Laborde. Also influenced by Victor Maurel and the actress Eleanora Duse. Début Brussels, M, 1881 (Marguerite). Paris from 1884; Milan, S, from 1887; Rome 1891; London, CG, 1894–1904; New York, M, 1893–1904; Manhattan OC 1907–8. Then retired, but gave concerts until after 1918. One of the great actress-singers who came to the fore with verismo opera, her technique and range enabled her to sing soprano and mezzo roles. She also possessed a high, 'disembodied' voice which Massenet employed in Sapho, which she created, together with La navarraise. She sang Pamina, Amina, and Lucia, but became especially associated with Santuzza, Ophelia, and Carmen (to which she brought a disturbing brand of realism; Shaw, though a keen admirer, was shocked by her portrayal); created Suzel (Amico Fritz). Her voice was rich and alluring, while her singing, according to Hahn, was 'always of the most perfect beauty'. (R)

Calzabigi, Ranieri de' (b Livorno, 23 Dec. 1714; d Naples, July 1795). Italian librettist. He is famous as the author of three librettos for Gluck, Orfeo ed Euridice (1762), Alceste (1767), and Paride ed Elena (1770). These constitute a reform, away from the narrow conventions and artificiality of opera seria, in favour of 'a beautiful simplicity' and greater dramatic truth, seen at its purest in Orfeo. He was the motivator, perhaps the actual author, of the famous Preface to *Alceste.

Cambert, Robert (b Paris, c.1628; d London, Feb. or Mar. 1677). French composer. His collaboration in 1659 with Perrin on the Pastoral d'Issy was not, as claimed, 'la première comédie française en musique', but it did represent only the second setting of a French

text with genuine operatic pretensions. Following its success, Perrin and Cambert began work immediately on a 5-act opera, Ariane, ou Le mariage de Bacchus, though this remained unperformed until 1674.

On 28 June 1669 the partnership were granted a royal privilege for 'L'établissement des Académies d'opéra ou représentations en musique et en langue françoise' and on 3 Mar. 1671 staged their latest work Pomone in the Salle du Jeu de Paume de la Bouteille, effectively the first home of the Paris Opéra. Though the venture was successful, the backers of Pomone retained all the profit and Perrin was imprisoned for debt. Cambert went on to write another opera, Les peines et les plaisirs de l'amour the following year, but soon afterwards Lully successfully conspired to obtain the imperial privilege. Forced to leave Paris, Cambert came to London, where little is known of his later life.

Though most of his music is lost, Cambert is recognized as one of the founding fathers of French opera, and the most significant of Lully's predecessors.

Cambiale di matrimonio, La (The Bill of Marriage). Opera in 1 act by Rossini; text by Rossi, after Camillo Federici's comedy (1790). Prem. Venice, T San Moisè, 3 Nov. 1810.

An English town, 18th cent. Sir Tobias Mill (bs), an English merchant, has promised the hand of his daughter Fanny (sop) to Slook (bar), a Canadian merchant. Fanny, however, is in love with Edoardo (ten), and Slook helps them outwit Sir Tobias.

Rossini's first opera to be performed. The duet 'Dunque io son' was later used in Act I of Il barbiere di Siviglia.

Cambreling, Sylvain (b Amiens, 2 July 1948). French conductor. Studied with Pierre Dervaux in Paris; début Lyons O, 1975 (Cenerentola). Paris, OC, 1975 (Rake's Progress); Paris, O, 1980 (Hoffmann); Gly. 1981 (Barbiere di Siviglia). Music dir., Brussels, M, 1981–92. Milan, S, 1984 (Lucio Silla); New York, M, 1985 (Roméo et Juliette). Music dir., Frankfurt O, 1993: Elektra, From the House of the Dead, Wozzeck. A sympathetic interpreter of a wide repertory. (R)

Cambridge. City in England. The Cambridge University Musical Society has done much for English opera (including for Handel), above all in the period 1902–41 under E. J. Dent, lecturer at King's Coll. from 1902 and Professor of Music from 1926. A production with far-reaching consequences was the 1911 *Magic Flute* in Dent's translation, with a cast including Steuart Wilson, which paved the way for the acceptance of Mozart into the English repertory. Other works produced by Dent included Purcell's *King Arthur* (1928) and *The Tempest* (1938), and Handel's *Samson* (1932), *Susanna* (1935 and 1938), and *Saul* (1937). Post-war productions included Handel's *Solomon* (1948) and *Athalia* (1954), and Vaughan Williams's *The Pilgrim's Progress* (1954). In 1954 the Cambridge University Opera Group was formed, largely to stage works less 'academic' than the official ones. Works produced included *Il matrimonio segreto* (1955), *The Rake's Progress* and Vaughan Williams's *Sir John in Love* (1956), Liebermann's *The School for Wives* (1958), and Bizet's *Don Procopio* (1959). It was from the group that the *New Opera Company was formed in 1956.

Cambridge Theatre. Theatre in Seven Dials, London (cap. 1,285). Opened in 1930, it has staged opera including a run of *Hänsel und Gretel* (1934) and a 2-year unbroken series (1946–8) by Jay Pomeroy's New London OC under Dino Borgioli with Alberto Erede conducting an Italian repertory. The British prem. of *The Consul* with the original New York cast was given in 1951.

Camden Festival. Annual arts festival in the London Borough of Camden, founded in 1954 and devoted especially to operatic revivals and first performances, given first in St Pancras TH and after 1970 in the Collegiate T of London U. Disbanded when funding was withdrawn by Camden Council in 1987. Productions (many of them British prems.) included Haydn's *Orfeo* (1955), *Il mondo della luna* (1961), *L'infedeltà delusa* and *L'incontro improvviso* (1966), and *La fedeltà premiata* (1971); Rossini's *La pietra del paragone* (1963), *Il turco in Italia* (1965), *Elisabetta, regina d'Inghilterra* (1968), and *Tancredi* (1971); Donizetti's *Maria Stuarda* (1966), *Marino Faliero* (1967), *Torquato Tasso* (1974), and *Francesca di Foix* and *La romanziera* (1982); Verdi's *Un giorno di regno* (1961), *I masnadieri* (1962), *Aroldo* (1964), and *Il corsaro* (1966); also Leoncavallo's *La bohème* (1970), Cilea's *Adriana Lecouvreur* (1971, 1984), Smetana's *The Secret* (1972), Rakhmaninov's *Aleko* (1972), Massenet's *La navarraise* (1972), Meyerbeer's *L'étoile du nord* (1977), Delius's *Village Romeo and Juliet* (1979) and *Margot la rouge* (1984), Grétry's *Zémire et Azor* (1980), the

Riccis' *Crispino e la comare* (1981), Sacchini's *Renaud* (1981), Cavalli's *Eritrea* (1982), Vivaldi's *Juditha triumphans* (1984), Caccini's *Euridice* (1985), Boito's *Nerone* (1985), Strauss's *Friedenstag* (1985), Mozart's *La finta semplice* (1985) and *La finta giardiniera* (1986), Weill's *Protagonist* and *Tsar* (1986) and *Silbersee* and *Happy End* (1987).

camerata (It.: 'society'). A term in vogue in the 16th cent., denoting a small body of intellectuals and creative artists which met for scholarly dialogue. Although only one of several such groups in Florence, the camerata which met during the 1580s at the house of Count Giovanni de' Bardi in Florence was of greatest importance for the development of opera, and is often known simply as the 'Florentine Camerata': its members included Jacopo Corsi, Vincenzo *Galilei (father of the astronomer), Piero Strozzi, *Peri, *Caccini, Emilio de' *Cavalieri, and *Rinuccini. The new *stile rappresentativo which the group developed was the bedrock of the earliest operas and the source of much scholarly debate.

Cammarano, Salvadore (*b* Naples, 19 Mar. 1801; *d* Naples, 17 July 1852). Italian librettist. From 1835 he was house poet of the Naples, C. He befriended Donizetti and wrote the texts for *Lucia di Lammermoor* (1835), *Belisario* (1836), *Pia de' Tolomei* (1837), *Roberto Devereux* (1837), and *Maria di Rudenz* (1838). For Verdi he wrote *Alzira* (1845), *La battaglia di Legnano* (1849), *Luisa Miller* (1849), and *Il trovatore* (1853). A careful and skilled craftsman, he was adept at fashioning an effective libretto in a robust traditional vein that would gratify composer, audience, and even censor, though often a good deal of the distinctive quality of his original source was thereby lost. He also wrote texts for Pacini and Mercadante.

Campana sommersa, La (The Sunken Bell). Opera in 4 acts by Respighi; text by Guastalla, after Gerhard Hauptmann's 'fairy-drama' *Die versunkene Glocke* (1896). Prem. Hamburg 18 Nov. 1927.

Heinrich (ten), a bell-founder, falls under the spell of the fairy Rautendelein (sop), and follows her to the mountains. He returns home on the death of his wife Magda (sop), but cannot forget Rautendelein, and on his own deathbed he calls for her and she returns to him.

Campanello di notte, Il (The Night Bell).
Also known as *Il campanello dello speziale* (The
Chemist's Bell). Opera in 1 act by Donizetti;
text by composer, after a vaudeville by Brun-
swick, Troin, and Lhérie, *La sonnette de nuit*.
Prem. Naples, N, 1 June 1836.

Foria, nr. Naples, 19th cent. Don Annibale
Pistacchio (bs), an elderly apothecary, has
married young Serafina (sop). Her former
lover Enrico (ten) disrupts their wedding
night by presenting himself at the apothecary's door, ringing the night bell and
demanding that various prescriptions are
dispensed by the frustrated bridegroom.

Campanini, Cleofonte (*b* Parma, 1 Sept.
1860; *d* Chicago, 19 Dec. 1919). Italian con-
ductor and violinist. Studied Parma, Scuola
di Musica, but expelled; then studied with
Rossi. Début as cond., Parma 1882 (*Carmen*).
Music staff New York, M, 1883–4; New York,
AM, 1888 (first US *Otello* (Verdi)). In Milan
from 1902: cond. prems. of *Adriana Lecouvreur*
(1902) at L, Giordano's *Siberia* (1903) and
Madama Butterfly (1904) at S (1903–6). London,
CG, 1904–12 (including *Manon Lescaut* with
Caruso, 1904, and first European *Fanciulla del
West* with Destinn, 1911). New York, Man-
hattan OC, 1906–9 (artistic dir.). Mounted
centenary cycle of Verdi at his own expense,
Parma 1913. Chicago 1910–19 (manager
1918–19). Married soprano Eva *Tetrazzini.
His brother **Italo** (*b* Parma, 30 June 1845; *d*
Corcagno, 22 Nov. 1896) was a tenor. Studied
Parma with Griffini, later Milan with Lam-
perti. Début Parma 1863 (Vitellozzo in *Lucrezia Borgia*). Sang in Russia for three years;
first Italian Lohengrin, Bologna 1871.
London, DL, 1872 (Gennaro); London, HM,
1878 (Don José). New York, M, 1883 (Gounod's
Faust at its opening). Idolized in his prime,
he used his limited but sweet-toned voice
with much feeling.

Campiello, Il (The Square). Opera in 3 acts
by Wolf-Ferrari; text by Ghisalberti, after Goldoni's comedy (1756). Prem. Milan, S, 12 Feb.
1936.

Venice, mid-18th cent. The Neapolitan
Astolfi (bar) is paying court to three girls,
Gasparina (sop), Lucretia (sop), and Gnese
(sop). The latter two already have lovers. Gasparina is unwilling to marry Astolfi, but her
uncle Fabrizio (bs) takes a liking to him.
Quarrels and confusions arise, involving
three old women who live in the square,
but all is eventually resolved and Gasparina

consents to marry Astolfi and move to
Naples.

Campra, André (*b* Aix-en-Provence, *bapt.* 4
Dec. 1660; *d* Versailles, 29 June 1744). French
composer of Italian descent. Already well
known as a composer of sacred music,
Campra inaugurated the new genre of opéra-
ballet with *L'Europe galante* in 1697. Its skilful
combination of music and dance paved the
way for works such as *Les fêtes vénitiennes*
(1710) and *Les âges* (1718), whose freshness
and vitality were to prove an important
ingredient for the later development of
*opéra-comique.

After release from his ecclesiastical duties
at Notre Dame in 1700, he devoted himself
fully to opera, producing *c.*40 dramatic
works ranging from full-scale operas to
shorter divertissements. The former, generally after Lully's model, were written for
the Opéra and based on familiar stories, such
as *Tancrède* (1702) and *Achille et Déidamie*
(1735), while in works such as *Le triomphe
de l'amour* (1705) the allegorical tradition of
both ballet de cour and early French opera
is clearly maintained. In general, Campra's
work falls midway between Lully and
Rameau, lacking the grandeur of the former
and the eloquence of the latter.

The libretto which he used for his highly
popular *Idoménée* was modified for Mozart's
opera on the same subject in 1780.

Canada. On 14 Nov. 1606 *Le théâtre de Neptune*,
a masque by Marc Lescarbot, was played from
small boats in the harbour of Port Royal on
the Bay of Fundy. But this enterprise had no
immediate successors. Towards the end of
the 18th cent. opera performances began in
Halifax, Quebec, and Montreal, and early in
the 19th cent. in Toronto. By the mid-18th
cent. a regular circuit of the main towns of
the provinces of Upper and Lower Canada
(now Ontario and Quebec) was travelled by
small touring companies, and by many
famous soloists from Europe and the US,
giving opera excerpts and concerts. From the
1850s full companies made regular visits to
Montreal and Toronto and often to many
smaller centres; by 1900 almost every town
had some acquaintance with opera and the
larger cities frequently saw a standard repertory, including Weber and Wagner.

Local productions were sporadic, and
there were no lasting established companies
until the mid-20th cent. The most successful

has been the Canadian O (1950), which in addition to seasons in Toronto and visits to Ottawa has, since 1958, sent out a touring company which visits every inhabited area of Canada and many towns in the US. Prems. have included Harry *Somers's *Louis Riel* (1967) and *The Shivaree* (1982) by John Beckwith (*b* 1927). In 1961 productions by the T-lyrique de Nouvelle-France began in Quebec. L'Opéra du Quebec was set up in 1971 to consolidate operatic production in Quebec, Montreal, and elsewhere, but closed in May 1975. A similar co-operative venture was established in 1972 in Western Canada by the Opera Associations of Vancouver, Edmonton, Calgary, and Winnipeg, all of which began regular local productions during the 1960s. Notable summer productions have been by the Stratford Fest., at the Nat. Arts Centre in Ottawa, and at the Guelph May Fest.

The Canadian Broadcasting Corporation formed its opera company in 1948 to present Canadian performers in live studio productions of a wide range of standard, unfamiliar, and contemporary works. It has also commissioned operas including Healey *Willan's *Transit through Fire* (1942) and *Deirdre* (1946), John Beckwith's *Night Blooming Cereus* (1959), Kelsey Jones's *Sam Slick* (1967), and Murray Adaskin's *Grant, Warden of the Plains* (1967).

Despite the absence of permanent companies, numerous operas and operettas have been written by composers in Canada from the early 19th cent.

See also MONTREAL, TORONTO, VANCOUVER.

Canadian Opera Company. See TORONTO.

Candeille, Pierre Joseph (*b* Estaires, 8 Dec. 1744; *d* Chantilly, 24 Apr. 1827). French composer and singer. Active in Paris 1767–71 and 1773–1827, he appeared as basse-taille in the choruses of the Académie Royale de Musique (Opéra) and the Concerts Spirituels and was involved in the production of dramatic works for various theatres. His only real success as a composer came with *Castor et Pollux* (1791), which received 130 performances up to 1800, and, after the failure of Peter von Winter's *Castor et Pollux* (1814), was revived and kept in the repertoire until 1817. As such it was one of the most enduring works of the Paris stage.

His daughter (Amélie) **Julie Candeille** (1767–1834) made her début in Gluck's *Iphigénie en Aulide* and, in addition to widely acclaimed appearances as a singer and actress, also enjoyed a more modest career as a composer of opera.

Caniglia, Maria (*b* Naples, 5 May, 1905; *d* Rome, 16 Apr. 1979). Italian soprano. Studied Naples with Roche. Début Turin 1930 (Chysothemis). The leading Italian lyric-dramatic soprano of the 1930s. Milan, S, 1931–51; London, CG, 1937, 1939, 1950; New York, M, 1938–9. Admired as Tosca and Adriana Lecouvreur; created Roxane (*Cyrano de Bergerac*) and Respighi's Lucrezia. A warm and vivid performer with a rich, vibrant voice. (R)

Canio. The leader (ten) of the strolling players, husband of Nedda, in Leoncavallo's *Pagliacci*.

Cantelli, Guido (*b* Novara, 27 Apr. 1920; *d* Paris, 24 Nov. 1956). Italian conductor. Studied Milan with Pedrollo and Ghedini. Début Novara 1943. Prod. and cond. *Così fan tutte* Milan, PS, 1956. His appointment as chief cond. at Milan, S, was announced a few days before his death in an air crash. (R)

Capecchi, Renato (*b* Cairo, 6 Nov. 1923). Italian baritone. Studied Milan with Carrozzi. Début Reggio Emilia 1949 (Amonasro). Milan, S, from 1950; New York, M, from 1952; London, CG, from 1962; also Aix, Edinburgh, Vienna, Chicago, etc. Has a repertory of almost 300 roles, including many contemporary works. A versatile, intelligent singer, and a thoughtful artist. (R)

Capobianco, Tito (*b* La Plata, 28 Aug. 1931). Argentinian producer. After working in the Argentine and Mexico, prod. and technical dir. Buenos Aires, C, 1959–62. Dir. Cincinnati Summer O, 1962; New York, CO, 1965; Hartford 1972; S Diego 1976; Pittsburgh 1983. Berlin 1972; Paris and Holland, 1973; Sydney 1974 (*Hoffmann* for Sutherland).

Cappuccilli, Piero (*b* Trieste, 9 Nov. 1929). Italian baritone. Studied Trieste with Donaggio. Début Milan, N, 1957 (Tonio). New York, M, 1959–60; Milan, S, from 1964; London, CG, from 1967; Salzburg from 1975. His large repertory includes many Verdi roles (Boccanegra, Germont, Renato, Macbeth, etc.), to which his strong, expressive voice is well suited. (R)

Capriccio. Opera in 1 act by Richard Strauss;

text by Clemens Krauss and the composer. Prem. Munich 28 Oct. 1942.

A castle nr. Paris, 1775. The opera is a dramatized conversation piece, set in Paris at the time of Gluck's operatic reforms. The countess Madeleine (sop) listens to a string sextet (which also serves as the overture to the opera) written for her by one of her admirers, Flamand (ten). Her other admirer, Olivier (bar), is a tragic poet, whose play is to be staged for the Countess's birthday. A debate arises as to whether music or words are the more important in opera. When they each have the opportunity, both suitors declare their love to the Countess. In a second discussion, a theatre impresario, La Roche (bs), declares that both Olivier's characters and Flamand's music lack sufficient drama. He sets them a challenge of writing an opera, taking as a plot the foregoing discussions and using the people present as characters. The guests all depart. The Countess has made assignments with both her suitors for the same time the next morning, but still cannot decide between them; as an opera character, she needs both words and music.

The old Italian tag from which the work takes its text, *Prima la musica e poi le parole* (First the music and then the words), is also the title of an opera by Salieri (1786).

Captain's Daughter, The. Opera in 4 acts by Cui; text by the composer, based on Pushkin's story (1836). Prem. St Petersburg, M, 27 Feb. 1911. The opera, which takes place during the reign of Catherine the Great (mez), concerns the love of Andrey Grinyov (bs) for Maria Ivanovna (sop). He is accused of treachery but Maria secures his pardon.

Captain Vere. The commander (ten) of *HMS Indomitable* in Britten's *Billy Budd*.

Capuana, Franco (*b* Fano, 29 Sept. 1894; *d* Naples, 10 Dec. 1969). Italian conductor. Studied Naples with De Nardis. Début Brescia 1919, then conducted in many Italian towns. Turin 1929–30; Naples, C, 1930–7; Milan, S, 1937–40, 1946–52 (from 1949 music dir.), conducting many prems., including works by Alfano, Refice, and Ghedini, Italian prems., and revivals of neglected works. London, CG (first post-war opera), with Naples, C, Co. 1946, 1951–2. Outside the Italian repertory, in which he was vivid and forceful, a fine conductor of Wagner and Richard Strauss. Died while conducting *Mosè*

on the opening night of the Naples, C, season. (R) His sister **Maria** (1891–1955) was a mezzo-soprano. Studied Naples. Début Naples 1918 (Urbain). Possessed a firm, dark voice, and specialized in Wagner, which she sang all over Italy, in Buenos Aires, Spain, and Africa. (R)

Capuleti e i Montecchi, I (The Capulets and the Montagues). Opera in 4 parts by Bellini; text by Romani, modified for Bellini from his libretto for Vaccai, after Matteo Bandello's ninth *novella*, in turn drawing on an earlier libretto by Foppa set by Zingarelli (1796). Foppa's sources drew not on Shakespeare but on Gerolamo della Corte's *Storie di Verona*. Prem. Venice, F, 11 Mar. 1830.

Verona, 13th cent. The opera tells of the love of Romeo (mez), head of the Montagues, and Giulietta (sop), daughter of Capellio (bs), head of the Capulets, in the face of a feud between the two families. Romeo has killed Capellio's son, and Giulietta's hand in marriage is promised to Tebaldo (ten) if he can avenge this. Romeo proposes a reconciliation between the families by his marriage to Giulietta but Capellio rejects the idea. Unable to persuade Giulietta to elope with him, Romeo intends to abduct her by force, but is meanwhile arrested. The sleeping potion which causes the appearance of death is given to Giulietta by Lorenzo (bs), the Capulet family's doctor. He is prevented from telling Romeo of the plan by his own capture by Capellio. News of Giulietta's death arrives as Romeo and Tebaldo are about to fight a duel. Romeo takes poison and, waking to find her lover dying, Giulietta herself dies of grief.

Carafa, Michele (*b* Naples, 17 Nov. 1787; *d* Paris, 26 July 1872). Italian, later French, composer. Following a distinguished military career, he had his first major success with *Gabriella di Vergy* (1816). In Naples, he formed a lifelong friendship with Rossini, to two of whose operas he contributed, *Adelaide di Borgogna* and *Mosè in Egitto*. From 1821 he had much success in Paris, especially with *Jeanne d'Arc à Orléans* (1821), *Le solitaire* (1822), *Le valet de chambre* (1823), and particularly *Masaniello* (1827), the last despite Auber's work on the same subject; he also had some success with *Le nozze di Lammermoor* (1829), *La prison d'Édimbourg* (1833), and finally *Thérèse* (1838). He became a French citizen in 1834, from 1837 was a member of the Académie des Beaux-Arts, and from 1840 professor of counterpoint at the Conservatoire. His music was much influenced by Rossini, latterly also by Cherubini. Though excellently written, his operas lack melodic individuality. In 1860 Rossini asked him to reshape the French text of *Semiramide* from two into four acts and to compose the ballet music compulsory at the Opéra, and, knowing Carafa to be impoverished, assigned to him all the rights.

Cardillac. Opera in 3 acts by Hindemith; text by Ferdinand Lion after E. T. A. Hoffmann's story *Das Fräulein von Scuderi* (1818). Prem. Dresden 9 Nov. 1926.

Paris, 17th cent. The plot concerns a master jeweller, Cardillac (bar), who murders his customers rather than part with his creations. An officer (bs) witnesses one of the attacks but blames an innocent party, since he hopes to win Cardillac's favour and marry his daughter (sop). Finally, threatened with arson to his workshop, Cardillac confesses and is torn to pieces by an irate crowd.

'Care selve'. Meleagro's (sop cas) opening arioso in Handel's *Atalanta*, when (as 'Tirsi'), he is seeking his love in the forests.

Carestini, Giovanni (*b* Filottrano, *c.*1704; *d* ?Filottrano, *c.*1760). Italian contralto castrato. Studied Bologna with Pistocchi and Bernacchi. Début Rome 1721 (in A. Scarlatti's *Griselda*) as soprano castrato. His voice later developed into 'the finest, fullest and deepest counter-tenor [*sic*] that has, perhaps, ever been heard' (Burney); also an 'animated and intelligent actor', he was considered by many to be the best singer of his time. Vienna 1723–5; Venice between 1724 and 1731; Rome 1727–30; sang for the Elector of Bavaria 1731–41. He was engaged by Handel in London 1733–5 as the answer to Senesino and later Farinelli, stars of Porpora's rival group, and created roles in *Ariodante*, *Alcina*, *Terpsicore*, and *Arianna in Creta*. (He sang in London again, 1739–40, in operas by Hasse and Pescetti.) In 1735 he returned to the Continent, appearing throughout Italy, and in 1747–8 at Dresden. He sang for Frederick the Great 1750–4, then at St Petersburg 1754–6, after which he retired. One of the foremost castratos of any age, he was admired universally for his virtuoso technique and expressive powers.

Carl Rosa Opera Company. English opera company founded in 1866 by Karl August Nicolaus Rose, a Hamburg violinist who came to England in 1866. After the death of his wife, the soprano Euphrosyne Parepa, in 1874, Rosa (as he became) founded the Carl Rosa OC to present opera in English, opening with *Figaro* in Sept. 1875 at the Princess's T, London. Rosa was associated with Augustus Harris of Drury Lane, and a prosperous five years followed. After Harris took over Covent Garden and Rosa died (1889), the company only toured. After a Balmoral performance in 1893, Queen Victoria conferred on the company the title 'Royal'. Alfred van Noorden was director 1900–16, Arthur Winckworth and Rosa's second wife co-directors 1916–23. After the First World War the company took over the Harrison-Frewin and Alan Turner companies; the former was managed by H. B. Phillips, who became director of the Carl Rosa OC in 1923. After Phillips's death in 1950 his widow directed the company, with Arthur Hammond as music director, until 1957, when she was succeeded by H. Procter-Gregg. Financial and other difficulties ensued, leading to Procter-Gregg's resignation and the withdrawal of Arts Council subsidy in 1958. Most of its personnel went to Sadler's Wells T. There was an unsuccessful attempt at a come-back in 1960.

The company gave the English prems. of *Manon* (1885), *La bohème* (1897), and *Andrea Chénier* (1903), and the prems. of British works including Goring Thomas's *Esmeralda* (1883) and *Nadeshda* (1885), Stanford's *The Canterbury Pilgrims* (1884), and Lloyd's *John Socman* (1951). Though the company's standards were sometimes rough and ready, it introduced opera to many parts of Britain and gave many artists valuable early experience.

Carlyle, Joan (*b* Upton-on-the-Wirral, 6 Apr. 1931). English soprano. After private study, made her début at London, CG, 1955 (Frasquita): remained with the company until 1976, with much success in such lyric roles as Nedda, Sophie, Mimì, Micaëla, and Arabella. Gly. 1965, Countess Almaviva. Salzburg 1968. Other roles incl. Jenifer (*Midsummer Marriage*), Donna Anna, Desdemona, Pamina.

Carmen. Opera in 4 acts by Bizet; text by Meilhac and Halévy, after Mérimée's novel (1845). Prem. Paris, OC, 3 Mar. 1875.

Spain, *c.*1820. In a square in Seville, Micaëla (sop) is looking for Don José (ten), a corporal. He arrives and, as the girls return to work in the cigarette factory, one of them, Carmen (mez), throws him a flower. Micaëla gives him news of his mother, and he puts Carmen out of his mind. After a quarrel in the factory in which Carmen wounds another girl, she is captured and Don José is set to guard her; quickly fascinated by her, he unties her hands so that she can escape.

Carmen is dancing in Lillas Pastia's inn with Frasquita (sop) and Mercédès (sop). When the famous bull-fighter Escamillo (bar) enters, he is immediately attracted to her. Carmen, however, waits for Don José, refusing to join the others on a smuggling expedition. Soon after he arrives, he is summoned back to barracks, but Carmen tries to persuade him to desert. Zuniga (bs), Don José's captain, bursts in, hoping to find Carmen alone. He and José are about to fight when Dancairo (bar) and Remendado (ten) enter and lead Zuniga away. Guilty of having threatened a senior officer, José now has to join the smugglers.

Carmen has tired of José and he thinks, with remorse, of how he has broken the promise to his mother to marry Micaëla. Reading her fortune in the cards, Carmen foresees death. When Escamillo arrives, he and José fight over Carmen, but Escamillo is saved by the smugglers. Micaëla, who has come to find José, is discovered. He leaves with her when she tells him that his mother is dying.

On the day of Escamillo's bullfight in Seville, Carmen is warned that José is in the crowd seeking revenge. Alone, the two encounter each other; Carmen refuses to return to José and, to the sound of Escamillo's triumph in the main ring, José kills her and gives himself up.

Modernized by Oscar Hammerstein II as *Carmen Jones* (1943).

Carnicer, Ramón (*b* Tárrega, 24 Oct. 1789; *d* Madrid, 17 Mar. 1855). Spanish composer. In 1816 he recruited an Italian company for the T de la Cruz, and in 1818 became director of the Coliseo T orchestra. He wrote three operas for Barcelona, moving to Madrid and then via Italy and France to London. Back in Madrid in 1827, he wrote four more operas. He was one of the founders of the Spanish national cons., remaining a prof. until his death. Much influenced by Rossini (for some of whose operas he wrote extra arias), he was nevertheless the most important Spanish opera composer of the early 19th cent. His works include *Cristoforo Colombo* (1831) and *Ismalia* (1838).

Caron, Rose (*b* Monnerville, 17 Nov. 1857; *d* Paris, 9 Apr. 1930). French soprano. Studied Paris with Masset and Obin; later with Sass. Début Brussels, M, 1883 (Alice in *Robert le Diable*). Here she created Brunehilde in Reyer's *Sigurd*, and title-roles in his *Salammbô* and Godard's *Jocelyn*. Paris, O, 1885–7, 1890–5. First French Sieglinde, Elsa, and Desdemona. Boschot portrays her 'indescribable poetic charm' as a performer. (R)

'Caro nome'. Gilda's (sop) aria in Act I of Verdi's *Rigoletto*, expressing her love for the 'student' Gualtier Maldé, who is in fact the Duke of Mantua.

Carré, Marguerite (*b* Cabourg, 16 Aug. 1880; *d* Paris, 26 Dec. 1947). French soprano. Studied Bordeaux and Paris Cons. Début (semi-prof.) Nantes 1899 (Mimì); real début Paris, OC, 1901/2 (Mimì) whose dir., **Albert Carré** (1852–1938) she married in 1901, divorced in 1924, and remarried in 1929. Here she created 15 roles, and was the first French Butterfly and Snegurochka. A popular singer, outstanding as Mélisande and Louise. Retired 1923. (R)

Carré, Michel (*b* Besançon, 21 Oct. 1822; *d* Paris, 27 June 1872). French librettist. Furnished most of the leading French composers of the second half of the 19th cent. with librettos, including Meyerbeer (*Dinorah*), Gounod (*Mireille, Faust, Roméo et Juliette*, and five more), Bizet (*Pêcheurs de perles*), Thomas (*Hamlet, Mignon*), Offenbach (*Contes d'Hoffmann*), often in collaboration with Jules *Barbier. Uncle of **Albert Carré**. Sometimes wrote under the name of Jules Dubois.

Carreras, José (*b* Barcelona, 5 Dec. 1946). Spanish tenor. Studied Barcelona with Puig. Début Barcelona 1970 (Flavio in *Norma*). A protégé of Caballé, with whom he sang *Lucrezia Borgia* and at his London début, in concert, 1971. London, CG, from 1974 (Alfredo, Rodolfo, etc.); New York, CO and M, from 1974; at S Francisco, Buenos Aires, Tokyo, etc. A gifted and popular lyric tenor with a highly appealing voice whose courageous struggle against leukaemia and come-back won him wide admiration. (R).

Carroli, Silvano (*b* Venice, 22 Feb. 1939). Italian baritone. Studied in Venice and with Mario del Monaco. Début Venice 1963

(Schaunard). Has sung widely in Italy, notably at Milan, S, and the Verona arena (Verdi's Ezio and Renato, 1985‒6). London, CG, from 1977 (Jack Rance, Nélusko, Iago). US appearances at Dallas (début 1972), Chicago and New York, M. Noted for his forthright performances of the major Verdi roles; other repertory incl. Escamillo, Gérard, Scarpia. (R)

Carte, Richard D'Oyly (b London, 3 May 1844; d London, 3 Apr. 1901). English impresario. Abandoned ambitions as a composer of light opera for management, first of Patti, Mario, Gounod, and others, then as theatre manager, introducing to England works by Lecocq, Offenbach, Serpette, and others at the Opera Comique T. Commissioned *Trial by Jury* from Gilbert and Sullivan, and its success led to his establishing the Comedy OC. Produced *The Sorcerer* and *H.M.S. Pinafore*, then formed his own company. Built and moved to the Savoy, opening with *Patience* 1881. Here the Gilbert and Sullivan partnership of 'Savoy Operas' flourished for ten years, and resumed with *Utopia Ltd* (1893) and *The Grand Duke* (1896). In 1891 he attempted to establish an English Grand Opera, and built the English OH (now Palace T), opening with *Ivanhoe*. The venture failed. At the Savoy he introduced electric lighting and abolished charges for programmes and cloakrooms. The D'Oyly Carte OC was revived after his death by his son Rupert then by his granddaughter Bridget. The company closed in 1982; a new company was formed in 1988 with the support of a bequest from Dame Bridget's estate and other sources, and benefited from a new artistic impetus.

Caruso, Enrico (b Naples, 25 Feb. 1873; d Naples, 2 Aug. 1921). Italian tenor. Studied Naples with Vergine. Début Naples, N, 1895 (in Morelli's *L'amico Francesco*). Pursued an unremarkable career in Italy until 1897, when he sang with success at Palermo in *La Gioconda*. This was consolidated in the following years and in 1901 a triumph at Milan, S, in *L'elisir d'amore*, assured his future. Created Federico (Cilea, *L'arlesiana*, 1897), Loris (Giordano, *Fedora*, 1898), Florindo (Mascagni, *Le maschere*, 1901), Federico (Franchetti, *Germania*, 1902). London, CG, 1902 (Duke of Mantua), 1904‒7, 1913‒14; New York, M, 1903‒20, where he sang in over 600 performances, among them creating Dick Johnson in *La fanciulla del West*. He possessed an astonishingly beautiful voice, rich and mellow in his youth and of an almost baritonal quality, then increasing in brilliance and smoothness in his middle years. His artistry, too, gained subtlety as he grew older, the abandoned gaiety of his earlier singing giving way to masterly phrasing and legato. His breath control was extraordinary. In 1908‒9 he suffered a temporary vocal setback, and subsequently his voice darkened, but without losing its expressive qualities. His range of roles was enormous, encompassing both the lyric and dramatic, and his acting was matched by his skill in make-up, especially in the roles of Radamès, Canio, and Eléazar. The first true 'gramophone' tenor, he began recording in 1902 and made his last record in 1920. His royalties apparently reached the region of £500,000. One of his most treasured recordings is 'Una furtiva lagrima' (1904). He died of pleurisy, and was mourned as a man of immense warmth and generosity as well as one of the greatest singers of the century. (R)

Carvalho, Léon (b Port-Louis, 18 Jan. 1825; d Paris, 29 Dec. 1897). French baritone and impresario. Studied Paris. Sang at the Paris, OC, 1851‒5, where he met Marie *Miolan, marrying her 1853. Dir. Paris, L, 1856‒68; prod., Paris, O, 1869‒75; dir., Paris, OC, 1876‒87. When Paris, OC, burnt down 1887 and 131 people died, he was fined and imprisoned for negligence; reinstated on appeal 1891. Dir. Cairo OH 1868‒72. Berlioz complained bitterly about his interference in the 1863 production of *Les Troyens*.

Casavola, Franco (b Modugno, 13 July 1891; d Bari, 7 July 1955). Italian composer and critic. Studied in Bari, Milan, and with Respighi in Rome. An early adherent of Futurism, he wrote a number of works for the movement, turning later to traditional opera. His greatest success was with the 1-act *Il gobbo del Califfo* (1929).

Casella, Alfredo (b Turin, 25 July 1883; d Rome, 5 Mar. 1947). Italian composer. Studied with his mother and in Paris piano with Diémer and composition with Leroux and Fauré. Returning to Italy in 1915, he associated himself with avant-garde ideas and was responsible for introducing much contemporary music to Italy. The greatest success of his three operas was *La donna serpente* (1932). This was based on the same fable used by Wagner for *Die Feen*; however, in reaction both to Wagner and to verismo, it is a fantastic opera built out of swiftly alternating dramatic and comic scenes.

Casken, John (*b* Barnsley, 15 July 1949). English composer. Studied Birmingham with Dickinson and Joubert, Warsaw with Dobrowolski. His first opera, the 1-act *Golem*, aroused much interest at its 1989 Almeida Festival prem., in particular for its concise and original dramatic sense and its rich orchestral colouring.

Caspar. A huntsman (bs) in Weber's *Der Freischütz*.

Cassandre. The Trojan seer (mez), daughter of Priam and Hecuba, in Berlioz's *Les Troyens*.

Cassilly, Richard (*b* Washington DC, 14 Dec. 1927). US tenor. After study in New York made his début on Broadway 1955 (Menotti's *Saint of Bleecker Street*). New York, CO, from 1956 (début as Vakula in Tchaikovsky's *Cherevichki*); New York, M, from 1973 as Radamès, Tristan, Samson. His strong stage presence and heroic voice were also admired as Laca, Otello, and Florestan (London, CG, from 1968). Last major role as Tannhäuser, Chicago 1988. (R)

Cassio. A captain (ten), whom Iago persuades Otello is Desdemona's lover, in Verdi's *Otello*.

'Casta diva'. Norma's (sop) aria with chorus in Act I of Bellini's *Norma*, praying to the moon for peace between Gaul and Rome.

Castelmary, Armand (*b* Toulouse, 16 Aug. 1834; *d* New York, 10 Feb. 1897). French bass. Paris, O, 1863–70, creating Don Diego (*L'Africaine*) Italy, 1873–9; S America, 1881; London, CG, 1889–96; New York, M, 1893–7. Was a refined and elegant Mephistopheles (Boito and Gounod); first Horatio in *Hamlet* (Thomas); Don Diego (*Africaine*). Though often credited with creating the Grand Inquisitor, he sang the Monk (Verdi, *Don Carlos*).

Castor et Pollux. Opera in a prologue and 5 acts by Rameau; text by Pierre-Joseph Bernard. Prem. Paris, O, 24 Oct. 1737.

Ancient Greece. Pollux (bs) is the son of Jupiter (bs) and is immortal, Castor (haut-contre) the son of Tyndareus and mortal. Castor has been killed, but when Pollux offers himself in Castor's place to Télaïre (sop), she is confused and insists instead that Jupiter must be persuaded to restore Castor

to life. Jupiter agrees on condition that Pollux take his place in Hades, while also revealing to him the delights of the Heavenly Pleasures on Olympus. Pollux remains firm, but at the gates of Hades he is met by Phoebe (sop), who loves him and tries to turn him back, while Télaïre spurs him on. With Mercury's help, he enters Hades; Castor agrees to return to earth and to tell Télaïre he cannot accept Pollux's sacrifice, But Jupiter declares that Castor and Pollux shall be taken up to Olympus; Télaïre will follow; Phoebe kills herself.

castrato (It.: 'castrated') or **evirato** (It.: 'unmanned') or **musico** (It.: 'musician', in the 18th cent. a virtual synonym for castrato). A male soprano or contralto whose unbroken voice has been artificially preserved by means of a surgical operation on the testicles before puberty. Although castrati were first employed exclusively for sacred music, the rise of opera in the 17th cent. provided them with another outlet for their talent. By the time of Metastasian opera seria in the mid-18th cent., castratos were a cardinal feature of operatic life: among the most famous were Senesino, Caffarelli, and Farinelli. Following the reforms of Gluck, the art of the castrato went into a decline; though they were still common in the early 19th cent., their activities were largely confined to Italy. Rossini composed *Aureliano in Palmira* for the last great castrato, Velluti, but did not repeat the experiment.

Castro, Juan José (*b* Avellaneda, 7 Mar. 1895; *d* Buenos Aires, 5 Sept. 1968). Argentinian composer and conductor, brother of musicians José Maria, Luis Arnoldo, and Washington. Studied Buenos Aires with Gaito and Fornarini, and Paris with D'Indy. Dir. Buenos Aires, C, 1933, giving Argentinian prem. of *L'heure espagnole* and other important performances. His three operas include *Proserpina y el extranjero* (1952), a modernization of the Persephone myth set in Buenos Aires which won the International Verdi Prize; the others reflect his admiration for his friend Lorca.

Catalani, Alfredo (*b* Lucca, 19 June 1854; *d* Milan, 7 Aug. 1893). Italian composer. Studied Lucca with Magi, Paris with Bazin. In Milan he also studied with Bazzini, graduating with the promising *La falce* (1875). Bazzini introduced him to the avant-garde Scapigliatura group, which included Boito and Faccio, and to the music publisher G. Lucca, who commissioned *Elda* (prod. 1880). When this was not immediately performed and *Dejanice* (1883) failed (uncharacteristically, one admirer was Puccini), he turned to Romantic subjects; but the absorption of Lucca into the firm of Ricordi placed Catalani in an inferior position to both Verdi and Puccini. His revision of *Elda* as *Loreley* (1890) was ignored by Ricordi, and when Catalani himself arranged a performance he found himself accused of Wagnerism (the work's orchestral skill in fact owes more to Weber). His fourth opera, *Edmea* (1886), was more popular; its prem. was the occasion of Toscanini's Italian début. Catalani next succeeded in obtaining a performance at Milan, S, of his masterpiece *La Wally* (1892), a work championed by Toscanini (who named a daughter after the heroine). The work has impressive and touching moments, and is carefully constructed, but its effective manner is insufficiently supported by enough strong inventive matter to give it more than occasional revivals in Italy. Nevertheless, Catalani was unlucky to make his career when Verdi was at the height of his fame, Puccini's star was rising, and the verismo movement was growing: Catalani's modest but distinct talent was of another order.

catalogue aria (It., *aria di catalogo*). One of the most characteristic aria forms in 18th-cent. opera buffa, consisting of a comically rapid enunciation of a list of items. The most famous example is in Act I of Mozart's *Don Giovanni*, where the servant Leporello (bar) enumerates his master's various sexual conquests country by country.

Catel, Charles-Simon (*b* Laigle, 10 June 1773; *d* Paris, 29 Nov. 1830). French composer and theorist. Studied Paris with Gossec. He joined the band of the Garde Nationale, also acting as répétiteur at the Opéra and as professor at the newly founded Cons. from 1795. His works for the Opéra, beginning with *Sémiramis* (1802), reflect the atmosphere of the Empire and of the emergent Romanticism, and helped to confirm the success of some genres and to explore novel techniques. His most spectacular work was *Les bayadères* (1810), which, though somewhat overshadowed by Spontini, was as effective in demonstrating the power of the evolving Grand Opera. With *Zirphile et Fleur de Myrte*

(1818) he explored the genre of magic opera, familiar from Grétry but handled with new effectiveness.

He was also successful as a composer of opéra-comique. *Wallace* (1817) draws on the Romantic fascination with Scotland that had absorbed opéra-comique composers including Méhul, but the others are light pieces that owe more to opera buffa. One of Napoleon's opera prize competitions in 1809 placed his *L'auberge de Bagnères* (1807) in joint second place with Cherubini's *Les deux journées*, behind Méhul's *Joseph*. He had only moderate success with *Les aubergistes de qualité* (1812). Though his music is often somewhat slender, with enterprising ideas that are not really sustained creatively, Catel is interesting as something of a pioneer and as one of the most intelligent and perceptive composers of French opéra-comique.

Caterina Cornaro. Opera in a prologue and 2 acts by Donizetti; text by Giacomo Sacchèro, after Vernoy de St Georges's libretto *La reine de Chypre* for Halévy. Prem. Naples, C, 18 Jan. 1844.

Venice and Cyprus, 1472. The wedding of Caterina (sop), daughter of Andreas (bs), to a young Frenchman, Gerardo (ten), is postponed when Mocenigo (bs) brings word that Lusignano, King of Cyprus (bs), wishes to marry her. After much intrigue, involving Lusignano being slowly poisoned by Mocenigo, Gerardo joins the Knights of the Cross to help Lusignano defend Cyprus against the Venetians. Lusignano is mortally wounded; as he dies he entrusts his people to Caterina's care. Gerardo then returns to Rhodes. (In a revised finale for the Parma production, Donizetti makes Lusignano inform Caterina that Gerardo has been killed in battle.)

Cavalieri di Ekebù, I (The Knights of Ekebù). Opera in 4 acts by Zandonai; text by A. Rossato, after Selma Lagerlöf's novel *Gösta Berlings saga* (1891). Prem. Milan, S, 7 Mar. 1925.

Ekebù, Sweden, 19th cent. The unfrocked priest Gösta Berling (ten) is given work with the 'Knights' of Ekebù by the Commander (mez), owner of the ironworks and castle of Ekebù. She is suspected of selling the knights' souls to the devil but is cleared by them. She pardons her accusers and dies, bequeathing her possessions to Gösta and his beloved, Anna (sop).

Cavalieri, Emilio de' (b Rome, c.1550; d Rome 11 Mar. 1602). Italian composer. From 1588 he was superintendent of musicians and actors at the Tuscan court and responsible for organizing many of the great celebrations of the Medici family: these included the famous 1589 intermedi, to which he was also a contributor. A member of the Bardi *camerata, he was also one of the first to experiment with the new *stile rappresentativo, and with his best-known work, La rappresentazione di anima, e di corpo (1600), initiated an operatic tradition in Rome which was to flourish in the 1620s and 1630s.

Unlike the early efforts of Peri and Caccini, La rappresentazione di anima e di corpo explores the interaction of allegorical figures rather than characters from classical mythology. Its didactic, overtly religious plot has often led to its being described as the first oratorio, though it should more accurately be considered a sacred opera. The preface to the score is one of the most important pieces of documentary evidence for an understanding of stile rappresentativo and confirms Cavalieri's position as a crucial figure in the early history of opera.

Cavalieri, Katharina (b Währing, 19 Feb. 1760; d Vienna, 30 June 1801). Austrian soprano. Studied with Salieri (becoming his mistress). Début Vienna, Italian O, 1775 (Sandrina in Anfossi's La finta giardiniera). Joined the National-Singspiel founded by Joseph II in 1778. In 1781 and 1783 created roles in two of Salieri's operas. Her voice was full and even throughout, and her technique excellent. Though not beautiful, she carried herself well and possessed 'considerable expression'. Mozart wrote Constanze (making concessions to her 'flexible throat'), and Mme Silberklang for her, as well as Elvira's 'Mi tradì' in the Vienna prem. of Don Giovanni. She also sang the Countess in 1789. One of the best in an array of very gifted singers in contemporary Vienna. She retired in 1793.

Cavalieri, Lina (b Viterbo, 25 Dec. 1874; d Florence, 7 Feb. 1944). Italian soprano. Of humble origins, she made a name for herself as a café-singer throughout Europe. Studied Milan with Mariani-Masi; début Naples, C, 1900 (Mimì). After appearances throughout Italy, in Lisbon and at St Petersburg, she created L'Ensoleillad in Massenet's Chérubin,

Monte Carlo 1905. New York, M, 1906–8; Paris, O, 1907 and 1909; London, CG, from 1908. Particularly successful in seductive roles (Manon Lescaut, Massenet's Salome, Giulietta, Violetta, etc.) by reason of her exceptional beauty and grace; in the US she was known as 'the kissing prima-donna'. Much admired by the aristocracy and royalty, she boasted over £500,000 of jewels, including gifts from the Tsar and the Prince of Monaco. She had four husbands, including the French tenor Lucien *Muratore; while married to him she made several films. She died in an air-raid on Florence, having turned back from the shelter in order to collect her jewellery. A film of her life, La donna più bella del mondo, was made in 1957 with Gina Lollobrigida. (R)

Cavalleria rusticana (Rustic Chivalry). Opera in 1 act by Mascagni; text by G. Menasci and G. Targioni-Tozzetti, after G. Verga's drama (1884) based on his story (1880). Prem. Rome, C, 17 May 1890.

A Sicilian village, 1880. Santuzza (sop), seduced by Turiddu (ten), is distraught when she finds he has deserted her in favour of Lola (mez), wife of the drover, Alfio (bar), his former sweetheart. A final appeal to Turiddu by Santuzza to return to her is of no avail, and so she tells Alfio all that has happened. Alfio swears vengeance, challenges Turiddu to a duel, and kills him. The action takes place in a small Sicilian village on Easter morning; the famous Intermezzo is played between the two scenes of the opera, while the stage remains empty.

Winner of the contest for a 1-act opera organized by Sonzogno in 1889, and a founding work of *verismo.

Cavalli, Francesco (orig. Pier Francesco Caletti) (b Crema, 14 Feb. 1602; d Venice, 14 Jan. 1676). Italian composer. An accomplished church musician, his first opera, Le nozze di Teti e di Peleo appeared in 1639, just two years after the opening of the first public opera-house in Venice. Over the next ten years he wrote nine operas for the T San Cassiano: his most important librettist was Faustini, with whom he shared the management of the theatre. In Egisto (1643), Ormindo (1644), and Doriclea (1645), the new style of Venetian opera was consolidated, though it was a setting of a libretto by Cicognini, Giasone (1649), which became his most popular work. Following the closure

of the T San Cassiano in 1650, Faustini and
Cavalli transferred to the smaller T San Apollinare, where four more operas were
produced, including *Rosinda* (1651) and
Calisto (1651).

Following Faustini's death in 1651 Cavalli
was unwilling to continue his association
with the theatre: anyway, his fame had by
now spread outside Venice, leading to such
commissions as *Orione* (1653) and *Veremonda*
(1652). In 1653 he became associated with
the T Santi Giovanni e Paolo and here *Serse*
(1655), *Statira* (1656), and *Artemisia* (1657)
were produced; in 1658 he returned to the T
San Cassiano as musical director. The apotheosis of his international fame was marked by
the commissioning of *Ercole amante* in 1660
for the wedding of King Louis XIV of France,
though its unfavourable reception dealt a
severe blow to Cavalli's morale. For much of
his later life he concentrated on his ecclesiastical duties as maestro di cappella at St
Mark's, while his operas were gradually
eclipsed by the work of a younger generation.

Cavalli occupies a central position in the
development of opera. Together with Monteverdi he was among the first to respond
to the new challenge of the public opera-
houses, with their socially and intellectually
more diverse audiences. This was achieved,
above all, by the exploitation of comic
figures (usually servants), whose simple,
appealing songs contrasted with the lofty
arias of the serious main characters. A gifted
melodist possessed of a sure dramatic touch,
he devised a winning formula (from both
the musical and managerial perspective) by
which the role of the chorus and size of
the orchestra were reduced, while individual
singers were given greater prominence. In
their sensitive exploration of pathos and
comedy, Cavalli's operas revealed an understanding of the human condition which captivated audiences in his day and, in modern
revival, have proved equally effective.

Cavaradossi. A painter (ten), lover of Tosca,
in Puccini's *Tosca*.

Cavos, Catterino (*b* Venice, 30 Oct. 1775; *d*
St Petersburg, 10 May 1840). Italian composer. His father Alberto, an important
figure in Venetian operatic life, was in charge
of La Fenice and arranged the début there of
Angelica Catalani. Caterino studied in
Venice with Bianchi, and made his mark
early as a composer of dramatic music. He

travelled to Russia in the winter of 1798–9,
and in April was made director of the
Imperial Theatres. Here he played a dominant part in the development of Russian
operatic life in the first decades of the 19th
cent.: he was responsible for bringing to
Russia Kauer's popular *Das Donauweibchen* in
an adaptation by Stepan Davydov as *Lesta,
dneprovskaya rusalka* (1804), with additional
music of his own; he followed this with a
second *Lesta* opera adding to Kauer's some of
his own music; two more parts were composed by Davydov. These successes encouraged Cavos to abandon trivial French works
in favour of a more indigenous and
ambitious opera. He was responsible for the
Russian prems. of *Der Freischütz* (1824), *Fra
Diavolo* (1831), *Robert le diable* (1834), and other
works. His many pupils, some of whom
formed the first generation of properly
trained Russian singers, included Osip
Petrov, Josephine Fodor-Mainvielle, and
Anna Vorobyova. He was Kapellmeister of the
Italian company (1828–31) and of the
German and Russian companies (1832–40).

However, his real influence on Russian
music was as a composer. From the first he
took an interest in Russian subjects (having
done so even while still in Italy), and beginning with a fairy opera, *Knyaz nevidimka* (The
Invisible Prince, 1805), he wrote a number of
works which set a fashion for later Russian
opera in their use of folk and patriotic, and
especially legendary and magical, subjects,
and also in their reliance on the fantastic
and spectacular in staging. These included
the successful *Ilya bogatyr* (1807) and *Kazak
stichotvorets* (The Cossack Poet, 1812). But his
major work is *Ivan Susanin* (1815), a *rescue
opera with dialogue on the same subject as
Glinka's *A Life for the Tsar* (though ending
happily). This is typical of his skill in grafting
Russian folk music and folk subjects onto
the Italian stock as one of the first moves
towards the growth of a national Russian
opera, though he generously welcomed Glinka's opera as superior to his own. Cui praised
his operas for their concern to assimilate
Russian elements, even if they remained fundamentally Italian. His wife **Camilla Bag-
lioni** was a singer of comic parts. Of their
sons, **Giovanni** was a respected conductor
in St Petersburg; and **Alberto** (1801–63) was
an architect who worked on theatre design,
being responsible for rebuilding the
Moscow, B, after the fire of 1853 and also
rebuilding the St Petersburg, M, and Mikhay-

lovsky; he wrote a *Traité de la construction des théâtres*. Alberto's daughter Camilla married Nikolay Benois; their son was Alexandre Benois.

Cebotari, Maria (*b* Kishinyov, 23 Feb. 1910; *d* Vienna, 9 June 1949). Bessarabian soprano. Studied Berlin with Oskar Daniel. Début Dresden 1931 (Mimì). Berlin, SO, 1936–44; London, CG, 1936, 1947; also appeared at Vienna and Salzburg. Roles ranged from Zerlina and Sophie to Turandot and Tatyana. Made several films, including *Maria Malibran*. Created Aminta (*Die schweigsame Frau*), Julia (Sutermeister's *Romeo und Julia*), and Iseut (Martin's *Le vin herbé*). An attractive performer with a clear, fresh voice. (R)

Cecchina, La. See BUONA FIGLIUOLA, LA.

'Celeste Aida'. Radamès's (ten) aria praising Aida's beauty in Act I of Verdi's *Aida*.

Cellini, Benvenuto. See BENVENUTO CELLINI.

Cenerentola, La (Cinderella). Opera in 2 acts by Rossini; text by Jacopo Ferretti, after Étienne's text for Steibelt's opera. Prem. Rome, Valle, 25 Jan. 1817.

The plot follows the familiar fairy story by Perrault. Angelina (mez), known as Cinderella, is ill-treated by her stepfather Don Magnifico (bs) and her two stepsisters Clorinda (mez) and Tisbe (sop). Prince Ramiro (ten), in search of a wife, changes places with his valet Dandini (bar), and falls in love with Angelina. Alidoro (bs), the Prince's tutor (the equivalent of the fairy godmother in the children's versions), helps Angelina to attend the ball at the palace. In place of the glass slipper there is a silver bracelet, by means of which the prince discovers the identity of Angelina and makes her his bride.

Cerha, Friedrich (*b* Vienna, 17 Feb. 1926). Austrian composer and conductor. Studied Vienna with Uhl. His association with the Second Viennese School through his work with the Viennese chamber ensemble Die Reihe led to him being invited by Berg's publishers to make a completion of *Lulu* (Paris, O, 24 Feb. 1979): this further confirmed the work's stature. He has also written *Baal* (1981) and *Der Rattenfänger* (1987).

Cesti, Pietro (*b* Arezzo, *bapt*. 5 Aug. 1623; *d* Florence, 14 Oct. 1669). Italian composer: sometimes wrongly referred to as Marc' Antonio. A choirboy in his native city, he

joined the Minorite friars in 1637. Studied Rome with Abbatini and Carissimi; by 1645 he was maestro di cappella at the seminary in Volterra and in charge of music at the cathedral. But he was already thinking of a career outside the Church and the production in Venice of *Alessandro* (1651) and *Cesare amante* (1651) soon brought him to attention. In 1652 he became Kapellmeister to Archduke Ferdinand Karl of Austria and moved to Innsbruck. During his time here he produced a number of operas, including *Orontea* (1656) and *Dori* (1657); 1666–9 he was at the imperial court in Vienna, where he produced five operas, including his most famous work, *Il pomo d'oro* (1668).

Cesti's works occupy a unique position in the early history of opera. Some were written for the Venetian public opera-houses, and aimed at a mixed audience, while for Innsbruck and Vienna he was obliged to compose operas in the lavish court tradition. Cesti learnt much from Cavalli (to whom he also provided the first serious challenge), not least about the choice of libretto and dramatic recitative style. The Innsbruck court operas share many points of similarity with the Venetian operas, but are characterized by a concentration on visual and aural spectacle and less emphasis on the role of the solo singer. *Il pomo d'oro*, written to celebrate the wedding of Emperor Leopold I with the Infanta Margherita of Spain, is usually regarded as Cesti's masterpiece, though its grandiose conception is remarkable even for a court celebration. The opening introductory sinfonia, which includes music from later scenes, was probably the first programme overture.

Chabrier, (Alexis-) **Emmanuel** (*b* Ambert, 18 Jan. 1841; *d* Paris, 13 Sept. 1894). French composer. His parents insisted that he follow a legal career, but he continued composing and his interest in poetry led him to form friendships with, among others, Catulle Mendès and Villiers de l'Isle Adam, to whom he taught music, and Verlaine, who provided him with the librettos of two operettas. He was also a close friend of Manet, and his musical gifts as pianist and improviser won him the entry to Paris salons and friendships with Fauré, Chausson, Duparc, and D'Indy. Parts of a projected opera, *Jean Hunyade*, were later used in *Gwendoline* (1886) and *Briséis* (1899). His vivid comic flair found expression in *L'étoile* (1877) and *Une éducation manquée*

(1879), though their liveliness does not exclude tenderness and some harmonic adventurousness. Through Duparc, he came to admire Wagner, and the experience of hearing *Tristan und Isolde* in Munich led him to resign the government post he had occupied and dedicate himself to music in 1880. The first opera to follow was *Gwendoline*, set in medieval England and filled with vigorous battles and some attractive love music; it is Wagnerian in its use of Leitmotiv and in its harmonic emancipation. He also composed quadrilles on themes from *Tristan*, in witty but appreciative vein; he was at this time a leading member of the group of French Wagnerians known as 'Le Petit Bayreuth'. He then produced an opéra-comique, *Le roi malgré lui* (1887), the work in which his gifts for elegant melody and lively characterization are most fully displayed.

Chailly, Riccardo (*b* Milan, 20 Feb. 1953). Italian conductor. Studied Italy with Guarino, Caracciolo, and Ferrara. Assistant cond. Milan, S, 1972–4. Chicago 1974 (*Butterfly*). Milan, S, from 1978; London, CG, 1979; New York, M, 1982; Vienna, S, 1983; Salzburg from 1984; music dir. Bologna, C, 1986–9. Repertory incl. *Cenerentola*, *Ricciardo e Zoroaide*, *Trovatore*, *Walküre*, *Fiery Angel*. (R)

Chalabala, Zdeněk (*b* Uherské Hradiště, 18 Apr. 1899; *d* Prague, 4 Mar. 1962). Czech conductor. Studied Brno with Neumann, also attending Janáček's master-classes. Brno O 1925–36, 1949–52; Prague 1936–45, 1953–62; Ostrava 1945–7. With his strong leadership and expressive artistry, he did much to establish a tradition of Czech and Russian opera in Brno and Prague. (R) His wife **Běla Rozumová** (*b* Příbram, 8 Feb. 1903) was a coloratura soprano; début Ljubljana 1923 (Mařenka), Brno 1925–36, Prague 1936–42.

Chaliapin, Fyodor. See SHALYAPIN, FYODOR.

chamber opera. A small-scale opera, or one of predominantly intimate character, calling for fewer vocal and instrumental resources than normally required, and often telling a simpler story than is customary. While many works of the 17th and 18th cents., e.g. Purcell's *Dido and Aeneas*, are often described as chamber operas, strictly speaking the term has no validity before the late 19th cent., for the concept of chamber music itself was not recognized until then. Among important chamber operas of the 20th cent. are the

second version of Strauss's *Ariadne auf Naxos*, Hindemith's *Cardillac*, Virgil Thomson's *Four Saints in Three Acts*, Britten's *The Turn of the Screw*, and Walton's *The Bear*.

Champagne Aria. See 'FINCH'HAN DAL VINO'.

Champs-Élysées, Théâtre des. Paris theatre planned by Gabriel Astruc to open in the Champs-Élysées but transferred to the Avenue Montaigne while retaining the name; opened 2 Apr. 1913 with a concert, then Berlioz's *Benvenuto Cellini* on 3 Apr. Comprises three auditoriums, the Grand T (cap. 2,100) for opera, Comédie (cap. 750) for drama, Studio (added 1923, cap. 250) for experimental work. The scene of Dyagilev's 1913 season and other important guest seasons, especially Russian, in the 1920s and 1930s. After the war the theatre's tradition of sometimes belated French prems. of important works continued, including visits from distinguished foreign companies. The theatre remains privately run.

Chance, Michael (*b* Penn, 7 Mar. 1955). English counter-tenor. Studied King's College, Cambridge. Début Buxton Fest. 1983 (Apollo in Cavalli's *Giasone*). His clear diction and well-projected voice are particularly admired in Handel roles, such as Andronico (*Tamerlano*), Julius Caesar (Scottish O), Otho (*Agrippina*). Modern repertory includes the creation of the Military Governor in Weir's *A Night at the Chinese Opera* (1987) and Orpheus in Birtwistle's *The Second Mrs Kong* (1994). (R)

'Chanson de la puce, La' (Song of the Flea). Méphistophélès's (bs or bar) aria in the second part of Berlioz's *La damnation de Faust*.

Chappelou. The postilion (ten) in Adam's *Le postillon de Lonjumeau*.

Charlotte. Albert's wife (mez), loved by Werther, in Massenet's *Werther*.

Charlottenburg. See BERLIN.

Charpentier, Gustave (*b* Dieuze, 25 June 1860; *d* Paris, 18 Feb. 1956). French composer. Studied Paris with Massenet. His most famous work is the opera *Louise* (1900). Its success, partly for its startling realism and liberal social views, partly for its lyrical fluency, was as great as the rapid failure of its sequel *Julien*. Charpentier also founded, in 1902, a Cons. Populaire Mimi Pinson, where working girls such as his Louise could study music and dance.

Charpentier, Marc-Antoine (b Paris, 1643, d Paris, 24 Feb. 1704). French composer. Studied in Rome with Carissimi. Following Lully's rift with Molière he collaborated with the playwright on comédies-ballets, incl. *Le mariage forcé* (1672) and *Le malade imaginaire* (1673). This initiated a period with the Comédie-Française which continued for the next 12 years, resulting in about 26 dramatic works of various kinds.

Charpentier was inevitably overshadowed by Lully, though Molière clearly had a high regard for his abilities, and only his death prevented further collaborations. Many of the small-scale pastorales which Charpentier wrote for the Comédie-Française, such as *Les amours d'Acis et de Galatée* (1678), remained in the repertoire until the middle of the 18th cent. His divertissements were equally popular, while the larger-scale works such as *Les plaisirs de Versailles* (early 1680s) followed in the tradition of the aristocratic ballet de cour and proved equally popular. Despite a weak libretto, the tragédie lyrique *Médée* (1693) was highly regarded.

Charton-Demeur, Anne (b Saujon, 5 Mar. 1824; d Paris, 30 Nov. 1892). French soprano. Studied Bordeaux with Bizot. Début Bordeaux 1842 (Lucia). London, DL 1846 and HM 1852 (Amina). Paris, OC, 1849, 1853. Created Béatrice (*Béatrice et Bénédict*), Berlioz being so impressed with her 'rare beauty of style' that he asked her to be the first Dido in *Les Troyens à Carthage*. This she performed with 'grandeur and dramatic force', and he declared himself 'overwhelmed' by Dido's monologue. She became his close friend, and was with him when he died. In 1870 she sang Cassandre in the first (concert) performance of *La prise de Troie*. Married the flautist Jules-Antoine Demeur.

Châtelet, Théâtre du. Paris theatre (cap. 2,500) on the site of the old T du Cirque Impérial, opened 1862 for drama and concerts but also housing opera and ballet. In the 1930s an important centre for operetta. Modernized and renamed Théâtre Musical de Paris 1980, it gives a mixed repertory from visiting companies.

Chausson, Ernest (b Paris, 20 Jan. 1855; d Limay, 10 June 1899). French composer. First studied law, later music with Franck and Massenet. Not needing to earn his living, he worked slowly, carefully, and diffidently at composition. He gained from his experience of Wagner a greater confidence of idiom which shows in his operas, though like many Frenchmen he was influenced by only a small part of Wagner's ideas. His early dramatic essays are slight works, though contemporaries found evidence of style and taste among the technical uncertainties. He contemplated scenarios for operas on Pushkin, Schiller, Shakespeare (*Macbeth*), Cervantes, and others, but his major work, on which he expended much time and care, is *Le Roi Arthus* (prod. 1903). An admirer of Celtic literature as well as of Wagner, he wrote his own skilful text in prose and verse on King Arthur's renunciation of life in the wake of Guinevere's betrayal of his love with Lancelot. The work makes a discreet and individual use of motive, and is eloquently scored; but the influence of Wagner is intelligently and discreetly applied, and comparisons with *Tristan* are not really appropriate.

'Che farò senza Euridice'. Orfeo's (con cas) lament at the loss of his wife Euridice in Act III (Act IV in some versions) of Gluck's *Orfeo ed Euridice*.

'Che gelida manina'. Rodolfo's (ten) aria to Mimì in Act I of Puccini's *La bohème*, making his first approach to her.

Chelard, Hippolyte (b Paris, 1 Feb. 1789; d Weimar, 12 Feb. 1861). French composer and conductor. Studied Paris with Fétis and Gossec, perhaps Méhul and Cherubini, later in Italy with Baini, Zingarelli, and Paisiello. He produced his first opera, *La casa da vendere* in Naples; but his first important opera, *Macbeth* (1827), failed in Paris, despite its skilful use of Grand Opera conventions, before succeeding in Munich from 1828; and after a second failure in Paris with *La table et le logement* (1829) he settled in Germany. In Munich he again had a success with a rewriting of *La table* as *Der Student*. *Macbeth* and *Der Student* were both given during his 1832–3 season directing the German Opera (with Schröder-Devrient) at London, DL, with little success despite the contribution of Malibran. His most important work is *Die Hermannsschlacht* (1835), in which full account is taken of the conventions of German Romantic opera. He was Liszt's predecessor in Weimar, was a loyal friend and supporter in Germany of Berlioz, to whose music his own has some resemblances, and had some influence on the young Wagner.

'Ch'ella mi creda libero'. Dick Johnson's (ten) aria in Act III of Puccini's *La fanciulla del West*, in which he asks that Minnie should be told not that he has been lynched but that he has been freed.

Chelleri, Fortunato (*b* Parma, June 1686/90; *d* Kassel, Dec. 1757). Italian composer. During an extremely itinerant life, which included spells in Florence, Würzburg, Kassel, and Stockholm, he composed 19 operas, including the highly popular *L'innocenza giustificata* (1711). He was in London 1726–7 and as a close friend of Bordoni and Cuzzoni participated fully in the musical life of the city and in the activities of the Royal Academy of Music.

Chelsea Opera Group. A group formed in 1950 by Colin Davis, David Cairns, and Stephen Gray to give concert performances of Mozart's operas. Their successful *Don Giovanni* in Oxford was followed by other Mozart performances, and by their first London appearance with *Fidelio* at St Pancras (1953). Other performances in the 1950s and 1960s helped to arouse interest in then rarely heard works, including *Les Troyens*, *Benvenuto Cellini*, *Guillaume Tell*, *Euryanthe*, and *Khovanshchina*. Conductors who made appearances early in their careers include Nicholas Braithwaite, Roger Norrington, and John Eliot Gardiner, and singers who first sang favourite roles include Peter Glossop (Don Giovanni), Derek Hammond-Stroud (Beckmesser, Act III), and Elizabeth Robson (Nannetta).

'Che puro ciel'. Orfeo's (con cas) arioso as he gazes on the beauties of the Elysian Fields in Act II of Gluck's *Orfeo ed Euridice*.

Chéreau, Patrice (*b* Lézigné, 2 Nov. 1944). French producer. Bayreuth 1976 (*Ring*); Paris, O, 1979 (*Hoffmann*, prem. of *Lulu* in its completed 3-act version). His production of *The Ring* (cond. Boulez) caused a scandal, its setting in 19th-cent. capitalist society, its emphasis on the brutal, and its reductiveness creating shock and sharp controversy at the time; nevertheless, critical opinion found much to respect in it, and its subsequent television broadcast reached a huge and appreciative audience. More recent but less controversial productions have included *Lucio Silla* (Milan, S, 1984), *Wozzeck* (Paris, C, 1992), and *Don Giovanni* (Salzburg 1994).

Cherevichki. See VAKULA THE SMITH.

Chernov, Vladimir (*b* Moscow, 22 Sept. 1953). Russian baritone. Studied Moscow and sang with the Kirov O from 1983 (Valentine, Figaro, Germont). First major role in West was Marcello at Boston 1988. London, CG, 1990 (Rossini's Figaro). He has won much acclaim for his portrayal of Verdi roles: Stankar (*Stiffelio*) and Boccanegra at New York, M (1994–5), Posa, and Don Carlo in *La forza del destino*. Further appearances at Los Angeles, Seattle, Vienna, and Verona. (R)

Cherubini, Luigi (*b* Florence, 8 or 14 Sept. 1760: *d* Paris, 15 Mar. 1842). Italian composer. Studied in Florence, at first with his father, later in Bologna and Milan with Sarti. He produced some church music and then his first operas, including *Quinto Fabio*. He visited London in 1784, then Paris. He had written 13 Italian operas by the time he established himself permanently in Paris in 1788; but with *Démophon* (1788) he broke away from this earlier vein and began developing the mature style that makes him a pioneer of French opéra-comique and Grand Opera, and a father figure of Romantic opera. This manner was first fully revealed in *Lodoïska* (1791), in which there is a new, richer handling of the orchestra, a more powerful and functional use of ensemble, a stronger sense of dramatic (and moral) motivation, and the emergence of character types that were to impress subsequent composers: the villain Dourlinski, for instance, is an operatic ancestor of both Beethoven's Pizarro and Weber's Caspar.

Meanwhile, Cherubini had directed an Italian opera in Paris; and in 1795 he joined the newly founded Conservatoire as an inspector of studies. Other early traits of Romantic opera begin to emerge in the works that followed in these years, e.g. *Éliza* (1794), in which the Alpine setting plays an important part in the action. A particular contribution was the use of natural forces to play a crucial role in the drama (a fire in *Lodoïska*, an avalanche in *Éliza*), as well as his more fully developed use of arias for secondary characters. An equally important ingredient for Romantic opera was the influence of Rousseau, not only in the handling of peasants or other simple people as embodying qualities of the highest virtue. In *Éliza*, the use of obbligatos, especially for horn and clarinet, was another characteristic that made its mark upon the Romantics.

Médée (1797) is an elevated tragedy, noble and somewhat cold; it is, none the less, an opera charged with forceful statements of passion, remote from human reality though the characters, even Médée herself, may seem to be. The work is in strong contrast to *Les deux journées* (1800), an opéra-comique making use of simple characters and consequently smaller forms such as *ariette and couplet. Bouilly's text was regarded as exemplary by Beethoven, and as a *rescue opera the work influenced him (including its use of melodrama): like the later *Faniska* (1806), another rescue opera, the work includes simple, ballad-like interpolations in a dark, dramatic plot, and makes rich use of the orchestra to carry the story and the emotions of the characters. Cherubini's methods here include a looser handling of set numbers, and even a suggestion of *Leitmotiv. Above all, it was his success in embodying in a novel operatic manner the idealization of simple life, in which servants or peasants are no longer comic figures or ingénus but human beings proposing righteous moral sentiments, that won him the admiration of both Beethoven and Goethe.

Though he wrote a number of further operas (including the interesting and underrated *Pimmalione* (1809), which uses Rousseau's text in an Italian version), and the better known *Les Abencérages* (1813), Cherubini turned away from opera in his later years in favour of sacred music. He was greatly admired in Paris, but his career there was not smooth. After a quarrel with Napoleon, he went to Vienna with *Faniska*, returning when the French occupied the city. He was director of the Cons. from 1821 to 1841. Though often derided—including, unkindly, by Berlioz—for his pedantry and for a distinct and self-confessed severity in his music, he was a master of technique, and at its finest his music possesses a brilliance, purity, and originality that make him one of the most important founders of Romantic opera and Grand Opera.

Cherubino. Countess Almaviva's page (sop, sometimes mez) in Mozart's *Le nozze di Figaro*.

chest voice. The lowest of the three main registers of the voice, the others being the 'middle' and the 'head'. So called because the tone of the lower notes in the singer's range, when using this voice, almost seems to go from the larynx into the chest. This method of production gives the richest notes, and is essential for strength and carrying power in the lower register. García considered that the chest voice predominated in men, and it is favoured especially by the Italians. See also REGISTER.

Cheval de bronze, Le (The Bronze Horse). Opera in 3 acts by Auber; text by Scribe. Prem. Paris, OC, 23 Mar. 1835.

A Chinese village and the planet Venus. Yanko (ten), Tao-chin (con), and Prince Yangyang (bar) are all turned into wooden pagodas after disclosing the secret of the planet Venus, where they have ridden on a magical bronze horse. Tao-chin's daughter, Peki (sop), breaks the spell, and is permitted to marry her beloved Yanko, while Yang-yang marries the beautiful Stella (sop), whom he met on Venus.

Chiara, Maria (*b* Oderza, 24 Dec. 1939). Italian soprano. Studied Venice with Cassinelli, Turin with Carbone. Début Venice 1965 (Verdi's Desdemona). Verona Arena from 1969; Munich and Vienna from 1970; Berlin, SO, 1971; Milan, S, 1972; Naples, C, 1974; New York, M, 1978–9; also London, CG; Paris; Rome; etc. Roles incl. Violetta, Aida, Odabella, Micaëla, Tosca, Butterfly. (R)

Chicago. City in Illinois, USA. The first opera given was a single performance of *Sonnambula* on 29 July 1850 in J. B. Rice's Chicago T. The theatre burnt down that year but was rebuilt (cap. 1,400). Arditi's company performed, with Rosa Devriès, 1852. In 1857 James McVicker built a new theatre (cap. 2,000), where Durant's English O Troupe gave *Trovatore* and *Daughter of the Regiment*. Uranus Crosby's OH was opened 1865 with *Trovatore* (to an audience including Generals Sherman and Grant), but burnt down 1871. Opera had no permanent home until 1889, when the Chicago Auditorium (cap. 4,250) opened with *Roméo et Juliette* (with Patti) and short seasons were given by companies including the Abbey, Grau, Damrosch, Savage, Mascagni, and Conried organizations. In 1910 the Chicago Grand Opera Co. was formed from elements of the Hammerstein Co., with *Campanini as music director. Mary Garden, who sang Mélisande on the second evening (4 Nov. 1910), became the dominating figure of opera in the city, singing here 1910–31 and acting as director 1921–2; her sole season led to the prem. of *The Love of the Three Oranges* and a deficit of over $1 m. The Chicago Civic OC's finances were guaranteed by Samuel Insull 1922–30, who before succumbing to the Depression also created the Civic OH (cap. 3,563) on the ground floor of a skyscraper. This opened 4 Nov. 1929 with *Aida*. Important Wagner seasons were given, and artists including Lotte Lehmann, Leider, Olczewska, Eva Turner, and Kipnis made their US débuts here, but the company was forced to close 1932. Other attempts to establish opera were by Paul Longone (1933–9), Fortune Gallo (1941–2), and Fausto Cleva (1944–6). Martinelli (who for a time assisted Gallo) sang his first Otello (1936) and only Tristan (1939) here.

The Lyric T of Chicago was formed 1952 by Carol Fox, Nicola Rescigno, and Lawrence Kelly, and a season included Callas's US début (*Norma*); this re-formed under Fox as the Lyric O of Chicago 1956, and guests have included Tebaldi, Nilsson, Di Stefano, Simionato, Del Monaco, Domingo, Pavarotti, Christoff, and especially Gobbi (début as producer, *Boccanegra*, 1956). The emphasis is now towards Italian opera. The Center for American Artists was founded 1973. Penderecki's *Paradise Lost* (1978) was commissioned for the 1976 US bicentennial and William Bolcom's *McTeague* was premiered 1992. Fox was succeeded by Ardis Krainik 1981. The artistic director from 1975 was Bruno Bartoletti (début there 1956).

'Chi mi frena'. The sextet in Act II of Donizetti's *Lucia di Lammermoor*, in which Edgardo (ten) finds his anger checked by the sight of Lucia's distressed condition, Enrico (bar) is torn between hatred for Edgardo and pity for Lucia (sop), who deplores her misery, while Raimondo (bs), Arturo (ten), and Alisa (mez) express their horror and pity.

chorus (Fr., *chœur*; Ger., *Chor*; It., *coro*). From the Greek *khoros*, a festive dance or those who performed it. The Attic drama first consisted of tales told by a single actor in the intervals of the dance; later the function of the chorus was to join in and comment upon the drama from the place before and below the stage known as the *orkhèstra* (orchestra). This function passed into opera.

Throughout the history of opera, the treatment of the chorus has been as much dependent on economic as on artistic factors. Hence, in the Venetian public opera of the later 17th cent. it was largely relegated on the grounds of cost, while for French tragédie lyrique of the same period it played a crucial role in demonstrating the omnipotence of the monarch. Not until Gluck did the chorus become a vital part of the drama; his example was followed in early-19th-cent. rescue opera and even more so in French Grand Opera, where it made a distinctive contribution to the visual and aural splendour. Particularly fine examples of massed choral handling can be found in Berlioz's *Les Troyens* (1858) and Meyerbeer's *Les Huguenots* (1836).

As the artificial separation of musical numbers was gradually supplanted by the writing of longer dramatic sequences, so the chorus gradually took part in the arias themselves: a famous instance occurs in Bellini's *Norma* (1831), during the heroine's 'Casta diva'. However, the use of the chorus to further the plot is relatively uncommon: more frequently it acts as a static point of repose, commenting on the action, summing it up, joining in to provide a bustle of activity parallel to it, and generally abetting the principals. A milestone in the history of the operatic chorus was provided by Verdi's *Nabucco* (1842), where the opposing factions of Babylon and Israel are represented by two choruses which participate so fully in the action that they rival the soloists in importance. A similar trait can be detected in the operas of Spohr, Marschner, and others, but particularly in Wagner. *Rienzi* (1842), *Tannhäuser* (1845), and *Lohengrin* (1850) all feature grand choral scenes, although in his slightly later theoretical writings, out of which grew the concept of *music drama, Wagner argued against the inclusion of the chorus. Hence it does not appear in *The Ring* until the Gibichungs' entry in *Götterdämmerung*: by this time Wagner had already revised his early views, and made the citizens of Nuremberg intrinsic to the plot of *Die Meistersinger*.

In the 20th cent. the handling of the chorus has been as diverse as the treatment of most other aspects of opera. Britten, for example, while using the chorus as the main dramatic force pitted against the hero in *Peter Grimes*, draws on Greek example to place his Male and Female Chorus in *The Rape of Lucretia* outside the action. A still more definite reversion to Greek method occurs in Stravinsky's *Oedipus Rex*.

An opera chorus is normally divided into the conventional soprano, contralto, tenor, and bass with the numbers varying according to requirements. It is maintained on the permanent staff of an opera-house under the direction of a chorus-master.

Chorus of Hebrew Slaves. See 'VA PENSIERO'.

Christie, John (b Eggesford, 14 Dec. 1882; d Glyndebourne, 4 July 1962). English operatic patron. Educated Eton, where he also taught, and Cambridge. Married the soprano Audrey *Mildmay in 1931, and in 1934 founded the *Glyndebourne Opera at his house in Sussex. A man of strong enthusiasms (originally for German music), his gift for allowing these to overrule common sense, and his innocent determination to secure the best, led to the realization of an idea that with lesser men would have remained merely an idea. His son (Sir) **George** (b Glyndebourne, 31 Dec. 1934) has acted as producer's assistant 1953, chairman from 1958. Operatic début and farewell as Fleance in *Macbeth*, 1947.

Christie, William (b Buffalo, NY, 19 Dec. 1944). US harpsichordist and conductor. Studied Tanglewood, Harvard, and Yale. First US prof. at Paris Cons. Founder and dir. of Les Arts Florissants (Paris 1978), which devotes its activities to the revival of Baroque music (especially French) in an authentic idiom. Edinburgh 1986; Paris, OC, 1987, London (Greenwich) 1987, CG 1995; also Florence, Montpellier, Aix. Staged repertory incl. Purcell's *Dido and Aeneas* and *King Arthur*, Lully's *Atys*, Charpentier's *Actéon* and *Médée*, Rameau's *Les Indes galantes*. The considerable accomplishments of the group, several of whose members are well known in their own right, derive from Christie's impeccable style and lively, clear direction. (R)

Christoff, Boris (b Plovdiv, 18 May 1914; d Rome, 28 June 1993). Bulgarian bass. Studied Rome with Stracciari, funded by King Boris, and Salzburg with Muratti. Début Reggio Calabria, 1946 (Colline). Milan, S, from 1947; London, CG, from 1949; S Francisco from 1956; Chicago 1957–63; also Paris, Salzburg, Edinburgh. Repertory included Rocco, King Mark, Gurnemanz, Hagen, Ivan Susanin, Dosifey, and the Verdi bass roles. A warm-voiced basso cantante with a rich variety of tonal colours, and masterly control and phrasing. Both dramatically incisive and sensitive, he was one of the great interpreters of Boris and King Philip. (R)

Christophe Colomb. Opera in 2 parts (27 scenes) by Milhaud; text by Claudel. Prem. Berlin, S, 5 May 1930.

Spain, late 15th cent. The opera recalls the events of Columbus's (bar) life in a series of scenes unrelated by time and space. Part 1 deals with the discovery of America; part 2 is concerned with Columbus's return to Spain, where he has a hostile reception. Finally, the old man is summoned by the dying Queen Isabella (sop). He sends her his mule, and she rides to Heaven on it, traversing a carpet which depicts America.

Milhaud links the scenes by use of a narrator, a chorus, and cinematographic projection.

Chrysothemis. The daughter of Klytemnästra (sop), sister of Elektra, in Strauss's *Elektra*.

Chukhadjyan, Tigran (b Constantinople, 1837; d Smyrna, 25 Feb. 1898). Armenian composer. Studied Constantinople with Mangioni, and in Milan (where he was much impressed by Verdi). On returning home he worked in various theatres, then wrote the first Armenian national opera, *Arshak II*. Only excerpts were performed in his lifetime; the complete prem. (after rediscovery and revision of the score) took place in 1945. In his operas, Chukhadjyan was the first Armenian composer to reconcile Western operatic techniques with the characteristics of his native folk melody; the ardent nationalism of his work played a part in encouraging Armenians in their liberation movement against Turkey. His comedies (such as *Arif* (1872), *Kyose kyokhva* (The Balding Elder, 1874), and *Leblebidji* (1876)) show a feeling for Armenian life and manners.

Chung, Myung-Whun (b Seoul, 22 Jan. 1953). Korean conductor and pianist. Studied conducting New York with Bamburger, and at Juilliard School. Operatic début New York, M, 1986 (*Boccanegra*). New York, M, 1990–1; Florence, C, 1987–9; Florence, Maggio Musicale, 1989. Also Monte Carlo; Geneva; Bologna; S Francisco; Paris, O. First music dir., Paris, B, 1989: he left in acrimonious circumstances in 1994. Repertory incl. *Idomeneo*, *Les Troyens*, *Boris Godunov*, *Queen of Spades*, *Fiery Angel*, Verdi's *Otello*, *Samson et Dalila*. A highly accomplished and refined musician, with an intensely lyrical style. (R)

church parable. A term coined by Britten for his *Curlew River* (1964), *The *Burning Fiery

Furnace (1966), and *The *Prodigal Son* (1968), works which derive from the example of the Noh Plays of Japan and in which a small group of singers and players present the dramatic fiction of monks staging an opera on a moral subject to a church congregation.

Ciccimarra, Giuseppe (*b* Altamura, 22 May 1790; *d* Venice, 5 Dec. 1836). Italian tenor. Naples, C, 1816–26, creating many roles in Rossini operas, including Iago, Goffredo (*Armida*), Aronne (*Mosè*), Ernesto (*Ricciardo e Zoraide*), Pilade (*Ermione*). Taught after retirement; his pupils included Joseph *Tichatschek.

Cicéri, Pierre-Luc-Charles (*b* Saint-Cloud, 17 Aug. 1782; *d* Saint-Chéron, 22 Aug. 1868). French painter and designer. Studied singing, later turning to painting and becoming an assistant at the Paris, O, 1810; *Peintre du roi* 1825. His designs include those for *Olympie* (1819), *La muette de Portici* (1828), *Guillaume Tell* (1829), and *Robert le diable* (1833). The greatest French designer of his day, with a strong historical and architectural sense, he opened up a new expressive range by his use of three-dimensional scenery and panoramic effects. His association with Louis *Daguerre was epoch-making, and set new standards of accuracy in historical detail and in grandeur of pictorial effect, matching and encouraging the grandiose ambitions of French *Grand Opera. For *La muette*, in a typical piece of work, he designed a view of Vesuvius seen through a splendid palace, with woods and houses in the middle distance; and he ended with an eruption that included fireworks. For *Robert* he imitated the cloister of Montfort l'Amaury, building three sides as his setting for the nocturnal scene of the ghostly nuns. In this, though his style had a Romantic fluency, he showed the influence of his Baroque forebears, and he also made skilful artistic use of the latest stage machinery and equipment (e.g. gaslight in Isouard's *Aladin, ou La lampe merveilleuse*, 1822). His designs extended the expressive possibilities of the panorama (blending into the scenery), as in Isouard's *Alfred le grand*, 1822. He also pioneered the mobile panorama, revolving drums turning a backcloth so as to produce an illusion of the characters on a journey along a river in the ballet *La belle au bois dormant* (1825), and from sky to earth in Auber's *Le lac des fées* (1839) (Wagner was to make use of both

ideas). Cicéri's four pupils Despléchins, Diéterle, Séchan, and Feuchères further developed his work in the years 1833–48, satisfying the French appetite for outdoor scenes, transformations, and thrilling special effects.

Cid, Le. Opera in 4 acts by Massenet; text by D'Ennery, Gallet, and Blau, after Corneille's drama (1637). Prem. Paris, O, 30 Nov. 1885.

Spain, 11th cent. Don Rodrigue (ten) kills Don Gormas (bs), father of his betrothed Chimène (sop), to avenge a wrong done to his own father. Before he can be punished, Rodrigue leaves to fight the Moors. On his return, he is acclaimed by all as the 'Cid', the master warrior. Chimène has the right to determine his sentence, but chooses to forgive him. Racked with guilt, Rodrigue attempts suicide but Chimène prevents him, and the couple are then united.

'Cielo e mar!' Enzo's (ten) aria, in which he declares his love for Laura by apostrophizing the sky and sea, in Act II of Ponchielli's *La Gioconda*.

Ciesinski, Katherine (*b* Newark, DE, 13 Oct. 1950). US mezzo-soprano, sister of below. Sang in Europe after study at the Curtis Institute. US début S Fe 1979 (Geschwitz in the completed version of *Lulu*). New York, M, 1988 (Nicklausse). Sang in the prems. of *The Aspern Papers* (Dallas 1988) and Ohana's *La Celestine* (Paris 1988). She is especially convincing in such dramatic repertory as Marina, Laura, Judith, and Cassandre (Scottish O). (R)

Ciesinski, Kristine (*b* Newark, DE, 5 July 1952). US soprano, sister of above. After study in Boston sang at the Salzburg Landestheater 1979–81, Bremen O, 1985–8. Sang Donna Anna with Scottish O (1985), Cassandre in *La prise de Troie* for O North and WNO (1986–7). Anna Maurant in *Street Scene* with ENO (1989) and achieved major success as Lady Macbeth on tour to USSR (1990). Other roles include Salome, Aida, Senta, and Tosca. (R)

Cigna, Gina (*b* Paris, 6 Mar. 1900). French-Italian soprano. Studied Paris with Calvé, Darclée, and Storchio. Début (as Genoveffa Sens) Milan, S, 1927 (Freia). Reverted to her own name, and sang there 1929–43. London, CG, 1933, 1936, 1937, 1939; New York, M, 1936–8; S Francisco and Chicago. A dramatic performer with a large repertory, particularly famous as Gioconda and Turandot. (R)

Cikker, Ján (*b* Banská Bystrica, 29 July 1911; *d* Bratislava, 21 Dec. 1989). Slovak composer. Studied Prague with Křička and Novák, conducting with Dědeček and in Vienna with Weingartner. Taught and worked in the opera in Bratislava from 1939. His vivid post-Romantic idiom, which owes something to Bartók and Janáček, has found its fullest expression in his operas, including *Hra o láske a smrti* (The Play of Love and Death, 1969) and *Coriolanus* (1974) which have won success in his own country and in Germany.

Cilea, Francesco (*b* Palmi, 26 July 1866; *d* Varazze, 20 Nov. 1950). Italian composer. Studied Naples with Serrao, producing his first opera, *Gina* (1889), with success soon after leaving the conservatory. A commission from Sonzogno led to a verismo work, *La Tilda* (1892), but its lesser success turned Cilea towards teaching, first in Naples and then in Florence. *L'arlesiana* (1897) fared a little better, in part due to the appearance of the young Caruso (whose career it also helped: the 'Lamento' was once a favourite tenor war-horse). His most enduring success was *Adriana Lecouvreur* (1902), more because of the work's skilful appeal to singers than for its melodic or dramatic strengths, though at its best his music has charm and style.

Cillario, Carlo Felice (*b* S Rafael, 7 Feb. 1915). Italian conductor. Studied Bologna and Odessa. Gly. and Chicago 1961; New York, M, 1972, 1985; Drottningholm 1982–4; S Francisco 1986; Sydney 1988 (principal guest cond.); also London, CG; Vienna; Milan, S; Buenos Aires; Paris; Berlin; Hamburg; Florence; etc. Repertory incl. *Magic Flute*, *Barber*, *Lucia*, *Aida*, *Otello*, *Falstaff*, *Werther*, *Walküre*, *Rheingold*. (R)

Cimarosa, Domenico (*b* Aversa, Naples, 17 Dec. 1749; *d* Venice, 11 Jan. 1801). Italian composer. Came to attention with *Le stravaganze del conte* (1772) and for the next 15 years divided his time between Naples and Rome, producing a string of popular successes, including *L'italiana in Londra* (1779) and *Il convito* (1782), mounting a worthy challenge to the supremacy of Paisiello and Piccinni. Moving to St Petersburg in 1787, he wrote *La vergine del sole* (1788) and *Cleopatra* (1789), and in 1791 was called to Vienna to succeed Salieri as Kapellmeister. Here in 1792 he produced *Il matrimonio segreto* which, according to legend, earned the cast a free Imperial

supper before an immediate repeat performance. During his later years, Cimarosa was attracted to opera seria too, but his enduring fame rests on his comic works, above all *Il matrimonio segreto*. Here, engaging melodies, a deep understanding of the conventions of the genre, and a sympathetic manipulation of the characters mark him as a composer of rare dramatic sensitivity.

Cinti-Damoreau, Laure (*b* Paris, 6 Feb. 1801; *d* Chantilly, 25 Feb. 1863). French soprano. Studied Paris with Plantade and Catalani. Début Paris, I, 1816 (Lilla, *Una cosa rara*). Paris, O, 1825–35; here she created leading roles in Rossini's *Le siège de Corinth*, *Moïse*, *Le Comte Ory*, and *Guillaume Tell*; also Isabelle (*Robert le diable*), and Elvira (*La muette de Portici*). At the Paris, OC, 1837–41, created roles in more of Auber's works, e.g. *Le domino noir*. London, H, 1822 and 1832. Toured US 1844. Taught singing at Paris Cons. 1833–56, and wrote a *Méthode de chant* (Paris, 1849). She had an exceptionally pure, clear, and accurate voice, and excelled in neat ornamentation. Stendhal called her 'that charming little singer'; Fétis acclaimed her 'beau talent'.

Cio-Cio-San. The Japanese name of Butterfly (sop) in Puccini's *Madama Butterfly*.

Cioni, Renato (*b* Portoferraio, 15 Apr. 1929). Italian tenor. Studied Florence. Début Spoleto 1956 (Edgardo). Milan, S, from 1957; London, CG, from 1964; S Francisco and Chicago from 1961: Berlin, D, 1965; New York, M, 1969–70; also Verona, Vienna, Munich, Buenos Aires, etc. Repertory incl. Bellini, Donizetti, Verdi (Duke of Mantua, Gabriele Adorno), Puccini (Pinkerton, Cavaradossi). Partnered Callas and Sutherland. (R)

Ciro in Babilonia (Cyrus in Babylon). Opera in 2 acts by Rossini; text by Francesco Aventi. Prem. Ferrara 14 Mar. 1812.

Amaria (sop), wife of Ciro, King of Persia (sop), is the object of the attentions of Baldassare, King of Babylon (ten). Ciro attempts to rescue Amaria and their son, who are held by Baldassare, but is captured himself. A storm seems to be a divine signal that Baldassare should sacrifice his three Persian captives. On the verge of their execution, the Persian army defeats Babylon, and Ciro is declared the new king.

City Center of Music and Drama. Home of the *New York City Opera 1944–65, when it moved with the New York City Ballet to the State T, Lincoln Center.

Claggart. John Claggart (bs), the master-at-arms in Britten's *Billy Budd*.

Clapisson, Louis (*b* Naples, 15 Sept. 1808; *d* Paris, 19 Mar. 1866). French composer. Son of a horn-player at the Naples, C; studied Bordeaux and in Paris with Rejcha, also playing the violin in opera orchestras. He had an early success with a comic opera, *La figurante* (1838), which he followed up with a long succession of works that caught the fancy of the Paris public. He defeated Berlioz in the election to a chair at the Institut by a large majority (to the indignation of Offenbach and to Berlioz's enduring hostility); and the appeal of his *Gibby-la-Cornemuse* (1846) was partly responsible for drawing audiences away from the prem. of *La damnation de Faust*. His large collection of instruments was the foundation of the Conservatoire museum.

Clark, Graham (*b* Littleborough, 10 Nov. 1941). English tenor. Studied London with Boyce. Début Scottish O 1975 (Verdi's Roderigo). London, ENO from 1978; Bayreuth 1981. Vienna, S; Munich, S; New York, M, 1985; Paris, B, 1991; also Barcelona, Zurich. Roles incl. David, Loge, Mime, Don Juan (*Stone Guest*), Gregor (*Makropoulos Case*), Mephistopheles (*Doktor Faust*), Captain Vere. Created Bégearss in *The Ghosts of Versailles* (New York, M, 1991). A performer of intelligence and vitality, with a bright tone. (R)

Clayton, Thomas (*bapt.* 28 Oct. 1673; *buried* 23 Sept. 1725). English composer and violinist. His *Arsinoe, Queen of Cyprus*, performed at Drury Lane in 1705, was described as 'an Opera after the Italian Manner: All Sung'; the libretto was a translation of an Italian text. It is the earliest full-length all-sung English opera extant, and the first wholly in the Italian style.

Clément, Edmond (*b* Paris, 28 Mar. 1867; *d* Nice, 24 Feb. 1928). French tenor. Studied Paris with Warot. Début Paris, OC, 1889 (*Mireille*). Remained there until 1910, creating many roles in contemporary works, including Bruneau's *L'attaque du moulin*. New York, M, 1909–11. A stylish and elegant singer. (R)

Clemenza di Tito, La (The Clemency of Titus). Opera in 2 acts by Mozart; text by Mazzolà, after Metastasio's text for Caldara (1734). Prem. Prague 6 Sept. 1791.

Rome, AD 80. Vitellia (sop) persuades Sesto (sop cas) to kill the Emperor Tito (ten) because he did not choose her as his empress. When the Emperor's wedding is postponed, Vitellia orders the assassination to be delayed. Annio (sop cas), a friend of Sesto's, wishes to marry Servilia (sop), Sesto's sister, but Tito announces that he plans to marry Servilia himself immediately. Servilia confesses to Tito that she loves Annio and he generously agrees not to come between them. Vitellia, believing she has been passed over again, has by now renewed her assassination order. When she learns of the change of Tito's plans she tries in vain to recall Sesto.

Sesto learns that Tito has not died and confesses his crime to Annio. But it emerges that Lentulus, whom Sesto stabbed by mistake, recognized his attacker and Sesto is taken before the Senate, where he is found guilty. Tito wants to save his friend but Sesto cannot explain his action without incriminating Vitellia. Filled with guilt, she throws herself at Tito's feet and confesses her part in the crime. Tito pardons everyone and the people rejoice in the clemency of their emperor.

Mozart's last opera, and the first to be performed in its entirety in London.

Cleonice. See DEMETRIO.

Cloches de Corneville, Les (The Bells of Corneville). Opera in 3 acts by Planquette; text by Clariville and Gabet. Prem. Paris, Folies-Dramatiques, 19 Apr. 1877.

Normandy, in the time of Louis XIV. The castle of Corneville stands empty following the banishment of the Duke. His descendant Henri (bar) wishes to prove his claim by fulfilling a local legend that the bells of the castle will ring spontaneously when the rightful heir approaches. However, a letter found in the castle, and wrongly interpreted, results in the house falling into the hands of a servant girl, Serpolette (sop). It emerges that the intended recipient is Germaine (sop), niece of a wealthy tenant Gaspard (bs). She loves Henri, who once saved her life, and the couple are happily united.

Planquette's most popular opera; at the end of a run of 461 performances the manager served the last audience with 2,000 rolls and free beer.

Cluytens, André (*b* Antwerp, 26 Mar. 1905; *d* Paris, 3 June 1967). French conductor of Belgian birth. Studied Antwerp. Antwerp O 1927–32; Toulouse 1932, also conducting much elsewhere in France. Paris, O and OC, 1947–66 (music dir. Paris, OC, 1947). First French cond. at Bayreuth, 1955–8, 1965. (R)

Clytemnestra. See KLYTEMNÄSTRA.

Coates, Albert (*b* St Petersburg, 23 Apr. 1882; *d* Cape Town, 11 Dec. 1953). English conductor and composer. Studied science in Liverpool, then in commerce in St Petersburg. Studied Leipzig with Nikisch. Début Leipzig (*Hoffmann*). Assistant to Nikisch 1904; cond. Elberfeld 1906–8; Dresden 1908–10; Mannheim 1910. St Petersburg, M, 1910, then chief cond. 1911–19, incl. *Boris* (prod. Meyerhold, 1911) and Taneyev *Oresteia* (1915), returning intermittently until 1934. London: CG, 1914 (*Tristan* and *Ring*), 1919–24; BNOC (*Ring*, with Shalyapin) 1929, 1935–8. His operas are *Samuel Pepys* (Munich 1929); *Pickwick* (CG 1936, in season by British Music Drama OC, organized by Coates with Vladimir Rosing): scenes from the latter were the first televised opera, Nov. 1936; and *Van Hunks and the Devil* (Cape Town 1952). (R)

Coates, Edith (*b* Lincoln, 31 May 1908; *d* Worthing, 7 Jan. 1983). English mezzo-soprano. Studied with Clive Carey and Dino Borgioli. Début London, Old Vic, 1924 (Giovanna, *Rigoletto*). London: SW 1931–46; CG 1937–9, 1947–63. Created Auntie (*Peter Grimes*), Mme Bardeau (*The Olympians*), Grandma (Grace Williams's *The Parlour*). Particularly striking as the Countess (*Queen of Spades*). (R)

Coates, John (*b* Girlington, 29 June 1865; *d* Northwood, 16 Aug. 1941). English tenor. Originally a baritone; sang with D'Oyly Carte Co. 1894. After further study emerged as tenor, and sang in light opera 1899–1900. London, CG, 1901 (Gounod's Faust). First Claudio in Stanford's *Much Ado about Nothing*. Toured Germany 1902–7, and US 1926–7. Sang with Moody-Manners and Beecham Cos. 1907–11. An intense, intelligent singer; one of the best British Tristans and Siegfrieds. (R)

Coccia, Carlo (*b* Naples, 14 Apr. 1782; *d* Novara, 13 Apr. 1873). Italian composer. His first opera, *Il matrimonio per lettera di cambio* (1807), was a failure, but with his teacher Paisiello's continued support he soon wrote the successful *Il poeta fortunato* (1808). In Venice, 1809–17, he developed his characteristic genre *opera semiseria, of which the most successful example was *Clotilde* (1815). The emergence of Rossini (whom he greatly admired) forced him to seek a new arena abroad, in Lisbon (1820–3) and London (1824–7). He conducted at the London, H, and in 1827 broke a six-year silence with *Maria Stuart* (with Pasta in the title-role). In the same year he returned to Italy, where he had new success especially with *Caterina di Guisa* (1833). A period of further study, especially of German music, during his silence led to a change in style, but the new seriousness in his work did not help him to retain popularity as fashion turned in new directions. He was director of the Turin Cons., 1836–40. He gave up opera in 1841. Verdi invited him to write the Lacrymosa and an Amen in the abortive Requiem for Rossini.

Cochran, William (*b* Columbus, OH, 23 June 1943). US tenor. Studied at the Curtis Institute: début S Francisco 1969 (Froh, *Rheingold*). Has sung at Frankfurt and elsewhere in Germany from 1970, in Heldentenor repertory and in operas by Busoni, Schreker, and Shostakovich. London, CG, 1974 (Laca in *Jenůfa*); New York, M, 1984 (Bacchus). A secure technique and clear diction have enabled him to become a convincing Siegfried (Frankfurt 1995). (R)

Cocteau, Jean (*b* Maisons-Laffitte, 5 July 1889; *d* Paris, 11 Oct. 1963). French writer and librettist. Collaborated with Honegger in *Antigone* and Stravinsky in *Oedipus Rex*, for which he also sometimes took the part of the narrator. Also provided librettos for Milhaud's *Le pauvre matelot* and Poulenc's *La voix humaine*. (R)

Coffey, Charles (*b* Ireland, late 17th cent.; *d* London, 13 May 1745). Irish playwright. Of his ballad operas, the most important was *The Devil to Pay* (music by Seedo, 1731). Initially a failure, it became when shortened from 42 to 16 airs a triumph, the most popular ballad opera after *The Beggar's Opera*. It was taken to Germany by the so-called English Players, or Englische Komödianten, and in a translation by Borcke, *Der Teufel ist los*, exerted a major influence on the development of *Singspiel. It was also the basis of a ballet by Adam, *Le diable à quatre* (1845).

Colasse, Pascal (*b* Reims, *bapt.* 22 Jan. 1649; *d* Versailles, 17 July 1709). French composer.

1677 at Paris, O, as assistant to Lully. Joined royal chapel 1683, rising to 'maître de la musique de la chambre' 1696. Wrote several works for the Paris stage: *Thétis et Pélée* (1689), the most successful, is notable for its advanced use of the orchestra.

Colbran, Isabella (*b* Madrid, 2 Feb. 1785; *d* Bologna, 7 Oct. 1845). Spanish soprano. Studied Madrid with Pareja, Naples with Marinelli and Crescentini. Début Spain 1806. Milan, S, 1808–9. Naples 1811–22, engaged by Domenico Barbaia, who became her lover. She was also admired by the King of Naples. In 1815 she began a relationship with Rossini that led to their marriage in 1822. He wrote several parts for her: Elisabetta, Desdemona, Armida, Semiramide, and the leading soprano roles in *La donna del lago*, *Mosè*, and *Maometto II*. She possessed a fine dramatic coloratura soprano with a range of nearly three octaves; her physique was imposing and her dramatic powers considerable, though Stendhal missed the element of pathos. One of the most famous singers in Europe; however, her reputation outlasted her voice, which began to weaken in 1815. She retired in 1824 after an unsuccessful *Zelmira* in London.

Coletti, Filippo (*b* Anagni, 11 May 1811; *d* Anagni, 13 June 1894). Italian baritone. Studied Naples with Busti. Début Naples, T del Fondo, 1834 (*Il turco in Italia*). During the next decade established himself as one of the leading exponents of Bellini and Donizetti. Lisbon 1836–9; London, HM, 1840. From 1844, when he sang Carlo in *Ernani* in Venice, F, became a prominent Verdi baritone, creating Gusmano (*Alzira*), and Francesco (*I masnadieri*) opposite Jenny Lind at London, HM, 1847. Rome 1851, the first Rigoletto there, when the opera was given as *Viscardello*. Also a distinguished Luna, Germont, and Boccanegra. Much admired by Verdi (who would have given him the title-role in *Re Lear*, had he written it). Also created roles in *Caterina Cornaro*, and Pacini's *Fidanzata corsa*. Possessed a sonorous, mellow voice capable of ringing high notes as well as subtle shading. Considered 'almost a genius' by Carlyle.

Colin. A village boy (ten), lover of Colette, in Rousseau's *Le devin du village*.

Colini, Filippo (*b* Rome, 21 Oct. 1811; *d* ? May 1863). Italian baritone. Studied Rome with Angiolini. Début Fabriano 1835, in *Aur-*

eliano in Palmira. After appearances in Italy and Vienna, sang with great success at Parma 1843, in *Nabucco*. Verdi wrote the leading baritone roles in *Giovanna d'Arco*, *La battaglia di Legnano*, and *Stiffelio* for him. A light rather than a true Verdi baritone, he was considered rather old-fashioned in his singing but had a fine legato and a beautiful tone.

Coliseum Theatre. Built by Sir Oswald Stoll in 1904; London's largest theatre (cap. 2,354) with the largest stage. Once a music-hall, with appearances by opera singers and ballet dancers an important feature. In June 1913 a series of living tableaux of *Parsifal* was presented with Wagner's music arranged and conducted by Henry Wood. SW Opera first appeared there in April 1959 with *Die Fledermaus*.

In Aug. 1968 the *Sadler's Wells company moved to the theatre as its permanent home. Charles Mackerras became music director 1970. Lord Harewood was director 1972–84. In 1974 the company was renamed English Nat. O. It has continued the enterprising policies of its predecessor on the larger scale which the size of the theatre and its stage invites. Among its early achievements were *The Ring* under Goodall, in a new translation by Andrew Porter, and other important productions included the British prems. of Prokofiev's *War and Peace* (1972), Penderecki's *The Devils of Loudun* (1973), and Henze's *The Bassarids* (1974). Among the singers who helped to give the company its distinctive character were Josephine Barstow, Rita Hunter, Valerie Masterson, Norman Bailey, Derek Hammond-Stroud, Eric Shilling, and Alberto Remedios. Charles Groves was music director 1977–9, succeeded by Mark Elder (to 1993) and Sian Edwards (1993–5). Notable events during these years were the prems. of Hamilton's *Royal Hunt of the Sun* (1977) and *Anna Karenina* (1981), and Blake's *Toussaint* (1977), also the British prems. of Martinů's *Julietta* (1978), and Jonathan Miller's production of *Figaro* (1978) and Goodall's *Tristan* (1981).

With the appointment of David Pountney to succeed Colin Graham as director of productions in 1982 (until 1993), and Peter Jonas to succeed Lord Harewood in 1985 (until 1993), emphasis changed towards the producer's dominant role, with results varying from the illuminating, even dazzling, to the self-indulgent and ludicrous, but ones greatly to the interest of an ever-widening operatic audience. Pountney himself produced *Rusalka* and *The Gambler* (1983), *The Midsummer Marriage* (1985), *Dr Faust* and *Carmen* (1986), *Lady Macbeth of Mtsensk* and *Hansel and Gretel* (1987), *Christmas Eve* (1988), and *Falstaff* (1989). Other producers included Jonathan Miller with *Rigoletto* (1982), *Don Giovanni* (1985), and *Tosca* and *Barber* (1987); and Nicholas Hytner with *Rienzi* (1983), *Xerxes* (1985), and *The Magic Flute* (1988). Other notable events of these years have included Goodall's performances of *Parsifal* (1986), the prems. of Birtwistle's *The Mask of Orpheus* (1986) and Holloway's *Clarissa* (1990), Oliver's *Timon of Athens* (1991) and Harvey's *Inquest of Love* (1993), and the British prem. of Reimann's *Lear* (1989). The theatre was bought by the company in 1992. Dennis Marks became general director in 1993.

Collatinus. A Roman (bs), husband of Lucretia, in Britten's *The Rape of Lucretia*.

Collier, Marie (*b* Ballarat, 16 Apr. 1927; *d* London, 8 Dec. 1971). Australian soprano. Studied Melbourne with Mme Wielaert. Début Melbourne 1954 (Santuzza). London, CG, 1956–71 (Marie (*Wozzeck*), Lisa, Chrysothemis, and created Hecuba in *King Priam*). London, SW (Emilia Marty, Minnie, etc.), S Francisco 1965; New York, M, 1967; created Christine in Martin David Levy's *Mourning becomes Electra*. A moving actress, with a highly charged voice and personality. (R)

Colline. A philosopher (bs), one of the four Bohemians in Puccini's *La bohème*.

Collingwood, Lawrance (*b* London, 14 Mar. 1887; *d* Killin, 19 Dec. 1982). English conductor and composer. Studied Oxford, then St Petersburg with Tcherepnin and Steinberg. Assistant to Coates, St Petersburg, M. London: Old Vic, 1920; chief cond. SW, 1931 (incl. first original *Boris* outside Russia, 1935), music dir. 1941–7. His operas are *Macbeth* (1938) and *The Death of Tintagiles* (concert, 1950).

Colón, Teatro. The leading opera-house of Argentina's capital, Buenos Aires, and of South America. For many years it gave the old-fashioned type of international opera season (May to Sept.) with French, German, and Italian works sung in their original languages by leading foreign artists. The first Colón was opened in Apr. 1857 (cap. 2,500) with *La traviata* (with Lorini and Tamberlik).

Opera was performed there regularly until 1888 by Italian and French ensembles which included Bellincioni, Boronat, Fricci, Borghi-Mamo, Battistini, De Lucia, Gayarre, Kaschmann, Stagno, and Tamagno. In 1887 the old Colón was sold to the National Bank for 950,000 pesos to be used for the building of a new opera-house. During the 20 difficult and controversial years before the present theatre was built, opera was given at the T de la O. The present building (cap. 2,478, with 1,000 standing) opened on 25 May 1908 with *Aida*. The first season, under Luigi Mancinelli, included Héctor Panizza's *Aurora*, commissioned by the government, and Shalyapin in *Mefistofele*. Cesar Ciacchi was the manager until 1914, and under his direction Serafin came, and Toscanini returned to Buenos Aires, where he had previously conducted some seasons at the T de la Opera, 1901–6. Toscanini's 1912 season sharply raised standards, and included the S American prems. of *Ariane et Barbe-bleue*, *Germania*, and *Königskinder* by a company that included Bori, Matzenauer, Amato, De Luca, and De Angelis. Saint-Saëns conducted his *Samson et Dalila* in 1916; other composers to conduct included Strauss, Respighi, Stravinsky, and Falla.

From 1915 to 1925 the seasons were directed by Walter Mocchi; as well as bringing Italian and French artists to the Colón, he engaged Weingartner and a German ensemble including Lotte Lehmann, Wildbrunn, and Schipper for *The Ring* and *Parsifal* in 1922. From 1926 to 1930 the Colón became a municipal theatre with a general manager and artistic director. The 1931 season included several operas conducted by Klemperer (his last complete *Ring* anywhere) and Ansermet. Busch conducted regularly 1933–6 and 1941–5; Erich Kleiber, 1937–41 and 1946–9; and Albert Wolff, 1938–46.

After 1949 financial difficulties during the Perón régime resulted in a lowering of artistic standards; but after the 1955 revolution the theatre regained its former traditions. In 1958, the theatre's 50th anniversary, Beecham conducted a season including *Fidelio*, *Otello*, and *Carmen*. In 1967 six complete *Ring* cycles were given, conducted by Leitner, who had been a regular visitor since 1960, with Nilsson, Windgassen, and David Ward. The change of government in 1973 resulted in a complete upheaval of the Colón's administration and artistic policy, and standards began improving again towards the end of the decade. *Peter Grimes* was given in 1979. A good general repertory is given under the present artistic director, Carlos Montero. The theatre closed for modernization in 1987, reopening with *Aida* in 1989.

Colonna. Stefano Colonna (bs), head of the Colonna family, in Wagner's *Rienzi*.

coloratura (derived from Ger., *Koloratur*; only by adoption an Italian musical term). Coloratura of itself means elaborate ornamentation of melody; thus a coloratura soprano is one who specializes in this type of music, formerly known as *canto figurato*, distinguished by light, quick, agile runs and leaps and sparkling *fioriture* (which is the correct Italian word for flourishes or ornaments). An aria which featured extensive use of such writing was known as an **aria di coloratura** (Ger., *Koloraturarie*), or an **aria di bravura**: classic examples are the Queen of the Night's two numbers in *Zauberflöte* and Constanze's 'Martern aller Arten' in *Seraglio*.

comédie-ballet (Fr.: 'comedy ballet'). An entertainment popular in France in the late 17th cent., in which ballet interludes were inserted into a spoken comedy. The architect of the genre was Molière, whose first such work was *Les fâcheux* (1661). With *Le mariage forcé* (1664) he began a distinguished collaboration with Lully, which lasted until *Le bourgeois gentilhomme* (1670) when, following their separation, Molière joined with Charpentier for *Le malade imaginaire* (1673). After his death in that year, and the rise of the *tragédie en musique*, the comédie-ballet lost its hold on the French public.

comédie mêlée d'ariettes (Fr.: 'comedy mixed with ariettes'). A type of French *opéra-comique*, which grew out of the earlier drame forain. It rose to popularity after the *Guerre des Bouffons and was in essence a light romantic comedy into which songs were inserted. While the text sometimes included political or social comment, the music was invariably direct, appealing, and not without a certain Italian influence. Examples include Gluck's *Le rencontre imprevue*, Philidor's *Tom Jones*, Monsigny's *Le déserteur*, and Grétry's *Zémire et Azor*.

Comedy on a Bridge (Cz.: *Veselohra na mostě*). Radio opera in 1 act by Martinů, text by the composer, after Klicpera. First given on Radio Prague, 18 Mar. 1937.

The scene of the opera is a bridge between two feuding villages, on which the characters become trapped. The plot recounts the many interactions which take place ranging from a schoolmaster attempting to solve a riddle to intimations of infidelity.

'Com'è gentil'. Ernesto's (ten) serenade in Act III of Donizetti's *Don Pasquale*. Said to have been provided by Donizetti at a late stage in the preparation of the opera for Mario to sing; he did so, with Lablache playing the lute in the wings.

Comelli, Adelaide. See RUBINI, GIOVANNI BATTISTA.

'Come scoglio'. Fiordiligi's (sop) aria in Act I of Mozart's *Così fan tutte* declaring that she will remain as firm as a rock against all temptations by her would-be seducer. In the manner, perhaps even a parody, of an opera seria aria.

'Come un bel dì di maggio'. Chénier's (ten) aria in Act IV of Giordano's *Andrea Chénier*, reflecting as he awaits execution.

comic opera. A general name for an operatic work in which the prevailing mood is one of comedy. Under this broad definition come works from the traditions of *opera buffa, *opéra-comique, *operetta, musical comedy, *ballad opera, and *Singspiel.

'Comme autrefois'. Leïla's (sop) cavatina in Act II of Bizet's *Les pêcheurs de perles*, in which she sings of the love that fills her heart.

comparsa (It.: 'extra actor'). Extra, walkeron: in operatic usage, it also signifies that the actor does not sing.

comprimario, comprimaria (It.: 'with the principal'). Sub-principal singer. Used mostly in relation to 19th-cent. Italian opera: although he could sing a romance, or participate in an ensemble, he was not allowed an individual aria.

Comte Ory, Le (Count Ory). Opera buffa in 2 acts by Rossini; text by Scribe and Delestre-Poirson, an expansion of a 1-act comedy (1817), after an alleged old Picard legend set down by Pierre-Antoine de la Place (1785). Prem. Paris, O, 20 Aug. 1828.

Fourmoutiers Castle, Touraine, 1250. The Countess Adèle (sop) is melancholy, her brother and the menfolk of Fourmoutiers having left for the Crusades. Ragonde (con), the Countess's companion, decides to consult the hermit: he is in reality the licentious Comte Ory (ten), who has encamped at the castle gates and offers interested advice on amorous matters. He is aided in his exploits by his friend Raimbaud (bar). Ory's tutor (bs) and his page Isolier (sop), who is in love with the Countess, arrive in search of Ory. Isolier's plan to enter the castle, disguised as a nun, so appeals to the Count that he and his followers disguise themselves in nuns' habits and lay siege both to the ladies in the castle and to the wine-cellars. The return of the crusaders, just as matters are getting out of hand, results in Ory's and Isolier's defeat in their pursuit of the Countess.

The first of Rossini's two French operas and his penultimate stage work; it contains much of the music of *Il viaggio a Reims* (including the overture) with 12 additional numbers.

Concepción. The wife (sop) of the clock-maker Torquemada in Ravel's *L'heure espagnole*.

Conchita. Opera in 4 acts (6 scenes) by Zandonai; text by Maurizio Vaucaire and Carlo Zangarini, based on Pierre Louÿs's *La femme et le pantin*. Prem. Milan, V, 14 Oct. 1911.

Seville, early 20th cent. The opera tells of the attempts of Mateo (ten), an elderly rake, to convince Conchita (sop), a poor cigar-maker and later flamenco-dancer, of the sincerity of his love for her. Eventually he succeeds, and she returns his affection.

Conforto, Nicola (*b* Naples, 25 Sept. 1718; *d* ?Madrid, after 1788). Italian composer. He came to notice as an operatic composer in Naples with *La finta vedova* (1746) and with *Antigono* (1750). In 1755 he settled permanently in Spain and was instrumental in establishing the taste there for Italian opera. Most of his operas employ librettos by Metastasio: they include the first attempt at *Nitteti* (1756), as well as settings of *L'eroe cinese* (1754) and *Adriano in Siria* (1754).

congiura (It.: 'plot, conspiracy'). The name sometimes given to scenes of conspiracy in Italian opera. Examples are 'Ad augusta!' in pt 3 of Verdi's *Ernani* and 'Dunque l'onta' in Act III of his *Un ballo in maschera*.

Conlon, James (*b* New York, 18 Mar. 1950). US conductor. Studied at Juilliard: début at Spoletto 1971 (*Boris Godunov*). Conducted

prem. of revised version of Barber's *Anthony and Cleopatra* (Juilliard 1975). New York, M, 1976 (*Zauberflöte*). Conducted *Macbeth* for Scottish O 1976; *Don Carlos* at London, CG, 1979. Other débuts include Paris, O, 1982 (*Tabarro* and *Pagliacci*); Chicago 1988 (*Forza del destino*); Milan, S, 1993 (*Oberon*). Music-dir. at Cologne O 1991, with début 1988, *Lady Macbeth of the Mtsensk District* (New York, M, 1995). (R)

'Connais-tu le pays?' Mignon's (mez) aria in Act I of Thomas's *Mignon*, the famous 'Kennst du das Land' of Goethe's *Wilhelm Meisters Lehrjahre*, trying to answer Wilhelm's questions about her origins.

Connell, Elizabeth (*b* Port Elizabeth, 22 Oct. 1946). Irish mezzo-soprano, then soprano. Studied London with O. Kraus. Début Wexford 1972 (Varvara). Sydney 1972–4; London: ENO from 1975, CG from 1976; Bayreuth 1980; Milan, S, 1982; New York, M, 1985; Munich, S, 1985. Roles incl. Eglantine, Ortrud, Kundry, Elisabeth, Leonore, Lady Macbeth, Leonora, Senta, Vitellia, Norma. (R)

Conradi, Johann Georg (*b* ?; *d* Oettingen, 22 May 1699). German composer. Held court appointments in Ansbach and Römhild; went to Hamburg *c*.1690. Here he was effectively resident composer at the opera-house and dominated its repertoire during the years 1690–3. Of the nine operas he wrote there, a few numbers from *Die Verstörung Jerusalems* (1692) and *Der wunderbar vergnügte Pygmalion* (1693) survive, as well as the complete score to *Die schöne und getreue Ariadne* (1691). This is the earliest surviving material from Hamburg's repertory and shows Conradi to be a composer of some considerable dramatic and musical abilities, much influenced by the prevailing styles of both Italian and French opera.

Conried, Heinrich (*b* Bielitz, 13 Sept. 1848; *d* Meran, 27 Apr. 1909). German operatic impresario and manager. Began career as an actor in Vienna; after holding managerial positions in a number of German cities went to US 1878. Managed various theatrical enterprises, then succeeded Maurice *Grau as dir. of New York, M, 1903–8. He engaged numerous celebrated artists, including Caruso; however, his controversial acts included the staging of the first US *Parsifal* 1903, before the expiry of the Bayreuth ban, and the first US *Salome* 1907. He resigned after dissensions with the New York M management.

Consul, The. Opera in 3 acts by Menotti; text by the composer. Prem. Philadelphia, Schubert T, 1 Mar. 1950.

The action takes place in a nameless police state in Europe and depicts the efforts of Magda Sorel (sop) to obtain a visa for herself and her husband John (bar), a revolutionary who is being pursued by the secret police. The Consul's Secretary (mez) frustrates all attempts to see the Consul by giving out innumerable forms. John is eventually arrested and Magda commits suicide by gassing herself; as she dies, she sees in a dream her husband and all the people she has met at the Consulate who urge her to join them on the journey to Death, whose frontiers are never barred.

Contes d'Hoffmann, Les (The Tales of Hoffmann). Opera in 3 acts with prologue and epilogue by Offenbach; text by Barbier and Carré, founded on the stories *Der Sandmann, Geschichte vom verlorenen Spiegelbilde*, and *Rat Krespel* by E. T. A. Hoffmann. Revision, recitatives, and part of orchestration by Guiraud. Prem. Paris, OC, 10 Feb. 1881.

Prologue. In Luther's wine-cellar in Nuremberg, a letter from the prima donna Stella to Hoffmann (ten), arranging a rendezvous, is intercepted by Councillor Lindorf (bar). Hoffmann arrives and is persuaded to tell the story of his three loves; each act of the opera is one of his tales.

His first love is Olympia (sop), a doll who seems human to Hoffmann since he views her through spectacles sold to him by one of her makers, Coppelius (bs-bar). Her other maker, Spalanzani (bar), has swindled Coppelius, who then smashes Olympia.

The next is Antonia (sop), a consumptive young singer. Dr Miracle (bs-bar) forces her to sing, thus causing her death.

Hoffmann's third love is the Venetian courtesan Giulietta (sop). She is in the power of the magician Dapertutto (bs-bar), who wishes to procure Hoffmann's shadow (i.e. his soul). Giulietta attracts Hoffmann, but abandons him as soon as Dapertutto's requirements have been fulfilled.

Epilogue. Back in Luther's tavern, the 'tales' are over. Hoffmann is drunk, and when Stella arrives it is Lindorf (who has also assumed the roles of Coppelius, Dr Miracle, and Dapertutto) who leads her away.

Offenbach died during rehearsals of *Hoffmann*, and it was rearranged (cutting the Giulietta act) by Guiraud for the prem.

Twelve years later the missing act was restored, but before the Antonia act. Correctly, the opera is largely with spoken dialogue, and in the order given above.

continuo. Abbr. of *basso continuo* (It.: 'continuous bass'). In 17th- and 18th-cent. opera, the bass part accompanying both *recitative and *aria. The continuo group (harpsichord and bass string instrument, such as viola da gamba or cello) was heard alone in recitative, but during other parts of the opera was part of the orchestral texture.

contralto (It.: 'against the high voice', i.e. contrasting with the high voice). In Ger., *Alt* (the voice), *Altistin* (the singer). The lowest category of female (or artificial male) voice. Several subdivisions exist within operahouses: the two commonest in general use (though seldom by composers in scores) are given below, with examples of roles and their approximate tessitura. In general, distinction is more by character than by tessitura: thus the examples of the roles give a more useful indication of the different voices' quality than any attempted technical definition.

German: dramatischer Alt (Erda); komischer Alt (Frau Reich in *Die lustigen Weiber von Windsor*).

Italian and French contralto roles are not generally further subdivided into categories, and have a similar tessitura to the German.

See also MEZZO-SOPRANO and CASTRATO.

contratenor. See COUNTER-TENOR.

Converse, Frederick (*b* Newton, MA, 5 Jan. 1871; *d* Westwood, MA, 8 June 1940). US composer and teacher. Studied Harvard with Knowles Paine. After abandoning a career in commerce studied privately with Chadwick and in Munich with Rheinberger. Returning to the USA he taught at the New England Cons., Boston, and at Harvard. In 1906 *The Pipe of Desire* was given in Boston; in 1910 it became the first opera by an American composer to be staged at the New York Met. Converse was vice-president of the Boston OC 1908–14: he wrote three further operas, two of which (*Sinbad the Sailor* (1913) and *The Immigrants* (1914)) were unperformed.

Cooper, Emil (*b* Kherson, 13 Dec. 1877; *d* New York, 16 Nov. 1960). Russian violinist and conductor of English descent. Studied Odessa, Vienna with Hellmesberger and

Fuchs, Moscow with Taneyev. Toured as violinist 1891–6; leader Kiev O 1896, début replacing regular cond. 1896 (*Fra Diavolo*). Kiev 1900–4; Moscow, Z (first *Golden Cockerel* and first Russian *Meistersinger*) and B. Russian seasons, Paris 1909–14. Petrograd 1919–24. Music dir. Riga 1925–8. Chief cond. Chicago 1929–32, 1939–44. Paris, O, and Milan, S, 1932–6. New York, M, 1944–50. His brother **Max Cooper** (1884–1959) conducted opera in Leningrad and Moscow.

Copland, Aaron (*b* New York, 14 Nov. 1900; *d* New York, 2 Dec. 1990). US composer. Studied with Wittgenstein and Rubin Goldmark, and with Nadia Boulanger in Paris (1921–4). In an attempt to encourage contemporary US music he promoted, with Roger Sessions, series of concerts in New York 1928–31. His first opera was *The Second Hurricane* (1937), a 'play opera' for high schools, which shows his early jazz-influenced style. His only other opera, *The Tender Land* (1954), illustrates his efforts to create an overtly US tradition of opera; he chose a subject concerning ordinary US people (a lower-middle-class farming community in the Midwest during the Depression years), and incorporated folk melodies, as he did in his ballet *Appalachian Spring* (1944).

Copley, John (*b* Birmingham, 12 June 1933). English producer. Studied London with Joan Cross. Appeared as the Apprentice, *Peter Grimes*, London, CG, 1950. Stage-manager, London, SW, producing *Tabarro* 1957. Resident prod. CG, where he has been responsible for many revivals as well as original productions, especially of Mozart; also London, C (*Carmen*, *Rosenkavalier* and *Julius Caesar*); Australian O; New York, M; Dallas; S Fe; and elsewhere. His productions are often highly inventive, but always undogmatic and responsive to the music and to singers' capabilities.

Coq d'Or, Le. See GOLDEN COCKEREL, THE.

Corder, Frederick (*b* London, 26 Jan. 1852; *d* London, 21 Aug. 1932). English conductor, composer, translator, and teacher. Studied London, Cologne with Hiller, Milan. His most successful opera was *Nordisa* (Liverpool 1887, by CR); but with the death of Carl Rosa he was forced to abandon his hopes of taking part in a revival of English opera, and turned to teaching and translation. His pupils at the London RAM included Bantock, Bax, and Holbrooke. Best remembered for the translations he made, with his wife Henrietta, of Wagner's *Parsifal* (1879), *Meistersinger* (1882), *Ring* (1882), *Tristan* (1882), and *Lohengrin* (1894). They were concerned to match Wagner's *Stabreim, which they did ingeniously but too often quaintly. These versions were performed at London, CG, and elsewhere.

Corelli, Franco (*b* Ancona, 8 Apr. 1921). Italian tenor. Studied Pesaro and Spoleto. Début Spoleto 1951 (José). London, CG, from 1957; Vienna, S, 1963; New York, M, 1961–75. Milan, S, 1954–65. A personable, large-voiced heroic tenor, especially successful as Calaf, Manrico, and Dick Johnson. (R)

Corena, Fernando (*b* Geneva, 22 Dec. 1916; *d* Lugano, 24 Nov. 1984). Swiss bass. Studied Milan with Romani. Zurich 1940–7; stage début Trieste 1947 (Varlaam). New York, M, 1954–78, succeeding Baccaloni as leading buffo bass. London, CG, 1960, 1969; also Vienna, Berlin, Buenos Aires. An accomplished and witty buffo, memorable as Bartolo (Mozart and Rossini), Leporello, Don Pasquale, Gianni Schicchi, and Falstaff. (R)

Cornelius, Peter (*b* Mainz, 24 Dec. 1824; *d* Mainz, 26 Oct. 1874). German composer. After an attempt at an acting career, he studied with Esser and in Berlin with Dehn. In Weimar he became a close friend and supporter of Liszt and Berlioz. But the production of *Der Barbier von Bagdad* (1858) met the organized opposition to the New German School from local musicians that was the final cause of Liszt's resignation. In Vienna he entered Wagner's circle of close friends, remaining loyal but never overwhelmed. *Der Cid* (1865) shows comparable signs of respect for Wagner but independence in its attempt to write an epic on a grand scale. The unfinished *Gunlöd* (1866–74) draws rather closer to Wagner. However, it is for his concern, almost alone of the New German School, to give German comic opera greater maturity than he found in the works of, for instance, Lortzing, that Cornelius is important. In the entertaining *Der Barbier von Bagdad* he shows an intelligent appreciation of how the example of Berlioz might be used to this end, and there are some influences of *Benvenuto Cellini* (which he had translated for Berlioz); but it is a work of no little charm in its own right.

Corregidor, Der (The Mayor). Opera in 4 acts by Wolf; text by Rosa Mayreder, after Alarcón's story *El sombrero de tres picos* (1874). Prem. Mannheim 7 June 1896.

Andalusia, 1804. Frasquita, the miller's wife (sop), dismissing her husband Tio Lucas's (bar) jealousy as groundless, uses the advances of the elderly Corregidor (ten) to obtain a post for her nephew. When this is achieved the Corregidor arrives, soaked from having fallen into the mill stream; Frasquita defends herself with a musket. Tio Lucas has meanwhile been summoned to town by the Corregidor; he realizes that this is a false errand, but passes Frasquita in the dark on his way home as she comes to find him. When Lucas finds the Corregidor asleep in bed, he dresses in the old man's clothes; on waking, the Corregidor is beaten by the officers who have come from the town. When he reaches his own house, his wife Mercedes (sop) refuses him admission, pretending that she has mistaken Lucas for him. Lucas, taken for the murderer of the Corregidor, is also beaten; and the opera ends with everyone even.

Corsaro, Il. Opera in 3 acts by Verdi; text by Piave, after Byron's poem *The Corsair* (1813). Prem. Trieste, 25 Oct. 1848.

An Aegean island, early 19th cent. Corrado, the pirate chieftain (ten), plans an attack against the Pasha Seid (bar). He announces his departure to his beloved Medora (sop).

Gulnara (sop), the Pasha's favourite concubine, longs to be free from him. He summons her to a banquet to celebrate certain victory over the pirates; Corrado and the pirates launch an attack. This misfires and Corrado is captured.

Gulnara has fallen in love with Corrado, which enrages the Pasha. She bribes a prison guard to allow her access to Corrado and offers to help him escape if he will kill the Pasha. As his conscience will not permit this, she murders Seid herself and the couple flee. Back on the island, Medora is dying after taking poison and longs to see Corrado. He appears with Gulnara, who confesses that she too loves Corrado. Medora dies in Corrado's arms and he flings himself into the sea.

Corselli, Francesco (*b* Piacenza, *c*.1702; *d* Madrid, 3 Apr. 1778). Italian composer. Maestro di cappella to the Duke of Parma 1727–33. Joined Madrid court 1734; maestro di cappella 1738. Wrote two early operas for Venice and six works for Madrid. The latter, including *Alessandro nell'Indie* (1738) and *Achille in Sciro* (1744), were among the most spectacular productions at the Spanish court during the 18th cent. and played an important part in the establishment of Italian opera there. Corselli was the most admired composer of Philip V, whose favourite castrato Farinelli performed in many of the prems.

Corsi, Jacopo (*b* Florence, 17 July 1561; *d* Florence, 29 Dec. 1601). Italian operatic amateur. It was in his house that the group later known as the Florentine *camerata met after Giovanni de' Bardi's departure in 1592. The discussions became more practical, and led to Peri's work completing Corsi's attempt at setting Rinuccini's *Dafne* (1598, lost, though surviving fragments include two Corsi songs). Peri's *Euridice* was also produced at his behest, 1600, with him at the harpsichord.

'Cortigiani, vil razza'. Rigoletto's (bar) aria in Act II of Verdi's *Rigoletto*, denouncing the courtiers who have abducted his daughter.

Cosa rara, Una. Opera in 2 acts by Martín y Soler; text by Da Ponte, after Luis Vélez de Guevara's story *La luna della sierra*. Prem. Vienna, B, 17 Nov. 1786.

A Spanish village, 18th cent. Lilla (sop) has been promised by her brother Tita (bs) as bride to Don Lisargo (bs), but she is in love with Lubino (bar), to whom she remains faithful though pursued by Prince Giovanni (ten) and his chamberlain Corrado (ten).

One of the great successes of its day, the opera drew the Viennese public away from *Figaro*, causing Mozart to quote from the Act I finale in the Supper Scene of *Don Giovanni* with Leporello's comment, 'Bravi! *Cosa rara*!'. Martín's use in the opera of a mandolin was copied by Mozart in Don Giovanni's serenade.

Così fan tutte (Women are Like That). Opera in 2 acts by Mozart; text by Da Ponte, probably after Ariosto's *Orlando furioso* (1516), perhaps in turn deriving from the story of Cephalus and Procris in Ovid's *Metamorphoses*, vii. Prem. Vienna, B, 26 Jan. 1790.

Naples, late 18th cent. Ferrando (ten) and Guglielmo (bar) boast of the fidelity of the two sisters to whom they are betrothed. Don

Alfonso (bs) maintains that all women are fickle and if the two men will act on his instructions for a day, he will prove it. He tells the sisters Fiordiligi (sop) and Dorabella (mez) that the two men have joined the army. There is a tearful farewell and the girls vow fidelity. Their maid Despina (sop) is persuaded to introduce the young men disguised as Albanian friends of Don Alfonso. Ferrando now courts Fiordiligi, and Guglielmo Dorabella. Next, the rejected 'Albanians' pretend to take poison. The girls weaken a little, but maintain their loyalty. Despina arrives disguised as a doctor and cures the men using magnets (a reference to Mozart's friend Dr Mesmer and his 'animal magnetism').

The sisters contemplate a little harmless flirtation. Dorabella and Guglielmo exchange love tokens but Fiordiligi still does not yield. When Ferrando learns that his Dorabella has given way, he is determined to conquer Fiordiligi, and she soon succumbs. A double wedding is arranged, with the disguised Despina as the notary. A military march signals the return of the army. The 'Albanians' flee and Ferrando and Guglielmo soon arrive. When they find the marriage contract Don Alfonso has dropped, they question the sisters angrily. They then reveal their trick. The supposed immorality of the plot led to many adaptations, often under different titles, in the 19th cent.

Cossotto, Fiorenza (b Crescentino, 22 Apr. 1935). Italian mezzo-soprano. Studied Turin Cons., and with Campogalliani. Début Milan, S, 1957, creating Sr. Mathilde (*Carmélites*). Milan, S, until 1973. London, CG, 1959; Chicago from 1964; New York, M, from 1968; Paris; Vienna; etc. Generally considered Simoniato's successor, with a warm, rich, and flexible voice. Repertory includes Rossini, Bellini, Donizetti; also successful in dramatic Verdi roles, e.g. Eboli and Amneris, which she sang at Buenos Aires (1990). (R)

Cossutta, Carlo (b Trieste, 8 May 1932). Italian tenor. Studied Buenos Aires with Melani and Wolken. Début Buenos Aires, C, 1958 (Cassio). London, CG, from 1964; Paris, O, 1975, 1979, and B, 1991; New York, M, from 1973; also Milan, S; Chicago; Moscow, B; Vienna; Verona; etc. A singer with a heroic style, successful as Pollione, Manrico, Radamès, Otello (Verdi), Samson (Saint-Saëns), Cavaradossi, Turiddu. (R)

Costa, (Sir) **Michael** (orig. Michele) (b Naples, 4 Feb. 1808; d Hove, 29 Apr. 1884). Italian, later British, composer and conductor of Spanish descent. Studied Naples with Zingarelli, singing with Crescentini. Settled in London, where he became a dominant figure in English music. Engaged as maestro al piano, London, H, 1830; dir. and cond. 1833–46, bringing orchestra and ensemble to an unprecedented state of efficiency. Cond. Philharmonic Society from 1846; music dir. new Royal Italian O, London, CG, 1847–69; London, HM, 1871–9. His discipline brought high standards into the institutions he directed with despotic control; he was, however, less strict about fidelity to scores, which he unhesitatingly adapted and augmented with extraneous music. His own work was on the whole coolly received.

Cotogni, Antonio (b Rome, 1 Aug. 1831; d Rome, 15 Oct. 1918). Italian baritone. Studied Rome with Fontemaggi and Faldi. Début Rome, T Metastasio, 1852, Belcore (*L'elisir d'amore*). Milan, S, from 1860; London, CG, 1867–89; St Petersburg 1872–94. His vast repertory encompassed Mozart, Bellini, Donizetti, Verdi, Wagner, Puccini, and Bizet. A virtuoso singer, whose voice was brilliant, richly coloured, and extended to a'. Particularly outstanding as Posa, and said to have made Verdi weep. After his retirement (1898) he taught in Rome. His pupils included Battistini, J. De Reszke, De Luca, Gilly, Lauri-Volpi, Galeffi, Viglione-Borgese, Stabile, and Gigli. (R)

Cotrubas, Ileana (b Galaţi, 9 June 1939). Romanian soprano. Studied Bucharest with Elenescu and Stroescu. Début Bucharest 1964 (Yniold). Frankfurt 1968; Gly. from 1969; London, CG, from 1971; Chicago 1973; Paris, O, 1974; Milan, S, from 1975. New York, M, 1977–84. Repertory included Susanna, Gilda, Violetta, Mélisande, Mimì, Tatyana. An intense performer with a strong, lyrical voice particularly well suited to conveying pathos. Retired 1989. (R)

Count. Among many operatic counts, the best known is Count *Almaviva (bar) in Mozart's Le nozze di Figaro.

counter-tenor. The term originally denoted the 'contratenor' line in Renaissance polyphony lying directly above the tenor. Later it came to mean a high male falsetto voice, also known as 'male alto', with a contralto or mezzo-soprano range, occasionally extending to soprano. (Some very high countertenors today have described themselves as 'male soprano'.) The term has sometimes been used to mean haute-contre, which is more generally taken, however, to be a very high, light tenor. The counter-tenor declined during the 18th and 19th cents., apart from in church choirs, to be revived in modern times by Alfred Deller, initially for singing English 16th- and 17th-cent. music, e.g. Dowland, Purcell. Others following him, including James Bowman and Jochen Kowalski, have sung in operas by Handel and Gluck, in roles conceived for castratos. Nowadays composers are increasingly interested in writing for the counter-tenor voice, often for other-worldly or ambiguous characters, e.g. Britten's Oberon, his Apollo (*Death in Venice*), and Glass's Akhnaten.

Countess. Among many operatic countesses, three are especially well known.

1. Countess Almaviva (sop) in Mozart's *Le nozze di Figaro*.

2. The Countess (mez) in Tchaikovsky's *The Queen of Spades*.

3. The Countess (sop), loved by Flamand and Olivier, in Strauss's *Capriccio*.

Covent Garden. The name of three theatres that have occupied roughly the same site in Bow Street, London, since 1732 on what was originally a convent garden.

The first was opened on 7 Dec. by John Rich with Congreve's *The Way of the World*; the first musical work was *The Beggar's Opera*. Most events in the first 100 years were dramatic, though some *Handel operas and Arne's *Artaxerxes* were premiered there. Burnt down 19 Sept. 1808. The second theatre opened 1809. The Old Price riots followed as a result of increased ticket prices. In 1826 the manager, Charles Kemble, invited Weber to compose *Oberon*. Important events 1833–47 included Alfred Bunn's 1833 season with Malibran and Schröder-Devrient; 1835 with Malibran in *Sonnambula* and *Fidelio* (same night); the artistically successful but financially disastrous 1839–42 seasons with Adelaide Kemble in *Norma* and other works; the Brussels Co. in 1845 with 'unmutilated and meritorious performances' (Chorley) of *William Tell*, *Les Huguenots*, and *La muette de Portici*. In 1847 the theatre became the Royal Italian O, with a company including artists from Her Majesty's including *Costa and

opening with *Semiramide*. Frederick Gye was the influential manager 1851–79, introducing Verdi, including *Aida* with Patti, and *Tannhäuser* with Albani (1876). The theatre burnt down in 1856, and the present building opened 15 May 1858 with *Les Huguenots*.

From 1858 to 1939 (except during the First World War) opera was given annually and virtually every artist of international repute appeared. Opera was first sung in the original language (as opposed to Italian) under the management of Augustus Harris (1888–96). In 1892 Covent Garden became the Royal Opera, and Mahler conducted the Hamburg company in the first CG *Ring*. Until 1924 the theatre was controlled by the Grand O Syndicate: Grau managed both the New York, M, and London, CG, 1897–1900, Messager the Paris, OC, and London, CG, 1901–4; and Percy Pitt, Richter, and Neil Forsythe were in partial or full control until 1914. Beecham first conducted there 1910, introducing the major Strauss operas to London. Closed 1914–18. The BNOC occupied Covent Garden for seasons 1922–4. German opera prospered 1924–31 under Walter with Wagner and Strauss performances including Leider, Lehmann, Schumann, Olczewska, Melchior, Schorr, Jansen, and Kipnis. Beecham was artistic adviser then director 1932–9, staging Rossini with Supervia, Mozart with Lemnitz, Berger, and Tauber, and Wagner under Beecham, Furtwängler, Reiner, and Weingartner, with Flagstad, Thorborg, Bockelmann, and Weber. Strauss conducted *Ariadne* with the Dresden O, 1936.

The theatre was a dance hall 1939–45, reopening 1946 (cap. 2,250) as the home of a permanent company with a government subsidy. Karl Rankl was music director 1946–51, Rafael Kubelik 1955–8, Georg Solti 1961–71, Colin Davis 1971–86, then Bernard Haitink. General directors have included David Webster 1946–70, John Tooley 1970–88, Jeremy Isaacs 1988–97. English operas receiving prems. have included *Billy Budd* (1951), *Gloriana* (1953), *Troilus and Cressida* (1954), *The Midsummer Marriage* (1955), *The Knot Garden* (1970), *The Ice Break* (1977), *Taverner* (1972), and *Gawain* (1991). British prems. have included *Wozzeck* under Erich Kleiber (1952), *Jenůfa* under Kubelik (1956), a complete *The Trojans* under Kubelik (1957); other important productions have included Visconti's prem. of *Don Carlos* under Giulini (1958), *Fidelio* under Klemperer (1961), Zeffirelli's prem. of *Tosca* with Callas and Gobbi

(1964), *Moses und Aron* under Solti (1965), *Pelléas et Mélisande* under Boulez (1969), Friedrich's prod. of the centenary *Ring* under Davis (1976), and *Meistersinger* under Haitink (1993). Singers whose careers grew with the company include Joan Sutherland, Geraint Evans, Michael Langdon, Jon Vickers, and Donald McIntyre.

Cowen, (Sir) **Frederic** (*b* Kingston, Jamaica, 29 Jan. 1852; *d* London, 6 Oct. 1935). English composer, conductor, and pianist. When only 8 he composed an operetta, *Garibaldi*, to a text by his 17-year-old sister. Studied with Goss and Benedict, later Leipzig with Moscheles and Reinecke, Berlin with Tausig. He joined Mapleson's Italian OC in 1871, also working at London, HM, under Costa. Among his operas, *Signa* (1893) was composed as a potential successor to Sullivan's *Ivanhoe* in D'Oyly Carte's project for an English Nat. O; when this failed, Cowen secured a production in Milan, but there were only two performances owing to sharp dissensions (which nearly led to a duel between Boito and Sonzogno), and the unfortunate opera was finally produced in a third version by Augustus Harris (London, CG, 1894).

Cox, Jean (*b* Gadsden, AL, 16 Jan. 1922). US tenor. Studied Alabama, Boston, and Rome with Luigi Ricci. Début Boston 1951 (Lensky). Spoleto 1954 (Rodolfo). Kiel 1954–5, Brunswick 1955–9, Mannheim 1959. Bayreuth 1956, Steersman, later Lohengrin, Parsifal, Walther, Siegfried. Chicago 1964, 1970, 1973 as Bacchus, Erik, Siegfried. Repertory included Števa, Apollo (*Daphne*), Sergey (*Lady Macbeth of Mtsensk*), Cardinal (*Mathis der Maler*). (R)

Cox, John (*b* Bristol, 12 Mar. 1935). English producer. Studied Oxford, where he produced the British stage prem. of *L'enfant et les sortilèges*, 1958; professional début, same work, London, SW, 1965. Assistant to Rennert Gly. 1959, returning 1970; dir. of productions 1972. London, SW, from 1969, and ENO; Frankfurt 1971; Australian O 1974; Munich; S Francisco; Scottish O 1981–6; London, CG, from 1988; Wexford; New York, M; Milan, S; Vienna, V; and many other cities. With Alexander Goehr, Cox was dir. of the Music T Ensemble. A highly gifted producer, with a quick eye for detail and a lively sense of drama in a wide repertory of composers incl. Strauss, Mozart, Massenet, Rossini, Wagner, Cavalli, and Puccini.

Craig, Edward Gordon (*b* Stevenage, 16 Jan. 1872; *d* Vence, 29 July 1966). English designer, producer, and actor. Son of designer E. W. Godwin and actress Ellen Terry. He was, with Appia, among the first to create designs intended not as conventional settings but to give the performer a planned role in the total theatrical experience. For the Purcell Operatic Society, 1900–3, he produced *Dido and Aeneas* using only a huge sky-cloth against which the singers moved, and Handel's *Acis and Galatea*, in which lighting effects and projections removed the action from the particular to the universal. He was an isolated figure, but a profound influence on the succeeding generation of producers.

'Credo in un dio crudel'. Iago's (bar) aria in Act II of Verdi's *Otello*, in which he declares his belief in a cruel god who has fashioned him in his own likeness. There is no Shakespeare original for the words. Boito's most substantial and personal addition to the opera.

crescendo (It.: 'growing'). Increasing in loudness. Now a basic part of music, the crescendo was once a controversial novelty. Its use in opera largely mirrors its gradual acceptance in instrumental music, where new methods of construction permitted greater dynamic flexibility. According to Burney, the first opera using it was Terradellas's *Bellerofonte* (1747), which refutes Mosca's claim for his *I pretendi delusi* (1811). The innovation was often credited to Rossini, with whom it bordered on a mannerism. His finest use of it is in *Barbiere* to suggest the rising gale of slander in Don Basilio's 'La calunnia'.

Crescentini, Girolamo (*b* Urbania, 2 Feb. 1762; *d* Naples, 24 Apr. 1846). Italian mezzo-soprano castrato. Studied Bologna with Gibelli. Début Padua 1782 in Sarti's *Didone abbandonata*. Created Romeo in Zingarelli's *Giulietta e Romeo*, Milan, S, 1796; Cimarosa also wrote an opera for him, *Gli Orazi ed i Curiazi*. Though not a success in London (1785), he was fêted throughout Europe, and sang in all the major opera-houses. The many admirers of his 'heavenly voice' and 'noble art' (*AMZ*, 1804) included Schopenhauer, E. T. A. Hoffmann, and Napoleon, who, having heard him sing in Vienna, 1805, engaged him as singing-teacher to his family in Paris (1806–12). Here he also sang at court, and was one of the few castratos ever to be well received by the French. Returning to Italy, he then settled in Naples, where he taught. Colbran was one of his pupils.

Crespin, Régine (*b* Marseilles, 23 Mar. 1927). French soprano. Studied Paris with Jouatte and Cabanel. Début Mulhouse 1950 (Elsa). Paris, O, from 1950; Bayreuth from 1958; London, CG, from 1960; New York, M, 1962–83; Chicago 1964. Equally at ease in French and German repertory, with particular success as Sieglinde and Marschallin. Created New Prioress in *Dialogues des Carmélites*. From 1975 began to sing mezzo-soprano roles, e.g. Carmen. A sensitive and eloquent singer, with a voice both voluptuous and dramatic. Retired 1989. (R)

Cressida. The Trojan High Priest Calkas's daughter (sop, in later version mez), lover of Troilus, in Walton's *Troilus and Cressida*.

Crimi, Giulio (*b* Paterno, 10 May 1885; *d* Rome, 29 Oct. 1939). Italian tenor. Studied Catania with Adernò. Début Palermo 1910 (Manrico). London, CG, 1914; Milan, S, 1916; Chicago and New York, M, 1916–24. Created Luigi (*Il tabarro*), Rinuccio (*Gianni Schicchi*), and Paolo (Zandonai's *Francesca da Rimini*). Retired 1928. His good looks and warm, generous voice were ideal for romantic, and particularly verismo, roles. His pupils included Gobbi. (R)

Crispino e la comare (Crispino and the Fairy). Opera in 3 acts by Federico and Luigi Ricci; text by Piave. Prem. Venice, B, 28 Feb. 1850.

Venice, 17th cent. The poor cobbler Crispino (bs) acquires fame and wealth thanks to the amazing healing powers given him by a fairy. He becomes so arrogant that he reveals to him that she is Death and has now come to claim him. However, Crispino repents and she allows him to return to his family.

Crociato in Egitto, Il (The Crusader in Egypt). Opera in 2 acts by Meyerbeer; text by Rossi. Prem. Venice, F, 7 Mar. 1824.

Damietta, *c*.1250. Armando d'Orville (orig. cas, later mez), a knight of Rhodes, assumed dead in Egypt during the Sixth Crusade; but under the name of Elmireno, he has become the confidant of the Sultan Aladino (bs). He falls in love with Palmide (sop), Aladino's daughter, and converts her to Christianity. Adriano (ten), Armando's uncle, arrives to sue for peace, but Emireno's true identity is discovered and he and the other captured Christians are sentenced to death. Armando, however, saved the Sultan's life after a plot to overthrow him; Armando and Palido are reunited, and a peace treaty is signed.

Cross, Joan (*b* London, 7 Sept. 1900; *d* Aldeburgh, 12 Dec. 1993). English soprano. Studied London with Freer. Joined chorus of Old Vic 1924, soon singing Cherubino and First Lady. London: SW, 1931–46; CG, 1931, 1934–5, 1947–54. Founder member of the EOG 1945. Created Britten's Ellen Orford, Female Chorus, Lady Billows, and Queen Elizabeth (whose birthday she shared) in *Gloriana*. Other roles included Mimì, Snegurochka, Micaëla. After 1955 devoted herself to teaching, especially at the National School of O, which she founded with Anne Wood in 1948. She also produced opera for CG and SW. One of Britain's great operatic artists, an exceptionally gifted musician, with a pure, true voice that she used with great sensitivity and feeling for line; also a fine, sympathetic actress. As director of SW during the Second World War, she did much to sustain the company and was instrumental in securing the prem. of *Peter Grimes*. (R)

Crosse, Gordon (*b* Bury, 1 Dec. 1937). English composer. Studied Oxford with Wellesz, Rome with Petrassi. His first opera was a powerful, strongly atmospheric setting of Yeats's *Purgatory* (1966), using a freely declamatory style closely connected to the orchestral expression. *The Grace of Todd* (1969) confirmed this dramatic instinct, and an exceptional musical intelligence, though the work was hampered by a somewhat laboured comic text; his qualities were more richly revealed in *The Story of Vasco* (1974). Crosse has also interested himself in music theatre, as with *Potter Thompson* (1975); this was written to involve children, for whom he has also composed the Nativity opera *Holly from the Bongs* (1974).

Crown. A tough stevedore (bar) in Gershwin's *Porgy and Bess*.

Crown Diamonds. See DIAMANTS DE LA COURONNE, LES.

Crozier, Eric (*b* London, 14 Nov. 1914; *d* France, 7 Sept. 1994). English writer and producer. With Benjamin Britten and John Piper, co-founder of the EOG (1947). Librettist of Britten's *Albert Herring* and *Let's Make an Opera*, and (with E. M. Forster) *Billy Budd*; also of Berkeley's *Ruth*. Produced new version of *The Bartered Bride* (made by him with Joan Cross), London, SW, 1943, and prems. of *Peter Grimes*, SW 1945, and *Rape of Lucretia*, Gly. 1946; first US *Grimes*, Tanglewood 1946.

'Cruda sorte'. Isabella's (con) cavatina in Act I of Rossini's *L'italiana in Algeri*, lamenting her separation from her lover Lindoro when she is captured by pirates, but then realizing she can use her charm as a woman to deal with her captors and master the situation. The original version, with its amorous *double entendres*, was censored after the 1813 Venice prem. for Milan.

Cruvelli, Sophie (*b* Bielefeld, 12 Mar. 1826; *d* Monaco, 6 Nov. 1907). German soprano. Studied Paris with Bordogni, Milan with Lamperti. Début Venice 1847 (Odabella, *Attila*). London, HM, 1848, Elvira (*Ernani*), Abigaille, and Mozart's Countess, which brought her little success; Milan 1850 (Luisa Miller); Paris, I, 1851–3 (Norma, Semiramide); London, CG, 1854, this time evoking enthusiasm as Donna Anna, Leonore, Desdemona (Rossini). Paris, O, 1854–6, Valentine, Rachel, and Hélène, which she created in *Les vêpres siciliennes*. One of the finest dramatic sopranos of her time, especially in the operas of Verdi, whose music Fétis considered 'faite pour la cantatrice'. Her voice was powerful and rich, though rather uneven, and she possessed great dramatic flair. Her sister **Friederika Marie Crüwell** (1824–68), mezzo-soprano, studied with Roger and sang in France and Italy.

Cuberli, Lella (*b* Austin, TX, 29 Sept. 1945). US soprano of Italian origin. Studied Dallas and Italy. Début Budapest 1975 (Violetta). Milan, S, from 1977; Pesaro 1984; Aix 1985; Paris, O, 1985–6; Salzburg 1986; New York, M, 1990. Repertory incl. Mozart's Countess, and roles in many revivals of Rossini, Bellini, and Donizetti. (R)

Cuenod, Hugues (*b* Corseaux-sur-Vevey, 26 June 1902). Swiss tenor. Studied Basle, and Vienna with Fr. Singar-Burian. Originally a baritone, trained as tenor, as which made

début Paris 1928 in *Jonny spielt auf*. Milan, S, 1951; Gly. from 1954; London, CG, 1954, 1956, 1958. Tall, humorous, and energetic, a character tenor of great individuality and intelligence. His career spanned over 60 years and the friendship of many composers, particularly Poulenc and Stravinsky, for whom he created Sellem (*The Rake's Progress*) and subsequently many major concert works. Memorable for his Erice (*Ormindo*), Linfea (*Calisto*), Triquet, Don Basilio (Mozart) and Vašek; at an indefatigable 85, made his début at New York, M, as the Emperor in *Turandot*. (R)

Cui, César (*b* Vilnius, 18 Jan. 1835; *d* Petrograd, 26 Mar. 1918). Russian composer and critic of French descent. Studied with Moniuszko, later moving to St Petersburg and studying engineering. In 1856 he met Balakirev, and became one of the five composers of the 'moguchaya kuchka' (mighty handful). Encouraged (and helped with his orchestration) by Balakirev, he wrote two operas before embarking upon what was to be his greatest success, *William Ratcliff* (1869). Its lengthy gestation is in part responsible for its great stylistic unevenness, which embraces some fairly conventional adaptation of the text for operatic purposes and, in the second half, musical diction close to that of Dargomyzhsky. It also makes some enterprising use of reminiscence motive. Not surprisingly, the work divided critics: among those who greatly admired it were Tchaikovsky and Rimsky-Korsakov, in sharp contrast to Serov. *Angelo* (1876), Cui's next opera, was an adaptation of Hugo's drama to match the contemporary interest in setting personal drama against a vividly depicted social background, though the intended influence of Musorgsky is less evident than that of Parisian grand opera. His next opera was actually French, *Le flibustier* (1894), and its successor, *The Saracen* (1899), was to a Dumas subject. *A Feast in Time of Plague* (1901) is another setting of one of Pushkin's 'little tragedies', one of which had inspired Dargomyzhsky's *The Stone Guest*, and attempts to follow that work in its manner of melodic declamation, while also imposing standard musical forms upon the poetry. His one full-length opera on a Russian subject was a setting of Pushkin's *The Captain's Daughter* (1911). Thereafter, disillusioned, he turned to children's operas. As a critic, he was a fervent upholder of nationalist ideals, using his notoriously sharp tongue and pen in defence of his friends and to attack those unsympathetic to his aims. His fiercest attacks were intended to kill Wagnerism in Russia, and thereby wound Serov.

Cunning Little Vixen, The (Cz., *Příhody Lišky Bystroušky*: lit. 'The Tales of Vixen Sharpears'). Opera in 3 acts by Janáček; text by the composer, after Rudolf Těsnohlídek's verses for drawings by Stanislav Lolek, published serially in the Brno newspaper *Lidové Noviny* during 1920. Prem. Brno 6 Nov. 1924.

A Moravian village and surrounding woods. Sharpears the vixen (sop) is caught by the Forester (bar) and kept as a pet. She laments her lot to the dog Lapák (mez or ten) and, having incited rebellion among the hens against their cock (sop), she manages to escape.

Having dispossessed the badger (bs) by fouling his lair, she settles in. In the world of men, the Priest (bs) is gloomy because he is to be transferred, while the Forester sighs for the mysterious girl Terynka, who has also fascinated the Schoolmaster (ten); and though they play cards together in the inn, disorder threatens. They leave, rather drunk, and confused about the allure of Terynka; Sharpears watches them. She takes a fox, Goldenmane (sop or ten) as mate; they are married by the woodpecker.

Harašta the poacher (bs) comes upon the fox family, and shoots Sharpears. Back in the inn, the Forester is sad that he cannot now find the vixen whose image haunts him; and the marriage of Terynka to Harašta does nothing to cheer the men up. They feel their ageing emphasized by the coming of spring. Alone in the woods, the Forester falls into a doze; waking, he observes the animals, among them a foxcub exactly like her mother, and taking new comfort from this vision of nature always renewing itself, he lies back at peace.

Curlew River. Church parable in 1 act by Britten; text by William Plomer, after Jūro Motomasa's Noh play *Sumida-gawa* (early 15th cent.). Prem. Orford Parish Church 12 June 1964.

The first of Britten's *church parables, it is cast in the dramatic metaphor of monks processing into church to enact a mystery play. The Ferryman (bar) is waiting to convey passengers across the river. A Madwoman (ten) arrives, on a search for her lost son; unwillingly, the Ferryman agrees to take her across. During the crossing, he relates a story of a young boy who, fleeing from robbers, crossed the river a year previously but was so exhausted that he died on reaching the far bank. The Madwoman realizes that this was her son and, taking pity on her, the Ferryman leads her to the boy's grave.

Curtin, Phyllis (*b* Clarksburg, WV, 3 Dec. 1921). US soprano. Studied Wellesley Coll. with Regneas. New England OT 1946 (Lisa, Lady Billows); New York, CO, from 1953 (début in US prem. of *Der Prozess*); New York, M, 1961; also Milan, S; Vienna; Buenos Aires; Scottish O. Created Cathy in Floyd's *Wuthering Heights* and title-role in his *Susannah*. Successful in contemporary works, but also as Salome, Mistress Ford, and in Mozart. (R)

Curtis, Alan (*b* Mason, MI, 17 Nov. 1934). US conductor and musicologist. Studied at U of Illinois and with Gustav Leonhardt in Amsterdam. Taught U of California at Berkeley from 1960; prof. 1970. He has made editions of *Poppea* and Jommelli's *La schiava liberata*, giving the first modern performance in 1982. Other revivals, all with a high regard for historical detail, include Landi's *Sant Alessio* (Rome 1981), Cesti's *Tito* (Innsbruck 1983), Handel's *Floridante* (Toronto 1990) and Traetta's *Buovo d'antona* (Venice 1993). (R)

Cuzzoni, Francesca (*b* Parma, 2 Apr. 1696; *d* Bologna, 19 June 1778). Italian soprano. First known appearance Parma, 1716. After successes in Bologna and Venice, engaged by London H in 1772 at £2,000 p.a.: début 1723, creating Teofane in Handel's *Ottone*; also created several other Handel roles, including Cleopatra (*Giulio Cesare*) and Rodelinda. Her notorious rivalry with Faustina *Bordoni (engaged London, 1726) culminated in a brawl on stage during Bononcini's *Astianatte* in 1727. Left London for Italy, but returned 1734–6, engaged by Porpora for Lincoln's Inn Fields. Though physically unprepossessing and regarded as a bad actress, she was by all accounts a singer of the highest quality. Quantz describes her 'clear and agreeable soprano, pure intonation, and a fine shake' and declares that her singing 'took possession of the soul of every auditor'. Her range was c'–c'''.

cycle. A group of works telling a more or less consecutive story, but, partly for reasons of length, partly for dramatic effect, separable and performable on different nights. The earliest cycle is Sartorio's *La prosperità di Elio Seiano* and *La caduta di Elio Seiano*, both in 3 acts with text by Nicolò Minato (Venice 1667). The best-known, and greatest, cycle remains Wagner's *Der *Ring des Nibelungen*. Upon this others were modelled, e.g. Bungert's *Homerische Welt* (based on the *Odyssey*) and Holbrooke's *The Cauldron of Annwyn*.

Cyrano de Bergerac. 1. Opera in 4 acts by Alfano; text by Henry Cain, after Rostand's drama (1897). Prem. Rome, R, 22 Jan. 1936.

Paris and Arras, 1640. Cyrano (ten), the poet-soldier, is disfigured by a huge nose that makes him repulsive to women. He falls in love with the beautiful Roxane (sop) and pays court to her through the mouth of Christian (ten), who also loves her. Only when Cyrano is on his deathbed does Roxane learn the truth and realize that she loves him.

2. Opera in 4 acts by Damrosch; text by W. J. Henderson, after Rostand. Prem. New York, M, 27 Feb. 1913.

Czech Republic. The name under which the rump of Czechoslovakia (formed in 1918 from the union of Bohemia, Moravia, and Slovakia) has been known, following the establishment of Slovakia's independence in 1992. Opera was first given in 1627, when Italian singers came from Mantua to perform a *commedia pastorale cantata* by G. B. Buonamente and Cesare Gonzaga for the coronation of Ferdinand III. Italian opera was thereafter given by visitors, including in 1702 Bartolomeo Bernardi's *La Libussa* (the first work on a Czech subject in Czech lands). In 1723 Fux's *Costanza e Fortezza* was produced for the 4,000 visitors to the coronation of Charles VI. Later, opera (including prems. of Vivaldi's works) was given in a theatre built by Count František Špork in his Prague residence in Na Poříčí in 1701, and open to the public. From 1739 Italian companies played in the new Kotzen T, which was adapted from the old town's medieval cloth market and remained the chief public theatre. The Gräflich-Nostitzsches Nationaltheater (1783), then the Königliches Ständestheater in the Old Town (Staré Město), and Count Thun's theatre in the Malá Strana (1781) replaced it.

The expansion of Italian opera in the 18th cent. led to the building of theatres in nobles' castles, where opera was given by Italian companies augmented by domestic musicians. Important castle centres included Špork's Kuks, Český Krumlov, and in Moravia Rottal's Holešov, Schrattenbach's Vyškov and Kroměříž, and especially Questenberg's Jaroměřice, where in 1730 *L'origine di Jaromeriz in Moravia*, by František Míča, was staged (revived then 1980). This, whether or not sung in Czech, was the first opera to be given a printed Czech translation. The Italian opera buffa and baroque drama influenced the simple Hanatic operas (from the district of Haná), composed in dialect, and *Pargamotéka* (1747) by Alanus Plumlovský (1703–59), performed in the Premonstratensian monastery of Hradiště from 1747; they also influenced the *Opera de rebellione Boëmica rusticorum* (Opera on the Bohemian Peasants' Revolt, 1775–7) by the East Bohemian teacher Jan Antoš (fl. 2nd half 18th cent.) and *Opera Bohemica de Camino* (The Bohemian Chimney O) by Karel Loos (1724–72), one of a number of 'craft' operas written in Czech. The Italian travelling companies visited Prague and elsewhere: Denzio settled in Prague and presented opera, the Mingottis brought opera buffa, and G. B. Locatelli introduced Gluck conducting his own works. In the second half of the 18th cent. these were gradually replaced by German companies, producing Singspiels, vaudevilles, and plays using songs and dances in Czech and German. As elsewhere, Italian opera appealed mainly to connoisseurs, Singspiel (often very simple) to a wider public. The castle productions died out during the first half of the 19th cent.; some were given in Náměšť, where works by Naumann, Gluck, and Handel were staged, mostly in German translations by Count Haugwitz and performed by his domestic musicians.

During these years, most Czech musicians lived abroad and worked in the main operatic languages of the day. Those working chiefly in Italian included Florian Gassmann (1729–74), Josef *Mysliveček (1737–81), and J. A. Koželuh (Kozeluch) (1738–1814); in German, Jiří Benda (1722–95), Pavel Vranický (Paul *Wranitzky) (1756–1808), and Vojtěch Jírovec (Adalbert *Gyrowetz) (1763–1850); in French, Josef Kohaut (1738–?1793) and Anton Rejcha (1770–1836). Ferdinand *Kauer (1751–1831) and Wenzel *Müller (1767–1835) worked mainly in Viennese Singspiel. Jan Rösler (1771–1813) and Václav *Tomášek (1774–1850) remained in Prague but wrote to German or Italian texts. Despite the earlier amateur operas in Czech, the first real Czech opera composer was František *Škroup (1801–62), with *Dráteník* (The Tinker, 1826). There is little influence of Weber (who had worked in Prague, 1813–16, introducing a wider repertory, and whose *Der Freischütz* was given there in 1824), and the work is closer to pre-Romantic Singspiel; whereas *Žižkův dub* (Žižka's Oak, 1841), by František Kott (1808–84), despite Italian influence, is in various ways Weberian. Škroup's lead was not decisively followed, and his own later operas were mixed in language and genre. The most successful German-language Czech opera was *Bianca und Giuseppe* (1848; text by Richard Wagner) by Jan Kittl (1806–68).

It took Bedřich *Smetana (1824–84) to recognize that a more mature method than a simple musical play using folk-songs was demanded as a basis for the development of a true national opera. In 1868–74 he was conductor of the Provisional T (opened 1862). He impressed his audiences with *Braniboři v Čechách* (The Brandenburgers in Bohemia, 1866), the prize-winner in Count Harrach's 1861 competition for the best Czech historical and comic opera; but he won their hearts with *Prodaná nevěsta* (The Bartered Bride, 1866). He further set an example of how to treat heroic as well as folk themes in a Czech idiom with *Dalibor* (1868). In the same year building began of the Nat. T, intended as a symbol of the nation's independent spirit. Smetana's *Libuše* was produced there in June 1881, before the completion of the building, which shortly burnt down. Of *Dvořák's operas (by which he set considerable store), only *Rusalka* has entered the international repertory; other of his works, especially *Jakobín* (The Jacobin, 1889) and *Čert a Káča* (The Devil and Kate, 1899), have remained in Czech repertories, but though wholly Czech in spirit and of much charm in their handling of history, character, and legend, they lack Smetana's dramatic qualities.

Smetana's immediate successor was Zdeněk *Fibich, who absorbed some Romantic, including Wagnerian, influences into a Czech national idiom and drew upon European literature for his subjects. Others who successfully built upon Smetana's example included Richard Rozkošný (1833–1913), Vilém *Blodek (1834–74), Karel *Bendl (1838–97), Josef Nešvera (1842–1914), Karel *Šebor (1843–1903), and Karel Weiss (1862–1944). The first outstanding Czech conductor was Karel *Kovařovic (1862–1920),

who introduced *Rusalka* and ran the National T 1900–20. Here he introduced French opera, Strauss, Musorgsky, and Wagner. His most successful opera was *Psohlavci* (The Dogheads, 1898).

Outstanding among composers of the period before the emergence of Janáček, however, was J. B. *Foerster (1859–1951), whose *Eva* made a great impression in 1899. By now opera was securely established in Czechoslovakia, and a flourishing, independent genre: 102 new operas were given between 1900 and 1925. It still held no interest for some leading composers: Suk wrote no operas, Vítězslav *Novák (1870–1949) few, though his *Lucerna* (The Lantern, 1923) is impressive. Work of greater significance came from Otakar *Ostrčil (1879–1935), who was influenced by Fibich, in *Honzovo království* (Johnny's Kingdom, 1934); by Otakar Zich (1879–1934), with *Malířský nápad* (The Painter's Whim, 1910); and later by Rudolf Karel (1880–1945), with *Smrt kmotřička* (Godmother Death, 1933). But the period is dominated by Leoš *Janáček (1854–1928), although *Jenůfa*, performed in Brno in 1904, did not gain proper recognition until the Prague production of 1916. He is one of the greatest figures in the history of opera, and the first Czech composer to absorb completely what his country had to offer and to make of it a mature, modern idiom.

He has somewhat overshadowed his successors. Alois *Hába (1893–1973) experimented with microtonal music, notably in *Matka* (The Mother, 1931). Otakar *Jeremiáš (1892–1962) wrote *Bratři Karamazovi* (1928). Jaromir *Weinberger (1896–1967) had an international success with *Švanda dudák* (Shvanda the Bagpiper, 1927). Emil František *Burian (1904–59) had a more local success with *Maryša* (1940). But the most important composer to win international fame was Bohuslav *Martinů (1890–1959), a substantial part of whose work was done outside Czechoslovakia. A later generation of important composers included Iša Krejčí (1904–68), especially successful in his *Comedy of Errors* setting, *Pozdvižení v Efesu* (1946), Jan Hanuš (b 1915), Zbyněk Vostřák (1920–85), Jiří Pauer (b 1919), Jan F. Fischer (b 1921), Ilja Hurník (b 1922), and Ivo Jirásek (b 1920). The Brno composer Josef Berg (1927–71) made some interesting experiments in the 1960s with his mini-operas.

See also BRNO, PRAGUE, SLOVAKIA.

D

da capo aria. Although 18th-cent. arias could embrace a wide variety of moods and emotions, they were usually constructed according to a uniform tripartite scheme, in which the third section was a repetition of the first and which the singer was expected to ornament. This form is thus generally referred to as the da capo aria, a term deriving from the Italian for 'from the head' (i.e. beginning). Though its supreme master was Hasse, examples can be found in composers from Monteverdi to Mozart and beyond. See also ARIA.

Daguerre, Louis (*b* Corneilles, 18 Nov. 1787; *d* Bry-sur-Marne, 10 July 1851). French physicist, painter, and designer. Though widely known as a pioneer of photography and inventor of the Daguerrotype (1839), he was also an influential scenic designer. After working in the theatre, he moved to the Paris Opéra in 1822, where in his first designs (with *Cicéri), for Isouard's *Aladin, ou La lampe merveilleuse*, he exploited the theatre's installation of gaslight with his own gift for lighting effects. At the Diorama, the theatre he also opened 1822, he developed a number of new pictorial and mechanical effects, and he made use of these at the Opéra to support Cicéri in giving French *Grand Opera a new scenic realism and splendour. He was largely responsible for banishing the old Italian system of wings, with their formation of a series of corridors and denial of perspective; and his contribution to the heightened realism of Cicéri's sets included the creation of the illusion of moving clouds, perhaps covering and then revealing the moon (which might move slowly during a scene), trees casting shadows when the sun came out, and many similar devices. He was responsible for the introduction of the panorama, especially exploited by Cicéri.

Daland. A Norwegian sea captain (bs), father of Senta, in Wagner's *Der fliegende Holländer*.

Dalayrac, Nicolas-Marie (*b* Muret, 8 June 1753; *d* Paris, 26 Nov. 1809). French composer. His first stage works date from 1781, but his real success came with the production of *Nina* in 1786; this set a fashion for sentimental comedy, and already contains the seeds of the greater human and musical subtlety he was to bring into opéra-comique. It influenced Paisiello in his setting of the same story (1789), which in turn influenced the development of *opera semiseria. During the 1790s his works were among the most significant to reflect the perilous and alarming times in their plots, their handling of character, settings frequently gloomy or sinister, and in the new attention to moral issues. *Camille* (1791) concerns a wife's unjust imprisonment. *Léon* (1798) and especially *Léhéman* (1801) similarly treat imprisonment and freedom in the *rescue opera genre, and are also significant for their pioneering use of *reminiscence motive to draw music and plot into a closer dramatic relationship. This new development, with its consequent greater attention to the role of the orchestra in opera, helped to win Dalayrac a significant following in Germany, where his works figured in many repertories and helped to provide example and stimulus to the development of German Romantic opera. As well as writing memorable short romances, he was able to use ensemble and chorus with a new dramatic fluency. In these matters, especially in his intelligent and inventive use of motive, he influenced Méhul and hence the next generation of French and German opera composers, Berlioz and Weber among them.

Dalibor. Opera in 3 acts by Smetana; text by Josef Wenzig, after the legend, translated from German into Czech by Ervín Špindler. Prem. Prague, Novoměstské T, on the occasion of the laying of the foundation stone of the Prague, N, 16 May 1868.

Prague, late 15th cent. Dalibor (ten) has been captured by his enemies and imprisoned for his assassination of the Burgrave in revenge for the killing of his friend Zdeněk. The Burgrave's daughter Milada (sop) begins to feel pity for him. Disguising herself as a boy, she apprentices herself to the gaoler Beneš (bs), and takes Dalibor's beloved violin to his dungeon. She is wounded in the attempt to rescue Dalibor and dies in his arms; he stabs himself.

In Czechoslovakia the work has been regarded as a *rescue opera with a significance for national liberty comparable to that of *Fidelio*.

Dalila. The Philistine temptress (mez) in Saint-Saëns's *Samson et Dalila*.

Dallapiccola, Luigi (*b* Pisino, 3 Feb. 1904; *d* Florence, 19 Feb. 1975). Italian composer. One of the leading dodecaphonist composers of his country, he successfully used the formal demands of the technique to give expression to an innate lyricism and love of the voice. *Volo di notte* (1940) is a skilful attempt to put contemporary ideas and incidents on the operatic stage without severing connections with tradition. *Il prigioniero* (1950) is a more powerful work in which Dallapiccola's intense sympathy with prisoners finds strong expression in the theme of the Inquisition captive almost allowed to escape. Dallapiccola declared that his operas concern 'the struggle of man against some force much stronger than he', and this finds final expression in his philosophical quest opera *Ulisse* (1968).

Dalla Rizza, Gilda (*b* Verona, 12 Oct. 1892; *d* Milan, 5 July 1975). Italian soprano. Studied Bologna with Ricci and Orefice. Début Bologna 1912 (Charlotte). Created Magda (written for her by Puccini) in *La rondine*, and leading roles in many other operas, including *Il piccolo Marat* (Mascagni), *Giulietta e Romeo* (Zandonai). Rome 1919 (Suor Angelica and Lauretta); London, CG, 1920; Milan, S, from 1923. With her clear, agile voice and versatile dramatic skills, she was notable in Verdi (especially as Violetta) and the verismo repertory. Retired 1939; taught at Venice Cons. 1939–55. (R)

'Dalla sua pace'. Ottavio's (ten) aria in Act I of Mozart's *Don Giovanni*, declaring that his own joy or sorrow depends on that of Donna Anna.

Dal Monte, Toti (*b* Mogliano Veneto, 27 June 1893; *d* Treviso, 26 Jan. 1975). Italian soprano. Studied Venice with Marchisio, later with Pini-Corsi. Début Milan, S, 1916 (Biancofiore, *Francesca da Rimini*). Appearances in the provinces, then regularly at Milan, S, from 1922; Chicago 1924–8; New York, M, 1924–5; London, CG, 1925; Melbourne, Tokyo, Berlin. After retiring in 1943, she appeared in several films. Her voice was pure and remarkably agile, and she possessed a touching quality in both her singing and charac-

terization. Celebrated as Gilda, Lucia, and Amina, she later sang Butterfly and Mimì. (R)

Dalmorès, Charles (*b* Nancy, 21 or 31 Dec. 1871; *d* Hollywood, 6 Dec. 1939). French tenor. Studied Rouen with Vergnet. Stage début Rouen 1899 (Siegfried). Brussels, M, 1900–6; Paris, T du Château d'Eau, 1902 (Tristan); London, CG, 1904–11; New York, Manhattan OC, 1906–10; Bayreuth 1908 (Lohengrin); Chicago 1910–18. Famous for his Faust (Gounod), Pelléas, Samson, and Herod. A good musician and actor, he possessed a large, resonant, and sometimes plangent voice. (R)

Damase, Jean-Michel (*b* Bordeaux, 27 Jan. 1928). French composer. Studied Paris with Busser. His skilfully written, eclectic, but also effective works include a number of operas, several to texts by Jean Anouilh, including *Eurydice* (1972).

Dame blanche, La (The White Lady). Opera in 3 acts by Boieldieu; text by Eugène Scribe, after Scott's novels *The Monastery* (1820) and *Guy Mannering* (1815). Prem. Paris, OC, 10 Dec. 1825.

Count Avonel's castle, Scotland, 1759. George Brown (ten), an English officer, asks the Scottish farmer Dickson (ten) for lodging, and relates his half-forgotten origins and his life as a soldier. Jenny (sop), Dickson's wife, tells him that the neighbouring castle is to be sold since the owners are Jacobites who must flee to France: the farmers hope to combine to buy the castle, and Dickson has sworn to serve a mysterious white lady said to be in the castle. She has summoned Dickson, but George offers to go instead. In the castle Gaveston (bs), the former steward, enters with his ward Anna (sop), who has promised to reveal the family secret. George is admitted, and eventually is left alone. He falls into a doze, and sees the white lady: it is in fact Anna, who has recognized him as a young officer she once nursed, but he believes her to be a ghost. Next morning, at the sale of the castle, Anna approaches George, and on her instructions from the 'white lady' he outbids his rivals. Later, in the castle, he is led to the treasure hidden in the pedestal of the statue of the white lady by Anna, who has taken the statue's place: he turns out to be the rightful heir, and when Anna is unveiled they fall into one another's arms.

Damnation de Faust, La. *Légende dramatique* in 4 parts by Berlioz; text by the composer, after Goethe's *Faust*, pt 1 (1773–1808), in Gérard de Nerval's translation (1828 and 1840), including contributions from Almire Gandonnière. Completed 1846, incorporating *Huit scènes de Faust* (1828) in altered form. Concert perf. Paris, OC, 6 Dec. 1846; prem. Monte Carlo 18 Feb. 1893.

The plot makes use of episodes from Goethe, with Méphistophélès (bar or bs) tempting Faust (ten) to bargain his soul in exchange for renewed youth. Faust grows sated with the pleasures provided by Méphistophélès, which include drunken companionship in Auerbach's Cellar, military glory (Berlioz introduces his version of the Rákóczy March), nature, and love for Marguerite (mez), whom he betrays: finally he is borne off to Hell in a Ride to the Abyss, while Marguerite is saved.

There have been many subsequent attempts at staging a work that was originally entitled 'opéra de concert' and not conceived for the theatre (though Berlioz had the intention of rewriting it for staging), e.g. by Béjart at the Paris, O, in 1964, and by Geliot at the London, C, 1969.

'D'amor sull'ali rosee'. Leonora's (sop) aria in Act IV of Verdi's *Il trovatore*, in which she sings of her love for Manrico as she stands beneath the tower in which he is imprisoned.

Damrosch, Leopold (*b* Posen, 22 Oct. 1832; *d* New York, 15 Feb 1885). German violinist and conductor. Studied Berlin with Ries, Dehn, and Böhmer, and gained experience as concert conductor. In 1871 moved to New York, where his many activities included, after the disastrous 1883–4 Italian season at the M, organizing a German season 1884–5. He conducted all the performances, which included the first M *Walküre*. His elder son **Frank** (*b* Breslau, 22 June 1859; *d* New York, 22 Oct. 1937) studied with his father and Moszkowski; chorus-master, New York, M, 1885–91. His younger son **Walter** (*b* Breslau, 30 Jan. 1862; *d* New York, 22 Dec. 1950) studied with Bülow. Assistant cond. to his father 1884–5, continuing at the New York M under Seidl. Cond. many US prems., especially of Wagner, 1885–91. Formed his own opera company 1894, returning to Metropolitan, 1900–3. His operas included *Cyrano de Bergerac* (1913) and *The Man without a Country* (1937).

Danaïdes, Les. Opera in 5 acts by Salieri; text by F. L. G. Lebland du Roullet and L. T. Tschudi, partly trans. from a libretto by Calzabigi. Prem. Paris, O, 26 Apr. 1784.

Greece, mythological times. All except one of the 50 Danaïdes, the daughters of Danaus (bs), obey their father and kill their husbands, the sons of Aegyptus, Danaus' brother, on whom he seeks vengeance. The exception, Hypermnestra (sop), flees to Memphis with her husband Lynceus (ten). A flash of lightning destroys Danaus' palace; he himself is chained to a rock in Tartarus, with a vulture gnawing at his entrails. The Danaïdes are also tormented, by evil spirits and fire.

Dance of the Apprentices. Dance by the Nuremberg apprentices and the girls from Fürth in Act III of Wagner's *Die Meistersinger von Nürnberg*.

Dance of the Blessed Spirits. Dance in Act II of Gluck's *Orfeo ed Euridice*.

Dance of the Comedians. Dance in Act III of Smetana's *The Bartered Bride* in which the clowns and dancers of the travelling circus are put through their paces.

Dance of the Hours. The entertainment put on by Alvise Badoero for his guests in Act III of Ponchielli's *La Gioconda*, in which the eternal struggle between dark and light is symbolized.

Dance of the Seven Veils. Salome's dance before Herod in Strauss's *Salome*, for which he has promised her anything: she chooses the head of John the Baptist.

Dance of the Tumblers. Dance of the *skomorokhi* (itinerant dancers, tumblers, and singers) before Tsar Berendey in Act III of Rimsky-Korsakov's *The Snow Maiden*.

Dance round the Golden Calf. Act II (scenes 3 and 4) of Schoenberg's *Moses und Aron*, in which the people indulge in an orgy at Aaron's instigation.

Danchet, Antoine (*b* Riom, 7 Sept. 1671; *d* Paris, 21 Feb. 1748). French librettist. Best known for his collaboration with Campra, for whom he produced many texts, including *Les fêtes vénitiennes* (1710), and *Achille et Déidamie* (1732). Their partnership, comparable to that of Lully and Quinault, conquered the French stage with spectacular and forceful works which vividly reflect the spirit of French classical tragedy. Danchet's libretto for *Idoménée* (1712) was adapted by Varesco for Mozart's *Idomeneo* (1781).

Danco, Suzanne (*b* Brussels, 22 Jan. 1911). Belgian soprano. Studied Brussels Cons. and Prague with Carpi. Début Genoa 1941 (Fiordiligi). Success throughout Italy, incl. at Milan, S, 1947–8; Naples, C, 1949; Gly. 1948–9; London, CG, 1951; also Vienna, Aix, Edinburgh, etc. A versatile singer of great musicality, successful as Donna Elvira, Mimì, Mélisande, Marie (*Wozzeck*), Jocasta, Ellen Orford. (R)

Dandini. Prince Ramiro's valet (bar) in Rossini's *La Cenerentola*.

Daniel, Paul (*b* Handsworth Wood, 5 July 1959). English conductor. Studied London GSMD, Italy with Ferrara, London with Boult and Downes. Staff cond. London, C, 1981–5; London, O Factory, founder cond. 1981, and music dir. 1987–90; music dir. O North from 1990; also Nancy (Fr. prem. *King Priam*) and London, CG, *Mitridate* (1993). Repertory incl. *Calisto*, *Return of Ulysses*, *Così*, *Don Giovanni*, first British *Jérusalem*, *Attila*, *Tosca*, *Mahagonny*, *Stone Guest*, *Akhnaten*, *Punch and Judy*, *Mask of Orpheus*. (R)

Daniels, Barbara (*b* Grenville, OH, 7 May 1946). US soprano. After study in Cincinnati, made her début with West Palm Beach O 1973 (Susanna). Sang at Innsbruck from 1974, Kassel 1976; roles included Manon, Fiordiligi, and Mozart's Countess. London, CG, 1978 (Rosalinde); New York, M, 1983 (Musetta). Most effective as a sympathetic exponent of Puccini roles: Minnie (New York, M, 1991); Butterfly, Mimì. (R)

Danon, Oskar (*b* Sarajevo, 7 Feb. 1913). Serbian conductor. Studied Prague with Křička and Dědeček. Cond. Sarajevo 1938–41. Dir. Belgrade O 1945–59, doing much to establish the company's national and then international reputation with performances of, in particular, the Russian repertory. Though himself a composer, he was less committed to building up a modern repertory. From 1960 he concentrated on conducting, and appeared in most European countries, the US, and Japan. (R)

Dantons Tod (Danton's Death). Opera in 2 parts by Gottfried von Einem; text by the composer and Blacher, after Büchner's drama (1835). Prem. Salzburg 6 Aug. 1947.

Paris, 1794. Danton (bar) is disillusioned by the French Revolution but sees little hope of changing the present situation. He and Desmoulins (ten), whose views accord with those of Danton, are arrested by Robespierre (bs) after disagreeing with him. Before the revolutionary tribunal, Danton makes a speech censuring the imminent dictatorship; he is sentenced to death. The mob greets his execution with singing and dancing.

Dapertutto. The evil sorcerer (bar) in the Giulietta episode of Offenbach's *Les contes d'Hoffmann*.

Daphne. Opera in 1 act by Richard Strauss; text by Josef Gregor, after the classical legend. Prem. Dresden 15 Oct. 1938.

By the hut of Peneios, mythological times. Daphne (sop), daughter of Peneios (bs) and Gaea (mez), is reprimanded by her mother for rejecting the shepherd Leukippos (ten), who loves her. The god Apollo (ten) comes down to earth disguised as a shepherd; he falls in love with Daphne, but she refuses to yield to him. Having revealed himself as the sun, Apollo kills Leukippos. Daphne is distraught, and Apollo begs Zeus to transform her into one of her laurel trees.

Da Ponte, Lorenzo (orig. Emanuele Conegliano) (*b* Ceneda, 10 Mar. 1749; *d* New York, 17 Aug. 1838). Italian librettist and poet. He studied for the priesthood, but was expelled from his seminary for adultery. In 1783 he settled in Vienna and, despite having written no librettos, was appointed poet to the Imperial Theatres. For several years he played a major role in Viennese operatic life, writing for all the major composers active there, including Gazzaniga, Martín y Soler, and Salieri. He is rightly immortalized, however, by the three masterpieces he produced for Mozart, *Le nozze di Figaro*, *Don Giovanni*, and *Così fan tutte*, which represent one of the great partnerships of operatic history. Though these are firmly rooted in the conventions, social distinctions, and attitudes of the day—many of which he satirized—the characters invariably convey a timeless message as relevant to a modern audience as to that of Enlightenment Vienna. In 1791 he was ordered to leave the city, having fallen foul of Leopold II. He became poet at London, H, then established himself as a printer, but was eventually forced to flee secretly to America in 1805 because of debt. From 1826 to 1837 he held a chair in Italian at Columbia U and also wrote his entertaining, Casanovesque autobiography.

Darclée, Hariclea (*b* Brăila, 10 June 1860; *d* Bucharest, 10 Jan. 1939). Romanian soprano. Studied Bucharest, and Paris with Faure. Début Paris, O, 1888 (Marguerite). Milan, S, from 1890; Moscow; St Petersburg, 1893–6; Buenos Aires, and New York, Academy T, 1896. Possessing physical and vocal beauty, she had success in a repertory ranging from Bellini and Donizetti heroines, Gilda, and Violetta, to Aida, Desdemona, and Valentine; she also sang many verismo roles, though her rather cold temperament was not ideally suited to the dramatic demands of the genre. She created La Wally, Tosca, and Iris. Though rich when she retired in 1918, she was forced to spend her declining years in the Verdi Home, Milan, and died penniless. (R) Her son **Ion Hartulary-Darclée** (*b* Paris, 7 July 1886; *d* Bucharest, 2 Apr. 1969), composer and conductor, studied Paris with Leroux and Widor, Milan with Amedeo and Victor de Sabata. Conducted in Italy, France, Switzerland, and Spain 1915–30. His operas include *Jaretiera* (1909), *La signorina sans-façon* (1920), and *Atlantic-City* (1930).

Dardanus. Opera in 5 acts by Rameau; text by Le Clerc de la Bruyère. Prem. Paris, O, 19 Nov. 1739.

Asia Minor, Antiquity. Teucer (bs) is at war with Dardanus (ten), son of Jupiter, and has promised to marry his daughter Iphise (sop) to Antenor (bs-bar), a neighbouring king. With the help of the magician Ismenor, Dardanus meets Iphise; they reveal their love for each other. He is saved from being killed through the intervention of Venus (sop); and other gods join her. A monster is sent to ravage Teucer's coasts, but Dardanus now comes to his enemy's aid and destroys the monster just as it is attacking Teucer. Peace is made between them, and Dardanus and Iphise are united.

Dargomyzhsky, Alexander (*b* Troitskoye, 14 Feb. 1813; *d* St Petersburg, 17 Jan. 1869). Russian composer. Originally destined for the Civil Service, he won himself a reputation in St Petersburg as a pianist and attempted his first opera, a setting of Hugo's *Lucrèce Borgia*. Abandoning this, he turned to another Hugo novel and completed *Esmeralda* in 1841. Though he later dismissed it as weak and trivial, over-influenced by Halévy and Meyerbeer (he might have added Auber), he was depressed by its failure to find a production and by the growing reputation of Glinka. In the 1850s he turned to the study of Russian folk-song, interesting himself especially in its dramatic and comic aspects, where Glinka had been drawn by its lyrical qualities. This led to a striking vividness in the recitative passages of *Rusalka* (1856) alongside the more immediately captivating songs: the comic role of the Miller was to become a favourite of singers including Shalyapin, and helped to win the opera wide popularity. However, dissatisfied with his artistic aims, he found himself drawn to the artists and writers associated with the satirical journal *Iskra* who were influenced by the Realist critics Belinsky and Chernyshevsky. Attempting to follow their precepts of an art that directly reflected truth in human behaviour, with as little intervention by artistic forms and formulas as possible, he began work on *Rogdana*, only to abandon it in dissatisfaction. For a time he travelled, and concentrated on orchestral music; but returning to Russia he found that some of his songs, each of which offers a vivid and immediately recognizable representation of a particular human character, had attracted the interest of Balakirev and his circle. These helped to give him a technical basis when he turned for his last opera to one of Pushkin's 'little tragedies', *The Stone Guest* (1872). Though already fatally ill, he worked at the opera with much support from his friends (at regular meetings to try out what he had written, Musorgsky would sing Leporello and the composer Don Juan, with Rimsky-Korsakov's future wife Nadezhda accompanying). He all but finished the work on his deathbed, leaving Cui to complete the last 60 bars of vocal score and Rimsky-Korsakov to orchestrate it.

Apart from two interpolated songs, *The Stone Guest* is a virtually complete setting of Pushkin's poem, composed with the aim of enhancing the verbal music and expressing the poetry musically, rather than subjecting it to compositional forms of any kind. In practice, some kind of compromise inevitably results; but Dargomyzhsky is ingenious in avoiding the risk of monotony in his unending recitative, and can move from simple parlando to a more lyrical manner, choosing his verbal emphases subtly and providing discreet but well-judged orchestral support. This, together with the use of a whole-tone scale motive for the Stone Guest, led to misjudged accusations of Wagnerism; but Dargomyzhsky's manner is radically different. *The Stone Guest* directly colours Rimsky-Korsakov's *Mozart and Salieri*, as well as the declamatory manner of Cui's *Feast in Time of Plague* and Rakhmaninov's *The Miserly Knight*. It has won a lasting place in Russian music as the classic of the Realist genre.

Dauvergne, Antoine (*b* Moulins, 3 Oct. 1713; *d* Lyons, 11 Feb. 1797). French violinist, composer, and theatrical director. A staunch supporter of Gluck, and an admirer of Italian music, he was director of the Paris, O, on four occasions between 1766 and 1790, for a total of 14 years.

His most famous opera was the 1-act *Les troqueurs* (1753), whose success was instrumental in concluding the *Guerre des Bouffons. Historically, it is important as the first French work on the model of the Italian intermezzo, using recitative instead of spoken dialogue, and it enjoyed popularity in many European countries. Dauvergne's other important works include *Hercule mourant* (1761) and *Polyxène* (1763): he also arranged many operas by other French composers, including Campra.

Davenant, (Sir) William (*b* Oxford, *bapt.* 3 Mar. 1606; *d* London, 7 Apr. 1668). English dramatist and theatre manager. His *The Siege of Rhodes* (1656), given at Rutland House with music (now lost) by various composers including Locke, is often cited as the first English opera, despite being preceded by Flecknoe's *Ariadne* (1654). By announcing *The Siege of Rhodes* as 'music and instruction' Davenant managed to evade the contemporary ban on stage plays. The work was notable for including the first appearance of a woman on stage in England.

David. Hans Sachs's apprentice (ten) in Wagner's *Die Meistersinger von Nürnberg*.

David. Opera in 5 acts by Milhaud; text by Lunel. Prem. (concert version in Hebrew) Jerusalem 1 June 1954 for 3,000th anniversary of foundation of Jerusalem. First stage perf. Milan, S, 2 Jan. 1955.

The opera is based on the events chronicled in I and II Sam. David (bar), a warrior and poet, is chosen to succeed Saul (bar) as King of Israel. The giant Goliath (bs) challenges the Israelites to send a champion to fight him. David slays Goliath, and Saul's jealousy is such that he attempts to murder David. Saul and his son Jonathan are killed in battle shortly afterwards. As the new King of Israel, David chooses the site for the new city of Jerusalem. He takes another wife, Bathsheba, and their second son Solomon eventually succeeds David as King, thus fulfilling the prophecy.

David, Félicien (*b* Cadenet, 13 Apr. 1810; *d* Saint-Germain-en-Laye, 29 Aug. 1876). French composer. Studied Aix-en-Provence with Michel and Roux, Paris with Millault and Fétis. He espoused Saint-Simonism, and when the sect was dispersed in 1832 he left for Egypt. Here he found inspiration for his 'oriental' works, which included operas. *Herculanum* (1859) is in Grand Opera vein, and naturally ends with the eruption of Vesuvius; but he won greater popularity with the more modestly atmospheric *Lalla-Roukh* (1862). He also stimulated more distinguished contemporaries (among them Gounod, Bizet, and especially Delibes) in their oriental operas. His delicate, tuneful music was much admired by Bizet, whose most immediate predecessor he was.

Davies, Arthur (*b* Wrexham, 11 Apr. 1941). Welsh tenor. Studied at the RNCM, and sang with WNO from 1972: Nemorino, Rodolfo, Don José, Ferrando. London, CG, from 1976, as Alfredo, Pinkerton, and Foresto (*Attila*). Notably successful as the Duke of Mantua in Jonathan Miller's Mafia *Rigoletto*; also admired as Faust, Cavaradossi, and Don Ottavio. Sang Gaston (*Jérusalem*) for O North, 1990. (R)

Davies, Dennis Russell (*b* Toledo, OH, 16 Apr. 1944). US conductor. After study at Juilliard, led the prem. of Berio's *Opera*, S Fe 1970. Bayreuth 1978 (*Fliegender Holländer*). Music dir. at Stuttgart 1980–7; Bonn from 1987. A leading exponent of the modern repertory, he conducted Henze's original version of *König Hirsch* (Stuttgart 1985); prems. of *The English Cat* (Schwetzingen 1983), *Akhnaten* (Stuttgart 1983) and Bolcom's *McTeague* (Chicago 1992).

Davies, (Sir) Peter Maxwell (*b* Manchester, 8 Sept. 1934). English composer. Studied Manchester, Rome with Petrassi. Early in his career he became interested in the dramatic presentation of music, sometimes using a single costumed performer (as with the startlingly Expressionist *Revelation and Fall* (1968) and *Eight Songs for a Mad King* (1969)) or a dancer (*Vesalii Icones* (1969)). These brilliantly effective pieces draw on a wide range of sources, medieval music and Lehár waltzes in the first, free and controlled improvisation in the second (whose published score reflects the cage which on the stage partly represents the King's madness), Victorian hymns in the last. These diverse kinds of music are brought together sometimes for dramatic contrast or shock, sometimes for the shedding of mutual light, sometimes curdled by parody. There is throughout a powerful feeling for dramatic effect that by no means excludes doing violence to the music parodied as well as to the audience's sensibilities. There is even an underlying note of blasphemy, disclosed also in the opera *Taverner* (Christ set against Antichrist (1972)), where despite some excellent and characteristic music, drawing on Taverner's own, the stage convention did not seem ideal for Davies's imagination.

After Davies moved to Orkney in the early 1970s, the religious element that he had been contesting came to the fore, and the challenge of working with amateurs and children (which he had brilliantly met early in his career at Cirencester Grammar School) led to the highly effective chamber opera *The Martyrdom of St Magnus* (1977), which contains elements of mystery play and also dislocation of music as well as of time and place; also to a charming piece for children, *The Two Fiddlers* (1978), requiring the young soloists both to play and to sing. The experience of living in a remote, bare landscape stimulated much in his art (even though his compelling personality drew audiences from far and wide to take part in his musical events), and one of his strongest stage works resulted in the taut, compelling opera *The Lighthouse* (1980). As before, diverse musics, including banjo songs and Victorian ballads, are used in a score of frightening claustrophobic power as the drama of vanished lighthousemen becomes a parable of extremes of metaphysical experience.

His most recent works include *Resurrection* (1988), *Redemption* (1988), and *The Doctors of Myddfai* (1996).

Davies, Ryland (*b* Cwm, Ebbw Vale, 9 Feb. 1943). Welsh tenor. Studied Manchester with Freddie Cox. Début WNO, 1964 (Rossini's Almaviva). Gly. 1968; London, CG, from 1969;

Salzburg 1970; Paris 1974; New York, M, 1975. Repertory includes Belmonte, Don Ottavio, Ernesto, Hylas, Lensky. Possesses a pleasing light tenor, and a sympathetic stage presence. (R)

Davies, Tudor (*b* Cymmer, 12 Nov. 1892; *d* Penarth, 2 Apr. 1958). Welsh tenor. Studied London with Gustave García. Joined London, BNOC at its inception; CG, début 1921 (Rodolfo). Created Hugh the Drover, and leading roles in Holst's *At the Boar's Head* and Smyth's *Fête galante*. S Francisco 1928 (Lohengrin). London: Old Vic and SW 1931–41; CR, 1941–6; then retired. Possessed a fresh, warm voice that later deteriorated through singing the wrong roles. (R)

Davis, Andrew (*b* Ashridge, 2 Feb. 1944). English conductor. Studied Rome with Ferrara. Début Gly. 1973 (*Capriccio*). Music director, Gly., 1988. New York, M, from 1981; also Milan, S; London, CG. Repertory incl. *Figaro*, *Barber*, *Salome*, *Ariadne*, *Kátá Kabanová*, *Jenůfa*. (R)

Davis, (Sir) **Colin** (*b* Weybridge, 25 Sept. 1927). English conductor. Studied clarinet at London, RCM. Début as cond. with London, COG, 1949 (*Impresario*, concert). After appointment with BBC Scottish Orch., London, SW, 1958, music dir. 1961–4. Gly. 1960 (*Zauberflöte*). London, CG, 1965 (*Figaro*), music dir. 1971–86. New York, M, 1967 (*Peter Grimes*). Bayreuth 1978 (*Tannhäuser*: first British cond.). He first made his name in Mozart, and his clarity of line but passionate feeling have been no less manifest in the composer with whom he became even more closely associated, Berlioz. His performances of Tippett won the trust of the composer, as well as the admiration of the audiences, for their lucidity in articulating textures and meanings that had often proved confusing. He conducted the prems. of *The Knot Garden* (1970) and *The Ice Break* (1977). (R)

Davydov, Stepan (*b*?, 1777; *d* St Petersburg, 22 May 1825). Russian composer. Studied St Petersburg with Sarti. He worked in the St Petersburg Drama School 1800–4 and 1806–10. He was music director of Count Sheremetyev's private theatre from 1815, and also taught singing at the Moscow Drama School. He is best known for his work on *Lesta* (1803). Basically a German Singspiel, which had been brought to Russia by *Cavos, the piece was reworked and augmented by Davydov.

Making use of both town and country songs, he gave it a distinctive Russian flavour and at the same time a distinctive Romantic colouring. He is one of the most important Russian opera composers before Glinka, who knew *Lesta* and may have been influenced by it.

Dean, Stafford (*b* Kingswood, 20 June 1937). English bass. Studied at London, RAM, and toured with Opera for All before Gly. début in 1964 (Lictor in *Poppea*). London: SW, from 1964 as Zuniga, Sparafucile, Daland; CG, from 1969 (début as Masetto). He has given particular distinction to such roles as Leporello (more than 300 performances) and Mozart's Figaro (New York, M, 1976). (R)

De Angelis, Nazzareno (*b* Rome, 17 Nov. 1881; *d* Rome, 14 Dec. 1962). Italian bass. Studied with Ricci and Prati. Début Aquila, 1903 (Podestà, *Linda di Chamounix*). S America 1909–25; Chicago 1911–12. Repertory included *La vestale*, *Medea*, *Barbiere*, *Don Carlos*, *Tristan*, and *Walküre*. Created Archibaldo in Montemezzi's *L'amore dei tre re*. A moving and noble actor, he was the best Italian bass of his generation. His most famous role was Mefistofele (Boito), which he sang 987 times. (R)

Death in Venice. Opera in 2 acts by Britten; text by Myfanwy Piper, after Thomas Mann's novella *Der Tod in Venedig* (1912). Prem. Snape 16 June 1973.

Munich and Vienna. Aschenbach (ten), a famous writer, leaves Germany for Venice. Here he succumbs to the allure of a boy, Tadzio (dancer), who represents the Dionysiac side of his character which he has hitherto suppressed beneath a cool Apollonian view of life. He tries to leave the cholera-stricken city, but is frustrated by an accident to his luggage, and returns to indulge his solitary and self-devouring obsession. Watching Tadzio playing on the beach with other boys, he collapses and dies.

The opera is cast in scenes connected by interludes, and makes prominent use of dance; the roles of the figures (such as an Elderly Fop) who contribute to Aschenbach's downfall are all taken by the same baritone.

De Bassini, Achille (*b* Milan, 5 May 1819; *d* Cava dei Tirreni, 3 July 1881). Italian baritone. Studied Milan with Perelli. Début possibly Voghera 1837 in *Belisario* (Donizetti) and then *Norma*. Padua 1838 and 1842; Milan, S, from 1842. Rome 1844, creating Francesco in

I due Foscari. Repeated this success at Milan S, where he also sang in *Ernani*, *Attila*, and *Alzira*, as well as many new operas by Rossi, Ricci, etc. Created Seid in *Il corsaro* (Trieste 1848); Miller in *Luisa Miller* (Naples 1849). Verdi, seeing in him 'a certain humorous vein', despite his talent for noble and suffering characters, wrote Fra Melitone in *La forza del destino* for him; he had also thought first of him when conceiving *Rigoletto*. St Petersburg 1852–63. London, CG, 1859 (Germont, Luna, etc.). His wife, the soprano (really mezzo-soprano) **Rita Gabussi** (*b* Bologna, *c*.1815; *d* Naples, 26 Jan. 1891), made her début Milan 1830 (Rosina). Successful throughout Italy, particularly as Giovanna in Ricci's *La prigione di Edimburgo*, and Mercadante's Medea (roles she created). Her gift for portraying violent, dramatic women caused Verdi to request her, unsuccessfully, as the first Azucena. Her voice declined prematurely through singing roles too high for her. Their son **Alberto** (*b* Florence, 14 July 1847; *d* ?) was a tenor, later baritone. Début Venice 1869 (*Belisario*). After success in Rossini and Donizetti, specialized in French repertory, 1880–90. Emigrated to US 1898. (R)

De Begnis, Giuseppe (*b* Lugo, 1793; *d* New York, Aug. 1849). Italian bass. Début Modena 1812 (Pavesi's *Ser Marcantonio*). Became leading buffo; engaged by Rossini 1817 as first Dandini. Paris, I, 1819–22. London, H, 1821–3, with his wife, in *Il turco in Italia*, and *Mosè*. Directed opera at Bath 1823–4, and Dublin 1834–7. A distinguished Dr Bartolo (*Barbiere*). His wife was the soprano **Giuseppina Ronzi de Begnis** (*b* Milan, 11 Jan. 1800; *d* Florence, 7 June 1853). Début Bologna 1816. After successes in Italy (including Nina in *La gazza ladra* under Rossini), Paris, I, 1819–22, where she was a notable Donna Anna. London 1821–3, in Rossini. Separating from De Begnis in 1825, she returned to Italy and sang at Naples, and Milan, S. Created Donizetti's Fausta, Sancia di Castiglia, Gemma di Vergy, Elisabeth in *Roberto Devereux*, and Maria Stuarda (during the rehearsals for this she attacked her rival Anna del Serre, who had to retire to bed for a fortnight). London, CG, 1843 (Norma). An admirable singer, she was also 'a superb figure of a woman' (Cottrau), and was reputedly the mistress of several younger men, including Donizetti (who compared her, as an artist, favourably with Malibran), and Ferdinand II of Sicily.

Debora e Jaële. Opera in 3 acts by Pizzetti; text by the composer, after Judges 4 and 5. Prem. Milan, S, 16 Dec. 1922.

Israel, c.1100 BC. Jaële (sop) is accused by the Hebrews of friendship with their enemy, Sisera (ten). Debora (mez) promises them victory and persuades Jaële to go to the enemy's camp and kill Sisera; but when the moment comes, Jaële cannot bring herself to do this. The Hebrews launch a successful battle and Sisera seeks refuge with Debora, who kills him to save him from more horrible tortures at the hands of his captors.

Debussy, (Achille-) **Claude** (b Saint-Germain-en-Laye, 22 Aug. 1862; d Paris, 25 Mar. 1918). French composer. Studied Paris with Lavignac, Guiraud, and others including, briefly, Franck. Despite plans for operas on the subject of Tristram and Yseult and on As You Like It, among other projects, Debussy's only completed opera is Pelléas et Mélisande (1902). His attraction to Maeterlinck (he had previously unsuccessfully sought permission to set La Princesse Maleine) was in part for the opportunity its shadowy, Symbolist world offered as a counter to Wagner and verismo. The score is certainly non-Wagnerian in its discretion, its understatement, and its very French attention to niceties of language-setting; but the shadow of Parsifal falls (constructively) across the work, and Debussy's very personal use of motive (generally evoking atmosphere or states of mind) would not have evolved as it did without the example of Wagner to resist. No less strong an influence was Boris Godunov, whose declamatory style and episodic structure also impressed Debussy. His command of atmosphere lends strength to the rather slender Symbolist structure of Maeterlinck, who was unwise enough to oppose the opera and even threaten Debussy with assault when the role of Mélisande was removed from his wife Georgette Leblanc, and given to Mary Garden by Carré, director of the Opéra-Comique. Further problems during the work's preparation for production arose when it was discovered that more time was needed for the scene changes: from this arose the interludes now generally regarded as a vital part of the musical fabric.

Of Debussy's other operatic projects, the two that most occupied him were both attempts at setting Poe, who greatly influenced his ideas. Le diable dans le beffroi suggests a novel approach to operatic choral writing (and has a whistling part for the Devil); La chute de la maison Usher was a further exploration of a world of morbid melancholia implicit in Pelléas and here made the emotional centre of what survives of the work.

Decembrists, The. Opera in 4 acts by Shaporin; text by Vsevolod Rozhdestvensky, using verses by A. N. Tolstoy and based on events of the Dec. 1825 rising. Prem. Moscow, B, 23 June 1953.

Russia, 1825. Dmitri Shchepin-Rostovsky (ten) is discontented with the system of ownership and serfdom, and joins forces with young aristocrats who also want to see an end to the system. The Decembrists plan an attack to capture the new Tsar, but the leaders, including Dmitri, are arrested, and sentenced to exile in Siberia. He is followed there by Yelena (sop), who loves him.

'Deh, vieni alla finestra'. Don Giovanni's (bar) serenade to Elvira's maid in Act II of Mozart's Don Giovanni, in which he sings to his own mandolin accompaniment (often played pizzicato on an orchestral violin).

'Deh, vieni non tardar'. Susanna's (sop) aria in Act IV of Mozart's Le nozze di Figaro, in which she tantalizes Figaro.

De Lara (orig. Cohen), **Isidore** (b London, 9 Aug. 1858; d Paris, 2 Sept. 1935). English composer. Studied Milan with Mazzucato, Paris with Lalo. Maurel suggested that he should rewrite his cantata The Light of Asia as an opera, which was performed as La luce dell'Asia at London, CG, 1892. His Amy Robsart was given a single performance there the following year. His compositions owe much to Massenet and Saint-Saëns. He constantly campaigned for the establishment of a permanent British opera company.

Delibes, Léo (b Saint-Germain-du-Val, 21 Feb. 1836; d Paris, 16 Jan. 1891). French composer. Studied Paris, with Tariot and Adam, whose opéras-comiques much influenced him. His first stage work, described as an 'asphyxie lyrique', was Deux sous de charbon (1856), staged at the Folies-Nouvelles. This initiated a long series of operettas that continued with the hugely successful Deux vieilles gardes (1856). He first attempted opéra-comique with Le jardinier et son seigneur; this was given in 1863 at the Lyrique, where he worked as chorus-master before moving on to the Opéra, first as accompanist and then as chorus-master under Massé. This turned his interests towards ballet, and he won fame with *Sylvia* and *Coppélia*. But opera drew him back, and he wrote three works for the Opéra-Comique, *Le roi l'a dit* (1873), *Jean de Nivelle* (1880) (a work close to Grand Opera style), and his masterpiece *Lakmé* (1883). In keeping with the current vogue for the East, an opéra-comique tradition refreshed by the Romantic poets' fascination, and stimulated further by the example of Félicien *David, Delibes set his tale of the English lieutenant and the Indian girl with a wealth of delightful mock-oriental melody. It is chiefly for the charming tunefulness and the decorative scoring that *Lakmé*, which owes much to Bizet, and the ballets retain an appeal which led Tchaikovsky to prefer Delibes to Brahms and Wagner.

Delius, Frederick (*b* Bradford, 29 Jan. 1862; *d* Grez-sur-Loing, 10 June 1934). English composer. Studied privately during his time working on an orange grove in Florida, later in Leipzig (less beneficially) with Sitt, Reinecke, and Jadassohn. Delius's operas belong to the earlier part of his career. *Irmelin* (comp. 1890–2) has few of his mature characteristics apart from harmonic felicity and a feeling for orchestral colour; but more personal experiences, especially those deriving from his Florida period, show in the more vivid score of *Koanga* (1904). His most striking work, however, is *A Village Romeo and Juliet* (1907). Here his acute sense of chromatic harmony (deriving in part from Grieg) and his expressive orchestration are at the service of a pessimistic tale of doomed young love that owes something to aspects of Wagner. *Margot-la-rouge* (comp. 1902) was a verismo attempt to win an international Sanzogno competition. His last opera, *Fennimore and Gerda* (1919), reflects his love of Scandinavia and is a lighter-textured work than *A Village Romeo and Juliet*, whose techniques it in other ways reflects. In part through Beecham's advocacy, the characteristic short orchestral pieces that are a feature of Delius's operas have entered the concert repertory.

Della Casa, Lisa (*b* Burgdorf, 2 Feb. 1919). Swiss soprano. Studied Zurich with Haeser. Début Solothurn-Biel 1941 (Butterfly). Zurich 1943–50; Gly. 1951 (Mozart's Countess); Bayreuth, 1952 (Eva); Vienna, S, 1952–74; New York, M, 1953–68; London, CG, 1953, and 1965 in her most famous role, Arabella. Created roles in Burkhard's *Die schwarze Spinne*, and Einem's *Der Prozess*. Retired 1974. An outstanding Richard Strauss and Mozart singer with a controlled legato and finely spun vocal line. (R)

Deller, Alfred (*b* Margate, 31 May 1912; *d* Bologna, 16 July 1979). English countertenor. Self-taught. While a member of Canterbury Cathedral choir, was heard by Tippett, who arranged his London début, Morley Coll. 1943. Founded Deller Consort, 1950. Influential in the revival of the counter-tenor voice, he performed neglected music of the 16th and 17th cents., but also contemporary works. Inspired many composers, including Rubbra, and Britten, who was drawn by the other-worldly quality of his voice to write Oberon in *A Midsummer Night's Dream* for him. Highly musical and intelligent, he used his pure tone to lyrical and expressive effect. (R)

Delle Sedie, Enrico (*b* Livorno, 17 June 1822; *d* La Garenne-Colombes, 28 Nov. 1907). Italian baritone. Studied with C. Galeffi and Persanola. Début S Casciano 1851 (Nabucco). Milan, S, 1859; Vienna 1859; London, L, 1861, first Renato. Paris, I, 1861–74, in Donizetti, Rossini, and Verdi. London, CG, 1862 (Don Giovanni, Germont, Malatesta). Though possessing a limited voice, he was a sensitive artist, exceptional in style and taste. After his retirement, 1874, taught at Paris Cons., and wrote a significant and comprehensive singing method.

Dello Joio, Norman (*b* New York, 24 Jan. 1913). US composer. Studied New York with Wagenaar, also with Hindemith. His most important dramatic music has been concerned with Joan of Arc. His first opera *The Triumph of St Joan* (1950) was withdrawn after its prem.; rev. version for TV as *The Trial at Rouen* (1955); this was further revised as *The Triumph of St Joan* (1959). Other operas have been *The Ruby* (1955) and *Blood Moon* (1961).

Delmas, Francisque (Jean-François) (*b* Lyons, 14 Apr. 1861; *d* Saint-Alban de Monthel, 29 Sept. 1933). French bass-baritone. Studied Paris with Bussine and Obin. Début Paris, O, 1886 (Saint-Bris, *Les Huguenots*). Sang there until 1927, creating more than 50 roles, including parts in *Thaïs*, *Monna Vanna*, and D'Indy's *L'étranger*. The first

French Wotan (his most famous role), Hagen, and Gurnemanz, and first Paris Sachs. A noble actor with a large, smooth, and even voice, his versatility encompassed Gluck, Mozart, and Weber. (R)

Del Monaco, Mario (*b* Florence, 27 July 1915; *d* Mestre, 16 Oct. 1982). Italian tenor. Studied Pesaro with Melocchi; later taught himself, studying records of the great singers of the past. Official début Pesaro 1941 (Pinkerton). London, CG, 1946, 1961. S Francisco 1950; New York, M, 1950–9; also Milan, S; Buenos Aires, C; Verona. Gifted with a powerful and vigorous voice, he was popular in the verismo and Verdi repertory, particularly as Canio, Chénier, and Otello. (R) His son **Giancarlo Del Monaco** (*b* Venice, 27 Dec. 1943) is a successful producer of opera in Europe and at New York, M (*Simon Boccanegra*, 1995).

De Los Angeles, Victoria. See LOS ANGELES, VICTORIA DE.

De Luca, Giuseppe (*b* Rome, 25 Dec. 1876; *d* New York, 25 Aug. 1950). Italian baritone. Studied Rome with Persichini and Cotogni. Début Piacenza, 1897 (Valentin). Milan, L, 1902, creating Michonnet (*Adriana Lecouvreur*); Milan, S, 1903–4, creating Sharpless, and Gleby in Giordano's *Siberia*. London, CG, 1907, 1910, 1935; New York, M, 1915–35, 1939–40, 1945–6. Here he appeared over 700 times in 50 operas, creating Paquiro in *Goyescas* and Gianni Schicchi. A classic exponent of the bel canto style, his repertory covered Malatesta, Rossini's Figaro, and Alberich; he was also an admired Rigoletto. Retired 1947. (R)

De Lucia, Fernando (*b* Naples, 11 Oct. 1860; *d* Naples, 21 Feb. 1925). Italian tenor. Studied Naples. Début Naples, C, 1885 (Gounod's Faust). London, DL, 1887. Rome 1891. Created Amico Fritz 1891, and Osaka (*Iris*) 1898. Florence 1892, and Milan 1895, in first *I Rantzau* and *Silvano* (Mascagni). London, CG, 1892–6, 1900 (Fritz, Canio, Cavaradossi, Turiddu); New York, M, 1893–4. Retired Naples 1917, and taught; pupils included Németh, Pederzini, and Thill. An excellent actor, and a master of bel canto, he was a distinctive and memorable singer, renowned for his Rossini, Bellini, and Verdi, but also enormously successful in the verismo roles. (R)

De Lussan, Zélie (*b* New York, 21 Dec. 1861;

d London, 18 Dec. 1949), US soprano. Studied with her mother. Début Boston 1885. London: CR, 1889, CG, 1895–1902; Beecham OC, 1910. New York, M, 1894–5 (first US Nannetta), and 1898–1900. Highly acclaimed as Carmen (which she sang over 2,000 times), Mignon, Cherubino, and Nedda. (R)

Demetrio. Opera in 3 acts by Hasse; text by Metastasio. Prem. Venice, GG, Jan. 1732. Rev. Vienna 1734 as *Cleonice*; also given as *Cleonice* Dresden 8 Feb. 1740.

Demetrio (sop cas) is brought up not knowing that his father was the exiled King of Syria; Cleonice (sop), daughter of the usurper Alessandro, falls in love with him. Alessandro is killed in an uprising and Cleonice, now heir to the throne, must find a husband. Eventually, Demetrio re-emerges, having been fighting on Alessandro's side; his identity is revealed and he marries Cleonice, regaining possession of his father's throne.

'De' miei bollenti spiriti'. Alfredo's (ten) aria which opens Act II of Verdi's *La traviata*, in which he sings of his happiness with Violetta.

Demofoonte. Opera in 3 acts by Jommelli; text by Metastasio. Prem. Stuttgart 11 Feb. 1764.

Demophoön (ten), King of Chersonnesus, seeks to put an end to the annual sacrifice of a virgin demanded of him by the gods. The oracle of Apollo (bs) replies that the practice may cease 'when the innocent usurper of a kingdom is recognized by himself'. Demophoön selects Dircea (sop) for sacrifice, not realizing that she is secretly married to his own son, Timante (sop). When Demophoön discovers this he at first condemns them both to death, but then pardons them.

Demon, The. Opera in 3 acts by Anton Rubinstein; text by Pavel Viskovatov, after Lermontov's poem (1841). Prem. St Petersburg, M, 25 Jan. 1875.

Caucasus, legendary times. The Demon (bar), a human with satanic traits, falls in love with Tamara (sop), daughter of Prince Gudal (bs), who is to be married the following day. In the hope of winning her, he has her lover Synodal (ten) killed. Tamara hides herself away in a convent but is pursued there by the Demon. As she begins to yield, the Angel (sop) intervenes, and she is borne off to Heaven.

Dempsey, Gregory (*b* Melbourne, 20 July 1931). Australian tenor. Studied as baritone, but sang Don Ottavio at Melbourne 1954. London, SW, from 1962 (prem. of *The Mines of Sulphur* 1965). His admirable diction and strong acting made him particularly successful in Janáček roles: Shuratov (*From the House of the Dead*); Gregor (*Makropoulos Case*); Števa (London, CG, 1972) and Brouček (ENO 1978). Also memorable as David, Peter Grimes, and Dionysus in *The Bassarids* (British prem., 1974). (R)

Denmark. Opera was first given in the mid-17th cent., and attempts were made to initiate Danish opera with librettos by N. H. Bredal set by Sarti. These and other works were Italianate. The first opera by a Dane was *Der vereinigte Götterstreit* (1698; lost) by Poul Schindler (1648–1740). The most important composers of the 18th cent. who tried to establish Danish opera were J. E. Hartmann (1726–93) and Friedrich *Kunzen (1761–1817); the latter's *Holger Danske* (1789, after Wieland's *Oberon*) won respect. The German J. A. P. *Schulz (1747–1800) attempted a form of Danish Singspiel based on the popular French opéra-comique; he had some success with *Host-geldet* (Harvest Festival, 1790) and *Peters Bryllup* (Peter's Wedding, 1793). Romanticism was slow to influence the young tradition, but is apparent in some of the six operas by Christoph *Weyse (1774–1842); these include some to texts by Oehlenschläger and Hans Andersen. The influence of Cherubini, and through him Weber, shows in the operas of Friedrich *Kuhlau (1786–1832).

The real influence of Romanticism is revealed in the work of J. P. E. Hartmann (1808–1900; grandson of J. E. Hartmann). He collaborated with Oehlenschläger on *Korsarerne* (The Corsairs, 1835) and with Hans Andersen on *Liden Kirsten* (Little Kristina, 1846). Niels Gade (1817–90) wrote the somewhat Mendelssohnian *Mariotta* (1850) (and left a fragmentary *Siegfried og Brunhilde*), and Peter *Heise (1830–79) *Drot og Marsk* (King and Marshal, 1878), in which there is an influence of Wagner; Berlioz is suggested in *La vendetta* (1870) by Asger Hamerik (1843–1923). Folklore and folk music are drawn upon by Peter Lange-Müller (1850–1926) in *Vikingeblod* (The Blood of the Vikings, 1900). A more eclectic composer was August *Enna (1859–1939). The dominating talent of the later period was Carl *Nielsen (1865–1931),

with *Saul og David* (1902) and *Maskarade* (1906). Other successful works have included *Den kongelige gæst* (The Royal Guest, 1919) by Hakon Børresen (1876–1954); *Fête galante* (1931) by Paul Schierbeck (1888–1949), also composer of *Tiggerens opera* (1936, a version of *The Beggar's Opera*); and *Marie Grubbe* by Poul Olsen (1922–82); *Labyrinten* (1963) and *Gilgamesh* (1973) by Per Nørgård (*b* 1932); and *Sandheddns Hævn* (The Revenge of Truth, 1985) by Ib Nørholm (*b* 1931).

Denzler, Robert (*b* Zurich, 19 Mar. 1892; *d* Zurich, 25 Aug. 1972). Swiss conductor. Studied Zurich with Andreae. Répétiteur Zurich and Bayreuth. Music dir., Zurich O, 1915–27, 1934–47. Cond. first *Lulu* (1937) and *Mathis der Maler* (1938). (R)

'Depuis le jour'. Louise's (sop) aria in Act III of Charpentier's *Louise*, recalling the day when she first yielded to Julien.

De Reszke, Édouard (*b* Warsaw, 22 Dec. 1853; *d* Garnek, 25 May 1917). Polish bass, brother of Jean. Studied Warsaw with Ciaffei, Italy with Steller and Coletti. Début Paris, O, 1876 as the King (*Aida*), under Verdi. Milan, S, 1879–81, Fiesco in revised *Boccanegra*, and created roles in works by Ponchielli and Gomez. London, CG, 1890–4; Chicago 1891. With his brother Jean was a key member of the Paris, O, London, CG, and New York, M, companies during the last decade of the 19th cent.; they often appeared together, e.g. in *Don Giovanni*, *Faust* (Gounod), *Hérodiade*, *Roméo et Juliette*, and first *Le Cid*. A distinguished Méphistophélès (Gounod), Frère Laurent, and Leporello, he later added Wagner to his vast repertory, including Sachs (one of his greatest interpretations), Gurnemanz, Mark, and Hagen. Retired 1903, and after unsuccessful attempts to teach in London and Warsaw, withdrew to his Polish estate. Here, after the outbreak of war in 1914, he lived in extreme poverty and seclusion, first in his cellar and then in a cave. One of operatic history's great basses: a huge man with an imposing dramatic presence, possessing a voluminous, rich, and flexible voice. (R)

De Reszke, Jean (*b* Warsaw, 14 Jan. 1850; *d* Nice, 3 Apr. 1925). Polish tenor. Brother of Édouard. Studied Warsaw with Ciaffei, Rome with Cotogni. Début as baritone, Venice, F, 1874 (Alfonso, *La favorite*). London, DL, 1874 (Alfonso, Don Giovanni, Valentin). Paris 1876 (Fra Melitone and Rossini's Figaro). After further study with Sbriglia, made début as tenor, Madrid 1879 (Robert le diable), with little success. Paris, I, 1884 re-emerged triumphantly as John the Baptist (*Hérodiade*). Paris, O, 1885–1902, Radamès, Vasco da Gama, etc., and Roméo (under Gounod) and Rodrigue (*Le Cid*), which he created. London, DL, 1887 (Radamès, Lohengrin). London, CG, 1888–1900 (Raoul, Gounod's Faust, Walther, Siegfried, Werther). Chicago from 1891; New York, M, 1891–1901. His last appearance was his only one as Canio, Paris 1902. After retiring, he taught in Paris and Nice, his pupils including Edvina, Sayão, Slezak, and Teyte. Vocally in direct descent from Mario, and with a handsome physique, he was ideal for French and Italian romantic roles, but later also achieved huge success in the heavy Wagner repertory (acclaimed for his impeccable declamation of the German text as much as for the beauty of his singing). His astonishing versatility enabled him to sing such disparate roles as Lohengrin, Roméo (Gounod), Don José, Faust (Gounod), Radamès, and Tristan, all within days of each other. A unique figure in history, he stands at the pinnacle of operatic achievement. A record label exists, suggesting that he may have recorded. Sister to the De Reszke brothers was **Joséphine** (*b* Warsaw, 4 June 1855; *d* Warsaw, 22 Feb. 1891), soprano. Studied with Nissen-Salomon. Début Venice 1874 (*Il Guarany*). Madrid 1879 (Alice, with Jean as Robert). Paris, O, 1874–84, very successfully as Marguerite, Rachel, Valentine, etc., and created Sita in *Le roi de Lahore*. Sang with Édouard and Jean in *Hérodiade*, Paris 1884; then retired, having married Baron Leopold de Kronenburg, and sang for charities in Warsaw.

'Der Hölle Rache'. The Queen of the Night's (sop) aria in Act II of Mozart's *Die Zauberflöte*, swearing revenge upon Sarastro. Famous for the top Fs it requires of the singer.

D'Erlanger, Frédéric. See ERLANGER, FRÉDÉRIC D'.

Dermota, Anton (*b* Kropa, 4 June 1910; *d* Vienna, 22 June 1989). Slovene, later Austrian, tenor. Studied Vienna with Rado. Début Cluj 1934. Vienna 1936–80 (First Armed Man, then Alfredo, Lensky, Rodolfo, Jeník, Des Grieux (Puccini), David, Flamand, Florestan); later sang character parts. Salzburg from 1935 (Ferrando, Belmonte, Don Ottavio). London, CG, 1947 (Ferrando,

Narraboth). Also Milan, Paris, etc. A fine artist, with a sweet-timbred, distinctive voice; memorable as a Mozart singer. (R)

Dernesch, Helga (*b* Vienna, 3 Feb. 1939). Austrian soprano. Studied Vienna Cons. Début Berne 1961 (Marina, *Boris*). Wiesbaden 1963–5; Bayreuth 1965–8; Scottish O from 1969; Salzburg 1969–74; London, CG, from 1970. Roles include Leonore, Marschallin, Cassandre, Isolde, Brünnhilde, Sieglinde. Created Goneril (Reimann's *Lear*), title-role in Fortner's *Elisabeth Tudor*. From 1979 sang mezzo-soprano parts, e.g. Fricka, Herodias, Dyer's Wife. Created Hecula in Reimann's *Troades* (1986). An intense performer with a warm, full tone. (R)

'Der Vogelfänger bin ich, ja'. Papageno's (bar) aria introducing himself as the bird-catcher in Act I of Mozart's *Die Zauberflöte*.

De Sabata, Victor (*b* Trieste, 11 Apr. 1892; *d* S Margherita Ligure, 11 Dec. 1967). Italian conductor and composer. Studied Milan with Saladino and Orefice. His *Il macigno* (The Boulder) was prem. Milan, S, 1917. Cond. Monte Carlo 1918 (*Traviata*); appointed cond. 1919–29, giving first *Enfant et les sortilèges* (1925). Milan, S, 1930–9, 1941–3, 1947–53, artistic dir. 1953–7. Bayreuth 1939 (*Tristan*, very widely praised). London, CG, 1950 with Milan S. Was working on a second opera at the time of his death. A brilliant, masterful conductor, whose incandescent and exciting readings suggested comparisons with Toscanini's; they were perhaps less instinctive, but more intellectually penetrating. (R)

Désaugiers, Marc-Antoine (*b* Fréjus, 1742; *d* Paris, 10 Sept. 1793). French composer. A friend of Gluck and Sacchini, he first came to attention in 1776 with a translation of a famous treatise on vocal technique by Giovanni Battista Mancini, and three years later had his first stage success with *Le petit Œdipe*, a verse comedy with ariettes and vaudevilles. This paved the way for the production of about ten successful operatic works 1780–92. Most popular were *Erixène, ou L'amour enfant* (1780) and the 1-act *Les deux jumeaux de Bergame* (1782).

Deschamps-Jehin, Blanche (*b* Lyons, 18 Sept. 1859; *d* Paris, June 1923). French mezzo-soprano. Studied Lyons and Paris. Début Brussels, M, 1879 (Mignon). Sang there until 1885, creating Massenet's Hérodiade, and

Uta in Reyer's *Sigurd*. Paris: OC, 1885–91, O, 1891–7, then OC until 1902. London, CG, 1891–2 (Carmen and Fidès). Created Margared (*Le roi d'Ys*), and the Mother (*Louise*). A particularly successful Amneris and Dalila; possessed a rich and unusually homogeneous voice. (R)

Desdemona. Otello's wife (mez) in Rossini's and (sop) in Verdi's *Otello*.

Desderi, Claudio (*b* Alessandria, 9 Apr. 1943). Italian baritone and conductor. Studied in Florence and made début at Edinburgh 1969, as Gaudenzio in *Il signor Bruschino*. Sang with the company of Milan, S, at London, CG (1976), returning for Royal O début 1987 (Mozart's Figaro). His comic gifts have been admired at Gly. from 1981, as Rossini's Bartolo, Don Magnifico, Don Alfonso, and Falstaff. Début as cond. with *Rigoletto* at Belfast 1977; *Figaro* and *Così fan tutte* in Turin 1989. (R)

Des Grieux. The Chevalier Des Grieux (ten), lover of Manon in Massenet's *Manon* and Puccini's *Manon Lescaut*.

Desmarets, Henry (*b* Paris, Feb. 1661; *d* Lunéville, 7 Sept. 1741). French composer. He began a successful career at the Paris, O, in 1693 with *Didon*, but in 1699 was forced to leave France because of a secret marriage and did not return until 1722. One of the most important figures of the generation which preceded Rameau, his operas show a generally good understanding of the tragédie lyrique and at times rank with those of Destouches and Campra in their dramatic and expressive qualities, even though they are usually marred by weak librettos. The most successful was *Iphigénie en Tauride* (1704).

Désormière, Roger (*b* Vichy, 13 Sept. 1898; *d* Paris, 25 Oct. 1963). French conductor. Studied Paris with Koechlin. Début Paris 1921. Paris: T Pigalle, 1931; OC, 1937, dir. 1944–6; O, assistant cond. 1945–6. London, CG, 1949 (*Pelléas*). An intelligent, versatile artist much of whose work lay outside opera, where his clear mind and enterprising taste were also manifest. Retired through ill health 1952. (R)

Despina. Fiordiligi's and Dorabella's maid (sop) in Mozart's *Così fan tutte*.

Desprez, Louis-Jean (*b* Auxerre, 9 Jan. 1742; *d* Stockholm, 17 Mar. 1804). French architect and designer. Studied Paris. Worked in Rome, then Stockholm for Gustav III at Royal OH. In his vivid, strongly charged, architecturally detailed designs, e.g. for Naumann's national opera *Gustaf Wasa* (1786), he anticipates some of the manner developed by *Cicéri and his followers in Paris in the 1820s and 1830s.

Dessau, Paul (*b* Hamburg, 19 Dec. 1894; *d* Berlin, 27 June 1979). German composer and conductor. Studied violin in Berlin, conducting and composition (with Loewengard) in Hamburg. Music dir. Hamburg Kammerspiele T 1912; from 1919 under Klemperer in Cologne; Mainz 1923; Berlin, SO, from 1925. Left Germany 1933 for US, where he began working with Brecht, returning to (East) Berlin 1948. The collaboration led to his most important stage works, including *Die Verurteilung des Lukullus* (The Condemnation of Lucullus, 1951), *Einstein* (1973), and *Leonce und Lena* (1979), in which he sought to support and interpret Brecht's ideas in dramatic music. Though highly eclectic, his style has a forcefulness and a sense of purpose that won him a keen following especially in the former East Germany.

Dessauer, Josef (*b* Prague, 28 May 1798; *d* Mödling, 8 July 1876). Bohemian composer. Studied Prague with Tomašek and D. Weber. Admired as a song composer by Liszt and Berlioz, he was also a friend of Chopin. His operas, which make use of various Romantic conventions, include *Lidwina* (1836), *Ein Besuch in St Cyr* (1838), *Paquita* (1851), *Dominga* (1860), and an unprem. *Oberon*. In Paris in 1842 he persuaded Wagner to draft him a libretto on Hoffmann's *Die Bergwerke zu Falun*, which was turned down by the Opéra.

Destinn (orig. Kittlová), **Emmy** (*b* Prague, 26 Feb. 1878; *d* České Budějovice, 28 Jan. 1930). Czech soprano. Studied Prague with Marie Loewe-Destinn, adopting her name for professional purposes. Début Dresden 1897 (Santuzza). London, CG, 1904–14, 1919; New York, M, 1908–16, 1919–21. Bayreuth, 1901 (Senta). Berlin, 1898–1908. Prague, 1914 (Libuše). After internment during the war, her powers declined, and she retired after 1921. Created Minnie. Her wide repertory included Donna Anna, Aida, Salome, Lisa, Mařenka, Butterfly. A fine actress, especially in tragic roles, while her very individual voice was well produced, even, and wide-ranging in colour. (R)

Destouches, André Cardinal (*bapt.* Paris, 6 Apr. 1672; *d* Paris, 7 Feb. 1749). French composer. After study with Campra, his career was launched with *Issé* in 1697; he went on to compose *c.*10 large-scale dramatic works. An important figure in the post-Lully generation, Destouches is sometimes compared favourably with Rameau on account of his carefully crafted melodic lines and richly expressive harmonic vocabulary. Though he concentrated on tragédie lyrique, early works such as *Amadis de Grèce* (1699) and *Omphale* (1701) contain an element of pastoral relief which also demonstrate the influence of Campra's lighter *opéra-ballet style.

Destouches's reputation rests on his trio of grand tragic works: *Callirhoé* (1712), *Télemaque et Calypso* (1714), and *Sémiramis* (1718). It is here that he shows himself to be no mere imitator of Lully's tragédies lyriques, but an intelligent composer with a unique and distinctive voice. Even to describe him as the most important forerunner of Rameau does not do justice to the originality of his style and approach, for he was perhaps the first French composer to appreciate the breadth of operatic structure and its potential, supplanting the independence of the individual acts with a bond of common dramatic purpose.

Deux journées, Les (The Two Days; formerly known in England as *The Water Carrier*). Opera in 3 acts by Cherubini; text by Jean Nicolas Bouilly. Prem. Paris, T Feydeau, 16 Jan. 1800.

Paris, *c.*1640. Count Armand (ten) and his wife Constance (mez) are hidden in the house of an old water-seller, Daniel Mikéli (bar); Mikéli recognizes Armand as the man who once rescued him from starvation. When a policeman arrives, Mikéli pretends Armand is his sick father. Constance succeeds in crossing the barricade to the next village by using a pass belonging to Mikéli's daughter; Armand is smuggled through in a water-barrel. Once safely across, the fugitive Armand is helped to hide by Antoine (ten) (Mikéli's son) and his betrothed; unfortunately, Constance reveals her husband's whereabouts and the couple are arrested. However, they are freed when Mikéli arrives with a royal pardon.

One of Cherubini's most important works. Beethoven regarded the libretto as the best of any contemporary opera, and kept a copy on his desk. An outstanding example of *rescue opera.

Devil and Daniel Webster, The. Opera in 1 act by Douglas Moore; text by composer, after Stephen Vincent Benét's story (1937). Prem. New York, Martin Beck T, 18 May 1939.

New Hampshire, 1840. At his wedding to Mary (sop), Jabez Stone (bs) is rescued from a pact selling his soul to the devil by Daniel Webster's (bar) brilliant defence before a jury of famous villains of history.

Devil and Kate, The (Cz., *Čert a Káča*). Opera in 3 acts by Dvořák; text by Adolf Wenig, after the folk-tale included in Božena Němcová's *Fairy Tales* (1845). Prem. Prague, N, 23 Nov. 1899.

Bohemia and Hell, legendary times. Kate (con) fails to secure a dancing partner at a country fair, so says she would dance with the Devil himself, Marbuel (bar), who now carries her off. Her garrulity oppresses even hell, which gladly relinquishes her to a rescuer. Marbuel returns to earth to capture the domineering lady of the manor, but vanishes at the sight of Kate.

Devils of Loudun, The (Pol., *Diabły z Loudun*). Opera in 3 acts by Krzysztof Penderecki; text by the composer, after John Whiting's drama *The Devils* (1961) based on Aldous Huxley's historical study *The Devils of Loudun* (1952), examining a celebrated 17th-cent. case. Prem. Hamburg, S, 20 June 1969.

Loudun, 1734–5. The plot describes how the priest Urbain Grandier (bar) engenders a diabolic obsession in a convent of Ursuline nuns, above all in the prioress Jeanne (sop). He is eventually tortured and burnt at the stake.

Devil's Wall, The (Cz., *Čertova stěna*). Opera in 3 acts by Smetana; text by E. Krásnohorská. Prem. Prague, C, 29 Oct. 1882.

Bohemia, 12th cent. The Devil, Rarach (bs), persuades the Bohemian ruler Vok (bar) to enter a monastery, in order that a vow made by Vok's friend Jarek (ten) will be broken. He has sworn not to marry before Vok. Despite the arrival of Hedvika (sop), with whom Vok has fallen in love, he departs for his monastic life, since he believes she cannot return his love. However, Hedvika follows him, much to the annoyance of the Devil, who summons his spirits to build a dam to drown the monastery. The Abbot, Beneš (bs), drives the Devil away and destroys the wall by making the sign of the cross, and Vok and Hedvika are free to marry.

Devin du village, Le (The Village Soothsayer). Opera in 1 act by Jean-Jacques Rousseau; text by the composer. Prem. Fontainebleau 18 Oct. 1752.

A French village, 18th cent. Colette (sop) learns that her beloved Colin (ten) has been unfaithful to her and seeks the aid of a Soothsayer (bar) who advises her to display utter indifference to Colin's advances. At the same time, the Soothsayer tells Colin that Colette has fallen in love with someone else. The trick works and the lovers are reunited.

One of the most successful and influential works of its age, and Rousseau's most famous composition: see GUERRE DES BOUFFONS. Of its innumerable parodies, imitations, and adaptations, the most famous is Mozart's *Bastien und Bastienne (1768).

Devrient, Eduard (b Berlin, 11 Aug. 1801; d Karlsruhe, 4 Oct. 1877). German baritone, librettist, and theatre historian. Nephew of the actor Ludwig Devrient; brother of Karl Devrient, who married Wilhelmine *Schröder. Studied Berlin with Zelter. Début Berlin Royal O 1819 (Thanatos, Alceste). Sang there until 1822, then Dresden, Leipzig, Frankfurt 1822; later Prague and Vienna. A refined performer with excellent declamation, he was successful as Papageno, Figaro (Mozart and Rossini), Orestes, etc. Created Bois-Guilbert in Marschner's Der Templer und die Jüdin, and title-role in Hans Heiling, for which he wrote the libretto. Lost his voice 1834. Actor and prod. Dresden Court T until 1846; dir. Karlsruhe Court T 1856–70, initiating many reforms. His writings include two other librettos (set by Taubert), plays, and several works on his ideal of a national theatre, e.g. Geschichte der deutschen Schauspielkunst. Responsible for (and sang in) the performance of St Matthew Passion, Berlin 1829, that began the Bach revival under his close friend Mendelssohn.

Dew, John (b Santiago de Cuba, 1 June 1944). British stage director. After study with Felsenstein and Wieland Wagner directed Rake's Progress at Ulm, 1971. Staged operas by Mozart and Wagner at Krefeld, then modern repertory at Bielefeld from 1981; Hindemith's Neues vom Tage, Brand's Maschinist

Hopkins, Nixon in China, works by Krenek and Schreker. Les Huguenots (Berlin, D, 1987; transferred to London, CG, 1991). His work is frequently provocative, not least by his challenge to audience expectations when operas are dislocated from their original time and place.

Dexter, John (b Derby, 2 Aug. 1925; d London, 23 Mar. 1990). English producer. After directing films and theatre, turned to opera with Benvenuto Cellini, London, CG, 1966. Hamburg from 1969. Prod. British prem. of Penderecki's The Devils of Loudun, London, C, 1973. Dir. of productions, New York, M, 1974–85. A gifted and stimulating producer, with original responses to many different works.

Dezède, Nicolas (b ?, c.1740–5; d Paris, 11 Sept. 1792). French composer. Came to attention with his opéra-comique Julie at the Paris CI, 1772; over the next 20 years composed six operas and 15 opéras-comiques for the Parisian stage. The success of Julie was repeated with its two sequels, L'erreur d'un moment (1773) and Le stratagème découvert (1773). In his opéras-comiques, including Les trois fermiers (1777) and Les trois noces (1790), he proved himself the natural successor to Monsigny and Philidor, writing in an appealing and undemanding style, though moments of tenderness and expressiveness did much to enhance the quality of the genre during this period. Dezède's last opéra-comique, Le véritable Figaro (comp. 1784), was banned by the censor. His serious operas, including Péronne sauvée (1783) and La fête de la cinquantaine (1796) appear anaemic when viewed against the rich tradition of Lully, Campra, Destouches, and Rameau, and have been overshadowed by his opéras-comiques.

Diaghilev, Serge. See DYAGILEV, SERGEY.

Dialogues des Carmélites (Dialogues of the Carmelites). Opera in 3 acts by Poulenc; text by Ernest Lavery, after the drama by Georges Bernanos, adapted from Gertrude von Le Fort's novel Die Letzte am Schafott (1931) and a film scenario by Fr. Brückberger and Philippe Agostini, in turn on the recollections of one of the original nuns of Compiègne, Sister Marie of the Incarnation. Prem. Milan, S, 26 Jan. 1957.

Paris, 1789. As a consequence of the Revolution, Blanche (sop), the daughter of the Marquis de la Force (bar) decides to enter a

Carmelite convent. There she meets Constance (sop), who foresees that the two will die together. The convent is attacked by a rabble and all are captured and sentenced to death except Blanche, who has already fled to her home. However, when she sees Constance approaching the guillotine, she is inspired with divine strength and goes to join her in martyrdom.

Diamants de la couronne, Les (The Crown Diamonds). Opera in 3 acts by Auber; text by Scribe and Vernoy de Saint-Georges. Prem. Paris, OC, 6 Mar. 1841.

Portugal, 1777. Don Enriquez (ten) is captured by a gang of forgers, but is saved by Theophila (sop), heiress to the crown of Portugal; she has set one of the forgers, Rebolledo (bs), the task of copying the crown jewels, in order that she may sell the original gems to pay off her debts. News breaks out that the jewels have been stolen, but Enriquez, who has fallen in love with Theophila, protects her, aided by his cousin Diana (sop). When Theophila's identity is disclosed, she chooses to marry Enriquez; Rebolledo is appointed head of the secret police.

Díaz, Justino (*b* San Juan, Puerto Rico, 29 Jan. 1940). US bass-baritone. Studied at New England Cons. and made début with local opera theatre 1961 (Giorgio). New York, M, from 1963 (Colline, Don Giovanni; created Antony in Barber's *Antony and Cleopatra*, 1966). His well-schooled technique has brought him success in roles including Escamillo (Salzburg 1966; London, CG, 1976), Amonasro (Cincinnati 1990) and Iago (in Zeffirelli's filmed *Otello*, 1986). Sang Franchetti's Cristoforo Colombo (Miami 1992). (R)

Dibdin, Charles (*b* Southampton, *bapt.* 15 Mar. 1745; *d* London, 25 July 1814). English composer, singer, and musical factotum. He is best remembered for his collaborations with Bickerstaffe, notably *Love in the City* (1767) (an unsuccessful parody of Arne's *Love in a Village*), *Lionel and Clarissa* (1768), which originally included a substantial proportion of music by Galuppi and other Italians, and *The Padlock* (1768).

'Dich, teure Halle'. Elisabeth's (sop) aria opening Act II of Wagner's *Tannhäuser*, in which she greets the Hall of Song in the Wartburg where the song contest is to take place.

Dick Johnson. The alias of the bandit Ramerrez (ten), lover of Minnie, in Puccini's *La fanciulla del West*.

Dido and Aeneas. Opera in a prologue and 3 acts by Purcell; text by Nahum Tate, after Book 4 of Virgil's *Aeneid* (unfin. 19 BC). Comp. ?1685 or earlier, but first known perf. Chelsea, Josias Priest's School for Young Gentlewomen, spring 1689.

Carthage, after the Trojan war. Dido (sop or mez) cannot bring herself to declare her love for Aeneas (bar). Belinda (sop) and the court succeed in making her yield, and a chorus celebrates the triumph of love and beauty.

The Sorceress (mez or male alto) summons the Witches to her cave to plot the downfall of Dido and of Carthage. They agree to conjure up a storm so as to force the royal lovers, out hunting, to take shelter in the cave; here the Spirit of the Sorceress (mez), disguised as Mercury, will remind Aeneas of his duty to go on to Italy. Dido and Aeneas are entertained with a masque of Diana and Actaeon: the storm drives Aeneas alone to the cave, where he is deceived by the false Mercury.

At the harbour, Aeneas plans to leave, while the Witches exult in their success: they plan to sink his fleet and fire Carthage. When Dido appears she silences Aeneas's explanations, and in the famous lament 'When I am laid in earth' she takes her leave of life; Cupids mourn above her tomb.

Didur, Adam (*b* Wola Sękowa, 24 Dec. 1874; *d* Katowice, 7 Jan. 1946). Polish bass. Studied Lwów with Wysocki, Milan with Emmerich. Début Rio 1894 (Gounod's Méphistophélès). Warsaw O 1899–1903; Milan, S, 1903–6; London, CG, 1905 (Colline, Leporello); Buenos Aires 1905–8; New York, M, 1908–32, succeeding Édouard De Reszke. Created Ashby (*La fanciulla del West*) and the Woodcutter (*Königskinder*); also first US Boris. His sonorous, dark-timbred voice was suited to both Rossini and Wagner, to whose music he brought great energy and subtlety, vocally as well as dramatically. He was much admired by Mahler. After retiring, he returned to Poland and formed an opera company in Katowice, where he also taught. (R)

'Die Frist ist um'. The Flying Dutchman's (bar) soliloquy in Act I of Wagner's *Der fliegende Holländer*, in which he reflects that once again the term of seven years' wandering, to which he is sentenced by a curse, is at an end and he may land to seek the redeeming love of a woman who will sacrifice herself for him.

'Dies Bildnis ist bezaubernd schön'. Tamino's (ten) aria in Act I of Mozart's *Die Zauberflöte*, declaring his love for Pamina at first sight of her portrait.

Dietsch, Louis (*b* Dijon, 17 Mar. 1808; *d* Paris, 20 Feb. 1865). French conductor and composer. Studied Paris with Rejcha. Played double bass at Paris, I and O. Chorus-master at O on Rossini's recommendation, 1840; cond., 1860–3; left after an argument with Verdi. Also quarrelled with Wagner, who wrongly accused him of plagiarism for the text of *Le vaisseau fantôme* (Paris 1842). Conducted the notorious 1861 Paris prem. of *Tannhäuser*, against Wagner's wishes and incompetently though not, as Wagner asserted, maliciously so as to encompass the disaster that occurred.

Dikoj. Savel Prokofjevič Dikoj (bs), uncle of Káťa's lover Boris, in Janáček's *Káťa Kabanová*.

Di Luna. The Conte di Luna (bar), a nobleman of Aragon, in Verdi's *Il trovatore*.

Dimitrova, Ghena (*b* Beglej, 6 May 1941). Bulgarian soprano. Studied Sofia with Dyakovich, Zagreb with Lunzer. Début Sofia 1966 (Abigaille). Belgrade, Zagreb from 1969; successes in Italy from 1970, incl. Milan, S; Dallas 1981; London, CG, 1983; New York, M, 1988; also Buenos Aires, C; Salzburg; Moscow; Verona; Berlin, D; etc. With her full, ample tone, an acclaimed Lady Macbeth, Odabella, Aida, Tosca, Turandot, Santuzza, Leonora (*Trovatore* and *Forza*). (R)

D'Indy, Vincent. See INDY, VINCENT D'.

Dinorah, ou Le pardon de Ploërmel. Opera in 3 acts by Meyerbeer; text by Barbier and Carré. Prem. Paris, OC, 4 Apr. 1859.

Brittany, 19th cent. The goatherd Hoël (bar) puts off his wedding to Dinorah (sop) and goes in search of treasure, which will enable them to live more comfortably. At the specified site, Dinorah appears and, after a mad fit, is revived by Hoël. Her mind is cleared of all memories of his desertion and the couple are reunited.

D'Intino, Luciana (*b* San Vito al Tagliamento, 1959). Italian mezzo-soprano. Studied at the Marcello Cons., Venice, making her début 1983 as Azucena. Has sung at Naples from 1984; Milan, S, from 1987, notably in *Nabucco*, Jommelli's *Fetonte* and *Don Carlos* (Eboli, 1993). New York, M, 1991 as Frederica (*Luisa Miller*). Her warm and well-focused voice has brought her particular success as Amneris (London, and elsewhere) and Rosina. (R)

'Dio, mi potevi scagliar'. Otello's (ten) monologue in Act III of Verdi's *Otello*, the equivalent of 'Had it pleased heaven to try me with affliction' in Act IV of Shakespeare's *Othello*.

'Di Provenza il mar'. The elder Germont's (bar) aria in Act II of Verdi's *La traviata*, in which he tries to persuade his son Alfredo to return to the parental home and give up his life with Violetta.

'Di quella pira'. Manrico's (ten) aria in Act III of Verdi's *Il trovatore*, a rousing call to his followers to join him in saving his mother Azucena from being burnt alive. The high C which many tenors interpolate in the line 'O teco almeno, corrir a morir' is not in the score, but was introduced by Enrico Tamberlik, with Verdi's permission.

'Di scrivermi ogni giorno'. The quintet in Act I of Mozart's *Così fan tutte*, in which the sisters Dorabella (mez) and Fiordiligi (sop) exchange promises with their lovers Ferrando (ten) and Guglielmo (bar) that they will write to one another every day during their absence, while Don Alfonso (bar) fears he will die of laughter.

Di Stefano, Giuseppe (*b* Motta Santa Anastasia, 24 July 1921). Italian tenor. Studied Milan with Montesanto. Début Reggio Emilia 1946 (Massenet's Des Grieux). Milan, S, from 1947. New York, M, 1948–52, 1955–6, 1964–5. London, CG, 1961 (Cavaradossi). In his early days, as Nadir, Elvino, Fritz, etc., his voice had a pure yet velvety tone, and a ravishing pianissimo. It changed when he began to sing heavier roles (Turiddu, Don José, Alvaro), and he appeared less frequently, although he partnered Callas on her final tour, 1973–4. (R)

'Di tanti palpiti'. Tancredi's (con) love-song in Act I of Rossini's *Tancredi*. It was perhaps the most popular aria of its day, sung and whistled in the streets all over Europe. In

Venice it was known as the *aria dei risi* (Rice Aria) as Rossini was alleged to have composed it in four minutes while waiting for the rice to cook—an impossible time for either event, as the gastronome Rossini would have been the first to appreciate.

'Dite alla giovine'. Part of the duet between Violetta (sop) and the elder Germont (bar) in Act II of Verdi's *La traviata*, in which she begs him to make her sacrifice known to his daughter.

Dittersdorf, Karl Ditters von (*b* Vienna, 2 Nov. 1739; *d* Neuhof, 24 Oct. 1799). Austrian composer. His *c*.40 Singspiels enjoyed great success in their day on account of their lively, tuneful music and largely comic plots. The first, *Doktor und Apotheker* (1786), proved especially popular and was successful throughout Europe: Stephen Storace made an English adaptation of it. Dittersdorf contributed to the development of Singspiel through the introduction of elements from opera buffa, notably the *ensemble finale. Particularly significant is the Act I finale of *Doktor und Apotheker*: this was the first time such a long multi-sectional finale movement had been introduced into Singspiel. His other works included *Hieronymus Knicker* (1789) and *Das Gespenst mit der Trommel* (1794).

'Divinités du Styx'. Alceste's (sop) aria in Act I of Gluck's *Alceste*, invoking the gods of the underworld and defying them to do their worst.

Djamileh. Opera in 1 act by Bizet; text by Louis Gallet, after Alfred de Musset's poem *Namouna* (1832). Prem. Paris, OC, 22 May 1872.

A palace in Cairo, 19th cent. Haroun (ten) pensions off his old mistress once a month and is bought a new one in the market by his servant Splendiano (bar). Djamileh (mez), the current mistress, falls in love with Haroun, and bargains with Splendiano to be readmitted disguised: this ruse wins Haroun's heart.

Dmitry. The Pretender to the throne of Russia (ten) in Musorgsky's *Boris Godunov* and Dvořák's *Dmitrij*.

Dobroven, Issay (*b* Nizhny-Novgorod (Gorky), 27 Feb. 1891; *d* Oslo, 9 Dec. 1953). Russian, later Norwegian, conductor, pianist, and producer. Appeared as pianist aged 5. Studied Moscow with Yaroshevsky

and Taneyev, Vienna with Godowsky. Début Moscow, Kommisarzhevsky T, 1919 (*Hoffmann*); Moscow, B, 1921–2. Left Russia 1923. Dresden 1923; Berlin, V, 1924–5, and SO as prod., 1928–9; Frankfurt 1930. Sofia 1927–8, where he did much for the opera. Frequent visitor to Budapest 1936–9. Settled in Norway 1932. Stockholm 1940–9 as cond. and prod. (incl. prem. of Sutermeister's *Raskolnikoff*, 1948). From 1949 cond. and prod. Russian works at Milan, S. London, CG, 1952–3 (*Boris*). (R)

Docteur Miracle. The evil doctor (bs-bar) in the Antonia episode of Offenbach's *Les contes d'Hoffmann*.

Docteur Miracle, Le. 1. Operetta in 1 act by Bizet; text by Battu and Halévy. Prem. Paris, BP, 9 Apr. 1857.
2. Operetta in 1 act by Lecocq; text by Battu and Halévy. Prem. Paris, BP, 8 Apr. 1857.

Padua, 19th cent. In order to win the hand of Laurette (sop), daughter of an anti-military official (bs), a young officer, Silvio (ten), disguises himself as a chef and cooks a remarkable omelette. It tastes so amazing that the official believes himself to be poisoned and summons a doctor (again Silvio in disguise) who proclaims that the only cure is to let him marry the official's daughter.

Both works were entries in a competition arranged by Offenbach (who offered 1,200 F. and a gold medal), being awarded the joint first prize among 78 entrants by a jury headed by Auber, Halévy, Scribe, and Gounod.

Doctor Bartolo. The old doctor of Seville (bs) in Paisiello's and Rossini's *Il barbiere di Siviglia* and Mozart's *Le nozze di Figaro*.

Dodon. King Dodon (bs) in Rimsky-Korsakov's *The Golden Cockerel*.

Doese, Helena (*b* Gothenburg, 13 Aug. 1946). Swedish soprano. Studied in Rome and Vienna before début at Gothenburg 1971 as Aida. Sang with Berne O 1972–5. London, CG, and Gly. débuts 1974, as Mimì and Mozart's Countess respectively; has returned to London as Gutrune, Agathe, Amelia Boccanegra. Has sung Eva at the Royal O, Stockholm (member there from 1975) and Sydney. US début S Francisco 1982. Frequent appearances at Frankfurt; other roles include Tosca, Ariadne, Fiordiligi. A versatile performer, equally at home in the lyric and dramatic repertories. (R)

Dohnányi, Christoph von (*b* Berlin, 8 Sept. 1929). German conductor. Studied Munich, later US with his grandfather, Ernő Dohnányi, and Bernstein. Frankfurt 1953, chorusmaster and cond. Music dir. of Lübeck 1957–63, of Kassel 1963–6, of Frankfurt 1968–75, and of Hamburg 1975–84. Chicago 1969; London, CG, 1974; New York, M, 1972; also Munich, Vienna, S Francisco. Repertory incl. *Fidelio, Fliegender Holländer, Meistersinger, Falstaff, Rosenkavalier, Salome, Wozzeck, Moses und Aron,* and prems. of Henze's *Bassarids* and *Der junge Lord.* Cond. *Der Ring des Nibelungen* at Vienna, S, 1994. Married soprano Anja *Silja. (R)

Doktor Faust. Opera in 2 prologues, an interlude, and 3 scenes by Busoni (completed by Jarnach); text by the composer after the Faust legend and Marlowe's treatment of it in *Dr Faustus* (1589), also the 16th-cent. German puppet play. Prem. Dresden 21 May 1925.

Wittenberg and Parma, 16th cent. Faust (bar) invokes the help of Mephistopheles (ten) to help him regain his lost youth. Faust elopes with the Duchess of Parma (sop) shortly after her marriage to the Duke (ten). At an inn in Wittenberg, Faust hears of the Duchess's death, and he too longs to die. He meets a beggar woman, who turns out to be the Duchess, clasping the corpse of a child. Faust offers his own life if the child can be revived. As Faust dies, a young man rises from the body of the dead child.

Doktor und Apotheker. Opera in 2 acts by Dittersdorf; text by G. Stephanie, after a French drama *L'apothicaire de Murcie* by 'le Comte N...'. Prem. Vienna, B, 11 July 1786.

A small German town, 18th cent. Gotthold (ten) and Leonore (sop) are forbidden to marry because of the hatred between their fathers, the doctor Krautmann (bs), and the apothecary Stössel (bs), who wants his daughter to marry an invalid soldier, Sturmwald (ten). Leonore's cousin Rosalie (sop) and her lover Sichel (ten) help the couple in a series of intrigues which involve disguises as Sturmwald and as a lawyer, and result in the drawing up of a marriage contract. The fathers are at first furious, but all is finally resolved by a miraculous change of heart on the part of Stössel's wife, Claudia (mez), who ensures that the lovers are united.

Dolukhanova, Zara (*b* Moscow, 5 Mar. 1918). Armenian mezzo-soprano. Studied Moscow with Belyayeva-Tarasevich. Début Erevan 1939. Engagements throughout USSR. Though she then spent most of her career as a concert singer, her championing of Rossini did much to establish his mezzo-soprano roles in the repertory, with broadcasts as Rosina, Cenerentola, Arsace, etc. A highly accomplished singer with a wide stylistic range. (R)

Domgraf-Fassbaender, Willi (*b* Aachen, 19 Feb. 1897; *d* Nuremberg, 13 Feb. 1978). German baritone. Studied Berlin with Stückgold, Milan with Borgatti. Début Aachen 1922 (Mozart's Almaviva). Berlin, Düsseldorf, and Stuttgart, then Berlin, SO, 1928–46. Gly. 1934 (opening night) (Mozart's Figaro), 1935, 1937 (Guglielmo, Papageno). Salzburg 1937. After the war, Vienna, Munich, and Nuremberg, where he was Oberspielleiter 1953–62, and also taught. Pupils included his daughter Brigitte *Fassbaender. A fine Mozart singer, with a warm, attractive voice; also an impressive Wozzeck. (R)

Domingo, Plácido (*b* Madrid, 21 Jan. 1941). Spanish tenor and conductor. Studied piano, conducting, and singing, Mexico City. Début as baritone Mexico City 1957 in Caballero's zarzuela *Gigantes y cabezudos.* Monterrey, O, 1961 (first major tenor role, Alfredo); Dallas, 1961 (Arturo, *Lucia di Lammermoor*). Israeli Nat. O, 1962–5. New York, M, from 1966; Milan, S, from 1969; London, CG, from 1971. Also S Francisco, Paris, Vienna, Berlin, etc. A leading lyric-dramatic tenor of great gifts, with a strong dramatic personality. His large repertory includes Cavaradossi, Don José, Turiddu, Samson, Aeneas (Troyens), Radamès, and Otello (Verdi), and, more recently, Heldentenor roles: Lohengrin, Parsifal, Siegmund. Cond. *Attila,* Barcelona 1973, and *Die Fledermaus,* London, CG, 1983. (R)

Domino noir, Le (The Black Domino). Opera in 3 acts by Auber; text by Scribe. Prem. Paris, OC, 2 Dec. 1837.

Two friends, Horatio (ten) and Juliano (ten), attend the Christmas ball given annually by the Queen in the hope of seeing once again a beautiful woman who comes dressed in a black domino. She is Angela (mez). After many deceptions and confusions, Angela chooses Horatio as her husband, and regains a large inheritance.

Donalda, Pauline (*b* Montreal, 5 Mar. 1882; *d* Montreal, 22 Oct. 1970). Canadian soprano. Studied Montreal, and Paris with Duvernoy. Born Lightfoot, she took her stage name from the 'Donaldas', the first women allowed on the McGill Campus, named after Sir Donald Smith. Début Nice 1904 (Manon). London, CG, 1905, sponsored by Melba, singing Micaëla, Zerlina, Gilda, Violetta, etc. First London Concepción (*Heure espagnole*), 1919, delaying her retirement at Ravel's request for the purpose. New York, Manhattan O, 1906, Paris. Taught Paris 1922–37, then Montreal, founding the O Guild of Montreal 1942. (R)

Don Alfonso. The philosopher (bar) who engineers the plot of Mozart's *Così fan tutte*.

Donath, Helen (*b* Corpus Christi, TX, 10 July 1940). US soprano. Studied Corpus Christi with Dapholl, New York with Novikova. Début Cologne 1960 (Inès). Hanover 1963; Frankfurt 1965–7; Munich from 1967; Vienna from 1970; Salzburg from 1971; Milan, S, 1972. New York, M, 1990. Roles incl. Pamina, Marzelline, Micaëla, Sophie, Eva. (R)

Donauweibchen, Das (The Danube Sprite). Opera in 3 acts by Ferdinand Kauer; text (*Ein romantisches komisches Volksmärchen mit Gesang nach einer Sage der Vorzeit*) by K. F. Hensler. Prem. Vienna, L, 11 Jan. 1798. Kauer's most popular work, and one of the most popular of all operas in the first half of the 19th cent. all over Central and Eastern Europe. A second part followed, Vienna, L, 13 Feb. 1798, and a third, *Die Nymphe der Donau*, text by Berling, music by Bierey, Altona, 25 July 1801. Also *Das Waldweibchen*, by Kauer and Hensler, Vienna, L, 1 Apr. 1800. *Das Donauweibchen* was translated into Russian by N. S. Krasnopolsky and given in St Petersburg, 1803, set as *Lesta, dneprovskaya rusalka* (Lesta, the Dnyepr Rusalka), after Kauer, by Davydov (1803), Cavos (1804), Davydov (1805), and (to a new text by Shakhovskoy) Davydov (1807). These works influenced Pushkin's *Rusalka*, originally intended as a Singspiel, and hence Dargomyzhsky's **Rusalka*. Davydov's settings also influenced Glinka, especially in their orchestration and their use of folk music.

Don Basilio. The priest and music-master (bs) in Paisiello's and Rossini's *Il barbiere di Siviglia* and (ten) in Mozart's *Le nozze di Figaro*.

Don Carlos. Opera in 5 acts by Verdi; text by Méry and Du Locle, after Schiller's drama (1787), Cormon's drama (1849), and Prescott's history (1856). Prem. Paris, O, 11 Mar. 1867. Rev. in 4 acts (omitting Fontainebleau act) 1884 by Du Locle, trans. Zanardini, based on orig. version by De Lauzières: prem. Milan, S, 10 Jan. 1884.

France and Spain, 1568. In the Forest of Fontainebleau, Don Carlos (ten), the son of Philip II of Spain, meets Elisabeth de Valois (sop), to whom he is betrothed by arrangement. The couple declare their instant love for each other; Elisabeth's father then decrees that she is to marry King Philip (bs) instead.

In the monastery of San Yuste in Spain, Carlos confesses his hopeless love for Elisabeth to his friend Rodrigo (bar). Rodrigo advises him to try to forget his passion by taking up the cause of Flanders. Elisabeth joins the court ladies, followed by Rodrigo who begs her to see Carlos. Rodrigo leads the others away and Carlos bids farewell to Elisabeth, declaring his undying love for her. King Philip returns to find the Queen alone; he is suspicious about the relationship of Elisabeth and Carlos and asks Rodrigo to watch them.

Having received an anonymous note, Carlos goes to meet a veiled woman. He assumes it will be Elisabeth but it is in fact the Princess Eboli (mez), who is in love with him. Realizing the object of Carlos's passion, she decides on revenge. Rodrigo arrives and persuades Carlos to hand over all documents incriminating him as a supporter of Flanders. At the *auto-da-fé* (a burning of heretics), a voice from Heaven is heard welcoming the 'heretics' to heaven and Flemish officials, led by Carlos, arrive to ask for an end to the persecutions in Flanders. When Philip orders their arrest, Carlos threatens him with a sword but Rodrigo intervenes and saves the King.

Philip sits alone in his study and broods on his loveless state. Compelled by the Grand Inquisitor, he resolves to put his son to death and agrees to hand over Rodrigo as a heretic. Elisabeth interrupts, agitated because her jewel casket has been stolen. Philip produces it and makes her open it in his presence; it contains a portrait of Carlos. Eboli confesses to Elizabeth that it was she who stole the casket and also that she has been the King's mistress. Repentant, she vows to enter a convent. Rodrigo visits Carlos in his cell. He has implicated himself as the leader of the

Flemish rebels and hopes that Carlos will be set free. Two of the King's men enter and Rodrigo is shot. Before he dies, he manages to tell Carlos that the Queen will wait for him at the monastery of San Yuste the next day.

At San Yuste, Carlos and Elisabeth bid each other a final farewell. Philip and the Grand Inquisitor have entered silently; they now seize Elisabeth and Carlos and it seems that all is lost. However, a figure who seems to be Charles V appears at the gates of his tomb and takes Carlos with him to safety.

Don Carlos. The lover of Laura (bar), and rival of Don Juan, in Dargomyzhsky's *The Stone Guest*. See also above.

Don Carlos di Vargas. Leonora's brother (bar) in Verdi's *La forza del destino*.

'Donde lieta uscì'. 'ADDIO SENZA RANCOR'.

Don Giovanni (orig. *Il dissoluto punito, ossia Il Don Giovanni*). Opera in 2 acts by Mozart; text by Da Ponte, after the Don Juan legend and particularly after Bertati's libretto for Gazzaniga's *Don Giovanni Tenorio* (1787). Prem. Prague, Nostic T, 29 Oct. 1787.

Seville, *c*.1600. Leporello (bs) is waiting outside a house where his master Don Giovanni (bar) is trying to seduce Donna Anna. She calls for help and her father, the Commendatore (bs), appears; Don Giovanni kills him. Donna Anna fetches her betrothed, Don Ottavio (ten), and they find the Commendatore dead; Don Ottavio vows to avenge the murder.

Donna Elvira (sop) arrives in search of Don Giovanni. He recognizes her as a former lover, and escapes, leaving Leporello to show her the catalogue of his master's conquests. She swears vengeance. Don Giovanni happens upon a peasant wedding and begins to flirt with the bride Zerlina (sop). She is about to succumb when Elvira intervenes. Don Ottavio and Donna Anna arrive and, not recognizing Don Giovanni, ask for his assistance in finding the Commendatore's murderer. As Don Giovanni departs, Anna recognizes him as the culprit. Three masked figures arrive and are invited to join the party with which Giovanni is celebrating the wedding of Zerlina and Masetto (bs); they are Elvira, Anna, and Ottavio. They discover him attempting further seduction and reveal their identities, vowing to disclose his behaviour to everyone.

Don Giovanni has exchanged costumes with Leporello and serenades Elvira's maid outside an inn. Elvira herself comes down to the street and departs with 'Don Giovanni' (actually Leporello). Masetto comes in search of Don Giovanni, who pretends to be Leporello but then beats Masetto. In a dark courtyard, Zerlina and Masetto encounter Leporello, whom they take for Don Giovanni. So as to escape, he sheds his disguise. Don Giovanni and Leporello meet in a cemetery, where the statue of the Commendatore seems to speak. Don Giovanni invites him to supper. The statue arrives and orders Don Giovanni to repent of his crimes. When he refuses, the flames of hell engulf him. Elvira, Anna, and Don Ottavio enter to confront Don Giovanni and are told of the events by Leporello. The opera ends with the cast addressing the audience with the moral of the story.

Donizetti, Gaetano (*b* Bergamo, 29 Nov. 1797; *d* Bergamo, 8 Apr. 1848). Italian composer. Studied Bergamo with Mayr and others, Bologna with Mattei. His first student operas were unproduced, but at Mayr's instigation he wrote some for Venice. The success of *Zoraide di Granata* (1822) led to a contract from Barbaia for Naples. His early successful comedies, which include *L'ajo nell'imbarazzo* (1824), *Olivo e Pasquale* (1827), and *Il giovedì grasso* (1829), belong, despite glimpses of individuality, to the world of Italian opera dominated by Rossini. With some later works, among them *L'esule di Roma* (1828), *Alina* (1828), *Il paria* (1829), and *Elisabetta* (1829), the influence of Rossini's French style is felt, as well as that of Bellini, though Donizetti's own mature style is also beginning to emerge. However, this is fully revealed in 1830 with *Anna Bolena*, his first great tragedy and the work with which he won international recognition.

In 1832 he broke his contract with Naples so as to broaden his field of activity, signing a new and more favourable contract there in 1834. Of works written in the 1830s, *L'elisir d'amore* (1832) remains a classic of sentimental comedy, while *Torquato Tasso* (1833) and *Lucrezia Borgia* (1833) broke new ground as Romantic melodramas. A visit to Paris and the discovery of Grand Opera in 1835 influenced *Lucia di Lammermoor* (1835), which, for all its familiarity as an example of Donizetti's style, is in fact uneven, including both original Romantic elements and pages (some of them the most famous) of routine post-Rossini vocalization. Donizetti was always happy to write so as to give the best expression to the leading vocal talents of the day; hence the virtuosity of Fanny Tacchinardi-Persiani is reflected in parts of *Lucia*, while the dramatic gift of Pasta marks *Anna Bolena* and that of Ronzi di Begnis *Roberto Devereux* (1837), the directness of Rosine Stolz *La favorite* (1840), and the noble example of Ronconi the writing for baritone in *Maria di Rohan* (1843) and *Maria Padilla* (1841).

By the mid-1830s Donizetti was in full command of his dramatic gift, and though always willing to amend the content of his works to suit conditions, or to write to accommodate singers, he had begun to subordinate mere display to the needs of the drama. A striking example from this period is *Roberto Devereux*, a powerful work to contrast with the flimsiness of *Pia de' Tolomei* (1837) or the awkward dramatic effect of *Maria de Rudenz* (1838). Commissions from Vienna and Paris encouraged him to develop his style to the needs of these new audiences. When in 1838 he was denied the directorship of the Naples Conservatory in favour of Mercadante, and *Poliuto* was banned by the Neapolitan censor, he left for Paris to produce the opera as *Les martyrs*.

In Paris he met with mixed success. He reworked some of his Italian operas and wrote *La fille du régiment* (1840), a highly successful work, Italian in essence and only lightly coloured with Gallicisms; however, also in 1840 he was obliged to withdraw *Lucrezia Borgia* when Hugo objected to Romani's adaptation of his tragedy. The initially unsuccessful *La favorite* of the same year is a French Grand Opera. *Linda di Chamounix* (1842) (though written for Vienna) manages by contrast to reconcile the Italian *opera semiseria genre with that of French opéra-comique. Declining health progressively limited his ability to travel, though he kept up a frantic round of activity and travel. In Milan in 1841 he was depressed by censorship troubles with *Maria Padilla*. In Vienna in 1842 he was appointed Kapellmeister to the Austrian court. Other works of his last years suggest further developments: *Maria Padilla* is much more freely composed, like the later stricter and more compact *Maria di Rohan* varying formal aria and recitative in a manner that virtually achieves continuous composition. *Caterina Cornaro* (1844) is concentrated and intense in manner, whereas *Don Pasquale* (1843), his comic masterpiece, is a relaxed and witty piece that almost wholly conceals his failing health. *Maria di Rohan* proved on its Vienna production in 1844 to be one of his most powerful Romantic dramas. He was disappointed by the failure of his last work, *Dom Sébastien* (1843), a French Grand Opera of sombre grandeur. His illness, syphilitic in origin, caused eventual paralysis, and he was moved to Bergamo, where he was looked after by friends until his death.

A versatile and practical musician, Donizetti ranged widely in his subjects. The early works are typically comedies, his most characteristic later ones Romantic tragedies; and it was the latter genre that he regarded as his most important. Here, though always prone to relapse into triviality, he developed a gift for characterization and for dramatic momentum that can still be strongly effective in the theatre. This was partly achieved by loosening the old firm divisions of recitative and aria, and interspersing arioso sections, perhaps varied with choral comments, that allow a much freer expressive range; yet even his most original moments could be followed by a scintillating but cold display of soprano fireworks. Aware of the problem, he evolved the slow cabaletta, which allowed the singer more effective dramatic expression, with coloratura that remained satisfying to the singer's vanity but was more respectful of the audience's intelligence. Towards the latter part of his career, he also found ways of enriching his accompaniments (which can be feeble) and of chromatically inflecting his vocal lines subtly for expressive purposes without loss of tunefulness or singability. At the same time, he explored a richer vein of orchestration, and experimented with novel combinations of voices to vary the conventional ensemble patterns. In these matters, as in a good deal else, Donizetti is the most important direct forerunner of Verdi. The tunefulness of his 70 stage works, not to mention their superiority, even at their most erratic, over most contemporary operas, long ensured their place in the repertory; and in modern times they have won new audiences for their dramatic power as well as for their melodic charm and skilful stagecraft.

Don José. The corporal of dragoons (ten), lover of Micaëla and of Carmen, in Bizet's *Carmen*.

Don Magnifico. Cenerentola's stepfather (bs) in Rossini's *La Cenerentola*.

Donna Anna. The Commendatore's daughter (sop), lover of Don Ottavio, in Mozart's *Don Giovanni*.

Donna del lago, La (The Lady of the Lake). Opera in 2 acts by Rossini; text by Tottola, after Walter Scott's poem (1810). Prem. Naples, C, 24 Oct. 1819.

Scotland, first half of 16th cent. James V of Scotland—Giacomo in the opera (ten)—loses his way and seeks shelter in the house of his enemy Douglas (bs), whose daughter Ellen (Elena, sop) has been forced to marry Roderick Dhu (Rodrigo, ten). In an uprising against the King, Roderick is killed, and Elena pleads with the King for her father's life and obtains his permission to marry her lover Malcolm (mez).

Donna Elvira. A lady of Burgos (sop), one of Don Giovanni's deserted lovers, in Mozart's *Don Giovanni*.

'Donna non vidi mai'. Des Grieux's (ten) aria in Act I of Puccini's *Manon Lescaut*, in which he voices his feelings of rapture as he sets eyes on Manon for the first time.

Donne curiose, Le (The Inquisitive Women). Opera in 3 acts by Wolf-Ferrari; text by Luigi Sugana after Goldoni's play of the same name. Prem. Munich, N, 27 Nov. 1903.

Set in 18th-cent. Venice, the opera tells of the suspicions of two married women and their friend, who believe that their husbands and lover are taking part in regular orgies at their men's club; they gain admission to the club and discover that all their menfolk are doing is indulging in gourmet meals.

Donner. The God of Thunder (bs-bar) in Wagner's *Das Rheingold*.

Don Ottavio. Donna Anna's lover (ten) in Mozart's *Don Giovanni*.

Don Pasquale. Opera in 3 acts by Donizetti; text by Ruffini and the composer after Anelli's libretto for Pavesi's *Ser Marc'Antonio* (1810). Prem. Paris, I, 3 Jan. 1843.

Rome, 19th cent. Don Pasquale (bs), a rich and crusty old bachelor, has decided to marry so that his nephew Ernesto (ten) will not inherit his fortune as he disapproves of his choice of a bride, the attractive young widow Norina (sop). The young couple, helped by Doctor Malatesta (bar), a friend of them both as well as of Pasquale, arrange for the old man to go through a mock marriage with 'Sofronia', Norina in disguise, who is presented as Malatesta's sister, fresh from a convent. No sooner is the wedding ceremony over, than Sofronia reveals herself in her true colours and makes the old man's life a misery. Malatesta suggests that the marriage be annulled; Pasquale agrees and, admitting he has been fooled, forgives them all.

Don Procopio. Opera in 2 acts by Bizet; text by Paul Collin and Paul de Choudens, translated from a libretto by Carlo Cambiaggio. Written 1859. Prem. (posth.) Monte Carlo, T du Casino, 10 Mar. 1906.

A country house in Spain, *c*.1600. To general disapproval, Don Andronico (bs) has agreed to marry his niece Bettina (sop) to Don Procopio (bar), a rich old miser. Her brother and aunt convince Don Procopio that Bettina would spend all his money and so he cancels the wedding, enabling Bettina to marry her beloved Eduardo (ten).

Don Quichotte. Opera in 5 acts by Massenet; text by Henri Cain, after Jacques Le Lorrain's play *Le chevalier de la longue figure* (1904), based in turn on Cervantes's novel (1605, 1615). Prem. Monte Carlo, T du Casino, 19 Feb. 1910.

Don Quixote (bs) is a naïve champion of goodness, charged by the sophisticated Dulcinea (con) to recover her necklace from brigands. He sets off with Sancho Panza (bar) and, after attacking the windmills, is seized by the bandits. His innocence wins his release with the necklace, but, rejected by Dulcinea, he dies broken-hearted.

Don Rodrigo. Opera in 3 acts by Ginastera; text by Alejandro Casona. Commissioned and prem. Buenos Aires, C, 24 July 1964.

The opera tells of the brief reign of Don Rodrigo (ten), the last Visigoth King of Spain, whose defeat at Guadalete led to the fall of Spain to the Saracens.

Don Sanche. Opera in 1 act by Liszt; text by Emmanuel Guillaume Théaulon de Lambert and De Rancé after a tale by Florian. Prem. Paris, O, 17 Oct. 1825.

Don Sanche (ten) wishes to enter a moated castle, owned by the magician Alidor (bar), but is told that only those who love and are loved may be admitted. He loves Princess Elzire (sop), but she does not love him. Alidor promises to help him, and raises a storm, enabling him to come to Elzire's aid. Don Sanche prevents her abduction by the knight Romualde, but is wounded: Elzire's indifference towards him is transformed into love. It emerges that 'Romualde' was Alidor in disguise; he cures Don Sanche's injuries and the happy couple may now enter the castle of love.

Liszt's only completed opera, written when he was 12. The score was lost until 1903.

Dorabella. Fiordiligi's sister (mez) in Mozart's *Così fan tutte*.

Dorati, Antal (*b* Budapest, 9 Apr. 1906; *d* Gerzensee, 13 Nov. 1988). Hungarian, later US, conductor. Studied Budapest with Bartók, Kodaly, and Weiner. Début Budapest O 1924. Dresden, assistant cond. to Busch, 1928–9; Münster 1929–33. London, CG, 1962 (*Golden Cockerel*). He conducted some notable recordings of Haydn's Esterházy operas, which did much to revive the composer's reputation for dramatic music.

Dorfbarbier, Der (The Village Barber). Opera in 1 act by Schenk; text by J. and P. Weidemann. Prem. Vienna, B, ? 6 Nov. 1796.

A small village, late 18th cent. The village barber and local quack, Lux (bs), wishes to marry his ward Suschen (sop). However, she loves Josef (ten), and the couple plan a trick on Lux, aided by the schoolmaster, Rund (bs). Suschen pretends to spurn Josef, who consequently takes poison. Since she has been named as Josef's beneficiary, Lux agrees to a deathbed marriage. The instant he has given his consent, Josef leaps up 'cured'.

Schenk's most popular work, it was seen on virtually every German stage.

Dorliak, Xenia (*b* St Petersburg, 11 Jan. 1882; *d* Moscow, 8 Mar. 1945). Russian soprano. Studied St Petersburg with Gladkaya, later Iretskaya. Sang Paris, Prague, Berlin. Paris, O, 1911 (Elisabeth, Elsa, Brünnhilde). St Petersburg and other major Russian houses. A prominent Wagner singer, she was also admired as Aida, Amelia, Tosca, Tatyana. Retired 1914. Her pupils incl. her daughter the soprano **Nina Dorliak** (*b* St Petersburg, 7 July 1908), later wife of Svyatoslav Richter.

Dorn, Heinrich (*b* Königsberg, 14 Nov. 1804; *d* Berlin, 10 Jan. 1892). German conductor and composer. Studied Berlin with Berger, Klein, and Zelter. Königsberg 1828; Leipzig 1829–32; Riga 1832–43; Cologne 1844–7; Berlin 1849–69. His Riga friendship with Wagner turned to hostility; and he anticipated Wagner by composing an opera *Die Nibelungen* (Weimar 1854) to a text rejected by Mendelssohn. Much admired as conductor and teacher.

Dorus-Gras, Julie (*b* Valenciennes, 9 Sept. 1805; *d* Paris, 9 Feb. 1896). Belgian soprano. Studied Paris with Henri and Blangini, then Paer and Bordogni. Début Brussels, M, 1826. Début Paris, O, 1830 (Angèle, *Le Comte Ory*), where she succeeded Cinti-Damoreau as prima donna 1835–45. (Her departure from the O was precipitated by the victimization of Rosine Stoltz.) London, DL, 1847 (Lucia); London, CG, 1849, Alice (*Robert le diable*), and Marguerite de Valois (*Les Huguenots*), two roles which she had created. Others included Eudoxie (*La Juive*), Pauline (Donizetti's *Les martyrs*), and Teresa (*Benvenuto Cellini*). Also a famous Elvira (*Muette de Portici*), which she sang in the performance in Brussels, Sept. 1830, that sparked off the revolt of the Low Countries. Like Cinti-Damoreau, she was a brilliant and accurate singer, with a pure voice. She had to endure lampooning for the sobriety of her private life.

Dosifey. Dositheus (bs), leader of the Old Believers in Musorgsky's *Khovanshchina*.

Dourlinski. Baron Dourlinski (bs), owner of the castle in which Lodoïska is imprisoned, in Cherubini's *Lodoïska*. He was a model for Beethoven's *Pizarro.

'Dove sono'. The Countess's (sop) aria in Act III of Mozart's *Le nozze di Figaro*, mourning the loss of her husband's love.

Downes, (Sir) Edward (*b* Birmingham, 17 June 1924). English conductor. Studied Birmingham, and with Scherchen. Début with CR, London, 1950. With CR until 1952; CG, 1952–69 (Solti's assistant from 1966), and subsequently; Australian O 1970–6; WNO 1975. Principal cond. CG 1992. Repertory incl. *Freischütz*, *Attila*, *Flying Dutchman*, *The Ring*, *Katerina Ismaylova*, *Turandot*, *Salome*, *War and Peace*, *Fiery Angel*. Completed and cond. first performance of Prokofiev's *Maddalena* (BBC 1979). Translations incl. *Khovanshchina*, *Katerina Ismaylova*, *Jenůfa*. (R)

Down in the Valley. Opera by Kurt Weill; text by Arnold Sundgaard. Prem. Bloomington, Indiana U, 14 July 1948.

In a series of flashbacks, the opera tells the story of a young couple, Brack Weaver (ten) and Jennie Parsons (sop). Brack is awaiting execution for the killing, in self-defence, of Thomas Bouché (bs), an unpleasant rival for Jennie's affections.

D'Oyly Carte Opera Company. See CARTE, RICHARD D'OYLY.

Draghi, Antonio (*b* Rimini, 1634/5; *d* Vienna, 16 Jan. 1700). Italian composer. Though he began his career as an opera singer in Venice, he is best remembered as the composer of *c*.120 dramatic works for the Viennese court, where he was appointed Kapellmeister in 1669. Like Cesti and Ziani before him, he proved adept at transforming the typical musical and dramatic devices of Venetian public opera into a style appropriate to a courtly entertainment, typically involving heroic subjects. His operas include *Rodogone* (1677), *La magnanimità di Marco Fabrizio* (1695), and *Gundeberga* (1672), one of the first to be based on a German historical subject.

Draghi, Giovanni Battista (*b* ?, *c*.1640; *d* London, 1708). Italian harpsichordist and componist. His music for Shadwell's *Psyché* (1675), for which he collaborated with Matthew Locke, represents some of the earliest operatic writing in England.

Dramaturg (Ger.). The member of staff of a German opera-house who combines the duties of adapter of librettos, editor of programmes, and press officer, sometimes also producer and even actor. The term (usually spelt dramaturge) is now also in wide use in the UK.

dramma giocoso (It.: 'jocular drama'). A development of *opera buffa, the dramma giocoso was created by *Goldoni around 1750 through the addition of serious roles (*parti serie*) to the stock figures of the genre. Classic examples are provided by the librettos set in Galuppi's *Il filosofo di campagna* and Piccinni's *La buona figliuola*, where the addition of serious characters and episodes lends a more poignant aspect to the drama. Most of Haydn's comic operas, including *Le pescatrici*, *Il mondo della luna*, and *La vera costanza*, were also of this variety. The most famous dramma giocoso, and the only such work regularly performed today, is Mozart's *Don Giovanni*.

dramma per musica (It.: 'drama for music'). The term used by many 17th-cent. Italian librettists to describe their text, reflecting the fact that it had been written with the express purpose of being set to music. By extension the resultant opera, invariably serious, could also be known as a dramma per musica, or sometimes a dramma in musica, a term preferred by composers, since it stressed the primacy of the music. These terms continued into the 18th cent., when they effectively became interchangeable with that of *opera seria.

Dreigroschenoper, Die (The Threepenny Opera). Opera in a prologue and 3 acts by Weill; text a modern interpretation of *The *Beggar's Opera*, based on a translation by Hauptmann, with lyrics, drawn also from Kipling and Villon, by Brecht, with Elisabeth Hauptmann. Prem. Berlin, T am Schiffbauerdamm, 31 Aug. 1928.

London *c*.1900. The prologue presents the scene of thieves, beggars, and prostitutes at a Soho fair.

J. J. Peachum (bs) hires costumes out to beggars to arouse the public's pity. When he discovers that his daughter Polly (sop) has secretly married the robber Mack the Knife (Macheath in *The Beggar's Opera*), Peachum threatens to hand him over to the police.

Mack flees but, through bribery from Mrs Peachum (sop), is captured and taken to prison. Mack has pretended to marry Lucy (sop), the daughter of Tiger Brown, the commissioner of the police; an angry scene ensues when both girls visit him. He denies having married Polly and, with Lucy's help, escapes.

The Peachums are again informed of Mack's whereabouts. He is arrested and sentenced to hang; he tries, unsuccessfully, to escape by bribing a policeman. As Mack goes to the gallows, a royal pardon arrives for him, and the Queen makes him a peer.

Drei Pintos, Die (The Three Pintos). Unfinished opera begun by Weber; text by Theodor Hell, after Seidel's story *Der Brautkampf* (1819). Completed and scored by Mahler, with additions, using other music by Weber and with an interlude composed on themes in the opera by Mahler. Prem. Leipzig 20 Jan. 1888.

Madrid, 19th cent. Don Pinto (bs) is intercepted by Don Gaston (ten) on his way to Seville to marry Clarissa (sop). Gaston, with the help of his servant Ambrosio (bar), first tries to teach the inane Pinto the art of wooing and then makes him drunk. Taking his papers off him, thus becoming Pinto no. 2, Gaston sets off for Seville. When he finds that Clarissa is secretly in love with Gomez (ten) but cannot marry him, he passes on the Pinto papers: Gomez thus becomes the third Pinto. Eventually the real Don Pinto turns up and discloses himself to Clarissa's furious father Don Pantaleone (bar); but all ends happily.

Dresden. City in Saxony, Germany. In 1617 Heinrich *Schütz reorganized the Kapelle on Italian models, and his *Dafne*, the earliest German opera (music lost), was produced for a court wedding nearby at Torgau in 1627. After the Thirty Years' War he was succeeded by Giovanni Bontempi and Vincenzo Albrici, and the line of opera that began with the opening of the Kurfürstliches Opernhaus in 1667 with *Teseo* (Moniglia) was Italian. Under the directorship of C. *Pallavicino, Dresden court opera developed in the late 17th cent. into a generally lavish and opulent manner, following the main musical precepts of the Venetian style. In 1707 this theatre was converted by Friedrich August into the Hofkirche, and performances were given in the Riesensaal of the Castle; the enlarged Grosses Opernhaus (cap. c.1,500–2,000: largest in Europe) opened 1719 with *Giove in Argo* by Antonio *Lotti. Admission was to the public, and free. Under Friedrich August II, Dresden became one of the most important operatic centres in Germany: characteristic at this time were lavish productions calling for the very best musical resources. Particularly significant was Johann *Hasse, and his wife Faustina *Bordoni worked here 1731 and 1734–56. Pietro Mingotti's company performed 1747 (with Gluck as conductor). The opera-house was altered by *Galli-Bibiena 1750. The Komödienhaus (Kleines Hoftheater) was completed 1755 and lasted until 1841; a small wooden theatre opened in the court of the Zwinger for more popular opera (burnt down 1748): operatic performances were also staged at the summer palace Schloss Moritzburg. Three Dresdeners, Johann *Naumann, Joseph Schuster, and Franz Seydelmann, visited Italy 1765–8 to study. The most popular and established form with court and nobility was Italian, and companies under Locatelli, Moretti, and Bustelli made successful visits. Singspiel was also popular; from 1770 works by Hiller, Benda, Schweitzer, and others were given by J. C. Wäser. On his appointment in 1786

Naumann did much to influence taste in a German and French direction, but unsuccessfully proposed a German opera. Opera semiseria began to appear. Joseph Seconda opened his theatre on the Linckesches Bad 1790, and E. T. A. *Hoffmann was director of the company run by the Seconda brothers in Leipzig and Dresden 1813–14.

In 1817 Carl Maria von *Weber became royal Kapellmeister; Francesco *Morlacchi was in charge of Italian opera 1810–41. Weber instituted searching reforms in the style of opera presentation, making a crucial shift towards the concept of music drama. He was succeeded by Karl *Reissiger in 1827. The Semper Opernhaus opened 1841. After the success of *Rienzi* here in 1842, Wagner succeeded Morlacchi as Hofkapellmeister, and produced his *Fliegender Holländer* and *Tannhäuser*. He had to flee after his part in the 1848 Revolution. In 1868 the opera-house burnt down; rebuilt on Semper's plans, it reopened 1878. Ernst von *Schuch was conductor from 1882, artistic director 1889–1914. A distinguished ensemble included Malten, Schuch-Proska, Sembrich, Schumann-Heink, Burian, Scheidemantel, later Siems, Von der Osten, Perron, and Plaschke. Fifty-one prems. included Strauss's *Feuersnot* (1901), *Salome* (1905), *Elektra* (1909), and *Rosenkavalier* (1911). Schuch was succeeded by Fritz *Reiner. In 1918 the theatre became the Staatsoper. Fritz *Busch was appointed 1922: his régime saw the prems. of more Strauss and Hindemith's *Cardillac* (1926), and the beginning of the German Verdi revival. Karl *Böhm succeeded 1934–42, Karl Elmendorff 1943–5; the company had included Seinemeyer, Cebotari, Rethberg, Höngen, T. Ralf, Tauber, Schoeffler, Boehme, and Frick.

On 14 Feb. 1945 the theatre was gutted during the bombing of Dresden. The company was housed in the Town Hall 1945–8, under the direction of Joseph Keilberth, then moving to the rebuilt Schauspielhaus (cap. 1,131). Rudolf Kempe was music director 1950–2, Franz Konwitschny 1953–5, Lovro von Matačić 1956–8, Otmar Suitner 1960–4. The rebuilt Semper opera-house reopened 13 Feb. 1985 with *Freischütz*. The ensemble included Schreier, Adam, and Bär.

Drottningholm. Palace near Stockholm, Sweden. The theatre was built by Queen Lovisa Ulrika in 1754; burnt down 1762; reopened 1766 (cap. 400). It still preserves stage machinery, a curtain, and some 30 18th-cent.

stage sets used in the present annual summer seasons. Period instruments are regularly used in the performances.

Drum-Major. Marie's seducer (ten) in Berg's *Wozzeck*.

Drury Lane, Theatre Royal. There have been four theatres on the site in London. The first opened in 1663, the second, designed by Wren, in 1674; this saw the prems. of several of Dryden's plays and masques with Purcell's music, and of many ballad operas. Arne, Dibdin, Linley, and Storace were all connected with the theatre. The third theatre (1794–1809) had Bishop as music director 1806–9. The fourth opened Oct. 1812. Tom Cooke was principal tenor 1813–35 and music director from 1821. Alfred Bunn took over in 1831, and presented Malibran singing *Fidelio* and *Sonnambula* in English. Bunn tried to establish English opera on a permanent basis 1835–47, producing works by Balfe, Benedict, and Wallace. In the mid-1850s seasons of English and Italian opera were given by E. T. Smith, including the English prem. of *Les vêpres siciliennes* (in Italian). The theatre was the home of Mapleson's Her Majesty's Opera 1867–77, and in 1870 saw the first English prem. of a Wagner opera, *Der fliegender Holländer* (as *L'olandese dannato*).

In 1882 Richter and a German company gave performances including the first London *Tristan* and *Meistersinger*, and from 1883 Drury Lane saw London seasons of the Carl Rosa OC. Augustus Harris began his Italian opera revival 1887, transferring to Covent Garden 1888 but using Drury Lane for some German opera 1892–3. There were English seasons 1894–1913, and Sir Joseph Beecham's Russian seasons 1913–14; these included the English prems. of important Russian works including *Boris Godunov*, *Khovanshchina*, *Prince Igor*, *Ivan the Terrible*, *May Night*, *The Golden Cockerel*, and *The Nightingale*. Thomas Beecham's English OC gave some London seasons there during 1914–18. Opera was not heard again until Gorlinsky's Italian season in 1958, including *William Tell* (English prem. of an arrangement there 1830).

Dublin. Capital of Republic of Ireland. Opera was first given in 1705–6 at the Smock Alley T (D. Purcell's *The Island Princess*). Italian opera was first performed in 1761 by a company under Antonio Minelli that included the De Amicis family, beginning with Scolari's *La cascina*. After seven years of English opera (1770–7), Italian opera returned, in the Fishamble Street T and again Smock Alley T, where works by Paisiello, Anfossi, etc. were given. Gluck's *Orfeo* (in English) had its first Dublin performance in 1784 with Mrs Billington as Euridice: she appeared regularly for the next 13 years. Many performances were described by Michael *Kelly, who appeared throughout the 1780s. In the 19th cent. the T Royal was the scene of outstanding seasons with artists from the Italian opera-houses in London, including Persiani, Grisi, Rubini, Mario, and Pauline Viardot, who sang Lady Macbeth in the only production of Verdi's opera in the British Isles before 1938. In 1871 the Gaiety T opened, and was the home of seasons given by touring companies including the Carl Rosa, Mapleson, Harris, and O'Mara. From 1928 to 1938 the Irish Opera Society performed at the Gaiety T. In 1941 the Dublin Grand Opera Society was formed, giving two seasons each year; normally chorus and orchestra are local, with soloists from England and the Continent, or sometimes whole visiting ensembles.

Duca d'Alba, Il (The Duke of Alba). Opera in 4 acts by Donizetti; text by Scribe. Originally written for Paris, O, in 1840 but not produced; the libretto was later altered by Scribe and became the text of *Les vêpres siciliennes*. Donizetti's score was recovered at Bergamo in 1875 and completed by Matteo Salvi, prem. Rome, Ap., 22 Mar. 1882.

Brussels, 1573. In this complicated tale about the oppressed Flemings suffering under Spanish tyranny, Amelia (sop), daughter of Egmont, is in love with Marcello (ten), who is revealed to be the missing son of the Duke of Alba (bar). Amelia, in an attempt to murder the Duke, instead kills Marcello, who has intervened to save his father's life. As he dies he begs the Duke to forgive Amelia.

Due Foscari, I. Opera in 3 acts by Verdi; text by Piave, after Byron's drama *The Two Foscari* (1821). Prod Rome, Arg., 3 Nov. 1844.

The Doge's Palace, Venice, 1457. The Council of Ten assemble for the trial of Jacopo Foscari (ten) for murder. Jacopo's wife Lucrezia (sop) is dissuaded from going to his father Francesco (bar), the Doge, to beg for his life. The Council condemns Jacopo to exile.

Lucrezia visits Jacopo in his cell to tell him

his sentence. The Doge feels unable to help his son because of the laws of Venice and tries to explain this to Lucrezia. Loredano (bs), an enemy of the Foscaris, insists that Jacopo should leave at once.

News emerges of a confession which clears Jacopo's name. The Doge is delighted, but Lucrezia rushes to say that Jacopo has collapsed and died as he was boarding the prison galley. At the instigation of Loredano, the Council of Ten 'invite' the Doge to abdicate. He agrees reluctantly. With Loredano exulting, the Doge dies as the bells announce his successor.

Due Litiganti, I (The Two Litigants). Correctly, *Fra due litiganti il terzo gode*. Opera in 3 acts by Sarti; text an altered version of Goldoni's *Le nozze*. Prem. Milan, S, 14 Sept. 1782.

The Count and Countess each have in mind a different husband for their maid Dorina. After many confusions and surprises, she marries a third suitor, but all is resolved satisfactorily.

In its day immensely popular; Mozart not only used the aria 'Come un agnello' for a set of piano variations (K460), but quoted it, with certainty of recognition, in Don Giovanni's supper scene as the wind band's second piece—whereupon Leporello exclaims, 'Evvivano I Litiganti!'

Duenna, The, or The Double Elopement. 1. Opera in 3 acts composed and compiled by Thomas Linley, sen. and jun.; text by Sheridan. Prem. London, CG, 21 Nov. 1775. One of the most successful English comic operas of the 18th cent., surpassing even *The Beggar's Opera* on its first run (75 performances as against 63).

2. Opera in 4 acts by Prokofiev (sometimes known, from the translation of Prokofiev's Russian title, as *Betrothal in a Monastery*); text by Prokofiev with verses by Mira Mendelson, after Sheridan. Prem. Prague, N, 5 May 1946.

Seville, 18th cent. Louisa (sop), daughter of Don Jerome (ten), has been promised to old Mendoza (bs), but she wants to marry Antonio (ten). Disguised as her duenna Margaret (con), Louisa runs away; she encounters her brother Ferdinando (bar) eloping with Clara d'Almanzo (mez). Clara agrees to hide in a convent so that Lousia may disguise herself and take Clara's place. Meanwhile, Margaret, disguised as Louisa, has managed to persuade Mendoza to elope with her. Fer-

dinando and Antonio have also been taken in by the deceptions and when all parties meet at the convent, the two propose to fight a duel. Eventually all is resolved and Don Jerome allows his children to make the marriages of their choice.

3. Opera in 3 acts by Roberto Gerhard; text by the composer, after Sheridan. Prem. Madrid 21 Jan. 1992.

Dufranne, Hector (*b* Mons, 25 Oct. 1871; *d* Paris, 4 May 1951). Belgian bass-baritone. Studied Brussels. Début Brussels, M, 1896 (Valentin). Paris, OC, 1899–1909, creating Marquis de Saluces (Massenet's *Grisélidis*), and Golaud, among other roles. Paris, O, from 1909, where he was 'un Jokanaan superbe' (*L'éclair*). Chicago 1913–22, where he created the Magician in *Love of Three Oranges*. London, CG, 1914. His sonorous, wide-ranged voice enabled him to sing a variety of parts. Retired 1939.

Dugazon, Louise (*b* Berlin, 18 June. 1755; *d* Paris, 22 Sept. 1821). French mezzo-soprano. Began life as a dancer, then studied with Favart. Grétry composed an air for her to sing in his *Lucille* (1769), but her mature début was as Pauline in his *Sylvain*, 1774. Sang at Paris, I, and later the OC, until 1804, creating more than 60 roles, especially in operas by Boieldieu, Grétry, and Isouard; her most famous was Dalayrac's Nina. Though her voice was unexceptional, and she was untrained musically, she was astonishingly versatile, possessing an instinctive feel for drama, and a moving intensity on stage that inspired odes, paintings, and general adoration. The genres in which she excelled came to be known as 'jeunes Dugazons' and 'mères Dugazons'.

Dukas, Paul (*b* Paris, 1 Oct. 1865; *d* Paris, 17 May 1935). French composer and critic. Both his first attempts at composition and his early critical writings were much influenced by Wagner. He wrote himself a libretto for *Horn et Rimenhild*, but composed no more than one act (1892). He abandoned another operatic project, *L'arbre de science* (1899), when Maeterlinck gave permission for use of *Ariane et Barbe-bleue* (1907). The first major opera to be influenced by *Pelléas et Mélisande*, it differs in its broader structural scheme, its scope for more elaborate musical development, its more extrovert scoring, and its simpler emotional appeal: some qualities of *Pelléas* are present but dispersed into a more conventional kind of opera. Other unrealized operatic projects included a setting of *The Tempest*. Dukas also helped Saint-Saëns to complete Guiraud's *Frédégonde*, and edited several of Rameau's operas.

Duke Bluebeard's Castle (Hung., *A Kékszakállú herceg vára*). Opera in 1 act by Bartók; text by Béla Balázs. Prem. Budapest 24 May 1918.

Bluebeard (bs) is not the Gilles de Rais monster of the *Ma Mère L'Oye* fairy-tale and Dukas's *Ariane et Barbe-bleue*, but a sorrowing, idealistic man. When his newest bride, Judith (sop), discovers his innermost secret and joins his other hidden wives, he is left with his loneliness once again.

Duke of Mantua. The licentious duke (ten) in Verdi's *Rigoletto*.

Dulcamara. The quack (bs) in Donizetti's *L'elisir d'amore*.

Du Locle, Camille (*b* Orange, 16 July 1832; *d* Capri, 9 Oct. 1903). French librettist and theatre director. His first libretto was for Duprato's *M'sieu Landry* (1856). Paris: O, joint dir. 1869; OC, joint dir. with Leuven 1870–4, sole dir. 1874–6. He continued the text of Verdi's *Don Carlos* after Méry's death, and made a preliminary draft of *Aida* with Verdi before it was passed to Ghislanzoni; he also translated *Simon Boccanegra*, *La forza del destino* (with Nuittier), and the first two acts of *Otello*. His other librettos include those for Reyer's *Sigurd* and *Salammbô*. He gave encouragement to Bizet at the time of *Carmen*, though he disliked the work.

Duni, Egidio Romualdo (*b* Matera, *bapt.* 11 Feb. 1708; *d* Paris, 11 June 1775). French composer. Studied Naples with Durante. In the 1735 Rome Carnival his first opera, *Nerone*, proved a greater success than the established Pergolesi's *L'Olimpiade*. After some travels, including to London for *Demofoonte* (1737), he had various successes in Italy, concluding his career as an opera seria composer with his own *L'Olimpiade* in 1755. At Parma, where he was maestro di cappella from 1749, he came to appreciate French music, and may then have set or contributed music to two Favart librettos (including *Ninette à la cour*). His first opera for Paris was *Le peintre amoureux de son modèle* (1757), popular partly for its refutation of Rousseau's denial of the French language's suitability for music. With the series of works that followed, Duni established himself as one of the most important founding composers of opéra-comique. The introduction of Italian arias and recitatives into French ensembles, dances, and divertissements proved a brilliantly successful mix, his Italian liveliness and tunefulness helping to give the French *comédie mêlée d'ariettes* greater substance than it had hitherto enjoyed. In the best of his work, the characters have a pathos and eloquence that greatly contributed to elevating the genre above the merely frivolous.

Dunn, Geoffrey (*b* London, 13 Dec. 1903; *d* London, 6 Sep. 1981). English tenor, producer, and librettist. Sang with Nigel Playfair's Co., Lyric T Hammersmith, in hitherto little-known works, e.g. *Idomeneo*. Formed Intimate OC 1930 (with Margaret Ritchie and Frederick Woodhouse), for which he revived several 18th-cent. English operas by Arne, Dibdin, and Carey. Translated many foreign librettos, including *Poppea*, *Serse*, *Der Corregidor*, *La vie parisienne*, and Rimsky-Korsakov's *Mozart and Salieri*. Also wrote librettos for Malcolm Williamson, e.g. *Dunstan and the Devil*. Producer for London, SW, *Don Giovanni* (1949) and *Dido and Aeneas* (1951). After giving up singing, turned to acting.

'Dunque io son'. The duet between Rosina (mez) and Figaro (bar) in Act I of Rossini's *Il barbiere di Siviglia*, in which he spins a story about his cousin, a poor student, who is in love with a certain girl, and eventually is given a letter already written for the disguised Almaviva.

Duprez, Gilbert(-Louis) (*b* Paris, 6 Dec. 1806; *d* Paris, 23 Sept. 1896). French tenor. Studied Paris with Choron. Début Odéon 1825 (Rossini's Almaviva). Further study in Italy, where he sang 1829–35, creating Edgardo (*Lucia*) at Naples. During this time his voice developed from a small, light tenor to one of considerable power, though with the sacrifice of agility and range of colour. Returned to Paris, replacing Nourrit as leading tenor at the Opéra, 1837–49. Here he created Benvenuto Cellini, Fernando (*La favorite*), and Polyeucte (*Les martyrs*), and took over much of Nourrit's repertory. Credited with being the first tenor to produce the *ut de poitrine*, or chest voice top C (to the delight of Paris audiences, but not of Rossini), he strongly influenced succeeding generations of tenors in this respect. Caricatured for his small size and gaping mouth, he performed with unrelenting commitment. Chorley praised his 'dramatic truth', and Roger described his singing, even at the end, as 'molten ore'. His voice declined early; Berlioz also regretted the coarsening of his style. After retiring, he was a notable teacher. Among his pupils were Miolan-Carvalho, Nantier-Didier, and Albani. He also wrote several operas, and two books on singing. His wife **Alexandrine Duperron** (1808–72) sang in Paris 1827–37, often with Duprez; their daughter **Caroline Vandenheuval-Duprez** (1832–75) was a light soprano, who sang 'exquisitely' (Berlioz) with Viardot, and also appeared with her father.

Durastanti, Margherita (*b*? Venice; *fl.* 1700–34). Italian soprano, later mezzo-soprano. First known appearance Venice, 1700, in a pasticcio. From 1707, engaged by Prince Ruspoli at Rome, where she worked with Caldara, and Handel. Venice, 1709–12, in operas by Lotti, etc.; created Handel's Agrippina. Dresden 1719. London, Royal Academy of Music: 1720–1, creating Handel's Radamisto and Clelia in *Muzio Scevola*; 1722–4, creating Sesto in *Giulio Cesare*; 1733–4, helping Handel in his struggle against Porpora (creating Tauride in *Arianna*). She was a fine singer and dramatically effective, despite her size (Rolli called her 'an elephant') and earned extremely high fees.

'Durch die Wälder'. Max's (ten) aria in Act I of Weber's *Der Freischütz*, in which he reflects how once he wandered happily through the countryside before misfortune befell him.

'Durch Zärtlichkeit und Schmeicheln'. Blonde's (sop) aria in Act II of Mozart's *Die Entführung aus dem Serail*, in which she declares that a girl's heart may be won by tenderness, never by force.

Duval, Denise (*b* Paris, 23 Oct. 1921). French soprano. Début Bordeaux 1941 (Lola). Paris, O and OC, 1947–65, when she retired. The first Thérèse (*Les mamelles*), and Blanche in the prem. of the original *Dialogues des Carmélites*, of which she is also the dedicatee. Created Elle (*La voix humaine*), written specially for her, with great success. Edinburgh 1960; Gly. 1962–3. A beautiful and impressive singing actress, also notable as Thaïs and Mélisande. (R)

Dvořák, Antonín (*b* Nelahozeves, 8 Sept. 1841; *d* Prague, 1 May 1904). Czech composer. Studied Zlonice with Liehmann, Prague with Pitsch and Krejčí. His interest in opera was first aroused when a violist in the Prague Provisional Theatre Orchestra, where he had been impressed with Wagner. Though some of his operas are popular in the Czech Republic, they have not won acceptance in foreign repertories. Even in their own country, the early works have languished, though the sentimental humour of *Jakobín* (1889) is appreciated, as are the folk charms of *Tvrdé palice* (The Stubborn Lovers, comp. 1874) and *Šelma sedlák* (The Cunning Peasant, 1878). *Čert a Káča* (The Devil and Kate, 1899) has had some success abroad, as to a lesser extent has *Dmitrij* (1882), whose plot begins where *Boris Godunov* ends. Dvořák's greatest success has always been *Rusalka* (1901), a work of much charm which is as popular with Czech children as *Hänsel und Gretel* is with Germans. In general, Dvořák lacked a strong sense of drama and characterization, so that it is for incidental numbers or general expressions of atmosphere that his operas can be appreciated. His earliest works show the influence of Wagner, to which he returned in his later works after allowing the nationalist spirit of Smetana to be felt.

Dvorsky, Peter (*b* Partizánske, 25 Sept. 1951). Slovak tenor. Studied with Černecká. Début Bratislava 1972 (Lensky). Vienna from 1976; New York, M, and Munich 1977; Milan, S, 1978; London, CG, 1979; Salzburg 1989 (Cavaradossi), also Moscow, B; Verona; Prague; etc. Roles incl. Edgardo, Alfredo, Duke of Mantua, Rodolfo, Cavaradossi, Jeník. (R)

Dyagilev, Sergey (*b* Selichev, 31 Mar. 1872; *d* Venice, 19 Aug. 1929). Russian impresario. Though renowned as founder of the Russian Ballet Co. that bore his name, he was also an important figure in opera, especially in Paris 1907–9, Paris and London 1913–14, and Paris and Monte Carlo 1922–4. In 1907 he presented scenes from *Sadko*, *Boris*, and *Ruslan* in concert at the Paris, O, and in 1908 the first fully staged *Boris* outside Russia, with Shalyapin. He gave *Ivan the Terrible* in Paris 1909; the first *Khovanshchina* outside Russia, Paris, CE, 1913; the first Russian season at London, DL, 1913. With Beecham, he gave seven Russian operas (*Boris, Ivan, Igor, Golden Cockerel, Nightingale, May Night*, and *Khovanshchina*). In Paris gave the prem. of *Mavra* (1922) and *Oedipus Rex* (1927); in Monte Carlo gave Gounod's *Médecin malgré lui* with Satie recitatives

(1924), *La colombe* with Poulenc recitatives, and *Philémon et Baucis* and Chabrier's *Une éducation manquée* with Milhaud recitatives.

Dybbuk, The. 1. Opera in a prologue and 3 acts by Lodovico Rocca (*Il Dibuk*); text by R. Simoni, after Shelomoh An-Ski's drama (1916). Prem. Milan, S, 24 Mar. 1934.

Chanon (ten) is fascinated by the mysteries of the Kabala and tries to discover the means of winning riches so that he can marry Leah (sop). He dies, but his spirit enters Leah's body.

2. Opera in 3 acts by David Tamkin; text by Alex Tamkin. Comp. *c*.1931; prem. New York, CC, 4 Oct. 1951.

Dyck, Ernest van. See VAN DYCK, ERNEST.

Dyer's Wife, The. The (anonymous) wife (sop) of Barak the Dyer in Strauss's *Die Frau ohne Schatten*.

Dzerzhinsky, Ivan (*b* Tambov, 9 Apr. 1909; *d* Leningrad, 18 Jan. 1978). Russian composer. Studied Moscow with Gnesin, Leningrad with Ryazanov and Asafiev. When still a student he entered his opera *The Quiet Don* (1935) in a competition organized by the Bolshoy T and the journal *Komsomolskaya Pravda*, unsuccessfully. Revised, with help from Shostakovich and others, it was produced in Leningrad under Samosud, when it was praised by Stalin as an example of an immediately comprehensible patriotic opera and hence became an instant paragon of Socialist Realism. The music's simplemindedness ensured that this success was particular and temporary.

E

Eaglen, Jane (*b* Lincoln, 4 Apr. 1960). English soprano. After study at the RNCM appeared with London, ENO from 1984, as Donna Elvira, Elizabeth I (*Maria Stuarda*), Eva and Leonora (*Trovatore*). Her ample resources have made her widely admired as Brünnhilde (Scottish O; Seattle; and Milan, S). Other roles include Matthilde in *Guillaume Tell* (London, CG, 1990), Norma, Sieglinde, and Fata Morgana (*The Love of the Three Oranges*). New York, M, 1995. (R)

Eames, Emma (*b* Shanghai, 13 Aug. 1865; *d* New York, 13 June 1952). US soprano. Studied Paris with Marchesi. Début Paris, O, 1889 (Juliette). London, CG, 1891–1901, arousing Melba's jealousy with her successes as the Countess (Mozart), Elsa, Sieglinde, Eva, Aida, etc. New York, M, 1891–1909; Boston 1911 (Tosca, Verdi's Desdemona), after which she appeared only in concert. Her voice, thought by some more beautiful than Melba's, was full, even, flexible, and accurate. She was handsome, but somewhat cold: Shaw refers to her 'casting her propriety like a Sunday frock over the whole stage'. (R)

'È amore un ladroncello'. Dorabella's (mez) aria in Act II of Mozart's *Così fan tutte*, in which she reflects on how love gives both imprisonment and release.

Easter Hymn. The Resurrection Hymn for the chorus led by Santuzza (sop), 'Inneggiamo, il Signor non è morto', in Mascagni's *Cavalleria rusticana*.

Easton, Florence (*b* Middlesbrough, 25 Oct. 1882; *d* New York, 13 Aug. 1955). English soprano. Studied London, RCM, and Paris with Haslam. Début Newcastle 1903 (Shepherd, *Tannhäuser*). London, CG, 1903, 1909, 1927 (Turandot), 1932 (Brünnhilde). Henry Savage Co., 1905. Berlin, H, 1907–13; Hamburg 1913–15. New York, M, 1917–29, 1935–6: created Lauretta (*Schicchi*) and Aelfrida (in Deems Taylor's *The Henchman*). Had a repertory of over 100 roles in four languages, and was able to take over a part, new or old, at only hours' notice. In one week in 1922 she sang Isolde, Kundry, Fiordiligi, and Sieglinde. Her voice, pure-toned and powerful, was still magnificent at her farewell in 1936. (R)

Ebert, Carl (*b* Berlin, 20 Feb. 1887; *d* Santa Monica, 14 May 1980). German producer and manager. Studied acting with Reinhardt, and after engagements in Berlin and Frankfurt became general director of the Darmstadt State T 1927. General director and producer, Berlin, SO, 1931, where his productions came as a revelation to critics and public. Left Germany 1933. Produced opera Florence, Buenos Aires. With Fritz Busch founded *Glyndebourne Opera, where together they established its reputation for the highest international standards. Organized Turkish Nat. T and O, 1936–47; dir. opera dept. U of S California 1948–56. Gly. 1947–59. Returned to former Berlin post 1956–61. New York, M, 1959–62. His productions of Mozart and Verdi set particularly high standards of intelligent dramatization and faithfulness to the composers' intentions. Staged prem. of *The Rake's Progress*, Venice 1951. His son **Peter** (*b* Frankfurt, 6 Apr. 1918) has also worked at Glyndebourne. Scottish O: dir. of productions 1963–75, general administrator 1977–80; Augsburg 1968–73; Wiesbaden 1975–7.

Eboli. Princess Eboli (conceived as low mez, written as high mez for Lauters-Gueymard), former mistress of King Philip and lady-in-waiting to Elisabeth de Valois in Verdi's *Don Carlos*.

Ebrahim, Omar (*b* London, 6 Sept. 1956). English baritone. Sang with Gly. Touring O from 1980, after study in London, and joined O Factory in 1982 (Don Giovanni, Mel (*The Knot Garden*), and Birtwistle's Punch). Created roles in *Yan Tan Tethera* (1986), *Gawain* (London, CG, 1991), and *The Second Mrs Kong* (1994). His strong stage presence was also seen to advantage in operas by Osborne (*The Electrification of the Soviet Union*), Berio (*Un Re in ascolto*, London, CG, 1989) and Tippett (*New Year*, Gly. 1990). (R)

Eccles, John (*b* ?London, *c*. 1668; *d*. Hampton Wick, 12 Jan 1735). English composer. He rapidly established himself as one of the leading theatre composers of the day. For

Lincoln's Inn Field's T he composed two 'all-sung' masques (*The Loves of Mars and Venus*, 1696, and *Acis and Galatea*, 1700) and a full length 'dramatic opera', *Rinaldo and Armida* (1698, lost). A setting of Congreve's masque *The Judgement of Paris* (1701) won second prize in a famous competition. His significance as an opera composer rests, ironically, on a work which was not performed. *Semele* (1707), setting the Congreve text later used by Handel, was a unique example of an attempt to fuse English and Italian styles of opera. It also contains elements of masque. Owing to delays he did not complete the work until the opportunity for performance had passed; it received a belated prem. in London in 1972.

'Ecco l'orrido campo'. Amelia's (sop) aria opening Act II of Verdi's *Un ballo in maschera*, expressing her fear and horror as she comes to the deserted spot where she is to pick the herb that will subdue her love for the King.

'Ecco ridente in cielo'. Count Almaviva's (ten) aria in Act I of Rossini's *Il barbiere di Siviglia*, in which, disguised as Lindoro, he serenades Rosina (or, strictly, sings her a morning song).

Eda-Pierre, Christiane (*b* Fort-de-France, Martinique, 24 Mar. 1932). Martinique soprano. Studied Paris Cons. Début Nice, 1958 (Leïla). Paris, O, from 1962; London, CG, 1966; Chicago, Berlin, Moscow, etc. Repertory includes Elettra, Teresa (*Cellini*), Zerbinetta; also Rameau, Wagner, and contemporary works (creating the Angel in Messiaen's *François d'Assise*). A musical, often vocally dramatic, singer with a limpid tone. (R)

Edelmann, Otto (*b* Brunn am Gebirge, 5 Feb. 1917). Austrian bass-baritone. Studied Vienna with Lierhammer and Graarud. Début Gera 1937 (Mozart's Figaro). Vienna, S, from 1947; Salzburg 1948; Bayreuth 1951–2; New York, M, 1954–70; Gly. 1965. Also Milan, S; Berlin; Munich; S Francisco. Roles incl. Leporello, Rocco, Sachs, Amfortas, Ochs, Kecal. (R)

Edgar. Opera in 3 acts by Puccini; text by Ferdinando Fontana, after Alfred de Musset's verse drama *La coupe et les lèvres* (1832). Prem. Milan, S, 21 Apr. 1889.

A village in Flanders, 1302. Fidelia (sop) and Tigrana (mez) both love Edgar (ten). Fid-elia's brother Frank (bar) loves Tigrana but she spurns him. While the peasants gather in worship, Tigrana sings a profane song and they condemn her behaviour. Edgar defends her and flees with Tigrana, having set fire to his house. Frank tries to prevent them, but is injured in the fight.

Edgar sings of his disillusionment with his new life of pleasure and longs to be back in his village with Fidelia. A platoon of soldiers approaches; their captain turns out to be Frank, and Edgar soon joins the ranks. He and Frank turn on Tigrana.

Edgar is believed killed in battle and is mourned by Fidelia. As Frank delivers the eulogy, a monk reminds the people of how Edgar set his home on fire and chose a life of debauchery. Fidelia defends his memory. Tigrana enters and, having been bribed with jewels, proclaims in front of the people that Edgar planned to betray his country. The crowd storms the coffin, but they find only an empty suit of armour. The monk reveals himself to be Edgar; he denounces Tigrana, who then stabs Fidelia. As Edgar throws himself on Fidelia's dead body, Tigrana is led away.

Edgardo. Edgar of Ravenswood (ten), lover of Lucia, in Donizetti's *Lucia di Lammermoor*.

Edinburgh. Capital of Scotland. Apart from touring companies, Edinburgh had little opera before the First World War, though it was the birthplace of the *Denhof OC. In 1947 the Gly. Society Ltd. founded the annual summer festival at the instigation of Audrey *Mildmay and Rudolf *Bing (who was artistic director 1947–50). Despite the city's enduring resistance to providing an opera-house, opera has played a central part in the festival; it has had to be staged in the King's T and various even less suitable venues. Visiting companies first were Gly. (1947–55); Hamburg (1952, 1956); Milan, PS, (1957); Stuttgart (1958); and Stockholm (1959). Lord Harewood's régime (1961–5) saw visits by London, CG, and Belgrade (1962); Naples, C (1963); Prague (1964); Munich (1965); and Holland Festival O (1965). Companies to have visited since include Stuttgart (1966); Scottish O regularly since 1967; Hamburg (1968); Florence (1969); Frankfurt and Prague (1970); Berlin, D (1971); Palermo and Deutsche O am Rhein (1972); Budapest (1973); Stockholm (1974); Berlin, D (1975); Deutsche O am Rhein (1976); Zurich (1978);

Kent (1979); Cologne (1980–1); Milan, PS, and WNO, and Dresden (1982); Hamburg and St Louis (1983); Washington (1984); Lyons, Connecticut, and Les Arts Florissants (1985); Leningrad Maly (1986); Stockholm Folk O (1986–9); Helsinki (1987); Houston (1988); Jutland (1989); Moscow, B, and Bratislava (1990); Moscow, and Leningrad, M (1991); Australia (1994); Kirov (1995). The festival has itself staged Rossini and Mozart, and *Carmen* (1977). The many British stage prems. have included *Mathis der Maler* (1952); *The Rake's Progress* (1953); *Oedipus Rex* and *Mavra* (1956); *La vida breve* (1958); *Aniara* (1959); *La voix humaine* (1960); *Love of Three Oranges* and *The Gambler* (1962); *Dalibor*, *From the House of the Dead*, and Cikker's *Resurrection* (1964); *Intermezzo* (1965); Malipiero's *Sette canzoni* (1969); Reimann's *Melusine* (1971); Zimmermann's *Die Soldaten* (1972); Szokolay's *Blood Wedding* (1973); Werle's *Vision of Thérèse* (1974); Orr's *Hermiston* (1975); Musgrave's *Mary, Queen of Scots* (1977); Maxwell Davies's *The Lighthouse* (1980); Merikanto's *Juha* (1987); Adams's *Nixon in China* and Turnage's *Greek* (1988). Other outstanding events have included the first version of *Ariadne auf Naxos* under Beecham (1950); Callas in *La sonnambula*, replaced when she left by Scotto (1957); Janet Baker in *The Trojans* (1973); *Moses und Aron* (1976); and the Zurich Monteverdi cycle (1978). The Fringe has also seen a variety of events of many shapes and sizes.

From 1963 Scottish O have given annual spring seasons at the King's T and 1969–74 short winter seasons. ENO also pay regular visits. The U O Club has staged enterprising productions in various locations.

Éducation manquée, Une (A Defective Education). Operetta in 1 act by Chabrier; text by Leterrier and Vanloo. Prem. Paris, Cercle de la Presse, 1 May 1879.

France. The reign of Louis XVI. Count Gontran de Boismassif (sop) arrives home with his new bride Hélène (sop), totally uninstructed by his tutor Pausanias (bs) in the facts of life. Aged relatives are reluctant to enlighten them but the problem is resolved when a violent storm drives the two into each other's arms.

Edvina, Louise (*b* Montreal 28 May 1878; *d* London, 13 Nov. 1948). Canadian soprano. Studied Paris with J. De Reszke. Début London, CG, 1908 (Marguerite). Sang there until 1914; also 1919–20, 1924. First London

Louise, Thaïs, Francesca da Rimini. Boston 1911–13; Chicago 1915–17; New York, M, 1915 (Tosca). A 'born actress' (*The Globe*), and an affecting singer, she was particularly successful as Louise and Mélisande. (R)

Edwards, Sian (*b* West Chiltington, 27 Aug. 1959). English conductor. Studied London with Groves and Del Mar, Holland with Järvi, Leningrad with Musin. Début Scottish O 1986 (*Mahagonny*). Gly. from 1987 (*Traviata*); London, CG, from 1988 (*Knot Garden*)—first woman cond. there; Munich and Edinburgh 1988, with prem. of *Greek* (Turnage); London, ENO, 1990 (*The Gambler*). Repertory incl. *Rigoletto, Trovatore, Carmen, Káťa Kabanová, New Year, Jenůfa, Khovanshchina*. Music Director, ENO, from 1993. (R)

Egisto. Opera in 3 acts by Cavalli; text by Giovanni Faustini. Prem. Venice, C, 1643.

The island of Zakynthos, mythological times. Egisto relates to Climene how he and Clori were captured by Corsican bandits; Climene says she and Lidio endured a similar experience. Both are upset at the unfaithfulness of their respective lovers and go to Amor to seek revenge. When Venus sees that Egisto now has the means of release, she begs Amor to drive him mad.

Egisto meets Clori, who wishes to have nothing more to do with him. He advises Lidio to break with Clori since she brings nothing but sorrow. Climene's brother Hipparco also loves Clori. He encourages his sister to stab Lidio, but she hesitates, asking the gods to forgive him. Lidio then appears, declaring his love for Climene is unaltered; the couples are reunited by Amor.

Egk, Werner (*b* Auchsesheim, 17 May 1901; *d* Inning, 10 July 1983). German composer. Studied Frankfurt, and Munich with Orff. His first stage opera was *Die Zaubergeige* (1935), using numbers based on popular tunes. *Peer Gynt* (1938) became successful after receiving Hitler's approval. His operas have been widely staged in Germany, where his dramatic flair and his capacity for drawing on the most readily acceptable aspects of his predecessors, notably Stravinsky, have made him popular.

Eglantine. Eglantine von Puiset (mez), a rebel's daughter and Lysiart's lover, in Weber's *Euryanthe*.

'E il sol dell'anima'. The Duke's (ten) aria

declaring his love to Gilda in Act I of Verdi's *Rigoletto*, leading to the love duet.

Einem, Gottfried von (*b* Berne, 24 Jan. 1918). Swiss, later Austrian, composer. Studied Plön. Répétiteur Berlin, S, 1938. Further study with Blacher during the war, when he also suffered arrest and persecution for aiding escapes from the Nazis. Composer in residence Dresden O, 1944. He won fame with his first opera, *Dantons Tod* (1947), consolidating this with *Der Prozess* (1953). In these he made use of separate numbers and a light, allusive style that includes the influence of jazz by way of Stravinsky and Blacher. The sentimental comedy *Der Zerrissene* (1964) is an emptier work, and Einem's eclecticism proved inadequate to the content of *Kabale und Liebe* (1976). He has also achieved popularity with *Der Besuch der alten Dame* (1971), in which he confirms his ability to confront sharp moral problems in music whose popular appeal need not weaken the issues. *Tulifant* (1990), a parable about the enslavement and destruction of the world, makes use of a small orchestra to create lucid textures and atmospherics as well as to provide rhythmic dance sections.

'Ein Mädchen oder Weibchen'. Papageno's (bar) aria in Act II of Mozart's *Die Zauberflöte*, in which he sings of his longing for a wife.

'Einsam in trüben Tagen'. Elsa's (sop) aria, sometimes referred to as 'Elsa's Dream', in Act I of Wagner's *Lohengrin*, in which she recounts her dream of a rescuing hero.

'Ein Schwert verhiess mir der Vater'. Siegmund's (ten) narration in Act I of Wagner's *Die Walküre*, in which he relates how he has been promised a sword in his hour of need by his father (Wotan).

Einstudierung (Ger.). Production.

Eire. See IRELAND.

Eisenstein. Gabriel von Eisenstein (ten), husband of Rosalinde, in Johann Strauss's *Die Fledermaus*.

Elder, Mark (*b* Hexham, 2 June 1947). English conductor. Début Melbourne 1972 (*Rigoletto*). Sydney O 1973; London, ENO, 1974, music dir. 1979–93; CG, 1976 (*Rigoletto*); Bayreuth 1981 (*Meistersinger*); New York, M, 1988 (*Figaro*). His period at the Coliseum was characterized by the exploration of opera as contemporary entertainment, in conjunction with David Pountney, and the revival of neglected works (*Rusalka*, *Lady Macbeth of Mtsensk*, *Mazeppa*), as well as the introduction of new ones (British stage prems. incl. *The Stone Guest*, *Osud*, *Doktor Faust*, *Le Grand Macabre*, *Lear*, *Pacific Overtures*, *Akhnaten*). A brilliant and versatile conductor, who provides sympathetic leadership to both singers and orchestra. (R)

Eléazar. The Jewish goldsmith (ten), supposed father of Rachel, in Halévy's *La Juive*.

Elegy for Young Lovers. Opera in 3 acts by Henze; text by W. H. Auden and Chester Kallman. Prem. Schwetzingen 20 May 1961.

An Alpine hotel, 1910. Gregor Mittenhofer (bar), the self-centred and egoistic poet, goes every year to the 'Schwarzer Adler' in the Austrian Alps, to seek inspiration for his work from the hallucinations of Hilda Mack (sop). She is forever awaiting the return of her husband, who disappeared 40 years earlier on their honeymoon. When his body is recovered from the glacier, the poet has to look elsewhere for inspiration and turns to the young lovers, Toni, his stepson (ten), and Elisabeth (sop). He sends them to the Hammerhorn to gather edelweiss, and there lets them die. Their death inspires his greatest poem 'Elegy for Young Lovers', which he reads silently before the audience in the closing scene of the opera.

Elektra. Opera in 1 act by Richard Strauss; text by Hugo von Hofmannsthal, after his drama (1903), in turn after Sophocles' tragedy (411 or 410 BC). Prem. Dresden, H, 25 Jan. 1909.

Elektra (sop) mourns the death of her father Agamemnon; she tries to persuade her sister Chrysothemis (sop) to help her avenge it. Her mother Klytemnästra (mez), Agamemnon's murderer, is plagued by nightmares and fears, but finds some comfort in news of the death of Elektra's absent brother Orest. Alone, Elektra begins to dig up the axe that had slain Agamemnon, but is interrupted by a stranger in the courtyard: it is Orest (bs-bar), not dead but secretly returned. He enters the palace and kills Klytemnästra; when Klytemnästra's lover Aegisth (ten) appears, Elektra lights his way into the palace and to his own murder. She dances in triumph, and collapses dead.

Eletsky. A prince (bar), in love with Lisa and

Hermann's rival, in Tchaikovsky's *The Queen of Spades*.

Elettra. The Greek princess Electra (sop), in love with Idamante, in Mozart's *Idomeneo*.

Elgar, (Sir) **Edward** (*b* Broadheath, 2 June 1857; *d* Worcester, 23 Feb. 1934). English composer. Elgar's only engagement with opera came late in his career, with a projected setting of a libretto by Barry Jackson, *The Spanish Lady*, on Jonson's *The Devil is an Ass*. Copious fragments survive and were given in a performing version by Percy Young at Cambridge U O, 1994.

Elisabeth. The Landgrave's niece (sop), Tannhäuser's 'sacred' love in Wagner's *Tannhäuser*.

Elisabeth de Valois. King Philip II of Spain's Queen (sop), who loves and is loved by his son Carlos, in Verdi's *Don Carlos*.

Elisabetta, regina d'Inghilterra (Elizabeth, Queen of England). Opera in 2 acts by Rossini; text by Giovanni Schmidt, after Carlo Federici's drama (1814). Prem. Naples, C, 4 Oct. 1815.

London, late 16th cent. Queen Elizabeth I (sop) learns from the Duke of Norfolk (ten) that her favourite, Leicester (ten), has secretly married Mathilde (sop). Unable to persuade Leicester to give up Mathilde, she has him imprisoned; when Norfolk's intrigues eventually lead to his arrest, the Queen shows her magnanimity by pardoning Leicester and Mathilde.

The overture and finale were taken over from *Aureliano in Palmira*, and the former now replaces the lost overture to *Il barbiere di Siviglia*.

Elisir d'amore, L' (The Love Potion). Opera in 2 acts by Donizetti; text by Romani, after Scribe's libretto for Auber's *Le philtre* (1831). Prem. Milan, T della Canobbiana, 12 May 1832.

A Tuscan village, early 19th cent. Inspired by the story of Tristan and Isolde, the shy young Nemorino (ten) buys potion from a quack, Dulcamara (bs), in the hope of winning Adina (sop). She seems to prefer Belcore (bar), a sergeant of the garrison, and, irritated by Nemorino's now apparent indifference towards her, she promises to marry Belcore immediately. Convinced that the elixir will take effect within 24 hours, Nemorino begs her to wait, but she refuses.

Nemorino joins the army, using his enlisting bonus to buy another bottle of elixir. Finding himself suddenly surrounded by village girls, he presumes the elixir is working, unaware of the rumour that his uncle has died leaving him a large fortune. Adina feels intense envy and realizes that it is Nemorino she really loves. Learning of his sacrifices, she redeems him from the army and the couple are married. Dulcamara capitalizes on the apparent success of his elixir and does a roaring trade.

'Ella giammai m'amo'. Philip II's (bs) aria in Act IV of the Italian version of Verdi's *Don Carlos*, grieving over his loneliness as a man, having never been loved by his wife, and as a king.

'Elle a fui, la tourterelle'. Antonia's (sop) aria at the piano, in the 'Antonia' act of Offenbach's *Les contes d'Hoffmann*.

Ellen Orford. The schoolmistress (sop) who befriends Peter in Britten's *Peter Grimes*.

Elmendorff, Karl (*b* Düsseldorf, 25 Oct. 1891; *d* Hofheim, 21 Oct. 1962). German conductor. Studied Cologne with Steinbach and Abendroth. Début Düsseldorf 1916. Berlin and Munich 1925–32. Bayreuth 1927–42. Wiesbaden 1932–5, 1952–6; Mannheim 1935–42; Dresden 1942–5; Kassel 1948–56. A distinguished Wagnerian; cond. Wagner widely in Italy and also introduced Italian operas to Germany. (R)

Elming, Poul (*b* Aalborg, 1949). Danish tenor. After study at Århus, sang baritone roles from 1979 (Posa, Germont and Onegin with Stockholm O). Retrained as tenor and sang Parsifal at Copenhagen 1989; also at Bayreuth, 1992–4. London, CG, 1991 and 1994, as Siegmund in *Ring* productions by Götz Friedrich and Richard Jones. His secure technique and good sense of style makes him a successful Lohengrin and Max. (R)

Elsa. Elsa von Brabant (sop), bride of Lohengrin in Wagner's *Lohengrin*.

Elsner, Józef (*b* Grodków, 1 June 1769; *d* Warsaw, 18 Apr. 1854). Polish composer and teacher of German origin. After schooling in Breslau, where he sang in the opera chorus, studied Vienna. Cond. Brno 1791–2; Lwów 1792–9. From 1799 he was dir. of the Warsaw O, where he developed the repertory and improved standards. His teaching activities included a period as Rector of the Cons. from 1821: his pupils included Chopin. Among the most important of his many operatic pieces are *Andromeda* (1807; written in honour of Napoleon, who attended the second performance) and *Leszek Biały* (1818; King Łokietek). The latter was encouragingly reviewed by his friend and colleague E. T. A. Hoffmann. His operas are characteristic of an early phase of nationalism in that they graft local plots, characters, and folk-songs on to an established tradition, in his case Viennese Singspiel. His activities helped to provide a creative base for the succeeding generation of Polish composers.

'E lucevan le stelle'. Cavaradossi's (ten) aria in Act III of Puccini's *Tosca*, in which he reflects on his love for Tosca as he writes his last letter before his execution.

Elvino. A young farmer (ten), bridegroom of Amina, in Bellini's *La sonnambula*.

Elvira. 1. See DONNA ELVIRA.
2. The Bey of Algiers's about-to-be-discarded wife (sop) in Rossini's *L'italiana in Algeri*.
3. The daughter of Gualtiero Valton (Lord Walton) (sop) in Bellini's *I Puritani*.
4. Silva's kinswoman (sop), lover of Ernani in Verdi's *Ernani*.

Emilia. Iago's wife and Desdemona's companion (mez), in Rossini's and in Verdi's *Otello*. Also Emilia Marty, the singer (sop) in Janáček's *The Makropoulos Case*.

Emmanuel, Maurice (*b* Bar-sur-Aube, 2 May 1862; *d* Paris, 14 Dec. 1938). French composer and musicologist. Studied Paris with Delibes, who, outraged by his experiments, forbade him to enter for the Prix de Rome; privately with Guiraud. His scholarly interest in Greek and medieval modes is reflected in his writings and in his music, including in his two operas, *Prométhée enchaîné* (comp. 1916–18) and *Salamine* (1929).

Emperor Jones, The. Opera in 2 acts by Louis Gruenberg; text by Kathleen de Jaffa, after Eugene O'Neill's drama (1921). Prem. New York, M, 7 Jan. 1933.

Brutus Jones (bar), an ex-Pullman porter and escaped convict, rules his island in the Caribbean, with all the outward trappings of royalty. He has systematically fleeced his people and is making preparations to flee, warned by Henry Smithers (ten) that the tribesmen are about to revolt. Jones flees into the jungle and is confronted (in hallucinations) by his past victims. He begs God for forgiveness; but, discovered by the witch-doctor who has summoned the tribesmen, he kills himself with his last bullet, a silver one he has saved for this purpose.

encore (Fr.: 'again'). The word called by members of a British audience to demand the repeat of a number, hence the word applied to the actual repeat. On the Continent, the word *bis* (Fr. and It., from Lat.: 'twice, again') is used, and can similarly be formed into a noun (It., *chieder un bis*: 'to call for an encore') or a verb (Fr., *il fut bissé*: 'he was encored').

Énée. See AENEAS.

Enescu, George (*b* Liveni Vîrnav (now George Enescu), 19 Aug. 1881; *d* Paris, 3 or 4 May 1955). Romanian composer, conductor, violinist, and teacher. Studied Vienna with Fuchs. His only opera was *Œdipe* (1936), a work neglected outside Romania but one which includes some of his most powerful, somewhat Expressionist music in an ambitious treatment of the whole of Oedipus' life.

Enfant et les sortilèges, L' (The Child and the Enchantments). Opera in 2 parts by Ravel; text by Colette. Prem. Monte Carlo 21 Mar. 1925.

A country house in Normandy. A child (mez) is punished by his mother (con) for not doing his homework. In a fury, he tears the wallpaper and pulls the cat's tail. Armchair, clock, toys, and other objects come to life and express their scorn at the child's behaviour; even Arithmetic (ten) taunts him.

At night in the garden, the child finds the animals and trees equally hostile. A squirrel is accidentally wounded in the rumpus and, when the animals see how gently the child cares for its wounds, they relent. The child is returned home to his mother and the disturbing enchantments end.

'En fermant les yeux'. Des Grieux's (ten) aria in Act II of Massenet's *Manon*, in which he describes how he saw Manon in a dream.

English Music Theatre Company. Formed in 1947 as the English O Group by Benjamin Britten, John Piper, and Eric Crozier to encourage new operas, especially on a chamber scale, bringing poets and playwrights together with composers. Its enterprise also lay behind the foundation of the Aldeburgh Festival, and the O Studio in London, which in turn became the O School, Nat. School of O, and London O Centre. The group commissioned and performed works including several by Britten, also Berkeley, Williamson, Birtwistle, Gardner, Crosse, and Musgrave. It also revived works by Purcell, Mozart, Handel, Tchaikovsky, and Holst. Steuart Bedford and Colin Graham became music director and director of productions in 1971. In 1975 it was renamed to reflect its wider range of activities. It toured widely, and was able to draw upon the services of the best English singers of the day, including Baker, Ferrier, Harper, Vyvyan, Pears, Tear, and Brannigan. Disbanded 1980.

English National Opera. See COLISEUM, SADLER'S WELLS.

English Opera Group. See ENGLISH MUSIC THEATRE COMPANY.

Enna, August (*b* Nakskov, 13 May 1859; *d* Copenhagen, 3 Aug. 1939). Danish composer of Italian descent. Studied Copenhagen with Rasmussen. His first success as an opera composer came with *Heksen* (1892), which won a certain international reputation, and this was confirmed with *Kleopatra* (1894). His natural skill and graceful, late-Romantic melodic manner ensured him popularity in his own country, though his works have not generally exported well.

Enrico. Henry Ashton (bar), Lucia's brother in Donizetti's *Lucia di Lammermoor*.

ensemble finale. The closing scene of an act, usually of an opera buffa, during which the characters assemble gradually on stage, until the full or near-full cast is present. Having its origins in 17th-cent. Venetian opera, the ensemble finale proper was developed in the mid-18th cent.—by Pergolesi, Piccinni, and Paisiello especially—and reached its apotheosis in Mozart's mature opere buffe. The second act finale of *Figaro* (1786) provides a particularly fine example.

Entführung aus dem Serail, Die (The Abduction from the Seraglio). Opera in 3 acts by Mozart; text by Gottlieb Stephanie the Younger, altered from Christoph Friedrich Bretzner's libretto for André's *Belmont und Constanze* (1781), in turn adapted from one of various English and Italian plays and comic operas on the subject. Prem. Vienna, B, 16 July 1782.

The palace of the Pasha Selim, Turkey, mid-16th cent. Constanze (sop) is a captive of the Pasha (spoken), together with her servant Blonde (sop) and Pedrillo (ten). Belmonte (ten), a young Spanish nobleman and Pedrillo's original master, comes in search of his beloved Constanze. In the garden of the palace, he encounters Osmin (bs), the Pasha's steward, who flies into a rage at the mention of Pedrillo. Osmin leaves, and Pedrillo forms a plan to introduce Belmonte to the Pasha as an architect. A chorus of Janissaries signals the arrival of the Pasha with Constanze. Once alone, he pleads with her to consider giving him her love, but says will not yet force her. She reminds him of her pledge to Belmonte and departs sadly. Pedrillo introduces Belmonte.

Osmin is trying, without success, to force Blonde to love him. She stubbornly stands up for the rights of an Englishwoman to choose. Constanze resolves to refuse the Pasha and to die rather than be unfaithful to Belmonte. Pedrillo manages to inform Blonde of the escape plans for that night. He gets Osmin out of the way by making him drunk. The four lovers are reunited.

It is midnight and, as a signal to the women to start the escape, Pedrillo sings a serenade. Osmin catches them and the captives are brought before the Pasha. Belmonte turns out to be the son of the man who was responsible for sending the Pasha into exile. Instead of exacting vengeance on the son of his enemy, the Pasha decides to be magnanimous and to set all four captives free.

entr'acte (Fr.: 'between acts'). In opera, a piece of orchestral music played between the acts or scenes; also called an *intermezzo or interlude. It sometimes erroneously appears, in writings about music, as a synonym for *intermède.

Enzo. A Genoese noble (ten), Laura's lover, in Ponchielli's *La Gioconda*.

'Era la notte'. Iago's (bar) narration in Act II of Verdi's *Otello*, in which he pretends to substantiate his accusations against Desdemona by alleging that he once heard Cassio talking in his sleep about her and their love.

Erb, Karl (*b* Ravensburg, 13 July 1877; *d* Ravensburg, 13 July 1958). German tenor. Self-taught. Début Stuttgart 1907 (Kienzl's *Der*

Evangelimann). Stuttgart 1910–12. Munich, N, 1913 (Lohengrin), and subsequently member until 1925, created *Palestrina* (title-role), 1917. London, CG, 1927 (Belmonte, with his wife Maria Ivogün as Constanze). Retired from opera 1930, but continued career as recitalist. The model for Erbe in Mann's *Dr Faustus*, the intelligent 'tenor with the voice of a eunuch'. (R)

Ercole amante (Hercules in Love). Opera in a prologue and 5 acts by Cavalli; text by Francesco Buti. Prem. Paris, T des Tuileries, 7 Feb. 1662.

In the allegorical prelude, important royal families, including the French, are presented by the goddess Diana.

Diana promises Ercole Beauty as his bride if he will continue his tasks. The remainder of the opera is concerned with the love of both Ercole and his son Hyllo for Iole. The action involves extensive use of machines in 'heaven' and at sea (Act IV). At the conclusion of the opera, Ercole is awarded Beauty, and Hyllo marries Iole.

Erda. The Earth Goddess (con) and mother, by Wotan, of the Valkyries in *Rheingold* and *Siegfried* in Wagner's *Der Ring des Nibelungen*.

Erede, Alberto (*b* Genoa, 8 Nov. 1909). Italian conductor. Studied Genoa, Milan, Basel with Weingartner, Dresden with Busch. Début (concert) Rome 1930. Gly. music staff 1934; cond. 1938–9. Dir. Salzburg O Guild 1935–8. Music dir. New London OC 1946–8. New York, M, 1950–5. Deutsche O am Rhein 1956, music dir. 1958–61. A fine trainer of young singers, and a strong ensemble leader. (R)

Erhardt, Otto (*b* Breslau (Wrocław), 18 Nov. 1888; *d* San Carlos de Bariloche, 18 Jan. 1971). German producer. Studied music and history of art; began career as violinist. Staged German prem. of Monteverdi's *Orfeo* (Breslau 1913). Düsseldorf 1918–20; Stuttgart 1920–7, where his *Boris* was an early Expressionist prod. and he also prod. *Doktor Faust* (1927) using film sequences; Dresden 1927–31, incl. prem. of Strauss's *Ägyptische Helena* (1928). Chicago 1930–2. London, CG, 1933–5, incl. British prems. of *Arabella* and *Shvanda* (1934). Buenos Aires, C, 1939–56. New York, CC, 1954–6, 1967; also Vienna, Milan, Munich.

Erik. A huntsman (ten), rejected lover of Senta, in Wagner's *Der fliegende Holländer*.

'Eri tu'. Anckarstroem's (Renato's) (bar) aria in Act III of Verdi's *Un ballo in maschera*, resolving to punish not his supposedly unfaithful wife but his friend and king, Gustavus (Riccardo).

Erkel, Ferenc (*b* Gyula, 7 Nov. 1810; *d* Budapest, 15 June 1893). Hungarian composer, conductor, and pianist. Studied Pozsony with Klein. Moved to Kolozsvár, where he first heard some early attempts at Hungarian opera; later settled in Buda as opera conductor of the Hungarian T Co. (*c*.1835). He gave up a developing career as a pianist on hearing Liszt, and turned increasingly to composition, achieving early success with his first opera, *Bátori Mária* (1840). He followed this up with *Hunyadi László* (1844), the most successful of his operas in Hungary. Though drawing on Viennese and Italian elements, it achieves a genuinely Hungarian character by its use of Hungarian-inflected recitative and by the incorporation of national dances. Erkel also tried to develop a Hungarian equivalent of the English ballad opera known as *népszínmű*, in which were incorporated both ballads and original songs: these included *Két pisztoly*, and became very popular. Other commitments and the need to earn a living prevented him from returning to opera for some years; but in 1861 he produced *Bánk bán*, based on a previously censored play and written in collaboration with his two sons Gyula and Sándor. Here the experiments of *Hunyadi László* are taken a stage further, with Hungarian elements more fully incorporated into fluent and original structures, and with more vivid and penetrating characterization. This was also the first composed work to make use of the cimbalom.

None of Erkel's subsequent operas achieved comparable success. He attempted comic opera on the one hand, with *Sarolta* (1862) and *Névtelen hősök* (1880), in which there is copious use of popular tunes and rustic scenes; and national music drama on the other, with *Dózsa György* (1867) and *Brankovics György* (1874), in which Hungarian musical characteristics are absorbed into a continuous musical flow, with the orchestra taking a prominent role. Though there are in them anticipations of Liszt and even of Bartók, the shadow of Wagner falls more heavily across them, and deepens with Erkel's last opera, *István király* (1885; mostly by Gyula Erkel). He left the Nat. T in 1874, being succeeded by Richter, though he continued to conduct his own works and to play in public. *Hunyadi László* and *Bánk bán* have remained in Hungarian repertories, and have occasionally been performed abroad. With them Hungarian national opera was effectively founded.

Erlanger, (Baron) **Frédéric d'** (*b* Paris, 29 May 1868; *d* London, 23 Apr. 1943). English composer of French and German descent. Studied Paris with Ehmant. His *Inès Mendo* was given at London, CG, 1897 (under the anagram Ferd. Regnal). His greatest operatic success was in 1906 with *Tess*, at Naples, C, with Destinn, Zenatello, and Sammarco. A banker by profession, he gave much financial support to CG and for many years was a director.

Ermler, Mark (*b* Leningrad, 5 May 1932). Russian conductor. Studied in Leningrad and made début there 1953 (*Entführung*). Conductor at the Bolshoy from 1956 (début with *Fidelio*), leading the company on tour to Japan, Italy and the USA (1975). London, CG, from 1986 (*Carmen, Onegin, Médée, Butterfly*). Conducted *War and Peace* at Seattle and Bolshoy forces in Tchaikovsky's *The Oprichnik* at Edinburgh 1992. He brings a firmly-disciplined approach to a wide repertory. (R)

Ernani. Opera in 4 acts by Verdi; text by Piave, after Victor Hugo's tragedy *Hernani* (1830). Prem. Venice, F, 9 Mar. 1844.

Spain, 1590. Ernani (ten) (the outlawed Don Juan de Aragon, now a bandit) and Don Carlo, King of Spain (bar), both love Elvira (sop) and want to prevent her marriage to her elderly kinsman Don Ruy Gomez de Silva (bs). Ernani has vowed to avenge the death of his father at the hands of the king.

On her wedding-day, Don Carlo takes Elvira as a hostage since the laws of hospitality will not allow Silva to yield Ernani to him. Ernani tells Silva that he is willing to die at his hand, but only after he has rescued Elvira. He gives Silva a horn, promising to kill himself when it is sounded.

Conspirators meet to plot the death of Don Carlo. Ernani will not surrender his right to strike the fatal blow even in return for release from his promise to Silva. A cannon sounds, indicating the election of Don Carlo as Holy Roman Emperor, and he emerges from a hiding place having witnessed the conspiracy. The traitors are captured, but

Don Carlo frees them at Elvira's intervention and offers her to Ernani in marriage.

In the middle of the wedding festivities, the horn sounds. Ernani is obliged to fulfil his promise; he stabs himself and dies.

'Ernani, involami'. Elvira's (sop) aria in Act I of Verdi's *Ernani*, in which she hopes that Ernani will flee with her.

Ernesto. Don Pasquale's nephew (ten) in Donizetti's *Don Pasquale*.

Ero the Joker (Srb-Cr., *Ero s onoga svijeta*: lit. 'Ero from the Other World'). Opera in 3 acts by Jakov Gotovac; text by Milan Begović, after a Dalmatian folk-tale. Prem. Zagreb 2 Nov. 1935.

A village in the Dinara mountains. Mischa (ten) appears from a hayloft to land among a group of girls, who include Djula (sop). He claims to be Ero, and to have fallen from heaven because it was boring there. Djula's stepmother Doma (mez) tries to chase him away, but he convinces her that her mother is doing badly in heaven and needs financial help. Doma fetches money and gives it to Ero. With the help of the miller Sima (bar), Ero and Djula escape. They return at the time of the village fair, and Ero discloses that he is not a poor good-for-nothing but the son of a wealthy farmer, and wanted to test Djula's love. Her father gives the couple his blessing.

Ershov, Ivan (*b* Novocherkassk, 20 Nov. 1867; *d* Leningrad, 21 Nov. 1943). Russian tenor. Studied Moscow with Alexandrova-Kochetova; St Petersburg with Gabel and Paleček. Début St Petersburg, M, 1893 (Gounod's *Faust*). Sang there 1895–1929, in a wide repertory including Mozart, Wagner, Verdi, and many Russian roles, among them Sobinin (*A Life for the Tsar*), Golitsyn (*Khovanshchina*); also Sadko, and the first Grishka Kuterma (*Kitezh*). Told Rimsky-Korsakov he wrote awkwardly for the voice, and would do better to consult the singers. An excellent declaimer, and an actor preferred by many to Shalyapin, with a ringing tone. Taught Petrograd (Leningrad) Cons. 1916–41. His dramatic conviction was especially significant for its contribution to Wagner's popularity in Russia: 'he could claim immortality just for his interpretations of Tannhäuser, Tristan, Siegmund, and Siegfried' (Eduard Stark). (R)

Erwartung (Expectation). Monodrama in 1 act by Schoenberg; text by Marie Pappenheim. Prem. Prague, Neues Deutsches T, 6 June 1924.

Written for a single voice and full orchestra, the work concerns the semi-deranged ravings of a woman (sop) searching for her lover in a forest at night; she hears weeping, mistakes a log for a corpse, imagines she is being watched, and thinks she is being pursued by the moon. In the fourth scene, the longest in the opera, she arrives at the house of her rival, who she finds has murdered her lover. Hysterically, she falls upon his body, smothering it with kisses. At length she departs.

Escamillo. The toreador (bar) in Bizet's *Carmen*.

'È scherzo od è follia'. Quintet in Act I of Verdi's *Un ballo in maschera*, in which Oscar (sop), Mam'zelle Arvidson (Ulrica) (mez), Gustavus (Riccardo) (ten), Ribbing (Sam) (bs), and Horn (Tom) (bs) react variously to the prophecy that Gustavus will die at the hand of a friend.

Esclarmonde. Opera in 4 acts (8 tableaux) by Massenet; text by Alfred Blau and Louis de Gramont, after a medieval romance, *Partenopeus of Blois*. Prem. Paris, OC, 14 May 1889.

Byzantium and France, early Middle Ages. Esclarmonde (sop), daughter of Phorcas, King of Byzantium (bs), falls in love with a French knight, Roland (ten), despite her father's statement that her inheritance of his throne and magical powers depends on her keeping away from men. She uses her own magical powers to lure Roland who, with her assistance, accomplishes heroic deeds. When her father states that she is endangering Roland's life and her magical powers by her love, she relinquishes him. Her husband is to be the champion of a tournament organized by her father; this turns out to be Roland, and Phorcas gives his approval for their marriage.

'Es gibt ein Reich'. Ariadne's (sop) aria in Richard Strauss's *Ariadne auf Naxos*, in which she dreams of a land where everything is pure—the land of death.

'È sogno'. Ford's (bar) monologue in Act II of Verdi's *Falstaff*, reflecting upon his jealousy at the prospect of Falstaff seducing his wife.

Esswood, Paul (*b* West Bridgford, 6 June 1942). English counter-tenor. Studied at London, RCM. Début in Cavalli's *Erismena* at Berkeley, CA, 1968; further Baroque repertory in operas by Monteverdi, Purcell, and Charpentier; title-roles in Handel's *Riccardo Primo* (English Bach Fest. at London, CG, 1991) and *Admeto*. His well-projected singing lends distinction to modern works including Penderecki's *Paradise Lost* and Glass's *Akhnaten* (both prems., 1978, 1984). (R)

Estes, Simon (*b* Centreville, IA, 2 Feb. 1939). US bass-baritone. After study at Juilliard, sang in Europe from 1965 (Ramfis at Berlin, D). S Francisco 1967 (Schuller's *Visitation*); Gly. 1972 (Pane in *Calisto*). New York, M: sang Oroveso with co. at Vienna 1976; from 1982 as the Landgrave, Porgy, and Wotan. First Black male singer at Bayreuth (*Dutchman* 1978). Also admired for his well-focused tone in operas by Verdi (Philip II), Musorgsky (Boris), and Gounod (Méphistophélès). (R)

'Esultate!' Otello's (ten) proclamation of victory over the Turks in Act I of Verdi's *Otello*.

Etcheverry, Bertrand (*b* Bordeaux, 29 Mar. 1900; *d* Paris, 14 Nov. 1960). French baritone. Studied Paris. Début Bordeaux 1925 (Le Bailli, *Werther*). Paris: O, 1932 (Ceprano, *Rigoletto*); OC, from 1937. London, CG, 1937, 1949. An outstanding Golaud; also popular as Boris. Created several roles, e.g. in Hahn's *Le marchand de Venise*. (R)

Étoile, L' (The Star). Opera in 3 acts by Chabrier; text by E. Leterrier and A. Vanloo. Prem. Paris, BP, 28 Nov. 1877.

King Ouf (ten) is seeking a victim for execution and so wanders, disguised, among his people, attempting to provoke a rebellion. He finds a victim in Lazuli (ten), a pedlar who insults the King after his suit for Princess Laoula is rejected. However, when the court astrologer, Siroco (bs), reveals that King Ouf will die 24 hours after Lazuli, the execution is cancelled, and Lazuli taken into luxurious confinement.

Lazuli and Laoula escape and news soon arrives of a shipwreck in which Lazuli has perished. King Ouf awaits his own death. The appointed hour passes, with the King still alive. Such is his rejoicing that he forgives Siroco's incompetence and permits the union of Laoula and Lazuli, whose reappearance is joyfully celebrated.

Étoile du nord, L' (The Northern Star). Opera in 3 acts by Meyerbeer; text by Scribe, after Rellstab's text for *Ein Feldlager in Schlesien*, based in turn on an episode in the life of Peter the Great. Prem. Paris, OC, 16 Feb. 1854.

Tsar Peter (bar) loves the village girl Katherine (sop). She substitutes herself for her brother George (ten) in the Russian Army, and informs the Tsar of a conspiracy. Disguised as a carpenter, the Tsar woos Katherine and makes her his Tsarina.

Originally composed as *Ein Feldlager in Schlesien* to open the new Berlin O, 7 Dec. 1844, with Tuczek: eight days after the prem., she was replaced by Jenny Lind, who sang the work widely, in the rev. version for Vienna (1847) under the new title *Vielka*.

Eugene Onegin. Opera in 3 acts by Tchaikovsky; text by the composer and Konstantin Shilovsky, after Pushkin's poem (1823–31). Prem. Moscow, Maly T, by Cons., 29 Mar. 1879.

The Larins' country estate, early 19th cent. Tatyana (sop), the young and impressionable daughter of Mme Larina (mez), falls in love with Onegin (bar), a friend of her sister Olga's betrothed, Lensky (ten). Tatyana stays up all night writing an impassioned letter to Onegin. Next morning he reproves her for her forwardness and urges her to forget him.

At Tatyana's birthday party, some of the elderly women gossip about her and Onegin as they dance together. Annoyed, Onegin dances with Olga (mez), who had promised the dance to Lensky (ten). When Lensky reproaches her, she petulantly gives another dance to Onegin. Monsieur Triquet (ten), the French tutor, sings a song in praise of Tatyana. When the dancing is resumed, Lensky quarrels with Onegin and challenges him to a duel. Early next morning the two men meet beside an old mill. Lensky is killed.

Six years have passed and Onegin, who has been abroad, returns to St Petersburg. A ball is in progress at the palace of Prince Gremin (bs), now married to Tatyana. Onegin sees Tatyana again and realizes that he loves her. She agrees to meet him. He urges her to flee with him: at first she responds ardently; but then she reminds Onegin of her duty, and sends him away for ever.

Euphrosine. Opera in 5 (rev. to 3, finally 4) acts by Méhul; text by F. B. Hoffman. Prem. Paris, CI, 4 Sept. 1790. The plot concerns the eventually successful efforts of Euphrosine (sop) to win the misogynist Coradin (ten) in spite of the efforts of the bitter, rejected Countess (sop). The duet 'Gardez-vous de la jalousie' became famous for its pioneering use of motive (a simple rocking figure of thirds) to express jealousy and its workings, and was much admired by Berlioz. Méhul's second opera, the first to be performed.

Euridice. 1. Opera in a prologue and 6 scenes by Peri; text by Ottavio Rinuccini. Prem. Florence, Pitti Palace, 6 Oct. 1600.

The plot follows the pattern of Poliziano's *Orfeo* (1480), differing only in that the opera has a happy ending. In the prologue, the spirit of Tragedy presents the subject of the opera and greets the important members of the audience.

Euridice is dancing with her companions. While Orfeo is singing of the beauties of nature, Dafne arrives to announce Euridice's death from a snake bite. In despair, Orfeo wishes to kill himself. However, Venus appears and allows him to descend to Hades to beg Pluto for his bride. He persuades Pluto and Proserpine to release Euridice, and a chorus of Shades accompanies the couple on their return to earth. The plot omits the famous condition whereby Orfeo must not look behind him as he leads Euridice back to the world.

2. Opera in prologue and 6 scenes by Caccini; text by Ottavio Rinuccini. Prem. Florence, Pitti Palace, 5 Dec. 1602.

Euryanthe. Opera in 3 acts by Weber; text by Helmina von Chezy, after a medieval French romance. Prem. Vienna, K, 25 Oct. 1823.

France, 1100. Lysiart (bar), angered by Adolar's (ten) protestations of love for Euryanthe (sop), wagers that he can seduce her. She has meanwhile given away a family secret about a suicide to the evil Eglantine (mez), who has won her confidence. When Lysiart accuses her of infidelity before the court, she fails to deny it, and the miserable Adolar leads her into the desert to kill her. But when she saves his life, he abandons her instead, to be found by the King (bs) and a hunting-party. Lysiart, who has won Adolar's possessions and estate in the wager, is about to marry Eglantine when Adolar arrives; the plot is disclosed, and he is reunited with Euryanthe.

Eva. Opera in 3 acts by Foerster; text by the composer, after Gabriela Preissová's drama *Gazdina roba* (The Innkeeper's Daughter). Prem. Prague, N, 1 Jan. 1899.

Slovakia, late 19th cent. Mánek (ten), the

son of a wealthy farmer, loves Eva (sop), a poor seamstress. Despite her love for Mánek, Eva agrees to marry Samko (bar), a tailor.

Eva grieves over the loss of her baby. Mánek is by now married, but still thinks only of Eva. They decide to abandon their families and flee.

At the harvest festival, Eva insults Zuzka (mez), and is inconsolable. Mánek's mother arrives, saying that the authorities disapprove of their relationship. Mánek is unconcerned by this, but Eva is greatly troubled and, after seeing a vision of her dead parents and child, hurls herself into the Danube.

Eva. Pogner's daughter (sop), lover of Walther, in Wagner's *Die Meistersinger von Nürnberg*.

Evangelimann, Der (The Evangelical). Opera in 2 acts by Kienzl; text by the composer, after L. F. Meissner's story (1894). Prem. Berlin, H, 4 May 1895.

St Othman and Vienna, 1820–50. The opera relates how jealousy leads Johannes (bar) to commit acts which ruin the love of Mathias (ten), his brother, and Martha (sop). The innocent Mathias is sent to prison; during his sentence Martha commits suicide. On his release, Mathias becomes an evangelical preacher; Johannes comes to him and confesses, not recognizing his brother, who absolves him.

Evans, Anne (b London, 20 Aug. 1941). English soprano. Studied London with Packer and Harford, Geneva and Rome with Ricci. Début Geneva 1967 (Countess Ceprano). London SW/ENO 1968–77, and from 1986; WNO from 1978; London, CG, from 1986; Bayreuth 1983 (Brünnhilde, 1989); New York, M, 1992 (Elisabeth, *Tannhäuser*); also S Francisco, Berlin, Paris, Turin, Zurich, etc. Repertory incl. Donna Anna, Leonore, Violetta, Elisabeth de Valois, Tosca, Elsa, Senta, Brünnhilde (with WNO at London, CG, 1986), Kundry, Marschallin, Dyer's Wife, Chrysothemis, Milada (*Dalibor*). A musicianly singer whose attractive voice encompasses the lyrical as well as the dramatic, most notably in the role of Isolde (from 1993). (R)

Evans, (Sir) **Geraint** (b Pontypridd, 16 Feb. 1922; d Aberystwyth, 19 Sept. 1992). Welsh baritone. Studied Hamburg with Hermann, Geneva with Carpi. Début London, CG, 1948

(Nightwatchman). Sang there 1949–84. Gly. 1950–61; Milan, S, 1960; Vienna 1961; New York, M, 1964–72. Created the roles of Flint (*Billy Budd*), Mountjoy (*Gloriana*), Antenor (*Troilus and Cressida*). Other roles include Figaro, Leporello, Beckmesser, Don Pasquale, Falstaff. Possessed a warm voice with a wide range, admirable diction, and lively dramatic skills. Produced for WNO, and in Chicago and S Francisco. Autobiography, *A Knight at the Opera* (London, 1984). (R)

Evans, Nancy (b Liverpool, 19 Mar. 1915). English mezzo-soprano. Studied with Teyte. Début London 1938 (Sullivan's *The Rose of Persia*). London, CG, 1939. Joined EOG 1946. Gly. 1946 (sharing title-role in first *Rape of Lucretia* with Ferrier), 1957, 1959–60. Also created Nancy (*Albert Herring*, written specially for her warm, silvery voice. (R)

Everding, August (b Bottrop, 31 Oct. 1928). German producer and administrator. Studied Bonn and Munich. Dir. Hamburg 1973–7; Munich 1976. Vienna, S Francisco, Bayreuth (*Flying Dutchman* 1969, *Tristan* 1974). Savonlinna, *Magic Flute*, 1973–89, regularly. First Warsaw *Ring* 1988–9. A skilful and highly practical prod., with a gift for using many different theatrical conditions to successful effect.

Ewing, Maria (b Detroit, 27 Mar. 1950). US soprano, later mezzo-soprano. Studied Cleveland with Tourel and Steber. Début Ravinia Fest. 1973. New York, M, 1976 (Cherubino); Milan, S, 1978 (Mélisande); Brussels, M, 1980; Salzburg 1980; Paris, O, 1981; Geneva 1982; London, CG, 1988. Gly. regularly from 1978, where she scored a memorable success as Carmen (1985). One of the most attractive and dramatic stage personalities of her generation; her roles include Susanna, the Composer, Zerlina, and Salome. (R)

Excursions of Mr Brouček, The (Cz., *Výlety páně Broučkovy*). Opera in 2 acts by Janáček; text by the composer, with suggestions, contributions, and amendments by F. Gellner, V. Dyk, and F. S. Procházka, after Svatopluk Čech's novels (1888, 1889). Pt 1, *Výlet pana Broučka do měsíce* (Mr Brouček's Excursion to the Moon); pt 2, *Výlet pana Broučka do XV. století* (Mr Brouček's Excursion to the 15th cent.). Prem. Prague, C, 23 Apr. 1920.

Prague and the moon. In the first of Mr Brouček's magic excursions, to the moon, he encounters a fantastic aesthetic world:

though the work's ostensible purpose is to lampoon his bourgeois complacency and philistinism, he actually emerges in a more sympathetic light than the posturing moondwellers. His second excursion is to the 15th cent., where he behaves in a cowardly fashion before being restored to the present.

Ezio. The Roman general (bar) in Verdi's *Attila*.

F

Faccio, Franco (*b* Verona, 8 Mar. 1840; *d* Monza, 21 July 1891). Italian conductor and composer. His first opera, *I profughi fiamminghi* (1863), led both to accusations of Wagnerism and to his friend Boito's claim in a celebratory ode that he would 'cleanse the altar of Italian opera, now stained like the walls of a brothel'—a remark taken personally by Verdi to Boito's disadvantage. His greatest success was with *Amleto* (1865), which benefits greatly from Boito's libretto and responds with some vivid scenes, but is scarcely able to rise to the demands of the subject. Taking up a career as a conductor, he toured Germany and Scandinavia with Lorini's OC 1867; Milan, T Carcano, 1868; Milan, S, 1869, assistant cond. when he made warm friends with Verdi, chief cond. 1871–90, conducting prems. of *Gioconda* (1876), *Otello* (1887), and *Edgar* (1889), as well as many important Italian prems., especially of Wagner. Cond. first English *Otello* (1889) and Italian *Meistersinger* (1889). He would have been chosen by Verdi for the first *Falstaff*, but a syphilitic condition led to his mental decline and death. A pioneering figure as a conductor, he brought new quality to the Scala orchestra and thereby set new standards to which composers could respond. His sister **Chiarina** (1846–1923) was a soprano who sang in Trieste.

Fach (Ger.: 'division', hence 'subject' or 'speciality'). The term used, strictly in Germany and more loosely internationally, to describe the range of roles that a singer may be expected to perform.

Fafner. With Fasolt, one of the two giants (bs) in Wagner's *Das Rheingold*. He has turned into a dragon by *Siegfried*.

Fair Maid of Perth. See JOLIE FILLE DE PERTH, LA.

Fairy Queen, The. Semi-opera in a prologue and 5 acts by Purcell; text an anon. adaptation (? by Thomas Betterton) of Shakespeare's comedy *A Midsummer Night's Dream* (1595–6). Prem. London, Dorset Garden T, 2 May 1692.

Falcon, Cornélie (*b* Paris, 28 Jan. 1812; *d* Paris, 25 Feb 1897). French soprano. Studied Paris with Henri and Pellegrini, later with Bordogni and Nourrit. Début Paris, O, 1832 (Alice, *Robert le diable*). Her career lasted only until 1838, when she lost her voice through overwork, and had to retire; an attempted come-back in 1840 ended badly. Created Mme Anckarstroem (*Gustave III*), Rachel (*La Juive*), Valentine (*Les Huguenots*), and many other roles; also a famous Donna Anna and Julie (*La vestale*). She possessed a full, resonant voice, and, like Nourrit, exceptional dramatic talent (they were together responsible for improving the artistic standing of the Opéra). Her name, then synonymous with the dramatic soprano parts in which she was unapproachable, still survives as a description of her voice type.

Falla, Manuel de (*b* Cádiz, 23 Nov. 1876; *d* Alta Gracia, 14 Nov. 1946). Spanish composer. As a young man, he wrote a number of zarzuelas. *La vida breve* (The Short Life, 1913) is an early work, with a weak plot; but already Falla's authentic voice is to be heard behind the different manners he adopts. Despite unevenness, it is a work of genuine dramatic power. *El retablo de Maese Pedro* (Master Peter's Puppet Show, 1923) handles an incident in *Don Quixote*, turning Falla's understanding of contrasting styles to skilful use in a piece of puppet music theatre treating different levels of reality and illusion. The forces are miniature, but there is a disciplined refinement and intensity now present in Falla's mature style. *L'Atlántida* (1962) is closer to dramatic oratorio than opera, and Falla did not wish it to be staged; but it is his most ambitious dramatic work, and stage performances have proved effective.

falsetto (It., lit. dim. of *falso*: 'false, altered'; or poss. from Lat. *fauces*: 'throat'). An artificial method of voice production employed by male singers, using only a partial vibration of the vocal chords. Normally used in opera only for special effects, whether for extreme refinement and softness of tone, as perhaps at the end of the romance in *Les pêcheurs de perles*, or satirically, as usually by Falstaff imitating Mistress Ford allegedly sighing, 'Io son di Sir John Falstaff'. There is a long passage in Weber's *Die drei Pintos*. In the 19th cent. a singer who specialized in a version of falsetto singing was sometimes known in Italy as *falsettone*, or *falsetto rinforzato*. The technique, when highly developed, now normally refers to *counter-tenor.

Falstaff. Opera in 3 acts by Verdi; text by Boito, after Shakespeare's comedy *The Merry Wives of Windsor* (1600–1) and *Henry IV* (pt 1, 1597; pt 2, 1598). Prem. Milan, S, 9 Feb. 1893.

Windsor, in the reign of Henry IV. In the Garter Inn, Sir John Falstaff (bar) defends himself and his retainers Bardolfo (ten) and Pistola (bar) against the accusations of Dr Cajus (ten), and tells his men he intends to seduce Ford's and Page's wives. When they refuse to bear letters to the women, on grounds of honour, Falstaff lectures them on the subject. In Ford's garden, Alice Ford (sop) and Meg Page (mez) read identical letters from Falstaff, with Nannetta Ford (sop) and Mistress Quickly (mez) listening. While Nannetta exchanges a quick kiss with Fenton (ten), the women resolve to teach Falstaff a lesson, and Ford (bar) another one for his jealousy.

In the Garter, Mistress Quickly encourages Falstaff to pursue his wooing of Alice. Ford, disguised as 'Fontana', pretends to be asking Falstaff to seduce Alice so as to smooth his own path, and, alone, gives vent to his jealousy. In Ford's house, Alice receives Falstaff. When Meg arrives, Falstaff hides in a laundry basket. The others arrive and begin searching the house for Falstaff. When he is tipped out of the window into the Thames, Ford realizes the unworthiness of his suspicions.

Outside the Garter, Falstaff is gloomily recovering from his ordeal when Mistress Quickly comes with the promise of a new assignation with Alice, this time in Windsor Forest at midnight. By Herne's Oak in the Forest, Nannetta invokes 'spirits', in fact the people and children of Windsor, who pinch and prick Falstaff as they enact the masque of the Fairy Queen with various marriages. When the plot is revealed, it emerges that in the confusion Fenton has actually married Nannetta. All is forgiven, and in a final fugue Falstaff suggests that they have all been duped and that all the world's a jest.

Fancelli, Giuseppe (*b* Florence, ?24 Nov. 1833; *d* Florence, Dec. 1887). Italian tenor. Début Milan, S (Fisherman, *Guglielmo Tell*). London, CG, 1866–8, 1870–2. Milan, S, 1866,

and in 1872 first Italian Radamès (Verdi commented, 'a good voice but nothing else', and went so far as to assault him in rehearsal). Extraordinarily gifted vocally (with a top C unsurpassed even by Tamberlik or Caruso, according to Klein), he was musically illiterate, and declared he could not sing and act at the same time.

Fanciulla del West, La (The Girl of the [Golden] West). Opera in 3 acts by Puccini; text by Civinini and Zangarini, after Belasco's drama *The Girl of the Golden West* (1905). Prem. New York, M, 10 Dec. 1910.

The Californian Gold Rush of 1850. Miners are playing cards at the Polka Saloon and are about to lynch one of their number for cheating when the Sheriff, Jack Rance (bar), intervenes. Rance is in love with Minnie (sop) and proposes to her. She refuses, reminding him that he already has a wife. A stranger, Dick Johnson (ten), arrives and Minnie recognizes him as the man she once knew and hoped to meet again. He is in fact the bandit leader Ramerrez, and he and his band have a plan to steal the miners' gold which Minnie guards. She shows him where it is hidden, but Johnson is so attracted to her that he ignores a signal from his band to attack.

In her cabin, Minnie receives Johnson and the couple confess their love. Outside, a blizzard rages and Johnson agrees to stay. Suddenly there is a knock at the door. Minnie hides Johnson and lets Rance and his group in. Rance shows her a photograph and Minnie realizes that Johnson is Ramerrez. When they are alone Johnson admits it and Minnie orders him to leave. A shot is heard; Johnson is injured and Minnie drags him back in, hiding him in the loft. Rance enters and finds the bandit when drops of blood fall from the loft; but Minnie persuades him to play poker, with Johnson as the prize. She wins by cheating and Rance has to abandon his pursuit.

A few days later, the miners capture Ramerrez and propose to hang him. As the noose is slipped over his head, Minnie arrives and shields him, holding the miners at bay with a gun. She persuades them to release Johnson and the couple leave together.

'Fanget an!' Walther's (ten) trial song in Act I of Wagner's *Die Meistersinger*, taking the marker Beckmesser's instruction to begin as words describing how spring begins everything anew.

Faninal. A wealthy, newly ennobled merchant (bar), Sophie's father, in R. Strauss's *Der Rosenkavalier*.

farewell. The name commonly given to the last performance in public of a favourite artist. Some singers, especially sopranos, have announced their farewell seasons years before taking their actual leave of the stage—Grisi is a notable example. Melba's farewell, including her speech, at London, CG, in 1926, was recorded by HMV. German provincial houses give 'Abschied' performances for a favourite singer when he or she leaves to take up an engagement in another theatre.

Farinelli (orig. Carlo Broschi) (*b* Andria, 24 Jan. 1705; *d* Bologna, 15 July 1782). Italian soprano castrato. Studied with Porpora. Début Naples 1720, in his teacher's serenata *Angelica e Medoro*. Two years later he won a famous competition of skill with a trumpeter. After triumphs in Italy and Vienna, he had another brilliant contest in 1727 with Bernacchi; he lost, but learned much from the other singer. By now he was famous all over Europe for his astonishing vocal feats; however, accused in 1731 by Charles VI of seeking more to 'surprise' than 'please', he modified his style. Engaged London 1734–7 as the star attraction in Porpora's rival company to Handel's, to ecstatic acclaim. Senesino, moved by his beautiful singing, once embraced him during an opera; women frequently fainted at his performances. In Madrid, 1737, he sang to the melancholic Philip V, with such success that he was asked to stay at the court for 50,000F a year. This led to his retirement from the stage. For 25 years, he sang the same four songs every night to Philip. Under his successor Ferdinand VI, Farinelli established an Italian Opera in Madrid, importing the best singers of the day, and his friend the librettist Metastasio. Also active in public works and as a diplomat. In 1750 he received the Order of Calatrava. On Charles III's accession, 1759, he left Spain for political reasons, with a large pension, and retired to Bologna, where he was visited by Burney in 1770. A highly cultured and agreeable man, and one of the greatest singers of all time.

Operas on him are by Barnett (1839), Espin y Guillén (1854), Zumpe (1886), and Bretón (1901).

Farinelli, Giuseppe (orig. Giuseppe Francesco Finco) (*b* Este, 7 May 1769; *d* Trieste, 12 Dec. 1836). Italian composer. Active in Naples, Turin, and Trieste, he was one of the most popular composers in Italy around the turn of the 19th cent.; his music, which owed much to Cimarosa's example, is firmly rooted in the late 18th-cent. tradition of opera buffa. Farinelli's decline came only with the rise to prominence of Rossini after 1812. At first the two composers were performed side by side—in 1813 Farinelli's *Il matrimonio per concorso* (The Marriage Contest) shared the season with Rossini's *L'italiana in Algeri* at the T San Moisè in Venice—but the greater talent of Rossini was soon perceived by audiences and, in an action reminiscent of that of the younger composer, Farinelli retired from opera composition in 1817. His other successes included *Il dottorato di Pulcinella* (1792), *Chi la dura la vince* (Who Endures, Wins, ?1803), and *La contadina bizzarra* (The Weird Peasant Girl, 1810).

Farlaf. A Varangian warrior (bs) in Glinka's *Ruslan and Lyudmila*.

Farley, Carol (*b* Le Mans, IA, 29 Nov. 1946). US soprano. Studied at Indiana U and with Marianne Schech in Munich. A specialist in the modern repertory, she sang Lulu with WNO (1971) and at New York, M, 1978; she also brings a vivid stage presence to such roles as Salome, Jenny (*Mahagonny*), and Marie (*Wozzeck*; Buenos Aires, 1989). Created the Maid of Orleans in *Le passion de Gilles* by Boesmans (Brussels 1983). Other roles incl. Offenbach's Hélène (New York, CO, 1976), Donna Anna, Violetta. (R)

Farrar, Geraldine (*b* Melrose, MA, 28 Feb. 1882; *d* Ridgefield, CT, 11 Mar. 1967). US soprano. Studied Boston with Long, New York with Thursby; later with Lilli Lehmann. Début Berlin, H, 1901 (Marguerite). New York, M, 1906–22; then retired. Created Goosegirl (*Königskinder*), Madame Sans-Gêne, and Suor Angelica; an outstanding Butterfly and Manon Lescaut (Puccini) and Manon (Massenet). Beautiful and a committed singer and actress, she was idolized by the public. (R)

Fasano, Renato (*b* Naples, 21 Aug. 1902; *d* Rome, 3 Aug. 1979). Italian composer and conductor. Studied Naples. Founded the Collegium Musicum Italicum in Rome (1941), later reformed as the Virtuosi di Roma; and in 1957 the Piccolo T Musicale Italiano, which has appeared throughout Europe and the US, giving performances of operas by Galuppi, Cimarosa, Paisiello, Pergolesi, Rossini, etc. (R)

Fasolt. With Fafner, one of the two giants (bs) in Wagner's *Das Rheingold*.

Fassbaender, Brigitte (*b* Berlin, 3 July 1939). German mezzo-soprano and producer. Studied Nuremberg with her father, Willi *Domgraf-Fassbaender. Début Munich, Bavarian SO, 1961 (Nicklausse). London, CG, 1971; New York, M, 1974–94; also San Francisco, Salzburg, Paris, etc. Roles include Cherubino, Octavian, Amneris, Brangäne, Charlotte, Carmen. Vivid on stage, with a warm, burnished tone; also a fine Lieder singer. Has latterly worked as a producer, e.g. *Cenerentola* (Coburg, 1990), *Der ferne Klang* (Leeds, 1992). (R)

Fatima. Reiza's attendant (mez) in Weber's *Oberon*.

Fauré, Gabriel (*b* Pamiers, 12 May 1845; *d* Paris, 4 Nov. 1924). French composer, teacher, pianist, and organist. Studied Paris with Saint-Saëns; held various positions as an organist and teacher, before becoming director of the Paris Cons. in 1905. Though he had a consummate understanding of the potential of the human voice, Fauré composed only one true opera, *Pénélope* (1913). This was preceded by incidental music for several plays, including Dumas's *Caligula* (1888), Haraucourt's *Shylock* (1889), and Maeterlinck's *Pelléas et Mélisande* (1898). His most extensive dramatic work was the grand cantata *Prométhée*: as only some of the characters participate in the stage action it is scarcely an opera, though Fauré's conception of the work is at times more operatic than merely choral.

Pénélope shows similar traits, but also has an affinity with Saint-Saëns's *Samson et Dalila* (1877) and Debussy's *Pelléas et Mélisande* (1902). Written at the request of the dramatic soprano Lucienne *Bréval, who also suggested the subject of the faithful Penelope's vigil for her husband Odysseus. Fauré's treatment of her anguish and his insight into her isolation and despair result in the creation of an operatic character worthy to stand beside the greatest of Rameau's and Gluck's tragic heroines. Though couched in Fauré's inimitably dream-like style, it also owes much to the conventions of Romantic opera, with its opening spinning chorus and final 'Gloire à Zeus'. In its seamless dramatic progression and masterful construction it is the ultimate proof that Fauré was not, as so many claim, merely a musical miniaturist: perhaps more importantly, it is in this work that he comes closest to exemplifying the true connection between the French and Greek genius—a spare, brilliant quality of thought rather than the Hellenistic languor on which the comparison generally rests.

Faure, Jean-Baptiste (*b* Moulins, 15 Jan. 1830; *d* Paris, 9 Nov. 1914). French baritone. Studied Paris with L. Ponchard and Moreau-Sainti. Début Paris, OC, 1852 (Pygmalion, Massé's *Galathée*). Sang there until 1859. London, CG, between 1860 and 1876; also sang at London, DL and HM. Paris, O, 1861–9, 1872–6, creating Nelusko (*L'Africaine*), Posa, Hamlet, among other roles. Vienna 1878; Marseilles, Vichy, 1886, when he published his treatise *La voix et le chant*. Famous as Alphonse (*Favorite*), Guillaume Tell, Don Giovanni, Gounod's Méphistophélès. Taught at Paris Cons. 1857–60. An exceptional performer, with superb vocal control and great dramatic insight. Painted twice by Manet. (R) His wife, the soprano **Caroline Lefèbvre** (1828–1905), sang in Paris at the OC 1849–59, then at the L.

Faust. Opera in 5 acts by Gounod; text by Barbier and Carré, after Goethe's poem (pt 1, 1808; pt 2, 1832). Prem. Paris, L, 19 Mar. 1859.

Germany, 16th cent. Faust (ten) makes a bargain with Méphistophélès (bs): in return for eternal youth and the beautiful Marguerite (sop), he promises Méphistophélès his soul. Valentin (bar), Marguerite's brother, entrusts the care of his sister to the faithful Siebel (mez) while he goes off to the wars. On his return he finds Marguerite has been betrayed by Faust and, challenging him to a duel, is killed. Marguerite, in prison for killing her baby, refuses to go with Faust and Méphistophélès; as she ascends to Heaven, Faust is dragged down to Hell by Méphistophélès.

Favart, Charles-Simon (*b* Paris, 13 Nov. 1710; *d* Belleville, 12 Mar. 1792). French librettist and impresario. Stage manager *Opéra-Comique, then summoned to Brussels by the Maréchal de Saxe to organize a theatre for the troops in Flanders. Succeeded Monet as dir. of the Opéra-Comique, 1758, holding the position until his retirement in 1769. In 1871 the Opéra-Comique assumed the name Salle Favart. He also wrote more than 150 librettos for different composers, among them Grétry, Philidor, and Gluck. These were generally characterized by their nimble pace and their ingenious tangle of intrigue; Favart was also largely responsible for a new naturalistic treatment of peasants and rustic life, often sentimental but more accurately observed and more respectful of simple people. He helped substantially to make possible the realism of later opéra-comique. His wife **Marie** (1727–72) was a celebrated soprano, actress, and dramatist who sang at Paris, CI, 1749–71; their son **Charles Nicolas Justin Favart** (1749–1806) was an actor and dramatist, who performed at Paris, CI, 1779–96, and wrote several vaudevilles. His son, **Antoine Pierre Charles Favart** (1780–1867) also wrote vaudevilles, including La jeunesse de Favart.

Favero, Mafalda (b Ferrara, 6 Jan. 1903; d Milan, 3 Sept. 1981). Italian soprano. Studied Bologna with Vezzani. Début (under name of Maria Bianchi) Cremona 1926 (Loia). Official début Parma 1927 (Liù). Milan, S, 1929–42, 1945–50; London, CG, 1937, 1939; New York, M, 1938. Created roles in Mascagni's Pinotta, Wolf-Ferrari's Il campanello and La dama boba. An expressive singer and actress, famous as Manon Lescaut, Mimì, and Adriana Lecouvreur. (R)

Favorite, La (The Favourite). Opera in 4 acts by Donizetti; text by Royer and Vaëz, after Baculard d'Arnaud's drama Le comte de Comminges (1764) and other material. Prem. Paris, O, 2 Dec. 1840.

Spain; San Giacomo and Seville, 1340. The novice Fernand (ten), though warned by the Prior Balthazar (b), abandons the monastic life because of his love for the mysterious Léonor (mez), who is actually the mistress of King Alphonse of Castille (bar). He resolves to win her through deeds of chivalry. Léonor begs for release from the King; Alphonse himself is excommunicated for abandoning his wife. Fernand, who has gained the King's favour, asks for Léonor's hand as a reward and the King agrees. The ceremony proceeds, but when Fernand learns of Léonor's relationship with the King, he is furious and storms out. Léonor seeks out Fernand, who has once again assumed his monk's habit, to beg his forgiveness. He pardons her but, before they can leave together, she dies in his arms.

Fedora. Opera in 3 acts by Giordano; text by Colautti, after Sardou's drama (1882). Prem. Milan, L, 17 Nov. 1898.

St Petersburg, Paris, and Switzerland, late 19th cent. The story of the tragic love of Count Loris Ipanov (ten), a Russian nihilist, for the Princess Fedora Romanov (sop).

Fedra. Opera in 3 acts by Pizzetti; text by D'Annunzio. Prem. Milan, S, 20 Mar. 1915.

The opera, based on Euripides' Hippolytus, tells how Phaedra (sop), the wife of Theseus (bar), falls in love with her stepson Hippolytus (ten) and when rejected by him hangs herself, leaving behind a letter falsely accusing Hippolytus of dishonouring her.

Feen, Die (The Fairies). Opera in 3 acts by Wagner; text by the composer after Gozzi's comedy La donna serpente (1762), first used in Himmel's Die Sylphen (1806; the first German Gozzi setting). Prem. Munich 29 June 1888.

Pursuing a doe, Prince Arindal (ten) plunges into a river and awakes in the castle of the fairy Ada (sop). They fall in love, and marry on condition that for eight years he shall not ask her origin. At the end of this time he does ask the question, and she and her castle and her children vanish; Arindal is cast back into the world of humans. Meanwhile his father has died and the city is threatened with invasion. Arindal does not know that Ada is subject to the fairies' insistence that she must remain one of them, and may only shed her immortality for Arindal by surviving a set of ordeals; she must lay dreadful tests upon him, and he must endure them without cursing her. Arindal is driven beyond his endurance and does curse her; and when the truth is revealed he goes mad when she turns to stone. But with the help of the magician Groma, Arindal pursues her into the underworld and overcomes the spirits who defend her; with his lyre, he melts the cold stone and wins back his bride. She must remain a fairy, but he can now join her in her realm.

Wagner's first complete opera, comp. 1833–4.

Feldlager in Schlesien. See ÉTOILE DU NORD.

Felsenstein, Walter (b Vienna, 30 May 1901; d Berlin, 8 Oct. 1975). Austrian producer. Studied Graz, and Vienna as actor. Début Lübeck 1923. Chief prod. Basle 1927; prod. Freiburg 1929–32; chief prod. Cologne 1932–4; Frankfurt 1934, then banned by

Nazis and worked largely freelance and in drama. Dir. Berlin, K, 1947–75. Here he found the conditions to develop his view of opera as music expressing a complete dramatic idea, with singing actors trained individually and as a closely knit ensemble. His 'realistic music theatre' was welcomed as according with the theories of 'Socialist Realism' demanded by the Communist régime; and, freed from commercial pressures, he was able to work with very long rehearsal periods. His productions, which were also taken abroad, included *Fledermaus* 1947, *Carmen* 1949, *Freischütz* 1951, and, one of the most famous, *The Cunning Little Vixen* 1956. His pupils and assistants included Götz Friedrich and Joachim Herz.

Female Chorus. The commentator (sop) who, with the *Male Chorus, introduces, comments upon, and sums up the action in Britten's *The Rape of Lucretia*.

Fenella. A poor Neapolitan girl, the dumb heroine of Auber's *La muette de Portici*.

Fenena. Nabucco's daughter (sop) in Verdi's *Nabucco*.

Fenice, Teatro La. See VENICE.

Fenton. A young gentleman of Windsor (ten), lover of Anne (Nannetta), in Nicolai's *Die lustigen Weiber von Windsor*, Verdi's *Falstaff*, and Vaughan Williams's *Sir John in Love*.

Feo, Francesco (*b* Naples, 1691; *d* Naples, 28 Jan. 1761). Italian composer. One of the most skilled Neapolitan composers of his generation, who did much to maintain the importance of the city as an operatic centre, he wrote *c*.16 operas: these include the first setting of Metastasio's *Siface* libretto (1723). He was also very active as a teacher.

Ferencsik, János (*b* Budapest, 18 Jan. 1907; *d* Budapest, 12 June 1984). Hungarian conductor. Studied Budapest with Fleischer and Lajtha. Hungarian SO; répétiteur 1927–30, cond. from 1930, music dir. 1953. Many guest appearances include Vienna 1948–50 and subsequently; S Francisco 1962–3; Edinburgh Fest. with Budapest Co. 1963, 1973. (R)

Fernand Cortez. Opera in 3 acts by Spontini; text by D. Esménard and Jouy, after Alexis Piron's tragedy (1744). Prem. Paris, O, 28 Nov. 1809.

Mexico, 1519. Alvaro (ten), brother of Cortez (ten) conqueror of Mexico, is to be sacrificed to the Aztec gods. Cortez has fallen in love with Amazily (sop), daughter of the Mexican king Montezuma (bs) and she, converted to Christianity, begs for forgiveness for the Spaniards.

Cortez puts down a mutiny, and when Telasco (bar), Amazily's brother, arrives at the camp to offer Alvaro's life in return for the Spaniard's departure, he is taken prisoner. Later he is released but refuses to free Alvaro unless Amazily is returned to the Mexicans. Cortez releases her, and Montezuma, persuaded of his sincerity, permits the marriage of the couple, thus ensuring peace.

Ferne Klang, Der (The Distant Sound). Opera in 3 acts by Schreker; text by the composer. Prem. Frankfurt 18 Aug. 1912.

Germany and Venice, present-day. The musician Fritz (ten) refuses to marry his beloved Grete (sop) until he has discovered the secret 'Distant Sound'.

Ten years later Grete reigns as Queen of the demi-monde, but still thinks longingly of Fritz. She has promised to marry whichever of her suitors can best stir her heart with his song. The winner is a stranger, whom Grete identifies as Fritz. On learning that she has become notorious, he once again abandons her.

Fritz finishes his opera *The Harp*, but the public is outraged by its finale. Grete, who has sunk to prostitution, is touched by the work. Fritz meditates on how he has destroyed not only his own but also Grete's life; he wishes desperately to see her. Grete arrives and, when the couple fall into each other's arms, Fritz at last hears the Distant Sound. He rewrites the end of his opera, but then dies in his beloved's arms.

Ferrandini, Giovanni Battista (*b* Venice, *c*.1710; *d* Munich, 25 Sept. 1791). Italian composer. After study in Venice, served at the Munich court 1722–60. On his return to Italy, his house in Padua was the scene of many notable concerts, including one in 1771 at which the young Mozart performed. He composed about ten operas for Munich, mainly opere serie, including *Catone in Utica* (1753) and *Talestri, Regina delle Amazoni* (1760). He was also a sought-after teacher: his pupils included the tenor Anton Raaff, who later created the title-role of Mozart's *Idomeneo*.

Ferrando. An officer (ten), lover of Dorabella, in Mozart's *Così fan tutte*.

Ferrani, Cesira (*b* Turin, 8 May 1863; *d* Pollone, 4 May 1943). Italian soprano. Studied Turin with Fricci. Début Turin, R, 1887 (Micaëla). Created Manon Lescaut and Mimì. A notable Elsa and Eva, and the first Mélisande in Italy. A handsome and sensitive singer, she was also highly cultured; after she retired in 1909, her salon in Turin became a focus of intellectual life.

Ferrarese, La (Francesca Gabrieli) (*b* Ferrara, *c*.1760; *d* ?Venice, after 1800). Italian soprano. Studied Venice with Sacchini. Known as La Ferrarese, and as Ferraresi del Bene after her elopement in 1783 with Luigi del Bene, whom she later married. London, H, 1785, sang in Luigi Cherubini's pasticcio *Demetrio*. Milan, S, 1787. Vienna 1788–91, where at her début she was praised for her voice (which Burney describes as 'fair, natural, and of extraordinary compass'), but not for her acting. Taken under the protection of Da Ponte, she sang in several operas with his librettos by Martín y Soler and Salieri. In 1789 she sang Susanna in the Vienna revival of *Figaro*, Mozart doubting her ability to sing the interpolated arias K577 and K579 (written specially for her) 'in an artless manner'. Though dismissive of her talent (describing Allegranti as 'far better than La Ferrarese, though I admit that is not saying much'), he wrote the role of Fiordiligi for her. Described even by Da Ponte as a trouble-maker, she was dismissed from court with him in 1791 after various scandals, and they went to Trieste (parting soon afterwards). Here in 1797 she sang in *Così*, and in 1799 she appeared at Bologna.

Ferrari, Benedetto (*b* Reggio Emilia, 1603 or 1604; *d* Modena, 22 Oct. 1681). Italian composer, librettist, impresario, and poet. He worked in Venice 1637–44 and made a crucial contribution to the development of opera there. In 1637 his *Andromeda* libretto was set by Manelli: the prem. of this work (at the T San Cassiano) was the first public performance of opera. In his next collaboration with Manelli, *La maga fulminata* (1638) he included a comic governess: this influenced later Venetian composers, who invariably featured a humorous role for a servant. In 1653 Ferrari provided the libretto for Bertali's *L'inganno d'Amore* and also wrote the librettos for five of his own operas (mostly lost). It is possible that he was also involved with the composition of Monteverdi's *Poppea*.

Ferrari, Giacomo (*b* Rovereto, *bapt.* 2 Apr. 1763; *d* London, Dec. 1842). Italian composer and theorist. After study in Italy and Switzerland, in 1787 went to Paris, where he was accompanist at the T de Monsieur. He was in London from Apr. 1792, supporting himself by teaching and writing popular vocal pieces. His first opera, *I due Svizzeri*, appeared in 1799, and was followed by a string of successes, including *Rinaldo d'Asti* (1802) and *L'eroina di Raab* (1814). He was well acquainted with a wide range of composers, including Haydn, Cherubini, and Clementi, as his operatic style suggests; he also showed an unusual concern for structural unity. His *Concise Treatise on Italian Singing* is an important source for information about the vocal technique of the period; his amusing autobiography (1830) was dedicated to King George IV.

Ferrario, Carlo (*b* Milan, 8 Sept. 1833; *d* Milan, 12 May 1907). Italian designer. Milan, S, 1853, and T Carcano 1881; also Rome and Naples. Art dir., Milan, S, 1889, incl. for Verdi on the first *Otello* and *Falstaff*. His designs for these and other Verdi productions (notably *Trovatore* 1865, *Forza del destino* 1876, *Aida* 1877, *Rigoletto* 1893) were welcomed by the composer, and by the public, for their new realism and fidelity to the works' settings, in reaction to more Romantic interpretations. Their colourful, detailed style, with its strong sense of time and place, was widely imitated. By their practicality and effectiveness they set an influential tradition. The many prems. for which he provided designs include *Mefistofele* (1868), *La Gioconda* (1876); he also designed a celebrated production of *Meistersinger* (1899).

Ferretti, Jacopo (*b* Rome, 16 July 1784; *d* Rome, 7 Mar. 1852). Italian librettist. After an early failure with his libretto for Fioravanti's *Didone abbandonata* (1810), a reworking of Metastasio, he made the brilliant version of the Cinderella story for Rossini (*Cenerentola*, 1817). He also wrote *Matilde di Shabran* for Rossini, and *Torquato Tasso* for Donizetti, as well as librettos for Zingarelli, Mayr, Guglielmi, Coccia, Mercadante, Pacini, L. Ricci, Coppola, and many others. His verses, especially for opera buffa, are distinguished by their verbal elegance and sharp social comment, and he was always willing to modify his own or other men's work to ensure a greater acceptability for the opera.

Ferrier, Kathleen (*b* High Walton, 22 Apr. 1912; *d* London, 8 Oct. 1953). English contralto. Studied with J. E. Hutchinson, then Roy Henderson. Sang Carmen in concert, Stourbridge 1944, but declined to repeat it for Gly. Stage début Gly. 1946, creating Britten's Lucretia. Gly. 1947, Orfeo (Gluck), which she also sang in Holland. London, CG, 1953 (Orfeo), though only able to perform twice before succumbing to illness. Memorable for her generous, deep voice, noble singing, and warmth of personality. (R)

Fervaal. Opera in a prologue and 3 acts by D'Indy; text by the composer. Prem. Brussels, M, 12 Mar. 1897.

The action, which takes place in the Midi of France at the time of the Saracen invasions, tells how Fervaal (ten), a Celtic Chief, wounded in battle, is nursed by Guilhen (mez), who, thinking herself betrayed, lures the Celts to their deaths.

Feuersnot (Fire-Famine). Opera in 1 act by Richard Strauss; text by Ernst von Wolzogen, after a Flemish legend, *The Quenched Fires of Oudenaarde*, in J. W. Wolf's *Sagas of the Netherlands* (1843). Prem. Dresden, H, 21 Nov. 1901.

Munich, 12th cent. Midsummer. Kunrad (bar), a magician, falls in love with Diemut (sop), the burgomaster's daughter. She humiliates him, so to punish the public, which laughs at him, he casts a spell which extinguishes all fires. He chides the people for their inability to comprehend the essential force of love. When Diemut accepts his love, he restores fire.

Février, Henry (*b* Paris, 2 Oct. 1875; *d* Paris, 8 July 1957). French composer. Studied Paris with Fauré, Leroux, Massenet, and Messager. His first opera, *Le roi aveugle* (1906), achieved moderate success; this was followed by *Monna Vanna* (1909), his most important work, which was produced in several countries. He wrote several more operas which were in the tradition of Massenet while showing the influence of Debussy and the Italian verismo school.

Fiakermilli. The pretty young girl who traditionally attends the annual ball of the Viennese cab drivers (*Fiaker*). She appears in Act II of R. Strauss's *Arabella*, where she sings one of the most brilliant of all coloratura arias.

Fiamma, La (The Flame). Opera in 3 acts by Respighi; text by Guastalla, after Hans Wiess-Jensen. Prem. Rome, R, 23 Jan. 1934.

Ravenna, late 7th cent. Silvana (sop), second wife of Basilio (bar), is persecuted by his mother Eudossia (mez). She hides Agnes de Carvia (mez), accused of sorcery, but is unable to prevent her from being hanged; Agnes prophesies on the scaffold that Silvana will meet the same fate. She falls in love with Basilio's son Donatello (ten), and is denounced to Basilio, who dies of shock. She is accused of sorcery, and also hanged.

Fibich, Zdeněk (*b* Všebořice, 21 Dec. 1850; *d* Prague, 15 Oct. 1900). Czech composer. Studied privately, Leipzig with Moscheles, Richter, and Jadassohn, and Mannheim with Lachner. Apart from a period as deputy conductor and choirmaster at the Provisional T in Prague (1875–8), Fibich's life was mostly devoted to teaching and composing. His interest in opera began early, and as with most of his music was strongly coloured by his German training and Romantic interests. His first surviving operas, *Bukovín* (1874) and *Blaník* (1881) are historical works that also, in part through his choice of two of Smetana's librettists, reflect nationalist ideas.

However, a more individual voice shows in *Nevěsta mesinská* (The Bride of Messina, 1884), a powerful work that achieves its grim, tragic effect in part by a dense network of motivic references, but also by its declamatory melodic style and even by such strokes as eliminating female voices from the choruses so as to darken the texture. He took his interest in declamation further with melodrama, whose effect he had admired in *Der Freischütz* and especially in the works of Benda, in his 'stage melodrama trilogy' *Hippodamia* (1888–91). His later operas were written to librettos by his pupil and mistress Anežka Schulzová, and are all to varying extents studies of women, and make central use of set numbers. His most successful and enduring work is *Šárka* (1897), a powerful and musically gripping treatment of the popular Czech legend. His second wife, **Betty Fibichová** (1846–1901) (whom he left for Anežka Schulzová), was a contralto who created several roles in his and Smetana's operas.

Fidelio, oder Die eheliche Liebe (Fidelio, or Married Love). Opera orig. in 3 acts by Beethoven; text by Josef Sonnleithner, a German version of Bouilly's *Léonore, ou*

L'amour conjugal, music by Gaveaux (1798) and then set, in an Italian version, by Paer (1804) and Mayr (1805). Altered and reduced to 2 acts by Stefan von Breuning in 1806; given final form by Georg Friedrich Treitschke in 1814. First version prem. Vienna, W, 20 Nov. 1805; 2nd version, Vienna, W, 29 Mar. 1806; 3rd version, Vienna, K, 23 May 1814.

A prison near Seville. Florestan (ten), a Spanish nobleman, has been thrown into prison. His wife Leonore (sop) has followed him disguised as a boy, Fidelio, in the hope of rescue. The kindly jailer Rocco (bs) employs 'Fidelio', with whom his daughter Marzelline (sop) falls in love, to the annoyance of her lover Jacquino (ten). The famous quartet expresses their reactions. The tyrannical governor Pizarro (bs-bar) decides to kill Florestan to prevent his discovery at an impending inspection. Leonore persuades Rocco to allow the prisoners out for a while; they emerge groping towards the sunlight. But Florestan is not among them.

Florestan is chained in his dungeon, whither Rocco comes with Leonore to dig the prisoner's grave. Pizarro tries to kill Florestan but is prevented by Leonore with a pistol. Far-off trumpets announce the arrival of the inspecting minister. The prisoners are all released; Pizarro is arrested, and Leonore herself unshackles Florestan.

The overture now usually played is entitled *Fidelio*. Three other overtures exist, *Leonore No. 1* (composed for a projected performance in Prague), *Leonore No. 2* (actually the first, played at the prem.), and *Leonore No. 3* (played for the 1806 revival). There is a long-standing tradition of using the last as an interlude between the final scenes; but it fits neither harmonically, instrumentally, nor dramatically, intruding an orchestral summary of parts of the drama.

Fidès. John of Leyden's mother (mez) in Meyerbeer's *Le prophète*.

Fieramosca. The Pope's sculptor (bar), Cellini's rival for Teresa's love, in Berlioz's *Benvenuto Cellini*.

Fiery Angel, The (Russ., *Ognenniy angel*). Opera in 5 acts by Prokofiev; text by the composer, after Valeriy Bryusov's historical novel, first published in the magazine *The Scales*, 1907–8. Prem. Venice, F, 14 Sept. 1955.

Cologne, 16th cent. At an inn, Ruprecht (bar or bs) meets Renata (sop) in a state of possession in which she mistakes him for Heinrich, a former lover whom she associated with her guardian angel. He agrees to take her to Cologne to look for Heinrich (mute), having fallen in love with her himself. The couple try by magic to find Heinrich; Ruprecht is equally disappointed by a visit to the magus Agrippa of Nettesheim. Renata has met and been repulsed by Heinrich; she urges Ruprecht to fight him. Ruprecht loses, but wins Renata. Renata threatens to leave Ruprecht, whose obsessive physical passion for her contrasts with memories of her 'guardian angel'. In a garden by the Rhine, Renata hurls a knife at Ruprecht, accusing him of being possessed by the Devil, as Faust (bs) and Mephistopheles enter. Ruprecht watches Mephistopheles (ten) angrily devour a slow-moving serving-boy and then resurrect him from a nearby rubbish dump. He joins the party. Ruprecht is in the suite of the Inquisitor (bs), who is investigating a story of diabolical possession in a convent. The source of the trouble is a new nun—Renata. Signs of possession appear; as the exorcism rite begins, hysteria seizes the community and the opera ends with the Inquisitor sentencing Renata to be burnt alive for having dealings with evil spirits.

Fiesco. A Genoese nobleman (bs) in Verdi's *Simon Boccanegra*.

Figaro. The barber of Seville (bar) in Paisiello's and Rossini's *Il barbiere di Siviglia*, subsequently Count Almaviva's manservant (bar) in Mozart's *Le nozze di Figaro*.

Figlia del reggimento, La. See FILLE DU RÉGIMENT, LA.

Figlia di Jorio, La (The Daughter of Jorio). Opera in 3 acts by Pizzetti; text, word-for-word setting of D'Annunzio's tragedy (1903). Prem. Naples, C, 4 Dec. 1954.

The Abruzzi, long ago. The sorcerer Jorio's daughter Mila (sop), fleeing from the peasants who think she is a witch, is saved by Aligi (ten), who falls in love with her. His father, Lazaro (bar), tries to prevent their liaison and has Aligi beaten and imprisoned. He escapes, and kills his father whom he discovers about to rape Mila; but she says she is the guilty one and is burned as a witch.

Figner (Mei-Figner), **Medea** (*b* Florence, 4 Apr. 1859; *d* Paris, 8 July 1952). Italian, later Russian, mezzo-soprano, later soprano.

Studied Florence with Bianchi, Carozzi-Zucchi, and Panofka. Début Sinalunga 1874 (Azucena). After successes in Italy, Barcelona, and Madrid as a mezzo-soprano, she met Nikolay *Figner, and (by now a soprano) sang with him in S America 1884–6. They married in 1889. St Petersburg 1887–1912, singing with her husband until their divorce in 1904. Here she created Lisa, Yolanta, and roles in Nápravník's *Dubrovský* and *Francesca da Rimini*. Officially retired 1912, but continued to appear as Carmen and Valentine until 1916. Her roles included Tatyana, Desdemona, Mimì, and Brünnhilde. She left Russia for Paris in 1919, though making return visits and recordings there until 1930. In 1949 (released 1975) she recorded (and even sang in) an interview in which she recalled working with Tchaikovsky. A handsome woman, she was much admired for her rich voice, excellent technique, and dramatic presence. (R)

Figner, Nikolay (*b* Nikiforovka, 21 Feb. 1857; *d* Kiev, 13 Dec. 1918). Russian tenor. Studied St Petersburg with Pryanishnikov and Everardi; Naples with De Roxas. Début Naples, T Sannazaro, 1882 (in Gounod's *Philémon et Baucis*). After engagements in Italy, he toured in S America 1884–6, singing in the performances which launched the young Toscanini. He later helped to secure the first Turin performance of Catalani's *Edmea* for the conductor. London, CG, 1887. St Petersburg 1887 (Raoul, with Medea Mei, his wife-to-be, as Valentine); he and Medea then became members of the Imperial O, he remaining until 1906. After singing in private companies (including his own), he became Narodny Dom O's soloist and dir. 1910–15. Repertory included Don José, Gounod's Faust, Turiddu, Radamès, Lohengrin, Lensky, Dmitry. He created roles in Nápravník's *Francesca da Rimini* and *Dubrovský*; also Vaudémont (*Yolanta*) and Hermann (*Queen of Spades*). Tchaikovsky wrote, 'I liked Figner very much, and imagined Hermann to be Figner'. Though not especially gifted vocally, his eloquent singing, versatility, and dramatic commitment made him Russia's outstanding tenor for many years.

Fille du régiment, La (The Daughter of the Regiment). Opera in 2 acts by Donizetti; text by Vernoy de Saint-Georges and Bayard. Prem. Paris, OC, 11 Feb. 1840.

Tirol, 1805. Marie (sop) has been brought up in a regiment by the kindly Sulpice (bs). She loves Tonio (ten), who has been following the regiment out of love for her. When Marie is suggested to the Marquise de Birkenfeld (sop or mez) as a travelling companion, it emerges that the girl is in fact the Countess's niece. This necessitates her leaving Tonio.

Marie, somewhat reluctantly, is taught correct social etiquette. French soldiers, among them Tonio, storm the castle where she lives and the couple reaffirm their love. The Marquise discloses that she is not Marie's aunt, but her mother; despite this, Marie cannot go along with an arranged marriage and her mother permits her marriage to Tonio.

finale (It.: 'end'). The last movement of a piece of music, in opera of an act. From the beginnning it tended to involve ensemble singing, from which developed, in 18th-cent. opera buffa, the *ensemble finale. By the 19th cent. the finale was almost invariably one of the most complex sections of the whole opera, involving any or all of solo aria, recitative, ensemble, chorus, and orchestral interludes.

'Finch'han dal vino'. Don Giovanni's aria in Act I of Mozart's *Don Giovanni*, in which he bids Leporello prepare for the party. Sometimes known as the Champagne Aria, from a tradition of the performer singing it with a glass of champagne in his hand.

Finnie, Linda (*b* Paisley, 9 May 1952). Scottish mezzo-soprano. Studied Glasgow with Busfield. Début Scottish O, 1976. WNO 1979; Bayreuth from 1988; also London, ENO and CG; Paris, O and C; Brussels, M; Lyons. With her strong characterizations and firm, warm tone, successful as Ulrica, Eboli, Amneris, Brangäne, Fricka, Waltraute. (R)

Finta giardiniera, La (The Feigned Gardener). Opera in 3 acts by Mozart; text possibly by Calzabigi for Anfossi's opera (1774), rev. Coltellini. Prem. Munich 13 Jan. 1775.

The house and garden of the Podestà of Lagonero, mid-18th cent. The Countess Violante Onesti (sop) is believed to have died at the hands of her lover Count Belfiore (ten) during a quarrel. He has fled, but she is seeking him forgivingly, and takes a post as a gardener under the name of Sandrina. Her employer, the Podestà Don Anchise (ten), has fallen in love with her, to the annoyance of his maid Serpetta (sop), who has designs on him herself. When Sandrina finds Belfiore paying court to the Podestà's niece Arminda (sop), she is determined to punish him. But when his arrest for the alleged murder of Countess Onesti is announced, she reveals her disguise; she then pretends to Belfiore that she is not Violante Onesti after all. After many fantastic confusions, all is resolved.

Finta semplice, La (The Feigned Simpleton). Opera in 3 acts by Mozart; text by Coltellini, after a libretto by Goldoni, first set by Perillo (1764). Prem. Salzburg, Archbishop's Palace, 1 May 1769.

Near Cremona, late 18th cent. Fracasso (ten), a Hungarian captain, is in love with Donna Giacinta (con); his lieutenant, Simone (bs), is in love with Giacinta's maid Ninetta (sop). It is arranged that Fracasso's sister, the Baroness Rosina (sop), who is coming to visit, will pretend to be a simpleton in order to divert the attention of Giacinta's two grumpy elder brothers, Don Cassandro (bs) and Don Polidoro (ten).

Both the brothers fall in love with Rosina. Giacinta and Ninetta disappear and the brothers, having been told that Giacinta has taken the family jewellery with her, promise Fracasso and Simone that they may marry the girls if they can bring them back, which they do.

Rosina marries Cassandro and everyone, except Polidoro, is happy.

Finto Stanislao, Il (The False Stanislas). Opera in 2 acts by Gyrowetz (Jírovec); text by Romani. Prem. Milan 5 Aug. 1818. Text set by Verdi in 1840 for *Un *giorno di regno*. Another opera on the subject is by Mosca (1812).

Fioravanti, Valentino (*b* Rome, 11 Sept. 1764; *d* Capua, 16 June 1837). Italian composer. He wrote some 77 operas; nevertheless, the last of them was entitled *Ogni eccesso è vizioso* (All Excess is Vicious). His first great success came with *Le cantatrici villane*, frequently revived including in Germany as *Die Dorfsängerinnen*. Its success took him to Lisbon and to the directorship of the S Carlos T (1802–6), whence he returned via a successful visit to Paris. His serious operas were eclipsed by his opere buffe, in which he shows a lively feeling for the manner of which Cimarosa (who admired him) was a master. His son **Vincenzo** (*b* Rome, 5 Apr. 1799; *d* Naples, 28 Mar. 1877) was obliged through parental opposition to study music

in secret (with his father's teacher Jannacconi); later, after he was discovered not to have been studying medicine, his reluctant father allowed him to take up music. He experienced many difficulties in his career as a composer; but his operas, like those of his father most successful when in buffo vein, were popular in Naples. *Il ritorno di Pulcinella dagli studi di Padova* (Pulcinella's Return from Study in Padua, 1837), which includes a scene in an asylum for mad musicians, had a wider success, and was even performed in London and America, due to adaptation by the singer Carlo Cambiaggio. A second son, **Giuseppe** (*b c*.1795; *d* ?) was one of the best buffo basses of his day: he took part in a number of prems., including those of Rossini's *Bianca e Faliero* and *Matilde di Shabran* and of some of Donizetti's works. Giuseppe's two sons **Valentino** (1827–79) and **Luigi** (1829–87) were also buffo basses, specializing in the same roles as their father.

Fiordiligi. Dorabella's sister (sop) in Mozart's *Così fan tutte*.

First Lady. The leader (sop) of the Three Ladies, attendants of the Queen of the Night, who save Tamino from the serpent in Mozart's *The Magic Flute*.

Fischer, Adam (*b* Budapest, 9 Sept. 1949). Hungarian conductor; brother of Ivan, below. Studied Vienna with Swarowsky and Siena with Ferrara. Won the Cantelli Competition 1973 and was cond. of the Finnish Nat, O until 1977. Freiburg 1981–3; Kassel from 1987. Has led a wide repertory in Vienna, S, and Munich. Paris, O, début 1984 (*Rosenkavalier*); London, CG, 1989 (*Fledermaus*). Prems. of operas by Tal (*Der Sturm*, 1987) and Schweinitz (*Patmos*, 1990). (R)

Fischer, Emil (*b* Brunswick, 13 June 1838; *d* Hamburg, 11 Aug. 1914). German bass-baritone. Studied with his parents, both singers. Début Graz 1857 (the Seneschal in Boieldieu's *Jean de Paris*). Danzig 1863–70; Dresden 1880–5. London, CG, 1884 (Sachs, a role in which he excelled). New York, M, 1885–91. The first American Lysiart, Sachs, King Mark, Wotan (*Rheingold*), Wanderer, Hagen.

Fischer, Ivan (*b* Budapest, 20 Jan. 1951). Hungarian conductor; brother of Adam, above. Studied Vienna with Swarowsky and Salzburg with Harnoncourt. Début Zurich 1977 (*Don Giovanni*). Cond. *Agrippina* with

Kent O 1982 and was music dir. 1984–9. ENO 1987 (*Zauberflöte*); Vienna, S, from 1988: *Don Giovanni*, *Figaro*, *Entführung*. Other repertory incl. *Bluebeard's Castle* (1992, London Proms), *La gazza ladra*, *Don Pasquale*. (R)

Fischer, Ludwig (*b* Mainz, 18 Aug. 1745; *d* Berlin, 10 July 1825). German bass. Studied with Raaff. Début Mannheim 1772 (Salieri's *Fiera di Venezia*). Vienna 1780–3, creating Osmin, written especially for him. Mozart admired his 'excellent bass voice' and 'beautiful deep notes', and arranged the aria K512 for him. He performed with success in Paris, Italy, Prague, and Dresden, and in 1789 took up a lifelong appointment at Berlin, Königliche Oper. London 1794, 1798, and 1812. The greatest German bass of his time, he possessed a range of two and a half octaves, a round, full tone, and unusual vocal agility. However, his Italianate training made him prone to outmoded ornamentation, and he was later criticized for continuing to embellish Sarastro's aria 'In diesen heil'gen Hallen'. He retired in 1815.

Fischer-Dieskau, Dietrich (*b* Berlin, 28 May 1925). German baritone. Studied Berlin with Georg Walter and Weissenborn. Début Berlin, SO, 1948 (Posa). Remained there as leading baritone; Vienna, S, and Bavarian SO, Munich from 1949; Salzburg from 1952. Bayreuth 1954–6 (Wolfram and Amfortas); London, CG, from 1965; Berlin, D, 1975–6. Repertory included Wagner (Hans Sachs, Kurwenal); Verdi (Falstaff, Rigoletto); Strauss (Mandryka, Olivier, Barak, Jochanaan); Mozart (Almaviva, Don Giovanni, Papageno, Don Alfonso); Wozzeck, Busoni's Doktor Faust, etc. Created Reimann's Lear, and Mittenhofer (*Elegy for Young Lovers*). The vocal mastery and sensitivity to words apparent in his Lieder singing were also impressive in his stage roles (particularly in the German repertory), to which was added an assured and commanding presence. Retired 1992. He is married to the soprano Julia *Varady. (R)

Fischietti, Domenico (*b* Naples, ?1725; *d* ?Salzburg, ?after 1810). Italian composer. His early promise was assured through his four collaborations with Goldoni in Venice: *Lo speziale* (The Apothecary, 1754), *La ritornata di Londra* (1756), *Il mercato di Malmantile* (1757), and *Il signor dottore* (1758). These were highly acclaimed, Fischietti's fame spread quickly beyond Italy and travels to Prague and Dresden followed. Appointed Kapellmeister

to the Archbishop of Salzburg, in preference to Leopold Mozart, 1772: he held the position until 1783, visiting Italy on several occasions to produce new operas, including *La molinara* (The Maid of the Mill, 1778). Fischietti's operas belong to the mainstream tradition of the mid-18th cent. and were performed in many European cities, including London. Together with Galuppi, Logroscino, and Piccinni, he is one of the most important composers of opere buffe before Mozart, who regarded him highly.

Fisher, Sylvia (*b* Melbourne, 18 Apr. 1910). Australian soprano. Studied Melbourne with Spivakovsky. Début Melbourne 1932 (Hermione in Lully's *Cadmus et Hermione*). London, CG, 1948–58, début Leonore. Also Sieglinde, and first British Kostelnička. Chicago 1959. London, EOG 1963–71, as Britten's Lady Billows, Female Chorus, Mrs Grose; created Mrs Wingrave (*Owen Wingrave*), BBC TV 1971, London, CG, 1973. Commanding yet warm on stage, with an intelligent approach to the study of the roles, she was particularly admired as the Marschallin. (R)

Flagstad, Kirsten (*b* Hamar, 12 July 1895; *d* Oslo, 7 Dec. 1962). Norwegian soprano. Studied Oslo with Jacobsen, and Stockholm with Dr Bratt. Début Oslo, 1913 (Nuri, *Tiefland*). Until 1933 she appeared only in Scandinavia, in a large repertory of opera and operetta, and was about to retire when she was engaged for small roles at Bayreuth. Here in 1934 she sang Gutrune and Sieglinde. New York, M, 1935 (Sieglinde, Isolde, Brünnhilde, Kundry), immediately establishing herself as a major artist. Remained at New York, M, until 1941, and returned there 1950–2. London, CG, 1936–7, and 1948–51 (Senta, Isolde, etc.), and Mermaid T, 1951, 1952 (Purcell's Dido). Retired in 1953, but continued to record. With her musical intuition, poise, and powerful, radiant voice, she was one of the greatest Wagner singers of the century. (R)

Flamand. A musician (ten), rival of the poet Olivier for the Countess's hand, in Strauss's *Capriccio*.

Fledermaus, Die (The Bat). Operetta in 3 acts by Johann Strauss II; text by Haffner and Genée, after a French *spirituel vaudeville*, *Le réveillon* (1872), by Meilhac and Halévy, based in turn on Roderich Bendix's comedy *Das*

Gefängnis (1851). Prem. Vienna, W, 5 Apr. 1874.

Vienna, 19th cent. Rosalinde (sop) is being serenaded by her former admirer Alfred (ten), an opera singer; her husband, Eisenstein (ten), is about to go to prison for having insulted the tax-collector. His friend Dr Falke (bar) comes supposedly to conduct him to prison, but suggests that they both should go to the party being given by Prince Orlofsky (mez, now often ten), and that Eisenstein should present himself at the prison the following morning. When the two men have gone, Alfred returns; his tête-à-tête with Rosalinde is disturbed by the arrival of Frank (bar), the prison governor who has come to conduct Eisenstein to jail. He mistakes Alfred for Eisenstein and takes him off to prison. Rosalinde, also invited to Orlofsky's party, arrives there masked, pretending to be a Hungarian countess; Eisenstein flirts outrageously with her. The plot is further complicated by the fact that Eisenstein's maid, Adele (sop), wearing one of her mistress's dresses, is also at the party. All misunderstandings are cleared up the following morning in the prison.

Fleming, Renée (*b* Rochester, NY, 14 Feb. 1959). US soprano. After study in New York made her début at the Salzburg Landestheater 1986 (Constanze). Her innate musicality and immaculate phrasing have made her admired as Mozart's Countess (S Francisco and Paris; Gly. 1994). London, CG, 1988 (Glauce in *Médée*); New York, M, 1991, as first Rosina in Corigliano's *The Ghosts of Versailles*. Other roles incl. Rossini's Armida, Donna Elvira (Milan, S), Thaïs (Washington, DC). (R)

Fleta, Miguel (*b* Albalate, 1 Dec. 1893; *d* La Coruña, 29 May 1938). Spanish tenor. Studied Barcelona Cons., and Italy with Pierrich. Début Trieste 1919 (Paolo, *Francesca da Rimini*). New York, M, 1923–5; Milan, S, 1924 and 1926, creating Calaf. Also first Romeo in Zandonai's *Giulietta e Romeo*. Possessed a velvety, expressive voice and sang with passion, but declined early. (R)

Fliedermonolog. The monologue in Act II of Wagner's *Die Meistersinger von Nürnberg*, in which Sachs (bs-bar) sits under the elder tree outside his workshop reflecting on the haunting novelty of the song Walther has sung at his trial before the Masters.

Fliegende Holländer, Der (The Flying Dutchman). Opera in 1 act, later 3 acts, by Wagner; text by the composer, after the legend as told in chapter 7 of Heine's *Aus den Memoiren des Herren von Schnabelewopski* (1831). First used as scenario for Dietsch's *Le vaisseau fantôme* (1842). Prem. Dresden, H, 2 Jan. 1843.

A Norwegian fishing village, 1650. The Dutchman (bar) has been condemned, for his blasphemy, to sail his ship until redeemed by a faithful woman. This salvation he is allowed to attempt once every seven years. In one of these periods he is driven by storms to a Norwegian harbour. He moors beside the ship of Daland (bs), who, impressed by the Dutchman's wealth, offers him shelter. Daland's daughter Senta (sop) sings to her friends, as they spin, the Ballad of the Flying Dutchman. Her lover Erik (ten) pleads his own cause, unsuccessfully. But when the Dutchman enters, she is confused by his declaration of love. The Dutchman overhears Erik being rejected again, but concludes that he too is to be deserted by Senta. He sets sail; but Senta leaps to him from a cliff-top. Her faith redeems him, and together they are seen rising heavenwards.

Floquet, Etienne (*b* Aix-en-Provence, 23 Nov. 1748; *d* Paris, 10 May 1785). French composer. He first came to public attention in 1773 with his opéra-ballet *L'union de l'Amour et des arts*, which received 60 performances. His opera *Le seigneur bienfaisant* (1780) is often described as the first French lyrical comedy; with its rejection of a heroic or mythological plot it stood, like *La nouvelle Omphale* (1782), in direct opposition to the reforms of Gluck. Though he was regarded as one of the main supporters of the Italianate faction in the struggle between the supporters of Gluck and Piccinni, his musical style was influenced as much by his compatriots Grétry and Philidor as by Piccinni.

Florence (It., Firenze). City in Tuscany, Italy. Home of the Florentine *camerata. Peri's *Dafne* was given 1598, his *Euridice*, 1600, in the Pitti Palace. Opera was also given (and still is) in the Boboli Gardens and in the Uffizi. The Accademia degli Immobili built the wooden T della Pergola, opened 1656 with Jacopo Melani's *La Tancia*, opened to the public 22 Jun. 1718 with Vivaldi's *Scanderbeg*; altered by Antonio Galli-Bibiena 1738; rebuilt 1857 (cap. 1,500). Scene of Italian prems. of Mozart's *Figaro* (1788), probably *Don Giovanni* (1792), and *Entführung* (1935), also prems. of Donizetti's *Parisina* (1833) and Verdi's original *Macbeth* (1847). The T Politeama Fiorentino Vittorio Emmanuele opened 1864 (open-air; covered 1883); renamed T Comunale 1932; rebuilt 1960; reopened (cap. 2,500) 1961.

The annual May Festival (Maggio Musicale) was established in 1933, largely due to Vittorio *Gui, who had in 1928 founded the Florence Orchestra around which the festival was built. Originally planned as biennial, it became annual in 1938 and has continued as such apart from 1943–7. Opera performed in the T Comunale, T Pergola, and the Boboli Gardens is the chief attraction. Verdi and Rossini are the composers who have contributed most to the festival's success, though the organizers have also used its renown to give a platform to lesser-known works by Bellini, Cherubini, Donizetti, and Spontini, as well as by contemporary composers, including Pizzetti, Dallapiccola, and Frazzi. There have also been many first Italian performances, and revivals of works by Cavalli, Peri, Gagliano, also Meyerbeer.

Florentine Camerata. See CAMERATA.

Florestan. A Spanish nobleman (ten), the unjustly imprisoned husband of Leonore in Beethoven's *Fidelio*. Also the Governor of Linz Castle (bs) in Grétry's *Richard Cœur de Lion*.

Flotow, Friedrich von (*b* Teutendorf, 27 Apr. 1812; *d* Darmstadt, 24 Jan. 1883). German composer. Studied Paris with Rejcha. He wrote part of Grisar's *Lady Melvil* in 1838 and *L'eau merveilleuse* in 1839, and his first public success was with a collaborative work, *Le naufrage de la Méduse* (Act I by Pilati): this was rewritten by Flotow as *Die Matrosen* (1845). He wrote several other operas for Paris, also *Alessandro Stradella* (1844). This was followed by his most enduring success, *Martha* (1847), which triumphed at its Vienna prem. and was promptly taken up by Liszt at Weimar. Few of his later operas achieved this popularity, though he had some success with *La veuve Grapin* (1859), *Zilda* (1866), and *L'ombre* (1870). He was Intendant at Schwerin, 1855–62.

Flotow's operas are cosmopolitan in style, in that the early influence of French opéra-comique was to be joined by an Italian lyricism in his vocal writing and an affection for the orchestra inherited from German Romantic opera. His music is light, dam-

agingly so when he tackles large subjects or serious issues (even in *Alessandro Stradella* it is the comic numbers which are the most memorable); but at its best his work has a grace, fluency, and charm that have continued to beguile audiences. He made a very successful Paris career by ingeniously modifying some of the more sentimental features of German Romantic opera to appeal to French taste. *Martha* has continued to survive the criticisms easily levelled at it, and the sweet Irish melody which he uses as a reminiscence motive, 'The Last Rose of Summer', is barely distinguishable from the manner of the rest of the score.

Flower Duet. The name sometimes given to the duet 'Scuoti quella fronda di ciliego', sung by Butterfly (sop) and Suzuki (mez) in Act II of Puccini's *Madama Butterfly* as they strew the house with flowers against Pinkerton's return.

Flowermaidens. The group of maidens (sop and alt) whom Klingsor sets to seduce Parsifal in Wagner's *Parsifal*.

Flower Song. See LA FLEUR QUE TU M'AVAIS JETÉE.

Floyd, Carlisle (*b* Latta, SC, 11 June 1926). US composer. Studied Syracuse U with Bacon. He first came to the fore with *Susannah* (1955), which transferred the biblical story of Susannah and the Elders to Tennessee, making effective use of folk idioms as well as of more advanced musical resources. His later operas have not met with the same success, though *Of Mice and Men* (1970) was praised for its ability to use simple musical means to good theatrical effect.

Flying Dutchman, The. See FLIEGENDE HOLLÄNDER, DER.

Foerster, Josef Bohuslav (*b* Prague, 30 Dec. 1859; *d* Nový Vestec, 29 May 1951). Czech composer. Studied Prague Organ School. He first taught in Prague, moving with his wife Bertha Foerstrová-Lautererová to Hamburg in 1893 and Vienna in 1903, and working in both cities as a critic. In 1918 they returned to Prague, where Foerster taught at the Conservatory and elsewhere. As a critic, he wrote civilized and perceptive essays in defence of Romantic and Nationalist music. His six operas show an increasing metaphysical interest. The first two reflect real life: *Eva* (1899), his greatest success, is a Moravian lyric tragedy that owes something to

Smetana. With *Srdce* (The Heart, 1923) and *Bloud* (The Simpleton, 1936) the characters are increasingly identified with moral states: the expression is inward, personal, and symbolic, the drama spiritual and embodied in music that is at its finest exalted and impressive.

Foerstrová-Lautererová, Bertha (*b* Prague, 11 Jan. 1869; *d* Prague, 9 Apr. 1936). Czech soprano. Studied Prague with Pold-ková-Panachová and Tauwitz. Début Prague, N, 1887 (Agathe). Sang many important Czech roles; also first Prague Desdemona (Verdi) and Tatyana (Tchaikovsky found her excellent). Hamburg, 1893–1901, becoming one of Mahler's favourite singers. He summoned her to Vienna, where, as Foerster-Lauterer, she sang 1903–13. Described in the *Neue Freie Presse* as 'a first-rate artist' and 'a pillar of the ensemble', she was impressive for her full, ripe voice and mature dramatic sense. Her repertory embraced Mozart, Bellini, Weber, Verdi, Richard Strauss, and Wagner. Married Joseph Bohuslav Foerster, 1888.

Foli (Foley), **A**(llan) **J**(ames) (*b* Cahir, 7 Aug. 1835; *d* Southport, 20 Oct. 1899). Irish bass. Studied Naples. Début Catania 1862 (Elmiro, Rossini's *Otello*). After appearances in other Italian cities, London début, HM, 1865 (Saint-Bris). Sang in over 60 operas at HM, DL, and CG; Daland in the first Wagner perf. in England, 1870. US with Mapleson's Co. 1878–9; also sang in Russia and Austria.

Fomin, Evstigney (*b* St Petersburg, 16 Aug. 1761; *d* St Petersburg, 28 Apr. 1800). Russian composer. Studied St Petersburg with Buini, Raupach, and Sartori, Bologna with Martini and Mattei. His first stage work was an opera-ballet, *Novgorodsky Bogatyr Boyeslavich* (The Novgorod Bogatyr Boyeslavich, 1788), to a text by Catherine the Great, in which he makes some use of folk tunes. From 1797 he was a répétiteur at the Imperial Theatres. *Yamshchiky na podstave* (The Post-Coach Drivers, 1787) is remarkable for its use of Russian folk polyphony as well as its vivid depiction of the life of the post-coach drivers, and is thus an important example for the development of Russian opera. However, his most important work is the melodrama *Orfey i Evridika* (Orpheus and Eurydice, 1791), an enterprising work that includes a number of technical and instrumental experiments (including a powerful Chorus of Shades). The

most talented Russian opera composer of the end of the 18th cent., even if he did not live to develop his gifts to the full, he brought genuinely Russian elements into opera of an essentially Italian vernacular.

Fontana, Ferdinando (*b* Milan, 30 Jan. 1850; *d* Lugano, 12 May 1919). Italian playwright and librettist. Best known as the author of two of Puccini's earliest opera texts, *Le villi* (1884) and *Edgar* (1889), a collaboration arranged by Ponchielli. Also librettist of Franchetti's *Asrael* (1888), and the Italian translator of *Tiefland* and *Die lustige Witwe*.

Foppa, Giuseppe (*b* Venice, 12 Aug. 1760; *d* Venice, 1845). Italian librettist. Apart from a brief period in Lisbon (1797–8), he lived largely in Venice, where he wrote over 80 works for composers including Andreozzi, Bertoni, Bianchi, Coccia, Farinelli, Fioravanti, Generali, Mayr, Nasolini, Paer, Pavesi, Rossini (*L'inganno felice*, *Il signor Bruschino*, and *Sigismondo*), Spontini (*Le metamorfosi di Pasquale*), and Zingarelli. His talent was for comedy, and his texts draw on the stock characters and situations of the 18th cent. and especially of the commedia dell'arte, somewhat under the influence of Goldoni. From the commedia dell'arte he selected and gave prominence to a number of scenes, including the *mad scene with flute obbligato. In his serious operas he showed more Romantic inclinations: he was one of the first librettists to introduce Shakespearian subjects into opera (though in the Ducis versions), e.g. *Giulietta e Romeo* for Zingarelli (1796).

Ford. A wealthy citizen of Windsor (bar), Alice's husband, in Verdi's *Falstaff* and Vaughan Williams's *Sir John in Love*. In Nicolai's *Die lustigen Weiber von Windsor* he is known as Herr Fluth (bar).

Ford, Bruce (*b* Lubbock, TX, 15 Aug. 1956). US tenor. Studied in Houston, singing there in 1981 prem. of Floyd's *Willie Stark*. Wuppertal O 1983–5, Mannheim O 1985–7 (Tamino and Fenton). A brilliant and secure technique informs his singing of Rossini: Argirio (*Tancredi*) at Wexford 1986, Agorante in *Ricciardo e Zoraide* (Pesaro), and Almaviva (London, CG, 1991). Other roles incl. Mozart's Mitridate and Ferrando (London, CG, 1991, 1995). (R)

Forest Murmurs (Ger., *Waldweben*). The name given to the scene in Act II of Wagner's *Siegfried*, in which Siegfried lies basking in the beauty of the forest just before his encounter with Fafner.

Foresto. An Aquileian knight (ten) in Verdi's *Attila*.

Forsell, John (*b* Stockholm, 6 Nov. 1868; *d* Stockholm, 30 May 1941). Swedish baritone. Début Stockholm 1896 (Rossini's Figaro). Sang there regularly until 1909. London, CG, 1909 (Don Giovanni); New York, M, 1909–10. Also sang in Berlin, Vienna. Dir. Stockholm O 1924–39. His enormous repertory included Germont, Amfortas, Sachs, Onegin, and Valentin, but he was most famous as Don Giovanni, which he was still singing in 1930 (Salzburg). Possessed a beautiful voice, excellent technique, and a refreshing vigour on stage. He taught J. Björling, T. Ralf, Berglund, and Svanholm. (R)

Fortner, Wolfgang (*b* Leipzig, 12 Oct. 1907; *d* Heidelberg, 5 Sept. 1987). German composer. Studied Leipzig with Grabner. A distinguished teacher, his many pupils included Henze. He first came to prominence as an opera composer with his Lorca setting *Die Bluthochzeit* (Blood Wedding, 1957), following this with the more lyrical *Don Perlimplin* (1962); both works have won considerable admiration in Germany. He has made use of a modern and personal version of Singspiel, with actors but also singers having speaking parts; and has a particularly sensitive feeling for the orchestra.

Förtsch, Johann Philipp (*b* Wertheim am Main, *bapt.* 14 May 1652; *d* Eutin, 14 Dec. 1732). German composer. He was one of the most influential figures in the early history of opera in Hamburg and while still a singer at the T am Gänsemarkt also wrote several librettos. From 1684–90 he was effectively house composer, when his works dominated the repertoire: these included *Croesus* (1684) and *Der irrende Ritter Don Quixote de la Mancha* (1690). Most of his music is lost, but that which survives suggests he was much influenced by the Venetian tradition of public opera.

Forza del destino, La (The Force of Destiny). Opera in 4 acts by Verdi; text by Piave, after the drama *Don Álvaro, o la fuerza del sino* (1835), by Angel de Saavedra Ramírez de Banquedano, Duke of Rivas, and on a scene from Schiller's drama *Wallensteins Lager* (1799). Prem. St Petersburg 10 Nov. 1862.

Spain and Italy, mid-18th cent. The Marquis of Calatrava (bs) surprises the elopement of his daughter Leonora (sop) and Don Alvaro (ten). Professing Leonora's innocence, Alvaro throws his pistol to the ground. It goes off, killing the Marquis.

In their escape, Leonora and Alvaro are separated. Disguised as a man, Leonora encounters her brother Don Carlo (bar), posing as a student, in a village inn. Carlo relates a story showing he is determined to kill his sister's seducer. Leonora believes that Alvaro has deserted her and asks the Father Superior (Padre Guardiano, bs) of a monastery if she may become a hermit nearby.

Alvaro, now a captain in the Spanish army, believes Leonora to be dead. He rescues a man who turns out to be Carlo, though neither reveals his real identity. At a call to arms, both men rush to join the fighting. Alvaro is wounded and it emerges that he is Leonora's seducer. He recovers, and Carlo reveals his identity and challenges him to a duel. A patrol discovers them fighting; Carlo is dragged away and Alvaro decides to enter a monastery.

Alvaro is living as Father Raphael. Carlo arrives, having been seeking him for five years, and provokes him to fight. Alvaro wounds Carlo mortally and seeks absolution from the hermit, who at first refuses. Leonora and Alvaro recognize each other. Alvaro confesses that he has just injured Carlo and Leonora rushes off to her brother. The dying Carlo stabs Leonora and she dies, believing she and Alvaro will meet again in heaven.

Forzano, Giovacchino (*b* Borgo S Lorenzo, 19 Nov. 1884; *d* Rome, 18 Oct. 1970). Italian librettist. Studied singing and appeared in baritone roles in the Italian provinces. Provided librettos for Mascagni (*Lodoletta*, *Il piccolo Marat*), Puccini (*Gianni Schicchi*, *Suor Angelica*), Wolf-Ferrari (*Sly*), Leoncavallo (*Edipo re*), Giordano (*Il re*), and Marinuzzi (*Palla de' Mozzi*), among others. Began producing operas in 1904, and worked at the Milan, S (1922–3), and other Italian cities, as well as in London (CG), Vienna, Berlin, Budapest, and Brussels. He was responsible for staging the world prems. of *Turandot* and Boito's *Nerone*, among other works. A fluent, skilful, and witty craftsman.

Foss (orig. Fuchs), **Lukas** (*b* Berlin, 15 Aug. 1922). US composer of German origin. Studied Berlin with Goldstein, Paris with Gallon, Philadelphia with Scalero and Thompson, later also with Hindemith. A gifted and versatile musician, he has composed music in many different manners, winning early success as an opera composer with his deft, appealingly written comedy *The Jumping Frog of Calaveras County* (1949). His comic gifts serve more serious points in the 'miracle play' *Griffelkin* (1955).

Fournet, Jean (*b* 14 Apr. 1913). French conductor. Studied at Paris Cons.; début Rouen 1936. Music dir. Paris, C, 1944- 57, and has appeared as guest cond. throughout the world: first *Pelléas* in Japan (1958), *Samson et Dalila* at New York, M, 1987. Often heard in Ravel and Berlioz, and in particular in Poulenc (*Les dialogues des Carmélites*).

Four Saints in Three Acts. 'An opera to be sung' in 4 (*sic*) acts by Virgil Thomson; text by Gertrude Stein. Prem. Hartford, by Society of Friends and Enemies of Modern Music, Avery Memorial T, 8 Feb. 1934.

The action takes place in Spain and takes the form of an allegory in which Saint Theresa (2 roles: St. Theresa 1 (sop) and St. Theresa 2 (mez)), surrounded by men, and Saint Ignatius (bar), surrounded by women, work together and help one another to become saints.

Fox, Carol (*b* Chicago, 15 June 1926; *d* Chicago, 21 July 1981). US manager. Studied singing Chicago, New York, and in Italy. With Nicola Rescigno and Lawrence Kelly founded Lyric O of Chicago 1952; general manager 1956–80. She dominated opera in Chicago by the force of her personality, raising standards to an international level; engaging outstanding singers, conductors, producers, and designers; and enlarging the repertory. Ill health, and unwillingness to bow to budgetary pressures, led to her resignation in 1980.

Fra Diavolo. Opera in 3 acts by Auber; text by Scribe. Prem. Paris, OC, 28 Jan. 1830.

Fra Diavolo (ten), a notorious bandit, passing himself off as the Marquis of San Marco, compromises Zerlina (sop), the daughter of an innkeeper, while engaged in an elaborate plot to steal the jewels of Lady Pamela (mez), wife of Lord Cockburn (bs). Betrayed by his associates, Fra Diavolo is shot,

having cleared Zerlina of any involvement and reunited her with her lover, Lorenzo (ten). An alternative ending has Fra Diavolo taken prisoner.

Fra due litiganti il terzo gode. See DUE LITIGANTI, I.

Fra Gherardo. Opera in 3 acts by Pizzetti; text by the composer after the Chronicles of Salimbene da Parma (13th cent.). Prem. Milan, S, 16 May 1928.

Parma, 1260. Gherardo (ten), a weaver, joins the order of the White Friars following a love affair with Mariola (sop). He leads a revolt of the oppressed people of Parma against the nobles and dies at the stake; Mariola is killed by a madwoman.

'Fra gli amplessi'. Duet in Act II of Mozart's *Così fan tutte*, in which Fiordiligi (sop) begins by trying to leave the disguised Ferrando (ten) to return to her lover and instead ends up in his arms.

Fra Melitone. A Franciscan friar (bar) in Verdi's *La forza del destino*.

Françaix, Jean (*b* Le Mans, 23 May 1912). French composer. Studied Paris with Boulanger. His lively, skilful invention has found expression principally in concert works, but he has also had success on the stage with his ballets and with an early chamber opera, *Le diable boiteux* (The Lame Devil, 1938). His most ambitious stage work is *La princesse de Clèves* (1965).

France. By the late 16th cent. various dramatic musical entertainments were fashionable at court, principally the *ballet de cour and its derivatives. These were distinguished by an emphasis on their dance content which has to varying degrees always marked the French approach to opera. During Louis XIV's minority, an attempt was made by Mazarin to establish Italian opera in Paris, probably beginning with Marazzoli's *Il giudizio* (perf. privately 1645); this was given impetus by the arrival of the exiled Barberini family from Rome in 1644. The performances of Italian opera which were given, including Cavalli's *Egisto* (1646) and Rossi's *Orfeo* (1647) were not well received: even the work which Cavalli wrote specially for Paris for Louis XIV's wedding, *Ercole amante* (1662), failed to please, despite his attempts to accommodate French taste. Under Benserade, ballet remained in the ascendancy; particularly significant was the series of *comédies-ballets for which *Lully collaborated with Molière. In these an embryonic form of French recitative was developed and the musical element gradually came to predominate.

The first attempts at a national genre based on the Italian example came with the foundation of the Académie Royale de Musique (as Académie Royale d'*Opéra) by P. *Perrin and *Cambert in 1669. They had already collaborated on a number of small-scale stage works; their *Pomone* (1671) has the best claim to being the first French opera. Following their next work, *Les peines et les plaisirs de l'amour* (1671), the couple were declared bankrupt and their monopoly on operatic performances was seized by Lully. Beginning with *Cadmus et Hermione* in 1673, he produced a series of *tragédies en musique which established a style of French opera that survived, modified, for almost a century. Lully's basic concept owed much to classical models: a prologue (in which the monarch was usually praised) and five acts; dance functional to the entertainment, drawing in part on the tradition of the ballet de cour; an individual and expressive vein of French recitative, and a skilful use of grandiose choral forces. It was difficult for a less imposing musician than Lully to develop French opera significantly, despite the work of M.-A. *Charpentier, *Campra, and *Destouches, until *Rameau, who in his *tragédies lyriques continued and developed his basic model, though placing less weight on the reflection of royal *gloire*. By now the grand formality and pomposity of the style was mocked in the drame forain, reflecting the no less French characteristic of wit and irreverence; this eventually developed into the *opéra-comique. The essentially French nature of this contrast, and of the love of forming factions, was shown when a troupe of Neapolitan opera buffa singers visited Paris in 1746 and 1752. There ensued the *Guerre des Bouffons. On the Italian side, *Rousseau wrote *Le devin du village* (1752). Though the liveliness of the Italians carried most Parisians with them, their style was soon absorbed into the French tradition. Having written *Orfeo* (1762) with Calzabigi under some influence of Rameau, *Gluck came to Paris in 1774 for *Iphigénie en Aulide* and French versions of *Orfeo* and *Alceste*. Gluck's success rekindled controversy, and *Piccinni was, against his will and

despite his admiration for Gluck, made the subject of a rival faction. French light opera continued as plays in which music had a subsidiary if essential role, though *Philidor (e.g. *Tom Jones*, 1765) and *Duni (e.g. *Les moissonneurs*, 1768) gave naturalism and freshness greater expressive weight in a pre-Romantic manner. A third important figure was *Monsigny (e.g. *Le déserteur*, 1769), who without loss of immediacy in treatment gave opéra-comique still more substance.

With the Revolution in 1789, opéra-comique replaced the high tragédie lyrique as the most important and popular form (and was to be the ancestor of Romantic opera). *Grétry, *Dalayrac, *Catel, and others brought into opera many new ideas, from different ages and exotic countries, from different social milieus, and from fairytale and the supernatural as well as Nature and a Rousseau-inspired respect for Natural Man. The most gifted and original of this group was *Méhul, who wrote some light works but whose real gift was for the passionate and tragic (e.g. *Euphrosine*, 1790). An important consequence, especially given the French attention to clarity of verbal expression, was the growth of interest in carrying on the action during a musical number. The orchestra took on a more functional character, and the opportunity for symphonic development led to a growth of interest in motive. Again it was an Italian, *Cherubini, who, together with Méhul, gave an important lead to opéra-comique, e.g. with *Lodoïska* (1791). Another important composer of dawning Romanticism was Le Sueur (e.g. *La caverne*, 1793). A significant genre to emerge as expressing the political and personal tensions of the period was *rescue opera.

The age of Napoleon gave France a renewed taste for grandeur and for demonstrations of *la gloire*, expressed now not to reflect aristocratic taste but, among other features, to celebrate the Hero, conquest, and the sweep of history; the audience, especially after the Restoration in 1815, was increasingly a prosperous bourgeoisie, uneducated in taste but impressed by pomp and spectacle. The style was, once again, set by an Italian, Napoleon's preferred composer *Spontini, with *La vestale* (1807); this initiated a genre of large, loud, long operas, usually on historical subjects, demanding elaborate spectacle and grandiose décor. Characteristic works which, in Spontini's wake, formed the new style of

*Grand Opera in the 1820s included *Auber's La muette de Portici (1828) and Rossini's Guillaume Tell (1829). This manner was brought to its highest point by *Meyerbeer, initally with Robert le diable (1831), and matched by *Halévy with La Juive (1835).

For the first half of the 19th cent. the supremacy of Paris as an operatic centre was unquestioned, and the style of the Opéra influenced composers from Verdi and Wagner to Tchaikovsky. Not all French composers were able to match its demands: Berlioz failed to obtain a footing at the Opéra with Benvenuto Cellini in 1838, and wrote Les Troyens without hope of French production. Once again in French operatic history, the grandeur and strength that impressed so many musicians brought with it an inflexibility that excluded too much. Not surprisingly, French vivacity found expression in comic opera. Auber had (to Wagner's dismay) moved on to a series of light, rather thin works, most successfully with Fra Diavolo (1830). *Adam won a great success with Le postillon de Lonjumeau (1836). A reconciliation between the two strains of opera was one of the reasons for the outstanding popularity of *Gounod's Faust (1859). A more significant step came with *Bizet's Carmen (1875), whose passionate naturalism captivated musicians all over Europe, and was an important example for *verismo. The sentimental strain in French opera exploited by Gounod was given a distinctive new colouring by *Massenet, especially in the combination of sex and religion in Hérodiade (1881) and Thaïs (1894), and in the romantic tragedies Manon (1884) and Werther (1892). *Saint-Saëns's operas, especially Samson et Dalila (1877), also won wide popularity. The realistic strain found new life in the work of *Bruneau (e.g. L'attaque du moulin, 1893), who had Zola as his librettist, and of Gustave *Charpentier in Louise (1900). Meanwhile, the love of farce had been indulged with a brilliant tradition of operetta that reached its most characteristic form in the irreverent, irresistible works of *Offenbach; also popular were *Audran, *Planquette, *Lecocq, and others.

The effect of Wagner went deeper in France that in any other country outside Germany, and a number of works were written either accepting or constructively rejecting the influence. *Debussy's Pelléas et Mélisande (1902) both rejects Wagner and is coloured by him; it is deeply French in its delicacy, its literary awareness, its care for good declamation, its subtle use of the orchestra. Wagnerisms had crept into the work of D'*Indy, *Chabrier, *Lalo, *Dukas, and C. Franck, too much so for their acceptance into the mainstream of French opera, despite many fine inventions. However, Chabrier also showed his light touch, as in his turn did *Ravel with two 1-act comedies. *Roussel, in Padmâvatî (1923), attempted a re-creation of *opéra-ballet. In modern times, the Grand Opera tradition has proved less adaptable to new ideas, despite the example of a few works, such as *Milhaud's Christophe Colomb (1930), than that of light opera. *Poulenc's talent was to be characteristically employed in Les mamelles de Tirésias (1947) but also embraced his deeply felt Dialogues des carmélites (1957); and Messiaen's powerful Christian faith took expression in St François d'Assise (1983). Important contributions to the French tradition have also been made by *Sauguet and *Tomasi. The youngest generation has shown an interest in experimenting with new dramatic forms in almost all kinds and directions.

See also PARIS.

Francesca da Rimini. Opera in 4 acts by Zandonai; text by Tito Ricordi, after D'Annunzio's tragedy (1902), after Dante. Prem. Turin, R, 19 Feb. 1914.

Ravenna and Rimini, late 13th cent. The story, based on the fifth canto of Dante's Inferno, tells how Francesca (sop) falls in love with Paolo (ten), thinking him to be his brother Gianciotto (bar) whom she is to marry; he has in fact sent Paolo to bring her to him. Malatestino (ten), another brother, who has made unsuccessful advances to Francesca, betrays the lovers. They are discovered in one another's arms by Gianciotto, who kills Paolo.

Franchetti, Alberto (Baron) (b Turin, 18 Sept. 1860; d Viareggio, 4 Aug. 1942). Italian composer. Studied Venice with Coccon and Maggi, Munich with Rheinberger, Dresden with Draeseke and Kretschmer. His private means enabled him to secure this thorough training and later to stage his operas under favourable conditions. His first opera, Asrael (1888), proved to be a work whose apocalyptic scale drew effectively upon French Grand Opera and upon Wagner. Verdi was sufficiently impressed to suggest Franchetti to the city of Genoa for a work to celebrate the fourth centenary of the Genoese Columbus's discovery of America. In *Cristoforo Colombo* (1892) Franchetti was again able to indulge his penchant for the grandiose to good effect. *Germania* (1902) (though also widely performed, initially under the direction of his defender Toscanini) is more manufactured, and less effectively so than the popular *La figlia di Jorio* (1906). His ambitious attempts to marry a native Italian idiom to a post-Wagnerian German manner he had learned from Draeseke foundered on a lack of real individuality in his often expert music.

Franck, Johann Wolfgang (*b* Unterschwaningen, *bapt.* 17 June 1644; *d* ?c.1710). German composer. At the court of the Margrave of Ansbach 1665–79, rising to be Hofkapellmeister, but forced to flee after murdering one of his musicians and wounding his wife. Already known as an opera composer through e.g. *Die drey Töchter des Cecrops* (the first extant German opera in full score), he settled in Hamburg, becoming musical director of the T am Gänsemarkt. Kapellmeister at Hamburg Cathedral 1682–6, then moving to London, in whose concert life he was an active participant.

Franck's 17 operas are an important contribution to the history of opera in Hamburg, and in the development of German opera. At Ansbach he had directed many Italian operas, particularly those of Ziani. His own works, including *Semele* (1681) and *Diocletianus* (1682), successfully reconcile the Venetian tradition of Cavalli and Cesti with that of Germany. At a time when most of his compatriots looked to Lully and to France for inspiration, Franck's preference for Italian music was noteworthy and played a crucial role in the development of a viable form of German recitative.

Franckenstein, Clemens von und zu (*b* Wiesentheid, 14 July 1875; *d* Hechendorf, 22 Aug. 1942). German composer and conductor. Studied Munich with Thuille, Frankfurt with Knorr. Cond. US 1901–2, England (Moody-Manners Co.) 1902–7, Wiesbaden 1907–8, Berlin 1908–12. Intendant Munich 1914–18, 1924–34, doing much to develop the city's operatic reputation. His operas included *Griseldis* (1898) and *Rahab* (1909).

Frank, Ernst (*b* Munich, 7 Feb. 1847; *d* Oberdöbling, 17 Aug. 1889). German conductor and composer. Studied Munich with

Lachner. He held conducting posts in Würzburg (1868), Mannheim (1872–8), Frankfurt (1878–9), and Hanover (1879–87). An energetic and intelligent musician, he did much to promote the works of his friend Goetz and of younger composers including Stanford. His own operas include *Adam de la Halle* (1880) and *Der Sturm* (1887).

Frankfurt (Ger., Frankfurt am Main). City in Hesse, Germany. The first opera given was Johann Theile's *Adam und Eva* by Johann Velten's company in the Haus zum Krachbein on 4 June 1698. In the 18th cent. the city was dependent on touring companies. Lacking a court, it had no tradition of opera seria and was more drawn to opera buffa, Singspiel, and opéra-comique. Theobald Marchand was the first to give opéra-comique in German 1770–7. The popularity of Singspiel extended to the young Goethe, whose first Singspiel text, *Erwin und Elmire* was set by Johann André 1777. Other visiting companies included those of Abel Seyler (with Neefe), Böhm, and Grossmann.

In 1782 the Städtisches Comödienhaus opened in the Paradeplatz (later Theaterplatz) with a repertory centring on Mozart; also popular were Winter, Weigl, Salieri, and Paer. Friedrich Kunzen was music director 1792–4, followed by Carl Cannabich 1796. Though there were chorus difficulties, Cannabich was able to form an orchestra from the dissolved orchestras of various Rhineland cities. The repertory continued to be based on Mozart and Singspiel, with an increasing amount of opéra-comique. There was also an emphasis on décor, with the use of perspective in splendid sets by Giorgio Fuentes (1796–1805), e.g. for *Clemenza di Tito*, Weigl's *Corsar*, and Salieri's *Palmira*: Goethe tried to win him for Weimar. Weber's *Silvana* was premiered 1810; and Spohr was music director 1818–19, premiering his *Zemire und Azor* 1819. The repertory was extended to include Auber, Halévy, and Meyerbeer, also Wagner and Verdi; singers included Sontag, Schröder-Devrient, Lind, and Tichatschek. In 1842 the theatre became private, and was enlarged 1855.

In 1880 an opera-house (the present Alte Oper) was opened by Kaiser Wilhelm I, with Otto Dessof as music director, then Ludwig Rottenberg (1889–1923). Under Rottenberg there were many prems., including that of Schreker's *Der ferne Klang*. Clemens Krauss was music director 1924–9, working with singers including his wife Viorica Ursuleac; high standards were maintained, but there was less emphasis on contemporary music. William Steinberg was music director 1929, conducting the prem. of Schoenberg's *Von Heute auf Morgen* (1930); he was restricted by the Nazis, and was succeeded by Franz Konwitschny 1938–49; prems. were given of works by Egk, Orff, and Reutter. The operahouse was bombed 1943. Opera was given in the Stock Exchange 1945–51, when the company moved to the rebuilt Schauspielhaus, with Georg Solti as music director 1952–61. He was succeeded by Lovro von Matačić (1961–6), Christoph von Dohnányi (1968–77), Michael Gielen (1977–87), Gary Bertini (1987–90), and Sylvain Cambreling (from 1993). An arsonist destroyed the operahouse in November 1987, and performances continued in the Schauspielhaus. The new O Frankfurt opened 7 Apr. 1991.

Franklin, David (*b* London, 17 May 1908; *d* Worcester, 22 Oct. 1973). English bass. Studied Vienna with Strasser. Début Gly. 1936 (Commendatore). Sang there until 1939; roles included Sarastro, Banquo. London, CG, 1947–50 (Rocco, Pimen, Ochs (one of his finest roles)). Retired from singing 1951. Librettist of Phyllis Tate's *The Lodger*. A warm, intelligent artist with a generous voice. (R)

Frantz, Ferdinand (*b* Kassel, 8 Feb. 1906; *d* Munich, 26 May 1959). German bass-baritone. Studied privately. Début Kassel 1927 (Ortel, *Meistersinger*). Hamburg 1937–43; Munich 1943–59; New York, M, 1949–51, 1953–4; London, CG, 1953–4. A distinguished Sachs, Wotan, and Kurwenal; also sang Daland, King Mark, Galitsky. (R)

Fraschini, Gaetano (*b* Pavia, 16 Feb. 1816; *d* Naples, 23 May 1887). Italian tenor. Studied Pavia with Moretti. Début Pavia (Tamas in Donizetti's *Gemma di Vergy*) 1837. Naples, C, 1840–8, creating Gerardo in *Caterina Cornaro*, and roles in numerous operas by Mercadante, Pacini, Battista, etc. Sang in many other Donizetti works; known as the 'tenore della maledizione' from his powerful rendering of the curse in *Lucia*. London, HM, 1847; Vienna, K, 1851; Paris, I, 1864. Greatly admired by Verdi, he created the leading tenor roles in *Alzira*, *Il corsaro*, *La battaglia di Legnano*, *Stiffelio*, and *Un ballo in maschera*. He was also successful in *Simon Boccanegra*, *La forza del destino*, *La traviata*, *Rigoletto*, and *I*

vespri siciliani. His voice, heroic and with a baritonal quality, sounded like 'a silver gong struck with a silver hammer' (Monaldi); yet Verdi and Donizetti appreciated his ability to sing softly and with sublety. His voice and technique were still intact at his retirement in 1873. The opera-house in Pavia is named after him.

Frate 'nnamorato, Lo (The Brother in Love). Opera by Pergolesi; text by Gennaro Antonio Federico. Prem. Naples, T dei Fiorentini, 27 Sept. 1732.

The complicated plot tells of the twin sisters Nena (sop) and Nina (mez), who love Ascanio (ten) rather than their intended husbands; he is loved by Lucrezia (con). Eventually he is discovered to be the twins' brother, to Lucrezia's delight.

Frau ohne Schatten, Die (The Woman without a Shadow). Opera in 3 acts by Richard Strauss; text by Hugo von Hofmannsthal, after his own story (1919). Prem. Vienna, S, 10 Oct. 1919.

The Empress (sop) is a supernatural being who lacks a shadow—a symbol of her inability to bear human children. A messenger (bar) announces that the Empress must return to her own world and the Emperor (ten) will be turned into stone unless she can acquire a shadow within three days. The Nurse (mez) takes her to the house of the dyer, Barak (bar), whose wife (sop) is willing to sell her own shadow and renounce motherhood in exchange for treasure. The Nurse and Empress promise to return the following day.

The Nurse tempts the dyer's wife by offering her a handsome lover. The Empress is distressed by the anguish she is causing the dyer, although he is not aware of what is happening. Barak's wife tells him she has been unfaithful, but when he makes as if to kill her she admits that she did not actually commit the act, though she had intended to.

Barak and his wife, in an underground cave but separated by a thick wall, each try to find a solution in their own mind to the problem. The Empress enters the cave but refuses to drink the Water of Life, which would give her the woman's shadow. The spirit world rewards her for this unselfish act by giving her the long-desired shadow.

Frazzi, Vito (*b* S Secondo Parmense, 1 Aug. 1888; *d* Florence, 7 July 1975). Italian composer and musicologist. Studied Parma with

Fano and Azzoni. A perceptive critic, he responded intelligently to the problems of setting *King Lear* (1939), though there is a more personal voice to be heard in his response to another masterpiece, *Don Quixote* (1952).

Freeman, David. See OPERA FACTORY.

Freia. The goddess of youth (sop) in Wagner's *Das Rheingold*.

Freischütz, Der (The Freeshooter, i.e. the marksman with magic bullets). Opera in 3 acts by Weber; text by Friedrich Kind, after a tale in the *Gespensterbuch* (1811) of Johann Apel and Friedrich Laun. Prem. Berlin, Sch., 18 June 1821.

Bohemia, after the Thirty Years' War. The huntsman Max (ten) is in love with Agathe (sop), daughter of the head ranger Cuno (bs). He is eager to win a shooting competition to decide the next head ranger and thereby become eligible to marry Agathe, but loses in a trial. Another huntsman, Caspar (bs), has sold his soul to the evil spirit Samiel (speaker), and must bring another victim; Max agrees to get magic bullets from Samiel.

Agathe (sop), apprehensive though soothed by Ännchen (sop), is interrupted by Max, who pretends he must fetch a stag he has shot in the haunted Wolf's Glen. Amid weird sights and sounds in the Glen, Caspar forges seven bullets for Max—the last to go where Samiel wills, though Max does not know this.

Preparing to marry Max, Agathe prays for protection; she has had bad dreams, but Ännchen again comforts her. Max amazes everyone at the shooting contest with his marksmanship. The Prince orders Max to shoot a passing dove with the seventh; Agathe's voice is heard begging him not to. Max fires. Agathe falls, but it is Caspar who is fatally wounded through Samiel's treachery. Max confesses his pact with Samiel, but on the intercession of the Hermit (bs) is promised forgiveness.

Other operas on the subject are by Neuner (1812), Rosenau (1816), and Roser (1816).

Fremstad, Olive (*b* Stockholm, 14 Mar. 1871; *d* Irvington, NY, 21 Apr. 1951). Swedish, later US, soprano. Studied Berlin with Lilli Lehmann. Début as mezzo-soprano, Cologne 1895 (Azucena). Sang there until 1898. Vienna, Bayreuth, and Munich (1900–3); repertory at this time included Brangäne, Carmen. London, CG, 1902–3 (Ortrud,

Venus). New York, M, 1903–14, by now a dramatic soprano (Sieglinde, Kundry, Brünnhilde, Isolde; also Selika, Tosca, and first US Armide (Gluck), and Salome). Chicago 1915–18, after which retired from stage but sang in concert until 1920. Intelligent and temperamental, versatile and cultivated, she was outstanding in her Wagner interpretations, to which she brought great vocal and dramatic gifts. Her popularity brought her 40 curtain calls when she left the Metropolitan in 1914. (R)

Freni, Mirella (*b* Modena, 27 Feb. 1935). Italian soprano. Studied Bologna with Campogalliani. Début Modena 1955 (Micaëla). Gly. 1960–2 (Zerlina, Susanna); London, CG, from 1961 (Nannetta, Violetta, Marguerite, Mimì); sang Fedora there 1994. Milan, S, from 1962; Chicago, 1963; New York, M, from 1965. With the ripening of her full, limpid tone, her repertory expanded with Butterfly, Desdemona (Verdi), Elisabeth de Valois, Tatyana. A highly musical and attractive artist; married to bass Nicolai *Ghiaurov. (R)

Frère Laurent. The holy man (bs) (Shakespeare's Friar Lawrence) who befriends Romeo and Juliet in the operas by Gounod and Sutermeister.

Fretwell, Elizabeth (*b* Melbourne, 13 Aug. 1920). Australian soprano. Studied London with Hislop. Début Australian Nat. O 1947 (Senta). Dublin O 1954; London, SW and CG, and the major British companies from 1955. A warm and forthright singer, acclaimed as Violetta and Leonora. (R)

Frezzolini, Erminia (*b* Orvieto, 27 Mar. 1818; *d* Paris, 5 Nov. 1884). Italian soprano. Studied with her father Giuseppe Frezzolini (1789–1861), a well-known buffo, and the first Dulcamara; later with D. Ronconi, Tacchinardi, and M. García jun. Début Florence 1837 (Beatrice di Tenda). Milan, S, from 1841; London 1842 and 1850. Paris, I, 1853–7. Toured US 1858–61. Her voice declined, and she retired in 1871. One of the most popular and fêted sopranos of her day. Admired by Verdi for her pure, sweet tone, legato singing, and simplicity of expression: she created Giselda (*Lombardi*, 1843), and Giovanna d'Arco, written with her in mind. Beautiful and dramatically affecting, she was also successful in *I Puritani*, *Lucrezia Borgia*, *Rigoletto*, and *Il trovatore*. She was engaged to the composer Nicolai, and married twice. Her first husband, **Antonio Poggi** (1806–75), was a tenor. He studied with Nozzari, and made his début, Paris 1827, as Giacomo in *La donna del lago*. Milan, S, 1834–6, 1845; created Carlo VII in *Giovanna d'Arco*. He and Frezzolini were married 1841–6.

Frick, Gottlob (*b* Ölbronn, 28 July 1906; *d* Pforzheim, 18 Aug. 1994). German bass. Studied Stuttgart with Neudörfer-Opitz. Début Coburg 1934 (Daland). Dresden 1940–50. Munich and Vienna from 1953. London, CG, 1951, 1957–67, 1971; Bayreuth 1957–64; New York, M, 1961. Officially retired 1970, though appeared occasionally thereafter. An expressive and powerful singer, with a large, black voice, strong and even throughout its considerable range. Repertory included Sarastro, Osmin, Caspar, Philip, and Falstaff, but especially famous for his Wagner roles: Hunding, Hagen, Daland, Gurnemanz, etc. (R)

Fricka. The goddess of wedlock (mez), Wotan's wife, in Wagner's *Der Ring des Nibelungen*.

Fricsay, Ferenc (*b* Budapest, 9 Aug. 1914; *d* Basle, 20 Feb. 1963). Hungarian conductor. Studied Budapest with Kodály and Bartók. Cond. Szeged 1936–44; Budapest from 1939, music dir. 1945. International career began 1947 after cond. prem. of Von Einem's *Dantons Tod* in place of the indisposed Klemperer. Music dir. Berlin, SO, 1949–52; Munich, Bavarian SO, 1956–8; returned to Berlin to open D, 1961 (*Don Giovanni*). Edinburgh 1950 with Gly. (*Figaro*). His clear, vigorous interpretations are preserved in a number of recordings, in the techniques of which he took special interest. (R)

Friedenstag (Day of Peace). Opera in 1 act by Richard Strauss; text by Gregor, after Calderón's drama *La redención de Breda* (1625). Prem. Munich 24 July 1938.

On the day that the Peace of Westphalia is signed in October 1648, the Commandant (bar) of Breda refuses to surrender to the Commander of the besieging army (bs), despite the latter's kind words and proferred hand. Only when the Commandant's wife Maria (sop) begs her husband to acknowledge that peace really has come and that brotherhood has replaced hatred, does he throw away his sword and embrace his former enemy. The opera ends with a paean to peace.

Friedrich, Götz (*b* Naumburg-Saale, 4 Aug. 1930). German producer. Studied Weimar. Berlin, K, first as assistant to Felsenstein, then chief prod. Début Weimar 1958 (*Così fan tutte*). Début at Berlin, K, 1959 (*Bohème*). Guest appearances Bremen, Kassel. Holland Fest., *Falstaff* 1972, *Aida* 1973. Left East Germany 1972. Bayreuth: *Tannhäuser* 1972, *Parsifal* 1982. Chief prod. Hamburg from 1973. London, CG: *Ring* 1974–6 and 1989–91, *Idomeneo* 1978, *Tristan* 1985, *Elektra* 1990; dir. of productions 1977–81. Dir. Berlin, D, 1981, where he strengthened the ensemble, included operetta, and introduced special chamber opera performances: also *Ring* 1984–5, *Turandot* 1986, prem. of Henze *Das verratene Meer* 1990. Houston, *Wozzeck* 1982. Salzburg, prem. of Berio *Un re in ascolto* 1984. London, C, *Tristan* 1985. Munich, *Forza* 1986. Los Angeles, *Otello* (Verdi) 1986, *Fidelio* 1990. Paris, O, *Kátá Kabanová* 1988. Stockholm, *Lohengrin* 1989. One of the most talented producers of the day, bringing a powerful theatrical sense and strongly argued ideas to productions that can seem didactic (and often argue a politically left-wing case) but that are rarely less than stimulating.

Fritz. See AMICO FRITZ.

Froh. The god of spring (ten) in Wagner's *Das Rheingold*.

From the House of the Dead. See HOUSE OF THE DEAD.

Fuchs, Marta (*b* Stuttgart, 1 Jan. 1898; *d* Stuttgart, 22 Sept. 1974). German mezzo-soprano, later soprano. Studied Stuttgart, Munich, and Milan. Début as mezzo-soprano, Aachen 1928. Dresden from 1931 (Octavian, Amneris). Bayreuth 1933–42 (Brünnhilde, Isolde, Kundry). London, CG, 1936 (Marschallin, Ariadne). Berlin, SO, 1936–42; Stuttgart 1949–51. A distinguished Wagner singer, possessing a big, dark-toned voice and dramatic intensity. (R)

Fugère, Lucien (*b* Paris, 22 July 1848; *d* Paris, 15 Jan. 1935). French baritone. Début 1870 at the Café-Concert Ba-ta-clan. Engaged by Paris, BP, in 1873, then Paris, OC, 1877–1910, where he sang over 100 roles, creating more than 30, including Le Père (*Louise*). A famous Figaro (Mozart), Papageno, and Leporello, which he sang at London, CG, 1897. Paris, Gaîté-Lyrique 1910–19, and OC 1919. Continued to sing till he was 85. An artist of exceptional qualities, possessing a large, rich, and resonant basso cantante, excellent technique, brilliant dramatic talent, and intuitive understanding of composers' intentions. (R)

'Fuor del mar'. Idomeneo's (ten) aria in Act II of Mozart's *Idomeneo*, in which he voices his despair that though now free from the dangers of the sea, he is menaced with a graver threat from Neptune as a consequence of his rash vow.

Furlanetto, Ferruccio (*b* Pordenone, Sicily, 16 May 1949). Italian bass. Début Vicenza 1974 (Sparafucile). Has sung widely in Italy, as Colline in Trieste, Banquo at Milan, S. US début New Orleans 1978 (Zaccaria); Gly. 1980, Melibeo in *La fedeltà premiata*. His keen sense of comic timing has made him a favourite as Leporello: at Salzburg under Karajan and at London, CG (1988) and New York, M (1990). (R)

Furtwängler, Wilhelm (*b* 25 Jan. 1886; *d* Baden-Baden, 30 Nov. 1954). German conductor and composer. Studied Munich with Beer-Walbrunn, Rheinberger, and Schillings. Répétiteur Breslau 1905–6; cond. Zurich 1906–7; Munich, N, 1907–9; Strasburg 1910–11. Music dir. Lübeck 1911–15; Mannheim 1915–20. Further study with Schenker, with whom he remained in close contact: to Schenker's analysis of structural fundamentals in a work may be attributed some of Furtwängler's security of structural grasp and resulting confident freedom of phrase and tempo. His questing mind and constantly renewed experience of a work set him to many as an antithesis to the objectivity of Toscanini (who greatly respected him). After a period spent largely in the concert-hall, he began winning admiration for his Wagner in Berlin and Paris from 1924. Bayreuth 1931, 1936, 1937, 1943, 1944; reopened Bayreuth (Beethoven's Ninth Symphony) 1951. Regular

guest Salzburg and Vienna, also Milan. London, CG, 1935 (*Tristan*), 1937, and 1938 (*Ring*). Though he remained politically independent, resigning all his posts over the Nazi banning of Hindemith's *Mathis der Maler* in 1934 and refusing to conduct in wartime occupied countries, he had to contend with post-war reproaches over his stance (his Jewish defenders included Schoenberg). He attached himself to what he saw as the highest German artistic and intellectual values, and these guided his music-making and gave it, at its finest, revelatory qualities. His notoriously imprecise beat was at least in part a demand for collaboration from his players and singers, deeply involving his listeners, in a creative search. (R)

Fux, Johann Joseph (*b* Hirtenfeld, 1660; *d* Vienna, 13 Feb. 1741). Austrian composer. Remembered for his treatise *Gradus ad Parnassum* (1725), one of the most influential of all counterpoint tutors, Fux embraced both secular and sacred music with equal ease and was recognized as one of the most skilled composers of his generation. Having risen to be principal Kapellmeister at St Stephen's Cathedral in Vienna, he reached the height of his career in 1715, when he succeeded Ziani as court Kapellmeister.

During his long career Fux composed 19 operas for the Austrian court, including *Julo Ascanio, Re d'Alba* (1708) and *Orfeo ed Euridice* (1715). Many of his works dealt, of necessity, with heroic themes, and many suffer from a dependence upon the heavy contrapuntal technique which was a mainstay of his religious music, thereby limiting dramatic possibilities. Such was his reputation that when gout prevented him from attending the performance of his *Costanza e Fortezza*, for the coronation of Charles VI as King of Bohemia in 1723, the Emperor arranged for him to be carried all the way to Prague in a litter.

G

Gabriele Adorno. A Genoese nobleman (ten), lover of Amelia Grimaldi, in Verdi's *Simon Boccanegra*.

Gabrielli, Francesca. See FERRARESE, LA.

Gadski, Johanna (*b* Anklam, 15 June 1872; *d* Berlin, 22 Feb. 1932). German soprano. Studied Stettin with Schröder-Chaloupka. Début Berlin, Kroll, 1889 (in Lortzing's *Undine*). Berlin, K, until 1894; New York, M, with Damrosch's Co., 1895, as Co. member 1900–17 (except 1904–6); London, CG, 1898–1901; Bayreuth 1899; Munich Fest. 1905, 1906; Salzburg 1906, 1910; Chicago 1910–11. Toured US 1929–31 in Wagner. Repertory incl. Pamina, Amelia, Aida, Valentine, Eva, Isolde, Brünnhilde, Santuzza. A fine singer and actress, with a beautiful voice and a lyrical, bel canto style; highly popular in US until the First World War, when there was anti-German hostility to her and her husband. (R)

Gaetano (Kajetan) (*b* Warsaw, 1st half 18th cent.; *d* Warsaw, *c*.1793). Polish composer and violinist. From 1764 played in the royal orchestra in Warsaw, which he conducted 1779–93. Composed several operas, including *Żółta szlafmyca* (The Yellow Nightcap, 1783), one of the first operas to incorporate elements from Polish folk music. *Les amours de Bastien und Bastienne* (1788) uses the libretto which Mozart had set in an adapted form 20 years earlier.

Gagliano, Marco da (*b* Florence 1 May 1582; *d* Florence, 25 Feb. 1643). Italian composer. Maestro di cappella to the Grand Duke of Tuscany from 1609, he was one of the founding fathers of opera. *Dafne*, first performed in Mantua in 1608, was an immediate success; even Peri judged it superior to his own earlier setting of the same libretto. Gagliano's preface to the score (pub. 1608) is one of the most important documents in the early history of opera; the instruction that an instrumental sinfonia should be played before the stage action is the earliest mention of the operatic overture.

Most of Gagliano's later operas are lost. However, *Dafne*, with its adumbration of the later split between arioso and recitative and sure dramatic touch, is one of the most impressive monuments from the very earliest phase of operatic history.

Gailhard, Pierre (*b* Toulouse, 1 Aug. 1848; *d* Paris, 12 Oct. 1918). French bass and manager. Studied Toulouse, and Paris Cons. Début Paris, OC, 1867 (Falstaff in Thomas's *Le songe d'une nuit d'été*). Paris, OC until 1870 and O 1871–84; London, CG, 1879–83. A cultured man with a warm, sonorous voice. Created roles in works by Mermet, Joncières, and Thomas; also sang Leporello, Osmin, Saint-Bris, and Gounod's and Boito's Mephistopheles, giving sharp, impressive characterizations in both comic and serious parts. In 1884 became joint manager of the Opéra, with first Ritt, then Bertrand; sole manager 1899–1906. He was responsible for many French prems. (including *Otello*, *Lohengrin*, *Die Walküre*, *Siegfried*, *Tristan*, *Die Meistersinger*), and for the high quality of their productions. (R)

Gál, Hans (*b* Brünn (Brno), 5 Aug. 1890; *d* Edinburgh, 3 Oct. 1987). Austrian composer and musicologist. Studied Vienna with Mandyczewski. One of his first successes came with his opera *Die heilige Ente* (The Holy Duckling), widely performed in the 1920s. His idiom owes much to the Brahms tradition he absorbed from his teacher, something to neo-classicism, nothing to the Second Viennese School. *Die heilige Ente* is a Singspiel, eclectic, folk-like, and influenced by both Johann and Richard Strauss. He was also a stimulating writer and teacher.

Galeffi, Carlo (*b* Malamocco, 4 June 1882; *d* Rome, 22 Sept. 1961). Italian baritone. Studied Paris with Sbriglia, and Rome with Cotogni. Début Fermo 1907 (Don Alfonso, *La favorita*). New York, M, 1910; Milan, S, regularly between 1913 and 1940; Chicago 1914, 1919–21. Created leading roles in Boito's *Nerone*, Montemezzi's *L'amore dei tre re*, and Mascagni's *Isabeau* and *Parisina*. First Italian Amfortas, and also famous as Rigoletto, Nabucco, and Tell. Retired 1955. Possessed an unusually round and even tone, and an expressive legato line. (R)

Galilei, Vincenzo (*b* S Maria a Monte, prob.

late 1520s; *d* Florence, buried 2 July 1591). Italian lutenist, composer, theorist, singer, and teacher. Father of the astronomer Galileo Galilei and a prominent member of the *Camerata which met at the house of Count Bardi in Florence in the late 16th cent. It was Galilei who initiated study of the dramatic practices of the ancient Greeks: his correspondence with Girolamo Mei formed the basis for the *Dialogo della musica antica et della moderna* (1581), the seminal theoretical work of the Camerata. According to Doni, Galilei's lost cantata *Il conte Ugolino*, setting lines from Dante's *Inferno*, was the first work using the new *stile rappresentativo.

Galitsky. Prince Vladimir Yaroslavich Galitsky (bs), husband of Igor's sister Yaroslavna, in Borodin's *Prince Igor*.

Gall, Jeffrey (*b* Cleveland, OH, 19 Sept. 1950). US counter-tenor. Studied Yale. Début in Cavalli's *Erismena* (Brooklyn Acad. 1979). Has sung in Europe from 1980 in operas by Jommelli (at Milan S), Cesti, and Lully. First major counter-tenor role at New York, M (Tolomeo in *Giulio Cesare*, 1988). Other Handel roles incl. Polinesso (*Ariodante*) and Ruggiero (*Orlando*, S Francisco 1989). (R)

Galli, Filippo (*b* Rome, 1783; *d* Paris, 3 June 1853). Italian tenor, later bass. Début Naples 1801. Sang as tenor until 1811, when after a serious illness he re-emerged as a bass. Success in *La cambiale di matrimonio* (Padua 1811) led to an enduring association with Rossini, for whom he created the parts of Taraboto (*L'inganno felice*), Fernando (*La gazza ladra*), title-role of *Maometto II*, Mustafà (*L'italiana in Algeri*), Selim (*Il turco in Italia*), Assur (*Semiramide*), and roles in *La pietra del paragone* and *Torvaldo e Dorliska*, as well as singing many others. Paris, I, 1823; London, H, 1827–33; Milan, Carcano, 1830, creating Henry VIII in Donizetti's *Anna Bolena*. After a vocal decline, he taught at Paris Cons. 1842–8, and died in poverty. Gifted with a magnificent, flexible, and expressive voice, he was also a superb actor, exuberant and witty, yet capable of 'the finest heights of tragic acting...in a style worthy of Kean' (Stendhal, who is also the source of a story, probably apocryphal, that Rossini, furious at having lost a mistress to Galli, deliberately wrote a passage in *La gazza ladra* using his three worst notes). His brother **Vicenzo** (1798–1858) was a buffo bass. Début Milan, S, 1824. Sang Bellini and Donizetti, and in creations of many new works by Ricci, Rossi, Mercadante, etc.

Galliard, John Ernest (Johann Ernst) (*b* ?Celle, *c*.1687; *d* London, 1749). German oboist and composer. Studied under Steffani; came to England 1706. His *Calypso and Telemachus* (1712) was one of the most important attempts to establish opera in English, but was unsuccessful and only three performances were given.

Galli-Bibiena. Italian family of scene designers and architects of the Baroque era, whose work was seen all over Europe. The family name was Galli; Bibiena was added from the birthplace of their father, **Giovanni Galli** (*b* Bibbiena, 1625; *d* Bologna, 1665).

The brothers (1) **Ferdinando** (*b* Bologna, 18 Aug. 1656; *d* Bologna, 3 Jan. 1743) and (2) **Francesco** (*b* Bologna, 12 Dec. 1659; *d* Bologna, 20 Jan. 1737) studied at Bologna, Ferdinando also with Rivani, one of Louis XIV's stage machinists at Versailles. Ferdinando was engaged by the Duke of Parma and worked in the T Farnese and in Bologna; then went with his brother to Vienna, where they were responsible for the décor for the court fêtes and theatrical performances. They were the first to exploit the *scena per angolo*, or diagonal perspective, which replaced the traditional central perspective of Baroque theatre. One of the most important designers of Baroque opera, Ferdinando interested himself particularly in architectural stage designs, making skilful use of space and perspective, and much influencing later generations. Francesco also worked in Bologna and other Italian cities, travelling widely and designing for many different composers. His work has greater imaginative range than his brother's. He designed theatres in Bologna, also Vienna, Verona, and Nancy.

3. **Alessandro** (*b* ?Parma, 1686; *d* Mannheim, 5 Aug. 1748), son of (1), worked with his father in Spain and Vienna, then settling in Mannheim 1720 and designing theatres there. His sets are in the family tradition of architectural elegance and the exploitation of asymmetry and false perspective.

4. **Giovanni Maria** (*b* Piacenza, 19 Jan. 1694; *d* Naples, 1777), son of (1), worked first in Mannheim, then chiefly in Prague.

5. **Giuseppe** (*b* Parma, 5 Jan. 1695; *d* Berlin,

1757), son of (1), worked with his father in Vienna, succeeding him and also working in Prague. Designed the Bayreuth OH 1746, then the Dresden Zwinger OH 1747; later Berlin, under Frederick the Great from 1753. He was associated with many important Baroque composers, including Jommelli, Hasse, and Graun, and the librettists Zeno and Metastasio, and expressed their opera seria ideals closely in his work. He built upon the example of his father in developing greater subtleties of architectural design and perspective without losing hold of the essential formality of the genre. He was the first to make use of transparent scenery lit from behind.

6. **Antonio** (*b* Parma, *bapt.* 1 Jan. 1697; *d* Milan, 28 Jan. 1774), son of (1), worked with him in Bologna, with (5) in Vienna, and with (2) in Verona and Rome. He designed the Bologna C 1756–63 and many sets for it.

7. **Giovanni Carlo** (*b* ?Bologna, *c.*1720; *d* Lisbon, 20 Nov. 1760), son of (2), worked in Bologna, then designing theatres in Portugal (none extant).

8. **Carlo** (*b* Vienna, *bapt.* 8 Feb. 1721; *d* Florence, 1787), son of (5), completed his father's Bayreuth theatre, also working in various European cities including Berlin for Frederick the Great 1765, St Petersburg for Catherine the Great 1774, and Stockholm and Drottningholm (where some of his designs are extant) for Gustavus III.

Galli-Curci, Amelita (*b* Milan, 18 Nov. 1882; *d* La Jolla, CA, 26 Nov. 1963). Italian soprano. Studied Milan with Carignani and Dufes, but mainly self-taught. Début Trani 1906 (Gilda). Successes in Italy, Spain, Russia, and S America; Chicago 1916–24. New York, M, 1921–30. A throat tumour (removed in 1935) eventually led to her retirement in 1937. Famous for her Rosina, Elvira (*Puritani*), Lucia, Violetta, and Lakmé, to which her pure and astonishingly agile voice was ideally suited. (R)

Galli-Marié, Célestine (*b* Paris, Nov. 1840; *d* Vence, 22 Sept. 1905). French mezzo-soprano. Studied with her father, Félix Mécène Marié de L'Isle. Début Strasburg 1859. After engagements in Lisbon and Rouen (in the first French *Bohemian Girl*), appeared at Paris, OC, 1862–85, where she created Carmen (giving staunch support to Bizet during the difficult rehearsal period), Mignon, and Friday in Offenbach's *Robinson Crusoé*, among other roles. Repertory also included Gounod, Massenet, Massé, etc. London, HM, 1886. 'She is small and graceful and moves like a cat', wrote a critic; she was also a penetrating actress and an intelligent singer with a voice of unusual timbre. Her Carmen was much admired by Tchaikovsky, and his brother Modest appreciated her 'unbridled passion' and 'mystical fatalism'.

Galuppi, Baldassare (Burano, 18 Oct. 1706; *d* Venice, 3 Jan. 1785). Italian composer. After initial failure, his career on the Venetian stage was launched with *Gl'odi delusi da sangue* (1728) and *Dorinda* (1729). Over the following years he produced nearly 100 operas, sometimes five in one year; from 1738 he composed for other cities, including London. Returning to Venice in 1743, he divided his time between opera and sacred music: in 1748 he became vice maestro di cappella at St Mark's, rising to the principal position in 1762. During this time he was also developing his operatic skills: crucially, in 1749 he made his first setting of a Goldoni libretto, *L'Arcadia in Brenta*, effectively the first full-length comic opera.

This collaboration ushered in a string of popular successes, including *Il mondo della luna* (The World on the Moon, 1750), *Il mondo alla roversa* (The Topsy-Turvy World, 1750), and *Le virtuose ridicole* (The Ridiculous Virtuosos). In 1765 Galuppi went to St Petersburg at the invitation of Catherine II, where in 1768 *Ifigenia in Tauride* was performed: two years later he returned to Venice, after which he devoted himself almost exclusively to sacred music.

Although Galuppi's music was gradually supplanted by that of the younger generation, at the height of his powers he was one of the leading composers of the day. Of that generation which moulded opera buffa into one of the most potent vehicles of dramatic expression, he drew enormous benefit from his collaboration with Goldoni, whose librettos rejected the traditional *mélange* of contrived situations and stock characters in favour of a more realistic approach. This is seen at best in *Il filosofo di campagna* (The Country Philosopher, 1754) where the charm and wit of the libretto is matched by music of a similarly appealing and carefully crafted nature.

Galuppi made a particularly significant contribution to the development of the *ensemble finale.

Gambler, The (Russ., *Igrok*). Opera in 4 acts by Prokofiev; text by the composer, after Dostoyevsky's story (1866). Orig. projected prem., Petrograd 1917, cancelled due to Revolution; second projected Leningrad prem., postponed. Prem. Brussels, M, 29 Apr. 1929.

A European gaming resort, *c*.1865. Alexey (ten) is in the service of a General (bs) in the German spa of Roulettenburg. In love with the coquettish Mlle Blanche (sop), and, having gambled away most of his money, in debt to a French Marquis, the General anxiously awaits the death of his rich grandmother. But she turns up, and proceeds to lose her fortune at the tables. The General's daughter Pauline (mez), whom Alexey loves, is now faced with marrying the Marquis; to prevent this, Alexey tries to win some money and succeeds in breaking the bank. But when he presents her with the money, she hysterically flings it in his face.

García. Family of singers and teachers of singing, of Spanish origin. The dynasty was founded by **Manuel** (del Pópulo Vicente Rodríguez) (*b* Seville, 21 Jan. 1775; *d* Paris, 10 June 1832). Spanish tenor, composer, and teacher. Studied Seville with Ripa. Début Cádiz 1798, in a tonadilla. After successes in Spain (where he scandalously appeared on stage with both wife and mistress), he went to Paris in 1808, and soon became popular. Italy 1811–16, creating Norfolk (*Elisabetta, regina d'Inghilterra*), and Almaviva (Rossini), written for him. Paris, I, 1819–24; London, H, 1818, 1819, 1823–5. New York 1825, introduced Italian opera to US, including *Barbiere, Cenerentola, Otello* (Rossini), and *Don Giovanni* (with himself, wife, son, and daughter in the cast, and in the presence of Da Ponte). Mexico 1827–8; Paris 1829; retired 1830. A handsome man of astonishing energy and versatility, he played the guitar, wrote a large number of popular operas and songs (major contributions to Spain's influence throughout the world), and was a gifted teacher, his pupils including Nourrit, Méric-Lalande, and his daughters Maria (*Malibran) and Pauline (*Viardot). In Mexico, when much of his company's music was lost, he wrote out the entire scores of *Don Giovanni, Otello*, and *Barbiere* from memory. As a tenor he was best known for his Rossini, though he also sang Mozart (including Guglielmo and Don Giovanni), and his most famous role was Otello, in which 'his acting was full of fire and fury' (Stendhal), he was 'most truly the

Moor', and was even praised by Edmund Kean. Some, however, found his style lacking in taste. His son **Manuel** (*b* Madrid, 17 Mar. 1805; *d* London, 1 July 1906) was a baritone and teacher. Studied with his father. Début New York 1825 (Rossini's Figaro). Retired from stage 1829. Teacher at Paris Cons. 1847–50; London, RAM, 1848–95. First to undertake study of voice production; invented the laryngoscope. With his perfection of his father's methods, he was the most influential teacher of his time; among his pupils were Lind, E. Frezzolini, M. Marchesi, M. Schnorr von Carolsfeld, and Santley.

Gardelli, Lamberto (*b* Venice, 18 Nov. 1915). Italian conductor and composer. Studied Pesaro and Rome. Répétiteur Rome, R, under Serafin; début there 1944 (*Traviata*). Cond. Stockholm 1946–55. Berlin, Helsinki, Budapest 1961–5; Gly. 1964–5, 1968; New York, M, 1966–8; London, CG, 1968–9, 1970–1, 1975–6, 1979–80. A fine cond. of the Italian repertory. His operas include *Alba novella* (1937) and *Il sogno* (1942). (R)

Garden, Mary (*b* Aberdeen, 20 Feb. 1874; *d* Inverurie, 3 Jan 1967). Scottish soprano. Studied Chicago, then Paris with Trabadelo and Fugère. Début Paris, OC, 1900 (Louise (taking over half-way through a performance from Rioton, its creator)). London, CG, 1902–3; New York, Manhattan OC, 1907; Chicago O 1910–31, and its dir. 1919–20. Created the roles of Mélisande, Massenet's Sapho and Chérubin, and d'Erlanger's Aphrodite, among others. Repertory included Manon, Thaïs, Salome, Carmen, Ophélie, and Jean (*Le jongleur de Notre-Dame*). An intelligent, original singer-actress, remarkable for a complete identification with her roles and skilful use of vocal colour. As Mélisande, she amazed Debussy: 'That was indeed the gentle voice I had heard in my innermost soul.' (R)

Gardiner, John Eliot (*b* Fontmell Magna, 20 Apr. 1943). English conductor. Studied Cambridge with Dart, Paris with Boulanger. After early experience as choral conductor, début London, C, 1969 (*Magic Flute*). London, CG, 1973 (*Iphigénie en Tauride*) and C, 1979 (Monteverdi's *Orfeo*). His initial experience with early music, especially with his Monteverdi Choir and Orch., led to his revival of a number of neglected Baroque works, including a concert series of Rameau operas in his own editions, 1973–5. Orange 1981; Aix-en-Provence 1982 (stage prem. Rameau

Les Boréades). Music dir. Lyons 1983–8, where he strengthened and widened the repertory; Salzburg 1990 (*Poppea*). Has given many outstanding performances of Baroque and Classical operas, also of later French repertory incl. Chabrier's *L'étoile*, and Debussy's *Pelléas*. A demanding, highly intelligent conductor, with a gift for reanimating Baroque music through careful study of the scores and contemporary performance practice, also for sharply observed performances of Gluck, Mozart, Rossini, and Berlioz. (R)

Garrett, Leslie (*b* Thorne, Doncaster, 10 Apr. 1955). English soprano. Studied London, RAM. London, ENO, from 1980 as Despina, Susanna, Atalanta (*Xerxes*), Adele, and the Vixen; Wexford 1980 (Dorinda in *Orlando*); Gly. from 1984, in operas by Mozart. She is admired for her spirited stage personality. (R)

Garsington. Opera is staged in short summer seasons in the gardens of Garsington Manor, the house of Leonard and Rosalind Ingrams near Oxford. Beginning with *Orlando paladino* in 1990, the organization has made a speciality of operas by Haydn, including *Il mondo della luna* (1991), *La vera costanza* (1992), and *L'incontro improvviso* (1994). The latter year also saw *Capriccio* and *Il barbiere di Siviglia*. As well as staging its own performances, Garsington has been host to visits from touring companies, including English Touring O, Pimlico O, and O 80. Though threatened with closure in 1994 through neighbourly complaints about noise, the organization won the right to continue in 1995, with Haydn's *La fedeltà premiata*.

Gasdia, Cecilia (*b* Verona, 14 Aug. 1960). Italian soprano. Studied Verona; début Florence 1982 (Bellini's Giulietta). One of the leading lyric sopranos of her generation, she has sung Anna Bolena at Milan, S; Anis in *Moïse* at Paris, O; and Gilda at Philadelphia (US début 1984). Other roles incl. Juliette (New York, M, 1986), Rossini's Armida, and Violetta. (R)

Gasparini, Francesco (*b* Camaiore, 19 Mar. 1668; *d* Rome, 22 Mar. 1727). Italian composer. Studied with Corelli and Pasquini in Rome, where his first opera *Roderico* was revived in 1694. In 1702 he moved to Venice and for the next 20 years was one of the leading opera composers in the city. In 1716 he moved to Rome, where he produced his last dramatic work, *Tigrana*, in 1724.

Gasparini was one of the most prolific and respected composers of the pre-Metastasian era: his operas, which included *Tiberio* (1702) and *Tamerlano* (1711), were performed throughout Italy, and were also popular in Germany and England. One of his most successful works was *Ambleto* (1706): this was the first Hamlet opera, though it was not based on Shakespeare and uses a different plot and secondary characters.

Gasparini was also important as a teacher: his pupils included Benedetto Marcello, Quantz, and Domenico Scarlatti.

Gassmann, Florian Leopold (*b* Most, 3 May 1729; *d* Vienna, 20 Jan. 1774). Bohemian composer. Studied Bologna with Martini, but had his first operatic success in Venice in 1757 with *Merope*. In 1763 succeeded Gluck as ballet composer in Vienna, becoming court Kapellmeister in Vienna 1772. A leading figure in Viennese musical life, he also composed much sacred music and was an influential teacher: among his pupils was Salieri, whom he brought to Vienna in 1766. His early death was caused by a fall from his carriage: he was succeeded at court by *Bonno.

Gassmann composed more than 20 operas, including both serious and comic works. Many of the former are to librettos by Metastasio, including *Issipile* (1758) and *Achille in Sciro* (1766); though generally unadventurous, the best, notably *Ezio* (1761), reflect a sympathy for Gluck's reforms. His comic works are more distinctive and include settings of Goldoni, including *Filosofia ed amore* (1760) and a satire about the conventions of serious opera, *L'opera seria* (1769).

Gatti, Daniele (*b* Milan, 1962). Italian conductor. After study in Milan conducted throughout Italy from 1982 (début with *Giovanna d'Arco*). Milan, S, 1988 (*L'occasione fa il ladro*). US début Chicago 1991 (*Butterfly*; also at New York, M, 1995). Valued for his firm control of dramatic structure (London, CG, 1992, *I Puritani*). (R)

Gatti-Casazza, Giulio (*b* Udine, 3 Feb. 1869; *d* Ferrara, 2 Sept. 1940). Italian impresario. Studied as an engineer, then succeeded his father as director of Ferrara, T Municipale, 1893. His success led to his appointment as director of Milan, S, 1898–1908, where with

Toscanini he did much for the theatre's prestige; he gave the Italian prems. of *Pelléas* (1908) and *Boris* (1909), and helped to popularize Wagner. Assistant dir. of New York, M, 1908, dir. 1910–35, when he gave more than 5,000 performances of 177 works, fostering original-language productions. He increased the theatre's international fame by the standard of his productions and the galaxy of singers he assembled. Married first Frances *Alda, then the dancer Rosina Galli.

Gavazzeni, Gianandrea (*b* Bergamo, 27 July 1909). Italian conductor, critic, and composer. Studied Rome with Cristiani, Milan with Pizzetti and Pedrollo. Bergamo 1930, assistant to Antonicelli. Until 1940 mostly engaged in composition, also conducting; his opera *Paolo e Virginia* (1935) had a success. Parma 1940; Bergamo 1941; Rome, T dell'Arte, 1942; Genoa, CF, 1942; Milan: L, with S Co., 1945, and since at S; artistic dir., S, 1965–8, directing many important prems. Edinburgh Fest., with Milan, PS, 1957; Gly. 1965 (*Anna Bolena*). Chicago and New York, M, 1976. A thoughtful and acute critic.

Gaveaux, Pierre (*b* Béziers, 9 Oct. 1760; *d* Charenton, 5 Feb. 1825). French tenor and composer. Studied Béziers with Combès and Beck. He sang at the T de Monsieur in Paris, including such major roles as Floreski (*Lodoïska*), continuing at the Feydeau. Here he also began composing opéras-comiques, having immediate success with *Les deux suisses* (1792). A genuine liberal, he found himself in trouble with 'Le réveil du peuple', the most inflammatory song before 'La Marseillaise'. His most important works include *Sophie et Moncars* (1797) and especially *Léonore* (1798), the latter to the libretto that also inspired Beethoven. Though now completely overshadowed, the work has some vivid and affecting strokes of imagination. Gaveaux himself created his own Florestan, and received an ovation. His works are in a manner that reflected current interest in such genres as the fait historique, or opera based on a real event, and in a style that admitted ideas of some substance into an essentially light genre. They had considerable appeal for their use of local colour and their lively dramatic effects (anticipating the popular stage devices of the 1820s). Gaveaux was outstanding among opéra-comique composers of his generation for the wit and skill with which he used

the conventions (admitting a certain Italian influence into his vocal writing), and he did something to extend and give substance to the finale. Latterly his voice, described as pleasant, light, and fluent, lost its timbre. His wife **Emilie Gavaudan** (1775–1837, sister of the tenor **Pierre Gavaudan** (1772–1840)) was a successful soprano at the T Feydeau, where his brother **Simon** (1759–?) was a répétiteur and souffleur; the two men also collaborated in a publishing business.

Gawain. Opera in 2 acts by Harrison Birtwistle; text by David Harsent, after the anon 14th-cent. English poem *Sir Gawain and the Green Knight*. Prem. London, CG, 30 May 1991. Rev. and prem. London, CG, 14 Apr. 1994.

The Green Knight (bs) comes to the court of King Arthur (ten); his challenge to anyone to behead him is met by Gawain (bs), and he rides away bearing his own severed head. There follows a masque, 'The Turning of the Seasons'.

Gawain journeys to the Castle of Bertilak de Hautdesert to find the Green Knight, observed and manipulated by Morgan le Fay (sop). Bertilak's hunting expeditions and the Lady de Hautdesert's attempts to seduce Gawain are woven into another series of ritual repetitions as Gawain breaks faith with his host. Bertilak is now revealed as the Green Knight, and Gawain returns to King Arthur; but though welcomed as a hero, he is himself aware of having survived by deceit, and Morgan le Fay has succeeded in undermining the solidarity of Arthur's court.

Gay, John (*b* Barnstaple, *bapt.* 16 Sept. 1685; *d* London, 4 Dec. 1732). English poet, playwright, and theatre manager. He is best known as the founder of *ballad opera, of which his *The Beggar's Opera* (1728) was the first example. Its immense success encouraged Gay to write a sequel, *Polly* (comp. 1729, but not prem. until 1779, owing to a ban by the Lord Chamberlain) in which all the characters are transported to the West Indies. It was Gay himself who selected the airs for *The Beggar's Opera*, sometimes choosing tunes whose original texts bore some relation to his purpose. His third and last ballad opera was a dull, poorly constructed work, *Achilles* (1733), which enjoyed little popularity.

As a theatre manager, he obtained Davenant's letters patent, which enabled him to build the first *Covent Garden T in 1732.

Gay, Maria (*b* Barcelona, 13 June 1879; *d* New York, 19 July 1943). Spanish mezzo-soprano. Originally self-taught, later studied Paris with Adiny. Voice discovered in prison, following her arrest for singing a revolutionary song. Début Brussels, M, 1902 (Carmen). London, CG, 1906; Milan, S, 1906–7; New York, M, 1908–9; Chicago 1910–27. Roles included Dalila and Amneris, but most famous for her forceful, earthy Carmen. Married tenor *Zenatello 1913; they founded a singing school, New York 1927, and effected the engagement of Lily Pons at the Metropolitan. (R)

Gayarre, Julián (*b* Valle de Roncal, 9 Jan. 1844; *d* Madrid, 2 Jan. 1890). Spanish tenor. Studied Milan with Lamperti. Début Varese 1869 (*I Lombardi*). Successes in Italy (including as first Italian Tannhäuser); St Petersburg 1873–5; Milan, S, 1876. London, CG, 1877–81, 1886–7. Paris: I, 1884; O, 1886. Created Enzo in *La Gioconda*; repertory also included Meyerbeer, Donizetti, and Verdi. Regarded by many as the supreme tenor of his time, with outstanding powers of expression; much admired by Duprez and by Gounod, who, on hearing him perform in *Faust*, said, 'I have never heard my music sung like that'. A premature vocal decline was shortly followed by his death, after withdrawing from a performance in Madrid during which his voice failed.

Gayer, Catherine (*b* Los Angeles, 11 Feb. 1937). US soprano. Studied Los Angeles and Berlin. Début Venice, F, 1961 (the Companion, Nono's *Intolleranza 1960*). Berlin, D, from 1961. Appearances at Milan, S; Vienna; Salzburg; Edinburgh. Created Nausikaa in Dallapiccola's *Ulisse*, Christina in Orr's *Hermiston*, title-role in Reimann's *Melusine*. Sang in a version of Joplin's *Treemonisha* at the 1992 Schwetzingen Fest. Other roles include Constanze, Queen of Shemakha, Zerbinetta, Mélisande, Lulu. An outstanding performer of 20th-cent. music. (R)

Gaztambide, Joaquín (*b* Tudela, 7 Feb. 1822; *d* Madrid, 18 Mar. 1870). Spanish composer and conductor. Studied Pamplona with Guelbenzu, Madrid with Carnicer. Chorus-master Madrid, T de Santa Cruz, 1845, dir. T Español 1848; cond. T Real and elsewhere, introducing to Spain works by Meyerbeer and Wagner. Toured Cuba and Mexico with his own zarzuela company, but fell ill and died on his return home. One of

the most important zarzuela composers of the 19th cent., the most successful of his 44 works was *La Catalina* (1854).

Gazza ladra, La (The Thieving Magpie). Opera in 2 acts by Rossini; text by Gherardini, after the comedy *La pie voleuse* (1815) by Baudouin d'Aubigny and Caigniez. Prem. Milan, S, 31 May 1817.

An Italian village, early 19th cent. Ninetta (sop), a servant girl, is engaged to Giannetto (ten), the son of the farmer in whose house she works. She is accused of stealing a silver spoon, and the Podestà (bs), whose advances Ninetta has repulsed, brings her to trial and she is condemned to death. Only when she is on the way to execution is it discovered that the real thief was a magpie who flew into the farmhouse window.

Gazzaniga, Giuseppe (*b* Verona, 5 Oct. 1743; *d* Crema, 1 Feb. 1818). Italian composer. Studied with Porpora, and with Piccinni in Naples, where his first opera, *Il barone di Trocchia*, was performed 1768. Then moved to Venice; maestro di cappella at Crema Cathedral 1791. He wrote *c*.50 operas, mostly for Naples, Rome, and Venice, though through Sacchini he forged an important relationship with Vienna. The first of his works to be performed there, *Il finto cieco* (The Feigned Blind Man, 1786), was a setting of a Da Ponte libretto: though the poet did not regard it highly, it proved very successful and brought Gazzaniga to public attention.

Most of Gazzaniga's works were of the *dramma giocoso genre. Though conventional in approach, the light-hearted manner of *La locanda* (1771) and *La donna astuta* (1793) were highly popular and earned him a place in history as one of the minor forerunners of Rossini. His most influential work was *Don Giovanni Tenorio, o sia Il convitato di pietra* (1787). Bertati's libretto was known to Da Ponte when he and Mozart began their work later that year; it is unclear whether Mozart knew Gazzaniga's score, though there are a number of similarities, both musical and dramatic, between the two treatments.

Gazzaniga, Marietta (*b* Voghera, 1824; *d* Milan, 2 Jan. 1884). Italian soprano. Studied Milan with Cetta and Mazzuccato. Début Voghera 1840 (Jane Seymour, *Anna Bolena*). Created Luisa Miller, and Lina (*Stiffelio*). Milan, S, 1851–3, 1862; US 1857–69, 1871 as mezzo-soprano. Taught New York until 1876; Genoa 1881–2.

Gedda, Nicolai (*b* Stockholm, 11 July 1925). Swedish tenor. Studied Stockholm with Oehmann. Début Stockholm O, 1952 (Chapelou, *Le postillon de Lonjumeau*). Milan, S, from 1953; Paris, O, 1954; London, CG, from 1955; New York, M, 1957–83; also Vienna, Moscow, Chicago, etc. His wide repertory included Don Ottavio, Huon, Cellini, Gounod's Faust, Don José, Duke of Mantua, Lohengrin, Lensky, Hermann; created the roles of the Husband (Orff's *Trionfo d'Afrodite*) and Anatol (Barber's *Vanessa*). Sang at Stockholm 1991 as Christian II in Naumann's *Gustaf Wasa*. Outstanding for his beauty of tone, expert vocal control, and musical perception. (R)

Geliot, Michael (*b* London, 27 Sept. 1933). English producer. Studied Cambridge; prod. British prem. of Liebermann's *School for Wives* 1958. Stage manager London, SW, 1960–1: prem. Burt's *Volpone* for New OC 1961, *Mahagonny* 1963, *Cardillac* 1970. Scottish O, Wexford. WNO resident prod. 1965–8, dir. of productions 1969–78: *Lulu* 1971, *Greek Passion* 1981. London, CG, prem. of Maxwell Davies's *Taverner* 1972, *Carmen* 1973. Netherlands O, *Wozzeck* 1973. Munich, *Fidelio* 1974. Cassel, prem. of Cowie's *Commedia* 1979, *Figaro* 1980. Although he has produced Mozart, Verdi, and Berlioz (*Faust*, London, C, 1969), his greatest successes have been in contemporary opera, to which he brings an original intelligence. He has worked closely with Ralph *Koltai, with whom he shares an approach to opera by way of modern methods of music theatre.

Gencer, Leyla (*b* Istanbul, 10 Oct. 1921). Turkish soprano. Studied Istanbul with Arangi-Lombardi. Début Ankara 1950 (Santuzza). Naples, C, 1953; Milan, S, from 1956; London, CG, 1962; Gly. 1962–3, 1965; also Moscow, Buenos Aires, Vienna, etc. Repertory included Donna Anna, title-roles of *Alceste*, *Médée*, *Aida*, *Gioconda*, *Maria Stuarda*, *Anna Bolena*; also early Verdi operas. Created Mme Lidoine in *Dialogues des Carmélites*. An intelligent, dramatic performer, remarkable for her pianissimo singing. (R)

Genée, Richard (*b* Danzig, 7 Feb. 1823; *d* Baden, 15 June 1895). German conductor, librettist, and composer. Studied Berlin with Stahlknecht. Cond. Reval, Riga, Cologne, Düsseldorf, Danzig, Mainz, Schwerin, Prague. Cond. Vienna, W, 1868–78. Of his operettas, only *Der Seekadett* (1876) and *Nanon* (1877) had more than local success; but he is famous for his brilliant and witty librettos, especially for Johann Strauss II (*Fledermaus*, 1874, with Haffner), Suppé, and Millöcker, often in collaboration with F. Zell (Camillo Walzel) and deriving from French farces. He also translated works by Lecocq, Offenbach, and Sullivan.

Generali, Pietro (*b* Masserano, 23 Oct. 1773; *d* Novara, 3 Nov. 1832). Italian composer. He had a success with his first of some 50 operas, *Pamela nubile* (1804), and other comedies, turning with less success to opera seria in 1812 with *Attila*. Overshadowed by Rossini (there is evidence of a mutual influence between the two composers), he moved to Barcelona as director of the T Santa Cruz in 1817. Even here he had some difficulty in including his own works in a Rossini-dominated repertory. He moved to Paris in 1819, to Naples in 1821; he was director of the Palermo T Carolino from 1823 until replaced by Donizetti in 1825. He became maestro di cappella at Novara in 1827 and devoted himself to sacred music. His operas have an easy brilliance which at first won him popularity, but his music lacks the individuality of Rossini's; and his work, which met with a good deal of critical reproof in his own lifetime, suffered from an indolence which often led to him finishing music when it was already in rehearsal.

Generalintendant (or **Intendant**) (Ger.: 'superintendent'). The name given to the administrator of a German opera-house—often but not necessarily the artistic or musical director.

Gennaro. 1. A young nobleman (ten), son of Lucrezia, in Donizetti's *Lucrezia Borgia*.
   2. The blacksmith (ten) in Wolf-Ferrari's *I gioielli della Madonna*.

Genoveva. Opera in 4 acts by Schumann; text by Robert Reinick, altered by the composer, after Tieck's tragedy *Das Leben und Tod der heiligen Genoveva* (1799) and Hebbel's tragedy *Genoveva* (1843). Prem. Leipzig 25 June 1850.

Siegfried's castle in Strasburg, AD 730. Margareta (con) offers to help Golo (ten) woo Genoveva (sop), the wife of Count Siegfried (bar), during the Count's absence. Rejected by Genoveva, Golo plants his friend Drago (bar) in her bedroom so that she can be accused of adultery. Golo then goes to tell Siegfried, who has been injured in battle, of his wife's infidelity. Siegfried orders his men to take her to a forest, where she is to be executed. Golo makes a final attempt to persuade Genoveva to run away with him. She refuses, but her life is saved by the arrival of Siegfried, who has now learnt the truth.

Gentele, Göran (*b* Stockholm, 20 Sept. 1917; *d* Sardinia, 18 July 1972). Swedish producer and administrator. Stockholm: Nat. T, 1941–52; Royal O, 1952–63 as prod., 1963–71 as dir. His many productions included a famous *Ballo in maschera* in historical context (1960) and the prem. of Blomdahl's *Aniara* (1959). London, CG, 1961, *Iphigénie en Tauride*. Died in car crash before taking up new appointment as director New York, M.

George Brown. A young English officer (ten), lover of Anna, in Boieldieu's *La dame blanche*.

Gérald. An English officer (ten), lover of Lakmé, in Delibes's *Lakmé*.

Gérard. A Revolutionary leader (bar) in Giordano's *Andrea Chénier*.

Gergiev, Valery (*b* Moscow, 2 May 1953). Russian conductor. Studied Leningrad and assisted Temirkanov at the Kirov from 1977, succeeding him as chief cond. and artistic dir. 1988. Led Kirov co. at New York, M, 1992 (*The Queen of Spades* and *Boris Godunov*). Co-production between the Kirov and London, CG (*Boris, Otello, The Fiery Angel*). Largely through his work, the Kirov has become re-established as one of the world's major companies (Rimsky-Korsakov festival at St Petersburg 1994). (R)

Gerhard, Roberto (*b* Valls, 25 Sept. 1896; *d* Cambridge, 5 Jan. 1970). Spanish composer. Studied Barcelona with Granados and Pedrell, Vienna with Schoenberg. His only opera, *The Duenna* (comp. 1947, prod. 1992), is a brilliant and intelligent setting which suggests that in more favourable circumstances he might have developed this side of his talent more fully.

German, (Sir) **Edward** (orig. Jones, German Edward) (*b* Whitchurch, 17 Feb. 1862; *d* London, 11 Nov. 1936). English composer. Studied with Hay and at London, RAM.

Hopes that he might prove Sullivan's successor in the field of light music were aroused by his completion of *The Emerald Isle* (1901), and encouraged by the success of *Merrie England* (1902); but his gift was much slenderer, though *Tom Jones* (1907) and *Fallen Fairies* (1909) were popular in their day. His music has a simple melodiousness, reflecting simple dramatic situations; it can be pretty, even dainty, or robust and jingoistic, and is admirably written for the voice. Most of the numbers in his operettas are lyrical and decorative, and have no rhythmic or harmonic complication, though the Act I finale of *Merrie England* suggests that he had in him a vein of dramatic music that never found a true outlet.

Germania. Opera in a prologue, 2 acts, and epilogue by Franchetti; text by Illica. Prem. Milan, S, 11 Mar. 1902.

Set during the Napoleonic wars, the opera tells of the activities of a group of patriotic German students. Further conflict is created by Carlo's (bar) abduction of Ricke (sop) during the absence of her betrothed, Federico (ten). Eventually all are reunited in their patriotic cause but both Carlo and Federico are killed in action.

Germany. As a single political entity, Germany did not exist until 1871. The path of unification was tortuous, and of considerable influence for the development of German culture generally, and opera specifically. In the 17th cent. the country comprised a loose federation of about 1,700 independent states, ranging from free imperial cities (e.g. Frankfurt) and principalities and electorates (e.g. Mannheim) to minor aristocratic holdings. The larger of these courts maintained a musical establishment which was frequently involved in dramatic productions, while commercial opera was established in a number of cities. Germany's highly fragmented political structure makes the drawing of large-scale cultural lines of development very difficult. Between the 17th and 19th cents. the fortunes of opera ebbed and flowed in these cities and courts, reflecting changes in their political and economic circumstances, but not necessarily according to any general plan. A further complication is that for much of this period a common operatic heritage was shared with other German-speaking lands, principally those which combined to form the Austro-Hungarian Empire. After the Second World War, during which many opera-houses were destroyed, Germany suffered a unique blow through its partition. While operatic life in the Federal Republic (West Germany) was rebuilt and developed along Western European lines, those regions which formed the German Democratic Republic (East Germany) were forced to embrace Marxism-Leninism in their cultural life, placing political constraints on composers and producers alike. Following the reunification of Germany in 1990 it became possible once more to consider the country as a single whole.

The early history of German opera is, in effect, the history of Italian opera in Germany. Following the first experiments in Italy, opera was soon introduced into the South German courts: Salzburg in 1614, Vienna in 1626, and Prague the following year. The first opera by a German composer was probably *Schütz's *Dafne* (music lost), which set a translation of Rinuccini's libretto for Peri and was staged at Torgau near Dresden in 1627; the earliest German opera extant in full score is *Bontempi's and Peranda's *Dafne* (1671). Under Bontempi and C. *Pallavicino opera was firmly established at Dresden by the late 17th cent., and at Vienna, under *Cesti, *Draghi, and others. Other courts, such as those at Munich and Hanover, at both of which *Steffani worked, followed suit, and a lavish style of opera developed, taking the Venetian model as a point of departure, but with the addition of a sumptuousness and splendour appropriate to the setting.

Despite this domination, many attempts were made to foster German-language opera. The earliest work for which music survives is *Staden's *Seelewig*, a setting of a libretto by Harsdörffer which was privately performed Nuremberg 1644: but the balance of music and text in this staged religious work is such that it barely merits description as an opera. The native German Singspiel developed slowly, initially on the basis of songs inserted into a play performed often by travelling companies who might later settle in a single place, or of music for the Reformation, and then the Counter-Reformation, school dramas. Progress towards an indigenous tradition was severely hampered by the Thirty Years' War (1618–48), which spelt economic ruin for many courts, while its destruction of the vague semblance of German unity which

had obtained hitherto served to encourage the influx of even stronger foreign influence. Within the realm of the court, there were few notable centres of German opera by the beginning of the 18th cent.: important exceptions were Wolfenbüttel (under G. C. *Schürmann) and Weissenfels (under Johann Philipp *Krieger).

Crucial for the development of German opera was the establishment of the first public opera-house outside Italy in 1678 in the free Hanseatic city of Hamburg. Away from courtly pressure, a repertoire developed in which elements of the German school drama were used in conjunction with features of French and Italian opera: many of the earliest Hamburg operas mixed German and Italian texts together, the title often being given in both languages. The works of the first generation, represented by *Franck, *Förtsch, and *Strungk, thus demonstrate a certain cosmopolitanism, which was carried further by *Conradi and *Kusser, and above all by *Keiser, under whose guidance German opera was for a while elevated to the standard of its rivals. Of later composers who spent time at Hamburg most important were *Handel, *Telemann, and *Mattheson: in 1738 the theatre closed and with it all hope of the establishment of serious German opera for several decades.

By the middle of the 18th cent. the supremacy of Italian opera seria in Germany seemed assured. *Agricola and *Graun in Berlin, *Caldara and *Predieri in Vienna, and especially *Hasse in Dresden, placed their talents at the service of the Metastasian libretto, a vehicle uniquely appropriate for courtly opera. Attempts were made, notably by *Gluck, to reform some of the more stultifying conventions of the genre, but a more serious challenge was presented by opera buffa, which proved increasingly popular. Yet more significant was the rise of a new Singspiel tradition, which drew on English *ballad opera and *opéra-comique. It began with *Der Teufel ist los* (1752), a setting of C. F. Weisse's translation of *The Devil to Pay* by J. C. Standfuss, and was followed by many works, most importantly the Weisse settings by J. A. *Hiller. Though the action is still in prose, with interpolated songs and other music, there are sometimes ensembles and finales; the subjects are generally rustic and comic, with a love interest. Other important composers were Jiří *Benda, Johann *André, J. F. *Reichardt, and Johann *Zumsteeg. Music played a significant part in early 18th-cent. Viennese Singspiel, but a crucial event was Joseph II's 1778 establishment of a German National-Singspiel designed to encourage vernacular works. This opened with Ignaz *Umlauff's Die Bergknappen, but did not prosper and closed 1783. Composers working in Vienna included Wenzel *Müller and especially Karl von *Dittersdorf, later Johann *Schenk and Josef *Weigl, in all of whose works there is more substantial and vital musical content. However, the condition of German opera in the late 18th cent. is seen in the attention *Mozart gave to Italian opera. His Entführung aus dem Serail (1782) is a Singspiel; the Viennese Singspiel provides the basis for the greatest work in the genre, Die Zauberflöte (1791). North German Singspiel was the basis, with the example of French *rescue opera, for *Beethoven's Fidelio (orig. 1805).

Early 19th-cent. German composers were concerned above all to develop a native tradition free from Italian influence. They included Peter von *Winter, Louis *Spohr, Franz *Schubert, Johann von *Poissl, and E. T. A. *Hoffmann. However, it was Carl Maria von *Weber who grasped most fully that the real example for German Romantic opera lay not with Singspiel but with French Revolutionary opéra-comique, since it was here that a more advanced technique had developed for the handling of popular subjects, with increased use of the orchestra and hence the greater dramatic possibilities for *reminiscence motive, free from the formalities of opera seria. The performance of his Der Freischütz (1821) was a turning-point in the history of German opera, and Weber took his reforms further in Euryanthe (1823). His death in 1826 left the field principally to Heinrich *Marschner, Albert *Lortzing, Otto von *Nicolai, and Peter *Lindpaintner, who took up a number of the themes Weber had identified as distinctively German. These included the supernatural, Nature, medievalism, popular settings, melodies deriving from folk-song, and stories based on folk legend. Musically there was an increased tendency towards continuity, and to structures based on motive and whole scenes, and with this came increased depth in the portrayal of character and psychology.

These elements and much else were the basis of the growth of the art and reforms of Richard *Wagner, whose life and work culminated in the first Bayreuth Festival

(1876). By now a German operatic tradition was thoroughly established, with theatres in all important towns and composers working in them or independently. Wagner's example divided musical Germany, with some consciously following it and others reacting against it, but none ignoring it. The most successful of his followers were minor figures such as Peter *Cornelius. His inspiration fired Richard *Strauss, and continued after the First World War in the work of Franz *Schreker and Hans *Pfitzner; more characteristic was the reaction manifest in Paul *Hindemith and Kurt *Weill. Among the most important composers to emerge after the Second World War were Wolfgang *Fortner, Aribert *Reimann, Wolfgang *Rihm, and especially Hans Werner *Henze.

Modern German operatic life remains as rich and solidly grounded as that of any country in the world, welcoming new ideas while acknowledging the strength of tradition: out of the contest between the two much stimulus continues to come.

See also BAYREUTH, BERLIN, DRESDEN, FRANKFURT, HAMBURG, MUNICH.

Germont. Giorgio Germont (bar), Alfredo's father, in Verdi's La traviata.

Gershwin, George (b Brooklyn, 26 Sept. 1898; d Hollywood, 11 July 1937). US composer. After an early career as pianist and song-writer for a Tin Pan Alley publisher, he wrote his first musical, La La Lucille (1919) and had his first success with the song 'Swanee'. During the 1920s and 1930s he wrote over 30 musicals, among them Lady, Be Good! (1924), Strike Up the Band (1927), and Girl Crazy (1930), many to lyrics by his brother Ira.

Gershwin's first opera, in which popular songs are connected by enterprising jazz-style recitative, was written as an interlude in George White's revue Scandals of 1922. Subtitled 'Opera Ala Afro-American', the Harlem setting of the 1-act Blue Monday Blues capitalized upon a vogue for African art and literature, but was quickly dropped from the musical comedy because of its tragic ending.

In Porgy and Bess (1935) Gershwin attempted to mix the idioms and techniques of jazz and classical music. At first he was attacked from both sides and forced to make extensive revisions and cuts, which were later reinstated. However, the popularity of such numbers as 'Summertime' and 'Bess, You is My Woman Now' has made Porgy and

Bess one of the most popular operas of the 20th cent., while the skilful, almost symphonic manipulation of musical motives provides a degree of unity which refutes the charge that the opera is merely a succession of popular songs.

Gerster, Ottmar (*b* Braunfels, 29 June 1897; *d* Leipzig, 31 Aug. 1969). German composer. Studied Frankfurt with Sekles. His *Enoch Arden* (1936) uses popular tunes in separate numbers as well as Leitmotiv. Together with *Die Hexe von Passau* (1941), later banned by the Nazis, this was his most successful opera.

Gerusalemme. See LOMBARDI, I.

Gerville-Réache, Jeanne (*b* Orthez, 26 Mar. 1882; *d* New York, 5 Jan. 1915). French contralto. Studied Paris with Laborde and Viardot. Début Paris, OC, 1899 (Gluck's Orfeo); OC till 1903. London, CG, 1905. New York, Manhattan OC, 1907–10. Chicago, Boston, Canada 1910–15. Created Geneviève (*Pelléas*); also sang Dalila, Hérodiade, first US Klytemnästra. A true contralto with impressive dramatic qualities. (R)

Gesamtkunstwerk (Ger.: 'unified work of art'). A term, associated with Wagner and discussed by him in *Das Kunstwerk der Zukunft* (The Artwork of the Future, 1849) and in other places, to describe a dramatic form in which all the arts—poetry, drama, the visual arts, music, song—should be united so as to form a new and complete work of art.

Ghedini, Giorgio (*b* Cuneo, 11 July 1892; *d* Nervi, 25 Mar. 1965). Italian composer. An intelligent artist with an understanding of the Baroque, his early operas were somewhat static in nature, a condition which marks even the intense and violent *Le Baccanti* (1948). He also had some success with *Billy Budd* (1949).

Gheorghiu, Angela (*b* Adjud, 7 Sept. 1965). Romanian soprano. Studied at the Budapest Academy. First major role in the West as Zerlina at London, CG, 1992; has returned to London as Mimì, Nina (*Chérubin*) and a highly-acclaimed Violetta. Other roles incl. Adina (Vienna, S), Juliette (Washington, DC), Desdemona. A natural actress, with a beautifully controlled voice. (R)

Ghiaurov, Nicolai (*b* Lidjene, 13 Sept. 1929). Bulgarian bass. Studied Sofia with Brambarov; then Leningrad and Moscow. Début

Moscow opera studio 1955 (Don Basilio, *Barbiere*), then Sofia 1956 (same role). Vienna, S, and Moscow, B, from 1957; Milan, S, from 1959; London, CG, from 1962 (Gremin 1993); Chicago from 1963; New York, M, and Salzburg from 1965; also Paris; etc. Repertory includes Ramfis, Créon, Gremin, Pimen, and Massenet's Don Quichotte. A notable basso cantante with a rich, expressive voice, and an imposing dramatic presence, outstanding as Boris, Philip, Gounod's and Boito's Mephistopheles; married to soprano Mirella *Freni. (R)

Ghiringhelli, Antonio (*b* Brunello, 5 Mar. 1903; *d* Aosta, 11 July 1979). Italian administrator. Studied law in Genoa. Supervised rebuilding of Milan S, 1945, then becoming its dir. till 1972. Built the Milan PS, and organized successful tours notably to London, Vienna, and Moscow. Established the Scala schools for young singers and stage designers, and developed the ballet school.

Ghislanzoni, Antonio (*b* Lecco, 25 Nov. 1824; *d* Caprino Bergamasco, 16 July 1893). Italian librettist and baritone. As a singer, he made his début in Sanelli's *Luisa Strozzi* in 1846, and sang in various Italian towns before being arrested for revolutionary activities in 1849 and deported to Corsica; resuming his career on his release, he sang Don Carlo in *Ernani* (Paris 1851). He also formed a company and began writing librettos. The loss of his singing voice compelled him to turn to writing novels and criticism as well as further librettos, and to editing periodicals. His 85-odd librettos, which earned him much respect, include works for Petrella, Ponchielli, Gomes, Cagnoni, Braga, and Catalani. He is most famous for his work on *Aida*, with which Verdi was very pleased. In it, he makes some attempt to loosen rhyme and metre.

Giacosa, Giuseppe (*b* Colleretto Parella, 21 Oct. 1847; *d* Colleretto Parella, 1 Sept. 1906). Italian playwright and librettist. After practising law, he turned to writing, also holding various teaching posts including that of professor of drama at the Verdi Conservatory. As a dramatist, he is one of the most important representatives of verismo; he is also remembered as collaborator with Luigi *Illica on three operas by Puccini, for which he provided the versification, *La bohème*, *Tosca*, and *Madama Butterfly*.

Giannini, Ferruccio (*b* Ponte all'Arnia, 15 Nov. 1868; *d* Philadelphia, 17 Sept. 1948). Italian, later US tenor. Emigrated to US 1885. Studied Detroit with De Campi, a Lamperti pupil. Début Boston 1891. Member of Mapleson's Co. for several years. Made the first operatic records, 1896, for Berliner. (R)

Gianni Schicchi. Opera in 1 act by Puccini; text by Forzano, after an episode (perhaps based on fact) in Dante's *Inferno*, xxx. 32 (*c*.1307–21). The third part of Puccini's *Trittico*. Prem. New York, M, 14 Dec. 1918.

The bedchamber of Buoso Donati, Florence, 1299. Buoso has recently died. Rumour leaks out that he has left most of his money to the monks and so his relatives start a frantic search for his will. Rinuccio (ten) finds it, but will not hand it over until his Aunt Zita (con) agrees that he may marry Lauretta (sop), daughter of Gianni Schicchi (bar), if the contents are favourable. The relatives' worst fears are confirmed, and as they are deciding what can be done, Gianni Schicchi arrives. He devises a plan to help the family: he pretends to be the dying Buoso Donati and summons a lawyer to make another will. Each member of the family offers Gianni large bribes to allocate them a substantial portion of the inheritance. When Gianni dictates the will, he leaves something to each of the relatives but keeps the best things for himself. The relatives are furious but helpless. After the lawyer has left, they turn on Schicchi and carry away from the house all they can. Rinuccio and Lauretta pledge their love, and Gianni begs the audience not to think too badly of him.

Gibert, Paul-César (*b* Versailles, 1717; *d* Paris, 1787). French composer. Studied in Naples; made an important journey around Italy recruiting singers for the French royal chapel, including the castrato Albanese, then settled in Paris *c*.1750. Earned a reputation as a singing-teacher and composer of opéras-comiques, including *La Sybille* (1758) and *La fortune au village* (1760). Remembered chiefly as the composer of music for Favart's *Soliman II, ou Les trois sultanes* (1761), which was popular throughout Europe. A proponent of the Italian style, his only (and lost) tragédie lyrique, *Deucalion et Pyrrha* (1772), was so well received that he was awarded a valuable gold medal.

Gibichungs. The tribe to whose stronghold on the Rhine Siegfried comes in Act I of Wagner's *Götterdämmerung*. Their lord is Gunther; his sister is Gutrune. Their half-brother is Hagen, son of Alberich.

Gibson, (Sir) **Alexander** (*b* Motherwell, 11 Feb. 1926; *d* London, 14 Jan. 1995). Scottish conductor. Studied Glasgow, London with Austin, Salzburg with Markevitch, Siena with Van Kempen. London, SW: répétiteur, 1951–2; cond. 1954–7; music dir. 1957–9, conducting a wide repertory incl. prem. of Gardner's *Moon and Sixpence*. London, CG, 1957. Founded *Scottish O 1962, conducting most of its productions, including *The Trojans* and *The Ring*, and acting as an invigorating force on the company; music dir. until 1987, leading the prem. of Orr's *Full Circle* (1968) and Hamilton's *The Catiline Conspiracy* (1974). London, Col. 1994 (*Tosca*). A versatile and sensitive musician, with a particular care in accompanying singers. (R)

Gielen, Michael (*b* Dresden, 20 July 1927). Austrian, later Argentinian, conductor and composer, son of producer Josef Gielen. Studied Buenos Aires with Leuchter, Vienna with Polnauer. Répétiteur Buenos Aires, C, 1947–50; Vienna, S, 1950–1. Début Vienna 1954. Chief cond. Stockholm 1960–5. Cologne 1965 (incl. prem. of Zimmermann's *Die Soldaten*). Chief cond. Netherlands O 1972–7. Music dir. Frankfurt 1977–87. A musician of sharp and clear intellect, he has made a particular reputation with modern music (*Moses und Aron* at Salzburg). (R)

Gigli, Beniamino (*b* Recanati, 20 Mar. 1890; *d* Rome, 30 Nov. 1957). Italian tenor. Studied Rome with *Cotogni and Rosati. Début Rovigo 1914 (Enzo, *Gioconda*). Milan, S, 1918 (Faust, *Mefistofele*) in Boito celebrations under Toscanini. New York, M, 1920–32, 1938–9, being regarded as Caruso's successor. London, CG, 1930–1, 1938–9, 1946; in 1946 sang with his daughter Rina in *Bohème* and *Pagliacci* and also sang Turiddu and Canio on the same evening. Left US for Italy in 1932 in protest against salary cuts at the New York, M.

His voice was one of the most beautiful of the century, with a technique secure well into his sixties and an exquisite cantilena. His taste was sometimes questionable, his acting often rudimentary, but his presence on the stage always assured the occasion a popular following. His best roles included the Duke of Mantua, Canio, Cavaradossi, Lionel, and Chénier. The concert tours he undertook in his last years crowned his immense popularity.

Gilbert, W. S. (Sir William Schwenk Gilbert) (*b* London, 18 Nov. 1836; *d* Harrow Weald, 29 May 1911). English poet, playwright, and librettist. His earliest dramatic work was a burlesque of Donizetti's *L'elisir d'amore* entitled *Dulcamara, or The Little Duck and the Great Quack* (1866). His long collaboration with *Sullivan on the *Savoy operas provided English opera with a vein of comedy which has never been consistently excelled. Idiosyncratic and ingenious, he was a versifier of matchless brilliance, with a mastery of the patter song that is the equal of anything in the whole of opera buffa. His satire of various British institutions—the Navy, the House of Lords, the Police—is as apt as that of more exotic manifestations such as the Japanese Exhibition (in *The Mikado*) and the aesthetic movement (in *Patience*), and ultimately as inoffensive. His extraordinary technical proficiency was always musically stimulating to Sullivan.

Gilda. Rigoletto's daughter (sop) in Verdi's *Rigoletto*.

Gilly, Dinh (*b* Algiers, 9 July 1877; *d* London, 19 May 1940). French baritone. Studied Rome with Cotogni, and Paris Cons. Début Paris, O, 1899 (Priest; *Sigurd*). Paris, O, 1902–8; New York, M, 1909–14. London, CG, 1911–14, 1919–24. Created Sonora in *La fanciulla del West*; first London Jack Rance. Also sang Athanaël (*Thaïs*), Amonasro, Germont, Rigoletto, Silvio, etc. A communicative, musical singer and actor. Married the contralto Edith Furmedge, and opened a singing school in London. Taught Walter Widdop. (R)

Giménez, Jerónimo (*b* Seville, 10 Oct. 1854; *d* Madrid, 19 Feb. 1923). Spanish composer and conductor. Studied Seville with his father; Paris with Alard, Savart, and Thomas. Dir. Madrid: T Apolo, 1885, then T de la Zarzuela (conducting first Spanish *Carmen*). One of the most important zarzuela composers of his day, he developed especially the 1-act *género chico*, making much use of Spanish song and dance. He wrote over 100 zarzuelas, including *Tannhauser el estanquero* (Tannhauser the Shopkeeper, 1890), *El barbero de Sevilla* (1901), *Los viajes de Gulliver* (Gulliver's Travels) (1911), and *Tras Tristán* (After Tristan) (1918).

Ginastera, Alberto (*b* Buenos Aires, 11 Apr. 1916; *d* Geneva, 25 June 1983). Argentinian composer. Studied at the Williams and Buenos Aires Cons. Held various academic posts in Argentina and US; on several occasions was forced to leave his native country because of disagreements with the Perón régime. Came to notice with his ballet *Estancia* (1943); was subsequently regarded as the father of an Argentinian national style of composition.

He wrote three operas, all of them during a period when he was experimenting with a kind of neo-Expressionism. The most important was *Bomarzo* (1967): at first banned in Buenos Aires because of its sex-ridden plot, it was taken up elsewhere and enjoyed brief fame; musically it combines the techniques of Leitmotiv and serialism in an original fashion. *Beatrix Cenci* (1971) develops Ginastera's fascination with the macabre, drawing on serial and aleatory techniques and producing some powerful dramatic climaxes.

Gioconda, La (The Joyful Girl). Opera in 4 acts by Ponchielli; text by 'Tobia Gorrio' (Arrigo Boito), after Hugo's drama *Angelo, tyran de Padoue* (1835). Prem. Milan, S, 8 Apr. 1876.

Venice, 17th cent. La Cieca (mez), the mother of the street-singer La Gioconda (sop), is accused of witchcraft, but is saved by the interception of Enzo Grimaldi (ten), a Genoese prince, whom La Gioconda loves. Barnaba (bar) is in love with La Gioconda and he offers to help Enzo elope with Laura Adorno (mez), wife of Alvise Badoero (bs). La Gioconda resolves to kill her rival, but when she realizes Laura was instrumental in obtaining the release of La Cieca, she alters her plan and helps the lovers; however, their escape attempt is foiled. When Alvise orders his wife to drink poison, La Gioconda substitutes a sleeping potion. Enzo, however, believes her to be dead and is arrested after an angry outburst. La Gioconda promises to yield to Barnaba in order to save Enzo. When he is released, Enzo disregards La Gioconda's sacrifice. As she pretends to give herself to Barnaba, she stabs herself, too late to hear Barnaba say that he has just killed La Cieca.

Gioielli della Madonna, I (The Madonna's Jewels). Opera in 3 acts by Wolf-Ferrari; text by Golisciani and Zangarini, German version *Der Schmuck der Madonna* by Hans Liebstöckl. Prem. Berlin, Kurfürstenoper, 23 Dec. 1911.

Raffaele (bar) is willing even to steal the Madonna's jewels to prove his love for Mariella (sop); but Gennaro (ten) wins her by this very deed. Remorsefully she confesses to the enraged Raffaele and rushes away to drown herself; Gennaro returns the jewels to an image of the Madonna, then stabs himself.

Giordano, Tommaso (*b* Naples, *c*.1733; *d* Dublin, 23 or 24 Feb. 1806). Italian composer. Active in London from 1753, he composed over 30 dramatic works, many of them collaborations, and played an important part in the flourishing musical life of both London and Dublin. Giordano also adapted the works of others, notably Gay's *The Beggar's Opera* (1765) and Hasse's *Artaserse* (1772).

Giordano, Umberto (*b* Foggia, 28 Aug. 1867; *d* Milan, 12 Nov. 1948). Italian composer. Studied Naples with Serrao. While still a student, won sixth place in the 1889 Sonzogno competition with *Marina* (1889), which led to the commission for *Mala vita* (1892). The scandal caused by this outspoken piece of verismo led to it being later watered down (though it also won admiration, including from Hanslick), and Giordano turned to what he hoped would be the safer paths of Romantic melodrama with *Regina Diaz* (1894). On its failure, he moved to Milan and achieved his most enduring success with *Andrea Chénier* (1896). Though the post-verismo, Puccinian effects are carefully calculated, the best pages of the score have genuine strength and passion. *Fedora* (1898) was initially almost as successful; and *Siberia* (1903) had a certain initial following. Giordano continued in verismo vein with *Madame Sans-Gêne* (1915), then tried once again to change course with *La cena delle beffe* (The Supper of Jests, 1924) and with a lighter work, *Il re* (1929), which had some success due to its appeal to coloratura sopranos.

Giorgetta. Michele's wife (sop) in Puccini's *Il tabarro*.

Giorgi-Banti, Brigida (*b* Crema, *c*.1756; *d* Bologna, 18 Feb. 1806). Italian soprano. Began life as a street-singer. Made a spectacular début at the Paris O, 1776, having made her way to the city by singing in cafés. London 1779–80 and 1794–1802; toured Europe 1780–94, appearing in Vienna, Italy, Warsaw, and Madrid. She was stupid, lazy, and never learned to read music, but enjoyed enormous popularity because of her glorious voice and spirited acting. Though Da Ponte found her coarse and ignorant, composers inspired to write for her included Haydn (his *Scena di Berenice*), Paisiello, Zingarelli, and Anfossi. Critics described her singing as 'charming', 'perfect', and 'impassioned'. In 1779 she married the dancer Zaccaria Banti. She left her immensely large larynx to the city of Bologna, though it has never been traced.

Giorgi-Righetti, Geltrude (*b* Bologna, 1793; *d* Bologna, 1862). Italian contralto. Studied Bologna. Début Bologna 1814. Married the lawyer Giorgi 1815. Created Rosina and Cenerentola, 1817, both of which reflect her gift for coloratura singing. Also highly successful as Isabella (*L'italiana*). Her voice was 'full, powerful, and of rare extension' (Spohr), and she was a good actress. Retired early in 1822; in 1823 published her well-known reply to an article by Stendhal on Rossini: *Cenni d'una donna già cantante sopra il Maestro Rossini*.

Giorno di regno, Un (King for a Day) (later known as *Il finto Stanislao*). Opera in 2 acts by Verdi; text by Romani, after A. V. Pineu-Duval's comedy *Le faux Stanislas* (1808). Prem. Milan, S, 5 Sept. 1840.

Baron Kelbar's Castle, near Brest, 1733. The King of Poland has had to depart on a secret mission, leaving the Cavalier Belfiore (bar) to impersonate him for a day. At court, there is to be a double marriage; Kelbar's daughter Giulietta (mez) is to marry La Rocca (bs), though she is in love with his nephew Edoardo (ten); the Marchesa del Poggio (sop) is to marry the Count Ivrea (ten). She plans to do this because she believes she was deserted by her lover, Belfiore.

Belfiore is dismayed to learn of the Marchesa's marriage but cannot reveal his identity. After many delaying tactics and amorous complications, the situation is finally resolved: Kelbar (bs) gives his consent for Giulietta to marry Edoardo. When the King succeeds in his mission, Belfiore reveals his identity and professes his love for the Marchesa. She forgives him and they are married.

Giovanna d'Arco (Joan of Arc). Opera in a prologue and 3 acts by Verdi; text by Solera, after Schiller's tragedy *Die Jungfrau von Orleans* (1801). Prem. Milan, S, 15 Feb. 1845.

France, 1429. Carlo VII (ten), King of France, is intending to abdicate. He visits a statue to the Virgin and lays his weapons beneath it. Giovanna (sop), who was asleep nearby, wakes to find them, and persuades Carlo to accompany her into battle.

The French army is victorious and Giovanna wants to return to her simple life. Carlo declares his love for her, and she in turn admits that she loves him. Angelic visions warn her against worldly love.

At Carlo's coronation, Giacomo (bar), Giovanna's father, who has been watching them, accuses Carlo of blasphemy and Giovanna of witchcraft. A thunderclap seems to confirm his statement. She is handed over to the English to be burned at the stake.

Giacomo, overhearing Giovanna's prayers, realizes that he was mistaken and frees her from her chains. She returns to battle and leads France to victory, but is mortally wounded in the fight.

Giraldoni, Leone (*b* Paris 1824; *d* Moscow, 1 Oct. 1897). Italian baritone. Studied Florence with Ronzi. Début Lodi 1847 (High Priest, Pacini's *Saffo*). Milan, S, 1850–85. Created Donizetti's Duca d'Alba, and Verdi's Boccanegra and Renato. Retired 1885, and taught in Italy and Moscow. Possessed a warm, even voice, and was an effective actor, especially in noble and dignified roles.

Giraud, Fiorello (*b* Parma, 22 Oct. 1870; *d* Parma, 28 Mar. 1928). Italian tenor. Son of the tenor **Ludovico Giraud** (1846–82). Studied Parma with Barbacini. Début Vercelli 1891 (Lohengrin). First Canio and Italian Pelléas; highly successful career in Wagner (above all as Siegfried) and in verismo opera. Possessed a robust voice and excellent declamation. (R)

Girl of the Golden West. See FANCIULLA DEL WEST, LA.

Giuditta. Operetta in 5 acts by Lehár; text by Paul Knepler and Fritz Löhner. Prem. Vienna, S, 20 Jan. 1934.

Sicily and Libya, early 20th cent. Giuditta (sop) leaves her husband to accompany Octavio (ten), an army officer who has seduced her, to Africa. When he departs with his regiment, Giuditta becomes a dancer. Octavio deserts from the army and becomes a pianist in a restaurant. The two meet again in the restaurant, where Giuditta is supping with her new admirer; as they leave, Octavio remains playing the piano as a waiter turns out the lights.

Giulietta. 1. The courtesan (sop), one of Hoffmann's lovers, in Offenbach's *Les contes d'Hoffmann*.

2. Juliet (sop) in Bellini's *I Capuleti e i Montecchi* and other Italian *Romeo and Juliet* operas.

Giulini, Carlo Maria (*b* Barletta, 9 May 1914). Italian conductor. Studied Rome with Molinari. Début Rome, 1944 (concert); became music director of Italian Radio 1946–51, broadcasting many little-known operas; operatic début Bergamo 1950 (*Traviata*). Milan, S, 1951; chief cond. 1953–6, working closely with Visconti and Zeffirelli, and with Callas. Edinburgh Festival, with Gly., 1956. London, CG, 1958 (*Don Carlos*), establishing his fame in England. From 1967 turned his attention to concert work, returning to opera 1981 with *Falstaff*, Los Angeles and London, CG. One of the most thoughtful and sensitive of contemporary Italian conductors. (R)

Giulio Cesare (Julius Caesar). Opera in 3 acts by Handel; text by Nicola Francesco Haym, after libretto by Bussani, set by Sartorio (1677) and Kusser (1691). Prem. London, H, 20 Feb. 1724.

The Roman general Giulio Cesare (con cas) has conquered Pompey in battle; Sesto (sop), Pompey's son, vows to avenge his father's assassination. Achilla (bs), a captain in the Egyptian army, falls in love with Pompey's widow, Cornelia (con), but she is taken into the harem of Tolomeo, King of Egypt (con cas). Having reported (falsely) the death of Caesar at his hand, Achilla hopes he may marry Cornelia, but Tolomeo now plans to marry her himself. In a second battle, Achilla is fatally wounded and confesses to Sesto that it was he who killed Pompey. Caesar leads a revolt against Tolomeo during which Sesto kills the Egyptian king; Tolomeo's sister Cleopatra (sop), who is Caesar's lover, is crowned queen.

Giuramento, Il (The Oath). Opera in 3 acts by Mercadante; text by Gaetano Rossi, based on Hugo's drama *Angelo* (1835). Prem. Milan, S, 11 Mar. 1837.

Syracuse, 14th cent. Manfredo (bar) commands his wife Bianca (mez) to take poison because she has committed adultery with Viscardo (ten). However, Elaisa (sop), who also loves Viscardo, substitutes a sleeping potion. Viscardo believes Elaisa to have murdered Bianca and kills her.

Gläser, Franz (*b* Obergeorgenthal (Horní Jiřetín), 19 Apr. 1798; *d* Copenhagen, 29 Aug. 1861). Bohemian composer and conductor. Studied Prague with D. Weber. Worked in Vienna 1817–30 (L, 1817–18; J, 1819–27: W, 1827–30), then in Berlin. Of his many works (over 50 for the stage), most are occasional pieces of transient interest. The most important was *Des Adlers Horst* (The Eyrie, 1832), once in most German repertories and known to Wagner; it includes 'pre-Wagnerian' features such as an apostrophe to the sun and the use of insistently repeated short figures for creating dramatic tension. In 1842 he moved to Copenhagen, being appointed court cond. in 1845. Here he wrote three more operas, two to texts by Hans Andersen: *Brylluppet ved Como-søen* (The Wedding on Lake Como, 1849) and *Nøkken* (The Water-Sprites,1853).

Glasgow. City in Strathclyde region, Scotland. Glasgow was for long dependent on visits from touring companies, such as the London CR from 1877. The amateur Glasgow Grand O Society, formed in 1905, staged some enterprising productions, including the first British *Idomeneo* (1934), *Les Troyens* (1935), and *Béatrice et Bénédict* (1936) under Erik Chisholm. It also revived MacCunn's *Jeanie Deans* (1951). Opera was finally put on a permanent professional footing with the formation of *Scottish O in 1962. Renovated and newly equipped Theatre Royal was opened 1975.

Glass, Philip (*b* Baltimore, 31 Jan. 1937). US composer. Studied at the Juilliard School in New York and with Nadia Boulanger in Paris. Early conservative works were later withdrawn, as Glass adopted a more radical style of music, now termed Minimalist. The static simplicity of his writing may be seen as a reaction; but a primary root of its evolution was his interaction with Indian music. This led to the development of a repetitive style with rippling arpeggiations and pattering percussion accompaniment.

This made its first appearance in opera in *Einstein on the Beach* (1976), which comprises scenes representing one of three visual images. Unnamed characters sing or speak words which present no narrative, and verbal communication is unimportant, with much of the text taken up by random repetition of numbers or meaningless prose. By *Satyagraha* (1980) Glass's approach was somewhat less radical and much of the music

based on a chaconne structure. The third work in his 'Portrait Trilogy' is *Akhnaten* (1983), whose three acts concern episodes from the rise, reign, and fall of the Egyptian King Akhnaten, though there is again no continuous narrative.

The chamber opera *The Juniper Tree* (1985) was Glass's first work written entirely in English. He aimed to write vocal lines as close as possible to the natural speaking range so that vowel sounds should not be distorted. This technique is also employed in *The Making of the Representative for Planet 8* (1988), where a definite narrative thread may now be discerned. With his adoption of a conventional opera orchestra and a more lyrical style of music, Glass seems to have reached a point closer to traditional opera, as with his Columbus opera, *Voyage* (1992). His increasing conventionalism is also indicated by his quest to infuse his works with allegorical 'meaning', as in *Orphée* (1993), for which the libretto is the script of Cocteau's screen treatment.

In so far as they are large scale with continuous music and, especially latterly, a narrative thread, Glass's more recent works conform to many of opera's expectations, though the composer himself continues to refer to his stage output as 'music theatre' while looking forward to a time when the opera-house will be revitalized by a breaking down of rigid barriers between traditional and contemporary forms.

Glastonbury. See BOUGHTON, RUTLAND.

Glière, Reinhold (*b* Kiev, 11 Jan. 1875; *d* Moscow, 23 June 1956). Ukrainian composer. Studied Moscow with Taneyev, Arensky, and Ippolitov-Ivanov. His music, skilfully crafted and cast in a post-Romantic vein, includes several operas that make use of Asian national subjects and folk music. The first, *Shekh-senem* (1927), was commissioned in 1923 by the Azerbaijani Composers' Union. *Leyli i Medjnun* (1940) recasts the popular folktale with a Communist slant, and uses Uzbek folk scales and rhythms with Westernized harmony. In his work Glière gave an example and much encouragement to musicians working in their own traditions.

Glinka, Mikhail (*b* Novospasskoye (now Glinka), 1 June 1804; *d* Berlin, 15 Feb. 1857). Russian composer. Studied casually, gaining most in St Petersburg from Mayer, especially later in Berlin from Dehn. He briefly contemplated two operatic projects, the second to a text by Zhukovsky, who suggested to him instead the story of Ivan Susanin. *A Life for the Tsar* (1836) was accepted by the Imperial Theatres partly through Cavos, himself the composer of an opera on the subject, and the interest aroused in rehearsals led to the Tsar suggesting the new title to replace *Ivan Susanin*. The work has long been regarded as the foundation stone of Russian historical opera, and as well as being on a heroic national subject includes much essentially Russian music recomposed: examples are Glinka's use of *podgolosok* (folk polyphony) and of balalaika sounds woven into the musical fabric, together with his use of Russian melodic contours and a recitative based on the inflections of the Russian language. But it also depends much on examples Glinka had heard in his childhood and on his travels, especially French Grand Opera and Italian vocal writing (Bellini in particular), and the reconciliation is incomplete. It also set an example in its clear, individual orchestration.

The success of his first opera led to Glinka being appointed imperial Kapellmeister and to contemplating *Ruslan and Lyudmila* (1842). Pushkin's death prevented their collaboration, and the confused and inadequate libretto was prepared by several hands. Despite this, the strength and individuality of the music show in the more consistent melodic quality, the skill in developing tunes according to his famous 'varying background' technique (which influenced numerous later Russian composers), the original rhythmic and harmonic pungency (especially in the orientalisms), and the dazzling colour of the orchestration. By contrast with its predecessor, *Ruslan* is the founding work of Russian magic opera. Later 19th-cent. Russian opera composers who acknowledged Glinka's influence include Tchaikovsky, Musorgsky, Dargomyzhsky, Borodin, and Rimsky-Korsakov; and this influence was not extinct by the time Stravinsky began composing.

'Glitter and be gay'. Cunegonde's (sop) aria in Act I of Bernstein's *Candide*, reconciling herself without much difficulty to the material consolations of her dissipated life.

Gloriana. Opera in 3 acts by Britten; text by William Plomer, after Lytton Strachey's study *Elizabeth and Essex* (1928). Com-missioned by the Arts Council for the coronation of Elizabeth II, and prem. London, CG, at a Gala Performance in her presence, 8 June 1953.

The plot describes the events of the later years of Queen Elizabeth I's reign. Elizabeth (sop) reassures Sir Robert Cecil (bar) of her total allegiance to the state, but in the next scene displays her affection for the Earl of Essex (ten); he pleads to be allowed to fight the rebel Tyrone in Ireland but the Queen is reluctant to let him go. However, he does depart on the mission with her blessing. When he returns defeated, she accuses him of betrayal and he falls from favour. Despite the pleas of his wife Frances (mez), he is condemned to death. The opera ends with episodes showing scenes leading up to Essex's beheading and Elizabeth's own death.

Glossop, Peter (*b* Sheffield, 6 July 1928). English baritone. Studied Sheffield with Mosley and Rich, later with Hislop. Début Sheffield O Soc. 1947 (Coppelius and Dr Miracle). Principal with London, SW, from 1953; London, CG, from 1961; Milan, S, 1965; New York, M, 1966–85; also Vienna, Buenos Aires, etc. Roles include Rigoletto, Iago, Billy Budd, Jochanaan. A vigorous performer, possessing a true Verdi baritone. (R)

Glover, Jane (*b* Helmsley, 13 May 1949). English conductor. Studied Oxford, where she gained experience conducting for the OUOC. Début Wexford 1975 (Cavalli's *Eritrea*). Gly. since 1982; London, CG, 1988 (*Entführung*) and C from 1989 (début with *Don Giovanni*); Canadian OC 1991. Though her initial interests were in Baroque opera, she has given some outstanding performances of Mozart and Britten, in particular. Her scholarly work has centred on Baroque opera, especially with her *Cavalli*. (London, 1978).

Gluck, Christoph Willibald, Ritter von (*b* Erasbach, 2 July 1714; *d* Vienna, 15 Nov. 1787). German composer. After study in Prague and Vienna, he worked in Milan. The success of his first opera *Artaserse* (1741) led to seven more operas in Italy before he left for London in 1745. Both political and musical circumstances militated against a comparable success, though he formed a friendship with Handel and an increased taste for simplicity in music. Busy years of travel followed from 1746, taking him, perhaps with the Mingotti company, through Germany, first to Vienna. Here *Semiramide riconosciuta* (1748) seems to have pleased everyone except the librettist, Metastasio. He then toured Germany, Denmark, and Bohemia, returning to Vienna in 1750, where marriage brought him good contacts with the Viennese court.

After success in Naples with *La clemenza di Tito* (1752), he took a post in Vienna as Kapellmeister to an aristocratic family. When Durazzo, manager of the Vienna Imperial Theatres, sought to capitalize on the success of a visiting French company, he engaged Gluck to make suitable adaptations; but soon Gluck was responding to his own interest in French opera by composing original material. His first complete opéra-comique was the successful *La fausse esclave* (1758). The no less successful *Le cinesi* (1754) attracted the admiration of the Emperor, from whom came several commissions, including *L'innocenza giustificata* (1755). He also wrote *Antigono* (1756) for Rome, where he was awarded the papal title of Cavaliere. He composed operas, serenatas, and ballet music (as well as chamber music), much of it at the encouragement of Durazzo, who now also introduced him to *Calzabigi. Their first collaboration, which included the dancer Angiolini, was with the ballet-pantomime *Don Juan* in 1761. This unified music, dance, and mime, and though a success in its own right, more significantly led to a further collaboration on *Orfeo ed Euridice* (1762).

Orfeo, the first of Gluck's so-called 'reform operas', elevates the fusion of different dramatic ingredients on to a new expressive plane and draws from the composer the fullest expression of his gifts so far. Though it retains conventional aspects, such as the irrelevant overture, it has in ample measure both the energy and the calm sublimity that are among his greatest characteristics. It also shows the greatly increased reliance on orchestration that was to mark his mature style.

At the beginning of 1763 Gluck went to Italy with Dittersdorf, where he had a limited success with a work of mixed achievement, the Metastasian *Il trionfo di Clelia* in Bologna. Cancelling an intended visit to Paris, he then returned to Vienna for a revival of *Orfeo*, to revise *Ezio*, and to write *La rencontre imprévue* (1764). This was to be the most successful work of his own day, and to influence even Mozart's *Entführung*.

The preface to *Alceste* (1767), his next important work, is one of the most famous documents of operatic reform. In it, Gluck attacks the domination of the singer, and the limitations imposed by the formalities of opera seria and by its constrictive plots. He was by no means the first in this field, and the terms he used well matched the ideals of the Enlightenment; and for all its quality, *Alceste* is not so consistent in its application of reform principles as its predecessor *Orfeo* or especially *Iphigénie en Tauride* (1779). It was not immediately the success it later became. His next reform opera, *Paride ed Elena* (1770), had a similar reception, with praise again given to Noverre's dance contribution.

Various other activities continued to keep Gluck busy. His next major work was *Iphigénie en Aulide* (1774). With plans to set Du Roullet's text, he arrived in Paris late in 1773. Its triumphant first run was interrupted by the death of Louis XV, and during the period of mourning Gluck revised *Orfeo*, to some extent loosening the structure in the interests of adding expressive music to suit French taste. On a second visit he made a French version of *Alceste*. A third visit brought him into conflict, unsought by either composer, with the defenders of Piccinni over the latter's *Roland* and his own *Armide* (1777). The intrigues were intended to lead to a confrontation between the settings of *Iphigénie en Tauride* by Gluck and Piccinni; but Gluck had left Paris by the time Piccinni's not unsuccessful work appeared. His own work is his masterpiece. Not only does he now completely fuse dance, action, chorus, and solo arias into a single imaginative whole, but the fluency of movement between them is guided entirely by the drama.

Gluck left Paris for Vienna in 1779. He had had a stroke during rehearsals for *Echo et Narcisse* (1779), and suffered two more while continuing work, including on a German revision of *Iphigénie en Tauride*. He was forced to abandon further plans for travel, and died after a fourth stroke.

Gluck's influence in revitalizing the traditions of tragédie lyrique shows immediately in the work of Cherubini, also in that of Méhul and Spontini. Further, if it was Gluck's grace, simplicity, and poise, and his heroic passion in treating classical legend that deeply impressed Berlioz, Wagner (who made a not very successful version of *Iphigénie en Aulide*) admired above all the dramatic fluency and urgency of his music.

Strauss's version of *Iphigénie en Tauride* was given at New York, M, 1916.

Glückliche Hand, Die (The Favoured Hand). Opera in 1 act by Schoenberg; text by the composer. Prem. Vienna, V, 14 Oct. 1924.

The subject is the artist's isolation in the contemporary world and his quest for happiness, represented by various scenes in which a man is plagued by a monster and exhorted by a green-faced chorus to abandon his reliance on his senses. He is also frustrated in his quest for a woman.

The work is scored for a solo baritone, mixed chorus, and orchestra, and alternates use of singing and *Sprechgesang. Following Kandinsky's theories, in this work Schoenberg placed particular stress on the symbolism of colours.

Glyndebourne. The house and estate of the Christie family near Lewes, Sussex, where the Glyndebourne Festival Opera was launched in 1934. John Christie, encouraged by his wife, the soprano Audrey Mildmay, built an opera-house in the grounds with the intention of giving performances of opera in ideal surroundings and conditions.

The first Glyndebourne Fest. opened on 28 May 1934 with *Le nozze di Figaro*, followed the next evening with *Così fan tutte*. The conductor was Fritz Busch, the producer Carl Ebert, who between them set new standards in English opera. The pre-war repertory consisted chiefly of Mozart, though *Macbeth* and *Don Pasquale* were also staged. Although the repertory is now much wider, Mozart remains at its centre, the modest scale of the house being particularly apt for his operas. By 1939 the theatre had nevertheless been enlarged (from a capacity of 300 to 600); it was enlarged again in 1952 to a capacity of 800. The back-stage facilities were also then extended. From the outbreak of war, when the house served as a school for evacuees, no performances were staged; however, the company toured with *The Beggar's Opera*. In 1946 the *English Opera Group gave the prem. of *The Rape of Lucretia* under Ansermet, and in 1947 *Albert Herring* under Britten. 1947 also saw Ebert's production of *Orfeo ed Euridice* with Ferrier, which helped to establish Gluck's place in the repertory.

Glyndebourne resumed its own annual summer festival, under the management of Rudolf Bing in 1949, when Busch returned to work with Ebert. On Busch's death in 1951,

his place was taken by Vittorio Gui, who brought several Rossini works into the repertory. In 1959 Ebert was succeeded by Rennert, who with Gui became artistic counsellor. Gui resigned this position to John Pritchard in 1963, though he continued to conduct. Rennert resigned in 1968, and Moran Caplat (assistant manager since 1945, then general manager) became general administrator, with Pritchard as music director. Pritchard was succeeded by Bernard Haitink in 1977, and Sir Peter Hall director of productions 1984–90. Brian Dickie, previously administrator of Glyndebourne Touring O, succeeded as general administrator in 1982, leaving in 1988.

The expansion of Glyndebourne's repertory during these years took an important turn with the performances of Venetian opera in editions by, and conducted by, Raymond Leppard. The first was *L'incoronazione di Poppea* (1962), which proved such a revelation to a new public that it was followed by Cavalli's *Ormindo* (1967) and *Calisto* (1970), and Monteverdi's *Il ritorno d'Ulisse in patria* (1972). Though Leppard's methods came in for scholarly rebuke, he and Glyndebourne were more than anything responsible for awakening a wider appreciation of Venetian opera. Another broadening of the repertory into 20th-cent. music led to Janáček's *The Cunning Little Vixen* (1975) and *Káťa Kabanová* (1988), *The Love of Three Oranges* (1982), a return of *The Rake's Progress* (orig. 1953; 1975 with designs by Hockney), and *Porgy and Bess* (1986). World prems. have included Maw's *The Rising of the Moon* (1970). Since 1984 a New O Policy has resulted in a Fest. prem. every two years: this has led to Knussen's *Where the Wild Things Are* (1984) and *Higglety, Pigglety, Pop!* (1985), Nigel Osborne's *The Electrification of the Soviet Union* (1987), and the English prem. of Tippett's *New Year* (1990). Glyndebourne's work has become more widely known through recordings, radio and TV broadcasts, videos, Prom concerts, and foreign tours.

The number of performances each season has gradually been extended. The season now lasts from mid-May to mid-August, and since 1987 has comprised six productions (two new and two revivals). Works are generally performed in their original language, exceptions including *Intermezzo* (1974) and *The Cunning Little Vixen* (1975); *Surtitles were introduced for *Káťa Kabanová* (1988). The RPO was resident 1948–63, being replaced by the

LPO in 1964. The chorus traditionally recruits from young singers likely to progress to solo careers. In 1976 a chorus scheme was launched to sponsor its financing; there are also awards for singers for study periods. Glyndebourne continues to draw all its subsidy from private and business sources. In 1953 the Glyndebourne Arts Trust was formed to relieve the Christie family of the financial burden of the festival, and now about 65% of the income derives from ticket sales, 35% from business, private, and other sources. In 1990 Sir George Christie announced plans to enlarge the opera-house to cap. 1,150 by 1994; the completely new house opened with a production of *Figaro* marking Glyndebourne's 60th anniversary.

Glyndebourne Touring Co. was founded in 1967 with the intention of taking productions to the regions making use especially of younger artists. It opened in Newcastle on 25 Mar. 1968, and continues to tour England with established singers and conductors as well as emerging talent.

Glyndebourne has been successful in preserving its unique atmosphere of operagoing in a large country house, with a famous feature being picnics in the beautiful gardens during the 'Long Interval'. Though criticized for catering too exclusively to the rich and to prosperous firms with greater social or commercial than artistic concerns, an effective reply is the maintenance of distinctive and distinguished artistic standards without which its reputation would not continue to stand so high; and the enlargement brought about by the new theatre has meant the availability of many more cheap seats. Prems. of operas by British composers have been given at Glyndebourne in October and repeated at the Fest. the following summer (Birtwistle's *The Second Mrs Kong*, 1994/5).

Gobatti, Stefano (*b* Bergantino, 5 July 1852; *d* Bologna, 17 Dec. 1913). Italian composer. Studied Bologna with Busi, Parma and Naples with Rossi. The astounding success of his first opera, *I goti* (1873), which had 52 curtain calls, won him the honorary citizenship of Bologna and the claim by anti-Verdi circles that he was Italy's new musical laureate. The enthusiasm quickly faded, and Verdi himself called the work 'the most monstrous musical abortion ever composed'. The failure of his other operas—which included *Cordelia* (1881) and *Masias* (comp. 1900)— coupled with misfortune, debt, and slander

(he was accused of having the evil eye), led to persecution mania, and after retreating to a monastery he died in an asylum.

Gobbi, Tito (*b* Bassano del Grappa, 24 Oct. 1913; *d* Rome, 5 Mar. 1984). Italian baritone. Studied Rome with Crimi. Début Gubbio 1935 (Rodolfo, *Sonnambula*). Milan, S, from 1942; London, CG, 1951–74; Chicago from 1954; New York, M, 1956–75; also Vienna, S Francisco, etc. His repertory of *c.*100 roles included Rossini's Figaro, Rigoletto, Posa, Falstaff, Scarpia, Wozzeck, Jack Rance, Schicchi. Also made many films, and produced at Chicago and London, CG, 1965. Using his voice with great intelligence, he was an outstanding and unusually versatile singing actor whose characterizations were direct and humane. Autobiography, *My Life* (London, 1979). (R)

Godard, Benjamin (*b* Paris, 18 Aug. 1849; *d* Cannes, 10 Jan. 1895). French composer. Studied Paris with Reber. After winning an early reputation with concert music, he turned to opera in 1880, with little success until achieving it posthumously with *La vivandière* (1895). His operatic music now survives only in the tenor Berceuse from *Jocelyn* (1888).

Goehr, Alexander (*b* Berlin, 10 Aug. 1932). German, later English, composer, son of below. Studied Manchester with Richard Hall, founding the New Music Manchester Group with *Birtwistle, *Davies, Elgar *Howarth, and the pianist John Ogdon; later studied Paris with Loriod. Professor of Music Leeds 1971, Cambridge 1976. His first opera, *Arden Must Die* (1967), was commissioned by the Hamburg, S, and stormily received for political reasons; it is a remarkable achievement, making intelligent use of both traditional and more Brechtian means and drawing upon different musical manners without loss of artistic control or integrity. He was director of the Music T Ensemble from 1967, contributing to their repertory his own sharply observed *Naboth's Vineyard* (1968), in which the stylistic resources were from the earliest days of opera; this was joined in a triptych by *Shadowplay-2* (1970) and *Sonata about Jerusalem* (1971). *Behold the Sun* (1985), on the subject of the Anabaptists, continues the move away from Goehr's early Expressionism and draws upon a number of musical sources, including the Baroque oratorio but also an appreciation of Stravinsky that had marked his music theatre pieces. *Arianna (lost opera by Monteverdi)* (1995) is an ingenious and imaginative composition of Rinuccini's text, taking Monteverdi's operatic manner as a creative starting-point.

Goehr, Walter (*b* Berlin, 28 May 1903; *d* Sheffield, 4 Dec. 1960). German, later English, conductor and composer; father of above. Studied Berlin with Schoenberg. Wrote the first radio opera, *Malpopita* (1930). Moved to England, becoming an influential conductor, teacher, and editor, including of Monteverdi's *Poppea* (1954). One of the first conductors in England to arouse wider interest in Baroque music, especially Purcell and Monteverdi, through the sympathetic, stylish quality of his performances.

Goethe, Johann Wolfgang von (*b* Frankfurt, 28 Aug. 1749; *d* Weimar, 22 Mar. 1832). German poet and dramatist. Goethe's deep interest and involvement in music included early experience singing bass in a choir, learning some instruments, and attending with admiration operas and Singspiels, especially those by Hiller. He was also much impressed by the visit of Marchand's company to Frankfurt, 1771–7, and came to know the composer Johann André. His own Singspiel texts were *Erwin und Elmire*, *Claudine von Villa Bella*, *Lila*, *Die Fischerin*, *Jery und Bätely*, and *Scherz, List und Rache*; he also wrote a second part to *Die Zauberflöte*. When he was director of the Weimar theatre, 1791–1817, his repertory included operas: his preferred composer was Mozart (280 perfs.) followed by Dittersdorf (139 perfs.), then French composers. Among the adaptations he made was one of Mozart's *Der Schauspieldirektor*. Beethoven began setting *Faust* several times.

Goetz, Hermann (*b* Königsberg, 7 Dec. 1840; *d* Hottingen, 3 Dec. 1876). German composer. Studied Königsberg with Köhler; Berlin with Stern, Bülow, and Ulrich. Tubercular from youth, he had a severe struggle in maintaining a musical career, and his most important work, *Der Widerspenstigen Zähmung* (The Taming of the Shrew, 1874), was written when he was already seriously ill. It is one of the few significant operas of its time to resist Wagner in positive terms. The separate numbers are elegant and well constructed, especially in the finales, with which Goetz hoped to create a modern equivalent of his beloved Mozart. The work, much admired by

Shaw, is one of the most successful German comedies of the mid-19th cent. He did not live to complete *Francesca da Rimini*.

Golaud. The grandson (bar) of King Arkel, half-brother of Pelléas and husband of Mélisande, in Debussy's *Pelléas et Mélisande*.

Goldberg, Reiner (*b* Crostau, 17 Oct. 1939). German tenor. Studied Dresden with Schellenberg. Début Dresden 1966 (Luigi, *Tabarro*). Dresden, S, 1969, and from 1972; London, CG, 1982; Milan, 1984; also Bayreuth 1988, New York, M, 1992, Vienna, Prague, Salzburg, Barcelona, etc. His roles include Erik, Tannhäuser, Walther, Siegfried; also as Florestan, Huon, Duke of Mantua, Hermann, Bacchus. (R)

Golden Cockerel, The (Russ., *Zolotoy petushok*). Opera in 3 acts by Rimsky-Korsakov; text by Vladimir Belsky, after Pushkin's poem (1834), after a folk-tale and Washington Irving (1832). Prem. Moscow, Z, 7 Oct. 1909.

The opera tells of the miraculous golden cockerel, given to old King Dodon (bs) by the Astrologer (ten), which crows at the sign of imminent danger. Dodon brings back the beautiful Queen of Shemakha (sop) to his capital; when the Astrologer demands payments for the cockerel he is killed by Dodon, and the cockerel kills the King.

Goldmark, Karl (*b* Keszthely, 18 May 1830; *d* Vienna, 2 Jan. 1915). Hungarian composer. Largely self-taught. A staunch supporter of Wagner, he was chiefly responsible for the founding of the Vienna Wagner Verein (1872). Hanslick's enmity did not prevent the success of his first (and most popular) opera, *Die Königin von Saba* (1875). Colourful and tuneful, it was taken up all over Germany and also in England and America. None of his later operas, which included *Das Heimchen am Herd* (The Cricket on the Hearth, 1896) and *Götz von Berlichingen* (1902) made a comparable effect. His eclectic style, drawing on influences as disparate as Mendelssohn and Hungarian folk music, was also influenced by Wagner. He was less successful when attempting monumental opera than when indulging his agreeable melodic vein in lighter pieces.

Goldoni, Carlo (*b* Venice, 25 Feb. 1707; *d* Paris, 6 Feb. 1793). Italian librettist and dramatist. A lawyer by training, Goldoni is credited with the invention of the opera buffa libretto, writing more than 100 texts, many under pseudonyms. To the traditions of the commedia dell'arte he added characters and situations drawn from everyday life, injecting a reality and earthiness into his librettos which made them popular throughout Italy.

The height of Goldoni's craft is represented in the many collaborations with Galuppi, beginning with *L'Arcadia in Brenta* (1749) and embracing *Il mondo della luna* (1750) and *Il filosofo di campagna* (1754): other important librettos included *La buona figliuola* (Piccinni, 1760, based on Richardson's *Pamela*) usually regarded as the first *opera semiseria, and *Lo speziale* (Pallavicini and Fischietti, 1754). After 1748 Goldoni designated many of his librettos as *dramma giocoso, indicating the presence of serious parts alongside the stock characters of opera buffa. A particular feature of his work was the opportunity he provided for ensemble writing, especially in the finale.

Almost no composer of the late 18th cent. remained untouched by his work: particularly noteworthy were Haydn's settings, but other composers attracted to his librettos included Gassmann, Alessandro Scarlatti, and Vivaldi. The effects of Goldoni's work were felt long after his death and profoundly influenced composers as diverse as Mozart, Rossini, Donizetti, and Wolf-Ferrari.

Goldovsky, Boris (*b* Moscow, 7 June 1908). Russian, later US, producer and conductor. Studied Moscow, Berlin with Schnabel, Budapest with Dohnányi, New York with Reiner. Dir. opera dept. Cleveland Institute, Berkshire Music Center, New England Cons. 1942–6. Founded Goldovsky O Institute 1946 and the touring Goldovsky Grand Opera T. Directed the US prems. of *Peter Grimes* and *Idomeneo* at Tanglewood, *Les Troyens* at Boston, 1955 (in nine scenes). A versatile musician with practical and administrative skills, also a lively commentator on opera.

Goldschmidt, Berthold (*b* Hamburg, 18 Jan. 1903). British composer and conductor of German birth. Studied Hamburg, and Berlin with Schreker. Assistant cond. Berlin, S, 1926–7; cond. Darmstadt 1927–9; artistic adviser Berlin, SO, 1931–3. Gly. at Edinburgh 1947. His *Beatrice Cenci* was a prize-winner in the 1951 Arts Council competition for the Festival of Britain, but was not produced until 1988, in concert, and then recorded,

1994. *Der gewaltige Hahnrei* (The Mighty Cuckold) was staged at Mannheim in 1932, but then banned by the Nazis. It was revived at Berlin, K, 1992.

Goldschmied von Toledo (The Goldsmith of Toledo). Pasticcio, compiled from music by Offenbach, by Stern and Zamara; text by Zwerenz, after Hoffmann's story *Das Fräulein von Scuderi* (1818). Prem. Mannheim 7 Feb. 1919.

The goldsmith Malaveda (bar) is driven by a desire to repossess all the jewels he has made. To this end, he commits four murders. His prize piece, a pearl necklace, is owned by the Marquesa Almedina (sop); unable to resist the demonic force driving him, Malaveda also murders her, only to discover too late that his own daughter Madalena (sop) had taken the Marquesa's place.

See also CARDILLAC.

Goltz, Christel (*b* Dortmund, 8 July 1912). German soprano. Studied Munich with Ornelli-Leeb. Début Fürth 1935 (Agathe). Dresden, S, 1936–50; London, CG, 1951; New York, M, 1954; also Munich, Vienna, Berlin until 1970. Created title-role of Liebermann's *Penelope*; large repertory included Leonore, Isolde, Elektra, Dyer's Wife. Impressive for her clear tone, 3-octave range, and powerful acting ability. (R)

Gomatz. A young Spaniard (ten), prisoner of Soliman and lover of Zaide, in Mozart's *Zaide*.

Gomes, Carlos (*b* Campinas, 11 July 1836; *d* Belém, 16 Sept. 1896). Brazilian composer. Studied with his father, Rio de Janeiro with J. Giannini, then, after the success of his first two operas, Milan with Rossi. He then developed an Italianate manner which had its most successful expression in *Il Guarany* (1870), a work whose powerful, quasi-exotic appeal won it an international reputation. Despite Verdi's admiration, he was soon identified with foreign influences on bel canto opera, a reproach he refuted with some success with the second version of *Fosca* (1878). Though he made use of Brazilian subjects and melodies, his music remains essentially in the Italian Romantic and veristic traditions.

Gomez, Jill (*b* New Amsterdam, 21 Sept. 1942). British soprano. Studied London, RAM and GSMD. Début Cambridge U O 1967 (Mermaid, *Oberon*). Gly. 1969; London, CG,

1970 (first Flora, *The Knot Garden*). Created Countess in Musgrave's *The Voice of Ariadne*. Wexford Fest. 1974 (Thaïs). Also Scottish O, Frankfurt O, London, ENO. Roles include Fiordiligi, Mélisande, Governess. An accomplished actress with a pure, silvery tone. (R)

Gomis y Colomber, José (*b* Onteniente, 6 Jan. 1741; *d* Paris, 4 Aug. 1836). Spanish composer. After producing *La Aldeana* (1821) in Madrid, he became music director of the royal guard but was forced for political reasons to flee to Paris. Here he was befriended by a number of important musicians, among them Rossini. He was briefly in London in 1826. Berlioz, who was to write a cordial obituary, praised, perhaps over-praised, his opéras-comiques (especially *Le revenant* (1833)) for their attempts to raise standards, in particular for their individual rhythmic and melodic nature.

Gonzaga, Pietro (*b* Longarone, 25 Mar. 1751; *d* St Petersburg, 6 Aug. 1831). Italian designer. Scene painter Milan, S, 1779, then in other Italian cities. Visited Russia to build a private theatre for Prince Yusupov 1789, returning to help the inauguration of the Venice, F. Back in Russia, he worked in various theatres, where he developed his interest in architectural scenery and perspective in sets that foreshadow much in Romantic practice.

Goodall, Reginald (*b* Lincoln, 13 July 1901; *d* Bridge, 5 May 1990). English conductor. Studied London. Début London 1936 (*Carmen*). Répétiteur with Coates in British Music Drama OC, at London, CG, 1936. London, SW, 1944–6, cond. prem. of *Peter Grimes* (1945; superior to Britten's own later performances, according to Pears). EOG at Gly. 1946. CG 1946, conducting *Manon*, *Meistersinger*, *Fidelio*, and much Italian repertory during Rankl's directorship, then only rarely works incl. *Walküre*, *Tristan*, *Parsifal*, *Salome*. This neglect became the more culpable when his conducting of *Meistersinger*, SW 1968, revealed to a wide public the existence of one of the great Wagner conductors of the day. It led to his no less successful *Ring* (London, C), and to further superlative Wagner performances with the WNO and at CG (*Parsifal*, 1971). His early years of studying Wagner in Germany bore fruit in interpretations whose care of preparation—he was a long, slow, and painstaking coach and rehearser—laid the foundations of performances which at their greatest set him in the tradition of Furtwängler and Knappertsbusch, the two conductors he most admired. Very influential as a vocal coach. (R)

Good Friday Music. The scene (Ger., *Karfreitagszauber*) in Act III of Wagner's *Parsifal* as Parsifal, returning from his wanderings, is anointed in preparation for his entry into the Castle of the Grail.

Goossens. English musical family, of Belgian origin, three generations of whom named Eugene were conductors.

1. **Eugene** (*b* Bruges, 25 Feb. 1845; *d* Liverpool, 30 Dec. 1906). Studied Bruges. Came to England 1873. London, CR, 1882, cond. first English *Manon*, 1885. Command perf. of *Fille du régiment* before Queen Victoria, 1892.

2. **Eugene** (*b* Bordeaux, 28 Jan. 1867; *d* London, 31 July 1958). Studied Bruges and Brussels. Worked under his father in CR; then chief cond. of Burns-Crotty, Arthur Rouseby, and Moody-Manners companies. Chief cond. CR 1899–1915, maintaining high standards set by his father, and making many additions to the repertory. Joined Beecham OC, Birmingham 1917, and cond. in Beecham season at London, HM. Opened Beecham season, London, DL (*Ivan the Terrible*). Married **Annie Cook**, former contralto of CR and daughter of bass T. Aynsley Cook.

3. **Eugene** (*b* London, 26 May 1893; *d* London, 13 June 1962). Studied Bruges, Liverpool, and London with Wood and Stanford. Began career as violinist. Début as conductor London 1916 (Stanford's *The Critic*). Cond. BNOC, CR. Latterly cond. little opera, apart from his own *Judith* (London, CG, 1929) and *Don Juan de Mañara* (London, CG, 1937), also performances in Philadelphia and Cincinnati. Both operas are to texts by Arnold Bennett; Goossens's operatic expertise is evident in the dramatic presentation of librettos whose merits are primarily literary, though his own highly chromatic yet chaste style is itself not essentially operatic. Director NSW Cons. of Music 1947–56, helping many Australian singers at the start of their careers. (R)

Gorchakova, Galina (*b* Novokuznetsk, 1 Mar. 1962). Russian soprano. Studied Novosibirsk. Sang with Sverdlovsk O from 1988, notably as Yoroslavna, and Tamara in *The Demon*. Roles with St Petersburg, K, have included Leonora (*Trovatore*). Admired for the total commitment of her Renata (*Fiery Angel*) at London, CG, and New York, M, 1992. Sang Fevronia (*Invisible City of Kitezh*) with the Kirov at the Barbican, London, 1994. (R)

Gorr, Rita (*b* Ghent, 18 Feb. 1926). Belgian mezzo-soprano. Studied Ghent with Poelfiet, Brussels with Pacquot-d'Assy. Début Antwerp 1949 (Fricka). Paris, OC and O, 1952. Bayreuth from 1958; Milan, S, from 1960; New York, M, 1962–8; London, CG, 1959–71. Roles include Iphigénie, Medée, Eboli, Dalila, Amneris, Kundry, Charlotte, Mother Marie in first original *Carmélites* (1957). A dramatic performer with a rich, ample voice. (R)

Gorrio, Tobia. See BOITO, ARRIGO.

Goryanchikov. Alexander Petrovich Goryanchikov (bar), a political prisoner, in Janáček's *From the House of the Dead*.

Gossec, François-Joseph (*b* Vergnies, 17 Jan. 1734; *d* Passy, 16 Feb. 1829). French composer of Belgian descent. In Paris, he was helped by Rameau and Stamitz, and in 1762 became director of the Prince of Condé's theatre at Chantilly. His own first operas were unsuccessful, apart from an opéra-comique, *Les pêcheurs* (1766), and rivalry with the more successful Grétry was partly responsible for him turning to instrumental music. When he resumed opera composition, having continued to work at the O (and direct some of Grétry's works), he faced the still more formidable rivalry of Gluck: in 1774 his tragédie lyrique *Sabinus* (1773) was quickly forgotten in the success of *Iphigénie en Aulide*. Nevertheless, he supported Gluck in the controversy with Piccinni. In 1780 he became assistant director of the O. He resigned on the outbreak of the Revolution. The works which he composed for large-scale, often outdoor Republican ceremonies gave his orchestration, always enterprising, a particular range of sonorities which was to influence French operatic composers, especially Méhul and Spontini, who were seeking to give the orchestra a more significant place in opera.

Gotovac, Jakov (*b* Split, 11 Oct. 1895; *d* Zagreb, 16 Oct. 1982). Croatian conductor and composer. Studied Split with Dobronić, Hrazdira, and Hatze, Vienna with Marx. Cond. Zagreb O 1923–57. His most successful opera is *Ero s onoga svijeta* (known in English

as *Ero the Joker*, 1935). This is a consciously folk-influenced, eclectic work transferring tried Italian methods to a local setting.

Gotter, Friedrich Wilhelm (*b* Gotha, 3 Sept. 1746; *d* Gotha, 18 Mar. 1797). German librettist, dramatist, and poet. He wrote the text for many Singspiels, but is best remembered for his two Shakespeare treatments, *Romeo und Julie* (1776; the earliest operatic treatment of the Shakespeare play) and *Die Geisterinsel* (an adaptation of *The Tempest*, set by Reichardt, 1798). Highly regarded in its day, the latter represents the apotheosis of the 18th-cent. German libretto and was set by several other composers, including Zumsteeg (1798).

Götterdämmerung. See RING DES NIBELUNGEN, DER.

Gottlieb, Anna (*b* Vienna, 29 Apr. 1774; *d* Vienna, 4 Feb. 1856). Austrian soprano and actress. Daughter of an actor and a singer. Studied Vienna with Mozart. Début Vienna, B, as child actress, 1779. Created Barbarina (*Figaro*), 1786. Joined Schikaneder's Co. at Freihaus T as leading soprano. Mozart admired her professionally and personally; he wrote Pamina for her, which she created and sang often, greatly contributing to the success of *Die Zauberflöte*. From 1792 a successful singer-actress at T in der Leopoldstadt. Her vocal decline began in 1808; she was finally dismissed in 1828, and passed her remaining years in poverty and neglect. At her death she was found holding the fan Mozart gave her in 1790.

'Gott! welch' Dunkel hier'. Florestan's (ten) aria opening Act II of Beethoven's *Fidelio*, in which he laments the silence and darkness of his imprisonment and consoles himself with the knowledge of duty done and then with a vision of Leonore.

Gounod, Charles (*b* Paris, 18 June 1818; *d* Saint-Cloud, 18 Oct. 1893). French composer. Studied Paris with F. Halévy and Le Sueur. He considered taking holy orders, but after early successes with church music he was encouraged by Pauline Viardot to turn to opera, in which field he acknowledged that success for a French composer had to be sought. For Viardot he wrote *Sapho* (1851), a promisingly shapely piece which had only modest success despite Berlioz's praise (it is influenced by Gluck); and he fared no better with a less impressive Grand Opera for her, *La nonne sanglante* (1854). He found his own voice with a witty, alert opéra-comique, *Le médecin malgré lui* (1858), and then produced his masterpiece in *Faust* (1859). Aware in himself of the pull between sacred and profane love, Gounod concentrates on the love story of Faust and Gretchen, and her eventual redemption. This excludes much of Goethe (and the Germans refer to the work as *Margarethe*), but Gounod's delicate touch with character, the elegant lyricism of the vocal writing, not least the melodic verve and charm gave French opera a new sense of identity in the wake of Meyerbeer. The work's success was overwhelming, such that the entrée it gave him to the Opéra obliged him to rewrite it with recitatives and a ballet. *La reine de Saba* (1862) did not clinch this success at the Opéra, and he rediscovered his real touch with the colourful, invigorating *Mireille* (1864) and especially with *Roméo et Juliette* (1867), in which the copious love music is in his most sensuous and captivating vein. A visit to England rekindled his interest in sacred (and sentimental) choral music and extended his popularity (*Faust* was Queen Victoria's favourite opera), though this was tested by his notorious association with Georgina Weldon. Back in France, he returned to writing opera, but had little success with *Cinq-Mars* (1877), or even with *Polyeucte* (1878). However, the example he set was admired and imitated by an important succeeding generation of French composers, chief among them Massenet and Bizet, perhaps also Saint-Saëns and at a remove Fauré, though they did not always escape the characteristic sentimentality into which he easily fell, and by which he is too often remembered above his very real craftsmanship and sense of theatre.

Goyescas. Opera in 3 scenes by Granados, amplified and scored from piano pieces after Goya's paintings; text added by Fernando Periquet. Prem. New York, M, 28 Jan. 1916.

When he hears that Rosario (sop) has been invited to a ball by his rival, the toreador Paquiro (bs), Fernando (ten) decides to go too. He is fatally wounded by Paquiro in a duel, and dies in Rosario's arms.

Graener, Paul (*b* Berlin, 11 Jan. 1872; *d* Salzburg, 13 Nov. 1944). German composer and conductor. Largely self-taught. London, HM, 1896, then returning to teach in Austria and Germany before concentrating on composition in the 1920s. During this decade and the next he had a wide success in Germany with his operas, which had an appeal for their direct and craftsmanlike qualities. These included *Don Juans letzte Abenteuer* (Don Juan's Last Adventure, 1914) and *Der Prinz von Homburg* (1935).

Graf, Herbert (*b* Vienna, 10 Apr. 1904; *d* Geneva, 5 Apr. 1973). Austrian, later US, producer. Son of critic Max Graf. Studied Vienna. Held posts in Münster, Breslau, and Frankfurt. Salzburg 1936 (*Meistersinger* and *Magic Flute* for Toscanini). Philadelphia 1936. New York, M, 1936–60. London, CG, 1958–9. Dir. Zurich O 1960–3; Geneva, Grand T, 1965–73. A producer with a strong sense of tradition, remembered for his encouragement of young talent.

Graham, Colin (*b* Hove, 22 Sept. 1931). English producer and librettist. Studied London. Began producing opera 1954. London, EOG, 1958, dir. of productions 1963–75: staged prems. of Britten's *Noyes Fludde*, church parables, *Owen Wingrave*, *Death in Venice*. London: New OC and Handel OC from 1958, SW and ENO 1961–84 (dir. of productions 1977–82). Staged British prems. of *Cunning Little Vixen* 1961, *War and Peace* 1972, and prems. of Bennett's *Mines of Sulphur* (1965) and *A Penny for a Song* (1967; also librettist) and Josephs's *Rebecca* (O North, 1983). London, CG, 1961–73. English Music T Co. 1975–8. New York, M, 1982 (*Così*). St Louis 1982, prem. of Paulus, *The Postman always Rings Twice* (also librettist). Withdrew from the theatre 1984 to take holy orders. Artistic dir. St Louis 1985: Britten cycle, *Hoffmann* 1986, first US *Oliver, Beauty and the Beast* (1987). New York, M, 1991 (Corigliano's *Ghosts of Versailles*). Has staged over 200 operas, 25 for SW/ENO. One of the most gifted and musical of English producers, especially successful in his handling of the chorus and in his perceptive character realization. His close collaboration with Britten on the three *church parables was crucial in formulating their dramatic convention.

Graham, Susan (*b* Roswell, NM, 23 July 1960). US mezzo-soprano. After study in New York sang with Seattle O (Charlotte in *Werther*). She is an effective exponent of such 'trouser' roles as Massenet's Chérubin (first in US and UK, 1989, 1993), Cherubino, and Ascanio in *Les Troyens*. Sang Meg Page and

Cecilio (*Lucio Silla*), Salzburg 1993. New York, M, 1991. Other roles include Annius (*Clemenza di Tito*) and Dorabella (London, CG, 1995). (R)

Granados, Enrique (*b* Lérida, 27 July 1867; *d* English Channel, 24 Mar. 1916). Spanish composer. Studied Barcelona with Pedrell, also Paris. His zarzuela *Maria del Carmen* (1898) was an immediate success on its Madrid production, and was followed by five more before he revised some of his piano pieces based on Goya to make his masterpiece, *Goyescas* (1916). Though influenced by late 19th-cent. Central European Romantic traditions, the work is essentially Spanish both in atmosphere and in melodic techniques. His son **Edoardo** (*b* Barcelona, 28 July 1894; *d* Madrid, 2 Oct. 1928) composed 23 zarzuelas: the best known were *Bufón y hastelero* and *La Ciudad eterna*.

Grandi, Margherita (*b* Hobart, 4 Oct. 1894). Tasmanian soprano. Studied Paris with E. Calvé, Milan with Russ. Début as 'Djemma Vécla' (anagram of Calvé), Paris, OC (*Werther*). Second début Milan 1932 (Aida), under her married name of Grandi. Milan, S, 1934; Gly. 1939; Verona Arena, 1946; London, CG, 1949; also Egypt, S America, etc. Roles included Donna Anna, Lady Macbeth, Tosca; created title-role of Massenet's *Amadis*, and Diana (Bliss's *Olympians*). A performer in the 'grand' style, with a rich vocal palette. (R)

Grand Inquisitor, The. The Head of the Inquisition (bs) in Verdi's *Don Carlos* and (ten) in Dallapiccola's *Il prigioniero*.

Grand macabre, Le. Opera in 2 acts by Ligeti; text by Michael Meschke and the composer, after Michel de Ghelderode. Prem. Stockholm, Royal Opera, 12 Apr. 1978.

The opera tells of the attempts of Nekrotzar (bar) to destroy the world, having returned from the grave. The court astrologer Astradamor (bs) predicts that a comet arriving at midnight will devastate the earth. However, its arrival passes safely and Nekrotzar allows Prince Go-Go (sop) to lead him back to his grave.

Grand Opera. The term normally given to the genre that flourished in Paris from the early 1820s and remained influential beyond the frontiers of France throughout the 19th cent. and even into the 20th cent. Though it had its roots in the enduring aspect of

French taste that responds to grandeur, which can be found in the works of Lully, and though its immediate ancestors were some of the works of Le Sueur and Spontini as expressions of Napoleonic pride, Grand Opera found its distinctive form in the 1820s. During this decade the painter and set designer Pierre *Cicéri and the lighting expert (and pioneer of photography) Louis *Daguerre contributed their joint influence to a style that became firmly established in the 1830s with the work of the librettist Eugène *Scribe. The effective organizer of these talents and of the contributing composers was the manager of the Opéra, Louis Véron.

Grand Opera typically consisted of a work in four or five acts that included ballet sequences, made functional use of sets (usually historically and geographically accurate) which would be altered for each act, and culminated in a spectacular final scene perhaps involving stage machinery to depict a natural disaster such as fire, earthquake, avalanche, shipwreck, or volcanic eruption. The scenery would involve three-dimensional sets, subtle and ambitious lighting effects, and elaborate stage machinery that could include moving backcloths to give an illusion of movement. A large number of soloists would be employed, closely linked to a chorus that was dramatically and musically essential both as a characteristic entity and for processions, riots, battles, festivals, and other spectacular moments. As well as an enlarged and augmented orchestra, stage bands became common, sometimes using unfamiliar instruments such as saxhorns, tuned bells, organ, anvils, musettes, etc.

Famous and characteristic examples of the genre include Auber's *La muette de Portici* (1828), Halévy's *La Juive* (1835), and Meyerbeer's *Les Huguenots* (1836). Whatever the limitations of the genre, it proved irresistible to composers from several countries. Many 19th-cent. French composers attempted Grand Opera, the greatest of them all, Berlioz, finding acceptance neither with *Benvenuto Cellini* (which failed in 1838) nor with the rejected *Les Troyens* (1856–8). Composers of other nations who also wrote Grand Operas destined for Paris included Rossini (*Guillaume Tell*, 1829), Wagner (*Rienzi*, 1842), Verdi (*Don Carlos*, 1867), and Tchaikovsky (*The Maid of Orleans*, 1881). The influence endures in Verdi's *Aida* (1871); and though *Rienzi* was rejected by Paris, the influence of Grand Opera also survives in Wagner's work with such features as the interrupted wedding in *Lohengrin*, the processions in the *Festwiese* scene in *Die Meistersinger von Nürnberg*, the inundation of the Gibichungs' Hall at the end of *Götterdämmerung*, and the collapse of Klingsor's magic castle in *Parsifal*. That some of the most characteristic devices could still be effective in modern times is shown in some historical operas, especially Russian (e.g. Prokofiev's *Semyon Kotko*, 1940, and Shaporin's *The Decembrists*, 1953).

Grane. Brünnhilde's horse in *The Ring*. Seldom seen on stage since the war, but formerly ridden with effect into the flames by singers including Leider and Lawrence.

Grassi, Cecila. See BACH, JOHANN CHRISTIAN.

Grau, Maurice (*b* Brno, 1849; *d* Paris, 14 Mar. 1907). Czech impresario. In US organized tours of Bernhardt, Offenbach, and Kellogg OC. Joined Abbey for season at New York, M, 1890; director with Abbey and Scheffel 1891–7; director 1897–1903. Director London, CG, 1897–1900.

Graun, Carl Heinrich (*b* Wahrenbrück, 7 May 1703/4; *d* Berlin, 8 Aug. 1759). German tenor and composer. His early development was much influenced by the works of Lotti and Keiser which he encountered at Dresden and by the model of Fux, in the prem. of whose *Costanza e Fortezza* he played as cellist. In 1725 he joined the court at Brunswick as tenor, but his skill as a composer was soon recognized and in 1731 he was appointed Vizekapellmeister under Georg Caspar Schürmann. His first opera, *Sancho und Sinilde*, was produced in 1727 and was followed by four more German operas which in style broadly followed the model of the Hamburg repertory.

From 1740 Graun was Kapellmeister to the Prussian court where the Crown Prince charged him with establishing a top-class Italian opera company. Here, Graun found ample scope to develop his talents. Having trawled Italy for singers, he launched his Berlin career with *Rodelinda* in 1741; the next year his *Cesare e Cleopatra* opened the court opera-house. Over the next 14 years Graun composed nearly 30 dramatic works for Frederick the Great, including pastorales, intermezzos, and opere serie. Together they represent a fundamental shift of taste away from the older-style Hamburg librettos set during his Brunswick years and emphasize the primacy of Italian opera in Germany at this time, despite a certain French influence, in keeping with the taste of the court.

Graun's work dominated the Berlin repertory and represents the pinnacle of Baroque operatic achievement, with its firm emphasis upon the importance of the solo singer. However, in his later works, notably *Silla* (1753) and *Semiramide* (1754), there is some evidence of reform, while *Montezuma* (1755) is unusual for being based on a modern subject and for its avoidance of the stylized da capo aria.

Graupner, Christoph (*b* Kirchberg, 13 Jan. 1683; *d* Darmstadt, 10 May 1760). German composer. Harpsichordist at the Hamburg Opera under Keiser 1707–9 then joined the Darmstadt court. He was elected Kantor of the Thomasschule in Leipzig 1722, but was persuaded not to leave Darmstadt by a rise in his salary, so the position was taken by Bach instead.

The majority of Graupner's ten operas date from his Hamburg years and have something in common with Handel's contemporary early efforts. They include *Dido, Königin von Carthago* (1707) and *Bellerophon* (1708), composed for the wedding of the King of Prussia; in several of these works he was aided by Keiser and he in turn possibly contributed to some of Keiser's works, including *Der Carnaval von Venedig* (1707) and *Die lustige Hochzeit* (1708). At Darmstadt Graupner wrote three operas, including *La costanza vince l'inganno* (Constancy Conquers Deceit, 1715).

Graziani, Francesco (*b* Fermo, 26 Apr. 1828; *d* Fermo, 30 June 1901). Italian baritone. Brother of below. Studied with Cellini. Début Ascoli Piceno 1851 (in *Gemma di Vergy*). Paris, I, 1853–61; London, CG, 1855–80; St Petersburg 1861–71. One of the best Verdi singers of the time, he successfully created Don Carlo (*Forza*), and was a notable Luna, Posa, Amonasro, Germont, and Rigoletto. Possessed a full, mellifluous voice, and a fine technique, but was a limited actor.

Graziani, Lodovico (*b* Fermo, 14 Nov. 1820; *d* Fermo, 15 May 1885). Italian tenor. Brother of above. Studied with Cellini. Début Bologna 1845 (in Cambiaggio's *Don Procopio*). Paris, I, 1851; Venice, F, 1851–3; Milan, S, 1855; Vienna 1860. Created Alfredo (though Verdi, depressed by *Traviata*'s failure, referred to his singing as 'marmoreal' and 'monotonous'), and was a successful Duke of Mantua, Manrico, Riccardo (*Ballo*). His voice was clear and vibrant, but he lacked dramatic gifts.

Great Britain. Most development in opera before the 20th cent. was in England, rather than Wales, Scotland, or Ireland. For much of the 17th cent. the popular form of dramatic musical entertainment was the *masque, much influenced by the French ballet de cour. After *stile rappresentativo had been introduced into England in Dowland's lute songs, it was exploited in a number of masques, notably *Lovers made Men* (1617, music lost) by Ben Jonson and Nicholas Lanier (1588–1666). According to the libretto, it was sung throughout in stile recitativo: if so, this must be seen as the first English opera, though it is doubtful if the music was continuous. Up to 1642 English composers, of whom the most important were Henry Lawes (1596–1662) and his brother William (1602–45), continued to develop a declamatory style, although always in the context of hybrid entertainments, such as masques. In 1639 William *Davenant (1606–68) obtained a royal patent for theatrical performances, but his plans for dramatic music were severely curtailed following the closure of the theatres during the Protectorate (1653–60). Masques continued to be produced in private: the most important was Shirley's *Cupid and Death* (1653), with music by Matthew *Locke (1621/2–77) and Christopher Gibbons (1615–76).

In 1656 Davenant staged *The Siege of Rhodes*, a 'Representation by the Art of Perspective in Scenes, and the Story Sung in Recitative Music', given at Rutland House with music (lost) by composers including Lawes and Locke. Davenant's elaborate description was an obvious attempt to circumvent the Puritan ban on theatrical performance: from the libretto it is clear that *The Siege of Rhodes* has the best claim to be the first English opera. Ten performances were given: these are notable for including the first appearance of a woman on the stage in England. At the Restoration in 1660 interest in spoken drama was so strongly renewed that it was impossible for opera to make any impact. However, several important dramatic works featuring extensive use of music were seen during this period: in 1674 *Ariadne* by Louis Grabu (*fl.* 1665–94), an adaptation of the Cambert–Perrin collaboration, was performed for the marriage of the Duke of York, the year after Locke's music to Shadwell's *Psyche* had been given. Both of these works are eclipsed by *Venus and Adonis* (*c.*1682) which, although described by its composer John *Blow (1649–1708) as a masque, contains sufficiently continuous music to qualify as a true opera.

This served as the model for English opera's first masterpiece, *Dido and Aeneas* (?1685 or earlier) by Henry *Purcell (1659–95). Written for a girl's school, it is of miniature proportions and demonstrates the debt to both the French and Italian styles which was apparent in all English music of this period. Its modern fame has given it exaggerated historical importance: better known at the time was Purcell's incidental stage music, some of which, notably that for Dryden's *King Arthur* (1691), closely approaches authentic opera and is indeed known as *semi-opera. After Purcell's untimely death, Italian opera seria overtook London. Some early works set English translations of Italian texts, such as *Arsinoe, Queen of Cyprus* by Thomas Clayton (*c.*1665–*c.*1725), who later collaborated with Joseph Addison on *Rosamond* (1707). Productions of the pastoral *Gli amori d'Ergasto* (1705) (in Italian) by Jakob Greber (?–1731), *Il trionfo di Camilla* (1706) by Antonio Maria Bononcini (1677–1726) (in English, but the first Italian work to be performed in its entirety) and of *Pirro e Demetrio* (1708) by Alessandro Scarlatti (1660–1725) (in a mixture of English and Italian) prepared the way for the first performances of full-scale operas sung entirely in Italian, *Idaspe fedele* (1710) by Francesco Mancini and *Almahide* (1710) by Giovanni Bononcini (1670–1747). The first castrato appeared in London in 1706 in *Thomyris* (music adapted from Bononcini and Scarlatti), establishing a vogue which was fully exploited after the arrival of George Frideric *Handel (1685–1759) in 1710, who, beginning with *Rinaldo* (1711), produced almost 40 operas (including adaptations) for London over 30 years.

The first effective counter to the Italian domination came with *The *Beggar's Opera* (1728); its popularity triggered off a series of *ballad operas, including *The Devil to Pay* (1731) (which in turn played an important part in the growth of *Singspiel) and led to the eventual downfall of opera seria. In 1760 *Thomas and Sally* by Thomas Arne (1710–78) made use of modern characters in an all-sung opera, but his popular *Artaxerxes* (1762) did not find successors. For many years English operas, even strong examples such as *Lionel and Clarissa* (1768) by Charles *Dibdin (1745–1814) and *The Duenna* (1775) by Thomas *Linley sen. (1733–95) and jun. (1756–78), were with spoken dialogue and close to *pasticcio. But during the 18th cent. the London theatres continued to attract such Italian musicians as Gioacchino Cocchi (*c*.1715–1804), Tommaso Giordano (*c*.1733–1806), Antonio Sacchini (1730–86), Ferdinand Bertoni (1752–1813), and Francesco Bianchi (*c*.1720–*c*.1788). The most successful of all foreign composers was probably Johann Christian *Bach (1735–82), who from his arrival in London in 1762 dominated the stage with his elegant opere serie in the galant style until the new vogue for opera buffa made popular the works of Domenico Cimarosa (1749–1801), Baldassare Galuppi (1706–85), and Niccolò Piccinni (1728–1800). Even the first complete performance of a French opera in London, Grétry's *Zémire et Azor* in 1779, was given in Italian.

By the early 19th cent. the Italian domination (especially that of Rossini) was complete, while English opera was unable to escape from pasticcio, with plot, dialogue, scenery, and stage machinery taking precedence over music. One of the most successful composers of the day was Henry *Bishop (1786–1855), who wrote dramatic works in every vein. These conditions dismayed Carl Maria von Weber (1786–1826) when he accepted the commission for *Oberon* (1826), which is scarred by them but whose quality helped to pave the way for English Romantic opera. The first significant work in the genre was *The Mountain Sylph* (1834) by John *Barnett (1802–90). This was followed by *The Siege of Rochelle* (1835) by Michael *Balfe (1808–70): of his 30 operas, the most successful was *The Bohemian Girl* (1843). Another classic of the period was *Maritana* (1845) by Vincent *Wallace (1812–65). Also significant was Edward *Loder (1813–65), whose *Raymond and Agnes* (1855) shows an ability to build up continuous forms; and Julius *Benedict (1804–85) won a success with *The Lily of Killarney* (1862). Nevertheless, the most successful aspects of these works tended to be German- or French-influenced.

A more independent form of nationalist opera came with *Shamus O'Brien* (1896) by Charles *Stanford (1852–1924). Other works by Frederic Cowen (1852–1935) and Alexander Mackenzie (1847–1935) were staged;

but the most popular figure of the latter years of the century, and enduringly in the 20th cent., was Arthur *Sullivan (1842–1900), who drew upon much in recent operatic history to fertilize his clever, Romantic idiom in the famous series of *Savoy Operas (really operettas). A serious attempt to transfer the tried methods of German opera to the stage was made by Ethel *Smyth (1858–1944); and these also affect the operas of Frederick *Delius (1862–1934). Belated attempts at English Wagnerian opera were made by Rutland *Boughton (1878–1960) and Joseph *Holbrooke (1878–1958).

However, a new attempt to discover a more authentic English idiom was made, by way of folk-song and Tudor and Elizabethan music, by Gustav *Holst (1874–1934) and Ralph *Vaughan Williams (1872–1958). Some of Holst's early operas were heavily influenced by Wagner, but with *Savitri* (1908, prem. 1916) he discovered an original vein and in particular an English musical declamation. Vaughan Williams wrote an English national folk opera in *Hugh the Drover* (1911–14, prem. 1924); and both composers also wrote comedies. If these works revealed the belated state of English opera's growth in European terms, they served to open up new vistas. Without them, the achievement of Benjamin *Britten (1913–76) in *Peter Grimes* (1945) might have been harder. With this, English opera found new maturity; and its success encouraged Britten himself, and his seniors including William *Walton (1902–83), Lennox *Berkeley (1903–89), and especially the five operas of Michael *Tippett (*b* 1905). The following generation included Iain *Hamilton (*b* 1922), Thea *Musgrave (*b* 1928), Alexander *Goehr (*b* 1932), Peter Maxwell *Davies (*b* 1934), and Harrison *Birtwistle (*b* 1934). Other composers who have written successful operas include Nicholas *Maw (*b* 1935), Robin *Holloway (*b* 1934), Richard Rodney *Bennett (*b* 1936), Gordon *Crosse (*b* 1937), Judith *Weir (*b* 1954), Robert Saxton (*b* 1953), Nigel *Osborne (*b* 1948), John *Casken (*b* 1949), Oliver *Knussen (*b* 1952) and Mark Anthony Turnage (*b* 1960). Though continuing economic problems have led composers to explore chamber opera or music theatre, the last half-century has seen Britain develop an operatic life creatively as rich as any in the world; and it is now the rule rather than the exception for a composer to write opera. See also ALDEBURGH, ALMEIDA THEATRE, BIRMINGHAM,

BRITISH BROADCASTING CORPORATION, BUXTON, CAM-
BRIDGE, CARL ROSA OPERA COMPANY, EDINBURGH,
ENGLISH MUSIC THEATRE COMPANY, GLASGOW, GLYN-
DEBOURNE, HANDEL OPERA SOCIETY, KENT OPERA, LEEDS,
LIVERPOOL, LONDON, MANCHESTER, MOODY, OPERA
NORTH, OXFORD, SCOTTISH OPERA, WELSH NATIONAL
OPERA.

Gregor, Bohumil (b Prague, 14 July 1926).
Czech conductor. Studied Prague with
Klíma. Prague, 5th May O, 1947. Brno O 1949–
51; Music dir. Ostrava O 1958–62; Prague, N,
1962, touring with Co. to Edinburgh in first
British *From the House of the Dead*; Royal
Swedish O 1966–9; Hamburg 1969–72; S
Francisco from 1969. Specialist in Janáček;
repertory also incl. Verdi's *Otello*, *Bartered
Bride*, *Salome*, and prems. of works by Trojan,
Kašlik, Pauer, and Kelemen. (R)

Gregor, Joseph (b Czernowitz (Černovice),
26 Oct. 1888; d Vienna, 12 Oct. 1960). Austrian librettist and writer. His extensive literary activity included the writing of
librettos for Strauss's *Friedenstag*, *Daphne*, and
Die Liebe der Danae.

Greindl, Josef (b Munich, 23 Dec. 1912; d
Vienna, 16 Apr. 1993). German bass. Studied
Munich with Bender and Bahr-Mildenburg.
Début Krefeld 1936 (Hunding). Berlin from
1942, first S, then SO. Bayreuth 1943, 1951–
70. New York, M, 1952–3. London, CG, 1963.
Also Italy, US, S America. Repertory included
Don Alfonso, Sarastro, Hagen, Wanderer,
Sachs, Boris, Ochs. A versatile and
accomplished artist with a strong, warm
tone. (R)

Gremin. Prince Gremin (bs), Tatyana's
husband, in Tchaikovsky's *Eugene Onegin*.

Gretel. Hänsel's sister (sop) in Humperdinck's *Hänsel und Gretel*.

Grétry, André-Ernest-Modeste (b Liège, ?8
(bapt. 11) Feb. 1741; d Montmorency, 24 Sept.
1813). French composer of Walloon origin.
Studied Liège with Moreau. While further
studying in Rome, he had a success with a
pair of intermezzos, *La vendemmiatrice* (1765,
lost), but his aim was Paris and opéra-
comique, which already he conceived of as
serious in content. He arrived there in 1767,
and soon had a success with *Le Huron* (1768),
then the very popular *Lucile* (1769) and *Le
tableau parlant* (1769), in which his Italian-
trained melodic charm was placed at the
service of good declamation (which he had
discussed with Voltaire) and elegant taste.

He consolidated his public following
(which he carefully cultivated) in a group of
works in which, if there was greater variety
than range, the music expressed different
settings and emotional situations with
unfailing grace. This period is concluded
with an outstanding example, *Zémire et Azor*
(1771), a 'Beauty and the Beast' opera of pre-
Romantic sensibility in which the touching
quality of the story is never allowed to
deteriorate into sentimentality. The librettist, as in earlier works, was Marmontel,
with whom relations gradually declined
despite his contribution to a group of four
striking and diverse works, *Le magnifique*
(1773), *La rosière de Salency* (1773), *La fausse
magie* (1775), and *Les mariages Samnites* (1776).
A new collaborator was Thomas d'Hèle
(Hales), who provided him with texts for the
witty *Le jugement de Midas* (1778) and the Italianate *Les événements imprévues* (1779); on
D'Hèle's death he turned to Sedaine for a
more ambitious, Romantic work, *Aucassin et
Nicolette* (1779). *Andromaque* (1780) found him
over-stretched at the Opéra with a great
tragic subject; he returned to his own métier
with *Colinette à la cour* (1782), and conquered
the Opéra on his own terms. He later confirmed this with *La caravane du Caire* (1783),
one of his greatest triumphs, and *Panurge
dans l'île des lanternes* (1785).

The opera which followed, *Richard Cœur-de-
Lion* (1784), was perhaps Grétry's masterpiece. Though there are suggestions of
functional repetition of music in his earlier
operas, it has entered history as a work
which set an example in its use of a recurring
melody to unify both story and score. This
use of the air 'Une fièvre brulante' has been
cited as an early instance of *reminiscence
motive, for which it may have set an example
but from which, for all its dramatic skill, it
differs in that it is not worked in any symphonic manner. There followed a series of
failures, from which the excellent *Raoul
Barbe-bleue* (1789) stands out. Family difficulties may have been partly responsible; the
Revolution further unsettled, without
destroying, his position. He had some
success with *Pierre le Grand* (1790), also with
Guillaume Tell (1791), which includes some
attractive 'Swiss' music. But he did not effectively return to the stage, though he continued to write occasional operas and to
devote himself to essays and his very interesting memoirs.

Grétry's quality rests chiefly on his skill

and taste in using the Italian models he had learnt in youth to express French qualities of taste, sensibility, and poetic eloquence. His clarity of thought accorded well with French expectations, as did his ability to discover the latent emotion in an apparently conventional situation. If his orchestration was generally slim, it served to present the characters sympathetically and to their best advantage; and he sought to relate the overture to the succeeding opera (strikingly in *Le magnifique*) and to write descriptive dramatic entr'actes. Moreover, without laying claim to reform, he was an ambitious innovator in his theoretical writings, looking forward to an ideal theatre with no boxes and a covered orchestra. He narrowed the old division between tragedy and comedy in opera by his perceptive and truthful treatment of human situations. Each of his best works has its distinct individuality; seen as a whole, his œuvre is an essential contribution to the maturity of opéra-comique.

Grieg, Edvard (*b* Bergen, 15 June 1843; *d* Bergen, 4 Sept. 1907). Norwegian composer. Seven numbers survive of his sole attempt at opera, *Olav Trygvason* (1873).

Grisar, Albert (*b* Antwerp, 26 Dec. 1808; *d* Asnières, 15 June 1869). Belgian composer. Studied Paris with Rejcha; then, after success with his first opera, *Le mariage impossible* (1833), production of *Sarah* (1836) in Paris and six more operas, further study with Mercadante in Naples. Returning to Paris, he produced a number of successful light works, including *Gille ravisseur* (1848) and *Les amours du diable* (1853). These are melodically lively and possess a quick ear for comedy, being influenced by Grétry and Boieldieu and anticipating some of the features of Hervé, Lecocq, and occasionally even Offenbach.

Grisélidis. Opera in a prologue and 2 acts by Massenet; text by Silvestre and Morand. Prem. Paris, OC, 20 Nov. 1901.

Alain (ten) loves Grisélidis (sop), wife of the Marquis (bar). The Devil (bs) tries to persuade her of her husband's infidelity and to accept Alain. She resists, and he takes her child, which is eventually retrieved by the Marquis.

Grishka Kuterma. A drunkard (ten) in Rimsky-Korsakov's *The Invisible City of Kitezh*.

Grisi, Giuditta (*b* Milan, 28 July 1805; *d* Robecco, 1 May 1840). Italian mezzo-soprano, sister of below, and cousin of the famous dancer **Carlotta Grisi**. Studied Milan with her aunt, Grassini, and at Milan Cons. Début Vienna 1826 (Faliero, *Bianca e Faliero*). Appeared throughout Italy, particularly in operas by Bellini, who wrote the part of Romeo for her in *I Capuleti e i Montecchi*. Also sang in London, Paris, Madrid. Her elegant stage presence and pure, agile voice brought her success, but singing soprano roles (e.g. Norma) led to difficulties. She retired in 1838.

Grisi, Giulia (*b* Milan, 28 July 1811; *d* Berlin, 29 Nov. 1869). Italian soprano, sister of above. Studied Bologna with Giacomelli, Milan with Marliani, and with her sister, and aunt (Grassini). Début Bologna 1828 (in Rossini's *Zelmira*). Milan, S, 1831–2, creating Adalgisa (written for her) in *Norma*. Unhappy with conditions there, she fled to Paris, making her début with Rossini's help at Paris, I, 1832, as Semiramide. Sang there until 1846, and in 1857. London, H (later HM) 1834–46 and CG 1847–61. St Petersburg, 1849; US tour, 1854–5; Madrid 1859. Made several farewells from 1854–66. Created Elvira (*Puritani*), when according to Bellini 'she sang and acted like an angel'; Elena (*Marin Faliero*); Norina (*Don Pasquale*). Her famous tenor partners were Rubini, and Mario, with whom she had a lasting relationship, but was unable to marry. Beautiful and gifted, she was idolized by the public, including the young Queen Victoria; her well-controlled voice was remarkably even, rich, and flexible, and her dramatic ability convincing (though Chorley comments on 'a fierceness . . . which impairs her efforts'). Famous as Anna Bolena, Lucrezia Borgia, Norma, Valentine, Alice (*Robert le diable*), Leonora (*Trovatore*); but an unsuccessful Fidès, trying to eclipse its creator, Viardot.

Grist, Reri (*b* New York, 29 Feb. 1932). US soprano. Studied New York with Gelda. Début S Fe 1959 (Adèle and Blonde). Zurich 1961–4; London, CG, from 1962; New York, M, 1966; also Vienna; Salzburg; Gly.; Milan, S. Roles include Susanna, Blonde, Zerbinetta, Queen of Shemakha. A lively artist with a light, sweet tone. (R)

Grob-Prandl, Gertrud (*b* Vienna, 11 Nov. 1917). Austrian soprano. Studied Vienna with Burian. Début Vienna, V, 1938 (Santuzza). Zurich 1946–7; Vienna, S, 1948–

64; London, CG, from 1951; also Milan, S; Berlin; S America; etc. A notable Brünnhilde, Isolde, and Turandot, with a full, robust voice, and great authority on stage. (R)

'Grossmächtige Prinzessin'. Zerbinetta's (sop) recitative and aria in Strauss's *Ariadne auf Naxos*, in which she tries to convert Ariadne to her fickle view of love. One of the most difficult coloratura arias in opera.

Groves, (Sir) **Charles** (*b* London, 10 Mar. 1915; *d* London, 20 June 1992). English conductor. Studied London. Chorus-master BBC O Unit 1937–9; cond. BBC Northern Orch. 1945–51, giving studio performances of operas incl. Holst's *The Perfect Fool* and Dohnányi's *The Tenor*. Music dir. WNO 1961–3, conducting first British *Battaglia di Legnano*, among some other distinguished Verdi performances. London, SW/ENO, as guest from 1971, music director 1977–9; cond. prem. of Crosse's *Story of Vasco* (1974), and among other works *Euryanthe* (1977) and *Due Foscari* (1978). (R)

Gruberová, Edita (*b* Bratislava, 23 Dec. 1946). Slovak soprano. Studied Prague with Medvecká, Vienna with Boesch. Début Bratislava 1968 (Rosina). Vienna, S, from 1970; Salzburg 1974–81; Gly. 1973; New York, M, from 1977; also London, CG; Milan, S; Munich; etc. Slovak début as Bellini's Giulietta 1984. An excellent coloratura singer, admired as Constanze, Queen of the Night, Lucia, Amina, Gilda, Violetta, Zerbinetta. (R)

Gruhn, Nora. See GRÜNEBAUM, HERMANN.

Grümmer, Elisabeth (*b* Niederjeutz, 31 Mar. 1911; *d* Berlin, 6 Nov. 1986). German soprano. Originally an actress. Operatic début Aachen 1940 (First Flowermaiden). Berlin, SO, from 1946; London, CG, from 1950; Gly. 1954; Bayreuth 1957–61; New York, M, 1967–79; also Paris, O; Vienna; Buenos Aires; etc. Retired 1972. An outstanding Countess (*Figaro*), Pamina, Eva, Marschallin. A musical and aristocratic artist with a fresh, true voice, and an unaffected style. (R)

Grunebaum, Hermann (*b* Giessen, 8 Jan. 1872; *d* Chipstead, 5 Apr. 1954). German, later English, conductor. Studied Frankfurt with Humperdinck, and Berlin. Début Koblenz 1893. Chorus-master London, CG, 1907–33: assisted Richter with English *Ring*, 1908–9. With T. C. Fairbairn, founded

London School of O, cond. prem. of Holst's *Savitri*, 1916. Dir. of opera class London, RCM, 1924–46, incl. complete student *Parsifal* (1926, with Boult). His daughter **Nora Gruhn** (*b* 6 Mar. 1905) studied Munich and sang at London, CG 1929–32 and SW 1932–6, 1945–8.

Guadagni, Gaetano (*b* ? 11 Dec. 1729; *d* Padua, Nov. 1792). Italian contralto, later soprano, castrato. Originally untrained. Venice, T San Moisè, 1746. London, H, 1748–9, member of Italian burletta company. Handel engaged him to sing in *Samson* and *Messiah*, and composed Didimus (*Theodora*) for him. Lisbon 1754, when he studied with Gizziello; then Paris, and London again 1755, when he performed in *The Fairies* and was trained by Garrick. Venice 1757–8; Vienna 1762–4, singing in works by Hasse and Traetta, and creating the title-roles in Gluck's *Orfeo* and *Telemaco*. London, H, 1770 and 1771 (Orfeo). Italy, Munich, Potsdam, until 1776 when he retired to Padua, singing for several years at the Basilica di Sant'Antonio. Also produced operas on a puppet stage at home, himself (now a soprano) singing the part of Orfeo. Unusual in his refusal to ornament gratuitously, he was an intelligent singer entirely to Gluck's taste. Burney admired him as an actor 'who had no equal on any stage in Europe', and for his 'impassioned and exquisite' singing. However, his artistic pride (he demanded respect for the music as well as for himself) was not appreciated in his own time. His sister **Lavinia-Maria** (*b* Lodi, 21 Dec. 1735; *d* Padua, *c*.1790) was a soprano who sang in London 1756–74 with her husband Felice Alessandri.

Gudehus, Heinrich (*b* Altenhagen, 30 Mar. 1845; *d* Dresden, 9 Oct. 1909). German tenor. Studied Brunswick with M. Schnorr von Carolsfeld, Berlin with Engel. Début Berlin, 1871 (Nadori, *Jessonda*). Dresden 1880–90; Bayreuth 1882, 1886, 1888 (one of the first Parsifals, and considered a potentially ideal Tristan by the composer); London, CG, 1884; New York, M, 1890; Berlin until retirement in 1896. Contributed to the newly emerging Wagner tradition, as Tannhäuser, Walther, Siegfried, Tristan, etc. Essentially a lyric tenor, temperamentally at his best in serious roles.

Gueden, Hilde (*b* Vienna, 15 Sept. 1915; *d* Klosterneuburg, 17 Sept. 1988). Austrian soprano. Studied Vienna with Wetzelsberger.

Début Vienna 1939 (in Stolz's operetta *Servus servus*). Munich 1941. Vienna, S, from 1947; London, CG, 1947; New York, M, 1950–60. Repertory included Zerlina, Gilda, Zerbinetta, Sophie (at composer's suggestion), Anne Trulove. A sensitive singer and actress, with a light, clear voice. (R)

Guerre des Bouffons (Fr: 'War of the Bouffons'; Ger, *Buffonistenstreit*). The controversy that from 1752 to 1754 divided musical Paris into two parties, those upholding French serious opera (Lully, Rameau, Destouches, etc.) and those upholding Italian opera buffa (Pergolesi, etc.). It was sparked off by a performance in 1752 of Pergolesi's *La serva padrona* given by Eustache Bambini's troupe of Italian comic actors (*bouffons*) and quickly divided Parisian literati. Those supporting the Italian cause included Rousseau, whose *Le devin du village* (1752) sought to utilize the best features of Italian opera buffa for the setting of a French libretto: it was one of the most important forerunners of *opéra-comique.

Though serious opera finally emerged triumphant, the imitation by French musicians of the Italian buffo style aided the evolution of the *comédie mêlée d'ariettes. The episode is sometimes also referred to as the **Querelle des Bouffons** or the **Guerre des Coins** ('War of the Corners'), a reference to the habit of the supporters of French opera gathering by the King's box, while their opponents gathered by the Queen's.

Gueymard, Louis (*b* Chapponay, 17 Aug. 1822; *d* Corbeil, July 1880). French tenor. Début Lyons 1845. Paris, O, 1848–68. Sang the repertory of Nourrit and Duprez, and created several roles, including Henri (*Vêpres siciliennes*), Jonas (*Prophète*), and Adoniram (Gounod's *La reine de Saba*). London, CG, 1852. Verdi comments on his 'fine voice'. His wife **Pauline Lauters-Gueymard** (*b* Brussels, 1 Dec. 1834; *d* *c.*1876) was a soprano. Début Paris, L, 1854; O, 1857–76. Her wide range enabled her to sing Donna Elvira, Fidès, Leonora (French *Trovatore*); she created Eboli (necessitating many changes from Verdi's original part for a low mez), the Queen (*Hamlet*), and Balkis (*Reine de Saba*). An eminent singer of her time.

Guglielmi, Pietro Alessandro (*b* Massa, 9 Dec. 1728; *d* Rome, 18 Nov. 1804). Italian composer. His first opera was *Lo solachianello 'mbroglione* (1757): this was followed by a string

of popular successes, including *Il ratto della sposa* (1765) and *La sposa fedele* (1767). Engaged at London, H, 1767, where he spent five years as conductor and composer. In 1772 he returned to Italy, where he enjoyed renewed favour with *La virtuosa in Mergellina* (1785), *La pastorella nobile* (1788), and *La bella pescatrice* (1789).

Guglielmi composed about 100 operas, approximately two-thirds of them comic. Although less distinctive or influential than Paisiello's, they earned him fame throughout Europe, probably on account of what Burney called his 'Neapolitan fire'. His pedestrian opere serie are of little significance.

Guglielmo. A young officer (bar), lover of Fiordiligi, in Mozart's *Così fan tutte*.

Guglielmo Ratcliff. Opera in 4 acts by Mascagni; text by Andrea Maffei, a translation of Heine's tragedy (1822). Prem. Milan, S, 16 Feb. 1895.

William Ratcliff (ten) is haunted by the visions of a man and a woman; in Maria (sop), daughter of MacGregor (bs), he finds the realization of the woman, and swears to kill anyone who tries to marry her; Count Douglas (bar) so intends, and William challenges him to a duel, but Douglas spares his life. Maria prepares for her marriage to Douglas and learns from her nurse Margherita (mez) that her mother and William's father had once been in love but were prevented from marrying; she had, instead, married MacGregor, who had then killed William's father. William, himself wounded, bursts into Maria's room, kills her and then dies. When Douglas sees the two bodies he kills himself.

Gui, Vittorio (*b* Rome, 14 Sept. 1885; *d* Florence, 17 Oct. 1975). Italian conductor and composer. Studied Rome with Settacioli and Falchi. Début Rome, Ad., 1907 (*Gioconda*). Milan, S, 1923–5 (at Toscanini's invitation), 1932–4. Founded the T di Torino 1925. Established Florence Orch. Stabile 1928, from which developed the Florence Maggio Musicale, 1933. Here he cond. a wide and enterprising repertory, and gave the festival a strong and attractive character. Salzburg 1933. London, CG, 1938–9, 1952; Gly. 1952–65, where he conducted many distinguished performances. One of the finest Italian conductors of Gluck, Mozart, and Rossini, and responsible for revivals of a number of neglected operas in Italy. His own works include an opera, *Fata malerba* (Turin 1927). (R)

Guillaume Tell (William Tell). Opera in 4 acts by Rossini; text by Étienne de Jouy, Hippolyte Bis, and Armand Marrast, after Schiller's dramatic version (1804) of the legend first set down in a ballad (before 1474). Prem. Paris, O, 3 Aug. 1829.

Switzerland, 1307. Resistance to the tyranny of the Austrian Gessler (bar) is led by the patriot Guillaume Tell (bar); he has the support of the elderly Melcthal (bs), whose son Arnold (ten) loves the Austrian Princess Mathilde (sop). Tell saves Leuthold (bar), pursued by the Austrians, and escapes with him in a boat without being recognized.

Mathilde and Arnold declare their love, interrupted by Tell with news of Melcthal's death; Arnold agrees to join the conspirators, who now gather from different cantons.

Arnold and Mathilde realize that they must part. In the main square of Altdorf, Gessler demands obeisance to his hat. Tell alone refuses, and is condemned to shoot an apple from the head of his son Jemmy (sop). He succeeds but, when he reveals that a second bolt was reserved for Gessler in case of failure, he is arrested. Mathilde takes Jemmy into her care as Tell is removed to the Castle of Küssnacht in the middle of the Lake of Lucerne.

At the edge of the lake, Arnold rouses his companions to action and leads them into the fight. Jemmy is reunited by Mathilde to his mother Hedwig (mez), then lights a beacon to signal the start of the uprising. Tell's boat is driven ashore, and he shoots Gessler. Victory is assured, and the people hymn their new-won liberty.

Guiraud, Ernest (*b* New Orleans, 23 June 1837; *d* Paris, 6 May 1892). French composer. Studied Paris with Marmontel and Halévy, where he was a classmate of his lifelong friend Bizet. He is best known (and often abused) for the recitatives he added to *Carmen*, and for his completion of the orchestration of Offenbach's *Les contes d'Hoffmann*. Most of his operas, which include *Le Kobold* (1870) and *Madame Turlupin* (1872), are in light vein; the exception is *Frédégonde* (1895), a more grandiose work which was completed after his death by Saint-Saëns and orchestrated by his pupil Dukas. His *Traité pratique de l'instrumentation* (1892) was the first French

work of its kind to evaluate Wagner's scores.

Gulbranson, Ellen (*b* Stockholm, 4 Mar. 1863; *d* Oslo, 2 Jan. 1947). Swedish soprano. Studied Paris with M. and B. Marchesi. Début Stockholm 1889 (Amneris). Bayreuth 1896, and from 1897 to 1914 its only Brünnhilde; also sang Kundry. London, CG, 1900, 1907; also Berlin, Vienna, St Petersburg. Retired 1915. A powerful, solid singer with fine declamation, much admired by Melba. (R)

Guleghina, Maria (*b* Odessa, 9 Aug. 1959). Russian soprano. Studied Odessa and sang with the Minsk O from 1984: Rosina, Tatyana, Elisabeth de Valois. Milan, S, 1987 (Amelia). A versatile performer in the dramatic repertory, she has been successful as Lisa (*Queen of Spades*) with the Kirov O; Vienna, S, and New York, M, 1990–1 (Maddalena, Tosca). Other roles incl. Leonora in *Oberto* (Edinburgh 1993), Aida, Odabella, Santuzza. (R)

Gunsbourg, Raoul (*b* Bucharest, 25 Dec. 1859; *d* Monte Carlo, 31 May 1955). French composer and impresario of Romanian birth. After managing opera in Russia (from 1881) and in Lille (1888–9) and Nice (1889–91), became dir. of the Monte Carlo O in 1893, a position he held until 1951. Under his long and brilliant régime Monte Carlo saw the prems. of many important works, especially by Massenet, and the French prems. of many more. An inventive and forceful producer, he was also a cavalier adapter, initiating his régime with his stage version of Berlioz's *La damnation de Faust*, also transposing operatic roles to different voices (e.g. Almaviva in *Figaro* for tenor) and in many other ways altering original texts. A gifted discoverer of talent, he was among the first to promote Caruso and Shalyapin.

Gunther. The Lord of the Gibichungs (bar), Gutrune's brother and Hagen's half-brother, in Wagner's *Götterdämmerung*.

Guntram. Opera in 3 acts by Richard Strauss; text by the composer. Prem. Weimar 10 May 1894.

Germany, 13th cent. Guntram (ten) is sent by the Holy Society of Peace, a secret society of Minnesingers, to free the people under the oppressive rule of Duke Robert (bs). He saves the Duke's wife, Freihild (sop), from suicide and falls in love with her. Guntram takes part in a singing competition and, when his song is seen as threatening by the Duke, is challenged to a duel. Guntram torments himself with the thought that he wished the death of Freihild's husband and refuses to seek the judgement of the guild, punishing himself with a life of solitude instead.

Gura, Eugen (*b* nr. Žatec, 8 Nov. 1842; *d* Aufkirchen, 26 Aug. 1906). German baritone. Studied Munich with Herger. Début Munich 1865 (in Lortzing's *Der Waffenschmied*). Leipzig from 1870; here his Tristan d'Acunha (*Jessonda*) in 1875 impressed Wagner, who found his portrayal 'noble', and 'of a moving simplicity'. Bayreuth 1876 (Donner, and created Gunther, in first complete *Ring*) until 1892. London, DL, 1882; Munich 1882–96, when he retired. Possessing a warm tone and dramatic power, he was one of the best of the first generation of Wagner singers, especially moving as Sachs and Wotan. Also sang Lysiart, Falstaff, Iago (Verdi), Leporello. (R) His son **Hermann Gura** (1870–1944) was a baritone and producer. Début Weimar 1890 (Dutchman). Dir. Berlin, K, 1911. Prod. (and sang Faninal in) first London *Rosenkavalier*, 1913.

Guridi, Jesús (*b* Vitoria, 25 Sept. 1886; *d* Madrid, 7 Apr. 1961). Spanish composer. Studied Paris with Sérieyx and D'Indy. His early success with his Basque opera *Mirentxu* (1910) was followed by the popular *Amaya* (1920) and, his greatest triumph, *El Caserio* (1928). Other zarzuelas and sainetes confirmed his position as one of the most successful composers of Basque opera.

Gurlitt, Manfred (*b* Berlin, 6 Sept. 1890; *d* Tokyo, 29 Apr. 1973). German composer and conductor. Studied Berlin with Humperdinck and Kaun. After various appointments, music dir. Bremen 1914; Berlin 1924. Moved in 1939 to Japan, where he did much to make German opera known. His operas include a setting of *Wozzeck* (1926), made at about the same time as Berg's and independently successful in its day.

Gurnemanz. The veteran knight of the Grail (bs) in Wagner's *Parsifal*.

Gustafson, Nancy (*b* Evanston, IL, 27 June 1956). US soprano. Studied S Francisco. S Francisco (Freia); Colorado, Minnesota, S Fe, Edmonton; Paris, 1984; London CG, Gly., and Chicago, 1988; Scottish O 1989. Possesses a

radiant tone and a highly appealing stage personality. Roles incl. Elettra, Donna Elvira, Violetta, Marguerite, Leïla, Antonia, Amelia, Rosalinde, Rusalka, Káťa Kabanová. (R)

Gustavus III. The King of Sweden (ten) in the 'Swedish' version of Verdi's *Un ballo in maschera*.

Gutheil-Schoder, Marie (*b* Weimar, 16 Feb. 1874; *d* Weimar, 4 Oct. 1935). German soprano. Studied Weimar with Naumann-Gungl. Début Weimar 1891 (First Lady). Engaged by Mahler (who called her 'a musical genius') for Vienna, 1900; remained until 1926. London, CG, 1913; also Berlin, Munich, Dresden, etc. Though attacked by Viennese critics as 'the singer without a voice', her extraordinary dramatic gifts and artistry brought her great success. Roles included Cherubino, Donna Elvira, Carmen, Isolde, Nedda, Elektra, Octavian, and the Woman in *Erwartung*, which she created in 1924. Taught Risë Stevens. (R)

Guthrie, (Sir) **Tyrone** (*b* Tunbridge Wells, 2 July 1900; *d* Newbliss, 15 May 1971). English producer. Connected with Old Vic from 1933; dir. London, SW, 1941, prod. *Figaro*. When Joan Cross became dir. of opera, he remained dir. of the Vic-Wells, also prod. *Bohème*, *Traviata*, *Carmen*. London, CG: *Peter Grimes* 1946, *Traviata* 1948. New York, M: *Carmen* 1952, *Traviata* 1957. A gifted man of the theatre, expert at creating natural stage movement though sometimes at the expense of the music.

Gutrune. Gunther's sister (sop), and Hagen's half-sister in Wagner's *Götterdämmerung*.

Gwendoline. Opera in 2 acts by Chabrier; text by Catulle Mendès. Prem. Brussels, M, 10 Apr. 1886.

The English coast, 8th cent. The Viking King Harald (ten) loves Gwendoline (sop), daughter of his prisoner, the Saxon Armel (ten), who pretends to consent to their marriage but arranges for her to kill Harald. She refuses, and commits suicide when Harald dies.

Gye, Frederick (*b* London, 1809; *d* Dytchley Park, 4 Dec. 1878). English impresario. Manager London, CG, 1849–77. Introduced many operas to London, especially Verdi and Wagner, as well as some of the great singers of the day, including Patti, Lucca, Tamberlik,

Faure, Maurel, and Albani, who married his son **Ernest** (manager CG 1879–85).

Gyrowetz, Adalbert (orig. Vojtěch Matyáš Jirovec) (b České Budějovice, 20 Feb. 1763; d Vienna, 19 Mar. 1850). Austrian composer of Bohemian origin. After early successes in Vienna, Naples, and Paris, Gyrowetz arrived in London in 1789, where he was given a welcome scarcely less rapturous than that accorded Haydn. His first opera, *Semiramide*, was commissioned for the Pantheon, but the score was destroyed when the theatre burnt down in 1792, shortly after rehearsals had begun. Returning to Vienna, he spent ten years as a diplomat before becoming conductor and composer at the Hoftheater in 1804, a post he held until 1831.

He composed c.30 stage works, of which the most popular were *Agnes Sorel* (1806), *Ida die Büssende* (1807), and *Der Augenarzt* (1811): his *Robert oder die Prüfung* (1813) was reputedly much admired by Beethoven. Most of them were to German librettos, although he did set some Italian texts, including Romani's *Il finto Stanislao* (1818), later used by Verdi.

H

Hába, Alois (*b* Vizovice, 21 June 1893; *d* Prague, 18 Nov. 1973). Czech composer. Studied Prague with Novák, Vienna and Berlin with Schreker. The principal advocate of microtonal music, he wrote works, including operas, for specially constructed instruments. *Matka* (The Mother, 1931), in the quarter-tone scale, was a sensation on its first production, and was given in Germany and Italy as well as at home. *Nová zem* (New Land, comp. 1934–6) was in the normal semitonal system; but *Přijď království Tvé* (comp. 1936–40) requires the singers to master sixth-tones. Though much admired in his own country, Hába's works have not found wider favour, partly because of the obvious difficulty for most singers of pitching microtones accurately.

Hadjibekov. Azerbaijani family of musicians.

   1. **Zulfugar Abdul Hussein-ogly** (*b* Shusha, 17 Apr. 1884; *d* Baku, 30 Sept. 1950). Composer. His works include the opera *Ashug-Garib* (1916) and musical comedies.

   2. **Uzeir Abdul Hussein-ogly** (*b* Agjabedi, 17 Sept. 1885; *d* Baku, 23 Nov. 1948). Composer and conductor. Studied Gori, Moscow with Ladukhin, St Petersburg with Kalafaty. Founded first Azerbaijani music school 1922. Produced his opera *Leila and Mejnun* in Baku, 1908; others are *Sheikh Senan* (1909), *Rustum and Sohrab* (1910), *Asli and Kerem* (1912), *Shah Abbas and Hurshidbanu* (1912), *Harun and Leila* (1915), and—his most famous work—*Kyor-ogly* (1937). Also wrote many successful musical comedies.

   3. **Hussein Aga Sultan-ogly** (*b* Shemakha, 19 May 1898; *d* Baku, 10 Nov. 1972). Tenor. Studied Baku with Speransky. First appeared in Azerbaijani Singspiels, then in female roles, 1916. Azerbaijan O, 1920, in operas by the two above composers. Moscow 1938, with Baku O. Roles also included Almaviva (Rossini), Alfredo, Lensky.

   4. **Sultan Ismail-ogly** (*b* Shusha, 8 May 1919). Composer and conductor. Studied with Zeidman. Conducted Baku musical comedy company 1938–40. Wrote many musical comedies.

Hadley, Henry (*b* Somerville, MA, 20 Dec. 1871; *d* New York, 6 Sept. 1937). US conductor and composer. Studied Boston with Emery and Chadwick, Vienna with Mandyczewski. Held various symphonic conducting posts, including associate conductorship of NYPO (1920–7), and founded Manhattan Symphony. The easy, late Romantic appeal of his operas, which include *Nancy Brown* (1903) and *Cleopatra's Night* (1920), has not had lasting significance.

Hadley, Jerry (*b* Princeton, IN, 16 June 1952). US tenor. Studied Illinois, and with LoMonaco. Début Sarasota 1978 (Lionel). New York: CO 1979, M 1987; Vienna, S, 1982; Gly. and London, CG, 1984; also Chicago, Berlin, Munich, etc. Roles incl. Ferrando, Tamino, Duke of Mantua, Alfredo, Gounod's Faust, Werther, Nadir, Pinkerton, Tom Rakewell. (R)

Haefliger, Ernst (*b* Davos, 6 July 1919). Swiss tenor. Studied Vienna with Patzak, Prague with Carpi. Zurich O, 1943–52. Berlin, SO, 1952–74. Gly. 1956. Created Tiresias (Orff's *Antigonae*). Retired 1995. Distinguished in Mozart and modern music, and also for his care with words. (R)

Haenchen, Hartmut (*b* Dresden, 21 Mar. 1943). German conductor. Studied Dresden Hochschule. Music dir. Zwickau O 1972–3; Schwerin 1976–9. Frequent guest with Berlin, K, and in Vienna, Munich, Warsaw. Music dir. of Netherlands O from 1986; *Elektra*, *Salome*, *Tristan*, *Parsifal*. London, CG, from 1991: *Orfeo ed Euridice*, *Mitridate*. (R)

Hagen. A Gibichung (bs), half-brother of Gunther and Gutrune, in Wagner's *Götterdämmerung*.

Hager, Leopold (*b* Salzburg, 6 Oct. 1935). Austrian conductor. Studied Salzburg Mozarteum. Début Mainz 1958 (*L'italiana in Algeri*). Linz, Landestheater, 1962–4; Freiburg O 1965–9. Has conducted and recorded the early operas of Mozart, incl. first modern *Mitridate*, Salzburg 1971. Vienna, S, 1973 (*Fidelio*). New York, M, from 1976, with Mozart's Da Ponte operas. London, CG, 1978 (*Figaro*). (R)

Hahn, Reynaldo (*b* Caracas, 9 Aug. 1875; *d* Paris, 28 Jan. 1947). French composer, conductor, singer, and critic of Venezuelan origin. Studied Paris with Dubois and Massenet. Music critic of *Le Figaro* 1934–47. Cond. Salzburg 1910, Paris from 1913, incl. at O and OC. Though well known for his elegant drawing-room songs, he was also a successful opera composer. His lightness of touch and expert craftsmanship gave his operas, in particular *Ciboulette* (1923) and *Mozart* (1925), considerable popular following.

Haibel, (Johann Petrus) **Jakob** (*b* Graz, 20 July 1762; *d* Djakovar, ?27 Mar. 1826). Austrian tenor and composer. Moved to Vienna 1789 and joined Schikaneder's company, with whom he sang Monostatos in *Die Zauberflöte*. Among his many works for the Viennese stage, the most popular was the Singspiel *Der Tyroler Wastl* (1796), given 118 times by 1801.

Haitink, Bernard (*b* Amsterdam, 4 Mar. 1929). Dutch conductor. Studied Amsterdam with Hupka, later Leitner. Opera début Holland Fest. 1963 (*Flying Dutchman*). Gly. 1972–3, 1975, music dir. 1977–8; London, CG, 1977, music dir. from 1987. Repertory incl. *Entführung*, *Zauberflöte*, *Don Giovanni*, *Don Carlos*, *Lohengrin*, *Ring*, *Rake's Progress*, *Prince Igor*, *Káťa Kabanová*, *Die Frau ohne Schatten*. His sound musicianship and command of structure have, together with his sensitivity towards his singers and players, given him access to a wide range of music. His years at Covent Garden and Glyndebourne have done much to sustain and develop the companies' reputations. Returned to Gly. 1994 to lead *Figaro* at the opening of the rebuilt opera-house. (R)

Haizinger, Anton (*b* Wilfersdorf, 14 Mar. 1796; *d* Karlsruhe, 31 Dec. 1869). Austrian tenor. Studied Vienna with Mozzati; later with Salieri. Début Vienna, W, 1821 (Gianetto, *La gazza ladra*). Paris, I, 1829; London, CG, 1833; St Petersburg 1835. Repertory included first Adolar (written for him); also Max, Huon, Florestan, Tamino, all opposite Schröder-Devrient. Contributed greatly to the success of Weber's operas. Later established a singing school at Karlsruhe, and published a handbook. He was much praised for his intelligence and musicianship; P. A. Wolff admired 'his sympathetic voice, his moving delivery, his excellent technique'.

Hale, Robert (*b* Kerryville, TX, 22 Aug.

1943). US bass-baritone. Studied at the New England Cons. and New York. Début Denver 1965 (Mozart's Figaro). New York, CO, from 1967; European début Cologne 1983, as Escamillo. London, CG, 1988 (Jochanaan). One of today's leading singers of Wagner, he made his New York, M, début as the Dutchman (1990) and has sung Wotan at Vienna; S Francisco; Berlin, D; and Washington, DC. (R)

Halévy, Fromental (*b* Paris, 27 May 1799; *d* Nice, 17 Mar. 1862). French composer. Studied Paris with Berton, Méhul, and (most influentially) Cherubini. After some initial rejections and failures, he had his first operatic success in 1828 with *Clari* (written for Malibran), crowning this with *Le dilettante d'Avignon* (1829). However, his real fame dates from 1835, when his masterpiece *La Juive* (his first operatic collaboration with Scribe) was produced at the Opéra. One of the key works of French *Grand Opera, it anticipates Meyerbeer's *Les Huguenots* but has a wholly individual breadth and grandeur. Berlioz praised the orchestration; Wagner admired in it 'the pathos of high lyric tragedy' and Halévy's capacity for reconstructing the atmosphere of antiquity without recourse to many circumstantial details. Halévy went on to confirm his position in Paris musical life with his opéra-comique *L'éclair* (1835). He followed these with the powerful *Guido et Ginevra* (1838), then *La reine de Chypre* (1841), a work to which Wagner devoted laudatory articles: it contains suggestions of his own Tarnhelm and of the *Tristan* love potion, and is also pre-Wagnerian in its chromatic harmony and in its freedom of movement between numbers. Halévy continued with another Grand Opera, *Charles VI* (1843), before returning to opéra-comique with *Le lazzarone* (1844); with a sequence of works mostly in this genre, none of them matching his previous successes, he concluded his career.

Despite Berlioz's view that he was better suited to light opera, it is as one of the most important composers of Grand Opera that Halévy is remembered: especially with *La Juive*, he confirmed the pioneering work of Rossini and in particular Auber in giving the genre a European importance. He was able to work inventively within its limitations—which included a reliance on large, somewhat static choruses and grandiose effects at the expense of characterization—not least because these matched his own; but the best of his scores include originalities of harmony and orchestration that held much for his successors. His daughter Geneviève married Bizet, who completed his late opera *Noé*. He taught at the Conservatoire from 1827, his pupils including Gounod, Massé, and Bizet. His brother **Léon** (*b* Paris, 12 Feb. 1802; *d* Saint-Germain-en-Laye, 2 Sept. 1883) was an author and dramatist who helped him with revisions of librettos, and whose son **Ludovic** (*b* Paris, 31 Dec. 1833; *d* Paris, 7 May 1908) collaborated with Meilhac in writing librettos for Offenbach, Bizet, and Delibes, sometimes as 'Jules Servières' or 'Paul D'Arcy'.

Halka (Helen). Opera in 2 (later 4) acts by Moniuszko; text by Włodzimierz Wolski, after K. W. Wójcicki's story *Góralka*. Prem. Vilnius 18 Feb. 1854.

Cracow and Tatras, late 18th cent. As the wealthy nobleman Janusz (bar) is celebrating his betrothal to Zofia (mez), the peasant girl Halka (sop) arrives, determined to see Janusz, who swore her undying fidelity, and whose child she is carrying. Janusz sends her back to her village, where the peasants are up in arms when they hear how Janusz has treated her. Unable to bear her sorrow, Halka throws herself into the river. News of her death puts an end to the wedding celebrations and the couple are driven from the village by the peasants.

Hall, (Sir) **Peter** (*b* Bury St Edmunds, 22 Nov. 1930). English producer. Studied Cambridge, where he was dir. Arts T 1955. Managing dir. Royal Shakespeare T 1960–9. London, CG: *Moses and Aaron* 1965, *Magic Flute* 1966, *Knot Garden* 1970, *Eugene Onegin* 1971, *Tristan* 1971. Appointed co-dir. London, CG, with Colin Davis 1969, but withdrew before taking up post. Gly. 1970–90, artistic dir. 1984: 15 prods. incl. *Calisto* 1970, *Ritorno d'Ulisse* 1972, *Fidelio* 1979, *Orfeo* 1982, *Poppea* 1984, *Carmen* 1985, Mozart and Verdi series; resigned over lack of consultation. New York, M: *Macbeth* 1982, *Carmen* 1986. Bayreuth 1983, *Ring*: his return to a sensual and naturalistic staging, leaving interpretative options open, was not generally liked. Los Angeles 1986, *Salome* (with his then wife Maria *Ewing; also CG 1988). Houston 1989, *New Year*. His productions are notable for their keen sense of theatre and for a freshness of approach that is always musical, never wilful or doctrinaire; at his finest when working with major dramatic singers whom he admires, including Janet Baker and Hildegard Behrens.

Hallé, (Sir) **Charles** (*b* Hagen, 11 Apr. 1819; *d* Manchester, 25 Oct. 1895). German, later English, pianist and conductor. Though most famous for the foundation of the orchestra which bears his name, he also conducted opera seasons in Manchester 1854–5, and at London, HM, 1860–1.

Hallström, Ivar (*b* Stockholm, 5 June 1826; *d* Stockholm, 11 Apr. 1901). Swedish composer. While studying law at Uppsala, he wrote *Hvita frun på Drottningholm* (The White Lady of Drottningholm, 1847) with Prince Gustav of Sweden. He is best known for his operas, among which the most popular was *Den bergtagna* (The Girl Bewitched by a Mountain Spirit, 1874): this was widely performed, and its light, easy use of folk melodies won the composer a following abroad. Of his other works, one of the most successful was the operetta *Den förtrollade katten* (The Enchanted Cat, 1869). Répétiteur Stockholm Royal O, 1881–5.

Hamburg. City-state in North Germany. The first independent opera-house in Germany was the T auf dem Gänsemarkt, opened against church opposition in 1678 with *Adam und Eva* by Johann Theile (1646–1724). J. W. *Franck was Kapellmeister 1682–6, and the opera gained in artistic standing under Johann *Kusser from 1693. Under Reinhard *Keiser, who was in Hamburg from 1695, dir. 1703–6, and wrote over 100 stage pieces, the city developed a vigorous operatic life. Johann *Mattheson was active in various roles from the early 1690s to 1705, drawing G. F. *Handel to the city (and fighting a famous duel with him). Handel's first operas, *Almira* and *Nero*, were premiered 1705. G. P. *Telemann was in the city from 1721, and a number of his early operas were premiered here. After the venture failed in 1738 the city was, like others in Germany, dependent on visiting companies with an Italian repertory. A new opera-house opened in 1765. Under the drama director Friedrich Schröder, Mozart and Gluck were heard from 1771.

The T am Dammtor opened 1827 with Spohr's *Jessonda*. In 1851 the opera became the Grosse O. Bernhard Pohl (Pollini) was director 1874–97, raising standards and making the city an important Wagner centre: also given were the German prems.

of *Otello* (1888) and *Eugene Onegin* (1892, under Mahler, in Tchaikovsky's approving presence). The Stadttheater opened 1874, and conductors have included Bülow (1888–91), Mahler (1891–7), Klemperer (1910–12), Weingartner (1912–14), Pollak (1917–31), Böhm (1931–4), Jochum (1934–44), Ludwig (1951–71), and Dohnányi (1975–84). The theatre became the Staatsoper 1934, was bombed 1943, rebuilt (cap. 1,674) and reopened 1955. Günther Rennert was director 1946–56, Heinz Tietjen 1956–9, Rolf Liebermann 1959–72 (the latter developing a particularly adventurous policy towards modern opera), August Everding (1973–7). Prems. have included Henze's *Prinz von Homburg* (1960), Goehr's *Arden muss sterben* (1967), Searle's *Hamlet* (1968), Penderecki's *Devils of Loudun* (1969), and Rihm's *Die Eroberung von Mexiko* (1992). A fire in 1975 destroyed much of the theatre's scenery and costumes. Liebermann returned 1985–8 when Dohnányi left. Gerd Albrecht became music director 1989.

Hamilton, Iain (*b* Glasgow, 6 June 1922). Scottish composer. Studied London with Alwyn. An early interest in opera has led to a number of large-scale works, for example *The Royal Hunt of the Sun* (1977), in which he is not afraid to tackle major dramatic subjects and present them with music that scrupulously serves the issues, if not always also musically enhancing them. He relinquished his earlier serial techniques, and has latterly worked in a tonal idiom, for example with *The Tragedy of Macbeth* (1990) and *London's Fair* (1992); his operatic music also shows great care in writing for voices as part of his attention to the enunciation of the drama.

Hamlet. Opera in 5 acts by Thomas; text by Barbier and Carré, after a French version of Shakespeare's tragedy (1600–1) by Dumas *père* and Paul Maurice. Prem. Paris, O, 9 Mar. 1868.

When Hamlet, Prince of Denmark (bar), learns from the ghost of his father (bs) that he was murdered by his own brother Claudius (bs) in order to usurp the throne, Hamlet vows revenge, and exposes Claudius when the Players act a story of a murdered king. He pretends to be mad, thus driving his beloved Ophélie (sop) to commit suicide. Laertes (ten) reproaches him, and as they prepare to fight, the king and queen appear with the body of Ophelia. Hamlet kills Claudius and assumes the throne. For the CG revival in 1869 the ending was revised so as to draw slightly closer to Shakespeare, with Hamlet killing the king and then himself.

Hammerstein, Oscar (*b* Stettin, 8 May 1846; *d* New York, 1 Aug. 1919). German, later US, impresario. Emigrated to US and made a fortune from inventing a cigar-making machine. Wrote plays and built a number of theatres. Turned to opera 1906 when he built the *Manhattan OH, establishing a brilliant company and an interesting repertory which threatened to rival the New York, M. Built Philadelphia OH 1908. In 1910 the Metropolitan bought his interests, stipulating that he should not produce opera in the US for ten years. Built London OH (Stoll T) 1911, which failed to rival Covent Garden and collapsed after two seasons. Built Lexington OH in New York 1913, but was legally restrained from staging opera. His grandson **Oscar Hammerstein II** (*b* 12 July 1895; *d* 23 Aug. 1960) was a librettist and songwriter who collaborated with Friml (*Rose Marie*, 1924), Romberg (*The Desert Song*, 1926), Kern (*Show Boat*, 1927), and especially with Rodgers (*Oklahoma!*, 1943; *Carousel*, 1945; *South Pacific*, 1949; *The King and I*, 1951).

Hammond, (Dame) **Joan** (*b* Christchurch, 24 May 1912). New Zealand soprano. Studied Sydney Cons., Vienna, London with Borgioli. Début Sydney, J. C. Williamson Grand Opera Co., 1929 (Siebel). Vienna, S, 1938; London: CR 1942–5, CG from 1948. Also New York, Russia, Lisbon. Retired 1965. Roles included Verdi's Desdemona, Butterfly, Tatyana, Mlada, Salome, Rusalka. Possessed a strong, clear voice and direct style. (R)

Hammond-Stroud, Derek (*b* London, 10 Jan. 1926). English baritone. Studied London at TCM and with Gerhardt, Munich with Hüsch. Sang Pluto in the UK prem. (concert) of Haydn's *Orfeo* (London 1955). Stage début London, Impresario Soc., 1957 (Publius, *Clemenza di Tito*). London: SW/ENO, from 1962; CG, 1971. Gly. 1973; New York, M, 1977–83. Roles include Doctor Bartolo (Mozart), Alberich, Faninal, Beckmesser. An outstanding character actor with excellent enunciation. (R)

Hampson, Thomas (*b* Elkhart, IN, 28 June 1956). US baritone. Studied at UCLA and in S Barbara with Lotte Lehman. Début Düsseldorf 1981 (Marcello). Sang widely in

Germany, notably Henze's *Prinz von Homburg* at Darmstadt, 1982. Principal baritone at Zurich O; New York, M, 1986 (Mozart's Almaviva). His warm, evenly-produced voice is admired as Guglielmo, Don Giovanni (Berlin, D, 1989), Monteverdi's Ulisse (S Francisco, 1990) and Rossini's Figaro (London, CG, 1993). (R)

Handel, George Frideric (orig. Georg Friedrich Händel) (*b* Halle, 23 Feb. 1685; *d* London, 14 Apr. 1759). Naturalized English composer of German birth. Studied with Zachau, organist of the Liebfrauenkirche in Halle; in 1697 he became assistant organist, and in 1702, first organist. In 1703 he joined the Hamburg opera, first as violinist, later as harpsichordist, where he worked under Keiser, whose hybrid German/Italian style provided the model for his own early operas, including *Almira* (1705).

In 1706 Handel began a lengthy study visit to Italy, taking in most major music cities. His opera *Vincer se stesso è la maggior vittoria* was given in Florence in 1707: little of the score survives, but the work clearly drew on *Almira* and seems to have made little impact. A visit to Naples in 1708 saw the production of the serenata *Aci, Galatea e Polifemo*, while during a stay in Venice in the winter of 1709–10 he produced *Agrippina*, the crowning success of his Italian years and earliest real evidence of his operatic talent.

His apprenticeship over, Handel left Italy in Feb. 1710 and found employment with the Elector of Hanover, who readily granted him an immediate year's leave of absence to visit England. By late 1710 he had arrived in London, where he already had influential friends. Anxious to make an impact, Handel composed *Rinaldo* at great speed and with it gave new impetus to the cultivation of Italian opera in England. In 1712 he again took a leave of absence, on condition that he return within a reasonable time: he was reluctant to do so and suffered considerable embarrassment when the Elector succeeded soon afterwards to the English throne as King George I.

Shortly after he reached London, Handel's new opera *Il pastor fido* was performed in the Haymarket. Neither this work, nor its successors *Teseo* (1713) and *Silla* (1713) repeated *Rinaldo*'s success, though the composer's reputation did not suffer unduly. For the next 20 years Handel's life centred on the London stage and, whatever the fate of individual works, his position at the forefront of operatic activities was always assured.

Unlike many composers, his approach to opera did not develop in an evolutionary way, but was shaped largely by the need to retain the interest of a fickle audience in a harsh commercial environment; to this end he demonstrated unsurpassed imagination and ingenuity. Many of his operas were written for the Royal Academy of Music, a venture which enjoyed spectacular success before equally catastrophic failure. As music director, Handel not only composed his share of the scores, but was also involved with the recruitment of singers. His first work for the Royal Academy of Music, *Muzio Scevola* (1721), was a collaboration by way of contest with his fellow composers Amadei and Bononcini. It was followed by a string of notable successes: *Floridante* (1721) was received as enthusiastically as *Radamisto* (1720), while *Ottone* (1723) saw the first appearance of the famous soprano Francesco Cuzzoni. Only *Flavio* (1723) failed to excite the public, although by this time Handel's supremacy on the London operatic stage was assured.

The next few seasons mark the zenith of his operatic achievements. *Giulio Cesare* (1724) was a resounding success, as were *Tamerlano* (1724) and *Rodelinda* (1725). By now more singers had been attracted to the Royal Academy, notably the soprano Faustina Bordoni, and rivalry between her and Cuzzoni set the tone for the 1725–6 season. Partisanship led to rowdy scenes at the opera-house, lampoons were published, and a performance of Bononcini's *Astianatte* was interrupted by a fight on stage between the two prime donne. Such diversions, although serving to uphold the public interest in opera, camouflaged the true appeal of a string of masterpieces from Handel's pen, including *Scipione* (1726), *Alessandro* (1726), *Admeto* (1727), and *Riccardo Primo* (1727).

The fall of the Royal Academy was as quick as its rise. Despite the intense public interest and box office receipts they had generated, singers such as Bordoni and Cuzzoni were a substantial drain on the resources of the organization. Most significant, however, was the performance of Gay's *The Beggar's Opera* in January 1728. Almost overnight this first example of *ballad opera eclipsed the Italian opera of the Royal Academy, with its contrived plots and complicated arias. *Siroe* (1728) and *Tolomeo* (1728) were the last two operas which Handel wrote for the Royal Academy and after a revival of *Admeto*, the company closed down in June 1728.

An attempt to relaunch the venture at the King's T in 1729 was doomed to failure. The first production, *Lotario* (1729), was not successful, so for his next work Handel turned to a comic, anti-heroic libretto. *Partenope* (1730) fared no better, however, and for a while he tried to recapture his former public by mounting a series of revivals. The limited success of these productions encouraged him to place new works before his public, but once again the venture was ill-judged. *Poro* (1731) was given a lukewarm reception, as was *Sosarme* (1732); *Ezio* (1732) was a complete disaster and even *Orlando* (1733), considered by many his finest opera, lasted for only a few performances. Another threat had also arisen in the shape of a rival company, the O of the Nobility. With Porpora as its main composer, it engaged some of Handel's former star singers and attracted a large attendance to its performances. Despite the success of Handel's new *Arianna in Creta* (1734) and a well-received revival of *Il pastor fido*, his position had been almost fatally challenged. On shifting his activities to Covent Garden, his fortunes improved temporarily with *Ariodante* (1735) and *Alcina* (1735), but the operatic battle had proved costly and he had sustained enormous losses.

A revival of *Esther* in 1732 had already suggested to him that oratorio could provide a means of recapturing his lost opera audiences, and the success of *Deborah* in the following year confirmed this. Although it was to be several years before his complete retirement from the operatic stage, the 1730s saw Handel turn increasingly to the composition of oratorio. He attempted to keep his opera company afloat with *Atalanta* in 1736, but both it and the Opera of the Nobility had entered into a terminal decline. In 1737 two new operas were produced, *Arminio* and *Giustino*, but neither captured the imagination of the public. Despite the growing success of his oratorios, Handel became increasingly depressed and ill. A visit to Aix-la-Chapelle to take the cure rejuvenated him, and he returned to England in late 1737 determined to set his operatic public alight once more. But *Faramondo* (1738) was not the success he had expected, while *Serse* (1738) was an unmitigated failure. In its light-hearted and entertaining plot it taps a genuinely comic vein which Handel had scarcely exploited

before, although this proved no more appealing than the heroic exploits of mythological figures or the machinations of apparitions from the world of the supernatural. His last two operas, *Imeneo* (1740) and *Deidamia* (1741), were both spectacular failures and many observers considered that his career was finished. As far as his operatic career was concerned this was, in fact, correct: his works quickly left the repertoire and lay unperformed until the 20th cent. However, the enormous acclaim which greeted the oratorios *Messiah* and *Samson*, produced hard on the heels of this final operatic failure, set him on a new path.

Handel occupies a curious position in operatic history. Ostensibly, he belongs to that large body of early and mid-18th-cent. composers whose activities centred around the production of opera seria of an increasingly stereotyped mould. However, his German background, Italian training, and English place of work and domicile impart to him a degree of cosmopolitanism lacking in most of his contemporaries, while his innately greater gifts enabled him to approach his task in a more inventive and creative way. Crucially, he turned the *da capo aria, with its rigid conventions, into a vehicle of great flexibility and expression for his singers, giving them every opportunity to display their vocal talents, while at the same time allowing the opera itself to unfold in a manner which was dramatically satisfactory according to the precepts of the day. Though Handel was unable entirely to overcome the inherent artificiality of opera seria, he was one of the few to produce works with any serious claim to convince in the modern opera-house.

Handel Opera Society. The English Handel O Society was founded in 1955 at the instigation of E. J. Dent, and began with *Deidamia*, in his translation, under Charles Farncombe in St Pancras TH. Notable subsequent productions included *Alcina* with Joan Sutherland (1957), *Semele* and *Rodelinda* with Sutherland and Janet Baker (1959—the first annual season at London, SW), *Serse* and *Giulio Cesare* with Sutherland (1963), *Orlando* with Baker (1966). Many other distinguished singers took part, sometimes early in their careers, including Heather Harper, Geraint Evans, Richard Lewis, Benjamin Luxon, and Philip Langridge. The society also performed in Liège, Göttingen, Halle, and Drottningholm. The Society was renamed Handel O in 1980 and disbanded in 1985.

Hann, Georg (*b* Vienna, 30 Jan. 1897; *d* Munich, 9 Dec. 1950). Austrian bass-baritone. Studied Vienna with Lierhammer. Munich, S, 1927–50. Also London, CG; Paris; Berlin; Milan, S. Created La Roche (*Capriccio*). A distinguished buffo artist, famous for his Kecal, Ochs, Nicolai's Falstaff, Leporello; also sang Pizarro, Sarastro, Amfortas. Possessed a large, attractive voice. (R)

Hänsel und Gretel. Opera in 3 acts by Humperdinck; text by Adelheid Wette (composer's sister), after the story in the Grimm brothers' *Kinder- und Hausmärchen* (1812–14). Prem. Weimar 23 Dec. 1893.

Hänsel (mez) and Gretel (sop) are sent by their angry mother (sop) to collect strawberries in the wood. Their father (bar), returning home drunk, is worried for their safety, knowing of a wicked Witch who lures children and eats them; the parents go in search of the children.

Tired out, but afraid to return home because they have eaten all the strawberries, Hänsel and Gretel fall asleep in the woods, aided by the Sandman (sop); they are protected by guardian angels.

On being woken by the Dew Fairy (sop) the following morning, Hänsel and Gretel see a house made entirely of marzipan and sweets. Hungry, they start to eat, and are captured by the wicked Witch (mez). She puts Gretel to work and fattens Hänsel up ready for eating; but Gretel manages to trick the Witch, pushing her head-first into the oven. As the Witch dies, the house collapses and previously imprisoned children re-emerge. The Witch herself is baked into a huge cake, which Hänsel and Gretel, now reunited with their parents, share with the other children.

Hans Heiling. Opera in a prologue and 3 acts by Marschner; text by Devrient, after an old folk-tale. Prem. Berlin, H, 24 May 1833.

The Bohemian mountains, 14th cent. A spirit, Hans Heiling (bar), has found a human girl he loves and, ignoring the warnings of his mother, the Queen of the Spirits (con), decides to forgo the realm of spirits and marry her.

He brings to earth jewels for Anna, his bride (sop). He is, however, perturbed by the warmth of her affection for Konrad (ten).

At evening, Anna wanders distractedly in the forest; she loves Konrad and yet is married to Heiling. Suddenly the Queen of the Spirits appears and beseeches Anna to relinquish him. Anna faints, and is found by Konrad, who carries her home. She rejects Heiling's gifts and reveals that she knows he is a spirit. Irate, Heiling stabs Konrad and flees.

Heiling returns to the spirit world; however, on learning that Konrad is not dead but plans to marry Anna, he resolves to hide among the wedding guests. He grasps Anna's hand; as Konrad hastens to his wife's aid, his hunting knife shatters. When Heiling summons a throng of spirits to annihilate humanity, his mother appears and leads Heiling back to the spirit world.

Hans Sachs. See SACHS, HANS.

Harewood, Earl of (George Henry Hubert Lascelles) (*b* London, 7 Feb. 1923). English critic and administrator. Son of the former Princess Royal and first cousin of Queen Elizabeth II. Founded magazine *Opera* 1950, editor to 1953. Board of directors, London, CG, 1951–3, 1969–72, controller of opera planning 1953–60. Dir. Edinburgh Fest. 1961–5. Managing dir., London, SW, later ENO, 1972–85; his years here saw the expansion of the company's range and enterprise. Compiled and wrote revised edition of *Kobbé's Complete Opera Book* (1954, 1987). Has championed the EOG, O School, and other native operatic enterprises.

Harmonie der Welt, Die (The Harmony of the World). Opera in 5 scenes by Hindemith; text by the composer. Prem. Munich, P, 11 Aug. 1957.

Set during the Thirty Years' War, the opera concerns the quest of the astronomer Johannes Kepler (bar) and General Wallenstein (ten) for harmony in the universe; each seeks a different form. At the end of the opera, Kepler is transformed into the Earth, and Wallenstein into Jupiter and they, together with other humans transformed into symbols of the zodiac, shine in the heavens. This work is, like *Mathis der Maler*, a study of the artist's or philosopher's relationship to the political and social movements of his times.

Harnoncourt, Nikolaus (*b* Berlin, 6 Dec. 1929). Austrian conductor. Formed the Vienna Concentus Musicus 1953 and gave *Il ritorno d'Ulisse* at the 1971 Vienna Festival. Conducted a historically informed cycle of Monteverdi operas at Zurich (1975–9) and has recorded operas by Mozart using modern instruments. He is admired for his pragmatic approach to early operas, notably *Poppea* (Salzburg, 1993). (R)

Harper, Heather (*b* Belfast, 8 May 1930). Irish soprano. Studied London with H. Isepp and Husler. Début OUOC, 1954 (Lady Macbeth). Gly. 1957, 1960, 1963. London, EOG 1956–75, CG from 1962. Bayreuth 1967, 1968; Buenos Aires, C, 1969–72; also New York, M, 1976–8; S Francisco. Roles included Eva, Micaëla, Arabella, Ellen Orford, Governess; created Mrs Coyle (*Owen Wingrave*) and Nadia (*The Ice Break*). A musicianly singer with a well-controlled voice. Retired from the stage 1984. (R)

Harris, (Sir) **Augustus** (*b* Paris, 1852; *d* Folkestone, 22 June 1896). English impresario. Stage manager and producer Mapleson Co., then manager Drury Lane 1879. Brought Carl Rosa OC to London 1883, managing their seasons until 1887, when he gave an Italian season. This led to him taking Covent Garden, where he was manager 1888–96, achieving great financial and artistic success with a company including Melba and the De Reszkes. He introduced opera in the original language to Covent Garden, and did much to popularize Wagner.

Harrison, William (*b* London, 15 June 1813; *d* London, 9 Nov. 1868). English tenor and impresario. Studied London, RAM. Début London, CG, 1839 (in the prem. of Rooke's *Henrique*). After seasons at Drury Lane and Her Majesty's, creating leading roles in *The Bohemian Girl*, *Maritana*, etc., he formed an English opera company in 1856, with Louisa *Pyne. This performed every autumn and winter at CG, 1858–64, and gave the first performances of works by Balfe, Wallace, Benedict, and others.

Harshaw, Margaret (*b* Narberth, PA, 12 May 1909). US mezzo-soprano, later soprano. Studied New York, Juilliard School. Début as mezzo-soprano, New York, M, 1942 (Second Norn). Sang there until 1950 as Amneris, etc., then until 1964 as soprano, establishing herself as a leading Wagnerian. London, CG, 1953–6; Gly. 1954. An earnest singer with a firm, even tone, successful as Brünnhilde, Kundry, and Isolde. (R)

Hart, Fritz (*b* London, 11 Feb. 1874; *d* Honolulu, 9 July 1949). English conductor and

composer. Studied London with Stanford. Dir. of Melbourne Cons. 1915, where Melba taught, and many of his operas were produced. A gifted writer, he provided most of his own texts, favouring Celtic twilight subjects; and his intense practical sense (he had appeared as an actor) helped to make his operas theatrically effective.

Hartmann, Karl Amadeus (*b* Munich, 2 Aug. 1905; *d* Munich, 5 Dec. 1963). German composer. Studied Munich with Haas and Scherchen. His *Simplicius Simplicissimus* was composed in 1935 but, owing to his refusal to take part in musical life under the Nazis, not staged until after the war, when its vigorous and effective music won it a following in Germany.

Hartmann, Rudolf (*b* Ingolstadt, 11 Oct. 1900; *d* Munich, 26 Aug. 1988). German producer and manager. Studied stage design Munich, Bamberg with Berg-Ehlert. Prod. Altenberg 1924; Nuremberg 1928–34, 1946–52; Berlin, S, 1934–8, where he began his collaboration with Clemens Krauss; Munich 1938–44, dir., Munich, P, 1952–67. Staged prems. of *Friedenstag* (1938) and *Capriccio* (1942), and revivals of most of Strauss's works, also prem. of *Der Liebe der Danae*, Salzburg 1952. London, CG: *Elektra* 1953, *Arabella* 1965, *Frau ohne Schatten* 1967; new *Ring* 1954. A producer with a strong and effective sense of tradition.

Harwood, Elizabeth (*b* Barton Seagrave, 27 May 1938; *d* Fryerning, 22 June 1990). English soprano. Studied RNCM. Début Gly. 1960 (Second Boy, *Zauberflöte*). London: SW from 1961; CG from 1968. Salzburg from 1970; Milan, S, 1972; New York, M, 1975. Roles included Lucia, Zerbinetta, Musetta, Tytania, Fiordiligi. An expressive and elegant singer with a bright tone and a warm stage personality. (R)

Háry János (John Háry). Opera in prologue, 5 parts, and epilogue by Kodály; text by B. Paulini and Z. Harsányi, after János Garay's poem. Prem. Budapest 16 Oct. 1926.

Hasse, Johann Adolf (*b* Bergedorf, nr. Hamburg, 25 Mar. 1699; *d* Venice, 16 Dec. 1783). German composer. Sang as tenor at Hamburg under Keiser (1718) and at the court of Braunschweig-Wolfenbüttel (1719), where his first opera *Antioco* (1721) was produced. Sent to Italy, he studied with Alessandro Scarlatti and settled in Naples from 1724 to 1729, where his operas and dialect comedies, including *Sesostrate* (1726) and *La sorella amante* (1729), enjoyed great popularity, and made him a much sought-after social personality. In 1730 *Artaserse* was staged in Venice: together with Vinci's contemporaneous setting of the same libretto, it proved a turning-point in the history of opera. Metastasio's reform of the opera seria libretto was matched in a musical style which, while appropriate to its stylized conventions, embodied sufficient contrast and expressive content to maintain the interest of the audience, while also providing brilliant opportunities for the display of the singers' talents. The libretto was immediately taken up by many other composers; Hasse's *Artaserse*, like Vinci's, was performed in houses across Italy, and the composer immediately capitalized upon his success in another work in similar vein, *Dalisa* (1730).

A tour of Europe with his new bride, the soprano Faustina Bordoni, brought further triumphs and, in 1730, an appointment to the prestigious Dresden court. Beginning with *Cleofide* (1731), this was the venue for many of Hasse's most celebrated works, though he found the intrigues of the Italian musical retinue wearisome and took every opportunity to be absent. Most of these trips were connected with the many performances of his works throughout Italy during the 1730s, though after 1740 Hasse spent more time at the Saxon court, whose supremacy in Germany as an operatic centre was now rivalled only by that of Berlin. Over the next 20 years he produced at least one opera each year, most to Metastasian librettos, and many smaller dramatic works. Of particular importance was the second *Arminio* (1745), which led to an invitation to compose for the court of Frederick the Great in Berlin. Following the Siege of Dresden in 1760, in which most of Hasse's possessions, including musical manuscripts, were destroyed, the Elector was forced to disband the opera company. In 1763 Hasse moved to Vienna, where his works, especially *Egeria* (1764), were well received. In 1773 he finally settled in Venice, participating in the active musical life of the city until his death.

Hasse's contribution to the development of opera seria was crucial. Together with Graun he was one of the last composers to work mainly in a court rather than in a commercial context, and it is impossible to separate the spirit of his achievements from the flourishing cultural life of the setting for which most of them were conceived. The broad lines on which his *opere serie* were designed, the majestic sweep of the music, and the heroic characters around whose actions and emotions the drama unfold, are the perfect embodiment of the Metastasian ideal and the yardstick against which all 18th-cent. opera seria must be measured.

Hauer, Josef (*b* Wiener Neustadt, 19 Mar. 1883; *d* Vienna, 22 Sept. 1959). Austrian composer and theorist. His theories of atonal music, which preceded and were respected by Schoenberg, found expression in two operas, *Salambo* (1930) and *Die schwarze Spinne* (comp. 1932). The latter, staged in Vienna in 1966 largely as an act of homage, proved to have little theatrical feeling.

Hauk, Minnie (*b* New York, 16 Nov. 1851; *d* Tribschen, 6 Feb. 1929). US soprano. Studied New York with Errani, later with Strakosch. Début Brooklyn 1866 (Amina). London, CG, 1868; Paris 1869; Moscow, St Petersburg 1869–70; Vienna 1870–4; Berlin 1874–7; London, HM, 1878–81. New York, M, 1890–1, then organized her own company, but retired after one season, and went to live in Wagner's villa at Tribschen with her husband. Her repertory encompassed 100 roles, including Juliette, Manon, Selika. A famous Carmen, she was a considerable singer-actress, possessing a forceful character, a penetrating tone, and scrupulous attentiveness to detail.

Häusliche Krieg, Der. See VERSCHWORENEN, DIE.

'Ha! welch' ein Augenblick!' Pizarro's (bs-bar) aria in Act I of Beethoven's *Fidelio*, in which he determines to murder his prisoner Florestan.

Hawes, William (*b* London, 21 June 1785; *d* London, 18 Feb. 1846). English composer and conductor. From 1824 he was dir. of the London, L, where he introduced Weber's *Der Freischütz*, adapted and with some airs of his own (1824). Apart from staging his own operettas, he adapted many others for the English stage, among them *Cosi fan tutte*, *Don Giovanni*, and *Der Vampyr*.

Haydn, Joseph (*b* Rohrau, 31 Mar. 1732; *d* Vienna, 31 May 1809). Austrian composer. Despite a sustained attempt in recent years to revive interest in Haydn's dramatic music, his operas are still largely accepted as inferior in quality to his instrumental and symphonic music. Yet the composition of opera held a central place in his life: he himself considered the works he wrote for Eszterháza to be among the finest of his œuvre, and much of his time was taken up in supervising the production of opera. Despite the judgement of posterity, Haydn was one of the most highly regarded opera composers of his day and placed by some above Mozart.

His surviving operas are almost all associated with the Esterházy court, where he was employed from 1761. His first work, *Acide* (1763), was an opera seria, though Haydn was predominantly attracted to opera buffa. In 1768 *Lo speziale* opened the new opera-house at Eszterháza, while *Le pescatrici* (1770) was the highlight of the marriage festivities for his patron's niece. For the visit of the Empress Maria Theresa in 1773 Prince Nikolaus Esterházy mounted his most lavish festival, at which *L'infedeltà delusa* was given a rapturously received performance. *L'incontro improvviso* (1775) was first performed for a visit of the Archduke Ferdinand, while *Il mondo della luna* (1777) was given to celebrate the marriage of the prince's second son. Though the inevitable comparison with Mozart's opere buffe finds Haydn somewhat lacking, these works have much to commend them, not least their handling of ensembles and musical characterization.

In addition to composing opera, Haydn was also kept busy writing incidental music for the plays of the wandering theatrical troupes which gravitated towards the Esterházy court, as well as Singspiels for the marionette theatre which opened at Eszterháza in 1773. His last works for Eszterháza were *La fedeltà premiata* (1781), *Orlando paladino* (1782), and *Armida* (1784). In 1790 Prince Nikolaus died and the theatre closed, bringing to an end a spectacular period in the annals of opera: in addition to his own works, Haydn had also been responsible for conducting over 100 operas by other composers.

Haydn's last operatic endeavour, *L'anima del filosofo* (1791), a treatment of the Orpheus myth, was written during his first visit to London, but not performed. Its most striking feature is its debt to Gluck, manifested in the tragic chorus writing and restraint of the vocal lines. One of the last great opere serie of the 18th cent., it is a fitting final testament to his lifelong involvement with the stage.

Haymarket. See KING'S THEATRE.

Haymon, Cynthia (*b* Jacksonville, FL, 6 Sept. 1958). US soprano. After study in New York made her début at S Fe 1984 (Xanthe in *Liebe der Danae*) and in the first US *We Come to the River* (Henze). Created title-role Musgrave's *Harriet, the Woman called Moses* (Norfolk, VA, 1985). She is best known for her idiomatic portrayal of Gershwin's Bess (Gly. 1986 and at London, CG). Other roles incl. Mimì, Liù, Pamina (Paris, B, 1991), Euridice. (R)

head voice. A method of tone production in the upper register, so called from the sensation experienced by the singer of the voice functioning at the top of the head. The tone is light and clear. See also CHEST VOICE.

Heger, Robert (*b* Strasburg, 19 Aug. 1886; *d* Munich, 14 Jan. 1978). German conductor and composer. Studied Strasburg, Zurich, and Berlin under Schillings. Strasburg 1907; Ulm 1908; Vienna, V, 1911; Nuremberg, 1913; Munich 1920; Vienna, S, 1925; Berlin, S, 1933–4, and SO 1944–50; Zoppot (Sopot) regularly; music dir. Kassel 1935–44. London, CG, 1925–35, and with Munich Co. 1953, conducting first London *Capriccio*; Bayreuth 1964 (*Meistersinger*). A sound, reliable musician who had the confidence of more famous conductors in more prominent positions than he ever achieved. His five operas include *Der Bettler namenlos* (1932). (R)

Heilbronn, Marie (*b* Antwerp, 1851; *d* Nice, 31 Mar. 1886). Belgian soprano. Studied Paris with Duprez, London with Wartel. Début Paris, I (Marie, *Fille du régiment*). Paris, OC, 1878, 1884–6, and O, 1880; Milan, S, and London, CG, 1879. Despite faults, her attractive voice and lively singing brought success as Violetta, Juliette, and Manon, which she created (having sung in Massenet's first opera, *La grand'tante*). When the composer first played her Manon, she cried, saying 'It's the story of my own life'.

Heinrich. Heinrich der Vogler (Henry the Fowler) (bs), the King of Saxony in Wagner's *Lohengrin*.

Heise, Peter (*b* Copenhagen, 11 Feb. 1830; *d* Tårbæk, 12 Sept. 1879). Danish composer. Studied Copenhagen with Berggreen, Leipzig with Hauptmann. Though chiefly known for his songs, he became increasingly interested in the stage, and his *Drot og marsk* (King and Marshal, 1878) is regarded as one of the most important Danish national operas.

Heldy, Fanny (*b* Ath, 29 Feb. 1888; *d* Passy, 13 Dec. 1973). Belgian soprano. Studied Liège. Début Brussels, M, 1910 (Elena, Gunsbourg's *Ivan the Terrible*); sang there until 1912. Paris, OC, 1917–20, and O, 1920–39; London, CG, 1926, 1928. Created roles in Hahn's *Le marchand de Venise*, and Honegger and Ibert's *L'aiglon*, among others. A prominent singer-actress of great character and beauty, she was an outstanding Violetta, Manon, and Concepción. (R)

Hélène. The Duchess Hélène (sop), sister of Duke Frederick of Austria and lover of Henri, in Verdi's *Les vêpres siciliennes*.

Heming, Percy (*b* Bristol, 6 Sept. 1883; *d* London, 11 Jan 1956). English baritone. Studied London with King and Blackburn, and Dresden with Grosse. Début London, Beecham OC, 1915 (Paris, *Roméo et Juliette*). Sang with this Co. until 1919, then joined BNOC, 1922. London, SW, 1933–40, 1942. Director London, CG English Co., 1937–9. A highly versatile and impressive artist with a full, mellow tone; roles included Amfortas, Scarpia, Mozart's Dr Bartolo, Macheath. (R)

Hempel, Frieda (*b* Leipzig, 26 June 1885; *d* Berlin, 7 Oct. 1955). German, later US, soprano. Studied Berlin with Nicklass-Kempner. Début Breslau 1905 (Violetta, Pamina, Rosina); Schwerin, 1905–7; Berlin 1905, 1907–12; New York, M, 1912–19; Chicago 1914, 1920–1. Thereafter sang only in concert, giving Jenny Lind recitals in costume. An exceptionally gifted and refined singer, whose pure, rounded tone, brilliant technique, and dramatic sensitivity enabled her to shine in a wide repertory, incl. Queen of the Night, Lucia, Euryanthe, Eva. (R)

Hemsley, Thomas (*b* Coalville, 12 Apr. 1927). English baritone. Studied with Manén. Début London, Mermaid T (Purcell's Aeneas). Gly. 1953–71; Zurich 1963–7; Bayreuth 1968–70; London, CG, from 1970. Sang Demetrius in prem. of *A Midsummer Night's Dream*, Mangus (*Knot Garden*), Caesar (Hamilton's *Catiline Conspiracy*). With his excellent enunciation and strong stage presence, a distinguished Beckmesser, Malatesta, and Almaviva (Mozart). (R)

Henderson, Roy (*b* Edinburgh, 4 July 1899). English baritone. Studied London, RAM.

Début London, CG, 1929 (Donner). Almaviva (Mozart) in first Gly. season, and regularly until 1939 (Guglielmo, Masetto, Papageno). A sensitive, intelligent artist who also made a considerable reputation as a teacher, incl. of Kathleen Ferrier. (R)

Hendricks, Barbara (*b* Stephens, AR, 20 Nov. 1948). US soprano. Studied New York with Tourel. Salzburg 1981; Paris, O, and New York, M, 1982; also Berlin, Vienna, etc. Roles include Susanna, Nannetta, Gilda. Possesses a pure, clear, and expressive voice. (R)

Henri. A young Sicilian patriot (ten), lover of Hélène, in Verdi's *Les vêpres siciliennes*.

Henri VIII. Opera in 4 acts by Saint-Saëns; text by Détroyat and Silvestre. Prem. Paris, O, 5 Mar. 1883.

England, *c*.1534. The opera concerns the love of the King (bar) for Anne Boleyn (sop), whom he marries despite her love for Gomez (ten), the Spanish ambassador, and in the face of the Pope's disapproval.

Henze, Hans Werner (*b* Gütersloh, 1 July 1926). German composer. Initially self-taught, then studied Heidelberg with Fortner. His first opera was *Das Wundertheater* (1949); this was followed by the radio opera *Ein Landarzt* (1951) and by *Boulevard Solitude* (1952). The latter, a version of the Manon Lescaut story, was an instant success; it makes much use of ballet, in which Henze has shown great interest, and is constructed in separate numbers, as is the radio opera *Das Ende einer Welt* (1953). This first revealed, in the form of a puncturing satire on snobbish arty society, Henze's abiding interest in the problem of the artist's relationship and duty to his fellows.

In 1956 *König Hirsch* revealed Henze as a major operatic talent: it is a very large-scale treatment of a Gozzi fable concerning the conflicting claims on a king's duty, and initially aroused violent enthusiasm and antagonism. The score reveals a new power in absorbing the various influences and manners to which Henze has been dangerously subject by virtue of his sheer skill in mastering all forms of musical language and his extreme technical fluency, while the vein of fantasy is undiminished. *Elegy for Young Lovers* (1961) concerns a great poet who feeds his art with the lives of all those around him, callously destroying them in the process if need be; a further treatment of Henze's ideas about the relationship between the artist and society, here portrayed as predator and prey, it is more disciplined in manner without excluding an affecting lyricism. *Der junge Lord* (1965) is a tart little satire, by no means without a streak of cruelty, on the *kleinbürgerlich* element in German society which Henze despises.

The Bassarids (1966) returns to the voluptuous richness of *König Hirsch* without loss of disciplines meanwhile acquired. Instructed by his librettist, W. H. Auden, to 'make his peace with Wagner' before beginning work, it duly shows a stronger, less wary acknowledgement of the German tradition than previously, and includes some fine large-scale music. A number of music-theatre works followed. *We Come to the River* (1976) marked Henze's return to opera, after a 10-year absence, and to the theme of the individual in conflict with authority, with a work on a left-wing political subject using his familiar neo-Romantic language. *Pollicino* (1980) is described as a 'Märchen für Musik', *The English Cat* (1983) as a 'story'; *Das verratene Meer* (1990) marked his full return to the lyric theatre. (R)

Heppner, Ben (*b* Murrayville, British Columbia, 14 Jan. 1956). Canadian tenor. Sang lyric roles at Toronto from 1984, then restudied as a dramatic tenor: Bacchus at Melbourne (1988), Walther at Seattle. European début as Lohengrin at Stockholm, 1989. London, CG, 1990 as Walther; returned 1995 as Peter Grimes. Created McTeague in Bolcom's opera, Chicago 1992. He has a well-disciplined voice and a strong stage presence. (R)

Herincx, Raimund (*b* London, 23 Aug. 1927). English bass-baritone. Studied Belgium with Van Dyck, Milan with Valli. Début WNO 1950 (Mozart's Figaro). London: SW, 1956–66; subsequently with ENO; CG from 1968. Also Boston, Salzburg. Created Faber (*Knot Garden*), White Abbot (*Taverner*), Segura (Williamson's *Our Man in Havana*). A forceful singer with a powerful voice, successful as Wotan, Escamillo, and Macbeth. (R)

Her Majesty's Theatre. The *King's Theatre in the Haymarket, London, was renamed Her Majesty's Royal Italian OH on the accession of Queen Victoria in 1837, during *Laporte's management. Two years later, after refusing to re-engage Tamburini in protest against a

singer's clique known as *La vieille garde*, he was replaced by *Lumley. Mapleson followed 1862–7 and 1877–87. With the opening of Covent Garden in 1847 came the rivalry of a second Royal Italian O. The theatre burnt down in 1867; reopened 1869, it did not become an opera-house again until 1877. The Lumley and Mapleson managements saw the English prems. of operas including later Donizetti; early and middle Verdi; Gounod's *Faust*, *Carmen*, and *Mefistofele*. The Carl Rosa London seasons were given there in 1879, 1880, and 1882. Seidl gave the first London *Ring* in 1882. Galli-Marié sang her original role of Carmen in a French season 1886, and Patti made her sole appearance 1887. The theatre was pulled down 1891, and the present building opened in 1897 under the management of Beerbohm Tree. Beecham gave the English prem. of *The Wreckers* in 1909, an opéra-comique season in 1910, and the first London *Ariadne* in 1913. The BNOC gave its London seasons there after leaving Covent Garden in 1924. The theatre has rarely housed opera since.

Hermann. A young officer (ten), loved by Lisa, in Tchaikovsky's *The Queen of Spades*.

Hérodiade. Opera in 4 acts by Massenet; text by Paul Millet and 'H. Grémont' (Georges Hartmann), after Flaubert's story (1877). Prem. Brussels, M, 19 Dec. 1881.

Jerusalem, AD 30. Hérodiade (mez), married to Hérode (bar), abandons her daughter Salomé (sop), who loves the prophet Jean (ten). Hérode perceives Jean as a threat and throws him into prison, encouraged by the discovery of Salomé's love for Jean; Hérode himself desires Salomé. When Salomé vows to die with Jean, he accepts her love for the first time, seeing it to be sincere. Salomé is taken to a banquet at Hérode's palace, and throws herself at his feet, begging forgiveness for Jean. However, he has already been beheaded and Salomé kills herself.

Herodias. The wife of Herod Antipas. She appears (mez) in Massenet's *Hérodiade* and Strauss's *Salome*.

Hérold, Ferdinand (*b* Paris, 28 Jan. 1791; *d* Paris, 19 Jan. 1833). French composer of Alsatian origin. Studied Paris with his father, François-Joseph Hérold, later with Adam, Catel, and Méhul. Winning the Prix de Rome, he went to Italy and had his first opera, *La* *gioventù di Enrico Quinto* (1815) successfully produced in Naples. Back in Paris, he became maestro al cembalo at the T Italien. He collaborated with Boieldieu on *Charles de France* (1816), but had his first great success with *Les rosières* (1817), following this up with another success, *La clochette* (1817). Other short, light operas were composed while he continued working at the T Italien, 1820–7, including another great success, *Marie* (1826); this combined elements of Italian vocal writing and Singspiel within an essentially French framework. In 1827 he moved to the Opéra as répétiteur. Among some ballets and less successful operas, he produced the first of his last two masterpieces, *Zampa* (1831), a work which initially did not make its way chiefly because of the Opéra-Comique being forced to close three times during the year 1831. After an unsuccessful collaboration on *La marquise de Brinvilliers* (1831) with eight other composers, he wrote *Le pré aux clercs* (1832), whose triumph he barely lived to see.

With *Zampa* and *Le pré aux clercs* alone, Hérold earns a place as an important minor figure in the history of French opera. There are suggestions in his music of Rossini and (especially in *Zampa*) of Weber, not least in the increased importance given to the orchestra he would also have observed in Méhul; Wagner's admiration of the work is reflected in some details in *The Ring*. *Le pré aux clercs* shows Hérold moving into the arena of Grand Opera with a work that in some respects anticipates Meyerbeer's *Les Huguenots*. But he was essentially a follower of Boieldieu, with an individual vein of melody that attempts greater depths of Romantic feeling without forfeiting lightness of manner. His early death was a tragedy for French opera: he himself remarked in his last illness, 'I was just beginning to understand the stage.'

Hertz, Alfred (*b* Frankfurt, 15 July 1872; *d* S Francisco, 17 Apr. 1942). German, later US, conductor. Studied Frankfurt. Début Halle 1891; Altenburg 1892–5; Barmen-Elberfeld 1895–9; Breslau 1899–1902. Moved to US; New York, M, 1902 as cond. of German opera until 1915, including of the first US *Parsifal* (before the expiry of the Bayreuth copyright; he never cond. in Germany again). Cond. prems. of *Königskinder* (1910) and W. Damrosch's *Cyrano de Bergerac* (1913) and several others in the US. London, CG, 1910. Latterly turned to concert conducting.

Hervé (orig. Ronger, Florimond) (*b* Houdain, 30 June 1825; *d* Paris, 3 Nov. 1892). French composer, singer, and conductor. Studied Paris with Elwart and Auber. Though working as an organist under his baptismal name, he used the name Hervé for his theatrical career, which included the composition of over 100 light operettas. His first success was with *Don Quichotte et Sancho Pança* (1848). At the Odéon and Palais-Royal his experience in many roles, including as composer, conductor, producer, and tenor, led to the satire *Les folies dramatiques* (1853) and also to the opening of the Folies-Concertantes in 1854 (later renamed Folies-Nouvelles). He continued to write and appear in a stream of light works, of which the most famous was *Mam'zelle Nitouche*. He also worked in London, writing *Aladin the Second* for the Gaiety and acting as music director at the Empire from 1886. At their best, his fluent, skilful pieces have an immediate charm and appeal.

Herz, Joachim (*b* Dresden, 14 June 1924). German producer and administrator. Studied Dresden, conducting with Hintze, producing with Arnold, also acting as répétiteur at O School. Further studies Berlin 1949–51. Prod. Dresden-Radebeul Touring O 1951–3; Berlin, K, assistant to Felsenstein 1953–6; Cologne 1956–7. Chief prod. Leipzig 1957, dir. 1959–76: *Ring* 1976. London, C: *Salome* 1975, *Fidelio* 1980, *Parsifal* 1986. Dir. film *Fliegender Holländer* 1963 and Danish TV *Serse* 1973. Dir. Berlin, K, 1976–81: first revival original 2-act *Butterfly* 1978, *Peter Grimes* 1981. WNO: original *Butterfly* 1979, *Forza* 1981. Munich: *Ägyptische Helena* 1981. Dresden: *Freischütz* 1985 (reopening of Semper O), Mayer *Goldene Topf* 1989. Helsinki: *Così* 1989. A disciple of Felsenstein with his own sharp ideas about music theatre, he has written (of *Fidelio*), 'the individual case has a significance that is generally applicable'.

'Herzeleide'. Kundry's (sop) narration in Act II of *Parsifal*, in which she tells Parsifal of his mother Herzeleide.

Heuberger, Richard (*b* Graz, 18 June 1850; *d* Vienna, 28 Oct. 1914). Austrian conductor, critic, and composer. After a mildly distinguished career as a choral conductor he turned to criticism, writing for Viennese and Munich newspapers and succeeding Hanslick on the *Neue freie Presse* in 1896. Here, as in his later editorship of the *Neue musikalische Presse*, he propagated lively if sometimes irascible views on modern music. He composed four operas, including *Mirjam* (1894) and *Barfüssele* (1905), and five operettas. Of these the most famous was *Der Opernball* (1898): although Heuberger's music lacks the inventiveness or immediate appeal of that of his successors Kálmán and Lehár, it was much admired in its day and *Der Opernball* was taken up abroad, notably in the US, where it was given both in English and in German.

Heure Espagnole, L' (The Spanish Hour). Opera in 1 act by Ravel; text by Franc-Nohain, after his own comedy. Prem. Paris, OC, 19 May 1911.

Toledo, 18th cent. The clockmaker Torquemada (ten) goes off to attend to the town clocks, leaving a customer, the muleteer Ramiro (bar), in the shop to await his return. Concepción (sop), who is accustomed to receive her lovers in her husband's absence, sets him carrying clocks about. Gonzalve (ten), a poet, enters and serenades her protractedly. On the arrival of a second lover, Don Inigo Gomez (bs), Ramiro is made to carry Gonzalve, hidden in a clock, up to the bedroom. The same happens to Don Inigo, while the first clock is brought down. Annoyed by their ineffectualness, Concepción eventually admiringly orders Ramiro upstairs again—without a clock. Torquemada returns, finds the two lovers inside the clocks 'examining' them, and effects quick sales.

Hickox, Richard (*b* Stokenchurch, 5 Mar. 1948). English conductor. Studied Cambridge and London, RAM. Opera début London, ENO, 1985 (*Dido and Aeneas*); CG, 1985 (*Zauberflöte*). Spitalfields Fest., London, 1985 and 1988 (*Alcina, Poppea*). Brings clear accents and buoyant rhythms to Gluck (*La rencontre imprévue* at Wexford), Handel (*Giulio Cesare* for Australian Opera), and Britten (*Midsummer Night's Dream* at London, C). Cond. *Troilus and Cressida* for O North and at London, CG, 1995. (R)

Hidalgo, Elvira de (*b* Aragón, 27 Dec. 1892; *d* Milan, 21 Jan. 1980). Spanish soprano. Studied Barcelona with Bordalba, Milan with Vidal. Début Naples, C, 1908 (Rosina). Monte Carlo from 1910; Paris, O, from 1912; Milan, S, 1916; London, CG, 1924; New York, M, 1924–6; also Chicago, Buenos Aires, etc. Taught from 1933; the only teacher of Callas. A vivacious singer with a high, delicate soprano, she excelled as Rosina, Lakmé, Musetta, and Philine. (R)

Hidalgo, Juan (*b* Madrid, 28 Sep. 1614; *d* Madrid, 31 Mar. 1685). Spanish composer. Though he worked for most of his life as a church composer, his enthusiasm for Italian opera led him to incorporate an operatic style into his secular vocal settings and to collaborate with Calderón on the first Spanish opera, *La púrpura de la rosa* (*c*.1660), then on the first to survive, *Celos aun del aire matan* (Jealousy even of Air Kills, 1660). He also wrote the first surviving zarzuela, *Los celos hacen estrellas* (The Skies have Stars, 1672).

Hill, Alfred (*b* Melbourne, 16 Nov. 1870; *d* Sydney, 30 Oct. 1960). Australian composer and conductor. Studied Leipzig with Sitt, Schreck, and Paul. Returning to Australia in 1896, by way of New Zealand, he formed the Australian O League, which produced his *Giovanni, the Sculptor* (1914). His operas include works on Maori legend as well as on more familiar subjects.

Hiller, Johann Adam (*b* Wendisch-Ossig, 25 Dec. 1728; *d* Leipzig, 16 June 1804). German composer and writer. Studied in Dresden. More than any other composer, he was the founder of *Singspiel. He contributed original music to Weisse's versions of the texts *Die verwandelten Weiber* (1766) and its sequel *Der lustige Schuster* (1766), writing numbers in a simple, popular vocal style. In an attempt to create a more operatic genre, after the manner of Hasse and Graun, whom he admired, Hiller approached Schiebeler. Their first collaboration was the 'romantisch-comische Oper' *Lisuart und Dariolette* (1766), but neither this, nor *Die Muse* (1767), was well received, and Hiller returned to Weisse. The first three of their five subsequent works played a vital role in the establishment of a modern form of Singspiel and were widely imitated. The plots of *Lottchen am Hofe* (1767), *Die Liebe auf dem Lande* (1768), and *Die Jagd* (1770) were all drawn from French opéras-comiques, and followed Rousseau's ideology in glorifying the simplicity of country life in preference to the artificiality of the town. The music, too, draws on German songs and elements of opéra-comique, alongside the bel canto lines of opera seria and the chattering arias and ensembles of opera buffa. These characteristics are also demonstrated in his two subsequent collaborations with Weisse, *Der Dorfbalbier* (1771) and *Der Aerndtekranz* (1771).

Himmel, Friedrich Heinrich (*b* Treuenbrietzen, 20 Nov. 1765; *d* Berlin, 8 June 1814). German composer. A protégé of Frederick William II of Prussia, he studied in Dresden (with Naumann) and in Italy. His first opera, *La morte di Semiramide*, was given in Naples 1795, following which he succeeded Reichardt as Kapellmeister to the Berlin court. Although he wrote two further Italian opere serie—*Alessandro* (1799) for St Petersburg and *Vasco da Gama* (1801) for Berlin—his German works brought him to greater prominence. After *Frohsinn und Schwärmerey* (1801), a 1-act Liederspiel, he had his greatest success with *Fanchon, das Leiermädchen* (1804), a Singspiel reworking by Kotzebue of an old French *vaudeville. Such was its simple charm and captivating music that it was one of the most frequently performed stage works of the 19th cent. and was heard throughout Europe. *Die Sylphen* (1806) was also well regarded and is seen by some historians as a forerunner to Weber's *Der Freischütz*. Himmel was essentially a conservative composer: his German works show clearly the influence of Hiller and Weisse at a time when the genuine Singspiel tradition had largely been absorbed into the operatic mainstream.

Hindemith, Paul (*b* Hanau, 16 Nov. 1895; *d* Frankfurt, 28 Dec. 1963). German composer, conductor, and violist. Studied Frankfurt, violin with Hegner and Rebner, composition with A. Mendelssohn and Sekles. His first three operas, *Mörder, Hoffnung der Frauen* (1921), *Das Nusch-Nuschi* (1921), and *Sancta Susanna* (1922), were somewhat ephemeral 1-act pieces, though the scandal over the outspokenness of the first two helped to draw attention to his exceptional gifts. The first opera to hold the stage to any degree was *Cardillac* (1926), which treats Hoffmann's tragic subject of a master-jeweller's obsession with his creations, and murder on their behalf, in an ingenious reconciliation between set forms and Expressionist elements. To some extent, the next opera, *Hin und Zurück* (1927), belongs with the earlier group, in that it is a 1-act chamber opera of considerable irreverence, drawing upon jazz. Written for the 1927 Baden-Baden Festival, it reverses the action (though not the music) half-way through its 12 minutes.

Neues vom Tage (1929) is another so-called *Zeitoper in which the intensity of the style explored in *Cardillac* is brought together with the satirical sharpness of *Hin und Zurück*, not always happily. The work's determined modernity involves an aria sung by the heroine in her bath praising the merits of electric heating over gas: this brought an injunction from the local gas company. There was here the turning away from Romanticism and the embracing of Baroque ideals that increasingly marked his art. School works composed at this time included *Lehrstück* (1929), a teaching piece with a political message on the insignificance of the individual written with Brecht, and the children's play, written with children, *Wir bauen eine Stadt* (1930).

The political stance and the effectiveness in reaching new audiences shown by these last pieces contributed to Hindemith falling foul of the Nazis. He had also, in 1932, begun work on his most serious engagement with the theme of the artist's relationship with society, *Mathis der Maler* (1938). Hindemith's own dilemma between accommodation with unacceptable political views, some form of compromise, and isolation from the society he should serve, found apt expression in the story of the painter Matthias Grünewald. The work draws upon old German sources, including folk-song, and is essentially cast in a series of linked set numbers; and in its language it reaffirms the belief in tonality which he held as something of a bastion against serialism. The opera was the source of the material for his *Mathis der Maler* symphony. The success of *Mathis* proved unwelcome to the authorities: in 1934 his music was subjected to a partial boycott (against which he was publicly defended by Furtwängler), and in 1935 he was dismissed from his teaching post at the Berlin Hochschule. These events impelled him to ponder further his views on the position of the artist in society: a later revision of *Cardillac* was made on the basis of rejecting the idea of the artist as above morality.

Hindemith's last full-length opera, *Die Harmonie der Welt* (1957), was based on the life of the Renaissance astronomer Johannes Kepler, taking his work as an example of human intelligence discovering in the laws of planetary motion a 'harmony of the spheres' with direct musical relevance. There is here a further justification of his belief in music deriving from the natural order rather than artificial construction: the stance is once more against serialism. His only other opera, the 1-act *The Long Christmas Dinner* (1961), is also strongly tonal.

Hines, Jerome (*b* Hollywood, 8 Nov. 1921). US bass. Studied Los Angeles with Curci. Début S Francisco 1941 (Monterone). New York, M, from 1946; Gly. 1953; Milan, S, and Bayreuth 1958; Moscow, B, 1962. Also Paris, Munich, Vienna, etc. A notable Boris, Wotan, and Philip, among a large repertory, with a smooth and sonorous voice. He celebrated the 50th year of his career in 1991; sang Fiesco for Long Beach O, 1992. (R)

Hin und Zurück (There and Back). Opera in 1 act by Hindemith; text by Marcellus Schiffer, after an English revue sketch. Prem. (with works by Milhaud, Toch, and Weill) Baden-Baden 17 July 1927.

On discovering that she has a lover, Robert (ten) wounds his wife Helen (sop) fatally. Supernatural intervention then reverses the plot: Helen comes back to life and the original conversation takes place in reverse. The opera ends with Robert giving Helen a birthday present. The entire proceedings are witnessed by Helen's aunt, who takes no notice of any of the events around her.

Hippolyte et Aricie. Opera in prologue and 5 acts by Rameau; text by Abbé Pellegrin after Euripides and Racine (*Phèdre*). Prem. Paris, O, 1 Oct. 1733.

The plot concerns the incestuous love of Phèdre (sop), wife of Thésée (bar), for her stepson Hippolyte (ten); he, however, loves Aricie (sop). Thésée, persuaded that Hippolyte is guilty of assaulting his stepmother, banishes his son, who is then killed by a sea-monster while attempting to flee with Aricie. Phèdre kills herself; Hippolyte, exonerated, is resurrected, and reunited with Aricie.

Hislop, Joseph (*b* Edinburgh, 5 Apr. 1884; *d* Upper Largo, 6 May 1977). Scottish tenor. Studied Stockholm with Bratt. Début Stockholm 1916 (Gounod's Faust). Chicago 1920–1; London, CG, 1920–8; Milan, S, 1923; Paris, OC, 1926. Retired 1937; taught in Stockholm 1936–48, his pupils including J. Björling and B. Nilsson. Rich-voiced and handsome, he was called 'my ideal Rodolfo' by Puccini; also successful in Verdi and the French repertory. (R)

Hockney, David (*b* Bradford, 9 July 1937). English painter and designer. Début London,

Royal Court T, 1966 (*Ubu roi*, Jarry). Gly. 1975 (*Rake's Progress*), 1978 (*Magic Flute*); New York, M, 1981 (the triple bills *Parade* and *Stravinsky*); also Los Angeles (*Tristan*), Dallas (*Magic Flute*).

Hoddinott, Alun (*b* Bargoed, 11 Aug. 1929). Welsh composer. Studied Cardiff, London with Benjamin. *The Beach of Falesá* (1974) brought his lyrical, highly chromatic style to bear upon an exotic South Seas plot and included some fine orchestral writing. He followed this with *The Magician* (1976); *What the Old Man Does is Always Right* (1977), a Hans Andersen setting combining the talents of Sir Geraint Evans and local Fishguard schoolchildren; *The Rajah's Diamond* (TV, 1979); and *The Trumpet Major* (1981), a work of considerable dramatic strength.

Hoengen, Elisabeth (*b* Gevelsberg, 7 Dec. 1906). German mezzo-soprano. Studied Berlin with Weissenborn. Début Wuppertal 1933. Vienna, S, from 1943. London, CG, 1947, 1959–60; New York, M, 1951–2; Bayreuth 1951. An impressive singing actress; roles included Lucretia, Klytemnästra, Ortrud. (R)

Hofer, Josepha. See WEBER.

Hoffmann, E. T. A. (Ernst Theodor Amadeus, orig. Wilhelm) (*b* Königsberg, 24 Jan. 1776; *d* Berlin, 25 June 1822). German novelist, critic, conductor, and composer. One of the most famous and influential figures of the Romantic movement in literature. Dir. the Bamberg T Co. 1808, and the Seconda Co. in Leipzig and Dresden 1813–14. After a Singspiel, *Die Maske* (1799), he wrote *Scherz, List und Rache* (1801) for Posen. There followed other number operas with dialogue, though *Aurora* (comp. 1811–12) and *Undine* (1816) have important freely composed finales.

Undine anticipates much in later Romantic opera. It was greatly admired by Weber, whose review is famous for its statement of Romantic ideals, as an example of 'the opera Germans want, a self-contained work of art in which all elements, contributed by the related arts in collaboration, merge into one another and are absorbed in various ways so as to create a new world'. *Undine* also contains another curious anticipation of Wagner in its final destruction of the lovers in what is referred to as a Liebestod (though the music at this point is quite un-Wagnerian). As a critic Hoffmann took an equivocal position about Romanticism: he had a wary friendship with Weber, whose *Freischütz* was attacked in some notorious anonymous articles possibly by him; in Berlin in 1821 he translated the rival opera *Olympie* for Spontini. His writings influenced generations of Romantics, and are still valuable. They include some perceptive critical articles, but much of his most interesting work is in his imaginative writings, especially in the stories contained in the *Serapionsbrüder* collection. Among these are *Ritter Gluck*, a study of the nature of inspiration, and *Don Juan*. This makes a mysterious imaginative connection between the author and Donna Anna, and first suggested Mozart's *Don Giovanni* as a Romantic work with a strong association between love and death. In *Der Dichter und der Komponist* there is a discussion on the priorities of words and music in opera, with the hope that they may one day be written by the same man.

Hoffmann, Grace (*b* Cleveland, 14 Jan. 1925). US mezzo-soprano. Studied New York with Schorr, Stuttgart with Wetzelsberger. Début with US touring co., 1951 (Lola). Milan, S, 1955; Stuttgart from 1955 (Wagner's Mary, 1989); Bayreuth 1957–70; London, CG, 1959; Paris, O, 1962; New York, M, 1957–8, 1971–2. A successful Kundry, Brangäne, Eboli, and Cassandra. (R)

Hofmann, Peter (*b* Marienbad, 12 Aug. 1944). German tenor. Began as rock singer. Studied Karlsruhe with Seiberlich. Début Lübeck 1969 (Tamino). Stuttgart 1975; Paris, O, 1976; Bayreuth from 1976 (Tristan 1976; Siegmund 1988); London, CG, 1979; New York, M, 1980; also Vienna, Chicago, S Francisco, etc. His handsome physique contributed to his success as Siegmund; roles also incl. Lohengrin, Tristan, Loge, Parsifal. (R)

Hofmannsthal, Hugo von (*b* Vienna, 1 Feb. 1874; *d* Rodaun, 15 July 1929). Austrian poet, dramatist, and librettist. He met Richard Strauss while on holiday in Paris in 1900, beginning a relationship which was to result in six operas, while many more projects were discussed and eventually discarded. Their first collaboration, *Elektra* (1909), is recognized as one of the seminal works of Expressionism, perhaps betraying Hofmannsthal's early acquaintance with Stefan George. Its successor, *Der Rosenkavalier* (1911), occupied quite different emotional ground,

although this text shared the same concern for economy of language and precision of expression. The works which followed drew inspiration from a variety of sources: *Ariadne auf Naxos* (1st version, 1911–12; 2nd version, 1915–16), *Die Frau ohne Schatten* (1914–17), *Die ägyptische Helena* (1924–7; rev. 1933), and *Arabella* (1924–9). Hofmannsthal also drafted a sketch for *Die Liebe der Danae*: after his death this was worked into a libretto by Joseph Gregor.

Hofmannsthal also wrote the libretto for Wellesz's *Alkestis* (1924); his play *Die Hochzeit der Sobeide* was the source of Cherepnin's opera (1933); and his *Das Bergwerk zu Falun* of Wagner-Régeny's opera (1961).

'Ho-jo-to-ho!' The cry of Brünnhilde (sop) in Act II, and of the other Valkyries in Act III, of Wagner's *Die Walküre*.

Holbrooke, Joseph (*b* Croydon, 5 July 1878; *d* London, 5 Aug. 1958). English composer. Studied London with Corder. His first opera was a light work, *Pierrot and Pierrette* (1909). He then devoted himself to a massive commission to set Lord Howard de Walden's poem *The Cauldron of Annwyn* as a trilogy of operas, *The Children of Don* (1912), *Dylan* (1914), and *Bronwen* (1929). These achieved performance and, in the case of the first work, even some popularity, in days when Wagner's example still seemed a viable one to some composers working in different national traditions. Holbrooke makes use of some superficially Wagnerian characteristics—a national myth, a vast orchestra, symphonic motivic methods—without approaching Wagner's creative power, though there are sections which suggest a feeling for mythic opera.

Holland. In 1634 De Musijk Kamer, a group modelled on the Florentine Camerata, met to discuss musical drama, though no original works seem to have resulted. *De triomfeerende Min* (1678, to celebrate the Peace of Nijmegen), by Carolus Hacquart (*c*.1640–?1701), is often claimed as the first Dutch opera but is really a pastoral play with music. Attempts at Dutch opera were made by Hendrik Anders (1657–1714) and Servaas de Konink (?–1717 or 1718), especially in the latter's *De vrijadje van Cloris en Roosje* (1688, lost). Bartholomeus Ruloffs (1741–1801) was conductor at the rebuilt theatre from 1774, translating foreign works and inserting his own music in opéras-comiques. Slow to develop an independent tradition, Holland was for long dependent on visiting Italian, French, and German companies. The many short-lived Dutch national opera companies were shared between Amsterdam and The Hague. An early attempt at Dutch opera was by J. B. van Bree (1801–57) with *Saffo* (1834). However, despite encouragement for opera, little was composed, though an enlightened welcome was given to much foreign opera. The Wagner-Vereniging (1883) had great success in stimulating interest in its subject. A new impulse came in modern times, especially with the example of Willem Pijper (1894–1947) and his *Halewijn* (1933). Henk Badings (1907–87) had some success with *De Nachtwacht* (The Night Watch, 1942).

The Holland Fest., founded in 1947, is unique in being a nation-wide festival, centred on Amsterdam and The Hague (latterly, through budget cuts, more exclusively on Amsterdam). It embraces music, drama, and the visual arts as well as other entertainments. Opera has always played an important part, and the programmes have shown a high regard for quality as well as great enterprise. O Forum, based on Enschede, tours opera throughout the country.

See also AMSTERDAM.

Holloway, Robin (*b* Leamington Spa, 19 Oct. 1934). English composer and critic. Studied with Goehr, also at Oxford and Cambridge. His major operatic work is a sensitive and intelligently constructed setting of Richardson's *Clarissa*, composed 1968–76, which made a powerful impression on its production in London, C, 1990. A thoughtful critic, he has written a perceptive and influential study *Wagner and Debussy* (1979).

Holm, Richard (*b* Stuttgart, 3 Dec. 1912; *d* Munich, 20 July 1988). German tenor. Studied Stuttgart with Ritter. Début Kiel 1937. Munich, S, from 1948. Gly. 1950. New York, M, 1952–3. London, CG, 1953, 1958–60, 1964–6. Also Bayreuth, Vienna, Berlin. Created Kent in Reimann's *Lear*; also sang Belmonte, Flamand, David, Aschenbach. (R)

Holst, Gustav (*b* Cheltenham, 21 Sept. 1874; *d* London, 25 May 1934). English composer of Swedish origin. His first five operas represent attempts to build upon the slender traditions and imported conventions of 19th-cent. English opera. *Lansdown Castle* (1893), written for his home town and performed

there with piano, is one of many Sullivan-derived operettas of the day, though it includes some enterprising concerted numbers and an individual handling of magic scenes. *The Revoke* (1895), to a text by his friend Fritz Hart, was written and rehearsed at the London RCM. It retains Sullivanesque features (though the text lacks Gilbertian wit); however, it is continuously composed and shows awareness of the more ambitious operas being written by Stanford and Ethel Smyth, not least in the enterprising handling of the orchestra, some use of *Leitmotiv, and a skilful overture. Of some short children's operettas which followed, the only survivor is *The Idea* (*c*.1896), a return to Sullivanesque conventions.

Holst had meanwhile been introduced by Hart to Wagner. He had sketched part of a Wagnerian opera, *The Magic Mirror*, in 1896, and now began planning *Sita*. However, he broke off to write *The Youth's Choice* (comp. 1902), 'a musical idyll' in one act, to his own text. The latter is as feebly Wagnerian as much of the music, attempting to cover lack of characterization with turgid symbolism in pursuit of a trite moral.

Sita (comp. 1900–6), later dismissed by Holst as 'good old Wagnerian bawling', was his first full-scale opera. Its weaknesses include lame efforts at an English equivalent of *Stabreim, and some two-dimensional characterization; but Holst has, although intermittently, built on experience especially in the development of vivid orchestral commentary and an intelligent handling of Leitmotiv.

Only the Hindu subject-matter foretells the astonishing achievement of *Sāvitri* (comp. 1908). Set for only three singers and off-stage chorus with a 12-piece orchestra, not only does the text show an understanding of Hindu ideas far in advance of its time for a Western artist (Holst had by now studied Sanskrit seriously); it anticipates modern chamber opera in its simplicity and directness of means. Turning away from Wagnerian expansiveness, Holst draws on his more natural sense of musical economy, and makes skilful dramatic use of his characteristic mastery of bitonality to express the essence of his brief drama both swiftly and evocatively.

The Perfect Fool (1923) contrasts, less effectively, a somewhat remote, ethereal manner with an earthy directness that does not exclude the hearty and the bathetic; though, as the popular ballet excerpts reveal, there is some excellent music buried in a cumbersome structure. *At the Boar's Head* (1925) collects the Falstaff episodes from Shakespeare's Henry IV plays, and draws on Holst's love of early English dance music to make a technically ingenious and often touching score. *The Tale of the Wandering Scholar* (1934, later retitled *The Wandering Scholar*) is a 1-act chamber opera which returns with success to the comic style sought and only intermittently grasped in the previous two operas. Laconic and deft, it has a certain dryness, but at its best the dryness of good wit.

Holzbauer, Ignaz (*b* Vienna, 17 Sept. 1711; *d* Mannheim, 7 Apr. 1783). Austrian composer. Studied briefly with Fux, and in Venice. Held posts as Kapellmeister in Vienna (1744–6), Stuttgart (1750), and Mannheim (1753), after the success of *Il figlio delle selve* (1753). His most successful work, *Günther von Schwarzburg* (1777), was his only German opera, the remaining 16 stage works being in Italian or French, and including settings of Metastasio's texts *La clemenza di Tito* (1757) and *Adriano in Siria* (1768).

The text of *Günther*, by Anton Klein, takes an historical German theme: the work is significant as the first effort at using a German subject in a full-length German opera, and prompted a reawakening of interest in a national genre after a lengthy domination by French and Italian opera. Mozart described Holzbauer's music as 'very beautiful', adding 'the poetry doesn't deserve such music'. Despite the work's immense success, encouraged by its overt patriotism, Holzbauer wrote no further German operas.

Homer, Louise (*b* Pittsburgh, 30 Apr. 1871; *d* Winter Park, FL, 6 May 1947). US contralto. Studied Paris with Koenig. Début Vichy 1898 (Léonore, *Favorite*). London, CG, 1899; New York, M, 1900–19, 1927–9; Chicago 1920–5. Created Witch in *Königskinder*, and leading roles in Paderewski's *Manrù* and Converse's *The Pipe of Desire*; also sang Amneris, Gluck's Orfeo, Laura (*Gioconda*). A popular artist with a full-toned voice, she was particularly admired as Dalila, and in Wagner. Wife of the composer Sidney Homer, and aunt of composer Samuel Barber. (R)

'Home, Sweet Home'. Originally an aria in Bishop's *Clari, or The Maid of Milan* (called by the composer a 'Sicilian Air'); also occurs in altered form in Donizetti's *Anna Bolena*, which resulted in Bishop's bringing an action for 'piracy and breach of copyright'. It used to be sung by Patti, Melba, and other prima donnas in the Lesson Scene in *Barbiere*; they often accompanied themselves on a piano wheeled on to the stage for the purpose.

Honegger, Arthur (*b* Le Havre, 10 Mar. 1892; *d* Paris, 27 Nov. 1955). Swiss composer. Studied Zurich, Paris with Widor. His large output includes a number of works which show an original approach to the stage. His most substantial opera, *Antigone* (1927), is less remarkable than the stage oratorio *Jeanne d'Arc au bûcher* (1938), in which the skilful blend of speech, song, orchestral narration, and other effects makes a powerful dramatic presentation of the Joan story. He also wrote a number of operettas, notably *Les aventures du roi Pausole* (1930).

Höngen, Elisabeth. See HOENGEN, ELISABETH.

Hopf, Hans (*b* Nuremberg, 2 Aug. 1916; *d* Munich, 25 June 1993). German tenor. Studied Munich with Bender, Oslo with Bjärne. Début Augsburg 1936 with Bayerisches Landestheater. Dresden and Oslo, 1942–4. Bayreuth 1951, 1961–6. New York, M, 1952–65; London, CG, 1951–3, 1963. Also Milan, S; Buenos Aires; Moscow; etc. A solid singer, particularly successful in Wagner and as Strauss's Emperor. (R)

Horne, Marilyn (*b* Bradford, PA, 16 Jan. 1934). US mezzo-soprano. Studied with her father, and U of S California with Vennard. Début Los Angeles 1954 (Háta, *Bartered Bride*). Gelsenkirchen 1956–60; London, CG, from 1964; Milan, S, from 1969; New York, M, from 1970. A versatile singer with an opulent voice of enormous compass, and an excellent technique. A notable contributor to the revival of Rossini, Bellini, Donizetti, etc. Repertory includes Rinaldo, Orfeo (Gluck), Rosina, Arsace, Adalgisa, Eboli, Carmen, Marie (*Wozzeck*), Charlotte, Dalila. Her Isabella at London, CG, 1993 was announced as her last Rossini role. Also dubbed the voice of Dorothy Dandridge in the 1954 film of *Carmen Jones*. (R)

Hotter, Hans (*b* Offenbach-am-Main, 19 Jan. 1909). German bass-baritone. Studied Munich with Roemer. Début Opava (Troppau) 1929 (Speaker, *Zauberflöte*). Prague

1932–4; Hamburg 1934–7; joined Munich, S, 1937, and subsequently Vienna, S; London, CG, from 1947; New York, M, 1950–4; Bayreuth from 1952. Also Milan, S; Paris, O; Chicago; etc. Produced *The Ring* at London, CG, 1962–4. Retired 1972, though continued to appear at Munich and elsewhere as Berg's Schigolch. Created Kommandant (*Friedenstag*) and Olivier (*Capriccio*); also Jupiter in the abortive prem. of *Die Liebe der Danae*, 1944. A famous Pizarro, Almaviva (Mozart), Sarastro, Philip, and Amonasro, and the dominating Wagner Heldenbariton of his day, celebrated as Amfortas, Kurwenal, Sachs, and above all Wotan. Possessed a warm, eloquent voice and a powerful stage presence, and excelled in the noble, the tragic, and the contemplative. An artist of penetrating intelligence, he considerably influenced succeeding generations of singers. Pupils incl. David Ward, Cheryl Studer. (R)

House of the Dead, From the (Cz., *Z mrtvého domu*). Opera in 3 acts by Janáček; text by the composer, after Dostoyevsky's novel based on his prison reminiscences (1862). Prem. Brno 12 Apr. 1930.

The opera presents scenes of life in a Siberian prison camp. A political prisoner, Alexander Petrovich Goryanshikov (bar), arrives, and immediately arouses the anger of the Commandant (bar). The convicts are ordered to work; a few remain behind, listening to a story told by Luka (ten).

A year later Goryanshikov is teaching Alyeya (sop) to read; Skeratov (ten) tells of how he shot a rival for a girl's love. In celebration of Easter, the convicts perform two plays, watched by the townspeople. Alyeya is injured in a fight with another prisoner.

Goryanshikov visits Alyeya in the prison hospital; he overhears two convicts recounting their pasts. Luka dies, and one of the story-tellers, Shishkov (bs), recognizes him as his former rival. As Goryanshikov leaves the camp, having been pardoned by the Commandant, the other prisoners release a caged eagle as a symbol of the inability to suppress the human spirit.

Howarth, Elgar (*b* Cannock, 4 Nov. 1935). English conductor. Studied Manchester. Stockholm 1978, first *Grand Macabre* (Ligeti). Birtwistle prems.: London, ENO, 1986 (*Mask of Orpheus*); O Factory 1986 (*Yan Tan Tethera*); London, CG, 1991 (*Gawain*). Gly. Touring O 1994 (*The Second Mrs Kong*). Guest cond. O North 1985–8. A specialist in contemporary music.

Howarth, Judith (*b* Ipswich, 11 Sept. 1962). English soprano. After study at the Royal Scottish Academy sang at London, CG, from 1985: Oscar, Siebel, Elvira (*Italiana*) and Iris in *Semele*. An attractive stage presence and keenly projected voice have lent distinction to such roles as Marguerite de Valois (*Les Huguenots*), Susanna, and Zerlina. Salzburg début 1991, in *Der Schauspieldirektor*. O North 1995 as Walton's Cressida (also at London, CG). (R)

Howell, Gwynne (*b* Gorseinon, 13 June 1938). Welsh bass. Studied Manchester with Llewellyn, London with O. Kraus. Début London, SW, 1968 (Monterone). London, CG, and Gly., from 1969; London, ENO from 1986; Paris 1983; New York, M, 1985; also Chicago, S Francisco, Hamburg. Roles incl. Padre Guardiano, Landgrave, Sachs, Pogner, Gurnemanz, Pimen, Colline; created title-role of Maxwell Davies's *Taverner*. (R)

Hughes, Arwel (*b* Rhosllanerchrugog, 25 Aug. 1909; *d* Cardiff, 23 Sept. 1988). Welsh composer. Studied with Kitson and Vaughan Williams. Joined BBC in Wales 1935, which he headed 1965–71. His first opera *Menna* (1953) was one of the earliest Welsh operas on a national theme and was followed by a comic work, *Serch yw'r doctor* (Love's the Doctor, 1960). Hughes also appeared as cond. with the WNO.

Hugh the Drover. Opera in 2 acts by Vaughan Williams; text by Harold Child. Prem. London, RCM, 7 July 1924.

England, early 19th cent. Hugh the Drover (ten) and John the Butcher (bs-bar) are rivals for the hand of Mary (sop). She is in love with Hugh, but her father wishes her to marry the wealthy John. In a boxing match, Hugh wins but is accused by John of being a Napoleonic spy and put in the village stocks. He is released by the Sergeant, who turns out to be an old friend, and Hugh and Mary leave together happily.

Huguenots, Les. Opera in 5 acts by Meyerbeer; text by Scribe and Deschamps. Prem. Paris, O, 29 Feb. 1836.

Touraine, France, August 1572. A Huguenot nobleman, Raoul de Nangis (ten), is in love with a woman he assumes to be the mistress of the Catholic Comte de Nevers (bar). Raoul is summoned to a meeting with an undisclosed lady.

In the gardens at Chenonceaux, Valentine (sop), daughter of the Comte de Saint-Bris (bar), awaits the arrival of Raoul, whom she loves and wishes to marry. Raoul recognizes her as the woman he loves but, believing her to be Nangis's mistress, refuses her hand. The Catholics are furious and a fight breaks out.

Valentine is to marry Nevers, to whom she was originally betrothed; Raoul challenges him to a duel. Valentine overhears a plan to ambush Raoul on his way to the fight and warns him to go well protected; a riot between the two parties ensues.

The Catholics, led by Saint-Bris, resolve to launch a fierce attack against the Huguenots; their plans are overheard by Raoul.

Raoul warns the Huguenots, who are gathered for the marriage of Marguerite de Valois to Henri IV, of the impending attack. In a Huguenot churchyard, Valentine finds Raoul and his servant. She is now free since Nevers has died in combat, and wishes Raoul to adopt her faith and marry her. When he refuses to relinquish his religion, she vows to die with him. The couple survive an attack by Catholic troops and return to Paris, but are shot by her father's men.

Hummel, Johann Nepomuk (b Pressburg, 14 Nov. 1778; d Weimar, 17 Oct. 1837). Austrian pianist, conductor, and composer, son of **Joseph Hummel**, who during the late 1780s conducted Schikaneder's troupe in Vienna. A child prodigy whose talent was much admired by Mozart, Hummel made extensive concert tours through Europe, including Scotland and England in 1790–2, before returning to Vienna to study with Albrechtsberger, Haydn, and Salieri. Kapellmeister to the Esterházy family at Eisenstadt 1804; after 1811 worked independently in Vienna, before becoming Kapellmeister at Stuttgart in 1816. Took a similar post at Weimar 1819, where he became friendly with Goethe. During the 1833 season he conducted the German OC at London, H. In addition to several ballets he composed four operas, which owe much to Mozart in their dramatic method and musical language. He was also influenced to some extent by French rescue opera, especially in Die Rückfahr des Kaisers (1814), while in Mathilde von Guise (1810) his approach is coloured by anticipations of the Romantic style.

Humming Chorus. The name usually given to the hidden chorus which ends Act II of Puccini's Madama Butterfly as Butterfly, Suzuki, and the baby take up their stand at the shosi awaiting the return of Pinkerton.

Humperdinck, Engelbert (b Siegburg, 1 Sept. 1854; d Neustrelitz, 27 Sept. 1921). German composer. As a child he learnt the piano and began composing operas and Singspiels; studied Cologne with Hiller, Jensen, and Gernsheim. Meeting Wagner in Italy in 1880, he was asked to help prepare Parsifal for Bayreuth; his many tasks included the composition of some music to cover a scene change at the first performance. He also worked as an editor of music, critic, and teacher: he was partly responsible for turning Siegfried Wagner's interests from architecture to music. His own most famous opera (and the first to survive), Hänsel und Gretel (1893), began life as song settings before being made into a Singspiel and then into an opera. Ever since its successful prem. under Richard Strauss, it has remained his most popular work. Its simple nursery tunes are used in a superficially Wagnerian manner, though there is no systematic attempt to develop an association between persons or ideas and a musical motive. A work of unique charm, it has been an enduring success with German children, perhaps still more with nostalgic German parents.

Humperdinck's next work, Die sieben Geislein (1895), was also based on a fairy story; and this was followed by his second most popular work, Königskinder (1897), which made constructive use of melodrama; it was later revised as an opera (1910). Dornröschen (1902), a third attempt at fairy-tale opera, was less successful. Strauss was again the first conductor of Die Heirat wider Willen (1905), a work that looked back to an earlier tradition of pre-Wagnerian Romantic opera. Weak librettos were partly responsible for the failure of two later Spielopern, Die Marketenderin (1914) and Gaudeamus (1919). His son **Wolfram Humperdinck** (b Frankfurt, 29 Apr. 1893; d 16 Apr. 1985) worked as a producer in Detmold, Leipzig 1933–41, then was Intendant at Kiel 1941–5.

Hunding. A Neiding (bs), Sieglinde's husband, in Wagner's Die Walküre. His name derives from Old Norse hundr and Middle High German Hunt (dog).

Hungary. The Turkish occupation from

1541 to 1686 inhibited the development of national music, and Hungary's first opera performances were given in Pozsony by visiting Italian companies (Mingotti, 1740; Bon, 1760; Zamperini, 1764). The country was under Habsburg rule 1711–1919. From 1762 Haydn directed his operas at Kismarton (Eisenstadt); and in 1768 his *Lo speziale* opened Prince Esterházy's theatre at Eszterháza, where, especially from 1776, many of his operas were performed. Other nobles' theatres included that of Count Erdődy at Pozsony, where the first Mozart opera in Hungary was given (*Entführung*, 1785), and that of Bishop Patachich at Nagyvárad, where Dittersdorf worked (1764–9). In Buda and Pest performances were given in German (from 1787) and in Hungarian (1793–6, 1807–15). In 1719 the theatre of the Piarist School in Pest opened; from 1790 it began working towards national opera by staging Singspiels and opere buffe, but the first Singspiel in Hungarian was *Pikkó Herceg* (Prince Pikkó, 1793) by József Chudy (1751– or 1754–1813) (music lost).

In the early years of the 19th cent., the German company performed works, especially by Mozart, Beethoven, and Weber, which keenly interested Hungarian musicians. The inclusion of many Italian and French works (Rossini, Bellini, Donizetti, Verdi, Auber, Meyerbeer) soon after their prems. gave an example to the tentatively emerging Hungarian national opera. Some composers began using Hungarian elements in their operas, drawing on the national verbunkos tradition; others incorporated sections of foreign works into them. The first true Hungarian opera (though it includes German and Italian elements) was *Béla futása* (Bela's Flight, 1822) by József Ruzitska (c.1755–1823), which made use of verbunkos music, and became very popular. Other operas followed, notably Ruzitska's *Kemény Simon* (1822); *Csel* (The Ruse, 1839), by András Bartay (1799–1854); *Visegrádi kincskeresők* (The Treasure-Seekers of Visegrád, 1839), by Mark Rózsavölgyi (1789–1848); and *Benyovszky* (1847), by Ferenc Doppler (1821–83). These combine large dramatic scenes based on Italian and Viennese models with lyrical and heroic episodes deriving their style from the verbunkos.

The true founder of Hungarian opera was Ferenc *Erkel (1810–93), the first composer gifted enough to fuse the above elements into a vivid and personal musical language.

From 1838 he directed the opera company of the Nemzeti Színház (Nat. T), which had opened in Pest on 22 Aug. 1837. Hitherto Hungarian opera companies had worked in provincial towns, from 1799 in Kolozsvár (Cluj) and Debrecen, from 1818 in Székesfehérvár, from 1828 in Kassa (Košice). Erkel's most important fellow-composer was Mihály *Mosonyi (1815–70); others included Károly Thern (1817–86), Károly Doppler (1825–1900), György Császár (1813–50), Ignác Bognár (1811–1900), and Károly Huber (1828–85); but for all their useful experimental work, they could not match Erkel's example. A parallel development, to which Erkel contributed, was the *népszínmű*, or popular play, which had musical insertions similar to ballad opera.

In 1884 Erkel moved to the newly opened Operaház, where he directed a large repertory. His death opened the theatre to Wagner, whose music he had resisted; of a Wagnerian generation which followed, the most outstanding was Ödön Mihalovich (1842–1929), composer of Wagnerian operas including *Toldi szerelme* (Toldi's Love, 1893) and a founder of the Budapest Wagner Society. A number of composers found international careers, especially in Habsburg lands: those who continued to work for national opera at home included Ferenc Sárosi (1855–1913), Jenő Sztojanovics (1864–1919), and Emil *Ábrányi (1882–1970). Their work helped to pave the way for the major talents of Béla *Bartók and Zoltán *Kodály. Other successful opera composers of the inter-war years included Ferenc Farkas (b 1905), Leó Weiner (1885–1960), Albert Siklós (1878–1942), and Pál Kadosa (1903–83).

After the war, with massive state support, opera developed and spread further, and new companies were formed in a number of provincial and industrial centres. The composer to win greatest international fame has been György Ligeti (b 1923), whose *Le grand macabre* was produced in Stockholm 1978. Among other composers to emerge have been Emil Petrovics (b 1930), with *C'est la guerre* (1962), *Lysistrate* (comp. 1962, prem. 1971), and *Bűn és bűnhődés* (Crime and Punishment, 1969); Sándor *Szokolay (b 1931); Sándor Balassa (b 1935) with *Az ajtón kívül* (Outside the Door, 1978); and Attila Bozay (b 1939), with *Csongor és Tünde* (1984).

See also BUDAPEST.

Hunter, Rita (*b* Wallasey, 15 Aug. 1933). English soprano. Studied Liverpool with E. Francis, London with R. Llewellyn; later with E. Turner. London, SW, chorus, 1954–6; début in *Figaro* (First Bridesmaid). London: CR 1956–8; SW, 1959–66; CG, from 1963; ENO from 1968. New York, M, 1972–7. Also Munich, S Francisco, Sydney. A generous singer with an ample, brilliant voice, notable as Brünnhilde, Norma, Amelia, Elisabeth de Valois. (R)

Huntsmen's Chorus. The name usually given to the chorus in Act III of Weber's *Der Freischütz*, in which the huntsmen sing of the joys of the chase.

Hunyadi László. Opera in 4 acts by Erkel; text by Béni Egressy, after Lőrince Tóth's drama. Prem. Budapest 27 Jan. 1844.

Hungary, 15th cent. László Hunyadi (ten), leader of the Hungarian army, learns of a plan by the new king László V (ten) to massacre his troops. When confronted, the King feigns reconciliation. He is attracted to Maria (sop), László's beloved, and, with the support of her father, Gaga (bar), has László arrested in order that he may marry Maria. László is condemned to death and beheaded.

Huon. Sir Huon of Bordeaux (ten), lover of Reiza, in Weber's *Oberon*.

Huron, Le. Opéra-comique in 2 acts by Grétry; text by Jean François Marmontel, after Voltaire's story *L'ingénu* (1767). Prem. Paris, CI, 20 Aug. 1768.

A coastal village in Brittany. The daughter (sop) of Saint-Yves (bs) does not wish to marry Gilotin (ten), as their parents have arranged, since she has fallen in love with a Huron Indian (bar). However, Abbot Kerkabon (bs) and his sister (sop) recognize the Huron as the son of their brother, who died on an expedition to the Hurons. Kerkabon tries to instil socially acceptable behaviour in his nephew, but the latter is impatient to marry the girl he loves. In order to prevent what he sees as an unsuitable marriage, Saint-Yves decides to send his daughter to a convent, but she is forgiven and the couple are happily united.

Hüsch, Gerhard (*b* Hanover, 2 Feb. 1901; *d* Munich, 21 Nov. 1984). German baritone. Studied Hanover with Emge. Début Osnabrück 1923 (Liebenau in Lortzing's *Der Waffenschmied*). Berlin: SO, 1930–5; then S, 1937–44. London, CG, 1930; Bayreuth 1930–1. Roles included Papageno, Wolfram. Possessed a warm lyric baritone. (R)

Hvorostovsky, Dimitri (*b* Krasnoyarsk, Siberia, 16 Oct. 1962). Russian baritone. Début Krasnoyarsk 1986. Sang with the Kirov O 1987 and won the 1989 Cardiff Singer of the World Competition. Sang Yeletsky at Nice (1989) and Riccardo (*I Puritani*) at London, CG, 1992. US début Chicago 1993 (Germont); New York, M, 1995 (Eletsky). His voice is admirably well produced throughout its range. (R)

Hyde, Walter (*b* Birmingham, 6 Feb. 1875; *d* London, 11 Nov. 1951). English tenor. Studied London with G. García. Début Terry's T 1905 (in *My Lady Molly*). London, CG, 1908–24, singing Siegmund in Richter's *Ring*. New York, M, 1909–10. Member of Beecham OC, and BNOC, of which he became a dir. A distinguished Wagner singer, especially as Parsifal. Also created title-role in Holst's *The Perfect Fool*. (R)

Hylas. A young sailor (ten) in Berlioz's *Les Troyens*.

Hymn of the Sun. The chorus in Act I (repeated in Act III) of Mascagni's *Iris*.

Hymn to the Sun. The aria with which the Queen of Shemakha (sop) introduces herself in Act II of Rimsky-Korsakov's *The Golden Cockerel*.

Also aria in Glass's *Akhnaten*, in which Akhnaten declares his ideas for reform.

Hytner, Nicholas (*b* Manchester, 7 May 1956). English producer. Studied Cambridge. Début Kent O 1979 (*Turn of the Screw*). Kent O 1984–5; London, ENO, from 1983; Paris, O, 1987; London, CG, 1987 (first British *King Goes Forth to France*, Sallinen), 1988; Houston and Geneva 1989; Gly. 1991 (*Clemenza di Tito*). Prods. incl. *Giulio Cesare*, a much-praised *Xerxes*, *Figaro*, *Magic Flute*, a famous *Rienzi* on a nearly bare stage, *Knot Garden*, *King Priam*. A very self-critical producer, his intelligent, cool, yet vital productions combine a sharp originality with a sensitivity to the music.

I

Iago. A Venetian soldier, ensign to Otello, (ten) in Rossini's and (bar) in Verdi's *Otello*.

Ibert, Jacques (*b* Paris, 15 Aug. 1890; *d* Paris, 5 Feb. 1962). French composer. Studied Paris with Vidal, Pessard, and Gédalge. His wide cultural interests and his love of drama found expression in seven operas, two of them in collaboration with Honegger. Almost all are in light vein. The witty farce *Angélique* (1927), his most popular stage work, successfully re-creates the spirit of 19th-cent. French comic opera; he then turned with almost equal success to opéra-comique with *Le roi d'Yvetot* (1930). The more ambitious *L'aiglon* (1937) won more respect than popularity. Director, Union des Théâtres Lyriques from 1955.

Ice Break, The. Opera in 3 acts by Tippett; text by the composer. Prem. London, CG, 7 July 1977.

N America, present-day. The subject of the opera is stereotypes—their imprisoning characteristics and the need for rebirth. After 20 years in prison camps, Lev (bs) arrives in a new world to join his wife Nadia (sop), who had emigrated with their baby son Yuri. Also at the airport are Yuri's girl-friend Gayle (sop) and her black friend Hannah (mez), there to meet the black 'champion' Olympion (ten) together with his fan club. Out of a series of violent tensions, individual and collective, there develops a riot in which Olympion and Gayle are killed and Yuri (bar) is near-fatally injured. Nadia dies peacefully. During an interlude in which a group attempts a psychedelic 'trip', the messenger Astron (mez and high ten or counter-ten) is mistaken for God, though he disclaims his divinity. Yuri is operated on by Luke (ten), a young doctor, and, released from the cracking plaster, he finds reconciliation with his father.

'Ich baue ganz auf deine Stärke'. Belmonte's (ten) aria in Act III of Mozart's *Die Entführung aus dem Serail*, which he is instructed by Pedrillo to sing so as to conceal the placing of the escape ladders to the seraglio windows.

'Ich sah das Kind'. Kundry's (sop) narration in Act II of Wagner's *Parsifal*, in which she relates to Parsifal the grief of his mother Herzeleide when he left her never to return.

Idamante. Idomeneo's son (sop cas, or ten), lover of Ilia, in Mozart's *Idomeneo*.

Idomeneo, re di Creta. Opera in 3 acts by Mozart; text by G. B. Varesco, after Danchet's text for Campra's *Idoménée* (1712) and the ancient legend. Prem. Munich 29 Jan. 1781.

Sidon, in Crete, shortly after the end of the Trojan wars. Idomeneo, King of Crete (ten), has sent home from Troy captives including Ilia (sop), daughter of King Priam. She and Idomeneo's son Idamante (sop cas or ten) are in love, though he has not declared himself: Elettra (sop) also loves him. The impending return of Idomeneo is the sign for an amnesty of prisoners. But a sudden storm causes the King to vow to the sea-god Nettuno (Neptune, bs) a sacrifice of the first living thing he meets on shore. This is his son. Horrified, he hurries away without speaking; a joyful chorus welcomes the warriors.

The King tries to evade his vow by sending Idamante to escort Elettra home to Argos, much to the distress of Ilia. But a storm arises, and there appears a monster who ravages the island. The people hold that some unknown sinner has offended the gods, and Idomeneo admits his guilt and is ready to die.

Idamante and Ilia declare their love before he sets out to attack the monster. Elettra, mad with jealousy, interrupts, followed by the King, who is torn between guilt and anxiety for his son. He is forced, by the people's demand for a victim, to reveal the truth. On hearing that the monster has been killed by Idamante, the High Priest hesitates to make the sacrifice. Idamante nevertheless offers himself as a victim so as not to break his father's vow. But the voice of the god spares him, announcing that Idomeneo must abdicate. Idamante ascends the throne with Ilia at his side.

Mozart revised *Idomeneo* for what was probably a concert perf. in Vienna in 1786, rewriting the part of Idamante for a tenor (originally for sop cas), and it is in this version that the work is usually performed.

'I have attained the highest power'. Boris's (bs) monologue in Act II of Musorgsky's *Boris Godunov*.

'Il balen'. Di Luna's (bar) aria in Act II of Verdi's *Il trovatore*, in which he sings of the tempest raging in his heart.

Ilia. A Trojan princess (sop), daughter of King Priam and lover of Idamante, in Mozart's *Idomeneo*.

'Il lacerato spirito'. Fiesco's (bs) aria in the prologue of Verdi's *Simon Boccanegra*, in which he sings of his tortured soul.

Illica, Luigi (*b* Piacenza, 9 May 1857; *d* Colombarone, 16 Dec. 1919). Italian playwright and librettist. He wrote or collaborated on about 80 librettos for some of the leading composers of his day, beginning with Smareglia's *Il vassallo di Szigeth* (1889). Others include Catalani's *La Wally* (1892), Giordano's *Andrea Chénier* (1896), Mascagni's *Iris* (1898) and *Le maschere* (1901), and D'Erlanger's *Tess* (1906); but he is most famous for his collaboration on Puccini's *Manon Lescaut* (1893) and, with Giuseppe Giacosa, *La bohème* (1896), *Tosca* (1900), and *Madama Butterfly* (1904). A man of exuberant and violent passions, he was at his best at inventing strong characters and situations. He lacked Giacosa's sensibility, but complemented him well, and in Puccini's words 'he had plenty of imagination'. He reflected a French influence in his work, in the conflict of a powerful love element with social or political tensions, portrayed in plots of some accuracy in historical atmosphere and detail, and supported by thorough stage directions (a French practice which he introduced into Italian opera).

'Il mio tesoro'. Don Ottavio's (ten) love-song to Donna Anna in Act II of Mozart's *Don Giovanni*.

'Il segreto'. The *brindisi sung by Maffeo (con) in Act II of Donizetti's *Lucrezia Borgia* as the banqueters drink the wine poisoned by Lucrezia.

Immolation. The name generally given to the scene of Brünnhilde's death in Act III of Wagner's *Götterdämmerung* as she rides (or in most modern productions walks) into the flames of Siegfried's funeral pyre.

Immortal Hour, The. Opera in 2 acts by Boughton; text by 'Fiona Macleod' (William Sharp). Prem. Glastonbury 26 Aug. 1914.

Etain (sop), princess of the fairies, is travelling in the human world in search of some new, unidentified experience. The mortal King Eochaidh (bar) is also seeking such an experience: the 'immortal hour'. Dalua (bar), the Lord of Shadow, engineers the meeting of the couple; they fall in love and marry. A year later Midir (ten), prince of the fairies, arrives to take Etain back to her spirit world. As she departs, Dalua touches Eochaidh, who falls dead at this fatal contact.

impresario (from It. *impresa*: 'undertaking'). Organizer and/or manager of an opera company. The Italian equivalent of Ger. *Schauspieldirektor*, both in general use and as title for Mozart's opera.

'Improvviso'. The name generally given to the aria 'Un dì all'azzurro spazio' in Act I of Giordano's *Andrea Chénier*, in which Chénier composes a poem on the beauty of the world and man's inhumanity to man, and exhorts Maddalena not to scorn love.

Incoronazione di Poppea, L' (The Coronation of Poppea). Opera in a prologue and 3 acts, usually attrib. Monteverdi, though almost certainly composed with the assistance of others; text by G. F. Busenello, after Tacitus, *Annals*, xiii–xv. Prem. Venice, autumn 1643.

In the prologue the allegorical figures of Fortune and Virtue argue over which is the stronger, though Love claims he is more powerful than either, as the action of the opera will show.

Rome, AD 65. Nerone, the Roman Emperor, has taken as his mistress the scheming Poppea, much to the consternation of Ottone, who is in love with her himself. Ottavia, Nerone's wife, is grief-stricken at her husband's actions, and the efforts of her nurse Arnalta and page to comfort her are in vain, as are those of the philosopher Seneca. When Nerone announces that he is to banish Ottavia and marry Poppea, Seneca accuses him of insanity. This, together with Poppea's insinuations that Seneca is trying to usurp the Emperor's position, persuades Nerone to sentence the philosopher to death. Ottone takes a last chance at reconciliation with Poppea; when this is unsuccessful he resolves to kill her, and begins to woo Drusilla, a courtier who has long sought his attention.

Told by Mercurio that Nerone has ordered his death, Seneca commits suicide: the Emperor celebrates with the poet Lucano. Ottavia meets Ottone and persuades him, with some difficulty, that he must go ahead with his plan to kill Poppea. He borrows clothes for a disguise from Drusilla, who is overjoyed that he now desires her. Poppea prepares for bed, and will let only Arnalta sleep near her. After the nurse has sung a lullaby, Amore appears, to keep watch over Poppea. When the disguised Ottone enters to carry out the murder, Amore prevents him, singing a triumphant aria as he makes his escape.

Arrested for her apparent attempt on Poppea's life, Drusilla protests her innocence to Nerone, though when Ottone tries to admit his guilt she protects him by confessing to the plot. Nerone, not knowing who is speaking the truth, resolves to kill them both, but eventually relents and orders them to be exiled instead. Discovering Ottavia to have been involved in the plan, Nerone banishes her as well. After Ottavia's final distraught appearance, the coronation of Poppea concludes the opera, watched over by Venere and Amore.

'In diesen heil'gen Hallen'. Sarastro's (bs) aria in Act II of Mozart's *Die Zauberflöte*, in which he tells Pamina that no thought of violence is entertained within the sacred walls of the Temple of Isis and Osiris.

Indy, Vincent d' (*b* Paris, 27 Mar. 1851; *d* 2 Dec. 1931). French composer. Studied Paris with Lavignac. Apart from a number of projects and the unimportant 1-act *Attendez-moi sous l'orme* (1882), D'Indy's first opera was *Le chant de la cloche* (1912), heavily indebted to *Parsifal*. He further expressed his love of Wagner, his ancestral feeling for the Cévennes, and his discipleship of Franck in his most important stage work, *Fervaal* (1897). *L'étranger* (1903) continues in the same line while discovering a greater refinement of texture. Nevertheless, it came to stand for virtues opposite to those expressed in *Pelléas*. *La légende de St Christophe* (1920) continued to oppose the new values in an extraordinary, ambitious mélange of Wagner and medieval mysteries. His last stage work, *Le rêve de Cinyras* (1927), is an unambitious operetta.

Inès. The daughter (sop) of Don Diego in Meyerbeer's *L'Africaine*.

'In fernem Land'. Lohengrin's (ten) narration (Ger., *Gralserzählung*) in Act III of Wagner's *Lohengrin*, in which he discloses his identity and tells of the Holy Grail.

Inghilleri, Giovanni (*b* Porto Empedocle, 9 Mar. 1894; *d* Milan, 10 Dec. 1959). Italian baritone and composer. Début Milan, T Carcano, 1919 (Valentin). Successful career in Italy, including at Milan, S, after 1945; London, CG, 1928–35; Chicago 1929–30. Created leading roles in works by Casella, Malipiero, and Cattozzo. Roles included Scarpia, Gérard (*Chénier*), Amfortas. He also wrote an opera (*La burla*), a ballet, and several songs. (R)

'In quelle trine morbide'. Manon's (sop) aria in Act II of Puccini's *Manon Lescaut*, in which she tells of the chill in the splendour among which she lives, and wishes she were back in the humble dwelling where she and Des Grieux were once so happy.

'In questa reggia'. Turandot's (sop) narration in Act II of Puccini's *Turandot*, in which she recounts how the rape of her ancestress Princess Lo-u-Ling made her resolve to be revenged upon all men through her vow to set riddles to those seeking her love, with death as the price for failure.

Insanguine, Giacomo (*b* Monopoli, 22 Mar. 1728; *d* Naples, 1 Feb. 1795). Italian composer. Studied Naples with Abos, Feo, and Durante. Although not well known outside Naples, he was one of the most frequently performed composers there in the mid-18th cent. Of his *c*.20 operas most successful were the comic *Lo funnaco revotato* (1756) and the serious *Didone abbandonata* (1770). In 1785 became director of the S Onofrio Cons.

Intendant (Ger.: 'superintendent'). The administrator of a German opera-house; not necessarily the artistic or musical director.

interlude. See INTERMEZZO.

intermède (Fr.: 'interlude'). A term current in France in the 17th and 18th cents. with a variety of applications, but always carrying the connotation of a self-contained musical entertainment, invariably featuring dance, inserted between the acts of another, larger work. Molière used them as a means of introducing secondary plots into his *comédies-ballets (thereby influencing the eventual development of opéra-comique), while they also appeared frequently in Italian operas performed in Paris during the 17th cent., e.g. Cavalli's *Serse* (1660) and *Ercole amante* (1662).

intermedio (It.: 'interlude'). Following the renaissance of secular drama in Italy, which began with Poliziano's *Orfeo* (1480), it became customary to include musical interludes between the acts of the spoken plays. These intermedi frequently had an allegorical connection with the substance of the main plot and in their combination of drama and music were an important precursor of opera, since they often told a continuous, if interrupted, story. At aristocratic courts, such as those of Mantua, Ferrara, and above all Florence, intermedi were usually given for a celebration, such as a birthday or wedding, and called for elaborate choral and instrumental forces. Particularly important intermedi included those performed at Florence in 1539 and 1589. The latter occasion, at which the intermedi framed Bargagli's comedy *La pellegrina*, represented the high point of the genre, and among those who collaborated in its success were several of the important figures of early opera, such as Peri, Caccini, and Rinuccini, while Cavalieri also supervised the whole production. Although the intermedi are frequently cited as an important influence on the birth of opera, this somewhat overstates the case, for their grandiose scale, spectacular presentation, and general dependence on Renaissance musical gesture were quite at variance with the Bardi *camerata's ideas.

intermezzo (It.: 'interlude'). Originally, the intermezzo was a short, comic entertainment inserted between the acts of a serious opera, often including grotesque elements. The earliest instance probably occurred at Bologna in 1623, when intermezzi were interpolated into *L'amorosa innocenza*; despite their separation, they formed a continuous opera of their own, *La coronazione di Apollo*. This joining together of a serious and a comic entertainment was very popular throughout the 17th cent., and received impetus from the reforms of opera seria led by Zeno and Metastasio, in which comic scenes, a staple feature of Venetian opera, were excised. The intermezzo grew in importance and the appeal of the more realistic, popular genre in contrast to the gods, kings, and heroes of opera seria had become too strong to be contained.

Following the wave of interest in the genre occasioned by Pariati's librettos for *Pimpinone* (1708) and *Paspagnacco* (1708), Naples was established as the main centre for composition and performance of the intermezzo. By the time of the most famous example, Pergolesi's *La serva padrona* (1733), the genre was widely cultivated throughout Italy. Rather than the stilted da capo structure of opera seria, it employed a wide variety of aria forms, and made distinctive use of the bass voice. Classically, there would be two singing characters, each of whom would sing one or two arias and a duet, and a mute. If opera seria stood for the establishment of order and the importance of conformity to social and moral standards, the intermezzo satisfied the complementary wish not to conform and, drawing from the lively world of the commedia dell'arte, so came to make the larger entertainment seem artificial and stilted. Eventually it was subsumed, together with the wider tradition of non-serious operas such as Abbatini's *Dal male il bene* and Scarlatti's *Trionfo d'onore*, into the mainstream *opera buffa tradition.

In opera the word 'intermezzo' is also used in the sense of an interlude, a short piece of music, or even a short scene interpolated in the course of an opera. An orchestral intermezzo may be virtually a miniature tone-poem, perhaps denoting the passing of time (as between scenes 8 and 9 of Mascagni's *Cavalleria rusticana*) or describing or summarizing events between scenes (as between Acts II and III of Puccini's *Manon Lescaut*). A dramatic intermezzo, or interlude, may take the form of a scene to some degree outside the main plot (as with the choral interlude between Acts I and II of Schoenberg's *Moses und Aron*). Henze's 'opera seria' *The Bassarids* (1966), includes a dramatic intermezzo, *The Judgement of Calliope*, which though relevant to the main plot is a conscious reversion to the earlier practice of the 18th cent.

Intermezzo. Opera in 2 acts by Richard Strauss; text by the composer. Prem. Dresden 4 Nov. 1924.

While the famous conductor Robert Storch (bar) is away, his wife Christine (sop) is pursued by the young Baron Lummer (ten). However, she soon realizes that all he wants is her money. A letter arrives for her husband, a passionate love-letter, causing Christine to send her husband a telegram refusing to see him again.

Storch receives the telegram when in the company of another conductor, Stroh (ten), for whom the love-letter was intended. Stroh goes ahead to explain the situation to Christine, but she still receives her husband coldly. However, the couple are reconciled and appreciate the true happiness of their marriage.

The opera is based on incidents in Strauss's own life, when his marriage was threatened by his having received, by mistake, a love-letter from an unknown admirer.

Intolleranza 1960. Opera in 2 acts by Nono; text by Nono, after Ripellino, Brecht, Sartre, Fučik, and Mayakovsky. Prem. Venice, F, 13 Apr. 1961.

A woman (sop) turns against her lover, a refugee miner (ten), not understanding his homesickness. After becoming involved accidentally in a political demonstration he is sent to a prison camp, where he finds love and humanity despite the harsh conditions. The opera ends with a purifying flood across the land, symbolizing a new sympathy between men.

'Invano, Alvaro'. The duet between Carlo (bar) and Alvaro (ten) in Act IV of Verdi's *La forza del destino*, in which Alvaro (now Padre Raffaello) tries to dissuade Carlo from challenging him to a duel.

Invisible City of Kitezh, The (Full title: *The Legend of the Invisible City of Kitezh and of the Maid Fevronia*; Russ., *Skazaniye o nevidimom grade Kitezhe i deve Fevronii*). Opera in 4 acts by Rimsky-Korsakov; text by V. I. Belsky, after the legend. Prem. St Petersburg, M, 20 Feb. 1907.

While out hunting, Vsevolod (ten), Prince of Kitezh, falls in love with Fevronia (sop), the sister of a woodcutter, who goes to his aid when he is injured. Not knowing his identity, she agrees to marry him; only when he sends a wedding procession to fetch her does she discover who he really is.

The wedding festivities in the city of Kitezh the Less are interrupted when the Tartars ransack the city; only Fevronia and the drunkard Kutierma (ten) survive. He is obliged to direct the Tartars to Great Kitezh.

Vsevolod gathers men to fight the Tartars, but they are killed, and their city vanishes completely.

Fevronia and Kutierma escape to the forest. She falls, exhausted, and as she dies,

she sees a vision of Vsevolod guiding her to a rebuilt Kitezh.

In another world, the city stands again and its people celebrate the wedding of Vsevolod and Fevronia.

Iolanta. See YOLANTA.

Iphigénie en Aulide. Opera in 3 acts by Gluck; text by Du Roullet, after Racine (1674), after Euripides' tragedy (?406–405 BC, unfin.). Prem. Paris, O, 19 Apr. 1774.

The island of Aulis. The oracle of Diane has stated that the Greeks' journey to Troy, which has been interrupted, may continue only if Iphigénie (sop), daughter of the Greek King Agamemnon (bs-bar), is sacrificed. Iphigénie and her mother Clytemnestre (mez) have been summoned to Aulis, supposedly for Iphigénie's marriage to Achille.

Reports of Achille's infidelity, intended to encourage Iphigénie to leave the island, prove to be unfounded.

The wedding celebrations are suspended when Arcas (bs) informs the company that Agamemnon intends to kill his daughter at the altar. After a violent argument between Agamemnon and Achille, the King orders his wife and daughter to quit Aulis.

Iphigénie decides to submit to the sacrifice, but the ceremony is interrupted by Achille. The high priest Calchas (bs) finally announces that Diane has been moved by the sincerity of emotion displayed, and will permit the army to move on without any sacrifice.

Iphigénie en Tauride. Opera in 4 acts by Gluck; text by Guillard and Du Roullet, after Euripides' drama (414–412 BC). Prem. Paris, O, 18 May 1779.

Tauris. Iphigénie (sop) is unaware that her brother Oreste (bar) killed their mother Clytemnestre, after she had murdered her husband Agamemnon. As priestess to Diane, she is obliged by Thoas, King of Scythia (bs), to put all strangers to death. When Oreste and his friend Pylade (ten) arrive on Tauris, Iphigénie fails to recognize them.

Oreste is tormented by the thought that he is the cause of Pylade's death, and by memories of his crime. In a state of delirium, he tells Iphigénie the fate of the royal family, without disclosing his own identity.

Disconcerted by the stranger's resemblance to her brother, Iphigénie tries to save him by sending him with a message to her sister Electre. Oreste refuses to leave Pylade, and when he vows to commit suicide if his friend is sacrificed, Pylade agrees to go.

At the moment of sacrifice, Iphigénie recognizes her brother. Thoas demands the sacrifice, and Iphigénie swears she will die with Oreste. The situation is saved by a Greek party, led by Pylade. Thoas is killed; Diane appears, pardons Oreste, and returns to the Greeks her image, which had been stolen by the Scythians.

Ippolitov-Ivanov, Mikhail (*b* Gatchina, 19 Nov. 1859; *d* Moscow, 28 Jan. 1935). Russian composer and conductor. Studied St Petersburg with Rimsky-Korsakov. Cond. Tiflis O from 1884, also in Moscow at Mamontov O (1898–1906), Zimin O, and Bolshoy from 1925. He conducted a number of the prems. of operas by Rimsky-Korsakov, whose music, as well as Tchaikovsky's, much influenced his own conservative idiom. His operas include *Ruth* (1887) and *Izmena* (Treachery, 1910); he also wrote text and music of Acts II–IV in completion of Musorgsky's *The Marriage*.

Ireland. The success of *The Beggar's Opera* in Dublin in 1728 led to many imitations using Irish songs as well as other folk and art music. Irish composers of opera, including Balfe, Wallace, and Stanford, mostly worked abroad. The first opera with a Gaelic (as well as English) libretto was *Muirgheis* (1903) by O'Brien Butler, followed by *Eithne* (1910) by Robert O'Dwyer.

See also DUBLIN, WEXFORD.

Irene. Rienzi's sister (sop), lover of Adriano, in Wagner's *Rienzi*.

Iris. Opera in 3 acts by Mascagni; text by Illica. Prem. Rome, C, 22 Nov. 1898.

The opera, set in 19th-cent. Japan, tells of the vain attempt by Osaka (ten) to win the love of the pure young Iris (sop). He arranges with Kyoto (bar), the keeper of a brothel, to have her abducted, and her blind father (Il Cieco, bs), thinking she has gone there voluntarily, curses her and flings mud at her. Iris drowns herself in a sewer.

Irmelin. Opera in 3 acts by Delius; text by the composer. Prem. Oxford, New T, 4 May 1953.

The Princess Irmelin (sop) awaits her true love. Nils (ten), a prince disguised as a swineherd, is searching for the ideal woman; he is told he will find her at the end of the silver stream, and there he finds Irmelin.

Isaac, Adèle (*b* Calais, 8 Jan. 1854; *d* Paris 22 Oct. 1915). French soprano. Studied Paris with Duprez. Début Paris, T Montmartre, 1870 (Massé's *Les noces de Jeannette*). Brussels, M, 1872–3; Paris: OC, between 1873 and 1894; O, 1883–5. A brilliant coloratura singer, successful as Gounod's Juliette, Violetta, etc., she created Olympia and Antonia in the first *Tales of Hoffmann*, persuading Offenbach to rewrite the Doll's music to suit her skills. (He also altered the other roles for her, but died before completing a florid aria for Giulietta; this act was thus omitted in the prem.) First Minka in Chabrier's *Le roi malgré lui*.

Isabeau. Opera in 3 acts by Mascagni; text by Illica. Prem. Buenos Aires, Coliseo, 2 June 1911.

Cavaggio, the Middle Ages. Unwilling to choose a husband, the Princess Isabeau (sop) is made to ride naked through the streets in the middle of the day; anyone who dares look at her will be condemned to death. This edict is disobeyed by Folco (ten), a young forester, and Isabeau falls in love with him; the crowd, however, lynch him, and Isabeau kills herself over his dying body.

Isabella. (1) An Italian lady (con), lover of Lindoro, in Rossini's *L'italiana in Algeri*.

(2) The Princess Isabelle (sop), later married to Robert, Duke of Normandy, in Meyerbeer's *Robert le diable*.

Ismaele. The nephew (ten) of Sedecia, King of Jerusalem, lover of Fenena and loved by Abigaille, in Verdi's *Nabucco*.

Isolde. The Irish princess (sop), wife of King Mark and lover of Tristan, in Wagner's *Tristan und Isolde*.

Isolier. The Count's page (mez) in Rossini's *Le Comte Ory*.

Isouard, Nicolò [Nicolò de Malte] (*b* Malta, 18 May 1773; *d* Paris, 23 Mar. 1818). Maltese composer; known simply as 'Nicolò' because his family disapproved of his music. Studied Paris; abandoned commerce to study composition, notably with Sala and Guglielmi. His first opera, *L'avviso ai maritati* (1794), had some success, but it was *Artaserse* (1794) which launched him. Held ecclesiastical appointments Malta 1794–8, also composing seven operas for the theatre in Valetta, including *Il barbiere di Siviglia* (1796) and *Ginevra di Scozia* (*c*.1798). After the French occupation of Malta in 1798, he went to Paris, where he contributed numbers to his friend Rodolphe Kreutzer's *Le petit page*, 1800. Their unsuccessful *Flaminius à Corinthe* (1801) was followed by revivals of two of his Italian operas with rewritten librettos. These works, *Le tonnelier* and *L'impromptu de campagne* (both 1801), established him as a leading composer for the French stage.

His first original works for Paris were *La statue* (1802), initiating his collaboration with the librettist F. B. Hoffman, and *Michel-Ange* (1802). During 18 years in Paris he wrote 30 operas, the most successful being *Les rendez-vous bourgeois* (1807), *Cendrillon* (1810), *Joconde* (1814), and *Jeannot et Colin* (1814). In his early works, with their instant melodic charm and light-hearted spirit, he reflects the Neapolitan style in which he was reared, showing a special talent for the handling of ensembles. Later, in France, he developed the lyrical aspects of the opéra-comique in a series of comic operas best characterized as escapist: a distraction from current events, rather than a reflection or witty distortion. His initial popularity in France lay partly in the absence of any serious competitor: after Boieldieu returned from Russia in 1811, and Auber's first Parisian work was performed in 1813, Isouard lost some of his following. He was, however, appreciated abroad, especially in Vienna, where *Le billet de loterie* (1811) and *Le magicien sans magie* (1811) were given shortly after their Paris prems.

'It ain't necessarily so'. Sporting Life's (ten) cynical song in Act II of Gershwin's *Porgy and Bess*, casting doubt on the truths put forward by the Bible.

Italiana in Algeri, L' (The Italian Girl in Algiers). Opera in 2 acts by Rossini; text by Angelo Anelli, originally set by Luigi Mosca (1808). Prem. Venice, B, 22 May 1813.

Mustafà, the Bey of Algiers (bs), wishes to find an Italian wife, and force his present wife Elvira (sop) to marry an Italian slave, Lindoro (ten). By chance an Italian ship is wrecked off the coast, and Isabella (con)—who has been travelling with an elderly admirer, Taddeo, whom she passes off as her uncle—comes ashore. She is in fact seeking her long-lost lover, Lindoro. She persuades Mustafà to give her Lindoro as her personal slave.

Lindoro persuades Mustafà that Isabella will marry him if he joins the noble order of the 'Pappataci', whose primary rules are to eat and be silent. During the initiation ceremony, organized by the Italians, Isabella and Lindoro make their escape, and Mustafà is obliged to return to Elvira.

Italian overture. In contrast to the earlier practice of Venetian opera, where the overture (usually called 'canzona' or 'sonata') took the form of a slow introduction in duple metre, followed by a faster movement in triple rhythm, A. Scarlatti introduced a new form c.1680 (in *Tutto il mal non vien per nuocere*) in which the slow movement was framed by two fast outer movements. Usually known as the Italian overture, or 'sinfonia', this pattern suggests the later structure of the symphony and was in vogue, alongside the French overture, up to the middle of the 18th cent.

Italy. The emergence of opera as a distinctive art form is widely accepted as dating from the meetings of the Bardi *camerata in Florence in the late 16th cent., although the influence of earlier forms in which music and drama combined, notably the *intermedio and pastorale, must be acknowledged. The first opera produced by members of the Camerata was *Peri's *Dafne* (1598), but little of this survives. More significant therefore are the *Euridice* operas of Peri and Caccini (1600); also Cavalieri's *Rappresentazione di anima e di corpo* (1600), which introduced the new *stile recitativo to Rome, and Agazzari's *Eumelio* (1606).

One of the earliest composers to emerge was also to prove one of the art's greatest geniuses, Claudio *Monteverdi, then working at Mantua. Not only is his music of the highest inspiration, but his vision of opera as a drama in music has remained valid through all its history. The early operas had placed great emphasis on the stile recitativo, pursuing the intention of the Camerata to imitate (as they thought) ancient Greek drama, but Monteverdi greatly enriched the genre, both in form and in subtlety of characterization, giving the recitative expressive force, the orchestra eloquence, and the solo arioso numbers concentrated emotional power. His *Orfeo* (1607) represents a merging of the old tradition of the intermedio with the new practices of opera; particularly important was his skilful use of the choral or orchestral ritornello as a unifying element. Its success was repeated with *Arianna* (1608), of which only the famous lament survives.

Gradually opera spread to other Italian cities, notably Rome, where it flourished under the patronage of the Barberini family up to their exile in 1644. Roman composers continued the process begun by Monteverdi, and increasingly differentiated more clearly between aria and recitative: in the operas of Stefano *Landi there is an increased emphasis on melody in the arias, while in his *Sant'Alessio* (1632) a sinfonia before Act II suggests the arrangement of the later *Italian overture in its 3-movement structure. These works also made increased use of ensemble and, beginning with Landi's *La morte d'Orfeo* (1619), comic scenes and characters were introduced.

With the opening to the public of the T San Cassiano in Venice in 1637, opera was made available to a wider audience than the aristocracy. At the same time, the formality of the manner had begun to demand comic relief. Venetian opera of this period, as exemplified above all in the late works of Monteverdi, and those of *Cesti and *Cavalli, developed greater variety and expressiveness, with more complicated plots, livelier characterization, comic episodes, and numbers which displayed some of the favourite singers who had begun to make careers in opera and to cultivate the art of *bel canto. With firmer separation between recitative and aria, the latter developed greater formality, the *da capo form making its first appearance. Under the new commercial constraints, the role of both orchestra and chorus was much reduced. Opera continued to spread across Italy, back to Florence with Cesti, and to Naples with the work of Francesco *Provenzale. Among the first Italians to establish themselves in Germany were Agostino *Steffani, P. A. *Ziani, A. *Draghi, *Sances, and *Pallavicino.

By the beginning of the 18th cent. Italian opera had achieved a standardization that, though rigid, provided an example for native and now also for foreign composers. The genre *opera seria, frequently also called Neapolitan opera (though the validity of this connection has long been challenged), was established largely by the librettists Apostolo *Zeno and Pietro *Metastasio who, in organizing the free forms of 17th-cent. opera into a firm 3-act structure, dispensed with much that threatened dramatic logic, but provided a confining strictness. The subjects of opera seria were generally classical history and legend, with action and reflection scrupulously balanced in the course of recitative and aria: in general, the action took place in recitative, with the arias providing points of reflection and repose, also of musical expression and the chance of personal display by the singer. To this pattern the other operatic ingredients were subject; and great attention devolved upon the *aria. This form not only gave opera a strict framework in which composers could work; it encouraged the rise of a school of virtuoso singers, especially the *castrato. The major figure in the transition to opera seria was Alessandro *Scarlatti and the genre was firmly established with Antonio *Vivaldi, Nicola *Porpora, Leonardo *Leo, and Johann Adolf *Hasse. But the composer who produced the greatest and most original work in the convention was *Handel. Subsequent composers of opera seria include Nicolò *Piccinni, Antonio *Sacchini, Antonio *Salieri, and the young *Gluck and *Mozart. It was the strictness and high seriousness of opera seria that encouraged the development of separate comedies, sometimes ending an act or inserted as *intermezzos, hence the growth of *opera buffa.

Reaction against so strict a form was inevitable, and Nicolò *Jommelli and Tommaso *Traetta helped to pave the way for Gluck. By now, Italian opera had begun to establish itself firmly in most countries. Germany was long dependent on the many travelling companies that crossed Europe, such as those of the brothers Mingotti, for vernacular entertainment, but many courts also supported an Italian composer. France had developed its tragédie lyrique from the example of an Italian, Lully, and was to be frequently dependent upon great Italian composers such as Cherubini, Spontini, and Rossini. Though attempts to found a school of English opera in the late 17th cent. foundered, the influence of Italian works was equally strong here, and seen especially in Purcell's *Dido and Aeneas*. Russia cultivated its national tradition by the classic method of first importing Italians to show the way, then sending native composers to study in Italy, finally developing a national genre based on folksong and folk legend grafted at first on to Italian stock. By the early 19th cent. Germany and France were becoming determinedly independent of Italian example, and the Paris Opéra was forming a style, *Grand Opera, that in turn embraced Italians including Cherubini, Spontini, Rossini, and Verdi.

However, Italian opera continued as a central tradition, and Italian singers and singing teachers continued to set such a powerful example that much of the desire for reform sprang from a wish to diminish their influence in favour of a more dramatic art. Rossini, though happy to write for great singers, restrained them by writing out most of his notes as they were to be sung. He revealed the comic possibilities of opera buffa to a matchless degree, and confirmed a number of conventions in what has been called the Code Rossini; he was also a master of Romantic opera and Grand Opera. Italian Romantic opera reaches its fullest stature in *Bellini and *Donizetti; its greatest master was *Verdi. For all its advances, Italian opera remained grounded on its original principles—melody that was a stimulus to the finest vocal art, dramatic plots, clarity of presentation, and powerful emotions presented with a sense of theatrical effect.

Such was the strength of this tradition that little effective influence reached Italy, though there were composers (including Verdi) who felt the force of Wagner. But partly in reaction to the drama that dealt with grand and heightened emotions, there developed the manner known as *verismo, the so-called *squarcio di vita* or 'slice of life' referred to in an early classic of the genre, *Leoncavallo's *Pagliacci*. The emotions here, too, quickly tended to be extreme, as in *Mascagni, *Giordano, and *Puccini, whose work proved immensely popular and stimulating to other countries' composers. Puccini remains one of the last composers with a substantial body of work that features regularly in world repertories.

Italian opera continues to be vigorous, and to draw composers from Puccini's successors such as *Zandonai, G. F. *Malipiero, and many others, including Nono and Maderna, down to the youngest generation. In recent times the increasing diversity of musical drama has challenged the traditional Italian supremacy; but the art remains powerfully rooted in Italy, and the traditions that spring from much in Italian nature continue to be carefully cultivated in many cities and towns of the peninsula.

See also FLORENCE, MILAN, NAPLES, ROME, VENICE.

'Ite sull' colle'. Oroveso's (bs) aria opening Act I of Bellini's *Norma*, urging the Druids to go upon the hills to see when it is the new moon.

Ivanhoe. Opera in 5 acts by Sullivan; text by Julian Sturgis, after Scott's novel (1818). Prem. for inauguration of short-lived Royal English Opera House (now Palace T) in Cambridge Circus, London, 31 Jan. 1891.

England, late 12th cent. Ivanhoe (ten) is in love with Lady Rowena (sop), but her guardian Cedric (bar) wishes her to marry a descendant of the crown. Two knights Templar, De Bracy (ten) and Gilbert (bar), attend a tournament and are so enamoured of Rowena and a Jewish girl, Rebecca (sop), that they capture them, along with Cedric and Rebecca's father Isaac (bar), and imprison them in the castle of Torquilstone. Ivanhoe besieges the castle, but the knights escape, taking Rebecca with them. In a duel between Ivanhoe and Gilbert, the latter is killed. King Richard the Lionheart (bs) orders the disbandment of the Templars, and permits the marriage of Ivanhoe and Rowena.

Ivanov, Alexey (*b* Chizhovo, 22 Sept. 1904; *d* 1982). Russian baritone. Studied Tver, and Leningrad with Bosse. Leningrad, Maly T, 1932–6; Saratov O and Gorky O, 1936–8; Moscow, B, 1938–67. Roles incl. Pizarro, Prince Igor, Onegin, Escamillo, Bolkonsky (*War and Peace*); sang Ryleyev in first *The Decembrists* (Shaporin, 1953). (R)

Ivanov, Andrei (*b* Samostye, 13 Dec. 1900; *d* Moscow, 1 Oct. 1970). Ukrainian baritone. Studied Kiev with Lund. Début with travelling opera co. 1925. Baku 1926; Odessa 1928–31; Sverdlovsk, 1931–4. Kiev O 1934–49; Moscow, B, 1950–6. His large repertory incl. Rigoletto, Prince Igor, Onegin, Mazeppa, Mizgir. (R)

Ivan Susanin. A peasant (bs), father of Antonida, in Glinka's *A Life for the Tsar*. Sometimes used as the title of the opera.

Ivogün, Maria (*b* Budapest, 18 Nov. 1891; *d* Beatenberg, 2 Oct. 1987). Hungarian soprano. Studied Vienna with Schlemmer-Ambros, Munich with Schöner. Début Munich 1913 (Mimì). Sang there until 1925. London, CG, from 1924. Berlin, SO, 1925–34. Chicago 1922–3. Created Ighino (*Palestrina*). A musical singer with an exceptionally flexible voice, famous as Constanze, Norina, Gilda, etc. Strauss described her Zerbinetta as 'without rival'. Taught Rita Streich. (R)

Ivrogne corrigé, L', ou Le mariage du diable (The Drunkard Reformed, or The Devil's Marriage). Opera in 2 acts by Gluck; text by Louis Anseaume, after La Fontaine's fable *L'ivrogne en Enfer*. Prem. Vienna, B, Apr. 1760.

A vineyard, c.1760. Colette (sop) and her lover Cléon (bar) devise a scheme to outwit her Uncle Mathurin's plan to marry her to his old friend Lucas. When Mathurin (ten) and Lucas (bs) are drunk one evening, the couple simulate a scene in hell, terrifying the men into allowing Colette to marry Cléon. When the deception is revealed, Mathurin resolves to give up drinking, and to abandon Lucas.

J

Jacobin, The (Cz., *Jakobín*). Opera in 3 acts by Dvořák; text by Marie Červinková-Riegrová. Prem. Prague, C, 12 Feb. 1889.

The opera tells of how the Jacobin Bohuš (bar), returned from political exile, is helped to re-establish his position in the community by his friend Benda (ten), a musician.

Jacobs, René (*b* Ghent, 30 Oct. 1946). Belgian counter-tenor, conductor, and editor. Studied at the U of Ghent and with Alfred Deller. Début Amsterdam 1974 (Clerio in Cavalli's *Erismena*). From 1970 has directed the Concerto Vocale, giving historically accurate performances of operas by Cavalli (*Giasone* and *Serse*), Charpentier (*David et Jonatas*), and Cesti (*Orontea*); *L'incoronazione di Poppea* in his own edition at Montpellier 1989. His reputation as a major figure in the revival of early opera was enhanced with *Orfeo* at Salzburg 1993.

Jacquino. Rocco's assistant gaoler (ten) in Beethoven's *Fidelio*.

Jadlowker, Hermann (*b* Riga, 20 July 1877; *d* Tel Aviv, 13 May 1953). Latvian tenor. Studied Vienna with Gänsbacher. Début Cologne 1899 (Gomez in Kreutzer's *Nachtlager von Granada*). Karlsruhe 1906–9; Paris, C, 1910; New York, M, 1910–12; Berlin, H, 1909–21. Created King's Son (*Königskinder*), and Bacchus (*Ariadne auf Naxos*). Possessed a large, mellow voice and a superb technique; his repertory encompassed Rossini's Almaviva and Parsifal. (R)

Janáček, Leoš (*b* Hukvaldy, 3 July 1854; *d* Moravská Ostrava, 12 Aug. 1928). Czech composer. Studied Brno with Křížkovský, Prague with Skuherský, Leipzig with Paul and Grill, Vienna with Krenn.

Janáček always regarded opera as lying at the centre of his creative life. The opening of the Czech Theatre in Brno in January 1885 encouraged him to sketch an operatic synopsis on Chateaubriand's *The Last Abencerage*, but his first completed opera was *Šárka* (comp. 1887–8), to a text originally intended for Dvořák. When Dvořák turned it down, Janáček composed it without the author's permission. It is a remarkably assured and well-written work with some anticipations of his later style; and it is a stronger piece than its successor, *The Beginning of a Romance* (1894). Here, in an attempt to compose a light folk comedy, he reverted to an unsuccessful version of opera based on folk-songs and dances.

Through this work, however, he came to know Gabriela Preissová's story *Její pastorkyňa*, which provided the basis of his next opera. Better known outside Czechoslovakia as *Jenůfa* (1904), it was his first operatic masterpiece and has remained perhaps the best-known of them. The work's gestation was long, and shows in the move away from number-orientated opera (which lies behind the first act) to a more freely composed manner depending largely on monologue or soliloquy. This also enabled him to develop a more personal idiom by the use of speech-melodies, melodic curves which owed their shapes to his observations of Czech (especially Moravian) vocal inflections but their character to his own lyrical gift. They also enabled him to place this gift at the service of the truthful yet compassionate observation of human nature which is first fully revealed in *Jenůfa*. Further, he was able to make use of these identifying melodic phrases motivically (though not in any manner approaching Leitmotiv) so as to construct whole scenes. It is his first opera to a prose text, though he was obliged to give the text some metrical symmetries so as to match his musical intentions. The first performance of *Jenůfa* caused little widespread attention, and it was not until the Prague prem. of a revised version in 1916 that the work achieved real success.

Meanwhile, Janáček turned his attention first to *Osud* (comp. 1903–6), or *Fate*, a work which marks some musical advance but a reverse in its use of a clumsy, semi-autobiographical text. There are also problems with the text of *The Excursions of Mr Brouček* (1920). The opera is divided into two parts (a third was initiated but not completed). The adventures of the stolid burgher Brouček as he is precipitated first into a society of empty aesthetes on the moon, and then back into the Hussite wars, owe something to the Viennese magic comedy of Raimund, but are essentially local; yet the opera's musical inventiveness has earned it increasingly wide acceptance.

Among other subjects contemplated by Janáček, in his affection for all things Russian, was *Anna Karenina*; but he eventually turned to Ostrovsky for *Káťa Kabanová* (1921). Even more than in *Jenůfa*, he here develops a motivic identification with characters, including the expression of the subtlety of Káťa herself by the use of an exceptionally wide range of motives for her, and the dependence of some of the subsidiary characters on her by their assumption of her motives. He can also characterize more freely than in earlier works by means of elegance and charm of line for the suffering Káťa, light superficiality for certain others, a grim abruptness for the mother-in-law responsible for Káťa's downfall and death.

Janáček was by now internationally famous, and his operas were taken up especially in Germany. More favourable operatic conditions at home gave him encouragement; and he was sustained by a passionate friendship with a younger woman, Kamila Stösslová, with whom he identified the heroines of his operas. His next work, however, showed his ability to draw on unlikely sources, in his use of a strip cartoon for an opera on the life and death of a fox, *The Cunning Little Vixen*, as it is known in English: a more correct translation is 'The Adventures of Vixen Sharpears' (1924). The narrative is here somewhat disjunct, but the subject enabled Janáček further to refine and concentrate his idiom without loss of lyrical intensity. It is characteristic in its laconic yet passionate, as well as compassionate, invention, and in its nearly pantheistic devotion to nature and the forces binding men, animals, and the forest. (There is, however, no attempt to make human–animal equivalents in the plot, as in the German version by Max Brod.)

The Makropoulos Case (1926) turns from the life of the woods to an urban world of legal wrangles and the unnatural figure of a singer whose use of an elixir of life has condemned her to a tragic immortality; yet the theme is related in that Janáček is pointing to the justness of a natural life span, and insisting that it is the certainty of death that gives beauty and meaning to life. The musical idiom is sharper and more rapid than in previous works, with—until the final monologue—an even greater detachment between voice and orchestra. His final work was on another unlikely subject, Dostoyevsky's prison diaries *From the House of the Dead* (1930). There is no female part here, and the series of short narratives, deriving from multiple characterizations of the various prisoners, is made to build up an image of different conditions of men drawn together by suffering and rising above it. At the head of the score he set the words, 'In every human being there is a divine spark.'

Janowitz, Gundula (*b* Berlin, 2 Aug. 1937). German soprano. Studied Graz with Thöny. Début Vienna, S, 1960 (Barbarina). Regular appearances there, and at Salzburg from 1963. Gly. 1964; New York, M, 1967; Paris, O, 1973; London, CG, 1976 (Eva). Roles included Pamina, Donna Anna, Leonore, Sieglinde, Ariadne. Possesses a vibrant and expressive voice. (R)

Janowski, Marek (*b* Warsaw, 18 Feb. 1939). Polish conductor. Studied in Cologne and Siena. Assistant at Aachen and Düsseldorf, then guest in Cologne, Hamburg, and Paris. Music dir. at Freiburg O 1973–5; Dortmund O 1975–9. London début with Henze's *Junge Lord* (SW 1969, with Cologne O). Chicago 1980 (*Lohengrin*); New York, M, 1984 (*Arabella*). First CD recording of *The Ring*; *Meistersinger* at the Paris, C. (R)

Janssen, Herbert (*b* Cologne, 22 Sept. 1892; *d* New York, 3 June 1965). German, later US, baritone. Studied Berlin with Daniel. Début Berlin, S, 1922 (Schreker's *Der Schatzgraber*), S until 1938; London, CG, 1926–39; Paris, O, 1929; Bayreuth 1930–7; Buenos Aires 1938; New York, M, 1939–52. A fine singer with a warm tone and much dramatic intelligence, celebrated as Wolfram, Kurwenal, Kothner, Gunther, Amfortas; sang Sachs and Wotan less successfully. (R)

Jasager, Der (The Yea-Sayer). Opera in 2 acts by Kurt Weill; text by Brecht, after a 15th-cent. Japanese Noh drama. Prem. Berlin 24 June 1930.

A boy plans to accompany his teacher and three older students on a strenuous expedition in search of a wise man, in order to find a cure for his ailing mother. Unable to complete the journey, he agrees to submit to a tradition which demands that anyone failing to reach the goal must be thrown into the valley; he does so on condition that the teacher takes the medicine back to his mother.

Weill intended this as a didactic opera concerned with intellectual and moral matters characterizing it as a Lehrstück (teaching piece).

Jason. The leader of the Argonauts (ten), former husband of Medea, in Cherubini's *Médée*.

Jean de Paris (John of Paris). Opera in 2 acts by Boieldieu; text by C. Godard d'Aucour de Saint-Just. Prem. Paris, OC, 4 Apr. 1812.

A Pyrenean village, 17th cent. The young widowed Princess of Navarre (sop) is destined to marry the Crown Prince of France (ten), but intends first to spend some time travelling. At a Pyrenean inn, preparations for her arrival are interrupted by the arrival of the suite of 'Jean de Paris' (the Prince in disguise); they take possession of the inn. The Princess's Seneschal (bar) is outraged, but Jean declares that the Princess may be his guest. She recognizes him, but conceals this, telling him as they dance that she has already chosen him her husband; all is disclosed, and the Prince and Princess are united.

'Je crois entendre encore'. Nadir's (ten) aria in Act I of Bizet's *Les pêcheurs de perles*, in which he sings of his love for Leïla.

'Je dis que rien ne m'épouvante'. Micaëla's (sop) aria in Act III of Bizet's *Carmen*, in which she prays to God to deliver her from the fear that against her will has overcome her as she seeks Don José in the mountains.

Jenifer. A young girl (sop), bride of Mark, in Tippett's *The Midsummer Marriage*.

Jeník. A young villager (ten), son of Tobias Micha by his first marriage, in Smetana's *The Bartered Bride*.

Jenůfa (Cz., *Její pastorkyňa*: Her Foster-Daughter). Opera in 3 acts by Janáček; text by the composer, after Gabriela Preissová's drama (1890). Prem. Brno, N, 21 Jan. 1904.

Moravia, 1900. In the mill of Grandmother Buryjovka in the Moravian mountains lives the ne'er-do-well Števa Buryja (ten); his stepbrother Laca Klemeň (ten) is a farm-hand and their cousin Jenůfa (sop) helps in the house. She is the stepdaughter of Grandmother Buryjovka's daughter-in-law, who, from her position as sexton, is known as the Kostelnička (sop). Jenůfa is expecting Števa's child, and anxiously awaits the result of a conscription ballot to know whether he will

return and marry her. He returns, unrecruited but also drunk, and the Kostelnička forbids him to marry Jenůfa until he has proved his worth by a year's total abstinence. When Števa, who is only physically attracted by Jenůfa, leaves, Laca offers her flowers and tries to kiss her; on being repelled, he slashes her face with a knife.

Jenůfa has secretly had a son. The Kostelnička, tormented by the disgrace, sends for Števa to marry Jenůfa; but he denies responsibility, and says that he is engaged to the mayor's daughter Karolka (mez). Laca appears, penitent and willing to marry Jenůfa though shocked by hearing of the birth of Števa's child. The Kostelnička, hoping to help the marriage on, tells Laca that the child has died; she takes it and drowns it in a brook. When Jenůfa awakes, she is also told that the child has died.

Jenůfa and Laca are about to be married, as are Števa and Karolka. As the ceremony begins, news comes that the body of a baby has been found under the ice. Jenůfa realizes the truth and reveals whose baby it is. To save her from being accused, the Kostelnička steps forward and confesses her guilt. Comforted by Jenůfa's forgiveness, she is led away. Jenůfa now turns to Laca and gives him his freedom; but he is faithful, and as the curtain falls they pledge their love.

Jeremiáš, Otakar (*b* Písek, 17 Oct. 1892; *d* Prague, 5 Mar. 1962). Czech composer and conductor. Studied with his father, **Bohuslav Jeremiáš** (1859–1918), founder of the South Bohemian Cons., and in Prague with Novák. Among other activities, dir. Prague, N, 1945–7. The most important of his operas, Romantic and post-Janáček in manner, is a setting of *The Brothers Karamazov* (1928) that has won much respect in his own country. His older brother **Jaroslav Jeremiáš** (*b* Písek, 14 Aug. 1889; *d* České Budějovice, 16 Jan. 1919) was a pianist and the composer of a number of works including an opera *Starý král* (The Old King, 1919).

Jerger, Alfred (*b* Brno, 9 June 1889; *d* Vienna, 18 Nov. 1976). Austrian bass-baritone. Studied conducting, Vienna. Passau, Berlin, and Zurich as conductor. Singing début Zurich 1917 (Lothario, *Mignon*). Munich 1919; Vienna 1920–64; London, CG, 1924, 1934. A highly versatile artist; also a prod. and libretto reviser. Large repertory included Leporello, Don Giovanni, Sachs, Beckmesser,

Ochs, Barak, and Jonny (Krenek); created Mandryka (*Arabella*), and the Man (*Die glückliche Hand*). Appointed dir. of Vienna, S, 1945, and sang Almaviva (Mozart) in its reopening season. (R)

Jeritza, Maria (*b* Brno, 6 Oct. 1887; *d* Orange, NJ, 10 July 1982). Moravian soprano. Studied Brno, Prague with Auspitzer, later New York with Sembrich. Début Olomouc 1910 (Elsa). Vienna, S, 1912–35. New York, M, 1921–32; London, CG, 1925–6. Created title-role of *Ariadne auf Naxos* (in both versions), and Empress (*Die Frau ohne Schatten*); also the inspiration for *Die ägyptische Helena*. A glamorous and gifted singing actress who used her resources to full effect, she was a celebrated Tosca, Turandot, Minnie, and Salome. (R)

'Jerum! jerum!' Hans Sachs's (bar) cobbling song in Act II of Wagner's *Die Meistersinger von Nürnberg*.

Jérusalem. See LOMBARDI, I.

Jerusalem, Siegfried (*b* Oberhausen, 17 Apr. 1940). German tenor. Bassoonist until 1977. Studied Stuttgart with Kalcher. Début Stuttgart 1975 (Prisoner, *Fidelio*). Hamburg 1976. Bayreuth from 1977; Berlin, D, from 1978; New York from 1980; London, CG, from 1986; also Geneva, Munich, Zurich, etc. A gifted Wagner singer, combining a fine physique, dramatic conviction, and a well-projected, lyrical style. Roles incl. Erik, Lohengrin, Walther, Siegfried, Siegmund, Parsifal. (R)

Jessonda. Opera in 3 acts by Spohr; text by E. H. Gehe, after Antoine Lemierre's tragedy *La veuve de Malabar*. Prem. Kassel 28 July 1823.

Goa, early 16th cent. The Rajah's widow Jessonda (sop) must die, according to custom, on his funeral pyre. Nadori (ten), a young priest of Brahma, must announce this to her; but he falls in love with her sister Amazili (sop) and promises to help save Jessonda. Purifying herself for her ordeal, Jessonda is recognized by her former lover, the Portuguese general Tristan d'Acunha (bar), besieging Goa. A truce forbids him to attack and rescue her; but when he finds that the priest Dan-dau (bs) has broken the truce, he feels free to enter the temple by a secret passage and rescue Jessonda.

'Je suis Titania'. Philine's (sop) aria in Act II of Thomas's *Mignon*, sung as she remembers her role in the performance the strol-

ling players have been giving of *A Midsummer Night's Dream*.

Jewels of the Madonna, The. See GIOIELLI DELLA MADONNA, I.

'Jewel Song' (Fr., 'Air des bijoux'). Marguerite's (sop) aria in Act III of Gounod's *Faust*, admiring the jewels in the casket which has been brought her by Faust and Méphistophélès.

Ježibaba. The Witch (con) in Dvořák's *Rusalka*.

Jo, Sumi (*b* Seoul, 22 Nov. 1962). Korean soprano. Studied Seoul and Rome. Début Trieste 1986 (Gilda). Major career from 1989, when she sang Barbarina then Oscar under Karajan at Salzburg. Vienna, S, and New York, M, débuts 1989. She has gained wide recognition in such coloratura roles as Olympia (London, CG, 1991), the Queen of the Night, and Zerlina (*Fra Diavolo*) (Milan, S, 1992). (R)

Jobin, Raoul (*b* Quebec, 8 Apr. 1906; *d* Quebec, 13 Jan. 1974). Canadian tenor. Studied Paris. Début Paris, O, 1930 (Gounod's Tybalt). Paris, O, 1930–9, 1946–52, and OC from 1937; London, CG, 1937; New York, M, 1940–50; also Chicago, Buenos Aires, S Francisco, New Orleans. Roles incl. Lohengrin, Walther, Gounod's Faust, Don José, Werther, Pelléas, Radamès, Canio, Cavaradossi; created Fabrice (Sauguet's *Chartreuse de Parme*). (R)

Jochanaan. John the Baptist (bar) in Strauss's *Salome*.

Jochum, Eugen (*b* Babenhausen, 1 Nov. 1902; *d* Munich, 26 Mar. 1987). German conductor. Studied Augsburg, Munich with Waltershausen and Hausegger. Répétiteur Munich 1924–5, Mönchen-Gladbach 1925–6. Chief cond. Kiel 1926–9, Mannheim 1929–30; music dir. Duisburg 1930–2, Hamburg 1934–5. Bayreuth 1953 (*Tristan*), 1954 (*Tannhäuser*), 1971–3 (*Parsifal*). (R) His brother **Georg** (*b* Babenhausen, 10 Dec. 1909; *d* Mülheim, 1 Nov. 1970) was a cond. who worked at Frankfurt 1934–7, Plauen 1937–40, and as music dir. Linz 1940–5.

John of Leyden. The Anabaptist prophet and self-proclaimed Emperor (ten) in Meyerbeer's *Le prophète*.

Johnson, Edward (*b* Guelph, Ontario, 22

Aug. 1878; d Toronto, 20 Apr. 1959). Canadian tenor and manager. Studied New York with Feilitsch, Florence with Lombardi. Début (as Edoardo di Giovanni) Padua 1912 (Chénier). Milan, S, 1913–14, first Italian Parsifal. Between 1914 and 1919 he created leading tenor roles in works by Montemezzi, Pizzetti, and Alfano; was also the first Italian Rinuccio and Luigi, and an admirable Siegfried and Tannhäuser. Chicago 1919–22; New York, M, 1922–35, creating leading roles in The King's Henchman, Peter Ibbetson, and Merry Mount. London, CG, with BNOC, 1923 (Gounod's Faust). Was also a fine Pelléas. Manager New York, M, 1935–50. Then active in opera class, Toronto U. An intelligent and musicianly singer with a fine stage presence and a strong lyrical voice; latterly a skilful manager. (R)

Johnston, James (b Belfast 17 Aug. 1903; d Belfast, 17 Oct. 1991). Irish tenor. Début Dublin 1940 (Duke of Mantua). London: SW, 1945–50, as guest until 1957; CG, 1950–8. Created Hector in The Olympians (Bliss). Roles included Canio, Radamès, Manrico, first English Gabriele Adorno. Possessed a ringing, Italianate tenor. (R)

Jolie fille de Perth, La (The Fair Maid of Perth). Opera in 4 acts by Bizet; text by Saint-Georges and Adenis, loosely based on Scott's novel The Fair Maid of Perth (1832). Prem. Paris, L, 26 Dec. 1867.

Perth, c.1500. Henry Smith (ten), an armourer, gives shelter to the gipsy Mab (sop or méz); when his beloved Catherine Glover (sop) arrives, Mab is forced to hide, but her subsequent appearance makes Catherine suspicious of Henry's behaviour. The Duke of Rothsay's (bar or ten) plan to abduct Catherine, whom he also loves, is upset when Mab takes Catherine's place. Mab gives the Duke a golden rose, a gift from Henry which Catherine threw away in her previous anger with him. On arriving to announce his formal betrothal to Catherine, Henry sees the rose and suspects her of infidelity with the Duke. Ralph (bs or bar), the apprentice to Catherine's father, swears her innocence, and agrees to fight a duel with Henry to prove it. The Duke prevents the duel, and Catherine's temporary loss of her senses is cured by Henry's singing.

Jommelli, Nicolò (b Aversa, 10 Sept. 1714; d Naples, 25 Aug. 1774). Italian composer. Studied Aversa and Naples with Feo and Fago. Achieved success with his first two operas, L'errore amoroso (1737) and Odoardo (1738), and in 1740 travelled to Rome, where Ricimero (1740) and Astianatte (1741) were produced. Moved to Bologna 1741, where he composed Ezio (first version) and developed a close friendship with Martini; then Venice, where he was director of the Ospedale degli Incurabili 1743.

Now recognized as one of the leading composers of the day, he wrote works for most major Italian houses: particularly notable were Semiramide (1742), Tito Manlio (1743), Demofoonte (1743), and Sofonisba (1745). In 1747 he settled in Rome, becoming assistant maestro di cappella at St Peter's 1749: here his operas included Ifigenia in Aulide (1751) and Talestri (1751). In Vienna that year he composed two operas, Achille in Sciro (1749) and Didone abbandonata (1749), both to texts by the court poet *Metastasio, who admired him and with whom he became friends. In 1753 he became Kapellmeister to the Duke of Württemberg and in Stuttgart composed nearly 40 operas, some for other German courts, as well as for Italy, which he visited regularly. Among significant works of this period are Pelope (1755), Fetonte (1768, first version), La clemenza di Tito (1753), Il re pastore (1764), and Bajazette (1753). In 1769 he returned to Italy, where he composed Armida abbandonata (1770) and Ifigenia in Tauride (1771). These were found too German in style; but the four dramatic works written for Lisbon, including Le avventure di Cleomede (1772), a dramma serio-comico, and Il trionfo di Clelia (1774), were very successful. The failure of his last operas for Italy brought on a fatal fit of apoplexy.

Jommelli composed around 80 operas, although only 53 of them survive, including a number of comic operas and intermezzos. Of the generation following Alessandro Scarlatti, he was reared in the conventional tradition of Metastasian opera seria, and was much influenced by Hasse, who provided crucial support in his early career. However, like Traetta, he possessed a radical streak nurtured by his long stay outside Italy which enabled him to enrich the opera seria tradition with French and German elements. But although even his early operas show signs of reform, his friendship with Metastasio hindered an appreciation of more modern librettos, and his main innovations were restricted to matters of musical style.

Jommellino. See ANDREOZZI.

Jones, Della (*b* Neath, 13 Apr. 1946). Welsh mezzo-soprano. Studied London, RCM. Début Geneva 1970 (in *Boris*). London, ENO 1973, 1977–82, and subsequently; London, CG, 1990; WNO; Scottish O; also Paris, O; New York; Los Angeles; Venice; Geneva. Roles include Ariodante, Ruggiero (*Alcina*), Armide, Ottavia, Rosina, Cenerentola, Dorabella, Donna Elvira, Despina, Dido (Purcell and Berlioz), Carmen, Baba the Turk. A versatile performer with a firm tone and a vivid, engaging stage presence. (R)

Jones, (Dame) **Gwyneth** (*b* Pontnewynydd, 7 Nov. 1936). Welsh mezzo-soprano, later soprano. Studied London with Packer; Siena, and Geneva with Carpi. Début (as mezzo-soprano) London 1963, RCM (Gluck's Orfeo). Engaged as mezzo-soprano for Zurich O 1962; soprano début as Amelia (*Ballo*). London, CG, from 1963; Vienna and Bayreuth from 1966; New York, M, from 1972. Roles include Senta, Kundry, Brünnhilde, Leonore, Salome, Marschallin, Verdi's Desdemona, Tosca, Turandot, Dyer's Wife (S Francisco 1989; London, CG, 1992). Impressive in her dramatic commitment, and, at her peak, with a voice of golden tone. (R)

Jones, Parry (*b* Blaina, 14 Feb. 1891; *d* London, 26 Dec. 1963). Welsh tenor. Studied London, RCM, and with Colli, Scheidemantel, and John Coates. Début D'Oyly Carte O 1915; London, CR 1919–22; BNOC 1922–8; CG 1949–53. Also Italy, Germany, Belgium. A musicianly, intelligent singer outstanding in character roles, e.g. Captain (*Wozzeck*), Shuisky, Monostatos, Bob Boles. (R)

Jones, Richard (*b* London, 7 June 1953). English producer. Studied Hull and London. Scottish O from 1982; Kent O; Wexford 1986; O North; London, ENO, 1989; Scottish O *Rheingold* and *Walküre* (1989, 1991); also Stuttgart, Amsterdam, Bregenz. Productions include *Così*, *Carmen*, *Rigoletto*, *Mignon*, *Into The Woods*, prem. of Blake's *Plumber's Gift* and a much-admired *Love of the Three Oranges*. His iconoclastic and bizarre style is marked by a distinctive black humour, well demonstrated in his *Ring* at London, CG, 1994–5.

Jongleur de Notre-Dame, Le (Our Lady's Juggler). Opera in 3 acts by Massenet; text by Maurice Léna, after a story by Anatole France in *L'étui de nacre* (1892). Prem. Monte Carlo 18 Feb. 1902.

Cluny, 14th-cent. The juggler Jean (ten) is reprimanded by the Prior (bs) for singing a blasphemous song, and is told that he must abandon his juggling in order to gain the Virgin's forgiveness. He joins the monks in the abbey and, unable to sing in Latin, wishes to praise the Virgin through his juggling. The monks are divided as to the propriety of this, but when a statue of the Madonna moves and blesses Jean, they know his offering was acceptable. Unaware of the miracle, Jean dies.

Jonny spielt auf (Johnny Strikes Up). Opera in 2 parts (11 scenes) by Krenek; text by composer. Prem. Leipzig 10 Feb. 1927.

Jonny (bar), a jazz-band leader, steals a violin from Daniello (bar) and becomes so immensely successful that his performance from the North Pole sets the world dancing the Charleston.

Joplin, Scott (*b* Marshall, TX, or Shreveport, LA, 24 Nov. 1868; *d* New York, 1 Apr. 1917). US composer. His first opera, *A Guest of Honor* (1903), was lost on its way to the copyright office. His only surviving opera, *Treemonisha* (1911), was to his distress never adequately performed during his lifetime, and was only revived in 1972 (at Atlanta). It uses ragtime tunes within a conventional framework, and includes substantial use of chorus.

José. See DON JOSÉ.

Joseph. Opera in 3 acts by Méhul; text by Duval. Prem. Paris, OC, 17 Feb. 1807.

Memphis, biblical times. Under the assumed name of Cleophas, Joseph (ten or sop) has saved Egypt from famine; his blind father Jacob (bar) and brothers arrive in Memphis to beg for food, but do not recognize him. When he reveals his identity, he forgives his brothers and begs his father to do likewise.

Joubert, John (*b* Cape Town, 20 Mar. 1927). South African composer. Studied Cape Town and London, RAM, where his teachers included Howard Ferguson, before taking university appointments at Hull and Birmingham. His dramatic writing embraces children's operas (e.g. *The Prisoner* (1973)), as well as a radio opera, *Antigone* (1954) and a rare adaptation of George Eliot, *Silas Marner* (1961).

Journet, Marcel (*b* Grasse, 25 July 1867; *d* Vittel, 25 Sept. 1933). French bass. Studied Paris with Obin and Seghettini. Début

Béziers 1891 (in *La favorite*). Brussels, M, 1894–1900; London, CG, 1897–1909, 1927–8; New York, M, 1900–8; Paris, O, 1908–32; Chicago 1915–19; Milan, S, 1917, 1922–7. First Simon Mago (Boito's *Nerone*). A basso cantante with a voice of great beauty and versatility; his wide repertoire included Guillaume Tell, Golaud, Gounod's Méphistophélès, Dosifey, Fafner, Wanderer, Sachs, Tonio, Scarpia. (R)

Jouy, Étienne de (*b* Jouy-en-Josas, 12 Sept. 1764; *d* Saint-Germain-en-Laye, 4 Sept. 1846). French playwright, librettist, and journalist. As librettist at the Paris Opéra, he worked for some of the most successful composers of the day, including Méhul, Boieldieu, Catel, and Dalayrac; but his greatest and most characteristic collaborations were in the field of *Grand Opera with Cherubini (*Les Abencérages*), Rossini (*Guillaume Tell*), and especially Spontini (*La vestale*, *Fernand Cortez*, and *Milton*). His vivid appreciation of the sensational could go to extremes of literalism: he introduced into *Cortez* the same number of horses with which the conquistador had subdued Mexico on the ground that the shock of the occasion to the audience matched that of the original Aztecs. At his finest, as in *La vestale*, he responded to the demands of the heroic and spectacular in Grand Opera with some imposing scenes and verses.

Juch, Emma (*b* Vienna, 4 July 1863; *d* New York, 6 Mar. 1939). US soprano. Studied Detroit with Murio Celli. Début London, HM, 1881 (Philine). American OC (later Nat. OC) 1884. After its collapse, she founded the Juch Grand Opera Co., which toured US, Canada, and Mexico until 1891, when she retired from the stage. A champion of opera in English, she possessed impeccable diction, while her vocal abilities encompassed the Queen of the Night and Senta. (R)

Juive, La (The Jewess). Opera in 5 acts by Halévy; text by Scribe. Prem. Paris, O, 23 Feb. 1835.

Constance, 15th cent. Samuel (Prince Léopold in disguise) (ten) works in the shop of the Jewish goldsmith Eléazar (ten), whose daughter Rachel (sop) he loves. Assuming Samuel to be a fellow Jew, Rachel invites him to their Passover meal.

They are interrupted by Prince Léopold's wife Eudoxia (sop), who requests a gold chain for her husband; Léopold is filled with remorse. Eléazar is furious when the truth emerges.

In Eudoxia's presence, Rachel claims that she and Léopold are lovers. The Cardinal de Brogni (bs), persecutor of the Jews in Constance, condemns them to death.

Eudoxia persuades Rachel to confess that she lied, and that Léopold is innocent. Eléazar refuses the Cardinal's offer that Rachel will be saved if he renounces his own faith, reminding him that it was a Jew who rescued the Cardinal's daughter from a fire in their home many years previously.

Rachel, too, refuses to abandon Judaism and, as she is executed, Eléazar reveals that she was the Cardinal's daughter.

Julia. The eponymous Vestal Virgin (sop), lover of Licinius, in Spontini's *La vestale*.

Julien. Opera in a prologue and 4 acts by Charpentier; text by the composer. Prem. Paris, OC, 4 June 1913.

The dead Louise (sop) appears to Julien (ten) in a vision and attempts to rekindle his faith in art and beauty. Julien, however, is frustrated in the attempt to find his soul by this means, and dies.

Julietta. Opera in 3 acts by Martinů; text by the composer, after Georges Neveux's drama *Juliette, ou La clé des songes* (1930). Prem. Prague, N, 16 Mar. 1938.

The opera tells of the efforts of a Paris bookseller, Michel (ten), to find Julietta (sop), whom he encountered three years previously. He discovers that the inhabitants of her home town, including Julietta herself, have lost their memory; Michel also begins to be afflicted. When, impulsively, Julietta struggles to tear herself away from him, Michel shoots her and is thereafter tormented by the sound of her voice. He eventually recedes into a dream-world, still in quest of Julietta.

Juliette. Roméo's lover (sop) in Gounod's *Roméo et Juliette*.

Jullien, Louis (*b* Sisteron, 23 Apr. 1812; *d* Paris, 14 May 1860). French conductor. Studied Paris. Conducted in London from 1840, where his flamboyant personality attracted much attention to his concerts. Composed the unsuccessful *Pietro il grande* (London, CG, 1852, with Tamberlik). Originator of the disastrous speculation at Drury Lane when operas were to be conducted by, among others, Berlioz (who gives a sardonic but tolerant account of Jullien in his *Mémoires*).

Junge Lord, Der (The Young Lord). Opera in 2 acts by Henze; text by Ingeborg Bachmann, after a parable in Hauff's *Der Scheik von Alexandria und seine Sklaven* (1827). Prem. Berlin, D, 7 Apr. 1965.

'Hülsdorf-Gotha', c.1830. Sir Edgar (silent role) introduces his nephew, Lord Barrat (ten) to the inhabitants of the small German provincial town of Grünwiesel. The young lord shocks the local snobbish establishment, but his behaviour is sycophantically condoned until it is revealed that he is a circus ape dressed in man's clothing.

Jurinac, Sena (b Travnik, 24 Oct. 1921). Bosnian soprano. Studied Zagreb with Kostrenčić. Début Zagreb 1942 (Mimi). Vienna from 1945, Salzburg from 1947; Milan, S, from 1948; London, CG, 1947, 1959–63; Gly. 1949–56. An exceptionally sensitive artist, with a sweet-toned yet powerful voice, outstanding in Mozart (as Ilia, Pamina, Donna Elvira, Cherubino, Countess, Donna Anna, Fiordiligi), and as Octavian and the Composer. Roles also included Marschallin, Verdi's Desdemona, Leonore, Butterfly. (R)

K

Kabaivanska, Raina (*b* Burgas, 15 Dec. 1934). Bulgarian soprano. Studied Sofia with Prokopova, Milan with Fumagalli-Riva, Vercelli with Tess. Début Sofia 1957 (Tatyana). Milan, S, from 1961; London, CG, and New York, M, 1962–3, 1979–80; Paris, O, from 1975; also Vienna, Chicago, Buenos Aires, etc. An expressive singer and effective actress, notably in the verismo repertory, e.g. as Nedda, Adriana Lecouvreur, Butterfly, Tosca. (R)

Kabalevsky, Dmitry (*b* St Petersburg, 30 Dec. 1904; *d* Moscow, 14 Feb. 1987). Russian composer. Studied Moscow with Catoire and Myaskovsky. His successful career, including official positions in publishing and administration, also included composition in many genres, including opera. His first, *Colas Breugnon* (1938), has become well known for its sparkling overture; others include works responding to contemporary events, such as *In the Fire* (1943), on the defence of Moscow against the Germans. He also rewrote one work, *The Taras Family* (1947), in the wake of the 1948 decree, which he supported, attacking formalism in Soviet music.

Kabanicha. Marfa Kabanov (con), widow of the rich merchant Kabanov and hence known as Kabanicha, in Janáček's *Káťa Kabanová*.

Kálmán, Emmerich (orig. Imre) (*b* Siófok, 24 Oct. 1882; *d* Paris, 30 Oct. 1953). Hungarian composer. Studied Budapest with Koessler and first won attention as a composer of serious music. Music critic of the *Pesti Napló* 1904–8, before the success of a cabaret, written under a pseudonym, turned him towards lighter music. In 1908 his first operetta, *Tatárjárás* (1908), was given in Budapest, and shortly afterwards in Vienna, to great acclaim and was followed by other successes, including *Der Zigeunerprimas* (1912) and *Der kleine König* (1912).

Although Kálmán drew inspiration from stylized features of Hungarian life and music, his main model was the Viennese operetta of Johann Strauss and Lehár. Following his first successes he settled in Vienna and, while not as consummate a melodist as Lehár, secured a loyal and enthusiastic following. His greatest triumph and most enduring work was *Die Csárdásfürstin* (1915), which was followed by eight more operettas for the Viennese stage, of which *Gräfin Mariza* (1924) and *Die Herzogin von Chicago* (1928) were best received. After the rise of Nazism Kálmán emigrated, first to Paris, and then to the US, where he was already known through his music for *Golden Dawn* (1927) and where he found further favour with *Marinka* (1945). His last work, *Arizona Lady* (1954), was completed by his son **Charles Kálmán** (*b* Vienna, 17 Nov. 1929), himself a composer of musicals.

Kalniņš, Jānis (*b* Pernav, 3 Nov. 1904; *d* Riga, 23 Dec. 1951). Latvian composer. Studied with his father, the composer and organist **Alfréds Kalniņš** (1879–1951), and Riga with Vītols. Music advisor and cond. Riga, Nat. T, 1923–33; cond. Nat. O 1933–44; then emigrated to US.

Kalomiris, Manolis (*b* Smyrna, 14 Dec. 1883; *d* Athens, 3 Apr. 1962). Greek composer. Studied Athens with Xanthopoulos, Constantinople with Spanoudi, Vienna with Grädener. Very active and influential in the development of modern Greek music; founded Hellenic Cons. 1919, dir. until 1926; founded Nat. Cons. dir. until 1948; chairman Nat. O 1950–2. His most successful operas, *The Shadowy Waters* (1950) and *The Mother's Ring* (1917), show his warm Romantic idiom and his understanding of how the example of the Russian nationalists could help the cause of an independent Greek musical style.

Kamieński, Maciej (*b* ?Sopron or Magyar-Ovar, 13 Oct. 1734; *d* Warsaw, 25 Jan. 1821). Polish composer of Slovak origin. Composed the first publicly performed Polish opera, *Misery Made Happy*, in 1778. His music reflects contemporary European influences, with some native ingredients.

Kamenny Gost. See STONE GUEST, THE.

Kammersänger(in) (Ger.: 'chamber singer'). High honorary title given by German and Austrian governments to distinguished singers. Originally the title was bestowed by the various courts, hence the titles Hofkammersänger(in).

Kanawa, Kiri Te. See TE KANAWA, KIRI.

Kapellmeister (Ger.: 'chapel-master'). Originally the choirmaster in a court chapel, and formerly generally used in Germany for a conductor. Those who held appointments in a court would be known as **Hofkapellmeister**; assistants were often called **Vizekapellmeister**. The equivalent of the French *maître de chapelle* and Italian *maestro di cappella*.

Kappel, Gertrude (b Halle, 1 Sept. 1884; d Pullach, 3 Apr. 1971). German soprano. Studied Leipzig Cons. Début Hanover 1907 (Leonore). Sang there until 1924. London, CG, 1912–14, 1924–6; Vienna 1921–7; Munich, S, 1927–31; New York, M, 1928–36. Retired 1937. A highly distinguished Wagner singer, with a warm, powerful tone, celebrated as Brünnhilde and Isolde. (R)

Karajan, Herbert (orig. Heribert) **von** (b Salzburg, 5 Apr. 1908; d Anif, nr. Salzburg, 16 July 1989). Austrian conductor. Studied Salzburg Mozarteum with Schalk and Vienna Cons. Début Salzburg, Landestheater, 1927 (*Fidelio*). Ulm 1929–34; Aachen 1934–8; Berlin, S, 1938–45; Vienna, S, as artistic dir. 1956–64; Milan, S, 1948–68; Bayreuth 1951–2; artistic dir. Salzburg Fest. 1958–60, from 1964. New York, M, 1967–9. Established Salzburg Easter Fest. in 1967, giving one opera of *The Ring* each year, never a complete cycle; and then *Parsifal, Tristan, Meistersinger, Trovatore,* and *Don Carlos*. These performances with the Berlin Philharmonic were subsequently recorded, and were intended to be filmed, as part of Karajan's skilful and assertive use of all forms of modern media to further his intentions. He rarely worked with other producers, preferring to control everything himself, and subjugating dramatic meaning to the beauty of sound he was a master at creating with his orchestra. Some singers admired him and owed much in their careers to his power; but others suffered from early over-exposure in roles for which they were not ready but found it difficult to resist. He was probably a member of the Nazi party from 1933; he admitted to the date 1935, and to career opportunism rather than political conviction. From musicians' viewpoint, the indictment was the use of exceptional gifts for performances that dealt in a self-indulgent, predictable gloss as part of a success mechanism and evaded the spontaneity, adventure, and risks of great music-making. (R)

Karfreitagzauber. See GOOD FRIDAY MUSIC.

Kašlik, Václav (b Poličná, 28 Sept. 1917; d Prague, 4 June 1989). Czech producer, composer, and conductor. Studied Prague with Talich. Début Brno 1941, cond. and prem. Gluck's *Orfeo*. Music dir. Brno 1943–5; Prague, T of 5 May, 1945–8. Chief prod. Prague, N, from 1953: prem. of Martinů's *Mirandolina* 1959. Milan, S; Venice, F, prem. of Nono's *Intolleranza 1960* (1961). London, CG, prod. *Pelléas* 1969, *Nabucco* 1972, *Tannhäuser* 1973. Verona, *Boris* 1976. Berlin, S, Gounod's *Faust* 1977. Ottawa, *Idomeneo* 1981. He worked with Josef *Svoboda on the 'laterna magica' technique using film, stereophonic sound, and other media. He explored some original ideas in opera production. The most successful of his operas was *Krakatit* (1961), which draws on mixed genres and media; *La strada* (1982) is an adaptation of Fellini's film.

Kaspar. See CASPAR.

Káťa Kabanová. Opera in 3 acts by Janáček; text by the composer, after Ostrovsky's tragedy *The Storm* (1859). Prem. Brno 23 Nov. 1921.

Kalinov, second half 19th cent. Boris (ten) is in love with Káťa (sop), who is married to Tichon (ten). Káťa's mother-in-law Kabanicha (con) is jealous because her son pays more attention to Káťa than to her. As Tichon is about to depart on a journey, his mother insists that he admonish Káťa not to take a lover during his absence.

Káťa obtains a key to the garden and, uncertainly, agrees to meet Boris. At length she returns his expression of love.

Tichon returns unexpectedly, causing Káťa to become hysterical. She interprets a violent storm as a divine signal of knowledge of her sin, and confesses her affair to Kabanicha and Tichon. Boris is to be sent to Siberia and Káťa, convinced that she has no future, throws herself into the Volga.

Katerina Ismaylova. See LADY MACBETH OF MTSENSK, THE.

Kauer, Ferdinand August (b Klein-Thaya, 18 Jan. 1751; d Vienna, 13 Apr. 1831). Austrian composer of Moravian birth. Studied Znaim, Tyrnau, and Vienna; in 1781 joined Marinelli's newly formed company at Vienna L, as leader and conductor. From 1782 also composed music for the theatre, including Singspiels, operas, and incidental songs, mostly to texts by the house poet Karl Friedrich Hensler. Their first major success was *Das Faustrecht in Thüringen* (The 'Law of the Jungle in Thüringen', 1796–7), eclipsed two years later by *Das Donauweibchen* (1798), which was taken up throughout central and eastern Europe and followed by an even more popular sequel, *Das Waldweibchen* (1800). He was Kapellmeister in Graz 1810–11; he returned to Vienna L, but in 1814 succeeded Leopold Huber at Vienna J. Shortly afterwards the company was wound up and he was unable to find another position; most of his manuscripts were lost in the Danube flooding of Mar. 1830.

Kauer made an important contribution to the development of the Singspiel in Vienna, composing music for at least 160 dramatic works. Like the works of Dittersdorf, Wenzel Müller, and Schenk, these range from mere pantomimes with the occasional song to continuous opera. Despite his significant development of the Zauberposse, no other works matched *Das Donauweibchen* and *Das Waldweibchen* in popularity: these fairy-tale operas were among the most frequently performed German stage works of the 19th cent. and of some importance for the eventual formulation of a national style of opera. *Das Donauweibchen* was also important in the history of opera in Russia, where it was first given in 1803 in an adaptation by Stepan *Davydov as *Lesta, dneprovskaya rusalka*, with additional music by *Cavos.

Kavrakos, Dimitri (*b* Athens, 26 Feb. 1946). Greek bass. Début Athens O 1970 (Zaccaria). Sang with Greek Nat. O until 1980. New York, M, from 1979, as the Grand Inquisitor, Walter (*Ernani*), and Silva. Gly. 1982 (Commendatore); London, CG, from 1984 as Pimen, Douglas (*Donna del lago*), and Henry VIII (*Anna Bolena*). A distinguished performer of such roles as Rossini's Moïse, Oroveso, and Gremin. (R)

Kecal. The marriage broker (bs) in Smetana's *The Bartered Bride*.

Keenleyside, Simon (*b* London, 3 Aug. 1959). English baritone. Studied with John Cameron at RNCM and sang with Hamburg O from 1987. Scottish O as Papageno, Billy Budd, and Rossini's Figaro. His fluent deliv-

ery is particularly admired as Guglielmo, which he has sung in London (ENO and CG) and at Gly. Other roles include Olivier (*Capriccio*, S Francisco), Hamlet, Almaviva (Mozart). (R)

Keil, Alfredo (*b* Lisbon, 3 July 1850; *d* Hamburg, 4 Oct. 1907). Portuguese composer of German and Alsatian descent. Studied Lisbon with Soares, Cinna, and Vieira, Nuremberg with Kaulbach, returning in 1870 and exhibiting as a painter. He began writing light music, including the 1-act *Susana* (1883). This was followed by more serious operas, all on Portuguese subjects. The last of these, *Serrana* (1899), was the first substantial opera to be written in Portuguese (though the prem. was in Italian).

Keilberth, Joseph (*b* Karlsruhe, 19 Apr. 1908; *d* Munich, 20 July 1968). German conductor. Studied Karlsruhe. Répétiteur Karlsruhe 1925; music dir. 1935. Cond. Dresden 1945–50; Munich 1951, music dir. 1959–68. Bayreuth 1952–6 (incl. *Ring*). Edinburgh Fest. with Munich Co. 1952. A fine conductor especially of Wagner, Richard Strauss, and Pfitzner. His declared wish to die, as Mottl had, while conducting *Tristan*, was uncannily granted him. (R)

Keiser, Reinhard (*b* Teuchern, *bapt.* 12 Jan. 1674; *d* Hamburg, 12 Sept. 1739). German composer. His principal teacher was almost certainly Kuhnau; *c.*1693 became Kapellmeister at Brunswick in succession to Kusser, who moved to Hamburg and produced Keiser's first opera, *Basilius* (?1694). Further operas were written for Brunswick, but in 1696 Keiser followed his mentor to Hamburg, where he began a lengthy collaboration with the librettist Postel. *Adonis* (1697) ushered in a series of successful operas for the T am Gänsemarkt, sometimes five per season. In 1702 he took over the theatre with Drüsicke: shortly afterwards Handel arrived, several of whose early works were given under Keiser's régime, as were operas by Grünwald and Mattheson. Keiser was later sole director, and under him Hamburg became the most important commercial operatic centre in Germany. In 1707 he resigned through financial difficulties, but continued to write for the Hamburg stage. Among his most successful works were *Störtebecker und Jödge Michel* (1701), *Claudius* (1703), *Octavia* (1705), and *Croesus* (1710), which with their emotional and lyrical power for a while elevated German opera to a standard rivalling that of the Italian and French traditions. *Der Carnaval von Venedig* (1707) mirrored the contemporary Neapolitan tradition of dialect opera in its extensive use of Platt-Deutsch.

In 1718 Keiser left Hamburg, first for Stuttgart, where he failed to obtain a post with the Duke of Württemberg. In 1721–3 he divided his time between Hamburg and Copenhagen, where he directed a German company in two new operas, as well as in revivals. He was rewarded with the unsalaried title of Kapellmeister to the King of Denmark, but in 1723 returned to Hamburg. His late work here was gradually supplanted by that of Telemann, and he turned to sacred music, succeeding Mattheson as Kantor of Hamburg Cathedral 1728.

The number of Keiser's operas is variously estimated at between 75 and 125: only *c.*30 survive. Like so many of the great composers of the Baroque, his main achievement lay in transcending the distinct national styles of German, Italian, and French music and elements of all three may be discerned in his operas. He was highly regarded by his peers, especially for his rich orchestral writing and his skilled handling of the voices. Mattheson called him the first dramatic composer in the world, while Handel learnt much from him.

Kelemen, Zoltán (*b* Budapest, 12 Mar. 1926; *d* Zurich, 9 May 1979). Hungarian bass. Studied Budapest, and Rome with Pediconi. Début Augsburg 1959 (Kecal). Cologne 1961 until his death. Bayreuth from 1962; New York, M, from 1968; London, CG, from 1970. Made skilful use of his rich vocal palette in a variety of characters, e.g. Osmin, Verdi's Falstaff, Ochs, Rangoni, Pizarro, Klingsor. (R).

Kellogg, Clara Louise (*b* Sumterville, SC, 9 July 1842; *d* New Haven, CT, 13 May 1916). US soprano and impresario. Studied New York. Début New York, AM, 1861 (Gilda). London, HM, 1867, 1879; toured US 1868–72. In 1872 formed the short-lived Lucca-Kellogg Co. with Pauline Lucca; director of English OC 1873–6, also singing and supervising the staging, chorus, and libretto translations. Vienna 1880; St Petersburg 1881. Intelligent, and with a fine technique, she was successful as Marguerite, Philine, Violetta, Aida. One of the first internationally famous US singers. Her memoirs contain acute observations on contemporary artists, e.g. Patti, Nordica.

Kelly, Michael (*b* Dublin, 25 Dec. 1762; *d* Margate, 9 Oct. 1826). Irish tenor and composer. Studied Dublin with Passerini and Rauzzini, later Italy with Finaroli and Aprile. Début Dublin 1779 (Count in Piccinni's *La buona figliuola*). After singing in Italy 1779–83, he was engaged at the Court T, Vienna, 1783–7. Here he created Basilio and Curzio in *The Marriage of Figaro*, and became a close friend of Mozart, as well as meeting other famous composers of the time. London, DL from 1787, H from 1793, where besides being leading tenor he was acting manager for 30 years. Last appearance Dublin 1811 in *The Bard of Erin*, one of his many popular compositions. As a singer he had 'amazing power and steadiness' (James Boaden), and was among the first English tenors to sing high notes in full voice. With Nancy Storace, he considerably raised the standard of singing at Drury Lane. His *Reminiscences* (1826) give an amusing and valuable picture not only of the operatic scene of his day, but also of theatrical life in London.

Kemp, Barbara. See SCHILLINGS, MAX VON.

Kempe, Rudolf (*b* Niederpoyritz, 14 June 1910; *d* Zurich, 11 May 1976). German conductor. Studied Dresden with Busch. First oboe Dortmund O 1928, Leipzig Gewandhaus 1929–36. Début as cond. Leipzig 1935; répétiteur 1935–9. Chemnitz 1942; music dir. 1946–8; Weimar 1946–9; Dresden 1949–52; Munich 1952–4. London, CG, with Munich co. 1953; regularly cond. CG until 1974. New York, M, 1954–6. Bayreuth 1960 (new *Ring*), 1967 (*Lohengrin*). First made his name in Wagner and Strauss, but was also one of the few German conductors widely admired in Verdi and Puccini. A first-rate orchestra trainer, always obtaining beautiful, lucid playing. (R)

Kenny, Yvonne (*b* Sydney, 25 Nov. 1950). Australian soprano. Studied Sydney Cons. and Milan, S, O school. Début in concert, London, QEH, 1975 (title-role of Donizetti's *Rosmonda d'Inghilterra*). London, CG, from 1975; ENO 1977, Gly. 1985, Scottish O; also Paris, O; Vienna; Munich, S; Aix; Salzburg. Roles include Semele, Ilia, Constanze, Pamina, Aennchen, Micaëla, Oscar, Alcina, Countess (*Capriccio*). (R)

Kent Opera. Founded in 1969, with encouragement from Alfred Deller, by Norman and Johanna Platt, the company opened with Monteverdi's *L'incoronazione di Poppea* at Tunbridge Wells on 10 December. It was conducted in the Leppard edition by Roger Norrington, who as the company's music director made his own version for production in 1974. This was in support of Platt's concern to present operas as nearly as possible as the composers imagined them. Similar considerations were brought to bear on Mozart and Verdi, and the company quickly made a reputation not only for vigour, enterprise, and effectiveness, but for a style of performance based on authenticity as a means to the greatest dramatic impact. In 1970 the company followed up its initial success with the first modern performance of Handel's *Atalanta*. Next came *Figaro*, then *Dido and Aeneas* in 1971, both at Canterbury. That year also saw two new operas commissioned from Alan Ridout, *The Pardoner's Tale* and *Angelo*, to texts by Platt. Other important productions included Telemann's *Patience of Socrates* (1974), *Così fan tutte* (1974), *Rigoletto* (1975), *Eugene Onegin* (1977), *Il ritorno d'Ulisse* (1978), *The Turn of the Screw* (1979), *Falstaff* and *Figaro* (1981), *Agrippina* (1982), *Fidelio* (1983), and the prem. of Judith Weir's *A Night at the Chinese Opera* (1987). Many of the productions were in the hands of Norman Platt; from 1974, visiting producers included principally Jonathan Miller, taking charge of one production each year until 1981, also Elijah Moshinsky and Nicholas Hytner. Norrington left in 1982, having conducted over 30 operas. Ivan Fischer, music director since 1984, succeeded Norman Platt as artistic director in 1989. Singers who appeared with the company include Sandra Browne, Janice Cairns, Eiddwen Harrhy, Felicity Lott, Felicity Palmer, Anne Pashley, Rosalind Plowright, Laura Sarti, Sarah Walker, Alfred and Mark Deller, Graham Allum, Neil Jenkins, Thomas Hemsley, Benjamin Luxon, and John Tomlinson. The company's tours chiefly covered the southern part of England. Arts Council cuts reduced activities in 1985, and though there were those who felt that the company had lost something with the withdrawal of Miller and Norrington, there was widespread dismay at the council's threat to remove its grant in 1987. This threat became reality in 1989, and the company went into liquidation. There was a limited re-forming under Norman Platt in 1994, and semi-staged performances of Britten's *Prodigal Son* were given 1995.

Kern, Adele (*b* Munich, 25 Nov. 1901; *d* Munich, 6 May 1980). German soprano. Studied Munich. Début Munich 1924 (Olympia). Vienna 1929–30; Salzburg 1927–35. London, CG, 1931, 1934; Munich 1937–46. Member of the celebrated Clemens Krauss ensembles, and admired as Susanna, Zerlina, Sophie, Zerbinetta. (R)

Kern, Patricia (*b* Swansea, 4 July 1927). Welsh mezzo-soprano. Studied London with Parry Jones. Début O for All 1952 (Cenerentola). London, SW, 1959–69; and CG, 1967–72; also Spoleto, Dallas, New York CO. With her excellent coloratura singing and lively characterization, she was particularly successful in Rossini (Isabella, Rosina, etc.). Sang Mozart's Marcellina at Chicago 1989; Vancouver 1992. Created Josephine in Williamson's *Violins of St. Jacques*. (R)

Kertész, István (*b* Budapest, 28 Aug. 1929; *d* nr. Tel-Aviv, 16 Apr. 1973). Hungarian, later German, conductor. Studied Budapest with Kodály, Weiner, and Somogyi, Rome with Previtali. Cond. Györ 1953; Budapest 1954–6. Left Hungary 1956. Music dir.: Augsburg 1958–63; Cologne 1964–73. London, CG, 1966–8. Though he was notable for his Mozart, he covered a range that included Wagner, Bartók, Britten, and Prokofiev. (R)

Khaikin, Boris (*b* Minsk, 26 Oct. 1904; *d* Moscow, 10 May 1978). Byelorussian conductor. Studied Moscow with Malko and Saradzhev. Cond. Moscow, Stanislavsky T, 1928–35; Leningrad, Maly T, 1936–43, and Kirov, 1943–54; Moscow, B, 1954–78. Cond. many prems., incl. Prokofiev's *Story of a Real Man* (1948). Florence 1953 (*Khovanshchina*). Leipzig 1964 (*Queen of Spades*). (R)

Khanayev, Nikandr (*b* Pesochnya, 8 June 1890; *d* Moscow, 23 July 1974). Russian tenor. Studied Moscow with Zvyagina. Moscow, B, 1926–54. A striking singer with a powerful voice, particularly successful as Hermann, Sadko; also Sobinin, Shuisky, Siegmund, Verdi's Otello. (R)

Khan Konchak. A Polovtsian Khan (bs) in Borodin's *Prince Igor.*

Kharitonov, Dimitri (*b* Kuibyshev, 18 Oct. 1958). Russian baritone. After study in Leningrad sang with the Bolshoy O 1985–8, notably as Mazeppa. British début Edinburgh 1989 (Jochanaan). S Francisco O from 1991, Andrey (*War and Peace*), Escamillo, Renato. One of his most successful roles is

Yeletsky (Gly. 1992) which he sings with a natural warmth and grace. (R)

Khovanshchina (The Khovansky Affair). Opera in 5 acts by Musorgsky; text by the composer and Stasov. Left unfinished, completed and orchestrated by Rimsky-Korsakov. Prem. St Petersburg, Kononov T, 21 Feb. 1886.

The opera, based on the complicated political events of the time of the accession of Peter the Great in 1682, concerns the strife between various factions. The Streltsy, or Guards, are led by Prince Ivan Khovansky (bs), whose son Andrey (ten) in a sub-plot tries to rape a German girl Emma (sop), but is prevented by his former mistress Marfa (sop). The rival faction is led by Prince Golitsyn (ten). An important part is also played by the Old Believers, the ultra-orthodox group in the Church who had refused to accept the reforms of the 1650s: they are led by Dosifey (bs), and are eventually killed, together with the reconciled Marfa and Andrey.

Khrennikov, Tikhon (b Elets, 10 June 1913). Russian composer. Studied with Agarkov and Vargunina, Moscow with Gnesin and Shebalin. The success of his song-opera *Into the Storm* (1939), especially with Stalin, led to this type of simple, melody-orientated opera in separate numbers being associated with the doctrine of Socialist Realism in opposition to more ambitiously, continuously composed works such as Prokofiev's *Semyon Kotko*. Khrennikov became a spokesman for Socialist Realism, and in 1948 headed the musical opposition at the Zhdanov tribunal attacking Prokofiev, Shostakovich, and others for 'formalism' and other deviant sins. Nevertheless, he succeeded in giving the Composers' Union which he led great influence in Soviet society, and there is evidence of private helpfulness. His bureaucratic activities limited his time for composition, but he had a further operatic success with *The Mother* (1957).

Khromchenko, Solomon (b Zlatopol, 4 Dec. 1907). Ukrainian tenor. Studied Kiev with Engel-Krom. Moscow, B, 1934–57. With his pliant, soft-grained voice and clear diction, he was an admired Almaviva (Rossini), Gérald (*Lakmé*), Lensky, Berendey, Boyan, Simpleton. (R)

Kienzl, Wilhelm (b Waizenkirchen, 17 Jan. 1857; d Vienna, 19 Oct. 1941). Austrian composer. After extensive travels became first Kapellmeister at the German opera in Amsterdam; following posts in Hamburg and Munich he was director of the Steiermärkischer Musikverein, Graz 1897–1917, when he retired to Vienna. His first opera, *Urvasi* (1886), attracted some attention, despite its dramatic weaknesses: its successor, *Heilmar der Narr*, was not produced until 1892 because of staging difficulties. With *Der Evangelimann* (1895) Kienzl achieved his greatest success: its folk scenes proved particularly effective and it was favourably compared to Humperdinck's *Hänsel und Gretel*.

Kienzl belonged to that group of composers, including Humperdinck, which was reared in the shadow of Wagner, and which sought to apply Wagnerian techniques of music drama, especially Leitmotiv, to non-heroic subjects. To the modern audience his works appear over-sentimental and lacking in dramatic sincerity: they are rarely seen today.

Kiepura, Jan (b Sosnowiec, 16 May 1902; d Harrison, NY, 15 Aug. 1966). Polish tenor. Studied Warsaw with Brzeziński and Leliva. Début Lwów 1925 (Gounod's *Faust*). Vienna, S, from 1926; London, CG, 1927; Paris, O, 1928; Chicago 1931–2; New York, M, 1938–41. A famous Calaf, Don José, Cavaradossi, and Des Grieux (Puccini), and, with his striking good looks, later a successful film star. Married the soprano and film actress **Marta Eggerth** (b 1912), with whom he sang in numerous tours of *The Merry Widow*. (R)

Kindermann, August (b Potsdam, 6 Feb. 1817; d Munich, 6 Mar. 1891). German bassbaritone. No formal training. Début from chorus of Berlin, H, 1837 (in Spontini's *Agnes von Hohenstaufen*). Leipzig 1839–46, becoming a close friend of Lortzing, who wrote the title-role of *Hans Sachs* and Eberhardt (*Der Wildschütz*) for him. Munich 1846–91, singing in a wide repertory (e.g. Don Giovanni, Mozart's and Rossini's Figaros, Gounod's Méphistophélès, Sachs), and creating Wotan in *Das Rheingold* and *Die Walküre*. First Titurel, Bayreuth 1882. Possessed a powerful voice, musical sensitivity, and dramatic inspiration. Father of Hedwig *Reicher-Kindermann.

King Arthur, or The British Worthy. 'A dramatick opera' in prologue, 5 acts, and epilogue, by Purcell; text by Dryden. Prem.

London, Dorset Gardens T, prob. early June 1691.

Arthur, King of the Britons, and Oswald, King of the Saxons, are rivals for the hand of Emmeline, and resolve to fight a battle on St George's day. Each is supported by different spirits. The armies meet, and when Arthur has the opportunity of killing Oswald, he spares him, thus winning Emmeline's hand.

King, James (*b* Dodge City, KS, 22 May 1925). US tenor. Studied New York with Singher. Début 1961, as baritone; tenor début S Francisco 1961 (Don José). Berlin, D, from 1962; Bayreuth 1965–75; London, CG, 1966–76; New York, M, from 1966; Milan, S, 1968; Paris, O, 1972. Roles included Florestan, Manrico, Calaf; especially successful as Walther, Lohengrin, Parsifal, Bacchus. (R)

King Fisher. A businessman (bar), Jenifer's father, in Tippett's *The Midsummer Marriage*.

King Mark. See MARK.

King Priam. Opera in 3 acts by Tippett; text by the composer, after Homer's *Iliad*. Prem. Coventry T, 29 May 1962.

Troy, antiquity. Priam (bs-bar), supported by Hecuba (sop), orders the death of his baby son Paris, who (it is prophesied by the Old Man (bs)) will cause his father's death. But he is relieved to find, when out hunting, that the boy (sop) has been spared; he and Hector (bar) take him to Troy. Here Paris (ten) and Hector quarrel; Paris fetches Helen (mez) from Sparta. In the last scene of the act, Hermes (ten) arranges the Judgement of Paris; Aphrodite (i.e. Helen) is chosen.

In the war that ensues, Achilles (ten) is sulking in his tent; the Trojans drive the Greeks back and fire their ships, but are weakened by Hector and Paris quarrelling. Patroclus (bar) puts on Achilles' armour but is killed by Hector. The Trojans' rejoicing is interrupted by Achilles' war-cry.

The women reflect upon their role in the war. News of Hector's death at the hands of Achilles is brought to Priam. He goes to beg his son's body, and rouses Achilles' pity. He then withdraws into himself, and is killed before the altar by Achilles' son.

King Roger (Pol., *Król Roger*). Opera in 3 acts by Szymanowski; text by Jarosław Iwaszkiewicz and the composer. Prem. Warsaw 19 June 1926.

Sicily, 12th cent. Queen Roxane (sop) falls in love with a shepherd-prophet (ten), from India, denounced as a heretic. King Roger (bar), after initially denouncing the shepherd as a blasphemer, is finally converted. The opera ends with a bacchanal in the ruins of a Greek temple, at which the shepherd, now transformed into Dionysus, officiates.

King's Henchman, The. Opera in 3 acts by Deems Taylor; text by Edna St Vincent Millay. Prem. New York, M, 17 Feb. 1927.

Eadgar (bar), King of England, sends Æthelwold (ten) to win the Princess Ælfrida (sop) for him; Æthelwold marries her, sending word that she is ugly, but when Eadgar comes to visit them and finds how beautiful she is, Æthelwold kills himself in remorse.

King's Theatre. Built by Vanbrugh in the Haymarket, London, to house the Lincoln's Inn Fields T Co. and opened 9 Apr. 1705 as the Queen's T with Greber's *Gli amori d'Ergasto*, the first Italian opera in London. Opera alternated with drama until the end of 1707, when opera alone was given. At first works were sung some in English, some in Italian, and some mixed. After 1710 it was the London home of Italian opera. Renamed the King's T on the accession of George I in 1714. Heidegger was the manager 1710–34, sharing with Handel 1729–34. The prems. of more than 24 of Handel's operas, seven of his pasticcios, and some of his secular choral works and oratorios were given here, also the English prems. of works by Bononcini, Tarchi, and Cimarosa. The new King's T, then the largest in England (cap. 3,300), opened under the management of Storace and Kelly on 16 Jan. 1793 with Paisiello's *Il barbiere di Siviglia*. During 1793–1830 many major works had their English prems. there, with singers including Giorgi-Banti, Bellochi, Mrs Billington, Catalani, Fodor-Mainvielle, Grassini, Mara, Garcia, Kelly, and Naldi. During Ebers's régime, 1821–7, a number of works by Rossini had their English prems., also the first Meyerbeer opera in England, *Il crociato in Egitto*. Singers included Brambilla, Colbran, Caradori, De Begnis, Pasta, and Velluti. During the régime of Laporte (1828–42) the theatre became *Her Majesty's.

Kipnis, Alexander (*b* Zhitomir, 13 Feb. 1891; *d* Westport, CT, 14 May 1978). Ukrainian, later US, bass. Studied Berlin with Grenzebach. Though interned in 1914 as an enemy alien, he was released through the influence of an officer who had heard him sing. Début Hamburg 1915. Wiesbaden 1916–18; Berlin, SO, 1919–30, and S, 1930–4, after which he settled in US. London, CG, 1927, 1929–35; Gly. 1936; Chicago 1923–32; New York, M, 1940–6. Also Bayreuth, Salzburg, Buenos Aires. Outstanding in German opera (his Gurnemanz was especially celebrated), he was also notable as Arkel, Philip, and Boris. His voice possessed great flexibility and tonal variety, and a wide compass, while his dramatic versatility was equal to both Sarastro and Ochs, and also Hans Sachs. (R)

Kirkby Lunn, Louise. See LUNN, LOUISE KIRKBY.

Kirov Theatre. See ST PETERSBURG.

Kirsten, Dorothy (b Montclair, NJ, 6 July 1910; d Los Angeles, 18 Nov. 1992). US soprano. Studied New York, Juilliard School, and Rome with Pescia. Début Chicago 1940 (Pousette, *Manon*). New York, M, 1945–57, 1959–79. Possessor of a clear, confident voice; roles included Butterfly, Tosca, Violetta, Minnie, Louise. Appeared in several films, including *The Great Caruso*. (R)

Kiss, The (Cz., *Hubička*). Opera in 3 acts by Smetana; text by Eliška Krásnohorská, after the story (1871) by 'Karolina Světlá' (Joanna Mužáková). Prem. Prague, P, 7 Nov. 1876.

A North Bohemian village. The widower Lukaš (ten) is anxious to exchange a betrothal kiss with Vendulka (sop), but she stubbornly refuses him before they are married; such an act is said to rouse the ghostly wrath of a dead wife. After many tricks and much indignation, Vendulka agrees.

Kitezh. See INVISIBLE CITY OF KITEZH, THE.

Klafsky, Katharina (b Mosonszentjános, 19 Sept. 1855; d Hamburg, 29 Sept. 1896). Hungarian soprano. Studied Vienna with Marchesi, later Leipzig with Sucher. Début as mez, Salzburg 1875. Discovered by Neumann; Leipzig 1876–82, graduating from small roles to Brangäne, Venus, and Alice (*Robert le diable*). Sang with Neumann's Wagner Co. 1882–3. London: HM, 1882; CG and DL, 1892; DL, 1894. Hamburg 1886–95; US tour 1895–6 with Damrosch Co. under her third husband, the conductor Otto Lohse. Returned 1896 to Hamburg, where she died suddenly at the height of her powers. She was buried in her *Tannhäuser* Elisabeth costume. One of the foremost dramatic sopranos of her day, much admired (including by Mahler) as Leonore, Agathe, Eglantine, Isolde, Elisabeth, Brünnhilde (incl. the last three on consecutive nights).

Klebe, Giselher (b Mannheim, 28 June 1925). German composer. Studied Berlin with Wolfurt, Rufer, and Blacher. He was one of the leading opera composers to emerge in Germany after the Second World War. His dramatic idiom was influenced both by Blacher and by Expressionist elements deriving from Berg and Schoenberg. Often the dense ingenuity of the dodecaphonic music has made comprehensibility difficult in the theatre. Latterly his style simplified and clarified, and he has sometimes turned to number opera. He has always shown an interest in operas based on distinguished literary originals (e.g. *Die Räuber* (1957), based on Schiller), and his technique is often to let the story, or a reordered version of it, unfold in the dramatist's terms with musical commentary superimposed. His other operas include *Figaro lässt sich scheiden* (Figaro Gets Divorced, 1963), *Der jüngste Tag* (1980) and *Die Fastnachtsbeichte* (Shrove Tuesday Confession, 1983).

Kleiber, Carlos (b Berlin, 3 July 1930). Austrian, later Argentinian, conductor; son of below. Began musical studies Buenos Aires 1950. Début La Plata 1952. Studied chemistry Zurich, returning to music as répétiteur Munich, Gärntnerplatz, 1954–6. Cond. Potsdam, Deutsche O am Rhein, 1956–64, Zurich 1964–6, Stuttgart 1966. Also Munich (from 1968); Vienna, S (from 1973); Bayreuth 1974–6 (*Tristan*). Edinburgh Fest. 1966 (*Wozzeck*). London, CG, since 1974 (*Rosenkavalier, Elektra, Bohème*). Milan, S, 1977 (Verdi's *Otello*); New York, M, 1988. An individualist and a perfectionist, he demands long rehearsal periods and will refuse to conduct if dissatisfied; his grasp of a score is always serious and original, his handling of it passionate and lyrical. (R)

Kleiber, Erich (b Vienna, 5 Aug. 1890; d Zurich, 27 Jan. 1956). Austrian, later Argentinian, conductor; father of above. Studied Vienna and Prague. Cond. Darmstadt 1912–18; Wuppertal 1919–21; Mannheim 1922–3. Music dir. Berlin, S, 1923–34. Guest cond. at many opera-houses 1933–56, notably Buenos Aires, C, 1937–49; London, CG, 1938, 1950–3; Amsterdam 1933–8, 1949–50. His directorship in Berlin was one of the most brilliant in the theatre's history with prems. of *Wozzeck* (1925) and Milhaud's *Christophe Colomb* (1930) and the introduction of *Jenůfa* and *Shvanda* into the repertory. Resigned 1934 at the time of the **Mathis der Maler* controversy and did not return to Germany until 1950. Reappointed to Berlin, S, 1954, resigning as protest against political interference. His contribution to the development of the English company at London, CG, 1950–3 was crucial. A fine, sensitive orchestra trainer, with a sharp intellect and quick sensitivity. (R).

Klein, Peter (*b* Zündorf, 25 Jan. 1907; *d* Vienna, 3 Oct. 1992). German tenor. Studied Cologne Cons. Début 1930 in small roles, Cologne. Hamburg 1937–42; Vienna from 1942; Salzburg 1946–56; London, CG, from 1947; New York, M, 1949–51. A highly successful character tenor, acclaimed as Pedrillo, Don Basilio (Mozart), M. Taupe (R. Strauss), David, Mime. (R)

Klemperer, Otto (*b* Breslau (Wrocław), 14 May 1885; *d* Zurich, 6 July 1973). German conductor. Studied Frankfurt with Knorr, Berlin with Pfitzner. Début Berlin 1906 (*Orpheus in the Underworld*). Recommended by Mahler to the German T, Prague, where he cond. 1907–10. Hamburg 1911–12; Bremen 1913–14; Strasburg 1914–17. Music dir.: Cologne 1917–24; Wiesbaden 1924–7; Berlin 1927–33, first at the Kroll 1927–31, then S: prems. incl. Hindemith *Neues vom Tage* (1929) and many in Berlin. His work at the Kroll was vital in advancing the cause of new ideas in opera which the theatre represented. Goethe Medal 1933; shortly afterwards forced to leave Germany. Apart from a period at the Budapest O 1947–50, conducted little opera after the war, but made a belated London, CG, début conducting and producing *Fidelio* 1961; also *Magic Flute* 1962, *Lohengrin* 1963. His greatness as a concert conductor made the rarity of these distinguished late appearances the more regrettable. Operas and operatic projects include *Wehen* (Birth Pangs, 1915; rev. as *Das Ziel* (The Goal) 1929). (R)

Klenau, Paul von (*b* Copenhagen, 11 Feb. 1883; *d* Copenhagen, 31 Aug. 1946). Danish composer and conductor. Kapellmeister Freiburg O, 1907. Further study Stuttgart with Schillings, also working at the Hofoper. Freiburg 1912. His Icelandic *Kjarten und Gudrun* (1918) was premiered under Furt-

wängler. Still further study with Schoenberg, whose music influenced his later operas, which included *Die Lästerschule* (School for Scandal, 1926) and *Elisabeth von England* (1939). His tastes led him to keep one foot in Germany, and he held conducting posts in Vienna as well as Copenhagen, whither he finally retired in 1940.

Klimentova, Maria (*b* Kursk, 1857; *d* Paris, 1946). Russian soprano. Studied Moscow with Galvani. Moscow, B, 1880–9. Created Tatyana 1879, when Tchaikovsky, though admitting her lack of acting ability, liked her 'warmth and sincerity'. Also sang Oxana in the first *Cherevichki* (the revised *Vakula the Smith*). Later taught in Moscow.

Klingsor. The magician (bs) in Wagner's *Parsifal*.

Klose, Margarete (*b* Berlin, 6 Aug, 1902; *d* Berlin, 14 Dec. 1968). German mezzosoprano. Studied Berlin with Marschalk and Bültemann. Début Ulm 1927 (in Kálmán's *Gräfin Mariza*). Mannheim 1928–31. Berlin: SO, 1931–49, 1958–61; S, 1949–55. Bayreuth 1936–42; London, CG, 1935, 1937; S Francisco 1953. Also S America, etc. A distinguished singer, particularly effective in Wagner and Verdi, but also as Dalila, Klytemnästra, and the Kostelnička. Created Oona in Egk's *Irische Legende*. (R)

Kluge, Die (The Clever Woman). Opera in 6 scenes by Carl Orff; text by the composer, after Grimm's story *Die Geschichte von dem König und der klugen Frau*. Prem. Frankfurt 20 Feb. 1943.

The King (bar), tired of the wisdom of the Clever Woman (sop), whom he married after she had successfully answered his riddles, sends her away, telling her she can take with her whatever she wants from the palace. She sets off down the road, and opens the trunk from which the King emerges, he being the one thing she wanted above all else. Delighted at her choice, he offers to take her back, if she promises not to be clever any longer.

Klytemnästra. Agamemnon's widow (mez), mother of Elektra and Chrysothemis, in Strauss's *Elektra*.

Knappertsbusch, Hans (*b* Elberfeld, 12 Mar. 1888; *d* Munich, 25 Oct. 1965). German conductor. Studied philosophy at Bonn, then music at Cologne with Steinbach and Lohse.

Mülheim 1910–12, also spending summers assisting Richter and Siegfried Wagner at Bayreuth. Cond. Elberfeld 1913–18; Leipzig 1918–19; Dessau 1919, music director 1920–2; Munich 1922–36. Dismissed by the Nazis. Vienna, S, 1936–50. Returned to cond. in Munich, and was regularly at Bayreuth 1951–64. Guest appearances Paris; Milan; Rome; Zurich; London, CG, 1937 (*Salome*); but never sought international career. An 'aristocratic master of the art of conducting' (Hans Hotter). His art came from deep in the German tradition he so fully exemplified, and his finest interpretations, sober, grandly conceived, and gravely moving, were of Bruckner and Wagner: no conductor has more sensitively conveyed the spirituality of *Parsifal* (the last work he conducted, Bayreuth 1964). (R)

Knight, Gillian (*b* Redditch, 1 Nov. 1934). English mezzo-soprano. Studied London, RAM. Début with D'Oyly Carte Co. 1959 (in Gilbert and Sullivan). London: SW/ENO from 1968; CG from 1970. Paris, O, from 1978; also Pittsburgh, Tanglewood, Montreal, Vancouver, Nice. Roles incl. Ragonde (*Ory*), Ulrica, Olga, Carmen, Gertrude (Thomas's *Hamlet*). (R)

Knipper, Lev (*b* Tbilisi, 3 Dec. 1898; *d* Moscow, 30 July 1974). Georgian composer. After a brief army career, studied Moscow with Glier and Zhilyayev, Berlin with Jarnach. Also worked in Moscow Art T and Nemirovich-Danchenko Musical T. He maintained his army connections, also aligning himself at first with the Association of Contemporary Music in Moscow. His most important work from this period is the opera *The North Wind* (1930), a work whose iconoclastic manner was advanced for its day. He later embraced a more orthodox party idiom, also interesting himself in the music of the Soviet republics and writing an opera, *On Lake Baykal* (1948), on Mongolian themes.

Knote, Heinrich (*b* Munich, 26 Nov. 1870; *d* Garmisch, 15 Jan. 1953). German tenor. Studied Munich with Kirschner. Début Munich 1892 (Georg, *Der Waffenschmied*). Sang there until 1931. London, CG, 1901, 1903, 1907–8, 1913; New York, M, 1904–8. A much-acclaimed Heldentenor, with a clear, resonant voice, excellent diction, and handsome appearance, he was extremely successful as Siegfried, Tristan, Lohengrin,

and Tannhäuser. After retiring in 1931, he taught in Munich. (R)

Knot Garden, The. Opera in 3 acts by Tippett; text by the composer. Prem. London, CG, 2 Dec. 1970.

A walled garden, near a city. The analyst Mangus (bar) has been invited by Faber (bar) and Thea (mez) to treat their ward Flora (sop), but quickly perceives that the real trouble lies in the marriage: Faber has grown too far outward, Thea too far inward, and they no longer meet in a true marriage. A homosexual couple arrive: they are the Black writer Mel (bar) and the musician Dov (ten). A further arrival is Denise (sop), Thea's sister and 'a dedicated freedom fighter' who has suffered torture. Mangus contrives a series of devices to set their difficulties to rights, including an elaborate charade based on *The Tempest*; the stage devices include the revolving of the symbolic knot garden of the title, in which they meet and play out their relationships. Eventually Mel leaves with Denise, and Faber and Thea find renewed marriage: Flora has found adulthood and independence, and Dov is left to set off upon a journey (recorded in Tippett's *Songs for Dov*, which arose out of the opera).

Knussen, Oliver (*b* Glasgow, 12 June 1952). English composer. Studied London with Lambert, Tanglewood with Schuller. His first opera, *Where the Wild Things Are* (1980), revealed a strong stage instinct and the ability to reach both children and adults with witty and appealing music; this was joined in a double-bill by *Higglety Pigglety Pop!* (1984), and with the benefit of Maurice Sendak's entertaining fantasy monsters and other beasts has proved widely successful.

Koanga. Opera in a prologue, 3 acts, and epilogue by Delius; text by C. F. Keary, after George Washington Cable's novel *The Grandissimes* (1880). Prem. Elberfeld 30 Mar. 1904.

Louisiana, late 18th cent. On a Mississippi river plantation, Palmyra (sop) spurns the slave-driver Simon Perez (ten) and falls in love with Koanga (bar) a prince of her own tribe. The planter Don José Martínez allows the wedding, during which Palmyra is abducted by Perez. Koanga quarrels with the planter and flees into the forest, where he and a voodoo priest invoke a plague on their enemies. But Palmyra is also afflicted. Koanga arrives in time to save her from Perez, whom he kills before being himself killed. Palmyra stabs herself with Koanga's spear.

Kochubey. A rich Cossack (bs), Maria's father, in Tchaikovsky's *Mazeppa*.

Kodály, Zoltan (*b* Kecskemét, 16 Dec. 1882; *d* Budapest, 6 Mar. 1967). Hungarian composer. Initially self-taught, then studied Budapest with Koessler. His early and enduring friendship with Bartók led to researches into Hungarian folk music out of a shared wish to give their country musical maturity and independence. This is expressed in all his music, including his stage works: here he prefers number opera with dialogue to forms involving continuous development, in the belief that audiences must first be educated in Hungarian folk music before a more advanced language employing it could be used. *Háry János* (1926) is essentially a Hungarian Singspiel, drawing on the tales of an historical folk hero, a braggart soldier whose fantastic adventures celebrate Magyar virtues. At the centre of the concept is a contrast between natural Hungarian characters and the sophistication of the foreign court as it impresses them. *The Transylvanian Spinning-Room* (1932) brings together many of the songs and dances he had himself collected into seven scenes: there is no real plot, rather a celebration of village life in a complex situation involving the parting and reuniting of two lovers. *Czinka Panna* (1948) is an historical piece written to celebrate the centenary of the 1848 revolution, and makes greater use of dialogue at the expense of musical substance.

Kollo, René (*b* Berlin, 20 Nov. 1937). German tenor. Grandson of operetta composer **Walter Kollo** (1878–1940). After period as pop singer and in operetta, studied Berlin with Varena. Début Brunswick 1965 (in *Oedipus Rex*). Düsseldorf 1967; Bayreuth from 1969; London, CG, and New York, M, 1976–9. Roles include Tamino, Max, Lensky, Laca; also, despite an essentially light lyric voice, Lohengrin, Siegmund, Parsifal, Walther. A singer of great musicianship. (R)

Koltai, Ralph (*b* Berlin, 31 July 1924). Hungarian, later British, designer. Studied London. London: CG, *Tannhäuser* 1954, prems. of *Taverner* 1972 and *The Ice Break* 1977; SW, *Mahagonny* 1963; C, *Ring* 1973, *Seven Deadly Sins* (Weill) 1978, *Pacific Overtures* (Sondheim) 1987. Scottish O: *Elegy for Young Lovers* 1970,

Rake's Progress 1971. WNO: *Midsummer Marriage* 1976, *Don Giovanni* 1982. Munich: *Fidelio* 1974. Lyons: *Die Soldaten* 1983. Has often worked closely and successfully with Michael *Geliot; a pioneering designer with an interest in novel materials and structures, including tubular scaffolding.

Konchak. The Khan (bs), chieftain of the Polovtsians, in Borodin's *Prince Igor*.

Konetzni, Anny (*b* Ungarisch-Weisskirchen, 12 Feb. 1902; *d* Vienna, 6 Sept. 1968). Austrian soprano. Sister of below. Studied Vienna with Schmedes, Berlin with Stückgold. Début as contralto, Vienna, V, 1925 (Adriano, *Rienzi*). Berlin, S, 1931–6; Vienna, S, from 1933; London, CG, 1935–9, 1951; New York, M, 1934–5. Specialized in Wagner and Richard Strauss repertory. (R)

Konetzni, Hilde (*b* Vienna, 21 Mar. 1905; *d* Vienna, 20 Apr. 1980). Austrian soprano. Sister of above. Studied Vienna Cons., Prague with Prochaska-Neumann. Début Chemnitz 1929 (Sieglinde, with her sister as Brünnhilde). Prague 1932–8; Vienna, S, from 1936; London, CG, 1938–9, 1947, 1955; Gly. 1938. Like her sister, sang the Marschallin; also Donna Elvira, Leonore, Chrysothemis, Gutrune. A popular singer with a warm, lyrical voice, she continued to appear in cameo roles in Vienna well into the 1970s. (R)

König Hirsch (King Stag). Opera in 3 acts by Henze; text by Heinz von Cramer, after Gozzi's *fiaba*, *Re Cervo* (1762). Prem. Berlin, S, 23 Sept. 1956.

Abandoned in the forest as a child by the Governor (bs-bar), the King (ten) has been cherished by wild beasts. Grown up, he returns to claim his throne and choose a bride, but the Governor's scheming contrives that he shall renounce the crown and return to the forest from what he now believes to be a world of lies. After various adventures he enters the body of a stag, while the Governor takes his shape and returns to the city to initiate a reign of terror. But, driven by human longings, the Stag King returns to the city; the Governor is killed by his own assassins, and the King regains human form.

Königin von Saba, Die (The Queen of Sheba). Opera in 4 acts by Goldmark; text by Salomon Mosenthal. Prem. Vienna, H, 10 Mar. 1875.

Jerusalem and the Syrian desert, *c*.950 BC. The plot, based on a biblical source, relates the story of the Queen of Sheba's visit to King Solomon. Assad (ten), the King's favourite courtier, has fallen in love with the Queen (mez), which causes him to commit an act of profanation in the temple during his own pre-arranged wedding to Sulamith (sop). After his release, Assad seeks Salamith out in the desert, but the couple can only pledge their love briefly before Assad dies.

Königskinder (The Royal Children). Opera in 3 acts by Humperdinck; text by 'Ernst Rosmer' (Else Bernstein-Porges). As melo-drama, prem. Munich 23 Jan. 1897. Prem. as opera New York, M, 28 Dec. 1910.

A Prince (ten) falls in love with the beauti-ful Goose-girl (sop), but a Wicked Witch (con), in whose power the girl is held, refuses to release her. The miracle of a star falling on to a particular lily enables the girl to escape. The Prince has now become King, but the people refuse to accept the Goose-girl as their Queen and, ostracized, the couple die in each other's arms in the snow.

Konwitschny, Franz (*b* Fulnek, 14 Aug. 1901; *d* Belgrade, 28 July 1962). German con-ductor. Studied Brno and Leipzig. Répétiteur, then cond., Stuttgart 1926–30; Freiburg cond., then music dir., 1933–7; Frankfurt 1937–45; Hanover 1945–6; Dresden 1953–5; Berlin, S, 1955–62. London, CG, 1959 (*Ring*). His warm, expansive musicianship was heard at its finest in Richard Strauss and Wagner. (R)

Kónya, Sándor (*b* Sarkad, 23 Sept. 1923). Hungarian tenor. Studied Budapest with Székelyhidy, Detmold with Husler. Début Bielefeld 1951 (Turiddu). Berlin, SO, from 1955; Bayreuth 1958–60, 1967; Paris, O, 1959; Milan, S, 1960; New York, M, 1961–74; London, CG, from 1963. Roles incl. Max, Don Carlos, Calaf, Walther, Parsifal; particularly successful as Lohengrin. (R)

Korngold, Erich (*b* Brno, 29 May 1897; *d* Hollywood, 29 Nov. 1957). Austrian, later US, composer. Studied Vienna with Fuchs, Zem-linsky, and Grädener. Very precocious, he made his début as a stage composer with a ballet *Der Schneemann* (orch. Zemlinsky) aged 11. His first two (1-act) operas *Der Ring des Polykrates* (1916) and *Violanta* (1916) were produced when he was 19. However, his greatest success was with *Die tote Stadt* (1920), a mildly Expressionist work in which his rich, fluent, late-Romantic music, suc-culently orchestrated and carrying echoes of Puccini and even Richard Strauss (both of them admirers), is shown to good effect. Later moved to Hollywood, working as a film composer; one of his films, *Give Us This Night*, included an original 1-act opera.

Košler, Zdeněk (*b* Prague, 25 Mar. 1928). Czech conductor. Studied Prague with Ančerl. Répétiteur Prague, N, 1948, cond. 1951–8; Music dir. Olomouc 1958–62; Ostrava 1962–6; Berlin, K, 1966–8; Bratislava 1971. Chief cond. at Prague, N, 1980–5 and 1989–91. (R)

Kostelnička (Cz.: 'sexton's wife'). The name by which the widow (sop) of Toma Buryja is known in Janáček's *Jenůfa*. She looks after Jenůfa, her stepdaughter (and also her foster-daughter).

Kothner. Fritz Kothner (bs), a baker and Mas-tersinger, in Wagner's *Die Meistersinger von Nürnberg*.

Koussevitsky, Sergey (*b* Vishny-Volochek, 26 July 1874; *d* Boston, 4 June 1951). Russian, later US, conductor. Studied Moscow as bass player and had career as soloist. Began con-ducting 1907. Though primarily known as a concert conductor, he was one of the pion-eers in introducing Russian opera to Western Europe, in 1921 conducting *Boris*, *Kho-vanshchina*, *Igor*, and *The Queen of Spades* in Paris, and *Snow Maiden* and other works in Barcelona. Responsible for commissioning Britten's *Peter Grimes*.

Kovalev. Platon Kuzmich Kovalev (bar), a college assessor, in Shostakovich's *The Nose*.

Kovařovic, Karel (*b* Prague, 9 Dec. 1862; *d* Prague, 6 Dec. 1920). Czech conductor and composer. Studied Prague with Fibich. Cond. Brno 1885–6, Plzeň 1886–7. As opera dir. of the Prague N, 1900–20 he greatly influenced the development of Czech national opera, partly by the catholic choice of his repertory: he championed Czech opera, but also loved French opera, and introduced Bizet, Mas-senet, and Charpentier to Prague audiences, as well as Musorgsky, Wagner, and Richard Strauss. He was also a brilliant if con-troversial conductor who did much to raise orchestral and singing standards in the ensemble. He was particularly successful with the operas of Smetana and Dvořák, but was less enthusiastic for new music. The first Prague performance of *Jenůfa* led to the work's wider fame, but the revisions were his own and not Janáček's. As a composer, he had his greatest success with *The Dogheads* (1898), a patriotic work in the Smetana–Dvořák tradition and still popular.

Kowalski, Jochen (*b* Wachow, 30 Jan. 1954). German counter-tenor. Studied in Berlin and made adult début at Halle 1982 in Handel's *Muzio Scevola*. Berlin, K, from 1983; Orpheus at London, CG, with the company 1989. London, CG, as Orlofsky and Farnace (*Mitridate*). Sang Ottone (*Poppea*) at Salzburg 1993. A versatile performer with a dynamic stage personality, he also sings Britten's Oberon and Handel's Giulio Cesare. (R)

Krásová, Marta (*b* Protivín, 16 Mar. 1901; *d* Vráž, 20 Feb. 1970). Czech mezzo-soprano. Studied Prague with Borov-Valouškov, Vienna with Ullanovský. Début Bratislava 1924 (Julia, Dvořák's *Jakobín*). Prague, N, 1926, 1928–66. Appearances throughout Europe. Outstanding in Czech opera, e.g. as the Kostelnička, Isabella (Fibich's *Bride of Messina*), the Witch (*Rusalka*); also sang Eboli, Amneris, Carmen. Possessed a beautiful voice and dramatic flair. (R)

Kraus, Alfredo (*b* Las Palmas, 24 Sept. 1927). Spanish tenor of Austrian descent. Studied Barcelona, Madrid, and Milan with Llopart. Début Cairo 1956 (Duke of Mantua). Milan, S, and London, CG, from 1959; Chicago 1962; New York, M, from 1966. A highly regarded *tenore di grazia* with a warm, effortless voice and an elegant style. Roles include Arturo, Alfredo, Werther, Des Grieux (Massenet), Hoffmann, and Ernesto. (R)

Kraus, Ernst (*b* Erlangen, 8 June 1863; *d* Wörthsee, 6 Sept. 1941). German tenor. Studied Munich with Schimon-Regan, Milan with Galliera. Début Mannheim 1893 (Tamino). Damrosch OC 1896–8; Berlin, H, 1898–1924; Bayreuth 1899–1909; New York, M, 1903–4; London, CG, 1900, 1907, 1910. Also Paris, O; Milan, S; etc. An outstanding Wagner singer, with a large and expressive voice. Sang Siegfried, Siegmund, Walther, Erik, Herod. (R) His son **Richard Kraus** (1902–78) was a conductor. He held posts at Hanover; Stuttgart; Cologne; and Berlin, SO. Particularly associated with Mahler and R.

Strauss; conducted revival of Busoni's *Faust*, 1955.

Kraus, Joseph Martin (*b* Miltenberg am Main, 20 June 1756; *d* Stockholm, 15 Dec. 1792). Swedish composer and conductor of German origin. Studied with Vogler; went to Stockholm 1778, where he became conductor at the theatre. In 1781 he was promoted to second court Kapellmeister; in the same year his first opera, *Proserpin* (1781), was given. In 1782–8 he travelled through Europe on a study visit at the expense of King Gustav III, visiting London, Naples, Paris, Rome, and Vienna. On his return he succeeded Uttini as first court Kapellmeister, playing an important role in the establishment of Swedish opera. His operas, which include *Soliman II* (1789) and *Aeneas i Carthago* (1799), show the influence of both Gluck, who like Haydn held him in high regard, and Hasse, and are distinguished by his expressive handling of the orchestra, which is reminiscent of the style of the Mannheim school.

Kraus, Otakar (*b* Prague, 10 Dec. 1909; *d* London, 27 July 1980). Czech, later British, baritone. Studied Prague with Wallerstein, Milan with Carpi. Début Brno 1935 (Amonasro). Bratislava 1936–9. London: CR, 1943–5; EOG, 1946; CG, 1951–68. Bayreuth 1960–2. Created Nick Shadow (*Rake's Progress*), King Fisher (*Midsummer Marriage*), Tarquinius (*Rape of Lucretia*), Diomede (*Troilus and Cressida*). A forceful and daring actor-singer, memorable in dark roles, particularly as Pizarro, Alberich, Iago, Scarpia. Also an excellent teacher; pupils included Robert Lloyd, Gwynne Howell. (R)

Krause, Tom (*b* Helsinki, 5 July 1934). Finnish baritone. Studied Vienna and Hamburg. Début Berlin, SO, 1959 (Escamillo). Bayreuth 1962; Gly. 1963; New York, M, from 1967; Paris, O, from 1975; also London, CG; Milan, S; Salzburg (Frère Bernard in *St François d'Assise*, 1992); etc. Created Jason in Krenek's *Der goldene Bock*. Possesses a warm, virile tone; roles include Mozart's Almaviva, Don Giovanni, Pizarro, Germont, Amfortas. (R)

Krauss, Clemens (*b* Vienna, 31 Mar. 1893; *d* Mexico City, 16 May 1954). Austrian conductor. Studied Vienna with Graedener and Heuberger. Début Brno 1913 (*Zar und Zimmermann*). Riga 1913–14; Nuremberg 1915–16; Stettin (Sczeczin) 1916–22. Assistant cond. Vienna 1922–4. Music dir. Frank-furt 1924–9. Dir. Vienna, S, 1929–35; Berlin 1935–7; Munich 1937–44: some of his leading singers, including Adele Kern, Viorica *Ursuleac (whom he married), and Julius Patzak followed him from Vienna to Berlin to Munich. Vienna, W, 1947. A close friend of Strauss, and one of his most gifted interpreters, he conducted the prems. of *Arabella* (1933), *Friedenstag* (1938), *Capriccio* (1942, also collaborating with Strauss on the text), and *Die Liebe der Danae* (1952). London: CG, 1934 (*Arabella, Shvanda*), 1947 with Vienna, S (*Salome, Fidelio*); Stoll T 1949 (*Falstaff, Tosca*); CG 1951–3 (*Tristan, Fidelio, Meistersinger*); Bay-reuth 1953 (*Ring, Parsifal*). (R)

Krenek (orig. Křenek), **Ernst** (*b* Vienna, 23 Aug. 1900; *d* Palm Springs, CA, 23 Dec. 1991). Austrian, later US, composer. Studied Vienna and Berlin with Schreker. Worked at Kassel and Wiesbaden 1925–7, where his comic opera *Der Sprung über den Schatten* (1924) was composed. This employed a basically atonal idiom, as did the Expressionist opera *Orpheus und Eurydike* (1926). However, in the political climate of the day Krenek became increasingly concerned with the relationship between the individual and the community, as well as in the power of the state. This prompted a series of Zeitopern in which his musical language underwent radical reform.

The first of these, *Jonny spielt auf* (1927), was one of the greatest operatic successes of the 20th cent., although it caused scandal with its portrayal of the relationships between a Black musician and White women. But with its fantastical plot, exuberant staging (which called for a real train), and exploitation of such technical devices as radio, it was quickly taken up by opera-houses throughout Europe; much of its effect also derived from the skilled use of jazz. Although Krenek considered it to have a serious message, it was much misunderstood at the time and seen as a simple comedy: none the less, its commercial success enabled him to retire to Vienna.

None of the works which followed repeated the impact of *Jonny spielt auf. Der Diktator* (1928), *Das geheime Königreich* (1928), and *Schwergewicht* (1928) all contained a more overt political message, while the catchy rhythms and melodies of their predecessor were replaced with a more restrained, neo-Romantic style, described by the composer as 'Schubertian': this was also employed in

the self-styled Grand Opera *Leben des Orest* (1930). For political reasons *Kehraus um St Stephan*, a satire on post-war pre-Depression Vienna, could not be performed at Dresden in 1930. Its rejection hastened the composer's turn to serialism, used in *Karl V.* (1938), a 'play with music' uniting elements of opera, pantomime, and film: although commissioned by the Vienna, S, its prem. was banned by the Nazis. In 1938 Krenek emigrated to the US, where he made a distinguished reputation as a teacher. His later operas, which include *Cefalo e Procri* (1934), *Dark Waters* (1951), and notably *Der goldene Bock* (1964), return to themes which had already fascinated him, such as the modern treatment of mythic subjects. He also wrote two television operas, *Ausgerechnet und verspielt* (1962) and *Der Zauberspiegel* (1968).

Krenn, Fritz (*b* Vienna, 11 Dec. 1897; *d* Vienna, 17 July 1964). Austrian bass. Studied Vienna with Iro. Début Vienna, V (in *Cavalleria rusticana*). Vienna, S, 1920–5, 1934–42, 1946–59; Berlin, S, 1927–43; London, CG, 1935, 1938; New York, M, 1951. A famous Ochs; also distinguished in Verdi, Wagner, and R. Strauss. Created roles in Hindemith's *Neues vom Tage* and *Cardillac*. (R)

Kreutzer, Conrad (from 1799, Conradin) (*b* Messkirch, 22 Nov. 1780; *d* Riga, 14 Dec. 1849). German composer and conductor. His first stage work was an operetta, *Die lächerliche Werbung* (1800), in which he sang a leading tenor role. In 1804 went to Vienna, where he probably studied with Albrechtsberger and composed several operas, of which only *Jery und Bätely* (1810) was produced. The success of *Konradin von Schwaben* (1812) and *Feodora* (1812) in Stuttgart led to his appointment to succeed Danzi as court cond., 1812–16. After working in Schaffhausen and Donaueschingen as court cond. to the Prince of Fürstenburg, he returned to Vienna in 1822, where *Libussa* (1822) was successfully performed. He conducted at Vienna K, 1822–7, 1829–32, and 1835–40; from 1833–5 at Vienna J, where his most successful opera, *Das Nachtlager von Granada* (1834), was produced. He was music dir. in Cologne 1840–2, eventually settling in Riga with his daughter Marie, a singer. In 1823 he set Grillparzer's *Melusine* libretto (intended for Beethoven).

Kreutzer wrote almost 40 works for the stage, but is remembered today chiefly for

Libussa and *Das Nachtlager von Granada*, which offer a *rapprochement* between the spirit of the 18th-cent. Singspiel and that of German Romantic opera. Although in a light, popular style, with immediately appealing melodies, Kreutzer's works were thought undramatic even in their day and his death went largely unnoticed.

Kreutzer, Rodolphe (*b* Versailles, 16 Nov. 1766; *d* Geneva, 6 Jan. 1831). French violinist and composer. Studied with his father and Stamitz. Best known as a violinist (and the dedicatee of Beethoven's Op. 47 violin sonata). From 1790 had works produced at Paris I and OC, including *Paul et Virginie* (1791, notable in that Act III is virtually continuous) and *Lodoïska* (1791): the latter was initially rated above Cherubini's work of the same year. Continued to write many other operas, the most successful being *Astyanax* (1801), *Aristippe* (1808), and *Abel* (1810): the latter was thought 'belle' by Berlioz. In 1810 a fracture of his arm ended his solo career; but in 1816 he became second cond. of the Opéra, chief cond. 1817–24, dir. 1824–6. His music became outdated in his own day, and his last opera, *Matilde*, was rejected by the Opéra.

Krieger, Johann Philipp (*b* Nuremberg, *bapt.* 27 Feb. 1649; *d* Weissenfels, 6 Feb. 1725). German composer and organist. Studied Nuremberg and Copenhagen; *c.*1670 Kapellmeister to the Bayreuth court, then travelled 1673 to Italy. 1677 organist at Halle court; in 1680 he moved with the court to Weissenfels, becoming Kapellmeister. In 1680–1725 he directed opera there, with a repertory including Strungk and later Telemann. Composed *c.*18 operas for various German courts; some were also taken into the repertory of the Hamburg O. All are lost except for two collections of airs.

Krips, Josef (*b* Vienna, 8 Apr. 1902; *d* Geneva, 13 Oct. 1974). Austrian conductor. Studied Vienna with Weingartner. Répétiteur Vienna, V, 1921–4. Ústí nad Labem (Aussig) 1924–5. Music dir. Dortmund 1925–6; Karlsruhe 1926–33; Vienna, S, 1933–8, when dismissed by the Nazis. Cond. first postwar operas in Vienna at the Volksoper and T an der Wien, and under his direction the Staatsoper was restored to its previous eminence, 1945–50. Salzburg 1946, helping to re-establish the festival. London début, CG, 1947 with Vienna, S, Co. (*Don Giovanni*); 1963, 1971–4. Chicago 1960, 1964; New York, M,

1966–8, 1969–71; Bayreuth 1961. A warm, energetic man who contributed much to his country's musical traditions, which he cherished in many affectionate performances. (R)

Krivchenya, Alexey (*b* Odessa, 12 Aug. 1910; *d* Moscow, 10 Mar. 1974). Ukrainian bass. Studied Odessa with Selyavina. Sang in various Ukrainian theatres 1938–44; Novosibirsk 1944–9; Moscow, B, 1949. Roles incl. Mozart's Don Basilio, Ivan Susanin, Varlaam, Khovansky, Farlaf, Konchak, Kutuzov, Tkachenko (*Semyon Kotko*). (R)

Kroll Oper. See BERLIN.

Krombholc, Jaroslav (*b* Prague, 30 Jan. 1918; *d* Prague, 16 July 1983). Czech conductor. Studied Prague with Novák and Talich. Répétiteur Prague, N, 1940, début as cond. 1942 (Bořkovec's *Satyr*); music dir. Ostrava 1944–5; Prague, N, from 1945. Vienna 1959. London: CG, 1959 (*Boris*), 1961 (*Bartered Bride*); C, 1978 (*Don Giovanni*). Budapest, Stuttgart, Holland, and Edinburgh Fests. with Prague, N, Co. A fine conductor especially of Czech music, for which he did much as an ambassador as well as at home. (R)

Krull, Annie (*b* Rostock, 12 Jan. 1876; *d* Schwerin, 14 June 1947). German soprano. Studied Berlin with Brämer. Début Plauen 1898. Dresden 1900–12, where she created Diemut (*Feuersnot*); subsequently chosen by Strauss, who wanted 'the most dramatic soprano possible', to be the first Elektra. Repeated the role when *Elektra*, the first Strauss opera to be heard in Britain, was given in London, CG, 1910. (R)

Krushelnytska (or Krusceniski), **Salomea** (*b* Bilavyntsy (Pol., Biała), 23 Sept. 1872; *d* Lvov, 16 Nov. 1952). Ukrainian, later Italian, soprano. Studied Lvov with Wysocki, Milan with Crespi. Début Lvov 1893 (Léonore, *Favorite*). Warsaw 1898–1902; Naples, C, 1903; Milan, S, 1907, 1909, 1915; Buenos Aires 1906–13. A beautiful woman who possessed great dramatic and vocal gifts, she was described by Strauss as 'perfect as both Salome and Elektra'. Also an acclaimed Selika, Aida, Butterfly (in the revised, successful version at Brescia after its Milan fiasco), Tatyana, Isolde, and Brünnhilde, among a large repertory. Retired from stage 1920. (R)

Kubelík, Rafael (*b* Býchory, 29 June 1914).

Czech, later Swiss, conductor and composer. Studied Prague with Šín. After a period with Czech Philharmonic, Music dir. Brno 1939–41. Left Czechoslovakia 1948 when he went to Edinburgh to conduct *Don Giovanni*. London: SW, 1954 (*Káťa*). Music dir. CG 1955–8, when his successes included *Otello*, a superb first English *Jenůfa* (1956), and *Troyens*. Encouraged native singers, and tried to keep casts intact throughout the season. Guest appearances Hamburg, Munich. Music dir. New York, M, 1973 (first ever; début with first local *Troyens*), resigning over budget cuts 1974. S Francisco 1977. His operas include *Veronika* (Brno 1947) and *Cornelia Faroli* (Augsburg 1947). (R) His wife, the Australian soprano **Elsie Morison** (b Ballarat, 15 Aug. 1924), studied Melbourne with Carey, also with him in London. Début London, RAH, 1948 (Galatea). London: SW, 1948–54; CG, 1954–62. Gly. 1953, 1956–9. First English Anne Trulove, and Blanche (*Carmélites*). Also sang Fiordiligi, Susanna, Marzelline. (R)

Kuhlau, Friedrich (b Uelzen, 11 Sept. 1786; d Copenhagen, 12 Mar. 1832). Danish composer of German origin. After early success in Hamburg as a keyboard player, he fled to Copenhagen in 1810 to avoid conscription into Napoleon's army. Here he made frequent appearances as a pianist; from 1813 he was *Kammermusikus* to the king, playing flute in the court orchestra.

Beginning with Oehlenschläger's *Røverborgen* (The Robbers' Castle, 1814), Kuhlau composed much incidental music. In some of these dramas the music is of a quantity and quality which renders them close to genuine opera, as in *Elverhøj* (1828). With its use of folk-song, and an overture which ends with the national anthem, it was, not surprisingly, an instant success and played an important role in the foundation of Danish opera.

Kühleborn. A water spirit, father of Undine, (bs) in Hoffmann's and (bar) in Lortzing's *Undine*.

Kuhlmann, Kathleen (b S Francisco, 7 Dec. 1950). US mezzo-soprano. Studied in Chicago and made début there 1979 (Maddalena in *Rigoletto*). European début Cologne 1980 (Preziosilla). London, CG, from 1982 as Ino and Juno (Handel's *Semele*). Rosina, Carmen, and Bradamante (*Alcina*). Salzburg 1985 as Penelope in the Henze/Monteverdi *Ulisse*. She

has a voice of considerable range and warmth, and is an effective actress. (R)

Kundry. The messenger (sop) of the Grail, also in Klingsor's power, in Wagner's *Parsifal*.

Kunz, Erich (b Vienna, 20 May 1909; d Vienna, Sept. 1995). Austrian bass-baritone. Studied Vienna with Lierhammer and Duhan. Début Troppau (Opava) 1933 (Osmin). Vienna, S, from 1940. Bayreuth 1943–4, 1951; New York, M, 1952–4; London, CG, 1947; Gly. 1948, 1950; Salzburg 1942–60. Roles included Leporello, Figaro, Guglielmo; especially popular as Beckmesser and Papageno. (R)

Kunzen, Friedrich Ludwig Aemilius (b Lübeck, 4 Sept. 1761; d Copenhagen, 28 Jan. 1817). German composer, pianist, and editor. Studied with his father, the organist **Adolph Karl Kunzen** (1720–81). In 1787 worked at the Copenhagen O, where his first opera, *Holger Danske* (Oger the Dane, 1789), was given. This had only six performances, so he moved to Berlin, and joined Reichardt in editing the *Musikalisches Wochenblatt*. He then held theatrical posts at Frankfurt and Prague; returned to the Copenhagen O, succeeding Schulz as director 1795.

Kunzen was one of the most important figures in the history of Danish opera and responsible for introducing Mozart's dramatic works to Denmark. His style betrays their influence, as well as that of Gluck, and of Schulz: his most successful works, which included *Hemmeligheden* (The Secret, 1796), *Dragedukken* (The Dragon Doll, 1797), *Erik Ejegod* (1798), and *Kaerlighed paa Landet* (Love in the Country, 1810), represent a Danish branch of German Singspiel and treat many of the same themes, sometimes in a nationalist context.

Kupfer, Harry (b Berlin, 12 Aug. 1935). German producer and designer. Studied Leipzig. Début Weimar 1967, dir. 1967–72, then Dresden (*Hoffmann, Tristan, Parsifal, Moses and Aaron*). Bayreuth 1978 (*Flying Dutchman* staged as Senta's dream), 1988–92 (*Ring*). Dir. Berlin, K, 1981, where his striking productions included *Meistersinger*, and the prem. of Matthus's *Judith*. His work has shown a remarkable ability to present operas of different periods in a fresh and revealing light.

Kupper, Annelies (b Glatz, 21 Jul. 1906; d

Munich, 8 Dec. 1987). German soprano. Studied Breslau. Début Breslau 1935 (Second Boy, *Zauberflöte*). Hamburg 1940–6; Munich, S, 1946–61; Bayreuth 1944; London, CG, 1953. A sensitive singer and a good musician; roles included Aida, Tatyana, Eva, Chrysothemis, and Danae (promised to her by Strauss before his death) in the official prem. of *Die Liebe der Danae* (1952). (R)

Kurpiński, Karol (*b* Włoszakowice, 6 Mar. 1785; *d* Warsaw, 18 Sept. 1857). Polish composer and conductor. Studied with his father, the local organist. After holding various appointments, became deputy cond., and then principal cond., of the Warsaw O (1824–40). Founded and taught at his own schools of singing and drama, and founded the first Polish music journal, *Tygodnik muzyczny* (1820). Played an important part in Warsaw's concert life (he conducted Chopin's first concerts); also made a vital contribution to the development of Polish opera. He wrote 24 stage works, of which nine survive complete: these include *Czorstyn Castle* (1819), which has occasionally been revived. Most of them are on Polish themes, and graft nationalist ideas on to a more international and particularly Viennese idiom.

Kurt, Melanie (*b* Vienna, 8 Jan. 1880; *d* New York, 11 Mar. 1941). Austrian soprano. Studied Vienna with Müller, later Berlin with Lilli and M. Lehmann. Début Lübeck 1902 (Elisabeth). Brunswick 1905–8; Berlin, H, 1908–12; London, CG, 1910, 1914; New York, M, 1914–17; Berlin, V, 1920–5. Powerful of voice and presence, she was a successful Leonore, Isolde, Kundry, Brünnhilde, Marschallin, and Iphigénie (*Tauride*). (R)

Kurwenal. Tristan's retainer (bar) in Wagner's *Tristan und Isolde*.

Kurz, Selma (*b* Bielitz, 15 Nov. 1874; *d* Vienna, 10 May 1933). Austrian soprano. Studied Vienna with Ress, Paris with Marchesi. Début Hamburg 1895 (Mignon). Engaged by Mahler for Vienna 1899; sang there until 1927. London 1904–5, 1907; then, owing to Melba's jealousy, not again until 1924. Repertory included Tosca, Eva, Sieglinde, Violetta, Philine, and Gilda. Though not a good actress, she was a virtuoso singer, with an outstanding voice, and a superb trill, which she could sustain for 20 seconds. Greatly admired by Mahler for 'the incomparable gentleness of her personality, her

legato, and her vocal control', she was also Strauss's favourite Zerbinetta, which she sang in the first revised version of *Ariadne*, 1916. (R)

Kusche, Benno (*b* Freiburg, 30 Jan. 1916). German bass-baritone. Studied Karlsruhe, and Freiburg with Harlan. Début Koblenz 1938 (Fra Melitone, *Forza*). Augsburg 1939–44; Munich from 1946; London, CG, 1952–3; Gly. 1954, 1963–4; New York, M, 1971–2. A fine character and buffo singer, acclaimed as Papageno, Leporello, Beckmesser, Faninal, Schicchi. (R)

Kusser, Johann Sigismund (*b* Pressburg, *bapt.* 13 Feb. 1660; *d* Dublin, Nov. 1727). Austrian composer. Studied Paris with Lully between 1674–82; *c.*1690 became Kapellmeister at Brunswick, where he wrote seven German operas, including *Julia* (1690) and *Ariadne* (1692). Following a quarrel with his librettist Bressand, he moved to Hamburg 1694, taking over direction of the T am Gänsemarkt. In two years he produced new operas, such as *Erindo* (1694), *Scipio Africanus* (1694), and revivals of earlier works. After touring Germany with an opera company, he settled in Stuttgart 1698, composing three operas before leaving in 1704. Having visited London, he arrived in Dublin in 1709, where he had considerable success, rising to be chief composer and music-master at Dublin Castle.

Kusser made a distinctive contribution to the development of opera in Germany by following Conradi in the cultivation of the French style acquired during his stay in Paris. Little of his music survives, but it was highly regarded by his contemporaries and was an acknowledged influence upon Keiser and Mattheson.

Kutuzov. Fieldmarshal Mikhail Kutuzov, the commander of the Russian armies confronting Napoleon's armies in 1812. He appears (bs-bar) in Prokofiev's *War and Peace*.

Kuzhamyarov, Kuddus (*b* Kaynazar, 21 May 1918). Uighur composer. Studied Alma-Ata with Brusilovsky. His people's first professional composer, he has composed operas based on the music and history of Kazakhstan, and given the country a distinctive musical lead. His idiom draws on local song and dance styles, and seeks to incorporate these into a simple operatic framework. His works include *Nazugum* (1956) and *Zolotye gorye* (The Golden Mountains, 1960).

Kuznetsova, Maria (*b* Odessa, 1880; *d* Paris, 25 Apr. 1966). Russian soprano and dancer. Began career as ballerina, in St Petersburg. Studied singing St Petersburg with Tartakov. Début St Petersburg Cons. 1904 (Tatyana). St Petersburg, M, 1905–13; Paris, O, 1908, 1910, 1912; London: CG, 1909, 1910, 1920; DL, 1914. Chicago 1916. Founded her own Russian Co. 1927, with which she sang in London, Paris, Barcelona, and S America until 1933, introducing much Russian repertory to the West. Other parts included Norma, Violetta, Tosca, Thaïs, Carmen; also created Fevronia (*Invisible City of Kitezh*), and Massenet's Fausta (*Roma*) and Cléopâtre. A much-admired artist, with a strong, flexible, bell-like voice, she was committed equally to singing and acting. As a dancer she performed in Russia and Paris, and created Potiphar's Wife in Strauss's *Josephslegende*, Paris 1914. (R)

L

Lablache, Luigi (*b* Naples, 6 Dec. 1794; *d* Naples, 23 Jan. 1858). Italian bass. Studied Naples with Valente. Début Naples, T San Carlino, 1812 (Palma's *Erede senza eredità*). Palermo 1813–17; Milan, S, 1817–24; Vienna 1824; Naples, C, 1824–30; London, H and HM, 1830–2, 1835–52. Paris, I, 1830, and regularly until 1851; St Petersburg 1852; London, CG, 1854–6. A highly influential figure in the history of opera; his enormous repertory included Leporello; Geronimo (*Matrimonio segreto*); Rossini's Doctor Bartolo, Dandini, Figaro, Assur; Donizetti's Henry VIII, Podestà, Baldassare; the creation of numerous roles, including his celebrated Don Pasquale, Marin Faliero, Lord Walton (*Puritani*), Massimiliano (Verdi's *I masnadieri*); and leading parts in other works by Bellini, Donizetti, Mercadante, Pacini, Vaccai, Mosca, Balfe, etc. Magnificent of voice and person, he possessed a large range, great vocal flexibility, and a genius for both the comic and the tragic that led Lumley to declare him 'the greatest dramatic singer of our time'; Chorley also praised his sensitivity, and his 'entire avoidance of grossness'. Though becoming gigantically fat, he was still robust and vocally fresh at 60. Among his numerous admirers were Schubert (who dedicated three Italian songs, Op. 83, to him), Wagner, and several monarchs, Tsar Alexander I, Ferdinand I, and Queen Victoria (who took lessons from him). Of his 13 children, a son, **Federico**, was also an operatic singer, and a daughter, **Francesca**, married the pianist Sigismond Thalberg.

La Borde, Jean-Benjamin de (*b* Paris, 5 Sept. 1734; *d* Paris, 22 July 1794). French composer and violinist. Studied with Rameau and Dauvergne and wrote his first stage work, *La chercheuse*, aged only 14. His first success was *Gilles* (1758): 1758–73 he composed *c*.30 dramatic works which embraced both opéra-comique and tragédie lyrique. Always an amateur musician, he was briefly governor of the Louvre; during the French Revolution his home was destroyed and he was guillotined.

In his serious works, which included *Ismène* (1763) and *Amadis de Gaule* (1771), he demonstrated a clear debt to Lully, without approaching similar depths of expression. More successful were his opéras-comiques, such as *Candide* (1768), *Le billet de mariage* (1772), and *Jeannot et Collin* (1770), where the influence of the Italian style is noteworthy. Though popular, his works did not enjoy a good critical reception. Today he is remembered more for his seminal *Essai sur la musique ancienne et moderne* (1780).

Labroca, Mario (*b* Rome, 22 Nov. 1896; *d* Rome, 1 July 1973). Italian composer, administrator, and critic. Studied Parma with Respighi and Malipiero. Artistic dir. Florence Maggio Musicale 1936–44. Organized seasons of contemporary opera, Milan, S, and Rome, R, 1942. Administrator Venice, F, 1946–7, 1959–73; Milan, S, 1947–9. Dir. RAI 1949–58, during which period he arranged for Furtwängler to conduct *The Ring*. His music includes two children's operas.

Laca. Laca Klemeň (ten), stepbrother of Števa Burya, in Janáček's *Jenůfa*.

La calinda. Dance in Act II of Delius's *Koanga*. Sometimes also known as *calenda*, the original dance was regarded as obscene and was at times banned.

'La calunnia'. Don Basilio's (bs) aria in Act I of Rossini's *Il barbiere di Siviglia*, in which he describes the growth of slander from a tiny breeze to a gale that can blast a man's reputation.

Lachner, Franz (*b* Rain am Lech, 2 Apr. 1803; *d* Munich, 20 Jan. 1890). German conductor. Studied with his father, Vienna with Sechter. Assistant cond. Vienna, K, 1827, chief cond. 1829–34. Mannheim 1834–6. Munich 1836, music dir. 1852–68. The real fame of the Munich O dates from his directorship. At first a great opponent of Wagner and his music, he was persuaded to produce *Tannhäuser* 1855, *Lohengrin* 1858, and behaved generously to Wagner. He was also a prolific composer, his operas including *Catarina Cornaro* (1841) and *Benvenuto Cellini* (1849).

Lachnith, Ludwig (*b* Prague, 7 July 1746; *d* Paris, 3 Oct. 1820). Bohemian composer. Studied Paris with Philidor. He was notorious as an arranger of famous operas to suit them to the lowest common denominator of public taste. He made *The Magic Flute* begin with the finale and included Don Giovanni's 'Finch'han dal vino', arranged as a duet, as well as excerpts from other Mozart operas and from Haydn's symphonies: this entertainment was entitled *Les mystères d'Isis* (1801). Reichardt and Berlioz were among those who protested, to no avail at first: despite being known as 'les misères d'ici', the piece had 134 performances. Lachnith also wrote some operas unaided.

'Là ci darem la mano'. Duet in Act I of Mozart's *Don Giovanni* in which Don Giovanni (bar) woos the initially reluctant but then complaisant Zerlina (sop).

'La donna è mobile'. The Duke of Mantua's (ten) aria in Act III of Verdi's *Rigoletto* declaring his philosophy of fickleness in women. Verdi shrewdly anticipated its great fame by keeping it secret until the day of the prem.

Lady Billows. An elderly autocrat (sop) in Britten's *Albert Herring*.

Lady Macbeth of Mtsensk, The (or *The Lady Macbeth of the Mtsensk District* (Russ., *Ledy Makbet Mtsenskovo uyezda*), later revised and retitled *Katerina Izmaylova*). Opera in 4 acts by Shostakovich; text by A. Preis and the composer, after Leskov's story (1865). Prem. Leningrad, Maly T, 22 Jan. 1934.

Mtsensk, 1865. Katerina (sop), wife of a wealthy merchant Zinovy Izmaylov (ten), is bored, and is treated harshly by her father-in-law Boris (bs). When Zinovy has to go away on business, he makes Katerina swear to be faithful. Despite Boris's watchfulness, Katerina has an affair with the new servant, Sergey (ten).

When Boris discovers the secret and has Sergey beaten, Katerina poisons him. Sergey persuades Katerina also to murder Zinovy on his return.

During the wedding festivities of Katerina and Sergey, a peasant discovers Zinovy's body in the cellar. They are arrested.

Katerina and Sergey join other convicts on the road to Siberia. Bored with Katerina, he seduces another convict, Sonyetka (con), by bribing her with Katerina's stockings. In despair, Katerina throws herself into the river, dragging Sonyetka with her.

'La fleur que tu m'avais jetée'. Don José's (ten) aria, in Act II of Bizet's *Carmen*, telling Carmen how he has treasured the flower she threw him, and with it the hope of her love. Popularly known as the Flower Song.

Lakes, Gary (*b* Dallas, 26 Sept. 1950). US tenor. Studied Seattle; début Dallas O 1981, as Froh (*Rheingold*). Mexico City 1983 (Florestan). New York, M, from 1986, notably with powerful and well-projected portrayals of Siegmund and Aeneas (*Les Troyens*). Other roles include Tannhäuser, Lohengrin (Buenos Aires), Rienzi (Montpellier Fest. 1993), Emperor (*Frau ohne Schatten*). (R)

Lakmé. Opera in 3 acts by Delibes; text by Gondinet and Gille, after the former's *Le mariage de Loti*. Prem. Paris, OC, 14 Apr. 1883.

India, mid-19th cent. An Englishman, Gérald (ten), is captivated by Lakmé (sop), the daughter of a Brahmin priest Nilakantha (bs), but her father swears to kill the man who has violated his holy temple.

In order to identify the intruder, Nilakantha forces Lakmé to sing at the bazaar: when Gérald appears, she faints, indicating the depth of her feeling for him. The priest stabs Gérald.

Lakmé tends Gérald in her hut in the forest; she presses him to drink magical water which will ensure the couple eternal love, but Gérald hesitates, unable to decide between his love for her and his duty to his regiment, a claim which is pressed by his fellow officer Frédéric (bs). Lakmé makes the decision for him by eating a poisonous leaf.

Lalande, Henriette. See MÉRIC-LALANDE, HENRIETTE.

Lalo, Édouard (*b* Lille, 27 Jan. 1823; *d* Paris, 22 Apr. 1892). French composer. Studied Lille, Paris with Schulhoff and Crèvecœur. Originally a violinist, he initially composed mostly chamber music. His first opera, *Fiesque* (comp. 1866–8), failed to win the Paris L prize in 1866, which greatly discouraged him. However, the success of his instrumental works encouraged him to write another opera, and this proved to be his masterpiece, *Le roi d'Ys* (1888). Initially rejected by theatres including the Opéra, the work was eventually produced at the Opéra-Comique to great acclaim. Though in the manner of Grand Opera, and sometimes falling victim to its mannerisms, it is marked by Lalo's own personality, especially his capacity for elegant and charming melody and his vigorous sense of movement. His third opera, *La jacquerie*, was left with only one act completed.

'L'altra notte'. Margherita's (sop) aria in Act III of Boito's *Mefistofele*, as she lies in prison and describes the drowning of her child.

'La luce langue'. Lady Macbeth's (sop) aria in Act II of Verdi's *Macbeth*, welcoming the darkness of night that will shelter the murder of Duncan.

'La maja y el ruiseñor'. Rosario's (sop) aria, known in English as 'The Lover and the Nightingale', sung in Tableau III of Granados's *Goyescas* as she waits for her lover and reflects on the nature of love.

'La mamma morta'. Madeleine de Coigny's (sop) aria in Act III of Giordano's *Andrea Chénier*, in which she tells Gérard of the terrible death of her mother when their house was burned by the Revolutionary mob.

Lambert, Constant (*b* London, 23 Aug. 1905; *d* London, 21 Aug. 1951). English conductor, composer, and critic. Studied London with Vaughan Williams and R. O. Morris. Although primarily associated with the growth of ballet in England, had a great love of opera and cond. *Manon Lescaut* and *Turandot* at London, CG, also *Fairy Queen* (in his arrangement) and *Turandot* (1946–7).

'Lamento d'Arianna'. The title usually given to Ariadne's scena 'Lasciatemi morire', the only surviving part of Monteverdi's *Arianna* (1608), mourning her desertion by Theseus.

Lammers, Gerda (*b* Berlin, 25 Sept. 1915). German soprano. Studied Berlin with Mysz-Gmeiner and Schwedler-Lohmann. Spent 15 years as a concert singer. Stage début 1955 Bayreuth (Ortlinde). Kassel O from 1955; London, CG, 1957, 1959; New York, M, 1961–2; Hamburg 1959, 1967. A successful Senta, Brünnhilde, Isolde, Marie (*Wozzeck*), and Elektra, as which she scored a triumph when she replaced Goltz at London, CG, 1957. (R)

'L'amour est un oiseau rebelle'. Carmen's (mez) Habanera in Act I of Bizet's *Carmen*, singing of the capricious and dangerous nature of love.

Lampugnani, Giovanni Battista (*b* ? Milan, 1708; *d* Milan, 12 Jun. 1788). Italian composer. Studied Milan. Having had some success in his native city, where he composed ten operas, he succeeded Galuppi at the London, H, 1743, where he composed *Alfonso* (1744) and *Alceste* (1744). He returned to Milan *c*.1745, where he eventually became maestro al cembalo at the T Regio Ducale and helped in the production of Mozart's *Mitridate* 1770. He wrote works for many of the major Italian houses; he may have revisited London 1755, when *Siroe* was given.

Lampugnani's career began with the composition of opera seria in a style comparable to Hasse's, but after 1755 he concentrated on opera buffa after the model of Galuppi.

Lanari, Alessandro (*b* S Marcello di Jesi, 1790; *d* Florence, 3 Oct. 1862). Italian impresario. Lucca 1821, and other Italian towns. Florence, P, 1823–8, 1830–5, 1839–48, 1860–2. Commissioned Bellini's *Norma* and *Beatrice di Tenda*, Donizetti's *Elisir d'amore* and *Parisina*, and Verdi's *Attila* and *Macbeth*, also operas by Pacini and Mercadante. Though he had a somewhat stormy career, his expertise and command earned him the title 'the Napoleon of Impresarios'.

Lancaster, (Sir) **Osbert** (*b* London, 4 Aug. 1908; *d* London, 27 July 1986). English designer. Studied Oxford and London. Already distinguished as artist, cartoonist, and author, he turned to opera in 1952, designing *Love in a Village* for London EOG. For Glyndebourne he designed *The Rake's Progress* (British prem., 1953), *Falstaff* 1955, *L'italiana in Algeri* 1957, *La pietra del paragone* 1964, *L'heure espagnole* 1966, and *The Rising of the Moon* 1970. Also *Don Pasquale* for Sadler's Wells and *The Sorcerer* for D'Oyly Carte. The intelligent observation in his architectural books, coupled with the wit of his cartoons, made him especially well suited to the comedies he designed for Glyndebourne.

Landgrave. Hermann (bs), Landgrave of Thuringia, in Wagner's *Tannhäuser*.

Landi, Stefano (*b* Rome, *bapt.* 26 Feb. 1587; *d* Rome, 28 Oct. 1639). Italian composer. Studied at the Collegio Germanico in Rome. By 1618 maestro di cappella to the Bishop of Padua; the next year his *La morte d'Orfeo* was performed in Rome, whither he had returned by 1620. In 1624 he became maestro di cappella at S Maria ai Monti; in 1629 he joined the papal choir. Three years later *Il sant'Alessio* was produced for the opening of the opera-house in the Barberini palace.

La morte d'Orfeo was the first secular opera

given in Rome, inaugurating a tradition culminating in the works of Mazzochi, Marazzoli, and Rossi. Although clearly influenced by the Bardi Camerata and by Monteverdi, Landi opened a new path by his inclusion of grand choral scenes reminiscent of the intermedi. The ensemble, particularly the spectacular finale, became a hallmark of Roman opera and was used to even greater effect in *Il sant'Alessio*, which eschews mythology in favour of a plot centring on the life of a human character. This move towards greater realism on stage was heightened by the inclusion of comic as well as serious episodes, while the strict stile rappresentativo of earlier opera was handled in a more flexible fashion, suggestive of the later distinction between recitative and aria. The orchestral sinfonias which preceded each act were some of the earliest forerunners of the *overture proper.

Landowski, Marcel (*b* Pont-l'Abbé, 18 Feb. 1915). French composer of Polish descent. Studied Paris with Busser. Much influenced by Honegger, on whom he wrote a book. His operas, for which he wrote his own texts, generally treat serious subjects in an accessible modern language. The most successful has been *Le fou* (1956). His most recent opera is *Montségur* (1985).

Langdon, Michael (*b* Wolverhampton, 12 Nov. 1920; *d* Hove, 12 Mar. 1991). English bass. Studied Vienna with Jerger, Geneva with Carpi, London with O. Kraus. Début London, CG, 1950, in small roles. Remained member of the company. Gly. 1961, 1963, 1965, 1979. New York, M, 1964; Paris, O, 1971; also Vienna, Buenos Aires, Edinburgh. A versatile actor with a rich voice, successful as the Grand Inquisitor, Moses, Varlaam, Landgrave, Claggart, and especially Ochs, among a wide repertory. Created Mr Ratcliffe (*Billy Budd*), Recorder of Norwich (*Gloriana*), He-Ancient (*Midsummer Marriage*), and title-role of Orr's *Hermiston*. (R)

Lange, Aloysia. See WEBER.

Langridge, Philip (*b* Hawkhurst, 16 Dec. 1939). English tenor. Studied London with Boyce and Bizony. Début Gly. 1964 (Servant, *Capriccio*). London, SW 1972, EOG 1974; Gly. 1977; Milan, S, from 1979; Chicago 1981; London, CG, from 1983; London, ENO, and New York, M, from 1984; Salzburg 1987. A highly versatile singer, who has used his

exceptional intelligence, range, and projection to master a large repertory, e.g. Dardanus (Rameau), Scipio (Handel), Don Ottavio, Idomeneo, Otello (Rossini), Huon, Florestan, Aeneas (Berlioz), Shuisky, Laca, and Živný (Janáček), Aron (Schoenberg), Nero (Monteverdi), Benedict (Berlioz), Vere, Grimes, and Aschenbach. Married to the mezzo-soprano Ann *Murray. (R)

'Largo al factotum'. Figaro's (bar) aria introducing himself in all his versatility and popularity in Act I of Rossini's *Il barbiere di Siviglia*.

Larmore, Jennifer (*b* Atlanta, 21 June 1958). US mezzo-soprano. Studied Princeton and New York. Début Spoleto 1979 in Menotti's *The Egg*. European début Nice 1986, as Sesto (*Clemenza di Tito*). She is widely known for her brilliant portrayals of Rosina: Paris; Rome; London, CG (1991); New York, M (1995); she has recorded Rossini's Arbace (*Semiramide*) and performed Isabella and Adèle in Italy. Other roles include Dorabella (Salzburg 1993), Donna Elvira, Bellini's Romeo. (R)

Larsén-Todsen, Nanny (*b* Hagby, 2 Aug. 1884; *d* Stockholm, 26 May 1982). Swedish soprano. Studied Stockholm with Ljedström, also Berlin and Milan. Début Stockholm 1906 (Agathe). Sang there until 1923. Milan, S, 1923–4; New York, M, 1925–7; Bayreuth 1927–8, 1930–1; London, CG, 1927, 1930. Possessed a very powerful voice; successful as Isolde, Brünnhilde, Kundry, etc.

Laruette, Jean-Louis (*b* Paris, 7 Mar. 1731; *d* Paris, 10 Jan. 1792). French composer and singer. Joined the Paris OC as actor and tenor in 1752; beginning in 1753 he contributed single airs to vaudeville comedies for the T de la Foire. Together with Blaise and Duni he developed the comédie mêlée d'ariettes: among his many popular works was *L'ivrogne corrigé* (1759), whose libretto was later set by Gluck. Remained a member of the Paris CI (with which the OC amalgamated) until 1779. His wife **Marie-Thérèse Villette** (1744–1837) was a popular singer and actress on the Parisian stage.

La Scala (rightly, Teatro alla Scala). Theatre in Milan, built 1778 (cap. 2,800), after the T Regio Ducale burnt down 1776, on the site of the 14th-cent. church of S Maria della Scala (named after Regina della Scala, one of the Visconti family); opened 3 Aug. with the prem. of Salieri's *L'Europa riconosciuta*; renovated 1838. The theatre's reputation was established in the early 19th cent. with the prems. of important works by Rossini, Donizetti, Meyerbeer, and Mercadante: some 250 performances of Rossini works were given 1824–6 under the English impresario Joseph Glossop. Domenico Barbaia succeeded him, 1826–32, commissioning works from Bellini; and he was followed by Bartolomeo Merelli, 1836–50 and 1861–3, who commissioned Verdi's first surviving opera, *Oberto* (1839), and three more, including *Nabucco* (1842).

The Scala's greatest periods were under *Toscanini, who ruled the theatre despotically but brilliantly 1898–1903, 1906–8, and 1920–9, attracting the greatest singers of the day. During the first he brought Wagner into the repertory and gave the Italian prems. of *Eugene Onegin* (1900), *Salome* (1906), and *Pelléas* (1908); during the third he gave the prems. of works by Pizzetti, Boito, Respighi, Puccini (*Turandot*, 1926), Giordano, and Zandonai. Toscanini left over quarrels with the Fascists, and was succeeded by Victor *De Sabata, 1930–57. The theatre was bombed Aug. 1943; reopened (cap. 3,600) 11 May 1946, concert under Toscanini (with Stabile, Nessi, Pasero, and Tebaldi's début). Ghiringelli succeeded as director, 1946–72. De Sabata was succeeded by Gavazzeni, Sanzogno, and Votto; and the presence of *Callas, 1950–8, led to revivals including *Anna Bolena*, *Pirata*, and *Medea*, and Visconti's productions of *Sonnambula* and *Traviata* under Giulini. The Piccola Scala (cap. 600) opened 1955 with *Matrimonio segreto*. Paolo Grassi was administrator 1972–7, with Massimo *Bogianckino director, 1972–5, and Claudio *Abbado music director, 1968–86; together they tried to give the theatre greater accessibility to a younger and wider audience. Riccardo *Muti became music director 1986. He has further broadened the repertory, not always to the taste of an audience that remains, after that of Parma, one of the most demanding in Italy.

Lassalle, Jean (*b* Lyons, 14 Dec. 1847; *d* Paris, 7 Sept. 1909). French baritone. Studied Paris Cons. and with Novelli. Début Liège 1868 (Saint-Bris). Paris, O, 1872–6, 1877–92. Milan, S, 1879; London, CG, regularly 1879–93; New York, M, 1891–4, 1896–7. Retired 1901. Repertory included Guillaume Tell, Hamlet, Rigoletto, Flying Dutchman, Sachs; created roles in Massenet's *Roi de Lahore*, Gounod's *Polyeucte* and *Tribut de Zamore*, and Reyer's *Sigurd*, among others. Possessed a smooth and ample voice, and was at his best in noble and dignified roles. (R)

'Last Rose of Summer, 'Tis the'. An old Irish air, *The Groves of Blarney*, for which Thomas Moore wrote new words; in this form it was used by Flotow for Lady Harriet's (sop) song in Act II of *Martha*.

László, Magda (*b* Marosvásárhely, 1919). Hungarian soprano. Studied Budapest with Stowasser and Székelyhedi. Début Budapest 1943. Remained until 1946. Then settled in Italy, singing at Milan, S, Rome, etc. Gly. 1953–4, 1962–3; London, CG, 1954. Roles include Poppea, Alceste, Norma, Senta, Daphne. Created Mother in Dallapiccola's *Il prigioniero*, and Cressida in *Troilus and Cressida*. An intelligent and graceful singer. (R)

Latham-Koenig, Jan (*b* London, 15 Dec. 1953). English conductor. Studied London RCM with Norman Del Mar. Conducted opera at Henze's Montepulciano Fest. 1981–6; *Giulio Cesare* at Stockholm 1985. London, ENO, 1987 (*Tosca*); Wexford 1987 (*La straniera*). Gave the prems. of Bussotti's *L'Ispirazione* and *Fedra* (1988); operas by Magnard, Sacchini, and Graun at Montpellier, from 1990. London, CG, 1995 (*Bohème*). Has done much to revive interest in Weill's stage works. (R)

Laubenthal, Horst (*b* Eisfeld, 8 Mar. 1939). German tenor. Studied Munich and with Rudolf *Laubenthal, whose name he adopted. Début Würzburg 1967 (Don Ottavio). Stuttgart 1967–73; Bayreuth 1970; Gly. 1972; Berlin, D, from 1973. Also Paris, O; Munich; Vienna; Barcelona; etc. A successful Lensky, Palestrina, Belmonte. (R)

Laubenthal, Rudolf (*b* Düsseldorf, 10 Mar. 1886; *d* Pöcking, 2 Oct. 1971). German tenor. Studied Berlin with Lilli Lehmann. Début Berlin, Deutsches Opernhaus, 1913, and member until 1918. Munich, S, 1919–23. London, CG, 1922, 1926–30; New York, M, 1923–33. A handsome Heldentenor with a strong dramatic sense, he was much esteemed as Siegfried, Tristan, and Walther; also sang Arnold (*Guillaume Tell*), John of Leyden, Števa. (R)

Lauretta. Schicchi's daughter (sop), lover of Rinuccio, in Puccini's *Gianni Schicchi*.

Lauri-Volpi, Giacomo (*b* Rome, 11 Dec. 1892; *d* Valencia, 17 Mar. 1979). Italian tenor. Studied Rome with Cotogni, later with Rosati. Début (as Giacomo Rubini) Viterbo 1919 (Arturo). Rome 1920, as Lauri-Volpi. Milan, S, from 1922; New York, M, 1922–33; London, CG, 1925, 1936; Rome, R (singing at its opening), from 1928; Paris, O and OC, 1929. In 1959 was still making occasional appearances, and sang at a gala in Barcelona 1972. An extraordinarily gifted singer in the line of Tamberlik, he possessed a full, poised voice with a wide range, a superb legato, and the capacity for both lyrical, pianissimo singing, and ringing, dramatic incisiveness. He also had excellent diction. Successful as Rossini's Almaviva, Arturo, Nemorino, and Massenet's Des Grieux, he was particularly acclaimed as Radamès, Calaf, and Manrico, among a large repertory. (R)

'La vergine degli angeli'. Leonora's (sop) scene with chorus in Act II of Verdi's *La forza del destino*, in which she and the monks pray for her protection.

Lavrangas, Dionysios (*b* Argostolion, 17 Oct. 1860 or 1864; *d* Razata, 18 July 1941). Greek composer and conductor. Studied Naples with Scarano, Rossi, and Serao; Paris with Delibes, Massenet, and Dubois. Began conducting on his native island of Cephalonia, also toured. Returned to Greece 1894 and founded Greek Opera; also taught Athens Cons., Hellenic Cons. (dir. Opera School), and elsewhere, and worked as a publisher and critic. He was more influential in his work for Greek opera as an administrator, conductor, and teacher than as a composer; his works, which include *O lytrotis* (The Redeemer, comp. *c*.1902) and *Dido* (1909), reflect his Italian and especially his French training.

Lawrence, Marjorie (*b* Dean's Marsh, 17 Feb. 1907; *d* Little Rock, AR, 13 Jan. 1979). Australian, later US, soprano. Studied Melbourne with Boustead, Paris with C. Gilly. Début Monte Carlo 1932 (Elisabeth). Paris, O, 1932–6; New York, M, 1935–41, when she contracted polio. Resumed career in 1943, appearing seated in specially staged performances. Retired 1952. Possessed a vibrant, distinctive voice, and was successful as Brünnhilde, Isolde, Ortrud, Salome, Rachel, Alceste. (R)

Lazaridis, Stefanos (*b* Dire-Dawa, 28 July 1944). Greek designer. Studied Geneva and London. London, ENO, from 1970, in notable partnership with David Pountney: their productions incl. *Rusalka, Doctor Faust, Lady Macbeth of Mtsensk, Traviata, Hansel and Gretel, Macbeth, Wozzeck*. Also London (CG and Earl's Court), Houston, S Francisco, Berlin, Sydney, Bologna, Florence, Seville, etc. Other producers with whom he has collaborated incl. Copley (*Figaro, Seraglio, Don Giovanni*), Friedrich (*Idomeneo*), Miller (*Tosca*), Lyubimov (*Tristan, Rigoletto, Fidelio*). Début as prod. Scottish O, 1990 (Bartók's *Bluebeard*). His designs are characterized by a dramatic simplicity, startling use of colour, and striking, sometimes violent, imagery, closely connected to the producer's concepts.

Lázaro, Hipólito (*b* Barcelona, 13 Dec. 1887; *d* Barcelona, 14 May 1974). Spanish tenor. No formal training. Début Barcelona 1909 in operetta. Then studied Milan with Colli. London, C, 1912 (as Antonio Manuele). Milan, S, from 1913 (under own name); New York, M, 1918–20. Paris, O, 1929; also S America, Italy, Spain. Retired 1950. An exuberant singer with a brilliant tone, he was a highly acclaimed Arturo; also sang Radamès, Vasco da Gama, Duke of Mantua, etc. Much admired by Mascagni; created leading roles in *Parisina* and *Piccolo Marat*. Also first Giannetto in Giordano's *Cena delle beffe*. (R)

Lear, Evelyn (*b* Brooklyn, 8 Jan. 1926). US soprano. Studied New York, Juilliard School, and Berlin. Début Berlin, SO, 1959 (Composer), remained with company when it became Berlin, D, 1961. London, CG, 1965; New York, M, 1967–85 (last perf. as the Marschallin); also Munich, Hamburg, Paris O. Roles included Countess (Mozart), Fiordiligi, Tatyana, Emilia Marty, Lulu. Created roles in operas by Egk and Klebe. (R)

Lebrun, Louis-Sébastien (*b* Paris, 10 Dec. 1764; *d* Paris, 27 June 1829). French composer and tenor. Had an undistinguished singing career in Paris at the Opéra (1787–91; 1799–1807) and T Feydeau (1791–9), but as a composer was very popular. The most successful of his 16 works, mainly opéras-comiques, were *Marcelin* (1800) and *Le rossignol* (1816), which had more than 200 performances. In 1807 Lebrun joined Napoleon's private chapel as a singer, becoming director in 1810.

Lecocq, Charles (*b* Paris, 3 June 1832; *d*

Paris, 24 Oct. 1918). French composer. Studied Paris Cons. with Halévy; in 1856 was joint winner (with Bizet) of an operetta competition sponsored by Offenbach. Although his entry, *Le docteur Miracle* (1857), was well received, he spent several fruitless years before achieving full recognition. This eventually came with the success of *Fleur-de-thé* (1868), followed by a series of almost 40 operettas of a similar style: some of these were first given in Brussels, where he lived during the 1870s, before being seen in Paris. His most successful work was the opéra-comique *La fille de Mme Angot* (1872), which ran for 500 nights; other triumphs included *Cent vierges* (1872), *Giroflé-Girofla* (1874), and *Le petit duc* (1878). Although his operettas did not achieve the lasting popularity of Offenbach's, their skilled orchestration and captivating melodies put them among the best of the Parisian tradition. His sole attempt at a more serious vein, *Plutus* (1886), was a spectacular failure, and survived only eight performances.

Leeds. City in Yorkshire, England. The Grand Theatre and Opera House opened in 1878, and saw performances by visiting companies including the Carl Rosa OC. The first *Ring* in the English provinces was given by the Denhof OC in 1911, and other companies to visit regularly included the BNOC (from 1923) and CG (from 1955). The Grand was restored in the 1980s (cap. 1,550), and is now the home of *Opera North.

'Legend of Kleinzach, The'. Hoffmann's (ten) aria in the Prologue to Offenbach's *Les contes d'Hoffmann*, telling the story of the dwarf at the court of Eisenach.

Legend of the Invisible City of Kitezh, The. See INVISIBLE CITY OF KITEZH, THE.

Legrenzi, Giovanni (*b* Clusone, *bapt.* 12 Aug. 1626; *d* Venice, 27 May 1690). Italian composer. His first appointment was in Bergamo, at S Maria Maggiore (1645); in 1657 he became maestro di cappella at the Accademia dello Spirito Santo in Ferrara, where his first operas were composed, beginning with *Nino il giusto* (1662). Around 1665 he left Ferrara and after 12 years travelling through Europe settled in Venice as director of the Ospedali dei Mendicanti; vice maestro di cappella at St Mark's 1681. He also composed about 14 operas, many of them lost, for Venice, but after becoming first maestro di cappella at St Mark's in 1685 devoted himself entirely to church and instrumental music. He was very influential as a teacher: among his pupils were Caldara, Gasparini, Lotti, and Pollarolo.

Legrenzi's operas represent the culmination of the 17th-cent. Venetian tradition, and owe much to Cavalli and Monteverdi. He was particularly famed for his 'heroic-comic' works, notably *Totila* (1677), *Giustino* (1683), and *I due Cesari* (1683), in which a serious historical or quasi-historical theme was given elaborate musical and scenic treatment, with relief provided through the inclusion of comic scenes.

Lehár, Franz (*b* Komáron, 30 Apr. 1870; *d* Bad Ischl, 24 Oct. 1948). Austrian composer and conductor. Studied Prague Cons., then worked as a military band conductor in Losoncz, Pola, Trieste, Budapest, and Vienna. He had an early stage success with the serious opera, *Kukuška* (1896); leaving the army in 1902, he turned to operetta. Already known in Vienna through his popular waltz 'Gold und Silber', he had intended to join the T an der Wien as a conductor: so triumphantly received were his first two operettas, *Wiener Frauen* (1902) and *Der Rastelbinder* (1902), that he devoted himself to composition. After the failure of *Der Göttergatte* (1904) and *Die Juxheirat* (1904), he scored his greatest success with *Die lustige Witwe* (The Merry Widow, 1905), which rejuvenated the apparently doomed Viennese operetta tradition and opened the way for Oscar Strauss, Fall, and Kálmán. Some 30 works in similar vein followed, including *Das Fürstenkind* (1909), *Der Graf von Luxemburg* (1909), *Zigeunerliebe* (1910), and *Frasquita* (1922), although he gradually began to lose his hold over the Viennese public. His fortunes revived after 1925, thanks in part to the championship of Richard Tauber, but the focus of his activities shifted from Vienna to Berlin. Notable successes of the later years included *Paganini* (1925), *Der Zarewitsch* (1927), *Giuditta* (1934), and especially *Das Land des Lächelns* (The Land of Smiles, 1929), which rivalled *Die lustige Witwe* in its melodic wealth. His final work was a revision of *Zigeunerliebe* as a Hungarian opera, *Garaboncis dik*.

At its height, Lehár's following rivalled that of the earlier generation of the Strausses, Suppé, Millöcker, and Zeller. Although less sparkling than Johann Strauss II's, his operettas have comparable melodic charm, and his gentle waltzes are probably the ancestors of the modern dance-music slow waltz. His lavish use of dance, dominated always by the waltz, almost created a form of ballet-operetta, which was imitated, always less convincingly, by several later composers. During his lifetime, his operettas were staged throughout Europe and America: today only a handful of the more important receive regular performances outside Germany, although many of the most popular numbers have a firm place in the repertory of light music.

Lehmann, Lilli (*b* Würzburg, 24 Nov. 1848; *d* Berlin, 17 May 1929). German soprano. Studied Prague with her mother Marie Loewe. Début Prague 1865 (First Boy, *Zauberflöte*). Berlin, Court T, 1869, 1870–85. Bayreuth 1876 (in first *Ring*, as Woglinde, Helmwige, and the Woodbird), 1896; London: HM, 1880, 1882, and CG, 1884, 1899; New York, M, 1885–92, 1898–9. Also Paris, Vienna, and Salzburg, where she was both artistic director and a principal artist. Last appearance in opera 1909, replacing the suddenly indisposed Bahr-Mildenburg in *Tristan*, Act III; gave recitals until 1920. A singer of phenomenal versatility, technique, and stamina, she possessed a vast repertory (170 roles), including Pamina, Donna Anna, Leonore, Lucia, Norma, Violetta, Marguerite, Philine, Isolde, Fricka, Brünnhilde, and Carmen. Her voice, though not large or rich, was used with resourceful intelligence, and her artistry was supreme. Hanslick refers to her 'superior mind', and 'a personality predestined for tragic and noble roles'; Farrar, one of her pupils, called her 'a daughter of Wotan'. (R)

Her sister **Marie Lehmann** (*b* Hamburg, 15 May 1851; *d* Berlin, 9 Dec. 1931) was also a soprano. Studied with their mother. Début Leipzig 1867 (Aennchen). Bayreuth 1876, in first *Ring* (Wellgunde, Ortlinde), 1896; Vienna 1882–96. Retired 1897. A rather cool singer, though with an excellent technique, she sang Donna Elvira, Adalgisa, Marguerite de Valois (*Huguenots*). (R)

Lehmann, Lotte (*b* Perleberg, 27 Feb. 1888; *d* S Barbara, CA, 26 Aug. 1976). German, later US, soprano. Studied Berlin with Jordan, Reinhold, and Mallinger. Début Hamburg 1910 (Third Boy, *Zauberflöte*). London, DL, 1914; Vienna 1916–38; London, CG, 1924–35, 1938; Salzburg 1927–37; New York, M, 1934–

45; S Francisco 1946. Thereafter sang in concert until 1951. Her repertory included Leonore, Verdi's Desdemona, Charlotte, Tatyana, Sieglinde, Eva, Suor Angelica, Arabella, Ariadne, Octavian, and her most famous role, the Marschallin. Much admired by Strauss, she was the first Composer in the revised *Ariadne auf Naxos*, and created the Dyer's Wife (*Die Frau ohne Schatten*), and Christine (*Intermezzo*). An exceptional singer, possessing a warm and beautiful tone, musicality, generosity, and charm, she was also an actress who brought a telling psychology and humanity to her interpretations. (R)

Lehmann, Maurice (*b* Paris, 14 May 1895; *d* Paris, 17 May 1974). French producer and manager. Studied Paris. Paris, C, 1928, director 1931–66, himself producing a series of operettas. Also produced opéra-comique at the T Porte-Saint-Martin, including works by Auber and the prem. of Pierné's *Fragonard*. Reorganized Paris, O and OC, after the war; dir. Paris, O, 1945–6, 1951–5; was responsible for sumptuous productions of *Oberon*, *Magic Flute*, *Indes galantes*.

Lehnhoff, Nikolaus (*b* Hanover, 20 May 1939). German stage director. Assisted Wieland Wagner at Bayreuth and trained further in Berlin and New York. Début Paris, O, 1972 (*Die Frau ohne Schatten*). Orange Fest. 1973 (*Tristan*). *Ring* productions at S Francisco (1983–5) and Munich 1987. New York, M, 1987 (*Salome*). Janáček stagings at Gly. with *Káťa Kabanová* (1988), *Jenůfa* (1989), *Makropoulos Case* (1995). His work is notable for its strong delineation of character.

Leider, Frida (*b* Berlin, 18 Apr. 1888; *d* Berlin, 4 June 1975). German soprano. Studied Berlin with Schwarz. Début Halle 1915 (Venus). Hamburg 1919–23; Berlin, S, 1923–40; London, CG, 1924–8; Chicago 1928–32; New York, M, 1933–4. Bayreuth regularly 1928–38. A great artist with a large, attractive voice, a fine legato line, and intense dramatic conviction, she was the outstanding Isolde and Brünnhilde of her day. Repertory also included Armide, Donna Anna, Leonore, Kundry, Marschallin, Santuzza. (R)

Leiferkus, Sergey (*b* Leningrad, 4 Apr. 1946). Russian baritone. Studied Leningrad Cons. with Shaposhnikov. Début Leningrad, Operetta T, 1970 (small roles). Leningrad: Maly T, 1972–8; Kirov O from 1978. Wexford

1983, 1986; London: CG, 1987 (with Kirov O), and from 1988, ENO from 1987; S Francisco 1989; New York, M, 1992; also Toronto, Dallas, Buenos Aires, Barcelona, Salzburg, etc. One of the first Leningrad artists to sing extensively in the West. A musical singer, successful as Onegin, Tomsky, Iago, Rangoni, Prince Igor, Scarpia, Escamillo. (R)

Leigh, Walter (*b* London, 22 June 1905; *d* nr. Tobruk, 12 June 1942). English composer. Studied Cambridge and in Berlin with Hindemith, from whom he inherited a concern for practical music-making which influenced his many stage works. With his melodic gift and expert craftsmanship Leigh raised the standard of light opera in *The Pride of the Regiment* (1932), a clever parodistic piece, and *Jolly Roger* (1933), which originally ran for six months.

Leïla. The Brahmin priestess (sop), lover of Nadir, in Bizet's *Les pêcheurs de perles.*

Leinsdorf, Erich (*b* Vienna, 4 Feb. 1912; *d* Zurich, 11 Sept. 1993). Austrian, later US, conductor. Studied Vienna with Pisk. Salzburg 1934–7, assisting Walter and Toscanini. New York, M, début 1938 (*Walküre*); succeeded Bodanzky as chief cond. German repertory 1938–43. Music dir. New York, CC, 1956–7, when he tried to pursue enterprising policies; New York, M, 1944–5, 1956–62, 1965–6 and guest cond. from 1971. S Francisco 1938–41, 1948, 1951, 1955, 1957. Bayreuth 1959 (*Meistersinger*) and 1972 (*Tannhäuser*). A stimulating conductor of considerable nervous intensity. (R)

'Leise, leise'. Agathe's (sop) aria in Act II of Weber's *Der Freischütz*, in which she prays for protection for her lover Max.

Leitmotiv (Ger.: 'leading motif'; the form Leitmotif is often used in English). A term first used by F. W. Jähns in his *Carl Maria von Weber in seinen Werken* (1871) to denote a short musical figure identifying a person, thing, event, or idea in music and above all in opera. The origins of the device are disputed, and its history is controversial. There are suggestions of it in Gluck and Mozart, and a more consistent use of a musical figure to represent a character or idea in various early German Romantic operas and especially those of Weber, e.g. Samiel's diminished 7ths in *Der Freischütz*, Eglantine's theme in *Euryanthe*. Though instances in Weber caused

Jähns to coin the term, it has since been generally reserved for a rather more advanced use of the device, above all as first developed by Wagner. Taking the old *reminiscence motive, Wagner showed how a subtle and intelligent use of it could not only recall characters or objects to mind, and further serve as a powerful structural force, but could convey to the listener an intricate understanding of how they change with the course of the drama, the musical modification or development expressing a new psychological or dramatic state. What are in *Das Rheingold* essentially reminiscence motifs are by *Die Walküre*, and above all by *Götterdämmerung*, formed into a subtle expressive network of ideas working in the music. The Leitmotiv became an obsession with some of Wagner's followers, as it never had with him: its first use is popularly ascribed to Hans von Wolzogen in an article about the form of *Götterdämmerung* (1878), and it was employed in a study of *Tristan* by Heinrich Porges, written in 1866–77, although not published until 1902. Wagner's own preferred term (in 1867) was **Hauptmotiv**; he made use of other terms, but only once mentioned 'so-called Leitmotiv'. Later composers who adapted the principle of Leitmotiv to their own purposes include Richard Strauss, Humperdinck, and Kienzl.

Leitner, Ferdinand (*b* Berlin, 4 Mar. 1912). German conductor. Studied Berlin with Schreker and Prüwer. Assisted Busch, Gly. 1935. Cond. Berlin, Nollendorf T, 1943; Hamburg 1945–6; Munich 1946–7; Stuttgart 1947, music dir. 1950–69, giving the company new stature; Zurich since 1969. Guest appearances in many European cities and S America (especially Buenos Aires, C). US début at Chicago (1969, *Don Giovanni*). A versatile and efficient conductor, and an excellent accompanist for singers. (R)

Lemeshev, Sergey (*b* Knyazevo, 10 July 1902; *d* Moscow, 26 June 1977). Russian tenor. Studied Moscow with Raysky and Stanislavsky. Début Sverdlovsk 1926. Moscow, B, 1931–61. Repertory included Rossini's Almaviva, Gounod's Faust, Duke of Mantua, Lensky, Berendey, Vladimir (*Prince Igor* and *Dubrovsky*). Admired for his lyrical singing and intelligent acting. (R)

Lemnitz, Tiana (*b* Metz, 26 Oct. 1897; *d* Berlin, 5 Feb. 1994). German soprano. Studied Metz with Hoch, Frankfurt with

Kohmann. Début Heilbronn 1921 (Lortzing's *Undine*). Aachen 1922–8; Hanover 1929–33; Berlin, S, 1934–57; London, CG, 1936, 1938. Repertory included Eurydice, Agathe, Mimì, Aida, Sieglinde, Jenůfa; especially acclaimed as Octavian, Pamina. A sensitive, refined artist, called 'Piana' Lemnitz by her admirers on account of her exquisite pianissimo. (R)

Lemoyne, Jean-Baptiste (*b* Eymet, 3 Apr. 1751; *d* Paris, 30 Dec. 1796). French composer. Travelled with a wandering theatrical troupe to Germany, where he studied with Graun, Kirnberger, and Schulz. Appointed second Kapellmeister at the Berlin court, he also worked in Warsaw, where *Le bouquet de Colette* (1775) was given, before returning to Paris. His first Parisian opera, *Electre* (1782), was a failure; Gluck, whose style he had imitated, vigorously repudiated his claim to be a pupil. In revenge he attached himself to the camp of Sacchini and Piccinni and wrote his next work after their model. *Phèdre* (1786) was an outstanding success and was followed by about 12 further operas in similar vein, of which the most important were *Les prétendus* and *Nephté* (both 1789): at the prem. of the latter he was called out to acknowledge the applause, the first recorded instance of this happening in Paris.

Leningrad. See ST PETERSBURG.

Lensky. Vladimir Lensky (ten), a young poet and Olga's betrothed, in Tchaikovsky's *Eugene Onegin*.

Lenya, Lotte (*b* Vienna, 18 Oct. 1898; *d* New York, 27 Nov. 1981). Austrian, then US, singing actress. Began career as dancer. Zurich 1914–20; Berlin 1920, where she met and then married Kurt Weill. Sang in first (concert) performance of *The Rise and Fall of the City of Mahagonny* (Baden-Baden 1927); created Jenny in *The Threepenny Opera* (Berlin 1928), also appearing in the film (1931). Forced to flee Germany in 1933, she and Weill settled first in Paris (where she created Anna in *The Seven Deadly Sins*), then US. There she created roles in *The Eternal Road*, and *The Firebrand of Florence*; also sang in *Street Scene* and *Down in the Valley*. After Weill's death she devoted herself to the performance of his works. Her inimitable, gravelly voice, highly charged singing, and keen dramatic perception contributed much to Weill's reputation, as well as her own. Acting parts incl.

Rosa Klebb in the James Bond film *From Russia with Love* (1963). (R)

Leo, Leonardo (orig. Leonardo Ortensio Salvatore de) (*b* S Vito degli Schiavi, 5 Aug. 1694; *d* Naples, 31 Oct. 1744). Italian composer. Studied Naples with Basso and Fago, where his first opera, *Pisistrato*, was performed in 1714. His reputation was properly established with *Sofonisba* (1718), by which time he also held a post in the royal chapel. With the success of *La 'mpeca scoperto* (Confusion Exposed, 1723) he began a notable series of comic operas in Neapolitan dialect, including *L'ammore fedele* (1724), and *Amor vuol sofferenze* (1739).

Leo's fame gradually spread, and commissions from opera-houses outside Naples, mainly for opere serie, resulted in *Timocrate* (1723), *Trionfo di Camilla* (1726), *La clemenza di Tito* (1735), and *Siface* (1737). He continued to hold posts in Naples, rising to be maestro di cappella at the Conservatorio della Pietà dei Turchini, 1741. Among operas written for Naples were *Farnace* (1736, the last work to be given at the T San Bartolomeo), *L'Olimpiade* (1737, the second work given at the T San Carlo), and *Demofoonte* (1735).

Though many scores are lost, Leo may have written over 70 operas. In his serious works, he was much influenced by Alessandro Scarlatti, though never his pupil, and was not afraid to depart from his model, notably in *L'Olimpiade*. This, in contrast to much Neapolitan opera, includes a prominent part for the chorus. More original were his dialect comedies, to which he brought many of the techniques of opera seria: his contribution to the development of the *ensemble finale was very important.

Leoncavallo, Ruggero (*b* Naples, 23 Apr. 1857; *d* Montecatini, 9 Aug. 1919). Italian composer. Studied Naples with Ruta and Rossi, and shortly after graduating composed his first opera, *Chatterton* (1877). Its production was abandoned shortly before the prem., forcing him to teach and perform popular music. After travelling in Europe and Egypt, he returned home 1887 with plans for a vast Wagnerian trilogy embracing the Renaissance in Italy, *Crepusculum*, which he offered to Ricordi. Encouraged, he completed the first part, *I Medici* (1892), but when no performance materialized he offered his next work, *Pagliacci* (1892), to Sonzogno.

Together with Mascagni's *Cavalleria rus-*

ticana, this ushered in a new epoch in Italian operatic history, that of *verismo. Though *Pagliacci* made Leoncavallo famous overnight, it did not ensure the success of his earlier works. *I Medici*, although well received by the audience, was attacked by the critics, as was *Chatterton*. *La bohème* (1897) arose from a suggestion to Puccini that Murger's *Scènes de la vie bohème* would make a good libretto: when Puccini was unenthusiastic, Leoncavallo adapted it for himself. Though his work contains many excellent ideas, and was quite successful in its day, it has suffered from comparison with Puccini's opera, with which it eventually coincided.

Leoncavallo remained at the forefront of operatic life in Italy, and also achieved popularity in the UK and in the US, but none of his subsequent works had lasting success. *Zazà* (1900) won some praise from Fauré and others, but *Der Roland von Berlin* (1904), commissioned by Wilhelm II in imitation of *I Medici* as a celebration of the House of Hohenzollern, had no appeal beyond the German court. Most of Leoncavallo's later works, which included *Malbruck*, *Il primo bacio*, and *La candidata*, were operettas; his final operas, the patriotic *Goffredo Mameli* (1916) and the 1-act *Edipo re* (1920), attempted unsuccessfully to recapture his youthful grand style.

The best of Leoncavallo's music is in *Pagliacci*, the only opera by which he is remembered. One of the seminal works of verismo, it has a strong dramatic flair, sharp characterization, and direct melodic appeal. He drew inspiration from a wide variety of sources, including Wagner, Bizet, and Massenet as well as his Italian forebears. Like Boito, he wrote skilful librettos for many of his own works. Despite his achievements, his work, like that of all his Italian contemporaries, was quickly overshadowed by the greater talents of Puccini, hastening the rapid eclipse of everything save *Pagliacci*.

Léonor. Léonor de Guzman (sop), mistress of King Alfonso XI of Castile, in Donizetti's *La favorite*.

Leonora. 1. Oberto's daughter, rejected lover of Riccardo, in Verdi's *Oberto*.

2. The lady-in-waiting (sop) to the Princess of Aragon, and lover of Manrico, in Verdi's *Il trovatore*.

3. Donna Leonora de Vargas (sop), lover of Don Alvaro, in Verdi's *La forza del destino*.

Leonore. Florestan's wife (sop), known as Fidelio, in Beethoven's *Fidelio*; also the title of the opera's original version. Also Léonore (sop), lover of Alonze, in Grétry's *L'amant jaloux*.

Leonova, Darya (*b* Vishny Volochuk, 21 Mar. 1829; *d* St Petersburg, 6 Feb. 1896). Russian contralto. Studied St Petersburg. Début St Petersburg 1852 (Vanya, *Life for the Tsar*). She was then taught by Glinka, and may have been his mistress; he certainly admired her and her 'beautiful voice'. Sang in Moscow and St Petersburg until 1874. Toured Europe 1857–8; toured Russia, China, US, and W Europe 1875–9. A great champion of Russian music, she created the Princess in Dargomyzhsky's *Rusalka*, Serov's *Rogneda*, the Hostess in *Boris Godunov*, Vlasevnya in *The Maid of Pskov*, and Margaret in Cui's *Ratcliff*. Other roles included Gluck's Orfeo, Azucena, Ortrud. Her voice was clear and sonorous, and she was a good actress. As a friend, she gave much practical help to Musorgsky, who was also her accompanist. She sang at his memorial service.

Leporello. Don Giovanni's servant (bs) in Mozart's *Don Giovanni* and Dargomyzhsky's *The Stone Guest*.

Leppard, Raymond (*b* London, 11 Aug. 1927). English conductor and musicologist. Studied Cambridge. Répétiteur Gly. 1954–6. Returned to Cambridge 1957 as lecturer, also beginning his exploration and editing of 17th- and early 18th-cent. music, especially Monteverdi and Cavalli, but including Rameau (*Dardanus*, Paris, O, 1981). London, CG, 1958 (*Samson*), 1972 (*Figaro*, *Così*); Gly. 1964 (*Poppea*), 1967 (*Ormindo*), 1970 (*Calisto*; prem. of Maw, *Rising of the Moon*), 1972 (*Ritorno d'Ulisse*), 1975 (*Cunning Little Vixen*); London, SW, 1965 (Monteverdi's *Orfeo*), 1971 (*Poppea*); S Fe 1974 (*Egisto*); New York, M, 1978 (*Billy Budd*). His realizations, which include additions from other works and some original composition, have been attacked for their inauthenticity, but served to introduce once-neglected music to a wide general audience, and were skilfully judged in theatrical effect. (R)

Le Roux, François (*b* Rennes, 30 Oct. 1955). French baritone. Studied Paris O Studio. O-Lyon 1980–5, in operas by Mozart. Gly. 1987, Ramiro (*L'heure espagnole*). London, CG, from 1988: Papageno, Malatesta, and created Birtwistle's Gawain. His fluent delivery and natural stage manner are well suited to Pelléas, which he has sung at Milan, S (1986), Vienna (1988), and London, CG (1993). (R)

Lescaut. A sergeant of the King's Guards (bar), Manon's cousin in Massenet's *Manon* and her brother in Puccini's *Manon Lescaut*.

Le Sueur, Jean-François (*b* Drucat-Plessiel, 15 Feb. 1760; *d* Paris, 6 Oct. 1837). French composer. Studied Abbeville and Amiens choir schools, Paris with Roze. Worked for a time as a choirmaster, usually controversially owing to his advanced ideas for a more theatrical church music. Turning to opera, with help and advice from Spontini, he began work on *Télémaque* (1796), but then caught the temper of the Revolutionary times with *La caverne* (1793). This made him, with Cherubini and Méhul, the most prominent composer of the day in France. A *rescue opera, *La caverne* is a powerful, even harsh work, formally pioneering for its successful reconciliation of elements from opera seria, opera buffa, and opéra-comique. *Paul et Virginie* (1794) and *Télémaque* followed, the former adumbrating some of the manner of Grand Opera.

This is the form of his greatest success, *Ossian, ou Les bardes* (1804). The presence of Napoleon as patron helped to win the work favour, as did the current fascination with all things to do with 'Ossian'. Le Sueur's old love of choral music (evident in *La caverne*) tends to dominate the work and give it the semblance of oratorio; nevertheless, the most famous section, the tableau 'Ossian's Dream', is finely conceived and boldly written. Le Sueur also makes use in the work of some originally composed 'barbaric' melodies and textures, a fluent movement between recitative and aria, and certain devices (such as tense off-beat rhythmic figures and some effects of sonority) which impressed his pupil Berlioz. Two works written with Persuis followed before *La mort d'Adam* (1809), a wildly ambitious work that demands a huge cast (including the entire population of heaven and hell) but that not surprisingly fails to match its theme with music of comparable majesty. *Alexandre à Babylone* (1814) takes some of the fluency of *Ossian* further, and anticipates the continuous manner of later 19th-cent. opera. Le Sueur was a teacher well loved by his pupils, among them Gounod, Thomas, and above all Berlioz, who failed to persuade him to accept

even Beethoven, let alone the Romantics whose music his own in fact often anticipates.

Let's Make an Opera. Opera in 2 parts by Britten; text by Eric Crozier. Prem. Aldeburgh, Jubilee H, 14 June 1949.

In the first part the preparations for the opera are discussed by the children and grown-ups taking part, and the audience is rehearsed for its role in four songs. The second part, *The Little Sweep*, is set in 1810 and tells the story of the encounter of Sammy (treb), an 8-year-old apprentice sweep, with the children who live at Iken Hall. The children manage to free Sammy from Black Bob (bs), his master.

Letter Duet. The Duettino 'sull'aria' between the Countess and Susanna (sops) in Act III of Mozart's *Le nozze di Figaro*, in which the Countess dictates to Susanna the letter to be sent to the Count making the assignation that evening in the garden.

Letter Scene. A favourite scene in 17th-cent. opera in which a character reads out a letter brought to him. The device long survived (e.g. in Massenet's *Werther*, where Charlotte rereads letters from the hero in the 'Air des lettres'), but is nowadays usually taken to refer to the extended scene for Tatyana (sop) in Tchaikovsky's *Eugene Onegin*, in which she sits up all night writing to Onegin declaring her love.

Levasseur, Nicolas (*b* Bresles, 9 Mar. 1791; *d* Paris, 7 Dec. 1871). French bass. Studied Paris with Garat. Début Paris, O, 1813 (Grétry's *Caravane du Caire*). London, H, 1815–16; Paris, I, 1819–28; Milan, S, 1820; Paris, O, 1827–45, 1849. Retired 1853. His repertory included much Rossini, and he created numerous roles: Bertram (*Robert le diable*), Marcel (*Huguenots*), Zacharie (*Le prophète*), Governor (*Ory*), Fürst (*Guillaume Tell*), Balthazar (*Favorite*), and Brogni (*La Juive*), among others. He was also the first Mosè in the Paris version. He possessed a magnificent true bass, and a refined style; he was, however, uninspired dramatically, and was at his best in austere, dignified roles.

'Le veau d'or'. The song in praise of gold, sung by Méphistophélès (bs) in Act II of Gounod's *Faust*.

Levi, Hermann (*b* Giessen, 7 Nov. 1839; *d* Munich, 13 May 1900). German conductor.

The son of a rabbi; studied Mannheim with Lachner, Leipzig with Hauptmann and Rietz. Music dir. Saarbrücken, 1859–61; cond. Mannheim 1861; Rotterdam 1861–4; Music dir. Karlsruhe 1864–72, where he cond. Schumann's *Genoveva* and impressed Wagner with his *Meistersinger* and *Rienzi*. Cond. Munich 1872–6. He was in Bayreuth as Wagner's supporter from early days; cond. prem. of *Parsifal* 1882. His choice was successfully urged on Wagner, who greatly admired him but nearly wrecked the collaboration by his crude behaviour especially over the notion of a Jew conducting a work that centres on the representation of Christian ideas. Upset, Levi withdrew with dignity but was persuaded back when Wagner (largely on King Ludwig's urging) made peace. Their friendship survived, and Levi became, in Wagner's words, 'the ideal Wagner conductor'. He conducted at Wagner's funeral. Accounts speak of his great personal qualities, and the 'spiritual' nature of his interpretations. He made new versions of *Così fan tutte*, *Don Giovanni*, and *Figaro*; though now discredited, they helped to win a following for Mozart at a time when his operas were little known and much misrepresented. He also translated *Les Troyens* and Chabrier's *Gwendoline*.

Levine, James (*b* Cincinnati, 23 June 1943). US conductor. Studied Cincinnati with Levin, New York with Lhévinne, Morel, Serkin. Assistant cond. Cleveland Orch. 1964. Début New York, M, 1971 (*Tosca*), principal cond. 1973, music dir. 1975, artistic director 1986. WNO 1970, *Aida*; Hamburg 1975, *Otello*; Salzburg from 1976 (début with *La clemenza di Tito*); Bayreuth 1982–93 (*Parsifal*) and 1994 (new *Ring*); etc. His most distinguished achievement has been to sustain and develop the position of the Met. as an opera-house of world standing, in part thanks to his own wide repertory and catholic tastes. In 1991 led the first new work there in 24 years (Corigliano's *The Ghosts of Versailles*); also gave the New York, M, prem. of *Porgy and Bess* (1985). At his best, an inspiring and dramatically exciting conductor. (R)

Lewis, Richard (*b* Manchester, 10 May 1914; *d* Old Willingdon, 13 Nov. 1990). English tenor. Studied Manchester and London with Allin. Début Gly. 1947 (Male Chorus, *Rape of Lucretia*). London, CG, from 1947, SW, from 1948; S Francisco from 1953. Also Paris, O; Berlin; Buenos Aires; etc. Created Walton's Troilus, Tippett's Mark (*Midsummer Marriage*) and Achilles (*King Priam*), and Klebe's Amphitryon (*Alkmene*). Roles included Ferrando, Idomeneo, Florestan, Pinkerton, Dmitri, Herod, Tom Rakewell. A versatile and intelligent artist. (R)

Lexington Theatre. New York theatre on Lexington Avenue and 51st St. built by Oscar *Hammerstein to evade the 1910 Metropolitan contract which prevented him from giving opera for ten years. Sold, then scene of Boston Nat. OC 1916 season, Chicago O visits 1917–19, German OC 1923–4.

'Libiamo, libiamo'. The *brindisi sung by Alfredo (ten) and Violetta (sop) in Act I of Verdi's *La traviata*.

libretto (It.: 'little book') (Fr., *livret*; Ger., *Textbuch*). The name generally given to the book of the words of an opera, hence the text itself. Though the earliest were some $8\frac{1}{2}$ in. in height, the diminutive was always used and the term has been current in English since about the mid-18th cent.

Early librettos usually began with a title-page succeeded by a preface in which the writer made his dedication to his patron, then by a few words addressed to the reader. The argomento was a summary of the events preceding the action of the opera: these tended to increase in complexity, and even to take their place in the opera itself as a prologue. After the list of the characters in the opera came a catalogue of the scene-changes, dances, perhaps also the scenic effects; until about the end of the 18th cent. there would also be a protesta, in which the author affirmed his sound Roman Catholic faith despite the pagan references to *numi*, *fati*, etc. Though some were published with care, as part of a poet's collected works, most were hurriedly printed for practical use by the audience in the theatre so as to enable them to follow the plot and, especially with opera seria, to appreciate the poetry of an aria that the composer had set and the singer was performing.

In the 17th and 18th cents. the established pattern of recitative, aria, and chorus made special demands upon the librettist, and determined the course of the action. Changing musical conventions have similarly shifted the demands, with the precedence of words or music remaining a topic argued in many theoretical works and dramatized in operas as diverse as *Prima la musica poi le parole*

(Music first and then words) by Salieri (1786) and Strauss's *Capriccio* (1942). The vital element has remained dramatic potency as it charges a composer's imagination, and a strong literary content in a libretto may prove obtrusive.

The sources of successful librettos have ranged from great dramatic masterpieces (*Othello* for Verdi) and great novels (*War and Peace* for Prokofiev) to sentimental novels (*Scènes de la vie de Bohème* for Puccini) and narrative poems (*Eugene Onegin* for Tchaikovsky), from classical and heroic legend (most of Zeno and Metastasio) or Romantic legend (Wagner's *The Flying Dutchman*) to real-life incident (supposedly *Pagliacci*, Janáček's *Osud*), from questions of belief (Wagner's *Parsifal*) to farce (most of Offenbach), from great painting (Hindemith's *Mathis der Maler*) to comic strip (Janáček's *Cunning Little Vixen*), from historical or biographical incident (much Grand Opera) to fairy-tale (much French, German, and Russian opera). In days when the conventions were firm, masters of them such as Zeno and Metastasio provided composers with material that could be used repeatedly, sometimes more than once by the same composer: 27 of Metastasio's works did duty for at least 1,000 settings by at least 50 composers. Collaboration between a librettist who understands, and will respond to the demands of, his composer has regularly proved successful, though it is no guarantee of quality. However, particularly fruitful results have come from the careful mutual planning of Quinault and Lully, Calzabigi and Gluck, Da Ponte and Mozart, Boito and Verdi, Gilbert and Sullivan, Hofmannsthal and Strauss. Among the most successful composers to fashion their own librettos have been Menotti, Tippett, Berlioz, and above all Wagner, who more than any other artist thought out creatively ideas about the interaction of words and music.

Libuše. Opera in 3 acts by Smetana; text (orig. German) by Josef Wenzig, trans. into Czech by Ervín Špindler. Prem. Prague, for the inauguration of the Czech Nat. T, 11 June 1881.

Libuše (sop), Queen of Bohemia, settles a dispute between two brothers, Chrudoš (bs) and Šťáhlav (ten), over the division of their father's inheritance. Chrudoš is unhappy and insults Libuše, saying she is unfit to rule. Distraught at this, she marries a wise

peasant, Přemysl (ten), to whom she abdicates power. The two brothers are reconciled and Přemysl founds the first Bohemian dynasty, the Přemyslids.

Licette, Miriam (*b* Chester, 9 Sept. 1892; *d* Twyford, 11 Aug. 1969). English soprano. Studied Paris with Marchesi and J. De Reszke, and Milan with Sabbatini. Début Rome 1911 (Butterfly). Beecham OC 1916–20; London: BNOC 1922–8, CG 1919–29. Possessed a pure and even voice, and a wide repertory including Donna Elvira, Marguerite, Mimì, Verdi's Desdemona, Gutrune, Louise. (R)

Liebe der Danae, Der (The Love of Danae). Opera in 3 acts by Richard Strauss; text by Josef Gregor, after a sketch by Hofmannsthal. Prem. Salzburg 14 Aug. 1952.

Danae (sop), daughter of Pollux (ten), King of Eos, is visited in her dreams by Jupiter (bar). He takes the form of her lover Midas (ten), and, deceiving Danae, successfully woos her.

Despite Jupiter's warnings that he will lose his golden golden touch if he disobeys him, Midas touches Danae, and she turns to gold. Danae is allowed to choose between Jupiter and the mortal Midas, and selects the latter.

Midas reveals to Danae how he lost his wealth through his agreement with Jupiter. In order to try to regain her, Jupiter disguises himself as a poor tramp, but Danae rejects his promises of wealth and, impressed by her loyalty, Jupiter gives the couple his blessing.

Liebermann, Rolf (*b* Zurich, 14 Sept. 1910). Swiss composer, critic, and opera manager. Studied Zurich, then Budapest and Vienna with Scherchen, later Ascona with Vogel. His style extends from serial music to jazz, and, though freely experimental, is based on knowledge of practical effect. He virtually abandoned composition on taking up his appointment as Intendant of the Hamburg, S (1959–73), one significant for his championship of many new works. At the Paris O, 1973–80, he greatly raised the standard of performances. His works include *Leonore 40/45* (1952), *Die Schule der Frauen* (1955), and *La forêt* (1987).

Liebestod (Ger.: 'love-death'). The first appearance of the term is in Hoffmann's *Undine* (1816), where it is used near the end of the work by Heilmann to describe the lovers' union in death. However, it is now always taken to refer to Isolde's death scene at the end of Act III of Wagner's *Tristan und Isolde*, beginning 'Mild und leise'. Wagner himself sometimes referred to the Prelude as 'Liebestod', and to Isolde's 'Transfiguration' (Verklärung), though without formally naming it as such.

Liebesverbot, Das (The Ban on Love). Opera in 2 acts by Wagner; text by composer, after Shakespeare's drama *Measure for Measure* (1604–5). Prem. Magdeburg 29 Mar. 1836.

Lied (Ger.: 'song'). In German opera, the term has generally been used for a number rather simpler than an aria, sometimes interpolated by a character and outside the plot. The May song in Weber's *Euryanthe* is described as 'Lied mit Chor', though other numbers in the work are described as Aria, Romanze, etc.

Life for the Tsar, A (Russ., *Zhizn za tsarya*). Opera in 4 acts and epilogue by Glinka; text by Baron Georgy Fyodorovich Rosen. Prem. St Petersburg, B, 9 Dec. 1836.

Russia and Poland, winter 1612. Ivan Susanin (bs) refuses to let his daughter Antonida (sop) marry her betrothed, Bogdan Sobinin (ten), until the future of Russia is secure and a new Tsar has been elected.

News of the election of Mikhail Romanov reaches the enemy Polish camp; the officers decide to launch an immediate attack.

While preparations for Antonida's wedding are under way, Polish soldiers burst into her home and compel her father to lead them to the Tsar. Secretly, Susanin tells his adopted son Vanya (con) to run ahead and warn the Tsar.

Susanin leads the Poles into the depths of the enchanted forest. They guess his trick and he prepares himself for death.

In the square of the Kremlin, the new Tsar praises his supporters and rejoices in their victory over the Poles; all lament the death of Susanin.

Ligeti, György (*b* Dicsöszentmárton (Tîrnă veni), 28 May 1923). Hungarian, later Austrian, composer. Studied Kolozsvár (Cluj) with Farkas, Budapest with Kadosa and Veress. His major stage work is *Le grand macabre* (1978), in which his wide-ranging and highly original language find brilliant dramatic expression.

Lily of Killarney, The. Opera in 3 acts by Benedict; text by John Oxenford and Dion Boucicault, after the latter's drama *Colleen Bawn* (1860). Prem. London, CG, 10 Feb. 1862.

Ireland, 19th cent. In order to solve his family's financial problems, Hardress Cregan (ten) is encouraged to marry the heiress Ann Chute (sop); however, he is already secretly married to a peasant, Eily O'Connor (sop), the Colleen Bawn. Mrs Cregan (con), without realizing the consequences of her action, passes to Danny Mann (bar) a glove from Hardress: this is the signal for Danny to kill Eily. He takes her out in a boat and pushes her under the water, but she is rescued by Myles na Coppaleen (ten). Corrigan (bs), believing Eily dead, has Hardress arrested. However, Myles and Eily suddenly appear and the truth about her marriage is disclosed.

Lima, Luis (*b* Córdoba, 12 Sept. 1948). Argentine tenor. Studied Buenos Aires and Madrid. Début Lisbon 1974 (Turiddu). Milan, S, 1977 as Egardo (*Lucia*); New York, M, 1978 (Alfredo). A handsome appearance and assured vocal style make him effective in such roles as Nemorino, Don Carlos, and Don José (all at London, CG, from 1984). (R)

Lincoln Center. The New York arts complex which houses the State T (home of the New York CO) and the *Metropolitan Opera House, also Avery Fisher Hall and the Juilliard School.

Lincoln's Inn Fields Theatre. The first theatre on the London site was the Duke's T, opened 1661 with *The Siege of Rhodes*. The second, 1695–1705, saw the first public *Dido and Aeneas*, 1700. The third, built by Christopher Rich and opened by his son John in 1714, saw the first *Beggar's Opera*, 1728. It was the home of the O of the Nobility, the Italian opera company set up in rivalry to Handel with Porpora as composer and Senesino as singer, 1733–4. Handel's last opera, *Deidamia*, was given there 1741. Later became a barracks; site now occupied by the Royal College of Surgeons.

Lind, Jenny (*b* Stockholm, 6 Oct. 1820; *d* Wynds Point, 2 Nov. 1887). Swedish soprano. Studied Stockholm with I. Berg. After many appearances as a child, she made her operatic début Stockholm 1838 (Agathe). By 1841 she had sung Euryanthe, Lucia, Norma, Donna Anna, and Julia (*La vestale*), and was in vocal trouble. Further study Paris with M. García jun. Returned triumphantly to Stockholm 1842–4. At Berlin, 1844, she was to have created Vielke (written specially for her) in Meyerbeer's *Ein Feldlager in Schlesien*; it was given instead to the soprano Tuczec. However, her Norma won high acclaim, as did her subsequent performances as Vielke. After further triumphs in Germany and Vienna, she was engaged by Lumley for London, HM, 1847, and sang there (creating Amalia in *I masnadieri*) until her retirement from the stage in 1849. Thereafter she performed only in concert. She married the pianist Otto Goldschmidt in 1852, and lived in England from 1858 until her death. One of the 19th cent.'s most famous prima donnas, and known as 'the Swedish nightingale', she was inordinately idolized by the general public, and much admired by Mendelssohn, Hans Andersen, the Schumanns, Prince Albert, and Hanslick. The quality of her voice was remarkably fresh, pure, and sympathetic. Its upper register was especially brilliant and powerful, and though its lower half, according to Chorley, was 'husky, and apt to be out of tune', its deficiencies were disguised by her skill in vocal colouring, while her breath control was extraordinary. Inimitable in roles of pathos and innocence, she was a celebrated Amina, Marie (*Fille du régiment*), and Alice (*Robert le diable*); however, her Norma, lacking in fire and grit, was not a great success in England.

Linda di Chamounix. Opera in 3 acts by Donizetti; text by G. Rossi. Prem. Vienna, K, 19 May 1842.

France, *c*.1760. When a tenant farmer, Antonio (bar), and his wife Maddalena (sop) find themselves in financial difficulties, their landlord's brother, the Marchese de Boisfleury (bar), offers to help by educating their daughter Linda (sop) at his château. However, the Prefect (bs) warns against this scheme, for the Marchese has designs on Linda, and she and some friends go to Paris in search of work instead.

The painter Carlo (ten) wishes to marry Linda, but his mother disapproves of the match since he is, in fact, the Visconti di Sirval, and the nephew of the Marchese. Although she does not yield to him, Linda occupies an apartment owned by Carlo. Misunderstanding the situation, Antonio curses her. When Pierotto (con) tells Linda that Carlo is to marry a rich girl this causes her to lose her reason.

Linda has returned to Chamounix and Carlo arrives there to look for her, having rejected his mother's choice of a match, and persuaded her to give her blessing to his marriage to Linda.

Lindoro. 1. A young Italian (ten), lover of Isabella, in Rossini's *L'italiana in Algeri*.

2. Assumed name of Count Almaviva in Rossini's *Il barbiere di Siviglia*.

Lindpaintner, Peter von (*b* Koblenz, 9 Dec. 1791; *d* Nonnenhorn, 21 Aug. 1856). German composer. Studied Munich with Winter. He became conductor at the new Isartortheater in Munich, 1812–19, also renewing his studies, with Grätz. When the opening of the Munich Hoftheater put the Isartortheater into difficulties, he was forced to resign, and moved to Stuttgart; here he remained until his death, much admired as a conductor, including by Mendelssohn and Berlioz.

Lindpaintner's early operas are in Singspiel manner; later he became interested in Grand Opera and especially in Romantic opera, to which he made an interesting contribution. *Der Bergkönig* (1825) shows the strong influence of Weber, especially of *Euryanthe*, in the sensational use of tremolo and the appeal to the spirits of darkness. *Der Vampyr* (1828, on the same subject as Marschner's opera, but with a different librettist) is still more Weberian, particularly in its use of the popular polacca rhythm, its chromatic harmony, a Cavatine in the manner of Aennchen, and a Bridesmaids' Chorus; but it also anticipates Wagner with its powerful use of running figures under tense triplets, its choral prayer (suggesting that in *Lohengrin*) when the heroine Isolde is abducted, and the Paris-influenced collapse of a palace in ruins. *Die Macht des Liedes* (1836) represents a reconciliation with Singspiel, and shows Lindpaintner's gift with simple song forms, where he was really most at home. In *Die sizilianische Vesper* (1843), described as a 'grosse romantische Oper', his talent and range fail to match his intelligent understanding of what Grand Opera and German Romantic opera had to offer each other.

Linley, Thomas (*b* Badminton, 17 Jan. 1733; *d* London, 19 Nov. 1795). English singing teacher and composer. Studied Bath with Chilcott. Wrote *The London Merchant* (London, CG, 1767). Joint dir. London, DL, 1774–94. Composed, mostly for DL, a large number of operas, ballad operas, pantomimes, and farces. The best-known was *The Duenna* (CG, 1775), a composition and compilation of music for his son-in-law Sheridan's play in collaboration with his eldest son **Thomas** (*b* Bath, 5 May 1756; *d* Grimsthorpe, 5 Aug. 1778). A friend of Mozart, Thomas jun. showed precocious musical gifts, but was drowned in a boating accident, leaving a 3-act opera *The Cady of Bagdad* (1776).

Lipkowska, Lydia (*b* Babino, 6 June 1882; *d* Beirut, 22 Mar. 1958). Bessarabian soprano. Studied St Petersburg with Iretskaya. Début St Petersburg, M, 1906; St Petersburg, M, until 1908, 1911–13; Paris: C, O, and OC, 1909; New York, M, 1909–11; Chicago 1910; London, CG, 1911–12; Petrograd, T of Musical Drama, 1913–15; Rome 1915; left Russia 1919, continuing appearances in Europe and US; USSR tour 1927–9; Odessa 1941. Retired to the Lebanon. An appealing singer with a bright, pure tone. Roles incl. Rosina, Lucia, Gilda, Violetta, Mimì, Snow Maiden, Tatyana, Yolanta, Susanna (Wolf-Ferrari). (R)

Lipovšek, Marjana (*b* Ljublana, 3 Dec. 1946). Slovene mezzo-soprano. Studied Graz and Vienna. Munich, S, from 1983, notable as Konchakovna (*Prince Igor*). Salzburg from 1981, in the prems. of *Baal* (Cerha) and *Die schwarze Maske* (1986) and as Ottavia in *Poppea* (1993). Other roles incl. Klytemnästra (London, CG, 1990), Fricka (New York, M, 1990), Nurse (*Frau ohne Schatten*). Also admired as Dalila and Carmen (Bregenz Fest.). (R)

Lisa. The Countess's granddaughter (sop), lover of Hermann, in Tchaikovsky's *The Queen of Spades*.

Lisenko, Nikolay. See LYSENKO, MYKOLA.

Lisinski, Vatroslav (*b* Zagreb, *bapt.* 8 July 1819; *d* Zagreb, 31 May 1854). Croatian composer. Studied Zagreb with Sojka and Wisner von Morgenstern. His first opera, *Ljubav i zloba* (Love and Malice, 1846), was also the first Croatian opera. Its success encouraged him to devote himself wholly to music, and he studied further in Prague with Kittl and Pitsch. Returning to Zagreb, he found it impossible to make a living in music, and became a clerk. However, he left a second opera, *Porin* (comp. 1851), in which he not only makes use of Croatian folk music but shows an awareness of Glinka's example in

giving such ingredients a wider context and further makes some use of Leitmotiv.

Lisitsyan, Pavel (*b* Vladikavkaz, 6 Nov. 1911). Armenian baritone. Studied Leningrad Cons. Début Leningrad 1935. Moscow, B, from 1940. New York, M, 1960; the first Soviet singer to appear there. Also S Francisco, Prague, Budapest. An impressive artist with a particularly warm and beautiful voice. Repertory includes Escamillo, Amonasro; also Onegin and many other Russian roles. (R)

List, Emanuel (*b* Vienna, 22 Mar. 1888; *d* Vienna, 21 June 1967). Austrian, later US, bass. Studied New York with Zuro. Début Vienna, V, 1922 (Gounod's Méphistophélès). Berlin: SO, 1924; S, 1925–33. London, CG, from 1925; Bayreuth 1933; New York, M, 1935–50; also Chicago, Buenos Aires, Salzburg. Possessed a deep, full tone and a strong stage presence. Roles included Osmin, Rocco, Pogner; especially distinguished as Hunding, Hagen, and Ochs. (R)

Liszt, Franz (Ferenc) (*b* Raiding, 22 Oct. 1811; *d* Bayreuth, 31 July 1886). Hungarian composer, pianist, and conductor. His sole completed opera was *Don Sanche* (1825), a 1-act piece written perhaps with some help over orchestration from his teacher Paer. It was produced in Paris in 1825, with Nourrit in the title-role, and after four performances lay neglected until modern times. On a fashionable subject of emotional trials and magic confusions, the work shows, unsurprisingly, little sign of individuality but includes some effective music (including for a storm). Of other operatic projects, the most ambitious, and one which absorbed Liszt for a considerable time, was *Sardanapale*.

Among Liszt's services to opera was his popularizing of works by many of his contemporaries with the piano transcriptions, paraphrases, and fantasias he played all over Europe during his years as a travelling virtuoso. In 1848 he became Kapellmeister in Weimar, where he championed, with characteristic generosity, many composers, including Wagner, whose *Lohengrin* had its prem. under him in 1850, and Berlioz, whose *Benvenuto Cellini* he gave in the revised 3-act version in 1852. He also gave the first performance of Schubert's *Alfonso und Estrella* in 1854, backing it up with a critical article, and of Rubinstein's *The Siberian Huntsmen* in the same year. Other pioneering productions included Schumann's *Genoveva* (1855). A plan to stage Wagner's as yet uncompleted *Ring* and make Weimar into what Bayreuth eventually became never materialized. Liszt's position eventually became difficult, partly for personal reasons, and matters came to a head in his confrontations with the reactionary elements in the town over Cornelius's *The Barber of Bagdad* in 1858: he felt compelled to resign.

Litvinne, Felia (*b* St Petersburg, 11 Oct. 1860; *d* Paris, 12 Oct. 1936). Russian, later French, soprano. Studied Paris with Barthe-Banderali and Viardot. Début Paris, I, 1883 (Amelia, *Boccanegra*). New York, Mapleson Co., 1885–6; Paris, O, from 1889; Milan, S, 1890; New York, M, 1896–7; London, CG, 1899, 1902, 1905, 1907, 1910. Also St Petersburg; Brussels, M; Monte Carlo. Retired from stage 1916. An impassioned singer with a large, brilliant, and supple voice, she was famous as Alceste, Donna Anna, Aida, Isolde, and Brünnhilde, among many other roles. Her sister Hélène was married to bass Edouard *De Reszke. (R)

Liù. A slave girl (sop), in love with Calaf, in Puccini's *Turandot*.

Liverpool. City in Lancashire, England. Largely dependent on touring companies, the city has also fostered local amateur groups. The most notable has been the Liverpool Grand OC, which has staged the British prems. of Bizet's *Ivan IV* (1956) and Gounod's original *Mireille* (1981), as well as productions of *Hérodiade*, *Macbeth*, *La Gioconda*, and *Eugene Onegin*. Beecham staged *The Bohemian Girl* as part of the Fest. of Britain in 1951. In 1971 the university gave the prem. of Elaine Murdoch's *Tamburlaine*. English prems. given in Liverpool include *Manon* (Carl Rosa OC, 1885) and *Mazeppa* (Russian Touring Co., 1888).

Livigni, Filippo (*fl.* 1773–86). Italian librettist. He was one of the most successful Venetian comic librettists. Of his 13 works, the most famous were *La molinara* (Fischietti, 1778), *Il convito* (Cimarosa, 1782), and *Il due castellani burlati* (Valentini, 1785): these were set many times in the 18th cent. and followed the model of Goldoni.

Ljungberg, Göta (*b* Sundsvall, 4 Oct. 1893; *d* Lidingö, 28 June 1955). Swedish soprano. Studied Stockholm with Bratt. Début Stock-

holm 1918 (Elsa). Berlin, S, 1926. London, CG, 1924–9; New York, M, 1932–5, when she retired. Created roles in operas by Goossens, D'Albert, and Hanson. With her great beauty, clear voice, and dramatic acting, a much admired Salome; also sang Elektra, Chrysothemis, Brünnhilde, Sieglinde, Kundry. (R)

Lloyd, Robert (*b* Southend-on-Sea, 2 Mar. 1940). English bass. Studied London with O. Kraus. Début London, U Coll. O, 1969 (Minister, Beethoven's *Leonore*). London, SW, 1969–72, CG, from 1972; New York, M, 1988; also Paris, Boston, etc. Repertory includes Sarastro, Gurnemanz, Leporello, Philip II, Frère Laurent, Don Giovanni. Kirov O 1990, as Boris (first British performer of the role there). (R)

Lloyd-Jones, David (*b* London, 19 Nov. 1934). Welsh conductor, translator, and editor. Studied Oxford. Coached *Boris* in Russian, London, CG, 1959. New OC 1960–4. Scottish O 1967; WNO 1968; London, SW/ENO from 1969, CG 1971; first artistic dir. O North 1977–90, greatly contributing to its success and developing a wide repertory, including first British *Jonny spielt auf* (1984) and *Daphne* (1987). Cond. first British staged *War and Peace*. A specialist in Russian opera: his translations incl. *Onegin* and Rakhmaninov's *Francesca da Rimini*. His authoritative edition of *Boris*, using the full score of the original versions, has been welcomed and performed in Russia. (R)

Locke, Matthew (*b* ?Devon, 1621 or 1622; *d* London, Aug. 1677). English composer. He contributed the fourth entry to Davenant's *The Siege of Rhodes* and sang the role of the Admiral of Rhodes in the first performance. *Cupid and Death* (1653, part-written by Christopher Gibbons) was described by Locke as a masque, although it resembles a full opera in having songs, recitative, short choruses, and dances: its score is the only complete extant copy of a 17th-cent. English masque.

After the Restoration in 1660, a strong French influence came to bear on Locke's work. *Psyche* (1675) was modelled on Molière's play and clearly emulates the form of the tragédie-ballet; it contains more music than any of his other stage works. Locke also wrote incidental music for many plays, including songs for Shadwell's famous version of *The Tempest*.

Lockhart, James (*b* Edinburgh, 16 Oct.

1930). Scottish conductor and pianist. Studied London. London: SW, 1960–2; CG, 1962–8; EOG, 1967. Music dir. WNO 1968–73, contributing much to its establishment and progress; music dir. Kassel 1972–80, also Koblenz O. London, ENO from 1984 (incl. at New York, M); also Hamburg, Munich, Florence, etc. Repertory incl. *Ring*, *Trovatore*, *Boris*, first *Lulu* by British co. (WNO), *War and Peace*, *Grimes*, first *Bear* (Walton). (R)

Loder, Edward (*b* Bath, 1813; *d* London, 5 Apr. 1865). English composer. Studied Frankfurt with Ries. His first opera, *Nourjahad*, opened the English OH (Lyceum) in 1834, and was acclaimed as a founding work of English opera. Other stage works followed, some little more than separate songs linked with dialogue, some ballad operas or something approaching English Singspiel. *The Night Dancers* (1846) was a characteristic example of English fairy opera, and like others failed to survive the satire of Sullivan's *Iolanthe*. His most important work was *Raymond and Agnes* (1855), which reveals his melodic gift and his command of vivid orchestration, as well as a certain dramatic power. In more favourable conditions, and with stronger librettos, he might have achieved considerable stature as a composer of English Romantic opera. His sister **Kate Loder** (*b* Bath, 21 Aug. 1825; *d* Headley, 30 Aug. 1904) was a pianist and composer: her works include an opera *L'elisir d'amore* (1844).

Lodoïska. Opera in 3 acts by Cherubini; text by C. F. Fillette-Loraux, after Louvet de Couvray's *Les amours de Faublas*. Prem. Paris, T Feydeau, 18 July 1791.

Poland, 1600. Count Floreski (ten) goes in search of Lodoïska (sop), whom he wishes to marry. She is the prisoner of Dourlinski (bar), who also plans to wed her. The Tartars, under Titzikan (ten), attack the castle where she is held, enabling Floreski to rescue her.

Lodoletta. Opera in 3 acts by Mascagni; text by Forzano, after Ouida's novel *Two Little Wooden Shoes* (1874). Prem. Rome, C, 30 Apr. 1917.

Holland and Paris, 19th cent. Antonio (bs) gives Lodoletta (sop) a pair of new red shoes. After his death she falls in love with a painter, Flammen (ten), and follows him from Holland to Paris. She is afraid to enter his house, where a party is in progress, and dies in the snow. Flammen finds her and laments that he has always loved her.

Loewe, Carl (*b* Loebjuen, 30 Nov. 1796; *d* Kiel, 20 Apr. 1869). German composer and singer. Though famous for his songs, especially his ballad settings, Loewe also wrote some sacred and instrumental music and six operas, two based on Scott (*Malek-Adhel* (1832) on *The Talisman*, *Emmy* (1842) on *Kenilworth*).

Loewe, Sophie (*b* Oldenburg, 24 Mar. 1815; *d* Budapest, 28 Nov. 1866). German soprano. Daughter of the actor Ferdinand Löwe. Studied Vienna with Ciccimarra, Milan with Lamperti. Début Vienna, K, 1832 (Elisabetta in Donizetti's *Otto mesi in due ore*). Berlin 1837; London 1841; Milan, S, 1841; Venice 1843–4. A highly strung, dramatic singer, she created the title-role of Donizetti's *Maria Padilla* (written for her), Elvira in *Ernani* (when she sang badly, possibly annoyed that Verdi, striking a blow for composers' independence, had refused to write the usual rondo-finale for her), and Odabella in *Attila*. She retired in 1848 on her marriage to Prince Ferdinand of Liechtenstein; by then her voice was already in decline.

Loge. The god of fire (ten) in Wagner's *Das Rheingold*.

Logroscino, Nicola (*b* Bitonto, *bapt*. 22 Oct. 1698; *d* ?Palermo, 1765). Italian composer. Studied Naples with Veneziano, Perugino, and Mancini; expelled from his conservatory for vice 1727. Organist to the Bishop of Conza 1728–31, also becoming known as an opera composer: especially successful were *Quinto Fabio* (1738) and *Inganno per inganno* (Deceit for Deceit, 1738).

Though records suggest that he was one of the most important and prolific composers of Neapolitan comic opera in the 1730s, 1740s, and 1750s, only the music for *Il governatore* survives. This suggests that his description as 'il dio dell'opera buffa' ('the god of opera buffa') was justified, and is important for the development of the *ensemble finale.

Lohengrin. Opera in 3 acts by Wagner; text by the composer, after the anonymous German epic. Prem. Weimar, Court T, 28 Aug. 1850.

King Henry the Fowler (bs), who has been visiting Antwerp to raise an army, holds court. He asks Frederick of Telramund (bar) why the kingdom of Brabant is torn by strife. Telramund accuses his ward Elsa (sop) of having murdered her young brother

Gottfried in order to obtain the throne. Elsa describes a dream in which a knight in shining armour has come to defend her. The King's Herald (bar) twice calls for a champion. A swan-drawn boat bearing a knight in shining armour arrives. The knight (Lohengrin, ten) bids the swan farewell, and agrees to champion Elsa, offering her his hand in marriage on condition that she will never ask him his name or origin. Lohengrin defeats Telramund, generously sparing his life.

In the courtyard of the castle in Antwerp, Telramund, who has been banned as a traitor by the King, and his wife Ortrud (sop), are brooding on the state of events. Elsa appears on a balcony and sings a song to the night breezes. She descends, and Ortrud, offering her friendship, begins to sow distrust of Lohengrin in her mind. Dawn breaks, and processions form for the marriage of Elsa and Lohengrin. On the steps of the Cathedral, Ortrud accuses Lohengrin of having defeated Telramund by evil means, and then Telramund repeats his wife's accusation. Elsa assures the knight that she trusts him; but the seeds of suspicion have taken root.

A brilliant orchestral prelude and the celebrated Wedding March open a scene set in Elsa's bridal chamber. Elsa's happiness gives way to hysteria and she demands to know her husband's name. Telramund and four of his followers break into the room to attack Lohengrin, who immediately kills Telramund. He bids the nobles to bear the body to the King, and tells Elsa that he will reveal his secret to them all. The scene changes to the banks of the Scheldt. The King and court assemble, and Lohengrin tells them that he has come from the Temple of the Holy Grail in Monsalvat; his father was Parsifal, and Lohengrin is his name. He bids Elsa a sad farewell, and then turns to greet the swan which has brought the boat for him. Ortrud rushes on and reveals that the swan is in reality Gottfried, Elsa's brother. Lohengrin falls on his knees and prays. The swan becomes Gottfried, and a white dove of the Grail flies down and draws the boat away.

Lola. Alfio's wife (sop), lover of Turiddu, in Mascagni's *Cavalleria rusticana*.

Lombardi alla prima Crociata, I (The Lombards at the First Crusade). Opera in 4 acts by Verdi; text by Solera. Prem. Milan, S, 11 Feb. 1843.

Milan, Antioch, Jerusalem, late 11th cent. Two brothers, Pagano (bs) and Arvino (ten), both loved Viclinda (sop). She preferred Arvino but on the day of her wedding to him, Pagano tried to kill him. At the start of the opera, Pagano returns from exile to Milan and seems to be reconciled with his brother and Viclinda, and their daughter Giselda (sop). Still seeking revenge on his brother, however, Pagano plans an attack but murders his father by mistake. He is exiled to the Holy Land where he lives as a hermit.

Giselda accompanies her father on a crusade and is captured by Acciano (bs), the tyrant of Antioch. His son Oronte (ten) is in love with Giselda and wants to espouse her Christian faith. In a battle between the Christians and Moslems, it appears that Oronte is killed. Giselda curses her people for allowing the war, so her enraged father tries to kill her. Pagano, whom neither of them now recognizes, prevents him.

Mortally wounded, Oronte escapes with Giselda. He is baptized by Pagano shortly before dying in Giselda's arms. Pagano leads an attack on Jerusalem and is also wounded. He discloses his identity to his brother who forgives him.

I Lombardi was adapted by Verdi for the Paris Opéra in 1847 (prem. 26 Nov). The libretto was refashioned in French by Gustav Vaëz and Alphonse Royer as *Jérusalem*. In this version Roger (bs), the uncle of Hélène (sop), engages a mercenary to kill Gaston (ten), to whom she is betrothed. By mistake he kills her father, the Count of Toulouse. Gaston is blamed but he and Hélène are reunited at the end when Roger confesses his guilt.

London. Capital of Great Britain. Masques were popular in the 17th cent., but opera began with *The Siege of Rhodes*, at Rutland House in Sept. 1656. Blow's *Venus and Adonis* was given during the 1680s, and many other works followed at the city's many theatres. In 1689 Purcell's *Dido and Aeneas* was given in Chelsea. After his death, opera in London was for long almost entirely Italian. The first operatic work sung in Italian was the pastorale *Gli amori d'Ergasto* (1705) by Jakob Greber (?–1731), and the first complete Italian opera given was Bononcini's *Camilla* (1706), although this was sung in English. In 1710 Handel arrived, producing almost 40 operas between *Rinaldo* (1711) and *Deidamia* (1741). The first Mozart opera heard was *La clemenza di Tito* (1806); and his operas, together with Rossini's, dominated repertories during the 1820s. The popularity of *Der Freischütz* (of which six versions were current in the 1820s) led to the invitation to Weber to compose and conduct *Oberon* (1826); this helped to encourage native composers to write for London theatres, whose taste remained largely centred on pasticcios or other light musical entertainments. Italian opera remained popular. Wagner was first heard regularly in the 1870s, the complete *Ring* in 1882. Opera developed rapidly after the turn of the century, and several new companies were formed. As London, with its long and powerful dramatic tradition, has always been well furnished with theatres, it is chiefly by way of their histories that the course of opera in the city is best followed.

See also ALMEIDA THEATRE, CAMDEN FESTIVAL, CHELSEA OPERA GROUP, COLISEUM THEATRE, COVENT GARDEN, DRURY LANE THEATRE ROYAL, HER MAJESTY'S THEATRE, KING'S THEATRE, LINCOLN'S INN FIELDS THEATRE, LONDON OPERA HOUSE, LYCEUM THEATRE, NEW OPERA COMPANY, OLD VIC, PANTHEON, ROYAL ITALIAN OPERA, SADLER'S WELLS, SAVOY THEATRE.

London, George (*b* Montreal, 30 May 1919; *d* Armonk, NY, 24 Mar. 1985). Canadian bass-baritone. Studied Los Angeles with Strelitzer and Stewart. Début (as George Burnson) Hollywood Bowl 1941 (Doctor, *Traviata*). Vienna 1949; Gly. 1950; Bayreuth 1951–64; New York, M, 1951–66; Milan, S, 1952; Moscow, B, 1960 (the first non-Russian to sing Boris there). Cologne 1962–4 (Wotan). Retired 1967. Opera prod. from 1971, including *Ring*, Seattle and S Diego, 1973–5; dir. Washington O Soc. from 1975. Prem. 1st US English-language *Ring*, Seattle 1975. Roles included Don Giovanni, Scarpia, Amfortas, Flying Dutchman, Mandryka. A dramatically intense performer with a rich and resonant voice. (R)

London Opera House. Built by Oscar *Hammerstein in 1911 and opened 13 Nov. with Nouguès's *Quo vadis?*, followed by prems. of works by Massenet and Holbrooke. Closed 1912. As the Stoll, became a variety theatre and cinema. Short seasons of opera were given in the First World War, including the first English *Queen of Spades* and *Aleko*. Seasons were resumed after the Second World War, from 1949, including by touring Italian and Yugoslav companies, also the first English *Porgy and Bess* (1952) and Honegger's *Jeanne d'Arc* with Ingrid Bergman (1954). Later demolished.

Loreley. Opera in 3 acts by Catalani; text by Zanardini and D'Ormeville. Prem. Turin, R, 16 Feb. 1890.

The Rhine, *c*.1500. The orphan girl Loreley (sop) has fallen in love with Walter (ten), but he spurns her advances in favour of Anna (sop). Loreley makes a pact with the king of the Rhine, Alberich, promising herself to him if he will transform her into an irresistible seductress. As such she interrupts the nuptials of Walter and Anna; he falls for her and abandons Anna, who dies of grief. The Loreley is about to embrace Walter when spirits carry her away to her rock, thereafter to lure sailors to their deaths. In despair, Walter hurls himself into the Rhine.

Lorengar, Pilar (*b* Saragossa, 16 Jan. 1928). Spanish soprano. Studied Barcelona Cons. Début Barcelona 1949 (in zarzuela). Aix 1955; London, CG, from 1955; Gly. 1956–60; Berlin, D, from 1958; New York, M, 1966–82. Roles include Euridice (Gluck), Donna Elvira, Donna Anna, Countess (Mozart), Alice Ford, Eva, Mélisande. Particularly esteemed in the classical repertory. Sang Valentine at Berlin, D, 1987; Maddalena at Lyons 1989; retired 1991. (R)

Lorenz, Max (*b* Düsseldorf, 17 May 1901; *d* Salzburg, 11 Jan. 1975). German tenor. Studied Berlin with Grenzebach. Début Dresden 1928 (Walther von der Vogelweide, *Tannhäuser*). New York, M, 1931–4, 1947–50; Bayreuth, and Berlin, S, from 1933; London, CG, 1934; Vienna, S, from 1937; also Milan, S; Paris, O; etc. Created several roles, including Joseph K in Einem's *Der Prozess*. An expressive singer with exceptional declamation, famous for his Wagner roles, especially Siegfried, Walther; also an outstanding Otello (Verdi). (R)

Lortzing, Albert (*b* Berlin, 23 Oct. 1801; *d* Berlin, 21 Jan. 1851). German composer, conductor, librettist, singer, and actor. Son of an actor; studied Berlin with Rungenhagen, later by himself when obliged by his father's profession to travel extensively. He played children's parts on the stage as both actor and singer.

Lortzing's first opera was *Ali Pascha von Janina* (comp. 1824), a conventional work which includes a strong vengeance aria making use of four trumpets. For this he wrote his own text, as he did throughout his career: he is the most important German composer before Wagner to do so. He followed this with some works that confirmed his attraction to Singspiel (he was a lifelong defender of opera with spoken dialogue) and his devotion to the language of Mozart: *Szenen aus Mozarts Leben* (comp. 1832) uses only Mozart's music. He then turned to comedy: *Die beiden Schützen* (1837) made a reputation later confirmed with *Zar und Zimmermann* (1837). These two works, enduringly popular in Germany, display his characteristic vein of light tunefulness (deriving from the manner of German popular song), his easy control of the stage, his lighthearted, sentimental approach to character, and a distinct individuality in the handling of the conventional ingredients of German musical comedy. *Caramo* (1839) and *Hans Sachs* (1840) proved less durable. Nevertheless, *Hans Sachs* includes some attractive music, and is remarkable for some anticipations of Wagner's *Die Meistersinger von Nürnberg*, while his next work, *Casanova* (1841), contains suggestions of Leitmotiv. *Der Wildschütz* (1842), which followed, was his greatest triumph, and remains popular in Germany; it is characteristic of Lortzing's easy, attractive musical manner in drawing on the German feeling for the countryside which Weber had first aroused in opera.

Lortzing was now also working as producer, singer, and conductor: he became Kapellmeister in Leipzig, 1844–5, but was forced to leave and suffered great difficulty in providing for his large family. His next work, *Undine* (1845), was a magic opera on the popular Romantic legend. It includes some striking effects: the conclusion, with rising waters and a palace crashing in ruins, was a common inheritance of Parisian Grand Opera in German Romantic opera up to and including Wagner. The work also includes some early use of true Leitmotiv.

In 1846 he moved to Vienna, where *Der Waffenschmied* (1846) was given. This strengthened his popularity, and at the same time confirmed the pattern of opera he had made his own—a lightly romantic comedy, to his own text, often turning on the disguise of an aristocrat as a workman, and expressed in engaging and tuneful songs culminating in rather stronger finales. *Zum Grossadmiral* (1847) followed; and then Lortzing attempted to capitalize on the revolutionary events of 1848 with *Regina* (comp. 1848). Though the work contains some enterprising ideas, it is in no sense revolutionary musically but repeats Lortzing's well-tried

formulas; and he discovered to his cost that the idea was in uneasy times found too subversive. He lost his post, but was nevertheless called to Leipzig to supervise his *Rolands Knappen* (1849), an impressive work which has a heroine named Isolda and also contains some harmonic glimpses of the world of *Tristan*. However, Lortzing's chromatic excursions, though often advanced, are hardly ever more than decorative or incidental. An appointment in Leipzig fell through, and in 1850 he moved to Berlin as conductor of a small theatre. Here his family lived in poverty despite the frequent performance of his works, and he died when about to be dismissed from even this humble post. His last work was *Die Opernprobe* (1851), which satirizes some of the stage and operatic conventions he knew so well, especially the Italianate recitative for which he retained a lifelong dislike.

Lortzing's music has a simple charm that fits it well to the kind of romantic comedy he preferred, though he can hardly be categorized as a Romantic: he was really always more concerned with effective singer types in his roles rather than subtlety of characterization. If not a sophisticated composer, and sometimes an over-sentimental one, he was capable of some remarkably enterprising strokes, and his works represent the most agreeable type of German comic opera.

Los Angeles. City in California, US. Visiting companies in the 1880s and 1890s included the Abbott, Juch, and Del Conti (1st US *Bohème*). The New York Metropolitan made its first West Coast appearance 1900. In 1906 the Lombardi (later San Carlo) Co. began visits, and the Chicago O came for 15 years from 1914. Other visitors included the Scotti Co. and a Russian company with Shalyapin. The Los Angeles Grand O Association was formed 1924 with Gaetano Merola as director, working with the S Francisco O. Merola formed the rival California Grand O Association 1925, rejoining 1927, and seasons were given at the Shrine Auditorium until 1932. The S Francisco O visited 1938–65, when the Dorothy Chandler Pavilion (cap. 3,098) was opened. Operatic activity increased during the 1980s, and the Los Angeles Music Center O Association was founded in 1985 with Peter Hemmings as director, opening in Oct. 1986 with Domingo (later artistic consultant) in Verdi's *Otello*. Since then operatic activity has put down strong and healthy roots. The Wiltern T (cap. 2,300) was reopened 1985, and productions have included Jonathan Miller's *The Mikado* with Dudley Moore. Opera has also been given in the Hollywood Bowl, beginning with Parker's *Fairyland* in 1915.

Los Angeles, Victoria de (*b* Barcelona, 1 Nov. 1923). Spanish soprano. Studied Barcelona Cons. Début Barcelona 1941 (Mimì). Paris, O, 1949; London, CG, 1950–61; New York, M, 1951–61; Bayreuth 1961–2. Also Vienna; Milan, S; Buenos Aires; Scandinavia; Australia; etc. A soprano held in much affection for her clear-toned, flexible voice, rich vocal palette, and the touching quality of her singing. Highly acclaimed as Rosina, Donna Anna, Mimì, Salud, Marguerite, Eva, Santuzza, Manon, Verdi's Desdemona, and Carmen. (R)

Lott, Felicity (*b* Cheltenham, 8 May 1947). English soprano. Studied London, RAM. Début London, ENO, 1975 (Pamina). London, CG, from 1976; Gly. Touring O 1976; Gly. Fest. O from 1977; Chicago 1984; New York, M, 1990 (Marschallin). Also Paris, O; Brussels, M; etc. Roles include Fiordiligi, Mozart's and Strauss's Countesses, Arabella, Christine, Anne Trulove, Louise, Eva. Possesses a radiant tone and an elegant style. (R)

Lotti, Antonio (*b* Venice or Hanover, *c*.1667; *d* Venice, 5 Jan. 1740). Italian composer, organist, and singer: studied Venice with Legrenzi. St Mark's as singer 1689, second organist 1692, first organist 1704, maestro di cappella 1736. He also composed 16 opere serie for Venice theatres 1706–17, of which *Porsenna* (1713) and *Alessandro Severo* (1717) were especially well received. In Dresden 1717–19 with his wife, the soprano Santa Stella, to establish an Italian company for the Crown Prince, also producing *Giove in Argo* (1717), *Ascanio* (1718), and *Teofane* (1719). Returning to Venice, he wrote no further operas, but was active as a teacher, his pupils including Bassani and Galuppi.

Lotti's operas fall into the period between the decline of the Venetian and the rise of the Neapolitan school, and he set librettos from both traditions. From Cavalli, Cesti, and late Monteverdi he inherited his basic understanding of dramatic procedures, although the use of da capo aria, especially with obbligato instrument, looked forward to the later style of Scarlatti. A skilled craftsman capable of deeply expressive writing,

Lotti was much admired by Hasse, whose operas owe something to his example.

Louise. Opera in 4 acts by Gustave Charpentier; text by the composer. Prem. Paris, OC, 2 Feb. 1900.

Paris, *c*.1900. Louise (sop) is in love with Julien (ten), but her parents (mez and bs) refuse to allow them to marry. They set up house together in Montmartre, but when Louise's mother comes to tell her that her father is seriously ill she returns home to help nurse him back to health on condition that she be allowed to return eventually to Julien. But when her father has recovered, Louise's parents refuse to allow her to rejoin Julien; she quarrels with her father and he throws her out of the house, accusing the city of Paris of destroying his life.

Love of the Three Oranges, The (Russ., *Lyubov k tryem apelsinam*). Opera in 4 acts by Prokofiev; text (in Russian) by the composer, after Gozzi's comedy (1761). Prem. (in French version by Vera Janacopoulos) Chicago, Auditorium, 30 Dec. 1921.

A mythical land. An opera is being presented in which the King of Clubs (ten) instructs his Prime Minister, Leandro (bar), to organize an entertainment to cure the Prince's (ten) fatal melancholy by making him laugh. Leandro is secretly plotting the Prince's death.

When the Prince offends the wicked witch Fata Morgana (sop) with his laughter, he is sent to find three oranges from another witch, Creonte (bs).

Truffaldino the jester (ten) cuts open two, but two princesses contained within die of thirst. The Prince opens the third orange and the Princess Ninetta is saved by some of the stage audience producing a bucket of water. But Smeraldina (mez), Fata Morgana's servant, turns Ninetta into a rat and takes her place.

The good magician Celio (bs) restores Ninetta to her original form and, having disposed of the plotters, the couple are united.

'Love, too frequently betrayed'. Tom Rakewell's (ten) aria in Act I of Stravinsky's *The Rake's Progress*, calling on love to remain with him even as he betrays it in Mother Goose's brothel.

Lualdi, Adriano (*b* Larino, 22 Mar. 1885; *d* Milan, 8 Jan. 1971). Italian composer, conductor, and critic. Studied Rome with Falchi,

Venice with Wolf-Ferrari. From 1909 very active as conductor, especially in Trieste, and then as critic and musical correspondent both nationally and internationally. His fervent nationalism led him to embrace Fascism, and he was elected to parliament in 1929. Dir. Naples Cons. 1936–43, Florence Cons. 1947–56. His political sympathies and the uneven nature of his advanced musical ideas led to his being first overrated as a composer and then rejected. The most significant of his operas, for which he mostly wrote his own texts, is perhaps *La figlia del re* (The King's Daughter, 1922), a version of the Antigone story set in India. For the rest, he tended to prefer comic or satirical subjects, with very erratic success: in a number of these, for instance the 1-act opera-ballet *La Grançeola* (1932), he made ingenious use of updated 18th-cent. styles, but his ingenuity could also be self-defeating, as in the stylistic jumble of *Il diavolo nel campanile* (The Devil in the Belfry, 1925).

Lubin, Germaine (*b* Paris, 1 Feb. 1890; *d* Paris, 27 Oct. 1979). French soprano. Studied Paris with Isnardon and Martini, later Litvinne and Lilli Lehmann. Début Paris, OC, 1912 (Antonia). Paris, O, 1914–44; London, CG, 1937; Bayreuth 1938–9; also Salzburg, Vienna, Berlin, etc. An excellent singer, with a full tone and great nobility of presence, highly acclaimed as Alceste, Iphigénie (*Aulide*), Donna Anna, Leonore, Aida, Isolde, Brünnhilde, Kundry, Elektra, Marschallin, Ariane (Dukas). Career ended prematurely when she was imprisoned for collaboration with the Nazis. (R)

Lucca, Pauline (*b* Vienna, 25 Apr. 1841; *d* Vienna, 28 Feb. 1908). Austrian soprano. Studied Vienna with Uffmann and Levy. Début Vienna, K, 1859 (Second Boy, *Zauberflöte*). Berlin 1861; London, CG, 1863–82; Russia 1868–9; Paris, O, 1872; US 1872–4; Vienna, K, 1874–89. Though not endowed with a beautiful voice, she had a wide range and was a colourful, uninhibited actress, known as 'the demon wild-cat'. Her varied repertory included Donna Anna, Zerlina, Valentine, Eva (which she studied with Wagner), Selika (written for her, though she did not create the part); also Leonora (*Trovatore*) and Azucena (once singing both in the same performance). Her Carmen caused a sensation, as did her appearances off-stage with Bismarck: Cosima Wagner, lamenting

their public familiarity, wrote, 'Such things do no honour to the crown or to art.'

Luchetti, Veriano (*b* Viterbo, 12 Mar. 1939). Italian tenor. Studied Milan with Piazza and Capuano. Début Wexford 1965 (Alfredo). Spoleto 1967; London, CG, from 1973; Milan, S, 1975; also Paris, O; Berlin, D; Brussels, M; Vienna; S America; Budapest; etc. Roles include Pinkerton, Rodolfo, Don Carlos, Don José. A sensitive singer with a firm, rich tone. (R)

Lucia di Lammermoor. Opera in 3 acts by Donizetti; text by Cammarano, after Scott's novel *The Bride of Lammermoor* (1819). Prem. Naples, C, 26 Sept. 1835.

Scotland, late 16th cent. Lord Enrico Ashton (bar) wishes his sister Lucia (sop) to marry Arturo Bucklaw (ten) in order to strengthen his own political alliances. She, however, loves Sir Edgardo Ravenswood (ten), an enemy of the family. He proposes to ask for Lucia's hand as a gesture of reconciliation.

In an attempt to encourage her to abandon Edgardo, Enrico shows Lucia a letter supposedly from her lover to another woman. Lucia consequently agrees to marry Arturo. Edgardo interrupts the wedding ceremony, cursing Lucia for betraying him.

Edgardo and Enrico have agreed to fight a duel when news arrives that Lucia has lost her senses and has killed Arturo. Edgardo resigns himself to death at Enrico's hand, but then learns that the mad Lucia is now dead. In grief, Edgardo kills himself.

Lucio Silla. Opera in 3 acts by Mozart; text by G. de Gamerra, rev. Metastasio, poss. after Plutarch's *Parallel Lives* (AD *c*.100). Prem. Milan, RD, 26 Dec. 1772.

Rome, *c*.80 BC. Cecilio (sop cas) has been banished by the dictator Silla (ten), but has returned illegally to Rome. He seeks news of his wife Giunia (sop) from his friend Cinna (sop cas). Cinna tells Cecilio that she mourns him, for Silla, who is enamoured of Giunia, has told her that her husband is dead. Cecilio meets Giunia at the family tombs.

Silla is discussing his plans to marry Giunia when Cecilio rushes in, sword drawn. Celia (sop), Silla's sister, joins a conspiracy to murder Silla. She loves Cinna but cannot tell him because his hatred of Silla is so great. Cinna tells Giunia that she is to be forced to marry Silla. Giunia resolves to plead with the Senate for her husband's life; if they refuse, she would prefer to die with him rather than marry Silla. As she rejects Silla before the Senate, Cecilio enters, again with his sword drawn. Silla orders both husband and wife to be arrested.

Celia and Cinna wish to save Cecilio and Giunia. In a sudden act of magnanimity, Silla pardons the couple and the people unite in singing his praises.

Lucrezia Borgia. Opera in a prologue and 2 acts by Donizetti; text by Romani after Victor Hugo's tragedy (1833). Prem. Milan, S, 26 Dec. 1833.

Venice and Ferrara, early 16th cent. Lucrezia Borgia (sop) alone knows that Gennaro (ten) is her son. Her fourth husband Alfonso (bar) suspects the couple of having an affair and orders Gennaro's arrest. Lucrezia arranges his escape.

At a party at the Princess Negroni's, Gennaro and his friends are given wine which, Lucrezia announces as she enters to the accompaniment of funeral music, is poisoned. She is insulted because one of them has mutilated the name Borgia on her family crest to read 'Orgia'. Finding Gennaro among them, she offers him an antidote, which he refuses; he dies having learnt the identity of his mother.

Ludwig, Christa (b Berlin, 16 Mar. 1928). German mezzo-soprano. Studied with her mother, Frankfurt with Hüni-Mihacsek, New York with Milanov. Début Frankfurt 1946 (Orlovsky). Salzburg from 1954; Vienna from 1955; New York, M, 1959–94; London, CG, 1969, 1976; also Milan, Chicago, Berlin, etc. A highly expressive and intelligent artist with a ripe, firm voice, even throughout its wide compass. Large repertory included Dorabella, Rosina, Eboli, Dido (Berlioz), Kundry, Brangäne, Octavian, Carmen; also Leonore, Dyer's Wife, Lady Macbeth, Marschallin. Created roles in operas by Einem (*Der Besuch der alten Dame*), and Martin. Retired 1994 (last role as Klytemnästra at Vienna, SO). (R)

Luigi. A young stevedore (ten), lover of Giorgetta, in Puccini's *Il tabarro*.

Luisa Miller. Opera in 3 acts by Verdi; text by Cammarano, after Schiller's tragedy *Cabale und Liebe* (1784). Prem. Naples, C, 8 Dec. 1849.

Tyrol, early 18th cent. Rodolfo (ten), the son of Count Walter (bs), is expected to marry Federica (mez), but is in love with Luisa (sop). In order to save her father, who threatened the Count, Luisa has to write to Wurm (bs), an employee of the Count, saying she loves him. Rodolfo makes Luisa admit that she wrote the letter. Rodolfo poisons himself and Luisa, and also succeeds in killing Wurm before dying.

Lully, Jean-Baptiste (Giovanni Battista Lulli) (b Florence, 23 Nov. 1632; d Paris, 22 Mar. 1687). French composer of Italian birth. Brought to France in 1646 to the court of Mlle de Montpensier. He soon made a reputation as a singer, dancer, and violinist, and entered the service of Louis XIV 1653, where he held various appointments and produced much ballet music.

In 1662, beginning with *Le mariage forcé*, he entered into collaboration with Molière on a series of *comédies-ballets, many of which approach genuine opera in the quantity and quality of their music. In *L'amour médicin* (1665) and especially *Le bourgeois gentilhomme* (1670) Lully served an apprenticeship for his later career as an opera composer, experimenting with different styles of recitative and air, and perfecting his instrumental technique.

Since the exile of the Barberini family to Paris in 1644, there had been a number of unsuccessful attempts to establish opera in France. Despite Louis XIV's preference for ballet, Lully followed such experiments with great interest and the success of Perrin's *Pomone* in 1671 eventually convinced him that this was where the future lay. When Perrin was imprisoned in 1672, the everdevious Lully moved swiftly to purchase his opera privilege and, using his considerable influence at court, achieved an almost complete monopoly of French stage music. Recruiting the theatre machinist Vigarani and the librettist Quinault, he founded the Académie Royale de Musique, which was soon offered the theatre in the Palais-Royal as its base.

The first significant production of the new group was *Cadmus et Hermione* (1673), with which Lully and Quinault may be said finally to have established French opera; over the next 12 years they were to collaborate in a series of such *tragédies en musique in which the same basic formula was replicated with considerable success. At the heart of such works, of which *Thésée* (1675), *Amadis*

(1684), and *Armide* (1686) are particularly fine examples, was the glorification of the monarch. The prologue, which only rarely had any connection with the tale following, was essentially intended as a homage to Louis XIV, while many of the stories—sometimes chosen by the King himself—were presented as an allegory of the royal character. The conflict between *amour* and *gloire*, with its attendant obligations, was explored through treatments of well-known mythological or chivalric plots in which the spirit of classical French tragedy, seen most notably through the intervention of the *merveilleux*, was tempered by an emphasis on spectacle and celebration reminiscent of the ballet de cour.

The synthesis of Italian and French musical styles which had already begun in the comédies-ballets was brought to full fruition in the tragédies en musique, which demonstrate a remarkable unity of approach. In particular, Lully must be credited with the invention of a style of recitative suitable for the French language, while his development of the air in its several guises confirmed the importance of a uniquely French form which was to influence composers up to Berlioz. Significant, too, was Lully's exploitation of choral and orchestral resources, which in Italian opera were of only secondary importance at this time.

Lully's claim to be the true founder of French opera is beyond dispute. His works demonstrate a consummate command of the vocal and instrumental resources at his disposal, as well as a sympathetic understanding of the native love for tragedy and ballet, genres with which the new French opera had to compromise. Under Lully's supervision the individual elements of music, poetry, drama, dance, and staging were welded together into an indivisible whole: he was no mere composer, but played a central role in the creation of each opera, particularly in the shaping of the libretto. By the time of his death—from gangrene caused by hitting his foot with a cane while beating time at a concert—Lully was acknowledged at home and abroad as the leading French composer of his generation. In France his works retained a certain following up to the French Revolution and were not totally dislodged either by Rameau, or by the *Guerre des Bouffons, one side of which they partly represented.

Lulu. Opera (unfinished) by Alban Berg; text by the composer, after Wedekind's dramas *Erdgeist* (1895) and *Die Büchse der Pandora* (1901). Prem. Zurich 2 June 1937. Completed version (orchestrated by Cerha), Paris, O, 24 Feb. 1979.

Prague, *c*.1930. A ring-master (bs) announces his show to the audience, presenting Lulu as one of the acts.

Lulu's (sop) elderly husband, Dr Goll, dies of a heart attack when he finds her in a compromising position with the Painter (ten). The Painter, now her husband, kills himself with a razor when Lulu's former lover, Dr Schön (bar), tells him of her past. Lulu forces Dr Schön to break off his engagement by threatening to run away with a Prince (ten), who loves her.

Lulu has married Schön, but continues to receive her many admirers, including Schön's son Alwa (ten). After an argument, Lulu kills Schön. In a filmed trial, Lulu is convicted of murder. She is helped to escape from prison by the lesbian Countess Geschwitz (mez).

In order to escape being sold as a prostitute to an Egyptian, Lulu flees to London with Alwa, the Countess Geschwitz, and the elderly Schigolch (bs). One of her clients is Jack the Ripper, who murders first Lulu and then the Countess.

Lumley, Benjamin (*b* Birmingham, 1811; *d* London, 17 Mar. 1875). English manager. Legal adviser to Laporte, whom he succeeded as manager of London, HM, 1841–52; forced to close by success of London, CG. Reopened 1856; retired 1859. Also manager Paris, I, 1850–1. Gave British prems. of many works by Donizetti and Verdi, commissioning *I masnadieri*, and brought to London singers incl. Lind, E. Frezzolini, Cruvelli, Piccolomini, Tietjens, Staudigl, Giuglini, and G. Ronconi. His company also included Grisi, Mario, Persiani, Tamburini, and Lablache; his quarrel with the first four led to the establishment of the Royal Italian O at London, CG. His *Reminiscences of the Opera* (1864) gives a vivid, if one-sided, picture of London operatic life in the 1840s and 1850s.

Lunn, Louise Kirkby (*b* Manchester, 8 Nov. 1873; *d* London, 17 Feb. 1930). English mezzo-soprano. Studied Manchester with Greenwood, London with Visetti. Début, as student, London, DL, 1893 (Margaret, *Genovéva*). London: CG, 1896, 1901–14, 1919–

22; CR, 1897–9. New York, M, 1902–3, 1906–8. Possessed of a large, well-controlled voice, she was somewhat cool dramatically. A successful Fricka, Brangäne, Ortrud, Dalila, and Amneris. (R)

Lussan, Zélie de. See DE LUSSAN, ZÉLIE.

Lustigen Weiber von Windsor, Die (The Merry Wives of Windsor). Opera in 3 acts by Nicolai; text by Mosenthal, after Shakespeare's comedy (1600–1). Prem. Berlin, Court T, 9 Mar. 1849.

Very much the same plot as Verdi's *Falstaff*, but without Bardolph and Pistol, and with Slender and Master Page. The Wives are given German names: Frau Fluth (Alice), Frau Reich (Meg).

Lustige Witwe, Die (The Merry Widow). Operetta in 3 acts by Lehár; text by Viktor Léon and Leo Stein, after Meilhac's comedy *L'attaché*. Prem. Vienna, W, 30 Dec. 1905.

The complicated plot deals with the attempts of Baron Zeta (bs) to obtain the Merry Widow Hanna Glawari's (sop) fortune for his impoverished country of Pontevedro by getting his compatriot Danilo (ten or bar) to marry her. A sub-plot is concerned with the flirtation between Zeta's young wife Valencienne (sop) and an officer, Camille (ten).

Lutyens, Elisabeth (*b* London, 6 July 1906; *d* London, 14 April 1983). English composer, daughter of Edwin Lutyens. Studied Paris and London. She first turned to opera with two chamber works, *The Pit* (1947) and *Infidelio* (1954), by which time her individual style was already well developed. An important trilogy of larger-scale works was composed during the 1960s: *The Numbered* (1967); *Time Off!—not a Ghost of a Chance* (1972); *Isis and Osiris* (1970). However, in *The Waiting Game* (1973) and *The Goldfish Bowl* (1975) she returned to the more intimate character of her early operas.

Luxon, Benjamin (*b* Redruth, 24 Mar. 1937). English baritone. Studied London with Grüner. Début in EOG's tour of USSR 1963 (Sid, *Albert Herring*, and Tarquinius). London, CG, and Gly. from 1972; London, ENO from 1974; Milan, S, 1986. Created title-role of *Owen Wingrave*, Jester and Death in Davies's *Taverner*. Roles include Almaviva (Mozart), Don Giovanni, Onegin, Posa, Ford, Wolfram,

Falstaff. Possesses a warm, round tone, and a strong stage personality. (R)

Luzzati, Emanuele (*b* Genoa, 3 July 1921). Italian designer. Studied Lausanne. Began theatrical career 1947, and has designed for most leading Italian houses, especially with the producer Franco Enriquez, who brought him to Glyndebourne 1963 for *Magic Flute*. Also for Glyndebourne designed *Macbeth* 1964, *Magic Flute* 1966, *Don Giovanni* 1967, *Entführung* 1968, *Così* 1969 (and Munich), *Turco in Italia* 1970. Florence, *Gazza ladra* 1965. London, EOG, *Midsummer Night's Dream* 1967. Scottish O, *Cenerentola* 1970. Many Italian cities, esp. Genoa, *Don Giovanni* 1976, *Figaro* 1979, *Salome* 1980, Tutino's *Pinocchio* 1985, *Turco in Italia* 1987; Bologna, *Fledermaus* 1978; Venice, *Attila* 1986; Pesaro, *Turco in Italia* 1986, *Scala di seta* 1988; Florence, *Káťa Kabanová* 1989. St Louis, *Oberon* 1988. His ingenious sets for Glyndebourne lent a consistency to the Mozart series, but his colourful, sometimes fantastic, invention has been most appreciated in Italy, where he has successfully designed a wide range of works.

Lvov, Alexey (*b* Reval (Tallinn), 5 June 1798; *d* Kovno (Kaunas), 28 Dec. 1870). Russian composer and violinist. Great-nephew of **Nikolay Lvov** (1751–1803), author of the text of Fomin's *The Postdrivers*. Studied privately before joining the army. After holding various appointments, including adjutant to the Tsar, director of Imperial Court Chapel, 1837. He won an international career as a violinist, and wrote a large amount of sacred music as well as some not very successful operas. Tchaikovsky used the text of *Undina* (1848) for his own abortive opera. Composer of the Tsarist national anthem.

Lyatoshinsky, Boris (*b* Zhitomir, 3 Jan. 1895; *d* Kiev, 15 Apr. 1968). Ukrainian composer and conductor. Studied Kiev with Glière. A prominent figure in Ukrainian music, his many and varied activities included the composition of two operas, both on heroic national themes and making use of Ukrainian folk music: *Zolotyy obruch* (The Golden Ring, 1930) and *Shchors* (1938).

Lyceum Theatre. Theatre in Wellington Street, London, built in 1772 for exhibitions and concerts; converted for opera 1792 by Samuel Arnold. He did not obtain a licence until 1809, when the theatre housed the English OC after Drury Lane burnt down.

From 1812 known as the English OH. Rebuilt 1815. Staged works by Bishop, Braham, Loder, etc. First English *Freischütz* 1824; English *Così* 1830 (as *Tit for Tat*). Burnt down 1830; rebuilt 1834. A long series of English Romantic operas began with Barnett's *The Mountain Sylph*. Balfe, who sang there 1839, became manager 1840. As the Royal Italian O, housed Gye's company during the rebuilding of Covent Garden 1856–7. Mapleson took the theatre 1861, wrongly believing he had Patti under contract, and gave the first English *Ballo in maschera*. Seasons by the Carl Rosa OC were given 1876–7, also in the 1920s and 1930s. The La Scala, Milan, company gave the first English *Otello* (Verdi) 1889. Beecham gave his last Russian opera season 1931 with Shalyapin. In 1945 the theatre became a dance hall.

Lysenko, Mykola (*b* Hrynky, 22 Mar. 1842; *d* Kiev, 6 Nov. 1912). Ukrainian composer, conductor, and pianist. Studied Kiev with Panochini, Dimitryev, and Wilczek, Leipzig with Reinecke and Richter. His operas and operettas were very popular in the Ukraine, and were admired by Rimsky-Korsakov (who gave him some orchestration lessons) and Tchaikovsky. Many of them are based on Gogol. Attempts by Tchaikovsky and others to have his operas staged in Moscow were frustrated by his refusal to have them translated into Russian. His works include *Rizdvyana nich* (Christmas Eve, comp. 1874) and *Taras Bulba* (comp. 1880–90).

Lysiart. The Count of Forest (bs), lover of Eglantine, in Weber's *Euryanthe*.

Lyudmila. Prince Svetozar of Kiev's daughter (sop), lover of Ruslan, in Glinka's *Ruslan and Lyudmila*.

M

Maag, Peter (*b* St Gallen, 10 May 1919). Swiss conductor. Studied Zurich, Basle, and Geneva, with Hoesslin and Marek. Répétiteur and chorus-master Biel-Solothurn 1943, cond. 1945–6; Düsseldorf 1952–4; music dir. Bonn 1954–9, incl. *Rappresentazione di anima e di corpo* and *Genoveva*; Vienna, V, 1964. London, CG, 1958, 1977. New York, M, 1972–9. After successful appearances in various Italian theatres, including Venice and Parma, music dir. Turin, R, 1974–6. Especially successful in Mozart. (R)

Maazel, Lorin (*b* Neuilly, 6 Mar. 1930). US conductor. Studied Pittsburgh with Bakaleinikoff. Début as conductor aged 9. Bayreuth 1968–9; New York, M, 1962; Rome 1965; Artistic dir. Berlin, D, 1965–71; London, CG, 1978; dir. Vienna, S, 1982–4, from which he resigned amid controversy. Repertory incl. *Don Giovanni*, *Lohengrin*, *Ring*, *Luisa Miller*, *Otello* (Verdi), *Rosenkavalier*, *Thaïs*, first *Ulisse* (Dallapiccola). A talented, efficient, highly successful conductor. (R)

Mabellini, Teodulo (*b* Pistoia, 2 Apr. 1817; *d* Florence, 10 Mar. 1897). Italian conductor and composer. Studied Florence with Pillotti and Gherardeschi. Following his early success with *Matilda e Toledo* (1836), the Grand Duke Leopold II provided funds for him to study with Mercadante. His next opera, *Rolla* (1840), confirmed his promise; settled in Florence 1843, where he conducted the Società Filarmonica, and became maestro di cappella to the Tuscan court (1847), and director of the T alla Pergola (1848). His nine operas, which include *I Veneziani a Costantinopoli* (1844) and *Fiametta* (1857), owe much to Mercadante's style, and enjoyed some popularity.

Macbeth. Opera in 4 acts by Verdi; text by Piave, after Shakespeare's tragedy (1605–6). Prem. Florence, P, 14 Mar. 1847. For the 1865 Paris prem., Verdi made a revised version whose principal features were the addition of 'La luce langue' for Lady Macbeth, alterations to Act III including 'Ora di morte' for Macbeth and Lady Macbeth, and in Act IV new choruses at the opening and close. This is the version usually now performed.

Scotland, 11th cent. A chorus of witches greets Macbeth (bar) as Thane of Cawdor and King of Scotland, and Banquo (bs) as the father of kings. Macbeth is duly announced Thane of Cawdor. Lady Macbeth (sop) persuades her husband to murder King Duncan (silent), when he stays with them at Dunsinane that night, so as to gain the throne for himself.

Macbeth is named King of Scotland and orders that Banquo and his son Fleance (silent) be killed in order to prevent the remainder of the witches' prophecy coming true. However, Fleance escapes, and Macbeth is haunted, during a banquet, by images of Banquo.

The witches tell the anxious Macbeth that he will be safe until Birnam Wood comes to Dunsinane.

Lady Macbeth walks in her sleep, to the alarm of her maid and the doctor. The English army, under Duncan's son Malcolm (ten), advances, disguised with branches taken from Birnam Wood. Macduff (ten) kills Macbeth.

McCabe, John (*b* Huyton, 21 Apr. 1939). English composer. Career as a concert pianist, then dir. of the London Coll. of Music. An eclectic composer, he has drawn inspiration from Stravinsky, Hindemith, and Bartók among others. His stage works, usually written with the abilities of specific performers in mind, include the children's opera *The Lion, the Witch, and the Wardrobe* (1969) and the chamber opera *The Play of Mother Courage* (1974).

McCormack, John (*b* Athlone, 14 June 1884; *d* Dublin, 16 Sept. 1945). Irish, later US, tenor. Studied Milan with Sabatini. Début Savona 1906 (Fritz). London, CG, 1907–14; New York: Manhattan OC, 1909; M, 1910–18. On his own admission a poor actor; retired from opera 1923, devoting himself to concert work. An outstanding singer, with a sweet, limpid tone, formidable breath control, and exquisite phrasing. Celebrated as Don Ottavio, Elvino, Rodolfo, Edgardo, and Duke of Mantua. (R)

McCracken, James (*b* Gary, IN, 11 Dec. 1926; *d* New York, 30 Apr. 1988). US tenor. Studied New York with Ezekiel and Pagano, later

Milan with Conati. Début Central City O, 1952 (Rodolfo). New York, M, 1953–7, and from 1963; London, CG, from 1964; also Vienna, Salzburg, Zurich, etc. A powerful performer with an imposing physique. Roles included Verdi's Otello, Don José, Samson, Calaf, Hermann, Florestan, Tannhäuser. (R)

MacCunn, Hamish (*b* Greenock, 22 Mar. 1868; *d* London, 2 Aug. 1916). Scottish composer and conductor. Studied London with Parry, Stanford, and Taylor. Director opera class London, GSM, from 1912. Later conducted for London CR (including the first English-language *Tristan*), also with the Moody-Manners Co., Savoy T, and Beecham OC. As a composer, he was basically German-influenced; and his talent, though distinctive, was not profound enough to reconcile this with the Scottish musical cause dear to his heart. The *rapprochement* is most successfully achieved in *Jeanie Deans* (1894), to a lesser extent in *Diarmid* (1897). He later moved away from Scottish interests, and two later operas are unremarkable.

Macfarren, (Sir) **George** (*b* London, 2 Mar. 1813; *d* London, 31 Oct. 1887). English composer and conductor. Studied with his father and Lucas, later with Potter. Conducted at London, CG, from 1845. His ambition to succeed as an opera composer was only partly realized, principally with *King Charles II* (1849) and *Robin Hood* (1860).

McGegan, Nicholas (*b* Sawbridgeworth, 14 Jan. 1950). English conductor and keyboard player. Studied London, TCM. A leading figure in the modern revival of Baroque opera, he has led Handel's *Teseo* at Boston (1985), *Ariodante* at S Fe and London, C (1986, 1993), *Giustino* at S Francisco (1989), and *Agrippina* at Washington (1992); music dir. Göttingen Festival 1991. Has also given US prem. of Landi's *Il sant' Alessio* (Los Angeles 1988) and *La clemenza di Tito* for Scottish O (1991). (R)

Macheath. The highwayman (ten) in Pepusch's *The Beggar's Opera* and in subsequent versions including Weill's *Die Dreigroschenoper* (where he is also known as Mackie Messer (Mack the Knife)).

McIntyre, (Sir) **Donald** (*b* Auckland, 22 Oct. 1934). English bass-baritone. Studied London with Keeler, Essen with Kaiser-Breme. Début WNO 1959 (Zaccaria, *Nabucco*). London, SW,

1960–7; London, CG, and Bayreuth from 1967 (first British Wotan there 1973); New York, M, 1975. Also Vienna; Paris, O; Milan, S. Repertory includes Guglielmo, Pizarro, Caspar, Attila, Amfortas, Wotan, Hans Sachs, Golaud. Possesses a rounded, substantial tone and a strong stage presence. (R)

Mackenzie, (Sir) **Alexander** (*b* Edinburgh, 22 Aug. 1847; *d* London, 28 Apr. 1935). Scottish composer. Studied Sondershausen with Stein, London with Lucas. His first opera, *Colomba* (1883), was criticized as being superficially Wagnerian; his other operas are *The Troubadour* (1886), *Phoebe* (unprem.), *The Cricket on the Hearth* (comp. 1900), and an operetta, *The Knights of the Road* (1905).

Mackerras, (Sir) **Charles** (*b* Schenectady, 17 Nov. 1925). Australian, later British, conductor. Studied Sydney, and Prague with Talich. Début London, SW, 1948 (*Fledermaus*). Principal cond. Hamburg O 1966–9; music dir. London, SW, 1970–7; music dir. WNO, 1987–92. Also New York, M; Vienna, S; Chicago; S Francisco; Berlin, D; Paris; Geneva; Zurich. Wide repertory incl. Handel, Mozart (e.g. *Così*, *Figaro*, *Flute*), and Czech composers, notably Janáček (e.g. *Cunning Little Vixen*, *Káťa Kabanová*). His early reputation was largely made in Mozart, when his scrupulous approach to texts involved the restoration of appoggiaturas, and especially in Janáček. He did much to establish Janáček's stature in England. A versatile, intelligent conductor, with a strong sense of structure and phrasing and a careful regard for singers. (R)

McLaughlin, Marie (*b* Hamilton, 2 Nov. 1954). Scottish soprano. Studied Glasgow with Alexander, and London O Centre. Début as student (Susanna). Scottish O; WNO; London, ENO from 1978, CG from 1980; Hamburg; Berlin, D; Paris, O; Munich Fest.; New York, M; Gly. Roles include Despina, Marzelline, Norina, Violetta, Nannetta, Micaëla, Tytania. (R)

McNair, Sylvia (*b* Mansfield, OH, 23 June 1956). US soprano. Studied Indiana U. Stage début New York 1982, as Sandrina in Haydn's *L'infedeltà delusa*. Swetzingen 1984, as Ophelia in the prem. of Kelterborn's opera. Gly. 1989, Anne Trulove; London, CG, 1990 (Ilia). Her vivacious personality and beautifully produced voice have made her in demand as Pamina, Marzelline (New York, M, 1991),

Morgana (*Alcina*), and Poppea (Salzburg 1993). (R)

MacNeil, Cornell (*b* Minneapolis, 24 Sept. 1922). US baritone. Studied Hartford with Schorr, New York with Lazzari and Guth. Début Philadelphia 1950 (first John Sorel, *The Consul*). New York, CC, 1952–5; Chicago 1957; Milan, S, 1958; New York, M, from 1959; London, CG, 1964; also Vienna; Buenos Aires; Paris, O; etc. A technically accomplished singer with a smooth, mellow tone, especially successful in Verdi, e.g. as Nabucco, Macbeth, Rigoletto, Carlo (*Ernani*), Luna. (R) His son **Walter MacNeil** (1949) is a tenor; father and son have appeared together as the Germonts.

'Ma dall'arido stelo divulsa'. Amelia's (sop) aria opening Act II of Verdi's *Un ballo in maschera*, when she has come to a lonely spot to pick a herb to cure her love for King Gustavus (Riccardo).

Madama Butterfly. Opera in 2 acts by Puccini; text by Giacosa and Illica, after David Belasco's drama (1900) on the story by John Luther Long, based on real events. Prem. Milan, S, 17 Feb. 1904. New version (in 3 acts) prem. Brescia, T Grande, 28 May 1904.

Nagasaki, early 20th cent. The geisha Cio-Cio-San, Madam Butterfly (sop), marries an American naval officer, Pinkerton (ten), who, despite the warnings of the American consul Sharpless (bar), treats the matter lightly.

Deserted by Pinkerton shortly after the wedding, Butterfly awaits his return; she now has a son, 'Trouble'. She remains insistent that Pinkerton will return, and Sharpless has not the heart to read her a letter from her husband saying he now has an American wife. The harbour cannon announces the arrival of Pinkerton's ship; Butterfly and her servant Suzuki (mez) decorate the house with petals, happily anticipating his return.

The following morning Pinkerton approaches the house with his wife Kate (mez), but, suddenly filled with guilt, cannot bring himself to face Butterfly. She tells Kate that she will hand over the child if Pinkerton will come and fetch him. Rather than face a life without honour, she kills herself with her father's ceremonial sword; Pinkerton arrives to find her dead.

Madame Chrysanthème. Opera in a prologue, 4 acts, and epilogue by Messager; text by Hartmann and André Alexandre, after Pierre Loti's novel (1888). Prem. Paris, T Renaissance, 26 Jan. 1893.

A French warship, Nagasaki, late 19th cent. The opera tells of the brief marriage of Pierre (ten), a French naval officer, to a Japanese geisha, Madame Chrysanthème (sop). He abandons her lightly, but is touched by the sincerity of a letter which he receives on board ship on his return voyage to France, and thinks with affection of the wife he has left behind.

'Madamina'. Leporello's (bs) *catalogue aria in Act I of Mozart's *Don Giovanni* enumerating Giovanni's conquests to Donna Elvira.

Maddalena. Sparafucile's sister (con) in Verdi's *Rigoletto*.

Madeleine de Coigny. The Comtesse de Coigny's daughter (sop), lover of Chénier, in Giordano's *Andrea Chénier*.

Maderna, Bruno (*b* Venice, 21 Apr. 1920; *d* Darmstadt, 13 Nov. 1973). Italian conductor and composer. Studied Venice with Malipiero, Milan with Pizzetti, Vienna with Scherchen. Cond. prems. of Nono's *Intolleranza* (1961), Berio's *Passaggio* (1963), and his own *Satyricon* (1973); its companion theatre piece *Hyperion* had been given at Venice in 1964. Florence, Maggio Musicale, 1964, 1970. Holland Festival 1965–8, 1973. Milan, S, 1967. New York: Juilliard School, 1970 (*Il giuramento*), 1971 (*Clemenza di Tito*); CO 1972 (*Don Giovanni*). As well as being expert at presenting difficult new scores to maximum dramatic effect, had a special interest in Monteverdi and Rameau. (R)

'Madre, pietosa vergine'. Leonora's (sop) aria in Act II of Verdi's *La forza del destino*, begging the Virgin Mary for forgiveness as she arrives at the Monastery of Hornachuelos.

Madrid. Capital of Spain. Opera was first given in the private royal theatres, initially in the Palacio Real Buen Retiro for Philip IV. At the Real Sitio del Buen Retiro, an island was used for open-air performances. An Italian company played in 1703 and 1708, then at the T de los Caños del Peral. Philip V arranged for Farinelli to come and sing to him as a cure for his melancholy. From 1740 the theatre gave performances in Spanish. The T del Real Palacio was opened in 1849, the T Real in 1850. Theatres that opened in the 19th cent. included the T del Liceo, T del

Instituto (1839) where zarzuela was given, T del Circo (originally for equestrian performances but also used by Italian singers), T del Museo, T de Variedades (1842), Circo del Príncipe Alfonso (as an opera-house renamed the Circo de Rivas, 1863), and the T Rossini (1864). The important T de la Zarzuela opened in 1856. The T Lírico opened in 1902 with the intention of paying special attention to Spanish opera. Many of these and other theatres later closed, but the principal theatres continued to house short seasons, often with Italian singers as well as Spanish. The T Real closed in 1925, to reopen in 1966. It is currently being renovated. The T de la Zarzuela (cap. 1,242) is meanwhile the company's home, and the country's second house after the Liceu, Barcelona. Between 1987 and 1994 eight new operas were commissioned on an annual basis, a policy now discarded. Madrid also holds an annual opera festival, extended in 1984 to include zarzuela and ballet.

mad scene (Fr., *folie*; Ger., *Wahnsinnsszene*). A scene in which the hero or heroine goes mad, generally with tragic results. Its first use was in 17th-cent. Venetian opera: there are many examples in Cavalli, notably in *Egisto*. The mad scene became a common feature of opera seria, as in Handel's *Orlando*, where the hero, *furioso* ('mad'), suffers a vision of Hell in which the disturbance of his reason is expressed by irregular rhythms including probably the first use of quintuple metre (which Burney thought would have been intolerable in any sane context). Handel later makes satirical use of the convention in *Imeneo* as the heroine feigns madness. The mad scene was a common element in 19th-cent. opera: the most famous is in Donizetti's *Lucia di Lammermoor* ('Ardon gl'incensi'), and others occur in his *Anna Bolena* and *Linda di Chamounix*, in Bellini's *I Puritani*, and in Thomas's *Hamlet*. This phase of the convention was satirized by Sullivan with Mad Meg in *Ruddigore*, and in Britten's *Midsummer Night's Dream*. Madness or mental derangement of one sort or another is also depicted in Strauss's *Elektra*, Berg's *Wozzeck*, Stravinsky's *The Rake's Progress*, and Britten's *Peter Grimes*.

Madwoman, The. The mother (ten) of the dead boy in Britten's *Curlew River*.

maestro (It.: 'master'). A courtesy title given to composers, conductors, and even impre-

sarios in Italy, sometimes more colloquially in other countries. The **maestro di cappella** (of the chapel) was originally the equivalent of the German *Kapellmeister, with duties that included presiding at the keyboard.

Magdalene. Eva's nurse (sop), lover of David, in Wagner's *Die Meistersinger von Nürnberg*.

Magda Sorel. The wife (sop) of John Sorel in Menotti's *The Consul*.

Maggio Musicale. See FLORENCE.

Maggiore, Francesco (*b* ?Naples, *c*.1715; *d* ?Holland, ?1782). Italian composer. Studied Naples with Durante. During an itinerant life was involved with opera composition in many European cities, including Verona and Frankfurt. Wrote *c*.12 operas, both comic and serious, but is remembered as the first Neapolitan opera buffa composer to write for Venice with *I rigiri delle cantarine* (1745).

Magic Fire Music. The name generally given to the music accompanying the final scene of Wagner's *Die Walküre* as Wotan conjures up the fire which will defend Brünnhilde as she sleeps on her rock, and through which only a hero can pass.

Magic Flute, The. See ZAUBERFLÖTE, DIE.

Magnard, Albéric (*b* Paris, 9 June 1865; *d* Baron, 3 Sept. 1914). French composer. After hearing *Tristan* at Bayreuth, studied Paris with Dubois and Massenet, then D'Indy. His first opera, *Yolande* (1892), met with little success. *Guercœur* (comp. *c*.1900) concerns a liberating hero who returns from heaven to earth to find himself betrayed both by his widow and by the people he has liberated and who now, unable to make a success of a free society, are turning back to dictatorship. It reflects Magnard's exalted pessimism, as well as his admiration for Wagner (by way of D'Indy) in his use of Leitmotiv and his rich chromatic vein. In the long preface to *Bérénice* (1911), he openly declared that Wagner's style suited his classical tastes and traditional musical culture; and there is in the work a feeling for what Wagner had admired in Gluck, another of Magnard's heroes.

Mahagonny. See AUFSTIEG UND FALL DER STADT MAHAGONNY.

Mahler, Gustav (*b* Kalischt (Kaliště), 7 July

1860; *d* Vienna, 18 May 1911). Austrian composer and conductor. Studied Vienna with Fuchs and Krenn. Début as cond., Summer T, Bad Hall, 1880. Appointments followed at Ljubljana 1881; Olomouc 1882–3; Kassel 1884; Prague 1885 (where Seidl was first cond. and where Mahler gave notable performances of *The Ring*); Leipzig 1886–8 (under Nikisch); Budapest 1888–91 (as dir.—originally engaged for ten years, but resigning after two owing to insuperable difficulties); Hamburg 1891–7; Vienna, H, 1897–1907 (appointed cond. in May 1897, dir. July 1897, artistic dir. Oct. 1897). Also conducted London: CG, 1892, first *Ring* cycle there, and other German works; New York, M, 1908–10, including first professional US performances of *The Bartered Bride* and *The Queen of Spades*.

It was during his ten years at the Vienna Hofoper (which later became the Staatsoper) that Mahler's true greatness as a conductor and director was revealed. He was an ardent perfectionist and innovator: he remarked at the outset, in famous words, 'Tradition ist Schlamperei' (Tradition is slovenliness). He built up an ensemble of singers who brought to the Hofoper some of its greatest glories; they included Gutheil-Schoder, Kurz, Mildenburg, Weidt, Mayr, Slezak, Schmedes, Winkelmann, and Weidemann; and his chief designer was Alfred Roller. Mahler's new productions in Vienna included *Rheingold* and *Walküre*; also *Figaro*, *Così fan tutte*, *Die Entführung*, *Don Giovanni*, and *Die Zauberflöte* (these five for the 150th anniversary of Mozart's birth); *Fidelio*, *Aida*, *Falstaff*, *Die lustigen Weiber*, *Louise*, *Der Corregidor*, *The Taming of the Shrew*, and *Iphigénie en Aulide*. He had many enemies during his period in Vienna—he was Jewish, dictatorial, and he spent lavishly on productions—yet he succeeded in wiping out the deficit which the Staatsoper had accumulated, and in raising the performances to a standard that has remained exemplary.

His early operas *Herzog Ernst von Schwaben* and *Die Argonauten* were destroyed, probably unfinished, and *Rübezahl* was abandoned, its music perhaps absorbed into other projects. He completed, from fragments and by adding other pieces, Weber's *Die drei Pintos* (1888), and made new performing versions of *Euryanthe* (1904) and *Oberon* (1906), and of Mozart's *Figaro*.

Maid of Orleans, The (Russ., *Orleanskaya deva*). Opera in 4 acts by Tchaikovsky; text by the composer, after Zhukovsky's version of Schiller's tragedy. Prem. St Petersburg, M, 25 Feb. 1881.

The opera relates the story of Joan of Arc's (mez or sop) recognition of King Charles VII of France (ten) at Chinon, of her love for a Burgundian knight, Lionel (ten), of her denouncement by her father (bs) at the coronation at Rheims, and her eventual sentence to be burnt at the stake.

Maid of Pskov, The (sometimes also known as *Ivan the Terrible*) (Russ., *Pskovityanka*). Opera in 4 acts by Rimsky-Korsakov; text by the composer, after Lev Mey's drama (1860). Prem. St Petersburg, M, 13 Jan. 1873.

Russia, late 16th cent. Tsar Ivan the Terrible (bs) has ransacked the city of Novgorod, whose citizens have rebelled against him; the people of Pskov fear a similar fate. He promises to leave the city in peace if he can take with him Olga (sop), niece of Prince Tokmakov (bs), Governor of Pskov. Olga plans to elope with her beloved Tucha (ten), but the couple are surprised, and Olga taken to the Tsar, who she learns is her father. As Tucha fights his captors, Olga is hit by a stray bullet, and dies as a sacrifice to Pskov.

Maillart, Aimé (*b* Montpellier, 24 Mar. 1817; *d* Moulins-sur-Allier, 26 May 1871). French composer. Studied Paris Cons. with Halévy 1833–41; won Prix de Rome with cantata *Lionel Foscari*. Beginning with *Gastibelza* (1847), contributed a series of works to the Paris stage, of which *Les dragons de Villars* (1856) was most popular. His success derived in part from a gift for writing light, captivating melodies; he was also helped by his choice of colourful librettos. Several works, including his last, *Lara* (1864), were given abroad, including London.

Maître de Chapelle, Le. Opera in 2 parts by Paer; text by Sophie Gay, after Duval's comedy *Le souper imprévu* (1796). Prem. Paris, OC, 29 Mar. 1821.

Barnabé (bs) tries to enlist the help of his French cook Gertrude (sop), in a performance of his opera *Cléopâtre*. At first she tricks him and his nephew Benedetto (ten) in order to delay the singing, but eventually succumbs and manages to sing the words and music correctly.

Majo, Gian Francesco di (*b* Naples, 24 Mar. 1732; *d* Naples, 17 Nov. 1770). Italian com-

poser. Studied with his father Giuseppe di
*Majo, his uncle Manno, his great-uncle Feo,
and later with Martini. Joined his father at
the Neapolitan court as organist 1747. His
first opera, *Ricimero* (1759), was well received
and his fame assured with *Cajo Fabricio* (1760).
This led to commissions from many Italian
cities, from Vienna (for which *Alcide* (1764)
was written), and from Mannheim (where he
produced *Ifigenia in Tauride* (1764)).

Majo wrote over 20 dramatic works, many
of them opere serie to Metastasian librettos.
These were popular and much praised in
their day, employing a fluent and sensuous
melodic line: Mozart spoke of their 'bellis-
sima musica'. His most striking modification
of contemporary practice came in *Ifigenia*,
which is a pioneering adumbration of some
of Gluck's later reforms. But like Jommelli's
and Traetta's, Majo's contribution to the
reform of opera seria in the mid-18th cent.
has been largely overshadowed by that of
Gluck, and despite their considerable originality his works have remained neglected.

Majo, Giuseppe di (*b* Naples, 5 Dec. 1697; *d*
Naples, 18 Nov. 1771). Italian composer.
Father of above. Studied Naples under Fago
and Basso; a contemporary of Leo and Feo.
Joined Neapolitan court, rising to become
first maestro di cappella (1744). His earliest
stage works, including *Lo vecchio avaro* (The
Old Miser, 1727), were opere buffe; like his
two later opere serie, *Arianna e Teseo* (1747)
and *Semiramide* (1751), these were conventional in conception.

Makropoulos Affair, The (Cz., *Věc
Makropulos*). Opera in 3 acts by Janáček; text
by the composer, after Karel Čapek's drama
(1922). Prem. Brno 18 Dec. 1926.

The famous singer Emilia Marty (sop)
intervenes in the lawsuit of Gregor v. Prus,
and shows first-hand knowledge of the
actions, a hundred years previously, of Elian
MacGregor, the mistress of the deceased
Baron Prus.

It gradually emerges that she is not concerned with the outcome of the case, but
only to recover an old Greek document
which contains the formula for giving 300
years of life. Emilia was, as Elina Makropoulos, used as a guinea-pig for an elixir
of eternal life 337 years previously, and is
now longing for death; throughout many
generations and changes of name she has
always retained the same initials.

Prus (bar) reluctantly hands over the document in return for spending the night with
her. Now in possession of the secret, she can
end her life, which has become an intolerable burden. The others long to know the
formula, but Marty wisely burns the parch-
ment, and dies.

Malanotte, Adelaide (*b* Verona, 1785; *d*
Salò, 31 Dec. 1832). Italian contralto. Début
Verona 1806. After successes in Turin and
Rome, created title-role in Rossini's *Tancredi*.
Stendhal relates how, when she rejected her
entrance aria the day before the prem.,
Rossini produced the famous 'Di tanti palpiti'. Impressive on stage, especially in travesti roles, she sang with 'perfect intonation
and refined taste', according to Hérold,
though he disliked her voice—'too like a cor
anglais'.

Malatesta. Dr Malatesta (bar), Pasquale's
friend, in Donizetti's *Don Pasquale*.

Maldere, Pierre van (*b* Brussels, 16 Oct.
1729; *d* Brussels, 1 Nov. 1768). Belgian composer. Studied Brussels with Fiocco. His *Le
déguisement pastoral* (1756), though produced
in Vienna, is an early Belgian opera.

Male Chorus. The commentator (ten) who,
with the *Female Chorus, introduces, comments upon, and sums up the action of Britten's *The Rape of Lucretia*.

Malfitano, Catherine (*b* New York, 18 Apr.
1948). US soprano. Studied New York with J.
Malfitano. Début Central City O, 1972
(Nannetta). New York: CO, 1974–9, M, from
1979. Paris, OC, 1984; London, CG, 1988
(Butterfly; Salome 1995). Also Salzburg;
Vienna; Munich Fest.; Florence; Amsterdam;
Brussels, M. Roles incl. Poppea, Zerlina,
Amelia, Violetta, Juliette, Manon, Mimì. (R)

Malgoire, Jean-Claude (*b* Avignon, 25 Nov.
1940). French conductor. Studied Paris Cons.
A leading exponent of Baroque opera, with a
practical approach to performance practice,
he founded La Grande Ecurie et la Chambre
du Roy, 1966; also formed L'Atelier du Tourcoing and has given operas by Lully and
Rameau throughout Europe. English Bach
Festival from 1974, with Rameau's *Indes Galantes*, *Hippolyte et Aricie*, and *Platée*; Gluck's
Orphée 1994. Revived Campra's *Tancrède* at
Schwetzingen (1988), Rossini's *Ciro in Babilonia* at Perugia 1992. (R)

Malheurs d'Orphée, Les (The Sorrows of Orpheus). Opera in 3 acts by Milhaud; text by Armand Lunel. Prem. Brussels, M, 7 May 1926.

A modernized version of the Orpheus and Eurydice legend. Orphée (bar), an animal healer, plans to marry the gypsy girl Eurydice (sop). When she develops a serious illness, Orphée tries in vain to cure her, and Eurydice dies. He is killed by her sisters, who blame Orphée for Eurydice's death.

Malibran, Maria (*b* Paris, 24 Mar. 1808; *d* Manchester, 23 Sept. 1836). Spanish mezzo-soprano. Elder daughter of Manuel *García, and sister of Pauline *Viardot. Studied with her father. Appeared aged 5 in Naples, 1814, in Paer's *Agnese*. Début London, H, 1825 (Rosina). New York, with her father's Italian OC, 1825–6. While there married Eugène Malibran, to escape from her father's domination, but returned to Europe without him, 1827. Paris, I, 1828; London, H, 1829; performed at both until 1832. Bologna, Naples, 1832–3; Milan, S, 1834–5; London, CG, 1835. In 1836 she married the violinist Charles de Bériot, by whom she had already had a son. She was the embodiment of Romanticism, in her brilliant yet melancholic personality, free and feverish life-style, and charismatic, impassioned performances. Even her early death was, as Rossini put it, an 'advantage'. Her genius was appreciated not only by an often-hysterical public, but also by many great figures of the age, e.g. Lafayette, Vigny, Musset, Hans Andersen, Donizetti, Bellini, Chopin, Moscheles, and Paganini. Liszt and George Sand were both profoundly influenced by her. Fétis (like Verdi) found her 'sublime' if 'unequal', and declared her 'the most astonishing singer of her century'. She excelled and fascinated as an actress; her voice, though peculiar and uneven, had an exciting quality, while its weakness in the middle register was disguised with an incomparable technique. A wide range enabled her to sing a variety of roles, including Norma, Cenerentola, Amina, Rossini's Desdemona, Semiramide, Leonore, Maria Stuarda. She created no major roles, but she was, as Legouvé said, 'one of those artists who cause art to advance, because they are always seeking'. When she was thrown from a horse in June 1836, she refused to concede to her injuries and went on performing as usual; she died three months later.

Malipiero, Gian Francesco (*b* Venice, 18 Mar. 1882; *d* Treviso, 1 Aug. 1973). Italian composer and editor. Studied Venice with Bossi, Bologna, and Vienna. Taught composition at Parma Cons. 1921–3; 1932 joined Liceo Musicale in Venice, where he established a formidable teaching reputation; dir. 1939–52. One of the most eclectic and prolific 20th-cent. opera composers, with a style shaped by influences as diverse as verismo, Expressionism, and neoclassicism. Though he rejected serialism, Malipiero's outlook was fundamentally that of a spirited avant-gardist; his distinctive musical language owes most to modal harmony and to a dislike of counterpoint and thematic development, while his vocal lines exhibit great rhythmical freedom following syllabic declamation.

Malipiero destroyed or subsequently rejected most of his music written before 1913, including his earliest operatic attempts, such as the 1-act *Canossa* (1914). In the trilogies *L'Orfeide* (1925) and the *Tre commedie goldoniane* (1926) he reveals a love of old music, reflecting his studies of earlier Venetian masters: this eventually resulted in an important complete critical edition of Monteverdi, and significant work on Vivaldi. Elements of the bizarre and fantastic, which form an integral part of the Venetian dramatic tradition, also appear in many early works. With the rise of Mussolini, Malipiero turned to more heroic gestures: *Giulio Cesare* (1936) was in part a celebration of the Duce's achievements. After a series of works on a similar scale, including *Antonio e Cleopatra* (1938) and *Ecuba* (1941), he returned to the fantastical style of his earlier works with *I capricci di Callot* (1942), *L'allegra brigata* (1950), and *Mondi celesti e infernali* (1951). The latter works are both cyclic: *L'allegra brigata* is based on a collection of six novels fashioned into a single drama, while the *Mondi celesti e infernali*, described as 'three acts with seven women', offers portraits of seven female dramatic figures, including Medea and Poppea. Of his later operas the most interesting are the *Rappresentazione e festa di Carnasciale e della Quaresima* (1970), whose inclusion of dance episodes recalls the *intermedio tradition, and the Pushkin-based *Don Giovanni* (1963).

Malipiero, Riccardo (*b* Milan, 24 July 1914). Italian composer, nephew of above. Studied Milan (with Dallapiccola) and Venice (with his uncle). Working largely in a serialist idiom, he has written three operas: *Minnie la* *candida* (1942); the comic *La donna è mobile* (1957), which caricatures traditional operatic forms; and a television opera, *Battono alla porta* (1962). Also active as a critic and writer.

Malten, Therese (*b* Insterburg, 21 June 1855; *d* Neuzschieren, Saxony, 2 Jan. 1930). German soprano. Studied Berlin with Engel. Début Dresden 1873 (Pamina). Sang there for 30 years. Admired by Wagner, who hoped to hear her as Isolde. He chose her as one of the three singers of Kundry (with Brandt and Materna) in the first performances of *Parsifal*. Bayreuth 1882–94; London, DL, 1882; Moscow 1889. Repertory included Armide, Leonore, Isolde, Eva, Sieglinde, Brünnhilde. A handsome and talented actress, she possessed a powerful voice with a wide range.

Mamelles de Tirésias, Les (The Breasts of Tiresias). Opera in 2 acts by Poulenc; text by Guillaume Apollinaire. Prem. Paris, OC, 3 June 1947.

When Thérèse (sop), fed up with her submissive life as a woman, casts aside her breasts and adopts a masculine life as Tiresias, her husband (ten) has to take her place as a woman, but soon tires of her arrogant behaviour. Declaring he will produce children without her, he proceeds to bring 40,000 children of varying ages into the world. A policeman (bar) consults a fortune-teller as to how the children are to be supported, but is nearly strangled by her, when he attacks her after having been accused of being sterile. The husband saves him, and it emerges that the fortune-teller is none other than Thérèse. She begs her husband's forgiveness and the couple are reunited.

Manchester. City in Lancashire, England. The first theatre in Manchester was built in 1753 and in 1775 the first T Royal was approved by Parliament. Opera was provided by touring companies and operatic excerpts in the 'Gentleman's Concerts' until Hallé conducted a season of operas at the T Royal in 1855, including *Fidelio*, *Don Giovanni*, *Der Freischütz*, *Robert le diable*, *Les Huguenots*, *Lucrezia Borgia*, and *La favorite*. He followed this with concert performances at the Free Trade Hall of *Fidelio* and *Die Zauberflöte*, and Gluck's *Armide*, *Iphigénie en Tauride*, which he also took to London, and *Orfeo ed Euridice*. The performances of *Iphigénie* and *Orfeo* were the first in English. Opera was also provided by the Rouseby and Parepa-Rosa Cos. The latter began its existence in England with a per-

formance in Manchester of *Maritana* on 1 Sept. 1873. After Hallé's death opera was again provided only by touring companies and by ambitious amateurs, though in 1897 Cowen conducted a concert perf. of *Les Troyens à Carthage* after giving the first British concert perf. at Liverpool earlier the same year. Between 1916 and 1919 Thomas Beecham presented an ambitious series of opera seasons at the New Queen's T, and it seemed as though Manchester would rival London as an operatic centre until Beecham's enforced withdrawal in 1920, when touring companies again took over. Since then amateur opera has flourished, and seasons have been given by London CG and SW, and Italian companies, at the Palace T, OH, and occasionally at the Hippodrome, Free Trade Hall, and suburban theatres.

Mancinelli, Luigi (*b* Orvieto, 6 Feb. 1848; *d* Rome, 2 Feb. 1921). Italian conductor and composer. Studied Orvieto with his brother Marino, Florence with Mabellini. Led cellos at Florence, P, and Rome, Ap., where in 1874 he was called upon to fill the place of a drunk conductor in *Aida*. After engagements in various Italian cities, conducted a concert in London in 1886, on the strength of which he was engaged by Harris as chief conductor London DL 1887, and CG 1888–1905, where he conducted many English prems., and many of the De Reszke Wagner performances in Italian. Music dir. Madrid, T Real, 1888–95. Chief Italian cond. New York, M, 1893–1903. His own operas included *Ero e Leandro* (1896) and *Paolo e Francesca* (1907). The most important Italian conductor between Faccio and Toscanini, he anticipated the latter in his powerful authority, personal magnetism, and deep fidelity to the score. His Italian Wagner performances were controversial, but not without German admirers (including Weingartner). As a composer, he resisted verismo in favour of a classicism he associated with Boito, who in 1877 called him the ideal conductor of *Mefistofele*.

Mancini, Francesco (*b* Naples, 16 Jan. 1672; *d* Naples, 22 Sept. 1737). Italian composer. Studied Naples with Provenzale and Ursino; his first opera was *Ariovisto* (1702). Joined the Neapolitan court as first organist 1704; became maestro di cappella 1707. Less than a year later was forced to cede the post to its former holder, A. Scarlatti: he became vice maestro di cappella, but was guaranteed the right to succeed Scarlatti, which he did in 1725. 1720–35 dir. of the Cons. S Maria di Loreto, where he was succeeded by Fischietti.

Mancini composed *c.*20 operas for Naples, and is generally regarded as Scarlatti's most important contemporary there. His works, which included *Lucio Silla* (1703), and *Trajano* (1723), enjoyed some popularity abroad.

Mandikian, Arda (*b* Smyrna, 1 Sept. 1924). Greek-Armenian soprano. Studied Athens with De Hidalgo and Trianti, Oxford with Wellesz. Début OUOC, 1950 (Berlioz's Dido). Created title-role *Incognita* (Wellesz) OUOC, 1951. Paris, CE, 1952; London, CG, 1953; EOG 1954. Her strong and individual dramatic powers contributed to the character of Miss Jessel, which Britten wrote for her in *The Turn of the Screw*. This she created and often sang. Other roles incl. Savitri and Elettra. Assistant general dir. Athens O 1974–80. (R)

Mandryka. A rich young landowner (bar) in Strauss's *Arabella*.

Manelli, Francesco (*b* Tivoli, after 13 Sept. 1594; *d* Parma, July 1667). Italian composer and bass. Though active as a singer in Tivoli, Rome, and Venice, before joining Parmese court in 1653, he is best remembered for his collaboration in 1637 with Ferrari on *Andromeda*. This was produced, with Manelli himself taking the parts of Nettuno and Astarco Mago, to inaugurate the first Venetian public opera-house in the T San Cassiano. It was followed by several more works, including *La maga fulminata* (1638) and *Alcate* (1642), which consolidated the new commercial opera: *Delia* was performed for the opening of Venice GP, in 1639. None of these works survives, but they probably followed the Roman style of Landi and Rossi, as did the lost works, including *Le vicende del tempo*, he wrote for the Parmese court.

Manfredini, Vincenzo (*b* Pistoia, 22 Oct. 1737; *d* St Petersburg, 16 Aug. 1799). Italian composer. Brother of the castrato **Giuseppe Manfredini**, he studied with his father, the violinist **Francesco Manfredini** (1688–1744), and with Perti and Fiorino. Travelled to Russia with his brother 1758, succeeding Raupach as court composer; here he wrote five operas, including *Carlo Magno* (1763) and *L'Olimpiade* (1762). Returned to Italy 1769, having been replaced at court by Galuppi. Living in Bologna and Venice, he worked for a time as a literary editor and wrote several important theoretical works. He returned to St Petersburg 1798 at the request of Tsar Paul I, whom he had earlier instructed on the harpsichord. His operas, though important contributions to the St Petersburg repertoire, were cast in a conventional mould.

Manhattan Opera Company. New York co. founded by Oscar *Hammerstein in 1906 at the Manhattan OH on W 34th St. Opened 3 Dec. 1906 with *Puritani* under the dir. *Campanini. The first season included appearances by Calvé and Melba. The 1907–8 season saw the first US *Thaïs*, *Louise*, and *Pelléas*, all with Mary Garden; the final season, 1909–10, saw the first US *Elektra*, *Sapho*, and *Grisélidis*. Artists included Nordica, Schumann-Heink, Tetrazzini, Cavalieri, Zenatello, McCormack, and Dalmorès. The company gave 463 performances of 49 operas in its four seasons, also appearing in Philadelphia in a theatre built by Hammerstein. From 1908 to 1910 the Philadelphia Co. had its own chorus, orchestra, and conductors, with singers commuting from New York. The company also visited Boston, Cincinnati, Pittsburgh, and Washington.

Such was its success that in 1910 the Metropolitan offered Hammerstein $2,000,000 if he refrained from giving opera in New York for ten years. He tried to break the agreement in 1913 by building the *Lexington Theatre, but was legally restrained. The Manhattan OH was used for the Chicago O's seasons, but later sold, becoming New York's leading opera recording studio for RCA and the Metropolitan recordings.

Manners, Charles (*b* London, 27 Dec. 1857; *d* Dundrum, Co. Dublin, 3 May 1935). Irish bass and impresario. Studied Dublin; London, RAM; and Italy. Début London with D'Oyly Carte Co. 1882 (creating Pte. Willis, *Iolanthe*). Joined London, CR, then CG, in 1890. First English Gremin, 1892. US 1893. Toured S Africa 1896–7 with his wife Fanny Moody. In 1898 they founded the Moody-Manners Co., which lasted until 1916. Manners promoted British opera by both producing it and awarding prizes to the best works. He was largely responsible for establishing the Glasgow Grand O Soc., which later gave the first British *Idomeneo* and *Les Troyens*. Retired from singing 1913.

Manolov, Emanuil (*b* Gabrovo, 7 Jan. 1860;

d Kazanlǔk, 2 Feb. 1902). Bulgarian composer and conductor. Studied Moscow. Composer of the first Bulgarian opera, *Siromakhkinya* (The Poor Woman) to his own text, after Vasov. Though unfinished, amateur production under his direction Kazanlǔk, 1900; later completed by others and produced Sofia 1910. Italianate in style, it also makes use of Bulgarian urban folk-songs.

Manon. Opera in 5 acts by Massenet; text by Meilhac and Gille, after Prévost's novel *L'histoire du chevalier des Grieux et de Manon Lescaut* (1731). Prem. Paris, OC, 19 Jan. 1884.

France, second half 18th cent. The Chevalier Des Grieux (ten) falls in love with Manon (sop), whom he meets as she stops at an inn in Amiens with her cousin Lescaut (bar) on her way to a convent.

The young lovers elope to Paris. De Bretigny (bar), a friend of Lescaut, persuades Manon to go away with him.

Des Grieux, in despair, decides to enter the priesthood, despite pleas from his father, the Comte Des Grieux (bs). Manon comes and persuades Des Grieux to go off with her.

At a gambling house Des Grieux is accused of cheating and Manon is arrested as a prostitute and condemned to deportation.

Des Grieux bribes an officer for permission to speak to her and tries to persuade her to run away with him. She is too weak to do so and dies in his arms.

Manon Lescaut. Opera in 4 acts by Puccini; text by Illica, and Oliva, after Prévost's novel *L'histoire du chevalier des Grieux et de Manon Lescaut* (1731). Prem. Turin, R, 1 Feb. 1893.

France, second half 18th cent. The young Chevalier Des Grieux (ten) sees Manon Lescaut (sop) in an inn on her way to a convent; they fall in love and elope, stealing the carriage of Géronte de Ravoir (bs).

Encouraged by her brother Lescaut (bar), Manon has abandoned Des Grieux and is living lavishly as Géronte's mistress. Des Grieux makes his fortune gambling and persuades Manon to escape with him again; she takes with her jewels she received from Géronte, who sends the police after her and has her arrested for theft and prostitution.

At Le Havre, Des Grieux and Lescaut try in vain to secure Manon's release; she has been sentenced to deportation. In desperation, Des Grieux pleads with the captain to be allowed to sail with her.

Manon and Des Grieux escape from New Orleans but Manon collapses from exhaustion and dies in her lover's arms.

Manrico. A chieftain (ten) under the Prince of Biscay, lover of Leonora and the eponymous troubadour of Verdi's *Il trovatore*.

Manru. Opera in 3 acts by Paderewski; text by Nossig, after Kraszewski's novel *The Cabin Behind the Wood* (1843). Prem. Dresden 29 May 1901.

Against her mother's wishes, Ulana (sop) marries the gypsy Manru (ten). She revives his love with a potion, but the gypsy girl Asa (sop) lures him back to his people. Ulana commits suicide and Manru, now chief of the tribe, is killed by Oros (bs), the man he had deposed who himself loves Asa.

Man without a Country, The. Opera in 2 acts by Damrosch; text by Arthur Guiterman, based on Edward Everett Hale's story (1863). Prem. New York, M, 12 May 1937.

Philip Nolan (ten), a young US Army officer, is deported for his impulsive shouts of treason in a courtroom. For 50 years he travels without a country, and gradually becomes a fanatical patriot. His bravery in a battle secures his return to his homeland, but the official pardon never arrives and he dies clutching the Stars and Stripes.

Mapleson, James Henry (*b* London, 4 May 1830; *d* London, 14 Nov. 1901). English singer, violinist, and impresario. Studied London. Sang Verona 1854 as Enrico Mariani; unsuccessfully under his own name London DL, once. Played London, HM, 1848–9. London: manager DL 1858; L 1861, incl. British prem. *Ballo*; HM 1862–7; DL 1868; joined *Gye at CG 1869–70; DL 1871–6; HM 1877–81; CG 1885, 1887; HM 1887, 1889. New York, AM, 1878–96. 1896–7, also touring other US cities. Gave many British and US prems., and brought to London Di Murska, Gerster, C. Nilsson, Trebelli, Hauk, Nordica, Campanini, Jean De Reszke (as baritone), Pandolfini. Known as 'the Colonel'; *The Mapleson Memoirs* (1888) give an amusing and colourful account of his activities.

'M'appari'. The Italian translation of Lionel's (ten) 'Ach, so fromm' in Act III of Flotow's *Martha*, in which he sings of his hopeless love for Martha.

Marais, Marin (*b* Paris, 31 May 1656; *d* Paris, 15 Aug. 1728). French composer and viola da gamba player. Studied with Lully. A gifted performer, he is best known for his instrumental music, though he also composed four highly regarded operas after the model of Lully's tragédies en musique. Most innovative was *Alcyone* (1706), which contains one of the earliest operatic representations of a storm. All his operas were successfully revived in the 18th cent.

Mařák, Otakar (*b* Esztergom, Hungary, 5 Jan. 1872; *d* Prague, 2 July 1939). Czech tenor. Studied Prague with Paršova-Zikešov. Début Brno 1899 (Gounod's Faust). Prague, N, 1900–7, 1914–34; Vienna 1903; Berlin, H, 1906; London, CG, 1908, and HM, 1913; Chicago 1914. Dubbed 'the Czech Caruso', he was a distinguished Canio; also sang Bacchus, Parsifal, and Gennaro in the first *Gioielli della Madonna*. After retiring in 1934, he became destitute in Chicago; funds were raised in Prague to enable its former star to return. He died soon after. (R)

Marazzoli, Marco (*b* Parma, *c*.1602 or *c*.1608; *d* Rome, 26 Jan. 1662). Italian composer, singer, and harpist. Possibly studied with Allegri; 1637 joined the papal choir as tenor. Travelled throughout Italy and in 1644 brought to Paris, where *Il capriccio* was probably given; stayed until 1645 and was involved with efforts to establish Italian opera there.

In 1637 he produced, with Mazzochi, the first comic opera, *Il falcone* (usually known by its title upon revival 1639, *Chi soffre, speri*). This includes some of the earliest *recitativo secco, but otherwise follows closely the style of earlier operas. *Dal male il bene* (1654), written jointly with Abbatini, is a more original work, and set a standard for later comic opera composers, especially in its use of ensembles.

Marcellina. A duenna (sop) in Mozart's *Le nozze di Figaro*.

Marcello. The Bohemian painter, lover of Musetta, (bar) in Puccini's and (ten) Leoncavallo's *La bohème*.

Marchesi, Mathilde (née Graumann) (*b* Frankfurt, 24 Mar. 1821; *d* London, 17 Nov. 1913). German mezzo-soprano and teacher, wife of **Salvatore Marchesi** (1822–1908). Studied Paris with García jun. Mainly a concert singer, appearing often with Salvatore, whom she married in 1852; only operatic appearance Bremen 1853 (Rosina).

Taught Vienna Cons. 1854–61 and 1868–78; Paris 1861–4; Cologne 1865–8; established own studio in Paris 1881–1908. Her method, based on García's, drew on the traditions of bel canto, and aimed for evenness throughout the register, precise attack, excellent intonation, brilliance and ease at the top of the voice, and vocal longevity. Among her numerous prima donna pupils were Krauss, Di Murska, Calvé, Sanderson, Kurz, Eames, Garden, and Melba. Farrar declined to learn with her, preferring not to sacrifice 'all dramatic expression . . . to sound only'.

Marchetti, Filippo (*b* Bolognola, 26 Feb. 1831; *d* Rome, 18 Jan. 1902). Italian composer. Studied Naples with Lillo and Conti; also helped by Mercadante. The success of his first opera, *Gentile da Varano* (1856), in Naples was not matched by that of *La demente* (1856) in Turin and elsewhere, and the difficulties of finding a stage for his third opera, *Il paria* (comp. 1859), coupled with the rise of Verdi, led him to withdraw from composition. He moved to Rome in 1862 and began work on *Romeo e Giulietta*, which was initially a failure in Trieste in 1865 but had a success in Milan two years later. He fully regained his popularity with *Ruy Blas* (1869) when it was staged in Florence after a poor initial reception in Milan; the work then swept Europe, and was even staged in Cairo, Sydney, and in N and S America. One of the only Italian operas apart from Verdi's to achieve real success in these years, it was followed by two more failures, *Gustavo Wasa* (1875) and *Giovanni d'Austria* (1880). Though of the second rank, Marchetti's work was intermittently popular in its day for its melodic charm (the duet 'O dolce voluttà' from Act III of *Ruy Blas* was long famous); to some extent it anticipates verismo.

Marcoux, Vanni (also known as Vanni-Marcoux) (*b* Turin, 12 June 1877; *d* Paris, 22 Oct. 1962). Italian–French baritone. Studied Turin with Collini, Paris with Boyer. Début Turin 1894 (Sparafucile). Bayonne 1899. London, CG, 1905–12, 1937. Paris: O, from 1908; OC, 1918–36. Milan, S, 1910; Boston 1911–12; Chicago 1913–14, 1926–32. His repertory of 240 roles included Don Giovanni, Don Basilio (Rossini), Hunding, Iago (Verdi), Scarpia, Golaud, Ochs, a much-acclaimed Boris, and many creations, e.g. Guido Colonna (*Monna Vanna*). He was also a celebrated Don Quichotte, a part which though created by Shalyapin was written for him by Massenet. An outstanding artist, he never allowed his moving and powerful dramatic sense to distort his superb singing. Retired from stage 1940, though sang Quichotte at Paris, OC, 1947. Taught Paris Cons. 1938–43; dir. Grand T, Bordeaux, 1948–51. (R)

Maréchal, Adolphe (*b* Liège, 26 Sept. 1867; *d* Brussels, 1 Feb. 1935). Belgian tenor. Studied Liège. Début Liège 1891. Paris, OC, 1895–1907. Monte Carlo and London, CG, 1902. Created several roles, e.g. Julien (*Louise*), Jean in *Le jongleur de Notre-Dame*. One of the Paris OC's foremost singers, he possessed a warm lyric tenor. Lost his voice in 1907. (R)

Mařenka. The daughter (sop) of Krušina and Ludmila, the eponymous intended bride of Jeník, in Smetana's *The Bartered Bride*.

Marfa. A young widow (sop), one of the Old Believers and lover of Andrey Khovansky, in Musorgsky's *Khovanshchina*.

Marguerite. A young girl (sop), lover of Faust, in Gounod's *Faust*.

Marguerite de Valois. Henri of Navarre's Queen (sop) in Meyerbeer's *Les Huguenots*.

Maria. 1 The daughter (sop) of Kochubey and Lyubov, lover of Mazeppa, in Tchaikovsky's *Mazeppa*.
  2 The daughter (sop) of Gara, lover of László, in Erkel's *Hunyadi László*.

Maria di Rohan. Opera in 3 acts by Donizetti; text by Cammarano and Lillo, after Lockroy's *Un duel sous le cardinal de Richelieu* (orig. *Il Conte di Chalais*). Prem. Vienna, K, 5 June 1843.

France, early 17th cent. Maria (sop) is secretly married to Henri, duc de Chevreuse (bar), but later falls in love with the comte de Chalais (ten), after interceding with him on behalf of her husband, who has been arrested for killing Richelieu's nephew. Chevreuse challenges Chalais to a duel and kills him; Maria too wants to die, but her husband decrees that she live a life of disgrace.

Mariani, Angelo (*b* Ravenna, 11 Oct. 1821; *d* Genoa, 13 June 1873). Italian conductor. Studied Ravenna with Roberti. His music attracted the interest of Rossini, with whom he became friends. Cond. Messina 1844–5, where he tried to develop the orchestra in opera against some opposition. Milan, RD,

1846 (*Due Foscari*). Gave performances of *I Lombardi* and *Nabucco* so exciting that he was threatened with imprisonment for stirring up rebellion. Copenhagen 1847–8; Constantinople 1848–51; Genoa, CF, 1852 (*Robert le diable*), where he made the orchestra the best in Italy. First worked with Verdi, Rimini 1857 (*Aroldo*), when they became close friends. Bologna 1860, opening a long series of Verdi performances with *Ballo* and also giving the first Italian *Lohengrin* (1871) and *Tannhäuser* (1872). His great contribution was, by unremitting attention to detail and thoroughness of preparation, to make opera more genuinely integrated as a total theatrical experience. His refusal when seriously ill to conduct the prem. of *Aida* in Cairo caused a breach with Verdi.

Mariani-Masi, Maddalena (*b* Florence 1850; *d* Erba, 25 Sept. 1916). Italian soprano. Studied Florence with Cortesi, Vienna Cons. Début Florence 1871. Milan, S, 1872. Created title-role in *La Gioconda*. Also sang Agathe, Lucrezia Borgia, Elena (*Vespri siciliani*). Capable of great variety in her singing, and imposing on stage. Retired in 1890, having forced her voice, and taught; her pupils included Lina Cavalieri. She appeared frequently with her sister **Flora Mariani de Angelis**, a talented mezzo-soprano who sang in Italy 1871–90.

Maria Padilla. The daughter (sop) of Don Ruiz de Padilla in Donizetti's *Maria Padilla*.

Maria Stuarda. Opera in 3 acts by Donizetti; text by Bardari after Schiller's tragedy (1800). Prem. (as *Buondelmonte*, with libretto changed by Salatino) Naples, C, 18 Oct. 1834.

London and Fotheringhay, 1587. Elizabeth's (mez) favourite, Leicester (ten), and Talbot (bs) have received a request for help from her rival for the throne, Mary Stuart (sop). Leicester persuades Elizabeth to visit Mary in prison at Fotheringhay.

On Leicester's advice, Mary is submissive to the Queen, but nevertheless finds herself accused of treachery. She insults Elizabeth and is sentenced to death.

Learning of her sentence, Mary makes a full confession, denying any involvement in the murder of her husband. As a last wish, granted by Elizabeth, Mary asks that her maid may accompany her to the steps of the scaffold. She goes to her death, still protesting her innocence.

Marie. 1. A *vivandière* (sop), the eponymous 'daughter of the regiment' and lover of Tonio, in Donizetti's *La fille du régiment*.

2. Wozzeck's wife (sop) in Berg's *Wozzeck*.

Marina. Marina Mnishek (sop), daughter of a Sandomir nobleman, in Musorgsky's *Boris Godunov*.

Marino Faliero. Opera in 3 acts by Donizetti; text by E. Bidèra, after Casimir Delavigne's tragedy (1829) and also Byron's tragedy (1821). Prem. Paris, I, 12 Mar. 1835.

Venice, 1355. The Doge Marino Faliero (bs), is enraged at the leniency of the sentence imposed on Michele Steno (bs), who has accused his wife Elena (sop) of infidelity. She has, in fact, fallen in love with his nephew Fernando (ten). Marino's conspiracy against the Council is betrayed; as he is led to his death he forgives her.

Marinuzzi, Gino (*b* Palermo, 24 Mar. 1882; *d* Milan, 17 Aug. 1945). Italian conductor and composer. Studied Palermo with Zuelli. Palermo, T Massimo, conducting German as well as Italian repertory (first *Tristan* there, 1909), also in Italy and Buenos Aires (first *Parsifal* there, 1913). Cond. prem. of Puccini's *La rondine*, Monte Carlo 1917. Chicago 1919–21. Chief cond. Rome, R, 1928–34. London, CG, 1934. Milan, S, with De Sabata 1934–44, dir. 1944. He wrote three operas, *Barberina* (1903), *Jacquerie* (1918), and *Palla de' Mozzi* (1932). (R)

Mario, Giovanni (*b* Cagliari, 17 Oct. 1810; *d* Rome, 11 Dec. 1883). Italian tenor. Of aristocratic birth, was an officer until he deserted the army for political reasons. Studied Paris with Bordogni and Ponchard. Début Paris, O, 1838 (title-role, *Robert le diable*). London, HM 1839–46, and CG 1847–71; Paris, I, from 1840; St Petersburg 1849–63, 1868–70; New York 1854; Madrid 1859, 1864. Retired from stage 1871; toured US with Patti 1872–3. Then, having spent all his considerable earnings, lived in poverty until his death. Considered Rubini's successor, he was elegantly handsome, with a winning stage presence, and an extraordinarily sweet-toned voice. Chorley, however, wrote that he 'fascinated everyone . . . into forgetting incompleteness and deficiency which study might have remedied'. He was acclaimed in a wide repertory, e.g. Don Ottavio, Rossini's Otello and Almaviva, Arturo (*Puritani*), Raoul, John of Leyden, Eléazar, Duke of Mantua, Manrico, Edgardo,

and first Ernesto in *Don Pasquale*. Verdi wrote an extra cabaletta for him in *I due Foscari*. His partnership with Grisi from 1839 was one of the most successful in operatic history; their personal relationship lasted until she died, but they were never able to marry.

Maritana. Opera in 3 acts by Wallace; text by Edward Fitzball, after the drama *Don César de Bazan* by D'Ennery and Dumanoir. Prem. London, DL, 15 Nov. 1845.

Madrid, early 19th cent. The opera tells of the complicated efforts of Don José (bar) to try to gain the attentions of the Queen of Spain. They revolve around the street-singer Maritana (sop), whom he persuades Don Caesar (ten) to marry on the eve of his execution; he subsequently implies to the Queen that the King (bs) is rather too fond of Maritana. However, plans go awry when Don Caesar's 'execution' fails to use real bullets and he returns to claim his bride. Don José is killed and Maritana and her husband live happily.

Mark. 1. King Mark of Cornwall (bs), husband of Isolde, in Wagner's *Tristan und Isolde*.

2. A young man of unknown parentage (ten), bridegroom of Jenifer, in Tippett's *The Midsummer Marriage*.

Marmontel, Jean François (*b* Bort, 11 July 1723; *d* Abloville, 31 Dec. 1799). French dramatist, librettist, and critic. His many librettos include four for Rameau, seven for Grétry, and others for composers including Cherubini (*Démophon*, 1788) and Zingarelli (*Antigone*, 1790). Here, he initiated a number of ideas that were to prove attractive to his contemporaries and successors. His enthusiasm for Rousseau, whom he knew personally, marks his libretto *Le Huron* for Grétry (1768), with its adulation of the Noble Savage; he helped to give impetus to the interest in the medieval; and his story *Soliman Second*, made into a Favart libretto and then a verse play, helped to kindle interest in the oriental. It even directly influenced a number of more famous librettos, including that of Mozart's *Die Entführung aus dem Serail*.

Mârouf, Savetier du Caire (Mârouf, the Cobbler of Cairo). Opera in 4 acts by Rabaud; text by Népoty, after a story in Mardrus's French version of the *1,001 Nights*. Prem. Paris, OC, 15 May 1914.

The cobbler Mârouf (ten) escapes his wife Fattoumah (sop) by going to sea. Shipwrecked, he is introduced by his friend Ali (bar) to the Sultan (bs) as a wealthy merchant; he marries the Sultan's daughter Saamcheddine (sop) and rifles his treasury, continually promising that his caravans will soon arrive. The princess loves him even when he confesses to her, and they flee. A magic ring brings Mârouf the service of a genie, and the pursuing Sultan forgives Mârouf when his rich caravans do indeed arrive.

Marquise de Brinvilliers, La. Opera in 3 acts by Auber, Batton, Berton, Blangini, Boieldieu, Carafa, Cherubini, Hérold, and Paer; text by Scribe and Castil-Blaze. Prem. Paris, OC, 31 Oct. 1831.

The most famous of several collective works of the period, treating the life and loves of the famous poisoner.

Marriage, The (Russ., *Zhenitba*). Opera (unfinished) by Musorgsky; text after Gogol's comedy (1842). Only one act (four scenes) completed in 1868; concert perf. at Rimsky-Korsakov's house, 1906; stage perf. with piano, rev. Rimsky-Korsakov, St Petersburg, Suvorin School, 1 Apr. 1908; first full prem., orch. Rimsky-Korsakov and Gauk, Petrograd 26 Oct. 1917. Completion (Acts II to IV) by Ippolitov-Ivanov, 1931; new completion in 1 act by Cherepnin, 1933.

St Petersburg, 1830. Councillor Podkolesin (bar) decides to marry. The marriage-broker Fekla (con) tries to do a deal with him for Agafya's hand. His friend Kochkarev (ten) intervenes and tries to precipitate matters. (In Gogol's play, and in the revisions, Agafya (sop) is so alarmed by Podkolessin's attempts at proposal that she jumps out of the window. Podkolessin also vanishes leaving Kochkarev laughing triumphantly.

Also opera in 1 act by Martinů; text by the composer, after Gogol. Prem. NBC TV, 7 Feb. 1953.

Marriage of Figaro, The. See NOZZE DI FIGARO, LE.

Marschallin, Die. The Princess von Werdenberg (sop), wife of the absent Field Marshal and lover of Octavian, in R. Strauss's *Der Rosenkavalier*.

Marschner, Heinrich (*b* Zittau, 16 Aug. 1795; *d* Hanover, 14 Dec. 1861). German composer. Studied Bautzen with Hering, Prague with Tomášek, Leipzig with Schicht. Apart from an early attempt, *Titus* (comp. 1816), and a work, *Der Kiffhaeuser Berg* (comp. 1816), in the manner of Viennese Singspiel, his first opera was *Heinrich IV und d'Aubigné* (1820). This was staged by Weber, who backed the performance up with an appreciative article. By then Marschner had already written a Romantic opera, *Saidar und Zulima* (1818), which Weber was unable also to perform in Dresden, whither Marschner moved in 1821. In 1824 he became Weber's assistant (as director of both Italian and German companies), though their initially cordial relationship had by now deteriorated, partly because Weber felt that Marschner was at once imitating his style and using it for commercial purposes rather than in the cause of German opera. *Der Holzdieb* (1825), written in such time as he could find from his duties, is another Viennese-style Singspiel with anticipations of Lortzing. That year, 1826, Weber died, and on being passed over for the succession to his post, Marschner left Dresden.

His first new post was as music director in Danzig, where he produced an unsuccessful and stylistically jumbled attempt at Spontini's Grand Opera manner in *Lucretia* (1827) (with his wife Marianne Wohlbrück in the title-role). Moving to Magdeburg on their way to Leipzig, where Marianne was engaged, he began work with his brother-in-law on his first great success, *Der Vampyr* (1828). The work takes much from *Der Freischütz*, both in the treatment of horror and in the form and melodic nature of the music, while lacking its predecessor's distinction especially in orchestration. It does, however, anticipate aspects of Wagner's *Der fliegende Holländer* in the handling of the accursed hero and his relationship with the pure heroine. Especially, Marschner here develops the idea of the character containing both good and evil, and divided against himself. He followed some of these ideas up in *Der Templer und die Jüdin* (1829), which reflects the more elevated, courtly manner of *Euryanthe* and anticipates much in *Lohengrin* and *Tannhäuser* both in the functional use of orchestration and in the self-divided character of Bois-Guilbert.

In 1831 Marschner became Kapellmeister in Hanover, where he first wrote the inflated *Des Falkners Braut* (1832) before turning to the third of his great successes, *Hans Heiling* (1833). Weber's influence, and that of E. T.

A. Hoffmann, remain in the treatment of a character torn between the real and the magic world, and in such details as the use of melodrama, but the opera shares with *Der Vampyr* and *Der Templer und die Jüdin* an individual voice that absorbs the influences effectively. None of his five remaining operas matches these achievements. The dramatic weakness of *Das Schloss am Aetna* (1836) is only partly due to a poor libretto, though this affected the work and, more seriously, *Der Bäbu* (1838), which contains some fine music in a cumbersome plot. *Kaiser Adolf von Nassau* (1845), reluctantly rehearsed by Wagner and deplored by him as superficial, was Marschner's first attempt at a continuously composed opera. *Austin* (1852) again suffers from a confused plot and poor characterization, as does his last opera, *Sangeskönig Hiarne* (comp. 1857–8).

Marschner did not really depart from Singspiel structure, and was more concerned with extending the range of set forms and finding links between them than in developing a continuous drama based on motive (of which he made inventive use within scenes). But he is capable of striking dramatic strokes, of the strong characterization of his hero/villains with divided souls, of some powerful orchestral writing and some expressive chromatic harmony. With his three most successful works, he makes an individual contribution to German Romantic opera, in the history of which he earns a place as more than a link between Weber and Wagner.

Marshall, Margaret (*b* Stirling, 4 Jan. 1949). Scottish soprano. Studied Glasgow and with Hotter in Munich. Début Florence 1978 (Gluck's Euridice). Milan, S, 1979 in Vivaldi's *Tito Manlio*; London, CG, 1980 (Mozart's Countess). Salzburg from 1982 as Fiordiligi, Ilia, and Vitellia. Her well-schooled voice is also admired in such roles as Violetta, the Countess in *Capriccio* (Scottish O), and the Marschallin (Cologne 1986). (R)

'Martern aller Arten'. Constanze's (sop) aria in Act II of Mozart's *Die Entführung aus dem Serail*, in which she declares that neither torture nor death itself will make her yield to the Pasha. Written for Katharina Cavalieri.

Martha, oder Der Markt von Richmond (Martha, or Richmond Market). Opera in 4 acts by Flotow; text by W. Friedrich (Friedrich Wilhelm Riese), after Vernoy de Saint-Geor-

ges's ballet-pantomime *Lady Harriette, ou La servante de Greenwich*, to which Flotow had contributed some music. Prem. Vienna, K, 25 Nov. 1847.

Richmond, *c.*1710. Lady Harriet (sop), maid of honour to Queen Anne, is tired of court life, and so she and her maid Nancy (mez) disguise themselves as country girls. Under the names of Martha and Julia they go to Richmond Fair, where they are hired as servants by two young farmers, Lionel (ten) and Plunkett (bs). The two men fall in love with the girls; when they later return to court life, Lady Harriet realizes that she loves Lionel. A replica of Richmond Fair is set up in her own garden and there, once again, Lionel sees 'Martha' in her humble clothes and the two couples are happily united.

Martin, Frank (*b* Geneva, 15 Sept. 1890; *d* Naarden, 21 Nov. 1974). Swiss composer. His two operas are *Der Sturm* (1956), a word-for-word setting of Schlegel's translation of Shakespeare's *The Tempest*, and *Monsieur de Pourceaugnac* (1963) after Molière, which moves from song by way of recitative and melodrama to unaccompanied speech in the interests of serving the drama.

Martin, Jean-Blaise (*b* Paris, 24 Feb. 1768; *d* Ronzières, 28 Oct. 1837). French baritone. Studied Paris with Dugazon. Début Paris, T de Monsieur, 1788. Paris: T Favart, 1794–1801; OC, 1801–23, 1826, 1833. Taught Paris Cons. 1816–18, 1832–7. With his range of E♭–a', plus an octave falsetto extension, he gave his name to the voice type known as *baryton Martin* (see BARITONE) that became an important feature of opéra-comique thereafter. He created numerous roles in works by Dalayrac, Méhul, Boieldieu, Halévy, etc. and was an excellent comic actor.

Martinelli, Giovanni (*b* Montagnana, 22 Oct. 1885; *d* New York, 2 Feb. 1969). Italian tenor. Studied Milan with Mandolini. Début Milan, V, 1910 (Ernani). London, CG, 1912, 1913–14, 1919, 1937. Milan, S, 1912. New York, M, 1913–46. Also Chicago, S Francisco. Last appearance Seattle 1967 (Emperor, *Turandot*). Enormously popular, and an artist of high calibre; possessed a ringing tone, a superb legato and breath control, and impeccable style. Admired by Puccini, and by Barbirolli, who refers to his 'unfailing musicality'. Roles included Guillaume Tell, Faust (Gounod), Eléazar, Don José, Lensky, Manrico, Don Carlos, Rodolfo, Dick Johnson,

Cavaradossi, Calaf, Otello (Verdi), and one Tristan. (R)

Martinpelto, Hillevi (*b* Alvalden, 9 Jan. 1958). Swedish soprano. Studied Stockholm; début with Folks-opera there (Pamina). Royal O Stockholm 1987 (Butterfly). Drottningholm 1988–90, as Gluck's two Iphigénies. She has given strongly committed performances of Wagner's Eva (Berlin, D), Freia at Chicago (1993), and such Mozart roles as Elettra and the Countess (both with John Eliot Gardiner); Donna Anna at Gly. 1994. (R)

Martinů, Bohuslav (*b* Polička, 8 Dec. 1890; *d* Liestal, 28 Aug. 1959). Czech composer. Initially largely self-taught, then studied Prague with Suk and Paris with Roussel. His first opera was a 3-act comedy, *The Soldier and the Dancer* (1928). There followed *Les larmes du couteau* (comp. 1928), a 1-act jazz opera, and *Trois souhaits* (comp. 1929), a 3-act film opera also making use of jazz. *The Miracles of Mary* (1935) consists of a cycle of four mystery plays. Martinů's first real success on the stage came with *Julietta* (1938), which concerns the relationship of dream and reality, and of reality and memory, in which his invariably fluent idiom achieves considerable lyrical intensity. *Mirandolina* (1959) was an attempt to update the spirit of Goldoni. A serious work followed, *The Greek Passion* (1961), but the steadily cumulative intensity of the original proved difficult to translate to the stage in short scenes lacking true dramatic power. Martinů also wrote three radio operas, *The Voice of the Forest* (1935), *Comedy on a Bridge* (1937), and *What Men Live By* (1953); the pungent wit of *Comedy on a Bridge*, one of his most attractive works, has successfully transferred to the stage.

Martinucci, Nicola (*b* Taranto, 28 Mar. 1941). Italian tenor. Studied Milan with Sforni. Début Milan, N, 1966 (Manrico). Milan, S; Venice, F; Florence; etc. Deutsche Oper am Rhein from 1973; Verona from 1982; London, CG, 1985; New York, M, 1988. Repertory incl. Radamès, Calaf, Dick Johnson, Poliuto, Pollione, and Enzo. (R).

Martín y Soler, Vicente (*b* Valencia, 2 May 1754; *d* St Petersburg, 10 Feb. 1806). Spanish composer. After early training as a choirboy and some success as a composer in Madrid, moved to Italy, producing both serious and comic works for Lucca, Parma, Turin, Venice, and above all Naples. Encouraged to Vienna

by Nancy Storace 1785: here he collaborated with Da Ponte on three operas: *Il burbero di buon cuore* (The Moaner with a Heart of Gold, 1786), *L'arbore di Diana* (1787), and his greatest triumph, *Una cosa rara* (1786). Such was its success that it supplanted *Figaro* which had been premiered earlier in the year; Mozart later quoted an aria from it ('O quanto si bel giubilo') in the banquet scene of *Don Giovanni*. Invited to St Petersburg by Catherine the Great 1788, replacing Sarti as court composer. Here he wrote two operas, *Gore Bogatyr Kosometovich* (1789) and *Pesnolyubie* (Beloved Songs, 1790), directed many productions, and played a significant role in the early cultivation of Russian opera. Da Ponte engaged him as composer at the London Haymarket 1794–6 but *c*.1796 he returned to St Petersburg and was inspector of the Italian court theatre 1800–4.

Although his works have been largely neglected, Martín y Soler was one of the most gifted and popular opera buffa composers of the late 18th cent., rivalling Cimarosa, Paisiello, and even Mozart. He possessed a sure gift for captivating melody, dramatic pace, and sharp musical characterization, talents recognized by Da Ponte, who much admired his work.

Marton, Eva (*b* Budapest, 18 June 1943). Hungarian soprano. Studied Budapest with Rösler and Sipos. Début Budapest 1968 (Queen of Shemakha). Frankfurt 1974–7; Bayreuth 1977–8; Milan, S, from 1978; New York, M, from 1981; Chicago 1980; London, CG, 1987. S Francisco, Buenos Aires, Vienna, etc. Possesses an even, powerful, dramatic soprano. Roles include Donna Anna, Elsa, Brünnhilde, Ariadne, Salome, Elektra, Turandot, Tosca. (R)

Martyrs, Les. Opera in 4 acts by Donizetti; text by Scribe, after Corneille's tragedy *Polyeucte*, orig. composed to an Italian libretto by S. Cammarano, *Poliuto*, in 3 acts, and written for Nourrit in Naples (rehearsed 1838) but banned by the censor. Prem. Paris, O, 10 Apr. 1840.

For plot see POLIUTO.

Mary Stuart. See MARIA STUARDA.

Marzelline. The daughter (sop) of the gaoler Rocco, in love with Fidelio, loved by Jacquino, in Beethoven's *Fidelio*.

Masaniello. Tommaso Aniello (ten), a Nea-

321 MASCOTTE

politan fisherman and brother of Fenella, in Auber's *La muette de Portici*.

Mascagni, Pietro (*b* Livorno, 7 Dec. 1863; *d* Rome, 2 Aug. 1945). Italian composer and conductor. Studied Livorno with Soffredini and Milan Cons. with Ponchielli and Saladino, where his friends included Puccini. Despite early recognition of his talent, he found the training stultifying and left before completing his formal studies. For a while he travelled Italy with a touring opera company; joined the orchestra of the Milan V 1884; conducted an operetta season in Parma 1885; eventually settled at Cerignola as a piano teacher.

Mascagni's first operatic work, *Pinotta* (comp. 1883), which he mislaid for 50 years, was an adaptation of a cantata; his next attempt, the romantic tragedy *Guglielmo Ratcliff*, remained unfinished when he was unable to find a theatre willing to stage it. But in 1890 he won first prize in a competition sponsored by the publishers Sonzogno with his 1-act opera *Cavalleria rusticana* (1890). At its prem. this melodramatic opera of love and hatred in Sicily was given a tumultuous reception, making its composer famous overnight; it was quickly taken up across Europe (Berlin 1890; London 1891; Paris 1892) and began a vogue for similar 1-act works. With Leoncavallo's *Pagliacci* of 1892 it represented the beginning of *verismo opera and attracted numerous admirers, including Verdi and Puccini, partly because it was generally regarded as a brilliantly successful counter to the principles of Wagnerian music drama.

The rest of Mascagni's career was effectively spent trying to recapture the success of *Cavalleria rusticana*, but to no avail. *L'amico Fritz* (1891) was quickly produced, but despite some charming pastoral passages failed to convince; the works which followed, *I Rantzau* (1892), the completed *Guglielmo Ratcliff* (1895), and *Silvano* (1895) were all soon forgotten. By the time that *Zanetto* (1896) was performed Mascagni had moved to Pesaro as director of the conservatory; modest in conception, it fared no better. With the orientally inspired *Iris* (1898), Mascagni fleetingly regained some of his former popularity, not least because of his inventive orchestration. The short-lived success of *Isabeau* (1911) apart, this was the last of his works to achieve serious recognition. The bold concept of *Le maschere* (1901), with its

six simultaneous prems., was fundamentally flawed and the opera had a brief and stormy career, while *Amica* (1905) was equally short-lived. *Il piccolo Marat* (1921), which many consider Mascagni's best work, found few admirers; none of the other late operas, which include *Parisina* (1913), *Lodoletta* (1917), and the rediscovered *Pinotta* (prod. 1932), have had any following.

Although Mascagni enjoyed some fame as an opera conductor, he was not highly regarded by his peers. His precarious position foundered completely when he allowed himself to become too closely associated with Fascism, composing his *Nerone* (1935) for Milan S with Mussolini in mind, as well as choral and orchestral works for various political occasions. As a result he was ostracized by many Italian musicians including Toscanini, and spent the last few years of his life in comparative poverty and disgrace in a Rome hotel. Of his works, only *Cavalleria rusticana* has found a permanent place in the present-day repertory. Although easily dismissed as a rather tawdry piece of melodrama, it was strikingly original and daring in its time, and shows Mascagni to have possessed, at his best, considerable dramatic skill. (R)

Maschere, Le (The Masks). Opera in a prologue and 3 acts by Mascagni; text by Illica. Prem. simultaneously in six Italian cities, 17 Jan. 1901.

In a plot of commedia dell'arte characters, Florindo (ten) and Rosaura (sop), aided by Columbina (sop) and Arlecchino (ten), attempt to prevent the marriage which Rosaura's father, Pantalone (bs), has planned for her. They eventually succeed.

Mascheroni, Edoardo (*b* Milan, 4 Sept. 1892; *d* Como, 4 Mar. 1941). Italian conductor and composer. Studied Milan with Boucheron. Cond. Brescia 1880; Rome, Ap., 1884–8. Chief cond. Milan, S, 1891–4, conducting prems. of *La Wally* (1892) and, at Verdi's request, *Falstaff* (1893), the latter with such effect that Verdi called him the 'third author'. Cond. Germany, Spain, S America. His *Lorenza* (text by Illica) was prem. Rome 1901, and *La perugina* (Illica) Naples 1909.

Mascotte, La. Operetta in 3 acts by Audran; text by Duru and Chivot. Prem. Paris, B, 28 Dec. 1880.

Piombino, 17th cent. The goose-girl Bettina (sop), sent as a good luck mascot to the farmer Rocco, is loved by the shepherd Pippo (bar). Prince Laurent (ten) takes her away to his castle, leaving his daughter Fiametta (sop) to try to seduce Pippo. Pippo agrees to marry Fiametta but, at the last moment, escapes with Bettina. After a war, in which Laurent is on the losing side, the Prince agrees to the marriage of Pippo and Bettina.

Masetto. A peasant (bar), betrothed to Zerlina, in Mozart's *Don Giovanni*.

Masini, Angelo (*b* Forlì, 28 Nov. 1844; *d* Forlì, 28 Sept. 1926). Italian tenor. Studied with Minguzzi. Début Finale Emilia 1867 (Pollione). Appearances in Venice, Rome, Florence, etc. until 1875; sang the first performances of Verdi's Requiem under his direction in Paris, London, and Vienna. Cairo 1875–6; St Petersburg 1879–1903; Madrid, 1881–2, 1884–5; Barcelona 1886; retired 1905. A virtuoso singer, he possessed what Tamagno called 'un voce di paradiso', a ravishing mezza voce, and superb breath control. Successful as Don Ottavio, Almaviva (Rossini), Nemorino, Duke of Mantua (having seven different endings for 'La donna è mobile'). Verdi thought there would have been 'no one better' as the first Fenton, but Masini accepted a more lucrative contract in Russia (where he became the Tsar's favourite tenor).

Maskarade. Opera in 3 acts by Nielsen; text by Vilhelm Andersen, after a play by Holberg. Prem. Copenhagen 11 Nov. 1906.

Copenhagen, 1723. Leander (ten) has fallen in love with an unknown woman at a masked ball, and vows to marry her, although his father Jeronimus (bs) has already arranged another marriage for him. Against Jeronimus's instructions, Leander goes to the masquerade; he is sighted by Mr Leonard (ten or bar), the father of his intended wife. Leander's beloved, Leonora (sop), turns out to be none other than Leonard's daughter, so the predestined couple are now happy to be united.

Mask of Orpheus, The. Opera in three acts by Birtwistle; text by Peter Zinovieff, after the classical legend. Prem. London, C, 21 May 1986.

Each major role is taken by three performers, representing different aspects of the character as man (or woman), hero, and myth—Orpheus (ten, ten, dancer/mime),

Eurydice (mez, mez, dancer/mime), and Aristaeus (bs-bar, bs-bar, dancer/mime)—and the three acts treat different aspects of the legend.

Maslennikova, Leokadia (*b* Saratov, 3 June 1918). Russian soprano. Studied Minsk, and Kiev with Yevtushenko. Kiev 1944–6; Moscow, B, 1946–59. Roles incl. Parasya (*Sorochintsy Fair*), Tatyana, Lisa, Yolanta, Marguerite, Micaëla, Nedda, Tosca. (R)

Masnadieri, I (The Robbers). Opera in 4 acts by Verdi; text by Maffei, after Schiller's drama *Die Räuber* (1781), after C. F. D. Schubart's story (1777). Prem. London, HM, 22 July 1847.

Germany, early 18th cent. Carlo (ten) is, through the machinations of his brother Francesco (bar), disinherited by their father Massimiliano Moor (bs) after leaving home and his lover Amalia (sop) and becoming chief of a robber band. Francesco announces Carlo's death, and also that of his father (whom he has imprisoned). But Amalia learns the truth, and also repels Francesco's advances. The lovers meet in a forest, and Carlo frees his father without, from loyalty to the robbers, disclosing his identity. He is later recognized by his father, but kills Amalia rather than bind her to his life of crime.

masque (sometimes also **mask**). A 16th- and 17th-cent. English stage entertainment combining poetry, music, singing, dancing, and acting, often setting mythological subjects in elaborate scenery. It grew out of the French *ballet de cour, but in England was not restricted to courtly performance: masques were, for example, sometimes given in the Inns of Court. The most important early writer was Ben Jonson with, e.g. the *Masque of Blackness* (1605) and *Lovers Made Men* (1617). As an art-form uniting music and drama, the masque was an important precursor of the short-lived English opera. It reached its most lavish form in such spectacular works as Shirley's *The Triumph of Peace* (1634; music by Ives) and *Britannia triumphans* (1638; music by William Lawes). The masque survived into the 18th cent.: important works were Congreve's *The Masque of Paris*, the subject of famous competition in 1701 to find the best setting of its text, and Handel's *Semele*. The masque form has occasionally been revived in modern times, for example in Britten's *Gloriana* and Harrison Birtwistle's *The Mask of Orpheus*.

Massé, Victor (*b* Lorient, 7 Mar. 1822; *d* Paris, 5 July 1884). French composer. Studied Paris Cons. with Halévy, winning the Grand Prix de Rome. Began his career with *La chambre gothique* (1849); this was followed by a string of popular comic works beginning with *La chanteuse voilée* (1850) and including *Galathée* (1852) and *Les noces de Jeannette* (1853, his most successful opera: 1,000 performances by 1895). For a while Massé was seen as the successor to Auber, but his later works, which included *La reine Topaze* (1856) and *Les saisons* (1855), did not prove enduring, though they are always charmingly tuneful.

He became chorus-master at the Opéra 1860, and professor of composition at the Conservatoire, 1866. After *Le fils du brigadier* (1867) he wrote no stage music for a while, but in 1876 produced a serious work, *Paul et Virginie*, which was well regarded. The same year he resigned from the Opéra because of illness; during his declining years he wrote another work in similar vein, *Une nuit de Cleopâtre* (1885). Ambitious in scope, neither recaptured the success of his earlier comic operas, the best of which stayed in the repertoire long after his death.

Massenet, Jules (*b* Montaud, 12 May 1842; *d* Paris, 13 Aug. 1912). French composer. Studied with his mother, Paris with Thomas. On his return from Italy, where he spent three years as a Prix de Rome winner, he had sufficient success with *La grand'tante* in 1867 for him to be commissioned, once the Franco-Prussian War was over, to write *Don César de Bazan* (1872). However, his career was really set on its course by Pauline Viardot's championship of his 'sacred drama' *Marie-Magdeleine*, whose theme of the reformed courtesan touched off the vein of what D'Indy called 'a discreet and pseudo-religious eroticism' that was to mark much of his work. *Le roi de Lahore* (1877) was carefully tailored to the demands of the newly opened Opéra (Palais Garnier) and to an audience that had learnt to appreciate the orientalisms of Bizet's *Les pêcheurs de perles*. Its triumph made Massenet's name, and led to his establishment at the Conservatoire as the most influential teacher of his generation. He was as popular in this role as he saw to it that he remained with the public as a composer. Though *Hérodiade* (1881) shows

some Wagnerian influences, and in its free melodic declamation anticipates aspects of Debussy's *Pelléas et Mélisande*, the style is essentially sweet and appealing whatever the dramatic situation. His capacity to charm and captivate under all circumstances, remarked upon by Fauré, was even more successfully deployed in *Manon* (1884): though the orchestration and some use of motive were to lead to jibes about 'Mlle Wagner', the work put him in a commanding position as the most successful French opera composer of the day, with large and enthusiastic audiences.

Nevertheless, three comparative failures followed, *Le Cid* (1885), *Esclarmonde* (1889), and *Le mage* (1891); Massenet's preference for *Esclarmonde* above all his other works is perhaps in part connected to the young Sybil Sanderson, who sang the title-role and who played an important part in his life. In *Werther* (1892) the sentimental aspect of the novel touched his own, and his mastery of an elegant declamatory vocal line, subtly reinforced by the orchestra, is at the service of powerful and touching scenes handled with a sure dramatic instinct. With *Thaïs* (1894), he returned to the contrast between sacred and profane love in *Hérodiade*, and to the treatment of the vulnerable courtesan of *Manon*; and though he does not portray in much depth either the sacred or the profane, or make Thaïs much larger than the touching Manon, the work has its now-familiar skill and charm. *Le portrait de Manon* (1894) was a conscious return to the earlier theme with a sequel; a more original departure was *La navarraise* (1894), a highly successful attempt to bring verismo back to its origins in France. *Sapho* (1897) again returns to formula in a work contrasting rural innocence with urban sophistication, once more depicting the two in elegant tones rather than entering seriously into their characterization. Not for the first time, there is here repaid a debt which Tchaikovsky had incurred to Massenet in some of his own operas (especially *The Maid of Orleans* and *Eugene Onegin*).

Sapho was Massenet's last major success, though *Cendrillon* (1899), a skilful confection of tried devices written for Carré's new reign at the Opéra-Comique, proved popular; and Massenet's mastery of the pretty was re-invoked with *Grisélidis* (1901), whose plot it suits less well. With *Le jongleur de Notre-Dame* (1902) he abandoned the female portraiture in which he had excelled for an all-male opera, and with all his old skill brings off a subject that tests even his ability with the religiously sentimental. Few of his remaining works showed such command, and the times were at last turning against him; but there is a genuinely affecting quality in *Don Quichotte* (1910), in part through a subtle refinement of his skills to a moving simplicity. *Chérubin* (1905) has been successfully revived (London, CG, 1994).

Master Peter's Puppet Show. See RETABLO DE MAESE PEDRO, EL.

Mastersingers of Nuremberg, The. See MEISTERSINGER VON NÜRNBERG, DIE.

Masterson, Valerie (*b* Birkenhead, 3 June 1937). English soprano. Studied London with Clinton and Asquez, Milan with Saraceni. Début Salzburg 1963 (Frasquita). D'Oyly Carte Co. 1966–70. London, SW/ENO from 1971, and CG from 1974; Paris, O, from 1978. Also Gly., Buenos Aires, Barcelona, Prague. Roles include Semele, Countess (Mozart), Constanze, Adèle (*Ory*), Marguerite, Violetta, Sophie, the Marschallin (Liège 1993). A singer of poise and distinction, especially successful in Handel, Mozart, and the French repertory. (R)

Matačić, Lovro von (*b* Sušak, 14 Feb. 1899; *d* Zagreb, 4 Jan. 1985). Croatian conductor and producer. Studied Vienna with Schalk, Herbst, and Nedbal. Chorus-master Cologne 1917, cond. 1919. Cond. Novi Sad 1919; Ljubljana 1924–6; Belgrade 1926–32, 1938–42; Zagreb 1932–8; Vienna, V, 1942–5. Guest appearances Germany and Italy from 1953. Music dir. Dresden 1956–8, jointly with Konwitschny Berlin, S, 1956–8. Chicago 1959. Frankfurt 1961–6. Bayreuth 1959 (*Lohengrin*). Also produced many operas, including *Orfeo*, *Poppea*, *Parsifal*, and *Turandot*. (R)

Materna, Amalie (*b* St Georgen, 10 July 1844; *d* Vienna, 18 Jan. 1918). Austrian soprano. Studied Graz. Début Graz 1864 (Suppé's *Light Cavalry*). Vienna, H, 1869–94. Bayreuth 1876, 1882–91; New York, M, 1885. A leading Wagnerian of her time; sang Brünnhilde in the first complete *Ring* (Bayreuth 1876); also created Kundry. Much admired by Wagner, who declared her the one woman capable of singing Brünnhilde; he also found her 'sympathetic' and visually convincing. Other roles included Elisabeth,

Rachel (*La Juive*), Valentine. Created title-role of Goldmark's *Königin von Saba*. Possessed a large, bright voice and immense stamina.

Mathis, Edith (*b* Lucerne, 11 Feb. 1938). Swiss soprano. Studied Lucerne, and Zurich with Basshart. Début Lucerne 1956 (Second Boy, *Zauberflöte*). Cologne 1959–63; Berlin, D, from 1963; Gly. 1962–3, 1965; Hamburg 1960–72; New York, M, 1970–4; London, CG, 1970, 1972; Salzburg and Munich Festivals. Successful as Zerlina, Pamina, Nannetta, Mélisande, Zdenka, and particularly as Sophie; sang the Marschallin at Berne 1990. (R)

Mathis der Maler (Mathis the Painter). Opera in 7 scenes by Hindemith; text by the composer, after Matthias Grünewald's life and his altar-piece at Colmar. Prem. Zurich 28 May 1938.

In the Peasants' War of 1542, Grünewald (bar) leads the peasants against the church. Losing faith in his cause, he escapes with Regina (sop). He renounces the outside world in favour of his art.

Matinsky, Mikhail (*b* Pokrovsk, 1750; *d* St Petersburg, *c*.1820). Russian librettist. Studied Moscow and in Italy. In 1782 he wrote the text for Pashkevich's *Sanktpeterburgsky gostiny dvor* (St Petersburg Market). This only survives in its revised version (1792) as *Kak pozhivyosh, tak i proslyvyosh* (As you live, so shall you be judged), and makes much use of folk music and of the chorus (including a remarkable and effective sequence of seven wedding choruses) to give one of the earliest operatic pictures of Russian life.

Matrimonio segreto, Il (The Secret Marriage). Opera in 2 acts by Cimarosa; text by Bertati, after the comedy *The Clandestine Marriage* (1766) by Colman and Garrick. Prem. Vienna, B, 7 Feb. 1792.

Bologna, 1780. The opera tells of the attempts of Geronimo (bs), a wealthy citizen of Bologna, to marry off his daughter Elisetta (sop) to an English 'Milord', Count Robinson (bs). The latter prefers Geronimo's other daughter Carolina (sop), who is secretly married to Paolino (ten), a young lawyer and business associate of Geronimo. Geronimo's sister Fidalma (mez), who rules the household, is herself in love with Paolino. Carolina and Paolino plan an elopement, and after a bedroom scene of mistaken identities, all ends happily with the Count agreeing to marry Elisetta.

Matters, Arnold (*b* Adelaide, 11 Apr. 1904; *d* Adelaide, 21 Sept. 1990). Australian baritone. Studied Adelaide with Bevan and Carey, London with Johnstone-Douglas. Début London, SW, 1932 (Valentin). London: SW, 1932–9, 1947–53; CG, 1935–9, 1946–54. Created Pilgrim (*Pilgrim's Progress*), Cecil (*Gloriana*). Roles included Don Giovanni, Sachs, Wotan, Falstaff (Verdi), Scarpia, and a memorable Boccanegra. Returned to Adelaide 1954 to teach. (R)

Mattheson, Johann (*b* Hamburg, 28 Sept. 1681; *d* Hamburg, 17 Apr. 1764). German composer, singer, harpsichordist, and organist. Joined the chorus of the Hamburg O while still a boy; by 1700 he was established as one of the leading figures in Hamburg's operatic life, variously taking principal roles, directing performances from the harpsichord, and contributing new works to the repertoire. In 1703 his friendship with Handel began: though on one occasion they fought a famous duel, the two composers maintained a generally cordial relationship. Appointed director of the Hamburg cathedral (1715), and Kapellmeister to the Duke of Holstein (1719).

Mattheson occupied an important pivotal position in the history of opera in N Germany, standing midway between the earlier tradition of Kusser and Keiser, an influence readily detectable in much of his vocal music, and the later developments of his near-contemporary Telemann, whose career in the city began somewhat later. He was a particularly important influence on Handel at a formative stage in his career, assisting with the composition of *Almira*; several of Handel's operas later borrowed from Mattheson's music. Full appreciation of his operatic talents is not possible: of his eight works, only one, *Die unglückselige Cleopatra* (1704), survives.

Mattila, Karita (*b* Somero, 5 Sept. 1960). Finnish soprano. Studied Helsinki; début Savonlinna 1981 (Donna Anna). Finnish Nat. O début 1982 (Mozart's Countess). Won Cardiff Singer of the World Competition and made US début at Washington DC (Donna Elvira) 1983. London, CG, from 1986, as Fiordiligi, Agathe, Pamina. An attractive stage presence lends distinction to such roles as Ilia (S Francisco 1989), Eva (New York, M,

1993), and Amelia Grimaldi (Geneva 1991). (R)

Matzenauer, Margarete (*b* Temesvár, 1 June 1881; *d* Van Nuys, CA, 19 May 1963). Austro-Hungarian soprano and contralto. Studied Graz with Janushovsky, Berlin with Mielke and Emmrich. Début Strasburg 1901 (Fatima, *Oberon*). Munich 1904–11; Bayreuth 1911; New York, M, 1911–30; London, CG, 1914. Possessed a rich voice of extraordinary range, singing Isolde, Erda, Brünnhilde, Amneris, Aida, Fidès, Brangäne, Dalila, Kostelnička, etc., with equal ease. (R)

Mauceri, John (*b* New York, 12 Sept. 1945). US conductor. Studied Yale and Tanglewood; début Wolf Trap 1973 (Menotti's *The Saint of Bleecker Street*). British début with WNO 1974 (*Don Carlo*); Scottish O 1976 (*Otello*). New York, CO, 1977–82, incl. *Candide*. Appeared with London, CG comp. at Manchester 1983 (*Butterfly*). An innovative and committed conductor, he was music director of Scottish O 1987–93, giving *Les Troyens*, the British prem. of Weill's *Street Scene* (1989), and his own version of Blitzstein's *Regina* (1991). (R)

Maurel, Victor (*b* Marseilles, 17 June 1848; *d* New York, 22 Oct. 1923). French baritone. Studied Paris with Vauthrot and Duvernoy. Début Marseilles 1867 (*Guillaume Tell*). Paris, O, 1868, 1879–94. Milan, S, from 1870; London, CG, 1873–9, 1891–5, 1904; New York, M, 1894–6, 1898–9. Roles included Don Giovanni, Rigoletto, Amonasro, Hamlet, Telramund; Boccanegra in the revised 1881 version (when Verdi lowered the tessitura for him); first Iago, Falstaff (described by W. J. Henderson as 'one of the great creations of the lyric stage'), and Tonio, persuading Leoncavallo to write the Prologue for him. One of the greatest singing actors of his time: intelligent, subtle, and cultivated, possessing a wide variety of vocal colour, and an exceptional dramatic instinct. Shaw, while admiring him, sometimes found him 'artificial' (e.g. as Don Giovanni), but Lilli Lehmann was once so moved by his Valentin that she was 'speechless for hours'. Designed sets for *Mireille* at New York M (1919). Taught New York 1909 until his death. (R)

Mavra. Opera in 1 act by Stravinsky; text by B. Kochno, after Pushkin's poem *The Little House at Kolomna* (1830). Prem. Paris, O, 3 June 1922.

A Russian village, *c*.1800. In order for her

lover Vassily (ten) to gain entry to her house, Parasha (sop) persuades her mother (con) to accept him (in disguise) as a new maid, Mavra, to replace their recently deceased servant. When she returns slyly to check on the maid's work, the mother finds 'Mavra' shaving; neighbours chase Vassily away.

Maw, Nicholas (*b* Grantham, 5 Nov. 1935). English composer. Studied London with Berkeley and Steinitz, Paris with Deutsch. An early comedy, *One Man Show* (1964), was notable for some engaging music whose promise was fulfilled in *The Rising of the Moon* (1970), a well-crafted work, witty and lyrical, showing that an understanding of the strengths of Romantic opera (in particular Strauss) need not involve either pastiche or anachronism.

Max. A huntsman (ten), lover of Agathe, in Weber's *Der Freischütz*.

Maxwell, Donald (*b* Perth, 12 Dec. 1948). Scottish baritone. Studied Edinburgh U. Début Scottish O 1977 (in Musgrave's *Mary, Queen of Scots*); further roles as the Forester (*Cunning Little Vixen*) and Rossini's Figaro. Verdi repertory incl. Falstaff and Rigoletto, with WNO. London, CG, début 1987; Gunther 1990. Other strongly characterized performances as the Dutchman and Scarpia (O North); Wozzeck for ENO (1990). (R)

Maxwell Davies, Peter. See DAVIES, PETER MAXWELL.

May Night (Russ., *Mayskaya noch*). Opera in 3 acts by Rimsky-Korsakov; text by the composer, after Gogol's story (1831–2). Prem. St Petersburg, M, 21 Jan. 1880.

Ukraine. Levko (ten) and Hanna (mez) are in love, but his father the Mayor (bs) disapproves. Levko tells her the legend of Pannochka (sop) who drowned herself to escape from her stepmother and become a rusalka (water sprite): the stepmother was also drowned, but cannot be distinguished now from the good rusalki. Levko is furious to find his father later serenading Hanna.

Great complications ensue at a drinking orgy of the Mayor, leading to his sister-in-law being mistaken for the Devil and nearly burnt.

Near the castle by the lake, Levko is singing in praise of Hanna when the rusalki appear; in return for his identifying the disguised stepmother, they provide him with evidence that leads to the Mayor being outwitted and his own wedding to Hanna being celebrated.

Mayr, Johann Simon (*b* Mendorf, 14 June 1763; *d* Bergamo, 2 Dec. 1845). German composer. Studied with his father, then Bergamo with Lenzi, Venice with Bertoni. On the death of the patron who supported him, he was urged by Piccinni to try his hand at opera, and the success of his *Saffo* in 1794 led to many commissions. His first opera for Milan was the 1799 revision of *Lodoiska*, though his national fame really dates from the success of *Ginevra di Scozia* (1801), which opened the T Nuovo in Trieste in 1801. Thereafter he wrote operas for Naples and Rome as well as Milan and Venice, and his fame also spread internationally with productions in Germany and also in London, St Petersburg, New York, and elsewhere.

Mayr's chief model in *Saffo* was Gluck, whose mastery of the chorus and orchestra the work reflects, as well as a dramatic fluency not then familiar in Italian opera. Most of his works are in buffo style, and he brought a new vividness of orchestration to the genre, with the addition of harps to the orchestra and a novel virtuosity of wind writing (as well as regular use of the stage band). He introduced orchestral numbers depicting storms, earthquakes, and other natural phenomena, and was one of various composers to anticipate the so-called 'Rossini crescendo'. His most celebrated work, *Medea in Corinto* (1813), makes pioneering advances in continuity between numbers, and it is chiefly for this greater emphasis on dramatic content and fluency that he was influential on the succeeding generation of Italian composers, among them Rossini.

Mayr, Richard (*b* Henndorf, 18 Nov. 1877; *d* Vienna, 1 Dec. 1935). Austrian bass-baritone. Studied Vienna Cons. Début Bayreuth 1902 (Hagen). Vienna 1902–35. Frankfurt from 1905; London, CG, 1911–13, 1924–31; New York, M, 1927–30. With his round tone, sensitive singing, and versatile dramatic gifts, an outstanding artist; acclaimed as Sarastro, Leporello, Gurnemanz, etc. Created several roles, notably Barak (*Die Frau ohne Schatten*). Though not the first Ochs, as Strauss and Hofmannsthal had hoped, he later became the fulfilment of their ideal: 'Falstaffian, comfortable, laughable'. (R)

Mazeppa. Opera in 3 acts by Tchaikovsky; text by the composer and V. P. Burenin, after Pushkin's poem *Poltava* (1829). Prem. Moscow, B, 15 Feb. 1884.

Ukraine, 18th cent. Maria (sop), daughter of Kochubey (bs), loves Mazeppa (bar) and rejects Andrey (ten). When Mazeppa is refused her hand by Kochubey, he abducts her; Andrey offers to approach the Tsar with information about Mazeppa's treachery in siding with the Swedes.

But the Tsar believes Mazeppa, and Kochubey is arrested; torture fails to break him or to part him from his treasure. Maria is told of this and pleads with Mazeppa, who is absorbed in his plans to set up a separate state under his rule. Kochubey is led to execution.

After the symphonic picture *The Battle of Poltava*, the last act shows Andrey pursuing the fleeing Swedes; however, he is shot by Mazeppa, and Maria, now gone mad, sings a lullaby over his body.

Mazurok, Yury (*b* Krasnik, 18 July 1931). Polish baritone. Studied Moscow with Sveshnikova. Moscow, B, from 1963; London, CG, from 1975; New York, M, from 1978 (Scarpia 1993); also Vienna, S; Berlin; Prague; Budapest; etc. Possesses an attractive tone and stage presence. Repertory incl. Figaro (Rossini), Germont, Luna, Escamillo, Onegin, Yeletsky, Andrey (*War and Peace*). (R)

Mazzocchi, Domenico (*b* Civita Castellana, *bapt.* 8 Nov. 1592; *d* Rome, 21 Jan. 1665). Italian composer, brother of below. His only surviving opera, *La catena d'Adone* (1626), was one of the first to be performed in Rome and both libretto and score adumbrate many later features of its tradition.

Mazzocchi, Virgilio (*b* Civita Castellana, *bapt.* 22 July 1597; *d* Civita Castellana, 3 Oct. 1646). Italian composer, brother of above, with whom he studied in Rome. Together with Marazzoli composed *Chi soffre, speri* (1637) for performance at the Barberini palace, one of the most characteristic works of the Roman tradition of the 1630s.

Médecin malgré lui, Le (Doctor Despite Himself). Opera in 3 acts by Gounod; text a slight alteration of Molière's comedy (1666) by the composer, Barbier, and Carré. Prem. Paris, L, 15 Jan. 1858.

France, 17th cent. The doctor Sganarelle (bar) is summoned to attend Lucinde (sop), daughter of a wealthy neighbour Géronte (bs). She is, her lover Léandre (ten) explains to the audience, pretending to be dumb in order to avoid having to marry a rich suitor. To help the couple, Sganarelle passes Léandre off as his apothecary; Lucinde is cured. The couple elope, and when news arrives that Léandre had inherited a large fortune, Géronte is happy for the marriage to proceed.

Médée (Medea). Opera in 3 acts by Cherubini; text by F. B. Hoffman, after Corneille's tragedy (1635). Prem. Paris, T Feydeau, 13 Mar. 1797.

Corinth, mythological. After helping Jason (ten) to recover the Golden Fleece, Médée (sop) returned with him to Corinth, and there bore him two sons. Having abandoned her in order to marry Glauce (sop), Jason fears Médée's vengeance; she curses him.

Glauce's father Créon (bar), King of Corinth, orders Médée to leave the city; she feigns acceptance and sends Glauce a wedding gift of a nightgown and magic diadem, which she has covered with poison.

Médée's gifts kill Glauce and the people clamour for her life. She takes refuge in the Temple of Juno and, having killed her sons, sets fire to the temple and burns to death.

Medium, The. Opera in 2 acts by Menotti; text by the composer. Prem. New York, Columbia U, 8 May 1946.

US, today. The Medium, Madame Flora (con), helped by her daughter Monica (sop) and the mute Toby, cheats her clients. During a seance she feels a hand on her throat and confesses to her clients that she is a fraud. They refuse to believe her, but she loses her nerve, beats Toby and throws him out of the house; she then turns to the whisky bottle. Toby, in love with Monica, returns to find her and hides behind a puppet theatre. A noise awakens Madame Flora, and seeing the closed curtain move she shoots at it, killing Toby. 'I've killed the ghost!' she screams.

Mefistofele. Opera in a prologue, 4 acts, and epilogue by Boito; text by the composer. Prem. Milan, S, 5 Mar. 1868; but not a success. Rev. and prem. Bologna 4 Oct. 1875.

Unlike Gounod in his *Faust*, Boito based his opera on both parts of Goethe's work. Prologue: Mefistofele (bs) wagers God that he can win Faust's soul. Faust (ten) is followed by a sinister grey friar who reveals himself to be Mefistofele. He persuades Faust to sell his soul in return for one moment of perfect happiness.

Faust, under the name of Enrico, courts Margherita (sop). Mefistofele later takes him to witness the Witches' Sabbath, where Faust is distressed by an apparition of Margherita in chains.

Margherita, delirious, is in prison after poisoning her mother and murdering the son she had by Faust. Mefistofele offers to free her but she rejects his help. She regains her sanity briefly and dies.

In Greece, Faust admires Helen of Troy who, flattered, offers him her love. The epilogue depicts a disillusioned Faust near death. He dies repenting his bargain; God pities him and frustrates Mefistofele's attempts to claim his soul.

Mehta, Zubin (*b* Bombay, 29 Apr. 1936). Indian conductor. Studied Vienna with Swarowsky. Début Montreal 1964 (*Tosca*). New York, M, 1965–71; London, CG, 1977; also Vienna, Florence. Repertory incl. *Trovatore*, *Aida*, *Otello* (Verdi), *Tosca*, *Turandot*, *Carmen*, first *Mourning becomes Electra*, *Ring* (Chicago 1993), *Fanciulla del West*. (R)

Méhul, Étienne-Nicolas (*b* Givet, 22 June 1763; *d* Paris, 18 Oct. 1817). French composer. Studied Givet with a local organist, Monthermé with Hanser, Paris with Edelmann. His first opera, *Cora* (comp. 1789), was unperformed until after his next and more representative work, *Euphrosine* (1790), an opéra-comique mixing serious and comic elements. It became immediately and enduringly famous for its duet 'Gardez-vous de la jalousie', in which a simple motive of alternating thirds identifies jealousy and its working both here and motivically elsewhere in the opera. The more severe *Stratonice* (1792) also contained a popular number, 'Versez tous vos chagrins'. Set in ancient times, and consciously simple in a Gluckian manner, it shows the care for achieving a vivid and individual setting that was to mark Méhul's operatic work: much of this he achieved by means of carefully devised orchestration. *Le jeune sage et le vieux fou* (1793) was a comedy, with an overture that like many others has had an independent life.

With the establishment of the new political régime, Méhul was appointed to the Institut National de Musique in 1793, and his next opera, *Horatius Coclès* (1794), used a classical theme to make a political point in what Méhul himself drily called his 'style de fer', or 'iron style'. He was more successful with *Mélidore et Phrosine* (1794), in which he takes still further his use of motive, making use of a motto theme associated with the guiding force of love, and also with his other major work of the decade, *Ariodant* (1799). The latter's ambitious structures and knightly setting, as well as the opposition of a 'dark' and a 'light' couple, anticipates Weber's *Euryanthe*, which it also influenced in its remarkable use of dark-hued orchestration as a functional expressive device. In 1795 Méhul was granted a pension by the Comédie-Italienne, and in 1794 he was made a director of the Conservatoire. Possibly at the command of Napoleon, with whom he had many contacts, he wrote *La prise du Pont de Lodi* (1797), celebrating the Austrian defeat of 1796.

From 1800 there followed a series of comedies, beginning with *Bion* (1800) and including *Une folie* (1802) and *Le trésor supposé* (1802), both also popular in Germany, as well as *Héléna* (1803), some of whose features (such as a dramatic trumpet call) influenced *Fidelio*. In the Ossianic *Uthal* (1806), Méhul's care for an individual atmosphere shows in the banishing of violins and trumpets from the orchestra; the most original part is an overture that is virtually non-thematic and includes a mysterious voice calling through the mist. His last major success was *Joseph* (1807), in which many of his gifts, including his melodic grace and his feeling for atmosphere and situation, are powerfully and movingly displayed. It was immediately successful, being as much admired in Germany and other European countries as in France, influencing a number of composers and surviving in repertories into the 20th cent. A few opéras-comiques followed, but Méhul never again gave himself so concentratedly to a dramatic subject. Though trained in the classical school, his Romantic impulses led him to explore the dramatic role of the orchestra, and with it of motive, and thereby to influence (especially through Weber's music and his advocacy) the course of German Romantic opera.

Meier, Waltraud (*b* Würzburg, 9 Jan. 1956). German mezzo-soprano. Studied Cologne with Thiesen and Jacob. Début Würzburg

1976 (Cherubino). Mannheim 1978–80; Dortmund 1980–3; Buenos Aires 1980; Cologne 1983; Bayreuth from 1983; London, CG, from 1985; New York, M, 1988; also Vienna, S; Paris, C; etc. A gifted singer and actress with a sensuous tone, successful as Venus, Brangäne, Fricka, Isolde, Azucena, Eboli, Carmen, Octavian, Sieglinde, Tchaikovsky's Maid of Orleans, and particularly Kundry. (R)

Mei-Figner, Medea. See FIGNER, MEDEA.

Meilhac, Henri (*b* Paris, 21 Feb. 1831; *d* Paris, 6 July 1897). French dramatist and librettist. Most of his librettos were written in collaboration, with Millaud for Hervé's *Mlle Nitouche*, with Gille for Massenet's *Manon* and Planquette's *Rip*; but by far the most important collaboration of his career was with Ludovic *Halévy. Their most famous libretto is certainly *Carmen*, for Bizet; but their more characteristic vein was operetta, especially as shown in Offenbach's *La belle Hélène*, *Barbebleue*, and *La vie parisienne*. Frequently by means of a classical setting, they satirized contemporary society in the guise of mocking an old myth, also parodying some of the conventions of opera. At a time when the Paris Opéra enshrined the pomp of the most elevated manner of Grand Opera, Meilhac and Halévy provided the necessary corrective of laughter at human foibles and the shortcomings of society.

'Mein Herr Marquis'. Adele's (sop) laughing song in Act II of Johann Strauss's *Die Fledermaus*, in which, disguised at Orlofsky's party, she flirts with her employer Eisenstein.

Meistersinger von Nürnberg, Die (The Mastersingers of Nuremberg). Opera in 3 acts by Wagner; text by the composer. Prem. Munich 21 June 1868.

Nuremberg, mid-16th cent. Walther von Stolzing (ten), falling in love with Eva (sop), daughter of the goldsmith Veit Pogner (bs), learns that she is to be betrothed next day to the winner of a singing contest held by the Guild of Mastersingers. The apprentice David (ten) explains the rules to Walther, who seeks to join the Mastersingers. He is invited to sing a trial song; Beckmesser (bs-bar), the town clerk, also in love with Eva, marks it harshly but Hans Sachs (bs-bar), the cobbler, discerns its originality and value.

On Midsummer Eve, Eva makes her way to Sachs's shop to question him about the competition. Despite being half in love with her himself, he resolves to help Eva and Walther, who have met and plan to elope. Beckmesser arrives to serenade Eva; Sachs, who is working on shoes for him, hammers every time he makes a mistake in his song. Sachs prevents Eva and Walther from escaping and takes the latter into his own house as a riot develops over the noise made by Beckmesser, who suffers a beating.

Sachs soliloquizes on the world's follies, as exemplified in the riot, and resolves to mend matters. When Walther relates the dream he had, Sachs writes down the words of two stanzas, sensing that it will be a prize song. The arrival of Eva, who visits on a pretext, inspires Walther to his final stanza. Beckmesser comes to see Sachs, finds the song, and is permitted by Sachs to make use of it. The company departs for the festal meadow. Beckmesser sings Walther's song disastrously, and Walther himself is summoned to show how it should be sung. He wins the prize and Eva's hand. He accepts membership of the Mastersingers after Sachs has reminded him of their purpose of preserving the art of German song.

Melani, Jacopo (*b* Pistoia, 6 July 1623; *d* Pistoia, 18 Aug. 1676). Italian composer. Wrote *c*.10 operas, mostly for Florence; one of the most important composers of comic opera in the 17th cent. The most interesting is *La Tancia* (1657) which contains a famous parody of the incantation scene from Cavalli's *Giasone*: other works include *Il pazzo per forza* (1658) and *Il Girello* (1668), whose performance in Rome in 1668 was responsible for rejuvenating comic opera there in the late 17th cent.

Melba, (Dame) **Nellie** (*b* Richmond, Melbourne, 19 May 1861; *d* Sydney, 23 Feb. 1931). Australian soprano. Studied Paris with Marchesi. Début Brussels, M, 1887 (Gilda). London, CG, 1888–1914 (except 1909, 1912), 1919, 1922–4, 1926; Paris, O, 1888; Milan, S, 1892–4; New York, M, 1893–7, 1898–1901, 1904–5, 1910–11. Also Chicago, Sydney, Melbourne. Retired 1928. At first a high coloratura famous for her Lucia, Gilda, Violetta, etc. she later sang the lyric repertory: Marguerite, Ophélie, Verdi's Desdemona, and her most famous role, Mimì. Also Aida, Elsa, Nedda, and her one failure, Brünnhilde (*Siegfried*). One of the most consummate technicians of her era, she dazzled with her runs, trills, staccato singing, impeccable intonation, and ease of attack. Her voice, with a range of b♭–f‴ and absolute evenness throughout the scale, had a pure, incandescent quality, remaining fresh because never forced. She was an indifferent actress, but possessed a strong, queenly presence. At Covent Garden, the *prima donna assoluta* ruled off-stage as well as on it, deciding the castings of operas and the engaging (or not) of other artists. Her popularity with the public was enormous; in England she was considered an institution.

Melbourne. City in Victoria, Australia. Melbourne was long dependent on touring companies, especially the Lyster 1861–80, with performances normally given in the Princess T. There were various visits by companies under *Melba (born in, and taking her professional name from, the city). The Nat. Theatre OC of Melbourne was founded in 1950, merging with the New South Wales Nat. O of Sydney in 1952. The Sidney Meyer Music Bowl (cap. 2,000, lawn seating for 30,000) opened 1959. The Victoria OC (Victoria State O since 1977) has also been very active in the face of financial and other difficulties. The Melba Memorial Centre opened 1973. The Globe OC was formed in 1979. The State Theatre (cap. 1,984) opened 1985.

Melchior, Lauritz (*b* Copenhagen, 20 Mar. 1890; *d* S Monica, CA, 18 Mar. 1973). Danish, later US, tenor. Studied Copenhagen with Bang. Début as baritone, Zwicki OC, 1912 (Germont). Official début Copenhagen 1913 (Silvio, *Pagliacci*). Retrained as tenor with Herold; second début Copenhagen 1918 (Tannhäuser). Further study Munich with Bahr-Mildenburg. London, CG, 1924 (Siegmund). Then Bayreuth 1924–31; London, CG, 1926–39; New York, M, 1925–7, 1928–50. Also Buenos Aires, Paris, Berlin, etc. Though a limited actor, and not always musically accurate, he was one of the most extraordinary Heldentenors in history, impressive as much for his eloquent singing as for his astonishing vocal endurance. His voice, plangent and dark, yet possessed of ringing top notes, had a moving quality, and his enunciation was exemplary. Famous as Siegmund, Siegfried, Parsifal, Tannhäuser, Lohengrin, and Tristan (which he sang more than 200 times); also sang Verdi's Otello. (R)

Mélisande. Golaud's second wife (sop), lover of Pelléas, in Debussy's *Pelléas et Mélisande*.

Melitone. Fra Melitone (bar), a comic priest, in Verdi's *La forza del destino*.

Melnikov, Ivan (*b* St Petersburg, 4 Mar. 1832; *d* St Petersburg, 8 July 1906). Russian baritone. Studied St Petersburg with Lomakin, Italy with Repetto. Début St Petersburg, M, 1867 (Riccardo, *I Puritani*). Sang there until 1890; producer there 1890–2. Celebrated as Ruslan, the Miller (Dargomyzhsky's *Rusalka*), Susanin (*Life for the Tsar*). Created title-roles of *Boris Godunov* (as which he was much acclaimed), *Prince Igor*, and *The Demon*; Don Juan *(The Stone Guest)*; roles in Rimsky-Korsakov's *May Night* and *Maid of Pskov*, and Tchaikovsky's *The Oprichnik*, *Vakula the Smith*, *The Sorceress*, and *The Queen of Spades*. Also sang Onegin, and Kochubey (*Mazeppa*). Tchaikovsky's favourite baritone, and a friend of Musorgsky; highly praised by Stasov for his dramatic interpretations, and by Modest Tchaikovsky for his declamatory and legato singing.

Melot. One of King Mark's courtiers (bar) in Wagner's *Tristan und Isolde*.

Mendelssohn (-Bartholdy), **Felix** (*b* Hamburg, 3 Feb. 1809; *d* Leipzig, 4 Nov. 1847). German composer. As a boy, Mendelssohn wrote a number of operas, mostly based on French vaudevilles and all in the Liederspiel manner that well suited his light, elegant gift. The first of these that can stand modern revival is *Die beiden Pädagogen* (comp. 1821), a witty satire on the arguments between rival educational methods (Pestalozzi and Basedow) that must have been only too familiar to the young composer. Others of these early works include some delightful and effective numbers, sometimes well matched to dramatic situations, that do not, however, suggest a larger operatic gift. Mendelssohn's most important opera is *Die Hochzeit des Camacho* (1827), a setting of an episode from *Don Quixote*. Despite some charming and amusing numbers, and in the woodland scenes a manner suggesting that the example of Weber had not been lost on him, there is a tendency for the musical forms to dominate the drama rather than the other way about. The work's failure greatly depressed him, but he continued to search for operatic subjects. In his next work, *Die Heimkehr aus der Fremde* (1829), he returned to his earlier Liederspiel manner, making effective use of his mature musical style and not least of his gifts as a Romantic orchestrator. His search for librettos led him to contemplate many subjects, and to embark upon various collaborations; but the fact that these all ran into the sand led his friends to suspect a deeper problem. The surviving fragments of his last operatic project, *Die Loreley*, do not suggest that this was being solved.

Menotti, Gian Carlo (*b* Cadegliano, 7 July 1911). US composer of Italian birth. Having written two operas in childhood, he studied Milan, then Philadelphia with Scalero. His first surviving opera is *Amelia al ballo* (1937), in which his light fertility of invention admirably serves the buffo plot. A more powerful dramatic vein was attempted in *The Old Man and the Thief* (1939); and this was followed by a thriller, *The Medium* (1946), which has often shared a double bill with one of his most successful works, the comedy *The Telephone* (1947). However, *The Consul* in 1950 showed Menotti at his most theatrically powerful and won him a world-wide audience, though it was noticeable that the power and sincerity of the dramatic plea was sharply at odds with the sub-Puccini lyricism of the score. Experience gained in filming *The Medium* stood Menotti in good stead in TV: *Amahl and the Night Visitors* (1951) has often been screened at Christmas. *The Saint of Bleecker Street* (1954) marked a return to blood-and-thunder verismo; but *The Unicorn, the Gorgon and the Manticore* (1956) was a satire on the vagaries of social fashion. In *Maria Golovin* (1958) Menotti tackled the deeper theme of personal imprisonment: his hero is blind and tormented by jealousy. A brilliantly skilled man of the theatre, quick and versatile, he has found it difficult to sustain the invention and theatrical power of his modern dramatic ideas with music that really belongs to a past verismo age.

He was librettist for Barber's *Vanessa*. In 1958 he founded the successful Fest. of Two Worlds in *Spoleto, later (1977) in Charleston, SC, designed to give openings to young musicians. He has also produced opera in Scotland, which became his home.

Mentzner, Susanne (*b* Philadelphia, PA, 21 Jan. 1957). US mezzo-soprano. Studied Juilliard, New York. Début Houston 1981 (Albina in *Donna del lago*). Sang Cherubino at Wash-

ington and Rosina with New York, CO. London, CG, from 1985, as Jane Seymour and Dorabella. Possesses a warm voice and an attractive stage presence, used to good advantage as the Composer and Octavian (New York, M, from 1989), Idamante, Adalgisa. (R)

Méphistophélès. The Devil (bs) in Gounod's *Faust* and in Berlioz's *La damnation de Faust*.

Mercadante, Saverio (*b* Altamura, *bapt.* 17 Sept. 1795; *d* Naples, 17 Dec. 1870). Italian composer. Studied Naples with Furno and Tritto, later Zingarelli. Here he attracted the attention of Rossini, who may have encouraged him to take up opera: *L'apoteosi d'Ercole* was well received in 1819. He followed this with others in quick succession, having his first great success with the seventh, *Elisa e Claudio* (1821), in Milan and abroad. After failing to establish himself in Vienna, he renewed his success with *Caritea, regina di Spagna* (1826) in Venice. A proposed Spanish appointment having fallen through, he wrote *Ezio* (1827) for Turin, returned to Spain for *I due Figaro* (whose production was postponed from 1827 to 1835 on political grounds), then moved to Lisbon and back to Cadiz before settling in Italy in 1831. Here he had a triumph in Turin with *I Normanni a Parigi* (1832). Invited to Paris by Rossini in 1835, he experienced a failure with *I briganti* (1836), despite the presence in the cast of Grisi, Rubini, Tamburini, and Lablache. But his contact with Meyerbeer's *Les Huguenots* gave him decisive encouragement (though not a stylistic model) for his next and most famous work, *Il giuramento*, which triumphed in Milan in 1837. The striking expansion in his style, coupled with the withdrawal from the scene of Rossini and the death of Bellini, led to further successes with *Le due illustri rivali* (1838), *Elena da Feltre* (1839), *Il bravo* (1839), and *La vestale* (1840). Appointed director of the Naples Cons., he continued to compose busily, his later operas including notably *Il reggente* (1843) and *Orazi e Curiazi* (1846).

Having begun in the heyday of Rossini, Mercadante's career extended well into the middle of Verdi's. His earliest operas are 18th cent. in manner, four of them deriving from Metastasio, and only later was he drawn to Cammarano and especially Romani as librettists, exchanging the manner of Rossini for lyrical melodrama and eventually, in *Il giuramento*, for music drama of considerable breadth and originality. Though this, and his succeeding works, are a clear bridge to Verdi, they have a strength of their own; structurally and harmonically they can be fluent and closely geared to the drama, while not losing a grasp of essentially Italian melody, and they impressed no less a judge of new music than Liszt. Verdi, who had been a victim of Mercadante's jealousy but forgave him, was fruitfully influenced (notably by *La vestale* in *Aida*). Though his later operas do not always maintain the ambition or quality of his best work, Mercadante is an important figure in 19th-cent. Italian music drama.

Méric-Lalande, Henriette (*b* Dunkirk, 4 Apr. 1799; *d* Chantilly, 7 Sept. 1867). French soprano. Début Nantes 1814. Then studied Paris with García sen. and Talma; Milan with Bonfichi and Bandeali. Paris, T du Gymnase Dramatique, 1823. Venice, F, 1823–5; Naples, C, 1826; Milan, S, 1827–9, 1833; Paris, I, 1828; London, HM, 1830; Trieste 1838. One of Bellini's preferred singers; created Bianca (*Bianca e Gernando*), Imogene (*Il pirata*), title-role of *Zaira*, and Alaide (*La straniera*); also Palmide (Meyerbeer's *Crociato in Egitto*), and title-roles in Donizetti's *Elvida* (which demonstrated her virtuosity) and *Lucrezia Borgia* (when she demanded an inappropriate final bravura aria that he later cut). A remarkable dramatic soprano d'agilità, and an effective actress, she was successful in Rossini's *Semiramide*, *Donna del lago*, etc. By 1830, however, Chorley thought her appearance in London 'too late'.

Merikanto, Aarre (*b* Helsinki, 29 July 1893; *d* Helsinki, 29 Sept. 1958). Finnish composer and teacher, son of below. Merikanto's reputation as an operatic composer rests on *Juha* (comp. 1920), a setting of a libretto rejected by Sibelius. It was not staged until long after its completion, largely owing to difficulties with the Finnish Nat. O, but is gradually receiving recognition as a seminal work in the country's opera.

Merikanto, Oskar (*b* Helsinki, 5 Aug. 1868; *d* Oitti, 17 Feb. 1924). Finnish composer and organist, father of above. Studied Leipzig and Berlin; Kapellmeister of Finnish O 1911–22. Although known mainly as a composer of salon music, Merikanto was responsible for the first opera to a Finnish text, *The Bothnian Maiden* (comp. 1899). Like his two later operas, this work was composed in a popular, Romantic style, although the libretto is heavily coloured by national folk legend.

Merli, Francesco (*b* Milan, 27 Jan. 1887; *d* Milan, 12 Dec 1976). Italian tenor. Studied Milan with Negrini and Borghi. Début Milan, S, 1916 (Alvaro, *Fernand Cortez*). Sang there until 1942, sharing roles with Pertile. London, 1926–30; New York, M, 1931–2. Retired 1948. Roles included Don José, Calaf, Verdi's Otello, Walther; created roles in works by Respighi and Favara. (R)

Merola, Gaetano (*b* Naples, 4 Jan. 1881; *d* S Francisco, 30 Aug. 1953). Italian conductor and manager. Studied Naples. Assistant cond. New York, M, 1899; Henry Savage and Hammerstein's Manhattan Co. 1906–10. London OH, 1910–11. Toured US with Naples San Carlo Co. Dir. S Francisco Co. 1923–53, raising it to rank second only to New York, M, and bringing many famous artists to the USA for the first time.

Merrie England. Opera in 2 acts by German; text by Basil Hood. Prem. London, Savoy T, 2 Apr. 1902.

England, late 16th cent. The plot turns on the rivalry of the Earl of Essex (bar) and Sir Walter Raleigh (ten) for the favour of Queen Elizabeth I (mez), who discovers that Raleigh's true affections are with Bessie Throckmorton (sop), but whose attempts to have Bessie murdered are frustrated by a plot of Essex's.

Merrill, Robert (*b* Brooklyn, 4 June 1917). US baritone. Studied with his mother, and New York with Margolis. Début Trenton 1944 (Amonasro). New York, M, 1945–76, 1983–4; Milan, S, 1960; London, CG, 1967; also Chicago, S America, Italy. With his generous, Italianate sound, vocally very successful as Germont, Posa, Renato, Carlo (*Forza*), etc. (R)

Merriman, Nan (*b* Pittsburgh, 28 Apr. 1920). US mezzo-soprano. Studied Los Angeles with Bassian and Lotte Lehmann. Début Cincinnati 1942 (La Cieca). Aix from 1953; Milan, S, 1955; Gly. 1956; also Chicago; Vienna; Paris, O. Repertory included a highly acclaimed Dorabella, Laura (*The Stone Guest*), Baba the Turk. Chosen by Toscanini for several broadcasts, including Gluck's *Orfeo* (title-role). (R)

Merritt, Chris (*b* Oklahoma City, 27 Sept. 1952). US tenor. Studied Oklahoma. Début S Fe 1975 (*Fenton*). New York CO 1981; Paris, O,

1983; London, CG, 1985; Milan, S, 1988; New York, M, 1990. Also Vienna, S; Florence; Amsterdam; Naples; S Francisco; etc. Roles include Otello (Rossini), Rodrigo (*Donna del lago*), Arnold, Arturo, Nemorino, Cellini, Aeneas (Berlioz), Robert le diable, Leukippos. Particularly admired in Rossini. (R)

Merry Widow, The. See LUSTIGE WITWE, DIE.

Merry Wives of Windsor, The. See LUSTIGEN WEIBER VON WINDSOR, DIE.

Mesplé, Mady (*b* Toulouse, 7 Mar. 1931). French soprano. Studied Toulouse with Isar-Lasson, Paris with Micheau. Début Liège 1953 (Lakmé). Paris, OC from 1956, and O from 1958; Moscow, B, 1972; New York, M, 1973; also Naples, Aix, Holland Fest., etc. Roles incl. Queen of the Night, Rosina, Lucia, Norina, Philine, Sophie, Zerbinetta. (R)

Messager, André (*b* Montluçon, 30 Dec. 1853; *d* Paris, 24 Feb. 1929). French composer and conductor. Studied Paris with Fauré, Saint-Saëns, and others. Organist at St Sulpice, then began writing operettas and ballets (including *Les deux pigeons*). His first success came with *La béarnaise* (1855), which was popular both in Paris and in London. After several more works in similar vein, he achieved his greatest hit with *La basoche* (1890), which set a new standard at the Opéra-Comique; in London its performance followed that of Sullivan's *Ivanhoe* at the English OH and led to a commission for *Mirette* (1894). During the 1890s he produced a string of operettas which were highly popular in their day, notably *Madame Chrysanthème* (1893), *Les p'tites Michu* (1897), and *Véronique* (1898).

Messager's works soon left the repertoire, but his importance as a conductor was more lasting. Coming under Wagner's influence in the 1880s, he made a name as a Wagner conductor; he was also music director of the Opéra-Comique 1898–1903, during which time he conducted the prem. of *Pelléas et Mélisande* (1902). He was manager of the Grand Opera Syndicate at London, CG, 1901–7; dir. of the Opéra 1907–14; music dir. of the Opéra-Comique again 1919–20. After the First World War, when he toured N and S America, he gave more time again to composition: works of this period include *Monsieur Beaucaire* (1919; prem. with Maggie Teyte) and *La petite functionnaire* (1921). He did much to introduce Wagner into France,

conducting the French prems. of the *Ring, Parsifal*, and *Meistersinger*. He is also famous for his support of Russian music and Mozart; he revived Gluck and Rameau, as well as encouraging his contemporaries and introducing Charpentier's *Louise* and Massenet's *Grisélidis*. At Covent Garden he conducted a wide repertory that included prems. of Saint-Saëns's *Hélène* and Massenet's *Le jongleur de Notre-Dame*. His music is unfailingly elegant and deft, with a theatrical flair and tunefulness that are the product of much musical learning lightly worn.

Messel, Oliver (*b* Cuckfield, 13 Jan. 1904; *d* Barbados, 13 July 1978). English designer. Studied London with Tonks. Began to work for theatre 1926. Designed ballets in London for Sadler's Wells, and for Covent Garden, where he also had a brilliant success with *The Magic Flute*, 1947. Here he also designed *The Queen of Spades* 1950, the prem. of *Gloriana* 1953, *The Golden Cockerel* 1954, *Samson* 1958. Edinburgh Fest. (Gly. Touring O), *Ariadne auf Naxos* 1950. Gly.: *Idomeneo* 1951, *Cenerentola* 1952, *Barbiere, Comte Ory* 1954, *Figaro* 1955, *Entführung, Magic Flute* 1956, *Rosenkavalier* 1959. Also designed post-war proscenium arch for Glyndebourne. New York, M, 1953. His beautiful, colourful sets and costumes, of which those for *The Magic Flute* were outstanding, were sensitively designed to give each opera an atmosphere in which its music could best flourish.

Messiaen, Olivier (*b* Avignon, 10 Dec. 1908; *d* Clichy, 28 Apr. 1992). French composer. Messiaen did not consider writing an opera until commissioned by Rolf Liebermann, and the text and music of *St François d'Assise* (1983) took him seven years. Subtitled 'Franciscan scenes', it is an interior drama tracing the progress of the state of grace in Francis's soul, employing seven principal singers and a large chorus and orchestra; it lasts some five hours, and draws extensively on the birdsong (including the birds of Assisi) which was one of Messiaen's enduring preoccupations, and is here celebrated in some of his richest orchestral writing.

Metastasio (orig. Trapassi), **Pietro** (*b* Rome, 3 Jan. 1698; *d* Vienna, 12 Apr. 1782). Italian librettist and poet. Adopted by a Roman literary dilettante, Gravina, who gave him the name Metastasio and eventually bequeathed him his fortune, he received a rigorous classical education. He moved to Naples and trained for the law, but was soon drawn into theatrical life there: he also studied with Porpora, and provided texts for some of his smaller dramatic works. With his first wholly original libretto, *Didone abbandonata* (set by Domenico Sarro, 1724), Metastasio rose to overnight fame; returning to Rome, he capitalized upon its success by producing a series of works in similar vein. In 1729 he was invited to Vienna, where he succeeded Zeno as Imperial Poet to Charles VI, arriving there the following year. 1730 also saw the first settings of his *Artaserse* libretto, marking a watershed in operatic history. Although all of his work to date had included a certain element of reform, it was *Artaserse* which provided the clearest expression of the new ideals of opera seria, and in Hasse's setting, which followed on shortly from that of Vinci, Metastasio's libretto found its ideal musical match.

During his half-century at Vienna, Metastasio's reputation grew to make him not only the most famous Italian poet of his day, but also the most frequently set librettist of all time. Excluding the texts he provided for oratorios and smaller dramatic pieces, he wrote 27 large-scale opera librettos, among the most famous of which were *Demofoonte*, *La clemenza di Tito*, *Alessandro nell'Indie*, and *Adriano in Siria*. Metastasio's librettos were set by composers throughout Europe, some being used 60 or 70 times, and retained a certain following right into the 19th cent. With plots which eschewed all comedy in favour of a love/duty conflict, opportunity in the arias for stylized emotional display, and elegant verses, they represented an ideal *rapprochement* between Baroque procedure and Enlightenment ideals and were a seminal ingredient of mid-18th-cent. opera seria.

Metropolitan Opera. New York's leading opera-house formerly stood on Broadway between 39th and 40th Streets. It was opened 1883 when some New York business men, unable to get boxes at the Academy of Music, subscribed $800,000; the Metropolitan (cap. 3,045) opened 22 Oct. 1883 with Gounod's *Faust*. Heavy losses under Henry Abbey led to stockholders appointing Leopold *Damrosch as director; dying before the end of his first season, he was succeeded by his son Walter *Damrosch (till 1891). Operas were sung in German, with US prems. of much Wagner. The theatre was rebuilt after a fire in 1892 (cap. 3,849). Abbey returned 1891,

with Maurice *Grau and Edward Schoeffel until 1897, with Grau as manager 1897–1903, Heinrich *Conried 1903–8. Singers included the De Reszkes, Eames, Lilli Lehmann, Nordica, Sembrich, Schumann-Heink, Ternina, Maurel, Plançon, and Van Dyck; then Caruso, Farrar, and Fremstad, with Mahler and Mottl as conductors. Conried enraged Bayreuth by giving the first US *Parsifal* before expiry of copyright, and public opinion in New York with *Salome*.

He was succeeded by *Gatti-Casazza (till 1935), whose shrewd and constructive policies included engaging Toscanini as chief conductor and staging the prems. of *La fanciulla del West*, *Il trittico*, *Königskinder*, *Madame Sans-Gêne*, *Goyescas*, and, the first US opera here, Converse's *Pipe of Desire* (1910), and many US prems. including *Queen of Spades*, *Boris Godunov*, and *Rosenkavalier*. Singers included Destinn, Alda, Tetrazzini, Bori, Hempel, Martinelli, Amato, and Renaud, with conductors including Hertz, Mahler, and Polacco; later virtually all the great singers of the century appeared (including the début of Rosa Ponselle, 1918). Edward *Johnson was manager 1935–50, and encouraged American singers including Warren, Peerce, Tucker, Traubel, Kirsten, Steber, and Harshaw, with guest conductors including Beecham, Walter, Busch, Stiedry, Szell, and Reiner; he also built up a Wagner tradition with the greatest Wagner singers of the day. He was succeeded by Rudolf * Bing, whose régime was conservative but who modernized stage techniques and brought in theatre producers including Alfred Lunt and Tyrone Guthrie, with operetta and a greater emphasis on the Italian repertory. The new Metropolitan (cap. 3,500) opened in the Lincoln Center on 16 Sept. 1966 with the prem. of Barber's *Antony and Cleopatra*. Kubelík became music director 1972, resigning 1974 and being succeeded by James Levine. The repertory has expanded under Levine's direction to include prems. of operas by Glass and Corigliano, the first complete Met. *Ring* for 90 years, and the house prems. of *Lulu*, *Idomeneo*, and *Porgy and Bess*.

Meyer, Kerstin (*b* Stockholm, 3 Apr. 1928). Swedish mezzo-soprano. Studied Stockholm with Sunnegard, New York with Novikova. Début Stockholm 1952 (Azucena). New York, M, and London, CG, from 1960; Gly. 1961; Bayreuth 1962–5; also Salzburg, Edinburgh, etc. Roles included Dorabella, Carmen, Brangäne, Berlioz's Dido, Britten's Lucretia; created Carolina in first original language *Elegy for Young Lovers*, Agave (*The Bassarids*), Mrs Arden (Goehr's *Arden Must Die*). A notable singing actress of great warmth, vitality, and perception. (R)

Meyerbeer, Giacomo (orig. Jakob Meyer Beer) (*b* Vogelsdorf, 5 Sept. 1791; *d* Paris, 2 May 1864). German composer of Jewish descent. Studied Berlin with Lauska, Zelter, and B. A. Weber, Darmstadt with Vogler. During his time with Vogler he wrote his first two operas, *Jephtas Gelübde* (1812) and *Wirth und Gast* (1813): the former, more oratorio than opera, was a failure; and the latter, a comedy, also failed on its first performance and when it was revised for Vienna as *Die beyden Kalifen* in 1814. A Singspiel, *Das Brandenburger Tor*, missed its occasion, the return of the victorious Prussian army in 1814. He was at this stage better known as a piano virtuoso; but still nursing ambitions as an opera composer, he sought the advice of Salieri, who suggested he should go to Italy to study the voice. Here he wrote six Italian operas, with such success that he was even compared with Rossini. This brought him little approval in Germany: his former fellow-student Weber did produce some of his operas, but complained of his Italian 'aberration'. The success of *Il crociato in Egitto* (1824), especially, encouraged him to turn his thoughts to Paris, where the work triumphed in 1825.

Though Meyerbeer travelled widely pursuing his career, this was centred henceforth on Paris, where he was to become the most important composer of French *Grand Opera. He spent some time assimilating French art, history, and literature, and, guided by his most important librettist, Scribe, planning his assault on the Opéra. His first conquest came in 1831 with *Robert le diable*, in which he successfully combined his German soundness of technique, Italianate melodies skilfully written for particular singers, and his shrewd understanding of the implications for a composer of the lavish staging of the Opéra. Even this triumph was overtaken in 1836 with the new commission from the Opéra's influential director Louis *Véron, *Les Huguenots* (1836). Plans were laid for *L'Africaine*, but shelved when the intended prima donna, Marie *Falcon, lost her voice, in favour of *Le*

prophète (1849) for Gilbert *Duprez. In 1842 Meyerbeer was appointed Prussian Generalmusikdirektor in Berlin. For the reopening of the theatre after a fire he wrote *Ein Feldlager in Schlesien* (1844), with Jenny Lind. Controversies with the Intendant, Küstner, eventually led to his dismissal in 1848. He resumed work on *Le prophète*, remodelling it for Pauline *Viardot, and had another triumph with its prem. in 1849. With a new text by Scribe, he revised the music of *Ein Feldlager* for *L'étoile du nord* (1854), successfully performed in 1854 at the Opéra-Comique, following this with another opéra-comique, *Le pardon de Ploërmel*, in 1859. He resumed work on *L'Africaine*, despite Scribe's death in 1851 and his own deteriorating health; the work went into rehearsal, but he died before preparations were complete.

Meyerbeer's contribution to Grand Opera was the most important of any single composer. His models were to a large extent Spontini, Auber, and Rossini's *Guillaume Tell*, though these were not really influences: what inspired him were the opportunities which Auber, Rossini, and others had found in the conventions developed at the Opéra in the 1820s by *Cicéri and *Daguerre and fostered by the astute management of Véron. His individual qualities included the mastery of orchestration which may be attributed in part to his German training and background, but which was extended to match particular dramatic demands. His inventiveness with the orchestra was much admired by Berlioz, and influenced Wagner (who bit the hand that had fed him help in Paris with some unpleasant references, including by implication in the anti-Semitic *Das Judentum in der Musik*). His collaboration with Scribe, who had a shrewd understanding of the Opéra and of the public, continued the tradition of Grand Opera in the use of historical subjects on a vast scale; it also gave him splendid musical opportunities, both for dazzling vocal writing carefully tailored for the greatest singers of the day and for grandiose scenes, or 'tableaux', in which they and massed choruses would conclude an act. He rarely made use of motive: his operas are constructed in a series of carefully planned numbers, and rely on individual and cumulative effect. Wagner described them as 'effects without causes'; and he has been by no means alone in finding in Meyerbeer's works too much calculation so as to achieve public success. That success can still be won by a production matching the works' nature.

Meyerhold, Vsevolod (*b* Pensa, 9 Feb. 1874; *d* Moscow, 2 Feb. 1940). Russian producer. His work in opera began at the St Petersburg M in 1909 with enterprising productions including *Tristan und Isolde* 1909, *Boris Godunov* 1911, *Elektra* 1913, and *The Nightingale* 1917. One of his most famous productions attempted a reconciliation between Pushkin's and Tchaikovsky's *Queen of Spades* (1935). He worked closely with Shostakovich and with Prokofiev (whose *Love of the Three Oranges* took an example from Meyerhold's view of the commedia dell'arte). He briefly took over Stanislavsky's company in 1938.

mezzo-contralto. A term first applied to the singer Rosine Stoltz (1815–1903), whose voice was characterized by an especially strong lower register. More a description of timbre than of range.

mezzo-soprano (It.: 'half-soprano'). The middle category of female (or artificial male) voice. Though closer to soprano than to contralto, it is marked more by quality of tone (darker or richer than soprano) than by range, which may include many of the soprano's high or the contralto's low notes. Many roles lying in the upper range, such as Poppea, Dido (Purcell and Berlioz), Cherubino, Charlotte, Eboli, Kundry, and the Kostelnička, are sung by both sopranos and mezzos. Parts written for castratos are now often taken by female mezzos, e.g. Handel's *Serse* and Gluck's *Orfeo*. Some mezzosoprano roles given as such by composers in scores are as follows:

England: Hermia (*Midsummer Night's Dream*), Thea (*Knot Garden*).

France: Cassandre, Dalila, Fidès, Hérodiade, Carmen.

Germany: Ortrud, Octavian, Gräfin Geschwitz (*Lulu*).

Italy: Emilia (Rossini's and Verdi's *Otello*), Teresa (*Sonnambula*), Azucena, Amneris.

Russia: Hostess (*Boris*), Mme Larina and Filipyevna (*Onegin*).

Micaëla. A peasant girl (sop), in love with Don José, in Bizet's *Carmen*.

Michaels-Moore, Anthony (*b* Grays, 8 Apr. 1957). English baritone. Studied Glasgow. Début O North 1987, Messenger in *Oedipus Rex*. London: CG, from 1987; roles with ENO

incl. Marcello, Almaviva (Mozart), Zurga. US début Philadelphia 1988 (Guglielmo). One of the most promising baritones of his generation, he has sung Posa with O North (1993) and Licinius in *La Vestale* at Milan, S (1993). Other roles incl. Don Giovanni (New Israeli O), Gluck's Oreste (Paris, B, 1995), Lescaut (Puccini and Massenet). (R)

Micheau, Janine (*b* Toulouse, 17 Apr. 1914; *d* Paris, 18 Oct. 1976). French soprano. Studied Toulouse, and Paris with Carré. Début Paris, OC, 1933 (La Plieuse, *Louise*). Paris, OC until 1956, and O 1940–56; London, CG, 1937; also Chicago, Buenos Aires, Florence. Roles included Violetta, Juliette, Mélisande, Sophie, Zerbinetta, Anne Trulove; created Milhaud's Creusa (*Medée*), and Manuela (*Bolivar*). (R)

Michele. A Seine bargee (bar), husband of Giorgetta, in Puccini's *Il tabarro*.

'Mi chiamano Mimì'. Mimì's (sop) aria in Act I of Puccini's *La bohème*, in which she describes herself to Rodolfo.

Midsummer Marriage, The. Opera in 3 acts by Tippett; text by the composer. Prem. London, CG, 27 Jan. 1955.

England, the present. Morning. Midsummer Day, the wedding-day of Mark (ten) and Jenifer (sop). Her father King Fisher (bs), a businessman, wishes to prevent the marriage. Before they can discover each other in marriage, each must first discover their true selves, so Jenifer goes in search of the physical reality and Mark in search of the imaginative intuition they each feel they lack.

Afternoon. In an acknowledged analogy with *The Magic Flute*, the couple are matched by an uncomplicated second pair, Jack (ten), a mechanic, and Bella (sop), secretary to King Fisher. They affirm their love. A series of ritual dances takes place.

Evening and Night. Madame Sosostris (con), a clairvoyante, arrives; King Fisher wishes her to return Jenifer to him. However, she sees a vision of Mark and Jenifer loving one another. When King Fisher unveils Sosostris, since Jack has refused to do so, he discovers Mark and Jenifer hidden inside a huge flower-bud. He attempts to prevent their union, but dies. During a ritual fire dance the couple are transfigured and appear, reborn, ready to celebrate their wedding.

Midsummer Night's Dream, A. Opera in

3 acts by Britten; text by the composer and Peter Pears, after Shakespeare's comedy (c.1593–4). Prem. Aldeburgh 11 June 1960.

The plot follows Shakespeare closely, with the characters separated musically into three groups: the fairies Oberon (counter-ten), Tytania (sop), and Puck (spoken acrobat); the lovers Lysander (ten) and Demetrius (bar), initially both in love with Hermia (mez), who is in love with Lysander, and Helena (sop), who is in love with Demetrius; and the rustics, Bottom (bs-bar), Quince (bs), Flute (ten), Snug (bs), Snout (ten), and Starveling (bar). The high sound of the fairies' voices (often associated by Britten with the exceptional or strange) is reinforced by the chorus of fairies, led by Cobweb, Peaseblossom, Mustardseed, and Moth (trebles). The playlet of *Pyramus and Thisbe* in Act III parodies various devices of Romantic opera.

Migenes, Julia (b New York, 13 Mar. 1945). US soprano. Early career on Broadway. Studied Cologne with Ultman. Début New York, CO, 1965 (Musetta). Vienna, V, 1973–8; S Francisco 1978; New York, M, from 1979; London, CG, 1987. Also Los Angeles; Houston; Geneva; Vienna, S; Berlin. Repertory incl. Blonde, Susanna, *Hoffmann* roles, Carmen, Tosca, Esmerelda (*Notre Dame*), Manon, Eurydice (Offenbach), Nedda, Salome, Lulu. (R)

Mignon. Opera in 3 acts by Thomas; text by Barbier and Carré, after Goethe's novel *Wilhelm Meisters Lehrjahre* (1795–6). Prem. Paris, OC, 17 Nov. 1866.

Germany and Italy, late 18th cent. Lothario (bs), a wandering minstrel, is searching for his long-lost daughter. A band of gypsies arrives; they try to make one of their number, Mignon (mez), dance. When she refuses they start to beat her; she is rescued by Wilhelm Meister, who engages her as his servant and then falls in love with her.

Mignon is saved from a burning castle by Wilhelm who, with Lothario, nurses her back to health.

Lothario, who had lost his memory when Mignon was first kidnapped, now remembers that he is Count Lothario, and recognizes Mignon as his long-lost daughter Sperata.

Mihalovich, Ödön (b Feričance, 13 Sept. 1842; d Budapest, 22 Apr. 1929). Hungarian composer. Studied Pest with Mosonyi, Leipzig with Hauptmann, Munich with Cornelius. Much influenced by Wagner whose cause he promoted in Hungary: he even set a version of Wagner's libretto *Wieland der Schmied* after it had been rejected by Berlioz, among others. Director Budapest Music Academy from 1887, and responsible for engaging Mahler at the Royal Hungarian OH.

Mikéli. The water-carrier (bs) in Cherubini's *Les deux journées*.

Mikhaylov, Maxim (b Koltsovka, 25 Aug. 1893; d Moscow, 30 Mar. 1971). Russian bass. As child, sang in church choir; deacon in Omsk, Kazan, and Moscow. Moscow, B, 1932–56. Roles incl. Pimen, Varlaam, Konchak, Gremin, Miller, and his most famous, Ivan Susanin. (R)

Mikhaylova, Maria (b Kharkov, 3 June 1866; d Molotov (Perm), 18 Jan. 1943). Russian soprano. Studied St Petersburg Cons., Paris with Saint-Yves-Bax, Milan with Ronconi. Début St Petersburg, M, 1892 (Marguerite de Valois, *Huguenots*). Sang there until 1912; Prague 1903; Tokyo 1907; also Moscow, Kiev, etc. Repertory included Zerlina, Juliette, Nannetta, Lakmé, Lyudmila, Tamara (*Demon*), first Electra (Taneyev's *Oresteia*). A prolific recording artist, she achieved international fame though singing mainly in Russia. (R)

Milan (It., Milano). City in Lombardy, Italy. Staged musical works were given in the Salone Margherita of the Palazzo Ducale in the 16th cent. When this burnt down in 1708 it was replaced by the T Regio Ducale, 1717; burnt down 1776. Mozart visited there in the early 1770s and was much fêted. The 96 box-holders appealed directly to the Empress Maria Theresa, who gave permission for the building of *La Scala, opened 3 Aug. 1778 with Salieri's *L'Europa riconosciuta*. Opera has also been given at the T della Cannobiana, the T Carcano, the T Lirico, and the T dal Verme.

The Cannobiana (cap. 2,000) was built at the same time as La Scala on land given by Maria Theresa; opened 1779 with Salieri's *Fiera di Venezia* and *Il talismano*. *L'elisir d'amore* was prem.d here 1832. Demolished 1894, replaced by T Lirico. Reopened 1894 with Samara's *Le martire*. Caruso made his Milan début here in the prem. of Cilea's *L'arlesiana*, 1897, and the theatre saw other important prems. by Cilea, Giordano, and Leoncavallo, and Italian prems. of works by Massenet and Berlioz (*La prise de Troie*). The T Lirico was demolished 1938, rebuilt 1939.

The T Carcano opened Sept. 1803 with Fed-
erici's *Zaira*. Scene of the prems. of *Anna
Bolena* (1830) and *Sonnambula* (1831). The T dal
Verme opened 1872, replacing the Politeama
Ciniselli (1864), with *Les Huguenots*. Primarily
the home of drama, but saw the prems. of
Puccini's *Le villi* (1884), Leoncavallo's *Pagliacci*
(1892), and Zandonai's *Conchita* (1911).

Milanov, Zinka (*b* Zagreb, 17 May 1906; *d*
New York, 30 May 1989). Croatian soprano.
Studied Zagreb with Ternina, Prague with
Carpi. Début Ljubljana 1927 (Leonora,
Trovatore). Zagreb 1928–35; Prague, German
T, 1936; New York, M, 1937–41, 1942–7, 1950–
66; Buenos Aires, C, 1940–2; London, CG,
1956–7. Repertory included Donna Anna,
Norma, Tosca; excelled in Verdi, e.g. as
Leonora (*Forza* and *Trovatore*), Amelia, and
Aida, and as Gioconda and Santuzza. Her
voice possessed beauty of tone, power, and
an unforgettable pianissimo. (R)

Milde, Hans Feodor von (*b* Petronell, 13
Apr. 1821; *d* Weimar, 10 Dec. 1899). German
baritone. Studied Vienna with Hauser, Paris
with García jun. Sang as guest, Weimar 1845;
remained there for the rest of his career,
staying because of Liszt. Retired 1884. Sang
Flying Dutchman, Sachs, Kurwenal; created
Telramund, and the Caliph (*Barber of Bagdad*).
He married in 1851 the soprano **Rosa Agthe**
(*b* Weimar, 25 May 1825; *d* Weimar, 25 Jan.
1906). Studied Weimar with Götze. Début
Weimar 1845; sang there until 1867. Roles
included Pamina, Lucia, Leonore, first Elsa,
and first Margiana (*Barber of Bagdad*).
Adelheid von Schorn praised husband and
wife for their 'magnificent voices', 'wonderful artistry', and 'inspired acting'. Liszt
held them both in high esteem as artists
and friends, and wrote many of his songs for
them.

Mildenburg, Anna von. See BAHR-MILD-
ENBURG, ANNA.

Milder-Hauptmann, Pauline Anna (*b*
Constantinople, 13 Dec. 1785; *d* Berlin, 29
May 1838). Austrian soprano. Studied Vienna
with Tomaselli and Salieri (on Schikaneder's
advice). Début Vienna 1803 (Juno, Süssmayr's
Der Spiegel von Arkadien). Created Leonore in
1805 and in the two subsequent versions
(persuading Beethoven to change 'unbeauti-
ful, unsingable' passages in Leonore's aria
for 1814). Though at first not dramatically
impressive, she later achieved many tri-

umphs in the role. Berlin 1812, 1816–29.
Further engagements in Vienna; retired
1836. One of the first of the German dramatic
sopranos who propagated and influenced
the ideas of Romanticism in the theatre, she
also created leading roles in Cherubini's
Faniska and operas by Spontini. Her nobility
and emotional intensity were greatly
admired in her Alceste, Armide, and
especially Iphigénie (both *Aulide* and *Tauride*),
as which she was praised by Goethe in verse.
Her powerful voice ('like a house', as Haydn
put it) was pure and expressive, and inspired
Schubert's 'Shepherd on the Rock', and
'Suleika II'. Beethoven had hoped to write
another opera for her.

Mildmay, Audrey (*b* Herstmonceux, 19 Dec.
1900; *d* London, 31 May 1953). English
soprano. Studied London with Johnstone-
Douglas, Vienna with Strasser. London, CR,
1928–31. Married John *Christie, with
whom she founded Gly. Fest. Sang there at
its opening, 1934, then 1935–6, 1938–9.
London, SW, 1939; Gly. 1940; Montreal 1943,
then retired. Roles included Polly Peachum
(*Beggar's Opera*), Zerlina, Susanna, Norina.
Founded Edinburgh Fest. 1947 with Rudolf
Bing. Vivacious and witty on stage, and an
inspiration behind the scenes. (R)

Milhaud, Darius (*b* Aix-en-Provence, 4 Sept.
1892; *d* Geneva, 22 June 1974). French composer. Studied Aix-en-Provence, and at the
Paris Cons. with Dukas, Gédalge, Leroux,
Widor, and D'Indy. His studies interrupted
by the First World War, he left the Cons.;
made a formative visit to Brazil 1917–18.
Returning to Paris, he became part of the
avant-garde group known as 'Les Six'; like his
colleagues, he drew inspiration from a wide
range of musical traditions, including jazz
and folk music, particularly that of Latin
America.

For his first mature work he turned to the
well-worn Orpheus theme, although *Les
malheurs d'Orphée* (1926) treats the subject in
the ironic fashion which was to characterize
much of his later music: like the satirical
work which followed it, *Le pauvre matelot*
(1927), it uses slender resources to maximum
effect. Yet more concentrated expression is
found in the three opéras-minutes, *L'en-
lèvement d'Europe* (1927), *L'abandon d'Ariane*
(1928), and *La délivrance de Thésée* (1928),
where the action is compressed into the
space of 10–15 minutes. The ability to work

on a larger canvas was demonstrated in the next work, *Christophe Colomb* (1930), for which an impressive army of ten principal and 35 secondary soloists was marshalled with great skill; among other technical devices the opera calls for the use of cinema. In the works which followed, such as *Bolivar* (1950) and *David* (1954), Milhaud returns to many of the same dramatic and musical techniques, while his three children's operas demonstrate a certain concern with *Gebrauchsmusik*. One of his last works is a setting of the little-known third play of Beaumarchais's Figaro trilogy, *La mère coupable* (1965).

Miller, Jonathan (*b* London, 21 July 1934). English producer. First operatic production *Noyes Fludde*, London, Round House, then SW, New OC; Goehr's *Arden Must Die* 1974. Kent O 1974–82, in a series of enterprising productions working closely with Roger *Norrington, notably *Falstaff* and *Eugene Onegin*. At London, C, his inventive stagings included a clever siting of *Rigoletto* in Mafia territory, *Tosca*, *The Mikado*, *Rosenkavalier*. New York, M, 1991 (*Káťa Kabanová*); London, CG, 1995 (*Così fan tutte*).

Millo, Aprile (*b* New York, 14 Apr. 1958). US soprano. Studied Juilliard School, New York. Début Salt Lake City 1982. Milan, S, 1982 and WNO 1984, both as Elvira (*Ernani*). New York, M, 1984 (début as Amelia (*Simon Boccanegra*)). Has made a mark especially as a Verdi singer: roles incl. Amelia (*Ballo*), Aida, Elvira (*Ernani*), Luisa Miller, Leonora (*Trovatore*), Elisabetta. (R)

Millöcker, Karl (*b* Vienna, 29 Apr. 1842; *d* Baden, nr. Vienna, 31 Dec. 1899). Austrian composer. Studied Vienna; became conductor at the Thalia T, Graz 1864, on Suppé's recommendation, where he composed his first operettas. Returned to Vienna 1866; was briefly conductor at the Vienna W, then the Harmonie T. Conductor of the Deutsches T in Budapest 1868–9, before returning once again to Vienna, W. A succession of operettas, including *Abenteuer in Wien* (1873) and *Apajaune der Wassermann* (1880), brought him to public attention and in 1882 he had his greatest triumph with *Der Bettelstudent*. Taken up throughout Europe and the US, such was its success that he was able to retire from conducting. None of his subsequent works was as popular or highly regarded, although *Der arme Jonathan* (1890) had some following.

Together with Johann Strauss II and Suppé, Millöcker was one of the founding fathers of Viennese operetta, skilfully blending the style of Offenbach with the local tradition of light dramatic music. An immensely skilled craftsman, he possessed a surer theatrical instinct than most of his contemporaries, though his scores generally lack their characteristic Viennese verve and charm. Only *Der Bettelstudent* has survived the test of time; it is still popular in the German and Austrian operetta repertory today.

Milnes, Sherrill (*b* Downers Grove, IL, 10 Jan. 1935). US baritone. Studied Tanglewood with Goldovsky. Début Boston OC 1960 (Masetto). Milan, N, 1964; New York, M, from 1965; London, CG, from 1971; also Chicago, Buenos Aires, Vienna, etc. Roles include Don Giovanni, Figaro (Rossini), Escamillo, Jochanaan, Scarpia, Falstaff, Jack Rance, Hamlet. His warm, incisive tone and excellent legato line particularly suit Verdi roles, e.g. Rigoletto, Di Luna, Posa, Macbeth, Germont. (R)

Mime. A Nibelung (ten), brother of Alberich, in Wagner's *Siegfried*.

Mimì. A seamstress (sop), lover of Rodolfo, in Puccini's and Leoncavallo's *La bohème*.

Minkowski, Marc (*b* Paris, 4 Oct. 1962). French conductor. Studied Hague Cons. Formed Les Musiciens du Louvre 1984, playing a major part in the recent revival of Baroque opera: *Dido and Aeneas* and Handel's *Teseo* in Paris; Lully's *Phaeton* at Lyons O; Monteverdi's *Orfeo* in Valencia. English Bach Fest. at London, CG (*Riccardo Primo* and *Iphigénie en Tauride*). Other repertory incl. Mondonville's *Titon et L'Aurore* and *Alcyone* by Marais (both in first modern performances). (R)

Minnie. The so-called 'Girl of the Golden West' (sop) and the owner of the Polka Saloon, lover of Dick Johnson, in Puccini's *La fanciulla del West*.

Minton, Yvonne (*b* Sydney, 4 Dec. 1938). Australian mezzo-soprano. Studied Sydney with Walker, London with Cummings and Cross. Début London, City Literary Institute, 1964 (Lucretia). London, CG, from 1965; Milan, S, and Chicago 1970; New York, M, 1973; Paris, O, 1976; Australian O 1972–3; Bayreuth 1974–7. Created Thea (*The Knot Garden*). Repertory includes Sesto, Cherubino, Dorabella, Marina, Dalila, Brangäne, Fricka, Orfeo, and, with her handsome stage presence and smooth tone, a highly acclaimed Octavian. (R)

Miolan-Carvalho, Marie (*b* Marseilles, 31 Dec. 1827; *d* Château-Puys, 10 July 1895). French soprano. Studied with her father F. Félix-Miolan, then Paris with Duprez. Toured France with him 1848–9. Début Brest 1849 (Isabella, *Robert le diable*). Paris: OC, 1849–55, 1868–85 (when she retired); L, 1856–67; O, 1868–79. London, CG, 1856, 1859–64, 1871–2; also Berlin, St Petersburg. Married the impresario Léon *Carvalho. One of the most celebrated singers of the time, with an attractive voice covering nearly three octaves, she created Marguerite, Baucis, Juliette, and Mireille for Gounod, and roles in operas by Halévy, Thomas, Massé, etc. Though a dazzling virtuoso, she could also rise to the demands of Mozart, e.g. as Pamina, Zerlina, Countess, Cherubino. Halévy wrote of her: 'No words can express such talent, such charm, such artistry!'

'Mira, o Norma'. The duet in Act II of Bellini's *Norma*, in which Adalgisa (sop) pleads with Norma (sop) not to give up her children.

Mireille. Opera in 5 acts by Gounod; text by Carré, after Mistral's poem *Mireio* (1859). Prem. Paris, L, 19 Mar. 1864.

Arles, 19th cent. The opera tells of the love of Mireille (sop) for Vincent (ten); this is opposed by Mireille's father Ramon (bs), and complicated by a rival for Mireille's affections in the bull-tender Ourrias (bar). The original 5-act version ended tragically with Mireille's death. The 1889 revised version ends with Vincent and Mireille happily united.

'Mir ist so wunderbar'. The canon quartet in Act I of Beethoven's *Fidelio*, in which Leonore (sop), Marzelline (sop), Jacquino (ten), and Rocco (bs) express outwardly similar emotions of wonder for inwardly different reasons.

'Miserere'. Properly the opening word ('Have mercy') of Psalm 51 (50 in the Vulgate). In opera, generally referring to the scene in Act IV of Verdi's *Il trovatore* in which a chorus of monks prays for the soul soon to depart as Leonora (sop) wanders beneath the tower in which her doomed lover Manrico (ten) is held.

Mistress Quickly. See QUICKLY, MISTRESS.

'Mi tradì'. Donna Elvira's (sop) aria in Act II of Mozart's *Don Giovanni*, in which she expresses her conflicting emotions of vengeance and pity towards Giovanni. Composed for Katharina Cavalieri in answer to her protest that she had too little to sing for the Viennese prem. of the opera.

Mitridate, re di Ponto. Opera in 3 acts by Mozart; text by V. Cigna-Santi, after G. Parini's translation of Racine's *Mithridate* (1673). Prem. Milan, RD, 26 Dec. 1770.

The Crimea, *c*.135 BC. Sifare (sop cas) and his half-brother Farnace (con cas), both love Aspasia (sop), betrothed to their father Mitridate (ten). News arrives that reports of Mitridate's death were false and that his fleet is approaching. Mitridate returns, defeated, with Ismene (sop), a princess betrothed to Farnace. He is suspicious of his sons' feelings for Aspasia.

Farnace tells Ismene he no longer loves her. Mitridate questions Aspasia and is convinced that Farnace has designs both on his throne and on his wife. Alone, Aspasia confesses to Sifare that she loves him and he is torn between love for her and loyalty to his father. Mitridate imprisons Farnace for conspiring with the Romans. When he learns of Sifare and Aspasia's love, he curses them and imprisons them.

Ismene pleads in vain for Mitridate to be merciful, while Aspasia prepares to take poison. She is prevented by Sifare, who has been released by Ismene, and who now joins his father in a new fight against the Romans. A Roman helps Farnace to escape, but he repents of his treachery and joins his father's army. Mitridate is wounded but, before he dies, is reconciled with his sons. Begging Aspasia's forgiveness, he gives her hand to Sifare, and Farnace is united with Ismene.

Mitropoulos, Dmitri (*b* Athens, 1 Mar. 1896; *d* Milan, 2 Nov. 1960). Greek, later US, conductor and composer. Studied Athens, Brussels, Berlin with Busoni. Répétiteur Berlin, S, 1921–5. Cond. some opera in Athens, but not again until the 1950s, when he gave concert performances of *Wozzeck* and *Elektra* with the New York Philharmonic. New York, M, 1954–60, including prem. of Barber's *Vanessa* (1958). His opera *Sœur Béatrice* was premièred Athens Cons. 1919.

Miura, Tamaki (*b* Tokyo, 22 Feb 1884; *d* Tokyo, 26 May 1946). Japanese soprano. Studied Tokyo with Junker, Germany with

Petzold and Sarcoli. Début Tokyo 1909 (Gluck's Euridice). London OH 1915; Chicago 1918, 1920; Italy, including Rome, C, 1921; 1924 toured US with S Carlo OC; S Francisco 1924. Roles included Butterfly, Iris, Marguerite, Mimì, Santuzza. Created title-role of Aldo Franchetti's *Namiko-San* (written for her), Chicago Civic O 1925. The first Japanese-born singer to make an international career. (R)

Mlada. Opera-ballet in 4 acts by Rimsky-Korsakov; text by the composer, based on a text by Viktor Krylov for an earlier opera to be written with Borodin, Cui, and Musorgsky. Prem. St Petersburg, M, 1 Nov. 1892.

Slav lands, 9th–10th cent. Voyslava (sop) poisons Mlada (silent dance role) in order to replace her in Yaromir's (ten) affections. Morena, Queen of the Underworld (mez), causes Yaromir to fall in love with Voyslava, but the ghost of Mlada intervenes; she tells Yaromir what happened. A priest advises Yaromir to question spirits sent by Morena to taunt him; they confirm that Voyslava was the murderess. When Voyslava is condemned to death, Morena raises a furious storm in which Yaromir dies, thus uniting him forever with his beloved Mlada.

Mödl, Martha (*b* Nuremberg, 22 Mar. 1912). German mezzo-soprano, later soprano. Studied Nuremberg Cons. Milan with Mueller. Début Remscheid 1943 (Hänsel). Düsseldorf 1945–9 as mezzo-soprano. Hamburg from 1949; London, CG, from 1950; Berlin 1950–1 (by now singing soprano roles); Bayreuth 1951–67; Vienna from 1952; New York, M, 1957–60. Also Paris, O; Milan, S; Berlin; Salzburg; etc. Created Mumie in Reimann's *Gespenstersonate* 1985 and was still singing 1990 (Countess in *The Queen of Spades*). Sang Carmen, Eboli, Marie, Octavian; also an outstanding Kundry, Isolde, Sieglinde, Gutrune, Brünnhilde, particularly in association with Bayreuth. An intensely dramatic performer, she used her warm, vibrant voice with artistry and intelligence. (R)

Moïse. See MOSÈ IN EGITTO.

Molinara, La, ossia L'amor contrastato (The Maid of the Mill, or Lovers' Rivalry). Opera in 3 acts by Paisiello; text by Giovanni Palomba. Prem. Naples, T dei Fiorentini, autumn 1788.

The lawyer Pistofolo (bs), the jilted Caloandro (ten), and the elderly Governor Ros-polone (bs) all write letters proposing marriage to Rachelina (sop), a beautiful mill-owner. In order to avoid being pursued by the Governor, Pistofolo dresses as a miller and Caloandro as a gardener. When Rachelina chooses Pistofolo, Caloandro, in a rage of disappointment, tries to kill him. The Governor then implies that Pistofolo is also mad so, rather than be the wife of a lunatic, Rachelina decides not to marry at all.

Molinari Pradelli, Francesco (*b* Bologna, 4 July 1911). Italian conductor. Studied Bologna, Rome with Molinari. Cond. Bologna 1939, Bergamo, Brescia. Milan, S, 1946. London, CG, 1955, 1960. Vienna, S, from 1959. S Francisco 1957–66; New York, M, 1966–73. Vienna since 1959. (R)

Moll, Kurt (*b* Buir, 11 Apr. 1938). German bass. Studied Cologne, and Krefeld with E. Müller. Début Aachen 1961 (Lodovico, Verdi's *Otello*). Aachen until 1965. Bayreuth from 1968; Milan, S, and Paris, O, from 1972; New York, M, from 1976; London, CG, from 1977; Vienna, Berlin, Buenos Aires, etc. Firm in tone and line; a successful Hunding, Fafner, King Mark, Pogner, Gurnemanz, also Osmin, Caspar. (R)

Mona Lisa. Opera in 2 acts by Schillings; text by Beatrice Dovsky. Prem. Stuttgart 26 Sept. 1915.

Florence, late 15th cent. A Carthusian monk (ten) relates to a young honeymoon couple in Florence the story of Mona Lisa (sop). Her jealous husband Francesco del Giocondo (bar) shuts her lover Giovanni de Salviati (ten) in a cupboard, where he suffocates. In turn, Mona Lisa shuts Francesco in the cupboard. The opera's three characters are revealed to be the modern counterparts of the people in the story.

'Mon cœur s'ouvre à ta voix'. The duet in Act II of Saint-Saëns's *Samson et Dalila*, in which Dalila (mez) almost overcomes the resolve of Samson (ten) not to part with the secret of his strength.

Mond, Der (The Moon). Opera in 3 acts by Orff; text by the composer, after Grimm. Prem. Munich 5 Feb. 1939.

Fairyland. The narrator (ten) tells the story of four boys (ten, 2 bars, bs) who steal the moon, each taking a quarter to their graves. The world grows dark and the four stick the pieces of the moon together and hang it up as a lamp. This wakes up all the dead, who create such a tumult that it is heard in heaven; St Peter descends to the underworld, takes the moon away, and hangs it up on a star.

Mondo della luna, Il (The World on the Moon). Opera in 3 acts by Haydn; text by Goldoni, adapted by P. F. Pastor. Prem. Eszterháza 3 Aug. 1777.

Venice, 1750. Bonafede has two daughters, Clarice (sop) who loves Ecclitico (ten) and Flaminia (sop) who loves Ernesto (sop); he opposes their marriage, also that of Ernesto's servant Cecco (ten) to Lisetta (mez). When Ecclitico tells Bonafede that he has received an invitation to visit the moon, Bonafede begs to go with him. Ecclitico and his friend Ernesto transform a garden into a lunar landscape and, waking from a sleeping potion, Bonafede believes himself to be on the moon. The others join in the charade, and marry their true loves 'on the moon'. Bonafede discovers the trick and is furious, but is eventually reconciled to the three marriages.

Mondonville, Jean-Joseph Cassanéa de (b Narbonne, bapt. 25 Dec. 1711; d Belleville, 8 Oct. 1772). French violinist and composer. Active as a court musician, his first opera, Isbé (1742), was a failure, though Bacchus d'Erigone (1747) fared better. During the *Guerre des Bouffons he was chosen to represent the French tradition; the production of Titon et l'Aurore (1753) is said to have hastened the departure of the Italian troupe from Paris. His later operas included a popular work in Languedoc dialect, Daphnis et Alcimadure (1754), and a controversial resetting of a libretto made famous by Lully, Thésée (1765). Mondonville's rise to fame was aided by his court connections—he was a protégé of Mme de Pompadour—but at his best he was a worthy, if less skilful, imitator of the dramatic techniques of Lully and Rameau, with a gift for writing graceful and pleasing melodies.

Mongini, Pietro (b Rome, 29 Oct. 1828; d Milan, 27 Apr. 1874). Italian tenor. Began career as bass (Ascoli Piceno 1851) but was singing tenor by 1853 (Genoa). Paris, I, 1855; Milan, S, 1858, 1868–9; St Petersburg 1857–8, 1861–2, 1870–1; London: HM, 1858–67, DL and CG, 1868–73; Cairo, 1871, 1873–4. Created Radamès, and was a notable Alvaro, Don Carlos, Manrico; also Don Ottavio, Otello (Rossini), Arnold (Guillaume Tell). An ex-dragoon who cut an exciting figure on stage (and once nearly cut off Charles Santley's finger in Forza), he possessed a voice both powerful and flexible, if one not used with great subtlety.

Moniuszko, Stanisław (b Ubiel, 5 May 1819; d Warsaw, 4 June 1872). Polish composer. Studied Warsaw with Freyer, Minsk with Stefanowicz, Berlin with Rungenhagen. His first important opera, after some early operettas, was his best-known, Halka (comp. 1846–7). On its delayed production in Warsaw, this was hailed as the first significant Polish national opera, and won international acclaim. Standing half-way between the old tradition of separate numbers and the new music drama, Halka makes use of an idiom that is recognizably Polish (without drawing on folk music). It was considerably influenced by Auber, whose music Moniuszko admired and conducted often during his period at the Teatr Wielki (from 1859). His other most successful opera was The Haunted Manor (1865), a less even work that suffers from an awkward plot but that contains some excellent music: its setting and its powerful atmosphere, no less than its use of Polish dance rhythms, fostered nationalist loyalties to such an extent that it was banned from the Teatr Wielki by the Tsar.

Monnaie, Théâtre royale de la. See BRUSSELS.

Monna Vanna. Opera in 4 acts by Février; text by Maeterlinck. Prem. Paris, O, 10 Jan. 1909.

Pisa, late 15th cent. Monna Vanna (sop), a childhood friend of Prinzivalle (ten), commander of the Florentine army, succeeds in getting him to lift the siege of Pisa. However, her husband Guido (bar), the Pisan commander, refuses to believe that she has achieved this innocently. When Prinzivalle is imprisoned, Monna Vanna sides with him, declaring her love for him, and the couple escape.

monody (from the It. stile monodico). See STILE RAPPRESENTATIVO.

Monostatos. A Moor (ten) in the service of Sarastro in Mozart's Die Zauberflöte.

Monpou, Hippolyte (b Paris, 12 Jan. 1804; d Orléans, 10 Aug. 1841). French composer and organist. Spent his early years as assistant at the Institution de Musique Religieuse, composing only sacred music. When this closed he turned to writing operas in order to support his family, quickly producing a series of comic works, including *Les deux reines* (1835), *Le luthier de Vienne* (1836), *Le Piquillo* (1837), and *Le planteur* (1839). Though popular in its day, his music soon passed out of fashion.

Monsigny, Pierre-Alexandre (*b* Fauquembergues, 17 Oct. 1729; *d* Paris, 14 Jan. 1817). French composer. After working in Paris as a clerk and in a private theatre, studied with Gianotti and began composing operas. Encouraged by the success of the first, *Les aveux indiscrets* (1759), he began collaborating with Sedaine on *On ne s'avise jamais de tout* (One Never Thinks of Everything, 1761). Anxious to give more substance to opéra-comique as it was practised by Philidor and Duni, he wrote *Le roy et le fermier* (1762), which not only gave scope to his melodic charm and sensitive response to situations, but concerned itself with political and social issues and made use of more elaborate musical techniques. The popular *Rose et Colas* (1764) was a simple pastoral comedy; but with *Le déserteur* (1769), his most famous and widely successful work, he used a dramatic subject to move away finally from the *comédie mêlée d'ariettes to what he described as opéra-comique larmoyant (or sentimental comedy). He strengthened his style still further in *La belle Arsène* (1773), and again in *Félix* (1777), his last opera. Impoverished by the removal of his aristocratic patrons in the Revolution, he withdrew from composition but survived on some pensions and lived to see his works recover their popularity. He had contributed to opéra-comique not only an individual melodic vein but a seriousness of purpose, some formal innovations (such as thematic relationships between final choruses and overtures), and an enhanced feeling for orchestration that anticipates Méhul.

Montague, Diana (*b* Winchester, 8 Apr. 1953). English mezzo-soprano. Studied Manchester with Cox, Tunbridge Wells with Bruce-Lockhart. Début with Gly. Touring O 1977 (Zerlina). London, CG, from 1978; Bayreuth from 1983; Chicago 1984; Salzburg 1986; New York, M, and Frankfurt 1987; Gly. 1989; also London, ENO; Scottish O; Edinburgh. Roles incl. Idamante, Cherubino, Dorabella, Sesto, Nicklausse, Orlovsky,

Wellgunde, Mélisande, Iphigénie (en Tauride), Orpheus (Gluck), Janáček's Fox. (R)

Montéclair, Michel Pignolet de (*b* Andelot, *bapt.* 4 Dec. 1667; *d* Aumont, 22 Sept. 1737). French composer. In service of Prince de Vaudémont, with whom he visited Italy; from 1699 in Paris; 1699–1737 double-bass player at the Opéra. His only opera, *Jephté* (1732), was banned at first because of its unprecedented use of a biblical plot. A considerable success, it was revived many times up to 1761 and is reputed to have turned Rameau, whose use of the chorus it adumbrates, towards the tragédie lyrique.

Montemezzi, Italo (*b* Vigasio, 4 Aug. 1875; *d* Vigasio, 15 May 1952). Italian composer. Studied Milan with Saladino and Ferroni. As a composer he stands closer to Boito than to his verismo contemporaries. His works have enjoyed more success abroad than in Italy, though his first opera, *Giovanni Gallurese* (1905), was given 17 times in its first season. His masterpiece is *L'amore dei tre re* (1913), a work which in Italy has been compared to *Pelléas*; however, the true influence is Wagner, and in *La nave* (1918) Richard Strauss. His eclectic late-Romantic style is also shown in his other operas.

Monterone. Count Monterone (bs), the nobleman who curses Rigoletto in Verdi's *Rigoletto*.

Monteux, Pierre (*b* Paris, 4 Apr. 1875; *d* Hancock, ME, 1 July 1964). French, later US, conductor. Studied Paris. Began conducting aged 12; violist Paris, OC, 1890; then gained much experience as concert and ballet cond. (incl. for Dyagilev's Ballets Russes). Paris, O, 1913–14, 1931. New York, M, 1917–19, 1953–6, conducting US prems. of *Golden Cockerel*, *Mârouf*, and between 1953 and 1956 authoritative performances of *Manon*, *Faust* and *Orfeo* (Gluck), *Hoffmann*, and *Samson et Dalila*. (R)

Monteverdi, Claudio (*b* Cremona, 15 May 1567; *d* Venice, 29 Nov. 1643). Italian composer. Though not the first opera, Monteverdi's *La favola d'Orfeo* is the earliest surviving work in the permanent repertory. Written for a private performance before the Accademia degli Invaghiti (Carnival 1607), it was inspired both by the *stile rappresentativo of Peri, Caccini, and other members of the Bardi Camerata, as well as by the more elaborate musical and ballet entertainments of the Gonzaga court at Mantua. Monteverdi's preface, and further instructions throughout the score, make apparently impressive instrumental demands: but the size of the probable venue for the first performance (the Galleria dei Fiumi in the ducal palace) meant that the orchestra must have been small, with performers doubling on several instruments. Despite the clear musical advances made through his handling of monody, and expansion of instrumental and choral material and resources, *Orfeo* is clearly rooted in the spirit of the Renaissance, rather than being a true harbinger of Baroque opera; with an intellectual audience clearly in mind, Monteverdi and Striggio produced a 5-act work whose classical derivation and Neoplatonic ideals are far more evident than any appeal to human emotion, the lifeblood of later opera.

Between *Orfeo* and *Il ritorno d'Ulisse in patria* (1640) Monteverdi was engaged on at least thirteen dramatic projects, yet of his operatic endeavours almost nothing is extant. *Arianna* (1608), written for a Gonzaga wedding, was an appropriately festive piece, quite different from *Orfeo*. Only one fragment survives, the famous 'Lamento d'Arianna', which achieved enormous popularity outside the opera. In 1612 Monteverdi was dismissed from Mantua: in 1613 he became maestro di cappella at St Mark's, Venice, where he was to remain until his death. However, his duties were sufficiently light to allow him to accept commissions from elsewhere; ironically the Mantuan court was to prove one of his best sources of income. Among important works written for Mantua were *Andromeda* (1620), and *La finta pazza Licori* (1627), which was apparently never completed. *Proserpina rapita* (1630) was, however, written to celebrate a wedding between two Venetian aristocratic families.

It was in Venice that Monteverdi achieved the crowning glory of his operatic career with at least two works written for the new public opera-houses; *Arianna* was also revived here. In *Il ritorno d'Ulisse in patria* Monteverdi rose admirably to the new challenge; with its constant twists of plot and frequent use of disguise the pace of the drama never flags and the earlier preoccupation with allegorical figures is here supplanted by a real interest in human emotion. Only the synopsis and scenario for *Le nozze d'Enea con Lavinia* (1641) survive, but they indicate that it too proceeded on much the same lines as *Ulisse* in being fundamentally tragic, yet with a happy ending. *L'incoronazione di Poppea* (1643) is cast on an even grander scale than *Ulisse*, requiring both a larger cast and more-skilled singers. Including such figures as nurses and servants, and provided with a simple, often comical style of music, it makes a direct appeal to the widest audience, while Poppea's conquest of Nero through the power of love and Nero's rejection of his wife Ottavia moved Monteverdi to compose some of his most passionate and lyrical vocal music, in particular the laments. *Poppea* established the standards by which later Venetian opera was to be measured; but though long considered the crowning glory of Monteverdi's career, it is now commonly accepted that at least some of the music was not by him. The most likely collaborators, if not composers of the whole opera, were Sacrati and Ferrari. Though Monteverdi's operatic abilities must be judged by a mere torso of his output, it is clear that he alone of the earliest operatic composers understood the problems of matching musical drama to its audience. That his powers were undiminished even in old age is proved by the hearty reception accorded him in Venice, while the many recent revivals of his operas have shown that his appeal has gone far beyond his own times.

Montreal. City in Quebec, Canada. The first opera to be heard was Dibdin's *The Padlock* in 1786. In the following years there were productions of Shield's *The Poor Soldier* (1787), Duni's *Les deux chasseurs et la laitière* (1789), and the prem. of Joseph Quesnel's *Colas et Colinette* (1790; the first Canadian opera). The T de Société opened in 1825, and saw opera from 1841. Throughout the 19th cent. Montreal was visited by touring companies giving a standard repertory of Italian opera, later also Wagner. The first attempt at a permanent company was the Société d'Opéra Français (1893–6). In 1910 the Montreal OC was formed and many famous singers were engaged, but it was forced to close in 1913. It was succeeded by the Nat. OC of Canada, 1913–14. Operetta then took precedence (Société Canadienne d'Opérette, 1921–33; Variétés Lyriques, 1936–52).

The Montreal Fest. began its summer performances in 1936 and for the following 30 years usually produced an annual opera, including many first Canadian performances. Beecham took part in the 1942 and 1943 festivals, conducting *Figaro, Roméo et Juliette*, and *Tristan*. In 1941 the O Guild of Montreal was formed by Pauline Donalda, and produced an opera a year until her death in 1969. In 1964 the Montreal Symphony Orch. under Zubin Mehta began staging two or three operas each season in its new home, the Salle Wilfrid Pelletier (cap. 2,874) at the Place des Arts. Expo' 67, the 1967 World Fair, brought many major visiting companies to the city, including the Moscow B, London EOG, Hamburg S, Milan S, Royal Stockholm O, and Vienna S. In 1971 the Provincial Government set up L'Opéra de Québec, intended not as a permanent company but to organize operatic activity with government support; it closed in 1975. L'Opéra de Montréal was founded in 1980.

Moody, Fanny (*b* Redruth, 23 Nov. 1866; *d* Dundrum, Co. Dublin, 21 July 1945). English soprano. Studied with Sainton-Dolby. Début Liverpool, with London CR, 1887 (Arline, *The Bohemian Girl*). CR until 1898. With her husband Charles Manners formed the Moody-Manners Co. 1898–1916, also singing as leading soprano. London, CG, 1902–3, and DL, 1904. Repertory included Marguerite, Juliette, Elsa, Senta, Santuzza, Tatyana; created title-role of Pizzi's *Rosalba*, and Militza (McAlpin's *The Cross and the Crescent*).

Moore, Douglas (*b* Cutchogue, NY, 10 Aug. 1893; *d* Greenport, NY, 25 July 1969). US composer. Studied Yale with Parker, Paris with D'Indy and Boulanger. He was one of the few to resist the latter's influence, though his operas reveal fine craftsmanship as well as a manner affected by D'Indy's harmonic style. Of his operas, the most successful have been *The Devil and Daniel Webster* (1939) and *The Ballad of Baby Doe* (1956), both of which have been regular items in US repertories. The latter, based on a true story of Colorado, recalls at times folk melodies and is a strong and effective work.

Moore, Grace (*b* Nough, TN, 5 Dec. 1898; *d* Copenhagen, 26 Jan. 1947). US soprano. Studied New York with Marafioti. Début in operetta. Further study Antibes with Berthélemy. Opera début, Paris, OC, 1928. Paris, OC, 1929, 1938, 1946. New York, M, 1928–32, 1935–46; London, CG, 1935. Glamorous and full of personality, she was extremely popular as Louise, Manon, Mimì,

Tosca, etc. Made several films, e.g. *One Night of Love, New Moon*. Died in an air crash. (R)

Moreira, António Leal (*b* Abrantes, 30 Jun. 1758; *d* Lisbon, 26 Nov. 1819). Portuguese composer. Studied Lisbon; joined the Brotherhood of S Cecilia 1777 and became known as a composer of sacred music. Began to write Italian operas for the Lisbon court 1783, including a resetting of the text Mozart had used for *Ascanio in Alba* (1785). Conductor at the T da Rua dos Condes 1790; at the T San Carlos 1793. Here he wrote the first two of the earliest operas to Portuguese librettos, *A saloià namorada* (1793) and *A vingança da cigana* (1794). A gifted melodist with a sure dramatic touch, Moreira made particularly effective use of the orchestra in his scores.

Morel, Marisa (*b* Turin, 13 Dec. 1914). Italian soprano and producer. Studied Turin. Début Milan, S, 1933 (Zerlina, Auber's *Fra Diavolo*). Further appearances at Milan, S, and elsewhere in Italy; New York, M, 1938–9. Roles included Amor (Gluck's *Orfeo*), Sophie. Formed (and sang with) Marisa Morel OC 1941 for the production of Mozart operas. This performed in Paris and elsewhere in Europe. Its singers included Danco, Simionato, Corena, Rothmüller; conductors included Ansermet, Böhm. (R)

Morena, Berthe (*b* Mannheim, 27 Jan. 1878; *d* Rottach-Egern, 7 Oct. 1952). German soprano. Studied Munich with Röhr-Brajnin and De Sales. Début Munich, N, 1898 (Agathe). Sang there until 1924. New York, M, 1908–12, 1925; London, CG, 1914; retired 1927. A distinguished, intelligent singer of great beauty, she excelled in Wagner, e.g. as Isolde, Brünnhilde, Eva. (R)

'Morgenlich leuchtend'. The opening words of Walther's (ten) Prize Song in Act III of Wagner's *Die Meistersinger von Nürnberg*.

Moriani, Napoleone (*b* Florence, 10 Mar. 1806 or 1808; *d* Florence, 4 Mar. 1878). Italian tenor. Studied with Ruga. Début Pavia, 1833 (Pacini's *Arabi nelle Gallie*). Successes throughout Italy, including Milan, S, 1839–40; Vienna 1842; Prague and Dresden 1843; London, HM, 1844; Paris, I, 1845, 1849–50. His voice deteriorated from 1844; retired 1851. One of the leading singers of his time, dubbed 'il tenore della bella morte', he inflamed audiences with his intensely acted death-scenes. Famous for his Donizetti, e.g.

in *Lucia di Lammermoor, Pia de' Tolomei, Lucrezia Borgia*; created Enrico (*Maria di Rudenz*) and Carlo (*Linda di Chamounix*). Also successful in Bellini and Verdi (who wrote an extra romanza for him in *Attila*, in 1847). Admired by Wagner, Mendelssohn, Fanny Mendelssohn ('He delighted me . . . he sings with such simplicity'), and Chorley, who appreciated his 'richly strong' voice even in its decline. He was very probably the father of his frequent partner *Strepponi's illegitimate children.

Morison, Elsie. See KUBELÍK, RAFAEL.

Morlacchi, Francesco (*b* Perugia, 14 June 1784; *d* Innsbruck, 28 Oct. 1841). Italian composer. Studied Perugia with Mazzetti (his uncle) and Caruso, Naples with Zingarelli, Bologna with Mattei. The success of his first opera, *Il poeta disperato* (1807), and then of *Il ritratto* (1807) and especially *Il corradino* (1808), led to commissions from Rome for *La principessa per ripiego* (1809) and *Le Danaidi* (1810), and also from Milan for *Le avventure di una giornata* (1809).

In 1810 Morlacchi succeeded Josef Schuster as Kapellmeister in Dresden, where he did much to improve standards, setting a fine example as a musician and as a virtuoso conductor and showing a capacity for selecting and training singers into an ensemble. His vanity and deviousness, and a tendency to indolence, were exacerbated by the rivalry with Weber, who arrived at the German opera in 1817. His first opera for Dresden was *Raoul di Créqui* (1811), regarded by some as his masterpiece, and others included *Il nuovo barbiere di Siviglia* (1816): of this, Weber remarked, 'The fellow has little musical knowledge, but he has talent, a flow of ideas, and especially a fund of good comic stuff in him.' The operas' greatest strength is in their handling of voices, especially in comic scenes; latterly Morlacchi showed an increasing response to German influences in his greater enterprise with orchestration, revealing some awareness of the work of Weber (with whom relations had improved). He also wrote a number of further operas for Italy. He was one of the last important Italian composers to work as Kapellmeister in a German theatre, and the closure of the Italian O in Dresden in 1832 was a step towards ending the supremacy of Italian opera in Germany.

Morris, James (*b* Baltimore, 10 Jan. 1947).

US bass-baritone. Studied Baltimore with R. Ponselle, New York with Valentino, Moscona, and with Hotter. Début New York, CO, 1969 (Crespel, *Contes d'Hoffmann*). New York, M, from 1971; Salzburg from 1982; London, CG, from 1988. Possesses a fine legato and a rich, mellifluous tone. Roles include Almaviva (Mozart), Don Giovanni, Philip, Amonasro, Gounod's Méphistophélès, Scarpia, Claggart, Boris, Iago, Flying Dutchman, and a much-acclaimed Wotan. (R)

'Morrò, ma prima in grazia'. Amelia's (sop) aria in Act III of Verdi's *Un ballo in maschera*, in which she accepts that she must die as the penalty for her accused adultery but begs to see her son first.

Mort d'Adam, La (The Death of Adam). Opera in 3 acts by Le Sueur; text by Guillard, combining Klopstock's drama *Der Tod Adams* (1757) with material from the Book of Genesis and Milton's *Paradise Lost* (1667). Prem. Paris, O, 21 Mar. 1809.

Approaching death, Adam (bs) is worried because his sons, including Seth (ten) and Cain (ten), will have to pay for his sins. Cain curses his father, but Adam forgives him. Prayers for Adam drive back Satan, who had come to bear him to hell; Adam rises to heaven.

Mosca, Giuseppe (*b* Naples 1772; *d* Messina, 14 Sept. 1839). Italian composer. Studied Naples with Fenaroli; first opera, *Silvia e Nardone*, performed there 1791. Worked for various Italian theatres; maestro al cembalo at Paris, I, 1803. Returned to Italy 1810; dir. of the T Carolino in Palermo 1817–20; dir. at Messina OH 1827–39. Composed over 40 operas, reminiscent in style of Rossini, including *Il finto Stanislao* (1812). Chiefly remembered for his famous attack on the latter's *La pietra del paragone* (1812), claiming that its use of the *crescendo had been stolen from his *I pretendenti* (1811).

Moscow. Capital of Russia, and of the USSR 1922–91. Though Italian troupes visited Moscow from 1731, the first opera-house in Russia was the Operny Dom (Opera House), opened in 1742 with *La clemenza di Tito*. In 1759 Locatelli opened another Operny Dom, which gave opera alternately with Russian drama. The opening of the Petrovsky T in 1780 by Prince Pyotr Urusov and the English ex-acrobat Michael Maddox was a major step: here most of the early Russian operas were given. When it burnt down in 1805, the independent theatres at which opera was also given absorbed the company.

In 1824 there opened the Maly T (Little T), so-called to distinguish it from the Bolshoy T (Grand T), which was also built by Osip Bove (on a project by A. Mikhaylov) and opened in 1825. The Maly (cap. 560, later 900) was primarily a dramatic theatre, but in the Bolshoy a mixed repertory included works by Verstovsky and Glinka. Reconstructed by Alberto Cavos (son of Caterino) after a fire in 1853, the new theatre opened in 1856 (cap. 2,000) and was reserved for opera and ballet. This was the home of a rising generation of great singers, and saw the prems. of many important Russian operas of the second half of the century. The production style (echoing French taste, as so much in Russian art) favoured an elaborate manner with large crowd scenes, histrionic gestures, and elaborately detailed sets, and this survives as a characteristic of the theatre. Among the most successful designers was Victor Vasnetsov (1848–1926), with his elaborate realistic sets. As all the Imperial Theatres were a Crown monopoly until a decree of Alexander III in 1882, no independent reform movement developed until the end of the century. In 1885 Savva Mamontov (1841–1918) opened his Moskovskaya Chastnaya Russkaya Opera (Moscow Private Russian Opera); when he was bankrupted and imprisoned in 1899, this was reorganized as the Tovarishchestvo Chastnoy Opera (Private Opera Society) under *Ippolitov-Ivanov. Among the singers it attracted was Shalyapin, and the enterprising production style served as a widely admired corrective to the official Bolshoy style. In 1904 this closed and was succeeded by the *Zimin Opera T, which worked (from 1908 at the Solodovnikov T, later Filial T) under Ippolitov-Ivanov and Emil *Cooper, with Pyotr Olenin as director from 1907 and Fyodor Komisarzhevsky from 1915. This arrangement lasted until 1917, when a disastrous fire destroyed the company's property. At the Revolution, the Bolshoy was temporarily directed by the tenor Leonid *Sobinov. The theatre was reorganized, reopening in April 1918 (cap. now 2,155) and also taking over the Filial T. The theatre remained throughout the succeeding years the bastion of Moscow operatic life, preserving, though not without cost to theatrical originality, an essentially 19th-cent. Russian tradition. In the late 1980s pro-

ductions (including by Elena *Obraztsova and the film director Sergey Bondarchuk) began to show more enterprise.

Also in 1919, Konstantin *Stanislavsky began working with the studio, which became the Stanislavsky O Studio in 1924 and was reorganized in 1926 and again, as the Stanislavsky OH, in 1928. The theatre known from 1926 as the Nemirovich-Danchenko Music T was founded in 1919; it specialized at first in opéra-comique and operetta, and later turned to the classics and to new Soviet works. Stanislavsky died in 1938, and the two groups were united in 1941, with *Nemirovich-Danchenko himself directing until his death in 1943. Though neither director had staged anything at the Bolshoy, their influence on the replacement of a fossilized style by vivid acting and staging was vital. The Stanislavsky-Nemirovich-Danchenko T is Moscow's second opera-house, where it still is that the more adventurous productions may be seen. From 1934 the Soviet O Ensemble gave concert performances of operas, including new ones (Prokofiev's *War and Peace*, 1944). Opera is also given, on a panoramic scale, in the vast Kremlin Palace of Congresses, built 1961 (cap. 6,000). The most advanced productions of all, however, are at the Kamerny Muzykalny T, opened in 1972 by Boris Pokrovsky and established in an old cinema in 1974, when Gennady Rozhdestvensky became music director. Early Russian opera and modern chamber works are given, including some pop opera; and works unsuccessful in larger theatres have found new careers (notably Shostakovich's *The Nose*).

See also RUSSIA.

Mosè in Egitto (Moses in Egypt). Opera in 3 acts by Rossini; text by Tottola, after Francesco Ringhieri's tragedy *L'Osiride* (1747). Prem. Naples, C, 5 Mar. 1818.

Near East, biblical times. Pharaon (bs) has decided to free the captive Hebrews, and Moïse (bs) hears a voice predicting that the Jews will at last reach their Promised Land. Pharaon's son Aménophis (ten) wishes to keep them in Egypt since he loves Moïse's niece Anaï (sop). Moïse obscures the sun to demonstrate his powers.

Aménophis's mother Sinaïde (sop) advises him to comply with his father's wishes and marry the King of Assyria's daughter.

Moïse and his people refuse to worship the god Isis; Moïse extinguishes the flame on the altar of the temple. Pharaon banishes the Jews.

The Hebrews, including Asaï, who was captured by Aménophis but has now been returned to her people, escape across the Red Sea, whose waves Moïse miraculously parts. The Egyptian troops in pursuit are drowned.

Moses und Aron. Opera in 2 acts (3rd uncompleted) by Schoenberg; text by the composer, after the Book of Exodus. Prem. Zurich 6 June 1957.

Near East, biblical times. Moses (spoken) receives the word of God but lacks the gift of communication possessed by his less visionary brother Aron (ten). While he is on Mount Sinai receiving the Ten Commandments, Aron encourages the Hebrews to erect a Golden Calf, as a tangible object they, as a simple people, can worship. The subsequent orgy is interrupted by Moses's return from Sinai: appalled, he shatters the tablets of stone and resolves to be released from his mission. The second act ends with him sinking to the ground mourning, 'O word, thou word, that I lack'. The (unset) third act was to show Moses triumphant in the desert.

Moshinsky, Elijah (*b* Shanghai, 8 Jan. 1946). Australian stage director. Studied in Melbourne and Oxford. Produced *Peter Grimes* at London, CG, 1975 and has returned for *Lohengrin*, *Samson et Dalila*, and a series of Verdi operas, incl. *Otello*, *Attila*, *Simon Boccanegra*, *Aida*. His work is characterized by strong musical values and a sense of period style: *Un ballo in maschera* at New York, M (1980), Ligeti's *Le grand macabre* and *Meistersinger* for London ENO.

Mosonyi, Mihály (orig. Michael Brand) (*b* Boldogasszonyfalva, *bapt.* 4 Sept. 1815; *d* Pest, 31 Oct. 1870). Hungarian composer and writer on music. Studied Poszony with Turnyi. During his first period he was entirely Germanic in his musical ideas: *Kaiser Max auf der Martinswand* (comp. 1856–7) was promised performance by Liszt but postponed and eventually abandoned; extensive revisions were planned, but Mosonyi had meanwhile turned his attention to Hungarian music. He Magyarized his name in 1859, but contined to champion Wagner and Liszt while also working by example and precept for Hungarian national music. *Szép Ilonka* (1861) was, in his words, 'written entirely in the Hungarian idiom to the exclusion of all foreign elements'. His last

opera, *Álmos* (comp. 1862), attempted to reconcile the two strains in his style; it is a Romantic opera incorporating Hungarian elements into a Germanic technique.

Mother, The (Cz., *Matka*). Opera in 10 scenes by Alois Hába; text by the composer. Prem. Munich 19 May 1931.

Moravia, early 20th cent. A year after the death of his first wife, the brutal smallholder Křen (ten) decides to take a new wife, Maruša (sop), to help him with his six children. When two years later she has still not had any children of her own, she blames her selfish husband. In successive years she does produce children and is an excellent mother to them all. Even when they flee the nest, she ensures that her marriage to Křen proves happy.

Mother Goose. A brothel-keeper (mez) in Stravinsky's *The Rake's Progress*.

Mother of Us All, The. Opera in 2 acts by Virgil Thomson; text by Gertrude Stein. Prem. New York, Columbia U, 7 May 1947.

The opera tells the story of Susan B. Anthony, US feminist leader and leading suffragette. Other historical characters appear, including Ulysses S. Grant, Andrew Johnson, and Daniel Webster.

motif (sometimes also **motive**) (Fr., *motif*; Ger., *Motiv*; It., *motivo*). A short musical figure of characteristic design, used as a unifying device in a composition, or section of a composition. In opera it has more specific uses, notably in the motto aria, the *reminiscence motive, and the *Leitmotiv.

Mottl, Felix (*b* Unter-Sankt-Veit, 24 Aug. 1856; *d* Munich, 2 July 1911). Austrian conductor and composer. Studied Vienna with Bruckner. One of Wagner's assistants at first Bayreuth Fest., 1876, and subsequently conductor there 1886–1906. One of the most important of the first Bayreuth conductors, with a particular clarity and flexibility. Conductor Karlsruhe 1881–1903, raising standards to great heights; gave the first near-complete performance of *Les Troyens* (on consecutive nights, Dec. 1890), as well as a revised version of Cornelius's *Barber of Bagdad*. London, CG, 1898–1900. New York, M, 1903–4. Munich 1904–11 (dir. from 1907). Collapsed while conducting *Tristan* and died shortly after. Composed three operas, including *Agnes Bernauer* (1880), and edited vocal scores of all Wagner's operas. Married soprano Zdenka Fassbaender (1879–1954).

Mouret, Jean-Joseph (*b* Avignon, 11 Apr. 1682; *d* Charenton, 22 Dec. 1738). French composer. In service of Duchess of Maine 1708–36, for whom he composed one of the earliest pastoral operas, *Le mariage de Ragonde* (1714), and the opéra-ballet *Le triomphe de Thalie*: its epilogue was revived 1722 as *La Provençale*, in which version it includes the first use in opera of Provençal dialect. Paris: dir. of the O 1714–18; dir. of the CI 1717–37, to whose repertoire he contributed. Dir. of the Concert Spirituel 1728–34. Mouret's later work included the tragédie lyrique *Ariane* (1717) and the opéra-ballet *Les amours des dieux*.

Mozart, Wolfgang Amadeus (*b* Salzburg, 27 Jan. 1756; *d* Vienna, 5 Dec. 1791). Austrian composer. Mozart's musical talents manifested themselves at an early age, and much of his childhood was spent making lengthy concert tours around Europe, mostly accompanied by his father, who was employed by the Archbishop of Salzburg. In 1767 he made his first serious attempt at operatic style, contributing the first act of a dramatic Lenten cantata, *Die Schuldigkeit des ersten Gebotes*, which may have been staged. *Apollo et Hyacinthus* (1767), his first true opera, was performed like an *intermezzo, between the acts of a play celebrating the end of the university year in Salzburg. In both works the music is already strikingly theatrical and couched in the grand style of opera seria. But both opera buffa and Singspiel were now claiming the attention of serious composers, and over the coming years he made his first attempts at these genres. *La finta semplice* (1769), a setting of a well-worn opera buffa libretto, demonstrated for the first time his powers of musical characterization, while in *Bastien und Bastienne* (1768) he showed his skill in adopting some of the features of German Singspiel.

While touring Italy in 1770, Mozart was commissioned to write an opera seria for the T Regio Ducale in Milan. Despite difficulties with the singers, *Mitridate, re di Ponto* (1770) was an enormous success and led to a commission for an archducal wedding in Milan in the following year. *Ascanio in Alba* (1771) further demonstrated his careful craftsmanship and understanding of the conventions of opera seria. These features also mark *Lucio Silla* (1772), in which he took his outstanding cast to the limits of its abilities, in music that is highly expressive and emotionally charged.

The other early operas are less significant. *La finta giardiniera* (1775) returns to the world of opera buffa, though the work uncharacteristically treats the darker and irrational side of human experience. However, the opera seria *Il re pastore* (1775) and the serenata *Il sogno di Scipione* (1772) can only be viewed as retrograde steps. The Singspiel *Zaide* (comp. 1779–80) held much promise, but was abandoned when it became clear to Mozart that he would be unable to arrange its performance.

Idomeneo (1781) marks a clear landmark not only in Mozart's operatic output, but also in his whole career. Commissioned by the Elector of Bavaria, it is the first of his operas in which individuality outweighs dependence on pre-existing models or conventions. He was especially fortunate to have the services of one of the best orchestras in Europe, the famous Mannheim band, which had moved to Munich in 1778. Although many arias have a static function, and features of Metastasian opera are retained, Gluck's influence is clearly discernible in the use of chorus, preference for accompanied recitative, and extensive instrumental writing.

Shortly after completing *Idomeneo*, Mozart was dismissed from the Archbishop's service after a series of disagreements and decided to settle in Vienna, living as a freelance teacher and composer. At the request of Gottlieb Stephanie, director of the National-Singspiel (Joseph II's newly-founded German opera company), Mozart was soon engaged on a Singspiel with a popular Turkish theme, *Die Entführung aus dem Serail* (1782). The exotic plot was mirrored in stylized imitations of Turkish music, including the use of quasi-oriental percussion instruments for the overture and choruses. Its success strengthened Mozart's growing reputation, but the demands of his subscription concerts, for which he wrote many of his piano concertos, left him little time for opera. Two opere buffe, *L'oca del Cairo* and *Lo sposo deluso*, were begun, but left incomplete, and it was four years before the next work was staged. This was the 1-act *Der Schauspieldirektor* (1786), a diverting trifle written for the small theatre in the grounds of the imperial summer palace at Schönbrunn, which pokes gentle fun at the world of opera and was first given with Salieri's *Prima la musica e poi le parole*.

Italian, rather than German, opera was now in vogue in Vienna, and it was in an optimistic and carefree mood that Mozart embarked upon *Le nozze di Figaro* (1786). The choice of a text by Vienna's most gifted comic librettist, Lorenzo Da Ponte, was bold, for the Beaumarchais play upon which it was based had been recently banned owing to its inflammatory content. In the hands of Da Ponte and Mozart, the political message and social satire were almost totally excised, however, and replaced instead by a concern for the interrelationships of the sharply contrasting characters, and their eventual reconciliation, in some profound and perceptive music.

The work became a success not only in Vienna, but also in nearby Prague, leading to a commission for the opera-house there in the following year. For his libretto Da Ponte turned to the familiar theme of Don Giovanni and the 'stone guest'; he and the composer again surpassed previous efforts, turning a hackneyed cautionary tale with the shallow characters of a morality play into a great dramatic work. Technically a *dramma giocoso*, *Don Giovanni* (1787) oscillates between moods of high comedy and deep tragedy, in a manner strongly tinged with irony. A revival of *Figaro* in Vienna in 1789 probably led to the commission for Mozart's next work, *Così fan tutte*. Da Ponte was naturally chosen as librettist, although this time he produced a more original work, yet one dealing with the familiar operatic theme of fidelity in love. In outward structure the plot is conventional, with two balanced pairs of lovers, manipulated by two more worldly wise confidants. But Da Ponte and Mozart again penetrate beyond the superficiality of amorous intrigues, with their stereotyped representations of blind passion and revenge, to reveal the essential humanity of their characters.

Die Zauberflöte (1791) comes from a quite different world. Commissioned by Schikaneder for his troupe at the T auf der Wieden, it clearly had its origins in Viennese Singspiel. Although the diversity of its musical expression was without parallel in the contemporary tradition, its plot capitalized upon the vogue for magic plays and operas. Much has been written about the clear, if only partly understood, Masonic subplot, but whether the opera is regarded as mystic ritual or childish pantomime is irrelevant against the enlightened humanism of Mozart's score. It was while engaged on *Die Zauberflöte* that he was commissioned to compose an essentially conventional Metastasian work for Prague to celebrate the coronation of Leopold. Work was thus interrupted for *La clemenza di Tito* (1791), though Mozart's pupil Süssmayr composed all the recitatives, and probably some of the arias as well.

The amalgam of the three main strands of contemporary opera in *Die Zauberflöte* forms a fitting apotheosis of Mozart's craft. His letters reveal it to be a work with which he identified closely, and herein perhaps lies a clue to his own character, for throughout his operas he speaks at one and the same time with the wit and natural charm of Papageno, while placing before his audience the lofty and worthy aspirations of Tamino. But to understand Mozart's mature operas also requires recognition of the strong cross-currents between his stage works and other genres. Though he demonstrated an acute appreciation of the conventions of all contemporary styles of opera, he developed them by adapting the formal and textural principles of the sonata, symphony, and concerto, which were themselves in turn imbued with the spirit of vocal music in their melodic shaping and expressive content. But Mozart rose above his contemporaries not only because of his mastery of musical craft. He possessed the supreme skill of being able to transform stock stage events into reflections of human life, mocking the vanity and folly of the proud and ignorant, and commiserating with the unfortunate and wronged. A shrewd observer of human life, like Shakespeare he reshaped the familiar themes of love, loyalty, revenge, and hatred in a manner which deepened and enriched the experience of audiences not only in his own lifetime, but for all succeeding ages.

Mozart and Salieri. Opera in 2 acts by Rimsky-Korsakov; text a setting of Pushkin's 'little tragedy' (1830). Prem. Moscow, private opera co., 7 Dec. 1898.

Vienna, end 18th cent. Salieri (bar) contemplates Mozart's (ten) genius in comparison to his own musical skills. He fears that such a gift is actually destructive to musical tradition, and decides that the only possible course of action is to poison Mozart's wine so as to ensure the future of music. Mozart dies, to Salieri's personal sadness but professional relief.

Mravina, Evgeniya (*b* St Petersburg, 16 Feb. 1864; *d* Yalta, 25 Oct. 1914). Russian soprano. Studied St Petersburg with Pryanishnikov, Berlin with Artôt. Début St Petersburg, M, 1886 (Gilda). Sang there until 1898. A highly attractive, intelligent woman, with a pure tone and exemplary diction, she was also influential as one of the first female singers in Russia to bring dramatic depth to her roles. These included Violetta, Elsa, Marguerite, Antonida (*A Life for the Tsar*), Lyudmila, Tatyana, first Fornarina (Arensky's *Raphael*), and first Oxana (*Christmas Eve*), when she 'sang and acted beautifully' (Yastrebtsev).

Mshevelidze, Shalva (*b* Tbilisi, 28 May 1904; *d* Tbilisi, 4 Mar. 1984). Georgian composer. An important ethnomusicologist and administrator, Mshevelidze's works for Georgian music included several operas based on national history and epic. The most successful has been *Ambavi Tarielisa* (The Legend of Tariel, 1946).

Muck, Carl (*b* Darmstadt, 22 Oct. 1859; *d* Stuttgart, 3 Mar. 1940). German conductor. Studied classics Heidelberg and Leipzig. Chorus-master Zurich; cond. there and Salzburg, Graz, and Brno. Engaged by Neumann for Prague 1886. Cond. Neumann's Wagner Co. in first performances of *The Ring* in Moscow and St Petersburg 1889. Berlin, H, 1892–1912 (music dir. from 1908): cond. 1,071 perfs. of 103 operas, of which 35 were novelties. London, CG, 1899. Bayreuth 1901–30, where he was considered the greatest *Parsifal* conductor of his generation: his interpretations were praised for their clarity and fidelity in slow tempos, and their strict rhythmic and formal control. (R)

Muette de Portici, La (The Dumb Girl of Portici). Opera in 5 acts by Auber; text by Scribe and Delavigne. Prem. Paris, O, 29 Feb. 1828.

Portici and Naples, 1647. When, during the wedding of the Spanish Princess Elvira (sop) and Alfonso (ten), son of the Duke of Arcos, the dumb girl Fenella (dancer) identifies Alfonso as her seducer, Elvira disowns him.

Fenella indicates to her brother, the fisherman Masaniello (ten), what has happened, though without naming the culprit; he and his friends vow revenge.

Elvira sends a messenger to fetch Fenella, and Masaniello realizes who his sister's seducer must have been.

Having incited the peasants of Portici to rebellion, Masaniello regrets their excessive action and helps Elvira and Alfonso to escape.

The revolutionaries gain control of the palace and declare Masaniello king. However, the Duke launches a counter-attack and Masaniello is killed while trying to save Elvira. After persuading Elvira to forgive Alfonso, Fenella hurls herself from the balcony of the castle as Vesuvius erupts.

Mugnone, Leopoldo (*b* Naples, 29 Sept. 1858; *d* Naples, 22 Dec. 1941). Italian conductor and composer. Studied Naples, beginning his career aged 12 with a comedy, *Il dottore Bartolo Sarsparilla*. Cond. Venice, F, aged 16. Cond. Rome, C, 1888, incl. prem. of *Cavalleria rusticana* (1890) and *Tosca* (1900); also did much to promote French opera in Italy. Milan, S, from 1880. London, CG, 1905, 1906, 1919, 1924, conducting first CG *Andrea Chénier* (1905), *Fedora* (1906), and *Iris* (1919). New York, Manhattan OC, 1922. His Verdi was much admired by Boito; and Beecham considered him the best Italian opera conductor of his period.

Mulè, Giuseppe (*b* Termini Imerese, 28 June 1885; *d* Rome, 10 Sept. 1951). Italian composer. Studied Palermo Cons., of which he was director 1922–5; then director S Cecilia Cons., Rome, till 1943. His operas were initially much influenced by verismo, in particular by Mascagni (as in *La baronessa di Carini*, 1912), but he later developed a more advanced style. His culminating work was *La zolfara* (The Mines of Sulphur, 1939).

Müller, Maria (*b* Litoměřice, 29 Jan. 1898; *d* Bayreuth, 13 Mar. 1958). Bohemian soprano. Studied Vienna with Schmedes. Début Linz 1919 (Elsa). After engagements in Prague and Munich, New York, M, 1925–35. Berlin: SO, 1926, 1950–2 (when she retired); S, 1927–45. Bayreuth 1930–44. London, CG, 1934, 1937. A warm-voiced, expressive performer with a wide repertory, e.g. Iphigénie (*Tauride*), Donna Elvira, Reiza, Marguerite, Amelia (*Boccanegra*), Jenůfa, and roles in works by Pizzetti and Weinberger. Particularly distinguished as Elsa, Elisabeth, Sieglinde, Eva. (R)

Müller, Wenzel (*b* Trnava, 26 Sept. 1767;

d Baden, nr. Vienna, 3 Aug. 1835). Austrian composer and conductor. Studied Johannisberg with Dittersdorf; joined Brno T as violinist 1782, also composing a Singspiel, *Das verfehlte Rendezvous* (1783); conductor 1785. Moved to Vienna, becoming conductor and composer at the Vienna L. Here he strove hard to improve musical and theatrical standards and with the demise of the National-Singspiel was able to give the theatre a position of great importance in Viennese musical life. During his career he produced *c*.250 works; his first major success came with *Das Sonnenfest der Braminen* (1790), equalled by *Das Neusonntagskind* (1793). Other important works included *Kaspar der Fagottist oder Die Zauberzither* (1791), reflecting a vogue for magic operas seen also in Mozart's contemporaneous *Die Zauberflöte, Die Schwestern von Prague* (1794), whose hit song 'Ich bin der Schneider Kakadu' forms the basis of a set of piano-trio variations by Beethoven, *Die zwölf schlafenden Jungfrauen* (1797), *Das lustige Beilager* (1797), and the exceptionally successful *Die Teufelsmühle am Wienerberg* (1799). Later works were less well received; in 1807 he moved to the German O in Prague, where his daughter the soprano Therese Grünbaum was also engaged.

Müller left in 1813, having been less successful than in Vienna at raising standards. But back at the Vienna L, he resumed activities with much success: among his most popular works were *Tankredi* (1817) and *Aline* (1822). He wrote several works with Raimund, including *Der Barometermacher auf der Zauberinsel* (1823), *Die gefesselte Phantasie* (1828), and *Der Alpenkönig und der Menschenfeind* (1828), some of which interested Wagner.

Müller was the most successful of all early 19th-cent. Viennese popular composers, and a few of his works with Raimund remain in the local repertory. Though early in his career he showed greater operatic ambitions, writing extended finales, it was in simpler songs and ensembles that he was most at ease. Witty and satirical numbers were his strong point, but he could also write in a more tender, reflective vein that charmed his audiences.

Mullings, Frank (*b* Walsall, 10 May 1881; *d* Manchester, 19 May 1953). English tenor. Studied Birmingham with Beard and Breedan. Début Birmingham 1913 (Tristan). Beecham OC 1916–20; London, BNOC 1922–

9; sang in concert 1930–45. A notable artist, memorable for his moving Otello (Verdi), Tristan, and Radamès. (R)

Munich (Ger., München; It., Monaco). City in Bavaria, Germany. Apart from Jesuit school dramas, the first 'opera' was Giovanni Macchioni's dramatic cantata *L'arpa festante* in Aug. 1653 in the Herkules-Saal of the Residenz. Johann Kaspar Kerll (1627–93) inaugurated the theatre on the Salvatorplatz (the Haberkasten, an old granary) with his *Oronte* (1656), and gave Munich standards as high as any in Europe; he left after disagreements over his progressive policies 1673. Kerll was succeeded by Ercole Bernabei 1674–87.

An important period began with Agostino *Steffani and his *Marco Aurelio* (1681); this was interrupted by the court's transfer to Brussels 1692, but resumed in 1701 under Pietro Torri (*c*.1650–1737), especially after the court finally settled in Munich again in 1715. A French influence was now felt beside the Italian. The new Residenztheater (cap. 436) was built by François Cuvilliés 1753 (bombed; reconstructed 1958), and saw the prems. of Mozart's *La finta giardiniera* (1775) and *Idomeneo* (1781). The Elector Carl Theodor forbade Italian opera 1787, and German opera was cultivated, with translations of foreign works, and Singspiels by composers including Franz Danzi, Ferdinand Fränzl (1767–1833), and especially Peter von *Winter. Joseph Babo became director 1799 and despite economic restraints further developed the repertory of French opera and Singspiel, with Italian opera returning 1805. Weber's *Abu Hassan* was prem.d 1811.

The T am Isarthor opened 1812 under Peter von *Lindpaintner (closed 1825), the Hof-und Nationaltheater 1818 (burnt down, rebuilt 1823; bombed 1943; rebuilt 1963, cap. 1,773). But standards declined until Franz Lachner took over as music director 1836; he extended the repertory and built up a strong ensemble. The Staatstheater am Gärtnerplatz (cap. 932) opened 1865.

Since 1945 the Staatstheater has been Munich's second opera-house; rebuilt 1969. Music directors since have included Georg Solti 1947–52, Rudolf Kempe 1952–4, Ferenc Fricsay 1956–9, Joseph Keilberth 1959–68, Wolfgang Sawallisch 1971–92, Peter Schneider from 1992.

Wagner was in Munich at Ludwig II's invitation from 1864, but his hopes for a festival theatre dedicated to his works were frustrated by the court. Nevertheless Hans von *Bülow (music director 1867–9) conducted the prems. of *Tristan und Isolde* (1865) and *Die Meistersinger* (1868), and many other Wagner performances (including a private one of *Parsifal* for the King). Franz Wüllner was music director 1869–71, Hermann Levi 1872–96. Karl von Perfall was an influential director 1867–93, as was his successor Ernst von Possart 1894–1905. Under Possart the Prinzregententheater (cap. 1,012) was built on the Bayreuth model; opened 1901 with *Meistersinger*. Felix Mottl was music director 1903–11, Bruno Walter 1913–22.

The Strauss tradition dates from 1919, when performances of his works became a feature of the season and of the summer festivals; Strauss had been Kapellmeister here 1886–9 and 1894–8, and *Friedenstag* (1938) and *Capriccio* (1942) were premiered here. The bombing of the opera-house in 1943 inspired his threnody *Metamorphosen*, and all 15 of his operas were given as a cycle 1988. Hans Knappertsbusch was music director 1922–35, Clemens Krauss 1937–44, both consolidating the company's reputation.

Muratore, Lucien (*b* Marseilles, 29 Aug. 1876; *d* Paris, 16 July 1954). French tenor. Studied Marseilles Cons., début as actor. Début Paris, OC, 1902 (King, Hahn's *Carmélite*). Paris: OC until 1904; O 1905–12. Chicago 1913–24. Paris: O, 1920; OC, 1923; retired 1931. Created many roles, e.g. title-role of Massenet's *Bacchus*, and Prinzivalle (Février's *Monna Vanna*). A skilful singer-actor, he was successful as Gounod's Faust, Puccini's Des Grieux, Strauss's Herod, and especially Don José. Married to soprano Lina *Cavalieri 1913–27. (R)

Murphy, Suzanne (*b* Limerick, 15 Aug. 1941). Irish soprano. Studied in Dublin. Sang with WNO from 1976, as Constanze, Elvira (*Ernani* and *Puritani*), Elisabeth de Valois, and Leonora (*Trovatore*). A sympathetic performer with a wide repertory, she has also been successful as Donna Anna and Tosca (London, ENO), Norma (New York, CO), Elettra in *Idomeneo* (Vienna, S, 1987) and Alice Ford. (R)

Murray, Ann (*b* Dublin, 27 Aug. 1949). Irish mezzo-soprano. Studied Manchester with Cox. Début Scottish O (in *Alceste*). London, ENO from 1975, and CG from 1976; Gly. 1979; Cologne, 1979–81; New York, M, 1984. Also Milan, S; Vienna; Salzburg; Moscow; Len-

ingrad. Roles include Xerxes, Cherubino, Donna Elvira, Dorabella, Sesto, Rosina, Charlotte, Octavian, Composer. A poised singer of vocal finesse, with a fine legato. Married to the tenor Philip *Langridge. (R)

Musetta. A *grisette*, lover of Marcello and others, (sop) in Puccini's and (mez) in Leoncavallo's *La bohème*.

Musgrave, Thea (*b* Barnton, 27 May 1928). Scottish composer. Studied Edinburgh with Gál, Paris with Boulanger. Apart from a chamber opera and a work for children, her first opera was *The Decision* (1967). This represented an expansion of already impressive creative powers, and brought a new warmth and humanity into her idiom and also, despite some Schoenbergian influences, a new individuality. *The Voice of Ariadne* (1974) accepts some of Britten's innovatory techniques in its use of the church parables, as well as making use of prerecorded tape; though it extends a Henry James short story over three acts, it successfully explores a complex and mysterious set of relationships. However, her major work has been *Mary, Queen of Scots* (1977), which reveals a more sure-footed dramatic pacing that also reflects some of Britten's control if not his idiom. She has also written a radio opera, *Occurrence at Owl Creek Bridge* (1982), and the powerful, impressive *Harriet, the Woman called 'Moses'* (1985).

music drama. The name given to works in which the musical and dramatic elements are (or are intended to be) entirely unified, with every other consideration (such as opportunities for display by singers) subjugated to this end. The term first came into general use with Wagner; he realized in his later works the ideal to which German opera had been moving since its beginnings.

music theatre. A term for works in which musical and dramatic elements are involved, not necessarily representationally. Thus instrumentalists may be costumed and on the stage, or a musician may use a mask, or a group of musicians operate in semi-dramatic conventions. Originally an attempt, deriving from Brecht, to infuse a new kind of dramatic immediacy into opera, it was taken up by a number of younger composers, especially Goehr, Birtwistle, Ligeti, and Maxwell Davies, with works in which a dramatic convention rather than a full staging is used, partly for reasons of economy but fundamentally in the wish to explore new relationships between music and drama.

Musorgsky, Modest (*b* Karevo, 21 Mar. 1839; *d* St Petersburg, 28 Mar. 1881). Russian composer. Studied with Herke, then entering the Cadet School of the Guards in St Petersburg, when he also began writing music. He came to know Balakirev, who gave him some lessons in form, and having resigned his Guards commission, took up music more seriously.

Though one of the great dramatic composers of history, Musorgsky completed only one opera, his masterpiece *Boris Godunov*; and all his operatic works present problems to editors and performers. His earliest projects were *Han d'Islande*, after Victor Hugo (1856) and *Noch na Ivanov den* (St John's Eve, after Gogol, 1858). Of *Oedipus in Athens* (comp. 1858–60) there survives only a single scene, later incorporated into *Salammbô*, *Mlada*, and *Sorochintsy Fair*, and some other choruses. *Salammbô* (comp. 1863–6) is also unfinished, and remains interesting chiefly for its lyrical elements and for a tough realism which hints at *Boris*. The latter quality is developed in the first and only completed act of *The Marriage* (comp. 1868): this is composed as a continuous drama based on speech-melody. It is a lively comedy of manners that includes some characterization by way of Leitmotiv. Musorgsky had also closely associated with the group of five composers comprising Rimsky-Korsakov, Balakirev, Cui, and Borodin as well as himself, dubbed by Stasov the *moguchaya kuchka* (mighty handful).

Musorgsky was by now growing interested in an opera on Pushkin's *Boris Godunov*; the original version was completed by 1869. Though *Boris* has antecedents in Romantic opera and Grand Opera, it is a unique and original product of them. It is also the greatest operatic outcome of the theories advocating realism in art that occupied Russian artists in these years. Examples are the opening crowd scene, which is not the conventional opening chorus but a musical depiction of the many groups and voices that make up a corporate crowd entity, and the Death of Boris, which, instead of being a conventional death aria, gradually fragments his vocal line against steady tolling and chanting until no music is left for it. There is some use of motive, though it is not developed after the manner of Wagnerian Leitmotiv. The vocal writing is still speech-

inflected, but also capable of strongly lyrical qualities; and there are some separate numbers within the continuous composition. When Musorgsky revised the opera, he added the so-called Polish acts and somewhat softened the original conception.

While negotiating the production of *Boris* in 1870, Musorgsky began a new opera, *Bobyl*, one scene of which was inserted in *Khovanshchina*; and in 1870 he was also considering an unidentified Gogol comic opera. He also collaborated with Rimsky-Korsakov, Borodin, and Cui on a projected opera-ballet, *Mlada*, using part of the *Oedipus* music and *A Night on the Bare Mountain*. He began planning another historical opera, *Khovanshchina* (1872–80). This suffers from a complex plot and a multiplicity of leading figures, but portrays with great power some clashing orthodoxies, such as the Slavophile–Westernizer opposition and that between the modern Church and the Old Believers; it also includes some powerful scenes between the main characters. One, the incantation scene, was taken over from the outline for *Bobyl*. Work on the opera was interrupted by yet another project destined to remain unrealized, the comedy *Sorochintsy Fair*. This draws heavily on Ukrainian folk music. For a possible *Pugachevshchina* (1877, on the Pugachev rebellion and partly based on Pushkin), Musorgsky had begun noting down Kirghiz, Transcaucasian, and other tunes; he also played his friends some ideas for another opera, *Byron*. However, his private life, always in a state of disarray, had now deteriorated into alcoholism, and he died with a number of his works incomplete.

Many attempts have been made to get Musorgsky's works into a performing condition. Rimsky-Korsakov made a standard version of *Boris Godunov*, rescoring, reharmonizing, and rewriting much of the music and reversing the order of the last two scenes, with the intention of making the work's originalities more generally acceptable; he claimed this to be a temporary measure, and it is Musorgsky's own music, sometimes with minor adjustments to the material included, which is now becoming accepted. Rimsky-Korsakov also made a performing version of *Khovanshchina*, but his smoothing out of Musorgsky's characteristics led both Boris Asafyev and Shostakovich to make new versions; there is also a completion by Ravel and Stravinsky. *The Marriage* has been completed for performance by Ippolitov-Ivanov, and *Sorochintsy Fair* by Lyadov, Karatygin, and others.

Mustafà. The Bey of Algiers (bs) in Rossini's *L'italiana in Algeri*.

Muti, Riccardo (*b* Naples, 28 July 1941). Italian conductor. Studied Milan with Votto. Début Naples 1970. Salzburg from 1971; Florence 1972; London, CG, 1977; music dir. Milan, S, from 1986, where he restored five Mozart operas to the repertory in addition to Wagner's *Walküre* and *Parsifal*, also reviving Cherubini's *Lodoïska* and Spontini's *La vestale*. Also Vienna, Munich, Paris, Rome, etc. Repertory incl. *Puritani*, *Attila*, *Ballo*, *Aida*, etc., and revivals incl. *Agnes von Hohenstaufen* and the first uncut *Guillaume Tell*. One of the finest Italian opera conductors of the day, he has given some powerfully dramatic performances of Verdi in particular, controlling the music strongly but with sympathetic encouragement to his singers. (R)

Muzio, Claudia (*b* Pavia, 7 Feb. 1889; *d* Rome, 24 May 1936). Italian soprano. Studied Turin with Casaloni, Milan with Viviani. Début Arezzo 1910 (Manon). Milan, S, 1913–14, 1926–7, 1929–30; London, CG, 1914; New York, M, 1916–22, 1933–4; Chicago 1922–3, 1931–2; Paris, O, 1923–5; also Buenos Aires, Rome. Created several roles, including a powerfully acted Giorgetta (*Il tabarro*) whose scream froze the blood. An unusually warm and communicative artist, called 'the divine Claudia' by her public, she possessed a voice of great beauty, superb vocal mastery, and an excellent command of style. Esteemed as Norma, Aida, Mimì, Tosca, Nedda, and Madeleine de Coigny (*Chénier*), and particularly cherished for her moving Violetta. (R)

Mysliveček, Joseph (*b* Prague, 9 Mar. 1737; *d* Rome, 4 Feb. 1781). Bohemian composer. Studied Prague with Habermann and Seeger, Venice with Pescetti. *Semiramide*, his first opera, was premiered Bergamo 1765, but he had an even greater success with *Bellerofonte* (1767). Some 30 operas followed, especially for Rome, Naples, Bologna, Milan, and Florence; his popularity was such that he became known to the Italians, unable to pronounce his name, as 'il boemo'. In 1773 he wrote *Erifile* for Munich, but he met with success only in Italy. Other triumphs included *Demofoonte* (1769), *Ezio* (1775), and *L'Olimpiade* (1778). Though admired and liked by Mozart, and praised by singers for his understanding of the voice, he accepted the conventions of opera seria though in his best works he tried to do more than merely fill them elegantly.

N

Nabucco (Nabucodonosor). Opera in 4 acts by Verdi; text by Solera, after the drama by Anicet-Bourgeois and Francis Cornue, *Nabucodonosor* (1836). Prem. Milan, S, 9 Mar. 1842.

Originally entitled *Nabucodonosor* (Nebuchadnezzar), the opera was first billed as *Nabucco* at the T San Giacomo, Corfu, in 1844, and has since been generally known by this abbreviation.

Jerusalem and Babylon, 586 BC. The Jews lament their defeat by Nabucco, and implore Jehovah to spare the Temple. Ismaele (ten) is holding Nabucco's daughter Fenena (sop) hostage; they declare their love. Abigaille (sop), her supposed sister and also in love with Ismaele, appears with soldiers and offers to save him. Nabucco (bar) now arrives; Zaccaria (bs), the High Priest, threatens Fenena's life so as to deny him the Temple, but Ismaele frustrates him and Nabucco sacks the Temple.

The Jews are captive in Babylon, with Fenena acting as Regent in Nabucco's absence. Abigaille discovers that she is not Nabucco's daughter but an adopted slave. She plans to kill Fenena, who has converted to the Jewish faith, and seize the throne. But Nabucco appears and seizes the crown, proclaiming himself divine; he is immediately struck down by a thunderbolt and made mad.

Abigaille is now Regent, as Nabucco is forced to acknowledge, and plans to kill the prisoners. By the Euphrates, they sing of their lost fatherland.

Nabucco, from prison, sees Fenena led to execution and prays to Jehovah. Freed by Abdallo (ten), Captain of the Guard, he rushes to the scaffold with his men, overthrows the false idols, and saves her. All join in prayer and thanks; Abigaille appears, having taken poison, and dies penitent.

Nachbaur, Franz (*b* Giessen, 25 Mar. 1830; *d* Munich, 21 Mar. 1902). German tenor. Studied Milan with Lamperti, Stuttgart with Pišek. Début Passau 1857. Hanover 1859; Prague 1860–3; Munich, N, 1867–90, when he retired; London, DL, 1882; Moscow 1887. A handsome, musical singer with a good technique, he pleased Wagner as the first Walther. Also first Froh; other roles included Rienzi, Lohengrin, Siegmund, Tannhäuser, Radamès, Gounod's Faust, Raoul, Chapelou (*Postillon de Lonjumeau*).

Nacht in Venedig, Eine (A Night in Venice). Operetta in 3 acts by Johann Strauss II; text by 'F. Zell' (Camillo Walzel) and Genée. Prem. Berlin, Friedrich-Wilhelm-Städtisches T, 3 Oct. 1883.

Venice, 18th cent. The old senator Delacqua (bs) decides to marry his ward Barbara (sop), who is being wooed by both Delacqua's nephew Enrico (ten or spoken) and the Duke of Urbino (ten or bar). The plot is further complicated by the fact that Annina, who had been brought up by the same nurse as Barbara, changes clothes with her during the Venetian Carnival, while Ciboletta (sop), engaged to Pappacoda (bar), pretends she is Barbara. By the end of the opera Caramello (ten), the Duke's barber, has married Annina, and Enrico has married Barbara.

Nachtlager von Granada, Das (The Night Camp at Granada). Opera in 2 acts by Conradin Kreutzer; text by K. J. Braun von Braunthal, after Kind's drama. Prem. Vienna, J, 13 Jan. 1834.

Spain, mid-16th cent. Disguised as a hunter, the Crown Prince of Spain (bar) is granted a night's shelter by shepherds, who decide, however, to kill and rob him when they find him kissing the shepherdess Gabriela (sop). She is loved by, and loves, Gomez (ten), but is also being pursued by Vasco (bs), whom her uncle Ambrosio (bs) wishes her to marry. She appeals to the 'hunter' for assistance, who promises to intercede for her with the Crown Prince. When she and Gomez, having found the Prince's followers, expose the plot, he reveals himself as the Prince and unites her and Gomez.

'Nacqui all'affanno'. Cenerentola's (mez) aria in Act II of Rossini's *Cenerentola*, rejoicing at the happy change in her fortunes and embracing her stepsisters and stepfather. One of the most difficult and brilliant of coloratura arias.

Nadir. A fisherman (ten), friend of Zurga and his rival for Leïla's love, in Bizet's *Les pêcheurs de perles*.

Nannetta. Ford's daughter (Anne) (sop), lover of Fenton, in Verdi's *Falstaff*.

Naples (It., Napoli). City in Campania, Italy. The first operas were given by visiting companies from Venice, probably invited by Count d'Oñate, Viceroy 1648–53, as part of a pacific policy after the revolt of Masaniello. These included Antonio Generoli's Accademia dei Febi Armonici, in a theatre in the grounds of the royal palace, 1651. *Ciro*, by Francesco *Provenzale, was probably given, 1653–4; then Francesco Cirillo's *Orontea*, 3 Apr. 1654. The T San Bartolomeo housed opera from 1654, with the Venetian repertory given by visitors. From 1676, under Filippo Coppola, operas were produced at the palace for royal occasions; he was succeeded by P. A. *Ziani, 1680, on whose death in 1684 Alessandro *Scarlatti was appointed. Under him, Naples became a great operatic centre, and the T San Bartolomeo was enlarged. Opera buffa also developed, the first known being Michelangelo Faggioli's *Cilla*, 1706, the first in public Antonio *Orefice's *Patrò Calienno de la Costa*, 1709 at the T dei Fiorentini (closed 1820). An important consolidation came with Domenico *Sarro's Metastasio setting *Didone abbandonata*, 1724. New theatres opened including the T Pace (1724–49) and T Nuovo (1724–1828). With a new impetus to cultural life at the accession of the Bourbon Charles III, the T San Carlo (built in 270 days) was opened 4 Nov. 1737 with Sarro's *Achille in Sciro*; enlarged 1777 and 1812. The T del Fondo (now T Mercadante) opened 1779, the T San Ferdinando 1790.

Naples was ruled by the French 1806–15, and French opera was influential. Domenico *Barbaia became manager 1809, bringing *Rossini in 1815 (until 1822) to manage the T Fondo and write two operas a year. Several were for Barbaia's mistress Isabella *Colbran, whom Rossini later married. The T San Carlo burnt down Feb. 1816; rebuilt in six months and reopened (cap. 3,500) 12 Jan. 1817; rebuilt 1844. Barbaia also helped the careers of *Donizetti (dir. of the royal theatres 1827–38) and *Bellini. *Mercadante was active from 1838. *Verdi had his operas produced, with mixed success, and also had censorship troubles.

The T San Carlo went through a long period of decline in the late 19th and early 20th cents. Bombed 1943, but quickly restored. Under the British occupation, operatic life was encouraged, and the theatre became very popular with the Allied troops, introducing many to opera for the first time. With Pasquale di Costanzo as director 1946–75, a more adventurous policy was developed, though the theatre has retained its long-standing reputation of having the noisiest and worst-behaved audience in Italy, well able to compete with events on the stage.

Napoli, Jacopo (*b* Naples, 26 Aug. 1911). Italian composer. Studied Cons. S Pietro, Naples; held directorships of Naples, Milan, and Rome Cons. His comic operas, which use Neapolitan songs, include *Il malato immaginario* (1939), *Miseria e nobiltà* (1946), and *Un curioso accidente* (1950), and have enjoyed a limited success. His *Mas'Aniello* (1953) was awarded one of the prizes in La Scala's Verdi competition.

Nápravník, Eduard (*b* Býšť, 24 Aug. 1839; *d* Petrograd, 23 Nov. 1916). Czech conductor and composer. Studied with Půhonný and Svoboda, then Prague with Blazek and Pitsch, also Kittl. Moved to Russia 1861 as director of Prince Yusupov's orchestra; when this was disbanded on the emancipation of the serfs in 1863, moved to St Petersburg, M, as répétiteur, becoming assistant conductor 1867, chief conductor 1869. Of his four operas, the most successful was *Dubrovsky* (1895); but though praised by Tchaikovsky, the music is skilful rather than inspired. His reputation rests on the work he did in presenting other men's operas with an efficiency that greatly helped their success and that of the cause of Russian opera. He was a well-trained, hard-working conductor, unfailingly clear in detail. He conducted over 4,000 performances during his career, and among some 80 works he premiered were Cui's *William Ratcliffe* (1869); Serov's *The Power of Evil* (1871); Dargomyzhsky's *Stone Guest* (1872); Rimsky-Korsakov's *Maid of Pskov* (1873), *May Night* (1880), and *Snow Maiden* (1882); Musorgsky's complete *Boris Godunov* (1874); Tchaikovsky's *Oprichnik* (1874), *Vakula the Smith* (1876), *Maid of Orleans* (1881), *Queen of Spades* (1890), and *Yolanta* (1892); and Rubinstein's *Demon* (1875). He did much, almost single-handedly, to raise standards of performance and company discipline in Russia, also concerning himself with improving the lot of singers and players.

Narraboth. A young Syrian (ten), the captain of the guard, in Strauss's *Salome*.

Nash, Heddle (*b* London, 14 June 1894; *d* London, 14 Aug. 1961). English tenor. Studied Milan with Borgatti. Début Milan, T Carcano, 1924 (Rossini's Almaviva). London, 1925, Old Vic, and with BNOC. London, CG, 1929–39, 1947–8; Gly. 1934–8; London, CR, during the war; New OC 1957–8. Highly gifted, with an excellent voice, technique, and stage presence, he was a notable Don Ottavio, Ferrando, Duke of Mantua, David, Faust (Gounod), Rodolfo. (R)

Nathan, Isaac (*b* Canterbury, 1790; *d* Sydney, NSW, 15 Jan. 1864). Australian composer of Polish-Jewish descent. Studied singing with Corri in London; appeared at Covent Garden and received some recognition as a song composer, especially for his settings of Byron's *Hebrew Melodies* (1815–19). He composed and produced two comic operas, *The Alcaid* (1824) and *The Illustrious Stranger* (1827), but financial problems eventually forced him to emigrate to Australia. Here his many activities culminated in the composition of the first two Australian operas, *Merry Freaks in Troublous Times* (comp. 1843), a comic opera on Charles II, and *Don John of Austria* (1847), a Spanish historical opera. Both are in the style of contemporary English ballad operas.

National Broadcasting Company. Formed in New York 1949–50 with Samuel Chotzinoff as producer and Peter Herman Adler as music director, the NBC opera department was launched with Weill's *Down in the Valley* Jan. 1950. It has given US prems. of many operas, commissioned works including Menotti's *Amahl*, and given the prem. of Martinů's *The Marriage*. Toured 47 US cities 1956, 55 cities 1957–8. In Oct. 1953 *Carmen* was the first opera to be televised in colour.

Naumann, Johann Gottlieb (*b* Blasewitz, 17 Apr. 1741; *d* Dresden, 23 Oct. 1801). German composer. Studied with Tartini and Martini in Italy, where he also met Hasse. His first opera, *Il tesoro insidiato*, was given in Venice 1762; in 1764 he joined the Saxon court, becoming Kapellmeister 1776, for which he wrote several operas, including *La clemenza di Tito* (1769). In 1777–8 and 1782–6 he was in Stockholm to assist King Gustav III in his plans for the reform of Swedish musical life. Here he composed two operas, *Cora och Alonzo* (1782), and *Gustaf Wasa* (1786): the latter, based on a sketch by Gustav III, was regarded in the 19th cent. as the first Swedish national opera. In 1785–6 he performed a similar function in Copenhagen, where *Orpheus og Eurydike* (1786) was produced: based on Calzabigi's libretto for Gluck, this was the first large-scale Danish opera.

Naumann was one of the last great exponents of the Neapolitan style in Germany, although in his opere serie the Baroque procedures of Hasse and Graun were gradually tempered with a certain adherence to a new Classical spirit of sensibility and elegance. His international career, particularly his seminal influence on the establishment of opera in Scandinavia, was of great significance, and gave prestige to Dresden, where his chief loyalties lay; he was the most important opera composer in the city between Hasse and Weber.

Navarraise, La (The Girl from Navarra). Opera in 2 acts by Massenet; text by Jules Claretie and Henri Cain, after the former's story *La cigarette*. Prem. London, CG, 20 June 1894.

Nr. Bilbao, Spain, *c*.1860. Anita (sop) is in love with Araquil (ten), but his father Remigio (bs) opposes the match as Anita has no dowry. In order to get some money, Anita decides to help General Garrido (bar), who is leading the royalist troops against the Carlist enemy Zuccaraga. When Araquil learns of this he follows Anita to Zuccaraga's camp, but is killed; Anita goes mad.

Neapolitan opera. See OPERA SERIA.

Neblett, Carol (*b* Modesto, CA, 1 Feb. 1946). US soprano. Studied with Vennard, Lotte Lehmann, and Bernac. Début New York, CO, 1969 (Musetta). New York, CO from 1969; Chicago from 1975; Vienna 1976; London, CG, 1977; New York, M, from 1979; also Leningrad, Salzburg, Sydney, etc. Roles incl. Mozart's Countess, Vitellia, Norma, Aida, Tosca, Senta, Musetta, Minnie, Marietta (*Die tote Stadt*), Louise, Thaïs. (R)

Nedda. Canio's wife (sop), lover of Silvio, in Leoncavallo's *Pagliacci*.

Neefe, Christian Gottlob (*b* Chemnitz, 5 Feb. 1748; *d* Dessau, 26 Jan. 1798). German conductor and composer. He wrote his first Singspiels in Leipzig, then becoming a conductor of travelling companies and subsequently court organist in Bonn (where he taught Beethoven) and music director at

Dessau (1796–7). He won a considerable following for his Singspiels, especially *Adelheit von Veltheim* (1780), an early and influential treatment of a Turkish subject. Admired for his melodic gift and neatness of characterization, he did much to enliven Singspiel conventions and give them dramatic life, preparing the way for a more continuously composed and wider ranging manner.

Neher, Caspar (*b* Augsburg, 11 Apr. 1897; *d* Vienna, 30 June 1962). German designer and librettist. Studied Munich with Pasetti, Vienna with Roller. Worked with Brecht, then 1924–6 Berlin with Reinhardt. Essen 1927 (*Idomeneo*). Designer at Berlin: Kroll under Klemperer 1928–31 (*Carmen, House of the Dead*), SO with Ebert 1931–3 (*Macbeth* 1931, *Ballo* 1932, cond. Busch). Wrote text and designed prem. of Weill's *Die Bürgschaft* (1932), and worked with Brecht and Weill on various productions. Frankfurt 1934–41. Designed *Macbeth* for Gly. 1938, *Ballo* (based on Berlin sets) for Gly. and Edinburgh, 1949. Wrote four texts for Wagner-Régeny, incl. *Persische Episode* with Brecht (1949–50, prem. 1963). *Wozzeck* London, CG, 1952. Salzburg 1947–62, Milan, Hamburg, Vienna, Berlin, Stuttgart, Cologne. New York, M, 1959 (*Macbeth*). Brecht called him the greatest designer of the day; though historically aware, including of his Baroque forebears, his designs were always planned as a functional and contemporary interpretation of the work.

Neiding. In Wagner's *Die Walküre*, one of Hunding's tribe, enemies of the Wölfing tribe to which Siegmund and Sieglinde belong. From Middle High German *nît* = hatred, modern *Neid* = envy.

Neidlinger, Gustav (*b* Mainz, 21 Mar. 1912; *d* Bad Ems, 26 Dec. 1991). German bass-baritone. Studied Frankfurt with Rottsieper. Début Mainz 1931. Hamburg 1936–50; Bayreuth 1952–75; London, CG, 1963, 1965; New York, M, 1972; Vienna; Paris, O; Milan, S; etc. Roles included Pizarro, Lysiart, Amfortas, Barak, and an outstanding Alberich. (R)

Nelepp, Georgy (*b* Bobruiky, 20 Apr. 1904; *d* Moscow, 18 June 1957). Ukrainian tenor. Studied Leningrad with Tomars. Leningrad 1929–44; Moscow, B, 1941, 1944–57. Full of nervous energy, and possessing a powerful, intense tone, he was considered the most impressive Hermann since the role's creator,

Figner; also sang Sadko, Golitsin, Dmitry, Florestan, Don José, Radamès, Manrico, and created Grigory Melekhov (*Quiet Don*), Kakhovsky (*The Decembrists*). (R)

Nelson, John (*b* S José, Costa Rica, 6 Dec. 1941). US conductor. Studied New York (Juilliard). New York, M, prem. of *Les Troyens* (1973), followed by *Jenůfa*. New York, CO, from 1972 (*Carmen* and *Poppea*). Cond. US prem. of *Owen Wingrave* (S Fe 1973) and was music dir. of the Opera T of St Louis, 1985–92. His brilliant style is well suited to Berlioz, whose *Benvenuto Cellini* he conducted for Lyons O (1989) and *Beatrice* for WNO (1993). (R)

Nelsson, Woldemar (*b* Kiev, 4 Apr. 1938). Russian conductor. Studied Novosibirsk Cons.; assistant to Kyril Kondrashin from 1971 and emigrated to West Germany 1977. Bayreuth 1980–5 (*Lohengrin* and *Fliegender Holländer*). Music dir. Kassel O 1980–7. Salzburg 1986 (prem. of Penderecki's *Schwarze Maske*); Copenhagen 1991 (*Lady Macbeth*). A fine exponent of the modern repertory. (R)

Nélusko. The slave (bar), in love with his fellow slave Sélika, in Meyerbeer's *L'Africaine*.

Németh, Maria (*b* Körmend, 13 Mar. 1897; *d* Vienna, 28 Dec. 1967). Hungarian soprano. Studied Budapest with Anthes, Naples with De Lucia. Début Budapest 1923 (Sulamith, *Die Königin von Saba*). Vienna, S, 1924–46; London, CG, 1931; Milan, S; Berlin; Paris; etc. Her considerable abilities encompassed Constanze, Queen of the Night, Donna Anna, Amelia (*Ballo*), Turandot, Brünnhilde (*Siegfried*). (R)

'Nemico della patria'. Gérard's (bar) monologue in Act III of Giordano's *Andrea Chénier*, accusing Chénier of being an enemy of the Revolution.

Nemirovich-Danchenko, Vladimir (*b* Ozurgety, 23 Dec. 1858; *d* Moscow, 25 Apr. 1943). Georgian-Armenian producer. Studied Moscow. Together with *Stanislavsky, he founded the Moscow Arts T in 1898. Its revolutionary methods and choice of works influenced the staging of opera in Russia and eventually abroad. In 1919 he founded a musical studio, which became in 1926 the Nemirovich-Danchenko Musical T. Bolder in his opera productions even than in the straight theatre, he was one of the first producers to conceive of the 'singing actor' (his phrase). He resisted the star system and developed abstract productions in which acting, movement, settings, and lighting were subject to the music (which, however, he would sometimes radically rearrange). Though admired for his productions of operetta, e.g. of Offenbach and Lecocq, it was in his avant-garde productions that his work was at its most characteristic, e.g. a very popular version of *Carmen* known as *Carmencita and the Soldier* (1924), Knipper's *North Wind* (1930), and the Moscow version in 1934 of Shostakovich's *The Lady Macbeth of Mtsensk*. He also staged a famous production of *La traviata* (1934).

Nemorino. A young peasant (ten), lover of Adina, in Donizetti's *L'elisir d'amore*.

Neri, Giulio (*b* Siena 21 May 1909; *d* Rome, 21 Apr. 1958). Italian bass. Studied Florence with Ferraresi. Début Rome, T delle Quattro Fontane, 1935. Rome, R, 1937–58. London, CG, 1953; Milan, S; Munich; Buenos Aires, C, etc. Large repertory included Verdi and Wagner; famous as Grand Inquisitor, Rossini's Don Basilio, Boito's Mefistofele. (R)

Nerone (Nero). Opera in 4 acts by Boito; text by the composer. Music unfin. at composer's death and completed by Tommasini and Toscanini. Prem. Milan, S, 1 May 1924.

The opera is a series of pictures of imperial Rome at the time of Nero (ten), in which the decadent civilization, corrupted by oriental influences represented by Simon Mago (bar) and Asteria (sop), is contrasted with the new world of Christianity, symbolized by Fanuel (bar) and Rubria (mez). The opera includes the scene of the burning of Rome.

Nessler, Victor (*b* Baldenheim, 28 Jan. 1841; *d* Strasburg, 28 May 1890). Alsatian composer. Studied theology in Strasburg, also music with Stern, but after the success of *Fleurette* (1864) he went to Leipzig to study with Hauptmann. Chorus-master Leipzig 1870, later conductor Carlos T. He won popularity, and the means to give up conducting, with *Der Rattenfänger von Hameln* (The Pied Piper of Hamelin, 1879), though his most enduring success came with *Der Trompeter von Säckingen* (1884). His operas reveal a gently nostalgic German Romanticism, and draw on old German tales and legends for their tuneful and highly effective scores.

'Nessun dorma'. Calaf's (ten) aria in Act III of Puccini's *Turandot*, in which he reflects that he alone can reveal his name, while Peking is searched all night to discover someone who can tell Turandot the secret.

Nesterenko, Evgeny (*b* Moscow, 8 Jan. 1938). Russian bass. Studied Leningrad with Lukanin. Début Leningrad, Maly T, 1963 (Gremin). Moscow, B, from 1971; Milan, S, from 1973; New York, M, 1975; London, CG, 1978. Possesses an expressive, rich voice, and a commanding presence; successful as Philip, Mazeppa, Basilio, Attila, Boris, Ruslan, Kutuzov, among many other roles. (R)

Netherlands. See HOLLAND.

Neues Deutsches Theater. See PRAGUE.

Neues vom Tage (News of the Day). Opera in 3 acts by Hindemith; text by Schiffer. Prem. Berlin, Kroll, 8 June 1929.

A modern city, present-day. A newly married couple, Edward (bar) and Laura (sop), decide to divorce after a fierce quarrel. Legal proceedings are so slow that they go to an agency to speed matters along. However, they are so irritated by the agency's methods that they are reconciled; but they are persuaded to act out their story in the agency's theatre, and are thus exploited by the gutter press.

Neuinszenierung (Ger.). New production.

Neumann, Angelo (*b* Vienna, 18 Aug. 1838; *d* Prague, 20 Dec. 1910). Austrian baritone and impresario. Studied Vienna with Stilke-Sessi. Début Cracow 1859. Vienna, H, 1862–76, when he gave up singing, owing to a heart condition. Roles included Don Giovanni; also sang in *Tannhäuser* and *Lohengrin* when produced by Wagner, whose dramatic talent made an indelible impression on him. Director, Leipzig O, 1876–82, opening with an unexpectedly successful *Lohengrin*; also gave other Wagner operas, including in 1878 the first complete *Ring* outside Bayreuth. After putting on another triumphant *Ring* in Berlin, 1881, and given exclusive rights until 1889 by Wagner, he formed his own company and toured with the *Ring* throughout Europe, 1882–3. Also gave it in St Petersburg and Moscow 1889. Dir. Bremen O 1882–5; Prague, Landestheater, 1885–1910. Wagner appreciated the indefatigable promoter of his work: 'You have done great things for me, and procured me an income on which I would never have counted' (1881).

Neumann, František (*b* Přerov, 16 June 1874; *d* Brno, 25 Feb. 1929). Czech conductor and composer. Studied Leipzig. Prague 1906–9; Brno 1919–29. Conducted prems. of Janáček's *Šárka*, *Káťa Kabanová*, *Cunning Little Vixen*, and *Makropoulos Case*, and Brno prem. of *The Excursions of Mr Brouček*. His compositions include eight operas, among them *Beatrice Caracci* (1922).

Neumann, Václav (*b* Prague, 29 Oct. 1920; *d* Vienna, 2 Sept. 1995). Czech conductor. Studied Prague with Dědeček and Doležil. After many concert engagements, engaged by Felsenstein for Berlin, K, 1956–64, where he conducted with great success *The Cunning Little Vixen* 1956. Leipzig 1964–8. Music dir. Stuttgart 1969–73. A sensitive, very musical conductor with a great care for dramatic truth.

Nevada (orig. Wixom), **Emma** (*b* Alpha, CA, 7 Feb. 1859; *d* Liverpool, 20 June 1940). US soprano. Mother of below. Studied Vienna with Marchesi. Début London, HM, 1880 (Amina). Milan, S, 1881; Paris, OC, 1883–4; New York, AM, 1884–5; London, CG, 1887; Berlin, H, 1907, when she retired. An excellent Bellini singer; her medallion is alongside Pasta's and Malibran's on the composer's statue in Naples. Also sang Lucia, Mignon, Mireille.

Nevada, Mignon (*b* Paris, 14 Aug. 1886; *d* Long Melford, 25 June 1971). English soprano, daughter of above, with whom she studied. Début Rome, T Costanzi, 1907 (Rosina). London, CG, 1910, 1922; Milan, S, 1923; Paris, OC 1920, O 1932. Successful as Zerlina, Marguerite, Lakmé, Mimì; her Desdemona (Verdi) was much praised by Beecham. (R)

Nevers. The Comte de Nevers (bar), a Catholic nobleman in Meyerbeer's *Les Huguenots*. Also the title of Adolar (Graf von Nevers, ten) in Weber's *Euryanthe*.

Neway, Patricia (*b* Brooklyn, 30 Sept. 1919). US soprano. Studied New York with Gesell. Début Chautauqua 1946 (Fiordiligi). New York CO, 1948; Paris, OC, 1952–4; Aix 1952. Created several parts, e.g. Menotti's Magda Sorel (*The Consul*) and title-role of *Maria Golovin*. Also sang Iphigénie (*Tauride*), Tosca, Marie (*La favorite*). (R)

New Opera Company. Founded in Cambridge in 1956, with Leon Lovett as music director, to stimulate interest in contemporary opera by promoting prems. of British works and British prems. of foreign works. In 1960–3 and from 1973 the company worked closely with Sadler's Wells, London. Prems. included Benjamin's *A Tale of Two Cities* (1957) and *Tartuffe* (1964), Joubert's *In the Drought* (1959) and *Under Western Eyes* (1969), Crosse's *Purgatory* (1966), Musgrave's *The Decision* (1967), and Lutyens's *Time Off? Not a Ghost of a Chance* (1972) and *Infidelio* (1973). British stage prems. included Egk's *Der Revisor* (1958), Dallapiccola's *Il prigioniero* (1959), Orff's *Die Kluge* (1959), Schoenberg's *Erwartung* (1960), Henze's *Boulevard Solitude* (1962), Prokofiev's *Fiery Angel* (1965), Hindemith's *Cardillac* (1970), Shostakovich's *The Nose* (1973), Goehr's *Arden Must Die* (1974), Szymanowski's *King Roger* (1975), Ginastera's *Bomarzo* (1976), and Martinů's *Julietta* (1978). Closed 1984.

New Orleans. City in Louisiana, US. Capital of French colonial Louisiana until 1762, in Spanish possession until 1800, under American control from 1803. The T St Pierre, built by the Henry brothers, opened 4 Oct. 1792, and gave the first recorded opera in the city, Grétry's *Sylvain*, 22 May 1796. The T St Philippe opened 30 Jan. 1808 with Méhul's *Une folie*. The first T d'Orléans opened 1815, but burnt down 1816; the second was opened by John Davis 27 Nov. 1819, with Boieldieu's *Jean de Paris*, and remained the city's leading opera-house for 40 years, with annual seasons usually from October to early spring. The auditorium included *loges grillées* (latticed boxes) for those in mourning or for other reasons not wishing to be seen. The repertory initially comprised Grétry, Méhul, Isouard, and Dalayrac, but later expanded to include important works by Cherubini and Rossini. From 1827 Davis also toured with works that were to be local prems. in New York, Philadelphia, and elsewhere. James Caldwell opened the rival Camp St T (cap. 1,100) on 1 Jan. 1824, with a repertory including opera; he then opened the lavish St Charles T (cap. 4,100) on 30 Nov. 1835, in further rivalry with Davis, importing Italian companies from Havana with US prems. of works by Rossini, Bellini, and Donizetti, 1836–42. The T d'Orléans countered, appealing to Creole audiences with French works by Adam, Auber, Halévy, and Meyerbeer, some of them also US prems.. The St Charles T burnt down 1842, but reopened on a more modest scale 1843, surviving until another fire 1899. Caldwell also managed the American T (opened 1840, rebuilt after fire 1842) until 1855; the mixed repertory included opera. Guest artists included Sontag and E. Frezzolini.

On 1 Dec. 1859 Charles Boudousquié opened the French OH (cap. 1,800) with *Guillaume Tell*; this was superior to any US theatre of its time. In its second season the 17-year-old Patti appeared as Lucia, Gilda, Rosina, Valentine, Dinorah, Lady Harriet, and Leonora (*Trovatore*). Activity declined during the Civil War, and an attempt to establish a resident company failed when the ship carrying the singers and musicians was lost in a hurricane. However, by the 1870s there was a rich and formal operatic life, supplemented by visits from travelling companies. During the 19th cent. over 400 operas received their US prems. in New Orleans (more than in any other American city), including 50 works by Bellini, Donizetti, Rossini, Spontini, Halévy, Auber, and Meyerbeer. The French OH, however, declined, closed 1913, was storm-damaged 1915, reopened 11 Nov. 1919, but burnt down 4 Dec. For over two decades the city was then dependent on visiting companies, including a Russian troupe. On 11 June 1943 the New Orleans O Association, founded by Walter Loubat, gave its first performance in City Park, moving to the unsuitable Municipal Auditorium (cap. 2,500) in the autumn to inaugurate 4- to 8-week autumn–winter seasons. Walter Herbert was Music Dir. 1943–54, Renato Cellini 1954–64, Knud Andersson 1964–70, Arthur Cosenza from 1970. In 1973 the Association began playing in the T for the Performing Arts (cap. 2,317).

New Year. Opera in three acts by Tippett; text by composer. Prem. Houston, Wortham T Center, 27 Oct. 1989.

The Presenter (ten) introduces the world of Somewhere and Today. Jo Ann (sop) is afraid of leaving her room to help the children of Terror Town; she is mocked by her delinquent foster-brother Donny (bar) and warned not to indulge him by their foster-mother Nan (mez). In the laboratory of Merlin (bar) in Nowhere and Tomorrow, Pelegrin (ten) is fascinated by the image of Jo Ann retrieved on a screen, but their boss Regan (sop), concerned with their voyage into the future, has it removed. However, Pelegrin leaves in his space ship to seek Jo Ann. When

he finds her, she believes she may discover courage.

During New Year's Eve celebrations, Donny is symbolically beaten as representing the bad Old Year. Merlin's space ship arrives, Regan having been tricked into travelling into the past. When Donny tries to board the space ship, it takes off; he is rescued by Jo Ann from a real beating as New Year strikes.

In Jo Ann's room, Nan arrives to take Donny into her care. Pelegrin arrives to take Jo Ann away, and in a ritual exchange she tastes forgetfulness and memory, choosing the latter; they declare their love. Back in her room, he gives her a rose. Eventually Merlin, Regan, and Pelegrin return to the future; Jo Ann is able to leave her room.

New York. City in US. Ballad operas were given during the early 18th cent. The first musical theatre was opened 1752, followed by the John St. T 1767. An early American opera, *Tammany*, by James Hewitt (1770–1827) was produced here 1794, followed in 1796 by *The Archers* by Benjamin Carr (1768–1831), the first American opera of which parts survive. The Park T opened 1798, and here García's company gave the first US *Don Giovanni*, 1826, and the first Italian opera in the US, *Barbiere*, 1828. Other New York theatres in which opera was given in the 19th cent. included the Italian OH (1833–9), the Astor Place OH (1847–57), the Broadway T, Richmond Hill T, Castle Gardens, Palmo's OH, and the Stadt T. See also CITY CENTER, LEXINGTON THEATRE, LINCOLN CENTER, MANHATTAN OPERA COMPANY, METROPOLITAN OPERA, NATIONAL BROADCASTING COMPANY, NEW YORK CITY OPERA, NIBLO'S GARDEN.

New York City Opera. A company founded in Feb. 1944 by the city's Mayor, Fiorello La Guardia, and by Newbold Morris, originally housed at the City Center. The aim was 'to present opera with the highest artistic standards, while maintaining the civic and democratic ideas of moderate prices, practical business planning and modern methods.' Lászlo Hálász was music director 1944–51, but was then summarily dismissed; he was succeeded by Joseph Rosenstock, who resigned in 1956, then Erich Leinsdorf, Julius Rudel 1957–79, Beverly Sills 1979–89, and Christopher Keene from 1989. The first seasons were short, with a popular repertory, but these were later extended, eventually to two or three months.

The company moved to the State T, Lincoln Center, in 1966, opening with Ginastera's *Don Rodrigo*. It is a rival to the Metropolitan, in that it offers an interesting repertory of classical and contemporary works, often in controversial productions; it has also welcomed distinguished guests, and given an early chance to young US artists. Prems. include Still's *The Troubled Island* (1949), Tamkin's *The Dybbuk* (1951), Copland's *The Tender Land* (1954), Kurka's *The Good Soldier Schweik* (1958), Weisgall's *Six Characters in Search of an Author* (1959), Floyd's *The Passion of Jonathan Wade* (1962), and Menotti's *The Most Important Man* (1971); it has also given many important foreign works, and continues to stage enterprising and original productions, including, under Keene's direction, the New York stage prems. of *Moses und Aron*, *From the House of the Dead*, and *Doktor Faust*.

New Zealand. Opera was first heard in 1864 (Lyster's company), and the country was long dependent on touring companies, including Pollard's Lilliputian OC with children and teenagers. The New Zealand OC was founded as a touring company in 1954 by Donald Munro, with James Robertson as artistic director. After some short works (in English, with local choruses), the company gave its first full-length production, *The Consul*, in 1957. Other productions followed, with the company benefiting from New Zealanders making international careers but returning to sing in productions. It was forced to close in 1972. The Nat. O of New Zealand opened in 1979, visiting Auckland, Christchurch, and Wellington, again under Robertson's musical direction, but financial problems in 1982 caused it to be effectively taken over by the Mercury T in 1984. However, in 1985 companies were formed in Dunedin, Wellington, and Canterbury, then some smaller ones including O Waikato, Perkel O, and O Boutique, leading to a healthy growth of regional opera. The International Fest. of the Arts in Wellington, founded in 1987, included a successful *Meistersinger* in 1990. Works by New Zealand composers have included *Plague upon Eyam* (1985) and *The Birds* (1986) by John Drummond and *Green Leaf* (1985) by Dorothy Buchanan.

Nezhdanova, Antonina (*b* Krivaya Balka, 16 June 1873; *d* Moscow, 26 June 1950). Ukrainian soprano. Studied Moscow with Masetti.

Début Moscow, B, 1902 (Antonida, *Life for the Tsar*). Leading soprano at Moscow, B, up to and after the Revolution; taught from 1936. Only stage appearance abroad, Paris 1912 (as Gilda, with Caruso and Ruffo). Repertory included Queen of the Night, Snow Maiden, Queen of Shemakha, Gilda, Violetta, Tatyana, Lisa, Elsa, Tosca, Lakmé. Her singing of Rimsky-Korsakov's roles, in particular, helped to form a tradition of their interpretation. An outstanding artist, who combined a well-centred voice and brilliant technique with sensitive acting. Nemirovich-Danchenko, with whom she worked, praised her 'candid simplicity and profound nobility'. (R)

Niblo's Garden. Originally a summer resort in New York, built by William Niblo at the corner of Broadway and Prince St. In 1828 Niblo built the Sans Souci T there, and it, and its two successors, later known as Niblo's Garden, were the scene of various opera seasons until 1895; these included Shireff's English Co. (1838), the New Orleans French Co. (1827–33), and the Havana Opera Co. (1848 and 1850). Important seasons were also given there in 1853 by a company that included Sontag, Badiali, and Pozzolini, and in 1858 by Strakosch's company, with Gazzaniga, Pauline Colson, and Marcel Junca. The theatre, which had a capacity of 1,700 with standing room for another 1,000, closed in 1895.

Nicholls, Agnes (*b* Cheltenham, 14 July 1877; *d* London, 21 Sept. 1959). English soprano. Studied London with Visetti. Début London, L, 1895 (Dido). London, CG, 1901–24; also sang with Denhof and Beecham Cos., and BNOC. Roles included Donna Elvira, Venus, Sieglinde, Brünnhilde (*Siegfried*). Married the conductor Hamilton Harty (1879–1941). (R)

Nicklausse. Hoffmann's friend (mez) in Offenbach's *Les contes d'Hoffmann*.

Nick Shadow. The Devil (bar) in Stravinsky's *The Rake's Progress*.

Nicolai, Otto (*b* Königsberg, 9 June 1810; *d* Berlin, 11 May 1849). German composer and conductor. After running away from home, studied Berlin with Zelter. While holding various posts in Italy, he interested himself in opera composition and worked in Vienna at the Hoftheater before returning to Italy. Here he had some success with his first operas. Back in Vienna, he conducted from 1841 at the Hofoper, where he was the first to introduce Beethoven's *Leonore No. 3* overture as an entr'acte in *Fidelio*. When what was to prove his most successful work, *Die lustigen Weiber von Windsor* (The Merry Wives of Windsor, 1849), was refused, he moved to Berlin as director of the Royal Opera.

Nicolai's most famous opera has survived competition even from Verdi's *Falstaff*, on the same subject, to remain a staple item in German repertories and an occasional one in those of other countries. In it the German tradition of comic opera is fertilized by the grace and fluency Nicolai had learnt in Italy. An intelligent and literate man, concerned to make a contribution to German Romantic opera, he here brought together qualities which included a fine feeling for the voice and a sensitive command of the orchestra. He was greatly admired as a conductor.

Nicolescu, Marianna (*b* Brașov, 28 Nov. 1948). Romanian soprano. Studied Rome and with Schwarzkopf. Début Cincinnati 1972 (Mimì). Sang Violetta at Florence (1976) and New York, M, 1978. Equally at home in the modern, bel canto, and Baroque repertory. Created Leonora (Berio, *La vera storia*) Milan, S, 1982; returned for Rossi's *Orfeo* (1985) and Jommelli's *Fetonte* (1988). Other roles incl. Mozart's Elettra (Salzburg 1990) and Donizetti's Elizabeth I (Monte Carlo 1992).

Nicolini, Ernest. See PATTI, ADELINA.

Nicolò. See ISOUARD, NICOLÒ.

Nielsen, Carl (*b* Sortelung, 9 June 1865; *d* Copenhagen, 3 Oct. 1931). Danish composer. Studied Copenhagen with Gade; worked as an orchestral violinist before making his reputation as a composer of symphonic music. In 1908 became conductor of the Royal O, resigning 1914. By the time of his death he was the most respected Danish composer of his generation.

His first opera, *Saul og David* (1902), took a decisively modernist approach and was initially controversial: in it the legacy of his symphonic apprenticeship is clearly apparent. Nielsen's only other completed opera, *Maskarade* (1906), was quite different in style: a light-hearted, whimsical comedy, it has won a position comparable to that of *Halka* or *The Bartered Bride* as a national opera.

Niemann, Albert (*b* Erxleben, 15 Jan. 1831; *d* Berlin, 13 Jan. 1917). German tenor. Studied Dessau with Nusch, later Paris with Duprez.

Début Dessau (1st Captain, *Le prophète*) 1849. Halle 1852; Hanover 1854–66; Berlin, H, 1866–88, when he retired. Paris, O, 1861; Munich, 1864; London, HM, 1882; New York, M, 1886–8. Possessed a huge physique and voice, and great powers of expression. Roles included Florestan, Gounod's Faust, Manrico, Rienzi, Lohengrin, and Tannhäuser in the 1861 Paris fiasco, when he caused Wagner much trouble with his intransigent arrogance. Later (though still causing trouble), he was highly successful as Siegmund in the first *Ring*; also as Walther, Tristan, and Siegfried.

Nightingale, The (Russ., *Solovey*; Fr., *Le rossignol*). Opera in 3 acts by Stravinsky; text by the composer and Stepan Mitusov, after Hans Andersen's story. Prem. Paris, O, 26 May 1914.

Fairyland. The famous nightingale (sop), whose song thrills all, sings to a poor fisherman (ten). The imperial court arrives in search of the bird, who agrees to sing for the Emperor (bar).

The nightingale refuses any reward save the pleasure of seeing tears of emotion in the imperial eyes. A mechanical nightingale arrives from the Emperor of Japan, but a comparison is prevented by the real bird's disappearance. The mechanical bird is installed at the royal bedside.

Death (con) sits by the Emperor's bed, but promises to return the crown when the nightingale returns and sings. This it does, and the Emperor's strength returns.

Nightwatchman. The watchman (bs) who goes the rounds in Nuremberg in Wagner's *Die Meistersinger von Nürnberg*.

Nile Scene. The name generally given to Act III of Verdi's *Aida*, which takes place by moonlight on the banks of the Nile.

Nilsson, Birgit (*b* West Karup, 17 May 1918). Swedish soprano. Studied Stockholm with Hislop and Sunnegaard. Début Stockholm 1946 (Agathe). Sang there regularly thereafter. Gly. 1951; Bayreuth 1954–70; London, CG, from 1957; Milan, S, from 1958; New York, M, 1959–83. Also Vienna, Rome, Munich, Chicago, etc. Retired 1984. One of the greatest Wagner singers of the century, she possessed an unusually ample, puretoned, and effortless voice, and a powerful stage presence. Repertory included Leonore, Lady Macbeth, Aida, Elsa, Sieglinde, Dyer's

Wife, Salome, Marschallin, Turandot; a famous Isolde, Brünnhilde, Elektra. (R)

Nilsson, Christine (*b* Sjöabol, 20 Aug. 1843; *d* Stockholm, 22 Nov. 1921). Swedish soprano. Studied Stockholm with Berwald, Paris with Wartel and Delle Sedie. Début Paris, L, 1864 (Violetta). Paris, L until 1867, and O 1868. London: HM, 1867, and then at CG and DL until 1882; New York, AM, 1871; also Moscow, St Petersburg, Brussels, Munich, etc. New York, M, at opening in 1883. Immensely popular for her beauty, charm, and vocal brilliance; her voice, which was sweet-toned and crystal-clear, extended to f‴. Was to have sung Catherine in the first *Jolie fille de Perth*, but broke her contract to create Ophélie (*Hamlet*), one of her best roles. Also successful as Queen of the Night, Lucia, Marguerite, Mignon, Martha, Valentine, Elsa.

Nimsgern, Siegmund (*b* St Wendel, 14 Jan. 1940). German bass-baritone. Studied Saarbrücken; début there 1967 (Lionel, *The Maid of Orleans*). London, CG, from 1973 (Amfortas; Dapertutto). New York, M, 1978 (Pizarro). Has an impressive range of Wagner roles, incl. Telramund (Salzburg 1976; Frankfurt 1991), Wotan (Solti–Hall *Ring* at Bayreuth, 1983–5), and the Dutchman. Other roles incl. Scarpia (Chicago 1982), Macbeth, and Boccanegra. (R)

Nina, ossia La pazza per amore (Nina, or The Girl Mad through Love). Opera in 2 acts by Paisiello; text (in French, *Nina, ou La folle par amour*) by Benoît Joseph Marsollier de Vivetières for Dalayrac, trans. by Giuseppe Carpani with additions by Giovanni Battista Lorenzi. Prem. Caserta, Royal Palace, 25 June 1789.

Italy, 18th cent. Nina (sop) goes mad after her lover Lindoro (ten) is shot in a duel by his rival; her father, the Count (bs), had decreed that the rival should have her hand and is consequently full of remorse.

Lindoro recovers from his wounds but is distraught to learn of Nina's madness. She gradually recognizes him and regains her sanity, happy that her father will now permit her marriage to Lindoro.

Nissen, Hans Hermann (*b* Zippnow, 20 May 1893; *d* Munich, 28 Mar. 1980). German bass-baritone. Studied Berlin with Raatz-Brockmann. Début Berlin, V, 1924 (Caliph, *Barber of Baghdad*). Munich, Bayerische SO, 1925–67. London, CG, 1928, 1934; Paris, O, 1930; Milan, S, 1936–8; New York, M, 1938–9; Bay-

reuth 1943; also Chicago, Vienna, Salzburg. Roles included Renato, Barak, Orestes; outstanding as Wotan and Sachs. (R)

'Niun mi tema'. Otello's death scene in Act IV of Verdi's *Otello*, in which he warns no one to fear him if they see him armed, for he is embarking upon his last journey, his own death.

Noble, Dennis (*b* Bristol, 25 Sept. 1899; *d* Javea, 14 Mar. 1966). English baritone. Studied London with Gilly. Début London, CG, 1924 (Marullo, *Rigoletto*). London: CG, until 1938, and in 1947; also CR and BNOC. Cleveland, US, 1935–6. Created several roles, e.g. Sam Weller (*Pickwick*, Albert Coates), and was a successful Verdi and Puccini singer. (R)

'Nobles seigneurs, salut!' The page Urbain's (sop) salutation in Act I of Meyerbeer's *Les Huguenots*, introducing his aria 'Une dame noble et sage' in which he brings a note from his mistress (Marguerite de Valois) to Raoul de Nangis.

Noni, Alda (*b* Trieste, 30 Apr. 1916). Italian soprano. Studied Trieste and Vienna. Début Ljubljana 1937 (Rosina). Vienna, S, 1942–5; London, Cambridge T, 1946; Gly. 1949–54. Also Milan, S; Paris, OC; Berlin, S; etc. An excellent soubrette with great comic gifts, successful as Blonde, Despina, Clorinda (*Cenerentola*), Nannetta, Zerbinetta. (R)

'Non lo dirò col labro'. Alessandro's (sop cas) aria in Act I of Handel's *Tolomeo*, known in English as 'Did you not see my lady?'

'Non mi dir'. Donna Anna's (sop) aria in Act II of Mozart's *Don Giovanni*, in which she bids Don Ottavio speak no more of his hopes of marriage so soon after her father's death.

Nono, Luigi (*b* Venice, 29 Jan. 1924; *d* Venice, 8 May 1990). Italian composer. Studied Venice with Malipiero, later with Maderna and Scherchen. His first opera, *Intolleranza 1960* (1961), drew on various 20th-cent. techniques, including serialism, in an intelligent dramatic plea, but ran into an organized demonstration from a Fascist group, Ordine Nuovo, at a stormy prem. whose notoriety has overshadowed the quality of the work. After various music theatre pieces, he wrote *Al gran sole carico d'amore* (1975), a large-scale celebration of the Paris Commune, and then an 'opera without action', *Prometeo* (1984), a piece performed in a Venetian church, S Lorenzo.

'No, no, Turiddu'. Santuzza's (sop) duet in Mascagni's *Cavalleria rusticana*, in which she begs Turiddu (ten) not to follow his new love Lola into the church but to return to her.

'Non più andrai'. Figaro's (bar) aria in Act I of Mozart's *Nozze di Figaro*, describing to the reluctant Cherubino his impending translation from civilian to military life. The melody is used for the last of the three numbers played by Giovanni's private band at supper in the penultimate scene of *Don Giovanni*, in recognition of the tune's popularity: Leporello exclaims, 'Questa poi la conosco purtroppo' ('I know this one only too well').

'Non più di fiori'. Vitellia's (sop) aria in Act II of Mozart's *La clemenza di Tito*, in which she reflects that the god of marriage she had hoped to welcome must now yield to death.

'Non so più'. Cherubino's (sop, sometimes mez) aria in Act I of Mozart's *Le nozze di Figaro*, in which he declares his bewilderment at the novel excitement of desire.

'No! Pazzo son! Guardate!' Des Grieux's (ten) appeal in Act III of Puccini's *Manon Lescaut*, in which he beseeches the ship's captain to allow him to accompany Manon on her journey into exile.

Nordica (Norton), **Lillian** (*b* Farmington, ME, 12 Dec. 1857; *d* Batavia, 10 May 1914). US soprano. Studied Boston with O'Neill, Milan with Sangiovanni, later Paris with Sbriglia. Début Milan, T Manzoni, 1879 (Donna Elvira). St Petersburg 1880; New York, AM, with Mapleson Co., 1883. London: CG, 1887–93, 1898–9, 1902; DL, 1888–93. New York, M, 1891–1909 (intermittently); Bayreuth 1894 (first US singer there); Paris, O, 1910. At first merely a skilful singer, she later became an artist of considerable dramatic expression, aided by both Cosima Wagner's tutelage and her own determined application. She possessed a pure style, a velvety tone, and a technique and versatility that enabled her to sing Brünnhilde and Violetta on consecutive nights. Other roles included Cherubino, Donna Anna, Norina, Marguerite, Philine, Selika, Aida, Elsa, Kundry, and a particularly triumphant Isolde with the De Reszke brothers. (R)

Norena, Eidé (*b* Horten, 26 Apr. 1884; *d* Lausanne, 19 Nov. 1968). Norwegian soprano. Studied Oslo with Gulbranson, London with R. von zur Mühlen. Début Oslo 1907 (Amor, Gluck's *Orfeo*). Oslo 1908–18; Milan, S, 1924; London, CG, 1924–5, 1930–1, 1934, 1937; Paris, O, between 1924 and 1937; Chicago 1926–8; New York, M, 1933–8. An accomplished and tasteful singer, especially successful as Gilda, Violetta, Desdemona, Mathilde, and the three sopranos of *Les contes d'Hoffmann*. (R)

Nørgård, Per (*b* Copenhagen, 13 July 1932). Danish composer. Studied Copenhagen and Paris with Boulanger. In 1961 won a prize at the Gaudeamus Festival (Holland), which brought him to international attention; in 1958–62 was music critic for the newspaper *Politiken*; from 1965 taught composition at the Conservatory in Århus. His operas include *Labyrinten* (1963) and *The Divine Circus* (1983).

Nørholm, Ib (*b* Copenhagen, 24 Jan. 1931). Danish composer. Studied Copenhagen and Darmstadt; music critic for the newspaper *Information* 1956–64; has held positions as organist and teacher in Denmark; from 1973 has taught at the Royal Cons. He has written a television opera, *Invitation til skafottet* (Invitation to a Beheading, 1967), a chamber opera, *Den unge Park* (The Young Park, 1970), and the opera *Truth's Revenge* (1986) on a comedy by Karen Blixen.

Norina. A young widow (sop), lover of Ernesto, in Donizetti's *Don Pasquale*.

Norma. Opera in 2 acts by Bellini; text by Romani, after Soumet's tragedy (1831). Prem. Milan, S, 26 Dec. 1831.

Gaul, during the Roman occupation. The Roman proconsul Pollione (ten) has abandoned the Druid high priestess Norma (sop), by whom he has two sons, in favour of another priestess, Adalgisa (sop). Norma protects Pollione by advising against war and, in 'Casta Diva', calls on the goddess of the moon for peace. Norma learns that Adalgisa's lover is none other than Pollione.

Norma intends to kill her sons, but cannot bring herself to do so. Adalgisa goes to Pollione to try to persuade him to return to Norma, but fails. In a rage, Norma incites the Gauls to war against the Romans. Pollione is captured near the Druids' temple and is sentenced to death. In a final attempt to save

Pollione, whom she still loves, Norma offers herself as a replacement for him and, having confided her children to her father's care, she mounts the pyre, where she is joined in death by Pollione.

Norman, Jessye (*b* Augusta, GA, 15 Sept. 1945). US soprano. Studied Washington with Grant, Michigan U with E. Mannion and Bernac. Début Berlin, D, 1969 (Elisabeth, *Tannhäuser*). Milan, S, and London, CG, from 1972; New York, M, from 1983; Paris, OC, 1984. Roles include Countess (Mozart), Dido (Purcell and Berlioz), Cassandre, Ariadne, Aida, Sieglinde, Selika. Possesses a large, opulent, and expressive voice, and a statuesque stage presence. (R)

Norrington, Roger (*b* Oxford, 16 Mar. 1934). Studied London with Boult. London COG as tenor, then conductor (*Rake's Progress*). First music director *Kent Opera 1969–82, with notable effect, conducting over 300 performances of 30 works, many in striking productions by Jonathan *Miller. London, SW, then ENO 1979, 1987; Milan, PS, 1982; Venice, F, 1983; Florence 1984; London, CG, from 1986 (Handel's *Samson*; *Peter Grimes*). Formed London Classical Players and Early Music Project (a company committed to historical stagings); has given highly successful performances, with an emphasis on composers' original intentions as well as an 'authentic' sound. A conductor of great musical subtlety, whose quick intelligence and infectious energy inform all his undertakings. (R)

Nose, The (Russ., *Nos*). Opera in 3 acts by Shostakovich; text by A. Preis, A. Zamyatin, G. Yonin, and the composer, after Gogol's story (1835), with extracts and suggestions from other works by Gogol and using Smerdyakov's song from Dostoyevsky's *The Brothers Karamazov*. Prem. Leningrad, Maly T, 18 Jan. 1930.

St Petersburg, 1850. An official, Major Kovalyev (bar), wakes one morning to find that his nose has disappeared. His barber, Ivan Jakovlevich (bs), is astonished to discover it in his bread. On his way to report his loss to the police, Kovalyev sights the nose, dressed as a state councillor, but it refuses to talk to him as a lower-ranking official.

Kovalyev tries to place an announcement in the newspaper, but is refused.

The nose is arrested by the police, but a surgeon is unable to sew it back in place.

However, one day, the nose reappears on Kovalyev's face just as suddenly as it disappeared.

'Nothung! Nothung!' Siegfried's (ten) song in Act I of Wagner's *Siegfried*, forging the sword 'Needful' which he knows his father (Wotan) has promised him in his hour of need. Its name derives from *Noth* = both affliction and need.

Nouguès, Jean (*b* Bordeaux, 25 Apr. 1875; *d* Paris, 28 Aug. 1932). French composer. Studied Bordeaux with Sarreau. His early operas were produced in Bordeaux, but he made a wider name with *Quo vadis?* (1909), which was championed by Battistini and chosen to open the London OH in 1911, though its shallowness may have contributed to the failure of this venture. Among later operettas, he had some success especially with *L'auberge rouge* (1910) and *L'aigle* (1912).

Nourrit, Adolphe (*b* Montpellier, 3 Mar. 1802; *d* Naples, 8 Mar. 1839). French tenor. Studied Paris with Manuel García sen. Début Paris, O, 1821 (Pylade, *Iphigénie en Tauride*). Paris, O, until 1837. Other roles included Orphée, Don Giovanni, Otello (Rossini). After 1824, further training with Rossini, to whom he in turn gave valuable advice on French style. Created the tenor roles in *Le siège de Corinthe, Moïse, Le Comte Ory*, and *Guillaume Tell*; also title-roles of *Robert le diable*, and Liszt's *Don Sanche*; Raoul in *Les Huguenots*, Masaniello in *La muette de Portici*, and Eléazar in *La Juive*, among others. In Italy studied further with Donizetti, who agreed to write *Poliuto* for him. However, its performance was prohibited by the Neapolitan censors (Duprez eventually created the title-role in Paris). Despite subsequent triumphs in Naples, severe melancholia drove him to suicide in 1839. An exceptionally intelligent, cultivated man, he was a highly influential artist of the Romantic movement.

Novák, Vítězslav (*b* Kamenice, 5 Dec. 1870; *d* Skuteč, 18 July 1949). Czech composer. Studied Jindřichův Hradec with Pojman, Prague with Knittl and Stecker, later Dvořák. He was initially influenced by the German Romantics, and only made a reputation after encounters with Moravian and Slovak folk music in the late 1890s fertilized a more individual style. In this, and in his devotion to nature, he at one time invited comparisons with Janáček. He did not write his first opera, *The Imp of Zríkov*, until 1915. The sharp irony in this work softened with *Karlštejn* (1916), which is a patriotic gesture that does not exclude comedy. His most successful opera, *The Lantern* (1923), draws on both fairy-tale and a feeling for the rococo. *Grandfather's Legacy* (1926) suffers from a cumbersome libretto, but includes some fine intermezzos.

Novotná, Jarmila (*b* Prague, 23 Sept. 1907; *d* New York, 9 Feb. 1994). Czech soprano. Studied Prague with Destinn. Début Prague 1926 (Violetta). Vienna, S, 1933–8; S Francisco 1939; New York, M, 1940–56. Also Milan, S; Buenos Aires, C; Paris, O. Successful as Pamina, Gilda, Butterfly, Octavian, Mélisande, and first Giuditta (Lehár). (R)

'No word from Tom'. Anne Trulove's (sop) aria in Act I of Stravinsky's *The Rake's Progress*, in which she grieves over Tom's absence in London and then, in a cabaletta, resolves to go to him.

Noyes Fludde. Miracle play in 1 act by Britten; text part of the Chester Miracle Play. Prem. Orford Parish church, 18 June 1958.

The Voice of God (spoken) tells Noye (bar) to build an ark and thus save his family, Mrs Noye (sop) and their children and wives (boy trebles and girl sops), from the Flood. Animals process in pairs into the ark, and the Flood rises. Eventually Noye releases a dove, which finds dry land; the ark's occupants leave.

The score, which is for a children's orchestra including recorders and bugles as well as a professional group, also involves the congregation with the use of three hymns: 'Lord Jesus, think on me', 'Eternal Father, strong to save', and 'The Spacious Firmament on High' (to Tallis's Canon).

Nozzari, Andrea (*b* Vertova, 1775; *d* Naples, 12 Dec. 1832). Italian tenor. Studied Bergamo with Petrobelli, Rome with Aprile. Probable début Pavia 1794. Milan, S, 1796–7, 1800, 1811–12; Paris, I, 1803, 1804; Naples, C, 1811–25. One of Rossini's greatest tenors, he created Leicester (*Elisabetta, regina d'Inghilterra*), title-role of *Otello*, Rinaldo (*Armida*), Osiride (*Mosè*), Agorante (*Ricciardo e Zoraide*), Pirro (*Ermione*), Rodrigo di Dhu (*La donna del lago*), Paolo Erisso (*Maometto II*), Antione (*Zelmira*). Also a famous Paolino (*Matrimonio segreto*). Possessed a strong voice, and an imposing, graceful stage presence.

Stendhal thought him 'one of the finest singers in Europe'. Rubini was his pupil.

Nozze di Figaro, Le (The Marriage of Figaro). Opera in 4 acts by Mozart; text by Lorenzo da Ponte, after Beaumarchais's comedy *La folle journée, ou Le mariage de Figaro* (1778, prem. 1784). Prem. Vienna, B, 1 May 1786.

Count Almaviva's castle near Seville, mid-18th cent. Figaro (bar) and Susanna (sop), servants of Count Almaviva (bar), are preparing for their wedding. Susanna realizes that their room is too close to that of the Count, who is pursuing her. Dr Bartolo (bar), the Countess's ex-guardian, and Marcellina (mez) wish to prevent Figaro's marriage by holding him to an agreement he made to marry Marcellina if he could not repay a loan. While the young page Cherubino (sop, sometimes mez) is telling Susanna of his hopeless love for the Countess, the Count arrives. Cherubino hides and his master flirts with Susanna. Don Basilio (ten) is heard and the Count also hides, forcing Cherubino to move from his place. Basilio enters and after proclaiming the Count's love for Susanna, gossips about Cherubino's love for the Countess. At this, the Count emerges and tells Susanna how he discovered Cherubino with Barbarina (sop), the gardener's daughter. He pulls back a cover and discovers Cherubino. Realizing that the boy has overheard his own indiscretions with Susanna, he despatches him to the army.

The Countess laments that her husband no longer loves her. She, Figaro, and Susanna devise a plan to trap him: Susanna will write to him agreeing to a rendezvous, but Cherubino will go instead, dressed in her clothes, and the Countess will interrupt. While he is being fitted with his costume, the Count knocks and Cherubino is hurriedly pushed into the dressing-room. The Countess tells her husband that the noise he hears is only Susanna trying on her wedding dress, but he is suspicious. He departs to fetch tools to force the door open, locking the main door as he leaves. As soon as he has gone, Cherubino leaps out of the window and Susanna takes his place. When the Count returns, she steps out and he has to apologize for having doubted his wife. The drunken gardener Antonio (bs) enters bearing a smashed flowerpot and a document (Cherubino's commission), dropped by the escapee. Figaro tries to cover up by taking the blame.

Figaro attempts to delay Marcellina's plans by saying that he cannot marry without the consent of his parents. As proof of his claim of noble birth, he shows a birthmark on his arm and Marcellina recognizes him as her long-lost son. Susanna enters and is furious to find Figaro embracing Marcellina. When the situation is explained, she joins in the rejoicing, and plans proceed for their wedding.

At night in the garden, Figaro comes across Barbarina, who unwittingly reveals that she is bearing a message from the Count to Susanna; Figaro believes his wife is already deceiving him. The Countess and Susanna appear in each other's clothes, and in the darkness there are many mistaken identities: Cherubino flirts with the Countess (thinking she is Susanna), and is succeeded by the Count, who does not realize he is paying court to his own wife. Figaro recognizes Susanna by her voice. When the Countess steps into the light, the Count realizes that he has been tricked and humbly begs his wife's forgiveness. All rejoice in the happy conclusion of the 'mad day'.

Nucci, Leo (*b* Castiglione dei Pepoli, 16 Apr. 1942). Italian baritone. Studied Milan with Marchesi, later Bizzarri. Début Spoleto 1967 (Rossini's Figaro). Padua 1975; Milan, S, from 1976; London, CG, from 1978; New York, M, 1980; Paris, O, 1981; also Chicago, Vienna, Tokyo, etc. Roles incl. Malatesta, Mercutio, Renato, Rigoletto, Posa, Onegin, Sharpless; particularly acclaimed as Rossini's Figaro. (R)

O

obbligato (It.: 'obligatory'). Strictly, a term for an instrumental part that cannot be omitted. (It is often used, paradoxically, for a part that may be omitted.) In vocal music it is essential but subordinate to the voice, e.g. the corno di bassetto obbligato in Vitellia's 'Non più di fiori' in Act II of Mozart's *La clemenza di Tito*.

Oberlin, Russell (*b* Akron, OH, 11 Oct. 1928). US counter-tenor. Studied New York, Juilliard School. Début as concert singer, New York 1951. Founder member of New York Pro Musica. New York 1956, sang title-role of Handel's *Giulio Cesare* (in concert). London, CG, 1961, Oberon (*A Midsummer Night's Dream*); first US Oberon, S Francisco 1961. Like Alfred Deller, a pioneer in the revival of the male alto voice and repertory. (R)

Oberon. Opera in 3 acts by Weber; text by James Robinson Planché, after William Sotheby's translation (1798) of Wieland's *Oberon* (1780), based in turn on a 13th-cent. *chanson de geste*, *Huon de Bordeaux*. Prem. London, CG, 12 Apr. 1826.

France, the Orient, and Fairyland, AD 800. Oberon (ten) has vowed not to meet Titania again until he has found a faithful pair of lovers. With some supervision and help from Puck (sop), and provision of a magic horn that can summon aid, he sends Sir Huon (ten), who has offended Charlemagne, to Baghdad to rescue Reiza (sop).

With the aid of the magic horn, Huon succeeds in releasing Reiza, while his squire Sherasmin (bar) carries off her attendant Fatima (sop). On their voyage to Greece, both couples are shipwrecked and captured by pirates.

Sherasmin and Fatima are sold as slaves to the Emir of Tunis. Huon appears and, when he refuses to concede to the Emir's wife's plans to murder the Emir and marry her, is sentenced to death. He is saved at the last moment by magic. Oberon accepts Huon's proof of his fidelity to Reiza, and the couple are restored to Charlemagne's court.

Oberspielleiter (Ger.: 'senior producer'). The name given to the chief resident producer of an opera company. He might sometimes also be the *Generalintendant.

Oberto, conte di San Bonifacio. Opera in 2 acts by Verdi; text by Piazza, revised by Solera, probably from the original text for Verdi's uncomposed or adapted *Rocester* and perhaps *Lord Hamilton*. Prem. Milan, S, 17 Nov. 1839.

Ezzelino's castle, near Bassano, 1228. Cuniza (mez) is to marry Riccardo (ten). Oberto (bs), the exiled Count of Bonifacio, has disowned his daughter Leonora (sop) because she was seduced by Riccardo. Oberto and Leonora reunite so as to be avenged on Riccardo. Oberto persuades Leonora to disclose the whole story to Cuniza. She is horrified and confronts Riccardo, telling him he must now marry Leonora.

Not satisfied with this revenge, Oberto challenges Riccardo to a duel. Riccardo kills Oberto and, filled with remorse, flees Italy, leaving Leonora in despair.

Obraztsova, Elena (*b* Leningrad, 7 July 1937). Russian mezzo-soprano. Studied Leningrad Cons. with Grigoryeva. Début Moscow, B, 1963 (Marina). Moscow, B, from 1964; New York, M, 1975 (with Moscow B), and from 1977; Milan, S, 1964, 1973 (with Moscow B), 1976; also Barcelona, Vienna, S Francisco, etc. Roles include Rosina, Countess (*Queen of Spades*), Marfa (*Khovanshchina*), Eboli, Carmen, Britten's Oberon. Possesses a deep, vivid tone and a vigorous style. (R)

O'Brien, Timothy (*b* Shillong, 8 Mar. 1928). English designer. Studied Cambridge. Has worked in TV and in the theatre, especially at Stratford, but has also made a reputation as an exceptionally intelligent, inventive, and practical designer for opera (often in collaboration with Tazeena Firth). Productions include London, SW: *Flying Dutchman* (1958), *Girl of the Golden West* (1962); London, CG: the prem. of Tippett's *Knot Garden* (1970), *Peter Grimes* (1975), *Rake's Progress* (1978), *Lulu* (1981), Verdi's *Otello* (1987); London, C: Henze's *Bassarids* (1974), *Meistersinger* (1984). *Wozzeck* (Adelaide 1976); *Turandot* (Vienna 1983); *Lucia* (Cologne 1985); *War and Peace* (Leningrad 1991).

'O Carlo, ascolta'. The introduction to Posa's (bar) aria in Act IV of Verdi's *Don Carlos*, telling Carlos that the Queen will wait for him on the following day outside the Monastery of San Yuste to see him for the last time.

'Ocean! thou mighty monster'. Reiza's (sop) aria in Act II of Weber's *Oberon*, in which she first apostrophizes the ocean and then hails the boat she believes to be coming to her rescue.

Ochs. Baron Ochs auf Lerchenau (bs), the Marschallin's cousin, in Strauss's *Der Rosenkavalier*.

Octavian. Count Octavian Rofrano (sop or mez), the Knight of the Rose in Strauss's *Der Rosenkavalier*. His full names, recited by Sophie in Act II, are Octavian Maria Ehrenreich Bonaventura Fernand Hyacinth; his nickname Quinquin was taken from Count Franz 'Quinquin' Esterházy, brother of Haydn's patron.

Odabella. The daughter (sop) of the Lord of Aquileia in Verdi's *Attila*.

'O don fatale'. Eboli's (mez) aria in Act IV of Verdi's *Don Carlos*, in which she curses the fatal beauty that has blighted her life.

'O du, mein holder Abendstern'. Wolfram's (bar) song to the evening star in Act III of Wagner's *Tannhäuser*.

Oedipus Rex (King Oedipus). Opera-oratorio in 2 acts by Stravinsky; text by Cocteau, after Sophocles' tragedy (c.435–425 BC), trans. into Latin by Jean Daniélou. Prem. Paris, SB, 30 May 1927, as oratorio; first stage prem. Vienna 23 Feb. 1928.

Thebes, mythological times. The people of Thebes seek the murderer of their former king, Laius, in order that their plague may be ended. The present king, Oedipus (ten), is disturbed to learn from the soothsayer that the killer was himself a king.

Jocasta (mez), Oedipus' wife who was previously married to Laius, assures the people that her first husband was killed by an unknown traveller. It then emerges that Oedipus' father was not Polybus, but Laius. Oedipus has fulfilled the prophecy of the oracle that Laius would be killed by his own son, though without knowing his victim's identity and Jocasta would marry her son. In final realization of the situation, Jocasta commits suicide and Oedipus blinds himself and departs for Colonus.

Oehmann, Carl Martin (b Floda, 4 Sept. 1887; d Stockholm, 26 Dec. 1967). Swedish tenor. Studied Stockholm with Gentzel, Milan with Oxilia and Quadri. Début Livorno, 1914 (Chénier). Göteborg 1917–23; Stockholm 1919–23, 1927–37; New York, M, 1924–5; Berlin, SO, 1925–37; London, CG, 1928. Roles included Tannhäuser, Walther, Hermann, Verdi's Otello, Bacchus. Retired from stage 1937, and taught; pupils included J. Björling, Gedda, and Talvela. (R)

Oestvig, Karl (b Oslo, 17 May 1889; d Oslo, 21 July 1968). Norwegian tenor. Studied Cologne with Steinbach. Début Stuttgart 1914. Stuttgart until 1919; Vienna, S, 1919–27; Berlin, SO, 1927–30. Retired 1932. Dir. Oslo O 1941. Described by Lotte Lehmann as 'a dazzling meteor'. A distinguished Lohengrin, Parsifal, and Walther, and 'positively ideal' (Strauss) as Bacchus. Created Giovanni (*Mona Lisa*) and Emperor (*Die Frau ohne Schatten*). (R)

Offenbach, Jacques (b Cologne, 20 June 1819; d Paris, 5 Oct. 1880). German, later French, composer and conductor. Son of a Cologne synagogue cantor from Offenbach originally named Eberst; studied with Alexander and Breuer, then from 1833 at Paris Cons. Forced to leave for financial reasons 1834; joined the orchestra of the T Ambigu Comique as cellist, moving to Opéra-Comique in 1837. In 1839 he composed his first dramatic work, the vaudeville *Pascal et Chambord* (1839), but first came to popular attention as a salon musician. During the 1840s his reputation in this field increased, though he failed to make any headway on the stage and for a while contemplated emigrating to the US. He became conductor of the T Français in 1850, and in 1855 rented the T Marigny in the Champs-Elysées which, renamed the Bouffes-Parisiens, was the venue for a season of operettas during the Exhibition of 1855. This was the turning-point of his career: with works like *Les deux aveugles* and *Le violoneux*, performed as part of a repertoire including Adam and Delibes, he won overnight successes.

For the winter Offenbach gave up his position at the T Français and moved to the T Comte. Here he gave the mock-oriental *Ba-ta-clan* (1855) and organized a competition for the best operetta, won by Bizet and Lecocq with their settings of *Le docteur Miracle*. In 1857 his company made a successful visit to London, though he was soon forced to flee Paris for a while because of debt. He returned with *Orpheus in the Underworld*, whose prem. in 1858 was his greatest triumph, quickly making him famous throughout France, Europe, and the US. In 1860 his first operetta was given at the Opéra-Comique, *Barkouf*, but in 1861 he gave up direction of the Bouffes-Parisiens in order to devote more time to composition. His greatest works date from this period, including *La belle Hélène* (1864), *Barbe-bleue* (1866), *La vie parisienne* (1866), *La Grande-Duchesse de Gérolstein* (1867), and *La Périchole* (1868). For the Vienna Hofoper in 1864 he produced the 'grand romantic' (in fact, comic) opera *Die Rheinnixen* which was much admired by Hanslick. But after the war of 1871, during which he had had to flee France, the new mood in Paris was against his frivolous manner, while his German ancestry also provoked hostility. He took over the T de la Gaité 1873–5, but lost a considerable amount of money and was forced to take a trip to the US to replenish his purse. During his last years he continued to write, and was still capable of securing a brilliant success, as with *La fille du tambour-major* (1879). His last work, *The Tales of Hoffmann*, lay unfinished at his death and was completed by Ernest Guiraud.

A brilliant man of the theatre, with a flair for epitomizing the wit of the day, Offenbach discovered a style which appealed irresistibly to the French taste of the 1860s. His opéras bouffes satirize the classics or contemporary politics and society, sometimes by reference one to the other, and with especial allusion to the modes and manners of the Second Empire. Similarly, familiar music is often pressed into service in absurd situations or made ludicrous by association with unexpected works. The impeccable *boulevardier* manner and exhilarating high spirits conceal the skill of these captivating pieces as well as the composer's literary erudition; they also distract from the lack of a true lyrical gift such as Johann Strauss could display. That he never lacked melodic appeal is shown not only in the frothiest of the operettas but also in *The Tales of Hoffmann*, though structural slackness and an absence of real musical substance weaken this, his one attempt at a larger-scale work with continuous music. At its best, his melodic manner could be touching (as with John Styx's aria in *Orpheus in the Underworld*, 'Quand j'étais roi de Béotie') as well as hilarious (the famous concluding Galop in the same work). There is, moreover, a recurrent cynicism and fatalism concealed beneath the Second Empire merriment which led Mauriac to write of *La Grande-Duchesse de Gérolstein*, 'The laughter I hear in Offenbach's music is that of the Empress Charlotte, gone mad.'

'O Isis und Osiris'. Sarastro's (bs) prayer to the Egyptian gods in Act II of Mozart's *Die Zauberflöte*.

Old Vic, The. Properly, The Royal Victoria Hall: the theatre in the Waterloo Road, South London, birthplace of the English opera company which later had its home at *Sadler's Wells. Built in 1818 as the Royal Coburg Hall by Joseph Glossop, who as Giuseppe Glossop was impresario at the Milan S and Naples C where he married one of the singers. Their son Augustus Glossop Harris was the father of Augustus *Harris, manager of London CG 1888–96. Renamed the Royal Victoria Hall 1833. In 1880 its lease was acquired by Emma Cons, and it was renamed the Royal Victoria Coffee Hall: opera was first heard as excerpts in costume. She was succeeded in 1898 by her niece Lilian *Baylis, who as well as Shakespeare gave opera twice a week and on alternate Saturday matinées. Even works on the scale of *Tristan* were heard, in drastically reduced versions by the music director, Charles Corri. After the First World War, Baylis invited the soprano Muriel Gough to produce *Figaro*; she declined in favour of Clive Carey, who persuaded Baylis to use E. J. Dent's translation. This was the beginning of the Dent–Carey Mozart revival in England, and of a move towards new standards of translation. By 1931, when Sadler's Wells opened, the repertory had widened to include Verdi and Wagner, with singers including Joan Cross, Edith Coates, Sumner Austin, Tudor Davies and Powell Lloyd, with Lawrance Collingwood as conductor. There were also ballet evenings under Ninette de Valois with Constant Lambert conducting. No opera was given at the Old Vic between 1935 and 1979, when the English Music T gave a short season; in 1991 *Carmen Jones* was performed there.

Olga. Olga Larina (mez), lover of Lensky, in Tchaikovsky's *Eugene Onegin*.

Oliver, Stephen (*b* Liverpool, 10 Mar. 1950; *d* London, 29 Apr. 1992). English composer. Studied Oxford with Leighton and Sherlaw Johnson. An intelligent and fluent composer with a strong theatrical instinct, he wrote many operas. Some of the most successful are brief, laconic pieces, e.g. the wordless squib *The Waiter* (1976); some approach the musical, e.g. *Jacko's Play* (1979) and *Blondel* (1983); others are more ambitious, e.g. *Tom Jones* (1976) and *Timon of Athens* (1991). He also wrote *Three Instant Operas* (1973) for children. Translated works by Sallinen, and made an arrangement of Peri's *Euridice*.

Olivero, Magda (*b* Saluzzo, 25 Mar. 1912). Italian soprano. Studied Turin with Gerussi and Simonetto. Début Turin 1933 (Lauretta). Successful career in Italy until 1941, when she married and left the stage. Returned 1951, at Cilea's request, to sing Adriana Lecouvreur, of which he considered her the ideal interpreter. London, Stoll T, 1952; Edinburgh 1963; New York, M, 1975. A notable singing actress; her successes included Medea, Fedora, Tosca, Minnie, Mimì, Liù. (R)

Olivier. A poet (bar), rival of the musician Flamand for the Countess, in Strauss's *Capriccio*.

Olszewska, Maria (*b* Ludwigsschwaige, 12 Aug. 1892; *d* Klagenfurt, 17 May 1969). German mezzo-soprano. Studied Munich with Erler. Début Krefeld 1915 (Page, *Tannhäuser*). Hamburg 1917–20; Vienna 1921–3, 1925–30; London, CG, 1924–33; Chicago 1928–32; New York, M, 1933–5. A dramatically intelligent singer with a glowing tone, celebrated as Ortrud, Brangäne, Herodias, Octavian. Created Brigitte in Korngold's *Die tote Stadt*. (R)

'O luce di quest'anima'. Linda's (sop) aria in Act I of Donizetti's *Linda di Chamounix*, in which she sings of her love for Arthur.

Olympia. The doll (sop), Hoffmann's first love, in Offenbach's *Les contes d'Hoffmann*.

Olympie. Opera in 3 acts by Spontini; text by M. Dieulafoy and C. Brifaut, after Voltaire's tragedy (1762). Prem. Paris, O, 22 Dec. 1819.

Ephesus, 332 BC. Antigone (bar) is reconciled to his former adversary Cassandre (ten); he has killed Alexander the Great, whose daughter Olympie (sop) he plans to marry. But she loves Cassandre, whom Arzana (mez) suspects of the murder. Arzana

discloses herself to the priests as Alexander's widow Statyre. Mortally wounded, Antigone confesses to the murder. The original version ends with Olympie's death and Statyre's suicide; the revision has Olympie marrying Cassandre and Statyre resuming the throne.

O'Mara, Joseph (*b* Limerick, 16 July 1861; *d* Dublin, 5 Aug. 1927). Irish tenor. Studied Milan with Moretti. Début London, Royal English OH, 1891 (Ivanhoe). London: CG and DL, 1894–5; Moody-Manners Co., 1902–8; CG, 1910 under Beecham. Formed O'Mara Co. 1912; sang with it until 1924. Large repertory included Walther, Lohengrin, Don José, and a famous Eléazar. Retired 1926. (R)

'Ombra mai fù'. Serse's (sop cas) aria in Act I of Handel's *Serse*, praising the tree that gives him shade. Though marked larghetto, it has become irrevocably known as 'Handel's Largo'.

'O Mimì, tu più non torni'. The duet between Rodolfo (ten) and Marcello (bar), mourning Mimì's fickleness, in Act IV of Puccini's *La bohème*.

'O mio babbino caro'. Lauretta's (sop) aria in Puccini's *Gianni Schicchi*, in which she appeals to her father to allow her to marry Rinuccio.

'O mio Fernando'. Léonor's (mez) aria in Act III of the Italian version of Donizetti's *La favorite*, in which she sings of her love for Fernando.

'O my beloved father'. See 'O MIO BABBINO CARO'.

'O namenlose Freude'. The duet of reunion for Leonore (sop) and Florestan (ten) in Act II of Beethoven's *Fidelio*.

Oncina, Juan (*b* Barcelona, 15 Apr. 1925). Spanish tenor. Studied Barcelona with Capsir. Début Barcelona 1946 (Massenet's Des Grieux). Sang widely in Italy 1946–52. Gly. 1952–61. A leading Donizetti and Rossini singer; also sang Ferrando, Don José, Cavaradossi. (R)

'One fine day'. See 'UN BEL DÌ VEDREMO'.

Onegin, Sigrid (*b* Stockholm, 1 June 1889; *d* Magliaso, 16 June 1943). Franco-German contralto. Studied Munich with Reiss, Milan with Di Ranieri. Début Stuttgart 1912 (Carmen). Munich 1919–22; New York, M,

1922–4; London, CG, 1927; Berlin 1926–31; Bayreuth 1933–4. Created Dryad in *Ariadne auf Naxos*; also successful as Gluck's Orfeo, Fidès, and especially, with her regal style, as Lady Macbeth, Amneris, and Fricka. Her excellent voice was of great range and richness. (R)

O'Neill, Dennis (*b* Pontardulais, 25 Feb. 1948). Welsh tenor. Studied RNCM. Début Wexford 1973 (*Ivan Susanin*). Sang with S Australia O 1974–6 (prem. of Sitsky's *Fiery Tales*). WNO début 1979 (Alfredo). Studied further in Italy; made London, CG, and Gly. débuts 1979–80. US début Dallas 1983 (Edgardo); New York, M, 1987 (Rodolfo). He brings musical perception and finely focused acting to such roles as Verdi's Foresto and Radamès (both at London, CG), Alfredo, Verdi's Otello, and Gabriele Adorno. (R)

'Ô paradis'. Vasco da Gama's (ten) apostrophe to the island of Madagascar in Act IV of Meyerbeer's *L'Africaine*.

'O patria mia'. Aida's (sop) aria in Act III (the Nile Scene) of Verdi's *Aida*, in which she mourns that she will never again see her beloved homeland.

opera (It.: 'work'; an abbreviation of *opera in musica*). A drama to be sung with instrumental accompaniment by one or more singers in costume; *recitative or spoken dialogue may separate musical numbers. See also GRAND OPERA, MUSIC DRAMA, OPERA BUFFA, OPÉRA-COMIQUE, OPERA SERIA, SINGSPIEL.

Opéra (Paris). The name by which the most important French operatic institution, and its building, have often been generally known, even when officially entitled Académie Royale de Musique, Théâtre des Arts, Théâtre de la Nation, etc., recently Opéra-Bastille, and when occupying various of 15-odd theatres during its history.

On 28 June 1669, Robert *Cambert and the Abbé Pierre *Perrin obtained a royal privilege from Louis XIV to perform 'académies d'opéra ou réprésentations en musique et en langue françoise, sur le pied de celles d'Italie'. They joined with the Marquis de Sourdéac as producer and Beauchamp as ballet-master to recruit singers in the Languedoc. In 1670 they rented the Salle du Jeu de Paume ('de la Bouteille') for five years, converted it into a theatre, and opened 3 Mar. 1671 with Cambert and Perrin's *Pomone*. *Lully secured the patent from Perrin in Mar. 1672, opening at the Salle du Jeu de Paume de Bel Air on 15 Nov. with *Les fêtes de l'Amour et de Bacchus*. He moved to the Palais-Royal 1674. Together with his librettist *Quinault he gave in 15 years some 20 works whose form and nature as 'tragédies mises en musique' (later described as *tragédie lyrique) set a style for the Opéra. The manner was given a new aspect by Lully's successors *Destouches and *Campra, later (in particular) *Rameau, who made his début at the Opéra with *Hippolyte et Aricie*, 1733, and had 24 of his operas produced by 1760. The theatre burnt down 6 Apr. 1763, and the company occupied the Salle des Tuileries 1764–9, returning to the renovated Palais-Royal (cap. 2,500) in 1770.

After Rameau's death in 1764, opera was principally in the hands of foreigners. The reign of *Gluck began with *Iphigénie en Aulide*, 1774; the arrival of *Piccinni, representing a more Italianate manner in contrast to Gluck's dramatic realism, precipitated a famous controversy. In 1781 the Palais-Royal again burnt down, and the Opéra transferred to the Salle des Menus-Plaisirs. The new theatre at the Salle de la Porte Saint-Martin (cap. *c*.2,000) was opened by Marie Antoinette Oct. 1781 with Piccinni's *Adèle de Ponthieu*. In 1794 the company moved again to the Salle Montansier (cap. 1,650: parterre audience seated for the first time). After various changes of name during and after the Revolution, it was established on a firmer footing with the title Académie Impériale de Musique. The repertory was widened, though the traditional emphasis on ballet remained.

In 1807 the era of *Spontini, Napoleon's favoured composer, opened with *La vestale*. Together with *Cherubini, he confirmed a style of *Grand Opera which marked the Opéra for many decades. In 1820 the company moved to the Salle Favart, opening 19 June with Kreutzer's *Clari*, briefly in 1821 to the Salle Louvois, and in 1822 to the Salle de la rue Peletier (cap. 1,954), opening 6 Feb. with *Isouard's *Aladin, ou La lampe merveilleuse*. In this work, suitably, gaslight was first used. Operas by *Rossini, *Donizetti, *Auber, *Meyerbeer, *Hérold, and *Halévy, in particular, were given in sumptuous stagings by *Cicéri and *Daguerre. The conventions of the Opéra dictated a 5-act work, with multiple soloists and choruses, an Act 2 ballet, and no spoken dialogue. In 1849

Meyerbeer, the most successful of his day in meeting these requirements, had his *Le prophète* produced with electric lighting. This was the period in which the Opéra, under Louis Véron, dominated Europe, setting a grand style, rewarding success with fame and fortune, imposing powerful but demanding standards as an orthodoxy, and thereby compelling composers as diverse as Wagner, Verdi, and Tchaikovsky to attempt the challenge. Wagner failed to achieve performance with *Rienzi*, and met a notorious scandal when his rewriting of *Tannhäuser* did not satisfy in 1861. Berlioz never had *Les Troyens* produced here in his lifetime.

In 1873 the Opéra again burnt down, and the company moved to the Salle Ventadour. Charles Garnier's sumptuous theatre was planned in 1867, but delayed by the Franco-Prussian War. The 'Nouvel Opéra' in the Salle du Boulevard des Capucines (or Palais Garnier) (cap. 2,156) opened 5 Jan. 1875, and was one of the largest and grandest theatres in the world. The auditorium was electrically lit 1881, the stage 1887. The policy was virtually that of a museum of French opera. Under the directorship of Jacques Rouché, 1915–45, this policy was extended; he preserved tradition, resisting innovation in its name, welcomed only the most orthodox composers, and isolated his singers from international careers while also generally excluding even the most distinguished foreign artists.

In 1939 the Opéra and Opéra-Comique were united as the Réunion des Théâtres Lyriques Nationaux. Rouché continued in office, and his policies endured after his retirement aged 82, though there was a gradual relaxation of the rule against spoken dialogue (finally admitting *The Magic Flute*, 1954) and then foreign languages. This, and a more adventurous policy about modern opera, did not halt the Opéra's decline. Rolf Liebermann was director 1973–80, placing the Opéra back on the world stage, even if losing it some of the old character while retaining some of the abuses. Among important events were the prems. of the complete *Lulu* (1979) and Messiaen's *St François d'Assise* (1983). After fierce public controversy, including the dismissal of the intended music director, Daniel Barenboim, in 1989, and amid technical troubles, the new Opéra-Bastille (cap. 2,716) opened 17 Mar. 1990 with the first almost complete French performance of *Les Troyens*, under the new music director, Myung-Whun Chung, who himself left amid much adverse publicity in 1994. It was intended as an 'opera for the people'; the building includes two smaller halls. The current director is Hugues Gall.

Opera 80. See OPERA FOR ALL.

opéra-ballet. A dramatic entertainment popular in France in the early 18th cent. in which operatic elements were combined with ballet. Its characteristic feature was a lack of dramatic continuity, for each entrée (scene) presented a discrete plot. Their most celebrated composer was Campra, who in works such as *L'Europe galante* (1697) and *Les fêtes vénitiennes* (1710) elevated lyrical comedy to the high status formerly only enjoyed by tragedy on the French stage.

opéra-bouffe (Fr.). A designation frequently given to satirical 19th-cent. French operetta: the classic example is Offenbach's *Orfée aux enfers*.

opera buffa (It.: 'comic opera'). Comic scenes first appeared in opera in Landi's *La morte d'Orfeo* (1619), but it was not until Mazzocchi's *Chi soffre, speri* (1639) and Abbatini's *Dal male il bene* (1653) that the exclusively comic opera was born. With the libretto reforms of Zeno and Metastasio in the early 18th cent., and the complete excision of comic elements from opera seria, there was an increased cultivation of the intermezzo, the genre of 1-act comic opera which had first been seen as early as 1623. Alongside the independent production of intermezzo there also developed the new genre of opera buffa, which shared its essential features, but was larger in scale and constituted a full-length entertainment in its own right. The earliest example was probably Orefice's *Patrò Calienno de la Costa*, though Pergolesi's *La serva padrona* (1733) is often regarded as the first great example of the genre. Like most later works, it deals with common, everyday characters, rather than the heroes and kings of opera seria, eschews the *castrato in favour of natural voices, particularly the bass, and places some emphasis on the ensemble. Pergolesi's work was supported by that of Logroscino, Leo, Vinci, Paisiello, Piccinni, Fischietti, and Cimarosa among others. The greatest composer of opera buffa was undoubtedly Mozart, who provided a fitting culmination to its development in his masterpieces *Le nozze di Figaro* (1786) and *Così* *fan tutte* (1790). Here, broad adherence to the main conventions of the genre is tempered by a uniquely enquiring, yet humane, approach to outwardly comic situations, allowing him to uncover the real unhappiness, even tragedy, which they actually conceal.

opéra-comique (Fr.: 'comic opera'). Despite its literal meaning, 'comic opera' conveys a false impression of this vague but generally accepted term: indeed, the French themselves understand different things by it according to the date of its use. Generally, it is taken to refer to the tradition of opera with spoken dialogue which developed during the 18th cent. under the influence of the librettist Favart and was given greater impetus through the appearance of Rousseau's *Le devin du village*. This inspired a new generation of opéra-comique composers, including Duni, Monsigny, and Philidor among many others, who wrote works in which musical numbers cast in a simple style were linked by spoken dialogue: this form was also known as the *comédie mêlée d'ariettes*. With the next generation a certain emphasis on the heroic may sometimes be discerned, especially in such works as Grétry's *Richard Cœur de Lion* and Boieldieu's *Jean de Paris*.

For a while opéra-comique developed along lines similar to those of the Italian *opera semiseria* and there are many similarities between the works of Paisiello and Cimarosa, and the French tradition of the early 19th cent., represented above all by Dezède and Dalayrac. Gradually the worlds of serious opera and opéra-comique began to blend, so that the remaining distinctive feature of the latter genre was its retention of spoken dialogue rather than sung recitative. In the 19th cent. the designation opéra-comique was thus applied to works which varied enormously in their physical and emotional scale. Serious, indeed tragic, themes were presented in such works as Méhul's *Joseph* and Cherubini's *Médée*, while Boieldieu, one of the most successful composers in the genre, showed a penchant for more Romantic themes, as in his masterpiece *La dame blanche*.

By the late 19th cent. the divide between serious opera and opéra-comique had all but disappeared, since spoken dialogue now made relatively rare appearances: one such was in Bizet's *Carmen*. However, with the strict traditions of the Paris *Opéra still largely observed, the rival house, the *Opéra-Comique, was the venue for a large number of more experimental works, which thus carried the generic description as well: among them may be included Delibes's *Lakmé* and Charpentier's *Louise*.

Opéra-Comique. Theatre in Paris, long the city's second opera-house; originally the home for French musical pieces with spoken dialogue. In 1714 an agreement between the Comédie-Française and the Académie Royale de Musique resulted in the setting up of the Opéra-Comique, inaugurating the T de la Foire Saint-Germain with the parody *Télemaque* (music by Gillier). Its success was so great that the Académie had it closed 1745; reopened 1752 at Saint-Germain, joined the Comédie-Italienne, 1762, first at the Hôtel de Bourgogne (rue Mauconseil), then 1783 at the Salle Favart, later known as Comédie-Italienne, Théâtre Italien, then Opéra-Comique. A rival 'Opéra-Comique' at the T Feydeau (which premiered Cherubini's *Médée*, 1797) bankrupted them both, and they merged to form the T Nat. de l'Opéra-Comique, 1801. In 1805 this moved to the Salle Feydeau. The company gave important prems. of works by *Spontini, *Méhul, *Dalayrac, *Boieldieu, *Isouard, and other composers whose opéras-comiques were pioneering examples of the genre and the most forward-looking operas of their day.

The company moved to the Salle Ventadour 1829, then to the T des Nouveautés, and in 1840 to the second Salle Favart. Here it maintained its reputation as a more open-minded, enterprising house than the convention-bound Opéra, welcoming many important new and foreign works, as well as being the home for opera with spoken dialogue when this was banned by the Opéra. Works by *Auber, *Hérold, *Massenet, and *Adam were prominent in the repertory, and prems. included *Carmen* (1875), *Hoffmann* (1881), *Lakmé* (1883), and *Manon* (1884). The theatre burnt down 1887, and Carvalho (director from 1876) was briefly imprisoned for negligence. The company eventually moved into the rebuilt Salle Favart (cap. 1,750), inaugurated 7 Dec. 1898, with Albert Carré as director (till 1925). Under him, prems. included *Louise* (1900), *Pelléas* (1902), and the Opéra-Comique became more of a rival to the Opéra. In 1939 the two were united as the Réunion des T

Lyriques Nationaux. Closed Apr. 1972 by the government, the Opéra-Comique housed the Opéra-Studio under Louis Erlo, Jan. 1973. It reopened with the old name Salle Favart, under Liebermann, in Dec. 1976.

Opera Factory. Company founded in Sydney 1973 by David Freeman (*b* Sydney, 1 May 1952); established Zurich 1976; sister co., in conjunction with London Sinfonietta, established 1981 with Freeman's production of *Punch and Judy*. Other O Factory successes were *Calisto* and *Knot Garden* (1984), the 1986 revival of *Così fan tutte*, and the prem. of *Yan Tan Tethera* (London, QEH, 1986). Freeman's work at London, C, includes *Orfeo*, *Ritorno d'Ulisse*, *Akhnaten*, and the prem. of *The Mask of Orpheus*; other important productions include *The Fiery Angel* (London, CG, and Kirov O, 1992). His demanding rehearsals and emphasis on the physical can produce remarkable performances from singers; his most striking productions can change a traditional view of the classical repertory (e.g. *Così*), though his strong ideas and inclination to the sensational can sometimes diminish the music.

Opera for All. A group founded in 1949 by the Arts Council of Great Britain to take opera to small towns, even villages, throughout the country. The initial group of six members expanded by 1966–7 into three groups of 12, touring in a minibus, based on the London Opera Centre, WNO, and Scottish O. By 1974 the Scottish and Welsh groups had expanded into autonomous ensembles, and Opera for All's London group remained the only one with the original name. In 1980 it was replaced by Opera 80, touring with a small orchestra and chorus.

opéra-lyrique (Fr.: 'lyric opera'). A term used, mostly outside France, for a style of opera that flourished in 19th-cent. France in distinction to *Grand Opera and *opéra-comique. In general, it was shorter and less rich in choral, scenic, and other effects than the former, while dispensing with the spoken dialogue of the latter. Beginning in the late 18th and early 19th cents., it developed in the works of Gounod and Thomas, and later Massenet, as a genre in which, on the whole, romantic elements were handled with a clarity, simplicity, and elegance that was at once more intense than opéra-comique in its more literally comic manifestations, and yet lighter in treatment than the most profound serious opera. Though it was not a term in general use among composers, Massenet did designate some of his operas as *drame lyrique*, *épisode lyrique*, *pièce lyrique*, and *conte lyrique*.

Opera North. Formed in Leeds in 1975, the company opened in 1978 as English National Opera North with *Samson et Dalila* under its music director, David Lloyd-Jones. It became independent in 1981, assuming its present name. Among productions that have won it a name for enterprise and high standards have been the prem. of Josephs's *Rebecca* (1983); the British prems. of Krenek's *Jonny spielt auf* (1984), Strauss's *Daphne* (1987), and Verdi's *Jérusalem* (1990); and productions of *Oedipus rex* (1981), *La traviata* (1985), *The Trojans at Carthage* (1986), Kern's *Show Boat* (1989), Dukas's *Ariane et Barbe-bleue* (1990), and Tippett's *Midsummer Marriage* (1985) and *King Priam* (1991). The company tours primarily in the north of England.

opera semiseria (It.: 'semi-serious opera'). The introduction of serious elements into opera buffa first occurred *c.*1750 in the librettos of *Goldoni. The style thus created, known as *dramma giocoso, gradually came to be more popular than the straight opera buffa, whose characters had always had a tendency to be mere comic stereotypes. During the later 18th cent., under the influence of the French comédie larmoyante, sentimental or melodramatic colouring became ever more popular, a characteristic which was formally recognized in the choice of such generic terms as **dramma di sentimento**, **dramma eroicomico**, and **dramma tragicomico**. From this tradition there developed opera semiseria, a term first used with reference to Paisiello's *Nina* (1789). Sharing their mixture of the comic and the sentimental, opera semiseria dealt with much of the same subject-matter, including the popular situation where the path of true love is thwarted by the conventions of society. A celebrated essay in the genre was Cimarosa's *Il matrimonio segreto* (1792).

opera seria (It.: 'serious opera'; sometimes also **melodramma serio**). The main operatic genre of the early and mid-18th cent., opera seria was born out of the libretto reforms of *Zeno and *Metastasio. At the heart of the genre lay two main concerns: to deliver, in an effective and appropriate manner, elegant verses and to provide a display vehicle for the talents of the solo singers whose presence now dominated opera. Unlike the Venetian style which it replaced, opera seria eschewed comic characters and scenes; these found their way into the *intermezzo, and thence eventually into *opera buffa. The earliest phase of opera seria has often been described as **Neapolitan opera**, a misleading term in that neither the developments which led to the formulation of the genre, nor the activities of the composers associated with it, were restricted to the city. Of a large school, which also included Porpora, Vinci, and Leo, the most important was undoubtedly Alessandro Scarlatti.

The full flourishing of the opera seria was reached in the music of Hasse, who in works such as *Cleofide* raised it to a supreme and confident reflection of 18th-cent. ideals. Around the same time, Handel was engaged in London concert life, to which he contributed a notable succession of opere serie. In the later 18th cent. several attempts were made to loosen or 'reform' the conventions of the genre: the most important of these were undertaken by Gluck, following earlier experiments by Jommelli and Traetta. Beginning in *Orfeo* and continuing in *Alceste*, whose famous preface provides a cogent explanation of his aims, he stripped opera seria of its musical excesses in an effort to provide a dramatically more satisfying work. Much has been made of his reforms, although their effect was short-lived. A certain influence can be traced in Mozart's *Idomeneo* and Haydn's *L'anima del filosofo*, but the eventual overthrow of opera seria's supremacy came not through reform, but as a result of the challenges laid down by opera buffa and Singspiel. Gradually, these became the most widely performed genres on the public stage, while opera seria retreated into the world of court opera. One of the last, and finest, opere serie is Mozart's *La clemenza di Tito*.

operetta (It.: 'little opera') (Fr., *opérette*). Originally used in the 17th cent. for a short opera, the term became associated by the 19th cent. with comic opera, to describe a play with an overture, songs, interludes, and dances. Beyond this, there is no single definition which is applicable to all the works usually thus described. In the 20th cent. a further development of operetta resulted in the musical comedy.

Two main strands of operetta may be identified. One was French, beginning with Offenbach, and continuing with such composers as Lecocq, and one Viennese. The latter, which drew inspiration from the established comic theatrical tradition in Vienna, may be traced back to Suppé and Johann Strauss II, although it achieved its most characteristic expression in the works of Lehár, Millöcker, Kálmán, and Ziehrer. In England the *Savoy operas of Gilbert and Sullivan are really operettas; in the US an indigenous tradition was established with the works of Victor Herbert and Reginald de Koven.

opérette. See OPERETTA.

Ophélie. Polonius's daughter (sop) in Thomas's *Hamlet*.

'Ora e per sempre addio'. Otello's (ten) farewell to his past glories in Act II of Verdi's *Otello*.

orchestra pit (Fr., *fosse d'orchestre*, Ger., *Orchestergraben*; It., *fossa d'orchestra*). The space before and below the stage which contains the opera orchestra. The partly hooded pit in the Bayreuth Festspielhaus, designed by Wagner and described by him as the 'mystic gulf' (mysticher Abgrund), allows an exceptionally faithful balance and a tonal blend especially suitable for his works, as well as an absence of visual distraction for the audience. Most opera-houses are now built with pits in sections of variable heights to assist the balance of different operas.

Orefice, Antonio (*fl*. Naples, 1708–34). Italian composer. A lawyer by profession; first came to attention with the opera seria *Maurizio* (1708). His *Patrò Calienno de la Costa* (1709) set a comic libretto in Neapolitan dialect; such was its success that several of Orefice's contemporaries, including Falco, Leo, and Vinci, were inspired to write similar operas. Composed *c*.14 further comic works for Naples; most of his music is now lost.

Orefice, Giacomo (*b* Vicenza, 27 Aug. 1865; *d* Milan, 22 Dec. 1922). Italian composer and critic. Studied Bologna with Mancinelli, offering *L'oasi* (1885) as his graduation exercise. Performed widely as a piano virtuoso before becoming professor of composition at Milan Cons. 1909; from 1920 music critic of the Milan *Secolo*. He was one of the first in Italy to encourage interest in older music and raise editorial standards, himself preparing versions of Monteverdi's *Orfeo* and Rameau's *Platée*.

Orefice wrote 11 operas which met with a mixed reception: they include *Chopin* (1901), based on the composer's life and using his music; *Mosè* (1905), his most successful work; and two based on Russian authors, *Il pane altrui* (1907) and *Radda* (1913). These technically proficient works belong to the verismo tradition.

Orest. Orestes (bs-bar), Elektra's brother, in Strauss's *Elektra*.

Oresteia. Opera-oratorios by Milhaud; texts by Paul Claudel, based closely on Aeschylus' tragedies. 1. *Agamemnon* prem. Paris 16 Apr. 1927. Clytemnestre greets her husband on his return from the war, but then kills him, in revenge for his sacrificing their daughter Iphigénie in order to gain victory.

2. *Les Choéphores* prem. Paris 8 Mar. 1927 (concert); Brussels, M, 27 Mar. 1935 (staged). This relates the story of Oreste, who kills his mother and her lover Aegisthe so as to avenge his father's death at his wife's hand. He is thereafter tormented by the Furies.

3. *Les Euménides* comp. 1917–22; prem. W Berlin Apr. 1963. This concerns Athene's and Apollon's pleas on behalf of Oreste and the eventual transformation of the Furies into the kindly Eumenides.

Orfeide, L'. Operatic triptych by Malipiero; text by the composer, comprising (1) *La morte delle maschere*, (2) *Sette canzoni*, and (3) *Orfeo, ovvero L'ottava canzone*. First complete prem. Düsseldorf 31 Oct. 1925.

Each of the three parts is independent. In *La morte delle maschere* masked commedia dell'arte figures are replaced with characters from real life. *Sette canzoni* consists of seven separate dramatic scenes, the majority of which depict one individual behaving harshly to another, or celebrating in the face of sorrow. Each is an expansion of a brief moment from life. The texts are drawn from old, mostly Renaissance, Italian sources. The third opera of the triptych, *Orfeo*, continues from the scenes of the previous opera; Orfeo sings a song which lulls everyone in a theatre to sleep, except the Queen, with whom Orfeo departs. This opera, like the first of the triptych, deals with the conflict between the artificiality of the theatre and reality.

Orfeo, La favola d' (The Legend of Orpheus). Opera in a prologue and 5 acts by Monte-verdi; text by Alessandro Striggio, after Ovid, *Metamorphoses* x. Prem. Mantua, Ducal Palace, before the Accademia degli Invaghiti, 24 Feb. 1607.

After a prologue, nymphs and shepherds are discovered rejoicing at the coming marriage of Orfeo and Euridice. In a wood, Orfeo sings to nature, but is interrupted by La Messaggera (the Messenger) bringing the news of Euridice's death. He descends to Hades to find her, and is comforted by Hope; lulling Charon with his song, he crosses the Styx and wins the agreement of Pluto and Pro-serpina that he may take her back to earth if he will not turn round to look at her on their journey. Unable to resist assuring himself that she is indeed there, he turns just as they reach the light, and she is snatched back to Hades. Orfeo laments his lot, but is consoled by Apollo with the promise of immortality with Euridice.

Orfeo ed Euridice. Opera in 3 acts by Gluck; text by Calzabigi, after the classical legend. Prem. Vienna, B, 5 Oct. 1762. French version, trans. Moline, and with title-role transposed for tenor, prem. Paris 2 Aug. 1774, with Legros, Arnould, Levasseur, cond. Francœur.

Greece, mythological times. Orfeo (con cas, in revision ten) mourns the death of his wife Euridice (sop). His grief is such that Zeus, the father of the gods, permits him to journey to Hades to try to reclaim her. If he can persuade Pluto through the power of his music, he may lead her home, but must not glance back at her until they have crossed the Styx.

The Furies try to block Orfeo's path and call on Cerberus, the triple-headed dog, to tear him to shreds. However, Orfeo charms them with his singing and continues on his way. In the Elysian fields he finds Euridice, and begins to guide her back to earth.

Euridice cannot understand her husband's strange behaviour, which he is forbidden to explain. Believing he no longer loves her, she says she would rather die. In desperation, Orfeo turns to face her; she falls dead. But Amor (sop), touched by the beauty of the lament Orfeo sings, restores Euridice to life.

Orff, Carl (*b* Munich, 10 July 1895; *d* Munich, 29 Mar. 1982). German composer. Studied Munich, where he wrote his first opera, *Gisei* (1913). Worked as répétiteur and then conductor at Munich, Mannheim, and Darmstadt. In 1920 he resumed study with Kaminski, who encouraged him in the study of old music, resulting in arrangements of Monteverdi, including his first of *Orfeo* (1925; other versions 1931 and 1940). In 1924 he founded (with Dorothée Günther) the Günther School in Munich; here a revolutionary approach was adopted, with musical gifts encouraged by their expression through gymnastics and dance. For this purpose Orff developed the concept of the *Schulwerk* (school-work), music dedicated to the pedagogical exercise, using recorders, percussion, and other technically straightforward instruments.

Carmina Burana (1937), called a scenic cantata since it is not staged but performed to the accompaniment of mime and dance, brought Orff immediate fame. Its methods were used, less successfully, in *Catulli carmina* (1943) and *Trionfo di Afrodite* (1953). These were the first works to explore Orff's so-called 'total theatre', the fundamental principles of which underpin all his dramatic music: a return to elementary rhythms and popular folk-song and the eschewal of counterpoint and thematic development. In practice this resulted in a series of works with such interrupted dramatic action and static settings that the description 'opera' may be but loosely applied. *Der Mond* (1939), a Bavarian fairy-tale, employs a narrator to tell the story, only three episodes of which are seen on the stage: it contains some of Orff's most lyrical music, as does the highly successful *Die Kluge* (1943). Similar techniques are used in *Die Bernauerin* (1947), *Oedipus der Tyrann* (1959), *Ludus de nato infante mirificus* (1960), *Prometheus* (1968), and *De temporum fine comoedia* (1973). Only in *Antigonae* does Orff approach the spirit of genuine opera in a sensitive and original treatment of Sophocles, tragedy which attempts to recreate the earliest operatic experiments.

Orgeni, Aglaja (*b* Rimászombat, 17 Dec. 1841; *d* Vienna, 15 Mar. 1926). Hungarian soprano. Studied Baden-Baden with Viardot. Début Berlin, 1865 (Amina). London, CG, 1866. Extensive career in Europe 1867–86, celebrated in coloratura roles, and as Agathe, Leonora (*Trovatore*), etc. Taught 1886–1914 Dresden Cons., where she was the first female Royal Professor.

Orlandini, Giuseppe Maria (*b* Florence, 4 Apr. 1676; *d* Florence, 24 Oct. 1760). Italian composer. Active at the Florentine Court, he composed *c*.44 operas. He is particularly remembered for the intermezzo *Il marito giocatore* (1719): possibly the most frequently performed operatic work of the 18th cent.— often as *Serpilla e Bacocco*—it reveals a light, witty touch and was important in the development of opera buffa.

Orleanskaya deva. See MAID OF ORLEANS, THE.

Orlovsky. The Russian prince (con, sometimes ten) in J. Strauss's *Die Fledermaus*.

Oroveso. The High Priest of the Druids (bs) in Bellini's *Norma*.

Orphée aux enfers (Orpheus in the Underworld). Operetta in 4 acts by Offenbach; text by Crémieux and L. Halévy, possibly from a German scenario by Cramer. Prem. Paris, BP, 21 Oct. 1858 (2 acts); Paris, Gaîté, 7 Feb. 1874 (4 acts).

In this parody of the Orpheus legend, Orphée (ten) is a violin-teacher in Thebes; his wife Eurydice (sop) has a lover Pluton (ten), disguised as the shepherd and bee-keeper Aristée. Pluton carries her away to the Underworld, so she leaves Orphée a note saying she is dead. Opinion Publique (mez) demands that he try and recover Eurydice from Hades. At Mount Olympus the gods are complaining about Jupiter's (bar) unacceptable behaviour, and of their unvarying diet of nectar and ambrosia. Orphée and Opinion Publique arrive and, at Jupiter's command, Pluton is compelled to hand back Eurydice. The gods decide to go to Hades to look for her.

In Hades, Eurydice sings a love duet with Jupiter, who has taken the form of a fly. Resuming his true shape, he turns her into a Bacchante and together they dance the cancan. Orphée enters and is warned that he must not look at his wife as he leads her back to earth. But Jupiter lets loose a thunderbolt which causes Orphée to jump round in fright, and so he has to forgo Eurydice, who stays as a Bacchante.

Orpheus in the Underworld. See ORPHÉE AUX ENFERS.

'Or sai chi l'onore'. Donna Anna's (sop) aria in Act I of Mozart's *Don Giovanni*, in which she reveals to Don Ottavio that it was Giovanni who tried to seduce her and upon him that he must take vengeance.

Orsini. Paolo Orsini (bs), a Roman patrician, in Wagner's *Rienzi*.

Ortrud. Telramund's wife (mez) in Wagner's *Lohengrin*.

Osborne, Nigel (*b* Manchester, 23 June 1948). English composer. Studied Oxford with Wellesz and Leighton, Warsaw with Rudziński. His first opera, *Hell's Angels* (1986) aroused little except distaste, but he drew much attention and admiration for *The Electrification of the Soviet Union* (the title is a quotation from Lenin, 'Communism is Soviet power plus the electrification of the whole country'). A Glyndebourne commission (1987), this makes use of songs, a powerful orchestral narrative, some electronic music, and cinematic devices to articulate a drama whose action proceeds at different levels. The novelty of the work, and initially the difficulty of grasping the words, caused a good deal of puzzlement, but also widespread interest. *Terrible Mouth* (1992) based on the life of Goya and set in a war hospital, aroused further distaste.

Oscar. The page (sop) to King Gustavus III (or Riccardo) in Verdi's *Un ballo in maschera*.

Osmin. The overseer (bs) of the Pasha Selim's estates in Mozart's *Die Entführung aus dem Serail*.

'O soave fanciulla'. The love duet between Rodolfo (ten) and Mimì (sop) ending Act I of Puccini's *La bohème*.

'O souverain! o juge!' Rodrigue's (ten) prayer in Act II of Massenet's *Le Cid*.

Ossian, ou Les bardes (Ossian, or The Bards). Opera in 5 acts by Le Sueur; text by Palat-Dercy and Deschamps. Prem. Paris, O, 10 July 1804.

Scotland, mythical times. The Scandinavians, led by Duntalmo (bs), have captured Caledonia. Rosmala (sop) is to marry Duntalmo's son Morval (ten), although she loves the Caledonian warrior Ossian (ten). About to be sacrificed to Odin by the Scandinavians, Ossian (in a famous tableau) dreams of bards and heroes of the past. Rosmala and her father Rosmor (bs) are also captured as sacrificial victims. However, all three are rescued by the Caledonians, and the opera ends with the marriage of Ossian and Rosmala.

Osten, Eva von der (*b* Heligoland, 19 Aug. 1881; *d* Dresden, 5 May 1936). German soprano and producer. Studied Dresden with Iffert and Söhle. Début Dresden 1902 (Urbain). Sang there until 1927. Berlin, H, from 1906; London, CG, 1913–14, and HM, 1913; USA, with German OC, 1922–4. Chosen as first Octavian; also sang Ariadne, Dyer's Wife (as which Strauss thought her 'magnificent'), Brünnhilde, Isolde, Kundry, Tatyana, Louise. Married the baritone Friedrich *Plaschke. After retiring, became producer at Dresden, and was artistic adviser for the first *Arabella*. (R)

Östman, Arnold (*b* Malmö, 24 Dec. 1939). Swedish conductor. Studied Paris and Stockholm. Music dir. of Vadstena Academy (1970–82), giving operas by Purcell, Provenzale, and Monteverdi. Best known for his performances at the Drottningholm Court Theatre (music dir. 1979–91), in which operas by Mozart, Kraus and Gluck have been given in convincing period style. London, CG, 1984 (*Don Giovanni*); Wexford 1986 (*Tancredi*); Vienna, S, 1990 (*Lucio Silla*). (R)

Ostrčil, Otakar (*b* Prague, 25 Feb. 1879; *d* Prague, 20 Aug. 1935). Czech composer and conductor. Studied Prague with Fibich. Though initially a teacher of philology, he conducted at the Nat. T from 1909 and was Dramaturg and conductor at the Vinohrady T 1914–18: here he introduced little-known operas by his contemporaries Foerster and Zich, also by Mozart, Weber, Berlioz, and Halévy. Director Nat. T from 1920 (when he conducted the prem. of *The Excursions of Mr Brouček*). An effective and influential director, he gave cycles of operas by Smetana (1924, 1927, 1934), Fibich (1925, 1932), and Dvořák (1929, 1934). He also introduced many new works, including by Janáček, and conducted the Czech prem. of *Wozzeck*, among other important works. His own operas show him to be a follower of Smetana and Fibich. The most successful of them has been *Honzovo království* (Johnny's Kingdom, 1934).

O'Sullivan, John (*b* Cork, 1878; *d* Paris, 28 Apr. 1955). Irish tenor. Studied Paris Cons. Début Geneva 1911 (Reyer's Sigurd). Paris, O, 1914, 1916–18, 1922, 1930–2; Chicago 1919–20; Milan 1924; London, CG, 1927. His fine top notes made him especially successful as Arnold, Raoul, and Manrico. Much admired by James Joyce. (R)

Otello. 1. Opera in 4 acts by Verdi; text by Boito, after Shakespeare's tragedy. Prem. Milan, S, 5 Feb. 1887.

Cyprus, 15th cent. The people of Cyprus anxiously await the safe return of the Moor Otello (ten), Venetian governor of the island. He lands unharmed, but Iago (bar) plots to kill him in revenge for Cassio's promotion over him. He obtains Cassio's (ten) dismissal by exaggerating reports of his involvement in a brawl.

Iago succeeds in making Otello believe that there is an affair between Desdemona (sop) and Cassio. So when, at Iago's instigation, she tries to secure Cassio's release, Otello refuses. Iago's wife Emilia (mez) helps him produce further 'evidence' which convinces Otello of his wife's guilt.

Otello again refuses Desdemona's plea for clemency for Cassio and, after further 'proof' supplied by Iago, decides to murder Desdemona that night. When a Venetian ambassador announces that Cassio is to succeed Otello as governor, Otello flies into a rage and flings his wife to the ground, cursing her. Prompted by Iago, Roderigo (ten), who was in love with Desdemona, attempts to kill Cassio.

Unable to understand her husband's behaviour, Desdemona recalls, in the 'Willow Song', one of her maid's tales of abandonment. Otello enters and, despite Desdemona's protests of innocence, suffocates her. Emilia reports Roderigo's death and exposes Iago's plot. Racked with guilt, Otello stabs himself, kissing Desdemona as he dies.

2. Opera in 3 acts by Rossini, text by Marchese Francesco Beria di Salsa, after Shakespeare's tragedy (1604–5). Prem. Naples, T del Fondo, 4 Dec. 1816. Rossini's opera includes material from the Venetian first act of Shakespeare's play, though in the opera Desdemona is pledged by her father Elmiro to Rodrigo. She has in fact pledged herself to Otello, but a love-letter to him is intercepted by Iago, who pretends it was meant for Rodrigo. Otello and Rodrigo fight. After Otello has murdered Desdemona in a jealous rage, Iago confesses his plot and commits suicide. Tormented by guilt and grief, Otello also kills himself.

'O terra, addio'. The closing duet between Aida (sop) and Radamès (ten) in Act IV of Verdi's *Aida*, in which they bid farewell to life on earth.

Otter, Anne-Sofie von (*b* Stockholm, 9 May 1955). Swedish mezzo-soprano. Studied Stockholm Cons., and London with Rozsa. Début Basle 1982 (Hänsel). London, CG, and Berlin, D, from 1985; also Geneva, Stockholm O, etc. New York, M, 1990. Roles include Cherubino, Dorabella, Sesto, Ramiro (*La finta giardiniera*), Composer, Romeo (Bellini). Possesses an outstanding voice and technique. (R)

Otto, Teo (*b* Remscheid, 4 Feb. 1904; *d* Frankfurt, 9 June 1968). German designer. Studied Kassel, Paris, and the Bauhaus in Weimar. Engaged by Klemperer for Berlin, Kroll O, 1927. Chief designer Berlin State Theatres 1927. Left Germany 1933; mostly Zurich until· 1945. Salzburg, Vienna, Zurich. New York, M, *Tristan* 1960. London, CG, *Figaro* 1963. Favoured real materials to give 'tactile excitements to the set' rather than the painted scenic object.

Ottokar. The Prince (bar) to whom the villagers owe allegiance in Weber's *Der Freischütz*.

'O tu che in seno agli angeli'. Alvaro's (ten) aria in Act III of Verdi's *La forza del destino*, in which he remembers Leonora, whom he believes dead.

'O tu, Palermo'. Procida's_(bs) aria in Act II of the Italian version of Verdi's *Les vêpres siciliennes* (orig. 'O toi, Palerme'), invoking the spirit of his homeland after his long absence.

overture. From the French *ouverture*, opening, the word normally used for the instrumental prelude to an opera, oratorio, play, ballet, or other work; later a concert work unconnected with the stage.

The earliest operas usually began with little more than a flourish of instruments, e.g. the Toccata opening Monteverdi's *Orfeo*, and sometimes had no overture at all. More elaborate introductions began to be used in Roman opera, such as the sinfonias which open the three acts of Landi's *Il sant'Alessio*; the familiar form of later Venetian opera was the canzona overture, usually cast with an introductory slow movement in duple rhythm and a fast movement in triple rhythm. This model was adapted by Lully into the French overture and supplanted in its native country by the *Italian overture around the turn of the 18th cent.

The idea of using material from the opera in the overture is anticipated by the introductory sinfonia to Cesti's *Il pomo d'oro*, where music from later scenes appears; the first important use of the technique occurs in Rameau's *Castor et Pollux*; despite earlier suggestions, it did not become accepted practice until Gluck. Mozart continued the practice, setting the mood of *Don Giovanni* and *Die Zauberflöte* or using some elements that recur, and in *Così fan tutte* using a motto theme to represent the words of the title. Beethoven took this principle of thematic anticipation further in the three *Leonore* overtures he wrote for *Fidelio*; and it reached its climax in Weber, who (taking his cue from Spohr's *Faust*) made his later overtures virtually epitomes of the ensuing opera, while adhering to sonata form. In Italy the overture was still designed chiefly to hush talkers and admit late-comers, only incidentally attempting to compose the audience's mind for the opera, e.g. Rossini's overture to *Aureliano in Palmira*, which was re-used for the tragedy *Elisabetta, regina d'Inghilterra* and the comedy *Il barbiere di Siviglia*. In French Grand Opera, the overture usually took the form of a freely composed selection of the most important tunes in the opera. Light composers have generally remained faithful to this pot-pourri style of overture. Wagner, though he came to prefer the term Vorspiel (prelude), at first pursued Weber's methods; later he composed still more subtle introductions to his dramas, preparing the audience thematically and psychologically for what was to come. The verismo composers on the whole preferred the brief introduction that had latterly become Verdi's habit, while Strauss sometimes even raised the curtain directly on the drama.

'O welche Lust'. The prisoners' chorus in Act I of Beethoven's *Fidelio*, praising the sun and freedom as they emerge from their cells for exercise.

Owens, Anne-Marie (*b* South Shields, 15 Aug. 1955). English mezzo-soprano. Studied London, GSMD with Laura Sarti. Début Gly. Touring O 1980 (Mistress Quickly). London, ENO, from 1981. Also Aix-en-Provence; Naples, London, CG; O North; Scottish O; Wexford; WNO; etc. Roles include Suzuki, Rosina, Charlotte, Baba the Turk, Adalgisa. Possesses a sumptuous voice deployed with great musicality. (R)

Owen Wingrave. Opera in 2 acts by Britten; text by Myfanwy Piper, after Henry James's story (1892). Written for TV and prem. BBC and NET (US), 16 May 1971.

London and Paramore, family home of the Wingraves. Owen (bar), the last of a military family, rejects his Army studies with Spencer Coyle (bs-bar) because of his pacifism, thus affronting both his family, in particular his aunt Miss Wingrave (sop) and his grandfather Sir Philip (ten), and also his betrothed, Kate (mez). Despite the sympathy of Coyle, they reject him, and to prove his courage to Kate he agrees to spend a night in the haunted room of the family seat. He is found dead in the morning.

'O, wie ängstlich'. Belmonte's (ten) aria in Act I of Mozart's *Die Entführung aus dem Serail*, in which he reveals the anxiety in his heart as he hopes once again to find Constanze.

Oxford. City in England. Apart from Sir Hugh Allen's productions of *Fidelio* and *Der Freischütz* before the First World War, there was no opera until the formation of the OUOC after J. A. Westrup's production of Monteverdi's *Orfeo* (1925). In 1927 *L'incoronazione di Poppea* had its British prem. Sumner Austin was adviser 1928–33, when productions included *The Bartered Bride*, *May Night*, and the first British *Devil and Kate*. Hans Strohbach supervised the productions 1931–3. Later productions have included *Idomeneo*, *Les Troyens*, *Khovanshchina*, *Ruslan and Lyudmila*, *Macbeth* (1954, Heather Harper's début), Cavalli's *Rosinda*, Spohr's *Jessonda*; the prems. of Wellesz's *Incognita* (1951) and Sherlaw Johnson's *The Lambton Worm* (1978); and the British prems. of *Hans Heiling* (1953), *The Secret* (1956, Janet Baker's début), *L'enfant et les sortilèges* (1958), Scarlatti's *Mitridate Eupatore* (1968), Schubert's *Fierrabras* (1986), Mendelssohn's *Hochzeit des Camacho* (1987), and (semi-staged) Hoffmann's *Undine* (1991).

Ozawa, Seiji (*b* Fenytien, 1 Sept. 1935). Japanese conductor. Studied Tokyo with Saito, Tanglewood, Berlin with Karajan. Début Salzburg 1969 (*Così*); London, CG, 1974; Paris, O, 1983 (first *Saint François d'Assise*), 1987. New York, M, 1992. Repertory incl. *Oberon*, *Carmen*, *Onegin*, *Elektra*, *Wozzeck*. Though possessing a lucid style and sympathy with his singers, he is less at home with the dramatic demands of opera than on the concert platform. (R)

'O zitt're nicht'. The Queen of the Night's (sop) aria in Act I of *The Magic Flute*, charging Tamino to rescue her daughter Pamina from Sarastro.

P

'Pace, pace mio Dio'. Leonora's (sop) aria in Act IV of Verdi's *La forza del destino*, opening with a long held note on sop B♭, in which she prays for peace of mind.

Pacini, Giovanni (*b* Catania, 17 Feb. 1796; *d* Pescia, 6 Dec. 1867). Italian composer. Son of Luigi Pacini, the first Geronio in *Il turco in Italia*; began to study singing with Marchesi at the age of 12, and also worked at composition with Mattei and Furnaletto. His first opera, *Don Pomponio* (1813), was not produced, but his second, *Annetta e Lucindo*, was given in the same year. He continued to pour out operas (a dozen comedies in four years); but his first real success was an opera semiseria, *Adelaide e Comingio* (1817).

In 1820 he went to Rome, where his easy Rossinian manner enabled him to help Rossini himself by composing three numbers for *Matilde di Shabran*. Many works followed; his Naples début was with *Alessandro nell'Indie* (1824), which had 70 consecutive performances, and after the success of *L'ultimo giorno di Pompei* in 1825 he became music director of the Naples C. Here he was contracted to compose two operas a year. By 1830 he was one of the most successful opera composers in Italy: in 16 years he had produced almost 40 operas, including *Il corsaro* (1831) for the inauguration of the rebuilt T Apollo in Rome. Especially after some failures in 1833, he realized that he was threatened by the growing reputation of Bellini and Donizetti. Accordingly he withdrew to found a music school at Viareggio, to which he devoted himself after the failure of *Carlo di Borgogna* in 1835. He made a comeback after the death of Bellini and retirement of Rossini with *Saffo* (1840), the most successful work in his new, more careful style and indeed his masterpiece. He continued to write successful works, especially *La fidanzata corsa* (1842), *Maria, regina d'Inghilterra* (1843), *Medea* (1843), *Lorenzino de' Medici* (1845), and *Bondelmonte* (1845); but with the rise of Verdi he was once more eclipsed. His last real success was *Il saltimbanco* (1858).

In his early works, Pacini took Rossini as his model, believing this to be the natural and successful way to write Italian opera, and he even copied Rossini's move towards a more serious manner. He was well aware of this, and of his carelessness; he relied on a fluency and dexterity which won him the respect of Rossini and Bellini, above all for his skill in writing singable melodies. In his middle works, he tried to improve on earlier weaknesses in harmony and orchestration; he helped to unify aria, ensemble, and chorus in the years before Verdi. For his pupils he wrote some theoretical treatises, and also left an entertaining autobiography.

Padilla y Ramos, Mariano. See ARTÔT, DÉSIRÉE.

Padmâvatî. Opéra-ballet in 2 acts by Roussel; text by Louis Laloy, after an event in 13th-cent. Indian history. Prem. Paris, O, 1 June 1923.

India, 1540. The Mogul sultan Alaouddin (bar) proposes an alliance with Ratan-sen (ten), King of Tchitor. He is well received, but demands Ratan-sen's wife Padmâvatî (mez) as a condition; to this Ratan-sen reluctantly consents. A Brahmin (ten) who later asks for her to be handed over is stoned to death by the crowd riots. Alaouddin defeats Ratan-sen in battle, but rather than have the sin of betraying her rest on her husband's conscience, Padmâvatî stabs him. She therefore has to die on his funeral pyre.

'Padre, germani'. Ilia's (sop) aria in Act II of Mozart's *Idomeneo*, expressing her guilt for loving a Greek, Idomeneo's son Idamante, whom as a Trojan princess she should hate.

Padre Guardiano. The Abbot (bs) of the monastery of Hornachuelos in Verdi's *La forza del destino*.

Paer, Ferdinando (*b* Parma, 1 June 1771; *d* Paris, 3 May 1839). Italian composer. Studied Parma with Fortunati and Ghiretti. He won early success with his operas, and was made honorary maestro di capella in 1792; his most important early work was *Griselda* (1798), in the semiseria style that he particularly cultivated. As director of the Vienna, K, 1797–1801, he came to know Beethoven. The most striking successes of this period were *Camilla* (1799) and *Achille* (1801), whose funeral march was not the only number in his music to impress Beethoven. He was in Dresden 1801–6: semiseria works composed here include *I fuorusciti di Firenze* (1802), *Sargino* (1803), and *Leonora* (1804), to the plot used by Beethoven. In 1806 he was taken up by Napoleon, at whose behest he soon settled in Paris. He became singing teacher to Napoleon's empress, Marie-Louise of Austria, and director of the Paris OC (1807) and I (1812) in succession to Spontini. He continued as a successful teacher after the fall of Napoleon, his pupils in the 1820s including Liszt. In 1824 Rossini (who had made his stage début as the boy Adolfo in *Camilla*) joined him at the Paris I in what was to prove a troublesome partnership.

Paer was expert at matching the taste of the day with fluent, singable melody. This gave him a dominating position in Italian music at the start of the 19th cent., and won him his many European appointments over the heads of local composers. His style was enriched by his contacts with Viennese music, and he even had some influence on Beethoven; but this did not spare him one of E. T. A. Hoffmann's most withering reviews, taking *Sofonisba* as an example of all that was unacceptable to Germans in Italian opera. Paer's real contribution is as a composer of *opera semiseria and *rescue opera, in which the mingling of a serious theme with often delightful elements of comic relief is agreeably expressed in music of great fluency and operatic efficiency. His originalities include a number of Romantic features, among them the Mad Scene and a concern for writing continuously composed opera, though his reach after these and other novelties was rather greater than his grasp of them. Together with Mayr, he was the most important Italian composer between the death of Cimarosa (who influenced his early operas) and the rise of Rossini (whom in turn he influenced, including in the use of the orchestral crescendo).

Pagliacci (Clowns). Opera in 2 acts (orig. 1 act) by Leoncavallo; text by the composer. Prem. Milan, V, 21 May 1892.

Montalto (Calabria), 15 Aug. 1865. In the Prologue, Tonio (bar) tells the audience that the story they are about to see is a real one about real people.

Canio (ten), the leader of a travelling troupe of players, warns that if he were to find his wife Nedda (sop) unfaithful, she would pay dearly for it. Tonio makes

advances to Nedda but she repulses him; however, he overhears Nedda and her lover Silvio (bar) planning to run away together, and he hurries to bring Canio back from the village inn.

Canio gives vent to his grief; and in the play put on for the villagers (in which he takes the part of Pagliaccio, Nedda that of Colombine, and Beppe (ten) that of Harlequin), he finds the situation so like reality that he stabs first Nedda, and then Silvio, who rushes to her aid.

Pagliughi, Lina (*b* Brooklyn, 27 May 1907; *d* Savigrano, 1 Oct. 1980). US, later Italian, soprano. Studied S Francisco with Brescia, Milan with Bavagnoli. Début Milan, T Nazionale, 1927 (Gilda). Milan, S, 1937, 1947; London, CG, 1938; Australian tour 1932; Rome 1949. Retired 1957. One of the leading light sopranos in Italy, celebrated as Queen of the Night, Lucia, Violetta, etc. (R)

Paisiello, Giovanni (*b* Taranto, 9 May 1740; *d* Naples, 5 June 1816). Italian composer. Studied Naples. His first successes were in opera buffa, beginning with *Il ciarlone* (1764) and *I francesi brillanti* (1764), above all with *L'idolo cinese* (1767). Performed in cities throughout Italy, these marked him out as a composer of rare talent, while the series of works written for Naples set him up as a worthy rival to Piccinni, later Cimarosa, and Guglielmi. He went to St Petersburg 1776 at the invitation of Catherine the Great; here he helped to establish Italian opera at the court, and composed *Lucinda ed Armidoro* (1777) and *Nitteti* (1777). A series of popular works followed, culminating in *Il barbiere di Siviglia* (1782), which became so popular as to prejudice the public against the setting by Rossini that was to oust Paisiello's work. Returned to Italy 1784, passing through Vienna, where he composed *Il re Teodoro in Venezia* (1784); became maestro di cappella to Ferdinand IV in Naples, where he wrote among other operas *L'amor contrastato* (or *La molinara*) (1788), which became one of his most popular works. For the opening of the Pantheon in London he wrote *La locanda* (1791); for the opening of Venice F, *I giuochi d'Agrigento* (1792). Other popular works of these years included *Nina* (1789) and *I zingari in fiera* (1789). He sided with Napoleon in the disturbances of 1799 and, out of favour at the Bourbon Restoration, went to Paris. He returned to Naples, but the Bourbons did not forgive his previous actions and he died in comparative poverty.

With some 80 operas to his credit, Paisiello was one of the most prolific composers of his generation. Though his works are distinguished more for their ease and accomplishment than for profundity, his elegant melodic manner is capable of much sensitivity, and his feeling for the orchestra is vivid. Together with that of Cimarosa, his work represents the highest peak of opera buffa before Mozart, particularly in the handling of the *ensemble finale.

Palestrina. Opera in 3 acts by Pfitzner; text by the composer. Prem. Munich, P, 12 June 1917.

Rome and Trent, 1563. The composer Palestrina (ten) refuses Cardinal Borromeo's (bar) commission to compose a mass for the Council of Trent and is imprisoned. However, urged by visions of past composers and by his wife Lucretia (con), he sets to work and completes the mass—the *Missa Papae Marcelli*—by the following morning.

The assembled Council of Trent discusses the role of music in the mass and learns that the Pope's approval depends on his receiving from Palestrina a work which conforms to his requirements.

Palestrina's mass is performed to great acclaim. Pope Pius IV (bs) congratulates him and the elderly Palestrina gives thanks to God.

Pallavicino, Carlo (*b* Salò, ?*c*.1640; *d* Dresden, 29 Jan. 1688). Italian composer. Worked first as a church musician in Padua. At the Dresden court, as Vizekapellmeister 1667–73; Kapellmeister 1672. Returned to Padua 1673; maestro di cappella at the Ospedali degli Incurabili in Venice 1674–85. Returned to Dresden 1687, as director of the first permanent opera troupe.

Beginning with *Demetrio* (1666), Pallavicino wrote *c*.20 works for the Venetian houses, including *Enea in Italia* (1675) and *Nerone* (1679); *Vespasiano* was given to open the Venice GG 1678. These belong in all essential respects to the tradition of Cavalli and Cesti, as does his best-known opera, *Gierusalemme liberata* (1687); though first seen in Venice, it was given a lavish performance at Dresden shortly afterwards to mark Pallavicino's return. Regarded by his contemporaries as an ingenious and capable composer, he showed a particular facility for effective orchestral writing; during his lifetime, several operas were revived in houses outside Venice.

Palmer, Felicity (*b* Cheltenham, 6 Apr. 1944). English soprano, later mezzo-soprano. Studied London, GSMD. Début Kent O 1971 (Purcell's Dido). London, ENO from 1975; London, CG, from 1985; Gly. 1985, 1988; also Lausanne, Houston, Zurich, Frankfurt. Roles include Handel's Tamerlano, Agrippina, Pamina, Donna Elvira, Marcellina, Lyubov (*Mazeppa*), Kabanicha, Witch (Humperdinck), Quickly. Created title-role in Gerhard's *The Duenna* (Madrid 1992). A zestful, imaginative performer with an incisive tone. (R)

Pamina. The daughter (sop) of the Queen of the Night in Mozart's *Die Zauberflöte*.

Pampanini, Rosetta (*b* Milan, 2 Sept. 1896; *d* Corbola, 2 Aug. 1973). Italian soprano. Studied Milan with Molaioli. Début Rome, T Nazionale, 1920 (Micaëla). After further study, second début Naples, C, 1923. Milan, S, 1925–30, 1934–7; London, CG, 1928–9, 1933; Paris, O, 1935; also Chicago, Berlin, Vienna, and throughout Italy. Retired 1943. Her warm tone and direct simplicity made her a celebrated Desdemona (Verdi), Mimì, Butterfly, Liù, Manon Lescaut, and Iris. (R)

Pandarus. The brother (ten) of the High Priest Calkas in Walton's *Troilus and Cressida*.

Pandolfini, Angelica (*b* Spoleto, 21 Aug. 1871; *d* Lenno, 15 July 1959). Italian soprano, daughter of below. Studied Paris with Massart. Début Modena 1894 (Marguerite). Malta and Italian provinces 1895–6; Milan, S, 1897–9, 1906, and L, 1902; Naples, C, 1898, 1901; also Buenos Aires, Cairo, Lisbon, Madrid. Retired 1909, after her marriage. A full-blooded yet sensitive singer, celebrated as Violetta, Eva, Mimì, Tosca, Butterfly. Created Adriana Lecouvreur. (R)

Pandolfini, Francesco (*b* Termini Imerese, 22 Nov. 1833; *d* Milan, 15 Feb. 1916). Italian baritone, father of above. Studied Florence with Ronconi and Vannuccini. Début Pisa 1859 (Conte di Vergy, *Gemma di Vergy*). Milan, S, 1871, 1873–4; Lisbon 1872–88; Paris, I, 1876; London, CG, 1877, 1882. Retired 1890. His powerful, sweet tone and noble style made him a successful Macbeth, Amonasro, and Renato. Also famous in Bellini and Donizetti.

Panerai, Rolando (*b* Campo Bisenzio, 17 Oct. 1924). Italian baritone. Studied Florence with Frazzi, Milan with Armani and Tess. Début Naples, C, 1947 (Pharaoh, *Mosè*). Milan, S, from 1951; New York, M, 1955; Salzburg from 1957; London, CG, 1960. Also Berlin, D; Moscow, B; S Francisco; etc. Roles include Guglielmo, Henry Ashton (*Lucia*), title-role of *Mathis der Maler*; particularly acclaimed as Figaro (Rossini), Luna, Germont, Ford. London, CG, 1990 (Dulcamara). (R)

Panizza, Héctor (*b* Buenos Aires, 12 Aug. 1875; *d* Buenos Aires, 27 Dec. 1967). Argentinian conductor and composer of Italian descent. Studied Milan with Ferroni. Début Rome, C, 1898, and had early success with his opera *Medioevo latino* (1900). Milan, V, 1902; Genoa 1902–3. London, CG, 1907–14, 1924. Turin 1912–17; Milan, S, 1916–17, 1921–9 (as Toscanini's assistant, cond. *Ring*), 1930–2, 1946–8. Vienna, Berlin, 1932. Chicago 1922–4; New York, M, 1934–42. Buenos Aires, C, 1908 (his *Aurora* for reopening), 1921–67 (incl. his *Bizancio*, 1939). One of the most highly regarded conductors of his day, especially of Italian opera, and admired by composers including Puccini and Richard Strauss. Introduced Wagner and Strauss into his repertories and gave the prems. of many operas, including Zandonai's *Francesca da Rimini* (1914), Wolf-Ferrari's *Sly* (1927), and Menotti's *The Island God* (1942).

Pantaleoni, Adriano (*b* Sebenico (Šibenik), 7 Oct. 1837; *d* Udine, 18 Dec. 1908). Italian baritone, brother of below. Studied Udine and Milan. Leading baritone Milan, S, 1871–2, 1875, 1877. Also Vienna; London, HM; New York. Large repertory included Rigoletto, Germont, Escamillo, and Donizetti roles.

Pantaleoni, Romilda (*b* Udine, 1847; *d* Milan, 20 May 1917). Italian soprano, sister of above. Studied Milan with Prati, Rossi, and Lamperti. Début Milan, T Carcano, 1868 (Foroni's *Margherita*). Turin 1875; Milan, S, 1883–7, 1889, 1891. Also Rome, Naples, Vienna, etc. Created Desdemona (not entirely to Verdi's satisfaction); Tigrana in Puccini's *Edgar*, and title-role of Ponchielli's *Marion Delorme*. Intelligent and cultured, she was an exceptional actress. Sang Aida, Amelia, Santuzza; famous for her Gioconda, Margherita (*Mefistofele*).

Pantheon. Building in Oxford Street, London: a rotunda based on S Sophia and much admired, it was described by Burney as 'the most elegant structure in Europe'. Opened Jan. 1772 and used mostly for concerts and appearances by singers including Aguiari and Giorgi-Banti. After the destruction of the King's T in 1789, adapted as a theatre and used for Italian opera 1791–2. In 1812 it became the home of a company composed of singers from the King's who had quarrelled with the management. In 1813 there was a short-lived attempt to establish an English OC.

Papageno and **Papagena**. The birdcatcher (bar) and his lover (sop) in Mozart's *Die Zauberflöte*.

Parasha. A village girl (sop), lover of the hussar Vasily, in Stravinsky's *Mavra*.

Pardon de Ploërmel, Le. See DINORAH.

Parepa-Rosa, Euphrosyne. See ROSA, CARL.

Pareto, Graziella (*b* Barcelona, 15 May 1888; *d* Rome, 1 Sept. 1973). Spanish soprano. Studied Milan with Vidal. Début Madrid 1908 (Amina). Buenos Aires 1907–9, 1926; Milan, S, from 1914; London, CG, 1920; Chicago 1921–2, 1923–5. Roles included Rosina, Norina, Gilda, Violetta, Leïla. Beecham admired her 'haunting pathos'. (R)

Paride ed Elena (Paris and Helen). Opera in 5 acts by Gluck; text by Calzabigi. Prem. Vienna, B, 3 Nov. 1770.

Greece, mythological times. Paris (ten) goes to Sparta to claim the fairest woman in the country as reward for having chosen Venus in his famous Judgement. He woos Helen (sop), at first unsuccessfully, and is eventually ordered to leave; but as he does so she confesses love, and they flee together, braving the anger of Pallas Athene (sop), but comforted by the support of Cupid (sop)(who has helped them, disguised as Erasto).

'Parigi, o cara'. The duet in Act III of Verdi's *La traviata*, in which Alfredo (ten) proposes to Violetta (sop) that they resume their life together far from the bustle of Paris.

Paris. Capital of France. At Mazarin's invitation, Italian companies played here, at the Petit-Bourbon, and at the Tuileries: the first Italian work was probably Macazzolì's *Il giudizio* (1645), the first French work Dassoucy's *Andromède*, Feb. 1650. Operatic life developed with the establishment of the Académie de Musique (*Opéra), *Opéra-Comique,

Comédie-Italienne (*Théâtre Italien), and over 20 other theatres, including the Colisée and Odéon, in which established or visiting companies played, or occasional enterprises and performances took place. It was in the 'official' institutions that French operatic life developed; but the busy activity of many others is no less characteristic.

These included, at an early stage, the T du Palais-Royal (cap. 650), opened 1784, and particularly the T de Monsieur, opened in the Tuileries 29 June 1789 with Viotti as director; this sheltered various companies, especially the Opéra-Comique, and was demolished 1829. The T de l'Odéon opened 1793, and provided a home to various companies, notably the T Italien. The T des Nouveautés (cap. 487) opened 1827, and was the home of the Opéra-Comique, 1839–69. The T des Variétés (cap. 1,100) was from 1855 a home of operetta. The T Marigny opened 1850, becoming later the *Bouffes-Parisiens. Various establishments at various times bore the name T de la Renaissance. The T de la Gaîté-Lyrique was an important centre of 19th-cent. operetta. The *Théâtre Lyrique (cap. 1,242) opened 1862 opposite the T du *Châtelet. Other theatres giving opera in the late 19th cent. included the T du Château d'Eau, opened 1866, and the Éden-T, opened 1884. Early 20th cent. theatres giving opera included the Trianon-Lyrique, Ranelagh, Petit Scène, Ambigu, for operetta the Apollo, Bobino, Casino Montparnasse, Casino de Paris, Empire, and Mogador. More important than these was the T des *Champs-Élysées (opened 1913). The Maison de la Radio, opened 1964, has concentrated on 20th-cent. works. Opera has also been given at the huge Palais des Sports. In 1990 the Opéra moved into its new home at the Bastille, becoming the Opéra-Bastille.

See also CHÂTELET, OPÉRA, OPÉRA-COMIQUE, THÉÂTRE DES NATIONS.

'Pari siamo'. Rigoletto's (bar) monologue in Act I of Verdi's *Rigoletto*, in which he reflects on the corrupt courtiers and the curse that he has drawn on himself.

Parisina. 1. Opera in 3 acts by Donizetti; text by Felice Romani, after Byron's verse tale *Parisina* (1816), 'grounded on a circumstance mentioned in Gibbon's *Antiquities of the House of Brunswick*'. Prem. Florence, P, 17 Mar. 1833.

Azzo d'Este (bar), Duke of Ferrara, marries Parisina (sop) after the death of his first wife.

But he rightly suspects that she and his son Ugo are in love, and when she murmurs Ugo's name in her sleep, he swears vengeance. The couple are caught trying to escape and Ugo is executed; Parisina collapses lifeless.

2. Opera in 4 acts (revised to 3 acts after first perf.) by Mascagni; text by Gabriele D'Annunzio, based on a historical event which took place in Ferrara at the time of Nicolò III. Prem. Milan, S, 15 Dec. 1913.

Ferrara, 1425. Nicolò d'Este (bar) abandons his mistress Stella de Tolomei (sop), by whom he has an illegitimate son, Ugo (ten), in order to marry Parisina Malatesta (sop).

On a pilgrimage, Parisina is rescued from pirates' attack by Ugo; she tends his wounds, and falls in love with him.

Parisina and Ugo are surprised by Nicolò, who sentences them to death.

Stella visits her son in prison and attempts to save him. Ugo rejects Parisina's pleas to leave her and be spared, and the couple are beheaded.

Parlamagni, Antonio (*b* 1759; *d* Florence, 9 Oct. 1838). Italian bass. Rome 1789–90, 1818, 1821; Florence 1795–6; Milan, S, from 1797. A celebrated Neapolitan buffo, he created Macrobio in Rossini's *La pietra del paragone*, when he was 'immensely successful' (Stendhal); also Isidoro in *Matilde di Shabran*, with his daughter **Annetta** creating Edoardo.

'Parmi veder le lagrime'. The Duke of Mantua's (ten) aria in Act II of Verdi's *Rigoletto*, in which he regrets the loss of Gilda.

Parsifal. Opera in 3 acts by Wagner; text by the composer, principally after Wolfram von Eschenbach's poem, *Parzival* (early 13th cent.). Prem. Bayreuth 26 July 1882.

In a forest near a lake at Monsalvat, Gurnemanz (bs) and his two Esquires watch a procession taking Amfortas (bar), son of Titurel (bs), on a stretcher to a nearby lake to bathe his wounds. Amfortas is guardian of the Holy Grail, the sacred cup which caught the blood of Christ on the Cross; it is the Grail which unites and sustains the brotherhood. A wild woman, Kundry (sop), brings Gurnemanz balsam. He relates to his knights how Amfortas was seduced by Kundry and wounded by the magician Klingsor after entering Klingsor's garden. In the struggle he lost possession of the Sacred Spear (said to be that with which the Centurion pierced

Christ on the Cross); his wounds need to be touched with the Spear in order to heal. Only a 'Pure Fool made wise through pity' can recover the Spear. A young man (Parsifal, ten) is dragged in, having killed a swan. Gurnemanz believes he may be the 'Pure Fool' and takes him to Amfortas's castle to witness the ceremony of the Holy Grail. Parsifal understands nothing of the ritual and is sent away by Gurnemanz.

Klingsor (bs) has recognized Parsifal as the only possible redeemer of Amfortas and instructs Kundry to seduce the youth. He remains indifferent to the charms of the Flower Maidens in Klingsor's magic garden but, when Kundry kisses him, is made aware of the nature of Amfortas's temptation, and becomes 'wise through pity'. Kundry realizes that her salvation, too, depends on Parsifal. Klingsor hurls the Sacred Spear at him, but it stops miraculously suspended in mid-air. When Parsifal seizes it and makes the sign of the Cross, Klingsor's domain falls in ruins.

Many years later, Gurnemanz is a hermit. On Good Friday Kundry goes to draw water for him and sees a knight in black armour approaching; it is Parsifal. He is recognized by her and later by Gurnemanz. After Kundry has bathed the knight's feet and dried them with her hair, Gurnemanz anoints Parsifal as the new King of the Holy Grail. He baptizes Kundry; the three go to the Hall of the Grail, where Amfortas is unable to celebrate the ritual uncovering of the Grail because of the pain of the wound. Parsifal heals it with the touch of the Sacred Spear. As the knights pay homage to their new King, Parsifal raises the Grail aloft; a white dove hovers over his head, and Kundry falls lifeless.

Pasero, Tancredi (b Turin, 11 Jan. 1893; d Milan, 17 Feb. 1983). Italian bass. Studied Turin with Pessina. Début Vicenza 1918 (Rodolfo, *Sonnambula*). Turin 1919; Milan, V, 1920, and S, 1926–43; New York, M, 1929–34; London, CG, 1931; Verona from 1933; Paris, O, 1935; Berlin, D, 1941. A moving artist with a rich, noble tone, and great dramatic authority. Wide repertory incl. Sarastro, Mosè, Philip, Mephistopheles (Gounod and Boito), Boris, Escamillo. (R)

Pashchenko, Andrey (b Rostov on Don, 15 Aug. 1885; d Moscow, 16 Nov. 1972). Russian composer. Studied St Petersburg with Witohl and Steinberg. His operas, conventional and straightforward in style, include *Orliny bunt*

(The Eagles Revolt, 1925) and *Tsar Maximilian* (1930).

Pashkevich, Vasily (b ?, c.1742; d St Petersburg, 20 Mar. 1797). Russian composer. He played the violin in the opera at St Petersburg in 1763, then working in various capacities in the Imperial Theatres. An important pioneer of Russian opera, he became well known with *Misfortune from Owning a Carriage* (1779): unlike many early nationalist operas, this includes only one folk-song. *The Miser* (1781) looks forward to later Russian opera in its pioneering use of natural speech rhythms; and other developments in Russian opera are anticipated in *Fevey* (1786), the first to make use of a fairy subject and to include exotic elements, also in one song using the technique of a repeated melody against a changing background which was to be developed by Glinka.

Pasini, Lina. See VITALE, EDOARDO.

Paskalis, Kostas (b Levadia, 1 Sept. 1929). Greek baritone. Studied Athens Cons. Début Athens 1951 (Rigoletto). Vienna, S, from 1958; Gly. 1964–5, 1967; New York, M, 1965– 7; Milan, S, from 1967; London, CG, 1969, 1971–2. With his warm tone and intense dramatic sense, a successful Macbeth, Renato, Iago (Verdi), and first Pentheus (*Bassarids*). Dir. of the Nat. T of Greece 1988; sang *Don Giovanni* with New Jersey O, in same year. (R)

Pasta, Giuditta (b Saronno, 26 Oct. 1797; d Blevio, 1 Apr. 1865). Italian soprano. Studied Como with Lotti, Milan with Asioli and Scappa. Début (under maiden name Negri) Milan, T Filodrammatici, 1815 (Scappa's *Le tre Eleonore*). Paris, I, 1816; London, H, 1817. By now married to the tenor Giuseppe Pasta. After further study with Scappa, engaged Venice 1818, then Padua, Rome, Brescia, Turin. First real success Paris, I, 1821. London, H, 1824; thereafter sang in both capitals until 1837. Naples, C, 1826; Vienna 1829; Milan, S, 1831; St Petersburg 1840. Her voice, always intractable, had by now deteriorated, but in 1850 she appeared twice in London. One of the great artists of the 19th cent., she was a 'consummate vocalist' (Chorley), and a dramatic genius who 'electrified the soul' (Stendhal). Her voice spanned a–d''' (though some considered her essentially a mezzo-soprano), and possessed a fascinating variety of colour. Though her passionate sincerity was unrestrained, her style was noble and majestic (in contrast with her rival Malibran, described by Legouvé as 'all fermentation'); she used embellishments with care and subtlety, and, unusually, kept the same ones throughout her career. She inspired and created the title-roles of Pacini's *Niobe*, Donizetti's *Anna Bolena* and *Ugo, conte di Parigi*, and Bellini's *Beatrice di Tenda*; also his Amina, and Norma (a role she found difficult, insisting on transposing 'Casta diva' down a tone to F, where it has remained). She also created Corinna in *Il viaggio a Reims*, and was a famous Desdemona (Rossini), Ninetta (*La gazza ladra*), Tancredi, Elisabetta, and Elcia (*Mosè*). Regrettably, she passed her peak before Verdi had the opportunity to write for her. Other celebrated roles were Mayr's Medea, and Bellini's and Zingarelli's Romeo.

pasticcio (It.: 'pie', hence 'hotchpotch'). In the 18th cent. the term was applied to a wide variety of music; more recently, writers have used it so loosely that a precise (and uncontroversial) definition is impossible. In its broadest sense, it may be applied to any 18th-cent. opera which is a collaborative effort on the part of more than one composer: a classic example is the *Muzio Scevola* opera produced in London in 1721, for which Mattei, Bononcini, and Handel each composed one act. Usually, however, the pasticcio was a looser structure, essentially a play with airs, ensembles, dances, and other movements assembled from one or more composers. A vintage example is *Thomyris* (1708), for which Pepusch adapted music by a number of composers.

patter song. A comic song in which the greatest number of words, delivered rapidly in conversational style, is fitted into the shortest space of time, with the music supporting their inflection.

Patti, Adelina (*b* Madrid, 19 Feb. 1843; *d* Craig-y-Nos Castle, 27 Sept. 1919). Italian soprano, daughter of the tenor **Salvatore Patti** (1800–69), a Donizetti singer, later opera manager in New York, and the soprano **Caterina Chiesa Barilli-Patti** (*d* 1870), who reputedly sang Norma the night before Adelina was born. Studied New York with E. Valentini, and Ettore Barilli (her half-brother). Singing début aged 7; stage début New York, AM, 1859 (Lucia). New Orleans, French OH, 1860–1. London, CG, 1861–95; Berlin 1861; Paris, I 1862 and O from 1872; Vienna 1863; Moscow, St Petersburg, 1869; Milan, S, from 1877; US tour 1881–4 with Mapleson Co.; New York, M, from 1887; Chicago 1889. Also Rome, Madrid, S America, etc. Retired 1906, but appeared occasionally until 1914. Roles included Zerlina, Rossini's Desdemona and Rosina; Amina, Lucia, Valentine, Violetta, Aida, Marguerite, Juliette, Lakmé. One of the greatest prima donnas in operatic history; her voice was astoundingly flexible, even, and sweet, and her technique superb. Verdi praised the balance between her singing and acting. Her contracts included exemption from rehearsals, as well as the highest fees of the day (after 1882, a minimum of $5,000 a performance), and a stipulation as to the size of her name on posters. Her jewel collection was so prodigious that she had to travel with several guards. But the beauty and charm of her singing won all hearts, including Hanslick's. Shaw admired her phrasing and her 'unerring ear'. She married three times; her second husband was the tenor **Ernest Nicolini** (1834–98), who sang in Milan, Paris, and especially London (DL and CG). (R) Her elder sisters were **Amalia** (1831–1915), who made her debut in 1848, later marrying Maurice *Strakosch, and **Carlotta** (1836–89), judged by some to be as good as Adelina (she sang the Queen of the Night's arias up a tone) but forced by her lameness to make a concert career.

Patzak, Julius (*b* Vienna, 9 Apr. 1898; *d* Rottach-Egern, 26 Jan. 1974). Austrian tenor. Studied Vienna: conducting with Adler, composition with Schmidt. Self-taught as singer. Début Reichenberg (Liberec) 1926 (Radamès). Brno 1927–8; Munich 1928–45; London, CG, from 1938; Vienna from 1946; also Berlin, Salzburg, Barcelona, etc. A great artist of rare intelligence, penetration, and subtlety. Large repertory included Belmonte, Tamino, Lohengrin, Hoffmann, Dmitry, Herod; particularly acclaimed as Florestan and Palestrina. Created several roles, e.g. the Private (Strauss's *Friedenstag*), Desmoulins (Von Einem's *Dantons Tod*), and Tristan (Martin's *Le vin herbé*). His excellent diction and care with words also made him a moving Lieder singer. (R)

Pauer, Jiří (*b* Kladno-Libušín, 22 Feb. 1919). Czech composer. Studied with Šín, then Prague with Hába and Bořkovec. Dir. Prague

O, 1953–5. His most successful work has been his opera *Zuzana Vojířová* (1958).

Paul Bunyan. Opera in a prologue and 2 acts by Britten; text by W. H. Auden. Prem. New York, Columbia U, 5 May 1941.

America, pioneer days. Dissatisfied trees anticipate the arrival of the lumberjack Paul Bunyan (spoken) who, the narrator (ten-bar) tells them, never ages but grows taller every day, so that he is as big as the Empire State Building.

He arrives at the camp and meets four Swedish workers, whose leader is Hel Helson (bar). Paul Bunyan marries Carrie but the marriage soon disintegrates and she returns to her home, taking their daughter Tiny (sop). When Carrie dies shortly afterwards, Paul Bunyan fetches Tiny back and she helps the new camp cook Slim (ten). Helson wants to leave the camp and become a farmer.

Helson, irritated at the manner in which Bunyan has taken command before his own departure, decides to kill the giant. However, on attempting an attack, he realizes his mistake and reconciles himself to working under Bunyan. The narrator tells how the characters all move on to new lives as time passes and the new age of the railroad and telephone arrives. Paul Bunyan reminds the audience of what can be achieved in a free country.

Pauly, Rosa (*b* Eperjes, 15 Mar. 1894; *d* Kfar Shmaryahn, 14 Dec. 1975). Hungarian soprano. Studied Vienna with Papier. Début Vienna, S, 1918 (Verdi's Desdemona). Berlin, Kroll O, 1927–31, and S, 1929–38; Vienna, S, 1929–35; Milan, S, 1935–9; New York, M, and London, CG, 1938. Retired 1943, then taught in Israel. Roles included Donna Anna, Leonore, Ortrud, Gutrune, Dyer's Wife, Marie (*Wozzeck*), and a famous Elektra. Admired by Strauss. (R)

Pauvre matelot, Le (The Poor Sailor). Opera in 3 acts by Milhaud; text by Cocteau, based on a newspaper report of an actual event. Prem. Paris, OC, 16 Dec. 1927.

A sailor (ten) returns home after a long absence and is not recognized by his wife (sop). He tests her fidelity by pretending to be her husband's rich friend, and showing her jewels to prove his wealth, tries to make love to her. When he is asleep she steals the jewels in order to help pay for her husband's voyage back home, and murders him.

Pavarotti, Luciano (*b* Modena, 12 Oct. 1935). Italian tenor. Studied Modena with A. Pola, Mantua with Campogalliani. Début Reggio Emilia 1961 (Rodolfo). London, CG, from 1963; Gly. 1964; Milan, S, from 1965; Miami 1965; New York, M, from 1968; Paris, O, from 1974. Also Vienna, Barcelona, Verona, Montreal, etc. A hugely successful, vastly popular singer, with a ringing, high lyric tenor of great beauty, an excellent technique, and a conquering personality. Repertory includes Elvino, Nemorino, Arturo (*Puritani*), Duke of Mantua, Alfredo, Rodolfo, Cavaradossi, Calaf, Edgardo. (R)

Pavesi, Stefano (*b* Casaletto Vaprio, 22 Jan. 1779; *d* Crema, 28 July 1850). Italian composer. Studied Naples with Piccinni, but was expelled from the conservatory for his republican sympathies and joined Napoleon's army as a serpent player; later studied Crema with Gazzaniga. In Venice he met the librettist Foppa, who helped to arrange for the staging of his second opera. Dir., Vienna Court O, for six months each year 1826–30. He was one of the most active and prolific Italian composers before the rise of Rossini, with a distinctive melodic vein and a stronger feel for the orchestra than many of his contemporaries. Among some 70 operas, the most successful was *Ser Marcantonio* (1810), on a subject similar to that of Donizetti's *Don Pasquale*, which had an initial run of 54 consecutive performances.

Pearl Fishers, The. See PÊCHEURS DE PERLES, LES.

Pears, (Sir) **Peter** (*b* Farnham, 22 June 1910; *d* Aldeburgh, 3 Apr. 1986). English tenor. Studied London with Gerhardt and Freer; US, with T. Schnabel and Mundy; later with Manén. Début London, Strand T, 1942 (Hoffmann). London, SW, 1943–5; Gly. 1946–7; founder member of EOG 1946–76; London, CG, regularly 1948–78; Aldeburgh 1952–79; New York, M, 1974, 1978. Last stage appearance Edinburgh 1979. One of the most cultivated and intelligent artists of his day, who used an elegant and individual voice with sensitive musicianship and skilful technique. His artistry profoundly influenced the music of Britten, his long-time companion, for whom he created the roles of Peter Grimes, Male Chorus, Albert Herring, Captain Vere, Essex, Quint, Flute, the Madwoman, Sir Philip Wingrave, Aschenbach. Also first Pandarus (*Troilus and Cressida*), and

Boaz (Berkeley's *Ruth*). Other roles included Don Ottavio, Ferrando, Rossini's Almaviva, Alfredo, Vašek, David, Oedipus Rex. His perceptive response to words also showed in his affecting Lieder partnership with Britten. (R)

Pêcheurs de perles, Les (The Pearl Fishers). Opera in 3 acts by Bizet; text by Eugène Cormon (Pierre-Étienne Piestre) and Michel Carré. Prem. Paris, L, 30 Sept. 1863.

Ancient Ceylon. Zurga (bar) is selected as king of the fishermen. His friend Nadir (ten) returns and, after a long estrangement caused by falling in love with the same priestess, Leïla (sop), they are reconciled. A new priestess arrives to pray to Brahma while the fishermen are at sea; she is sworn to a vow of chastity and is heavily veiled. However, when she removes her veil, Nadir recognizes her as Leïla, and their love is rekindled.

Leïla tells the high priest Nourabad (bs) how she risked death to save a fugitive and was rewarded with a gold chain. She hears Nadir singing a serenade; he joins her and the couple reaffirm their love. But Nourabad finds them, and the couple are accused of sacrilege. Zurga recognizes Leïla and vows revenge by refusing clemency.

Zurga refuses Leïla's pleas to spare Nadir's life; as she leaves, she hands Zurga her gold chain, asking that it may be sent to her mother. As Nadir and Leïla are about to mount the funeral pyre, Zurga rushes in shouting that the camp is ablaze; he recognized the chain Leïla gave him as his own and realized she was his rescuer. Zurga releases the couple, and they escape.

Berlioz admired the work, writing that 'it does M. Bizet the greatest honour'. However, it was subjected to various revisions, the most notorious but longest lasting being that of 1889; this ends with Zurga dying on the funeral pyre, and numbers among other musical mutilations the rewriting of a duet as a trio by Benjamin Godard.

Pechkovsky, Nikolay (*b* Moscow, 13 Jan. 1896; *d* Leningrad, 24 Nov. 1966). Russian tenor. Studied Moscow with Donsky. Début as actor, Moscow 1913; début there as tenor Sergyevsky T, 1918. Moscow, B (Stanislavsky's operatic studio), 1921–3; Leningrad 1924–41. A fine singing actor, whose best roles incl. Hermann, Golitsin, Manrico, Radamès, Otello (Verdi), Don José, Canio. (R)

Pederzini, Gianna (*b* Vò di Avio, 10 Feb. 1903; *d* Rome, 11 Mar. 1988). Italian mezzo-soprano. Studied Naples with De Lucia. Début Messina 1923 (Preziosilla). Milan, S, 1930–43, 1956–7; Rome 1939–52; London, CG, 1931 (Preziosilla, Maddalena); Buenos Aires 1937–9, 1946–7. One of the outstanding mezzo-sopranos of her day, her roles included Carmen, Mignon, and the Rossini heroines. She also sang the Countess in *The Queen of Spades* and Mistress Quickly, roles for which her vivid dramatic talents suited her admirably. Created the Prioress in *Les dialogues des Carmélites*, Milan 1957. (R)

Pedrell, Felipe (*b* Tortosa, 19 Feb. 1841; *d* Barcelona, 9 Aug. 1922). Spanish composer. Studied Tortosa with Nin y Serra. Assistant dir. at Barcelona, T Circo, 1873–4. His position as the father of Spanish music drama rests on his foundation of a Spanish national style. This took its inspiration only partly from folk music; his scholarly interests involved a profound study of earlier music, especially Victoria. Though he wrote some comic operas and zarzuelas, his major work was the consciously Wagnerian trilogy *Los Pirineos* (1902). There is a note of studiousness in his operas which, though they contain much fine music, inhibits wide acceptance.

Pedrillo. Belmonte's servant (ten), lover of Blonde, in Mozart's *Die Entführung aus dem Serail*.

Pedrotti, Carlo (*b* Verona, 12 Nov. 1817; *d* Verona, 16 Oct. 1893). Italian composer and conductor. Studied Verona with Foroni. The success of his first performed opera, *Lina* (1840), secured him the conductorship of the Italian O in Amsterdam. Worked there 1840–5; returned to direct the T Nuovo and the T Filarmonico in Verona. Here he wrote several operas, including his best-known work, *Tutti in maschera* (1856). Turin 1868 appointed dir. of the Liceo Musicale and cond. at the T Regio; 1882 dir. of the Liceo Musicale, Pesaro. Composed *c*.18 stage works, mostly opere buffe or opere semiserie of a conventional kind. Wrote nothing after 1872, feeling himself to have been eclipsed by the younger generation; this lack of self-esteem eventually drove him to suicide, by drowning in the River Adige. Although his works enjoyed some popularity in their day, they were soon forgotten. His activities as a conductor had more influence on Italian operatic life: under his régime the T Regio rivalled Milan S in the number, quality, and importance of its productions.

Peerce, Jan (*b* New York, 3 June 1904; *d* New York, 15 Dec. 1984). US tenor. Began career as violinist. Studied with Borghetti. Début Philadelphia 1938 (Duke of Mantua). Chicago 1940; New York, M, 1941–68. Moscow, B, and Leningrad 1956. Also S America, Canada, Germany, Austria, Holland, etc. Roles included Don Ottavio, Edgardo, Gounod's Faust, Rodolfo, Cavaradossi, Alfredo. (R)

Pell, William (*b* Baltimore, 1946). US tenor. Studied at Manhattan School of Music and sang first as baritone (Mozart's Figaro at Toronto; Germont at S Francisco). Tenor roles from 1975, singing at Berlin, D, from 1982 (as Siegfried and in the prem. of Rihm's *Oedipus*, 1987). Sang Parsifal with well-focused tone at Bayreuth 1989–91. Other roles incl. Alwa (Hanover 1988), Bacchus, and Gounod's Roméo. (R)

Pelléas et Mélisande. Opera in 5 acts, 12 tableaux, by Debussy; text a slight alteration of Maeterlinck's tragedy (1892). Prem. Paris, OC, 30 Apr. 1902.

Allemonde. Golaud (bar), grandson of King Arkel (bs), marries a mysterious girl, Mélisande (sop), he has found weeping in the forest. He is a widower and already has a son Yniold (sop) by his previous marriage. Geneviève (mez), Golaud's mother, reads to the almost blind Arkel a letter from Golaud to his half-brother Pelléas (ten or bar), telling of his marriage. Arkel instructs Pelléas to convey his acceptance to Golaud. The couple arrive in Allemonde.

Mélisande accidentally drops her wedding-ring into a fountain. Golaud, thrown from his horse at the moment the ring fell, is being tended by Mélisande. He notices the ring's absence, and tells her to go in search of it, taking Pelléas with her as it is night. Together they go to the gloomy grotto where she told Golaud she had lost the ring, and are frightened by three blind beggars.

At her window, Mélisande combs her hair and allows it to tumble around Pelléas, below; although they do not speak of love, it is clear that their emotions are closely entwined. In a sinister vault in the castle, Golaud warns Pelléas to let Mélisande alone. Later he holds his son Yniold (treb or sop) up to spy on the couple in a room: the child reports that they sit in silence, but Golaud's jealousy remains.

Pelléas has decided to leave the castle and arranges a final meeting with Mélisande. Golaud finds them and, enraged, drags Mélisande along the ground by her hair. Later, the couple meet by the fountain where Mélisande lost her ring; they confess their love for the first time. Golaud, who has been spying on them, kills Pelléas.

Arkel, Golaud, and the Physician wait by Mélisande's bed, where she is dying, having given birth to a child. Golaud, repentant but still jealous, questions her about her love for Pelléas—was it a 'forbidden' love? The castle servants enter, and fall on their knees as Mélisande dies without answering Golaud.

Pelletier, Wilfred (*b* Montreal, 20 June 1896; *d* New York, 9 Apr. 1982). Canadian conductor. Studied Paris with Philipp and Widor. New York, M, as répétiteur 1917. Cond. Met. Saturday Night O Concerts 1932, also directing the Met. French repertory. Also cond. Ravinia, S Francisco. Active in Montreal concert life, and dir. Montreal Cons. 1942–61.

Penderecki, Krzysztof (*b* Dębica, 23 Nov. 1933). Polish composer. Studied Cracow with Malawski and Wiechowicz. The strong grasp of dramatic effect and skill with diverse musical effects shown in his religious concert works was first revealed in opera with *The Devils of Loudun* (1969); here the effects are not always backed with sufficient musical substance and continuity. With the sacra rappresentazione *Paradise Lost* (1978) he stepped back from his earlier experimentation and drew upon influences that include Stravinsky, Berg, and even Wagner, though not their mastery of cumulative dramatic effect. *Die schwarze Maske* (1986), set in the Thirty Years' War, concerns the difficulty of transcending racial as well as political, national, and sexual types, in an idiom that returns to some of his most violent early music, with a strong dissonant and percussive impulse.

Pepusch, John Christopher (*b* Berlin, 1667; *d* London, 20 July 1752). English composer of German birth. After working at the Prussian court, he arrived in London *c*.1700, where he was employed as viola player and later harpsichordist at Drury Lane. He is best remembered for his contribution to *The Beggar's Opera* (1728), for which he wrote the bass lines to melodies selected by Gay, and the overture.

Perez, David (*b* Naples, 1711; *d* Lisbon, 30 Oct. 1778). Italian composer. Studied Naples with Mancini, Veneziano, and Galli. His first opera, *La nemica amante* (1735), established his reputation, which he confirmed with *Li travestimenti amorosi* (1740) and especially *Siroe* (1740). He also worked in Palermo until 1748, then moving to Lisbon. Here he was patronized by King José I, and his operas were sumptuously staged. He introduced the style of Neapolitan opera to Portugal, and helped to encourage the growth of opera there.

Perfect Fool, The. Opera in 1 act by Holst; text by the composer. Prem. London, CG, 14 May 1923.

The Princess's (sop) hand has been promised to any man 'who does the deed no other man can do'. Many suitors take part in a competition, among them a (Verdian) Troubadour (ten) and a (Wagnerian) Traveller (bar). However, the Princess's eye lights on the Perfect Fool (spoken), and asks to marry him. But he has no interest in her and refuses.

Pergola, Teatro alla. See FLORENCE.

Pergolesi, Giovanni Battista (*b* Jesi, 4 Jan. 1710; *d* Pozzuoli, 16 Mar. 1736). Italian composer. Studied Naples with Greco, Vinci, and Durante; employed there by various aristocrats as maestro di cappella. In 1732 his first stage work, the opera seria *Salustia*, was staged. It was unsuccessful but the warm reception accorded the comic *Lo frate 'nnamorato* (The Beloved Brother, 1732) later that year indicated where his real talents lay. While the opere serie which he wrote over the next few years are largely forgotten, the comic *intermezzos with which they were performed—*La serva padrona* (1733) and *La contadina astuta* (1734) respectively—are regarded as seminal for the development of *opera buffa. Likewise, though now considered one of the best 18th-cent. opere serie, *L'Olimpiade* (1735) was regarded with indifference in its day. Pergolesi's final stage work, the opera buffa *Flaminio* (1735), was given a triumphant reception.

Though a consummate master of opera seria, it was in comic works that he excelled. *La serva padrona* is the classic example of the early 18th-cent. intermezzo and adumbrates many of the features of later opera buffa. Taken up by comic troupes and performed throughout Europe, it brought Pergolesi posthumous fame and soon came to be regarded as the epitome of Italian style; it represents an important stage in the development of the *ensemble finale.

Peri, Jacopo (*b* Rome, 20 Aug. 1561; *d* Florence, 12 Aug. 1633). Italian composer, singer, and harpist. Studied Florence with Malvezzi; *c.*1588 joined the Medici court, where he won fame as a singer and participated in lavish court entertainments, such as the famous 1589 intermedi for Bargagli's *La pellegrina*, for which he also composed some music. An important member of the Bardi *camerata, he was closely involved in the intellectual debate out of which opera evolved. Though not the first to write in the new *stile rappresentativo, he was the first to use it for a complete dramatic work. His (mostly lost) setting of Rinuccini's *Dafne* libretto (1598), for which he collaborated with Corsi, is usually regarded as the first true opera; for its performance Peri took the part of Apollo. To celebrate the wedding of Henri IV of France to Maria de' Medici (1600) he was commissioned to write a work for public performance. This opera, *Euridice*, is the first for which complete music survives: it was published 1600. Peri again participated, taking the part of Orpheus. He planned two further operas, *Tetide* and *Adone*, but only the latter was written, and this was not performed.

Together with his arch-rival Caccini, it was Peri who gave effect to the deliberations of the Bardi camerata and by turning theory into practice demonstrated the full potential of the new art-form. In this he was aided by his background as a singer, his literary sensitivity, and a streak of true dramatic flair. *Euridice* was soon recognized as a work of considerable emotional force and originality and had a notable effect on the early history of opera.

Périchole, La. Operetta in 3 acts by Offenbach; text by Meilhac and Halévy, after Mérimée's drama, *Le carrosse de Saint-Sacrement* (1829). Prem. Paris, T des Variétés, 6 Oct. 1868.

Peru, mid-18th cent. A gypsy street-singer, La Périchole (mez), and her partner and lover Piquillo (ten), come to Lima. Don Andrès (bar), the viceroy of Peru, is charmed by La Périchole and engages her as a lady-in-waiting. After many intrigues and complications, including an escape from the local prison, the lovers are reunited.

Périer, Jean (*b* Paris, 2 Feb. 1869; *d* Neuilly, 6 Nov. 1954). French baritone. Studied Paris

with Taskin and Bussine. Début Paris, OC,
1892 (Monostatos). Paris, OC, 1892–4, 1900–
20. New York, Manhattan OC, 1908; also
Monte Carlo. Though possessing only a
limited voice, he was a very fine actor, and
had a successful career in films (1900–10,
1922–38). Created many leading roles,
including Ramiro (*L'heure espagnole*),
Rabaud's Mârouf, and Pelléas, a role to which
he gave 'admirable definition', with affecting simplicity (Inghelbrecht). Debussy, who
had reservations, attributed his growing
popularity to the fact that he had got better
and better because 'he has entirely given up
singing what I wrote'. (R)

Perlea, Jonel (*b* Ograda, 13 Dec. 1900; *d* New
York, 29 July 1970). Romanian conductor.
Studied Munich with Beer-Waldbrunn,
Leipzig with Lohse and Graener. Concert
début Bucharest 1919. Répétiteur Leipzig
1922–3; Rostock 1923–5. Cond. Cluj 1927–
8; Bucharest 1928–32, 1934–44, music dir.
1929–32, 1934–6. Gave Bucharest prems. of
many works, including *Meistersinger*, *Falstaff*,
and *Rosenkavalier* (all in Romanian). Berlin,
Vienna, Stuttgart from 1935; Milan, S, and
other Italian houses 1945–58, giving many
world and Italian prems. New York, M, 1949–
50. Afflicted by a stroke in 1957, he took to
conducting with his left arm. Taught cond.
New York, Manhattan School, 1952–69. (R)

Pernet, André (*b* Rambervilliers, 6 Jan.
1894; *d* Paris, 23 June 1966). French bass.
Studied Paris with Gresse. Début Nice 1921.
Paris: O, 1928–31, 1932–45, 1948; OC, 1931–
48. Created leading roles in many operas,
e.g. Milhaud's *Maximilien*, Hahn's *Marchand
de Venise*, Enescu's *Œdipe*. Played the Father in
the film of *Louise* directed by Charpentier. (R)

'Per pietà'. Fiordiligi's (sop) aria in Act II of
Mozart's *Così fan tutte*, her resistance weak-
ening in the face of the advances of her sister
Dorabella's disguised lover Ferrando.

Perrin, Émile-César-Victor (*b* Rouen, 19
Jan. 1814; *d* Paris, 8 Oct. 1885). French administrator. Dir. Paris: OC, 1848–57, 1862, and O,
1862–71. Persuaded Verdi to write *Don Carlos*
for the Opéra. His managements saw the production of many new works, incl. Thomas's
Mignon (1866), Massenet's first opera, *La
grand' tante* (1867), Saint-Saëns's first opera,
La princesse jaune (1872), *Carmen* (1875), and
works by Halévy, Adam, Massé, Auber, and
Offenbach.

Perrin, Pierre (*b* Lyons, *c.*1620; *d* Paris, 25
Apr. 1675). French librettist. Assumed the
title of Abbé. The first important French librettist, and the founder of the Académie
Royale de Musique et de Danse (the Paris
*Opéra). Previously, he had written an opera
for Cambert for performance at the small
royal theatre at Issy (*La pastorale d'Issy*, 1659),
'in an attempt to evolve a genre of opera
simpler than the current forms of Italian
opera'. He abandoned the alexandrines of
the French classical theatre in favour of short
lyric verses. His success led Louis XIV to consider the foundation of a national opera, and
in 1669 letters patent were granted to Perrin
for the formation of the Académie. In 1671
the work which has the best claim to be
the first French opera, Cambert's *Pomone* to
Perrin's text, was publicly given. But financial difficulties and malpractices led to
his imprisonment, and he died in poverty,
having sold his letters patent to Lully.
Though a mediocre versifier, Perrin is
remembered as a founder of French opera,
and also for his influence, directly on Quinault and later on the pastoral operas and
writings of Rousseau, in developing a
simpler and more popular folk-influenced
style.

Perron, Karl (*b* Frankenthal, 3 June 1858;
d Dresden, 15 July 1928). German baritone.
Studied Berlin with Hey, Frankfurt with
Stockhausen. Début Leipzig 1884 (Wolfram).
Leipzig till 1891; Dresden 1892–1924. Bay-
reuth 1889–1904. Also Munich, Amsterdam.
Roles included Don Giovanni, Wotan, King
Mark, Amfortas, Onegin. Created Jochanaan,
Orestes; also Ochs, though not the com-
poser's and Hofmannsthal's ideal choice (too
thin, refined, and humourless). Strauss none
the less considered him 'a first-class artist'.

Persiani, Fanny (*b* Rome, 4 Oct. 1812; *d*
Neuilly, 3 May 1867). Italian soprano. Studied
with her father, the tenor Nicola Tacchinardi. Début Livorno 1832 (Fournier's
Francesca da Rimini). Successes in Venice;
Milan; Naples; Paris, I, 1837–48. London: HM,
1838–46; CG, 1847–9. Vienna 1837, 1844; St
Petersburg 1850–2, after which she retired.
A considerable virtuoso, she possessed complete mastery of her clear and silvery voice
(which, however, Donizetti thought 'rather
cold'). With her delicate, angelic appearance
she epitomized the fragile heroines of contemporary opera. Created title-roles of Don-

izetti's *Lucia, Pia de' Tolomei*, and *Rosmonda d'Inghilterra*; also highly acclaimed as Zerlina, Amina, Adina, Linda di Chamounix, Lucrezia Borgia, etc. In 1830 she married the composer **Giuseppe Persiani** (1804–69). Her singing largely accounted for the success of his operas, though his most famous, *Inès de Castro* (1835), was written for Malibran. Husband and wife helped to establish London's Royal Italian O at Covent Garden, 1847, he putting up much of the money.

Pertile, Aureliano (*b* Montagnana, 9 Nov. 1885; *d* Milan, 11 Jan. 1952). Italian tenor. Studied Padua with Orefice, Milan with Bavagnoli. Début Vicenza 1911 (Lionel, *Martha*). Milan, S, 1915, 1918, 1921–37; New York, M, 1921–2; Buenos Aires, C, 1923, 1925–6, 1929; London, CG, 1927–9, 1931; also Verona, Berlin, Vienna, etc. Created title-roles of both Boito's and Mascagni's *Nerone*, and Wolf-Ferrari's *Sly*. Roles included Edgardo, Fernando (*Favorita*), Manrico, Radamès, Verdi's Otello, Rodolfo, Lohengrin, Chénier, Canio. Toscanini's favourite tenor, he was described by the critic Eugenio Gara as a 'sculptor of melody'. Though his tone could be hard (and aroused controversy), he used it expressively, and gave unforgettable performances of exceptional artistry and fervour. (R)

Pescetti, Giovanni Battista (*b* Venice, *c*.1704; *d* Venice, 20 Mar. 1766). Italian composer. Studied with Lotti. His first opera, *Nerone detronato* (1725), was for Venice; after some collaborations with Galuppi came to London where he replaced Porpora 1737. London: dir. CG 1739, H 1740. Operas produced here included a revival of *Demetrio* (1732), and *Aristodemo* (1744). Returned to Venice *c*.1745. His operas owe much to Galuppi in their elegance and poise.

Peter Grimes. Opera in a prologue and 3 acts by Britten; text by Montagu Slater, after Crabbe's poem *The Borough* (1810). Prem. London, SW, 7 June 1945.

The Borough, a small Suffolk fishing village, *c*.1830. At an inquest into the death of the apprentice of the fisherman Peter Grimes (ten) a verdict of accidental death is recorded, but Grimes is warned not to take on more boy apprentices.

Ellen Orford (sop), the schoolmistress, alone stands by Grimes, and goes to fetch his new apprentice. That evening, in The Boar, the village people accuse Grimes of being a murderer. As soon as Ellen arrives with the new boy, Grimes takes him off home through a raging storm.

Several weeks later Ellen discovers that Grimes has been ill-treating the boy; when she insists that he be allowed to rest as it is Sunday, she and Grimes quarrel. The villagers, coming out of church, hear this, and set off for Grimes's hut to see what is happening. Grimes's efforts to comfort the boy are interrupted by the arrival of the village deputation. Grimes pushes him out through a back entrance on to the cliff where, missing his footing, he plunges to his death.

The people of the Borough have not seen Grimes and the boy for several days and assume they are out fishing. However, Ellen recognizes a pullover washed up on the beach as the one she knitted for the boy. Grimes's boat has returned to harbour and a posse of villagers sets off to find him. Grimes has lost control of his senses and fails to recognize even Ellen for a while. Captain Balstrode (bar) advises Grimes to take his boat out to sea and sink it. This he does as the village comes to life for another, ordinary day.

Peter Ibbetson. Opera in 3 acts by Deems Taylor; text by the composer and Constance Collier, after the latter's play founded on George du Maurier's novel (1892). Prem. New York, M, 7 Feb. 1931.

England and France, 1855–87, Peter Ibbetson (ten) murders his tyrannical uncle, Colonel Ibbetson (bar), and is imprisoned for life in Newgate. He succumbs to dreams and visions, and conjures up his past, including memories of his childhood sweetheart Mary, now the Duchess of Towers (sop). After nearly 40 years in prison, he learns that she has died, and losing the will to live he also dies; the prison walls disintegrate and Peter, young once more, finds Mary waiting for him.

Petrassi, Goffredo (*b* Zagarolo, 16 July 1904). Italian composer. Studied Rome with Bustini and Donato. His operas form a comparatively minor part of his output. *Il cordovano* (1949) was bitterly attacked for a supposedly pornographic libretto at its first performance; it uses the voices in a somewhat instrumental, even concertante, manner. *Morte dell'aria* (1950) has also attracted attention for its thoughtful treatment of a real-life incident, the death of a would-be birdman falling from the Eiffel Tower. Intendant Venice, F, 1937–40.

Petrella, Clara (*b* Milan, 28 Mar. 1914; *d* Milan, 19 Nov. 1987). Italian soprano. Studied Milan with her sister Micaëla, and Giannina Russ. Début Alexandria 1939 (Liù). Milan, S, from 1947. Also Naples, C; Rome; Mexico City; etc. Created roles in numerous operas, e.g. *Maria Golovin* (Menotti), *Cagliostro*, *La figlia di Jorio* (Pizzetti). Highly acclaimed as a singing actress, especially as Manon Lescaut, Iris, Magda Sorel. (R)

Petrella, Errico (*b* Palermo, 10 Dec. 1813; *d* Genoa, 7 Apr. 1877). Italian composer. Studied Naples Cons. with Bellini and Zingarelli. Aged only 15 he wrote his first opera, *Il diavolo color di rosa* (The Roseate Devil, 1829): though a great success, it had been done against his teachers' will, so he was expelled from the Cons. He wrote five operas for Naples 1831–9, including *I pirati spagnuoli* (The Spanish Pirates, 1838), but ceased composing following a quarrel. Resumed his career with the successful *Le precauzioni* (1851), then with *Elena di Tolosa* (1852) and *Marco Visconti* (1854), the latter rivalling even Verdi's *Il trovatore* in the same season. Taken up by the firm of Lucca to compete with Ricordi's Verdi, he wrote his first commission for La Scala, Milan, *Elnava*, in 1856. This ushered in a number of well-received works, of which the most widely publicized and successful was *Jone* (1858).

Though his music had an appeal in its day, Petrella's success was ephemeral and his style remained firmly rooted in the 18th-cent. opera buffa tradition. He chose subjects that really demanded greater imaginative control than he could give them and, unlike his great contemporary Verdi, was unable to release himself from the restricting conventions and formulas of the day.

Petrograd. See ST PETERSBURG.

Petrov, Ivan (*b* Irkutsk, 29 Feb. 1920). Russian bass. Studied Moscow with Mineyev. Début with Kozlovsky's Co. 1939 (small roles). Moscow, B, from 1943; Paris, O, from 1954. An authoritative singer with a wide range, renowned for his Boris, Dosifey, Kochubey, Méphistophélès (Gounod), and Philip. (R)

Petrov, Osip (*b* Elizavetgrad, 15 Nov. 1806; *d* St Petersburg, 12 Mar. 1878). Russian bass. Initially self-taught, later studying with Cavos. Début Elizavetgrad 1826 (Cavos's *Cossack Poet*). Joined I. F. Stein's troupe, and was much influenced by the actor Shchep-

kin. St Petersburg 1830–78. The first of the great Russian basses, he at once set an example for composers of the emergent nationalist school, and became one of their finest interpreters. He was accordingly sought out to create most of the important bass parts of new operas performed in St Petersburg for nearly half a century: Glinka's Ivan Susanin and Ruslan; Dargomyzhsky's Miller (*Rusalka*) and Leporello (*Stone Guest*); Ivan the Terrible (*Maid of Pskov*); the Mayor (*Vakula the Smith*); and Varlaam (*Boris Godunov*); as well as works by Rubinstein and Serov. His warm, dark voice, versatility, and powerful dramatic perception were allied to artistic integrity and great generosity of spirit. At his funeral, Musorgsky mourned his 'Grandpa' as 'an irreplaceable instructor . . . who inspired me to creativity'. An unnamed critic wrote of him, 'He has shown us what nationality in art means.' His wife **Anna Vorobyeva** (*b* St Petersburg, 14 Feb. 1816; *d* St Petersburg, 26 Apr. 1901) was a contralto, the daughter of the bass **Yakov Vorobyev** (?1766–1809). Studied with Sapienza. Created Vanya (*A Life for the Tsar*). Though prevented by illness from singing the first Ratmir (*Ruslan*), she sang in the third performance, and Glinka considered that it was she who made the work a success. Her large voice was of 'irresistible charm' (Stasov), and she was a much admired performer, highly successful in the Italian repertory.

Pfitzner, Hans (*b* Moscow, 5 May 1869; *d* Salzburg, 22 May 1949). German composer and conductor. Studied Frankfurt with Knorr and Kwast, Wiesbaden with Riemann. Cond., Mainz Stadttheater, 1894–6, a post he took in order to speed the prem. of *Der arme Heinrich* (1895); Berlin, T des Westens, 1903–6; Strasburg 1908–18 (dir., Stadttheater, 1910–16, where his assistant from 1914 was Klemperer).

A great admirer of Wagner and Schopenhauer, Pfitzner expressed dislike for modernist tendencies in music and became a fervent nationalist. His early triumph with *Der arme Heinrich* was followed up in the no less successful *Die Rose vom Liebesgarten* (1901): this was given in several cities and among its admirers was Mahler who staged it in Vienna. *Christelflein* (1906) made less impact, but with *Palestrina* (1917) Pfitzner produced his greatest work. His treatment of the apocryphal legend of Palestrina's dealings with the Council of Trent, for which he wrote his own libretto, elevates it to a Wagnerian exploration of the conflict between old and new artistic ideals. Though well regarded in its day, when it was even claimed as the successor to *Parsifal*, the score fails sufficiently to articulate the taut dramatic structure of the libretto. His last opera, *Das Herz* (1931), found few supporters.

Philadelphia. City in Pennsylvania, US. The first opera heard was *Flora*, an anon. ballad opera, given by an English company on 7 May 1754 at Plumstead's Warehouse. The Southwark T opened 1766 with Arne's *Thomas and Sally*, and imported English comic opera. Most opera in the early 19th cent. was Italian, brought by Da Ponte to the Chestnut St. T ('Old Drury'). The first true opera was *Der Freischütz* in 1825. A French company from New Orleans appeared 1827–33, and the Havana OC gave the first Italian opera here, Mayr's *Che originali* in 1829. William Fry wrote 'the first publicly performed Grand Opera written by a native American', *Leonora*, libretto by his brother, given by the Seguin Co., 1845.

The Philadelphia Academy of Music, opened Jan. 1857, is the oldest opera-house in continuous use in US. Up to the end of the 19th cent. many works had their US prems. there, including *Luisa Miller*, Gounod's *Faust*, *Fliegender Holländer*, *Pagliacci*, *Cavalleria*, *Amico Fritz*, *Pêcheurs de perles*, and *Manon Lescaut*. Companies functioning included the Philadelphia O, which gave performances under Gustav Heinrichs 1891–6, under Damrosch 1896–7, and Damrosch and Ellis 1897–9. The New York M appeared 1899–1961 at the Academy of Music. The Chicago Grand Opera Co. was known as the Chicago–Philadelphia Grand O, as financial support came from both cities. Works receiving US prems. included Herbert's *Natoma* (1911), Goldmark's *Cricket on the Hearth* (1912), and Franchetti's *Cristoforo Colombo* (1913): seasons were given in the Metropolitan OH built by Hammerstein to house his Manhattan OC, originally known as the Philadelphia OH (cap. 4,000) (now abandoned).

The Philadelphia Civic OC, founded in 1923 with Alexander Smallens as music director, was renamed the Philadelphia Lyric OC in 1958; US prems. included *Feuersnot* (1927) and *Ariadne* (1928). The Pennsylvania Grand Opera Co. was active 1927–30, and gave the first US *Khovanshchina* (1928); this

became the Philadelphia La Scala Co., then the Philadelphia Grand Opera Co. The Lyric and Grand finally merged into the Philadelphia OC, Mar. 1975, and performs at the Academy (cap. 2,818). New directions in the 1980s took the company into enterprises that included *Carmen* set in Fascist Spain and a revival of Sousa's *The Free Lance*, also the staging of opera for PBS TV.

Other short-lived enterprises included the Philadelphia Grand O, 1926–32, which launched the careers of singers including Rose Bampton, and the Philadelphia Orch. OC, 1930–5, which gave the first US *Glückliche Hand*, *Wozzeck*, and *Mavra*, with Stokowski, Goossens, and Reiner conducting. In 1938 the Philadelphia OC was founded to give opera in English; it gave the prem. of Menotti's *The Old Maid and the Thief*. The Curtis Institute has staged student and semi-professional performances, and gave the prem. of Menotti's *Amelia goes to the Ball* (1937).

Philidor, François-André Danican (*b* Dreux, 7 Sept. 1726; *d* London, 31 Aug. 1795). French composer. Studied Versailles with Campra. His proficiency as a chess-player— he toured as a master and published a study of the game—was one facet of intellectual gifts that made him the first truly learned composer of opéras-comiques. From 1756, after his Italian style debarred him from the Opéra, he developed his career as a successful composer of opéra-comique. With *Le sorcier* (1764), he became the first composer to take a curtain call. He did much to develop the genre, by the greater character he gave to melody, by his richer harmonic palette (especially in modulation), and by novelties he introduced such as the unaccompanied canon quartet in *Tom Jones* (1765), his masterpiece (though it was originally booed). These were, however, more skilful extensions of existing forms and techniques than real originalities, together with a capacity for handling the familiar with panache; his success here can be attributed in part to his Italianate training. He was also influenced by Gluck, to the point of probable plagiarism in *Le sorcier* and *Ernelinde* (1767). He also had vivid imitative powers, and brought into his scores the sounds of a hammer, or a donkey, or other effects to underline the text wittily; and he gave the orchestra a more expressive role even in light works.

Philine. An actress (sop) in the theatrical

company joined by Wilhelm in Goethe's *Wilhelm Meister*.

Philip. Philip II, King of Spain (bs) in Verdi's *Don Carlos*.

Piave, Francesco Maria (*b* Murano, 18 May 1810; *d* Milan, 5 Mar. 1876). Italian librettist. He wrote librettos for Balfe, Cagnoni, Mercadante, and Pacini, among others, but is most famous for his collaboration with Verdi. He provided the librettos for *Ernani*, *I due Foscari*, *Macbeth*, *Il corsaro*, *Stiffelio*, *Rigoletto*, *La traviata*, *Simon Boccanegra*, *Aroldo*, and *La forza del destino*. A close friend and complaisant colleague, he saw his role as servant to Verdi's demands, and was prepared to listen to, and answer, the most detailed instructions about versification.

Piccaver, Alfred (*b* Long Sutton, 5 Feb. 1884; *d* Vienna, 23 Sept. 1958). English tenor. Studied New York, Milan with Rosario, Prague with Prohaska-Neumann. Début Prague 1907 (Gounod's Roméo). Vienna 1910–37; Chicago 1923–5; London, CG, 1924. A much-loved artist with a sweet, clear tone and a distinguished stage presence, his roles included Florestan, Radamès, Gounod's Faust, Walther, Lensky, Canio, Werther. (R)

Picchi, Mirto (*b* S Mauro, 15 Mar. 1915; *d* Florence, 25 Sept. 1980). Italian tenor. Studied Florence with Armani and Tess. Début Milan, Palazzo dello Sport, 1946 (Radamès). London, Cambridge T, 1947–8; Gly. 1949; London, CG, 1952–3. Milan, S, from 1954; also Rome, Naples, etc. Notable for his acting, and for his advocacy of 20th-cent. music. Created roles in works by Pizzetti, Testi, Lizzi, Castro; acclaimed as Grimes, Vere, Oedipus, Tom Rakewell, Drum-Major, and Tiresias (*The Bassarids*). (R)

Piccinni, Niccolò (*b* Bari, 16 Jan. 1728; *d* Passy, 7 May 1800). Italian composer. Studied Naples with Leo and Durante. Made his début 1754 with the highly acclaimed *Le donne dispettose*, whose popularity placed him on a level with Logroscino: this was followed by a series of well-received works, culminating in *La Cecchina, ossia La buona figliuola* (1760). One of the most successful opere buffe of its day, *La buona figliuola* (as it is usually known) found many admirers and imitators: it is still sometimes revived in Italy. While holding various positions in Naples, Piccinni wrote *c*.50 operas, including a masterful setting of

L'Olimpiade (1761): he was particularly well regarded in Rome, where *I viaggiatori* (1775) was received almost as enthusiastically as *La buona figliuola*, though his position was eventually usurped by Anfossi. In 1776 he was encouraged to travel to Paris by a faction that wished to counter the reforms of Gluck. Here he directed a company of Italian singers which performed on alternate nights at the Opéra. He made an attempt at a French opera (taking advice from Marmontel over the adaptation of the Quinault libretto) but *Roland* (1778) had not yet been staged when the feud, fostered not by the composers but by their supporters, became public. An enterprising director of the Opéra arranged for them both to compose an *Iphigénie en Tauride* (1781), but Piccinni's setting, though successful, could not rival Gluck's. After Gluck's departure a new rival arose in Sacchini following the success of his *Renaud* in 1783. Despite the triumph of *Didon* (1783), which ran until 1826, Piccinni's star was on the wane. At the outbreak of the Revolution (1789) he returned to Naples, where he was involved in political trouble. He was fêted on his eventual return to Paris 1798, but never regained his old position.

Among his *c*.120 works there are some fine opere serie, but Piccinni is chiefly remembered as a composer of opera buffa: with Paisiello, Cimarosa, and Guglielmi he represents the last of the great Neapolitan tradition. He had a mastery of detail and a rare talent for writing engaging melodies; his handling of the orchestra also surpassed the general level of the times, as did his command of harmonic resources (especially major-minor relationships) which impressed many later composers, including Bellini. His masterpiece was *La buona figliuola*, which is a milestone in the history of Italian opera buffa; particularly noteworthy is its highly developed use of the *ensemble finale.

Piccolo Marat, Il. Opera in 3 acts by Mascagni; text by Forzano and Targioni-Tozzetti. Prem. Rome, C, 2 May 1921.

Paris, *c*.1793. In order to free his mother from prison, Prince Jean-Charles de Fleury (ten) joins the Revolution and becomes known as the Piccolo Marat ('little Marat'). With the help of his lover Mariella (sop) and the Carpenter (bar), they force the President of the Revolutionary council (bs) to sign a release order for the imprisoned princess, and all escape to freedom.

Pierné, Gabriel (*b* Metz, 16 Aug. 1863; *d* Ploujean, 17 July 1937). French composer. Studied Paris with Lavignac and Massenet. His long list of works includes eight operas, in which the influence of Massenet shows in the direct emotional appeal and in the elegance and fluency of the vocal writing. Among the most successful were *La coupe enchantée* (1895), *On ne badine pas avec l'amour* (One Doesn't Jest with Love, 1910), *Sophie *Arnould* (1927), and his masterpiece, *Fragonard* (1934). In this, he shows a light touch with rococo stylization but also the ability to write skilfully effective arias and set pieces.

Pietra del Paragone, La (The Touchstone). Opera in 2 acts by Rossini; text by Luigi Romanelli. Prem. Milan, S, 26 Sept. 1812.

In a Tuscan village, early 19th cent. The wealthy Count Asdrubale (bs) puts to the test three young widows who want to marry him—Aspasia (sop), Fulvia (mez), and Clarice (con). Disguising himself as a Turk, he arrives at his own castle claiming that Asdrubale owes him a large sum of money. Only Clarice and Giocondo (ten) stand by their friend. Clarice in turn resolves to test the Count's faithfulness and appears in the guise of her twin brother, a soldier, threatening to remove Clarice. When Asdrubale begs for Clarice's hand, she reveals her identity and the couple swear their love, leaving Fulvia and Aspasia to find other lovers.

Pikovaya dama. See QUEEN OF SPADES, THE.

Pilarczyk, Helga (*b* Schöningen, 12 Mar. 1925). German soprano. Studied Hamburg with Dziobek, later Rennert. Début Brunswick 1951 (Irmentraud, *Der Waffenschmied*). Hamburg 1954–68; Berlin, SO, 1956–60; London, CG, and Gly., 1958; Milan, S, 1963; New York, M, 1965. A committed advocate of 20th-cent. opera, who brought intelligence and insight to the roles of Salome, Marie (*Wozzeck*), Lulu, the Woman (*Erwartung*), Jocasta, etc. (R)

Pilgrims' Chorus. The chorus of pilgrims, 'Zu dir wall ich' in Act I, and 'Beglückt darf nun dich' in Act III of Wagner's *Tannhäuser*.

Pilgrim's Progress, The. Opera in 4 acts, with prologue and epilogue, by Vaughan Williams; text by composer and Wood, after Bunyan's allegory (pt 1, 1674–9; pt 2, 1684) and the Bible. Prem. London, CG, 26 Apr. 1951.

John Bunyan (bs-bar) introduces the story of the journey of Pilgrim (bar) towards the Heavenly City. This is shown in a series of scenes depicting his most famous encounters, including that with Apollyon (bs).

Pilou, Jeannette (*b* Alexandria, July 1931). Greek, later Italian, soprano. Studied Milan with Castellani. Début Milan, T Smeraldo, 1958 (Violetta). Milan, S; Naples; Rome; Vienna 1965; Paris, O, 1973; New York, M, from 1967; London, CG, 1971; also Monte Carlo, Chicago, Buenos Aires, Wexford. Roles incl. Susanna, Nannetta, Marguerite, Manon, Manon Lescaut, Mélisande, Butterfly. (R)

Pimen. The old chronicler monk (bs) in Musorgsky's *Boris Godunov*.

Pimmalione. Opera in 1 act by Cherubini; text by Stefano Vestris, after Antonio Sografi's Italian version of Rousseau's *Pygmalion* (1770), after the classical legend. Prem. Paris, Tuileries, 30 Nov. 1809.

Greece, mythological times. The Cypriot sculptor Pygmalion (mez) creates an ivory statue so beautiful that he falls in love with it. In answer to his prayers, Aphrodite (sop) brings the statue Galatea (sop) to life.

Pini-Corsi, Antonio (*b* Zara, June 1858; *d* Milan, 22 Apr. 1918). Italian baritone. Studied with Ravasio. Début Cremona 1878 (Dandini). Berlin, H, 1889; Milan, S, from 1893; London, CG, 1894–6, 1902–3; New York, M, 1899, 1909–14. A born buffo singer with a powerful tone, he was a popular Leporello, Dr Bartolo (Rossini), and Pasquale; created Ford, Schaunard, Happy (*Fanciulla*), and the Innkeeper (*Königskinder*). Retired 1917. (R) His brother **Gaetano** (1860–after 1923) was a tenor. Milan, S, from 1898; roles included David, Mime, and first Goro (*Butterfly*). (R)

Pinkerton. The American naval lieutenant (ten), faithless husband of Butterfly, in Puccini's *Madama Butterfly*. Originally Sir Francis Blummy Pinkerton, but after the opera's disastrous prem. rechristened Benjamin Franklin Pinkerton (and further altered to Linkerton in Germany and Austria, to avoid a Teutonic indelicacy).

Pinza, Ezio (*b* Rome, 18 May 1892; *d* Stamford, CT, 9 May 1957). Italian bass. Studied Bologna with Ruzza and Vezzani. Début Soncino 1914 (Oroveso). Milan, S, 1922–4;

New York, M, 1926–48; London, CG, regularly 1930–9; also Buenos Aires, and all Europe's major opera-houses. After 1948 sang in musical comedy (e.g. a highly successful Broadway *South Pacific*) and films. One of the noblest bassi cantanti of the century, he possessed not only a voice of great warmth, plasticity, and beauty, but a 'magnetic charm' (Gilman) and excellent dramatic skills. His large repertory (over 95 roles) included Figaro (Mozart), a famous Don Giovanni, Don Magnifico, Philip, Boris, Pogner, Amfortas, Golaud, and first Tigellino (Boito's *Nerone*). (R)

Pipe of Desire, The. Opera in 1 act by Converse; text by George Edward Burton. Prem. Boston, Jordan H, 31 Jan. 1906. The first US opera to be prem. at the New York, M, 18 Mar. 1910.

A magic pipe belonging to the Elf King (bs) is selfishly used by Iola (ten) and brings disaster to himself and to his lover Naoia (sop). The King pipes, and they die.

Piper, John (*b* Epsom, Surrey, 13 Dec. 1903; *d* Fawley, 28 June 1992). English painter and critic. Studied Richmond and London. One of the founder members of the *English Opera Group, 1947. His sets and costumes for the revival of Vaughan Williams's ballet *Job*, London, CG, 1948, though not liked by the composer, led to further stage designs. He worked at Glyndebourne, Covent Garden, and Sadler's Wells; but his most distinctive stage work has been done for Britten's operas. His strong architectural sense, sometimes a use of tapestry effects in a semi-abstract manner, and his powerful feeling for light and for colour, have produced remarkable designs closely attuned to the music. His wife **Myfanwy** (*b* 1911) was librettist of Britten's *Turn of the Screw*, *Owen Wingrave*, and *Death in Venice*.

Pirata, Il (The Pirate). Opera in 2 acts by Bellini; text by Romani, after Raimond's drama *Bertram, ou Le pirate* (1826), after Maturin's *Bertram* (1816), possibly deriving from Scott's *Rokeby* (1813). Prem. Milan, S, 27 Oct. 1827.

Sicily, 13th cent. Imogene (sop), although in love with Gualtiero (ten), has been forced to marry Ernesto, Duke of Caldora (bar), in order to prevent her father's death. Now a pirate, Gualtiero is shipwrecked off the coast of Caldora and aided by Imogene. He is horrified to learn of her marriage to Ernesto and vows revenge.

When Ernesto accuses Imogene of infidelity, she admits she still loves Gualtiero. Ernesto secretly watches the lovers' assignment. Gualtiero kills Ernesto in a duel, but then gives himself up and is sentenced to death. As he mounts the scaffold, Imogene collapses from grief.

Pirogov, Grigory (*b* Novoselky, 24 Jan. 1885; *d* Leningrad, 20 Feb. 1931). Bass. Studied Moscow with Medvedyev and Donsky. Début Rostov-on-Don 1908. St Petersburg, M, 1909. Moscow, B, 1910–15, 1917–21. Also St Petersburg, Paris, Berlin, Prague. Retired 1930. His full-toned, even voice was of exceptional range; he sang the baritone roles of Tomsky, Escamillo, and Rubinstein's Demon, as well as Boris, Ruslan, Wotan, Dodon, and Don Basilio (Mozart).

Pitt, Percy (*b* London, 4 Jan. 1869; *d* London, 23 Nov. 1932). English conductor. Studied Leipzig with Reinecke and Jadassohn, Munich with Rheinberger. Music adviser Grand O Syndicate at London, CG, 1902; dir. 1907–24, helping Richter with the English-language *Ring*, 1908–9. Beecham OC 1915–20; BNOC 1920–4. Music adviser BBC 1922–30, and cond. first complete broadcast opera in Britain, *Hänsel und Gretel*, 6 Jan. 1923.

Pixis, Johann Peter (*b* Mannheim, 10 Feb. 1788; *d* Baden-Baden, 22 Dec. 1874). German pianist and composer, son and pupil of the composer Friedrich Wilhelm Pixis. One of the most brilliant pianists of his time, and the composer of much virtuoso piano music, he also wrote four operas. The first, *Almazinde* (1820), was said to have too noisy and busy an accompaniment for the singers. *Bibiana* (1829), written for Schröder-Devrient, failed.

Pizarro. The prison governor (bar) in Beethoven's *Fidelio*.

Pizzetti, Ildebrando (*b* Parma, 20 Sept. 1880; *d* Rome, 13 Feb. 1968). Italian composer. Studied Parma with Righi. Having written some operas when very young, including *Il Cid* (entered for the 1902 Sonzogno competition), he formed a friendship with D'Annunzio, who wrote *Fedra* (1915) with the intention of turning it into a libretto for him. It is, however, a wordy text, and the music lacks the freedom he later achieved. Conservative by nature, he evolved a free-flowing declamatory style that has certain obvious debts to Wagner and

Debussy but that is wholly Italian in its contours. He also wrote powerfully for the chorus, notably in his finest opera, *Debora e Jaële* (1922). Other works that have developed these methods successfully include *Vanna Lupa* (1949), *La figlia di Jorio* (1954), and *Assassinio nella cattedrale* (1958).

Pizzi, Pier Luigi (*b* Milan, 15 June 1930). Italian stage director and designer. Studied Milan Polytechnic. Début Genoa 1952 (designs for *Don Giovanni*). Designs for and staging for Baroque repertory incl. Handel's *Orlando* (Florence 1959), Gluck's *Alceste* (Milan, S, 1987), Rameau's *Castor et Pollux* (Aix 1991). London, CG, 1984 (*I Capuleti e i Montecchi*); *Les Troyens* at the opening of the Paris, B, 1990.

Planché, James Robinson (*b* London, 27 Feb. 1796; *d* London, 29 May 1880). English theatrical writer. Translated many operas for the English stage, including works by Rossini, Auber, Marschner, Bellini (*Norma*), Hérold, Offenbach, and Mozart (*Magic Flute* and *Marriage of Figaro*). His version of Weber's *Der Freischütz* led Kemble to engage him as the librettist for *Oberon*. The form this took reflects not only Planché's assessment of the contemporary English musical theatre, and what would be acceptable, but his own interest in pantomimes and in historical costume. His *Recollections and Reflections* give a detailed picture of the theatrical life of his day.

Plançon, Pol (*b* Fumay, 12 June 1851; *d* Paris, 11 Aug. 1914). French bass. Studied Paris with Duprez and Sbriglia. Début Lyons 1877 (Saint-Bris). Paris, T de la Gaîté, 1880, and O 1883–93; London, CG, 1891–1904; New York, M, 1893 regularly until 1908. Repertory included Sarastro, a highly acclaimed Méphistophélès (Gounod), Frère Laurent, Escamillo, Ramfis, Landgrave, Pogner; created several roles including Gormas (*Le Cid*). A highly polished artist, whose smooth, essentially profondo voice also possessed a baritonal high register and great flexibility. His florid singing and trill were exceptional. (R)

Planquette, Robert (*b* Paris, 31 July 1848; *d* Paris, 28 Jan. 1903). French composer. Studied Paris with Duprato. After trying to earn a living by making arrangements and by playing the piano in cafés, he had some 1-act operettas performed at the Eldorado Music Hall and the Délassements-Comiques; then achieved his greatest success with *Les cloches de Corneville* (1877), which had 400 consecutive performances at the Folies Dramatiques, and was widely staged abroad. He wrote *Rip van Winkle* (1882) for London, following this with *Nell Gwynne* (1884), and adapting other works for the English stage. Among his later works *Mam'zelle Quat'sous* (1897) is outstanding, but on the whole they were not well received. A careful and stylish composer, with a lively melodic vein, he lacked the ease and variety of invention to keep his name before a public notorious for tiring quickly of anything lacking novelty.

Plaschke, Friedrich (*b* Jaroměř, 7 Jan. 1875; *d* Prague, 4 Feb. 1952). Czech bass-baritone. Studied Prague with Dötscher and Sklenář-Mala, Dresden with Scheidemantel. Début Dresden 1900 (Herald, *Lohengrin*). Dresden until 1937; Bayreuth 1911; London, CG, 1914; toured US 1922–4 with German O. Created several Strauss roles, including First Nazarene (*Salome*), Altair (*Die ägyptische Helena*), Waldner (*Arabella*), Morosus (*Die schweigsame Frau*); also sang Kurwenal, Amfortas, Sachs, Barak. Married the soprano Eva von der *Osten. (R)

Plasson, Michel (*b* Paris, 2 Oct. 1933). French conductor. Studied Paris Cons. and in US with Leinsdorf and Stokowski. Music dir. Toulouse T du Capitole 1968–83, with *Parsifal*, *Aida*, and the prem. of Landowski's *Montségur* 1985. London, CG, from 1979: *Werther*, *Guillaume Tell*, *Tosca*. Noted for carefully detailed and well-structured recordings of Magnard's *Guercœur* and Roussel's *Padmâvatî*. (R)

Platée. Opera in a prologue and 3 acts by Rameau; text by Adrien Le Valois d'Orville, after Jacques Autreau's libretto after Pausanias' *Periegesis*, ch. 9 (*c.* AD 176). Prem. Versailles 31 Mar. 1745.

Greece, mythological times. The prologue depicts the birth of comedy: Thespis (ten) instigates the creation of an entertainment demonstrating the absurdities of the gods and thus reforming human behaviour. In the play itself, Jupiter (bar) feigns love for the grotesque nymph Platée (ten) in order to arouse the anger of Junon (sop). Duly furious at Jupiter's behaviour, she disguises herself and, as he is about to make his marriage vows, hurls herself at Platée and tears off her bridal veil, then collapsing in a fit of laughter. She and Jupiter are happily reconciled.

Plishka, Paul (*b* Old Forge, PA, 28 Aug. 1941). US bass. Studied New Jersey with Boyajian. Début New Jersey 1961. New York, M, from 1967; Milan, S, 1975; also Chicago, Paris, Berlin, Barcelona. Large repertory incl. Leporello, Oroveso, Silva, Philip, Varlaam, Boris, King Mark, Frère Laurent, Abimelech (*Samson et Dalila*), Falstaff. (R)

Plowright, Rosalind (*b* Worksop, 21 May 1949). English soprano. Studied Manchester. Début Gly. Touring O 1975 (Agathe). WNO, London ENO, Kent O 1975–8; London, CG, from 1980; Madrid, Hamburg 1982; Milan, S, 1983; Verona 1985; Paris, O, 1987; Vienna, S, 1990; also Munich, S Francisco, Rome, Buenos Aires, etc. Roles incl. Médée, Norma, Elizabeth (*Maria Stuarda*), Aida, Amelia, Rossini's Desdemona, Senta, Ariadne, Tosca, Madeleine (*Andrea Chénier*). (R)

Poggi, Antonio. See FREZZOLINI, ERMINIA.

Pogner. Veit Pogner (bs), the goldsmith and Mastersinger, and Eva's father, in Wagner's *Die Meistersinger von Nürnberg*.

Poisoned Kiss, The. Opera in 3 acts by Vaughan Williams; text by Evelyn Sharp, after Richard Garnett's story *The Poison Maid* in the collection *The Twilight of the Gods* (1888). Prem. Cambridge 12 May 1936.

Fairyland. The fantastic plot turns on the rivalry of a sorcerer and an empress; his daughter Tormentilla (sop) has been brought up on poisons so that when she meets the empress's son Amaryllus (ten) she will kill him with her kiss. In the end the sincerity of their love defeats the plot.

Poissl, Johann Nepomuk von (*b* Haukenzell, 15 Feb. 1783; *d* Munich, 17 Aug. 1865). German composer. Studied Munich with Danzi and Vogler. His first opera was the comic *Die Opernprobe* (1806), but his first real successes were the serious *Antigonus* (1808) and *Ottaviano in Sicilia* (1812). In 1811 he met Weber, from whose friendship and championship he greatly benefited. The success of *Athalia* (1814) and *Der Wettkampf zu Olympia* (1815) did not bring him much material reward, and his career was made difficult by his belonging to the nobility. He was further disappointed of hopes of an appointment to Darmstadt, for which he wrote the popular *Nittetis* (1817) and *Issipile* (comp. 1818). In 1823 he gained a court appointment in Munich, and in 1825 became director of the court theatre; but the theatre lost money and he was forced to resign in 1832. Though he seldom staged his own operas, he did reopen the Nationaltheater after the 1823 fire with *Die Prinzessin von Provence* (1825). He died in poverty.

Poissl is important as a transitional figure between Mozart and Weber, and was one of the first German composers to move away from Italian and French example in favour of a continuously composed German opera (as in *Antigonus*, which does, however, contain some Italian and French elements). Weber praised *Der Wettkampf* and *Athalia* (which makes some use of motive) for their melodic qualities, commending the latter as a national achievement. Poissl was ahead of his time in writing most of his own librettos, and he published criticism and essays on theatre organization.

Pokrovsky, Boris (*b* Moscow, 23 Jan. 1912). Russian producer. Worked in Gorky 1937–43, then in Moscow and Leningrad staging many distinguished productions. His most significant work has been at the Moscow Chamber Musical T from 1972. Here he was able even in restrictive times to stage unfamiliar works in pioneering and highly imaginative productions, drawing his repertory from both classical pre-Glinka opera, neglected or officially disregarded contemporary works, and foreign opera. His revivals, with the support of Gennady Rozhdestvensky as music director, have included Pashkevich's *The Miser* and Shostakovich's *The Nose* (1974), as well as works by Bortyansky, Kholminov, and Stravinsky (first Russian *Rake's Progress*), among many others.

Polacco, Giorgio (*b* Venice, 12 Apr. 1873; *d* New York, 30 Apr. 1960). Italian conductor. Studied Venice, Milan, St Petersburg. Répétiteur London, CG, 1890, cond. Lago's Co., Shaftesbury T, 1891 (Gluck's *Orfeo*). After engagements in Italy (prem. of *Zazà*, Milan 1900), and in Warsaw, Lisbon, and Brussels, also Russia, cond. four seasons in Buenos Aires and seven in Rio de Janeiro. New York, M, 1912–17, conducting 327 performances in five seasons. Chicago 1918–19, music dir. 1921–30, directing many memorable performances of French operas with Mary Garden, also Italian and German repertory. London, CG, 1913–14, 1930 (*Pelléas* with Teyte, who found him 'the ideal interpreter'). Forced by ill health to retire 1930.

Poland. Opera was first given in Poland in 1613, when Prince Stanisław Lubomirski invited an Italian company to his residence at Wiśnicz. In 1625 Prince Władysław Zygmunt visited the Grand Duchess of Tuscany and heard, in his honour, Francesca Caccini's *La liberazione di Ruggiero dall'isola d'Alcina*, which he may have brought home: a Polish libretto appeared in 1628. After he was crowned Władysław IV in 1632, he founded an Italian opera company (1634–48) with Margherita Cattaneo as prima donna; it included some young Poles. About 12 operas (probably adaptations) were performed and published, including one by a Pole, Piotr Elert (?–1653), *La fama reale, ovvero Il principe trionfante Ladislao IV* (1633). The librettos were mostly by Virgilio Puccitelli, the music to some operas by Marco Scacchi.

Frederick Augustus, Elector of Saxony, was crowned Augustus II in 1697, and brought in his retinue an ensemble directed by J. C. Schmidt and Jacek Różycki. In 1700 a company of 60, formed in Paris at his request by Angelo Costantini, was brought under Deschallières; other companies also toured. In 1725 a court theatre, the Operalnia, opened in Warsaw. Augustus III was crowned in 1733 and at once showed enthusiasm for opera; he provided large subsidies, and twice-weekly performances were given with an orchestra of over 100. Many Metastasian operas were given; the company included *Hasse and *Bordoni. From *c*.1725 private operas were also established in the residences of Polish nobles, e.g. in Nieświcz, Ołyka, Słuck, and Białystock, performing mostly French and Italian works.

The growth of Polish national opera dates from the reign (1764–95) of Poland's last King, the enlightened and intelligent Stanisław August Poniatowski, who summoned artists of every kind to Warsaw and encouraged the arts throughout the country. The opening of the first public theatre in Warsaw in 1765 under Karol Tomatis encouraged the popularity of opera; and from 1776 opera seria was added to opera buffa. The first Polish opera was *Nędza uszczęśliwiona* (Sorrow Turned to Joy, 1778) by Maciej Kamieński (1734–1821), consisting of 11 airs and two duets. In 1779 the T Narodowy opened, giving in its first year Kamieński's *Zośka* and *Prostota cnotliwa* (Virtuous Simplicity), also *Nie każdy śpi, co chrapi* (Not All who Snore, Sleep) by Gaetano (known as Kajetan Majer, ?–*c*.1793).

Despite the three partitions of Poland at the end of the 18th cent., Polish texts began superseding foreign ones, due largely to the 'father of the Polish theatre', Wojciech Bogusławski (1757–1829). An actor, producer, and singer (he was the first Antek in as well as the librettist of *Nędza uszczęśliwiona*) who also directed the theatre 1782–4 and 1799–1814, he translated many librettos and wrote others, including *Krakowiacy i Górale* (The Krakowians and the Highlanders, 1794) by Jan Stefani (1746–1829). In four acts, this is the first full-scale Polish opera, and was based on peasant life. In the period of national difficulties which followed, Bogusławski staged productions of foreign works, while Jószef Elsner (1769–1854) wrote a long series of Polish operas, including *Andromeda*: this was given on 14 Jan. 1807 before Napoleon, who followed the performance with a French translation. Other popular operas by Elsner, mostly on Polish historical themes, included *Leszek Biały* (Leszek the White, 1809), *Król Tokietek* (King Lokietek, 1818), and *Jagiełło w Tenczynie* (Jagiełło at Tenczyn, 1820). In 1810 Karol *Kurpiński (1785–1857) was appointed to the opera, and with his work and music helped to maintain a Polish opera free from Russian influence. He introduced works by himself, Elsner, Mozart, Rossini, later Weber, Auber, Donizetti, Bellini, and eventually Verdi. The T Wielki opened in Warsaw on 24 Sept. 1833.

Stanisław Moniuszko (1819–72) first had *Halka* given in Wilno in 1848, but it was kept out of Warsaw by the director Tomasz Nidecki; when Giovanni Quattrini took over in 1852, he immediately staged the work hailed as Poland's first great national opera. In his period as music director (1858–72), many new Polish works were staged, including those by Ignacy Dobrzyński (1806–67), Gabriel Rożniecki (1815–87), Adam Minchejmer (1830–94), Stanisław Duniecki (1839–70), and Moniuszko himself. In the decade 1858–67 some 40 new operas appeared, the most important being Moniuszko's own *Straszny dwór* (The Haunted Castle, 1865). Wagner was first given under Cesare Trombini. New composers included Władysław Zeleński (1837–1921), whose four operas included *Wallenrod* (1885) and *Goplana* (1896); and Ludomir Różucki (1884–1953), conductor at Lvov, whose *Bolesław Śmiały* (Bolesław the Bold, 1909) and *Meduza* (1912) show an ability to reconcile post-Wagnerian and verismo methods within a Slavonic manner, and whose most important work was *Eros i Psyche* (1917). Dominating them, however, was Karol *Szymanowski, whose sumptuous post-Romantic manner finds expression in *Hagith* (comp. 1913; prem. 1922) and *Król Roger* (King Roger, 1926).

After the First World War, there came a period of intense activity especially in Warsaw, Poznań, Lvov, Cracow, and Katowice, with many famous singers appearing; in composition, it was a reactionary period, and in the 1930s only about 30 new Polish operas appeared. After the Second World War, activity was quickly renewed. Warsaw's T Wielki, burnt down in 1939 and bombed in 1944, was rebuilt in 1965, but opera continued meanwhile and outside the capital a number of new companies were formed. 19th-cent. Polish opera remains popular in repertories that concentrate on Italian and Russian opera but are increasingly catholic in taste. Successful post-war Polish operas have included *Bunt żaków* (The Goliards' Revolt, 1951) and *Krakatuk* (1955) by Tadeusz Szeligowski (1896–1963); *Chłopi* (The Peasants, 1974) by Witold Rudziński (b 1913); *Jutro* (Tomorrow, 1966) by Tadeusz Baird (b 1928); *Cyrano de Bergerac* (1962), *Lord Jim* (1976), and *Mary Stuart* (1981) by Romuald Twardowski (b 1930); *Diabły z Loudun* (The *Devils of Loudun, 1969) by Krzysztof Penderecki (b 1933); and works by Joanna Bruzdowicz (*Bramy raju* (The Gates of Paradise, 1988)).

See also WARSAW.

Polaski, Deborah (b Richmond Center, WI, 26 Sept. 1949). US soprano. Studied Ohio Cons. and Graz. Début Gelsenkirchen 1976. Has sung throughout Germany in such dramatic repertory as Marie (*Wozzeck*), Elektra, and Katerina Ismaylova. Particularly strong in the middle register, she sang Brünnhilde at Bayreuth (new prods. 1988, 1994) and at London, CG (1994–5). Other roles incl. the Dyer's Wife (Amsterdam 1992), Kundry, Isolde. (R)

Poliuto. Opera in 3 acts by Donizetti; text by Cammarano, after Corneille's tragedy *Polyeucte* (1642). Comp. 1838 for Nourrit, for prod. in Naples, but not passed by censor. New 4-act version as Grand Opera, with French text by Scribe, prem. Paris, O, 10 Apr. 1840, as *Les martyrs*.

Mytilene, capital of Armenia, AD 257. Poliuto (ten) has become a secret convert to Christianity, and is arrested and condemned to death. His wife Paolina (sop), although still in love with Severo (bar), the Roman proconsul, decides to join her husband and die with him.

Pollak, Anna (b Manchester, 1 May 1912). English mezzo-soprano. Studied with Hislop, and London with Cross. Début London, SW, 1945 (Dorabella). London, SW, until 1961. London: EOG 1946, CG 1952; Gly. 1952–3; also Holland Fest. A versatile and stylish actress; sang Cherubino, Fatima, Orlovsky, Siebel. Created Bianca (*Rape of Lucretia*), Berkeley's Lady Nelson (*Nelson*) and title-role of his *Ruth*. (R)

Pollak, Egon (b Prague, 3 May 1879; d Prague, 14 June 1933). Austrian conductor. Studied Prague with Knittl. Chorus- master Prague, Landestheater, 1901. Cond. Bremen 1905–10; Leipzig 1910–12; Frankfurt 1912–17; music dir. Hamburg 1917–31. London, CG, 1914. Chicago 1915–16, 1929–32. Buenos Aires, C, 1928. Vienna, S, 1932–3. Admired for his Wagner and especially Richard Strauss (who thought him 'superb'). Collapsed and died while conducting *Fidelio*. (R)

Pollarolo, Carlo Francesco (b Brescia, c.1653; d Venice, 7 Feb. 1722). Italian composer. Studied Venice with Legrenzi. Active as a church musician in Venice, he also composed c.85 operas, many lost; 1691–1707 he was the most frequently performed composer at the Venice GG. His style shares some similarity with Pallavicino's and his works are notable for their increased use of the orchestra, suggesting the influence of Lully: this is seen also in his occasional use of the French overture, e.g. in *Faramondo* (1698). Pollarolo's works represent an important transitory phase leading to Neapolitan opera seria: his settings of Zeno, which also include *Gl'inganni felice* (1696), were among the first.

Pollet, Françoise (b Boulogne Billancourt, 10 Sept. 1949). French soprano. Studied Versailles Cons. and Munich. Lübeck O 1983–6 (début as Marschallin) and in operas by Wagner and Mozart. Paris, OC, as Mozart's Vitellia; Paris, C, as Dukas's Ariane. A leading exponent of the dramatic repertory, she has sung Magnard's Berenice at Montpellier, Valentine in *Les Huguenots* at London, CG, 1991, and Cassandre (*Les Troyens*) at Brussels and New York, M, 1994. (R)

Pollini, Bernhard (*b* Cologne, 16 Dec. 1838; *d* Hamburg, 27 Nov. 1897). German tenor, baritone, and impresario. Début Cologne 1858 (Arturo). Later sang as baritone with an Italian co., and became its manager. Dir. Lvov O 1864; dir. Italian O, St Petersburg, and Moscow; dir. Hamburg O 1874–97, where he worked closely with Bülow, then Mahler. Important for his promotion of Wagner's operas (taking *The Ring* to London, CG, 1892) and other new works including *Carmen*, Verdi's *Otello*, *Manon Lescaut*. Engaged the best singers of the day, e.g. Niemann, Klafsky, and the young Mildenburg.

Pollione. The Roman proconsul (ten), lover of Norma and of Adalgisa, in Bellini's *Norma*.

Polly. Polly Peachum (sop), Lucy Lockit's rival for Macheath's love, in Pepusch's *The Beggar's Opera*, and in Weill's version of it, *Die Dreigroschenoper*.

Polovtsian Dances. The dances in Act II of Borodin's *Prince Igor* with which the Khan Konchak entertains Igor.

Ponchielli, Amilcare (*b* Paderno Fasolaro, 31 Aug. 1834; *d* Milan, 16 Jan. 1886). Italian composer. Studied Milan with Frasi and Mazzucato. Composed his first operatic music, with fellow-students, for *Il sindaco babbeo*. Conducted at the T Carcano, Milan, 1860. His first opera was *I promessi sposi* in 1856, successful on its revival in 1872, as was the Ricordi commission *I lituani* (1874). But his greatest, and only enduring, triumph was *La Gioconda* (1876). His dramatic instinct here finds its best outlet: Boito's text combines many features of French Grand Opera and Italian Romantic melodrama, in a manner that suited the composer's gift for agreeable, warm music. The work's musical and dramatic styles were already exhausted in opera; but it contains celebrated passages, including the arias 'Cielo e mar' and 'Suicidio', and the Dance of the Hours ballet. In his other operas Ponchielli toyed with exotic styles, Slavonic in *I lituani*, oriental in *Il figliuol prodigo* (1880). His last work, *Marion Delorme* (1885), is closer to opéra-comique in style. Married the soprano **Teresina Brambilla** (1818–95).

Poniatowski, Józef (*b* Rome, 20 Feb. 1816; *d* Chislehurst, 3 July 1873). Polish composer and tenor. Great-nephew of Stanisław August, King of Poland 1764–95. Studied

Rome, then Florence with Zanetti and Ceccherini. Début Florence in title-role of his *Giovanni di Procida* (to his own text, 1838). His *Don Desiderio* (1840) was also widely successful; other operas include *Ruy Blas* (1843), *Bonifazio de' Geremei* (1843), *Malek Adel* (1846), and *Esmeralda* (1847). Became Prince of Monte Rotondo, 1848; Ambassador in Brussels, London, and Paris, where he also became a senator. His *Pierre de Médicis* was given at the Opéra, 1860, *Au travers du mur* at the Opéra-Comique, 1861. He followed Napoleon III into exile to London, where his *Gelmina*, written for Patti, was given in 1872.

Ponnelle, Jean-Pierre (*b* Paris, 19 Feb. 1932; *d* Munich, 11 Aug. 1988). French designer and producer. Studied Paris. Invited by Henze to design the prems. of *Boulevard Solitude* (1952) and *König Hirsch* (1956); then Germany, Italy, US. First prod. *Tristan* Düsseldorf 1962. Rapidly in demand as prod. in many theatres (also generally making his own designs) in a wide range of works, both classics, especially Mozart and Rossini, and new works, e.g. Reimann's *Lear*, Munich 1978. Bayreuth, *Tristan* 1981; Cologne, *Parsifal* 1983; Salzburg Mozart series and *Moses und Aron* 1987; Zurich Monteverdi from 1979 with Harnoncourt, *Carmen* 1982. Cologne, complete Mozart series. S Francisco over 20 productions from 1958, *Fliegender Holländer*, *Carmen* 1981; Houston, *Arlecchino* and *Pagliacci* 1982; New York, M, *Fliegender Holländer* 1979, *Titus* 1984. London, CG, designer *L'heure espagnole* 1962, designer-producer *Don Pasquale* 1973, *Aida* 1984, *Italiana* 1988. Gly., *Falstaff* 1977. Vienna, *Cavalleria* and *Pagliacci* 1984. Munich, *Lulu* 1985, prem. of Reimann *Troades* 1986. Also made many films for TV. One of the most gifted, hardworking, and stimulating producers of his day: many of his ideas excited controversy, e.g. his new angles on Mozart and his *Fliegender Holländer* prod. seen as a dream by the Steersman, but his theatrical sense was potent and musically based, and he unfailingly stimulated audiences, as well as performers and younger producers, without losing his sense that the work's importance was greater than his own.

Pons, Juan (*b* Ciutadella, Menorca, 1946). Spanish baritone. Studied Barcelona and soon became identified with the major Verdi baritone roles: Falstaff (Rome and S Francisco); Amonasro (Verona); Germont (Chicago 1988). New York, M, 1986 (Scarpia)

and 1993 (Rigoletto). Other roles incl. Alfio (London, CG, 1979), Tonio (Paris, O, 1983). (R)

Pons, Lily (b Draguignan, 12 Apr. 1898; d Dallas, 13 Feb. 1976). French, later US, soprano. Studied Paris with Gorostiaga. Début Mulhouse 1928 (Lakmé). New York, M, 1931–60; London, CG, 1935. Also Paris, O; Chicago; Buenos Aires; etc. Gifted with an unusually high and agile voice, and great vivacity, she had an extremely successful career on a very small repertory. This included Amina, Lucia, Gilda, Olympia, Philine. She also appeared in films. (R)

Ponselle, Rosa (b Meriden, CT, 22 Jan. 1897; d Green Spring Valley, MD, 25 May 1981). US soprano of Neapolitan parentage. Studied with Thorner and Romani. Early career in vaudeville. Discovered by Caruso; he sang at her début, New York, M, 1918 (Leonora, Forza), her first ever operatic performance. New York, M, until 1937; London, CG, 1929–31; Florence, Maggio Musicale, 1933. Described by Serafin as a 'miracle', and considered one of the most remarkable singers of the century, she possessed a phenomenal, powerful voice (Huneker called it 'vocal gold ... dark, rich, and ductile'), a seamless legato, and impeccable coloratura. Also striking were her intense musicality and dramatic authority. Her 23 roles included Julia (La vestale), Donna Anna, Reiza, Norma, Violetta, Aida, Gioconda, Santuzza, Romani's Fedra. Retired early, 1937; artistic dir. of Baltimore Civic O from 1954. (R) Her sister **Carmela** (1887–1977) was a mezzo-soprano who sang at New York, M, 1925–35 as Amneris, Azucena, etc. (R)

Ponziani, Felice (b ?; d ?, c.1826). Italian bass. Active in Parma 1784–5; Prague 1786, where he sang successfully as Figaro, and 1787, creating Leporello, which Mozart wrote for him. Evidently a gifted performer, he was described in a Prague newspaper as 'the favourite of connoisseurs, and of all who have heard him'. Venice 1792; Vienna 1792–8.

Popp, Lucia (b Uhorská Veš, 12 Nov. 1939; d Munich, 16 Nov. 1993). Czech soprano. Studied Bratislava and Prague with Hrušovska-Prosenková. Début Bratislava 1963 (Queen of the Night). Vienna, S, from 1963; London, CG, from 1966 (début as Oscar); New York, M, from 1967; Paris, O, from 1976, and B, 1991; Cologne, Salzburg, Munich, etc. An artist of charm, with a well-projected, bright, and vibrant voice. Roles included Susanna, Countess (Mozart), Aennchen, Eva, Mařenka, Sophie, Manon. (R)

Poppea. The lover and later crowned empress (sop) of Nero in Monteverdi's L'*incoronazione di Poppea*.

'Porgi amor'. The Countess's (sop) aria in Act II of Mozart's Le nozze di Figaro, in which she laments the loss of her husband's love.

Porgy and Bess. Opera in 3 acts by Gershwin; text by Du Bose Heyward and Ira Gershwin, after the drama Porgy by Du Bose and Dorothy Heyward. Prem. Boston, Colonial T, 30 Sept. 1935.

Catfish Row, Charleston, 1920s. Crown (bs), a stevedore, is obliged to flee after killing his friend Robbins (ten) in a fight over a dice game. He leaves behind him his girl Bess (sop); she is taken care of by Porgy (bs-bar), who has long loved her.

Porgy is happy in his new life with Bess. But while on a picnic, she meets Crown again and is persuaded to return to him. After a few days, however, she runs home to Porgy seeking shelter and declaring she loves him. Crown sets out to rescue some fishermen during a storm. The women weep for the dead lost at sea.

As he promised, Crown goes to Porgy's house in search of Bess, but Porgy stabs him dead and is arrested. Alone again, Bess is persuaded by Sporting Life (ten) to follow him to New York. When Porgy is released through lack of evidence, he sets off to New York after her.

Porpora, Nicola (b Naples, 17 Aug. 1686; d Naples, 3 Mar. 1768). Italian composer and singing teacher. Studied Naples with Grecos, Giordano, and Campaniles. His first operatic success came with Agrippina (1708), followed by Flavio Anicio Olibrio (1711) and Basilio (1713). Through Prince Philipp of Hessen-Darmstadt, whose service he had entered c.1707, his Arianna e Teseo was given to great acclaim at the Vienna court 1714. In 1715–21 he was maestro di cappella at the Cons. di S Onofrio, Naples, where he taught a number of celebrated singers, including Caffarelli, Farinelli, Porporino, Salimbeni, and (though unsuccessfully) Hasse. During the 1720s his fame as a composer began to increase both in Italy and elsewhere in Europe, especially Vienna. He began to set librettos by his pupil

Metastasio, of which the first was *Didone abbandonata* (1725). In 1726–33 he lived in Venice, writing *Siface* (1725) and *Semiramide riconosciuta* (1729). Having failed to secure the post of maestro di cappella at St Mark's, he travelled to London in 1733, where he had been invited as principal composer of the Opera of the Nobility. Here he became the main rival to Handel and produced five operas, including *Ifigenia in Aulide* (1735), and *Mitridate* (1736). Following the success of Handel's *Atalanta*, Porpora prudently left London, shortly before the collapse of the company. Returning to Italy, he held positions in Venice (1737), Naples (1739), and Venice (1742), but in 1747 went to Dresden as singing-teacher to Princess Maria Antonia Walpurgis. Appointed Kapellmeister in 1748, but shortly afterwards Hasse was appointed above him as Oberkapellmeister. In 1752 he moved to Vienna, where Haydn was his pupil, copyist, and accompanied his lessons. He finally returned to Italy, to Naples (1758), Venice (1759), and Naples again (1760), where he died in poverty. Porpora composed *c*.50 operas which were highly regarded in their day: together with Hasse's, they represent Metastasian opera seria in its purest form.

Porsile, Giuseppe (*b* Naples, 5 May 1680; *d* Vienna, 29 May 1750). Italian composer and singing-teacher. Held positions at Spanish court and Naples, before becoming singing-teacher to the Dowager Empress Amalia in Vienna 1715. Court composer 1720–40, writing *c*.30 dramatic works, including six opere serie. His style owes much to Fux and Caldara and he showed an appropriate fondness for heroic and noble themes, as in *Il ritorno d'Ulisse alla patria* (1707) and *Spartaco* (1726).

portamento (It.: 'carrying'). The smooth carriage of the voice from one note to another, momentarily sounding the pitches in between. The Fr. *porte de voix* is generally reserved, from *c*.1800, for an appoggiatura, generally from below: Ger., *tragen der Stimme*.

Portugal, Marcos António (da Fonseca) (orig. Ascenção; also known as Portogallo) (*b* Lisbon, 24 Mar. 1762; *d* Rio de Janeiro, 7 Feb. 1830). Portuguese composer. Singer and organist at the Seminário da Patricial. Music dir. of the T Siltre 1785, where he wrote five Portuguese operettas, including the popular *A castanheira* (The Chestnut Seller, 1788). In 1792 he went to Naples to study; here he

wrote 21 operas for various Italian cities. The first, *La confusione della somiglianza* (The Problems of Looking Alike, 1793), was one of his greatest successes and was revived shortly afterwards in Germany. His work embraced both opere serie and opere buffe: highly regarded were *Lo spazzacamino principe* (The Royal Chimney Sweep, 1794), *La vedova raggiratrice* (The Cheating Widow, 1794), and *Fernando nel Messico* (1798), which brought him fame throughout Europe. Dir. of the Royal O at S Carlos T, Lisbon, 1800: here he engaged Catalani 1801–6. When the court fled to Brazil following French occupation he stayed first in Lisbon but then followed (1810); opened the T São João in Rio de Janiero in 1813. Illness prevented him from returning to Lisbon with the court in 1821.

Portugal composed *c*.35 Italian operas and 21 1-act Portuguese comic operas. His style in the Italian works, predominantly that of the Neapolitan school, rarely goes beyond conventional gestures, but as one of the earliest to set librettos in his native language, he represents, together with Moreira, the first generation of Portuguese opera composers. Equally important for the establishment of his country's national opera were his activities outside Portugal and the international reputation which he achieved both as composer and as conductor.

Posa. Rodrigo, Marquis of Posa (bar), in Verdi's *Don Carlos*.

'Possente spirto'. The arioso section in Act III of Monteverdi's *Orfeo* in which he charms Caronte (Charon) to sleep. Famous for its skilfully contrasting instrumental accompaniment.

Postillon de Lonjumeau, Le. Opera in 3 acts by Adam; text by De Leuven and Brunswick. Prem. Paris, OC, 13 Oct. 1836.

The postilion Chapelou (ten) possesses a fine voice, and is engaged by De Courcy (bar), the manager of the royal amusements, to sing at Fontainebleau. Under the name of Saint-Phar he becomes a great singer, and promises marriage to the rich Madeleine (sop), whom he had previously married when he was a postilion and she the hostess of a village inn. All ends happily.

Poulenc, Francis (Jean Marcel) (*b* Paris, 7 Jan. 1899; *d* Paris, 30 Jan. 1963). French composer. Studied with Koechlin. Like other members of the group Les Six, Poulenc was eclectic in his inspiration and his music is imbued with a healthy irreverence for tradition which places him among the most original of his generation. Most of his music was not for the theatre: *Le gendarme incompris*, a *comédie-bouffe*, which he later withdrew, was not followed for nearly a quarter-century, until the witty and surrealist satire *Les mamelles de Tirésias* (1947). *Dialogues des Carmélites* (1957) is of an altogether different order, a deeply felt religious work written in a simple lyrical style. For its conception Poulenc owes much to Debussy and the model of *Pelléas*, seen not least in his handling of the orchestra. His final work, *La voix humaine* (1959), is a 45-minute monologue for soprano, written for Denise Duval: ironically described by him as a 'tragédie lyrique', it is a vocal *tour de force* which fails to satisfy dramatically.

Pountney, David (*b* Oxford, 10 Sept. 1947). English producer. Studied Cambridge: Scarlatti *Trionfo d'onore*, Cambridge O Soc. 1967 (cond. Elder), then Smetana *Kiss* 1969, British prem. Dessau *Lukullus* 1970, *Rake's Progress* 1971; latter also Scottish O 1971, Amsterdam 1972. Janáček cycle jointly with Scottish O/WNO, some later transferred to London, C. Houston: *Macbeth* 1974. Aldeburgh: *Savitri* and *Wandering Scholar* 1974. London, EOG: Puccini *Rondine* 1974. Scottish O: *Macbeth* 1977, *Meistersinger* 1977, *Onegin* 1979, *Don Giovanni* 1979, *Street Scene* 1989. London, C: prem. of Blake *Toussaint*, designed Bjørnson, cond. Elder, 1977, initiating a collaboration which gave the work of the Coliseum a particular stamp, with innovative, provocative, sometimes brilliant productions; dir. of productions 1982; *Flying Dutchman*, *Makropoulos Case*, 1982; *Queen of Spades*, *Rusalka*, *Gambler*, 1983; *Walküre* 1983; *Osud* 1984; *Midsummer Marriage*, *Orpheus in the Underworld*, 1985; *Dr Faust* 1986; *Carmen*, *Lady Macbeth of Mtsensk*, *Hänsel and Gretel*, 1987; *Cunning Little Vixen*, *Traviata*, *Christmas Eve*, 1988; *Falstaff* 1989; *Macbeth*, prem. Holloway *Clarissa*, *Wozzeck*, 1990; *Königskinder* 1992; *The Excursions of Mr Brouček*. Berlin, K: *Iolanthe* 1984. Bregenz: *Fliegender Holländer* 1989. New York, M, 1992 (prem. of Glass, *The Voyage*). A gifted and highly intelligent man of the theatre, with strong ideas articulated through his productions: these can be profoundly or wittily illuminating, often theatrically dazzling, but at their most wilful can cast only a selective spotlight and leave much of the work's quality in darkness.

'Pourquoi me réveiller?' Werther's (ten) aria in Act III of Massenet's *Werther*, in which he sings a song of tragic love from the verses of Ossian which in happier days he had translated with Charlotte.

'Poveri fiori'. Adriana's (sop) aria in Act IV of Cilea's *Adriana Lecouvreur*, in which she contemplates the faded bunch of violets (now poisoned by her rival, the Princesse de Bouillon) which she had given Maurizio.

Prague (Cz., Praha). Capital of Czechoslovakia from 1918, formerly capital of Bohemia. Opera was first given in 1627, when Italian singers came from Mantua to perform at the coronation of Ferdinand III. In 1723 Fux's *Costanza e Fortezza* was performed for the 4,000 visitors to the coronation of Charles VI in an amphitheatre with room for 1,000 performers. Visiting Italian companies performed first in the Estates Riding School, then in the home of Count František Špork, Na Poříčí. From 1739 opera was also given at the Kotzen (Kotce) T, the main public theatre until the 1780s. Pasquale Bondini's Italian co. played in a theatre built by Count Thun at his palace in the Malá Strana; and Karel Wahr's German co. played at the Gräflich-Nostitzsches Nationaltheater, built at his own expense by Count Nostic and opened in 1783 (cap. over 1,000). In 1784 Nostic replaced Wahr with Bondini, who after the sensational prem. of *Figaro* (said to be far superior to the original Vienna production) secured the commission for *Don Giovanni* in 1787. The Kotce T closed in 1783, and the Thun T burnt down in 1794. The 1790s saw operatic performances in Czech by the Patriotic T co. The Nostic T became the Královské stavovské divadlo (Royal Estates T) in 1789. The director of the German co. in 1803–13 was Wenzel Müller, and in 1813–16 it was Carl Maria von Weber, who did much to widen and develop the repertory and to improve theatrical standards. The playwright Jan Štěpánek revived the Czech professional co. from 1824, and in the face of restrictions built up opera in Czech. The theatre became the Královské zemské divadlo (Royal Provincial T) in 1861. In 1837 František Škroup was appointed conductor, and the theatre developed under the management of Josef Tyl (1846–51: since 1949 the theatre has been known as the Tylovo divadlo). Opera was also given in summer theatres, including the Novoměstské divadlo (New Town T) from 1858 (cap. over 3,000) and the Nové české divadlo (New Czech T) from 1876 (cap. over 3,000).

Another theatre being urgently required, in part as a national gesture, a newly formed association built the Prozatímní divadlo (Provisional T) in 1862 (cap. 900). Its methods and resources were initially primitive, with most of its singers amateurs and a tiny scratch orchestra under Jan Maýr. Smetana was director 1866–74, and six of his operas were produced here, as were the first stage works of Dvořák and Fibich. Practical and political disputes delayed its replacement, and the laying of the foundation stone of the new theatre in 1868 was a national event. In 1881 the Národní divadlo (Nat. T), incorporating the Provisional T, opened with *Libuše*; but shortly afterwards the theatre burnt down. Money was quickly found for another theatre, which opened in 1883 (cap. 1,598). This has remained at the centre of Prague operatic life. Chief conductors have included Adolf Čech (1883–1900), Karel Kovařovic (1900–20), Otakar Ostrčil (1920–35), Václav Talich (1935–44 and 1947–8), Zdeněk Chalabala (1953–62), Jaroslav Krombholc (1963–75), and Zdeněk Košler (1980–5 and 1989–91). Important prems. included Schoenberg's *Erwartung* (1924). The theatre was rebuilt 1977–83 (cap. 986, with Chamber T cap. 500).

Meanwhile, replacing the Novoměstské divadlo, the German minority built the Neues Deutsches T (opened 1887, cap. 1,554). The company was directed by Angelo *Neumann and Alexander *Zemlinsky (1911–27), in a line of distinguished German musicians who have developed their careers in Prague, including Mahler (1885), Klemperer (1907–10), and Szell (1929–37). After 1945 the theatre became first the Velká opera 5 května (Grand O 5th May), then in 1948, as filial of the Nat. T, the Smetanovo divadlo (Smetana T) (cap. 1,044). The theatre has won a name for enterprise, especially with the productions of Josef *Svoboda; renamed Prague State Opera 1992. Opera has also been given at the Městské divadlo na Král, Vinokradech (Vinokradské divadlo) opened in 1907; particularly under Ostrčil (1913–19), this was a pioneering centre of modern opera. Operetta has been given in various theatres but especially in the Variété in Karlín (built 1880–1), from 1962 known as the Hudebni divadlo v Karlíně, and the Velká Opereta. In 1934 Emil F. *Burian opened,

in the Mozarteum, an avant-garde theatre called D34 (Divadlo (theatre) 1934) where, especially in the 1950s, chamber operas and plays with music were given. In 1983 an experimental theatre, the Nová Scéna (New Stage), was opened next to the Nat. T.

Prati, Alessio (*b* Ferrara, 19 July 1750; *d* Ferrara, 17 Jan. 1788). Italian composer. Studied Ferrara and Rome; *c.*1775 travelled to Paris, where he had success with *L'école de la jeunesse* (1779). In 1782 he went to St Petersburg at the invitation of Grand Prince Paul; other travels took him to Warsaw, Dresden, Vienna, and Munich. Returned to Italy 1784, where *Ifigenia in Aulide* (1784) was given. Though not prolific by the standards of the day, with only *c.*10 operas to his credit, Prati was one of the most skilled composers of the mid-18th cent. and his work was highly regarded.

Pré aux clercs, Le. Opera in 3 acts by Hérold; text by Planard, after Mérimée's novel *Chronique du règne de Charles IX* (1829). Prem. Paris, OC, 15 Dec. 1832.

Girot (bar), host of the 'Pré aux Clercs', celebrates his betrothal to Nicette (sop), goddaughter of Marguerite de Valois (sop or mez). The ambassador Mergy (ten), searching for the queen, meets his childhood love Isabelle (sop), who is promised to Comminges (bar). Aided by Cantarelli (ten—*Trial role), the queen helps Isabelle: Mergy challenges Comminges, kills him, and marries Isabelle.

Predieri, Luca Antonio (*b* Bologna, 13 Sept. 1688; *d* Bologna ? 3 Jan. 1767). Italian composer. Member of the Accademia Filarmonica 1716; dir. 1723; also held ecclesiastical appointments in Bologna. Moved to Vienna 1737; appointed second Kapellmeister to Fux, in succession to Caldara 1739; first Kapellmeister 1746–51.

During his years in Italy Predieri composed for various Italian cities both opere serie and opere buffe, including *Lucio Papirio* (1714) and *La serva padrona* (1732), while in Vienna he contributed to the long-established tradition of court opera. Though apparently not as skilled or distinguished a composer as his predecessors Fux and Caldara, his works, which include *Astrea placata* (1739) share a similar fondness for grand themes and heroic gesture.

Preetorius, Emil (*b* Mainz, 21 June 1883; *d* Munich, 27 Jan. 1973). German designer.

After working as a book illustrator, he was suggested to Bruno Walter by Thomas Mann in 1912 for the Munich *Iphigénie en Aulide*. Berlin, Dresden, Madrid in the 1920s. Bayreuth 1932–41, all productions except *Parsifal*. Also *Tristan* Paris 1936, Florence 1941, Rome 1943, Amsterdam 1948, Munich 1958, Vienna 1959. *Ring* Berlin, S, 1936; Milan, S, 1938; Rome 1953–4. His three-dimensional sets derived from Wagner's instructions but were more stylized; he insisted that, 'for his penetratingly descriptive music Wagner needs a certain nearness to nature which should, however, not be literally naturalistic'. He asked for emphasis on the things carrying symbolic weight, and sought to combine 'inner vision and outward nature'. He managed to resist Nazi pressures to make his designs more literal and nationalistic.

preghiera (It.: 'prayer') (Fr., *prière*; Ger., *Gebet*). An aria or chorus of quiet or reverent character in which the singer or singers make a prayer to God or to supernatural powers. Designed to display mastery of soft vocalization and simple line, it became a very popular ingredient of Italian opera, especially in the 19th cent., and thence of French and German opera. Famous examples include Desdemona's 'Ave Maria' in Verdi's *Otello* and Rienzi's 'Allmächt'ger Vater' in Wagner's opera.

prelude (from Lat. *praeludium*: something played before another work) (Ger., *Vorspiel*). There is no clear distinction between the prelude and *overture, though in general the former may be shorter and may also run directly into the opera (or act of an opera) which it introduces.

'Prendi, l'anel ti dono'. Elvino's (ten) aria in the opening scene of Bellini's *La sonnambula* as he places the ring on Amina's finger.

'Près des remparts de Séville'. Carmen's (mez) aria in Act I of Bizet's *Carmen*, in which she tempts Don José to release her from arrest by proposing to spend the evening at Lillas Pastia's tavern drinking manzanilla and dancing the seguidilla with her lover.

Presentation of the Rose. The name generally given to the scene in Act II of Strauss's *Der Rosenkavalier* as Octavian comes to present Sophie with a silver rose as token of Baron Ochs's wooing.

Prêtre, Georges (*b* Waziers, 14 Aug. 1924). French conductor. Studied Douai, Paris with Cluytens and Dervaux. Début Marseilles 1946 (*Samson*). Marseilles 1946–8; Lille 1948–50; Toulouse 1951–4; Lyons 1955; Paris: OC, 1956–9 (*Mignon, Capriccio*, prem. of *Voix humaine*); O, 1959–71, music dir. 1970–1. Chicago 1959; S Francisco 1963–4; New York, M, from 1964. London, CG, 1965, 1976. Milan, S, 1965. Composed operetta *Pour toi* (1951). (R)

Prey, Claude (*b* Fleury, 30 May 1925). French composer. Studied Paris with Messiaen and Milhaud. His music is essentially theatrical, and he has explored a wide range of forms and media in the interests of making a bridge between stage and concert-hall. His most important work, *Les liaisons dangereuses* (1974), follows the epistolatory form of Laclos's novel, and makes use of an instrumental 'double' for each character who takes part in the action as the recipient of the letters. *Le rouge et le noir* (based on Stendhal) was given its prem. at Aix in 1989.

Prey, Hermann (*b* Berlin, 11 July 1929). German baritone. Studied Berlin with Prohaska, Baum, and Gottschalk. Début Wiesbaden 1952 (2nd Prisoner, *Fidelio*). Hamburg 1953; Vienna, S, and Berlin, SO, from 1956; Munich and Cologne from 1959; Bayreuth 1965–7, 1981–2, 1986; New York, M, from 1960; London, CG, from 1973; also Chicago, Buenos Aires, etc. An engaging performer with a warm, lyrical tone. Roles included Don Giovanni, Papageno, Wolfram, Beckmesser, Storch, Marcello. Also a fine Lieder singer. (R)

Preziosilla. A gypsy girl (mez) in Verdi's *La forza del destino*.

Přibyl, Vilém (*b* Náchod, 10 Apr. 1925; *d* Brno, 21 July 1990). Czech tenor. Studied Hradec Králové with Jakoubkova. Début Ústí nad Labem 1959 (Prince, Dvořák's *Rusalka*). Brno O from 1961 throughout his career; also Prague Nat. O. Edinburgh 1964 (with Prague); London, CG, from 1964; also Vienna, Barcelona, Holland, Vancouver, Scandinavia. Retired 1984. Roles included Admetus (*Alceste*), Florestan, Lohengrin, Don José, Radamès, Verdi's Otello, Turiddu, Shuisky, Laca, Boris (*Káťa Kabanová*), Sergey (*Lady Macbeth of Mtsensk*), Dalibor. Created Claudius (Horký's *The Poison of Elsinore*). Possessed a voice of great power and beauty, and was a highly expressive performer, outstanding in noble roles. (R).

Price, Leontyne (b Laurel, MS, 10 Feb. 1927). US soprano. Studied New York, Juilliard School, and with Page. Début Broadway 1952 (in Thomson's *Four Saints in Three Acts*). Toured Europe and Moscow as Gershwin's Bess, 1952–4. Chicago 1957; London, CG, and Paris, O, from 1958; Milan, S, 1960; New York, M, 1961–85, when she retired. Repertory included Poppea, Donna Anna, Tatyana, Manon Lescaut. Created Barber's Cleopatra. Her fine spinto soprano, with a burnished glow, shone especially in Verdi roles, e.g. Aida, Leonora (*Trovatore* and *Forza*), Amelia (*Ballo in maschera*). (R)

Price, (Dame) **Margaret** (b Blackwood, 13 Apr. 1941). Welsh soprano. Studied London, TCM. Début WNO 1962 (Cherubino). London, CG, 1963, 1968, 1973, 1980, 1988; EOG 1967; Gly. from 1968; Paris, O, from 1973; Cologne from 1971; Munich from 1972; Paris, O, and Vienna from 1973. New York, M, 1985. Also Chicago, Salzburg, etc. With her full, limpid tone, fine technique, and musical phrasing, a singer of great quality. Roles include Donna Anna, Pamina, Fiordiligi, Countess (Mozart), Norma, Tatyana, Amelia (*Boccanegra*), Desdemona (Verdi), Ariadne. (R)

prière. See PREGHIERA.

Prigioniero, Il (The Prisoner). Opera in prologue and 1 act by Dallapiccola; text by the composer, after Villiers de l'Isle-Adam's *La torture par l'espérance* (1883) and Charles Coster's *La légende d'Ulenspiegel et de Lamme Goedzak*. Broadcast RAI 1 Dec. 1949. Prem. Florence, C, 20 May 1950.

Saragossa, c.1570. The mother (sop) describes a recurrent dream in which she is haunted by the ghost of Philip II, who is gradually transformed into the symbol of death. A prisoner (bs-bar) of the Inquisition is treated kindly by his gaoler (ten), who calls him 'brother', but is subjected to harsh torture. Finding that the gaoler has left the door unlocked, the prisoner escapes, passing monks who seem not to notice him, and arrives in a garden. However, as he reaches out to embrace a cedar, the arms of his gaoler, the Grand Inquisitor, surround him. Approaching the execution pyre, he realizes that hope and the illusion of freedom have been used as the ultimate instruments of torture.

prima donna (It.: 'first lady'). The name given to the leading female singer in an opera, or the principal soprano of an opera company. In 19th-cent. Italy it carried specific connotations regarding the nature of the role and the amount of music to be sung.

Prima Donna. Opera in 1 act by Benjamin; text by Cedric Cliffe. Prem. London, Fortune T, 23 Feb. 1949.

Set in 18th-cent. Venice, the opera includes a comic duet between rival prima donnas 'La Filomela' and Olimpia, who try to outdo one another in a scene from *Ariadne desolata* much in the manner of *Le cantatrici villane*.

Prima la musica e poi le parole (First the Music, then the words). Opera in 1 act by Salieri; text by Casti. Prem. Vienna, Schönbrunn Palace, 7 Feb. 1786.

Vienna, 18th cent. A composer (bar) and a poet (bar) argue about an opera commissioned by their patron. The composer wishes the poet to write new texts for an old score he has discovered. They also disagree violently over the choice of performer for the principal female part, the poet selecting an actress, Tonina (mez), while the composer favours a prima donna, Eleonora (sop). The issue is resolved by the women sharing the role, taking the comic and tragic portions respectively.

The opera presents in witty, often sarcastic dialogue, the age-old argument of the respective importance of the various artistic components of opera. The subject is also treated in Strauss's *Capriccio.

Prince Igor (Russ., *Knyaz Igor*). Opera in prologue and 4 acts by Borodin; text by composer after a sketch by Stasov. Music completed by Rimsky-Korsakov and Glazunov. Prem. St Petersburg, M, 4 Nov. 1890.

Polovtsia, 1185. The opera tells of the capture of Prince Igor (bar), with his son Vladimir (ten), by the Polovtsians. Their leader, Khan Konchak (bs), entertains his captive like a royal guest, treating him to a display of oriental dances. He offers to let Igor go free if he promises not to fight the Polovtsians again. Igor refuses, but manages to escape, and rejoins his wife Yaroslavna (sop). Vladimir remains behind in the Polovtsian camp, having fallen in love with the Khan's daughter Konchakovna (mez), whom he is allowed to marry.

Printemps qui commence. Dalila's (mez)

aria in Act 1 of Saint-Saëns's *Samson et Dalila*, rejoicing in her conquest of Samson.

Prinzregententheater. See MUNICH.

Prinz von Homburg, Der. Opera in 3 acts by Henze; text by Ingeborg Bachmann, after the drama by Heinrich von Kleist (1821). Prem. Hamburg, S, 22 May 1960.

Fehrbellin and Berlin, 1675. The opera is set in the 17th cent. Prince Friedrich von Homburg (bar), the General of Cavalry, is a poet and dreamer. Confused by reality and imagination, he leads a nearly disastrous charge in a battle, and is court-martialled. His beloved, Princess Natalie (sop), pleads with her uncle, the Elector of Brandenburg (ten), for Friedrich's life. When Friedrich refuses to beg for mercy on the grounds that the judgement was just, the Elector magnanimously pardons him.

Prise de Troie, La. See TROYENS, LES.

Prisoners' Chorus. See 'O WELCHE LUST'.

Pritchard, John (*b* London, 5 Feb. 1921; *d* Daly City, CA, 5 Dec. 1989). English conductor. Studied with his father. Gly.: répétiteur 1947; chorus-master 1949; assistant cond. 1950, début 1951 (*Don Giovanni*); cond. 1951–78; music counsellor from 1963; music dir. from 1969. London, CG, from 1952, incl. prems. of *Gloriana* (1953), *Midsummer Marriage* (1955), and *King Priam* (1962, at Coventry). Vienna, S, 1952–3, 1964–5; Salzburg 1966. New York, M, from 1971. Music dir. S Francisco 1970–89, Cologne 1978–89, joint music dir. Brussels, M, 1981–9. A highly talented, versatile conductor, whose gift centred on Mozart but also embraced the Italian and French repertory and Strauss. His quick professionalism always enabled him to grasp new scores and to give sensitive support to singers and players, though it was on occasion not matched by a comparable energy. A well-loved figure especially at Glyndebourne, which both shaped his career and which, as George Christie wrote, was in later years significantly shaped by him. (R)

Prize Song. See 'MORGENLICHT LEUCHTEND'.

Probe (Ger.: 'trial, rehearsal'). Thus *Beleuchtungsprobe* (lighting rehearsal), *Hauptprobe* (main rehearsal), *Generalprobe* (final [dress] rehearsal). For *Das Rheingold* some German opera-houses call a *Schwimmprobe* for the Rhinemaidens.

Prodaná nevěsta. See BARTERED BRIDE, THE.

Prodigal Son, The. Church parable in 1 act by Britten; text by William Plomer, after Luke 15: 11–32. Prem. Orford Parish Church, 10 June 1968.

The Father (bs-bar), his Elder Son (bar), and Younger Son (ten), work in the fields, but the Younger Son is lured by the Tempter (ten: the Abbot in the dramatic fiction) to demand his inheritance and leave for the city. Here he is robbed by Parasites, and eventually returns home, where he is welcomed by his father and in the end reconciled to his brother.

producer (Fr., *metteur en scène*; Ger., *Spielleiter*; It., *regista*). In Germany and elsewhere the term *Regisseur* is used, but *régisseur* in France refers specifically to those working on stage matters, e.g. lighting. In the US the term 'general stage director' is normally used. The term for the artist responsible for the dramatic presentation of a performance. The English term 'production' is in Ger. *Inszenierung* or *Regie*, in It. *regia*, in Fr. *mise-en-scène*. The terms are comparatively modern, and did not appear in programmes regularly until the 1920s.

When opera was in its infancy, the dramatic presentation was controlled by the composer; but with the growth of spectacle as an aspect of opera, the designer played an increasing role. Still more important was the role of the ballet-master, who placed the chorus, generally symmetrically on either side of the stage or across the rear, and instructed its members in a limited amount of formal movement. He also controlled the principals: the stereotyped gestures still sometimes observed, recalling the conventions of mime, may derive from this. With dance an essential ingredient, Lully formed a strong set of production conventions with his ensemble of singing actors. The expressive grouping and movement of dance also influenced Gluck by way of the ideas of Noverre. With the development of opera buffa in the 18th cent., the principal bass often took over the stage direction, a convention that survived during the 19th (as with Tagliafico at Covent Garden, London) and even into the 20th cent. Mozart was one of the first musical stage directors who not only rehearsed his operas from the pit, but controlled his singers. He was followed in Germany by Spohr and especially Weber, who instructed his singers in the drama before rehearsing them in the music, and conducted the performance from a position close to the footlights. In Italy Verdi normally supervised every detail of the production. It was Wagner who worked most fully towards the *Gesamtkunstwerk*, or unified work of art, and used his considerable dramatic skills to rehearse his singers in every detail of gesture, movement, and expression. His influence increased the emphasis on opera as drama, whether by musicians (e.g. especially Mahler in Vienna, also Toscanini in Milan, later Klemperer in Germany and Karajan in Austria) or with men of the theatre establishing didactic principles and forming special ensembles (e.g. *Stanislavsky in Russia) or making individual contributions as producers. Wagner's pre-eminence reasserted itself in post-war Bayreuth with his grandson Wieland. Actors and men of the theatre who became distinguished opera producers include Ernst von Possart, Max Reinhardt, Carl Ebert, Günther Rennert, Walter Felsenstein, Jean Vilar, Jean-Louis Barrault, Jean Cocteau, Tyrone Guthrie, Peter Hall, and Sam Wanamaker; designers include Jean-Pierre Ponnelle and Filippo Sanjust; film-makers include Luchino Visconti and Franco Zeffirelli; ballet-masters include Margherita Wallmann and Maurice Béjart; singers include Tito Gobbi, Hans Hotter, Regina Resnik, and Geraint Evans.

The rise in importance of the producer has led to the widely held view that after the Age of the Singer, then the Age of the Conductor, opera entered the Age of the Producer. This in turn has led to the term 'producer's opera', used (generally pejoratively) when the producer's ideas are felt to have been wished upon an opera rather than to have arisen from it.

Prohaska, Jaro (*b* Vienna, 24 Jan. 1891; *d* Munich, 28 Sept. 1965). Austrian bass-baritone. Studied Vienna. Début Lübeck 1922. Nuremberg 1925–31; Berlin, S, 1931–53; Bayreuth 1933–44; Paris, O, 1936; Buenos Aires 1935, 1937. A notable Wotan, Sachs, Amfortas, Ochs. Pupils included Hermann Prey. (R)

Prokina, Elena (*b* Odessa, 16 Jan. 1964). Russian soprano. Studied as an actress before vocal studies in Leningrad. Joined Kirov O 1988, singing Emma (*Khovanshchina*) and Natasha (*War and Peace*). London, CG, 1994–5 (Kaťá Kabanová and Desdemona). She is

admired for the total conviction which she brings to her portrayals and her warm, true voice; Lina (*Stiffelio*) at Los Angeles; Tatyana at Gly. 1994.

Prokofiev, Sergey (*b* Sontsovka, 27 Apr. 1891; *d* Moscow, 5 Mar. 1953). Russian composer. Studied Sontsovka with Glière, by when he had already composed two operas, adding to these a third before studying St Petersburg with Lyadov and Rimsky-Korsakov; he was helped more, however, by Myaskovsky, and was also influenced by Tcherepnin, with whom he studied conducting. *Maddalena* (comp. 1911–13) to some extent anticipates both *The Gambler* (comp.1917) and *The Fiery Angel* (comp. 1923) in its treatment of male obsession for a woman who exercises an influence both benign and malign. However, his first mature opera is in fact *The Gambler*, consciously anti-Wagnerian and both a comedy and a study of obsession: though conversational in technique, it first fully revealed Prokofiev's lyricism, his ability to characterize sharply, and his fascination with abnormal or extreme states of mind.

Leaving Russia after the Revolution, Prokofiev began work on *The Love of the Three Oranges* (1921) en route for America, where initial success was gradually replaced with frustration. The new opera, composed for Chicago, ran into difficulties, though not for its quality. Impressed by *Meyerhold's theories, which included a diminution of the role of the actor and a challenge to conventional audience relationships, Prokofiev based the work on a play by Gozzi (then popular in Russian literary circles). It represents a change of course: the treatment is anti-Romantic, and the fantastic comedy provides the composer with the opportunity for some of his most pungent and wittily grotesque, also wry and tender, music, drawing much stimulus from the surrealist interaction of different planes of reality. Career difficulties impelled him to leave for Paris; he returned to the US for the opera's prem., retreating again when hopes faded for the production of his next opera, *The Fiery Angel*. Further difficulties surrounded the work, the opera Prokofiev not without reason thought his best. The fantastic strain wittily indulged in the previous opera is here turned to horrific ends. Based on a story of possession and sorcery, the work has its grotesque elements, but is openly Romantic and even Expressionist in its violence and its exploration of dark emotions and sinister experiences in music of unprecedented power. At its centre is the largest and most powerful role Prokofiev ever wrote, for the doomed heroine Renata. The problems over its production led him to develop some of its ideas in his Third Symphony.

By 1932 Prokofiev was considering returning to Russia, though he did not finally do so until 1936. This was the time of maximum Communist repression of artistic initiative. At first the constraints did not oppress him personally, though he had been attacked for his two previous operas' qualities of parody and Expressionism: he was not opposed to everything in Socialist Realism, but the official welcome given him as a returning prodigal was only partially extended to *Semyon Kotko* (1940). Nor was the work more widely admired. It has the broad approach and epic ambitions that make it perhaps Prokofiev's nearest approach to Grand Opera, by way of Glinka (there is even a Meyerbeerian dedication of the partisans' weapons): the grandiose gestures attempting to express optimistic Communist emotions are predictably less successful than the lyrical love music and colourful ensembles that are also to be found.

However, Socialist Realism is abandoned in *The Duenna* (comp. 1941, also known as *Betrothal in a Monastery*). The simplicity here is not artificial, and the composer responds unaffectedly with some of his most charmingly accomplished music. With *War and Peace* (comp. 1943) he returns to a grand manner that again acknowledges the example of Glinka (in particular, *A Life for the Tsar*), and includes some fine scenes of battle and desolation, sometimes recalling his expertise as a film composer; there is also some memorable handling of the 'peace' element in the plot in the detailed and lyrical portrayal of the Bolkonsky family and the love of Natasha and Andrey. Yet it was one of the works singled out by the notorious 1948 Zhdanov tribunal in the attack on Russia's leading composers for 'formalism' and other alleged errors. It is a remarkable achievement, with carefully opposed musical manners that succeed in contrasting the public and national with the private and lyrical in a way not representative of the novel. Its complete Russian rehabilitation was signalled by its choice, for the first time since 1842, as a work to open

the Bolshoy season in place of Glinka's *A Life for the Tsar*. In the wake of the Zhdanov tribunal, Prokofiev wrote *The Story of a Real Man* (1948), but failed to satisfy even the authorities it was designed to appease.

prompter (Fr., *souffleur*; Ger., *Souffleur*; It., *maestro suggeritore*). Whereas in the theatre the prompter only intervenes when the actor forgets his words or cue, in the opera-house the prompter helps the performers by giving them the opening words of every phrase a few seconds in advance. Especially in Italy, he may also act as a sub-conductor, relaying the conductor's beat, which he picks up from either a mirror or nowadays more commonly a TV monitor. Extra prompters are sometimes concealed on the stage, e.g. lying under Tristan's couch. The prompter is normally a member of the theatre music staff. One makes a rare stage appearance in Strauss's *Capriccio* in the person of M. Taupe ('Mr Mole').

prompter's box (Fr., *trou de souffleur*; Ger., *Souffleurkasten*; It., *buca*). The compartment containing the prompter, usually situated immediately before the footlights and covered over so as to conceal its occupant from the audience. Normally unobtrusive, but on occasion made part of the décor, even of the 'business' of comic opera.

Prophète, Le. Opera in 5 acts by Meyerbeer; text by Scribe. Prem. Paris, O, 16 Apr. 1849.
The plot concerns the love of John of Leyden (ten) for Bertha (sop). Count Oberthal (bar), ruler of Dordrecht, desires her for himself and has her abducted; she escapes back to John, but Oberthal threatens to kill Fidès (mez), his mother, if Bertha is not returned to him. John's loyalty to his mother prevails, but in revenge he is now ready to join the Anabaptists, whose incitement to revolt he has previously rejected. He is proclaimed a prophet of God, leads a bloody rebellion, and is crowned Emperor. Fidès, now reduced to poverty, and believing her son murdered by the Prophet, recognizes him at the coronation; he compels her to deny that she is his mother, however, fearing the wrath of his followers, who consider him divine. He meets her in secret, and she persuades him to repent of his deeds. They are joined by Bertha; she, having escaped from Oberthal once more and learning of John's 'death', has set fire to the palace to destroy the Prophet who she believes has killed her

lover. A captain arrives to tell John that he is betrayed by the Anabaptists. Discovering that the Prophet and John are the same man, Bertha kills herself. John and Fidès choose to die with the Anabaptists in the destruction of the palace.

Protschka, Josef (*b* Prague, 5 Feb. 1946). Czech tenor. Studied Cologne. Sang widely in Germany, becoming a member of Cologne O 1980: tenor leads in Jean-Pierre Ponnelle's Mozart cycle and as Max and Faust. Salzburg 1985, as Pisandro in *Ulisse*; Vienna, W, 1988 (Schubert's *Fierrabras*). A forthright performer of the lyrical and lighter dramatic repertory, he sang Florestan at London, CG, 1990.

prova (It.: 'rehearsal'). In normal Italian usage, a session of preparation preceding the performance of a work.

Provenzale, Francesco (*b* Naples, *c.*1626; *d* Naples, 6 Sept. 1704). Italian composer. Studied Naples with Sabino; held various appointments as maestro di cappella there, the last at the royal chapel. Wrote *c.*9 operas for Naples of which only two survive, *Lo schiavo di sua moglie* (His Wife's Slave, 1672) and *La Stellidaura vendicata* (1674). These reveal a gift for expressive melody combined with an effective use of harmonic resources. Though reared in the Venetian tradition, his style in part prefigures that of his pupil A. Scarlatti, which has led some to describe him, erroneously, as the father of Neapolitan opera.

Pryanishnikov, Ippolit (*b* Kerch, 26 Aug. 1847; *d* Petrograd, 11 Nov. 1921). Russian baritone and producer. Studied St Petersburg with Corsi, Milan with Ronconi. Début Milan 1876 (*Maria di Rohan*). St Petersburg, M, 1878–86. Singer, prod., and manager, Tiflis O, 1886–9; Kiev 1889–92; Moscow 1892–3, with own company, the Private O Partnership. Tchaikovsky, who admired and wished to help him, conducted Gounod's *Faust*, *The Demon*, and *Onegin* for him. Created Lionel (*Maid of Orleans*) and Mizgir (*Snow Maiden*); also sang Mazeppa. Productions included *Stone Guest*, *May Night*, *Pagliacci*. Taught Figner, Mravina, and Slavina, among others.

Puccini, Giacomo (*b* Lucca, 22 Dec. 1858; *d* Brussels, 29 Nov. 1924). Italian composer. Studied Lucca with his father (a pupil of Don-

izetti and Mercadante) and his uncle, then formally with Angeloni, later Milan with Bazzini and Ponchielli.

In 1883 the latter urged him to enter the *Sonzogno competition: despite failure, *Le villi* sufficiently impressed Boito and Ricordi for them to arrange for a performance in 1884. Its success confirmed Ricordi's admiration and led to his commission for *Edgar*, which failed in Milan in 1889. For all their promise, both works suffer from awkward librettos and show unevennesses that include the intermittent influence of Ponchielli. For *Manon Lescaut* (1893) he chose his own subject, in spite of the success of Massenet's opera, and five librettists eventually contributed to what was his first mature opera and the work that led Shaw to proclaim him as the heir to Verdi's crown. Some infelicities, notably heavy scoring, are outweighed by the wealth of melodic ideas, the sensitive musical characterization, above all a flexible approach to musical and dramatic structure.

Puccini's closeness to *verismo, evident here, is confirmed in his next opera, *La bohème* (1896). Despite his greater gifts as a melodist and his broader, symphonic conception of operatic form, much in Puccini's style here sets him alongside the verismo composers in their appeal to the prevailing taste of Italian audiences. Turning, after some hesitation and with numerous libretto revisions, to *Tosca* (1900), Puccini employed many of his by now familiar technical devices in a darker, still naturalistic, melodrama. Similarly, while *Madama Butterfly* (1904) inhabits another radically different emotional world, it is closely allied to its two predecessors in general approach. Yet problems with the libretto led to many difficulties in the work's composition, and the first night in 1904 was a disaster; only on its third revision did the opera achieve proper dramatic integration, with the heroine firmly at the centre of the action.

Considering and discarding many ideas for his next opera, Puccini eventually settled on *La fanciulla del West* (The Girl of the [Golden] West, 1910). Progress was slow, however, and the work was not ready until 1910. At first sight, he seemed merely to be supplanting the Japanese flavour of *Butterfly* with another exoticism: however, in its more fluent musical construction, *La fanciulla del West* is a major advance and the work triumphed when it became the first opera to receive its world prem. at the New York M in 1910.

Once again considering and discarding many ideas for librettos, Puccini was next guided by a commission from Vienna for an operetta; agreeing on a comic opera, he wrote *La rondine* (1917), which despite initial success has failed to hold its place in the repertory. He returned now to an earlier idea for a triptych of operas. A visit to Paris in 1912 led to the source of the strongly veristic *Il tabarro*; this was quickly followed by the all-female *Suor Angelica*; finally a comic foil to these two contrasting tragedies with *Gianni Schicchi*. A chance conversation next led to *Turandot*, but the now familiar drawn-out problems with constructing the libretto delayed work, and Puccini died before he could quite complete the score. At Toscanini's suggestion, Franco Alfano composed the final scene.

Puccini's immediate model was Verdi, especially the later operas in which the formal divisions between aria, recitative, and ensemble are dissolved. However, the influence of Wagner is also marked, since Puccini turned to his own account the practice of linking action to music by use of motive. Wagner also provides a point of departure for his rich harmonic language and vivid orchestration, which continues its development up to and including *Turandot*. While the bel canto tradition remains influential, and marks many of the famous setpiece arias, Puccini's ultimate goal was a flexible structure in which all the elements would be subordinated to the drama. However, his innate feel for dramatic situation was somewhat clouded by his fondness for absurd or trivial plots: of these, perhaps *Madama Butterfly*, with its faintly mawkish overtones, and *La fanciulla del West*, a somewhat sub-Wagnerian treatment of redemption in a mining camp, are the most dubious. But such criticism must defer to his powers of musical characterization, at their most vivid in *Tosca*, where it is achieved in an intense, almost violent fashion, and *Turandot*, where the heroine's personality is passionately illuminated musically by comparison with the pale Gozzi original. Even in his own time, these conflicting elements aroused contradictory views of his talent, not least in his own country, where critics deplored his decadence even as the public flocked to the opera-house. He remains a controversial figure, whose evident faults are readily forgotten in the overwhelming appeal of his works in the theatre.

Purcell, Henry (*b* London, 1659; *d* London, 21 Nov. 1695). English composer. Although he wrote only one stage work which may properly be described as an opera, *Dido and Aeneas* (?1685 or earlier), Purcell composed much dramatic music, contributing music to 44 plays, mostly comedies, mainly between 1690–5. Four of the stage works for which Purcell provided music use it in such an integrated or extensive way that they have come to be known as semi-operas, after first being so described by Roger North. Apart from *King Arthur* (1691), this term is misleading, for usually the musical contribution merely forms a self-contained episode surrounded by dialogue, as with the song 'I Attempt from Love's Sickness to Fly', in *The Indian Queen* (1695). However, in such passages as the Incantation Scene of the same work Purcell uses all the techniques of operatic music, including recitative and aria styles. Only in *King Arthur* is the musical material so extensive and continuous that the work approaches opera. The authenticity of the music for *The Tempest*, formerly counted among the semi-operas, is now questioned: it was probably written by John Weldon.

Much uncertainty surrounds the genesis of *Dido and Aeneas*. For long it was thought that Purcell composed it for performance at a girls' school in Chelsea, though recent evidence suggests it may have been written several years earlier. Previous attempts to found a tradition of English opera had been largely unsuccessful, and the fact that Purcell wrote no other opera after *Dido and Aeneas* suggests that it would be wrong to view it as anything other than an isolated masterpiece. Although it comprises three acts, *Dido and Aeneas* is cast on a small scale and makes modest demands on the performers. Its musical style betrays the influences of both French and Italian opera: the overture, use of the chorus, and intervention of the supernatural (in the shape of the witches) are strongly reminiscent of Lully, while the recitative, whose contours are uniquely moulded by the English language, owes much to the Italian monodic style.

With Purcell's early death and the invasion of Italian opera composers around the turn of the century, *Dido and Aeneas* came to occupy a unique place as the first surviving English opera. In its day it was largely without influence: it is as a rejuvenating force on modern English composers, especially Britten and Tippett, that it has made its greatest impact.

Puritani, I. Opera in 3 acts by Bellini; text by Pepoli, after the play *Têtes rondes et Cavaliers* (1833) by Ancelot and Saintine, in turn loosely derived from Scott's novel *Old Mortality* (1816). Prem. as *I Puritani e i Cavalieri* Paris, I, 24 Jan. 1835.

The opera is set in Plymouth at the time of the Civil War. Queen Henrietta (mez), widow of Charles I, is held prisoner in a fortress whose warden is the Puritan Lord Walton (bs). His daughter Elvira (sop) is in love with Lord Arthur Talbot (ten), a Cavalier, and permission for their marriage has been obtained, though she is also loved by the Puritan Sir Richard Forth (bar). Arthur helps Henrietta to escape by dressing her in Elvira's bridal veil. Elvira, believing herself betrayed, loses her reason. Arthur, now in danger from the Puritans both for his political crime and as the agent of Elvira's madness, returns to her, refusing to desert her although his capture will mean certain death. He is seized by his pursuers, and about to be executed when news arrives of the defeat of the Stuarts, and a pardon for all prisoners. The joyful shock of being reunited to Arthur restores Elvira's sanity.

Putnam, Ashley (*b* New York, 10 Aug. 1952). US soprano. Studied Michigan with Mosher and Patterson. Début Virginia O 1976 (Lucia). New York CO 1978; Gly. from 1978; New York, M, 1983; London, CG, 1986; also Aix, Amsterdam, Cologne, Brussels, S Fe, St Louis, Philadelphia, etc. Roles incl. Fiordiligi, Queen of the Night, Maria Stuarda, Gilda, Violetta, Musetta, Hanna Glawari (*Merry Widow*), Marschallin, Arabella, Danae. (R)

Pyne, Louisa (*b* ?, 27 Aug. 1832; *d* London, 20 Mar. 1904). English soprano. Studied London with Smart. Début Boulogne 1849 (Amina). London: DL, HM, CG, 1851; US tour 1854–6. In 1856, she and *Harrison formed the Pyne–Harrison Co., with which she appeared first at London, L and DL, then CG, 1858–64, creating many roles in operas by Balfe, Wallace, Benedict, and Glover. Known as 'the English Sontag', she also sang an impressive Queen of the Night and Arline (*Bohemian Girl*). She retired on her marriage to the baritone Bodda in 1868.

Q

Quaglio. Italian, later German, family of designers active from the early 18th to the 19th cents. Generally working in pairs, they made an important contribution to the visual aspect of German Romantic opera. Of the six generations, 15 members of the family were active as designers. The most important were:

1. **Giulio I** or **Giovanni Maria III** (*b* Laino, *c*.1700; *d* Vienna, 1765). Designed operas for Vienna, B and K, 1748–65, making considerable use of transparent backdrops, and responding to the reform movement in his designs for Gluck's *Cinesi* (1754), *Orfeo* (1762), and *Telemaco* (1765).

2. **Lorenzo I** (*b* Laino, 23 July 1730; *d* Munich, 2 May 1805). Worked in Mannheim and Schwetzingen from 1758, designing works by Salieri, Galuppi, Hasse, and Paisiello. Frankfurt, Dresden 1768–9; designed new Ducal T at Zweibrücken 1775–6, and new Schlosstheater at Mannheim (with Alessandro Bibiena) 1777. Munich from 1778; designed sets for prem. of *Idomeneo* (1781) and for Singspiels by Hiller, Schweitzer, and Holzbauer. His designs are preserved in the T Museum, Munich, and in the Uffizi Gallery, Florence.

3. **Giuseppe** (*b* Laino, 2 Dec. 1747; *d* Munich, 2 Mar. 1828). Second designer Mannheim and Schwetzingen, also worked at Ludwigsburg, Speyer, Frankfurt. Designed Redoutensaal in Mannheim. Munich from 1779; designs include those for *Don Giovanni*, *Magic Flute*, *Freischütz*, developing a more consciously Romantic approach.

4. **Angelo II** (*b* Munich, 13 Dec. 1829; *d* Munich, 5 Jan. 1890). Worked at Munich from 1849, designing Munich prems. of *Tannhäuser* 1855, *Lohengrin* 1858, prems. there of *Tristan* (1865), *Meistersinger* (1868), *Rheingold* (1869), *Walküre* (1870), and private productions of *Oberon* and Gluck's *Armida* for Ludwig II, all revealing a flair for epic architecture. The courtyard at Hohenschwangau is supposedly based on Act 2 of his 1867 Munich *Lohengrin*. Dresden 1865–80; also Prague, St Petersburg. Designs in the Munich T Museum and Ludwig II Museum at Herrenchiemsee.

'Qual cor tradisti'. The duet in Act II of Bellini's *Norma*, in which Norma (sop) reproaches the guilty Pollione (ten) for having betrayed her and now welcomes death with him.

'Quand'ero paggio'. Falstaff's (bar) arietta in Act II of Verdi's *Falstaff*, in which he recalls the days when he was a slender young page to the Duke of Norfolk.

'Quando le sere al placido'. Rodolfo's (ten) aria in Act II of Verdi's *Luisa Miller* grieving over the evidence in a letter that his wife Luisa has betrayed him with Wurm.

'Quando m'en vo'. Musetta's (sop) aria in Act II of Puccini's *La bohème*, hoping to recover Marcello's love as they meet in the crowd outside the Café Momus.

'Quanto è bella!' Nemorino's (ten) aria in the opening scene of Donizetti's *L'elisir d'amore*, which he sings as he gazes at the beautiful young Adina.

Quatro rusteghi, I (The Four Curmudgeons). Opera in 3 acts by Wolf-Ferrari; text by Sugana and Pizzolato, after Goldoni. Prem. in German as *Die vier Grobiane*, Munich, N, 19 Mar. 1906.

Venice, end of the 18th cent. Lunardo, Maurizio, Simon, and Cancian (all bs) try to control their wives' excesses, as they see it. Lunardo's daughter Lucieta (sop) is to marry Maurizio's son Filipeto (ten), but custom forbids them even to meet until the wedding. Aided by Riccardo (ten), Filipeto gains entry to Lucieta's house disguised as a girl and the young couple meet, but they are discovered. Cancian's wife Felice (sop) takes a hand, and the old men are persuaded that their best interests lie in permitting the marriage.

Queen of Shemakha, The. The Queen (sop) who comes to seduce King Dodon in Rimsky-Korsakov's *The Golden Cockerel*.

Queen of Spades, The (Russ., *Pikovaya dama*). Opera in 3 acts by Pyotr Tchaikovsky; text by Modest Tchaikovsky, with suggestions and contributions from the composer, after Pushkin's story (1834). Prem. St Petersburg, M, 19 Dec. 1890.

St Petersburg, 1790. Hermann, a young

officer (ten), loves Lisa (sop), granddaughter of the old Countess (mez), once a gambler known as the Queen of Spades. She is described in a ballad sung by Hermann's friend Tomsky (bar) as possessing the secret of winning at cards. Hermann goes to the Countess's bedroom at night to obtain the secret from her so as to win enough money to marry, but so terrifies her that she dies without speaking. Her ghost appears to him and reveals the secret: 'Three, seven, ace'. As Hermann becomes obsessed with winning, Lisa despairs, and drowns herself. Staking all in a gambling session with Prince Eletsky (bar), Lisa's original betrothed, he wins on the first two cards, but finds to his horror that the third, which he thinks will be the ace, is the Queen of Spades. The Countess's ghost appears once more, and Hermann, losing his reason, stabs himself.

Queen of the Night, The. Pamina's mother (sop), Sarastro's adversary, in Mozart's *Die Zauberflöte*.

Queen's Theatre. See KING'S THEATRE.

Querelle des Bouffons. See GUERRE DES BOUFFONS.

'Questa o quella'. The Duke of Mantua's (ten) aria in the opening scene of Verdi's *Rigoletto*, in which he declares that all women attract him.

Quickly, Mistress. A lady of Windsor (mez) in Verdi's *Falstaff* and Vaughan Williams's *Sir John in Love*.

'Qui la voce'. Elvira's (sop) Mad Scene in Act II of Bellini's *I Puritani*.

Quilico, Louis (*b* Montreal, 14 Jan. 1925). Canadian baritone. Studied New York with Singher, Rome with Pizzolongo. Début New York, CC, 1953 (Germont). S Francisco 1956–9; London, CG, and Paris, O, 1962; New York, M, from 1971. Also Moscow, B; Paris, OC; Buenos Aires, etc. Roles incl. Enrico (*Lucia*), Rigoletto, Falstaff, Golaud. (R) His son **Gino Quilico** (*b* New York, 29 Apr. 1955) is also a baritone. Studied with his father, and at Toronto Cons. Début Toronto 1978 (TV in *The Medium*). Paris, O and OC 1981, B 1991; London, CG, 1983; New York, M, 1987; Salzburg 1988 (Dandini); also Frankfurt, Hamburg, Aix, etc. Roles incl. Oreste (Gluck), Don Giovanni, Figaro (Rossini), Malatesta, Valentin, Lescaut (Massenet), Posa, Marcello. (R)

Quinault, Philippe (*b* Paris, 3 June 1635; *d* Paris, 26 Nov. 1688). French dramatist and librettist. Though an established playwright by the time he abandoned his career for opera, he was able to modify his technique with great skill to the requirements of his demanding (and sole) collaborator Lully. As servant of the composer who was directly subject to Louis XIV, he wrote formal scenes, expressing stereotyped noble sentiments, in lines whose stateliness and elegance reflected the court's expression of royal *gloire* (frequently remarked upon in a special Prologue). Quinault's characters, generally drawn from mythology or chivalry, can express themselves passionately, but normally do so within the terms of a classical restraint. His librettos for Lully included *Cadmus et Hermione*, *Thésée*, and *Amadis*.

Quivar, Florence (*b* Philadelphia, PA, 3 Mar. 1944). US mezzo-soprano. Studied at New York, Juilliard School, making her début there 1975, in *Rusalka*. New York, M, from 1977, as Marina, Fides, Isabella, and Serena (*Porgy and Bess*). Salzburg 1990 (Ulrica). Admired for her expressive singing in such roles as Carmen, Adalgisa, and Gluck's Orpheus. Sang Eboli at Seattle 1993. (R)

R

Raaff, Anton (*b* Gelsdorf, *bapt.* 6 May 1714; *d* Munich, 28 May 1797). German tenor. Studied Munich with Ferrandini, later Bologna with Bernacchi. Début Munich 1736 (in an opera by Ferrandini). Italy 1739; Bonn and Frankfurt 1742; Vienna 1749 (Metastasio commenting that he 'sang like an angel'); Italy 1752; Madrid 1755, singing for Farinelli, with whom he went to Naples 1759. Further successes there and in Florence. In 1770, he entered the service of the Elector Palatine, Carl Theodor, at Mannheim and from 1778 at Munich. In 1777 Mozart was at first dismissive of his singing and wooden acting, but later wrote (and 'tailored' for him) the aria K295 (1778), so impressing Raaff that he asked Carl Theodor to commission *Idomeneo*. Mozart, by now appreciative of the ageing tenor's still considerable artistry (though finding his style 'peculiar'), wrote the title-role with his qualities in mind. His vocal longevity was remarkable; Kelly notes that he was still in good voice in 1787.

Rabaud, Henri (*b* Paris, 10 Nov. 1873; *d* Paris, 11 Sept. 1949). French composer and conductor. Studied Paris with Gédalge and Massenet. His first opera was a historical piece, *La fille de Roland* (1904), but his greatest success came with *Mârouf, savetier du Caire* (Mârouf, the Cobbler of Cairo, 1914), an oriental comedy notable for its lightness of touch and its fine orchestration. None of his other works approached its success, though he continued to write works with an expert understanding of the stage and an indifference to fashion. Paris: O, cond. 1908–18, dir. 1914–18; dir. Cons. 1920–40.

Rachel. Éléazar's daughter (sop), lover of Léopold, the eponymous Jewess of Halévy's *La Juive*.

'Rachel, quand du Seigneur'. Éléazar's (ten) aria in Act IV of Halévy's *La Juive*, in which he struggles with his dilemma between letting Rachel die at the hands of the Christians or saving her life by telling Cardinal Brogni that she is in fact the latter's daughter.

Rachmaninov, Sergey. See RAKHMANINOV, SERGEY.

Radamès. The Captain of the Egyptian Guard (ten), lover of Aida, in Verdi's *Aida*.

Radford, Robert (*b* Nottingham, 13 May 1874; *d* London, 3 Mar. 1933). English bass. Studied London with Randegger, Haynes, and King. Début London, CG, 1904 (Commendatore). Sang Hunding and Hagen under Richter in English *Ring*; subsequently sang with Beecham OC, and with London BNOC, of which he was a founder and director. Admired in Mozart and as Boris. (R) His daughter **Winifred** (*b* London, 2 Oct. 1901; *d* Cheltenham, 15 Apr. 1993), also his pupil, sang as a soprano at Gly. 1934–8. Intimate O 1936; dir. 1956–75. (R)

Raff, Joachim (*b* Lachen, 27 May 1822; *d* Frankfurt, 24 or 25 June 1882). German composer. Self-taught; given guidance by Liszt. He left several unproduced operas; the only two to reach the stage were *König Alfred* (1851) and *Dame Kobold* (1870), which even Liszt thought a hotch-potch.

Raimondi, Ruggero (*b* Bologna, 3 Oct. 1941). Italian bass. Studied Rome with Pediconi, Piervenanzi, and Ghibaudo. Début Spoleto 1964 (Colline). Rome 1964; Venice 1965–7; Gly. 1969; Milan, S, and New York, M, from 1970; London, CG, from 1972; Paris, O, from 1979. A handsome performer, particularly acclaimed for his Verdi roles, e.g. Attila, Philip; also as Almaviva (Mozart), Don Giovanni, Mosè, Boris, Don Quichotte, Don Basilio (Rossini), Méphistophélès. (R)

Raisa, Rosa (*b* Białystok, 23 May 1893; *d* Los Angeles, 28 Sept. 1963). Polish, later US, soprano. Fled from a pogrom in Poland, settling in Naples. Studied there with Marchisio and E. Tetrazzini. Début Parma 1913 (Leonora, *Oberto*). Chicago 1913–14, 1916–36; London, CG, 1914, 1933; Milan, S, 1924, 1926. Also Paris, O; Buenos Aires, etc. Roles included Donna Anna, Norma, Aida, Tosca; created Asteria (Boito's *Nerone*) and Turandot. With an opulent, well-controlled voice, statuesque beauty, and impressive acting ability, she was one of the leading singers of her time. Opened singing school in Chicago, 1937, with her husband, the baritone **Giacomo Rimini** (1887–1952); he made his début in 1910 (Albert, *Werther*), sang Falstaff under Toscanini, Milan 1915, also Pong in the first *Turandot* (1926). (R)

Rake's Progress, The. Opera in 3 acts and epilogue by Stravinsky; text by W. H. Auden and Chester Kallman, after Hogarth's eight engravings (1735). Prem. Venice, F, 11 Sept. 1951.

England, 18th cent. Tom Rakewell (ten) declines the offer of a city position offered by Trulove (bs), father of his sweetheart Anne Trulove (sop), and is complaining of his lack of money when Nick Shadow (bar) appears with news of sudden wealth. Taking Shadow as his servant, to be paid after a year and a day, Tom leaves for London, where he quickly descends to a life of vice, initially in the brothel run by Mother Goose (mez).

His pleasures palling, he is easily tempted by Shadow to marry the fantastic bearded lady Baba the Turk (mez), and then to place his trust in a fake machine for turning stones into bread. He goes bankrupt, and all his effects are sold, under Sellem (ten), the auctioneer.

The time comes to pay Nick Shadow, who reveals himself as the Devil, and claims Tom's soul. They gamble for it; Tom wins, and Shadow sinks into the ground, but leaves Tom mad. The final scene is in Bedlam; Tom thinks he is Adonis, and Anne now takes her last leave of him.

The characters point the moral in the Epilogue: 'For idle hands And hearts and minds The Devil finds A work to do.'

Rakhmaninov, Sergey (*b* Semyonovo, 1 Apr. 1873; *d* Beverley Hills, CA, 28 Mar. 1943). Russian composer and pianist. His first opera, *Aleko* (1893), was the winner of a student competition, and on its production won some approval, including from Tchaikovsky (whose influence it reflects). Its lyrical qualities dominate its dramatic ones, though it includes some appealing genre music. *The Miserly Knight* (1906) has a stronger individuality, and adds the influence of Wagner. Written for an all-male cast, it is cast in three scenes, the central one consisting of a fine monologue for the Knight (intended for Shalyapin). For *Francesca da Rimini* (1906), Rakhmaninov had a libretto by Modest Tchaikovsky whose weaknesses he was unable to overcome with music of sufficient power.

Ralf, Torsten (*b* Malmö, 2 Jan. 1901; *d* Stockholm, 27 Apr. 1954). Swedish tenor. Studied Stockholm with Forsell, Berlin with Dehmlow. Début Stettin 1930 (Cavaradossi). Dresden 1935–43; London, CG, 1935–9, 1948; Stockholm from 1941; New York, M, 1945–8. Roles included Lohengrin, Walther, Parsifal, Radamès, Otello (Verdi); created Apollo (*Daphne*). (R) His elder brother **Oscar** (1881–1964) was leading tenor of Stockholm O 1918–30; Bayreuth and Paris, OC, 1927. Sang Siegmund, Tristan, and Verdi roles. Translated over 40 operas and operettas. (R).

Rameau, Jean-Philippe (*b* Dijon, 25 Sept. 1683; *d* Paris, 12 Sept. 1764). French composer and theorist. Taught first by his father, Rameau studied briefly in Italy before becoming organist at Avignon in 1702. His early career was devoted largely to church music and to the production of a seminal treatise on harmony. His entry into the world of opera came only in middle age: after many abortive attempts, including a collaboration with Voltaire, an introduction to the Abbé Pellegrin in 1730 resulted in a libretto which Rameau considered worthy of his music.

In *Hippolyte et Aricie* (1733) Rameau established at a stroke a new formula for French opera which served to rouse it from the stylistic torpor into which it had declined following Lully's death. From the outset he was viewed as a controversial figure by critics and academicians, who unanimously condemned the work; fortunately, he was no less strongly acclaimed by the public, who saw in *Hippolyte* a way forward for French music. Though the Lullian model had provided a point of departure, Rameau's greater emotional sensitivity enabled him to develop a richer and more vivid interpretation of the plot, in which he was aided by a skilful librettist. The former emphasis on *gloire* and rich spectacle is supplanted by a heightened dramatic awareness, and the classical myth is transmuted into a more engaging story, in which human emotions play their part.

Hippolyte was followed by a string of popular successes, in which many of the same techniques were employed: *Les Indes galantes* (1735), *Castor et Pollux* (1737), and *Dardanus* (1739). After a five-year break from opera, during which time he founded a school of composition, Rameau returned with the opulent *La princesse de Navarre* (1745), which was followed by two more works in serious vein, *Zoroastre* (1749) and *Linus* (comp. c.1752), in which his handling of the tragédie lyrique is further refined. By now Rameau was recognized as the most important composer of his generation, so that when a performance of Pergolesi's La serva padrona in 1752 sparked off the famous intellectual debate known as the *Guerre des Bouffons, it was only natural that he should become the main spokesman in defence of the conservative tradition. His lively promotion of French tragédie lyrique against the claims of lighter Italian opera eventually triumphed, and he went on to produce a final masterpiece in Abaris, ou Les Boréades (comp. 1763). He died a national hero and, like Lully, his works remained in the repertory until the French Revolution, and are now being revived.

Rameau's influence on the development of opera in Europe was profound and wide-ranging. For his own generation he provided an escape from the stasis of Lully's tragédie en musique by offering a genuinely dramatic entertainment focusing on human emotions in place of an outdated concentration on the glorification of royalty. Later he was to have an important rejuvenating influence on Italian opera seria, when Gluck took his work as a model for his first 'reform' opera, Orfeo ed Euridice, which itself shares several points of similarity with Castor et Pollux, including the opening choral scene. Finally, in the 19th cent. Berlioz found inspiration in Rameau for some of his grandest conceptions, including Les Troyens.

Ramey, Samuel (b Colby, KS, 28 Mar. 1942). US bass. Studied Wichita with Newman, New York with Boyajian. Début New York CO 1972 (Zuniga). New York CO for several seasons. Gly. 1976–8; Paris, O, from 1983; New York, M, from 1984; London, CG, from 1985. Also Milan, S; Salzburg; Florence; etc. Vocally gifted, and magnetic on stage. His unusually broad repertory includes Figaro (Mozart), Don Giovanni, Leporello, Mustafà, Moïse, Gounod's and Boito's Mephistopheles, Don Quichotte, Attila, Assur (Rossini's Semiramide), Philip, Pimen, Boris, Nick Shadow, Duke Bluebeard. One of the most prolific recording artists of his generation. (R)

Ramfis. The High Priest (bs) in Verdi's Aida.

Ramiro. The muleteer (bar), lover of Concepción, in Ravel's L'heure espagnole.

Rance, Jack. The sheriff (bar) in Puccini's La fanciulla del West.

Randegger, Alberto (b Trieste, 13 Apr. 1832; d London, 18 Dec. 1911). Italian/German, later British, conductor, teacher, and composer. Studied Trieste with Ricci. Composed operas and held appointments in Italy before moving to London 1854. Wrote The Rival Beauties (1864). A very influential professor of singing London, RAM, 1868, later RCM. Cond. London: J, 1857, CR, 1879–85; CG and DL, 1887–98, helping to promote Wagner; also admired in Verdi.

Randle, Thomas (b Hollywood, CA, 21 Dec. 1958). US tenor. Studied in Los Angeles and Germany. Sang in concert before opera début at London, ENO, 1988 (Tamino). Sang Monteverdi's Orfeo at Valencia and appeared on tour as Pelléas in the Peter Brook version of the opera. He brings strong acting and a keen musical intelligence to such roles as Ferrando (Scottish O) and the Earl of Essex (Gloriana for O North 1994). (R)

Randová, Eva (b Kolin, 31 Dec. 1936). Czech mezzo-soprano. Sang Eboli at Ostrava (1962) and joined Prague Nat. T 1968. Stuttgart O from 1971 (Azucena, Amneris, Santuzza). Bayreuth from 1973 (Fricka, Kundry, Ortrud). Salzburg début 1975; New York, M, 1981. She brings intense dramatic conviction to roles such as Janáček's Kostelnička and Kabanicha, which she sang at London, CG, 1986 and 1994. (R)

Rangoni. The Jesuit (bs), Marina's confessor, in Musorgsky's Boris Godunov.

Ránki, György (b Budapest, 30 Nov. 1907). Hungarian composer. Studied Budapest with Kodály. His interest in folk music is shown in a number of theatrical works, of which the most successful has been the opera Pomádé király új ruhája (King Pomádé's New Clothes, 1953).

Rankl, Karl (b Gaaden, 1 Oct. 1898; d St Gilgen, 6 Sept. 1968). Austrian, later British, conductor and composer. Studied Vienna with Schoenberg and Webern. Vienna, V, 1924; Liberec 1925; Königsberg 1927; Berlin, Kroll T, 1928–31, as chorus-master under Klemperer; Wiesbaden 1931–2. Graz 1932–7. Prague, Landestheater, 1937–9 (prem. of Krenek's Karl V). Music dir. London, CG, 1946–51, building up the new co.; this constructive work was more admired than his conducting. Music dir., Elizabethan O Trust,

Australia, 1958–60. His *Deirdre of the Sorrows* won a Fest. of Britain prize but was unprod. (R)

Raoul. Raoul de Nangis (ten), a Huguenot nobleman, lover of Valentine, in Meyerbeer's *Les Huguenots*.

Rape of Lucretia, The. Opera in 2 acts by Britten; text by Ronald Duncan, based on André Obey's play *Le viol de Lucrèce* (1931), in turn based on Shakespeare's poem *The Rape of Lucrece* (1594) and on Livy's history *Ab Urbe Condita*, i. 57–9 (*c*.26 BC–AD 17). Prem. Gly. 12 July 1946.

Rome, 510 BC. With a Male (ten) and Female (sop) Chorus commenting and eventually drawing a Christian moral, the opera relates the story of the proud, destructive Tarquinius (bar). He rides from the camp where news has arrived of the Roman wives' infidelity to make an attempt on the virtue of the sole exception, Lucretia (mez), wife of Collatinus (bs). Claiming hospitality, he later enters her room and rapes her. Unable to bear the burden of her shame, she kills herself the next day in the presence of her urgently summoned husband.

Rattle, (Sir) **Simon** (*b* Liverpool, 19 Jan. 1955). English conductor. Studied London. While a student, cond. *L'enfant et les sortilèges* (London, RAM, 1974). Début Gly. 1977 (*Cunning Little Vixen*). Gly. regularly, incl. *Don Giovanni* (1994); London, ENO, 1985; Los Angeles 1988 (*Wozzeck*); London, CG, from 1990. Repertory incl. *Idomeneo*, *Figaro*, *Cunning Little Vixen*, *Porgy and Bess*, *L'heure espagnole*. His brilliant, sensitive, and passionate musical direction has produced memorable performances, incl. concert versions of Janáček's *Osud* (1993) and *Idomeneo*, London, QEH, 1987, which had more dramatic vitality than many stage productions. Knighted 1994. (R)

Ravel, Maurice (*b* Ciboure, 7 Mar. 1875; *d* Paris, 28 Dec. 1937). French composer. His two operas are unique contributions to the art, calling for elaborate resources but focusing them on two themes that especially suited him. *L'heure espagnole* (The Spanish Hour, 1911) is a cynical, farcical romp with plenty of Spanish local colour, and treats with wit and poise the subject of a bored wife's afternoon infidelities. The sophistication of the means is, indeed, a necessary part of the worldly wise elegance of the treat-

ment. With *L'enfant et les sortilèges* (The Child and the Enchantments, 1925), the technical brilliance also helps to lend a detachment from the risk of sentimentality. The story of the bad child punished and returned to innocence is told by way of first some brilliantly parodistic music for his revengeful tormentors, then some ravishingly lyrical nature music in a garden scene. Ravel is known to have contemplated at least three more serious subjects: *La cloche engloutie* (on which he was working until 1914), *Jeanne d'Arc*, and *Don Quixote*.

Rebikov, Vladimir (*b* Krasnoyarsk, 31 May 1866; *d* Yalta, 4 Aug. 1920). Russian composer. Studied Moscow with Klenovsky, Berlin with Meyerberger. His style moved from a 19th-cent. Russian Romanticism by way of Impressionism towards Expressionism, and in his operas, some of which he entitled 'musico-psycholographic dramas', he attempted to place the music entirely at the service of the action, though this did not exclude a sense of fantasy. In this he was much influenced by the Moscow Arts T. Admired as avant-garde in its day, his work was found forced and pretentious under Communism, despite its lyrical qualities. His operas included *Into the Storm* (1894) and *Yolka* (1903).

Re cervo, Il. See KÖNIG HIRSCH.

recitative (Fr., *récitative*, or *récitatif*; Ger., *Rezitativ*; It., *recitativo*). The name given to the declamatory portions of opera, in which the plot is generally advanced, as opposed to the more static or reflective lyrical settings; it developed during the 17th cent. from the branching of *stile rappresentativo into two distinct styles, the other of which became *aria. Generally, two styles may be discerned: **recitativo secco** ('dry' recitative), in which the notes and rhythms of the vocal line follow the verbal accentuation, and **recitativo accompagnato**, in which the text is set in a more lyrical fashion, with the accompaniment of instruments other than the *continuo.

'Recondita armonia'. Cavaradossi's (ten) aria in Act I of Puccini's *Tosca*, in which he contrasts the dark beauty of his beloved Tosca with the fair beauty of the Marchesa Attavanti, the model for his painting of the Magdalen.

'Re dell'abisso'. Mam'zelle Arvidson's (Ulrica's) (con) aria in Act I of Verdi's *Un ballo in maschera*, invoking the spirits.

Refice, Licinio (*b* Patrica, Rome, 12 Feb. 1883; *d* Rio de Janeiro, 11 Sept. 1954). Italian composer and conductor. Studied Rome, S Cecilia, with Boenzi, Falchi, and Renzi. Most of his music is for the Church, but he also wrote two operas, *Cecilia* (1934) and *Margherita da Cortona* (1938). He died while conducting a performance of *Cecilia*, leaving incomplete a further opera, *Il mago*.

Regie. See PRODUCER.

Regisseur. See PRODUCER.

register. The tone quality in different parts of the voice: chest, middle, and head in women; chest, head, and falsetto in men. The difference in tone results from the variation of muscular tension in the larynx, arising from the vibration frequency of the note produced, but controllable by the singer. Chest tones have a weighty quality, head tones a light (and thus more flexible) nature. Ideal vocal production effects a seamless change between the registers, by combining the qualities of each.

'Regnava nel silenzio'. Lucia's (sop) aria in Act I of Donizetti's *Lucia di Lammermoor*, in which she recounts to Alisa the legend of the fountain.

rehearsal. A session of preparation preceding the performance of a work. In opera, first come the piano rehearsals, with a coach or *répétiteur first working privately with individual singers, then accompanying them, often under the direction of the conductor, in a studio. Then follow stage rehearsals, when the singers work on stage with the producer, sometimes with the conductor, accompanied by the piano. Orchestral rehearsals will meanwhile have been taken by the conductor, at first without the singers. The German term **Sitzprobe** is now widely used for the first (and any subsequent) unstaged rehearsal with seated singers and the orchestra, directed by the conductor. Stage and orchestra rehearsals follow, in which the work is rehearsed piecemeal. Technical rehearsals ('techs') are for the benefit of the lighting crew and stage staff, with the set and the producer, sometimes also with the singers in costume. However, the piano dress rehearsal may well be treated as the first stage and technical run-through. The pre-dress rehearsal is the first complete stage run-through with orchestra, possibly also the last before the dress rehearsal. 'Dress rehearsal' remains the normal term for the final rehearsal, though this is often virtually a trial performance, without interruptions, sometimes before an invited audience or (with a new work) even members of the Press. See PROBE, PROVA, RÉPÉTITION.

Reichardt, Johann Friedrich (*b* Königsberg, 25 Nov. 1752; *d* Giebichenstein, 27 June 1814). German composer and writer on music. In 1776, on Agricola's death, obtained the post of Kapellmeister to Frederick the Great in Berlin by sending him a copy of his *Le feste galanti*. Here he produced several Italian operas and conducted many works by Graun and Hasse. A visit to Paris in 1785 produced the French operas *Tamerlan* and *Panthée*, which were originally intended for the Opéra and were strongly influenced by Gluck. Returning to Berlin, he had one of his greatest successes with *Brenno* (1789), which one critic compared to Gluck. In 1794 he was dismissed for his subversive views and retired to Giebichenstein, near Halle, which became a meeting-place for many luminaries of the nascent Romantic movement.

The importance of Reichardt's songs has overshadowed consideration of his other works. However, his Singspiels, which included settings of three Goethe librettos, *Claudine von Villa Bella* (1789), *Erwin und Elmire* (1793), and *Jery und Bätely* (1801), were much admired at the time and their generally warm reception is indicative of the gradual shift in Berlin from Italian to German taste. Reichardt's German operas, of which *Die Geisterinsel* (1798), *Das Zauberschloss* (1802), and *Der Taucher* (1811) were the most successful, represent an important contribution towards the eventual formulation of a style of national opera.

Reicher-Kindermann, Hedwig (*b* Munich, 15 July 1853; *d* Trieste, 2 June 1883). German mezzo-soprano, then soprano. Studied with her father, the bs-bar August *Kindermann. Début Karlsruhe 1871. Munich, N, 1871–7. Bayreuth 1876, Grimgerde in first *Ring*. Vienna 1878–80; Leipzig 1880, then singing for Neumann in his European Wagner tour 1882–3. First English *Ring*, 1882. Ill for a part of this, she rejoined it in Italy, only to die a few weeks later. Thought by Neumann to be 'the greatest dramatic singer of the second half of the 19th century', she was a rare and gifted artist with a voice like 'a sword-blade flashing in the sunlight' (Weingartner), and a striking presence. Roles included Gluck's Orfeo, Fidès, Leonore, Agathe, Ortrud, and a breathtaking Brünnhilde and Isolde.

Reichmann, Theodor (*b* Rostock, 15 Mar. 1849; *d* Marbach, 22 May 1903). German baritone. Studied Berlin with Elssler, Milan with Lamperti. Début Magdeburg 1869 (Ottokar). Hamburg 1873–5; Munich 1875–82; Neumann's Wagner tour, 1882–3; Vienna 1883–9, 1893–1903. Bayreuth 1882–94, 1902; London, CG, 1884, 1892; New York, M, 1889–91. Roles included Don Giovanni, Pizarro, Guillaume Tell, Hamlet, Verdi's Iago, Flying Dutchman, Wolfram, Sachs, and first Amfortas. A highly regarded artist of great integrity and dramatic energy, he was notable for his carefully considered characterizations.

Reimann, Aribert (*b* Berlin, 4 Mar. 1936). German composer and pianist. Studied Berlin with Blacher. The early influences of Webern and particularly Berg remain in *Ein Traumspiel* (A Dream Play, 1965), and are absorbed in *Melusine* (1971). A modern treatment of the Melusine myth, concerning a failure of two characters to reconcile civilized and natural order, with Nature wreaking final revenge, the work makes intelligent use of the Romantic elements now more prominent in Reimann's idiom; this includes some lyrical vocal writing for the spirits contrasting with a more declamatory manner for the mortals. Fischer-Dieskau, whom he often accompanied, suggested *Lear* (1978) to him, and has been identified with the title-role. The music is post-Bergian, both in atmosphere and in some of its technical resources, but finds its own structural strengths and its own vein of lyricism. After the bleak, claustrophobic chamber work *Die Gespenstersonata* (The Ghost Sonata, 1984), he returned to full-scale opera with the more dramatic and approachable *Troades* (1986); his most recent work is *Das Schloss* (1992).

Reine de Saba, La (The Queen of Sheba). Opera in 4 acts by Gounod; text by Barbier and Carré, after Gérard de Nerval's *Les nuits de Ramazan* (in his *Le voyage en Orient*, 1851), in turn based on the Arab legend. (Nerval had originally submitted a libretto, now lost, to Meyerbeer.) Prem. Paris, O, 28 Feb. 1862.

Jerusalem, 950 BC. King Soliman's (bs) master architect Adoniram (ten) is in love with Balkis, the Queen of Sheba (sop); she leaves her betrothed, Soliman, but in the end Adoniram dies in her arms, killed by his own workmen and not, as she believes, by the vengeful Soliman.

Reiner, Fritz (*b* Budapest, 19 Dec. 1888; *d* New York, 15 Nov. 1963). Hungarian, later US, conductor. Studied Budapest with Kössler. Répétiteur Budapest, Comic O, 1909, cond. début 1909 (*Carmen*). Cond. Ljubljana 1910, Budapest 1911. Chief cond. Dresden 1914–21, where he was much influenced by Nikisch. Rome, Barcelona, 1921–2. In US 1922–35, mostly concert conducting. London, CG, 1936–7, incl. Flagstad's London début as Isolde. S Francisco 1936–8. New York, M, 1949–53 (first US *Rake's Progress*, 1953). A strong orchestral disciplinarian with a gift for exceptionally lucid performances: Stravinsky had a high regard for 'l'amico Fritz'. (R)

Reinhardt, Delia (*b* Elberfeld, 27 Apr. 1892; *d* Dornach, 3 Oct. 1974). German soprano. Studied Frankfurt with Strakosch and Schako. Début Breslau 1913. Munich, N, 1916–23; New York, M, 1922–4; Berlin, S, 1924–35; London, CG, 1924–7, 1929. Also Paris, O; Buenos Aires; etc. Sang Cherubino, Micaëla, Freia, Mimì, Verdi's Desdemona, Eva, Octavian, Empress, Christine. (R)

Reinhardt, Max (*b* Baden, 9 Sept. 1873; *d* New York, 31 Oct. 1943). Austrian producer, administrator, and actor. Although primarily a man of the theatre, he influenced operatic production in his collaboration with Roller on the prem. of *Der Rosenkavalier* (1911); he also staged the prem. of the original *Ariadne auf Naxos* (1912). He played a major part, with Strauss and Hofmannsthal, in the founding of the Salzburg Fest., 1920. His spectacular productions of *Hoffmann*, *La belle Hélène*, and *Die Fledermaus* were particularly remarkable for their close integration with the music.

Reining, Maria (*b* Vienna, 7 Aug. 1903; *d* Vienna, 11 Mar. 1991). Austrian soprano. Studied Vienna. Début Vienna, S, 1931 (soubrette roles). Vienna until 1933, 1937–58; Munich 1935–7; Salzburg from 1937; London, CG, and Chicago 1938. Milan, S; Paris, O; and New York, CO, 1949. A refined and aristocratic singer with a warm, silvery tone, acclaimed as Countess (Mozart),

Pamina, Euryanthe, Elsa, Eva, Tatyana, Butterfly, Marschallin, Ariadne, Arabella. (R)

Reissiger, Karl (*b* Belzig, 31 Jan. 1798; *d* Dresden, 7 Nov. 1859). German composer and conductor. Studied Leipzig with Schicht, Vienna with Salieri, Munich with Winter. Succeeded Weber as music dir. of the German O in Dresden, 1826; later he became Hofkapellmeister and also directed the Italian opera in place of Morlacchi. A vigorous supporter of Weber and Beethoven, he also championed Wagner and prepared the prem. of *Rienzi*; Wagner became his assistant, but they fell out over Reissiger's refusal to set Wagner's libretto *Die hohe Braut*, and Wagner then portrayed him as reactionary and indolent. Berlioz admired his work. Though a capable musician, he lacked distinctive talent as a composer: his operas mingle French and Italian styles with German Romantic elements. The most successful was *Die Felsenmühle zu Etalières* (1831).

Reiza. Haroun al Raschid's daughter (sop), lover of Huon, in Weber's *Oberon*.

Remedios, Alberto (*b* Liverpool, 27 Feb. 1935). English tenor. Studied Liverpool with Francis, and London, RCM, with Carey. Début London, SW/ENO, 1955 (small roles). London, SW/ENO, then ENO, from 1955; Frankfurt 1968–70; London, CG, from 1965; Cologne, S Francisco from 1973; New York, M, from 1976. Roles included Don Ottavio, Don José, Dmitri, Bacchus, Verdi's Otello, Mark (*Midsummer Marriage*). Combined lyricism and stamina to great effect, especially as Walther, and Siegmund and Siegfried in the SW *Ring*. (R)

reminiscence motive. A short theme identified with a person, place, object, or idea in an opera, which can then be reintroduced so as to recall its subject at a later stage of the drama. It is distinct from *Leitmotiv in that it does not normally change its shape very markedly, since its function is to represent and recall to mind, rather than to suggest dramatic progress. It was a feature of opera, especially French opéra-comique, particularly at the end of the 18th cent. and in the early years of the 19th cent., before the development of Leitmotiv as a stronger structural and expressive force.

Renard. *Histoire burlesque chantée et jouée* in 2 parts by Stravinsky; text by composer, after

Russian folk-tales, trans. into Fr. by C. F. Ramuz. Prem. Paris, O, 18 May 1922.

The fox (ten) persuades the cock (ten) down from his perch by preaching to him; but the cat (bs) and the goat (bs) rescue him. Renewing his efforts, the fox again lures the cock into his reach, and he is rescued again, just in time, by the others suggesting that Mrs Fox is unfaithful. They strangle the fox with his own tail.

Renaud, Maurice (*b* Bordeaux, 24 July 1861; *d* Paris, 16 Oct. 1933). French baritone. Studied Paris and Brussels Cons. Début Brussels, M, 1883. Brussels until 1890, 1908–14; Paris: OC, 1890–1, and O, 1891–1902; London, CG, 1897–9, 1902–4; New York: Manhattan OC, 1906–7, 1909–10; M, 1910–12. Roles included Chorèbe, Telramund, Alberich, Beckmesser, Hérode (*Hérodiade*); created Reyer's High Priest (*Sigurd*) and Hamilcar (*Salammbô*). Retired 1919. A skilful singer and distinguished artist, he possessed great dramatic flair. (R)

Rendall, David (*b* London, 11 Oct. 1948). English tenor. Studied London RAM and Salzburg Mozarteum. Début Gly. Touring O 1975 (Ferrando). London: CG from 1975 as the Italian Singer (*Rosenkavalier*), Rodolfo, and the Duke of Mantua; ENO from 1976 (Alfredo, Pinkerton, Cavaradossi). His fluent delivery and strong stage presence lend distinction to such roles as Don Ottavio (S Francisco 1978), Ernesto (New York, M, 1980), and Don Antonio (prem. of Gerhard's *Duenna*, Madrid 1992). (R)

Re pastore, Il (The Shepherd King). Opera in 2 acts by Mozart; text by Metastasio for Bonno (1751), rev. Varesco. Prem. Salzburg, Archbishop's Palace, 23 Apr. 1775.

Sidon, at the time of Alexander the Great (*c*.332 BC). After conquering Sidon, Alessandro (ten) decides to place on the throne a distant descendant of the royal house, Aminta (sop), who was brought up as a shepherd, and loves Elisa (sop), a shepherdess of noble Phoenician descent. Tamiri (sop), an exiled princess, is in love with Agenore (ten), a Sidonian noble and friend of Alessandro. Alessandro sends Agenore to offer Aminta the throne of Sidon and he is thus reunited with Tamiri.

But Elisa and Aminta fear that fate may ruin their happiness. Agenore persuades Aminta that as a king he cannot marry a shepherdess, and Alessandro, on hearing that Tamiri has been found, decides that Aminta shall marry her; Agenore renounces her. Rather than lose Elisa, Aminta gives up the throne, and Alessandro, impressed by their loyalty, makes them King and Queen of Sidon, promising to conquer new territory for Agenore and Tamiri.

répétiteur (Fr.: 'rehearser'). A pianist in an opera company who coaches and accompanies the singers. In France, however, the term normally used is *chef de chant*, in Italy *maestro collaboratore*, in Germany *Solo répétiteur* or sometimes *Korrepetitor*. A good 'rep' will be an excellent pianist and sight-reader, will correct musical and linguistic mistakes, and will be able to conduct a rehearsal.

répétition (Fr.: 'rehearsal'). In normal French usage, a session of preparation preceding the performance of a work.

rescue opera (Fr., *pièce à sauvetage*, also in It. usage; Ger., *Rettungsoper* or *Schreckensoper*). The name given to an opera in which an essential part of the plot turns on the rescue of a hero or heroine from prison or some other threatening situation. Examples are to be found at various times in the 18th cent., but it developed into an identifiable genre with the French Revolution and the close involvement of opera with real-life situations, often highly dramatic. The first Revolutionary rescue opera was Berton's *Les rigueurs du cloître* (1790), concerning the repression of monasticism. Other famous examples include Dalayrac's *Camille* (1791), Le Sueur's *La caverne* (1793), and Cherubini's *Les deux journées* (1800). Bouilly's libretto *Léonore* (1798) concerns the rescue of the hero more exclusively in its first setting by Gaveaux than in Beethoven's *Fidelio* (1805), in which the genre is raised to the level of the ideal of freedom.

Rescigno, Nicola (*b* New York, 28 May 1916). US conductor. Studied Rome. Co-founder and artistic dir. of Chicago Lyric O, 1954–6; Dallas O 1957–92, with US débuts of Sutherland, Caballé, and Domingo; also first US major co. stagings of *Poppea* and Handel's *Alcina*; prem. of Argento's *The Aspern Papers* 1988. New York, M (*Traviata*, *L'elisir d'amore*).

Residenztheater. See MUNICH.

Resnik, Regina (*b* New York, 30 Aug. 1922). US soprano, later mezzo-soprano. Studied New York with R. Miller. Début New York, New OC, 1942 (Lady Macbeth). New York, M, 1944–83; Bayreuth 1953. Roles included Donna Anna, Sieglinde, Ellen Orford, Alice Ford. Withdrew 1954 for further study with Danise. Mez début Cincinnati 1955 (Amneris). London, CG, 1957–72; also Chicago, Vienna, etc. A vivid dramatic imagination and firm, rich tone brought her much success as Carmen, Eboli, Klytemnästra, Mistress Quickly, Lucretia. From 1971 opera prod., e.g. *Carmen* (Hamburg), *Elektra* (Venice), *Falstaff* (Warsaw). (R)

Respighi, Ottorino (*b* Bologna, 9 July 1879; *d* Rome, 18 Apr. 1936). Italian composer. Studied with Torchi and Martucci in Bologna; in 1900 became violist in the opera orchestra at St Petersburg, where he studied with Rimsky-Korsakov; later attended lectures by Bruch in Berlin. His first operas, the comic *Re Enzo* (1905) and *Semirâma* (1910), made his name and led to an appointment at the conservatory in Rome in 1913, where he settled. Of the operas which followed, *Belfagor* (1923), *Maria Egiziaca* (1932), and *La fiamma* (1934) had some success, although none could match the popularity of *La bella dormente* (1922).

Respighi did not have a natural talent for dramatic composition and relied instead for effect upon his sumptuous scoring and lyrical inventiveness. His style owes much to his teachers, especially Rimsky-Korsakov, as well as to Richard Strauss, whose *Salome* provided the model for *Semirama*, and to Ravel.

Reszke, de. See DE RESZKE.

Retablo de Maese Pedro, El (Master Peter's Puppet Show). Opera in 1 act by Falla; text by composer after Cervantes's novel *Don Quixote* (1615). Prem. Paris, house of Princess Edmond de Polignac, 25 June 1923.

The piece was originally intended for performance with puppets taking all the parts, double-sized for the human beings. A boy narrator (treb) introduces the puppet show to an audience including Don Quixote (bar or bs) and Sancho Panza (silent). The interaction of reality and fiction characteristic of *Don Quixote* takes the form of the boy telling the story of Don Gayferos rescuing the fair Melisendra from the Moors, subject to interruptions from Don Quixote and Master Peter himself (ten). Eventually Don Quixote becomes confused about the reality of the puppets, and leaping forward, beheads the Moors and destroys the puppet show.

Rethberg, Elisabeth (b Schwarzenburg, 22 Sept. 1894; d New York, 6 June 1976). German, later US, soprano. Studied Dresden with Watrin. Début Dresden 1915 (Arsena, *Der Zigeunerbaron*). Dresden until 1922, then regularly; New York, M, 1922–42 (when she retired); London, CG, 1925, 1934–9. Also Milan, S; Salzburg, etc. Her enormous repertory included Constanze, Countess (Mozart), Pamina, Agathe, Marguerite, Selika, Eva, Sieglinde, Aida, Desdemona (Verdi), Marschallin, and first Helen (*Die ägyptische Helena*). An outstanding singer of impeccable style, she used her beautiful voice with consummate skill and musicality. Much admired by R. Strauss and Toscanini. (R)

Reutter, Hermann (b Stuttgart, 17 June 1900; d Heidenheim an der Brenz, 1 Jan. 1985). German composer and pianist. Studied with Courvoisier and Dorfmüller, before establishing a successful career as performer and teacher. Although his music is now seldom performed, in his day he was regarded as one of Germany's leading composers. His style owes much to the neo-Romanticism of Pfitzner, although in his early works he was also influenced both by the technique and spirit of Hindemith, while traces of Orff's music are also to be detected. Of his operas the most successful was *Dr Johannes Faustus* (1936), which like much of Reutter's music at this time took inspiration from German folk-song and contrasts sharply with its successor, the epic *Odysseus* (1942). Several works, including *Der verlorene Sohn* (1929), *Der Weg nach Freudenstadt* (1948), and *Der Lübecker Totentanz* (The Lübeck Death-Dance, 1948), explore Expressionist themes. More recent works include *Hamlet* (1980).

Revisor, Der. Opera in 5 acts by Egk; text by composer, after Gogol's story *The Government Inspector* (1836). Prem. Schwetzingen by Stuttgart O, 9 May 1957.

A small Russian town; c.1840. Khlestakov (ten), a penniless civil servant, is mistaken for the Government Inspector and lavishly entertained by the Mayor (bs), his wife (mez), and daughter (sop).

Reyer, Ernest (b Marseilles, 1 Dec. 1823; d Le Lavandou, 15 Jan. 1909). French composer. Studied Marseilles, Paris with Farrenc, but largely self-taught. Made an early reputation with his works, including two opéras-comiques and an opera, *Erostrate* (1862). His most famous work was *Sigurd* (1884), a success he almost equalled with *Salammbô* (1890). Though *Sigurd* is Wagnerian in subject-matter, and Reyer was a great admirer of Wagner (as of Berlioz and Weber), his work is not greatly coloured by any of their influences. His music does not reveal great individuality, though it shows an appreciation of the strengths of Grand Opera and is excellently scored, but reflects the intelligence and independence of mind which made him a witty and forceful critic. He defended Wagner and Berlioz eloquently, and travelled widely in the course of his work, making a visit to Cairo for the prem. of *Aida*.

Reyzen, Mark (b Zaytsevo, 3 July 1895; d Moscow, 25 Nov. 1992). Russian bass. Studied Kharkov with Bugamelli. Début Kharkov 1921 (Pimen). Leningrad, K, 1925–30; Moscow, B, 1930–54. Also Paris, O; Berlin, S; Dresden; Budapest; etc. Sang Gremin at Moscow, B, on his 90th birthday, still in good voice. A sensitive actor with a warm, solid tone, remarkable in a wide range of characters, e.g. Rossini's Don Basilio, Gounod's Méphistophélès, Philip, Susanin, Boris, Dosifey. (R)

Rezia. See REIZA.

Rezniček, Emil von (b Vienna, 4 May 1860; d Berlin, 2 Aug. 1945). Austrian composer and conductor. Studied Graz with Mayer, Leipzig with Reinecke and Jadassohn. He held many conducting posts, including at Mannheim (1896–9); Warsaw (1907–8); and Berlin (1909–11). Of his operas, the best known are *Donna Diana* (1894), especially for its sparkling overture, and *Till Eulenspiegel* (1902), though he also wrote a number of serious works.

Rheingold, Das. See RING DES NIBELUNGEN, DER.

Ricci, Federico (b Naples, 22 Oct. 1809; d Conegliano, 10 Dec. 1877). Italian composer. Studied Naples with Zingarelli and Raimondi, also with Bellini and his brother **Luigi** (b Naples, 8 July 1805; d Prague, 31 Dec. 1859), who studied Naples with Furno, Zingarelli, and Generali.

Apart from works written in collaboration with his brother, Federico had successes with *La prigione d'Edimburgo* (1838), *Luigi Rolla* (1841), and *Corrado d'Altamura* (1841). The latter, based on the same plot as Verdi's

Oberto, led to other commissions; but his serious operas fared less well than his comedies. *Il marito e l'amante* (The Husband and the Lover, 1852) was successful, but *Il paniere d'amore* (The Basket of Love, 1853) failed, and he accepted a post in St Petersburg. In 1869 he moved to Paris, where he had some success with an opéra-bouffe, *Une folie à Rome* (An Escapade in Rome, 1869). The most famous of the brothers' collaborations was *Crispino e la comare* (Crispino and the Fairy, 1850), to which he contributed the lighter numbers that reflect his elegant craftsmanship.

Luigi, the more imaginatively gifted brother, was also less successful as a serious composer than in comedy, though he first became popular with his *Chiara di Rosembergh* (1831). He had a great success with *Un avventura di Scaramuccia* (1834). In Trieste from 1836, he unwisely attempted *Le nozze di Figaro* (1838). He then moved to Odessa with his twin-sister mistresses, the sopranos **Francesca** and **Ludmilla Stolz** (*b* 8 May 1827; sisters of Teresa *Stolz). He wrote for them *La solitaria delle Asturie* (1845). They travelled together to Copenhagen and back to Trieste. Ricci had further successes with comic operas, before dying insane. His music has a lively tunefulness, and he was probably the leading spirit in the collaborations with his brother.

Ricciarelli, Katia (*b* Rovigo, 18 Jan. 1946). Italian soprano. Studied Venice with Adami-Corradetti. Début Mantua 1969 (Mimì). Milan, S, from 1973; Chicago 1973; London, CG, and New York, M, from 1975. Also Moscow, B; Barcelona; Berlin, D; Verona; etc. An attractive artist with a warm, ripe, lucent tone, capable of much emotional depth. Large repertory includes Imogene, Giulietta (Bellini), Lucrezia Borgia, Micaëla, Elisabeth de Valois, Desdemona (Verdi), Mimì, Luisa Miller. (R)

Richard, Cœur-de-lion. Opera in 3 acts by Grétry; text by Sedaine, after 13th-cent. fable. Prem. Paris, CI, 21 Oct. 1784.

Austria, end 12th cent. Blondel (ten), Richard's (ten) minstrel, wanders in search of his King disguised as a blind singer. Helped by Sir Williams (bs), his daughter Laurette (sop), and Marguerite of Flanders (sop), he manages first to make contact with Richard by means of his romance, 'Une fièvre brulante', and then to rescue him from the castle where he is held prisoner under Florestan (bs).

Richter, Hans (*b* Raab (Györ), 4 Apr. 1843; *d* Bayreuth, 5 Dec. 1916). Austro-Hungarian conductor. Studied Vienna with Sechter. Horn-player, Vienna, K, 1862–6. Worked with Wagner at Tribschen 1866–7 on fair copy of *Meistersinger* and 1870 on *Ring*; played trumpet in first performance of *Siegfried Idyll*. Wagner recommended him to Bülow as chorus-master for Munich. Cond. Munich 1868–9 (début *Guillaume Tell*), also singing at short notice Kothner in sixth performance of *Meistersinger*. Cond. *Lohengrin*, Brussels 1870. Chief cond. Budapest 1871–5. Vienna 1875–1900, music dir. from 1893. Bayreuth 1876–1912, cond. first *Ring*. London: DL 1882, first English *Tristan* and *Meistersinger*; CG 1884, 1903–1910, where, after his production of *The Ring* in English, his attempts to found a permanent English national opera in association with Percy *Pitt, were thwarted by the Grand O Syndicate at HM.

One of the greatest German conductors of his time, Richter was (with *Levi, *Mottl, and *Muck) in the first generation of Wagner conductors who worked with the composer in Bayreuth and founded a tradition. Accounts of his interpretations suggest gravity, a deep understanding of structure, and a strong lyrical flow that did not exclude lightness of touch. (R)

Ricordi. Italian firm of music publishers, founded in 1808 by **Giovanni** (1785–1853) who, benefiting from his close association with Milan S, built up the firm and secured himself a powerful commercial position. The most important member of the family was his grandson **Giulio** (1840–1912), who was dir. 1888–1912 and exercised a notable force on Italian opera. Himself a minor composer (his single opera, *La secchia rapita* (1910) was to a text by Renato Simoni, later librettist of *Turandot*), he combined shrewd musical judgement in his choice of composers with ruthless business acumen in furthering their and the firm's interests. Though he did attack Toscanini, and reject Bizet and Leoncavallo, he championed Verdi with a fervour based on personal friendship and belief in Verdi's supremely Italian genius (Wagner was an enemy so vile that Ricordi even continued the attacks after acquiring the composer's operas with Lucca's stock in 1887). Ricordi quickly recognized Puccini as the

'Crown Prince' to Verdi, and helped him incalculably in his early career. Librettos were bought in case Puccini might use them, and Ricordi was also able to persuade Franchetti, dissatisfied with Illica's *Tosca* text, to hand it over to Puccini. 'Don Giulio' became, for Puccini, 'The only person who inspires me with trust, and to whom I can confide what is going through my mind.' He was the first to advertise operas with illustrated posters (starting with *La bohème*), and these were later used for the early editions of the vocal scores.

Ridderbusch, Karl (*b* Recklinghausen, 29 May 1932). German bass. Studied Essen. Début Münster 1961. Deutsche O am Rhein from 1965; New York, M, 1967–9, 1976–7; Bayreuth from 1967; London, CG, 1971, 1973. Also Paris, O; Buenos Aires; Milan, S; Chicago; Berlin, D. Powerful of voice and build; repertory included Rocco, Daland, Hunding, Hagen, Sachs, Ochs, Boris, Doktor (*Wozzeck*). (R)

Ride of the Valkyries. The name generally given to the scene opening Act III of Wagner's *Die Walküre*, in which the warrior-maidens, Wotan's daughters, gather on a rocky peak.

Riders to the Sea. Opera in 1 act by Vaughan Williams; text, J. M. Synge's tragedy (1904). Prem. London, RCM, 1 Dec. 1937.

The setting is the west coast of Ireland, where Maurya (con) has lost her husband and four sons at sea. A fifth is also discovered to have been drowned when her daughters Cathleen (sop) and Nora (sop) identify some clothes brought in; and when her last son Bartley (bar) in turn is claimed by the sea as he is riding some horses to a fair, her grief finally turns to resignation and peace.

Riegel, Kenneth (*b* Womelsdorf, PA, 19 Apr. 1938). US tenor. Studied Manhattan School of Music. Début S Fe 1965 (US prem. of Henze's *König Hirsch*). New York, CO, 1969–74; New York, M, from 1973 as Iopas, Tamno, Hoffmann. Created roles incl. Painter in 3-act version of *Lulu* (Paris 1979) and the Leper in Messiaen's *St François d'Assise* (1983). A capable and musical performer, his acting skill was shown in the title-role of Zemlinsky's *Der Zwerg* at London, CG, 1985. Other roles incl. Don Ottavio, Dionysus (*The Bassarids*). (R)

Rienzi (orig. *Cola Rienzi, der letzte der Tribunen*).

Opera in 5 acts by Wagner; text by composer, after Mary Russell Mitford's drama (1828) and Bulwer Lytton's novel (1835). Prem. Dresden, H, 20 Oct. 1842.

Set in 14th-cent. Rome, the opera tells of the struggle between the Orsinis and the Colonnas. Paolo Orsini (bs) attempts to abduct Irene (sop), sister of Cola Rienzi (ten), but is interrupted by Stefano Colonna (bs), whose son Adriano (mez) appears to defend Irene. Rienzi, the papal legate, appears, and encouraged by Cardinal Raimondi (bs) urges the people to resist the tyranny of the nobles. The nobles swear allegiance to Rienzi as tribune, but they plot to murder him, and almost succeed. Condemned to death, they are spared through Adriano's intercession; but when they break their oath of submission, the people rise and kill them. However, the people in turn prove disloyal to Rienzi, and Adriano also tries to kill him. Rienzi is excommunicated, and Adriano now warns Irene of her brother's danger. She finds him at prayer in the Capitol, and refusing to flee with Adriano, remains with him as the mob fires the Capitol; Adriano rushes into the flames to perish with them.

Righetti-Giorgi, Geltrude. See GIORGI-RIGHETTI, GELTRUDE.

Righini, Vincenzo (*b* Bologna, 22 Jan. 1756; *d* Bologna, 19 Aug. 1812). Italian composer. Studied Bologna with Martini. His early career was as a singer, which took him to Parma and Prague. Here his first opera, *Il convitato di pietra* (1776), was given, a treatment of the Don Juan legend which predated that of Da Ponte and Mozart by ten years. In 1780 he was called to Vienna by Joseph II to become dir. of the Italian O. After seven years he moved to Mainz, and quickly on to Berlin, where the successful performance of *Enea nel Lazio* (1793) secured for him the post of Hofkapellmeister and dir. of Italian O in 1793. His career here was highly successful and with the librettist Filistri he produced a number of popular triumphs, including *Atalante e Meleagro* (1797) and *Tigrane* (1800).

Rigoletto. Opera in 3 acts by Verdi; text by Piave, after Hugo's drama *Le roi s'amuse* (1832). Originally entitled *La maledizione*. Prem. Venice, F, 11 Mar. 1851.

Mantua, 16th cent. Rigoletto (bar), the hunchbacked court jester, taunts Count Ceprano (bs), whose wife is the latest fancy of the licentious Duke. The courtiers resolve to abduct Rigoletto's 'mistress' in revenge. She is in fact his daughter Gilda (sop). Count Monterone (bar) bursts in to confront the Duke, who has seduced his daughter. He is arrested and curses Rigoletto, who is mocking him. On going home, Rigoletto is accosted by Sparafucile (bs), a professional assassin, who offers his services. The jester enjoins Gilda never to leave the house on her own. She does not tell him of the visits of the handsome young student she met in church (the Duke in disguise). The courtiers trick Rigoletto into helping them abduct Gilda.

In the ducal palace, the courtiers report their exploits with glee. The Duke is delighted to hear Gilda is there and rushes off to her. A despondent Rigoletto enters, and a series of lies leads him to realize that the Duke must be with Gilda. She runs in, having been seduced by the Duke, and throws herself into her father's arms. Even the courtiers are abashed to find that she is really Rigoletto's daughter. He swears vengeance.

Rigoletto and Gilda go to Sparafucile's inn outside the town, where Rigoletto has arranged for the Duke's murder. The Duke appears and flirts with Maddalena (con), Sparafucile's sister, singing to her. This distresses Gilda, who still loves him. Maddalena has grown fond of the Duke and tries to dissuade her brother from murdering him. They agree that any stranger coming to the inn before midnight should substitute for the Duke. Gilda, disguised in man's clothing, overhears this and resolves to sacrifice her life. Rigoletto returns and Sparafucile hands over a sack containing a body. As Rigoletto is about to throw it into the river, he hears the Duke singing his song again. Realizing that he has been deceived, Rigoletto opens the sack and a flash of lightning reveals Gilda's face. She is still alive, but dies in his arms, begging forgiveness. Monterone's curse is fulfilled.

Rihm, Wolfgang (b Karlsruhe, 13 Mar. 1953). German composer. Studied Karlsruhe, and with Stockhausen. After *Faust und Yorick* (1977), he had a striking success with *Jakob Lenz* (1979), in which he abandoned serialism for a freer manner (influenced by Berg) that included some extremes of vocal writing in an ultra-Expressionist manner. *Die Hamletmaschine* (1987) follows Stockhausen in seeking a total theatre of sound and non-narrative, ritualistic drama. *Oedipus* (1987)

fragments Sophocles in order to reconstruct the essence of the drama through music. *Die Eroberung von Mexico* was produced 1992.

Rimsky-Korsakov, Nikolay (b Tikhvin, 18 Mar. 1844; d Lyubensk, 21 June 1908). Russian composer. Studied piano with Canille, and had guidance from Balakirev.

With two exceptions, all Rimsky-Korsakov's operas are on Russian themes. Mythology attracted him, as did fantastic subjects, and his first opera, *The Maid of Pskov* (1873), is unusual in being an historical costume drama that treats human emotions. His gift for harmonic and orchestral colour, coupled with his love of legend and fairy-tale, drew him more to the type of opera of which *May Night* (1880) was the first. This is a Gogol-inspired work dealing with supernatural elements in a colourful folk setting, and characteristically it includes a good number of set pieces such as dances for wedding guests, skomorokhi, and rusalki, choruses, and a song for a blind bard.

In *The Snow Maiden* (1882), fairy and human worlds impinge; but the heroine's dilemma is expressed more by Rimsky-Korsakov's demonstration that they are irreconcilable than by anything beyond the very simplest characterization of the heroine, who is touching but not truly sympathetic. This was a weakness underlined when he reverted to village comedy with *Christmas Eve* (1895), which for all its entertaining brilliance lacks the warmth of Tchaikovsky's setting of the same subject (*Vakula the Smith*). This and *Mlada* were regarded as studies for *Sadko* (1898), in which he responds vividly to the picturesqueness of a story that affords ample opportunity for spectacle and the exotic. His idiom was by now slightly tinged by a Wagnerian influence and yet also a wish to strengthen his feeling for Russia's past by a use of a special bardic type of declamation.

However, his next work was *Mozart and Salieri* (1898), a neoclassical opera (the first) based on Pushkin's 'little tragedy' dramatizing the rumour that Mozart had been poisoned by his rival. It is a conscious descendant of Dargomyzhsky's *The Stone Guest*, though it is more openly melodic and includes some pastiche. But feeling that this was not a way forward, he turned in *The Tsar's Bride* (1899) back to the kind of historical costume drama with which he had begun his career. Less self-indulgently colourful, this represents a return also to a more lyrical manner, and is a bel canto opera with songs and ensembles; it is the peak of his achievement in melodic composition. *The Tale of Tsar Saltan* (1900) combines fantasy with satire, whereas *Kashchey the Immortal* (1902) is a short, magic opera in which the characters are represented as much by the orchestra as vocally, allowing the composer to indulge in some dazzling orchestration that had a distinct influence on his pupil Stravinsky's *The Firebird*. These qualities reappear in *The Legend of the Invisible City of Kitezh* (1907), a work involving the familiar dances and set pieces, but also combining a feeling for Orthodox sanctity and Dostoyevskyan mysticism with a somewhat Tolstoyan moral fervour: it includes his best single character, the spiritually tormented, drunken scoundrel Grishka Kuterma. *The Golden Cockerel* (1909) mixes the old fantastic elements with a vein of satire: that much is left obscure is of little importance since the air of mystery is without meaning and is no more than the magician's deception of his audience.

Rimsky-Korsakov was also responsible for completing, revising, and orchestrating a number of works by other Russian composers which he believed should see as friendly a light of day as possible. His revisions of Musorgsky's *Boris Godunov* have been much criticized, and his version has now been generally replaced in the theatre by the original, but it should be remembered that this was his expressed intention: at the time, he did not think the world would understand Musorgsky's originalities.

Rinaldo di Capua (*b* Capua or Naples, *c*.1710; *d* ?Rome, *c*.1780). Italian composer. Music to only six of his 32 operas survives. His most successful works were the drammi giocosi *La commedia in commedia* (1738) and *La libertà nociva* (1740), which were given throughout Italy. The former was heard in an abridged version in Paris (1752) as *La donna superba*, where it was also parodied as *La femme orgueilleuse*. Together with performances of the intermezzo *La zingara* it played an important role in the *Guerre des Bouffons.

Ring des Nibelungen, Der (The Ring of the Nibelung). A stage-festival play for three days and a preliminary evening (*Ein Bühnenfestspiel für drei Tage und einen Vorabend*)—sometimes called a tetralogy—by Wagner; text by the composer, based on the Nibelung Saga. Prem.

Bayreuth, Festspielhaus, 13, 14, 16, 17 Aug. 1876. The separate operas were produced as follows:

Das Rheingold (The Rhinegold). Prologue in 1 act to the trilogy *Der Ring des Nibelungen*. Prem. Munich, N, 22 Sept. 1869.

Die Walküre (The Valkyrie). Music-drama in 3 acts. Prem. Munich, N, 26 June 1870.

Siegfried. Music-drama in 3 acts. Prem. Bayreuth, Festspielhaus, 16 Aug. 1876.

Götterdämmerung (The Twilight of the Gods). Music-drama in 3 acts. Prem. Bayreuth, Festspielhaus, 17 Aug. 1876.

In *Rheingold*, the Nibelung dwarf Alberich (bs-bar) renounces love so that he may steal the Rhinegold, guarded by the three Rhinemaidens (sop, sop, mez), and by forging a Ring from it become master of the world. Wotan (bs-bar), ruler of the gods, has engaged the giants Fafner and Fasolt (basses) to build Valhalla for the gods; unable to pay for it, he has promised them Freia (sop), goddess of youth. Loge (ten), the fire god, persuades Wotan to accompany him to Nibelheim where by a trick Wotan obtains the Ring and the Rhinegold from Alberich; he intends to pay the giants with the gold, and keep the Ring himself. Alberich curses the Ring. The giants see the Ring on Wotan's finger and demand it as well as a magic helmet, the Tarnhelm. Wotan at first refuses, and the giants prepare to drag Freia away. Wotan's wife Fricka (mez) urges Wotan to comply; Erda (con), the earth goddess, warns Wotan of the consequences of retaining the Ring. He adds it to the gold, whereupon Fasolt and Fafner quarrel. Fafner kills Fasolt, and takes away the gold, the Tarnhelm, and the Ring. The gods, watched cynically by Loge, enter Valhalla as the curtain falls.

(In order to safeguard Valhalla, Wotan begets with Erda nine warrior daughters, the Valkyries, who bear the bodies of dead heroes to Valhalla, where they are revived and help to defend the castle. But in order to restore the Ring to the Rhinemaidens and rid the gods of the curse, Wotan has to engender human children. He descends to earth and begets Siegmund and Sieglinde, hoping that the former will one day kill Fafner and return the Ring to the Rhinemaidens. The pair are separated, Sieglinde being forcibly married to Hunding, and Siegmund driven to lead a wandering life of hardship.)

In *Die Walküre*, Siegmund (ten) is driven to shelter in Hunding's hut. He and Sieglinde (sop) feel a mysterious attraction. Hunding (bs) returns, and realizing that Siegmund is the murderer of his kinsmen, challenges him to fight the next day. Later, after she has drugged Hunding's drink, Sieglinde shows Siegmund the sword Nothung that Wotan had left embedded in the tree growing in Hunding's hut to be withdrawn by a hero. He pulls out the sword, and flees with Sieglinde. Fricka, the guardian of marriage vows, forces Wotan to side with Hunding in the coming combat. But Brünnhilde (sop), Wotan's favourite Valkyrie daughter, disobeys him and sides with Siegmund. Wotan intervenes and Siegmund is killed, Nothung being shattered by Wotan's spear. Brünnhilde gathers up the fragments and entrusts them to Sieglinde, who will soon bear Siegmund's child—the hero Siegfried. Wotan's punishment for Brünnhilde is to deprive her of her immortal status, putting her to sleep on a fire-girt rock until she is claimed by a man. He mitigates her fate, however, by granting her plea that only a true hero will win through the flames. The curtain falls on the magic fire.

(Sieglinde has died giving birth to Siegfried. The boy has been brought up by the dwarf Mime, brother of Alberich. Mime's dwelling is in the forest close to the cave where Fafner, who by means of the Tarnhelm has changed himself into a dragon, guards the Rhinegold. Mime hopes to weld the fragments of Nothung together so that Siegfried can kill Fafner; he means thereby to gain the Ring for himself.)

In *Siegfried*, Wotan, disguised as a Wanderer, visits Mime (ten) and prophesies that the sword will be forged by a hero. Mime recognizes Siegfried (ten) as this hero, and intends to kill him when his plan is accomplished. Siegfried successfully forges the sword Nothung, and with Mime sets out to seek Fafner. After Siegfried has aroused and killed Fafner, he burns his finger in the dragon's blood. Sucking it, he finds that he can understand the language of the birds, one of which (sop) warns him of Mime's treachery, and then tells him of the sleeping Brünnhilde. Siegfried kills Mime, and with the Ring and Tarnhelm follows the bird to the Valkyrie's rock. The Wanderer, although he has told Erda that he longs only for the end, tries to bar his path, but Siegfried shatters his spear with Nothung and, making his way through the fire, awakens Brünnhilde and claims her as his bride.

In *Götterdämmerung*, the Three Norns (con,

mez, sop) prophesy the end of the gods. Siegfried gives Brünnhilde the Ring, and leaving her, goes to seek adventure. He comes to the Hall of the Gibichungs, where Alberich's son Hagen (bs) lives with his half-brother Gunther (bar) and half-sister Gutrune (sop). Hagen, who knows all that has happened, devises a plot. He gives Siegfried a drug to make him forget Brünnhilde, and arranges for him to marry Gutrune, the price being that he will fetch Brünnhilde as Gunther's bride: thus Hagen will obtain the Ring. To Brünnhilde comes her sister Waltraute (mez), who urges her in vain to return the Ring to the Rhinemaidens. Siegfried, wearing the Tarnhelm and in the guise of Gunther, penetrates the fire again; he overcomes Brünnhilde, tears the Ring from her finger, and takes her back, an unwilling bride for Gunther. Hagen summons the Gibichungs for the double wedding. Gunther leads on Brünnhilde, unrecognized by Siegfried. Seeing the Ring on Siegfried's finger, she accuses him of treachery. With Hagen and the now suspicious Gunther she plans Siegfried's death in a hunt.

Siegfried is resting on the banks of the Rhine; the Rhinemaidens appear and plead with him to return the Ring. Hagen, Gunther, and the huntsmen now arrive. Siegfried is asked to relate his adventures. Hagen gives him a second drug to restore his memory, and he speaks of his love for Brünnhilde. Hagen spears him in the back. Siegfried's body is carried back to the Gibichung Hall, and in a quarrel over the Ring, Gunther is killed by Hagen. When Hagen approaches the dead Siegfried to remove the Ring, Siegfried's hand rises in the air and stops him. Brünnhilde orders a funeral pyre to be built, and taking the Ring from Siegfried's finger, places it on her own. On her horse Grane, she plunges into the flames. The Hall collapses, the Rhine overflows, and when Hagen tries to snatch the Ring from Brünnhilde, he is dragged below the waters by the Rhinemaidens. Valhalla rises in flames, and as the kingdom of the gods is destroyed, a new era of love dawns.

Rinuccini, Ottavio (*b* Florence, 20 Jan. 1562; *d* Florence, 28 Mar. 1621). Italian librettist. His text for Peri's *Favola di Dafne* (1598) was the first opera libretto, later set by Gagliano (1608) and Schütz (trans. Opitz, 1627; music lost—perhaps the first German opera). He also provided the libretto for *Euridice* (set by both Peri and Caccini in 1600) and later wrote the libretto for Monteverdi's *Arianna*. This was his most famous work and led to a further planned collaboration on *Narciso ed Ecco* (1608); Monteverdi did not set the libretto, disliking its unhappy ending.

Riotte, Philipp Jakob (*b* St Wendel, 16 Aug. 1776; *d* Vienna, 20 Aug. 1856). German composer and conductor. Studied with André; *c*.1805 Kapellmeister at Gotha. After travels to Danzig, Magdeburg, and Erfurt arrived in Vienna in 1808, taking up a post at the H. Worked at the Vienna W as music dir. 1818–20 and 1824–6. His reputation was achieved by many popular stage works, including the pantomimes *Staberl als Freischütz* (1822) and *Der Postillon von Stadt-Enzersdorf* (1838) and the Singspiel *Das Grenzstädtchen*. Of the *c*.50 works he produced, the most popular and lasting was the music for Raimund's *Moisasurs Zauberspruch* (1827).

Rise and Fall of the City of Mahagonny. See AUFSTIEG UND FALL DER STADT MAHAGONNY.

Ristori, Giovanni Alberto (*b* ?Bologna, 1692; *d* Dresden, 7 Feb. 1753). Italian composer. After early success in Italy, he went to Dresden in 1717 to become composer to the company directed by his father **Tommaso Ristori**. His first opera there was *Cleonice* (1718); in the late 1720s he again produced Italian opera, notably *Calandro* (1726). After the accession of Augustus II (1733) he was increasingly passed over in favour of Hasse, though he did compose Augustus's coronation opera, *Le fate* (1736). In 1731–2 he accompanied his father on a trip to Russia and was possibly Kapellmeister to the St Petersburg court briefly. The performance of *Calandro* in Moscow in Dec. 1731 was the first of an Italian opera in Russia.

Risurrezione (Resurrection). Opera in 4 acts by Alfano; text by Cesare Hanay, after Tolstoy's novel *Resurrection* (1900). Prem. Turin, V, 30 Nov. 1904.

Russia, *c*.1910. Katusha (sop) meets and falls in love with Prince Dimitri (ten), by whom she becomes pregnant. He has to join his regiment and fails to keep a rendezvous with her at a railway station. Katusha commits a murder and is sentenced to be deported to Siberia; Dimitri follows her there and obtains a free pardon for her; but she rejects him in favour of Simonson (bar), a fellow convict.

'Ritorna vincitor'. Aida's (sop) aria in Act I of Verdi's *Aida*, in which she struggles with her conflicting emotions as she longs for Radamès to return victorious from a war against her own father and country.

Ritorno d'Ulisse in patria, Il (The Return of Ulysses to his Homeland). Opera in a prologue and 5 acts by Monteverdi; text by Badoaro. Prem. Venice, C, Feb. 1640.

The opera relates the events of the closing book of Homer's *Odyssey*, with added comments from the gods and from allegorical figures (Human Frailty, Time, Fortune, and Love: these appear as a prologue). Penelope laments the continued absence of Ulisse to her nurse Ericlea. After a discussion of men's sins between Giove and Nettuno, Ulisse is put on shore at Ithaca and encouraged by Minerva to reclaim his palace, given over to the suitors of his wife Penelope. Eumete, his herdsman, is taunted by the jester Iro, and then welcomes the disguised Ulisse, who revives his hopes of his master's return. Eumete then welcomes Ulisse's son Telemaco, also returning home, and there is a joyful reunion, while Eumete tells Penelope that Ulisse may soon appear. The suitor Antinoo mocks Ulisse, disguised as a beggar, who first wins a contest with the suitors by being able to string his own bow, and then turns it upon them. Penelope's fear that he may not truly be Ulisse is overcome by Ericlea, and husband and wife join in a love duet.

Rizzi, Carlo (*b* Milan, 16 July 1960). Italian conductor. Début Milan, Angelicum, 1982 (Donizetti's *L'ajo nell'imbarrazzo*). A persuasive performer in a wide repertory, has given *Tancredi* and *Don Giovanni* throughout Italy. UK début at Buxton 1988 (*Torquato Tasso*). London, CG, from 1990 (*Cenerentola*, *Il viaggio a Reims*). New York, M, 1993 (*Barbiere di siviglia*). Other repertory incl. *Tosca* (O North), *Lucrezia Borgia* (Australian O). (R)

Robert le diable. Opera in 5 acts by Meyerbeer; text by Scribe and Delavigne. Prem. Paris, O, 21 Nov. 1831.

In 13th-cent. Palermo, Robert, Duke of Normandy (ten), the son of a mortal and a devil, falls in love with the Princess Isabella (sop). Disguised, and under the name of Bertram (bs), the Devil tries to gain Robert's soul; he prevents Robert from winning Isabella in a tournament, and Robert is then willing to use diabolical means. At a midnight orgy with ghostly nuns, Robert acquires a magic branch with which he gains access to Isabella; but she persuades him to break it. Robert denounces his father the Devil, and marries Isabella.

Roberto Devereux, ossia Il conte d'Essex. Opera in 3 acts by Donizetti; text by Cammarano, after F. Ancelot's tragedy *Elisabeth d'Angleterre*. Prem. Naples, C, 29 Oct. 1837.

London, early 17th cent. The Earl of Essex, Robert Devereux (ten), although loved by Queen Elizabeth (sop), is in love with Sara (sop or mez), Countess of Nottingham. Essex is accused of treason and sentenced to death by the Queen, whose reprieve comes too late to save him.

Robertson, James (*b* Liverpool, 17 June 1912; *d* Ruabon, 18 May 1991). English conductor. Studied Cambridge, Leipzig, and London. Répétiteur Gly. 1937–9; cond. London, CR, 1938–9; music dir. London, SW, 1946–54. Dir. London O Centre 1964–78. (R)

Robeson, Paul (*b* Princeton, NJ, 9 Apr. 1898; *d* Philadelphia, 23 Jan. 1976). US bass and actor. Studied law, Columbia U. Main career as actor, notably as Othello, but gave unforgettable performances as Joe (*Show Boat*), London DL 1928, and in New York (also appearing in the film), and as Crown (*Porgy and Bess*). His huge frame, magnificent voice, and the moving quality of his singing (especially in Spirituals) left indelible impressions on all who heard him. (R)

Robin, Mado (*b* Yseures-sur-Creuse, 29 Dec. 1918; *d* Paris, 10 Dec. 1960). French soprano. Studied Paris with Podestà. Début Paris, O, 1945 (Gilda). Appeared at Paris, O and OC; Brussels; S Francisco; and in Russia. Chiefly remarkable for her extraordinarily high range. Her most famous roles were Lucia and Lakmé. (R)

Robinson, Forbes (*b* Macclesfield, 21 May 1926; *d* London, 13 May 1987). English bass. Studied at Milan, La Scala school. Début London, CG, 1954 (Monterone). CG from 1954. Appearances with WNO, Berlin, Zurich, Buenos Aires, etc. Repertory of over 70 roles included Figaro (Mozart), Don Giovanni, Pizarro, Philip, Boris, Dodon, Kecal, Moses (*Moses und Aron*), Claggart, and first

Priam (*King Priam*). An excellent singing actor with a dark timbre and striking powers of expression. (R)

Robson, Christopher (*b* Falkirk, 9 Dec. 1953). Scottish counter-tenor. Studied London with Gaddarn, Esswood, and Mott. Début Birmingham 1979 (in Handel's *Sosarme*). Kent O; O Factory (Zurich and London); London, ENO from 1985 (Moscow, Leningrad, Kiev 1990) and CG from 1988 (début as Athamas in Handel's *Semele*); Houston and New York, CO, 1985 (creation of Glass's *Akhnaten*); also Frankfurt, Berlin, Houston, Aix, etc. Roles incl. Endymion, Sorceress (Purcell), Arsamene (*Serse*), Gluck's Orfeo, Akhnaten. (R)

Rocca, Lodovico (*b* Turin, 29 Nov. 1895; *d* Turin, 25 June 1986). Italian composer. Studied Turin, and Milan with Orefice. His fame rests chiefly on his third opera, *Il dibuk* (1934), a skilful and effective amalgam of various styles and techniques. Dir. Turin Cons., 1950–66.

Rocco. The gaoler (bs), Marzelline's father, in Beethoven's *Fidelio*.

Rode, Wilhelm (*b* Hanover, 17 Feb. 1887; *d* Icking, 2 Sept. 1959). German bass-baritone. Studied Hanover with Moest. Début Erfurt 1909 (Herald, *Lohengrin*). Munich 1922–30; Vienna 1930–2; Berlin, SO, 1932–45 (Intendant from 1934). Also Paris, O; London, CG; Madrid; Prague; etc. One of the leading Wagner baritones of his time, and much esteemed as Wotan and Sachs. (R)

Roderigo. A Venetian gentleman (ten) in Verdi's *Otello*.

Rodgers, Joan (*b* Whitehaven, 1959). English soprano. Studied RNCM. Début Aix 1982 (Pamina). London, CG, from 1983: Princess (*L'enfant et les sortilèges*), Zerlina, Servilia. A warm and sympathetic artist, she has also sung Susanna at Gly. (1989), Mozart's Countess (ENO), Cleopatra (*Giulio Cesare*) and Elvira, 1955, for Scottish O, and Iolanta (O North 1993). (R)

Rodolfo. 1. The Count (bs) in whose room Amina sleepwalks in Bellini's *La sonnambula*.

2. Count Walter's son (ten), lover of Luisa, in Verdi's *Luisa Miller*.

3. The Bohemian poet (ten), lover of Mimì, in Puccini's *La bohème*.

Rodrigo. 1. See POSA.

2. A Venetian gentleman (ten) in Rossini's *Otello*.

Rodzinski, Artur (*b* Spalato (Split), 1 Jan. 1892; *d* Boston, 27 Nov. 1958). Polish, later US, conductor. Studied Lvov, Vienna with Marx, Schreker, and Schalk. Début Lvov 1920 (*Ernani*). Cond. Warsaw 1924–8. Moved to US, conducting mostly concerts, but also US prem. of *Lady Macbeth of Mtsensk*, 1935, and Wagner and Richard Strauss in Cleveland and Chicago. Salzburg 1936, Vienna 1937. Florence 1953 (first non-Russian *War and Peace*), Milan, Rome, Naples. Chicago 1958 (*Tristan*). (R)

Roi de Lahore, Le. Opera in 5 acts by Massenet; text by Gallet. Prem. Paris, O, 27 Apr. 1877.

India, 11th cent. Alim (ten), King of Lahore, and his minister Scindia (bar) love Sita (sop). Scindia kills Alim, who is allowed by a god to return as a beggar. Sita kills herself so as to join him in Paradise.

'Roi de Thulé, Le'. The ballad 'Il était un roi de Thulé' sung by Marguerite in Act III of Gounod's *Faust* as she reflects upon her meeting with Faust.

Roi d'Ys, Le (The King of Ys). Opera in 3 acts by Lalo; text by Blau. Prem. Paris, OC, 7 May 1888.

Brittany, mythological times. So as to be reconciled to Karnac (bar), the king of Ys (bs) offers him the hand of his daughter Margared (sop). But she loves Mylio (ten), who loves the king's other daughter Rozenn (sop). Margared refuses Karnac. Mylio defeats Karnac, who conspires with Margared and they open the flood gates and submerge Ys. Mylio kills Karnac, and Margared drowns herself. The waters recede, and the town is saved.

Roi malgré lui, Le (The King despite himself). Opera in 3 acts by Chabrier; text by De Najac and Burani, after Ancelot. Prem. Paris, OC, 18 May 1887.

Poland, 1574. Henri de Valois (bar), about to be crowned King of France, learns from Minka (sop), his betrothed, that there is a plot to kill him. He disguises himself as his friend De Nangis (ten) and joins the plotters. De Nangis comes to the camp and is mistaken for Henri. The plot is foiled, and the lives of both men are spared. Henri is finally crowned King of France and Poland.

Rolfe Johnson, Anthony (*b* Tackley, 5 Nov. 1940). English tenor. Studied London with Keeler. Début London, EOG, 1973 (*Vaudémont, Yolanta*). Gly. 1974–6; Milan, S, 1984, 1986; London, ENO, CG. Salzburg 1987; New York, M, 1994 (Aschenbach); also Hamburg, Edinburgh. A fine performer with a warm, flexible voice and great vocal skill. Roles incl. Ulisse, Jupiter (*Semele*), Jason (*Médée*), Idomeneo, Ferrando, Don Ottavio, Tito, Lensky, Fenton, Aschenbach. (R)

Roller, Alfred (*b* Vienna, 2 Oct. 1864; *d* Vienna, 21 June 1935). Austrian designer. Studied Vienna. Worked with Mahler at the Vienna, H (later S); chief designer 1903–9, 1918–34, also Vienna, B, 1918–34. Designed prems. of *Rosenkavalier* (Dresden 1911) and *Frau ohne Schatten* (Vienna 1919), also many Salzburg prods. His powerful sets, atmospheric and carefully attuned to the music, were highly influential.

romance (Fr., *romance*; Ger., *Romanze*; It., *romanza*). In opera, an aria, generally amorous or soliloquizing, normally intended less for display than aria proper, and thus lacking ornamentation, cadenzas etc. However, the distinction is not precise: Verdi used the terms almost interchangeably. Examples are Pedrillo's 'Im Mohrenland gefangen war' in Mozart's *Entführung*, Matilde's 'Sombres forêts' in Rossini's *Guillaume Tell*, and Radamès's 'Celeste Aida' in Verdi's *Aida*.

Romanelli, Luigi (*b* Rome, 21 July 1751; *d* Milan, 1 Mar. 1839). Italian librettist. At Milan S, for over 30 years from 1799, he was one of the most prolific librettists of his day, producing over 60 texts and collaborating with a large number of composers. He drew on a wide literary and linguistic knowledge to develop a set of operatic conventions which proved flexible to different demands; and many of what were to become standard operatic expressions (and hence clichés) originated with him. Basically a classicist, he also treated the medieval and exotic subjects that were becoming an important part of Romantic feeling. Composers who set his texts included Fioravanti, Mayr, Mercadante, Nicolini, Pacini, and Rossini (*La pietra del paragone*).

Romani, Felice (*b* Genoa, 31 Jan. 1788; *d* Moneglia, 28 Jan. 1865). Italian librettist and critic. His first librettos were written in Milan for Mayr; moving to Turin to take up an editorship, he developed the skills which made him sought after by most important Italian composers: over 100 set his texts. Though he collaborated with Rossini (e.g. *Il turco in Italia*) and once with Verdi (*Un giorno di regno*), his most important work was done with Donizetti and Bellini. Classical in his training and in his sense of balance, he made use of Romantic ideas rather than being possessed by them. However, his quick dramatic instinct for the operatic essence of a subject and the musical elegance of his verse made him an outstanding librettist for Donizetti and little short of an ideal one for Bellini. The haste with which he worked on his numerous commissions meant that his work is not free from cliché, and can lack profundity; but as well as the pastoral idylls of *L'elisir d'amore* and *La sonnambula* he could achieve the nobility of *Anna Bolena* and especially *Norma*.

Romani, Pietro (*b* Rome, 29 May 1791; *d* Florence, 11 Jan. 1877). Italian composer, conductor, and teacher. Studied with Fenaroli; singing-master at the Reale Istituto Musicale; later cond. at Florence. He composed two operas, *Il qui pro quo* (1817) and *Carlo Magno* (1823). He is better known, however, for the aria 'Manca un foglio', which he wrote to replace Dr Bartolo's 'A un dottor della mia sorte' for a performance of *Il barbiere di Siviglia* in Rome in 1816 because it was beyond the capabilities of the singer Paolo Rosich.

romanza. See ROMANCE.

Romanze. See ROMANCE.

Rome (It., Roma). Capital of Italy. The first opera produced in Rome was *Cavalieri's Rappresentazione di anima e di corpo*: based on a religious theme, it is sometimes wrongly described as an oratorio. It introduced the new Florentine *stile rappresentativo, which was further exploited in *Agazzari's pastoral drama *Eumelio*, prem. by pupils of the Seminario Romano early 1606. Works by M. A. Rossi, Vittori, Mazzocchi, and Marazzoli were given in various palaces and noble houses, in many cases circumventing the papal ban on women on the stage which encouraged the rise of the castrato. The hall of the Palazzo Barberini was inaugurated

1632 with *Landi's *Sant'Alessio*, text by Giulio Rospigliosi (later Pope Clement IX); repeated 1634 for the visit of Alexander Charles, brother of Władisław of Poland. Other works given there included Marazzoli's and Mazzocchi's *Chi soffre, speri* (1639), an early comic opera (text by Rospigliosi); the last was Marazzoli's *La vita umana* (1656) in honour of Queen Christina of Sweden, resident in Rome 1654–89 and herself a patron of opera at her palace.

Clement IX authorized the first public opera-house, the T Torre di Nona (or T Tordinona), opened 1670 with Cavalli's *Scipio Affricano*; closed 1674 by Clement's less enthusiastic successors; reopened 1690; demolished by Innocent XII 1697; rebuilt 1733; burnt down 1781; rebuilt 1787; altered 1795 (22 rows of stalls and 174 boxes) and reopened as T Apollo. Staged prems. of Rossini's *Mathilde de Shabran*, cond. Paganini, Verdi's *Trovatore* and *Ballo*, and Donizetti's *Duca d'Alba*; demolished 1889 for a Tiber embankment, the Lungotevere Torre di Nona.

Other Rome theatres included the T Capranica, opened as private theatre 1679 (189 private boxes), publicly 1695. Staged mostly opera seria 1711–47, opera buffa from 1754 till closure 1881. The T delle Dame opened 1717, giving mostly opera seria. The T Valle, opened 1727, was originally a wooden structure in the courtyard of the Palazzo Capranica; gave prems. by Rossini (*Cenerentola*) and Donizetti. The T Argentina was built 1731–2 by the Duke Sforza-Cesarini, with 186 boxes; opened with *Sarro's *Berenice*, prem.d Rossini's *Barbiere* and Verdi's *Due Foscari* and *Battaglia di Legnano*. A leading theatre until the building of the T Costanzi, and continued to give seasons; now a concert hall and playhouse.

The T Costanzi was built by Domenico Costanzi, a rich builder, designed by Achille Sfondrini (cap. 2,293); opened 27 Nov. 1880 with *Semiramide*. The first act was interrupted for the Royal March as King Umberto and the Queen arrived late; the King left early, but the Queen remained. In 1888 the publisher Edoardo Sonzogno became manager, and announced his second competition for a 1-act opera: *Cavalleria rusticana* won, prem.d here 17 May 1890. Also scene of other *Mascagni operas, and prems. of *Tosca* and Zandonai's *Giulietta e Romeo*. Directed by the soprano Emma Carelli, 1911–25. Taken over by the city, enlarged, renovated, reopened as

T Reale dell'O (cap. 1,600) 28 Feb. 1928 with Boito's *Nerone*. Gino Marinuzzi was cond. 1928–34, Serafin 1934–43 (also artistic dir.). Mussolini hoped to challenge the supremacy of Milan S, and enticed singers back from the New York M: Gigli, Lauri-Volpi, Caniglia, Cigna, and Stignani were in the co. Serafin's achievements included cycle of *The Ring* in Italian, largely with Italian singers; also Verdi cycles 1940–1, and a cycle of contemporary opera, including the first Italian performance of *Wozzeck*, given during the German occupation though banned in Germany.

The theatre was renamed T dell'O in 1946, and developed a policy of encouraging new Italian works, welcoming works new to Italy (e.g. *Mathis der Maler*, 1951) and inviting foreign companies. Massimo Bogianckino was dir. 1963–8, when the theatre gave some of the best opera in Italy; Bruno Bartoletti was cond., with visits from Giulini and Gui, and from producers including Visconti. Alberto Antignani, dir. since 1988, has revived works by Spontini and Cherubini, and commissioned new works. The theatre also organized the summer seasons at the 3rd-cent. Terme di Caracalla (cap. 6,000), where large-scale productions used to be staged (from 1937).

'Romerzählung'. Tannhäuser's (ten) long narration of his pilgrimage to Rome in the last act of Wagner's opera.

Ronconi, Giorgio (*b* Milan, 6 Aug. 1810; *d* Madrid, 8 Jan. 1890). Italian baritone. Studied with his father, the tenor **Domenico Ronconi** (1772–1839), who had sung at Milan, S, Vienna, and Munich. Début Pavia 1831 (Valdeburgo, *La straniera*). Successes at Rome, Naples, and Venice, 1832–8; Milan, S, 1839, 1842; London: HM, 1842; CG, regularly 1847–66. Also Paris, I, 1843; St Petersburg 1852–5, 1858–9. Sang until 1870. Taught singing Madrid Cons. from 1874. Despite an early vocal decline, one of the great singers of his age; a superlative melodramatic performer who could 'chill the blood' and 'stop the breath' (Chorley, who 'owed some of his best opera evenings' to him), and led Donizetti to champion the baritone protagonist. Among the roles he created were Cardenio (*Il furioso all'isola di San Domingo*), title-role of *Torquato Tasso*, Enrico (*Il campanello*), Nello (*Pia de' Tolomei*), and a famous Chevreuse (*Maria di Rohan*). One of the earliest Verdi baritones;

created Nabucco, and sang the Doge (*I due Foscari*), Don Carlo (*Ernani*), and Rigoletto.

Rondine, La (The Swallow). Opera in 3 acts by Puccini; text by Adami, translated from a German libretto by A. M. Willner and H. Reichert. Prem. Monte Carlo 27 Mar. 1917.

Paris and the Riviera, 1850s. Magda de Civry (sop), mistress of the banker Rambaldo (bar), is giving a party in her Paris home. The poet-philosopher Prunier (bar, later ten) reads Magda's palm and predicts that, like the swallow, she will fly away from Paris, perhaps to find true love. A young man, Ruggero (ten), son of an old friend of Rambaldo's, arrives and Lisette (sop), Magda's maid, advises him to spend his first evening in Paris at Bullier's café. Magda decides to follow him, in disguise.

At Bullier's, Ruggero sits alone. When Magda arrives, however, he dances with her (though without recognizing her) and the couple are soon drinking a toast to their love. Suddenly Rambaldo storms in and demands that Magda return home. She refuses, saying she has found love.

Ruggero and Magda have been living together on the Riviera. He hopes that they may marry and has written to ask for his parents' consent. Magda admits her past and feels unfit to marry him. She departs for Paris, since Rambaldo has begged her to return, leaving behind the one love of her life.

Ronzi, Giuseppina. See DE BEGNIS, GIUSEPPINA.

Roocroft, Amanda (*b* Coppull, 1966). English soprano. Sang Alcina while still a student at RNCM; professional début WNO 1990 (Sophie). London, CG, 1991 (Pamina); Gly. 1991 (Fiordiligi). An exciting performer with a wide dramatic resource, she sang Ginevra (Handel's *Ariodante*) for London ENO in 1993, Donna Elvira at Gly. 1994, Fiordiligi at London, CG, 1995. (R)

Rooy, Anton van (*b* Rotterdam, 1 Jan. 1870; *d* Munich, 28 Nov. 1932). Dutch baritone. Studied Frankfurt with Stockhausen. Début Bayreuth 1897 (Wotan). Bayreuth until 1902; London, CG, 1898–1913; New York, M, 1898–1908. A sensitive and serious artist, he was impressive as Valentin, Escamillo, Jochanaan; above all as Wotan, Kurwenal, and Sachs. (R)

Rosa, Carl (*b* Hamburg, 22 Mar. 1842; *d* Paris,

30 Apr. 1889). German conductor and impresario, born Karl Rose. Studied Leipzig and Paris. After touring Europe and US as a violinist, met his wife **Euphrosyne Parepa** (*b* Edinburgh, 7 May 1836; *d* London, 21 Jan. 1874) who was a soprano. Studied with her mother Elizabeth Seguin. Début Malta 1852 (Amina). London: L, 1857; CG and HM regularly, 1859–65; CG, 1872. Toured US 1865 with Rosa, whom she married in 1867. They formed the Parepa-Rosa Co., 1867, with her as leading soprano; this had much success in US until 1872. Terminal illness prevented her appearing with it in London, 1873; after her death it was renamed *Carl Rosa OC. Her voice was strong and sweet-toned; roles included Donna Anna, Norma, Elvira (*Puritani*).

Rosalinde. Eisenstein's wife (sop) in J. Strauss's *Die Fledermaus*.

Rosbaud, Hans (*b* Graz, 22 July 1895; *d* Lugano, 29 Dec. 1962). Austrian conductor. Studied Frankfurt with Sekles. After a concert career in which he became a champion of new music, music dir. Münster 1937–41; Strasburg 1941–4. Chief cond. Aix Festival 1947–58. Cond. prem. of *Moses und Aron* Hamburg Radio 1954, then Zurich 1957; cond. *Erwartung* and *Von Heute auf Morgen* Holland Fest. 1958. (R)

Rosen, Albert (*b* Vienna, 14 Feb. 1924). Austrian-born conductor. Studied Prague and Vienna. Principal at Prague, Smetana T, 1964. Particularly effective in the Czech repertory, he has given *Káťa Kabanová* (1972) and *The Devil and Kate* at Wexford, *Jenůfa* at S Francisco (1980), *The Brandenburgers in Bohemia* for Chelsea O. Other repertory incl. *The Gambler* and *Hans Heiling* (Wexford), first British *Christmas Eve* (Rimsky-Korsakov) at London, ENO, 1988.

Rosenberg, Hilding (*b* Bosjökloster, 21 June 1892; *d* Stockholm, 19 May 1985). Swedish composer and conductor. Studied privately, Stockholm with Ellberg and Stenhammar. Worked with theatre dir. Per Lindberg from 1926. Studied conducting with Scherchen; assistant cond. Stockholm, Royal O, 1932–4, chief cond. 1934. His theatrical work led to much incidental music, then to several successful operas, including *Resa till Amerika* (Journey to America, 1932) that to some extent reflect his admiration for Schoenberg.

Later he simplified his style, and *Marionetter* (1939) is more neo-classical.

Rosenkavalier, Der (The Knight of the Rose). Opera in 3 acts by Richard Strauss; text by Hugo von Hofmannsthal. Prem. Dresden, H, 26 Jan. 1911.

After a prelude depicting passionate love-making, the curtain rises on the Marschallin (sop) and her young lover Octavian (sop or mez) in her bedroom. Hearing voices, Octavian hides and disguises himself as a maid. The Marschallin's boorish cousin Baron Ochs (bs) enters; he wants her to nominate a Knight of the Rose to present the traditional silver rose to his intended bride, the very young Sophie von Faninal (sop). Octavian emerges, dressed as 'Mariandel', and is instantly pursued by the lascivious Ochs. After the Marschallin's customary levée, Octavian reappears as himself, only to find her sombrely fatalistic that he will soon leave her. He cannot accept this, but their parting is subdued. Regretting that she did not kiss him goodbye, she sends the silver rose after him.

In the house of the newly rich merchant Faninal (bar), Sophie and her duenna Marianne (sop) are awaiting the presentation of the silver rose. When Octavian arrives with it, Sophie and he are immediately entranced by each other. Ochs follows shortly, repelling Sophie and outraging Octavian with his coarse behaviour. Octavian provokes him to a duel, and wounds him lightly; in the ensuing uproar, Faninal threatens Sophie with a convent if she refuses Ochs. Octavian, wanting her himself, hires Ochs's two intriguers, Annina (sop) and Valzacchi (ten). Later, Ochs receives a note via Annina from 'Mariandel' arranging a rendezvous.

'Mariandel' meets Ochs at an inn, with the intention of discrediting him as Sophie's suitor. The room is fitted with numerous devices enabling Annina and Valzacchi to frighten the Baron with strange apparitions; then Annina appears surrounded by children, pretending to be his deserted wife. Amid increasing tumult, the innkeeper and servants arrive, then the police, then the Faninals, and finally the Marschallin. She dispatches them all (including the discomfited Ochs). Gently yielding Octavian to Sophie, she leaves them alone in their happiness.

Rosina. Dr Bartolo's ward, lover of Count

Almaviva, (sop) in Paisiello's and (mez) in Rossini's *Il barbiere di Siviglia*.

Rosing, Vladimir (*b* St Petersburg, 23 Jan. 1890; *d* Los Angeles, 24 Nov. 1963). Russian, later US, tenor. Studied St Petersburg with Tartakov, Paris with J. De Reszke and Sbriglia. Début St Petersburg 1910 (Lensky). London OH 1915, directing and singing; US 1921; founded American OC, which toured US till 1929. In 1936 organized British Music Drama OC with Albert Coates. Possessed a powerful tone, and was considered by G. B. Shaw the best Russian singer of his time after Shalyapin. Roles included Hermann, Cavaradossi. (R)

Rossellini, Renzo (*b* Rome, 2 Feb. 1908; *d* Monte Carlo, 13 May 1982). Italian composer and critic. Was a pungently conservative critic for *Il messagero*. His operas, which include *La guerra* (1956), *La leggenda del ritorno* (1966), and *La reine morte* (1973), follow the examples of Zandonai, Respighi, and Alfano, and have been enjoyed by audiences content with that tradition.

Rossi, Gaetano (*b* Verona, 18 May 1774; *d* Verona, 25 Jan. 1855). Italian librettist. Worked at different times in Venice and Verona. He wrote over 120 librettos for composers including Carafa, Coccia, Donizetti (e.g. *Linda di Chamounix*), Mayr, Mercadante, Meyerbeer (four, incl. *Il crociato in Egitto*), Nicolai, Pacini, and Rossini (*La cambiale di matrimonio*, *Tancredi*, and *Semiramide*). Though of no great literary ambitions, he drew on a wide range of sources and put into operatic currency many of the themes of Romanticism. His plots were often taken from classical or historical drama, and embraced the fashionable Spanish, Nordic, and British subjects as well as more traditional material; and his techniques contributed to the loosening of set forms characteristic of the reforms of early 19th-cent. opera.

Rossi, Lauro (*b* Macerata, 19 Feb. 1812; *d* Cremona, 5 May 1885). Italian composer. Studied Naples with Zingarelli, Furno, and Crescentini. His first opera was the successful *Costanza e Oringaldo* (1830), followed by the comedy *Le contesse villane* (1831). The further success of three more comedies attracted the attention of Donizetti, who recommended him to the T Valle, Rome (1831–3). *La casa disabitata* (1834) was so successful that Malibran arranged for Barbaia to commission *Amelia* for her; but, through Malibran's insistence on dancing a pas de deux with the ballerina Mathis, the work was hissed. Rossi then toured Mexico, producing *Giovanna Shore* (1836) there; he returned suffering from yellow fever in 1843.

Settling in Milan, he revived *La casa disabitata* in 1844 as *I falsi monetari*, restoring his fame, and confirming this with *Il domino nero* (1849). Head of Milan Cons. 1849–70; head of Naples Cons. to 1880, where he was unpopular. His last opera, *Biorn* (1877), was a version of *Macbeth* transferred to Norway, written for London. Rossi was always more successful in comedy, where he was at his best—lively and inventive if not innovative, and was considered by some to be Donizetti's natural successor.

Rossi, Luigi (*b* Torremaggiore, *c*.1597; *d* Rome, 20 Feb. 1653). Italian composer and singing-teacher. In 1641 entered the service of the Barberini family, thereby participating in Rome's emergent operatic life. His *Il palazzo incantato* (1642), first given in the opera-house at their palace, was one of the most lavish of mid-17th-cent. Italian operas and one of the most highly regarded. In 1646 Rossi followed his patrons in their exile to Paris: here his second opera, *Orfeo*, was given 1647. Regarded as the apotheosis of the spectacular 17th-cent. Roman tradition, it also provided the French with one of their first and most widely discussed experiences of Italian opera.

Rossi, Michelangelo (*b* Genoa, 1601–2; *d* Rome, July 1656). Italian composer. In 1633 his *Erminia sul Giordano* was given at the Barberini theatre: its production was one of the most spectacular events in the history of 17th-cent. Roman opera.

Rossignol, Le. See NIGHTINGALE, THE.

Rossi-Lemeni, Nicola (*b* Istanbul, 6 Nov. 1920; *d* Bloomington, IN, 12 Mar. 1991). Italian bass. Studied with his mother Xenia Makadon. Début Venice, F, 1946 (Varlaam). Milan, S, 1947–60; London, CG, 1952; New York, M, 1953–4; Chicago 1954–6. Also Paris, O; Moscow; Leningrad; etc. Roles included Don Giovanni, Don Basilio (Rossini), Mephistopheles (Gounod and Boito), Philip, Boris, Claggart. Sang in Italian prem. of Gruenberg's *Emperor Jones*, and created Pizzetti's Becket. Though his voice declined early, he was notable for his intelligent and vivid characterizations. (R)

Rossini, Gioachino (b Pesaro, 29 Feb. 1792; d Paris, 13 Nov. 1868). Italian composer. In 1806 he entered the Bologna Cons., and during his student years wrote his first opera, *Demetrio e Polibio* (comp. before 1809), as well as working as a continuo player in local opera-houses. His first professional work for the stage was *La cambiale di matrimonio* (1810), which already reveals characteristics of wit and sentiment that were to mark his work. Two semiseria works, *L'equivoco stravagante* (1811) and *L'inganno felice* (1812), show the emergent range and versatility of his work. The latter was a particularly popular and artistic success, more so than the biblical *Ciro in Babilonia* (1812), a somewhat static work whose best music is to be found in the choruses, or the nimbly farcical *La scala di seta* (1812).

Further success came with *La pietra del paragone* (1812), whose warm lyrical content, together with a new feeling for nature, at the service of an ingenious and amusing plot, greatly appealed to a public that had by now learnt to relish his verve and melodic grace. Four works for Venice followed between Nov. 1812 and May 1813: *L'occasione fa il ladro*, *Il signor Bruschino*, *Tancredi*, and *L'italiana in Algeri*. *Tancredi* first made his name known outside Italy, partly through the wide popularity of 'Di tanti palpiti', but more deservedly for the manner in which he was able to give heroic virtues a new sensibility and hence accessibility to contemporary audiences. There is also a fresh approach to the handling of the orchestra, especially in the use of woodwind to add expressiveness to the vocal line. In his first comic masterpiece, *L'italiana in Algeri* (1813), Rossini displays his assurance not only in the music's lyrical eloquence but in the virtuosity with which he both uses and disturbs convention to comic effect. Having mastered the conventions inherited from an earlier generation, and transformed them, he was able to establish and further develop a range of formal procedures which subsequently became known as the Code Rossini. The modest *Aureliano in Palmira* (1813) had little success and *Il turco in Italia* (1814), his first collaboration with Romani, at first suffered from comparison with *L'italiana in Algeri*. *Sigismondo* (1814), by contrast, was a failure, and remains an improbable candidate for successful revival.

Rossini was now engaged by *Barbaia as music dir. of both the T San Carlo and the T del Fondo in Naples. His first opera to be written for Naples was the dramatically powerful *Elisabetta, regina d'Inghilterra* (1815), in which he drew on the T San Carlo's superb roster of singers. The next opera was the slight, but sharp and consciously Neapolitan, *La gazzetta* (1816), and this was followed by *Otello*. A public in 1816 unfamiliar with Shakespeare was disturbed by the latter's tragic ending, which was replaced for the Rome revival. With *Il barbiere di Siviglia* (1816), Rossini achieved his most enduring masterpiece. It marks a radical break with a past symbolized by the work of Paisiello, whose own setting of Beaumarchais is decisively outmanœuvred, though at its stormy prem. it was unfavourably compared with the earlier work. *La Cenerentola* (1817) shows a Rossini capable of genuine tenderness and pathos, as well as fine writing for the coloratura mezzo-soprano voice of which he was so fond. A degree of latent Romanticism again emerges both in the powerful and dramatically far-flung melodrama *La gazza ladra* (1817), and in the exotic and, for Rossini, remarkably sensuous score of *Armida* (1817). In both works, there is an increased range and sophistication in the use of orchestral colour, something that preoccupied Rossini in his later Naples period.

After the somewhat formal and monochrome *Adelaide di Borgogna* (1817), he completed the masterly *Mosè in Egitto* (1818), famous for Moses's Prayer in Act III, and memorable for the opening 'Scene of the Shadows', a piece of sustained music drama that makes the significant advance of dispensing entirely with the use of a curtain-raising overture. There followed the 1-act farce *Adina* (1818), and two further Naples works, *Riccardo e Zoraide* (1818) and *Ermione* (1819). *Eduardo e Cristina* (1819), written for Venice, is no more than a hastily cobbled together pasticcio.

Rossini's last six Italian operas exhibit no less variety. *La donna del lago* (1819) is the first major opera to exploit Europe's growing fascination with Scott, though *Maometto II* (1820) is a more consistently and powerfully sustained musical structure, imposingly written for soloists, chorus, and orchestra. Though startlingly difficult to sing, *Bianca e Faliero* (1819) presents a striking picture of internecine strife within war-threatened Venice, Rossini directing the fierce coloratura-writing towards the depiction of states of emotional excess. There is also a good deal of emotional belligerence in *Matilde di Shabran* (1821), Rossini's final essay in the semiseria genre and a rumbustiously diverting piece. His last Neapolitan opera, *Zelmira* (1822), suffers from a dull libretto by Tottola, set in ancient Greece and drawing from the composer somewhat formal, only occasionally exciting, music. Rossini's Italian career did, none the less, reach a fitting climax with *Semiramide* (1823), one of his longest and most ambitious works.

He was by now the most popular and prolific composer of his day, having in the ten years since *Tancredi* composed some 25 operas. Stendhal declared, 'The glory of the man is only limited by the limits of civilization itself, and he is not yet 32.' After visits to Vienna, where he met Beethoven, and London, where he conducted and sang in concerts with his wife, Isabella *Colbran, he settled in Paris as director of the Théâtre Italien. Under his influence, it underwent something of a renaissance. He retained Paer as maestro al cembalo, engaged the young Hérold as chorus-master, and introduced Meyerbeer to Paris with *I crociato in Egitto*. For the extravagant coronation of Charles X in 1825 he wrote for a star-studded cast of singers a long, sophisticated, and often brilliantly inventive entertainment, *Il viaggio a Reims* (1825). Commissioned by the French government to write a number of comic and serious operas for the Opéra, he bode his time, familiarizing himself with French prosody and training a hand-picked group of singers in the Italian bel canto manner. Initially, he provided theatrically elaborate revisions of two Neapolitan works, *Maometto II* and *Mosè in Egitto*, whose political overtones were a resonance of the interest of a public inflamed by news of the Greek War of Independence as surely as they met a new public taste for opera as spectacle. His first new work (though one that draws on *Il viaggio a Reims*) was *Le Comte Ory* (1828), a piece unique in its warmth, sensuous elegance, and good humour. It is also remarkable for the irony that chastens even the most tender moments, lending them a touch of wryness. His culminating masterpiece was to be one of the masterpieces of French Grand Opera, *Guillaume Tell* (1829). Though the scene setting in the first act is rather leisurely, and there are empty pages to be found in its great length, Rossini's sense of picturesque colour

reaches new heights in this score. This was Rossini's last stage work, though he lived for another 39 years, composing two religious works and a host of engaging trifles (the so-called *péchés de vieillesse*, or Sins of Old Age).

Rostropovich, Mstislav (*b* Baku, 27 Mar. 1927). Russian conductor and cellist. Began his career as a cellist 1942 and has conducted from 1968 (*Eugene Onegin* at the Bolshoy). US opera début S Francisco 1975 (*Queen of Spades*); Washington DC 1986 (*The Tsar's Bride*). Particularly distinguished in the modern repertory, he has led several prems.: Schnittke's *Life With an Idiot* (1992) and *Gesualdo* (1995), Gubaydulina's opera-oratorio *The Age of Aquarius*. Gave Prokofiev's *Duenna* at London, RAM, 1991. (R)

Roswaenge, Helge (*b* Copenhagen, 29 Aug. 1897; *d* Munich, 19 June 1972). Danish tenor. Début Neustrelitz 1921 (Don José). Berlin, S, 1929–45, 1949; Bayreuth, 1934, 1936; London, CG, 1938; Salzburg 1933–9; Vienna, S, 1936–58. Also Paris, O; Milan, S; etc. Large repertory included Belmonte, Tamino, Florestan, Huon, Duke of Mantua, Radamès, Parsifal, Calaf. A highly regarded singer, he possessed a warm, ringing tone and glorious top notes. (R)

Rota, Nino (*b* Milan, 3 Dec. 1911; *d* Rome, 10 Apr. 1979). Italian composer. Studied Milan with Orefice, Rome with Pizzetti and Casella. Held teaching posts in Taranto and Bari; dir., Bari Cons., from 1950. Composed much music for the cinema and radio. His operas are unabashedly tuneful and direct in appeal, and he won a particularly wide following with *Il cappello di paglia di Firenze* (A Florentine Straw Hat, comp. 1946) and *La visita meravigliosa* (The Visitation, 1970).

Rothenberger, Anneliese (*b* Mannheim, 19 June 1924). German soprano. Studied Mannheim with Müller. Début Koblenz 1943 (small roles). Hamburg 1946–56; Munich from 1955; Vienna from 1957; Salzburg 1954, 1957; Gly. 1959–60; New York, M, 1960–5. Roles incl. Ilia, Constanze, Susanna, Pamina, Sophie, Zdenka, Lulu; created Sutermeister's Madame Bovary, among other parts. An attractive and excellent actress, with a firm, light tone. (R)

Rothmüller, Marko (*b* Trnjani, 31 Dec. 1908; *d* Bloomington, IN, 20 Jan. 1993). Croatian baritone. Studied Zagreb, Vienna with

Weiss and Steiner (composition with Berg). Début Hamburg 1932 (Ottokar). Zurich 1935–47; London, CG, 1939, 1947–52; Vienna 1946–9; Gly. 1949–55; New York: CO, 1948, M, 1958–61, 1964–5. A well-rounded and intelligent artist with a warm, flexible voice. His repertory included Don Giovanni, Papageno, Rigoletto, Iago (Verdi), Kurwenal, Amfortas, Prince Igor, Tomsky, Doktor (*Wozzeck*); first Truchsess (*Mathis der Maler*). (R)

Rousseau, Jean-Jacques (*b* Geneva, 28 June 1712; *d* Ermenonville, 2 July 1778). Swiss philosopher, composer, author, and writer on music. Wrote his first opera, *Les muses galantes* (1745), in imitation of *Les Indes galantes* of Rameau, who had a poor regard for it. His most famous composition was *Le devin du village* (1752), where the use of simple melodies and accompaniments (all that Rousseau was really capable of) well expressed the victory of plain rustic virtue over aristocratic corruption. Siding with the Italians in the *Guerre des Bouffons, he published his important *Lettre sur la musique française* (1753), expounding his hostility to French opera and taking a strong stand for melody as a form of heightened speech. *Pygmalion* (1770) uses orchestral interludes between actual speech, and prompted a number of imitations. He also left parts of another opera, *Daphnis et Chloé* (1779), and six new arias for *Le devin*.

Roussel, Albert (*b* Tourcoing, 5 Apr. 1869; *d* Royan, 23 Aug. 1937). French composer. After an early naval career, studied music Paris 1894 with Gigout. His major stage work is the opéra-ballet *Padmâvatî* (1923), based on an Indian legend. In it he affirms his belief that opera was exhausted and that a renewed impulse could be found in the 17th- and 18th-cent. French tradition of the opéra-ballet. Accordingly he gives choruses, dances, and mime an integral rather than decorative role, finding thereby opportunity for the symphonic development of his musical ideas. The subject further allows him a sense of distance—of masking and ritualizing emotion—which suited his temperament and also his musical nature in his fondness for 'exotic' scales and rhythms. In his *conte lyrique*, *La naissance de la lyre* (1925), the element of ritual dance is turned to a classical legend, with the mask consciously, and by virtue of the subject, Apollonian. These qualities hardly equipped him for the comically racy intrigues of the plot of *Le testament de la tante Caroline* (1936).

Rousselière, Charles (*b* Saint-Nazaire, 17 Jan. 1875; *d* Joué-lès-Tours, 11 May 1950). French tenor. Studied Paris with Vaguet. Début Paris, O, 1900 (Saint-Saëns's Samson). Paris, O, until 1912; Monte Carlo 1905–14; New York, M, 1906–7; Milan, S, 1909; Buenos Aires, C, 1910. Roles included Roméo, Manrico, Siegmund, Parsifal; created leading roles in operas by Mascagni (*Amica*), Fauré (*Pénélope*), Charpentier (*Julien*). (R)

Royal Hunt and Storm. The name given by Berlioz to the choral and orchestral pantomime at the start of Act IV of his *Les Troyens* in which Dido and Aeneas take refuge in a cave from a storm while out hunting, and there consummate their love.

Royal Italian Opera. The name adopted by the annual subscription series of Italian opera given in London during the 19th cent.; these involved a variety of companies and theatres, including HM, CG, L and DL.

Royal Opera House. See COVENT GARDEN.

Rozkošný, Josef (*b* Prague, 21 Sept. 1833; *d* Prague, 3 June 1913). Czech composer and pianist. Studied Prague with Kittl. Became a banker, but was a significant figure in Prague cultural life, including as choral director. His first opera, *Mikuláš* (1870), was to a text by Smetana's librettist Karel Sabina, and shows the influence of Smetana (with whom he had an equivocal relationship). Few of the remainder had any sucess, apart from the Romantic *Svatojanské proudy* (1871), one of the few fairy-tale operas in a genre later to be distinguished by Dvořák, and *Stoja* (1894), the first Czech verismo opera.

rubato (It.: 'robbed'). The art (sometimes the abuse) of hurrying or slowing the pace within a given tempo in varying degrees for expressive effect.

Rubini, Giovanni Battista (*b* Romano, 7 Apr. 1794; *d* Romano, 3 Mar. 1854). Italian tenor. Studied Bergamo with Rosio, later Naples with Nozzari. Début Pavia 1814 (Generali's *Lagrime di una vedova*). Naples 1816–29; Milan, S, 1818, 1825–31; Paris, I, 1825, 1831–43; London, H (later HM), 1831–43; St Petersburg 1843, 1844. A supreme singer, celebrated in Mozart and Rossini, whose vocal gifts also influenced Italian Romanticism through Bellini, for whom he created roles in *Bianca e Gernando, Il pirata* (Gualtiero, which Tamburini said 'placed him above all known tenors'), *La sonnambula* (Elvino), and *I Puritani* (Arturo); and through Donizetti, for whom he created seven roles, most importantly Percy (*Anna Bolena*) and Fernando (*Marin Faliero*). Also admired by Glinka, Chopin, Liszt (with whom he sang on tour), and Rubinstein. Though lacking looks and dramatic presence, he was so brilliant, committed, and intense a performer that he 'entirely enchanted' his hearers (Chorley, who thought him a 'genius'). His range was high, his voice sweet, powerful, flexible, and capable of subtle gradations of colour and volume. He was also famous for his expressive musical sob. He retired in 1845, later going to sing to the dying Donizetti, who was unable to respond.

Rubinstein, Anton (*b* Vikhvatinets, 28 Nov. 1829; *d* Peterhof, 20 Nov. 1894). Russian composer and pianist. Studied with Villoing, later Berlin with Dehn. His operas show his concern for developing various Russian national characteristics, but suffer from a certain emotional coolness allied to a self-defeating fluency. When his first two nationalist operas, *Dmitry Donskoy* (1852) and *The Siberian Huntsmen* (1854), both failed, he attacked the whole concept of Russian opera and the amateur condition of Russian composers (he founded the Russian Musical Society, 1859, and the St Petersburg Cons., 1862). Even disregarding his own German-Jewish origins, this served to place him in the Westernizer camp against the more Slavophile Stasov and the 'Mighty Handful'. His most successful opera, *The Demon* (1875), is strongly influenced by French music, and its harmonic idiom is not recognizably Russian, though his lyrical vocal writing was of a quality to influence Tchaikovsky (who greatly feared and admired him). Nevertheless, it has some strongly written scenes, and the title-role was for many years regarded as one of the great Russian bass parts. The most successful of his other operas was *The Merchant Kalashnikov* (1880). He later turned to comedy and sacred opera.

Rudel, Julius (*b* Vienna, 6 Mar. 1921). Austrian, later US, conductor. Studied Vienna and New York. New York, CC: répétiteur 1943, cond. 1944, music dir. 1957–79. Pursued an enterprising policy including seasons devoted to US opera. Music dir. Kennedy Center, Washington, DC, 1971–6 (incl. prem. of Ginastera's *Bomarzo*, 1967). Dir. Caramoor

Fest. 1963–76. Paris, O, 1972. New York, M, from 1978. Chicago 1990 (*Hamlet*); Nice 1992 (*Don Carlo*). (R)

Ruffo, Titta (*b* Pisa, 9 June 1877; *d* Florence, 5 July 1953). Italian baritone. Studied Rome with Persichini, Milan with Casini. Début Rome, T Costanzi, 1898 (Herald, *Lohengrin*). London, CG, 1903; Chicago, frequently, 1912–26; New York, M, 1922–9. Also Buenos Aires; Milan, S; and the major European opera-houses. Gifted with an extraordinarily noble, ringing, and extensive baritone (described by both Serafin and De Luca as 'a miracle'), he was impressive, as a singer, for his compelling vigour and incisiveness; his critics, however, found him too aggressive. Famous for his Figaro (Rossini), Rigoletto, Don Carlos (*Ernani*), Scarpia, Hamlet, Leoncavallo's Tonio and Cascart (*Zazà*). (R)

Runnicles, Donald (*b* Edinburgh, 16 Nov. 1954). Scottish conductor. Studied Edinburgh and London. Début Mannheim 1980 (*Hoffmann*). Chief cond. at Mannheim 1984–7. New York, M, 1988 (*Lulu*). Music dir. at S Francisco 1990 (*Ring*). Successful in a wide repertory, he has led *Prince Igor* at Vienna, S; *Don Giovanni* at Gly. (1991); *Tannhäuser* at Bayreuth (1993). (R)

Rusalka. In Slavonic mythology, the water spirit which a drowned girl became. Generally, in northern lands the rusalki were less benign than in the south, where they would bewitch the passer-by and where death in their arms was an agreeable translation into a new world. The legend overlaps with that of *Undine and the *Donauweibchen.

  1. Opera in 4 acts by Dargomyzhsky; text by composer, after Pushkin's dramatic poem (1832). Prem. St Petersburg, Circus T, 16 May 1856.

Natasha (sop), daughter of a miller (bs), is betrayed by the Prince (ten) and drowns herself in the mill-stream. She becomes a Rusalka who lures men to their death. When the Prince marries, he hears her cries every time he approaches his bride. Wandering by the stream, he meets a child who reveals herself as his daughter. The miller hurls the Prince into the stream, where he joins Natasha and their child.

  2. Opera in 3 acts by Dvořák; text by Jaroslav Kvapil, based largely on Fouqué's *Undine*, with additions from Hans Andersen's *The Little Mermaid* and suggestions from Gerhard

Hauptmann's *Die versunkene Glocke*. Prem. Prague, N, 31 Mar. 1901.

The water spirit Rusalka (sop) falls in love with the Prince (ten), and with the help of the witch Ježibaba (mez) becomes human so as to marry him. But she must remain silent, and when the Prince tires of her and is unfaithful, a condition of her becoming human is violated and she dies together with the remorseful Prince.

Ruslan and Lyudmila (Russ., *Ruslan i Lyudmila*). Opera in 5 acts by Glinka; text by V. Shirkov, K. Bakhturin, and others, after Pushkin's poem (1820). Prem. St Petersburg, B, 9 Dec. 1842. Lyudmila (sop) disappears from a feast for her three suitors, the knight Ruslan (bar), the poet Prince Ratmir (con), and Farlaf (bs), a cowardly warrior. Her father Svyetozar (bs) promises her to the one who can find her. Ruslan learns that she has been stolen by the dwarf Chernomor (silent), and is warned by the Finn (ten) against the wicked fairy Naina (mez), who advises Farlaf to wait until Ruslan has rescued Lyudmila, and then abduct her. Ruslan meets a gigantic head on a battlefield, and subduing it, discovers a magic sword. In Naina's palace, Ruslan is saved from her sirens by the Finn. He comes to Chernomor's castle, and defeats the dwarf, who has put Lyudmila into a trance. Ruslan is only able to awaken her with the aid of a magic ring from the Finn.

Russia. Though various theatrical entertainments with songs and dances were given in the 17th cent., no true operatic influence was felt until the opening up of Russia to the West by Peter the Great (d 1725). Under the Empress Anna (reigned 1730–40), the first Italian opera troupes to arrive were those of Giovanni Ristori and Johann Keyser, and the first opera performed in Russia was the former's *Calandro* (Moscow 1731). Other Italian companies came in 1733 and 1734, and the excellent company under Francesco *Araia in 1736. His *La forza dell'amore e dell'odio* (in the 'new St Petersburg Imperial T', 1736) was a great success, and two more works followed. German Singspiel probably made its first appearance in Russia in 1740.

The Empress Elizabeth (reigned 1741–61), with her love of Italy, further encouraged opera, which soon began to put down Russian roots. The first opera in Russian was *Tsefal i Prokris* (Cephalus and Procris, 1755), an opera seria by Araia; this was followed,

also to a libretto by Sumarokov, by Raupach's *Altsesta* (Alceste, 1858). Peter III (reigned 1762) sent for Galuppi and Tartini, perhaps under the influence of his wife and successor Catherine the Great (reigned 1762–96), who encouraged French opéra-comique: the invitation to Italy, renewed by her, continued to support the century-long dynasty of foreign, principally Italian, composers in Russia: Araia, 1735–40, 1742–59, 1762; the German Raupach, 1755–62; G. B. Locatelli, 1757–62; Manfredini, 1758–69; Galuppi, 1765–8; Traetta, 1768–75; Paisiello, 1776–83; Sarti, 1784–6, 1792–6; Cimarosa, 1787–91; the Spaniard Martín y Soler, 1788–94; and Cavos, 1798–1840. French opéra-comique was first staged in the 1750s, English opera (Dibdin's *The Padlock*) in 1771. The late 18th cent. also saw the building of theatres in the provinces, and visits from companies whose repertories included opera.

Native Russian opera was slow to emerge with any true identity. An early piece was *Tanyusha* (1756), set by the actor and theatre director Fyodor Volkov (1729–63), who had also translated operas; but probably a more nearly operatic piece was *Anyuta* (1772: music lost, perhaps by Vasily *Pashkevich, c.1742–97). The first whose music has survived is *Pererozhdeniye* (Rebirth, 1777), by Dementy Zorin. This, and surviving librettos, indicate opéra-comique with spoken dialogue as the example, with ballad opera as the immediate model. The first significant Russian operas are *Melnik koldun* (The Miller-Magician) (1779) by Mikhail Sokolovsky (fl. 1750–80) (using folk-songs), and three by Pashkevich, *Neschastye ot karety* (Misfortune from Owning a Carriage, 1779), *Skupoy* (The Miser, 1781), and *Sankpeterburgsky gostiny dvor* (The St Petersburg Bazaar, 1782) (using town songs). Another important work of the period was *Sbitenshchik* (The Sbiten [a drink] Seller, 1784), by the Frenchman Antoine Bullant (?1750–1821).

Pashkevich's *Fevey* (1786) was to a text at least in part by Catherine herself. As an admirer of the *Encyclopédistes*, she believed in opera's role as social commentary; and her librettos include the patriotic, anti-Turkish *Nachalnoye upravleniye Olega* (The Early Reign of Oleg, music by Pashkevich, Canobbio, and Sarti, 1790), also domestic homily and satire, as in her attack on Gustav III during the Swedish war, *Gore Bogatyr Kosometovich* (The Unfortunate Hero Kosometovich, music by Martín y Soler, 1789). Other successful works were by Mathias Stabinger (c.1750–c.1815), (Shchastlivaya Tonya (Happy Tonya) and Baba Yaga, both 1786), and especially by *Fomin and Bortnyansky. Paul I severely censored and restricted opera, but with Alexander I's accession in 1801 interest was renewed, in a French direction. A fashion for German fairy opera followed, and successful examples were written by Stepan Davydov (1777–1825), part-composer of the popular Lesta (from 1803), by Alexander Titov (1769–1827) (at least 13), and especially by Caterino *Cavos and Alexey *Verstovsky. The influential Cavos's substantial reorganizations included the development of a native singing tradition.

It is with *Glinka that Russian opera attains maturity. In Zhizn za tsarya (A Life for the Tsar, 1836) and Ruslan i Lyudmila he found an authentic Russian voice that proved to be enduringly influential, the former work setting the example of the national epic, the latter that of the fantastic fairy-tale. After Alexander II's accession in 1855, steps were taken to improve the training of composers and singers, with the foundation of the conservatories of St Petersburg (1862) and Moscow (1864); and the strong influence of their respective founders, the brothers Anton and Nikolay *Rubinstein, gave a lead to such diverse composers as the 'Westernizers' *Serov and *Tchaikovsky, and the 'Slavophile' *Dargomyzhsky and the group dubbed by the critic Vladimir Stasov the moguchaya kuchka ('mighty handful'), Balakirev, *Musorgsky, *Rimsky-Korsakov, *Borodin, and *Cui. An important development was the breaking of the monopoly of the Imperial Theatres in 1882, allowing the growth of the enterprising private opera-companies such as those of Mitrofan Belyayev (1836–1904), Savva Mamontov (1841–1918), and Sergey *Zimin. After this great flowering of Russian opera, and of a school of singers to meet and encourage its standards, there was a brief recession in the early 20th cent. Interest turned elsewhere, despite the contributions of *Rakhmaninov, *Arensky, Grechaninov, Rebikov, and others. The line of lyrical, Italian-inspired opera was consciously reinvoked, and closed, by *Stravinsky with Mavra (1922).

After the 1917 Revolution, opera was threatened by Lenin's doubts about its importance in the social priorities, and by its aristocratic associations; but largely through the able arguments of the critic Boris Asafyev, and with the support of the arts commissar Anatoly Lunacharsky, opera was able to be viewed as based on national music and folk images, thus forming a foundation for the development of a Soviet operatic style. A reluctance to take opera seriously on the part of producers was overcome, and men of the stature of *Stanislavsky, *Nemirovich-Danchenko, Kommisarzhevsky, and Meyerhold were persuaded to apply their talents to opera. Fruitful contact between the Moscow Arts T and the Bolshoy led to the evolution of true actor-singers, though both Stanislavsky and Nemirovich-Danchenko preferred to work in their own studios. New life was infused into old productions, with more attention given to intelligent acting, less to vocal display; and the more ableminded singers, including Shalyapin and Ershov, were encouraged to produce operas in which they appeared. Sometimes, for lack of original Revolutionary operas, new librettos were provided for old works (Les Huguenots became The Decembrists). New Western operas were also introduced, including works by Schreker and Berg (Wozzeck, Leningrad 1927). The first attempts at genuinely modern Soviet opera, vigorously advocated by Asafyev, were Za krasny Petrograd (For Red Petrograd) by Arseny Gladkovsky and E. Prussak, Andrey Pashchenko's Orliny bunt (Eagles in Revolt), and Vasily Zolotarev's Dekabristi (The Decembrists) (all 1925).

The quarrel between restraint and adventure came to a head, inevitably, not over the many mediocre works that followed but over a major talent. *Shostakovich's Nos (The Nose, 1930) aroused both enthusiasm and opposition; and the opposition intensified with Ledy Macbeth Mtsenskovo uyezda (The Lady Macbeth of Mtsensk District, 1934). This precipitated a notorious Pravda article, 'Chaos instead of Music' ('Sumbur vmesto muzyky') (28 Jan. 1936), and the establishment of a hard, certainly Stalin-inspired, line which preferred Dzerzhinsky's Tikhy Don (The Quiet Don, 1935). Even *Prokofiev, though interested in working for Soviet opera, found it virtually impossible to satisfy the new demands, and his operas were misunderstood by officials; the willingness of lesser composers to toe the line assured their works of careers, but usually short ones. Great difficulties confronted composers anxious to reconcile an ideology they often did not share with their artistic integrity. Initial success was sometimes followed by violent rejection, most notoriously with *Velikaya druzhba* (The Great Friendship, 1947) by Vano Muradeli (1907–70). The nadir of state intervention was reached at the notorious 1948 congress (repudiated ten years later) at which leading Soviet composers were abused by the minister Andrey Zhdanov.

Since then there has been cautious evolution; but despite the enthusiasm for opera in Russia, the excellence of the singers' training, and the generous facilities available, few modern Russian operas, apart from those by Prokofiev and Shostakovich, have found a secure place in world repertories. Among those wartime and post-war composers most successful within Russia are Tikhon Khrennikov (*b* 1913), for long secretary of the Composers' Union, with *V buryu* (Into the Storm, 1939), Vissarion Shebalin (1910–63) with *Ukroshcheniye stroptivoy* (The Taming of the Shrew, 1957), Dmitry Kabalevsky (1904–87) with *Colas Breugnon* (1938), and Yury Shaporin (1887–1966) with *Dekabristy* (The Decembrists, 1953). The 'thaw' in Khrushchev's régime (1953–64) allowed some avant-garde productions but was too brief to give new composers serious encouragement; and even a composer with adventurous ideas such as Rodion Shchedrin (*b* 1932) settled for convention in *Mertviye dushi* (Dead Souls, 1977). With the reforms of Gorbachev in the interests of *glasnost* ('openness'), then of Yeltsin, new ideas and enterprises have developed, though the situation remains uncertain. Composers to benefit from access to wider performance include Alfred *Schnittke, the Tatar Sofia Gubaydulina (*b* 1931, with *The Age of Aquarius*) and Dmitry *Smirnov.

The principal opera-houses of Russia are in Chelyabinsk (Glinka O and Ballet T, opened 1956 (cap. 1205)); Gorky (Nizhny Novgorod) (Pushkin O and Ballet T, opened 1935 (cap. 1200); Kuybyshev (O and Ballet T, opened 1931); *St Petersburg; *Moscow; Novosibirsk (Novonikolayevsk) (O and Ballet T opened 1931); Perm (first season, 1894; Tchaikovsky O and Ballet T, opened 1920); Saratov (opera given from 1860s); Chernyshevsky (O and Ballet T, opened 1962 (cap. 1200); and Ekaterinburg (opera given from 1879; Lunacharsky O and Ballet T opened 1924 (cap. 1200). An important and valuable feature of post-Revolutionary Russia has been the operatic encouragement given to the republics that became part of the USSR, later the CIS.

Ruthven. Lord Ruthven (bar), the eponymous vampire in Marschner's *Der Vampyr.*

Ruzitska, József (*b* ?Pápa, *c.*1775; *d* ?, after 1823). Hungarian composer and conductor. Little is known of his life, except for records of theatrical appointments at Nagyvárad (1821) and Kolozsvár (1822), where he was Kapellmeister of the Hungarian theatre. He wrote three stage works: *Arany idők* (Golden Ages, 1821); *Béla futása* (Béla's Escape, 1822) and *Kemény Simon avagy dicsőség házáért meghalni* (Simon Kemény, or It is Glorious to Die for the Fatherland, 1822). The latter, which combines folk-music elements with traditional operatic procedures, is one of the earliest attempts at a national style of Hungarian opera.

Rysanek, Leonie (*b* Vienna, 12 Nov. 1926). Austrian soprano. Studied Vienna with Jerger, later Grossmann. Début Innsbruck 1949 (Agathe). Bayreuth regularly 1951–82; Munich from 1952; London, CG, 1953–5, 1959, 1963; New York, M, 1959–96. Also Paris, O; Berlin, SO; Salzburg; etc. Particularly effective, with her dramatic talent and strong, opulent tone, as Sieglinde, Kundry, Salome, Danae, Chrysothemis, Lady Macbeth, Empress (*Die Frau ohne Schatten*). Later career as mezzo, e.g. Kabanicha, Klytemnästra, Kostelnička, with great success. (R)

S

Sabata, Victor de. See DE SABATA, VICTOR.

Sabbatini, Giuseppe (*b* Rome, 11 May 1957). Italian tenor. Studied Accademia di S Cecilia, Rome. Début Spoleto 1987 (Edgardo). A well-placed voice and dignified stage-bearing have made him successful in such roles as Rodolfo, Werther, and Alfredo throughout Europe and in Chicago. London, CG, from 1990 (Duke of Mantua, Arturo, Lensky). (R)

Sacchini, Antonio (*b* Florence, 14 June 1730; *d* Paris, 6 Oct. 1786). Italian composer. Studied Naples with Durante, where his intermezzos *Fra Donato* (1756) and *Il giocatore* (1757) brought him to early attention. Taught Naples (Cons. S Maria di Loreto) 1756–62; dir. of the Cons. dell'Ospedaletto, Venice 1768–72. During this time he established a glowing reputation as an opera composer, above all with *L'Olimpiade* (1763) and *Il finto pazzo per amore* (The Lover Feigned Madman, 1765), both in Italy and elsewhere. In 1772–81 he worked in London, where his operas were well received; because of debt he fled to Paris in 1781, where he was quickly drawn into the controversy between Gluck and Piccinni. Though at first hailed as a new weapon for the Italian faction, fierce rivalry soon developed between him and Piccinni. Neither *Renaud* (1783) nor *Chimène* (1783), were well received, nor was *Dardanus*, in which he tried more consciously to imitate the style of the tragédie lyrique. Only after the posthumous performance of *Œdipe à Colone* (1786), a work which owes much to Gluck's example, were his talents recognized by the French public.

As a student, Sacchini was regarded by Durante as Italy's brightest operatic hope, a judgement which was borne out in part by his later popularity. But though his opere serie represent the culmination of the 18th-cent. tradition, they largely suffer from the same dramatic weaknesses as those of his contemporaries. The height of his art is seen in the French operas, particularly *Œdipe*, where skilful use of the chorus and a more flexible approach to the aria permit more satisfactory reconciliation of dramatic and musical aims.

Sachs, Hans (*b* Nuremberg, 5 Nov. 1494; *d* Nuremberg, 19 Jan. 1576). Poet and Mastersinger. He is the composer of 13 *Meistertöne* and the author of several thousand poems, prose dialogues, comedies, and tragedies. His poem *Die Wittenbergisch Nachtigall* hailing Luther and the Reformation, and beginning 'Wach auff! es nahent gen dem tag', is set in part by Wagner as a salute to Sachs himself in *Die Meistersinger von Nürnberg* (1868). Here Sachs appears as the wise old cobbler-poet (bs-bar). He is also, as a younger man, the hero of Lortzing's *Hans Sachs* (1840), which is based on the Deinhardstein play drawn on by Wagner. Also Singspiel by Gyrowetz, *Hans Sachs im vorgerückten Alter* (1834), and three *Hans-Sachs Spiele* by Behrend (1949).

Sack, Erna (*b* Berlin, 6 Feb. 1898; *d* Wiesbaden, 2 Mar. 1972). German soprano. Studied Berlin with Daniel. Début Berlin, SO, 1925 (as contralto). Coloratura soprano from 1930. Berlin, S, 1933; London, CG, 1936; Chicago 1937. Also Milan, S; Paris, O; and world-wide tours. Roles included Rosina, Lucia, first Isotta (*Die schweigsame Frau*). Had a voice of phenomenal range, for which Strauss wrote several cadenzas in Zerbinetta's aria. (R)

Sacrati, Francesco (*b* Parma, *bapt.* 17 Sept. 1605; *d* ?Modena, 20 May 1650). Italian composer. Worked in Venice from *c*.1640, where he composed five operas. 1648 moved to Bologna; 1649 maestro di cappella Modena Cathedral.

The rediscovery of Sacrati's *La finta pazza* (The Feigned Madwoman) brought to light one of the earliest works in the Venetian repertory, in which the style of Cavalli and Cesti is to some extent prefigured. Performed in Paris 1645, it was one of the first Italian operas to be seen in France. A case has been argued, with some conviction, that Sacrati was responsible for much of the *Poppea* score usually attributed to Monteverdi.

Sadko. Opera-legend in 7 scenes by Rimsky-Korsakov; text by composer and V. I. Belsky, after folk legends. Prem. Moscow, private theatre, by Solodovnikov Co., 7 Jan. 1898.

The wanderings of the minstrel Sadko

(ten) bring him to Volkhova (sop), Princess of the Sea, who promises that his net will be filled with golden fish. He wages his head against the wealth of the citizens of Novgorod that he can catch the golden fish; he succeeds, and sets sail with some merchants, the Viking (bs), the Indian (ten), and the Venetian (bar), to find their fortunes, leaving behind his wife Lyubava (mez).

Returning successfully 12 years later, they are becalmed, and throw gold overboard to pacify the King of the Sea (bs); but his daughter Volkhova tells Sadko that one of the company must be sacrificed. Sadko is set adrift, and sinks to the sea-bed, where his song wins Volkhova's hand. At the wedding Sadko's singing so arouses the sea that many ships are sunk; this brings down the anger of St Nicholas, who orders Sadko back to land. On the shore of Lake Ilmen Sadko bids farewell to Volkhova, who is transformed into the river that bears her name. Lyubava, still waiting, is reunited with Sadko, now the richest man in Novgorod.

Sadler's Wells. Theatre in Rosebery Avenue, North London. Originally a pleasure garden belonging to Sadler, who in 1684 discovered a medicinal well there. The first theatre was built 1765, and saw performances by Bland, the young Braham, and the Dibdins. Opera was sometimes given in the 19th cent., including the English prem. of *Luisa Miller* (1858); it then became a music-hall before falling into disuse.

In Mar. 1925 a move began to turn it into an *Old Vic for north London, and £70,000 was raised. The theatre (cap. 1,550) was reopened under Lilian *Baylis on 6 Jan. 1931. Opera and ballet alternated with Shakespeare until 1934, when it became the home of the opera and ballet companies. The repertory was enlarged and included the English prems. of *The Snow Maiden*, *Tsar Saltan*, and the original *Boris Godunov*, the first *Don Carlos* in English, and productions of Wagner and works by English composers including Benjamin, Smyth, and Stanford. Singers included Joan *Cross, Edith Coates, Sumner Austin, Powell Lloyd, and Arnold Matters, with Warwick Braithwaite and Lawrance Collingwood as conductors and Clive Carey and Sumner Austin as producers; the company also invited guest artists including Florence Austral, Miriam Licette, Heddle Nash, and the conductors Beecham, Barbirolli, and Coates. After 1940 a reduced

company toured, with short seasons at the New T.

The company was built up again by Joan Cross, with productions including *The Bartered Bride* and *Così fan tutte* and new artists including Owen Brannigan and Peter Pears. It reopened in Sadler's Wells on 7 June 1945 with the prem. of *Peter Grimes*. Joan Cross then resigned, to be succeeded by Clive Carey and in 1947 by Norman *Tucker: music directors were James Robertson 1946–54, Alexander Gibson 1957–9, Colin Davis 1961–5. Prems. included Berkeley's *Nelson* (1954), Gardner's *The Moon and Sixpence* (1957), and Bennett's *The Mines of Sulphur* (1965); British prems. included *Simon Boccanegra*, *Rusalka*, *Mahagonny*, and an influential Janáček series under Mackerras beginning in 1951 with *Káťa Kabanová*. Leading singers included Victoria Elliott, Amy Shuard, Charles Craig, James Johnston, Howell Glynne, David Ward, and Owen Brannigan. Producers included Denis Arundell, Basil Coleman, George Devine, Powell Lloyd, and Tyrone Guthrie; Glen Byam Shaw was director of productions from 1962. The strength of public feeling for the theatre and company was shown by the response to a financial crisis which threatened to close them in 1958, and it became recognized that a stable company providing sound but also enterprising repertory performances had at least as secure a claim on audiences as the more glamorous international fare offered at Covent Garden. Stephen Arlen became director 1966–72: his régime included the 1968 *Mastersingers* which marked the rediscovery of Reginald *Goodall as a great Wagner conductor.

Plans for a move to the South Bank site of the Nat. T in 1961 were abandoned, and the company moved in 1968 to the *Coliseum. In 1974 it was renamed *English National Opera. The theatre continued to play host to visiting opera companies from home and abroad, and has been the scene of the British prems. of *Die Frau ohne Schatten* and *Lulu*.

Saint-Bris. The Comte de Saint-Bris (bar), a Catholic nobleman in Meyerbeer's *Les Huguenots*.

Saint François d'Assise. Opera in 8 scenes by Messiaen; text by composer. Prem. Paris, O, 28 Nov. 1983.

The work describes various episodes in the life of St Francis, among them his healing of a leper, his preaching to the birds, his receiving of the stigmata, and his visitation by an angel.

St Petersburg

City in Russia, named St Petersburg 1703–1914, Petrograd 1914–24; Leningrad 1924–91, St Petersburg again from 1991: capital of Russia 1703–1917.

The first theatrical productions were given soon after Peter the Great's foundation of the city, but the first opera to be performed was *La forza dell'amore e dell'odio* (1736) by the company of Francesco *Araia; his *Cephalus and Procris* (1755) was the first opera in Russian. In 1757 the first public theatre was opened, and here a mixed repertory included opera: Karl Knipper's Volny T (Free T) of 1777 became the Bolshoy Kammeny T (Grand Stone T) in 1783, and was followed by the Maly T (Small T). Caterino *Cavos was conductor of the Bolshoy 1798–1840. Italian opera was given 1826–32, and 1840. In 1833 Nicholas I opened the Alexandrinsky T, built by Rossi. The Bolshoy was rebuilt in 1836, opening with Glinka's *A Life for the Tsar*. For many years this work opened every season, and by the end of the century had been given over 700 times. Giovanni *Rubini headed a company; government-supported opera then lasted until 1885. Opera was also given from 1855 at the T Tsirk (Circus T), opposite the Bolshoy: this burnt down in 1859 and was rebuilt by Alberto Cavos (son of Caterino) as the Maryinsky T in 1860. The influential conductor from 1863 (chief from 1869) to 1913 was Eduard *Nápravník. Prems. included *La forza del destino* (1862) as well as many of the operas of the leading Russian composers of the day. From 1860 visiting French operetta and Italian companies played at the T Mikhaylovsky (built by Bryullov 1831–3, rebuilt by Cavos 1859). The three Imperial Theatres of St Petersburg were the Maryinsky, Mikhaylovsky, and (for drama) Alexandrinsky.

At the Revolution there was more resistance to change in Petrograd than in Moscow, and the commissar, the enlightened Anatoly Lunacharsky, was obliged to bring pressure on the company to resume work. The Maryinsky reopened in 1919 as the State Academic T of O and Ballet (known as GATOB; cap. 1,780: some of the first Soviet operas were given here in 1925), the Mikhaylovsky in 1920 as the State Academic T of Comic O, and the Maly T in 1921 as the Little Petrograd Academic T, becoming in 1926 the State Academic Little Opera T (known as MALEGOT;

cap. 1,212). The latter was the home of most of the more advanced operatic experiments, and of the more advanced foreign works of the 1920s; but many smaller experimental groups flourished, among them the T Komichesky Opery (from 1920), the T Muzykalny Komedy, and the Palas-T (for operetta). In 1922 an opera studio was established in the conservatory, and here much enterprising and successful work was done; in 1928–9 they toured clubs and factories, and even gave a season in Salzburg. In 1935 the State Academic T was renamed the Kirov O and Ballet T. While this theatre upheld a traditional style, experimental work continued at the MALEGOT, including new works and productions (e.g. a Meyerhold production of *The Queen of Spades*). This was sharply interrupted by the 1936 attack on *Shostakovich's *The *Lady Macbeth of Mtsensk*. During the war the Kirov was evacuated to Perm, the MALEGOT to Orenburg, both returning in 1944. A group of artists who remained in the city formed an Opernobalety Kollektiv. After the war the Kirov and Maly set about re-establishing their reputations, which have continued to be more traditional for the former, more experimental for the latter. Under the conductor Yury Temirkanov, 1977–88, then Valery Gergiyev, standards at the Kirov have improved and the artistic enterprise widened. In the early 1960s the Leningrad Conservatory opened a section to train musicians as opera directors: there is also an opera training section at the State Institute of T Art. Following the dissolution of the USSR, many theatres have chosen to revert to their former names.

See also RUSSIA.

Saint-Saëns, Camille

(*b* Paris, 9 Oct. 1835; *d* Algiers, 16 Dec. 1921). French composer and pianist. Studied Paris with Maleden and F. Halévy, and made a very early mark as a child prodigy pianist. His long list of works includes 13 operas. The first, *La princesse jaune* (1872), showed a touch with operetta which he did not really pursue. The only one to survive at all regularly in repertories is *Samson et Dalila* (1877). Here his unfailing craftsmanship is supplemented by some sense of characterization for the two principals and the ability to create a unique and consistent emotional world. It was these qualities which led Liszt to secure it for production at Weimar when it was (temporarily) banned from the Paris stage because of its biblical subject-matter. *Henri VIII* (1883) is a Grand Opera making some use of motive. Other of his operas include some attractive numbers and show his fluency, sometimes his skill in pastiche, seldom much in the way of dramatic flair.

Salammbô. Opera in 5 acts by Reyer; text by Camille du Locle, after Flaubert's novel (1862). Prem. Brussels, M, 10 Feb. 1890.

Carthage, 240 BC. Matho (ten) has stolen the sacred veil from the shrine of the Carthaginian goddess Tanit. He is condemned to die at the hands of the priestess Salammbô (sop), who has fallen in love with him. She kills herself in his place, and Matho stabs himself.

'Salce, salce'. See WILLOW SONG.

Salieri, Antonio (*b* Legnano, 18 Aug. 1750; *d* Vienna, 7 May 1825). Italian composer. Studied with his brother Francesco, Venice with Pescetti and Pacini; during a visit Gassmann recognized Salieri's talents and brought him to Vienna 1766. Salieri's first surviving opera, the dramma giocoso *Le donne letterate* (The Cultured Ladies, 1770), was well received. In 1774 he became court composer and took charge of Italian opera at the court; in 1788 he succeeded Bonno as Kapellmeister.

Vienna remained the focus of Salieri's activities until his death. He composed over 30 operas there and exerted a considerable influence as a teacher, his pupils including Beethoven, Hummel, Schubert, Weigl, and Winter. His work embraced opera seria, e.g. *Palmira* (1796), and opera buffa, e.g. *Falstaff* (1799): less characteristically, for the National-Singspiel he wrote *Der Rauchfangkehrer* (The Chimney Sweep, 1781). The most interesting of his Viennese works are the settings of Da Ponte, largely opere buffe including *Il ricco d'un giorno* (A Rich Man for a Day, 1784), *Il talismano* (1779), and *La cifra* (1789). An effective writer in the comic style, Salieri turns these librettos into attractive and diverting works, though they lack Mozart's humane and sensitive insight. For a celebration at Schönbrunn, at which Mozart's *Der Schauspieldirektor* was also given, Salieri provided *Prima la musica e poi le parole* (First the Music, Then the Words, 1786), a satire on the rival claims of text and music. Following the death of Joseph II (1790) his influence at court declined; he relinquished directorship

of the opera (and was succeeded by Weigl), though he continued to compose for it up to 1804.

Outside Vienna, he scored notable successes in Italy during an extended visit 1778–80: *L'Europa riconosciuta* (1778) opened Milan S, and operas were also given in Rome and Venice. But his greatest triumph came in France, where *Les Danaïdes* (1784) proclaimed him Gluck's successor. Even more overwhelming was the reception of *Tarare* (1787), also well regarded when it was revised by Da Ponte for Vienna as *Axur*.

Salieri was a composer of the old school who found it difficult to adapt to the changing climate of the late 18th cent., which he explicitly acknowledged by his retreat from the operatic stage after 1804. Whether in comic or serious works, he rarely moved beyond the conventions of the genre, though he showed sensitivity to the notion of reform, and partly acknowledged it in *Tarare*. Highly regarded in his day, not least by Gluck, who eased his passage into Parisian musical circles, Salieri manifestly fails when the inevitable comparison is made with his near-contemporary Mozart. The claim that he poisoned Mozart (entirely without foundation) was dramatized first by Pushkin and thence advanced in opera by Rimsky-Korsakov's *Mozart and Salieri*; the story also occurs in Lortzing's pasticcio *Szenen aus Mozarts Leben*.

Salignac, Thomas (*b* Générac, 19 Mar. 1867; *d* Paris, 1945). French tenor. Studied Paris with Duvernoy. Début Paris, OC, 1893 (small roles). New York, M, 1896–1903; Paris, OC, 1905–13, 1923; London, CG, 1897–9, 1901–4; Brussels, M, 1919. Dir. Nice O, 1913–14. Toured Canada and US 1926 with an opéra-comique co. Roles included Don Ottavio, Don José, Gounod's Faust, Canio, Mârouf, Salammbô (Reyer), and creations in operas by Milhaud, Missa, and Falla (title-role of *El retablo de Maese Pedro*). (R)

Sallinen, Aulis (*b* Salmi, 9 April 1935). Finnish composer. Studied Helsinki with Merikanto and Kokkonen. His reputation as a concert composer was enhanced by the appearance of his first opera, *The Horseman* (1975), a tight-knit and powerful nationalistic work. This dramatic control was demonstrated anew with *The Red Line* (1978), which further developed an idiom owing something to Shostakovich in its direct, innovative traditionalism. *The King Goes Forth to France* (1984) was a part-commission from London CG: it is a powerful though enigmatic work, centring on the growth of irrational power as the main character deteriorates morally, and builds on the previous operas with lighter textures and a more economic use of material. Sallinen was originally commissioned to write *Kullervo* for the opening of the new Helsinki OH and it was performed there in 1993, after its Los Angeles prem. the previous year.

Salmhofer, Franz (*b* Vienna, 22 Jan. 1900; *d* Vienna, 22 Sept. 1975). Austrian composer and conductor. Studied Vienna with Schreker and Schmidt. Cond. Vienna: B, 1929–39; dir. S, 1945–55; V, 1955–63. He had successes in Vienna with *Dame im Traum* (1935), *Ivan Tarassenko* (1938), and *Das Werbekleid* (1943).

Salminen, Matti (*b* Turku, 7 July 1945). Finnish bass. Studied Helsinki, and Rome with Ricci. Début Finnish Nat. O 1966 (small roles). Cologne 1972–6; Milan, S, 1973; London, CG, 1974; Bayreuth 1976; Paris, O, 1977; New York, M, 1981; also Savonlinna, Budapest, Vienna, Munich, etc. Roles incl. Osmin, Sarastro, King Mark, Fafner, Hunding, Hagen, Philip, Gremin. (R)

Salome. Opera in 1 act by Richard Strauss; text, Oscar Wilde's tragedy (1893) in the Ger. translation of Hedwig Lachmann. Prem. Dresden, H, 9 Dec. 1905.

Herod's Palace in Jerusalem, AD 30. During Herod's banquet, Jochanaan (John the Baptist) (bar), proclaims—from the cistern where he is imprisoned—the coming of the Messiah. He is brought out for Salome (sop) to see, and repels her fascinated advances: he urges her not to follow the ways of her mother Herodias (mez). He is taken back to the cistern. Herod (ten), her stepfather, asks Salome to dance; she agrees on condition that he will grant her what she desires. After her Dance of the Seven Veils she demands the head of Jochanaan, which Herod is forced to have brought to her. She fondles and kisses it until the revolted Herod orders his soldiers to crush her with their shields.

'Salut, demeure chaste et pure'. Faust's (ten) apostrophe to Marguerite's house in Act III of Gounod's *Faust*.

Salvini-Donatelli, Fanny (*b* Florence, *c*.1815; *d* Milan, June 1891). Italian soprano. Début Venice, T Apollo, 1839 (Rosina). Vienna 1842; London, DL, 1858. Created Violetta, against Verdi's wishes; though she was a good singer, her comfortable nature and her plumpness contributed to the fiasco of the first *Traviata*. She was, however, praised in the role by some critics, and admired in *Macbeth*, *I due Foscari*, and *Ernani*.

Salzburg. City in Austria. On 10 Feb. 1614 a 'Hoftragicomoedia' was staged in the Archbishop's palace, probably the first opera performance outside Italy. Operas were then staged in the Steintheater in the gardens of Schloss Hellbrunn. The late 17th cent. saw operas and school dramas by Georg Muffat, Heinrich Biber, and Andreas Hofer, mostly lost. Antonio *Caldara was regularly in Salzburg 1716–27, and the Heckentheater in the gardens of Schloss Mirabell was probably opened with his *Dafne* (1719). Here Mozart (born in the city 1756) had his *La finta semplice* produced 1769, and *Sogno di Scipione* 1772. The Ballhaus was converted into the Hoftheater 1775, becoming the Nationaltheater 1806.

The first Mozart festival was held in 1842, with an important centenary festival in 1856 directed by Alois Taux, also an opera conductor and composer. The modern festival dates from 1877; concerts and operas were given under Richter, Mottl, Mahler, Richard Strauss, Muck, Schalk, and Weingartner. Lilli Lehmann arranged two *Don Giovanni* performances in 1901, singing Donna Anna, and there were performances of *Don Giovanni* and *Figaro* under Mahler, in the Roller settings and with Mayr as Figaro, 1906. From 1922 opera was given in the Stadttheater. The Festspielhaus (former Winterreitschule) was converted 1924, rebuilt 1926 (cap. 1,200), first staged opera 1927 (*Fidelio* with Lotte Lehman). The 1930s saw opera under Walter, Toscanini, Krauss, Furtwängler, and Knappertsbusch, though the German annexation in 1938 caused some to leave. The festival resumed 1945. The most influential conductors were Furtwängler, Böhm, and Karajan, who was director 1956–60 and 1964–89, and in 1967 founded an Easter Fest. annually including a new opera production; Claudio Abbado was artistic director from 1994. Opera has been given in the Felsenreitschule from 1949, altered 1970 (cap. 1,549); the Festspielhaus from 1927, rebuilt 1937 (renamed Kleines Festspielhaus 1960) (cap. 1,323); and the Grosses Festspielhaus (cap. 2,177), opened 1960 with *Rosenkavalier*.

The festival has included prems. of works by Strauss (*Liebe der Danae*, 1952), Von Einem, Orff, Egk, Liebermann, Henze, and Berio.

Samaras, Spiridon (*b* Corfu, 29 Nov. 1861; *d* Athens, 25 Mar. 1917). Greek composer. Studied Corfu with Xyndas, Athens with Stancabianco (with whom he wrote an opera), Paris with Delibes. His *Flora mirabilis* (1886) is a verismo work anticipating Mascagni's *Cavalleria rusticana* by four years, and was given throughout Greece with great success. A further verismo opera, *La martire*, confirmed his touch with the genre, and was chosen to open the Milan L in 1894. Though he composed several other operas, his only comparable success was with *Rhea* (1908).

Samiel. The devil (spoken) in Weber's *Der Freischütz*.

Sammarco, Mario (*b* Palermo, 13 Dec. 1868; *d* Milan, 24 Jan. 1930). Italian baritone. Studied Palermo with Cantelli, Milan with Emerich. Début Palermo 1888 (Valentin). Milan, S, 1895–6, 1902, 1905, 1913; Buenos Aires from 1897; London, CG, 1904–14, 1919; New York, Manhattan OC, 1907–10; Chicago 1909–13. Created Gérard (*Chénier*), Cascart (Leoncavallo's *Zazà*) among other roles; also sang Scarpia, Hamlet, Rigoletto, and Tonio, with a mellifluous tone and dramatic conviction. (R)

Sammartini, Giovanni Battista (*b* Milan, 1700 or 1701; *d* Milan, 15 Jan. 1775). Italian composer. The most important Milanese instrumental and church composer of his generation. Sammartini's music was widely disseminated throughout Europe and was crucial in the development of the Classical style. His three operas, of which *L'ambizione superata dalla virtù* (1734) was the most successful, are models of mid-18th-cent. opera seria. As a teacher he had a considerable influence on Gluck.

Samson et Dalila. Opera in 3 acts by Saint-Saëns; text by Lemaire, after Judges 14–16. Prem. Weimar (in German) 2 Dec. 1877.

Israel, 1150 BC. Samson (ten), the Hebrew warrior, leads a revolt against the Philistines. Dalila (mez), a Philistine beauty, is urged by the High Priest of Dagon (bar) to seduce Samson and discover the secret of his strength. Samson reveals to her that it lies in his hair, which Dalila then cuts off, rendering him powerless. He is taken prisoner by the Philistines, who put out his eyes. Brought to the temple of Dagon, where he is mocked by his captors, he prays to God for the return of his strength, and pulls down the temple, killing himself and his enemies.

San Carlo Company. US touring co. founded in 1919 by Fortune Gallo (1878–1970) which gave popular-priced opera throughout the US. It attracted distinguished guest singers, and many of its artists went on to major careers, including Jean Madeira, Dorothy Kirsten, Eugene Conley, and Nicola Rescigno. Disbanded 1955.

Sances, Giovanni Felice (*b* Rome, *c.*1600; *d* Vienna, *c.*12 Nov. 1679). Italian composer and singer. Studied Collegio Germanico, Rome. Held positions in Rome, Bologna, Venice, and possibly Padua. Joined the Vienna court as singer 1636; assistant Kapellmeister 1649; Kapellmeister 1669.

He wrote five operas: for the first, *Ermiona* (1636), he himself took the part of Cadmus. His other works were written for Vienna or Prague for imperial occasions and include the operas *Apollo deluso* (1669) and *Aristomene Messanio* (1670).

Sanderson, Sibyl (*b* Sacramento, CA, 7 Dec. 1865; *d* Paris, 15 May 1903). US soprano. Studied Paris with Sbriglia and Marchesi. Début The Hague 1888 (Manon). Paris, OC, 1889, and O, 1894; London, CG, 1891; New York, M, 1895, 1901. Adored by Massenet, who launched her career, and wrote the roles of Esclarmonde and Thaïs for her. Also created Saint-Saëns's Phryné; sang Juliette, Gilda, etc. Despite her beauty, dramatic talent, and impressive voice (rising to a g‴ nicknamed the 'sol Eiffel'), few thought her as 'superbly gifted' as Massenet did.

San Francisco. City in California, US. The first opera was *Sonnambula* at the Adelphi T by the Pellegrini Co. in 1851. Opera was performed in 11 theatres, including the Baldwin, Tivoli, Civic OH, and Auditorium. The largest was Wade's OH (cap. 2,500), built in 1876 and later expanded as the Grand OH (cap. 4,000). Visiting companies included those of Mapleson (from 1879, with Patti 1884 and 1889), Emma Juch, Del Conte, and Damrosch. The New York M first visited in 1890 (with Tamagno in *Otello* (Verdi) and *Trovatore* and Patti in *Semiramide*, *Sonnambula*, *Traviata*, and *Lucia*), returning in 1900 with a complete *Ring*. The 1906 earthquake struck only hours after Caruso, Fremstad, and Journet had been singing in *Carmen*.

Not until 1909 was recovery sufficient for a permanent company to be proposed by Gaetano Merola, conductor of W. A. Edwards's International Grand OC. The Italian community having raised some funds, Merola returned 1919–20 with the S Carlo Co. and staged *Pagliacci*, *Carmen*, and Gounod's *Faust* in Stanford University's football stadium 1922. He founded San Francisco O 1923. Operas were staged in the Civic Auditorium (cap. 12,000) until 1932, with a largely Italian and French repertory (though *Tristan* was given in 1927 and *Salome* in 1931), and a few rarities such as *Mârouf* and *L'enfant et les sortilèges*. Singers who appeared included Jeritza, Muzio, Rethberg, De Luca, Didur, Gigli, Journet, Lauri-Volpi, Martinelli, Pinza, Schipa, and Scotti. The company opened the War Memorial T (cap. 3,176) in 1932 with *Tosca*. Merola continued as director until his death in 1953, staging a popular, mainly Italian repertory, and engaging many European singers before the Metropolitan. German opera fared better from the 1930s; singers included Flagstad, Melchior, Schorr, later Traubel and Lotte Lehmann.

Merola was succeeded by Kurt Herbert Adler, who initiated a more adventurous policy with the US prems. of many works. Among singers making their US débuts were Tebaldi, Del Monaco, Simionato, Gobbi, Jurinac, Margaret Price, Nilsson, Rysanek, Schwarzkopf, Sciutti, Te Kanawa, Geraint Evans, and Richard Lewis. Artists singing roles for the first time included Martinelli (Otello) and Tibbett (Iago); Geraint Evans (Wozzeck); Björling (Riccardo, *Ballo*); Horne (Eboli); and Sutherland (Maria Stuarda). Terence McEwen succeeded Adler in 1982, restoring the company's fortunes with careful economies, but retired through illness in 1988 to be succeeded by Lotfi Mansouri.

In 1961 The Spring OC was founded to give popular operas with young US singers; gradually new US operas were added and new production styles encouraged. Western Opera T tours opera in English, in 1987 becoming the first US company to visit China.

Sanjust, Filippo (*b* Rome, 9 Sept. 1925; *d* Rome, Nov. 1993). Italian designer and producer. Collaborated with Visconti London, CG, *Don Carlos* 1958, and subsequently. Salzburg, prem. Henze's *Junge Lord* 1965 and *Bassarids* 1966. First prod., Frankfurt, *Magic Flute*

1968. London, C, *Semele* 1970. Hamburg, Berlin, Amsterdam, producing works as diverse as *Poppea*, *Lohengrin*, *Lulu*. A sensitive designer with a strong feeling for atmosphere.

Sanquirico, Alessandro (*b* Milan, 27 July 1777; *d* Milan, 12 Mar. 1849). Italian designer. Milan, S, 1817–32, designing prems. including *Gazza ladra* 1817, *Pirata* 1827, *Norma* 1831, also many works by Donizetti, Mercadante, and Pacini. Redecorated interior of La Scala 1829. His designs, most of which can be seen in the La Scala Museum and elsewhere in Milan, reveal an impressive neo-classical style, later a warmly Romantic one that included the architectural and historical realism associated with the comparable Grand Opera genre of the Paris O.

Santa Fe. Town in New Mexico, US. The O Association of New Mexico, later Santa Fe O, was founded in 1956 by John Crosby. Its opening 1957 season included *The Rake's Progress* (supervised by Stravinsky) and the prem. of Marvin David Levy's *The Tower*; and this commitment to 20th-cent. music has continued with the prems. of Floyd's *Wuthering Heights* (1958), Berio's *Opera* (1970), and Villa-Lobos's *Yerma* (1971). For ten years the company performed at an open-air theatre, which burnt down in 1967 after the US prem. of *Cardillac*; the season continued at the local High School. A new theatre (cap. 1,773) opened on the site 1968, with stage and pit covered but auditorium partly covered. The company has maintained its distinguished record for world and US prems. and its steadfast commitment to the operas—particularly the later ones—of Richard Strauss. Crosby continues as dir. and music dir.

Santi, Nello (*b* Adria, 22 Nov. 1931). Italian conductor. Studied Padua. Début Padua 1951 (*Rigoletto*). Zurich from 1959. Salzburg 1960. London, CG, 1960 (*Traviata*). New York, M, from 1962. Salzburg 1960 (*Don Carlos*). Guest appearances Hamburg, Munich, Vienna. A good 'singers' conductor'. (R)

Santini, Gabriele (*b* Perugia, 20 Jan. 1886; *d* Rome, 13 Nov. 1964). Italian conductor. Studied Perugia and Bologna. Début Rome, C, 1906. Cond. Buenos Aires (eight seasons) and Rio de Janeiro. Chicago; New York, Manhattan OC. Assistant cond. to Toscanini at Milan, S, 1925–9. Rome O, 1929–33, music dir. 1944–7. Milan, S, 1960–1. A champion of new works, and one of the leading Verdi conductors of his day. (R)

Santley, (Sir) **Charles** (*b* Liverpool, 28 Feb. 1834; *d* London, 22 Sept. 1922). English baritone. Studied Milan with Nava, later London with García jun. Début Pavia 1857 (Doctor, *Traviata*). London, CG from 1859, Pyne-Harrison Co. 1859–63, Mapleson Co. 1862–70; Milan, S, 1866; sang with London CR 1875–7, when he retired from the stage. Roles included Don Giovanni, Almaviva (Mozart), Nevers, Luna, Flying Dutchman, and Valentin (Gounod, impressed, wrote 'Avant de quitter ces lieux' for him). Also created roles in operas by Wallace (*Lurline*), Balfe (e.g. *The Puritan's Daughter*), and Benedict (*The Lily of Killarney*). A singer highly acclaimed for his inspired and polished performances, he also composed, sometimes under the name of Ralph Betterton. (R)

Santuzza. A village girl (sop), Turiddu's abandoned lover, in Mascagni's *Cavalleria rusticana*.

Sanzogno, Nino (*b* Venice, 13 Apr. 1911; *d* Milan, 4 May 1983). Italian conductor and composer. Studied Venice with Agostini and Malipiero, Brussels with Scherchen. Cond. Venice, F, 1937. Milan, S, 1939; opened Milan, PS, 1955 (*Matrimonio segreto*). Edinburgh Fest. 1957 with Milan, PS. Cond. many prems. and Italian prems. Milan and Venice, and was an outstanding advocate of modern opera, also of 18th-cent. Italian opera. Cond. Milan, S, 1962–5. (R)

'Saper vorreste'. Oscar's (sop) aria in Act III of Verdi's *Un ballo in maschera*, refusing to divulge the costume the King is wearing at the masked ball.

Sapho. Opera in 5 acts by Massenet; text by Henri Cain and Arthur Bernède after Daudet's novel (1884). Prem. Paris, OC, 27 Nov. 1897.

The opera tells of the unhappy love of Fanny Legrand (sop), an artist's model who has been posing as Sappho for the sculptor Caoudal (bar), and a country youth, Jean Gaussin (ten).

Sarastro. The High Priest (bs) of Isis and Osiris in Mozart's *Die Zauberflöte*.

Sargent, (Sir) **Malcolm** (*b* Ashford, 29 Apr. 1895; *d* London, 3 Oct. 1967). English conductor. Although primarily a concert con-

ductor, he worked with the London BNOC, conducting the prems. of Vaughan Williams's *Hugh the Drover* and Holst's *At the Boar's Head* (1925). D'Oyly Carte OC, 1926–8, 1951. London, CG, 1936 (*Louise*), 1954 (prem. of Walton's *Troilus and Cressida*). (R)

Šárka. 1. Opera in 3 acts by Janáček; text by Julius Zeyer, after his own drama (1887). Orig. version 1887; rev. 1888, 1918; final version rev. Chlubna, prem. Brno 11 Nov. 1925.

Bohemia, mythological times. After the death of Libuše, her husband Přemysl (bs) plans to dispense with her council of women. They revolt, under Šárka (sop), who falls in love with the warrior hero Ctirad (ten); nevertheless, she brings about his death, eventually hurling herself onto his funeral pyre.

Sarro, Domenico Natale (*b* Trani, 24 Dec. 1679; *d* Naples, 25 Jan. 1744). Italian composer. Active at the Naples court from 1704, he is particularly remembered for making the first setting of Metastasio's *Didone abbandonata* (1724), the latter's first wholly original libretto. Of the generation of Neapolitan composers which followed Scarlatti, Sarro is at his most characteristic in the *c.*25 heroic operas which he wrote both for Naples and other Italian houses. These brought him great popularity during the 1720s, but he was gradually eclipsed by Vinci. *Achille in Sciro* was given 1737 for the opening of the Naples C.

Sarti, Giuseppe (*b* Faenza, *bapt.* 1 Dec. 1729; *d* Berlin, 28 July 1802). Italian composer. Studied Padua with Valotti and Bologna with Martini. Organist of Faenza Cathedral, 1748–52; dir. of Faenza T, 1752–5. His first opera, *Il re pastore* (1753), brought him to attention; a visit to Copenhagen 1753 with Mingotti's troupe resulted in his appointment as Kapellmeister at the Danish court and dir. of the Italian O, 1755; dir. of court music 1763; dir. of court T, 1770–5. Sarti at first concentrated on composing Metastasian opere serie during his years in Copenhagen, including *Achille in Sciro* (1759) and *Didone abbandonata* (1762). Later he wrote some of the earliest Danish operas, including *Tronfølgen i Sidon* (The Succession to the Throne in Sidon, 1771) and *Aglae, eller Støtten* (Aglae, or the Column, 1774). Following political difficulties at court, Sarti returned to Italy 1775. He became maestro di cappella at Milan Cathedral 1779, but 1784 was appointed to direct the imperial chapel in St Petersburg, where he collaborated with Pashkevich and Canobbio on one of the first Russian operas *The Early Reign of Oleg* (1790), to a libretto by Catherine the Great. Later he founded a school of singing in the Ukraine and became head of the St Petersburg Cons.

An accomplished composer with dramatic flair and sure melodic gift, Sarti was one of the most important figures for the wider dissemination of Italian opera during the late 18th cent.: his influence was crucial for the establishment of opera in both Denmark and Russia. He was equally at home in comic or serious genres but the greatest successes of his *c*.70 works were the opere buffe *I finti eredi* (1785) and *Fra i due litiganti* (Between the Two Litigants, 1782). The latter contains the aria 'Come un agnello', quoted by Mozart in the banquet scene of *Don Giovanni*.

Sarti, Laura (*b* Trieste, 1925). Italian, later British, mezzo-soprano. Studied with Lucie Manén and Emmy Heim. First major appearance with Gly.: has also performed with Scottish O, Kent O, London SW, and at Drottningholm and Aix-en-Provence. One of her most celebrated roles is as Ottavia in Monteverdi's *Poppea*; others include Dido (Purcell), Emilia (Verdi's and Rossini's *Otello*), Principessa (*Suor Angelica*), and Signora Fabien (*Volo di notte*). Possessing a rich mezzo voice and a powerful stage presence, Sarti has also proved an influential and highly regarded teacher. (R)

Sartorio, Antonio (*b* Venice, 1630; *d* Venice, 30 Dec. 1680). Italian composer. Nothing is known of his life before the appearance of his first opera *Gl'amori infruttuosi di Pirro* (The Fruitless Loves of Pyrrhus) in Venice 1661. In 1666–75 he was Kapellmeister at the court of Duke Johann Friedrich of Brunswick-Lüneburg, though he made annual journeys back to Venice to recruit musicians and to arrange productions of his operas during the Carnival. In 1676 he was appointed vice maestro di cappella at St Mark's, Venice.

Together with the works of Pollarolo and Ziani, Sartorio's 15 operas represent the apotheosis of the 17th-cent. Venetian tradition and a crucial advance on the work of Cavalli and Cesti. Among his successes were *La prosperità d'Elio Seiano* (1667) and *Orfeo* (1672).

Sass, Marie Constance (*b* Oudenaarde, 26 Jan. 1834; *d* Auteuil, 8 Nov. 1907). Belgian soprano. Studied Ghent with Gevaert, Paris

with Ugalde, Milan with Lamperti. Début as Marie Sax (she was later forced by Adolphe Sax to change her name) Venice 1852 (Gilda). Paris, O, 1860–70; Milan, S, 1869–70; St Petersburg 1870–1. Also Brussels, M; Barcelona; Madrid, etc. Her voice was powerful, flexible, and appealing. As well as *falcon roles, her repertory included Donna Anna, Lucrezia Borgia, Elisabeth (first Paris *Tannhäuser*), Amelia, Valentine. Created Selika; also Elisabeth de Valois, with little conviction and much temperamental behaviour: Verdi refused to have her for either Aida or Amneris. Married to *Castelmary 1864–7; retired 1877; died in poverty.

Satie, Erik (*b* Honfleur, 17 May 1866; *d* 1 July 1925). French composer. Studied Paris with Taudou. His stage works include a puppet opera, *Geneviève de Brabant* (comp. 1899), and the operetta *Pousse l'amour* (comp. *c*.1905).

Sauguet, Henri (*b* Bordeaux, 18 May 1901; *d* Paris, 22 June 1989). French composer. Studied Bordeaux with Vaubourgoin and Canteloube. His first stage piece, *Le plumet du colonel* (1924), was a so-called 'opéra-bouffe militaire'; this was followed by another comedy displaying his urbane manner, *La contrebasse* (1930). His most substantial opera is *La chartreuse de Parme* (1939), which showed his ability to handle a major subject, though it lacks the sharp focus of his lighter works. His dextrous and eminently civilized manner is shown to admirable effect in *Les caprices de Marianne* (1954).

Saul og David. Opera in 4 acts by Nielsen; text by Einar Christiansen, after 1 Samuel. Prem. Copenhagen, Royal T, 28 Nov. 1902.

Israel, *c*.1006 BC. In this version of the biblical story, Saul (bs) is cast as a complex, questioning figure in contrast to the more straightforward David (ten). The events encompass David falling in love with Saul's daughter Michal (sop), the narrow defeat of Goliath, and the return of Jonathan (ten) with news of the victory over the Philistines, Saul's jealousy of David, and David's eventual accession as King.

Saunders, Arlene (*b* Cleveland, 5 Oct. 1930). US soprano. Studied New York with Barbour. Début Nat. OC 1958 (Rosalinde). New York, CO, and Milan, N, 1961; Hamburg 1963; Gly. 1966; New York, M, 1976; London, CG, 1980. Also Paris, O; Vienna; Munich; Washington; Edinburgh; Rome. Roles incl. Pamina,

Louise, Eva, Marschallin, Arabella, Countess (*Capriccio*), Minnie. Created Beatrix Cenci (Ginastera). (R)

Sãvitri. Opera in 1 act by Holst; text by composer, after an episode in the Mahabharata. Prem. London, Wellington H, by London School of O, 5 Dec. 1916.

India, legendary times. Death (bar) has come to claim Sãtyavan (ten), but agrees to grant his wife Sãvitri (sop or mez) any wish, excepting the life of Sãtyavan. She chooses that she herself shall have 'life in its fullness', thereby outwitting Death, because a full life will only be possible with her husband.

Savoy operas. The name given to the operettas by Gilbert and Sullivan, from the theatre at which many of them were first produced.

Savoy Theatre. Theatre in the Strand, London, built by Richard D'Oyly Carte to house the Gilbert and Sullivan operettas, consequently known as the Savoy Operas. Opened 1881 with *Patience*. Three seasons of opera were organized by Marie Brema 1910–11; she sang Gluck's Orfeo. The present theatre (cap. 1,122) opened 1930.

Sawallisch, Wolfgang (*b* Munich, 26 Aug. 1923). German conductor. Studied Munich with Haas. Répétiteur Augsburg 1947, later chief cond. until 1953. Music dir.: Aachen 1953–8; Wiesbaden 1958–60; Cologne 1960–3. Bayreuth 1957–62, conducting new productions of *Tristan* (1957), *Holländer* (1959), and *Tannhäuser* (1961). Music dir. Munich 1971–92. London, CG, with Munich co., 1972. An intelligent, judicious conductor with a particular feeling for Mozart and Strauss. (R)

Sayão, Bidú (*b* Rio de Janeiro, 11 May 1902). Brazilian soprano. Studied Nice with J. De Reszke. Début Rio de Janeiro 1924 (Rosina). Paris, O and OC, 1931; New York, M, 1937–51. Also Buenos Aires, San Francisco, Rome, etc. Retired 1958. Roles included Susanna, Adina, Juliette, Violetta, Mimì, Manon, Mélisande. An engaging performer with a refined style. (R)

Sbriglia, Giovanni (*b* Naples, 23 June 1829; *d* Paris, 20 Feb. 1916). Italian tenor and teacher. Studied Naples with Roxas. Début Naples, C, 1853. Successful in Italy; toured US and S America. New York 1860. From 1875, taught in Paris, becoming one of the most celebrated teachers of his time. Pupils

included the De Reszkes, Nordica, Sanderson, Plançon, Whitehill.

Scala, Teatro alla. See LA SCALA.

Scala de seta, La (The Silken Ladder). Opera in 1 act by Rossini; text by Foppa, after the play *L'échelle de soie* by François-Antoine-Eugène de Planard and possibly a libretto from it made for Gaveaux (1808). Prem. Venice, S Moisè, 9 May 1812.

Venice, early 19th cent. The silken ladder of the title is used nightly by Dorvil (ten) to rejoin his wife Giulia (sop), whom he has secretly married, but who is living in the house of her tutor Dormont (bs); the intrigues are complicated by Giulia being promised by Dormont to Blansac (bar), who is loved by her cousin Lucilla (mez).

Scaria, Emil (*b* Graz, 18 Sept. 1838; *d* Blasewitz, 22 July 1886). Austrian bass. Studied Vienna with Gentiluomo and Lewy. Later London with García. Début Budapest 1860 (Saint-Bris). Leipzig 1863; Dresden 1865. Vienna, H, 1873–86. Berlin 1881, and London, HM, 1882, with Neumann's co., when he had a mental collapse, and had to be replaced. But, recovering, he created Gurnemanz later that year and rejoined Neumann's co. touring Europe. US tour 1883. Supervised revival of *Parsifal*, Bayreuth, 1883. Died insane. He was much admired by Wagner, also by Hanslick. An excellent and musical singer, with crystal-clear declamation. Roles included Rocco, Dulcamara, Falstaff (Nicolai), King Mark, Wotan.

Scarlatti, (Pietro) Alessandro (Gaspare) (*b* Palermo, 2 May 1660; *d* Naples, 22 Oct. 1725). Italian composer. Little is known about Scarlatti's early training; in 1679 he came to attention with his first opera, *Gli equivoci nel sembiante* (Misunderstandings in Appearance), which was quickly taken up by houses outside Rome. Maestro di cappella to Queen Christina of Sweden, then Naples from 1684, as maestro di cappella to the Viceroy. The next eighteen years were highly productive: though Scarlatti's claim that he wrote over 80 operas while in Naples is almost certainly an exaggeration, at least 40 works dating from this period have survived. Many of these were for the Naples B, where he was director from 1684, but a number were first given elsewhere, among them *Statira*, produced for the reopening of the T Tordinona in Rome, 1690. Gradually becoming disenchanted with life in Naples, Scarlatti resigned his position there in 1702. The next year he moved to Rome, holding various positions, but in 1708 he resumed his post in Naples, where he composed a further 11 operas, including two of his greatest successes, *Tigrane* (1715) and *Cambise* (1719).

Scarlatti is often credited with being the founder of a new school of so-called Neapolitan opera, and he was indeed more responsible than any other single composer for the establishment of Naples as a centre of operatic activity at the beginning of the 18th cent. However, he gave his operas a dramatic and musical shape far closer to the Venetian tradition than to that of opera seria which followed, though some features of Metastasian opera seria are adumbrated in such forward-looking works as *Griselda* (1721). Perhaps his greatest contribution came through his handling of the orchestra, where the skilful use of obbligato instruments considerably enhanced the expressive potential of opera.

Scarlatti, Domenico (*b* Naples, 26 Oct. 1685; *d* Madrid, 23 July 1757). Italian composer, son of the above. Though he is remembered today principally for his keyboard works, his early career was dominated by fruitless efforts to emulate his father's success as a composer of opera. His *c*.15 works reveal a certain dramatic flair, though fail entirely to live up to the high standards of originality set by his father: most important for their influence on later composers were *Orlando* (1711) and *Ambleto* (1715).

Scarpia. Baron Scarpia (bar), the Chief of Police, in Puccini's *Tosca*.

scena. A solo operatic movement of primarily dramatic purpose, less lyrical or formally composed than an aria, though very similar, e.g. Leonore's 'Abscheulicher' in Beethoven's *Fidelio*.

scenario (It.: 'scenery', also used in the English sense of the word). An outline libretto indicating the characters and number and type of scenes. In German, *Scenarium* means a complete libretto with detailed indications of scenery and staging.

scene (from Gr. *skene*: lit. 'tent', or 'booth', hence 'stage'). The term used to denote the smaller subdivision of an *act.

Schaaf, Johannes (*b* Bad Cannstadt, 7 Apr.

1933). German producer. Produced plays in Stuttgart before opera début at Vienna, V (*Hoffmann*). *Idomeneo* at Vienna, S, and *Capriccio* at Salzburg (1995). His stagings of Mozart's Da Ponte operas at London, CG, from 1987 stressed the darker side of human nature. Geneva 1992 (*Frau ohne Schatten*).

Schack, Benedikt (*b* Mirotice, 7 Feb. 1758; *d* Munich, 10 Dec. 1826). Bohemian tenor and composer. Studied Vienna with Frieberth. Début with Schikaneder's co. 1786 (in Paisiello's *La frascatana*). Freihaus-T auf der Wieden, Vienna, 1789–93. Graz 1793; Munich, N, 1796–1814. Created Tamino (also playing the flute solos); first German-language Don Ottavio and Almaviva. Described by L. Mozart as an excellent singer with 'a beautiful voice' and 'a beautiful method'. As a composer (appreciated by Haydn, among others), he collaborated with F. X. Gerl on Schikaneder's 'Anton' Singspiels; also wrote several operas, in one of which, *Der Stein der Weisen*, Mozart assisted with the duet 'Nun liebes Weibchen'.

Schalk, Franz (*b* Vienna, 27 May 1863; *d* Edlach, 3 Sept. 1931). Austrian conductor. Studied Vienna with Bruckner. Cond. Reichenberg (Liberec) 1888; Graz 1890–5; Prague 1895–8; Berlin 1898–1900. Vienna, H, 1900, succeeding Gregor as dir. 1918, and shared first conductorship with R. Strauss 1919–24. Cond. first revised *Ariadne* (1916) and *Frau ohne Schatten* (1919). Differences arose, with the two eventually not on speaking terms, and the public generally siding with Schalk. Strauss resigned, leaving Schalk in control until 1929. London, CG, 1898, 1907, and (three highly successful *Ring* cycles) 1911. New York, M, 1898–9. A founder of the Salzburg Fest. Had the reputation of being a somewhat dour but extremely efficient conductor. (R)

Schaunard. The Bohemian musician (bar) in Puccini's *La bohème*.

Schauspieldirektor, Der (The Impresario). Opera in 1 act by Mozart; text by Gottlieb Stephanie the younger. Prem. Vienna, Schönbrunn Palace T, 7 Feb. 1786.

Vienna, late 18th cent. The plot describes the rivalries between two prima donnas, Madame Silberklang (sop) and Madame Herz (sop): each offers a sample of her ability, the former in sentimental vein, the latter with a brighter rondo. They then come to blows over which of them deserves the higher salary, and try to outsing each other in a trio with M. Vogelsang (ten) in the presence of the long-suffering Impresario (spoken).

Scheidemantel, Karl (*b* Weimar, 21 Jan. 1859; *d* Weimar, 26 June 1923). German baritone. Studied Weimar with Borchers, Frankfurt with Stockhausen. Début Weimar 1878 (Wolfram). Weimar until 1886; Dresden 1886–1911; London, CG, 1884, 1899; Bayreuth 1886–92; Milan, S, 1892. Roles included Pizarro, Kurwenal, Sachs, Amfortas, Scarpia; created Kunrad (*Feuersnot*), and Faninal, among other roles. Much admired and very popular, he was described by R. Strauss as 'wonderful'. Dir. Landestheater, Dresden, 1921–2; wrote two books on singing. (R)

Schenk, Johann Baptist (*b* Wiener Neustadt, 30 Nov. 1753; *d* Vienna, 29 Dec. 1836). Austrian composer. Studied Vienna with Wagenseil. From 1794 he was music dir. for Prince Auersperg, but never sought a career as a court musician. Five early works, written 1780–6, were given anonymously, but their success persuaded him to reveal his identity with *Im Finstern ist nicht gut tappen* (1787). His position in the court theatres of Vienna established by the mid-1790s with works such as *Achmet und Almanzine* (1795), Schenk went on to produce his most successful work, *Der Dorfbarbier*, in 1796. This Singspiel remained popular for over 25 years, receiving performances as far afield as Moscow and New York; it is still revived occasionally.

Schenk, Otto (*b* Vienna, 12 June 1930). Austrian producer. Début Salzburg Landestheater 1957 (*Zauberflöte*). Staged *Dantons Tod* and *Lulu* at Vienna, S, 1962; resident dir. there from 1964. Later Viennese prods. incl. *Rosenkavalier* (1969) and *Freischütz* (1972). London, CG, 1975 (*Ballo in maschera*). New York, M, 1968 (*Tosca*); returned 1986–91 with a *Ring* which pleased audiences by its realistic, unpolemical approach.

Scherchen, Hermann (*b* Berlin, 21 June 1891; *d* Florence, 12 June 1966). German conductor. Largely self-taught. Gained early experience as viola player, then conducting various ensembles and orchestras. Though primarily a concert conductor, he made some operatic appearances, generally with the new music he always championed; cond. prems. of Dallapiccola's *Il prigioniero*

(Florence 1950), Dessau's *Das Verurteilung des Lukullus* (Berlin 1951), Henze's *König Hirsch* (Berlin 1956). Also cond. successful prem. of *Moses und Aron* (Berlin 1959). Adapted Webern's Second Cantata for the stage as *Il cuore* (Naples 1958). (R)

Scherman, Thomas (*b* New York, 12 Feb. 1917; *d* New York, 14 May 1979). US conductor. Studied New York with Bamberger and Rudolf. Début Mexico City 1947; in same year formed New York Little Orch. Society, which has given many important concert performances of opera including *Ariadne auf Naxos, L'enfant et les sortilèges, Goyescas, Iphigénie en Tauride*, and *Euryanthe*. (R)

Schikaneder, Emanuel (*b* Straubing, 1 Sept. 1751; *d* Vienna, 21 Sept. 1812). German theatre manager, singer, actor, and playwright. Schikaneder's early life was spent as a wandering musician, but in 1773 he fell in with a travelling theatrical troupe in Augsburg, married the daughter of the manager, and eventually succeeded to the directorship of the enterprise himself. The company appeared widely in Germany and Austria and Schikaneder acquired a reputation as one of the best comic actor-singers of his day. In 1780, the troupe appeared in Salzburg, and here Schikaneder made acquaintance with the young Mozart. After appearances in 1784 at Vienna K and B, Schikaneder moved to Regensburg to take over the direction of the theatre there; he was soon recalled to Vienna by his wife to manage a small suburban theatre, the T auf der Wieden. For several years he encountered great difficulties in running it, but the success of Mozart's *Die Zauberflöte* in 1791 saved him from financial ruin. In 1800 he partnered a merchant in opening a new theatre, the T an der Wien, which he continued to manage until 1806. Although Schikaneder planned to build and manage other theatres in Vienna, his sudden decline into madness caused an abrupt departure from the Viennese operatic scene.

Schikaneder's reputation today rests upon the libretto which he provided for Mozart's *Die Zauberflöte*, in which he also took the part of Papageno. In total Schikaneder wrote the librettos for about 50 operas or plays with music: composers who set his texts include Schack, Süssmayr, Hoffmeister, Paisiello, Seyfried, Winter, Teyber, and Weigl, as well as Mozart.

Schillings, Max von (*b* Düren, 19 Apr. 1868; *d* Berlin, 24 July 1933). German composer, conductor, and manager. Studied Bonn with Brambach, and in Munich was influenced by Strauss. Assistant stage cond., Bayreuth 1892, chorus-master 1902. His first opera, *Ingwelde* (1894), was imitative of Wagner, and even the second, the comic *Der Pfeifertag* (Day of the Piper, 1899), did not escape this influence. Prof. at Munich, 1903 (his pupils included Furtwängler and Heger). Wagner's influence continues in his third opera, the religious *Moloch* (1906). Intendant, Stuttgart, 1908–18, Generalmusikdirektor 1911; was ennobled when the new opera-house opened in 1912. His régime was of great enterprise, and included the prems. of the original *Ariadne auf Naxos*, of his version of *Les Troyens*, and of his most successful opera, *Mona Lisa*. Intendant, Berlin, 1919–25, when productions included *Palestrina* and *Die Frau ohne Schatten*, among much else. Toured US as guest cond., 1924, 1931. His wife was **Barbara Kemp** (*b* Kochem, 12 Dec. 1881; *d* Berlin, 17 Apr. 1959). German soprano. Studied Strasburg Cons. Début Strasburg 1903 (Priestess, *Aida*). Berlin, H (later S), 1913–32. New York, M, 1922–4; Bayreuth 1914–27. Sang Isolde, Senta, Kundry; created title-role of her husband's *Mona Lisa*, and produced this and *Ingwelde* in Berlin, 1938–9. (R)

Schindelmeisser, Louis (*b* Königsberg, 8 Dec. 1811; *d* Darmstadt, 30 Mar. 1864). German conductor and composer. Studied Berlin with Marx, Leipzig with Dorn. Kapellmeister Salzburg, 1832, then occupying various other posts until settling in Darmstadt 1853. An early defender of Wagner, and conductor of his works. His own operas, which include *Melusine* (1861), are more directly Weberian.

Schinkel, Karl Friedrich (*b* Neuruppin, 13 Mar. 1781; *d* Berlin, 9 Oct. 1841). German architect and designer. Studied Berlin, Italy, and France. Worked as scene designer for Wilhelm Gropius 1807–15; chief designer at the Royal T 1815–28, initially for *Magic Flute*. These famous sets provided a panoramic background to the action, strongly atmospheric in mood and detail. He also designed some of Spontini's operas, in which his grasp of architectural design and ability to handle large structures were particularly appropriate (*La vestale*, 1818; *Olympie*, 1821).

Schipa, Tito (*b* Lecce, ?1888, birth cert. states 2 Jan. 1889; *d* New York, 16 Dec. 1965). Italian tenor. Studied Lecce with Gerunda, Milan with Piccoli. Début Vercelli 1910 (Alfredo). Milan, S, from 1915; Chicago 1919–22; New York, M, 1932–5, 1940–1. Also Buenos Aires, Monte Carlo, Rome, Italian provinces (never opera in England). Sang into the late 1950s. The outstanding *tenore di grazia* of his time; his sweet, slightly nasal, highly individual tone, superbly projected and controlled, was used with exceptional refinement and often with moving pathos. His roles included Don Ottavio, Elvino, Ernesto, Duke of Mantua, Werther, Mascagni's Fritz; created Ruggero (*La rondine*). Autobiography, *Si confessa* (Genoa, 1961). (R)

Schippers, Thomas (*b* Kalamazoo, MI, 9 Mar. 1930; *d* New York, 16 Dec. 1977). US conductor. Studied Philadelphia, and with Olga Samaroff. Début New York 1948 with Lemonade Co. New York, M, 1955–75. Cond. prem. of Copland's *The Tender Land* (1954), also many works by Menotti, including at Spoleto. Cond. prem. of Barber's *Antony and Cleopatra* opening New York, M, at Lincoln Center, 1966. Milan, S, 1967 (*Assedio di Corinto*). Bayreuth, 1963, first US cond. (*Meistersinger*). London, CG, 1968 (*Elektra*). (R)

Schira, Francesco (*b* Malta, 21 Aug. 1809; *d* London, 15 Oct. 1883). Italian conductor and composer. Studied Milan with Basili and wrote his first opera, for Milan S, aged 23. Music dir. Lisbon, S Carlos, 1834–42. Music dir., London, Princess's T, 1842. Succeeded Benedict at DL, 1844–7; cond. CG, 1848; DL, 1852. The good reception given his operas in London was far exceeded by the success of *Selvaggia* in Venice (1875).

Schlosser, Max Karl (*b* Amberg, 17 Oct. 1835; *d* Utting, 2 Sept. 1916). German tenor. After unsuccessful early career in operetta, became a baker, but returned to singing 1868 to create David. Munich 1868–1904. Also created Mime in *Rheingold* and *Siegfried*, much to the satisfaction of Wagner, who (though ambiguously describing him as 'every inch a dwarf') found in him a rare performer who actually fulfilled his ideal of a role. Saint-Saëns and Grieg (who praised his declamation) both declared him one of the most convincing in the cast of the first *Ring*. Toured Europe with Neumann's co. as Mime, 1880–2. Other roles included Almaviva (Rossini), Max, Lionel, and the baritone role of Beckmesser.

Schlusnus, Heinrich (*b* Braubach, 6 Aug. 1888; *d* Frankfurt am Main, 18 June 1952). German baritone. Studied Frankfurt, later Berlin with Bacher. Début Hamburg 1915 (Herald, *Lohengrin*). Berlin, S, 1917–50; Chicago 1927; Bayreuth 1933; Paris, O, 1937; Barcelona; etc. A singer of noble qualities, whose generous, Italianate sound, fine legato, and easy top notes made him an excellent Verdi baritone, e.g. as Rigoletto, Germont, Montfort (*Vêpres siciliennes*); also a successful Amfortas. (R)

Schmedes, Erik (*b* Gentofte, 27 Aug. 1866; *d* Vienna, 23 Mar. 1931). Danish tenor. Studied Berlin with Rothmühl, Paris with Artôt, later Vienna with Ress. Début Wiesbaden 1891 as baritone (Valentin). Nuremberg 1893–4; Dresden 1894–7, during when, after further study with Iffert, became tenor. Vienna 1898–1924; Bayreuth 1899–1902, 1906; New York, M, 1908–9. Also Paris, O; Berlin; Munich; Prague; etc. Roles included Florestan, Siegfried, Tristan, Parsifal, Palestrina. A blond giant with a huge voice, whose greatest musical achievements were reached under Mahler. (R)

Schmidt-Isserstedt, Hans (*b* Berlin, 5 May 1900; *d* Holm bei Wedel, 28 May 1973). German conductor. Studied Heidelberg, Münster, Berlin with Ertel and Schreker. Cond. Wuppertal 1928; Rostock 1928; Darmstadt 1931–3. Chief cond. Hamburg 1935–42; Berlin, Deutsches Opernhaus, 1942–5. Gly. 1958 (*Figaro*); London, CG, 1962 (*Tristan*). Composed *Hassan gewinnt* (1928). (R)

Schneider, Hortense (*b* Bordeaux, 30 Apr. 1833; *d* Paris, 6 May 1920). French soprano, later mezzo. Studied Bordeaux with Schaffner. Début Agen 1853 (Inès, *La favorite*). Paris from 1855 at various venues in works by Offenbach, Adam, etc. Created leading roles in Offenbach's *Belle Hélène*, *Grande-Duchesse de Gérolstein*, *Périchole*, with brilliant success. London 1867; St Petersburg 1872; retired 1878. An accomplished and captivating performer, with an exuberant temperament both on and off stage. Saint-Saëns once thought of her for Dalila.

Schneider, Peter (*b* Vienna, 26 Mar. 1939). Austrian cond. Studied Vienna with Swarowsky. Début Salzburg Landestheater 1959 (Handel's *Giulio Cesare*). Principal cond. Heidelberg O 1961–7; Deutsche O am Rhein 1968–77 (incl. Janáček cycle); Bremen O

1978–85; Mannheim 1985–7. Bayreuth from 1981 (*Fliegender Holländer*, *Lohengrin*, *Ring*). London, CG, 1986 (*Zauberflöte*). A reliable and perceptive conductor of the German repertory, he became music dir. of the Bayerische SO, Munich, 1993. (R)

Schneider-Siemssen, Günther (*b* Augsburg, 7 June 1926). German designer. Studied Munich with Preetorius. Bremen 1954–62; Vienna, S, from 1962; London, CG, *Ring* 1962–4; New York, M, from 1967, incl. *Ring*. Salzburg since 1965, *Boris*, *Don Giovanni*, *Frau ohne Schatten*, and all Karajan's Easter Fest. prods. Adept at traditional settings and using modern techniques with sparse scenery, and what he has called 'painting with light' (or, in some of the Easter productions, darkness).

Schnittke, Alfred (*b* Engels, 24 Nov. 1934). Russian composer. Studied privately in Vienna (1946–8) and the Moscow Cons. 1953–61; teacher of counterpoint and composition there 1962–72. Early influences included serialism and Stockhausen (worked at Moscow Experimental Studio of Electronic Music). His first opera, *The Eleventh Commandment* (1962) was unfinished. From the late 1960s has adopted a highly influential style, using pastiche, quotation, and programmatic material, which he describes as 'polystylistic'. His first completed opera, *Life With an Idiot* (1992), concerns a university lecturer ('I') whose life is ruined by a mental patient who comes to share his flat. A Faust project was initiated with the cantata *'Seid Nüchtern und Wachet ...'* (1982) and was fulfilled with the opera *Historia von D. Johann Fausten* (1995). His most recent opera is *Gesualdo* (1995), on the madrigalist who murdered his wife and her lover.

Schnorr von Carolsfeld, Ludwig (*b* Munich, 2 July 1836; *d* Dresden, 21 July 1865). German tenor. Studied Dresden with J. Otto, and Leipzig. Début Karlsruhe 1853 (in small roles). Karlsruhe until 1860; Dresden 1860–5; Munich 1865. Though corpulent, he was a heroic and affecting performer, intelligent, dramatically powerful, and vocally gifted. After triumphs as Lohengrin and Tannhäuser, created Tristan, with a dedication that contributed to his premature death within weeks. His loss profoundly affected Wagner. He had married 1860 the Danish soprano **Malvina Garrigues** (*b* Copenhagen, 7 Dec. 1825; *d* Karlsruhe, 8 Feb. 1904). She studied Paris with García. Début

Breslau 1841 (in *Robert le diable*). Karlsruhe 1854–60, where she met her husband. Created Isolde with him in Munich, to equal acclaim. She retired after his death, and taught; her pupils included Gudehus.

Schoeck, Othmar (*b* Brunnen, 1 Sept. 1886; *d* Zurich, 8 Mar. 1957). Swiss composer. Studied Zurich with Attenhofer. His sensitivity to poetry and love of the human voice led him to express himself most fully in song and opera. His first opera, *Erwin und Elmire* (1916), is written in somewhat Mozartian language and also shows the influence of Strauss's *Ariadne auf Naxos*, but its favourable reception gave Schoeck encouragement. He followed it with *Don Ranudo* (1919), a comedy whose lack of love interest did not prevent its initial success; there ensued two works on a theme that absorbed Schoeck, *Das Wandbild* (1921), a Hoffmannesque fantasy to a text by Busoni concerning a portrait that comes to life, and *Venus* (1922), in which it is a statue that comes to life.

His most important opera, however, followed in 1927 with *Penthesilea* (1927). Schoeck claimed to have learnt from Wagner, Strauss, and Ravel; its Expressionistic music is more advanced than that of *Elektra*, but does not go so far as *Lulu*. Despite his assertion that 'The artist must speak the language of his day', he reverted to a more tonally stable idiom with *Vom Fischer und syner Fru* (1930). His dislike of German nationalism did not leave him unaware of the advantages of maintaining cultural links with Hitler's Germany. *Massimilla Doni* (1937) was accordingly premiered with success under Karl Böhm in Dresden, where the critics eagerly emphasized the work's supposed 'Germanness'. Similar success attended *Das Schloss Dürande* (1943) in Berlin, though its run was abandoned shortly after Goering made a furious attack on the libretto. None of Schoeck's operas found a place in the repertory during his lifetime, though *Penthesilea* has enjoyed a revival in Germany since the late 1970s. However, the best of his work has a subtlety and also a Romanticism that in varying ways and to varying degrees of success reconciles itself to more modern styles.

Schoenberg, Arnold (*b* Vienna 13 Sept. 1874; *d* Los Angeles, 13 July 1951). Austrian composer. Studied Vienna with Zemlinsky. Schoenberg first turned to opera in 1909 with the composition of *Erwartung*, though its prem., like that of its successor *Die glückliche Hand*, was not given until 1924. Both are imbued with the spirit of the Expressionist movement and are among the earliest works in which tonality was definitely abandoned. *Erwartung*, which took him only 17 days to write, is a monodrama centring on the experiences of a woman who, wandering through the wood at night in search of her lost lover, discovers his dead body. To a generation which stood so much under the influence of Wagner's music dramas, the links between *Tristan* and *Erwartung*, which might be seen as an Expressionist version of its *Liebestod, were obvious. In his intense exploration of the woman's feelings and recollections, Schoenberg penetrates the depths of human experience, conveying the nightmare journey of her mind in music which eschews the use of obvious themes or their development. Despite its delayed production, *Erwartung* was known to the circle around Schoenberg and influenced a whole series of similarly Expressionist works by his fellow composers. He himself continued many of the same ideas in *Die glückliche Hand*, which again centres on one character, though it also calls for mimed dance and a chorus. Again, a re-interpretation of a characteristically Wagnerian theme is the basis for the action: the quest for truth by the artist, whose *glückliche Hand* is his individual, specially favoured touch.

Schoenberg's next opera, *Von Heute auf Morgen* (1930), was the first in which twelve-note, serialist principles were used. But those who were acquainted with his instrumental music in this style and expected something arid, or uncompelling, were disappointed. A brilliantly observed comedy of a witty and determined woman keeping hold of her husband, it is satirical and farcical, yet manages none the less to mirror the symmetry of the music with a plot and action which is contrived in a similarly balanced fashion. Freer serialist principles were used for Schoenberg's last opera, *Moses und Aron*, which remained uncompleted on his death and was not staged until 1957. His largest dramatic work, it is also his fullest expression of the quest theme that absorbed him so deeply. Concerning communication between God and Man, its action hinges around the distortion suffered by pure truth (received by Moses) when it undergoes exposition (by Aron) in terms comprehensible to

Man. Schoenberg's religious nature and his artist's concern over communication were profoundly touched by this theme, and the opera has by its emotional power done much to overcome prejudices against him. Of all Schoenberg's works composed after his discovery of serialism, it offers the closest *rapprochement* between new procedures and those of traditional tonal music.

Schöffler, Paul (*b* Dresden, 15 Sept. 1897; *d* Amersham, 21 Nov. 1977). German, later Austrian, baritone. Studied Dresden with Staegemann, Berlin with Grenzebach, Milan with Sammarco. Début Dresden 1925 (Herald, *Lohengrin*). Dresden until 1938. Vienna, S, 1938–65; London, CG, 1934–9, 1949–53; New York, M, 1949–53, 1954–6, 1962–5; Bayreuth 1943–4; Salzburg 1938–41, 1947, 1949–65. Highly regarded as a Wagner interpreter, especially as Sachs, he also sang Figaro, Don Alfonso, Pizarro, Iago; created Jupiter (*Liebe der Danae*), and Danton (*Dantons Tod*). (R)

School for Fathers, The. See QUATRO RUSTEGHI, I.

Schorr, Friedrich (*b* Nagyvárád, 2 Sept. 1888; *d* Farmington, CT, 14 Aug. 1953). Hungarian, later US, bass-baritone. Studied Vienna with Robinson. Début Chicago 1912 (small roles). True début Graz 1912 (Wotan). Graz until 1916; Cologne 1918–23; Berlin, S, 1923–31; New York, M, 1924–43; Bayreuth 1925–31; London, CG, 1924–33. Settled in US 1931. The dominating Wotan and Sachs of his generation, he could sing with warm, lyrical ease, yet also with arresting dramatic force, always with exemplary attention to words. Repertory included Pizarro, Amonasro, Scarpia, Jochanaan, Orestes, Doktor Faust. (R)

Schreier, Peter (*b* Meissen, 29 July 1935). German tenor and conductor. Studied Leipzig with Polster, Dresden with Winkler. Début as student Dresden, S, 1957 (Paolino, *Matrimonio segreto*). Dresden, S, 1959–63; Berlin, S, from 1963; Vienna, Salzburg, and New York, M, 1967–9; Milan, S, and Buenos Aires, C, from 1968. Also London, CG; Moscow, B; Budapest; Warsaw; etc. Large and varied repertory includes Belmonte, Ferrando, Tamino, Loge, David, Flamand, Lensky. An extremely intelligent singer and actor, with a fine legato line, and sympathetic feeling for the text. An excellent Lieder singer. (R)

Schreker, Franz (*b* Monaco, 23 Mar. 1878; *d* Berlin, 21 Mar. 1934). Austrian composer, teacher, and conductor. Studied Vienna with Fuchs; from 1912 taught composition at the Vienna Academy. He began work on his first opera, *Der ferne Klang*, as early as 1903, though it was not completed until 1912, when its prem. in Frankfurt marked him down as the most gifted operatic composer of his generation. Among the work's admirers were Schoenberg, who quoted passages of it in his *Harmonielehre*, and Berg, who made the piano score and was influenced (in *Wozzeck*) by its use of set forms. One of the first German works to acknowledge the impact of Debussy's music, it is an important essay in Expressionism and shares some of the same vision and musical language as Strauss's *Elektra* and Schoenberg's *Erwartung*.

Schreker's next work, *Das Spielwerk und die Prinzessin* (1913), caused an outrage when performed before the conservative Viennese audience 1913; a more experimental work, making some use of pan-tonality, both its music and libretto offended. More successful were *Die Gezeichneten* (1918) and *Der Schatzgräber* (1920), which confirmed his reputation as an avant-garde composer and led to the prestigious directorship of the Berlin Hochschule in 1920. During the 1920s and 1930s Schreker came increasingly under attack: from musicians, who began to revolt against the late Romantic style which he represented, and from the Nazis, because of his Jewish origins. The prem. of *Christophorus* (comp. 1924–7) was cancelled for fear of the Nazi demonstrations which later totally disrupted that of *Der Schmied von Gent* (1932). In 1932 Schreker was removed from his position at the Berlin Hochschule for political reasons.

Though perhaps the most original German opera composer after Berg and Schoenberg during the first decades of the 20th cent., Schreker did not have a lasting influence, due in no small measure to the rise of the Nazis. But the important emancipating effect which his works had for later composers, opening up a world beyond that of post-Wagnerian music drama, cannot be underestimated, while at their best they have real dramatic power in their own right.

Schröder-Devrient, Wilhelmine (*b* Hamburg, 6 Dec. 1804; *d* Coburg, 26 Jan. 1860). Daughter of **Friedrich Schröder** (1744–1816), the first German Don Giovanni, and the actress **Sophie Bürger Schröder** (1781–1868), 'the German Mrs Siddons'. Appeared in ballet, Hamburg and Vienna, as child, later as actress. Studied with her mother, and Vienna with Mozatti. Début Vienna, K, 1821 (Pamina). Vienna, K, until 1822; Dresden 1822–47; Berlin 1828; Paris 1831–2; London, H, 1832–3, 1837. By now her voice was declining, but she successfully created Adriano (*Rienzi*), Senta, and Venus. Last appearance Riga 1847. Though deficient in vocal technique, she was a powerful and moving actress, dubbed 'the Queen of Tears' when seen really weeping on stage. She was famous for her Donna Anna, Euryanthe, Reiza, Norma, Valentine; and Weber thought her the best of all Agathes, who revealed more than he had believed the role to contain. Beethoven, who had rehearsed her, thanked her personally for her Leonore. This was by all accounts the greatest interpretation of the age; Moscheles preferred her to Malibran, and Wagner was aroused by it to his sense of vocation as a composer, as he describes in *Mein Leben*. Her style later disturbed Berlioz with its exaggeration and vehemence, and she was criticized for declaiming rather than singing, but she was one of the principal performers to inspire and contribute to German Romantic opera with her committed and passionate approach. Her private life suffered: her first marriage to Karl Devrient ended with divorce; she remarried twice, and had a succession of lovers, defending her life as 'grist to her art'.

Schubert, Franz (*b* Vienna, 31 Jan. 1797; *d* Vienna, 19 Nov. 1828). Austrian composer. Studied Vienna with Ruzička and Salieri. For the whole of his life, Schubert hoped for, and frequently attempted to write, the successful opera that would have helped to establish his wider renown. The operas he saw in Vienna which most influenced him were those by Weigl and Gyrowetz, as well as the many lighter pieces with music by Wenzel *Müller. His own completed operas fall broadly into three categories: most are Singspiels, one is a melodrama, and three are true operas.

For all the Romantic absurdities of the plot of *Des Teufels Lustschloss* (comp. 1813–14), the music is said to have astonished Salieri with its quality and range, and does indeed contain some powerful invention, especially orchestral; but despite an impressive fluency between numbers, the work shows the lack

of true dramatic instinct that was to plague Schubert. In the following year, 1815, he completed four Singspiels. *Der vierjährige Posten* is a slight, amusing piece in simpler style, with separate songs in a manner very different from the Lied, of which Schubert was already making himself a great master. *Fernando* is somewhat weightier, and in its scoring again reflects Schubert's ability to conceive of orchestral effects that belong purely in the theatre. Despite use of a more skilful libretto (by Goethe), *Claudine von Villa Bella* is not very distinctive; but by the end of the year, with *Die Freunde von Salamanka*, Schubert's technique had greatly matured, and there are signs that he was trying to make the music interact with the (lost) dialogue.

Apart from the unfinished *Die Bürgschaft* (comp. 1816), which shows signs of growing out of hand, Schubert wrote no more theatre music until 1819 and the unfinished *Adrast* (which contains some splendid music) and *Die Zwillingsbrüder*; 1820 saw some delightful and well-planned music for a melodrama, *Die Zauberharfe*. In 1821 he was briefly appointed to a conducting post at the Court T, where his tasks included coaching Caroline Unger in *Così fan tutte*, but he soon resigned. In 1821–3 came the three works that crown his brief operatic career. Of all his stage works, Schubert set most store by *Alfonso und Estrella* (comp. 1822), his most lyrical opera though once again weakened by a fatally static quality. The only one of his operas to have achieved much posthumous success came next, *Die Verschworenen* (or *Der häusliche Krieg*) (comp. 1823): here, the lyrical gifts are more successfully matched to deft dramatic strokes. With *Fierrabras* (comp. 1823), there is not only orchestral mastery and some beautiful individual numbers, but a more expert use of *reminiscence motive and a freer dramatic construction. There are fewer set arias, more scenas that merge swiftly into one another, though Schubert's dramatic instincts are insufficiently strong to keep him from falling prey to banal situations and to numbers in which his genius for sustaining musical structures works against a true opera composer's sense of when these must be governed by dramatic considerations. At least some of the blame for Schubert's lack of operatic success can be attributed to the fact that only one of his operas was staged in his lifetime, *Die Zwillingsbrüder*, and this was withdrawn after about a dozen performances. *Fierrabras* contains enough achievement, and more promise, for his early death to seem tragic in the field of opera as in those of song, symphony, and chamber music where his genius is more fully revealed.

Schuch, Ernst von (*b* Graz, 23 Nov. 1846; *d* Kötzschenbroda, 10 May 1914). Austrian conductor. Studied Graz with Stolz, Vienna with Dessoff. Music dir., Lobe's T in Breslau 1867; répétiteur Würzburg 1868–70; Graz 1870–1; Basle 1871. Music dir. Dresden, Italian O, 1872; music dir., Dresden H, with Rietz from 1873, with Wüllner from 1879; in sole charge 1882–1914. Schuch made this one of the great periods in the city's operatic history. He was a cultivated, enterprising, and highly practical musician, with a belief in opera as music drama which he had inherited from his predecessors Weber and Wagner and a close control over all aspects of performance. It was only in the interests of greater orchestral control that he felt obliged to move the conductor's rostrum back from the old position near the footlights to the orchestra rail. He gave 51 prems., including several of Strauss's most important works: *Feuersnot* (1901), *Salome* (1905), *Elektra* (1909), and *Rosenkavalier* (1911). Strauss negotiated hard with him, but declared, 'Schuch is a wonder'. Also conducted prems. of Bungert's tetralogy *Odyssee* (1898–1903), Paderewski's *Manru* (1901), Dohnányi's *Tante Simona* (1912), and Wolf-Ferrari's *L'amore medico* (1913), gave some celebrated Wagner performances, and introduced Puccini to Dresden.

Schulz, Johann Abraham Peter (*b* Lüneburg, 31 Mar. 1747; *d* Schwedt an der Oder, 10 June 1800). German composer and conductor. Studied Berlin with C. P. E. Bach and Kirnberger. He was music director of the French O in Berlin from 1776, later taking an additional court appointment at Rheinsberg. His championship of new music, especially that of Gluck, brought him into disfavour, so he resigned 1787, taking a position in Copenhagen as Kapellmeister at court and director of the Royal Danish O.

Schulz wrote several operas for Berlin and Rheinsberg, including *La fée Urgèle* (1782) and *Athalie* (1785), but his most important stage works were given in Copenhagen. In his Singspiels *Høstgildet* (1790), *Indtoget* (1793), and *Peters bryllup* (1793), which follow in essential outline the main N German style of Singspiel of the day, he made an important contribution to the foundation of national opera in Denmark.

Schuman, William (*b* New York, 4 Aug. 1910; *d* New York, 15 Feb. 1992). US composer. Studied New York (Malkin Cons.) with Persin and Haubiel, Columbia U, Salzburg Mozarteum, Juilliard School. 1935–45 taught at Sarah Lawrence Coll.; 1945–62 president, Juilliard School; 1962–9 president of Lincoln Center. Though his reputation was established largely by his orchestral music, he wrote several ballets and the popular *The Mighty Casey* (1953), whose plot centres around a baseball hero.

Schumann, Elisabeth (*b* Merseburg, 13 June 1888; *d* New York, 23 Apr. 1952). German, later US, soprano. Studied Dresden with Hänisch, Berlin with Dietrich, Hamburg with Schadow. Début Hamburg 1909 (Shepherd, *Tannhäuser*). Hamburg until 1919; Vienna 1919–38; London, CG, 1924–31; New York, M, 1914–15. Settled in US 1938. Her fresh, silvery voice, used with unerring skill and intelligence, her immaculate phrasing, sensitivity, and purity of style, together with irresistible personal charm, made her a singer who inspired a rare affection in her listeners. Unforgettable as Blonde, Susanna, Zerlina, Eva, Adele, and especially Sophie, she was also treasured for her Lieder singing. Toured US 1921 with R. Strauss, her great admirer and supporter, performing his songs. (R)

Schumann, Robert (*b* Zwickau, 8 June 1810; *d* Endenich, 29 July 1856). German composer. His one opera, *Genoveva* (1850), includes some excellent music, but reveals his difficulty in thinking in dramatic terms: there is little characterization, and the effects tend to be muted, in part through his scorn of all he thought cheap in Italian opera. It reflects his admiration for *Euryanthe*, including in its more advanced use of motive, and harmonically approaches some of the practices of Wagner, who was bemused by Schumann's reluctance to take his advice about the work. He also left some fragments of a setting of Byron's *The Corsair*.

Schumann-Heink, Ernestine (*b* Lieben, 15 June 1861; *d* Hollywood, 17 Nov. 1936). Austrian, later US, contralto. Studied Graz with Leclair and Wüllner. Début (as Tini Rössler) Dresden 1878 (Azucena). Dresden until 1883, and in 1909; Hamburg 1883–97; Bayreuth

1896 regularly until 1914; London, CG, 1897–1901; New York, M, 1899–1903, and frequently until 1932. Had three husbands, taking her stage name from her first and second (Ernest Heink and Paul Schumann). Possessed a deep, powerful voice and a compelling artistic personality. Her outstanding achievements were in Wagner, e.g. Ortrud, Fricka, and especially with her extraordinary Erda (as which Cosima Wagner always addressed her), still impressive at 70; but also in Donizetti, and as Amneris, Fidès, Orlovsky, Carmen, Witch (*Hänsel*). Created Klytemnästra, pronouncing the opera 'a fearful din'. (R)

Schürmann, Georg Caspar (*b* Idensen, 1672 or 1673; *d* Wolfenbüttel, 25 Feb. 1751). German composer. Sang at Hamburg O from *c*.1692; 1697 joined Brunswick court as singer and conductor of opera. Studied in Italy 1701–2. Wrote *c*.40 operas (mostly lost), including *Die getreue Alceste* (1719); though originally intended for the Brunswick court, many of these were eventually taken into the repertory of the Hamburg O. One of the most highly regarded early composers of German opera, his works show both French and Italian characteristics and were an important influence on succeeding generations, surpassed only by that of Keiser.

Schütz, Heinrich (*b* Köstritz, *bapt.* 9 Oct. 1585; *d* Dresden, 6 Nov. 1672). German composer. Studied in Italy with Giovanni Gabrieli (1609–12). Dresden from 1614, rising to the position of Electoral Kapellmeister. Although known today as a composer of sacred music, Schütz produced several dramatic entertainments for festivities at the Dresden court; one, a setting of Martin Opitz's translation of Rinuccini's *Dafne*, is sometimes regarded as the first German opera. Written to celebrate a royal marriage in 1627, the score of *Dafne*, like that of all his stage works, is lost. It has been suggested that Schütz wrote another opera in Italy in the following year, but there is no concrete evidence to support this claim.

Schützendorf. German family of singers, all brothers.

1. **Guido** (*b* Vught, 22 Apr. 1880; *d* Apr. 1967). Bass. Studied Cologne. Sang with German OC throughout Germany and US. Title-role of silent film, *Der fliegende Holländer* (1919).

2. **Alfons** (*b* Vught, 25 May 1882; *d* Weimar,

Aug. 1946). Bass-baritone. Studied Cologne with Walter, Milan with Borgatti. Bayreuth 1910–12; London, CG, 1910; also Prague, Vienna, etc. (R)

3. **Gustav** (*b* Cologne, 1883; *d* Berlin, 27 Apr. 1937). Baritone. Studied Cologne Cons. and Milan. Début Düsseldorf 1905 (Don Giovanni). Berlin, H; Munich, N, 1914–20; New York, M, 1922–35. Roles included Alberich, Beckmesser, Faninal, and first Luna (*Palestrina*). His first wife was Delia *Reinhardt. (R)

4. **Leo** (*b* Cologne, 7 May 1886: *d* Berlin, 18 Dec. 1931). Bass-baritone. Studied Cologne with D'Arnals. Début Düsseldorf 1908. Engagements at Krefeld, Darmstadt, Wiesbaden; Vienna 1919–20; Berlin, S, 1920–9. A versatile actor, he sang in a wide range of parts, including Gounod's Méphistophélès, Boris, Ochs. Created Wozzeck, when Berg called him 'superb'. (R)

The four brothers performed together only once, in *Die Meistersinger*, Bremen 1916: Alfons sang Sachs; Leo, Beckmesser; Gustav, Pogner; and Guido, Kothner.

Schwanda the Bagpiper. See SHVANDA THE BAGPIPER.

Schwarzkopf, (Dame) **Elisabeth** (*b* Jarocin, 9 Dec. 1915). German soprano. Studied Berlin with Mysz-Gmeiner, later Ivogün. Début Berlin, SO, 1938 (Flowermaiden). Berlin until 1942; Vienna 1942–7; London, CG, 1947, 1948–51, 1959; Milan, S, 1948–63; Chicago 1959; New York, M, 1964–6. Created Anne Trulove. Roles included Marzelline, Violetta, Mimì, Mélisande; particularly associated with Donna Elvira, Countess (Mozart), Marschallin. A beautiful woman with a fine voice, whose interpretations were always contrived to give maximum effect. (R)

Schweigsame Frau, Die (The Silent Woman). Opera in 3 acts by Richard Strauss; text by Stefan Zweig, after Ben Jonson's drama *Epicœne* (1609). Prem. Dresden 24 June 1935.

London, 1780. Sir Morosus (bs), a retired English admiral, cannot abide noise of any kind. His nephew Henry (ten) is secretly married to Aminta (sop), and both are members of a group of travelling actors. With the help of the Barber (bar), they arrange a mock marriage between Morosus and 'Timida', the silent woman, actually Aminta in disguise. Once married, she emerges (like Norina in *Don Pasquale*) as a noisy termagant. Morosus gives the young couple his blessing, and adopts a more mellow attitude to life.

Sciutti, Graziella (*b* Turin, 17 Apr. 1927). Italian soprano. Studied Rome. Début Aix-en-Provence 1950 (Elisetta, *Matrimonio segreto*). Gly. 1954–9, 1970, 1977; London, CG, 1956–62; Milan, S, from 1956; also Salzburg, Vienna, Rome etc. An outstanding soubrette, vivacious, and with excellent diction. Roles included Susanna, Despina, Papagena, Rosina, Norina, Nannetta. Also producer (New York, Chicago, Coblenz, Gly.). (R)

Scotland. See EDINBURGH, GLASGOW, SCOTTISH OPERA.

Scotti, Antonio (*b* Naples, 25 Jan. 1866; *d* Naples, 26 Feb. 1936). Italian baritone. Studied Naples with Triffani Paganini. Début Naples 1889 (Cinna, *La vestale*). Appearances in Madrid, Buenos Aires, Moscow; Milan, S, 1898; London, CG, 1899–1910, 1913–14; New York, M, 1899–1933. Repertory included Don Giovanni, Posa, Scarpia, Sharpless, Iago (Verdi), Falstaff. In his prime, possessed a smooth, fine tone; always sang and acted with great artistry though his voice declined latterly. (R)

Scottish Opera. Founded in Glasgow in 1962 by Alexander Gibson, with Peter Hemmings as general administrator, the company began with two operas in its first season, *Madama Butterfly* and *Pelléas*. By 1975 it had staged 50 operas. Among its many achievements have been the completion of a *Ring* in 1971, *The Trojans* with Janet Baker, and commissions from Scottish composers including Musgrave (*Mary, Queen of Scots*) and Hamilton (*The Catiline Conspiracy*). Until 1975 the company toured Scotland and Northern England from a base in the Theatre Royal (opened 1867), which was restored and made its permanent home in 1976 (cap. 1,560); this was the first British opera-house to open since the war. From 1967 the company appeared regularly at the Edinburgh Fest. with a number of outstanding productions including *The Rake's Progress*. Its achievements also include a successful Janáček cycle. The faithful audience which had been built up found its loyalty tested by some productions in the late 1980s. Gibson was succeeded by John Mauceri in 1986. Richard Armstrong became music dir. 1993.

Scotto, Renata (*b* Savona, 24 Feb. 1933).

Italian soprano. Studied Milan with Ghirardini and Llopart. Début Milan, N, 1953 (Violetta). Milan, S, from 1953; London, Stoll T 1957, and CG from 1962; New York, M, from 1965. Also Vienna; Paris, O; Chicago; Buenos Aires; Moscow; etc. Roles include Amina (as which successfully replaced Callas, Edinburgh 1957), Norma, Lucia, Gilda, Amelia, Mimì, Butterfly, Gioconda. Possessing a full-toned, flexible lirico-spinto soprano, also very effective in her characterizations. (R)

Scribe, Eugène (*b* Paris, 14 Dec. 1791; *d* Paris, 20 Feb. 1861). French librettist. He began his theatrical career as a writer of comedies. His first great operatic success came with the text for Auber's opéra-comique *La dame blanche* (1825). However, by his skilful appreciation of the theatrical conditions of the Paris of his day, and of the sensibilities of the audiences, he reanimated the genre of French *Grand Opera as well as giving opéra-comique a new strength. He followed up his first success for Auber with *La muette de Portici* (1828), which gave Grand Opera a new stature and style: in all, Auber was to set 38 of his librettos. Among many other composers with whom he worked, Halévy and especially Meyerbeer stand out as central representatives of the genre of Grand Opera.

Scribe inherited the historical awareness of Jouy's librettos for Spontini, and capitalized on the opportunities for staging on the most elaborate scale afforded by the Opéra. If characterization was sacrificed to grandeur, the effectiveness of his texts assured him and his composers of the greatest success. His plots often draw on historical sources, but are thoroughly reworked rather than directly adapted from a literary original, and frequently deal in the clashing of religious, national, or political orthodoxies and the lives and loves of characters caught up in them: the chorus is thus made a more functional part of the drama. This did not preclude the use of collaborators, chiefly in order to polish or even write verses to suit the strong stage situations in which he specialized. He was also adept at accepting or inventing novel effects: examples in Meyerbeer are the scene of the ghostly nuns in *Robert le diable*, the bathing scene in *Les Huguenots*, and the skating scene in *Le prophète*. He gave Grand Opera a definitive form, and an influence that was potent even in those, such as Wagner, who most sharply attacked it.

Sea Interludes. The name generally given to the orchestral interludes in Britten's *Peter Grimes*. Though four are usually selected for concert performance, they are in fact six in number: 'Dawn' opening Act I, 'Storm' between scenes 1 and 2 of Act I, 'Sunday Morning' opening Act II, a passacaglia between scenes 1 and 2 of Act II, 'Moonlight' opening Act III, and a final interlude between scenes 1 and 2 of Act III.

Searle, Humphrey (*b* Oxford, 26 Aug. 1915; *d* London, 12 May 1982). English composer. Studied London with Jacob, Morris, and Ireland; Vienna with Webern. His first opera, *The Diary of a Madman* (1959), was a Berlin Fest. commission that made use of electronic music as well as a normal orchestra. *The Photo of the Colonel* (1964) confronts the question of making the serial technique of which Searle was one of the leading British exponents a real vehicle for comedy, solving it by extensive use of rapid parlando passages for the singers with the burden of the commentary in the orchestra. *Hamlet* (1968) matches contemporary operatic techniques to Shakespeare's tragedy, and provides some ingenious music (for instance in deriving all the material from the 'To be or not to be' series) that attempts to expose rather than interpret the issues at the centre of the play.

Sébastian, Georges (*b* Budapest, 17 Aug. 1903; *d* nr. Paris, 13 Apr. 1989). Hungarian later French, conductor. Studied Budapest with Bartók, Kodály, and Weiner, Munich with Walter. Répétiteur Munich 1922; New York, M, 1923–4. Cond. Hamburg 1924–5; chief cond. Berlin, SO, 1927–31. Moscow Radio 1931–7. S Francisco 1944–6. Chief cond. Paris, O, 1947–73, where he specialized in Wagner and Richard Strauss, also being much admired in Verdi and Puccini and for his *Carmen*; also Paris, OC. Frequent appearances in French provinces and Geneva. Mexico 1978. (R)

Šebor, Karel (*b* Brandýs nad Labem, 1843; *d* Prague, 17 May 1903). Czech composer. Studied Prague with Kittl. Kapellmeister, Erfurt 1863; chorus-master, Prague, P, 1865; returned after a period in Vienna and other cities to Prague, 1894. His operas, which include *Templáři na Moravě* (The Templars in Moravia, 1865) and *Nevěsta Husitská* (The Hussite's Bride, 1868), are important as early attempts at a Czech national style.

Secunde, Nadine (*b* Independence, OH, 21 Dec. 1953). US soprano. Studied with Margaret Harshaw. Sang at Wiesbaden from 1980; Cologne from 1985 (début as Káťa Kabanová). A spirited performer in the dramatic repertory, she has sung Elsa at Bayreuth (début 1987) and London, CG (1988). Other successful roles incl. Elisabeth, Cassandre (Los Angeles 1992), Chrysothemis (Chicago 1992). (R)

Secret, The (Cz., *Tajemství*). Opera in 3 acts by Smetana; text by Eliska Krásnohorská. Prem. Prague, C, 18 Sept. 1878.

A small N Bohemian town, end 18th cent. The plot concerns the separation through pride and poverty of two lovers, Rose (con), and Councillor Kalina (bar), who after many vicissitudes discover one another when Kalina, seeking a promised treasure, follows an underground passage that leads him into Rose's house.

Sedaine, Michel-Jean (*b* Paris, 2 June 1719; *d* Paris, 17 May 1797). French librettist. Originally a stonemason, he began writing vaudevilles for the Opéra-Comique after the *Guerre des Bouffons. His first successes were comédies mêlées d'ariettes, in the style of Favart but, as in his text for Philidor's *Le diable à quatre* (1756) and *Blaise le savetier* (1759), with greater attention to the detail of the action and the setting. His texts for Monsigny were particularly successful, and *On ne s'avise jamais de tout* (1761) was an example for Beaumarchais in *Le barbier de Séville*. The realism of his plots and incidents (as opposed to the idealized pastoral convention) impressed his contemporaries, despite the poor quality of the actual verse: his greatest strength is his instinctive grasp of theatrical character and situation. His librettos for Monsigny's *Le déserteur* (1769) and Grétry's *Richard Cœur-de-Lion* (1784) transform the *larmoyant* element from being merely a touch of colour for the ingénue into the atmosphere of the whole drama, and subdue the comic element: their mixture of comic and serious disconcerted audiences, but was influential on *rescue opera, and even on Romantic opera. Two more important librettos were for Grétry's *Raoul Barbe-bleue* (1789) and *Guillaume Tell* (1791). Sedaine helped to increase the importance of opéra-comique as a genre, and hence to give the Opéra-Comique a new stature *vis-à-vis* the Opéra.

Sedie, Enrico delle. See DELLE SEDIE, ENRICO.

Seefried, Irmgard (*b* Köngetried, 9 Oct. 1919; *d* Vienna, 24 Nov. 1988). Austrian soprano. Studied Augsburg with Mayer. Début Aachen 1940 (Priestess, *Aida*). Vienna, S, from 1943. London, CG, 1947–9; New York, M, 1953–4. Also Milan, S; Salzburg; Edinburgh; etc. Her warm tone and appealing personality made her a successful Susanna, Fiordiligi, Eva, Octavian, Composer (Strauss commenting, 'I never knew what a good part that could be'); also sang Cleopatra (*Giulio Cesare*), Marie (*Wozzeck*), Blanche (*Carmélites*). An admired Lieder singer. (R)

Segreto di Susanna, Il (Susanna's Secret). Opera in 1 act by Wolf-Ferrari; text by Golisciani and Zangarini. Prem. Munich, N (as *Susannas Geheimnis*), 4 Dec. 1909.
    Piedmont, early 20th cent. A slight but charming curtain-raiser about a jealous husband, Count Gil (bar), who, smelling tobacco in the house, suspects his pretty wife Susanna (sop) of secretly entertaining a lover. Susanna's secret is that she herself smokes.

Seidl, Anton (*b* Pest, 7 May 1850; *d* New York, 28 Mar. 1898). Hungarian conductor. Studied Leipzig. Much influenced by Richter, and went to Bayreuth 1872, helping Wagner with preparations for the first *Ring*. On Wagner's warm recommendation cond. Neumann's Wagner Co. in Leipzig 1879, then touring as chief cond. 1883. Cond. Bremen 1883–5. New York, M, 1885–92, 1893–7, US prems. of *Meistersinger* and *Tristan* 1886, *Siegfried* 1887, *Götterdämmerung* 1888, *Rheingold* 1889. London, HM, 1882, first English *Ring*; CG 1897. Bayreuth 1897, *Parsifal*. With *Richter, *Mottl, *Levi, and *Muck, one of the first generation of great Wagner conductors. In 1883 married the soprano **Auguste Kraus** (*b* Vienna, 28 Aug. 1853; *d* Kingston, NY, 17 July 1939), who then sang as Auguste Seidl-Kraus. Studied Vienna with Marchesi. Début Vienna, H, 1877 (small roles). Leipzig 1881–2. London, HM, 1882. Neumann's Wagner Co. 1883. Bremen 1883. New York, M, 1884–7. First US Eva, Woodbird, Gutrune.

Seidl-Kraus, Auguste. See SEIDL, ANTON.

'Se il padre perdei'. Ilia's (sop) aria in Act II of Mozart's *Idomeneo*, reflecting that if she had lost her father in Troy, Idomeneo would now be a father to her and Crete the place where she could be happy.

'Selig wie die Sonne'. The quintet in Act III of Wagner's *Die Meistersinger von Nürnberg*, in which Eva (sop) and Walther (ten) muse rapturously on the song which they hope will gain the prize in the coming contest, Magdalene (mez) and David (ten) reflect on the good fortune this is likely to bring them, and Hans Sachs (bs-bar) confides to himself his thoughts on the loss of Eva.

Sélika. The eponymous African slave (sop), in love with Vasco da Gama and loved by Nélusko, in Meyerbeer's *L'Africaine*.

Sellars, Peter (*b* Pittsburgh, 27 Sept. 1957). US producer. Studied Harvard U, where his highly original theatrical productions earned him early notoriety. On graduating formed his own company, the Explosives B Cabaret; first came to wider attention with Gogol's *The Inspector General* (1980). In 1983 he became director of the Boston Shakespeare Co., in 1984 director of the American Nat. T Co. at the Kennedy Center.
    Sellars's first important production for the opera-house was Handel's *Orlando* (American Repertory T, 1981). With its up-dated setting (the most notable feature of which was Orlando's transformation into an astronaut) and generally loose interpretation, it established Sellars as one of the most controversial figures in US opera. A production of *The Mikado* (transferred to present-day Japan) began his relationship with the Chicago Lyric O (1984); his most notable production here was that of *Tannhäuser* in 1988. For this Sellars not only employed *surtitles for the sung text, but also projected colour-coded lines of his own invention to convey the unsung thoughts of the characters. In John *Adams he found an ideal partner, and played a major role in the conception of both *Nixon in China* and *The Death of Klinghoffer*.
    In the UK Sellars was initially associated with Gly., where his decision, without prior consultation, to excise the spoken dialogue from a production of *The Magic Flute* was widely criticized and led to a management crisis. Salzburg 1992 (*St François d'Assise*); Amsterdam 1993 (*Pelléas*); London, CG, 1995 (*Mathis der Maler*). One of the most inventive and lively figures on the current scene, together with David Pountney he is the most striking practitioner of what may loosely be called 'producer opera'.

Sellem. The auctioneer (ten) in Stravinsky's *The Rake's Progress*.

Sembrich, Marcella (*b* Wiśniewczyk, 15 Feb. 1858; *d* New York, 11 Jan. 1935). Polish, later US, soprano. Taught piano and violin by her father, Kasimir Kochański (she later adopted her mother's maiden name for artistic purposes), and heard playing these, and singing, by Liszt. Though impressed by her talent in all three, he advised her to follow a singing career. Studied Milan with G. Lamperti, later with F. Lamperti. Début Athens 1877 (Elvira, *Puritani*). Dresden 1878–80; London, CG, 1880–5, 1895; New York, M, 1883, 1898–1909 (except one season); also Madrid, Hamburg, St Petersburg, where she so moved Alexander II with a Chopin song that he promised 'not to forget Poland' (but was dead within the week). A highly gifted artist, who gave concerts performing with equal virtuosity as violinist, pianist, and singer, she was universally admired, including by Patti, Clara Schumann, Brahms, Verdi, and Bernhardt; for Puccini she was 'the Mimì'. Repertory also included Zerlina, Rosina, Lucia, Marguerite, Violetta, Elsa, Eva. Using her warm, generous tone and technical brilliance with an exceptional musicality, she was mistress of every style. A pioneer of the song recital without operatic arias. (R)

Semenoff, Ivan (*b* Paris, 7 June 1917; *d* Paris, 14 June 1972). French composer of Russian descent. Studied Paris with Honegger. His operas, exploratory in nature and effectively written for the stage, have won a considerable following in France. They include a popular setting of Chekhov's *The Bear* (*L'ours*, 1958), *Évangéline* (1964), *Don Juan ou L'amour de la géométrie* (1969), and *Sire Halewyn* (1974).

semi-opera. A term used to describe a number of English works of the late 17th-cent. which approach genuine opera in the method of their union of drama and music, yet fall short of true opera since their main action is carried forward in speech. The earliest example is Thomas Betterton's *The Tempest* (1674); Purcell's *King Arthur* (1691) represents its most developed form. More typical is Purcell's *The Indian Queen*, which contains lengthy passages of dialogue into which occasional songs and other pieces are inserted, some of which, e.g. the 'Incantation Scene', exploit operatic procedures to the full.

Semiramide. Opera in 2 acts by Rossini; text by G. Rossi, after Voltaire's tragedy *Sémiramis* (1748). Prem. Venice, F, 3 Feb. 1823.

Babylon, 1200 BC. Semiramide (sop), Queen of Babylon, and her lover Assur (bar) murder the King. She later falls in love with a young man who turns out to be her son Arsace (mez). She receives a mortal blow that Arsace intends for Assur. Arsace is made king.

'Sempre libera'. The cabaletta to Violetta's (sop) aria 'Ah! fors' è lui' in Act I of Verdi's *La traviata*, in which she declares her intention of abandoning her dream of Alfredo's love and returning to her former life of pleasure.

Semyon Kotko. Opera in 5 acts by Prokofiev; text by Valentin Katayev and composer, after Katayev's story. Prem. Moscow, Stanislavsky T, 23 June 1940.

Ukraine, 1918. Semyon Kotko (ten) returns to the Ukraine after the First World War. He wishes to marry Sophia (sop), the daughter of a rich landowner, Tkachenko (bs-bar), who refuses his consent. Semyon's cottage is destroyed by a German detachment; he escapes, and leaves home to form a resistance movement. Returning several months later, he prevents Sophia's marriage to the rich Klembovsky (ten) by blowing up the church.

Seneca. Lucius Annaeus Seneca the Younger (*b* Corduba, *c*.4 BC; *d* Rome, 12 Apr. AD 65), the Stoic philosopher, appears (bs) in Monteverdi's *L'incoronazione di Poppea* in his historical role as Nero's mentor who obeys with dignity the command to commit suicide.

Sénéchal, Michel (*b* Tavery, 11 Feb. 1927). French tenor. Studied Paris with Paulet. Début Brussels, M, 1950. Brussels, M, until 1952. Aix from 1954; Milan, S, 1960; Gly. 1966; Paris, O and OC regularly, B 1990–1; Salzburg 1972–80; New York, M, 1985; also Rome, Toulouse, Marseilles, etc. His many roles incl. Platée (Rameau), Don Basilio (*Figaro*), Don Ottavio, Tamino, Idiot (*Boris*), M. Triquet, Quint, Oberon (Britten), and much French repertoire. A character-actor of great vocal and dramatic finesse. (R)

Senesino (orig. Francesco Bernardi) (*b* Siena, *c*.1680; *d* ?Siena, before 27 Jan. 1759). Italian mezzo-soprano castrato. Venice 1707–8; then at Bologna, Genoa, Naples; Dresden 1717–20. London, H, 1720–8 for Handel, with enormous success. Though his moodiness and arrogance enraged Handel (who called him 'a damned fool', according to Rolli), he was re-engaged 1730–3, until he deserted to the O of the Nobility. Sang with this co. 1733–6, to further acclaim, rivalling even Farinelli in popularity. His departure from London was much mourned by the ladies. Florence 1737–9; Naples 1739–40, though here his style was considered old-fashioned. Created 17 parts for Handel, including Ottone, Giulio Cesare, Bertarido (*Rodelinda*), Siroe, Orlando. With a voice described by Quantz as 'powerful, clear, equal, and sweet', he was remarkable for his singing of recitative, his tastefully ornamented adagios, and fiery allegros; also for his acting and expressiveness.

Senta. Daland's daughter (sop) in Wagner's *Der fliegende Holländer*.

Senta's Ballad. The ballad relating the legend of the Flying Dutchman sung by Senta (sop) in Wagner's *Der fliegende Holländer*, beginning 'Johohoe!'

'Senza mamma, o bimbo'. Angelica's (sop) aria in Puccini's *Suor Angelica*, grieving over the death of her illegitimate baby son and longing to join him in Heaven.

Serafin, Tullio (*b* Rottanova di Cavarzere, 1 Sept. 1878; *d* Rome, 2 Feb. 1968). Italian conductor. Studied Milan with Saladino and Coronaro. Played violin and viola in orchestra, Milan, S. Début (anagrammatically as Alfio Sulterni) Milan 1898 (*Elisir*). Répétiteur Milan, S, 1898, under Toscanini. Cond. Ferrara 1903; Turin 1904–5; also Brescia, Milan, Trieste, Venice, Palermo. London, CG, 1907. Chief cond. Milan, S, 1910–14, 1917–18, giving various prems. (incl. Montemezzi's *L'amore dei tre re* (1913) and *La nave* (1918) and many Italian prems.). Paris, O, 1912 (*Fanciulla del West* with Caruso); Madrid 1912. Inaugurated Verona Arena summer seasons 1913 (*Aida*). Buenos Aires, C, 1914–16. New York, M, 1924–34, giving various prems. (incl. Taylor's *The King's Henchman* (1927) and *Peter Ibbetson* (1931), Gruenberg's *Emperor Jones* (1933), Hanson's *Merry Mount* (1934)) and other US prems. London, CG, 1931. Rome 1934–43 (first Italian *Wozzeck*, with Gobbi, Italian-language *Ring*). Milan, S, 1939–40, 1946–7 (first Italian *Peter Grimes*, 1947). Chicago 1956–8. London, CG, 1952, 1959, 1960. Rome 1962. A conductor of great authority and understanding, with a versatility that centred on the Italian tradition of which he became a distinguished representative, he was particularly admired for his care with singers;

those who owed him much for his shrewdness and wisdom in coaching included Ponselle, Callas, Sutherland, and Gobbi (who thought him 'an infallible judge of voice and character' and 'the most complete man of the theatre of our time'). In no small part responsible for the revival of bel canto. (R)

Seraglio, The. See ENTFÜHRUNG AUS DEM SERAIL, DIE.

Serban, Andrei (*b* Bucharest, 21 June 1943). Romanian producer. Studied T Institute, Bucharest. After working on theatrical productions in New York (with Peter Brook) and Paris, made his début as an opera prod. with WNO 1981 (*Eugene Onegin*). Has worked with WNO on several subsequent occasions (*Puritani*, *Rodelinda*, *Norma*). London, CG, (*Fidelio*, *Prince Igor*); Nancy, 1979 (*Zauberflöte*); New York, CO (*Alcina*); prem. of Glass, *The Juniper Tree* (Cambridge, MA, 1985). Also Geneva, Los Angeles, Bologna.

serenade (It., *serenata*: 'evening song', from *sera*: 'evening'). By origin, a song sung under his lady's window by a lover, with or without instrumental accompaniment, which might in opera be provided by himself (as in Don Giovanni's 'Deh vieni') or by a hired band (as in Almaviva's 'Ecco ridente in cielo' in Rossini's *Barbiere*). The term was soon applied to any instrumental piece of a light nature.

Sergey. A workman (ten), Katerina Ismaylova's lover, in Shostakovich's *The Lady Macbeth of Mtsensk*.

Serov, Alexander (*b* St Petersburg, 23 Jan. 1820; *d* St Petersburg, 1 Feb. 1871). Russian composer and critic. Studied in St Petersburg, initially following a career in the Civil Service. He was greatly encouraged by Stasov, at whose suggestion he began an opera, *The Pagan*, in 1840; other abortive operatic projects included *The Merry Wives of Windsor* and Gogol's *May Night*. Frustrated by his lack of technique, he took correspondence lessons with Osip Hunke, but the problem dogged him all his life, as did his inability to get on with his librettists. His notoriously sharp tongue, coupled with his intellectual acuteness, helped to make him a feared but respected critic. In 1858 he was greatly impressed by a performance of *Tannhäuser* in Dresden, and this not only made him into Wagner's main advocate in a Russia resistant to Wagnerian music drama, but confirmed him in his own creative aims. He contemplated various Wagnerian projects (including an *Undine*). Eventually he settled on *Judith* (1863), paradoxically at first in an Italian treatment and then in a manner that recalls Parisian *Grand Opera rather than Wagner. He broke with Balakirev over *Judith*, and was also at odds with both the Slavophile and Westernizer groups, resisting what he saw as formlessness and subservience to the text (in Dargomyzhsky) in favour of expressive forms controlled by the composer. He took his Wagnerian precepts to the point of having a personal hand in the production of *Judith*.

The success of *Judith* established Serov artistically and materially, and enabled him to marry the pianist and composer **Valentina Bergmann** (1846–1924: she was the first female Russian opera composer, and her *Uriel Acosta* was prem. Moscow 1885, *Ilya Muromets*, with Shalyapin in the title-role, Moscow 1899). He followed this with *Rogneda* (1865), which initially achieved an even greater success than *Judith*. In it, he turned his attention to national legend, intending an opera that would appeal to some of the ideals of the Slavophiles and also be an organically satisfying entity. Ironically many preferred individual parts to the whole, in a work that is certainly very uneven. Once again, there is a spectacular element that suggests Grand Opera rather than Wagnerian ideals of any kind, and that vitiates Serov's own genuinely held ideals: the best of the work was to survive in its influence on Rimsky-Korsakov, Musorgsky, and Borodin.

Serov's last opera, *The Power of Evil* (1871), began as a collaboration with Ostrovsky, whom Serov replaced with a more complaisant librettist. Here, the nationalism is achieved more through use of folk music, leading to a style now deeply imbued with Russian folk styles in its declamation, its harmony, and its rhythmic and metrical characteristics. Though highly controversial, dividing Serov's critics, the work can be defended for its serious, thoroughgoing attempt to unify Russian musical characteristics with music drama on a substantial scale. Serov died leaving the work not quite finished: the score was completed by his wife and Nikolay Solovev.

Serpette, Gaston (*b* Nantes, 4 Nov. 1846; *d* Paris, 3 Nov. 1904). French composer. Studied Paris Cons. with Thomas. Won the Prix de Rome 1871, but failed to gain acceptance as a composer of serious opera. The success of *La branche cassée* at the Paris B. 1874 turned him in the direction of operetta and vaudeville. For the Parisian stage he composed *c*.30 such works, whose deft charm won them great popularity.

Serpina. Uberto's servant (sop), the eponymous maid-mistress of Pergolesi's *La serva padrona*.

Serra, Luciana (*b* Genoa, 4 Nov. 1946). Italian soprano. Studied Genoa Cons. Début Budapest 1966 (in Cimarosa's *Il convito*). Teheran O from 1969 and throughout Italy from 1974 (Bellini's Elvira and Giulietta; Rosina, Ophelia). Admired for her secure coloratura in such roles as Olympia (London, CG, 1980), the Queen of the Night, and Zerlina (*Fra diavolo*; Milan, S, 1992). (R)

Serva padrona, La (The Maid-Mistress). Intermezzo in 2 parts to the opera *Il prigionier superbo* by Pergolesi; text by Federico. Prem. Naples, B, 5 Sept. 1733.

The most famous of all *intermezzos describes how Serpina (sop) lures her master Uberto (bs) into marrying her by pretending to leave with a ferocious soldier, in fact another servant, Vespone (mute).

Servilia. 1. The sister (sop) of Sesto (Sextus), lover of Annio (Annius), in Mozart's *La clemenza di Tito*.

2. Soranus' daughter (sop), lover of Valerius Rusticus, in Rimsky-Korsakov's *Servilia*.

Sessions, Roger (*b* Brooklyn, 28 Dec. 1896; *d* Princeton, 16 Mar. 1985). US composer. Studied Harvard and Yale U, also privately with Bloch. Subsequently held teaching positions at Cleveland Cons., Princeton, Berkeley, and Harvard U. Sessions's music owes most to the models of Stravinsky and the Second Viennese School, whose intellectual clarity he shares; while not as overtly lyrical as that of many of his US contemporaries, notably Copland, it also reflects Bloch's influence in its expansive phrase structure and rich expressive content. Though *The Trial of Lucullus* (1947) was well received, Sessions's operatic reputation rests on the epic *Montezuma* (1964).

Sesto. 1. Sextus (sop cas), a young Roman patrician, Servilia's brother and lover of Vitellia, in Mozart's *La clemenza di Tito*.

2. Pompey's son (sop) in Handel's *Giulio Cesare*.

Séverac, Déodat de (*b* St-Felix-Lauragais, 20 July 1872; *d* Céret, 24 Mar. 1921). French composer. Studied Paris with D'Indy and Magnard. His first opera, *Le cœur du moulin* (1909), indicated his deep love of his native countryside, and in *Héliogabale* (1910), which had its first performance to a crowd of over 15,000 in an arena, he used some Catalan instruments. His style is restrained, and in some ways anticipates neoclassicism.

'Se vuol ballare'. Figaro's (bar) aria in Act I of Mozart's *Le nozze di Figaro*, in which he promises himself to pit his wits against those of Count Almaviva.

Seydelmann, Franz (*b* Dresden, 8 Oct. 1748; *d* Dresden, 23 Oct. 1806). German composer. Studied Dresden with Schürer and Naumann; toured Italy 1765–8. His career was spent entirely at the Dresden court, where he had an active involvement with opera: church composer 1772; Kapellmeister 1787. He wrote 12 stage works, including both Singspiel and opera buffa, the first being *La serva scaltra* (1773) and the most successful *Il mostro* (1786) and *Il turco in Italia* (1788).

Seyfried, Ignaz (*b* Vienna, 15 Aug. 1776; *d* 27 Aug. 1841). Austrian composer, conductor, and writer on music. Studied Vienna with Albrechtsberger, Kozeluch, Mozart, and Winter. He was cond. in Schikaneder's Freihaustheater, later at the T an der Wien, from 1797 to 1827. His career as a composer began with *Der Friede*: of his later works most successful were *Der Wundermann am Rheinfall* (1799), and the biblical music dramas, including *Saul* (1810) and *Noah* (1819). He also made many arrangements, among them the popular *Rochus Pumpernickel*, and provided incidental music for many plays, including the prem. of Grillparzer's *Die Ahnfrau* (1817).

's Gravenhage (Eng., The Hague). See HOLLAND.

Shade, Ellen (*b* New York, 17 Feb. 1944). US soprano. Studied New York, Juilliard School. Début Frankfurt 1972 (Liù). US début Pittsburgh 1972 (Micaëla). New York, M, 1976 (Eva); Chicago, Lyric O, 1978, as Eve in prem. of Penderecki's *Paradise Lost*. An extrovert performer of a wide variety of dramatic roles, she has sung Donna Elvira and Sieglinde in New York, Káťa Kabanová in Geneva, and the Empress (*Frau ohne Schatten*) at the 1992 Salzburg Fest. (R)

Shalyapin, Fyodor (*b* Kazan, 13 Feb. 1873; *d* Paris, 12 Apr. 1938). Russian bass. Of humble peasant origins, he had little formal education, and was self-taught. After difficult years touring with several theatrical troupes, making formal début with Semyonov-Smarsky's Co., Ufa, 1890 (Steward, Moniuszko's *Halka*), he studied briefly Tiflis with his only teacher, Usatov, who taught him free, and gave him invaluable support. Tiflis O 1893, learning over 14 roles in five months. St Petersburg, Panayev's Co. 1894, and M 1895–6. Left, feeling artistically constricted, to work in Mamontov's Private OC, 1896–9. This was a formative period, when he sang 19 roles with the freedom and encouragement to explore and experiment. Moscow, B, 1899–1920, also, unusually, singing for St Petersburg, M. Milan, S, 1901, 1904, 1908, 1912, 1929–30, 1933; Monte Carlo 1905–37; New York, M, 1907–8, 1921–9; London: DL, 1913–14; CG, 1926, 1928–9; L, 1931. Left Russia 1921. Repertory included Leporello, Mozart's Don Basilio, Konchak, Gounod's and Boito's Mephistopheles, Philip, Ivan Susanin, Ivan the Terrible, Miller (Dargomyzhsky's *Rusalka*), Varlaam, Boris, Dosifey; created Salieri (Rimsky-Korsakov) and Massenet's Don Quichotte. His talent was colossal. His natural gifts comprised a beautiful voice with an instinctive control (his mezza voce was much praised), an imposing physique, and plastic features. Combining these with an untiring search for knowledge, acute perception of physical detail and psychological truth, and painstaking costuming and make-up, he created characters with such depth that audiences were spellbound. His creativity extended not only to his own artistic expression (whether singing, acting, drawing, or writing), but also to any production in which he was involved, inspiring all concerned. The revelatory nature of his interpretations, particularly in his Russian roles, helped to bring Musorgsky to the world's attention. (R)

Shaporin, Yury (*b* Glukhov, 8 Nov. 1887; *d* Moscow, 9 Dec. 1966). Russian composer. Studied Kiev with Lyubomirsky, St Petersburg with Sokolov. Founded Grand Drama T with Gorky, Blok, and Lunacharsky, worked as music director, and continued to

work in experimental theatre music. A
project for an opera with Gorky, *The Mother*,
foundered with the writer's death. His only
opera, *The Decembrists*, began life as *Pauline
Goebbel*, and was eventually completed and
performed in 1953. It was found very acceptable to Soviet officialdom for its grandiose
treatment of the subject, but is nevertheless
a work of some power and individuality, cast
in the epic tradition of Glinka's *A Life for the
Tsar*.

Sharpless. The American consul (bar) in
Puccini's *Madama Butterfly*.

Shaw, Glen Byam (*b* London, 13 Dec. 1904;
d Wargrave, 29 Apr. 1986). English producer.
After a career as an actor and theatre producer, turned to opera in 1962 when
appointed dir. of productions at London, SW.
Staged many notable productions for
SW/ENO, including *Idomeneo*, *Rake's Progress*,
the 1968 *Mastersingers*, and, with John Blat-
chley, *The Ring*. His work is marked by an
economy of movement and a concentration
on the essentials of character.

Shepherds of the Delectable Mountains.
See PILGRIM'S PROGRESS, THE.

Sherasmin. Huon's squire (bar), lover of
Fatima, in Weber's *Oberon*.

Shicoff, Neil (*b* New York, 2 June 1949). US
tenor. Sang in the prem. of Virgil Thomson's
Lord Byron while a student at the Juilliard
School, New York. European début Munich
1976 (Maurizio, *Adriana Lecouvreur*). New
York, M, from 1976 (Werther, Hoffmann,
Lensky, Don Carlos, Faust). London, CG, 1988
(Duke of Mantua). With a voice of con-
siderable range, he is equally suited to the
lyric and dramatic Italian repertory. (R)

Shield, William (*b* Swalwell, 5 Mar. 1748; *d*
London, 25 Jan. 1829). English composer and
librettist. His first dramatic work, *The Flitch of
Bacon* (1778), was a considerable success and
launched him on a career during which he
wrote *c*.45 works, most of them for Covent
Garden, where he was house composer for
15 years. Together with Dibdin and Storace,
he dominated the London stage during the
1780s and 1790s and represent the apotheosis of 18th-cent. English comic opera.
Among his successes were *Rosina* (1782) and
The Poor Soldier (1783).

Shimell, William (*b* Ilford, 23 Sept. 1952).

English baritone. Studied London, GSMD,
and London O Centre. Joined London ENO
1980 and has sung Schaunard, Mercutio,
Papageno. US début S Francisco 1988 (Nick
Shadow). Widely admired for his Mozart
roles: Figaro (Geneva, Milan, and Vienna S);
Guglielmo (London, CG); Don Giovanni
(Zurich). Further appearances for Scottish O
and O North. (R)

Shirley, George (*b* Indianapolis, 18 Apr.
1934). US tenor. Studied Detroit with Eber-
sole and Boatner, Washington with Georgi.
Début Woodstock 1959 (Eisenstein). Spoleto
1961; New York, M, 1961–73; London, CG,
from 1967; Gly. 1967–74. Also New York, CO;
Buenos Aires, C; S Fe; Berlin, D; etc. Roles
included Ferrando, Tamino, Alfredo, David,
Loge, Pelléas, Apollo (*Daphne*), Alwa (*Lulu*). (R)

Shirley-Quirk, John (*b* Liverpool, 28 Aug.
1931). English baritone. Studied London
with Henderson. Début Gly. 1962 (Doctor,
Pelléas). London, EOG 1964–73; London, CG,
from 1973; New York, M, 1973; also Holland,
St Louis, Berlin, etc. Created leading roles in
Britten's church parables, the baritone roles
in *Death in Venice*, Coyle (*Owen Wingrave*); also
Lev (*The Ice Break*). Other roles included Guglielmo, Mozart's Almaviva, Golaud, Duke
Bluebeard, Wozzeck. Has used a firm, clean
tone with intelligence and musicality. (R)

Shostakovich, Dmitry (*b* St Petersburg, 25
Sept. 1906; *d* Moscow, 9 Aug. 1975). Russian
composer. Studied Petrograd with Steinberg.
Shostakovich is known to have contemplated
many operatic projects, including Gorky's
The Mother, Sholokhov's *The Quiet Don*, Chek-
hov's *The Black Monk*, Lermontov's *A Hero of
Our Time* (to a libretto by Meyerhold), and
Tolstoy's *Resurrection*. The latter was possibly
to be the second part of his projected trilogy
of operas about women, of which *The Lady
Macbeth of Mtsensk* (1934; second version as
Katerina Izmaylova, 1963) was the first.

Partly under the inspiration of Meyerhold,
to whom he was close in the 1920s, Shostakovich composed *The Nose* in 1927–8.
Gogol's satirical play provided him with a
vein of barbed grotesquerie that closely
matched the sharp, witty, iconoclastic
musical manner that he was still able to
indulge comically and openly. Influenced by
Prokofiev and especially Stravinsky, the work
also ingeniously uses a modern form of the
kind of musical declamation explored by
Shostakovich's admired predecessors Dar-

gomyzhsky and Musorgsky. Some of this manner survives into *The Lady Macbeth of Mtsensk*, notably in the scene in the police station; but it is absorbed into a more lyrical and expansive style that can skilfully contrast the composer's warmly expressed sympathy for the heroine, Katerina Izmaylova, and his scorn for the surrounding characters, venial, shallow, and corrupt, who bring about her sins and downfall. The work's first enormous success was sharply curtailed by a notorious *Pravda* article, 'Confusion instead of Music' (28 Jan. 1936). Inspired by Stalin, this abused the work for its ugliness, tunelessness, noisiness, and especially its treating of sex and violence. It marked not only a tragic turning-point in Shostakovich's career, but showed composers the constricting limits set by the doctrine of Socialist Realism that was imposed in the wake of the permitted arguments of the 1920s.

Shostakovich never completed another opera, though he wrote a single act setting Gogol's *The Gamblers* (comp. 1941–2) in a manner renewing his devotion to Musorgsky. He is said to have abandoned this when he realized it was growing too long and would never be staged. He also completed an operetta based on a local joke, *Moscow, Cheremushky*, and made new versions of Musorgsky's *Boris Godunov* (1940) and *Khovanshchina* (1960, also filmed).

Shuard, Amy (*b* London, 19 July 1924; *d* London, 18 Apr. 1975). English soprano. Studied London with Warren, later with Sacher and Turner. Début Johannesburg 1949 (Aida). London, SW 1949–55, and CG 1954–74; Milan, S, 1962; Bayreuth 1968. Also Buenos Aires, C; Vienna; S Francisco, etc. Roles included Cassandra (Berlioz), Eboli, Lady Macbeth, Kundry, Brünnhilde, Elektra, Turandot, Jenůfa, Káťa. A sensitive, telling performer with an expressive, dramatic voice. (R)

Shuisky. Prince Vassily Ivanovich Shuisky (ten), a boyar, in Musorgsky's *Boris Godunov*.

Shvanda the Bagpiper (Cz., *Švanda dudák*). Opera in 2 acts by Weinberger; text by Miloš Kareš and Max Brod, after the folk-tale by Tyl. Prem. Prague, N, 27 Apr. 1927.

Bohemia, legendary times. Babinsky (ten) persuades Shvanda (bar) to try to win Queen Ice Heart (mez) by means of his piping. Finding Shvanda to be already married, she orders his execution, but he is saved by his music and by Babinsky. A rash promise lands him in Hell, whence he is again rescued by Babinsky, who cheats the Devil (bs) at cards.

Sibelius, Jean (*b* Hämeenlinna, 8 Dec. 1865; *d* Järvenpää, 20 Sept. 1957). Finnish composer. His only opera is a youthful 1-act work, *Jungfrun i tornet* (The Maiden in the Tower, 1896), which owes much to the example of *rescue opera, allied to a nationalist musical style. Also wrote much incidental music.

Siberia. Opera in three acts by Giordano; text by Illica. Prem. Milan, S, 19 Dec. 1903.

Russia, early 19th cent. Vassili (ten), in love with Stephana (sop), mistress of Prince Alexis, has wounded him in a duel, and for this is exiled to Siberia; there he is joined by Stephana, and then Gleby (bar), her manager and former lover. They attempt to escape together, but are shot at by guards; Stephana is fatally wounded, and dies in Vassili's arms.

'Si colmi il calice'. Lady Macbeth's *brindisi in Act II of Verdi's *Macbeth*.

Siebel. A village youth (mez), in love with Marguerite, in Gounod's *Faust*.

Siegfried. 1. The third part of Wagner's *Ring* cycle. See RING DES NIBELUNGEN.

2. The young hero (ten), son of Siegmund and Sieglinde and lover of Brünnhilde, in Wagner's *Siegfried* and *Götterdämmerung*, in *Der Ring des Nibelungen*. His name derives from *Sieg* (victory) and *Friede* (peace or protection).

3. The Count Palatine (bar) in Schumann's *Genoveva*.

Siegfried's Journey to the Rhine. The name generally given to the orchestral interlude between the Prologue and Act I of Wagner's *Götterdämmerung* describing Siegfried's journey from Brünnhilde's fire-encircled rock to the castle of the Gibichungs.

Sieglinde. Hunding's wife, Siegmund's sister and lover (sop), in Wagner's *Die Walküre*. Her name derives from *Sieg* (victory) and *linde* (gentle, also the *Lindenbaum*, or lime tree, whose heart-shaped leaves symbolize love).

Siegmund. Sieglinde's brother and lover (ten) in Wagner's *Die Walküre*. His name derives from *Sieg* (victory), *Mund* (guardian).

Siehr, Gustav (*b* Arnsberg, 17 Sept. 1837; *d* Munich, 18 May 1896). German bass. Studied Berlin with Krause and Dorn. Début Neustrelitz 1863 (Oroveso). Prague 1865–70;

Wiesbaden 1870–81; Bayreuth 1876, 1882–4, 1886, 1889; Munich 1881–96. Repertory included Sarastro, Don Basilio (Mozart), Kaspar, Daland, King Mark. Created Hagen; alternated with Scaria as Gurnemanz in first *Parsifal*. Wagner found his singing and characterization excellent in *The Ring*. He later considered him for Wotan, telling him he had conceived the part for a bass, rather than baritone, voice.

Siems, Margarethe (*b* Breslau, 30 Dec. 1879; *d* Dresden, 13 Apr. 1952). German soprano. Studied Dresden with Orgeni, Paris with Viardot. Début Prague 1902 (Marguerite, *Les Huguenots*). Dresden 1908–20; London, CG, 1913, DL, 1914; also Berlin, Milan, St Petersburg. A singer of extraordinary versatility, she created Chrysothemis, Marschallin (pronounced 'magnificent' by Strauss), and Zerbinetta. Also sang Queen of the Night, Bellini and Donizetti coloratura parts, Amelia, Aida, Venus, Elisabeth, Isolde. Retired 1925. (R)

Siepi, Cesare (*b* Milan, 10 Feb. 1923). Italian bass. Self-taught. Début Schio 1941 (Sparafucile). Resumed career after the war; Milan, S, from 1946; London, CG, 1950, 1962–73; New York, M, 1950–73; also Salzburg, Verona, S America, etc. With a warm, even tone and handsome stage presence, successful as Figaro (Mozart), Don Giovanni, Philip, Mephistopheles (Gounod and Boito), Boris, Gurnemanz. (R)

Siface (orig. Giovanni Francesco Grossi) (*b* Chiesina Uzzanese, 12 Feb. 1653; *d* nr. Ferrara, 29 May 1697). Italian soprano castrato. Studied Rome with Redi. Début Rome 1672. Much early success in Italy, acquiring his nickname from his acclaimed performance of Syphax in Cavalli's *Scipione affricano*, Venice 1678. In the service of the Duke of Modena, 1679–97. Also taken up by Queen Christina, now living in Rome; further success at her theatre, 1679. England 1687, where he was much admired (Purcell writing a harpsichord piece, 'Sefauci's Farewell', lamenting his departure), though he did not sing in opera. Modena, Naples, Parma, Bologna 1688 until his murder by the family of his mistress, Contessa Elena Forni. A singer of great gifts, praised by Mary of Modena as 'the finest musico living', he was an arrogant, capricious, and insolent character whose indiscreet boasting undoubtedly

hastened his own end. As an artist, he was much mourned.

'Si, fui soldato'. Chénier's (ten) defence of his actions in the revolutionary tribunal in Act III of Giordano's *Andrea Chénier*.

Signor Bruschino, Il, ossia Il figlio per azzardo. Opera in 1 act by Rossini; text by Foppa, after a French comedy by De Chazet and Ourry. Prem. Venice, S Moisè, 27 Jan. 1813.

An Italian town, 1800. Sofia (sop), ward of Gaudenzio (bs), is being forced to marry Bruschino's (bar) son, whom she has never seen. Her lover, Florville (ten), passes himself off as the son; when Bruschino himself arrives, he helps the plot along for his own reasons.

'Signore, ascolta'. Liù's (sop) appeal to Calaf to give up his attempt to woo Turandot, in Act I of Puccini's *Turandot*.

Sigurd. Opera in 5 acts by Reyer; text by Du Locle and Blau, after the Nibelung legend. Prem. Brussels, M, 7 Jan. 1884.

The Rhine, legendary times. Hilda (sop), sister of King Gunther (bar), asks Uta (con) for magic aid to win the hero Sigurd (ten). He appears, and having drunk a love potion given to him by Hilda, agrees to obtain the Valkyrie Brunehild (sop) from her fire-encircled rock for Gunther in return for Hilda's hand. Sigurd, in the guise of Gunther, rescues Brunehild and gives her to Gunther, while he marries Hilda; but Brunehild loves Sigurd, sensing him to be her real saviour. Hilda reveals the truth; Sigurd, now free from the effect of the potion, realizes that he loves Brunehild. He is killed by Hagen (bs), Gunther's companion, Brunehild dying beside him. They rise from their funeral pyre to Odin's paradise.

Si j'étais roi (If I were King). Opera in 3 acts by Adam; text by Ennery and Brésil. Prem. Paris, L, 4 Sept. 1852.

A kingdom by the sea, 16th cent. The fisherman, Zephoris (ten), longs to marry the Princess Nemea (sop), whom he rescued from drowning. As a joke, the King (bar) transports him to his castle to lead a courtly life, but evicts him when he becomes betrothed to Nemea. Back in his hut, Zephoris believes the whole episode a dream, but Kadoor (bs), a scheming Prince who intends to murder the King and marry Nemea, arrives to challenge his rival. The King appears and banishes Kadoor, giving his blessing to Zephoris and Nemea.

Silja, Anja (*b* Berlin, 17 Apr. 1935). German soprano. Studied with her grandfather Egon van Rijn. Gave public recital aged 15. Début Brunswick 1956 (Rosina). Stuttgart 1958, and from 1965; Frankfurt 1959 (singing Constanze, Turandot); Bayreuth 1960–6; London, CG, from 1967; also Vienna, Cologne, Chicago, etc. Closely associated with Wieland Wagner, she rapidly made a reputation as a stimulating singing actress. Repertory includes Leonore, Lady Macbeth, Senta, Venus, Isolde, Salome, Elektra, Marie, Lulu, Kostelnička, Emilia Marty. (R)

Sills, Beverly (*b* Brooklyn, 25 May 1929). US soprano. Studied New York with Liebling. Début Philadelphia 1947 (Frasquita). New York, CO, 1955–79; Vienna 1967; Milan, S, 1969; London, CG, 1970; New York, M, 1975–9. Dir. New York, CO, 1979–89. Roles included Cleopatra (Handel), Lucia, Anna Bolena, Queen of Shemakha, Manon. A highly popular singer, effective on stage. (R)

Silva. Don Ruy Gomez de Silva (bs), a Spanish grandee, Elvira's uncle and guardian, in Verdi's *Ernani*.

Silvio. A villager (bar), lover of Nedda, in Leoncavallo's *Pagliacci*.

Sì, mi chiamano Mimì. See 'MI CHIAMANO MIMÌ'.

Simionato, Giulietta (*b* Forlì, 17 May 1910). Italian mezzo-soprano. Studied Rovigo with Lucatello, Milan with Palumbo. Début Florence 1938 (Pizzetti's *Orséolo*). Milan, S, 1939–66; London, CG, 1953, 1964; Chicago 1954; New York, M, 1959–65. Also Gly., Paris, Salzburg, etc. A versatile singer with a vibrant, rich-toned voice, excellent technique, and vivid stage personality. Highly acclaimed as Gluck's Orfeo, Cherubino, Servilia, Jane Seymour, Azucena, Eboli, Quickly; also the soprano role of Valentine. (R)

Simon Boccanegra. Opera in a prologue and 3 acts by Verdi; text by Piave, based on the drama by António García Gutiérrez. Prem. Venice, F, 12 Mar. 1857; rev. version Milan, S, 24 Mar. 1881.

Genoa, 14th cent. Simon Boccanegra (bar), a plebeian candidate, is elected Doge. He hopes this will enable him to marry Maria Fiesco, who already has a daughter by him,

though the child is lost. Maria dies and her father Jacopo Fiesco (bs) curses Boccanegra.

Twenty-five years later Simon's daughter Amelia (sop) has been brought up by his political enemies. In conversation with her, Simon discovers her identity. Paolo (bar), one of Simon's courtiers, loves Amelia, and when the Doge tells him that he must renounce her, he arranges to have her abducted.

Gabriele (ten), who also loves Amelia, murders her abductor and a riot breaks out, interrupting a meeting of the Doge's Council. Gabriele believes Simon was behind the murder and tries to kill him. Amelia intervenes to save her father.

Paolo gives Simon a slow poison and tries to blackmail Gabriele and Fiesco (now living unrecognized under the name of Andrea) into killing the Doge. Gabriele agrees, on being told that Amelia is the Doge's mistress. Simon's life is once again saved by his daughter's intervention. When he discovers that Amelia is Simon's daughter, Gabriele begs forgiveness. He agrees to fight on behalf of the Doge, who agrees that he can marry Amelia.

Paolo joins the rebel army. The plebeians win, and on his way to his execution, Paolo admits to Andrea that he abducted Amelia and tried to kill Simon. Simon meets and recognizes Fiesco (Andrea), joyfully announcing that he can now restore his granddaughter to him. When Amelia enters, he reveals this news to her. As he dies from the effect of Paolo's poison, Simon names Gabriele as his successor.

Simoneau, Léopold (*b* Quebec, 3 May 1916). Canadian tenor. Studied Montreal with Issaurel, later New York with Althouse. Début Montreal 1941 (Hadji, *Lakmé*). Paris, OC, 1949–54; Gly. from 1951; Paris, O, 1948–51; Chicago 1954, 1959; New York, M, 1963; also Vienna, Buenos Aires, Salzburg. Dir. O du Québec 1971. Outstanding, with his poignant, sweet tone and lyrical singing, as Ferrando, Don Ottavio, Tamino, Nadir, Wilhelm Meister (*Mignon*). (R)

Simpleton. The name usually given in English to the *yurodivy* or holy fool (ten) in Musorgsky's *Boris Godunov*.

Singspiel (Ger.: 'song-play'). A term for a German drama in which musical numbers are separated by dialogue. Although plays with inserted numbers were given the name (in various forms and spellings) as early as the 16th cent., it came into more general use in the 17th cent., e.g. with Staden's *Seelewig* (1644), but was not regularly applied to dramas with music in the 18th cent. The influence of French opéra-comique and English ballad opera helped to develop Singspiel as a genre of comic opera with spoken dialogue, especially with the translation *c*.1750 of Coffey's ballad opera *The Devil to Pay* (1731) and *The Merry Cobbler* (1735) by C. F. Weisse as *Der Teufel ist los* and *Der lustige Schuster*, with new music by J. C. Standfuss. Both texts were then set by J. A. Hiller, one of the most important Singspiel composers; he followed these with many more (e.g. *Die Jagd*, 1770), making the genre particularly distinctive in Leipzig. From here it spread to Berlin, where one of the most prominent composers was Benda (*Der Jahrmarkt*, 1775). The tradition thus established bore a strong relationship to opéra-comique in its emphasis upon sentimental, lyrical comedy and, with its frequent use of folk colour, was an important influence on the eventual development of German national opera in the early 19th cent. Other important composers of this tradition included André (*Das tartarische Gesetz*, 1789), Neefe (*Die Apotheke*, 1771), and Reichardt.

In Vienna, following the establishment of the National-Singspiel under Joseph II in 1778, the genre developed along markedly different lines. From Italian opera buffa there came a more lively, sometimes bravura melodic style, while the librettos were characterized by their sharp wit and not infrequent satire and farce. Magic and the supernatural were an important element in Viennese Singspiel, although they were often treated irreverently. Established by Umlauff (*Die Bergknappen*, 1778), the Viennese Singspiel found its most consummate exponent in Dittersdorf (*Doktor und Apotheker*, 1786). Later composers included Schenk (*Der Dorfbarbier*, 1796), Wenzel Müller (*Die Schwestern von Prag*, 1794), and Schubert (*Die Zwillingsbrüder*, 1820). The greatest Singspiel composer was Mozart, who composed two mature examples: *Die Entführung aus dem Serail* (1782) follows more closely the Viennese tradition, and is characterized by its Turkish flavour; *Die Zauberflöte* (1791), while having many points of contact with contemporary magic operas, is a musically more complex work, in which the traditions of Singspiel, opera buffa, and opera seria are all combined.

In the early 19th cent. aspects of Singspiel technique found their way into other genres, principally *rescue opera—the classic example is Beethoven's *Fidelio*—and German Romantic opera, notably Weber's *Der Freischütz*. A Danish branch of Singspiel, established in the late 18th cent. by Schulz and Kunzen, had an equally important influence on the development of national opera there in the 19th cent.

Sinopoli, Giuseppe (*b* Venice, 2 Nov. 1946). Italian conductor and composer. Studied Vienna with Swarowsky. Début Venice 1978 (*Aida*). London, CG, 1983 (*Manon Lescaut*). Bayreuth and New York, M, débuts 1985 (*Tannhäuser* and *Tosca*). Music dir. Berlin, D, 1990; Dresden, S, from 1993. His subjective approach to interpretation has brought him much popularity. His compositions include the opera *Lou Salomé* (1981). (R)

'Sì, pel ciel'. The duet in Act II of Verdi's *Otello*, in which Otello (ten) is joined by Iago (bar) in swearing vengeance on Desdemona for her alleged infidelity.

'Si può?' The prologue to Leoncavallo's *Pagliacci*, in which the singer, generally Tonio (bar), asks the audience to listen to his exposition of the situation before the curtain goes up.

Sir John in Love. Opera in 4 acts by Vaughan Williams; text selected by composer from Shakespeare's *The Merry Wives of Windsor*, *Love's Labour's Lost*, and *Much Ado about Nothing*; also from Thomas Middleton, Ben Jonson, Thomas Campion, *Gammer Gurton's Needle*, Christopher Marlowe, John Fletcher, Psalm 137, George Peele, Nicholas Udall, Philip Sidney, Richard Edwards, Philip Rosseter, and the song 'Greensleeves'. Prem. London, RCM, 21 Mar. 1929.

The plot follows the story of *The Merry Wives of Windsor* and their discomfiture of Falstaff (bar). Several of the minor characters are given larger parts than in Verdi's or Nicolai's operas, as part of the composer's attempt to fill out the vivid English background to the comedy.

Sitzprobe. See PROBE.

Škroup, František (*b* Osice, 3 June 1801; *d* Rotterdam, 7 Feb. 1862). Bohemian composer and conductor. Studied with his father Dominik, then after law studies in Prague was drawn into the movement for Czech national opera, first as an amateur and then as a professional répétiteur, conductor, and composer. With Josef Chmelenský as librettist, and basing his ideas on the established tradition of Czech Singspiel, he wrote the first Czech opera, *Dráteník* (The Tinker), and took the title-role at the very successful prem. (Prague 1826). Assistant Kapellmeister, Stavovské T, 1827; Kapellmeister, 1837. Here he introduced many new works, latterly including some by Verdi and Wagner. His own subsequent operas were unsuccessful, largely because he proved unwilling or unable to advance from the simple, charmingly naïve Singspiel manner of *Dráteník* to answer the demands of new expressive ideals. Cond., Rotterdam O, 1861.

Slavina, Maria (*b* St Petersburg, 17 June 1858; *d* Paris, 1951). Russian mezzo-soprano. Studied St Petersburg with Iretskaya, Everardi, Pryanishrikov. Début St Petersburg, M, 1877 (Amneris). St Petersburg, M, until 1917. Her repertory of over 50 roles included Ratmir (*Ruslan*), Lyubov (*Mazeppa*), Ortrud, Fricka, Fidès, Quickly, Dalila, and a famous Carmen; created Countess (*Queen of Spades*), Lyubasha (*Tsar's Bride*), and, alternating with Kaminskaya, Hanna (*May Night*). Possessed a deep, velvety voice and a forceful dramatic personality; at her best in heroic parts. Taught St Petersburg from 1917, Paris from the 1920s.

Sleepwalking Scene. The name usually given to the scene in Act IV of Verdi's *Macbeth*, beginning 'Vegliammo invan due notti', in which a doctor (bs) and a gentlewoman (mez) observe Lady Macbeth (sop) walking and talking in her sleep. See also SLUMBER SCENE.

Slezak, Leo (*b* Schönberg (Šumperk), 18 Aug. 1873; *d* Egern am Tegernsee, 1 June 1946). Austrian tenor. Studied Brno with Robinson, later Paris with J. De Reszke. Début Brno 1896 (Lohengrin). Breslau 1899; London, CG, 1900, 1909; Vienna 1901–12, 1917–27, 1933; New York, M, 1909–13; also Paris, Munich, Berlin. An immensely popular artist, of generous stature; his brilliant tone and deeply felt singing were much admired in his Guillaume Tell, Manrico, Radamès, Otello (Verdi), Walther, Tannhäuser, and Hermann, among a large repertory. His sense of humour was irrepressible: he once so convulsed the chorus at the Metropolitan during *Aida* that they were fined by the management (Slezak paid the fine). Later an effective character

tenor; appeared in films after leaving the stage. (R) His son **Walter** (1902–83) and daughter **Margaret** (1901–53) were both singers.

Slivinsky, Vladimir (*b* Moscow, 4 June 1894; *d* Moscow, 7 Aug. 1949). Russian baritone. Studied Moscow with Raysky. Moscow, Z, 1922–4; Leningrad 1924–35; Moscow 1930–48. With his attractive stage presence, a successful Onegin, Mazeppa, Eletsky, Demon, Germont; created Sandy (Yurasovsky's *Trilby*, 1924). (R)

Slobodskaya, Oda (*b* Vilna (Vilnius), 10 Dec. 1888; *d* London, 29 July 1970). Russian soprano. Studied St Petersburg with Iretskaya. Début St Petersburg, M, 1919 (Lisa). St Petersburg, M, until 1922; Paris 1922; London, L, 1931, CG, 1932, 1935; Milan, S, 1933; Buenos Aires, C, 1936. Settled in England, where she continued to sing into the 1960s. Repertory included Marguerite, Elisabeth de Valois, Sieglinde, and many Russian roles, e.g. Tatyana, Natasha (Dargomizhsky's *Rusalka*), Fevronia (*Invisible City of Kitezh*); created Parasha (*Mavra*). A moving interpreter, in recital as well as on stage, with a well-placed and beautiful voice. (R)

Slovakia. Slovak opera had been developing semi-independently since the formation of the Czechoslovak state in 1918. The first Slovak opera composer is Ján Bella (1843–1936) with *Kováč Wieland* (Wieland the Smith, 1890; prod. 1920), followed by Viliam Figuš-Bistrý (1875–1937) with *Detvan* (1928). The most significant has been Eugen *Suchoň (1908–93), whose *Krútňava* (The Whirlpool, 1949) has been widely staged, together with Jan *Cikker (1911–89) whose most important work has been *Vzkriesenie* (Resurrection, 1962). Among a younger generation, Juraj Beneš (*b* 1940) has attracted attention with more advanced techniques. Following the establishment of Slovak independence in 1992, the nationalist tradition has been given new impetus.

slumber scene (It., *sonno*). A stock scene in 17th-cent. Italian opera, in which a character is, or falls, asleep on stage. The character may fall asleep to a lullaby (e.g. Poppea, to Arnalta's lullaby, in Monteverdi's *Poppea*) or simply through exhaustion (e.g. Giustino, over his plough, in Legrenzi's *Giustino*, Gomatz in Mozart's *Zaide*). He or she may then risk murder (as in *Poppea*), or talk in his sleep revealing secret feelings, either of hatred for a tyrant or love for the astonished beloved, who has meanwhile arrived, or wake to overhear some plot, or be warned by a friendly shade of a course to pursue (a device that survives into the ombra scene).

Sly. Opera in 2 acts by Wolf-Ferrari; text by Forzano, developed from an idea in the Induction of Shakespeare's comedy *The Taming of the Shrew* (1593–4). Prem. Milan, S, 29 Dec. 1927.

London, 1603. Sly (ten), antagonizes the Duke of Westmoreland (bar) at an inn. He is taken to the Duke's castle, where he is told that he is a nobleman recovering from an illness; Dolly (sop), the Duke's mistress, is presented to him as his wife. When they fall in love, the Duke throws Sly into a dungeon, where he dies.

Smallens, Alexander (*b* St Petersburg, 1 Jan. 1889; *d* Tucson, AZ, 24 Nov. 1972). Russian, later US, conductor. Studied New York and Paris. Assistant cond. Boston 1911–14. Cond. Chicago 1919–23. Music dir. Philadelphia, Civic O, 1927–34. Cond. prem. of *Porgy and Bess*, Boston 1935, also on European tour 1952–3. Cond. US prems. of R. Strauss's *Feuersnot* (1927) and *Ariadne* (1928). (R)

'Smanie implacabili'. Dorabella's (mez) aria in Act I of Mozart's *Così fan tutte*, in which she swears to give the Furies that torment her with longings an example of doomed love.

Smareglia, Antonio (*b* Pola, 5 May 1854; *d* Grado, 15 Apr. 1929). Italian composer. Studied mathematics in Graz, turning to music after hearing Mozart, Beethoven, and especially Wagner: he came to blows with an opponent at the Milan prem. of *Lohengrin* 1873. Studied Milan with Faccio. His first opera, *Preziosa* (1879), had a success which led to sumptuous prems. of *Il vassallo di Szigeth* (1889) in Vienna under Richter and *Cornill Schut* (1893) in Dresden under Schuch. Their suggestions of German Romantic opera and early Wagner in their reliance on the orchestra may have helped their popularity in other German cities, but militated against it in Italy. However, his finest work, *Nozze istriane* (Istrian Nights, 1895), also successfully given in a number of European cities, is closer to verismo, and remains popular in his native Istria. Poverty and encroaching blindness impeded his career, which was rescued by Toscanini, who had conducted the prem. of his *Oceàna* (1903), and who arranged for the prod. of *Abisso* (1914) and commissioned Smareglia to complete Boito's *Nerone* (which he was unable to do).

Smart, (Sir) **George** (*b* London, 10 May 1776; *d* London, 23 Feb. 1867). English conductor and singing teacher. Although primarily a concert conductor he was closely associated with London CG in the 1820s, and accompanied Kemble to Germany to engage Weber as the theatre's music dir. and to commission *Oberon*; Weber died in his house. Much sought after as a singing-teacher; his pupils included Sontag and Lind.

Smetana, Bedřich (*b* Litomyšl, 2 Mar. 1824; *d* Prague, 12 May 1884). Czech composer. Studied privately, Prague with Proksch.

His first opera, *The Brandenburgers in Bohemia* (1866), was written for Count Harrach's national opera competition, which it won. It already declares the interests and abilities that were to make him the first great nationalist composer of his country. Among these were not only a quick ear for the cadences of spoken Czech (of which he was not initially complete master), but a command of orchestral music which was at the service of a strong dramatic instinct. He was thus from the first able to write continuously composed opera, within which room could be found for arias and ensembles. However, the first version of *The Bartered Bride* (1866) was with spoken dialogue, partly, he said, out of a reaction to accusations of Wagnerism levelled at him over *The Brandenburgers*. Later versions moved towards a continuous texture, without losing hold of the essentially Czech lyricism that has kept it one of the most popular operas in the repertory. Smetana draws on folk dances and characteristic rhythms from Czech folk-song, as well as plenty of local colour, but the elegance and skill with which it is handled come from his own imaginative qualities. In 1866 he became conductor of the Prague P.

Wagnerism was a charge Smetana had to face over other operas, including his next, *Dalibor* (1868). Also often compared to *Fidelio* because of its theme of imprisonment and freedom, and similarly often staged at moments of national liberation, *Dalibor* is in fact a very different work. It uses motive, but in a non-Wagnerian way, and it continues to draw on Czech musical characteristics while forming a continuous symphonic texture. Its nationalism is more overt in *Libuše* (comp. 1869–72), a festival work which celebrates the founding of the Czech nation in glowing terms; and Smetana ingeniously reconciles the personal with the heroic in his contrast of chromatic and diatonic harmony and in his discreet but expressive use of motive. Its production was delayed for the opening of the Prague N in 1881.

The remaining operas are lighter. *The Two Widows* (1874) is a delightful sentimental comedy, and especially in its revision brings a touch of French opéra-comique to a Czech milieu. The gains of the previous works include mastery of Czech prosody now expressed in light, rapid conversational exchanges, which also mark the warm characterization of *The Kiss* (1876). Smetana's sense of dramatic contrast is richer here, and is taken further forward in the more dramatic declamatory style and extended orchestral commentary of *The Secret* (1878). However, the deafness (caused by encroaching syphilis) which had descended on him by the time of *The Kiss* made work on *The Devil's Wall* (1882) difficult. Despite this, and the problematic nature of the plot, the work includes some impressive and ingenious music. He did not manage to compose more than 365 bars of *Viola*.

Smirnov, Dmitry (*b* Moscow, 19 Nov. 1882; *d* Riga, 27 Apr. 1944). Russian tenor. Studied Moscow with Krzhizhanovsky and Dodonov, later Pavlovskaya. Début Moscow 1903 (Gigi, Esposito's *Camorra*). Moscow, B, 1904–10; St Petersburg, M, 1910–17; New York, M, 1910–12; London, DL, 1914; sang throughout Europe from 1919, including Paris with Dyagilev's Co. A highly successful singer with a fine technique, and a warm, even, lyrical tone. Large repertory included Lensky, Hermann, Werther, Nadir, Lohengrin, Canio. (R)

Smirnov, Dmitry (*b* Minsk, 2 Nov. 1948). Belorussian composer. Studied Moscow with Sidelnikov and Denisov, privately with Gershkovich. His fascination with Blake's poetry and painting has found expression in two operas, *Tiriel* (1989) and its chamber companion *The Lamentations of Thel* (1989). One of the most significant composers to have emerged in Russia since *glasnost*, he has drawn from European influences, especially French and German, in the formation of his own neo-Romantic style.

Smith, Jennifer (*b* Lisbon, 13 July 1945). English soprano. Studied in Lisbon and London. Sang Mozart's Countess with WNO (1979) and Alphise in first staged production of Rameau's *Boréades* (Aix 1982). An outstanding interpreter of a wide range of Baroque roles, she sang Cybele in the New York prem. of Lully's *Atys* (1988) and the Taurean Iphigénie at London, CG, 1992 (English Bach Fest.). Has made important recordings of operas by Purcell, Rameau, Marais, Mondonville. (R)

Smyth, (Dame) **Ethel** (*b* London, 22 Apr. 1858; *d* Woking, 8 May 1944). English composer. Studied Leipzig with Reinecke and Jadassohn, then with Herzogenberg. Difficulties in making her way as a woman composer, especially of opera, led to *Fantasio* (1898) being first performed in Weimar; it is a light piece which she later repudiated. Her second opera, *Der Wald* (1902), had a wide success, and aroused admiration for its professionalism and its strong sense of atmosphere. However, her most important opera is *The Wreckers* (1906), which shows remarkable stagecraft and an ability to write strong roles in effective dramatic situations. The idiom is basically Germanic but makes use of English ballads and has distinct individuality. There followed her most striking comedy, *The Boatswain's Mate* (1916), which had considerable success in England.

Snegurochka. See SNOW MAIDEN.

Snow Maiden, The (Russ., *Snegurochka*). Opera in prologue and 4 acts by Rimsky-Korsakov; text by composer, after Ostrovsky's drama (1873) on a folk-tale. Prem. St Petersburg, M, 10 Feb. 1882.

The Snow Maiden (sop), who is safe from the sun only so long as she renounces love, begins the life of a mortal with Bobyl (ten) and Bobylikha (mez). She is attracted to the singer Lel (con), who resists her; but Mizgir (bar), come to marry Kupava (sop), falls in love with her, in vain. Tsar Berendey (ten), asked to judge the Snow Maiden's actions, is impressed by her beauty, and promises a reward to anyone who can win her love. At a feast, Lel prefers Kupava to her, and she flees from Mizgir. She appeals to her mother, Spring (mez), and then greets Mizgir lovingly. But the warmth of love is fatal to her:

she dies, and Mizgir throws himself into the lake.

'Soave sia il vento'. The trio in Act I of Mozart's *Così fan tutte*, in which Fiordiligi (sop) and Dorabella (mez) and Don Alfonso (bs) wish for a calm sea as Ferrando and Guglielmo pretend to set off for the wars.

Sobinov, Leonid (*b* Yaroslavl, 7 June 1872; *d* Riga, 14 Oct. 1934). Russian tenor. Studied Moscow with Dodonov and Santagano-Gorchakova. Début Moscow 1893, with a visiting Italian troupe (small roles). Moscow, B, 1897–1924; St Petersburg, M, from 1901; Milan, S, 1903, 1905, 1911; Berlin 1905. First elected dir., Moscow, B, 1917. Retired from stage, 1924; later artistic consultant for *Stanislavsky's Opera T. One of the idols of his time, with a strong romantic appeal in voice and appearance, and intelligent sensitivity, he was famous for his Ernesto, Sinodal (*Demon*), Berendey, Gounod's Faust, Werther, Nadir, and especially Lensky. (R)

Söderström, Elisabeth (*b* Stockholm, 7 May 1927). Swedish soprano and administrator. Studied Stockholm with Skilondz. Début Stockholm, Drottningholm T, 1947 (Bastienne). Stockholm, Royal O, from 1949; Gly. from 1957; New York, M, from 1959; London, CG, from 1960, and the major European opera-houses. One of the leading singing actresses of her day, whose intense and penetrating interpretations covered a wide range of roles, e.g. Susanna, Countess (Mozart and Strauss), Tatyana, Octavian, Jenůfa, Elena Makropoulos, Mélisande, Marie (*Wozzeck*). Dir., Drottningholm Court O from 1992. (R)

'Softly awakes my heart'. See 'MON CŒUR S'OUVRE À TA VOIX'.

Sogno di Scipione, Il (Scipio's dream). Opera in 1 act by Mozart; text by Metastasio, based on Cicero's 'Somnium Scipionis' in *De Republica* (54 BC), orig. written for Predieri (1735). Prem. Salzburg, ? early May 1772.

North Africa, *c*.200 BC. Scipio (ten) is visited in his sleep by the Goddess of Fortune (sop) and the Goddess of Constancy (sop), who ask him to choose one of them to guide him through life. Constancy guides him to his ancestors in Paradise, where his uncle, Scipio Africanus the Elder (ten), lectures on the immortality of man's soul and his father Emilio (ten) emphasizes the insignificance

of worldly pleasures. In order to join their heavenly company as he wishes, Scipio must save Rome. When Scipio chooses Constancy as his guide, Fortune summons a fierce storm. Scipio awakens, and the moral is made plain in a licenza.

Sokalsky, Pyotr (*b* Kharkov, 26 Sept. 1832; *d* Odessa, 11 Apr. 1887). Ukrainian composer and critic. Studied science at Kharkov. Best known for his journalism (sometimes under the pseudonym 'Fagot') and for his work for music in Odessa, but also wrote three operas which reflect another of his interests, folksong. They are *Mazeppa* (1858, unfin.), *Mayskaya noch* (May Night, 1876), and *Osada Dubno* (The Siege of Dubno, comp. 1878, unprod.).

'Sola, perduta, abbandonata'. Manon Lescaut's (sop) final aria in Act IV of Puccini's *Manon Lescaut*, in which she awaits her death near New Orleans.

Soldaten, Die. Opera in 4 acts (15 scenes) by Bernd Zimmermann; text by the composer from the drama by Jakob Michael Reinhold Lenz (1776). Prem. Cologne 15 Feb. 1965.

Flanders, yesterday, today, and tomorrow. Marie (sop), who is engaged to Stolzius (bar), is seduced by the Baron Desportes (ten), a high-ranking army officer; rejected, degraded, she eventually becomes the soldiers' whore.

Soldiers' Chorus. The name generally given to the chorus of soldiers, 'Gloire immortelle', in Act IV of Gounod's *Faust*, in which they vow to perpetuate the glory of their ancestors.

'Solenne in quest'ora'. The duet in Act III of Verdi's *La forza del destino*, in which Alvaro (ten) and Carlo (bar) swear eternal friendship.

Solera, Temistocle (*b* Ferrara, 25 Dec. 1815; *d* Milan, 21 Apr. 1878). Italian librettist and composer. He ran away from boarding-school in Vienna and joined a travelling circus, being eventually arrested by the police in Hungary. Admired as a poet by Merelli, he was given the libretto of *Oberto* to refashion and for three years remained Verdi's favourite librettist. His texts suited Verdi at this period, in their bold theatrical effects and vigorous, unsubtle verse. He worked on *Nabucco*, *I Lombardi*, *Giovanna d'Arco*, and *Attila*; with the latter not quite complete, he left for Spain to follow his wife, the singer Teresa

Rosmini. His subsequent adventures include periods as a manager in Madrid, as Queen Isabella's counsellor and perhaps lover, as editor of a religious magazine in Milan, as secret courier between Napoleon III and Cavour, and organizer of the Khedive of Egypt's police force, before he fell on hard times. He died in poverty and neglect. He composed five operas to his own texts including *Ildegonda* (1840), *Genio e sventura* (Talent and misfortune) (1843), and *La hermana de Pelayo* (The Sister of Pelayo) (1853).

Solti, (Sir) **Georg** (*b* Budapest, 21 Oct. 1912). Hungarian, later British, conductor. Studied Budapest, piano with Bartók and Dohnányi, composition with Kodály. Répétiteur Budapest O, 1930–3. Assistant to Toscanini, Salzburg 1936–7. Début Budapest 1938 (*Figaro*). Munich 1946; music dir. Munich, S, 1946–52; dir. Frankfurt 1952–61; Gly. 1954 (*Don Giovanni*). London, CG, 1959 (début with *Rosenkavalier*), dir. 1961–71, when he considerably raised the standards, as the house changed from the repertory system in English to the stagione system in the original language, facilitating the engagement of top international singers and conductors. CG subsequently; Bayreuth 1983 (*Ring*). Also New York, M (début with *Tannhäuser*) 1960–4; Chicago; Paris, O; etc. A conductor of intense energy with a gift for generating dramatic excitement. Distinguished in Verdi, Wagner, and Richard Strauss. Repertory also incl. *Zauberflöte*, *Fidelio*, first British *Moses und Aron*, *Billy Budd*. He was the first conductor to record all Wagner's mature operas. (R)

'Sombre forêt'. Mathilde's (sop) romance in Act II of Rossini's *Guillaume Tell*, in which she chooses the wild countryside above splendid palaces and begs the evening star to guide her.

Somers, Harry (*b* Toronto, 11 Sept. 1925). Canadian composer. Studied Toronto Cons. 1942–9 with Godden and Kilburn. Rejected a career as a concert pianist in favour of composition, supporting himself by casual employment, including broadcasting. His first large-scale theatrical work, and one of the finest by a Canadian, was *Louis Riel* (1967), commissioned for the Canadian OC in Toronto. It deals with the inflammatory situation which arose in Canada in 1869 when Riel, the visionary Métis leader in Manitoba, came into conflict with Sir John A. Macdonald, the Prime Minister. Riel was eventu-

ally executed for treason in 1885 but recent views have grown increasingly sympathetic towards him. The libretto is in both French and English as appropriate to the situation; Somers's score is eclectic but a personal and original blend of contemporary European techniques, including those of electronic music, and a distinctly Canadian musical heritage. Somers has also composed two 1-act operas, *The Fool* (1953) and *The Homeless Ones* (1955).

sommeil (Fr.: 'slumber'). The French equivalent of the *slumber scene. One of its earliest appearances is in Lully's comédie-ballet *Les amants magnifiques* (1670); the most famous example is in his *Atys* (1676).

Song to the Moon. The name generally given to Rusalka's (sop) aria 'Měsíčku na nebi' in Act I of Dvořák's *Rusalka*, in which she begs the moon to stay and reveal her lover to her.

'Son lo spirito che nega'. Mefistofele's (bs) aria in Act I of Boito's *Mefistofele*, in which he declares himself as the spirit of eternal denial (Goethe's 'Geist der stets verneint').

Sonnambula, La (The Sleep-walker). Opera in 2 acts by Bellini; text by Felice Romani, based on the scenario for *La somnambule, ou L'arrivée d'un nouveau seigneur*, a ballet-pantomime by Scribe, the choreographer Jean-Pierre Aumer, and Hérold (1827), in turn derived from the comédie-vaudeville *La somnambule* by Scribe and Delavigne (1819). Prem. Milan, T Carcano, 6 Mar. 1831.

In a quiet little Swiss village early in the 19th cent., Amina (sop), foster-daughter of Teresa (mez), owner of the mill, is to be betrothed to Elvino (ten), a young farmer. Lisa (sop), the proprietress of the local inn and herself in love with Elvino, gladly entertains Count Rodolfo (bs), the handsome lord of the castle recently returned to the village. Amina, unknown to her lover and friends, is a sleep-walker; she enters the Count's bedroom at night and is discovered asleep in his room.

The distraught Elvino is now ready to marry Lisa, but the Count tries to prevent this by explaining Amina's condition. The villagers scoff; but at that moment Amina is seen walking in her sleep along the edge of the mill roof (in some prods., the insecure bridge over the mill stream). Elvino gives her the ring he had taken back after she was discovered in the Count's room, and Amina awakes to find Elvino ready to marry her.

Sonnleithner, Joseph (*b* Vienna, 3 Mar. 1766; *d* Vienna, 25 Dec. 1835). Austrian writer, poet, editor, and librettist. Secretary to the court theatres 1804–14, he played an important role in Viennese musical life. Remembered today for his reworking of Bouilly's *Léonore, ou L'amour conjugal* for Beethoven's *Fidelio* (1805), later revised by Treitschke, and for his librettos for Cherubini's *Faniska* (1806) and Gyrowetz's *Agnes Sorel* (1806).

sonno. See SLUMBER SCENE.

Sontag, Henriette (*b* Koblenz, 3 Jan. 1806; *d* Mexico City, 17 June 1854). German soprano. Born into a theatrical family, she studied first with her mother. Earliest appearance Darmstadt aged 6. Studied Prague with Czegka. Début Prague 1821 (Princess, Boieldieu's *Jean de Paris*). Vienna 1822–3, creating Euryanthe, at Weber's request, after triumphing in *La donna del lago*. Berlin 1825, where her success led to 'Sontag-fever'. (Rellstab countered with a satirical article, and went to prison for libel.) Paris, I, 1826, 1828; London, H, 1828, again sweeping all before her, including the Duke of Devonshire, who proposed marriage; Berlin 1830, when she was forced to retire, having secretly married the diplomat Count Rossi in 1827. Known thereafter as the 'Rossi-gnol', she continued to sing privately, enchanting Tsar Nicholas I among others. Returned to the stage after Rossi's retirement, to undiminished acclaim in London, Paris, and Germany, 1849–51, and US, 1852. Died of cholera while still at the height of her powers. One of the most naturally gifted singers of her time, she possessed golden beauty, great personal charm, and a sweet, highly flexible voice that she used with consummate ease. She was admired for her 'brilliant, inventive, fresh ... and pleasing' qualities (J. E. Cox) but also 'something more' (Berlioz). Goethe wrote his poem 'Neue Siren' for her. Roles included Susanna, Donna Anna, Semiramide, Isabella, Lucrezia Borgia, Agathe; also created Miranda (Halévy's *Tempestà*), and soprano part in Beethoven's Ninth Symphony.

Sonzogno, Edoardo (*b* Milan, 21 Apr. 1836; *d* Milan, 14 Mar. 1920). Italian publisher. His firm was founded at the end of the 18th cent.

by his grandfather G. B. Sonzogno. He began to publish French and Italian music in 1874, and also established a series of competitions for new works in 1883, the second contest of 1889 being won by Mascagni's *Cavalleria rusticana*; the firm was an important promoter of verismo. Opened the T Lirico Internazionale, Milan 1894 (later TL).

Soot, Fritz (*b* Wellersweiler, 20 Aug. 1878; *d* Berlin, 9 June 1965). German tenor. Studied Dresden with Scheidemantel. Début Dresden 1908 (Tonio, *Fille du régiment*). Dresden until 1918. Stuttgart 1918–22; Berlin, S, 1922–4, 1946–52, and SO, 1946–8; London, CG, 1924–5. Created Italian Tenor (*Rosenkavalier*), Drum-Major (*Wozzeck*), and roles in operas by Pfitzner and Schreker. Repertory included Erik, Siegfried, Tristan, Otello (Verdi), Laca, Palestrina, Mephistopheles (*Doktor Faust*). (R)

Sophie. 1. Faninal's daughter (sop), lover of Octavian, in Strauss's *Der Rosenkavalier*.
2. Charlotte's sister (sop) in Massenet's *Werther*.

soprano (from It. *sopra*: 'above'). The highest category of female (or artificial male) voice. Many subdivisions exist within operahouses: the commonest in general use (though seldom specified by composers in scores) are given below, with examples of roles. These divisions often overlap, and do not correspond exactly from country to country. In general, distinction is more by character than by tessitura, especially in France: thus, the examples of the roles give a more useful indication of the different voices' quality than any technical definition.

French: soprano dramatique (Valentine, Alceste); soprano lyrique (Lakmé); soubrette or soprano léger (Despina, Zerline in *Fra Diavolo*); soprano demicaractère (Manon, Cassandre); *Dugazon, divided as jeune Dugazon (Bérénice in Thomas's *Psyché*), prem. Dugazon (Djelma in Auber's *Le premier jour de bonheur*), forte prem. Dugazon (La Comtesse in Thomas's *Raymond*), and mère Dugazon (Mistress Bentson in *Lakmé*); Falcon (Alice in *Robert le diable*).

German: dramatischer Sopran (Brünnhilde); lyrischer Sopran (Arabella); hoher Sopran or Koloratur Sopran (Zerbinetta, Queen of the Night); Soubrette (Blonde, Aennchen).

Italian: soprano drammatico (Tosca); soprano lirico (Mozart's Countess, Mimì);

soprano lirico spinto (Butterfly, Desdemona); soprano leggiero (Norina, Despina).

See also CASTRATO, MEZZO-SOPRANO.

Sorochintsy Fair (Russ., *Sorochinskaya yarmarka*). Opera (unfinished) by Musorgsky; text by composer, after Gogol's story *Evenings on a Farm near Dikanka* (1831–2). Musorgsky completed only the prelude, the market scene, and part of the sequel, most of Act II, a vision scene adapted from *A Night on the Bare Mountain*, an instrumental hopak, and two songs. The first editors were Lyadov (1904) and Karatygin (1912). A version from these editions, with Rimsky-Korsakov's version of *A Night on the Bare Mountain*, and additions from other hands, prem. St Petersburg, Comedy T, 30 Dec. 1911. Version by Cherepnin prem. Monte Carlo 17 Mar. 1923. In addition to these, a version by Shebalin was published 1933.

Sorochintsy, 19th cent. Cherevik (bs) has brought his daughter Parasya (sop) to the Fair, where she meets her lover Gritzko (ten), and obtains her father's consent to their betrothal. His wife Khivrya (mez) disapproves, but she is discovered to have taken a lover, the Priest's son (ten), and eventually all ends happily for the young couple.

Sotin, Hans (*b* Dortmund, 10 Sept. 1939). German bass. Studied with Hezel, Dortmund Cons. with Jacob. Début Essen 1962 (Police Commissioner, *Rosenkavalier*). Hamburg from 1964; Gly. 1968; Chicago 1971; New York, M, 1972; Bayreuth from 1972; London, CG, from 1974; Milan, S, 1976. Also Paris, O; Buenos Aires; Vienna, S; etc. Possesses a rotund, powerful tone and strong dramatic talent. Acclaimed as Sarastro, Hunding, Sachs, Gurnemanz, Grand Inquisitor, Ochs. (R)

sotto voce (It.: 'below the voice'). A direction to sing softly or 'aside'.

soubrette (Fr. from Old Fr., *soubret*: 'cunning or shrewd'). Used in opera for such roles as Serpina, Despina, Susanna etc.—the cunning servant-girl; then, more generally, to designate a light soprano comedienne, such as Marzelline (*Fidelio*), Adele (*Fledermaus*). In Italian opera the term *servetta* is also used.

Souez, Ina (*b* Windsor, CO, 3 June 1903; *d* S Monica, 7 Dec. 1992). US soprano. Studied Denver with Hinrichs, Milan with Del Campo. Début Ivrea 1928 (Mimì). London, CG, 1929, 1935; Gly. 1934–9; New York, New OC, 1941, and CO 1945; then left opera for jazz. Highly praised for her Donna Anna and Fiordiligi. (R)

souffleur. See PROMPTER.

Souzay, Gérard (*b* Angers, 8 Dec. 1918). French baritone. Studied Paris with Bernac, Croiza, Marcoux, and Lotte Lehmann. Distinguished principally as a concert-singer, he also appeared on the stage in Aix-en-Provence (Purcell's Aeneas, 1960) and Paris, OC, 1960 (Golaud), and O, 1963–6 (Don Giovanni). Outside France, he sang Mozart's Almaviva at Gly. and New York, M, 1965. Teacher at the U of Texas, Austin, from 1986. A subtle and perceptive artist, with a warm gift for characterization especially in the French and Italian repertoire.

Soviero, Diana (*b* St Paul, 19 Mar. 1946). US soprano. Studied St Paul and made début there 1974. New York, CO, 1976 (Manon), then performed throughout US in lyric repertory. Admired for her evenly produced tone in such roles as Juliette (New York, M, 1986); Nedda (London, CG, 1989); the *Trittico* (Dallas 1992); Marguerite.

sovrintendente (It.: 'superintendent'). The administrator of an Italian opera-house designated as ente autonomo: his functions are distinct from those of the artistic or music director though he will normally work in close artistic contact with them.

Spain. Popular musical dramas were successful from the Middle Ages, especially with religious subjects. The first Spanish opera whose music survives is to Calderón's text *Celos aun del aire matan* (Jealousy even of Air Kills, 1660), with music by Juan *Hidalgo (1612/16–85). Calderón was also the author of the text for some of the first *zarzuelas, e.g. *El jardín de la Falerina* (1684). However, developments were halted by the restraint on native works in favour of Italian opera by Philip V. In the 18th cent. a number of Spanish composers wrote opera in Italian, notably *Martín y Soler and Terradellas. The history of 18th-cent. Spanish opera is largely that of struggle between zarzuela and Italian-modelled serious opera. Then a royal decree of 1800 forbade all operas except those sung in Spanish by Spaniards; translations of foreign works were still preferred, though these now included French opéra-comique. Ramón *Carnicer (1789–1855) wrote popular and pioneering operas; by contrast, in the 19th cent. there developed rivalry between two versions of zarzuela, the *género grande* and the *género chico*. Great influence was exercised by Felipe *Pedrell, and in the early years of the 20th cent. Spanish works were given at the Teatro Real (which closed in 1925). Despite difficulties, Spanish operas of European popularity were composed by Isaac *Albéniz (1860–1909), Enrique *Granados (1867–1916), and Manuel de *Falla (1876–1946).

See also BARCELONA, MADRID, ZARZUELA.

Sparafucile. A professional assassin (bs) in Verdi's *Rigoletto*.

Speziale, Lo (The Apothecary). Opera in 3 acts by Haydn; text based by composer on a libretto by Goldoni. Prem. Eszterháza, autumn 1768.

Italy, 18th cent. Sempronio (bs), an old apothecary, wants to marry his ward Grilletta (sop). She is also loved by the frivolous Volpino (mez) and the serious young Mengone (ten), who eventually wins her hand.

Spielplan (Ger.: 'performance plan'). The published prospectus of the season's repertory. Also a monthly publication giving programmes in all German opera-houses.

Spieltenor (Ger.: 'acting tenor'). A light tenor in a German company who plays such character roles as Mime, David, and Pedrillo. See TENOR.

Spinning Chorus. The name generally given to the chorus 'Summ' und brumm'' sung by the girls in Wagner's *Der fliegende Holländer*, wishing that the spinning-wheels could drive their lovers back from the sea.

spinto (It.: 'pushed'). The description given to a voice, almost always tenor, but sometimes also soprano, of particular vigour and attack; the description may also be qualified, e.g. tenore lirico spinto.

'Spirto gentil'. Fernando's (ten) aria in Act IV of Donizetti's *La favorita*, in which he reflects on his love for Leonora as he is about to take his monastic vows.

Spohr, Louis (*b* Brunswick, 5 Apr. 1784; *d* Kassel, 22 Oct. 1859). German composer and violinist. Studied Seesen with Riemenschneider and Dufour, Brunswick with Kunisch and Hartung.

Spohr's first stage work was an operetta, *Die Prüfung* (1806), which received a concert performance during his leadership of the ducal band at Gotha. Its successor, *Alruna* (comp. 1808), was rehearsed at Weimar, when it won Goethe's admiration: it is a more advanced work, taking a supernatural subject and attempting continuous opera. The first production he achieved was of *Der Zweikampf mit der Geliebten* (The Duel with the Beloved, 1811), something of a reversion to convention while containing attractive music. This was followed in 1816 by *Faust*.

Faust is a landmark in German Romantic opera. The overture's use of leading themes from the opera was one of many devices admired by Weber, who conducted the prem. and whose review of it writes of 'a few melodies, carefully and felicitously devised, which weave through the whole work like delicate threads, holding it together intellectually'. Spohr strengthened this aspect of the opera when he revised it in 1852, adding recitatives.

The work's popularity was exceeded by that of *Zemire und Azor*, given at the Frankfurt O during Spohr's two years as conductor, 1817–19. Here, the system of reminiscence motive and Leitmotiv is taken even further, and the theme of redemption through love achieves new significance. In other ways, too, the work anticipates Wagner, e.g. in the atmospheric use of harmony and orchestration.

Among Spohr's operatic plans was one for *Der Freischütz*; he abandoned this, without later regrets, on learning that it was being set by Weber, who recommended him for the post of Hofkapellmeister at Kassel, 1822. Here he remained for the rest of his life: Generalmusikdirektor 1847. His greatest operatic success was *Jessonda* (1823). Spohr and his audiences were fascinated by the characteristically Romantic idea of an oriental subject: he was here also able to give his lyrical gift, and above all his mastery of chromatic music, their fullest effect. He also gave a new fluency to recitative and loosened the set forms of aria; some of the dramatic pacing of the sequence of arias is awkward, but the best of the work has an imagination ahead of its time.

Der Berggeist (1825), which followed, suffers from a poor libretto, though Spohr again anticipates Wagner (in *Der fliegende Holländer*) by constructing the music in linked scenes rather than arias and thereby achieving considerable dramatic pace. *Pietro von Abano* (1827) aroused predictable distaste for its treatment of necrophily, and returns to spoken dialogue between larger scene-complexes in which there is an awkward mix of convention and originality. More enterprisingly constructed numbers built into scene-complexes mark *Der Alchymist* (1830), together with a fashionable use of Spanish local colour. Like other of his operas, it was damned with faint praise as appealing chiefly to connoisseurs. His last opera, *Der Kreuzfahrer* (1845), did, however, achieve success, and is indeed one of his most effective works in its cohesive and continuous structure.

In 1842 Spohr became the first musician of importance to support Wagner, when he produced *Der fliegende Holländer* in Kassel only five months after the Dresden prem. He later staged *Tannhäuser* but was prevented from following this with *Lohengrin*.

Spoleto. Town in Umbria, Italy. Opera was given from 1667 in the T Nobile; rebuilt 1830 as T Caio Melisso (cap. 500). The T Nuovo (cap. 900) opened Aug. 1864 with works by Verdi and Petrella. In 1958 *Menotti established the Fest. of Two Worlds, giving young European and US artists chances to appear in his and Visconti's productions and also involving local talent. Thomas *Schippers was music director 1958–70. The first production was of Verdi's *Macbeth*, by Visconti; others have included Donizetti's *Duca d'Alba* (1959, using the original 1882 designs), *Carmen* (1962, with Verrett and George Shirley), *Salome* (1961), *Manon Lescaut* (1973), and *Parsifal* (1987). Revivals have been of works by Graun, Gagliano, Mercadante, and Salieri; there was later more emphasis on modern works and radical productions, including Polanski's production of *Lulu* (1974). Menotti's own works have also featured. He has also founded Spoleto festivals near Charleston, SC and Melbourne.

Spoletta. The police agent (ten) in Puccini's *Tosca*.

Spontini, Gaspare (*b* Maiolàti, 14 Nov. 1774; *d* Maiolati, 24 Jan. 1851). Italian composer and conductor. Studied Naples with Sala and Tritto.

An early commission led to the successful *Li puntigli delle donne* (1796), immediately followed by five more operas. When the Neapolitan court moved to Palermo before the advancing French in 1798, Spontini took on Cimarosa's post as conductor and in 1800 produced three deft Neapolitan operas. Shortly afterwards he left for Paris, where his light style was unsuited to the special demands of opéra-comique; but with the carefully composed *Milton* (1804) he won a success that carried his name to Germany and Austria.

One of *Milton*'s librettists was Étienne de Jouy, who, understanding better than the composer himself where his gifts lay, provided for *La vestale* (1807) a text that fully released Spontini's talent and led to his recognition as one of the leading opera composers of the day. Spontini intensified selected features of Gluck, Cherubini, and Méhul, and put them to novel use in his serious operas. These are founding works of Parisian *Grand Opera in their generous use of processions, rituals, oath-takings, ceremonies, and other imposing stage effects, with extra bands, large choral groupings, and tableaux. The Empress Josephine's patronage carried Spontini through all opposition; and after the constant rewriting that was his habit, *La vestale* triumphed. For *Fernand Cortez* (1809) the librettist was again Jouy, the patron now Napoleon (who felt that the subject might influence opinion more favourably in the Spanish Wars). A more polished work, it had a still greater success.

In 1810 Spontini took over the T Italien, and at the Odéon formed a distinguished and enterprising ensemble before his dismissal in 1812; his restoration in 1814 was brief and again controversial, for his undoubted gifts were allied to an overbearing personality. A few minor pieces followed before *Olyimpie*, another tragédie lyrique which again included much spectacle—processions, a Bacchanal, a battle, an apotheosis. Though carefully composed, and including original elements (such as a Grand March that directly influenced Berlioz's Trojan March), it was not well received in its first form in 1819; but assiduous revision brought success in Paris and Berlin, where Spontini was now summoned. Much impressed, Frederick William III of Prussia engaged him for the Berlin H, where he worked in uneasy co-operation with the Intendant, Brühl. His temper and haughtiness quickly caused difficulties, and when in 1821 the imposing spectacle of *Olympie* was succeeded in a few weeks by the thrilling new popular experience of Weber's *Der Frei-*

schütz, Berlin was divided, the court siding with Spontini, the public preferring the new German Romantic opera.

Spontini's painstaking methods of composition prevented him from producing as much as was now required of him. In *Nurmahal* (1822) and *Alcidor* (1825) he had to attempt German Romantic opera for Berlin; the works are actually closer in nature to French opéra-féerie. *Alcidor* in particular hardened the division of public opinion, and Spontini could not rally his scattering admirers even by a conscientious attempt at a German Grand Opera, *Agnes von Hohenstaufen*, in 1829. The sympathies of the new king lay elsewhere, but Spontini also hastened his own downfall: though fairly, even generously treated, he felt obliged to leave. He made occasional return visits to Germany: on one of them, he conducted at Dresden a *Vestale* prepared by Wagner, who admired much in Spontini and especially his command as a conductor. The admiration was fully shared by Berlioz, especially for his orchestration. He spent most of his remaining years in Paris, before returning to his native village.

Sporting Life. A dope peddler (ten) in Gershwin's *Porgy and Bess*.

Sprechgesang (Ger.: 'speech-song'). A type of vocalization first used by Humperdinck in early versions of *Königskinder* (1897), describing a form of musical declamation in which the actual pitch of the notes is indicated but the voice falls or rises in a manner between true speech and true song. It is used by Schoenberg, who preferred the term *Sprechstimme*, as in *Moses und Aron* and by Berg in *Wozzeck* and *Lulu*.

Staatsoper (Ger.). State opera.

Stabile, Mariano (*b* Palermo, 12 May 1885; *d* Milan, 11 Jan. 1968). Italian baritone. Studied Rome with *Cotogni. Début Palermo 1909 (Marcello). After modest successes in Italy and on foreign tours, Milan, S, 1921 (Falstaff: chosen and coached by Toscanini). Chicago 1924–9; London, CG, 1926–31; Gly. 1936–9; Salzburg 1934–9; London, Cambridge T and Stoll T, 1946–9; also Milan, S, until 1955. His extraordinary artistic achievements lay not in beauty of tone, but in subtlety of style and singing, and a psychological perception that made an individual mark on every role he interpreted. He was memorable in over 50 parts, e.g. Figaro (Mozart and Rossini), Don Giovanni, Malatesta, Beckmesser, Iago (Verdi), Scarpia, Gianni Schicchi. Of his greatest role it was said, 'La donna è mobile; Falstaff è Stabile.' (R)

Stabinger, Mathias (*b* ?, *c*.1750; *d* Venice, *c*.1815). Composer and conductor, probably of German origin. A shadowy figure, he worked first in France and then in Italy, where *Le astuzie di Bettina* was given 1780. This brought him considerable success: he travelled to Poland 1781, becoming maestro al cembalo at the Warsaw O, then on to Russia. He worked in St Petersburg with the Mattei-Orecia troupe and in Moscow at the Petrovsky T, staying until 1783. After a brief visit to Italy he was back in St Petersburg 1785–99, directing the orchestra at the Petrovsky T. He returned to Italy *c*.1800.

An important figure in late 18th-cent. Russian cultural life, he contributed four operas to the Moscow repertory, including *Baba Yaga* (1786) and *Pigmalion* (1787).

Stabreim (Ger.: 'alliteration'). The system of giving cohesion to verse, and also suggesting contacts in meaning, by alliterating key words in a line and perhaps also an adjacent line. Originating in Old English and German verse, it was taken up again and cultivated for use in mythic opera by Wagner, in *Tristan* but with especial emphasis in *The Ring*.

Stade, Frederica von (*b* Somerville, NJ, 1 June 1945). US mezzo-soprano. Studied New York with Engelberg. Début New York, M, 1970 (Second Boy, *Zauberflöte*). New York, M; Paris, O, from 1973; Gly. 1973; London, CG, from 1975; Milan, S, 1976; Holland, Houston, S Francisco, etc. Her attractive presence and clear, sensuous tone have brought her much success as Cherubino (Mozart and Massenet), Sesto, Dorabella, Rosina, Cenerentola, Composer, Octavian, Charlotte, Mélisande. (R)

Staden, Sigmund Theophil (*b* Kulmbach, *bapt*. 6 Nov. 1607; *d* Nuremberg, *c*.30 July 1655). German composer. Studied Nuremberg with his father and Augsburg with Paumann, then returned to Nuremberg 1623, where he held municipal and ecclesiastical appointments. He is remembered as composer of one of the earliest German musical dramas to have survived, *Seelewig* (1644), whose theme is the spiritual conflict between good and evil. The score mixes occasional attempts at *stile rappresentativo with strophic songs and short instrumental numbers.

Städtische Oper (Ger.). City opera.

stage design. Although the masques and other forms of elaborate entertainment which were forerunners of opera often required complex scenery, the first operas were simply staged. Not until the grandiose performances mounted in Cardinal Barberini's palace in Rome (c.1632–50), and the establishment of court theatres shortly after, did stage spectacle become the fashion.

It was in these court theatres, with their tiers of boxes, that stage became separated from audience by means of the proscenium frame. The perspective painting which characterized much Renaissance art was seized upon by theatre designers, and splendid two-dimensional scenery characterized the magnificent operatic productions of the Baroque. Even within this convention, the initial emphasis on central perspective soon gave way to angled perspectives, false perspective, trompe-l'œil effects, and other ingenuities. Pioneering work, particularly on machinery, was done by Giovanni Burnacini in Venice, and by Giacomo *Torelli, especially with indoor sets and swifter scene changes. Greater realism was encouraged, with influential designers including the *Mauro family. In France, Torelli's successor Gaspare Vigarani created a formal beauty to match Lully's demands, in turn influencing Jean Bérain. These influences spread to Germany, once the country began recovering its court operatic life in the mid-17th cent. after the Thirty Years War; while in England, Inigo Jones produced beautiful and elegant décor for Stuart masques.

More subtle approaches to illusion and realism began to appear with a changing ethos in the 18th cent. A new range of stage presentation by way of more sophisticated use of such devices as diagonal perspective, trompe-l'œil, and views from above or below, together with great architectural sophistication, characterized the epoch-making work of Ferdinando *Galli-Bibiena and his dynasty. The reforms of Gluck encouraged a sharper realism represented by the Galliari family (who increased the use of stage props), then by the important *Quaglio dynasty. Greater interest in Nature, decorative in the rococo, led to new methods, and with Revolutionary opera to a more functional use of scenery. In Germany, experiments in three-dimensional scenery were made by designers including Karl *Schinkel. In Paris, the emphasis on grandeur and a preoccupation with stage mechanics met in the work of *Cicéri and *Daguerre with their magnificent and ingenious sets. Their work also included sophisticated lighting and a greater concern for historicism, all reflecting the ethos of *Grand Opera. These interests influenced the Romantic designs of Alessandro *Sanquirico and Carlo Ferraio in Milan, and guided the ideas of artists working in countries where Romantic opera was associated with nationalism.

The developments in stage machinery in the 20th cent., together with new artistic movements, affected all countries. Among them was Russia, where the dazzling designs of Alexandre Benois captured European imagination, but where also Symbolist painters associated with the Mir iskusstva group evolved new approaches to the visual. Painters, including Alfred *Roller, were more often brought into the opera-house, and new concepts of stage design were explored by Edward Gordon *Craig and Adolphe *Appia. Opera design was affected by virtually every artistic movement, including Expressionism, Futurism, Surrealism, Cubism, Constructivism, neoclassicism, and the work of particular artistic groups such as Walter Gropius's Bauhaus. Among important designers of the 1930s were Emil *Preetorius. Further developments after the Second World War focused initially on the work of Wieland *Wagner at Bayreuth, but also on that of many talented artists for whom opera has provided encouragement for technical and artistic experiment. In England original and successful designers have included Oliver *Messel, John *Piper, Osbert *Lancaster, and Ralph *Koltai, among many; those who have made an impression internationally include Emanuele *Luzzati, Jean-Pierre *Ponnelle, Josef *Svoboda, Filippo *Sanjust, Luchino *Visconti, and Franco *Zeffirelli. These and other designers have often worked regularly in a successful partnership with a producer, or as producers themselves.

stagione (It.: 'season'). The *stagione lirica* is the opera season at any Italian theatre. The stagione system (as opposed to the repertory system) has come to mean putting on one opera for a series of performances within a few weeks with the same cast during its run.

Stagno, Roberto (*b* Palermo, 11 Oct. 1840; *d* Genoa, 26 Apr. 1897). Italian tenor. Studied Milan with Lamperti. Début Lisbon 1862 (Rodrigo, Rossini's *Otello*). Madrid from 1865, replacing Tamberlik with great success; Moscow, B, 1868, partnering Artôt; Buenos Aires from 1879; opening season of New York, M, 1883–4; Paris, I, 1884. Last appearance 1897. Impressive for his vocal control, he encompassed florid Rossini and Donizetti roles, also Faust (Gounod), Lohengrin, Radamès, Manrico, and Otello (Rossini and Verdi). Created Turiddu (with his wife Gemma *Bellincioni as Santuzza); famous as Robert le diable.

Standfuss, Johann (*b* ?; *d* after *c*.1759). German composer. He is remembered as composer of music for the first important German *Singspiel, Der Teufel ist los* (1752), a translation by Weisse of Coffey's ballad opera, *The Devil to Pay*. The score for this, and for its sequel *Der lustige Schuster* (1759), is now lost.

Stanford, (Sir) **Charles Villiers** (*b* Dublin, 30 Sept. 1852; *d* London, 29 Mar. 1924). Irish composer. Studied Dublin with Quarry, Leipzig with Reinecke, Berlin with Kiel. One of the few major British musical figures of his day to have faith in a national operatic revival, he wrote ten operas himself. It was symptomatic of the difficulties that the first two were produced in Germany. High claims have been made for a few of them, but the only one to achieve any success was *Shamus O'Brien* (1896).

Stanislavsky, Konstantin (*b* Moscow, 17 Jan. 1863; *d* Moscow, 7 Aug. 1938). Russian producer. Famous as actor and producer and director of the Moscow Arts T, and as developer of a new realism in acting, Stanislavsky also did much for opera. From 1885, with Tchaikovsky, Taneyev, Jürgenson, and Tretyakov, he was one of the directors of the Russian Musical Society. In 1898, with Vladimir *Nemirovich-Danchenko, he founded the Moscow Arts T, whose revolutionary methods and choice of works were also to influence the staging of opera in Russia and eventually abroad. He also sang in operetta with Savva Mamontov's company. In 1918 he founded the O Studio of the Bolshoy T, opening in 1919 with an act of *Eugene Onegin*; this separated from the Bolshoy in 1920.

Stanislavsky proposed to use the theatrical discoveries of the Moscow Arts T to refresh the tradition of staging opera in Russia, and hoped to develop a style of singing in which words and their meaning would be given new dramatic importance: to this he brought great system and powers of persuasion. His productions included *Werther* (1921), *Eugene Onegin* (1922: a famous 'workshop' production in everyday dress), *Il matrimonio segreto* (1925), works by Rimsky-Korsakov and Musorgsky, *The Barber of Seville*, and *Carmen*. In 1926 he moved his theatre to the Dmitrovsky T. The last production he supervised completely was *May Night* (1928). Becoming ill, he was obliged to conduct his rehearsals by summoning the cast to his bedside and even by use of the telephone. He organized a new Operatic-Dramatic Studio in 1938: the last production in which he took a personal part was *Madama Butterfly* (1938). *Meyerhold was director 1938–9.

Steber, Eleanor (*b* Wheeling, WV, 17 July 1914; *d* Langhorne, PA, 3 Oct. 1990). US soprano. Studied Boston with Whitney, New York with Althouse. Unofficial début Boston, Commonwealth O, 1936 (Senta). New York, M, 1940–66; Gly. (Edinburgh) 1947; Bayreuth 1953; also Salzburg, Vienna, etc. Created Barber's Vanessa. A gifted and intelligent artist, highly regarded as Fiordiligi, Pamina, Violetta, Desdemona (Verdi), Elsa, Arabella, Marschallin, Marie (*Wozzeck*). (R)

Steersman. Daland's steersman (ten) in Wagner's *Der fliegende Holländer*.

Steffani, Agostino (*b* Castelfranco, 25 July 1654; *d* Frankfurt, 12 Feb. 1728). Italian composer, diplomat, and cleric. Studied Munich with Kerll and Rome with Bernabei. Held various appointments at the Munich court from 1674, where he wrote his first operas, beginning with *Marco Aurelio* (1681). In 1688 he moved to the Hanover court as Kapellmeister, where eight of his own operas were given, including *Orlando generoso* (1691) and *La libertà contenta* (1693). By the later 1690s he was more actively engaged as a diplomat than as a musician.

Steffani made an important contribution to the establishment of opera in N Germany, for though his works were essentially Italian in style, they were translated and taken into the repertory of the Hamburg O, where they influenced the following generation of composers. Many of the operas take historical subject-matter, sometimes Teutonic (e.g. *Alarico il Baltha* (1687)) and eschew the concentration on mythology which was typical at the time. Particularly interesting is the influence of French opera, notably in the overture and in the occasional use of a 5-part string texture. Among the composers whose operatic style was directly influenced by Steffani the most important was Handel.

Stehle, Sophie (*b* Sigmaringen, 15 May 1838; *d* Hackerode, 4 Oct. 1921). German soprano. Studied Munich with Lachner. Début Munich 1860 (Emmeline, Weigl's *Schweizerfamilie*). Distinguished as Senta, Elsa, Elisabeth; created Fricka (*Rheingold*, 1869) and Brünnhilde (*Walküre*, 1870), but declined Brangäne. Also sang Pamina, Agathe, Selika, Marguerite. Hanslick admired her for her 'God-given talent', and for her persuasive, dark-hued voice.

Stehle-Garbin, Adelina (*b* Graz, 30 June 1860; *d* Milan, 24 Dec. 1945). Austrian, later Italian, soprano. Studied Milan Cons. Début Broni 1881 (Amina). Engagements in Bologna, Florence, Venice, S America; Milan, S, 1890–2, 1894; also appeared in Vienna, Berlin, Moscow, Madrid, etc. With her sweet tone, refined style, and dramatic skill, successful as Violetta, Manon, Ophelia; important as a verismo interpreter, e.g. as Adriana Lecouvreur. Created Nedda, Walter (*La Wally*), and first Nannetta, with her fiancé tenor Edoardo Garbin as Fenton; they were later much admired in *La Bohème*. (R)

Steibelt, Daniel (*b* Berlin, 22 Oct. 1765; *d* St Petersburg, 20 Sept. 1823). German composer. Studied with Kirnberger. Following desertion from the Prussian army he visited several European cities, settling in Paris 1790: here his first opera, *Roméo et Juliette* (1793), was successful only when revised as an opéra-comique. In 1810 he became dir. of the French O in St Petersburg, where he composed three operas, including *Cendrillon* (1810). A colourful, rakish character, Steibelt was a competent composer with some dramatic flair, though his scores contain few memorable moments.

Stein, Horst (*b* Elberfeld, 2 May 1928). German conductor. Studied Cologne with Wand. Répétiteur Wuppertal 1947–51. Cond. Hamburg 1951–5, 1961–3; Berlin, S, 1955–61; Mannheim 1963–70. S Francisco 1964–8. Chief cond. Vienna, S, 1970. Music dir. Hamburg from 1972. Bayreuth 1969–84, *Ring* and *Parsifal*. Paris, O, 1973, 1976. (R)

Stenhammar, Wilhelm (*b* Stockholm, 7 Feb. 1871; *d* Göteborg, 20 Nov. 1927). Swedish composer and conductor. Largely self-taught, Stenhammar was one of the central figures in Swedish music nationalism. As well as performing as a concert pianist, he had considerable success as a conductor and was briefly artistic director of the Royal Swedish O, 1900–1 and 1924–5. Though his musical style was forged, like that of many of his Scandinavian contemporaries, from the blending of nationalist folk influences into an essentially Romantic amalgam, Stenhammar showed greater interest than most in the more progressive music of Liszt and Wagner. This is seen nowhere better than in *Tirfing* (1898) and *Gildet på Solhaug* (1899): both works were written early in his career and their conspicuous lack of success turned him away from opera.

Stepanova, Elena (*b* Moscow, 17 May 1891; *d* Moscow, 26 May 1978). Russian soprano. Studied Moscow with Polli. Début Moscow, B, 1912 (Antonida, *Life for the Tsar*). Moscow, B, until 1944, also Stanislavsky's opera studio. Sang with Shalyapin, Sobinov, Nezhdanova, etc.; roles incl. Gilda, Tatyana, and she was particularly associated with Rimsky-Korsakov roles, e.g. Snegurochka, Queen of Shemakha. (R)

Stephanie, Gottlieb (der Jüngerer) (*b* Breslau, 19 Feb. 1741; *d* Vienna, 23 Jan. 1800). Austrian dramatist, librettist, and theatre director. After military exploits, he became director of the National-Singspiel in Vienna in 1779. His work here included the production of about 20 Singspiel librettos, including that for Mozart's *Die Entführung aus dem Serail* (1782).

Števa. Števa Buryja (ten), half-brother of Laca Klemeň and faithless lover of his cousin Jenůfa, in Janáček's *Jenůfa*; also the name given to the baby he fathers on Jenůfa.

Stevens, Risë (*b* New York, 11 June 1913). US mezzo-soprano. Studied New York with Schoen-René, later Vienna with Gutheil-Schoder and Graf. Début New York, Little Theatre OC, 1931 (small roles). Prague and Vienna 1936–8; Gly. 1939, 1955; New York, M, 1938–61; Milan, S, 1954. A talented singing actress, much acclaimed as Gluck's Orfeo, Cherubino, Mignon, Carmen, Dalila, Laura (*Gioconda*), Octavian. (R)

Stewart, Thomas (*b* S Saba, TX, 29 Aug. 1928). US baritone. Studied New York with Harrell. Début (as student) New York, Juilliard School, 1954 (La Roche in first US *Capriccio*). Appeared as bass with New York CO and Chicago O. Further study in Europe. Berlin, SO, 1958. London, CG, and Bayreuth from 1960; New York, M, from 1966; Paris, O, 1967; Orange 1974, 1980; S Francisco 1971, 1984–5. Roles include Don Giovanni, Escamillo, Kurwenal, Sachs, Wotan, Amfortas, Onegin. Married to the soprano Evelyn *Lear. (R)

Stich-Randall, Teresa (*b* West Hartford, CT, 24 Dec. 1927). US soprano. Studied Columbia U School of Music, singing Aida aged 15, and appearing in the prem. of Thomson's *Mother of Us All*. Sang in Toscanini's broadcasts of *Aida* (Priestess) and *Falstaff* (Nannetta) 1949–50. Vienna from 1952; Chicago from 1955; New York, M, 1961–6; also Milan, S, Salzburg. Roles include Constanze, Donna Anna, Pamina, Violetta, Sophie, Ariadne. (R)

Stiedry, Fritz (*b* Vienna, 11 Oct. 1883; *d* Zurich, 8 Aug. 1968). Austrian, later US, conductor. Studied Vienna with Mandyczewski. Recommended by Mahler to Schuch, who engaged him for Dresden, 1907–8. After appointments at Teplice, Poznań, Prague, Nuremberg, and Kassel, chief cond. Berlin, H, later S, 1914–23. Vienna, V, 1924–8 (prem. of Schoenberg's *Die glückliche Hand*, 1924). Berlin, SO, 1928–33, succeeding Walter as chief cond. 1929 and working with Ebert on important revivals of *Macbeth* and *Boccanegra*; cond. prem. of Weill's *Die Bürgschaft* (1932). Forced to leave Germany by the Nazis, he cond. in Russia 1933–7. New York, New OC, 1941; Chicago 1945–6; New York, M, 1946–58, principal Wagner cond. and also cond. important Verdi revivals. Gly. 1947 (Gluck's *Orfeo*). London, CG, 1953–4 (*Ring*, *Fidelio*). (R)

Stiffelio. Opera in 3 acts by Verdi; text by Piave, after the play by Émile Souvestre and Eugène Bourgeois, *Le pasteur, ou L'évangile et le foyer* (1849). Prem. Trieste, T Grande, 16 Nov. 1850.

Germany, early 19th cent. Stiffelio (ten), an evangelical priest, does not detect the affair his wife Lina (sop) is having with Raffaele (ten). Her father Stankar (bar) suspects it and forbids her to confess to her husband as she wishes. Stankar challenges Raffaele to a duel.

The sound of the duel brings Stiffelio to the scene. When Stankar reveals that Raffaele is Lina's lover, Stiffelio starts to attack him himself.

Stiffelio offers Lina a divorce so that she may spend her life with Raffaele; he will dedicate himself to God. Stankar enters and announces that he has killed Raffaele. Following the example of the parable of Christ and the adulterous woman, Stiffelio is moved to forgive Lina.

The opera was unsuccessful and was revised by Verdi as *Aroldo*, first performed at the T Nuovo, Rimini, 16 Aug. 1857.

England and Scotland, *c*.1200. Aroldo (ten) has just returned from a crusade. During his absence his wife Mina (sop) has been having an affair with Godvino (ten). Her father Egberto (bar) persuades her not to confess to Aroldo as the shock would kill him.

Egberto challenges Godvino to a duel. Aroldo interrupts the fight, but when he learns of Godvino's guilt attacks him himself. Briano (bs), Aroldo's spiritual mentor, reminds him of a Christian's duty to forgive.

Egberto, unable to live with the shame to his family's honour, is about to commit suicide when Briano enters and announces that Godvino has been recaptured. Aroldo has coerced Mina into signing a divorce agreement, when Egberto bursts in and announces that he has just killed Godvino.

Aroldo and Briano live in seclusion at Loch Lomond. During a storm on the loch, Egberto and Mina are washed ashore. Aroldo tries to drive Mina away but, after exhortations from both Briano and Egberto, forgives her.

Stignani, Ebe (*b* Naples, 11 July 1903; *d* Imola, 5 Oct. 1974). Italian mezzo-soprano. Studied Naples with Roche. Début Naples, C, 1925 (Amneris). Milan, S, 1926–56; London, CG 1937, 1939, 1952, 1955, 1957, and DL 1958; S Francisco 1948; also Verona, Gly., S America. A performer with a grand and fiery style, and a wide vocal range, famous for her Azucena, Ulrica, Eboli; also sang Orfeo (Gluck), Isabella (*L'italiana*), Adalgisa, Dalila, Ortrud. (R)

stile monodico. See STILE RAPPRESENTATIVO.

stile rappresentativo (It.: 'representative style'). The style of accompanied solo singing which developed around 1600 as a result of the deliberations of the Bardi *camerata. Apart from the experimental efforts of

Galilei and others, the first sustained use of this new approach (sometimes also called **stile moderno** to distinguish it from the polyphony of the preceding generations) was in the operas of Peri, Caccini, and Cavalieri. Caccini's collection *Le nuove musiche* (1602) provides the most extensive early exploration of stile rappresentativo, and contains an illuminating preface. Over the following decades the style gradually split into two branches which later came to be recognized as *recitative and *aria. Despite many attempts by later scholars to distinguish between the terms **stile rappresentativo**, **stile recitativo**, and **stile monodico**, contemporary usage by composers and writers suggests that they were broadly interchangeable.

stile recitativo. See STILE RAPPRESENTATIVO.

Still, William Grant (*b* Woodville, MS, 11 May 1895; *d* Los Angeles, 3 Dec. 1978). US composer. Studied at Wilberforce Coll. and Oberlin Cons., then moved to New York where for several years he earned a living playing in theatre orchestras. The first Black American composer to receive widespread recognition, he composed seven operas beginning with *A Bayou Legend* (1941). *Troubled Island*, given by the New York CO in 1949, was the first opera by an African-American to be staged by a major opera company.

Stilwell, Richard (*b* St Louis, MS, 6 May 1942). US baritone. Studied Bloomington and New York. Début St Louis 1962 (Silvio). His fluent delivery and impressive stage presence have been in the service of such roles as Pelléas (New York, CO, and London, CG, débuts, 1970, 1974); Guglielmo (New York, M, 1975); Monteverdi's Ulisse (Gly. 1973). Dallas O from 1988 in prems. of Argento's *Aspern Papers*, and as Malatesta and Mozart's Almaviva. (R)

Stockhausen, Karlheinz (*b* Burg Mödrath, 22 Aug. 1928). German composer and theorist. Studied Cologne Hochschule with Martin, and Cologne U; Paris with Messiaen. During the 1950s he was at the forefront of advances in electronic music; his influence spread through editorship of the journal *Die Reihe* (from 1954) and his directorship of summer composition courses at Darmstadt (from 1957). Taking Webern as a point of departure he developed the concept of 'total

serialism', i.e. music in which all parameters, not just pitch, but duration, timbre, intensity as well, are subject to serial principles: many of his works also involve the use of aleatory procedures.

Commencing in 1981, he has been involved with an operatic cycle of immense proportion, *Licht*, the first four parts of which, *Donnerstag*, *Samstag*, *Montag*, and *Dienstag* have appeared to date.

Stoll Theatre. See LONDON OPERA HOUSE.

Stoltz, Rosine (*b* Paris, 13 Feb. 1815; *d* Paris, 28 July 1903). French soprano. Studied Paris with Ramier and L. Ponchard, Brussels with Cassel. Début (as Mme Ternaux) Brussels, M, 1832 (small roles); (as Heloïse Stoltz), 1835–7. Paris, O, from 1837, where she so much abused her influence as the dir. Pillet's mistress (ruthlessly eliminating rivals, e.g. Dorus-Gras) that they were both forced to resign 1847. Sang in French provinces, Lisbon, Vienna, Turin, and Brazil; returned to Paris O 1854–5; Lyons 1860, when she retired from the stage. Her subsequent private life was rich in aristocratic protectors, some of whom she married. Though vocally imperfect, she was a passionate, striking, and intelligent performer. Created many roles, e.g. title-role of Halévy's *Reine de Chypre*, Ascanio (*Benvenuto Cellini*), when Berlioz found her 'delightful', Marguerite (Auber's *Lac des fées*), and (her most famous) Léonore (Donizetti's *Favorite*); also sang Donna Anna, Rossini's Desdemona, Rachel, Fidès.

Stolz, Teresa (*b* Kostelec, 2 June 1834; *d* Milan, 23 Aug. 1902). Bohemian soprano. Studied Prague with Cabouna, Trieste with Ricci, Milan with Lamperti. Début Tiflis 1857. Appearances in Odessa, Constantinople; Bologna 1863; Milan, S, 1865–72; Cairo 1873–4; Vienna 1875; St Petersburg, with Paris I, 1876. Roles included Mathilde (*Guillaume Tell*), Lucrezia Borgia, Alice (*Robert le diable*), Norma, Giovanna d'Arco, Amelia, Gilda, Elisabeth de Valois, Leonora (*Trovatore* and *Forza*). A beautiful woman with a powerful, 'diamond-like' voice (Blanche Roosevelt), and impeccable, long-breathed phrasing, she was one of the greatest Verdi singers of her time, and created the soprano part in his Requiem. Much admired professionally and (to Giuseppina Verdi's distress) personally by the composer, who considered her the ideal Aida. Giuseppina bequeathed her a watch and a bracelet.

Stolze, Gerhard (*b* Dessau, 1 Oct. 1926; *d* Garmisch-Partenkirchen, 11 Mar. 1979). German tenor. Studied Dresden with Bader and Dittrich. Début Dresden 1949 (Moser, *Meistersinger*). Dresden until 1953; Bayreuth regularly 1951–69; Berlin, S, 1953–61; Vienna and Stuttgart from 1956; London, CG, 1960; New York, M, 1968. Also Paris, O; Naples, C; Stockholm, etc. An acclaimed David, Mime, Herod; also Captain (*Wozzeck*), Oberon (Britten), and first Oedipus (Orff). (R)

Stone Guest, The (Russ., *Kamenny gost*). Opera in 3 acts by Dargomyzhsky; text Pushkin's 'little tragedy' (1830). Prem. St Petersburg, M, 28 Feb. 1872.

Spain, 17th cent. Don Juan (ten) has killed the Commandant (bs), husband of Donna Anna (sop), and now returns to Seville with Leporello (bs). Seeing Anna arrive at a monastery, he resolves to seduce her. Meanwhile he dines at the home of Laura (mez), a former lover now bored with her present lover Don Carlos (bar). Juan kills Carlos in a duel and makes love to Laura.

Disguised, he gains promise of admittance to Anna's house, also inviting the Commandant's statue to dine.

Despite discovering Juan's identity, Anna welcomes Juan. They are interrupted by the arrival of the statue. Anna faints, and Juan is dragged down to Hell.

Storace, Nancy (*b* London, 27 Oct. 1765; *d* London, 24 Aug. 1817). English soprano, sister of below. Studied London with Sacchini and Rauzzini. Début aged 10 (Cupid, Rauzzini's *Le ali d'amore*). Florence 1780; outsang the castrato Marchesi, and was obliged to leave. Vienna 1783–7, where her brilliant gift for comedy made her extremely popular. Here she married the composer John Abraham Fisher, and met Mozart, who began to write Emilia (*Lo sposo deluso*, unfinished) for her; also Susanna, which she created with enormous success, and the concert aria 'Ch'io mi scordi di te', K505. London, H, 1787–9, 1793; DL 1789–96, singing in her brother Stephen's operas. After his death in 1796, she toured the Continent with the tenor John Braham; they had a son, 1802, but could not marry with Fisher still living, and parted 1816.

Storace, Stephen (*b* London, 4 Apr. 1762; *d* London, 15/16 Mar. 1796). English composer, brother of above. His first two operas, *Gli sposi malcontenti* (1785) and *Gli equivoci* (1786), to a libretto by Da Ponte, were written in Vienna, where his sister Nancy and Michael Kelly sang in their prems.

The immediate success of *The Haunted Tower* (1789), which was one of the most popular full-length operas staged at Drury Lane during the entire 18th cent., established Storace as a leading theatre composer. His belief in the importance of collaboration between librettist and composer, demonstrated in *The Haunted Tower* and more strongly in *The Pirates* (1792), was continued in his later operas; he also made notable use of the long continuous finale movements he must have heard in Vienna. Storace's *The Cherokee* (1794) was the first English opera about the Wild West; Beethoven twice used what he assumed to be a Welsh folk tune taken from it.

Storchio, Rosina (*b* Venice, 19 May 1876; *d* Milan, 24 July 1945). Italian soprano. Studied Milan with Giovannini and Fatuo. Début Milan, V, 1892 (Micaëla). Milan: S, 1895–1904, and till 1918; L, 1900–6. Buenos Aires 1904–14; Rome 1917; New York, Manhattan OC, and Chicago 1921. Sang Mimì, Manon, and Sophie (Massenet); created Madama Butterfly, also Leoncavallo's Musetta (*Bohème*) and Zazà. A lyrical singer, and a sensitive exponent of vulnerable verismo heroines. (R)

Story of a Real Man, The (Russ., *Povest o nastoyashchem cheloveke*). Opera in 3 acts by Prokofiev; text by composer and Mira Mendelson, after the story by Polevoy. Prem. Moscow, B, 8 Oct. 1960.

Russia, 1942. The airman Alexey (bar) is shot down and after wandering for 18 days in the forest has to have both legs amputated. When told of another pilot who continued to fly after losing a leg, he resolves to return to service against doctors' orders. He is eventually reunited with his lover Olga (sop).

Stracciari, Riccardo (*b* Casalecchio sul Reno, 26 June 1875; *d* Rome, 10 Oct. 1955). Italian baritone. Studied Bologna with Masetti. Début Bologna 1900 (Marcello). Milan, S, 1904–6, 1908–9; London, CG, 1905; New York, M, 1906–8; Paris, O, 1909; Chicago 1917–19. Thereafter mainly in Italy, Spain, S America. Last stage appearance Milan 1944. Possessed an exceptionally fine, velvety, and well-projected voice, and an aristocratic style. Large repertory included a celebrated Figaro (Rossini), Rigoletto, Amonasro, Germont. Taught Boris Christoff. (R)

Stradella, Alessandro (*b* Nepi, 3 Apr. 1639; *d* Genoa, 25 Feb. 1682). Italian composer. Possibly a pupil of Bernabei, during the 1670s he composed many short dramatic pieces. In 1677 he was forced to leave Rome after quarrelling with the ecclesiastical authorities and, travelling via Venice and Turin, arrived in Genoa 1678. Here three of his operas were given at the T Falcone: *La forza dell'amor paterno* (1678), *Le gare dell'amor eroico* (1679), and, most innovatory, the comic *Trespolo tutore* (*c*.1677), one of the earliest operas in which the leading male part is taken by a bass. In many respects his work prefigures the early Neapolitan school epitomized by Alessandro Scarlatti.

Stradella's career was filled with amorous adventures, which nearly led to his murder for the abduction of a nobleman's mistress for whom he was engaged to teach music; he actually was murdered for an affair of which his mistress's brothers disapproved. His rakish behaviour is the subject of several operas.

Strakosch, Maurice (*b* Zidlochovice, ?15 Jan. 1825; *d* Paris, 9 Oct. 1887). Czech impresario. Studied Vienna; toured Europe and US as pianist. Managed Adelina Patti's concert tours. Undertook first opera season, New York 1857; Chicago 1859; Paris 1873–4. Rome, Ap., 1884–5 with his brother **Max** (1835–92), who succeeded him as Manager of the New York AM 1887. Another brother, **Ferdinando** (?–1902), directed opera-houses in Rome, Florence, Barcelona, and Trieste.

Straniera, La (The Stranger). Opera in 2 acts by Bellini; text by Romani, after V.-C. Prévôt, Vicomte d'Arlincourt's novel *L'étrangère*, possibly from its dramatization by G. C. Cosenza (1827). Prem. Milan, S, 14 Feb. 1829.

The Castle of Montolino, Brittany, *c*.1200. Arturo (ten), betrothed to Isoletta (sop or mez), falls in love with Alaide (sop), the stranger who is thought to be a witch. Discovering her with Valdeburgo (bar), in fact her brother, he suspects that she is betraying him and challenges his supposed rival to a duel. Valdeburgo is seen apparently drowning, and Alaide is accused of his murder although Arturo is ready to take the blame. Valdeburgo is found to be alive, and insists that Arturo marry Isoletta. Alaide is revealed as the morganatic wife of the French king, and in his grief Arturo kills himself.

Stratas, Teresa (*b* Toronto, 26 May 1938).

Canadian soprano. Studied Toronto with Jessner. Début Toronto 1959 (Mimì). New York, M, from 1959; London, CG, from 1961; Milan, S, 1962; Moscow, B, 1963; Paris, O, from 1967; also Berlin, Salzburg, Lisbon. An impressive singing actress, displaying intense dramatic commitment. Roles include Cherubino, Violetta, Liù, Lisa, Salome, Lulu, Jenny (*Mahagonny*). Created Marie Antoinette in Corigliano's *The Ghosts of Versailles* (New York, M, 1991). (R)

Strauss, Johann (II) (*b* Vienna, 25 Oct. 1825; *d* Vienna, 3 June 1899). Austrian composer, conductor, and violinist, eldest son of **Johann Strauss I** (*b* Vienna, 14 Mar. 1804; *d* Vienna, 25 Sept. 1849). Studied with Drechsler; made his spectacular début as a composer and conductor of waltzes with his own orchestra 1844. Soon established as the most important composer of light music in Vienna, where he was known as the 'King of the Waltz', Strauss amalgamated his orchestra with that of his father 1849. Appointed *Hofballmusikdirektor* 1863.

His success as a composer of dance music has tended to overshadow Strauss's importance as a composer of stage music. *Indigo und die vierzig Räuber* (1871) appeared at the Vienna W, 1871, and ushered in a series of operettas of which *Die Fledermaus* (1874) and *Der Zigeunerbaron* (1885) were the most successful. With these he founded, with Suppé and Millöcker, a tradition of Viennese operetta which continued into the next century in the works of Straus, Stolz, Kálmán, and above all Lehár.

Strauss, Richard (*b* Munich, 11 June 1864; *d* Garmisch-Partenkirchen, 8 Sept. 1949). German composer and conductor. His father **Franz** (1822–1905) was a leading horn-player at the Munich O, and is credited with having rendered playable Wagner's original version of Siegfried's horn call. His early musical endeavours were greatly assisted by Hans von Bülow, who arranged for him to become assistant music director at Meiningen in 1885; he also became acquainted with the prominent Wagnerian Alexander Ritter, under whose guidance he rejected the conservative tradition in which his father had reared him. Meanwhile, his conducting career was also advancing: in 1886 he was appointed sub-conductor at Munich, moving to Weimar in 1889. By the time that he composed his first opera, *Guntram*, in 1892–3 he already had a consummate understanding of both instrumental and vocal technique, as well as a sure appreciation of the problems of the opera-house.

In 1894 Strauss conducted at Bayreuth for the first time (*Tannhäuser*), while the unsuccessful prem. of *Guntram* marked out its composer as an avid disciple of Wagner. This was confirmed by his second opera, *Feuersnot*, produced in Dresden in 1901. Both works adhere strongly to the principles of music drama, particularly in their manipulation of *Leitmotivs, though Strauss's distinctive voice is already clearly discernible.

By the time that *Salome* was produced in 1905 Strauss's fame as a conductor had already made him a household name. In 1895 he had become conductor of the Berlin Philharmonic and in 1898 conductor of the Berlin O; in 1903 a Strauss Fest. was held in London. The public outcry which followed *Salomé*'s appearance thrust him to the forefront of musical avant-gardism. One of the earliest works to exhibit the Expressionist tendencies later associated with the Second Viennese School, it provoked violent opposition. Cast in one continuous act, it relies heavily upon Wagnerian principles in its construction, with the role of the orchestra assuming ever greater importance.

In *Elektra* (1909) he continued along this revolutionary musical path. With his first setting of a libretto by Hugo von Hofmannsthal, Strauss entered upon a long and active collaboration worthy of comparison with that of Mozart and Da Ponte; though the opera contains the same emphasis on the darker side of human emotion, Hofmannsthal's treatment of the story of the murdered Agamemnon develops a strain of genuine tragedy.

In 1910 Strauss resigned his post in Berlin; the following year *Der Rosenkavalier* received its first performance. Turning aside from the violence and horror of *Salome* and *Elektra*, Strauss and Hofmannsthal produced a comedy of manners concerning 18th-cent. Viennese society. Undoubtedly, this was Hofmannsthal's greatest libretto and Strauss responded with a score of unsurpassed warmth and tenderness. The striking move away from Expressionism was continued in *Ariadne auf Naxos*. Intended originally as a 1-act opera for the concluding celebration of Molière's *Le bourgeois gentilhomme* (for which Strauss had written the incidental music) it was first performed in 1912. The problems of

assembling a cast of actors and singers on the same evening soon persuaded the authors to make their second, and better-known, version (1916), in which the events preparatory to the performance of *Ariadne* become a separate operatic Prologue.

For his next opera, *Die Frau ohne Schatten* (1919) Strauss returned briefly to the Expressionist world of *Salome* and *Elektra*, though on this occasion the subject-matter was not concerned with physical horror, but intended as a complex psychological exploration of a kind later seen in Schoenberg's *Erwartung*. It is generally considered that this is the last opera in which an overt strain of genuine modernism may be detected. By now Strauss's musical language was firmly established and already sounding conservative. Over the remaining 30 years of his life there is little sign of any serious musical development and against the backdrop of increasingly severe economic and political problems in Germany, Strauss's inspiration flagged noticeably, though he did not help himself by choosing to set a succession of weak librettos, beginning with his own *Intermezzo* (1924).

The collaboration with Hofmannsthal, ended by his death in 1929, resulted in two further works: the classically inspired *Die ägyptische Helena* (1928), originally intended as an operetta, and the Viennese comedy *Arabella* (1933). For the libretto of *Die schweigsame Frau* (1935) Strauss turned to Stefan Zweig. In its handling of the well-worn themes of love and comic misunderstanding it stands together with *Der Rosenkavalier* and *Arabella*, and if less successful than either, it is only because Zweig, for all his other talents, lacked Hofmannsthal's superlative dramatic gifts and extensive theatrical experience. Further collaboration was prevented by intervention of the Nazis, who forbade any further work with Zweig, who was Jewish, and Strauss was forced to turn to the incomparably less gifted Josef Gregor, with whom he wrote three operas.

For *Daphne* (1938) Strauss produced one of his most ravishing scores, while *Friedenstag* (1938), though suffering from a noticeable paucity of dramatic and musical invention, received 100 performances. *Die Liebe der Danae* reached the stage of public dress rehearsal, but was not heard in Strauss's lifetime, owing to the sudden closing of all theatres by Goebbels in 1944. Strauss's last opera, *Capriccio* (1942), was based on an idea of his own, from which the conductor Clemens Krauss fashioned the libretto. Its theme is the age-old question of whether words or music should take precedence in an opera: it is perhaps significant that the conflict is left unresolved, for Strauss himself had grappled with this problem from *Salome* onwards without coming down firmly on either side of the argument.

The last years of his life were unhappy and dogged with controversy. Having held public office during the Third Reich, Strauss was forced to undergo de-Nazification after the Second World War. Despite formal acquittal, this political controversy did nothing to help the career of a composer who, by the time of his death, was frankly anachronistic. As a conductor, however, he had a reputation second to none in German opera, both in his own music and that of other composers. His repertoire was wide-ranging, but without doubt it was as an interpreter of Mozart that he achieved greatest fame: having completed 1,192 performances (including 200 of his own works) when he left Berlin, Strauss became co-director, with Schalk, of the Vienna S from 1919 to 1924, and conducted there regularly until 1942. He also conducted performances in Salzburg, Milan, London, Buenos Aires, and elsewhere, and after the end of the Second World War made an important visit to London at the encouragement of Thomas Beecham. (R) In 1894 he married the soprano **Pauline de Ahna** (1863–1950) who created Freihild in his *Guntram* (1894).

Stravinsky, Fyodor (*b* Novy Dvor, 20 June 1843; *d* St Petersburg, 4 Dec. 1902). Russian bass. Father of below. Studied St Petersburg with Everardi. Début Kiev 1873 (Count Rodolfo, *Sonnambula*). Kiev until 1876; St Petersburg, M, 1876–1902. Repertory of 60 roles included Bartolo and Basilio (Rossini), Sparafucile, Henry the Fowler (*Lohengrin*), Mephistopheles (Gounod and Boito). Outstanding in the Russian repertory, e.g. as Farlaf (*Ruslan and Lyudmila*), the Miller (Dargomyzhsky's *Rusalka*), Rangoni, Varlaam (inspiring Rimsky-Korsakov to write the drinking song in *Sadko* for him). Sang in first performances of *May Night* (Golova), and *Snow Maiden* (Frost); also created roles in Tchaikovsky's *Vakula the Smith*, *Maid of Orleans* (Dunois), *The Enchantress* (Mamirov). Possessed a two-octave range, and a powerful, even tone. In the line of Petrov, he was, with Figner, a singer who

approached his roles with an unusual care for detail and dramatic forcefulness, paving the way for Shalyapin. He was, however, also criticized for over-acting (Rimsky-Korsakov's biographer Yastrebtsev).

Stravinsky, Igor (*b* Oranienbaum, 17 June 1882; *d* New York, 6 Apr. 1971). Russian, then French, then US, composer. Studied St Petersburg with Kalafaty and Rimsky-Korsakov. Son of above.

Stravinsky's first opera, *The Nightingale* (1914), both covers and concludes the period of his early spectacular, lavishly composed stage works. The first act was written in Russia in 1909; the last two were completed in Switzerland in 1914. In between came the three great early ballets, *The Firebird*, *Petrushka*, and *The Rite of Spring*. Stravinsky was the first to recognize the perils of returning to a half-finished work after such experiences, and agreed to do so only under pressure. The change of idiom is in theory justified by the contrast between the scenes in the forest with the child who loves the nightingale's song and the later ornate luxury of the Chinese court; but the stylistic and technical development is marked, and despite great beauties the opera as a whole cannot manage to bestride two separate worlds.

Most of Stravinsky's later stage works reflect a doubt about traditional opera and place the singers in a special position with regard to the action. *The Soldier's Tale* (1918) has speech and acting but no singing, though to some extent it anticipates modern chamber theatre. *The Wedding* (1923) is a ballet, or song-and-dance ritual, with songs and choruses, and Stravinsky's ambiguous feelings towards the stage were further revealed in his next dramatic work, *Renard* (1922). Described as 'Une histoire burlesque chantée et jouée', this gives the action to dancers and places the singers (all male) in the orchestra. Written in 1915–16, it was not performed until 1922, in the same programme as the conventionally operatic *Mavra*. Based on a Pushkin story (and dedicated to him, Glinka, and Tchaikovsky), this was written in deliberate reaction against Wagner's 'inflated arrogance' in the form of a modern opera buffa, 'because of a natural sympathy I have always felt for the melodic language, the vocal style and conventions of the old Russo-Italian opera'. There is no recitative, but a succession of arias and ensembles with simple accompaniment figures, reminiscent of classical opera buffa.

Oedipus rex (1927) again places the singers on the stage, but all are masked in the interest of preserving the impersonal and universal sense of tragedy that led to the choice of a dead language, Latin, for the libretto: the chorus is confined to one position and the soloists are allowed only formal entries and restricted gestures and movements. A speaker using the audience's language introduces each of the six episodes which make up the 'opera-oratorio'. Despite the wide variety of influences, the music has a powerful artistic unity, and the self-imposed constraints serve to depersonalize and ritualize the story, responding to its mythic stature.

Two ballets, *Apollon Musagète* and *Le baiser de la fée*, followed before Stravinsky resumed his highly individual relationship with the lyric stage in *Perséphone* (1934); this is a 'melodrama' for reciter, tenor, chorus, dancers, and orchestra, closer to sung ballet than to danced opera. Two more ballets, *Jeu de cartes* and *Orpheus*, separate this from Stravinsky's next opera, *The Rake's Progress* (1951). (A later opera, on the rebirth of the world after atomic disaster, with Dylan Thomas, was prevented by the poet's death.) Here the influences are again diverse, and in this culminating work of Stravinsky's neoclassical period the forms serve both to make contact with the world of Hogarth and to contain some of his most compassionate music. *The Flood* (1962), a setting of part of the York miracle play, is a slighter work in Stravinsky's neo-Webern manner. (R)

Strehler, Giorgio (*b* Trieste, 14 Aug. 1921). Italian producer. Studied Milan. Early career as actor. Founded Milan, PS, 1947 (with Paolo Grassi). Début Milan, S, 1947 (*Traviata*). Milan, S and PS subsequently, as the base of his operatic activities; also Paris, O, and Salzburg. Much appreciated by Brecht for productions of his work, he mounted two memorable *Die Dreigroschenoper* at PS (1956, 1973). Repertory incl. *Entführung*, *Don Giovanni*, *Zauberflöte*, *Macbeth*, *Boccanegra*, *Otello* (Verdi), *Falstaff*, *Love of Three Oranges*. Combines elements of the past (with commedia dell'arte) and present (social and political comments); and seriousness with comedy in comic roles (Cherubino, Falstaff).

Streich, Rita (*b* Barnaul, 18 Dec. 1920; *d* Vienna, 20 Mar. 1987). German soprano. Studied Augsburg, Berlin with Ivogün and

Berger. Début Aussig (Ústi nad Labem) 1943 (Zerbinetta). Berlin, S 1946–50, SO 1950; Vienna 1953; London, with Vienna O, 1954; S Francisco 1957; Gly. 1958. An outstanding singer in Mozart and Strauss with coloratura roles (Queen of the Night, Zerbinetta), but also a fine, sensitive Constanze and Sophie. (R)

Strepponi, Giuseppina (*b* Lodi, 8 Sept. 1815; *d* Sant'Agata, 14 Nov. 1897). Italian soprano. Studied Milan Cons. Début possibly Adria 1834. Trieste and Vienna, K, 1835; Venice, Bologna, Rome, Florence, Verona, etc. 1836–42; Milan, S, 1839–42. With G *Ronconi and *Moriani (the probable father of two of her four, if not five, illegitimate children), she enjoyed a series of brilliant triumphs as Amina, Norma, Imogene, Elvira (*Puritani*), Lucia, Saffo (Pacini). She was highly praised for her attractive, smooth voice, and charming and spirited performances. However, overwork had led to a premature decline by the time she created Abigaille, 1842. She retired 1846, then taught. Her championing of Verdi's first opera, *Oberto*, contributed greatly to his recognition. She became his mistress, probably 1844, and in 1859 his second wife. A woman of extraordinary generosity and sensitivity, she loved Verdi with a devotion that survived even the difficult period of his relations with Teresa *Stolz.

stretta (It.: 'tightening or squeezing'). The passage at the end of an act, ensemble, or aria, in which the tempo is accelerated to make a climax.

'Stride la vampa'. Azucena's (mez) aria in Act II of Verdi's *Il trovatore*, in which she contemplates the grim, mysterious memories reflected in the fire at which she stares.

Striggio, Alessandro II (*b* Mantua, ?1573; *d* Venice, 15 June 1630). Italian librettist, musician, and diplomat. The son of the composer **Alessandro Striggio I** (*c*.1540–92), he took part in the famous Florentine intermedi of 1589 and provided librettos for small dramatic pieces by both Monteverdi and Gagliano. His most important work was the libretto written for Monteverdi's *Orfeo* in 1607.

Strungk, Nicolaus Adam (*b* Brunswick, bapt. 15 Nov. 1640; *d* Dresden, 23 Sept. 1700). German composer. Engaged at courts of Wolfenbüttel, Vienna, Celle, and Hamburg before becoming music director to the cathedral and city of Hamburg. Court composer in Hanover 1682–6; Vize-kapellmeister in Dresden 1688. In 1692 he founded an opera-house in Leipzig, where he lived from 1696: this opened 1693 with his *Alceste*. Strungk was one of the most important German opera composers of his generation: though most of his *c*.20 works are now lost, he made a significant contribution to the Hamburg O repertory in its earliest days and played a crucial role in the establishment of commercial opera elsewhere in Germany.

Studer, Cheryl (*b* Midland, MI, 24 Oct. 1955). US soprano. Studied Vienna with Hotter. Munich, S, 1980 (Mařenka). Darmstadt 1983–5; Berlin, D, and Bayreuth from 1985; Paris, O, 1986; New York, M, 1988, also Milan, S; Vienna; Philadelphia. Roles include Pamina, Elettra, Donna Anna, Lucia, Odabella, Micaëla, Aida, Empress (*Frau ohne Schatten*), Salome, Daphne, Elsa, Elisabeth, Eva, Chrysothemis. (R)

Sucher, Rosa (*b* Velburg, 23 Feb. 1847; *d* Eschweiler, 16 Apr. 1927). German soprano. Little formal vocal training. Début Munich, N, 1871 (Waltraute, *Walküre*). Berlin, H, 1875; Leipzig 1877–8; here she married the conductor Josef Sucher. Hamburg from 1878; London, DL, 1882 and CG, 1892; Vienna 1886; Bayreuth 1886, 1888, 1891, 1896; Berlin, H, 1888–98; New York, M, 1895, with Damrosch Co. Retired 1903. One of the finest of the first generation of Wagner singers, she was an intense performer with a splendid voice and stage presence. Her roles included Agathe, Euryanthe, Selika, Elsa, Eva, Brünnhilde, Isolde, Kundry, Desdemona (Verdi).

Suchoň, Eugen (*b* Pezinok, 25 Sept. 1908; *d* Bratislava, 5 Aug. 1993). Slovak composer. Studied Bratislava with Kafenda, Prague with Novák. His most successful work is *The Whirlpool* (1949), which has been widely performed. Superficially close to Janáček in its drawing on folk inflections for its declamatory melodic lines, and in the plot of a village drama of murder, jealousy, and forgiveness, it is in fact very different in nature. The characterization is less vivid, but the work has its own powerful atmosphere: this derives partly from strongly composed singing parts that owe much to Slovak folk music, partly from excellent writing for an orchestra that plays a powerful narrative role, also from the original use of a chorus:

this takes part (as in the wedding scene), comments, and acts as an abstract, somewhat pantheistic, exponent of the connection between Nature, music, and men's souls. Suchoň's other opera, *Svätopluk* (1960), has not matched the success of this work: it makes use of serial techniques without relinquishing a lyrical manner.

'Suicidio!' La Gioconda's (sop) dramatic monologue in Act IV of Ponchielli's *La Gioconda*, in which she contemplates suicide.

Suitner, Otmar (*b* Innsbruck, 19 May 1922). Austrian conductor. Studied Innsbruck, Salzburg with Krauss. Répétiteur Innsbruck 1942–4; music dir. Kaiserslautern 1957–60; chief cond. Dresden 1960–4; Berlin, S, from 1964. Bayreuth 1964 (*Tannhäuser*) and 1965 (*Fliegender Holländer*). S Francisco from 1969. Admired in Mozart, Wagner, and Richard Strauss, also the Italian repertory. (R)

Sullivan, (Sir) **Arthur** (*b* London, 13 May 1842; *d* London, 22 Nov. 1900). English composer. Studied London RAM with Sterndale Bennett, and Leipzig (1858–61) with Hauptmann and Rietz. His first stage works were to librettos by F. C. Burnand, a 1-act farce *Cox and Box* (1867) and the 2-act *Contrabandista* (1867). The first collaboration with W. S. Gilbert came in 1871 with *Thespis*, most of which is lost. In 1875 the impresario Richard D'Oyly Carte persuaded them to work together again on a piece to precede Offenbach's *La Périchole*: the result was the successful *Trial by Jury* (1875), unique as being their only operetta without spoken dialogue. In the same year Sullivan collaborated with B. C. Stephenson on *The Zoo*. It had a few performances, but Sullivan soon decided to join forces with Carte and Gilbert, and a theatre was taken.

Their first production was *The Sorcerer* (1877), which ran for 175 nights. This was followed by the immensely successful *HMS Pinafore* (1878) and *The Pirates of Penzance* (1879), which established the pattern of what have become known, from the theatre to which Carte transferred in 1881, as the Savoy operas. Selecting venue and target carefully, Gilbert contrived successions of ingeniously whimsical or paradoxical situations in verse whose wit and brilliance of invention have rarely been matched: the chief reproaches against him are a certain mawkishness and his notoriously cruel handling of the middle-aged spinsters who recur as a fixation in many of the operettas. Sullivan brought to these admirable librettos many apt qualities. Above all, his quick melodic ear responded to the lilt and patter of Gilbert's rhythms, and gave them new and often unexpected twists. Harmonically he was less original, and occasionally matches Gilbert's sentimentality too well; but his melodic elegance extends to a contrapuntal ingenuity that enabled him to combine tunes of different character with satisfying musical and dramatic effect. The essence of his success as an operetta composer, however, was at least as much in his vivid sense of parody and the sure instinct with which he seized and both guyed and used his models. Sometimes the parody is direct: more often he fastens on a composer (e.g. Handel) or form (e.g. madrigal) and absorbs as much of it as is needed to start his own invention running. His technical skill and wide knowledge of music, especially of Romantic opera, stood him in good stead here.

Patience (1881) turns these gifts on the cult of the aesthetic, and in particular upon Oscar Wilde: the quality of the invention is shown by the work's continuing popularity long after the target had vanished. *Iolanthe* (1882) is a skilful mixture of fairy-tale and satire on the peerage; but in *Princess Ida* (1884) the combination of satire (on women's rights) and never-never-land court romp is less happily managed by Gilbert. Sullivan, however, provided for it some of his most ambitious and original music. A return to formula came with *The Mikado* (1885), which was pure never-never-land, spiced as ever with topical allusions, though it took its impulse from the Victorian cult of *japonaiserie*. It was a brilliant success, running for 672 nights, and has remained the most popular of the series. *Ruddigore* (1887) followed, a comedy on country life with ghostly goings-on that reach their climax in one of Sullivan's finest extended scenes, 'The Ghosts' High Noon'. *The Yeomen of the Guard* (1888) was an attempt to break out into a more operatic manner; though it remains a vintage Savoy opera, it includes some of Sullivan's best numbers and successfully creates a pervading sense of grimness in the dominating presence of the Tower of London. *The Gondoliers* (1889) reverts brilliantly to the former type of success, and is further notable for the skilfully handled long introductions and finales without spoken dialogue.

During its run, Sullivan quarrelled with Gilbert, and having failed in his ambition to write a successful Grand Opera, *Ivanhoe* (1891), collaborated with Sidney Grundy on the operetta *Haddon Hall* (1892). Reconciliation with Gilbert followed, and the thirteenth of their operettas ensued, *Utopia Limited* (1893), a satire which fails partly through trying to fire at too many Victorian targets. After a remodelling of the old *Contrabandista* as *The Chieftain* (1894), the partners produced their last piece, *The Grand Duke* (1896).

Sullivan went on to write *The Beauty Stone* (1898), and with *The Rose of Persia* (1899) it was hoped that he had found his new Gilbert in Basil Hood. They began work on *The Emerald Isle*; after Sullivan's death it was completed by Edward German.

Sulpice. The sergeant (bs) of the 21st Grenadiers in Donizetti's *La fille du régiment*.

Summers, Jonathan (*b* Melbourne, 2 Oct. 1946). Australian baritone. Studied London with Otakar Kraus (1974–80). Début Kent O 1975 (Rigoletto). London, CG, from 1976 as Mozart's Figaro, Papageno, Ford, Malatesta. Admired for his forthright performances in a wide repertory, he has sung Mozart's Almaviva and Don Giovanni (Scottish O); Nabucco (O North); Marcello (New York, M, 1988). Other roles incl. Enrico (*Lucia* at Chicago 1990) and Posa (London, ENO, 1992). (R)

'Summertime'. Clara's (sop) lullaby to her baby in Act I of Gershwin's *Porgy and Bess*.

Suor Angelica. Opera in 1 act by Puccini; text by Forzano: pt 2 of *Il trittico*. Prem. New York, M, 14 Dec. 1918.

A Tuscan convent, late 17th cent. Sister Angelica (sop) was forced by her noble family to take the veil after giving birth to a son out of wedlock. Seven years later her aunt, the Princess (con), arrives to ask her to sign away her share of the inheritance. Angelica asks for news of her son, only to be told that he has been dead for two years. She gathers herbs to make a potion to kill herself; but having drunk it, she realizes she has committed a deadly sin and prays to the Virgin for forgiveness. As she dies, she has a vision in which the Virgin brings her son to her.

Supervia, Conchita (*b* Barcelona, 9 Dec. 1895; *d* London, 30 Mar. 1936). Spanish mezzo-soprano. Little musical training.

Début Buenos Aires 1910 (Bretón's *Los amantes de Teruel*). Rome 1911 (Octavian); Bologna 1912 (Carmen); Chicago 1915–16; Milan, S, from 1924; Turin 1925; Paris: CE, 1929; O, 1930; OC, 1933–4. London, CG, 1934–5. Died in childbirth at the height of her powers. An exceptional artist possessing an innate musicality and a *joie de vivre* that permeated her singing. Her voice was vibrant, very flexible, and had a range of g–b″. Famous as Carmen, and in Rossini, e.g. as Isabella, Rosina, Cenerentola. Also sang Cherubino, Adalgisa, Charlotte, Mignon. (R)

Suppé, Franz (von) (*b* Split, 18 Apr. 1819; *d* Vienna, 21 May 1895). Austrian composer of Belgian descent. Studied as a boy with a bandmaster, Ferrari, and with Cigalla, later Vienna with Seyfried and Sechter. Cond. Vienna: J, 1840–5 (also visiting Baden, Odenbürg, and Pressburg); W, 1845–62; Kaitheater, 1862–5; Carltheater from 1865. Inspired by the success of Offenbach's operettas, especially *Ba-Ta-Clan*, in Vienna, in 1860 he began, with *Das Pensionrat* (1860), the long series of works that was to give Viennese operetta its first classic form. His greatest successes in this manner were *Die schöne Galathea* (1865), under the influence of Offenbach's classical parodies, and *Leichte Kavallerie* (1866), a piece with a contemporary Austrian military setting. In a rather more ambitious manner, he had further success with *Fatinitza* (1876) and especially with his masterpiece, *Boccaccio* (1879). Here he comes closest to true opera, without sacrificing his typical melodic elegance and charm, his neat characterization, or his ability to develop musical ideas wittily and at some length. He had little success after *Boccaccio*; he was overshadowed by Johann Strauss II. Among his lesser-known works is a clever parody of Wagner's *Lohengrin, Lohengelb oder Die Jungfrau von Dragant* (1870).

surtitles (proprietary term). Also supertitles, supratitles. A device for screening a summary translation of an opera in the course of its performance, normally projected above the proscenium arch. Invented in 1983 by John Leberg.

Susanna. 1. Figaro's betrothed (sop) in Mozart's *Le nozze di Figaro*.

2. An Old Believer (sop) in Musorgsky's *Khovanshchina*.

3. Count Gil's wife (sop) in Wolf-Ferrari's *Il segreto di Susanna*.

Süssmayr, Franz Xaver (*b* Schwanenstadt, 1766; *d* Vienna, 16 Sept. 1803). Austrian composer. He had some lessons with Mozart, and with Salieri in vocal composition. From 1795 he conducted at the Vienna K, where he produced a number of his own operas. He is best remembered for his completion of Mozart's *Requiem*; he also probably wrote the secco recitatives for *La clemenza di Tito*.

Süssmayr's early works clearly follow the Singspiel vein of Hiller, but following the success of Cimarosa's *Il matrimonio segreto* (1792), he also came under the influence of the Neapolitan buffo style. Despite this enthusiasm, he completed only four Italian operas, in comparison with 21 German stage works, the most successful of which was the Singspiel *Der Spiegel von Arkadien* (1794).

Sutermeister, Heinrich (*b* Feuerthalen, 12 Aug. 1910; *d* Vaux-sur-Morges, 16 Mar. 1995). Swiss composer. Studied Munich with Courvoisier. Worked as répétiteur, Berne, before devoting himself to composition. His intention to make strong audience appeal an essential of opera composition was rewarded with the success of the radio opera *Die schwarze Spinne* (The Black Spider, 1936), and particularly with that of *Romeo und Julia* (1940). Subsequent operas proved thinner in content, their effects not being commensurate with their effectiveness, and the acknowledged influence of Orff providing insufficient substance.

Suthaus, Ludwig (*b* Cologne, 12 Dec. 1906; *d* Berlin, 7 Sept. 1971). German tenor. Studied Cologne. Début Aachen 1928 (Walther). Aachen until 1931; Stuttgart 1932–41; Berlin, S, 1941–8, and SO (later D), 1948–65; Vienna 1948–71; Gly. 1950; London, CG, 1952–3; Milan, S, 1954, 1958; also S Francisco, Buenos Aires, etc. Roles included Florestan, Erik, Tristan, Siegmund, Siegfried, Hermann, Otello (Verdi), Bacchus, Števa. A powerful, moving singer, much admired by Furtwängler. (R)

Sutherland, (Dame) **Joan** (*b* Sydney, 7 Nov. 1926). Australian soprano. Studied Sydney with her mother, later with John and Aida Dickens, London with Carey. Début Sydney 1951 (Goossens's *Judith*). Gly. 1959–60; London, CG, from 1952; New York, M, and Milan, S, from 1961. Also Vienna, S; Venice; Dallas; etc. Retired 1990. Gifted with a voice of outstanding flexibility, beauty, and ease in the upper register, and possessing a virtuosic technique (with a superb trill), she contributed greatly to the revival of the bel canto repertory. Though there were criticisms of her limited interpretative range and feeling for words, her extraordinary vocal abilities and attractive personality made her one of the most popular prima donnas of her day. Roles included Alcina, Donna Anna, Gilda, Desdemona (Verdi), Eva, the *Hoffmann* heroines; particularly famous for her Rossini (e.g. Semiramide), Bellini (e.g. Elvira, Norma), and Donizetti (e.g. Lucia, Anna Bolena). Created Jenifer (*Midsummer Marriage*). Married to Richard *Bonynge, who became her preferred conductor. Awarded Order of Merit 1991. (R)

Suzel. A farmer's daughter (sop), lover of Fritz in Mascagni's *L'amico Fritz*.

Suzuki. Madam Butterfly's servant (mez) in Puccini's *Madama Butterfly*.

Svanholm, Set (*b* Västerås, 2 Sept. 1904; *d* Saltsjö-Duvnäs, 4 Oct. 1964). Swedish tenor. Studied Stockholm with Forsell. Début (as baritone) Swedish Royal O, 1930 (Silvio). Début there as tenor 1936 (Radamès); permanently engaged from 1937. Vienna 1938–42; New York, M, 1946–56; Milan, S, 1942, 1950; Bayreuth, 1942; London, CG, 1948–57. Dir. Swedish Royal O 1956–63. An intelligent, musical and robust singer, he was highly acclaimed as Tristan, Siegmund, Parsifal; also sang Florestan, Otello (Verdi), Herod, Peter Grimes. (R)

Svoboda, Josef (*b* Čáslav, 10 May 1920). Czech designer. Leading designer Prague O from 1948, especially Czech repertory. London: CG, *Frau ohne Schatten* 1967, *Pelléas* 1969, *Nabucco* 1972, *Tannhäuser* 1973, *Ring* 1974–6; C, *Vespri* 1984. Ottawa, *Idomeneo* 1981. Creator of the 'Lanterna magika' combining cinema projection on multiple screens. Makes inventive use of gauzes and ingenious lighting effects; and has often used a staircase as a central feature of his designs.

Sweet, Sharon (*b* New York, 16 Aug. 1951). US soprano. Studied Curtis Institute. Début Munich 1985 (Aida). She uses her considerable resources to good effect in a dramatic repertory including Elisabeth de Valois (Paris 1987), Norma (Brussels 1988), Wagner's Elisabeth (Berlin, D). Other roles incl. Lina (*Stiffelio*; New York, M, 1994), Turandot (London, CG, 1994), Leonora (*Trovatore*). (R)

Sydney. City in New South Wales, Australia. Sydney was for many years dependent on touring companies, and the struggle to establish a permanent company in a properly equipped permanent home was long and difficult. In 1952 the New South Wales OC joined with the Nat. Theatre OC of Melbourne; this merger was completed under the auspices of the Elizabethan Theatre Trust in 1954. Warwick Braithwaite was music director 1955–6, resigning over managerial interference. In 1955 the NSW State government announced a competition for the design for a new Sydney opera-house. This was won by Jørn Utzon, whose design immediately aroused controversy for its originality, problems of construction, and then soaring costs (finally $120 m). Utzon resigned in 1966, and local architects completed the interior. In 1967 the large hall, intended for opera, was redesigned as a concert-hall (cap. 2,690) and the smaller hall became the opera theatre (cap. 1,547). In July 1970 the old opera theatre, Her Majesty's, burnt down, destroying most of the Opera's possessions. The new opera-house was opened on 20 Oct. 1973 by Queen Elizabeth II, but the first public performance was of *War and Peace*, conducted by the music director of Australian O, Edward Downes, on 28 Sept. He was succeeded in 1976 by Richard Bonynge, whose policies led to a crisis over which the general manager, Peter Hemmings, was forced to resign: this led to an official enquiry by the Australia Council in 1986. Bonynge was obliged to step aside to the post of chief guest conductor in 1984. A crisis of confidence and cash ensued. Since then morale and standards have revived.

Szell, George (*b* Budapest, 7 June 1897; *d* Cleveland, 29 July 1970). Hungarian, later US, conductor. Studied Vienna with Mandyczewski, Foerster, and Reger. Encouraged to conduct by Richard Strauss, joined Berlin, H, 1915. Cond. Strasburg 1917; Darmstadt 1921; Düsseldorf 1922; Berlin, S, 1924–9. Music dir. Prague German O 1929–37. New York, M, 1946, 1953–4, much admired in Wagner and Strauss. Salzburg 1949–64, incl. prems. of Liebermann's *Penelope* (1954) and Egk's *Irische Legende* (1955). A powerful and demanding conductor, who obtained performances of great energy and intensity. (R)

Szokolay, Sándor (*b* Kúnágota, 30 Mar. 1931). Hungarian composer. Studied Budapest with Szabó and Farkas. His first opera, *Blood Wedding* (1964), drew attention to him as an opera composer of great dramatic command, and the work was quickly taken up by a number of European theatres. Its dark, somewhat Expressionist nature was modified for *Hamlet* (1968), in which Szokolay found a more lucid and coherent style (including some skilful archaicism) upon which he was able to build with the colourful imagery of *Sámson* (1973). *Ecce homo* (1987), a setting of Kazantzakis's *Christ Recrucified*, develops this orchestral mastery and includes some fine choral writing, if sometimes at the expense of the solo vocal lines.

Szymanowski, Karol (*b* Tymoszówka, 6 Oct. 1882; *d* Lausanne, 29 Mar. 1937). Polish composer. Studied with his father and Neuhaus. Hopes of having his first opera, *Hagith* (1922), produced in Vienna under his friend Fitelberg were not realized. It has made less mark than his most ambitious stage work, *King Roger* (1926), an impressive attempt at treating the theme of the enticements and perils of Dionysus in a setting of the conflict between Christianity and paganism in 12th-cent. Sicily. Szymanowski's richly sensual orchestral style, and his skilful vocal writing, are at the service of an intelligent handling of a late-Romantic style.

T

Tabarro, Il (The Cloak). Opera in 1 act by Puccini; text by Adami, after Didier Gold's tragedy *La houppelande* (1910). Pt 1 of *Il trittico*. Prem. New York, M, 14 Dec. 1918.

A barge on the Seine, Paris, early 20th cent. The bargee Michele (bar) suspects his wife Giorgetta (sop) of unfaithfulness, but tries to win her back by reminding her of how she used to shelter under his cloak. She has arranged a meeting with her lover, the bargehand Luigi (ten), who mistakes Michele's lighting of his pipe for the signal that the coast is clear. Michele kills him and covers the body with his cloak. When Giorgetta appears, Michele invites her under the cloak again; he reveals Luigi's body and flings her down on top of it.

'Tacea la notte placida'. Leonora's (sop) aria in Act I of Verdi's *Il trovatore*, in which she muses to Inez on the mysterious troubadour with whom she has fallen in love.

Taddei, Giuseppe (*b* Genoa, 26 June 1916). Italian baritone. Studied Rome. Début Rome, R, 1936 (Herald, *Lohengrin*). Rome from 1942; Vienna 1946–86; London, Cambridge T 1947, and CG between 1960 and 1967; Milan, S, 1948–51, 1955–61; also New York, M, 1985–7, Chicago, Salzburg, etc. A versatile singer impressive as Papageno, Figaro (Mozart and Rossini), Germont, Macbeth, Falstaff (Verdi), Alberich, Sachs, Scarpia. (R)

Tadolini, Eugenia (*b* Forlì, 1809; *d* Naples, ?). Italian soprano. Studied with Favi, Grilli, and her husband, the composer **Giovanni Tadolini** (1785–1872). Début Florence 1828. Paris, I, 1830–2; Milan, S, 1833, 1836, 1838–40, 1846; Vienna, K, 1842–4; Naples, C, and London, HM, 1848. Retired 1851. Roles included Donna Anna, Rosina, Amina, Norma, Lucia, Anna Bolena, Norina, Odabella; created Linda di Chamounix, Maria di Rohan, Verdi's Alzira. Donizetti thought highly of her ('She is a singer, she is an actress, she is everything') as did Strepponi, also Verdi, though he found her too beautiful, her voice too 'stupendous, clear, and pure', and her singing too 'perfect' for his conception of Lady Macbeth.

Tagliafico, Joseph (*b* Toulon, 1 Jan. 1821; *d* Nice, 27 Jan. 1900). French bass. Studied Paris with Piermarini and Lablache. Début Paris, I, 1844. London, CG, 1847–76 (1877–82 as stage-manager); also St Petersburg, New York, Paris, etc. An extremely versatile performer with a huge repertory, including Mozart, Rossini, Bellini, Verdi, Berlioz, Gounod.

Tagliavini, Ferruccio (*b* Reggio Emilia, 14 Aug. 1913; *d* Reggio Emilia, 28 Jan. 1995). Italian tenor. Studied Parma with Brancucci, Florence with Bassi. Début Florence 1938 (Rodolfo). Milan, S, from 1940; New York, M, 1947–54, 1961–2; London, CG, 1950, 1955–6. Also Buenos Aires, C; Vienna; Paris; Chicago; etc. Retired 1965. A tenore di grazia outstanding as Arturo, Elvino, Edgardo, Nemorino, Werther, Fritz. (R) Married 1941 the Italian soprano **Pia Tassinari** (1903–95), with whom he often performed in *Bohème*, *L'amico Fritz*, etc. She studied Bologna with Vezzani. Début Casale Monferrato 1929 (Mimì). Milan, S, 1931–7, 1945–6; Rome 1933–43, 1951–2; New York, M, 1947–8. Later, her voice darkening, sang mez roles, e.g. Carmen, Charlotte. (R)

Tajo, Italo (*b* Pinerolo, 25 Apr. 1915; *d* Cincinnati, 29 Mar. 1993). Italian bass. Studied Turin with Bertozzi. Début Turin 1935 (Fafner). Milan, S, 1940–56; Rome 1939–48; London, CG, 1950; S Francisco 1948–56; New York, M, 1948–50, 1975–90. Also Edinburgh; Paris, O; Naples, C; etc. A gifted buffo singer, with a large repertory including Mozart's Dr Bartolo, Leporello, Don Pasquale, Dulcamara, Doktor (*Wozzeck*), Ochs, and creations in works by Berio, Bucchi, Lualdi, Malipiero, Nono. (R)

Taktakishvili, Otar (*b* Tbilisi, 27 July 1924; *d* Tbilisi, 22 Feb. 1989). Georgian composer, conductor, and writer; son of below. Studied Tbilisi with Barkhudaryan. His operatic works include a number of historical and patriotic pieces, such as *Mindiya* (1961) and *Sami novela* (Three Stories, 1967), which make use of an eclectic and popular style. His many official posts included that of Georgian Minister of Culture.

Taktakishvili, Shalva (*b* Kvemo Khviti, 27 Aug. 1900; *d* Tbilisi, 18 July 1965). Georgian composer and conductor; father of above. Studied Tbilisi with Barkhudaryan. He directed opera studies at the Tbilisi Cons., and his own pioneering operas, which include *Deputat* (The Deputy, 1940), helped to give stimulus to a younger generation.

Tal, Josef (*b* Pinne, 18 Sept. 1910). Israeli composer. Studied Berlin with Hindemith and others. Taught Palestine from 1934, dir. Israel Academy of Music 1948–52. Other important posts include with Hebrew U and Israel Broadcasting Authority. His most important opera is *Ashmedai* (1971), a work in the form of a Jewish morality play; composed in free serial technique, it also employs jazz rhythms. *Massada 967* (1973) uses electronic techniques (of which Tal has been an expert teacher), organically and not merely atmospherically, but is dramatically somewhat halting. A similar lack of theatricality affects *Die Versuchung* (1976); more recent works include *Der Turm* (1987) and *Joseph* (1995).

Tale of Tsar Saltan, The. See TSAR SALTAN.

Talich, Václav (*b* Kroměříž, 28 May 1883; *d* Beroun, 16 Mar. 1961). Czech conductor. Studied Prague with Mařák. Joined Berlin Philharmonic as violinist, becoming leader and thence being under the influence of Nikisch. After working in Odessa and Tbilisi as a violinist, conducted some opera in Ljubljana 1908–12, studied further Leipzig with Reger, Sitt, and Nikisch, Milan with Vigna. Cond. Plzeň 1912–15. Music dir. Prague, N, 1935–44, when the Nazis closed the theatre; cond. again 1947–8, again removed from post, and only restored to favour 1954. The greatest Czech cond. of his generation, he stood for much in his country's music both on the concert platform and in the operahouse, where his achievements included the advancement of Janáček's cause. His enterprising productions at the Prague N were frequently controversial. (R)

Talvela, Martti (*b* Hiitola, 4 Feb. 1935; *d* Juva, 22 July 1989). Finnish bass. Studied Lahti, and Stockholm with Oehmann. Début Swedish Royal O 1961 (Sparafucile). Bayreuth 1962–70; Berlin, D, from 1962; New York, M, from 1968; London, CG, 1970–3. Possessed a massive physique and voice, and a dramatic authority that could encompass both the frightening and the tender. Impressive as Osmin, the Grand Inquisitor, King Mark, Boris, Kecal, and Paavo Ruotsalainen (Kokkonen's *The Last Temptations*), written for him. Directed and performed in Savonlinna O Fest. 1972–7, raising it to an international level, and greatly contributing to the appreciation of opera in Finland. (R)

Tamagno, Francesco (*b* Turin, 28 Dec. 1850; *d* Varese, 31 Aug. 1905). Italian tenor. Studied Turin with Pedrotti. Début Turin 1870 (Nearco, *Poliuto*). Palermo 1874 with great success; Venice, F, 1875; Milan, S, 1877–87, 1899, 1901; Chicago 1889; New York, M, 1890, 1894–5; London, L, 1889, and CG, 1895, 1901; also Buenos Aires, Madrid, St Petersburg. Last appearance 1904. Repertory included Arnold, Poliuto, Edgardo, Radamès, Don Carlos, Don José, Samson. Created Verdi's Otello, and roles in works by Ponchielli, Leoncavallo, and De Lara; also sang Gabriele Adorno in first revised *Boccanegra*, 1881. One of the most idolized tenors of his time, he possessed a thrilling, stentorian voice (described by Bispham as 'enduring brass') that reached a tireless top C. This, together with a natural, passionate temperament and instinctive dramatic perception (providing an ideal contrast with Maurel's Iago), made his Otello incomparable, earning even Verdi's approbation. Left his large collection of butterflies to Varese. (R)

Tamberlik, Enrico (*b* Rome, 16 Mar. 1820; *d* Paris, 13 Mar. 1889). Italian tenor. Studied Naples with Zirilli and Borgna, Bologna with Guglielmi, Milan with De Abella. After a semi-public début Rome 1837, official début as Danieli, Naples 1841 (Tybalt, *I Capuleti e i Montecchi*). Naples, C, 1842–4 as Tamberlik; London, CG 1850–5, 1859–64, 1869, and HM 1877; St Petersburg, 1850–6, 1857–63 (creating Alvaro, *Forza del destino*, 1862); Paris, I, regularly 1858–77; toured Spain 1881–2; also Madrid, Buenos Aires, etc. An imposing man with a powerful, ringing, and virile tone, he was a highly sought-after artist who could sing lyrically as well as dramatically. His roles included Don Ottavio, Florestan, Arnold, Otello (Rossini), Poliuto, Cellini, Faust (Gounod). One of the first exponents of the high C# from the chest (to Rossini's dismay), he was also the first to interpolate the top Cs in 'Di quella pira' (with Verdi's approval). Retired to Madrid, and became an arms manufacturer.

Tamburini, Antonio (*b* Faenza, 28 Mar.

1800; d Nice, 8 Nov. 1876). Italian baritone. Studied with Boni and Osidi. Début Cento 1818 (Generali's *Contessa di colle erboso*). Milan, S, 1822, 1827–30; Naples, C, 1824, 1828–32; London, H, 1832–51, and CG 1847; Paris, I, regularly 1832–54. Also Vienna, K; Genoa; St Petersburg. He was 'singularly handsome', his voice 'rich, sweet, and equal' (Chorley), and he possessed a superb coloratura technique. Like Lablache, his frequent partner, he was a highly popular artist (his non-engagement in 1840 at London, HM, caused riots) with great comic gifts. His falsetto singing was, by all accounts, sensational. Created roles in Bellini's *Il pirata* (Ernesto), *La straniera* (Valdeburgo), and *I Puritani* (Sir Richard Forth), also in ten Donizetti operas, including *L'ajo nell'imbarazzo*, *Gianni di Calais*, *Marin Faliero*, *Don Pasquale* (Malatesta). Famous in Rossini's *L'italiana in Algeri*, *Barbiere*, *Tancredi*, *Cenerentola*, *Mosè*, *Semiramide*, *Otello*, and Donizetti's *Lucia di Lammermoor*, *Roberto Devereux*, *Lucrezia Borgia*, and as Mozart's Don Giovanni and Almaviva. Retired 1856, but sang Rossini's Figaro, Nice 1865.

Tamino. A Japanese prince (ten), lover of Pamina, in Mozart's *Die Zauberflöte*.

Tancredi. Opera in 2 acts by Rossini; text by G. Rossi, after Voltaire's *Tancrède* (1760). Prem. Venice, F, 6 Feb. 1813.

Syracuse, 11th cent. Returning from exile in Sicily, Tancredi (con) prevents the marriage of his beloved Amenaide (sop) to Orbazzano (bs). The latter, however, intercepts a letter from her to Tancredi, which he alleges is being sent to the Saracen Chief, the enemy of the Sicilians. Amenaide is thrown into prison and condemned to death unless a champion will fight for her honour.

Tancredi agrees to be her champion, although he believes her to be guilty of treason. He wins the duel, leads the Sicilians to victory, and finally learns that Amenaide was falsely accused. The lovers are reunited.

Taneyev, Sergey (b Vladimir, 25 Nov. 1856; d Dyudkovo, 19 June 1915). Russian composer. Studied Moscow with Langer and Hubert, more importantly with Tchaikovsky and N. Rubinstein. His only operatic work is a trilogy based on the *Oresteia*, which he began in 1887 and finished in 1894. His painstaking approach is shown in a letter to Tchaikovsky describing how he devised the entire work in outline before planning acts, then scenes, then numbers, and only finally writing the actual music. The work reflects above all Taneyev's care, skill, and intelligence, as well as his independence: neither 'Slavophile' nor 'Westernizer', he attempted a setting that would keep aloof from Russian influences and concerns in the interests of a timeless classicism, especially by way of its elegant contrapuntal techniques.

Tannhäuser und der Sängerkrieg auf Wartburg (Tannhäuser and the Song Contest on the Wartburg). Opera in 3 acts by Wagner; text by the composer, based on a Middle High German poem, the *Wartburgkrieg* (*c*.1250), and on the *Tannhäuserlied* (*c*.1515), probably suggested by L. Bechstein's *Der Sagenschatz und die Sagenkreise des Thüringerlandes* (1835–8), with ideas from L. Tieck's *Der getreue Eckhart und der Tannenhäuser* (1799), E. T. A. Hoffmann's *Der Kampf der Sänger* (1818), and Heine's *Der Tannhäuser*. Prem. Dresden 19 Oct. 1845.

The Wartburg, Thuringia, at the beginning of the 13th cent. Inside the Venusberg, Tannhäuser sings in praise of the pleasures offered him by Venus (mez). But sated, he longs to return to the world, and when he names the Virgin Mary, the Venusberg disappears and he finds himself in the valley of the Wartburg where a young shepherd (sop) is singing. A group of pilgrims passes on the way to Rome; then horns herald the Landgrave Hermann (bs), Tannhäuser's friend Wolfram (bar), and other knights. They welcome Tannhäuser after his year's absence, and he decides to return with them on hearing how sad the Landgrave's niece Elisabeth has been since his departure.

The Hall of Song in Wartburg Castle. Elisabeth (sop) greets the Hall, then welcomes Tannhäuser, who will not, however, reveal where he has been. The knights and their guests enter for the song contest; the Landgrave announces the theme as love. Wolfram sings of a pure, selfless love; but Tannhäuser follows with an outburst in praise of Venus. The knights threaten him, but Elisabeth intervenes. Tannhäuser promises atonement; he is banished to seek absolution from the Pope, and joins the pilgrims.

In the Valley of the Wartburg, several months later, Elisabeth is praying for Tannhäuser's forgiveness. When she sadly returns home, Wolfram prays to the evening star to guide and protect her. Tannhäuser returns, distraught at the Pope's refusal of absolution: he can now only return to Venus.

A funeral procession approaches: Elisabeth has died of a broken heart. Tannhäuser sinks dead beside her. Pilgrims arrive from Rome bearing the Pope's staff, which has sprouted leaves in token that God has forgiven him.

Tarare. Opera in prologue and 5 acts by Salieri; text by Beaumarchais, after a Persian tale (trans. Hamilton). Prem. Paris, O, 8 June 1787.

Ormus, Persia, 1680. In the Prologue, the Genius of Nature (ten) and Genius of Fire (bar) conjure up a crowd of human shades. The popularity of Tarare (ten), a captain, with his troops arouses the envy of King Atar (bs), who tries unsuccessfully to murder him. Atar then abducts Tarare's beloved Astasie (sop). Aided by Calpigi (ten), Tarare eventually rescues her, and, after a rebellion during which Atar is killed, Tarare is acclaimed king (in a 1790 version he becomes a constitutional monarch, in 1795 an overthrower of tyranny, and with the 1815 Restoration the general in charge of the reformed Atar's army).

Tarchi, Angelo (b Naples, c.1760; d Paris, 19 Aug. 1814). Italian composer. Studied Naples with Fago and Sala. Had his first success there with the comic operas L'archetiello (1778), I viluppi amorosi (The Entanglements of Love, 1778), and Il barbiere d'Arpino (1779). Three operas written for Rome, including Don Fallopio (1782), were also well received, as was the later opera seria Ariarte (1786). In 1789 he was at London, H, producing Il disertore francese (1789) and La generosità d'Alessandro (1789). From 1797 lived in Paris: wrote seven French comic operas for the Opéra-Comique of which the most successful was D'auberge en auberge (1800). Tarchi was a fluent representative of the Neapolitan opera buffa style whose works enjoyed great popularity in their day: his opere serie were generally less highly regarded.

Tarquinius. Sextus Tarquinius, Prince of Rome, son of Lucius Tarquinius Superbus, appears (bar) in Britten's The Rape of Lucretia.

Tassinari, Pia. See TAGLIAVINI, FERUCCIO.

Tate, Jeffrey (b Salisbury, 28 Apr. 1943). English conductor. Studied London O Centre; assistant to Boulez at Bayreuth and Paris O. Début Gothenburg 1978 (Carmen). New York, M, from 1980 with Lulu, Rosenkavalier, Lohengrin. London, CG, 1982

(Clemenza di Tito); principal cond. 1986–91. Salzburg 1985 (Henze/Monteverdi Ulisse); Geneva 1987 (prem. of Liebermann's La forêt). Noted for a sure command of structure, he conducted a successful Ring at Paris, C, 1994.

Tatyana. Tatyana Larina (sop), in love with Onegin and later married to Prince Gremin, in Tchaikovsky's Eugene Onegin.

Tauber, Richard (b Linz, 16 May 1891; d London, 8 Jan. 1948). Austrian, later British, tenor. Studied Freiburg with Beines. Début Chemnitz (where his natural father, the actor Richard Anton Tauber, was director) 1913 (Tamino). Dresden 1913–18; Berlin, S, from 1919; Vienna, S, from 1925; Paris, O, 1928; London, CG, 1938–9, 1947; also Salzburg, Munich, Canada, S America, Australia. An exceptionally popular singer, with a lucent, mellow tone and an exquisite lyrical style, he lavished as much care on works by Lehár, who wrote several roles for him (e.g. in Das Land des Lächelns), as on Mozart (Belmonte, Don Ottavio, Tamino). Other roles included Florestan, Calaf, Bacchus. Also a composer (incl. operettas) and conductor. (R)

Taylor, Deems (b New York, 22 Dec. 1885; d New York, 3 July 1966). US composer and critic. Studied New York, writing burlesques of opera and an original work, The Echo, before studying music seriously with Coon. Worked as a critic for the New York World (1921–5) and other journals, also as a broadcaster, especially on opera. Of his operas, both The King's Henchman (1927) and Peter Ibbetson (1931) were highly successful in their day, having more performances at the New York M than those of any other American composer. Their idiom is essentially European and late-Romantic.

Tchaikovsky, Pyotr (b Votkinsk, 7 May 1840; d St Petersburg, 6 Nov. 1893). Russian composer. Studied St Petersburg with Zaremba and A. Rubinstein.

Tchaikovsky declared that to refrain from writing opera was a heroism he did not possess. From his youth, the stage fascinated him: seeing a performance of Don Giovanni at the age of 10, he decided to devote himself to music, and throughout his life he returned to the writing of opera. His first serious attempts at composition came after the shock of his mother's death in 1854, but his operatic essays were all abortive until The Oprichnik (1874).

Though he has not yet found his individual touch, the opera contains some good numbers, some aptly handled motives, and passages in which convention gives way to genuine feeling. In *Vakula the Smith* (1876) he takes a much stronger operatic position, and develops a more personal vein of dramatic music. Though it lacks the comic realism and subtlety of character demanded by the plot, the work is well written, with some attractive lyrical love music and some delightful dances, and a neat contrast between peasant vigour and urban, aristocratic grace. It was later revised as *Cherevichki* ('The Slippers' or 'The Little Boots').

His impetus to write opera was renewed in Paris in 1876 by a hearing of *Carmen*; and in the same year, his attendance as a special correspondent at the first Bayreuth Fest. gave him an admiration for Wagner but no attraction to his ideas. The virtues disclosed in his earlier operas find full expression in his operatic masterpiece, *Eugene Onegin* (1879). Haunted by the predicament of Tatyana in her rejection by the subsequently remorseful Onegin, he began work on the famous *Letter Scene. He described the work as 'lyrical scenes', and hoped to get far from operatic convention as he knew it. Bringing together a story of frustrated love, scenes of Russian urban and country life, a feeling for the rococo and also for Russian folk music, *Onegin* touched on a great deal close to Tchaikovsky's nature, and the subject drew from him his freshest and most lyrical operatic music.

Turning from Russian subjects, Tchaikovsky next set a version of *The Maid of Orleans* (1881), making use of a text based on a version of Schiller. Again he was drawn above all to the heroine, and began by setting the scene of her narrative to the Dauphin and Count and her acclamation in Act II. His intention was to conquer the Paris O, and the work is therefore cast in Grand Opera vein, with touches of Gounod and Massenet and with the pervading influence of Meyerbeer in its grandiose crowd scenes. However, despite some fine strokes and effective passages, he is unable to give real emotional life to Joan.

Mazeppa (1884) returns to a Russian subject. Again, Tchaikovsky began by composing a central, crucial scene so as to achieve immediate emotional identification with the characters: this was the Act II duet. The work exhibits some familiar Russian operatic characteristics, such as the suffering heroine, the intransigent old man, and the use of dances, and these are now fluently handled; but though there are delightful episodes and some striking dramatic ideas, Tchaikovsky fails to characterize the agonized Maria and the harsh, impressive Mazeppa very fully. There was still less chance of success with *The Enchantress* (1887), to a confused plot that drew on inconsistent musical characterization.

The influence of *Carmen* returns in *The Queen of Spades* (1890), another Pushkin setting. Tchaikovsky's beloved Mozart, too, is evoked in some scenes re-creating the rococo past of Catherine the Great's Petersburg and its French elegance. The opera is permeated with the sense of Fate which obsessed Tchaikovsky, operating, as in *Carmen*, within a convention of lyrical elegance; and though the work is inconsistent, above all in juxtaposing Mozartian grace with some almost Wagnerian chromatic intensity in the scenes of horror, it contains some of his finest operatic writing.

Tchaikovsky's last opera was the 1-act *Yolanta* (1892), originally commissioned as a double bill with the ballet *The Nutcracker*. It has much delicacy and grace, with some Wagnerian elements both harmonically and in the prominence of the orchestra in articulating the drama. Yet for all the excellence of the music in this work, and especially in *The Queen of Spades*, it is above all in the 'lyrical scenes' of *Eugene Onegin* that Tchaikovsky's individual gift for the operatic stage finds its fullest expression.

Tear, Robert (*b* Barry, 8 Mar. 1939). Welsh tenor. Studied Cambridge with Kimbell. Début Birmingham 1963 (Rameau's Hippolyte). London, EOG, 1963–71, creating roles in Britten's church parables, and 1973. Edinburgh 1968; London, CG, from 1970; Paris, O, from 1976. Also Munich; Milan, S; Berlin, D; S Francisco; Los Angeles; Geneva; etc. A singer of penetrating intelligence, vocal subtlety, and dramatic flair, distinguished as Loge, Lensky, Golitsyn, Herod, Tom Rakewell, Grimes, Aschenbach. Created Dov (*Knot Garden*), and title-role Penderecki's *Ubu rex*. (R)

Tebaldi, Renata (*b* Pesaro, 1 Feb. 1922). Italian soprano. Studied Parma with Campogalliani, Pesaro with Melis. Début Rovigo 1944 (Elena, Boito's *Mefistofele*). Milan, S,

1946–7, 1949–55, 1959–60; Naples, C, 1949–54; London, CG, 1950, 1955; Paris, O, 1951; New York, M, 1955–73; Chicago 1956–69. Also Buenos Aires, C; Vienna; Rome; etc. Her full, smooth, glowing tone was capable of both great power and a ravishing pianissimo; and her emphasis on the vocal and lyrical led her supporters to foster a rivalry with Callas. Roles included Donna Elvira, Elsa, Eva, Tatyana; particularly impressive in Verdi, Puccini, and as Madeleine (*Andrea Chénier*) and Adriana Lecouvreur. (R)

Te Kanawa, (Dame) **Kiri** (*b* Gisborne, 6 Mar. 1944). New Zealand soprano. Studied Auckland with Leo, London with Rozsa. Début London, Camden Fest., 1969 (Elena, *La donna del lago*). London, CG, from 1970; Gly. 1973; New York, M, from 1974; Paris, O, from 1974; also Vienna, Brussels, S Fe, S Francisco, Sydney, etc. One of the most successful divas of the day, whose chief asset is a sumptuous, creamy tone. Roles include Donna Elvira, Countess (Mozart and R. Strauss), Marguerite, Micaëla, Amelia Grimaldi, Violetta, Elisabeth de Valois, Mimì, Arabella. (R)

Telemaco. Opera in 2 acts by Gluck; text by Coltellini, after Capece's text for A. Scarlatti (1718), in turn after the *Odyssey*. Prem. Vienna, B, 30 Jan. 1765.

Greece, antiquity. Ulisse (ten) is rescued from his capture on Circe's island by his son Telemaco (con), aided by Asteria (sop) and Merione (sop), son of King Idomeneo of Crete. In retribution, Circe (sop) conjures up before Telemaco's eyes images of his mother's death. However, all manage to escape from the island, which Circe then transforms to desert.

Telemann, Georg Philipp (*b* Magdeburg, 14 Mar. 1681; *d* Hamburg, 25 June 1767). German composer. Largely self-taught; his first opera, *Sigismundus* was written when aged 12. In 1700–4 he attended Leipzig U, where he founded the Collegium Musicum and wrote four operas. Held various positions in Sorau, Eisenach, Frankfurt, and Bayreuth before becoming music director of the principal churches in Hamburg 1721. Here he stayed for the rest of his career, though he made many journeys to Berlin and an important trip to France 1737.

Though roughly half of Telemann's 40 operas were composed for Leipzig, Eisenach, and Bayreuth, he is chiefly remembered for the *c*.20 works which he contributed to the

repertory of the Hamburg O. His activities there, which began with *Der geduldige Socrates* (1721), dominated the O until its closure in 1738 and represented the culmination of the first phase of Hamburg's operatic history. Though the influence of earlier German opera composers, especially Keiser, is apparent, Telemann was more cosmopolitan in style, drawing inspiration from France especially. Possessing more dramatic talent than Mattheson or Graupner, he was much the most adventurous German composer of his day, and enjoyed greater fame even than J. S. Bach. His most successful work was the intermezzo *Pimpinone* (1725), whose correct title is *Die ungleiche Heyrath*: other important works were *Der neumodische Liebhaber Damon* (1724) and *Flavius Bertaridus* (1729).

Telephone, The. Opera in 1 act by Menotti; text by composer. Prem. New York, Heckscher T, 18 Feb. 1947.

Lucy's apartment, present-day. Ben (bar) visits Lucy (sop) on the eve of his departure so as to propose marriage. His attempts are repeatedly frustrated by the telephone ringing. Eventually he finds the only recourse is to leave and ring her up himself; he is accepted.

Telramund. Friedrich von Telramund (bar), Count of Brabant, husband of Ortrud, in Wagner's *Lohengrin*.

Templer und die Jüdin, Der (The Templar and the Jewess). Opera in 3 acts by Marschner; text by W. A. Wohlbrück, after Scott's *Ivanhoe* (1820) and J. Lenz's *Das Gericht der Templer* (1824). Prem. Leipzig 22 Dec. 1829.

Tender Land, The. Opera in 2 acts by Copland; text by Horace Everett, after Johns. Prem. New York, CO, 1 Apr. 1954.

US, *c*.1950. Laurie Moss (sop), a farmer's daughter, graduates from high school and, despite being hampered by her over-protective mother (con), determines to embark fully upon adult life. She does so with the help of two strangers, Martin (ten) and Top (bar), from outside her close community. But Martin fails to keep a promise to elope with her, and the pain this causes her forces her at last to grow up.

tenor (It., *tenore*: 'holding'; in early times the voice which held the plainsong). The highest category of natural male voice. Many subdivisions exist within opera-houses: the commonest in general use (though seldom by composers in scores) are given below, with examples of roles. These divisions often overlap, and do not correspond exactly from country to country. In general, distinction is more by character than by tessitura, especially in France: thus, the examples of the roles give a more useful indication of the different voices' quality than any technical definition.

French: ténor (Don José); ténor-bouffe (Paris in *La belle Hélène*); Trial (Torquemada in *L'heure espagnole*).

German: Heldentenor (Huon, Bacchus); Wagnerheldentenor (Siegfried); lyrischer Tenor (Max); Spieltenor (Pedrillo, David); hoher Tenor (Brighella, *Rosenkavalier* tenor).

Italian: tenore (Radamès); tenore spinto (Rodolfo); tenore di forza (Otello); tenore di grazia (Nemorino); tenor-buffo (Dickson, *La dame blanche*).

See also CASTRATO, COUNTER-TENOR.

tenuto (It.: 'held'). A direction to hold notes for their full value, or very slightly longer. Consistently taken by singers as an invitation to hold them, especially if high ones, for as long as they please.

Teresa. The daughter (sop) of the papal treasurer Giacomo Balducci, lover of Cellini, in Berlioz's *Benvenuto Cellini*.

Terfel, Bryn (*b* Pantglas, 9 Nov. 1965). Welsh baritone. Studied London, GSMD. Début WNO 1990 (Guglielmo). One of the most successful of today's Mozart singers, he appeared as Figaro on his London, ENO, and New York, M, débuts (1991 and 1994). Masetto at London, CG (1992); Leporello at Salzburg. Other roles incl. Jochanaan (Salzburg 1992) and Mozart's Almaviva (Vienna, S, 1993). (R)

Ternina, Milka (*b* Vežišće, 19 Dec. 1863; *d* Zagreb, 18 May 1941). Croatian soprano. Studied Zagreb with Wimberger, Vienna with Gänzbacher. Début Zagreb 1882 (Amelia, *Ballo in maschera*). Leipzig 1883; Bremen 1886–90; Munich 1890–1906; Boston 1896; London, CG, 1898, 1900, 1906; Bayreuth 1899; New York, M, 1899–1904. Retired 1906, with a facial paralysis, and taught; her pupils included Zinka Milanov. A stupendous actress with a voice to match, she was triumphant in a wide range of roles, including Donna Anna, Reiza, Marguerite, Aida, Elsa, Ortrud, Sieglinde, Brünnhilde, Kundry, Tosca, and above all as Leonore and

Isolde. Henry James found her singing 'a devastating experience'.

Teschemacher, Margarete (*b* Cologne, 3 Mar. 1903; *d* Bad Wiessee, 19 May 1959). German soprano. Studied Cologne. Début Cologne 1924 (Micaëla). Aachen 1925–7; London, CG, 1931, 1936; Stuttgart 1931–4; Dresden 1935–46; Düsseldorf 1947–52; Buenos Aires, C, 1934. Roles included Senta, Sieglinde, Countess (*Capriccio*), Arabella, and a much-acclaimed Jenůfa and Minnie. Created Daphne, as which she was praised by Strauss. (R)

Tess, Giulia (*b* Milan, 19 Feb. 1889; *d* Milan, 17 Mar. 1976). Italian mezzo-soprano, later soprano. Studied Verona with Bottagisio. Début, as mezzo-soprano, Prato 1904. Venice and Prague 1909; also Vienna, St Petersburg, as Mignon, Amneris, Charlotte, etc. After further study, became soprano. Milan, S, 1922–36. Created Jaele (Pizzetti's *Deborah e Jaele*), Orsola (Wolf's *Il campiello*); also successful in verismo roles and as Salome, Elektra, and Honegger's Judith. Retired 1940, becoming a producer (e.g. Milan, S, 1946, *Cenerentola*) and teacher, her pupils including Tagliavini, Barbieri. (R)

tessitura (It.: 'texture'). A term indicating the prevailing range of a piece of music in relation to the voice for which it is written. Thus, Zerbinetta's aria in *Ariadne auf Naxos* has a particularly high tessitura.

Tetrazzini, Eva (*b* Milan, Mar. 1862; *d* Salsomaggiore, 27 Oct. 1938). Italian soprano, sister of below. Studied Florence with Ceccherini. Début Florence 1882 (Marguerite). New York, AM, 1888; Manhattan OC, 1908; London, CG, 1890. Roles included Aida, Valentine, Fedora, and first US Desdemona (Verdi). Married Cleofonte *Campanini. Recordings of 'E. Tetrazzini' refer to the third sister, **Elvira**, also a soprano. (R)

Tetrazzini, Luisa (*b* Florence, 29 June 1871; *d* Milan, 28 Apr. 1940). Italian soprano, sister of above. Studied Florence, and with her sister Eva. Début Florence, T Pagliano, 1890 (Inez, *L'Africaine*). After much success in Italy, Russia, Spain, and especially S America, she made a belated but spectacular début London, CG, 1907. London, CG, 1908–12; New York, Manhattan OC, 1908–10, and M, 1911–12; Chicago 1912–13. Then sang in concert until 1934. A superb coloratura artist, whose upper register was warm and rounded, she dazzled audiences with her clear, brilliant, and spirited singing. Even a rotund figure and eccentric taste in costume did not detract from her Rosina, Amina, Lucia, Violetta, Gilda, Lakmé, and Ophélie. E. M. Forster, in *Where Angels Fear to Tread*, describes a singer 'stout and ugly' but with a beautiful voice, later admitting that this was the then unknown Tetrazzini. She died in poverty, her enormous fortune having been dissipated by her third husband. (R)

Teyte, (Dame) **Maggie** (*b* Wolverhampton, 17 Apr. 1888; *d* London, 26 May 1976). English soprano. Studied London, and Paris with J. De Reszke. Début Monte Carlo 1907 (Tyrcis, Offenbach's *Myriame et Daphné*). Paris, OC, 1907–10; London, HM, 1910, and CG, 1911, 1914, 1922–3, 1930, 1936–8; Chicago 1911–14; New York, CC, 1948; London, Mermaid T, 1951, when she retired from the stage. Possessing a clear, firm tone and great interpretative gifts, she was admired as Zerlina, Blonde, Marguerite, Mimì, Butterfly, Cendrillon, and especially Mélisande—as which, however, Debussy thought her, while better vocally than Garden, 'an adorable doll' who sang the role with 'total incomprehension'. Created Princess, *The Perfect Fool*. Made celebrated recordings of French song. (R)

Thaïs. Opera in 3 acts by Massenet; text by Louis Gallet, after Anatole France's novel (1890). Prem. Paris, O, 16 Mar. 1894.

Egypt, 4th cent. Athanaël (bar), a young coenobite monk, resolves to persuade the courtesan Thaïs (sop) to return to a virtuous life. Eventually she allows him to take her to a convent. But unable to forget her, Athanaël returns to the convent, where Thaïs lies dying. As she expresses her gratitude to him for saving her soul, he collapses in anguish over the physical love for her that has overcome him.

The Méditation (properly Méditation réligieuse), the Act 2 intermezzo featuring violin and harp, has become well known as a concert piece.

Théâtre des Nations. The name of various Paris theatrical enterprises, initially the theatre opposite the Châtelet. The name of the T Sarah Bernhardt 1879–99. Various operatic seasons were given there, e.g. an Italian season in 1905 and some Dyagilev seasons. From 1957 the name of a theatrical festival

including operas, many of them French prems., often by distinguished visiting companies.

Thebom, Blanche (*b* Monessen, PA, 19 Sept. 1918). US mezzo-soprano. Studied New York with Matzenauer and Walker. Début New York, M, 1944 (Fricka). New York, M, 1964–7; Gly. 1950; London, CG, 1967. Paris, O; Milan; Brussels. Repertory included Mozart, Wagner, and an acclaimed Dido (Berlioz) and Amneris. (R)

'There's a boat dat's leavin' soon for New York'. Sporting Life's (ten) song in Act III of Gershwin's *Porgy and Bess*, trying to persuade Bess to flee with him.

Thieving Magpie, The. See GAZZA LADRA, LA.

Thill, Georges (*b* Paris, 17 Dec. 1897; *d* Draguignan, 15 Oct. 1984). French tenor. Studied Paris, and Naples with De Lucia. Début Paris, OC, 1918 (Don José). Paris, O, until after the war; London, CG, 1928, 1937; New York, M, 1931–2; Milan, S, 1928. Also Buenos Aires, C; Verona. Last stage appearance Paris, OC, 1953. Large repertory included Gluck, Cherubini, Méhul; also the roles of Aeneas (Berlioz), Don José, Werther, Lohengrin, Parsifal, Alfredo, Calaf. A considerable artist, impressive for his poised, full-toned singing and clarity of style. (R)

Thoma, Therese. See VOGL, HEINRICH.

Thomas, Ambroise (*b* Metz, 5 Aug. 1811; *d* Paris, 12 Feb. 1896). French composer. Studied privately, Paris with Zimmermann and Dourlen, also Barbereau, then Le Sueur. Between 1837 and 1843 he wrote nine stage works, most successfully *La double échelle* (1837). There followed a series of opéras-comiques: in the tradition of Auber, these are both more lively and more consciously Romantic, if not very markedly individual. The best of them was *Le songe d'une nuit d'été* (1850): non-Shakespearian, though it includes parts for Shakespeare, Falstaff, and Elizabeth I. Its success contributed to his election to the Académie in succession to Spontini (1851) and as professor at the Cons. (1856), where he was to exercise an influence on generations of students. He was director from 1871 until his death, maintaining a stoutly conservative régime in defiance of what he regarded as pernicious modern, especially Wagnerian, influences.

Himself always prone to the influence of

more distinctive (or more successful) composers, he produced *Psyché* (1857) in imitation of Gounod's classically inspired *Sapho*, *Le carnaval de Venise* (1857) in imitation of Massé, and—after a failure with *Le roman d'Elvire* and then a pause—his greatest triumph, *Mignon* (1866), in imitation of Gounod's *Faust*. He went on to repeat this with *Hamlet* (1868) in imitation of Gounod's *Roméo et Juliette*; but thereafter success largely eluded him. He was always willing to revise his works for changing audiences or conditions; and his careful eye for the main chance at the Opéra-Comique, supported by good craftsmanship and a certain gift for sentimental melodiousness, ensured his works popularity in their day, especially in France. These qualities were respected by many of his distinguished contemporaries, including Berlioz and Verdi.

Thomas, Arthur Goring (*b* Ratton Park, 20 Nov. 1850; *d* London, 20 Mar. 1892). English composer. Studied Paris with Durand, London with Sullivan and Prout, later Bruch. The success of *The Light of the Harem* (1879) brought a Carl Rosa commission, which produced his best-known and most successful work, *Esmeralda* (1883). This was performed abroad, though its handling of the drama could not guarantee it long life once its easy charm had worn off. His talent did not prove up to the dramatic demands of *Nadeshda* (1885), though there was admiration for his fluent recitative and for some of the lighter numbers.

Thomas, Jess (*b* Hot Springs, SD, 4 Aug. 1927; *d* San Francisco, 11 Oct. 1993). US tenor. Studied Stanford with Schulmann. Début San Francisco (Major-domo, *Rosenkavalier*). Karlsruhe 1958; Bayreuth 1961–9, 1976; Munich from 1961; New York, M, 1962–83; London, CG, 1969–71; Paris, O, 1967, 1972; also Salzburg, Munich, Vienna. Large repertory included Florestan, Tannhäuser, Walther, Tristan, Parsifal, and first Caesar (*Antony and Cleopatra*). (R)

Thomson, Virgil (*b* Kansas City, 25 Nov. 1896; *d* New York, 30 Sept. 1989). US composer and critic. Studied initially with Nadia Boulanger in Paris (1921–2), at which time he also met Les Six and Satie. Returning to Paris in 1925, he lived there until 1940, and worked with Gertrude Stein on his first opera, *Four Saints in Three Acts* (1934).

The score includes elements ranging from Gregorian chant to American folk hymnody, and incorporates features characteristic of many of Thomson's works, notably the quotation of familiar tunes and the attention paid to word setting. His second opera, *The Mother of Us All* (1947), composed while working as critic on the New York Herald Tribune, is based on the theme of women's suffrage: again the music draws on a wide range of sources—revival hymnody, popular 19th-cent. melodies, gospel tunes—to create a distinctly American style.

For his third opera, *Lord Byron* (1972), Thomson collaborated with librettist Jack Larson. This work, which took seven years to write, displays an emotional content entirely new to Thomson's generally muted language, expressed by increased lyrical expansiveness.

Thorborg, Kerstin (*b* Venjan, 19 May 1896; *d* Falun, 12 Apr. 1970). Swedish mezzo-soprano. Studied Stockholm. Début Stockholm 1924 (Ortrud). Swedish Royal O 1924–30; Vienna, S, 1935–8; London, CG, 1936–9; New York, M, 1936–50; also Paris, Buenos Aires, Berlin, etc. Roles included Eglantine, Orfeo, Klytemnästra, Dalila, Fricka, Brangäne; Newman thought her 'the greatest Wagnerian actress' of the day. (R)

Tibbett, Lawrence (*b* Bakersfield, CA, 16 Nov. 1896; *d* New York, 15 July 1960). US baritone. Studied Los Angeles with Ruysdael, New York with La Forge. Début New York, M, 1923 (Lovitsky, *Boris*). New York, M, until 1950. London, CG, 1937; also Vienna, Prague, Australia. Roles included Valentin, Boccanegra, Ford, Verdi's Iago; created parts in *The Emperor Jones*, *The King's Henchman*, *Peter Ibbetson*, among others. Handsome, dramatically talented, and a fine singer with an attractive tone 'as solid as a piston rod' (Beckmesser of *Gramophone*), he was also successful in light opera and films. (R)

Tichatschek, Joseph (*b* Ober-Weckelsdorf (Teplice), 11 July 1807; *d* Blasewitz, 18 Jan. 1886). Bohemian tenor. Studied Vienna with Ciccimarra. Début Vienna, K, 1835 (Raimbaud, *Robert le diable*). Graz 1837; Dresden 1838–70; London, DL, 1841. Repertory included Idomeneo, Tamino, Adolar, Éléazar, Fernand Cortez (Spontini), Lohengrin; created Rienzi and Tannhäuser. His impassioned delivery and heroic presence, together with a fine and brilliant tone, brought him much admiration from Berlioz,

Liszt, Nicolai, and Wagner (who appreciated his 'lively nature, glorious voice, and great musical ability' while deploring his lack of dramatic perception).

Tiefland (The Lowlands). Opera in a prologue and 3 acts by D'Albert; text by Rudolf Lothar, after the Catalan play *Terra Baixa* by Angel Guimeras. Prem. Prague, German T, 15 Nov. 1903.

The Pyrenees, 19th cent. The wealthy landowner Sebastiano (bar) has forced Marta (sop), whom he once found starving, to become his mistress. He now marries her off to a young shepherd, Pedro (ten), on condition that he abandon his mountain life for the lowlands; Sebastiano plans to continue his relationship with Marta under this cover. But Marta comes to love Pedro, and eventually she confesses the true situation to him. When Sebastiano tries to take her back, his marriage plans having collapsed when the story emerges, Pedro strangles Sebastiano and bears Marta off to the mountains.

Tietjen, Heinz (*b* Tangier, 24 June 1881; *d* Baden-Baden, 30 Nov. 1967). German conductor and producer. Prod. Trier 1904–22, dir. 1907–22; Saarbrücken 1919–22; Breslau 1919–22. Dir. Berlin, SO, 1925–7, 1948–55, Prussian State T 1927–45. Artistic dir. Bayreuth 1931–44, prod. from 1933, also cond. *Parsifal* (1933), *Ring* (1936, 1938, 1939, 1941), *Meistersinger* (1933–4), *Lohengrin* (1936–7). Dir. Hamburg 1955–9. London, CG, as prod. 1950–1. His Wagner prods. were traditional but not old-fashioned. Conducted Wieland Wagner prod. of *Lohengrin*, Hamburg 1958. Returned to Bayreuth to conduct 1959. (R)

Tietjens, Therese (*b* Hamburg, 17 July 1831; *d* London, 3 Oct. 1877). German, later British, soprano. Studied Vienna with Dellessie, Babing, and Proch. Début Hamburg 1848 (Erma, Auber's *Maçon*). Hamburg 1849, as Lucrezia. Vienna, 1853 and 1856. London, HM, 1858, making a great impression. London: DL, HM, L 1859 until her death; CG 1869. Paris, O, 1863; Naples, C, 1862–3, 1868–9. Possessed a generous, velvety tone, wide-ranging dramatic conviction, a magisterial presence, and great personal magnetism. Her superb technique encompassed the roles of Medea, Donna Anna, Elvira (*Puritani*), Norma, Lucia, Valentine, Fidès, Ortrud, and a particularly famous Leonore and Lucrezia; Wagner requested her in vain to create Isolde and to sing Sieglinde. She was adored by the British public; unusually for an international prima donna, she sang opera on stage in the provinces. Her last performance, as Lucrezia, was given in severe pain from cancer.

Tinsley, Pauline (*b* Wigan, 23 Mar. 1928). English soprano. Studied Manchester with Dillon, London with Keeler, Cross, Henderson, and Turner. Début London 1961 (Rossini's Desdemona). London, SW/ENO from 1963; CG from 1965; New York, CO, 1971–2; S Fe 1969; also WNO, Boston, Hamburg, Amsterdam, Zurich, Verona, etc. An indomitable performer with a powerful, distinctive tone. Wide repertory included Queen of the Night, Donna Anna, Zerlina, Anna Bolena, Leonora (*Trovatore* and *Forza*), Brünnhilde, Kundry, Elektra, Kostelnička, Lady Billows, Ortrud, Lady Macbeth. (R)

Tippett, (Sir) **Michael** (*b* London, 2 Jan. 1905). English composer. Studied London with Wood and Morris. His deep humanity, richly stocked mind, and fascination with elaborate concepts and literary and other cultural allusions mark each of his operas, which are among the most original and important contributions to the genre in the 20th cent. He has always written his own texts, following early advice from T. S. Eliot, and there is a close interlocking between on the one hand his searching ideas and allusive, sometimes colloquial, expression, and on the other the richness yet pungency and the lyrical exuberance of his music.

Through his operas there runs a thread of concern for reconciliation between opposing or sundered elements in human beings, epitomized in a line from his oratorio *A Child of Our Time*, 'I would know my shadow and my light, so shall I at last be whole.' *The Midsummer Marriage* (1955) takes as its metaphor a couple whose respective earthiness and airiness make them unfit for a full union until they have undergone various trials, conducted in semi-mythical English surroundings. Their search is expressed in some of Tippett's most ecstatic, haunting, and profusely lyrical music. Structurally, the work makes use of traditional arias, duets, and ensembles, and gives a particular importance to ballet (in the Ritual Dances). *King Priam* (1962) turns to an existing myth, that of the Trojan war, and, partly in response to criticisms of self-defeating prolixity in the earlier opera, now draws on a sparer, tauter idiom, a more declamatory vocal style, and sharper orchestral contrasts. The declared subject is 'the mysterious nature of choice'; and the plot is vividly dramatic, including some stunning *coups de théâtre* (such as the close of Act I on the wrath of Achilles) and some tenderly lyrical exchanges (as that between Achilles and Priam over Hector's body).

In *The Knot Garden* (1970), proposing *Così fan tutte* as his example, Tippett returned to his reconciliation theme; here his central subject is a marriage which has gone wrong through the partners growing the one too mundane and the other too isolated from reality. They are set in a psychological (but dramatically and musically active) maze, from which they and the other characters emerge in new or renewed emotional bonds. The music draws on both the richness of Tippett's first opera and the spareness of his second, and finds in its confrontations between personalities a new concentration of expression. His fourth opera, *The Ice Break* (1977), enlarges the reconciliation theme to wider issues, bringing into operatic context the divisions, acute but not unhealable, between East and West, Black and White, old and young, past and present. The attachment to the present (which includes some rather forced colloquialisms in the dialogue) shows in the enrichment of Tippett's lyrical language by his sympathy for blues and boogie-woogie, one that was already revealed in the previous opera.

Tippett's last opera, *New Year* (1989), shows no slackening of contemporary awareness or lyrical impulse. The opera gathers up many of his long-held ideals and preoccupations, here in the context of contacts between a contemporary 'Terror Town' and a Utopian future, and of the characters' need to find reconciliation with their own pasts. In a work as rich as ever in layers of meaning, and in resonances that touch and stimulate, Tippett has again found his own reconciliation between his intense and personal sound world and various forms of urban popular music. Dance plays an organic part in a work that has more than a few links with the musical. Not only does the orchestra use saxophones and electric guitars; jazz and pop styles, accepted as a genuine modern vernacular, are not merely imitated but fully composed in Tippett's own idiom. (R)

Titov, Alexey (*b* St Petersburg, 23 July 1769;

d St Petersburg, 20 Nov. 1827). Russian composer. Most of his works are for the stage, and based on a Mozartian idiom. About a dozen operas survive, including a 1-act comedy, *Yam* (1805). This proved so popular that he wrote two sequels, *Posidelky* (The Winter Party, 1808) and *Devichnik* (The Wedding Eve Party, 1809), to make up a trilogy. In them, he draws upon certain Russian musical characteristics and makes some use of folk-song (including the folk polyphony that was to be employed by Glinka and Tchaikovsky, among others).

Titurel. The former ruler (bs) of the Kingdom of the Grail, father of Amfortas, in Wagner's *Parsifal*.

Toczyska, Stefania (*b* Gdańsk, 11 Aug. 1943). Polish mezzo-soprano. Studied Gdańsk; début there 1973 (Carmen). Noted for her dramatically incisive performances of Verdi, she has sung Eboli and Ulrica at Vienna, S, from 1977. London, CG, from 1983 as Amneris and Azucena. New York, M, 1988. Other roles incl. Anna Bolena (Chicago 1986), Adalgisa (Houston 1987), Venus (*Tannhäuser*, Hamburg 1990). (R)

Todesverkündigung (Ger.: 'announcement of death'). The name usually given to the scene in Act II of Wagner's *Die Walküre* in which Brünnhilde comes on Wotan's orders to tell Siegmund of his approaching death.

Tomášek, Václav (*b* Skuteč, 17 Apr. 1774; *d* Prague, 3 Apr. 1850). Bohemian composer. Largely self-taught. His influence on Prague musical life in the first half of the 19th cent., especially as teacher, was powerful. The list of his works, in which the keyboard music and songs are most important, includes one completed opera, *Seraphine* (1811).

Tomasi, Henri (*b* Marseilles, 17 Aug. 1901; *d* Avignon, 13 June 1971). French composer and conductor. Studied Marseilles, and Paris with Caussade, Vidal, and D'Indy. Cond. Paris radio 1930–6. Music dir. Monte Carlo O, 1946–50. An important and honoured figure in France, he was influential as a cond. with a strong feeling for the theatre. His operas, which include *Miguel Mañara* (1952) and *L'Atlantide* (1954), are on the whole conventional in style, though theatrically effective; they found a following in French opera-houses during the years after the Second World War.

Tomlinson, John (*b* Accrington, 22 Sept.

1946). English bass. Studied Manchester with McGuigan, London with O. Kraus. Début Gly. Touring O 1971 (Second Priest, *Zauberflöte*). Kent O; London: SW (New OC) 1972–4, ENO 1974–80, CG from 1979 (*Ring* 1994–5); Bayreuth from 1988 (Wotan); New York, M, from 1991. Also O North (sang title-role and directed Verdi's *Oberto*, 1995); Berlin, D; S Francisco; Salzburg; Aix; etc. An impressively powerful performer with a large voice. Roles incl. Masetto, Padre Guardiano, Mosè, Attila, Hunding, Hagen, Wotan, Boris, Arkel; created Green Knight (Birtwistle's *Gawain*). (R)

Tomowa-Sintow, Anna (*b* Stara Zagora, 22 Sept. 1941). Bulgarian soprano. Studied Sofia with Zlatev-Cherkin. Début Stara Zagora 1965 (Tatyana). Leipzig 1967–72; Berlin, S, 1972–6; Salzburg from 1973; Paris, O, 1974; Milan, S, 1975; London, CG, from 1975; New York, M, from 1978; also Vienna, Munich, Moscow, Brussels, etc. Roles include Countess (Mozart and R. Strauss), Donna Anna, Elsa, Eva, Leonora (*Forza*), Desdemona (Verdi), Marschallin, Arabella. Possesses a strong, rich tone and a fine technique. (R)

Tom Rakewell. A young man (ten), lover of Anne, in Stravinsky's *The Rake's Progress*.

Tonio. 1. A Tyrolean peasant (ten), lover of Marie, in Donizetti's *La fille du régiment*.

2. A clown (bar) in Leoncavallo's *Pagliacci*.

Toreador Song. The name generally given to Escamillo's couplets in Act II of Bizet's *Carmen*, 'Votre toast, je peux vous le rendre', in which he acknowledges their toasts to him and sings of the toreador's life.

Torelli, Giacomo (*b* ?Fano, 1 Sept. 1608; *d* Fano, 17 June 1678). Italian designer and architect. Built T Novissimo, Venice's fourth public opera-house, including a new system for changing the sets in a single operation and thus increasing dramatic pace. Paris 1645, installing new stage machinery and working for the Italian troupe brought to Paris by Mazarin.

Toronto. City in Ontario, Canada. The first operas given were Coleman's *The Mountaineers* and Storace's *No Song, No Supper* in 1825 by an American company, when Toronto, of fewer than 1,700 inhabitants, was mainly a garrison town and administrative capital of Upper Canada. During the years of growth to a commercial centre, vis-

iting singers and small troupes appeared increasingly. In the second half of the century visiting singers included Sontag, Lind, and Patti (generally in concerts). Full-scale productions date from 1853, with Rosa Devriès in a *Norma* conducted by Luigi Arditi. Semi-staged performances were given, but little progress was made in resident production of opera until 1867, when the Holman English O Troupe leased the Royal Lyceum and installed itself as the city's permanent company for plays and opera until 1873. In 1867–80 the company gave many performances of about 35 operas and operettas. Visiting companies presenting major artists in leading roles included the Strakosch, Emma Abbott, Kellogg, English OC, New York M, and troupes headed by Melba (1895) and Sembrich (1901).

Local productions were sporadic until 1929, when Sir Ernest Macmillan organized the Cons. OC, playing at the Regent T; but owing to the financial crisis of the 1930s this never developed. In 1934 Harrison Gilmour, a wealthy financier married to a singer, organized the O Guild of Toronto, which gave opera until 1941. An O School was set up in 1946 as part of the Royal Cons. of Music. The Royal Cons. OC, formed in 1950, mounted three productions in the Royal Alexandra T (cap. 1,700), an opera festival so successful that it gradually severed ties with the Cons. and grew into the Canadian OC in 1959 (with Herman Geiger-Torel as director). In 1960 the company moved to the O'Keefe Center (cap. 3,200), where it mounted six or seven operas each autumn. *Die Walküre* was the first Wagner opera to be staged, and gradually other Wagner and Strauss works entered the repertory. The 17 performances in 1961 and 1962 increased to 36 by 1973 and 1974, with many full houses. Since 1958 a touring group has toured Canada and the US annually. From 1964 the O School has had its own theatre and workshops, and since 1969 has been a department of the university Faculty of Music, producing programmes of excerpts and two complete operas each year. Plans are in hand for a new theatre to replace the notoriously inadequate O'Keefe Center. Companies working locally include O Hamilton and O Atelier.

Torquato Tasso. Opera in 3 acts by Donizetti; text by Jacopo Ferretti, after Giovanni Rosini's drama *Torquato Tasso* (1832), Goldoni's drama *Tasso* (1755), Goethe's drama

Tasso (1790), and Byron's poem *The Lament of Tasso* (1817). Prem. Rome, T Valle, 9 Sept. 1833.

Ferrara, 16th cent. The poet Tasso (bar) has as rivals Roberto (ten) for his fame and Don Gherardo (bs) who believes that he loves Eleonora di Scandiani (mez): Tasso in fact loves another Eleonora (sop), sister of Duke Alfonso d'Este (bs). Gherardo steals a poem by Tasso in praise of his Eleonora. Plots and counterplots lead to the Duke declaring Tasso mad and having him confined in an asylum for seven years. When he is released, he learns that his Eleonora has died, and his mind now does give way; but he is urged to think of his future glory and to return to poetry.

Tosca. Opera in 3 acts by Puccini; text by Giacosa and Illica, after Sardou's drama *La Tosca* (1887). Prem. Rome, C, 14 Jan. 1900.

Rome, June 1800. Angelotti (bs), a political prisoner, has escaped and is hiding in the Attavanti Chapel. He recognizes the painter Cavaradossi (ten) as an old friend and Cavaradossi gives him the keys to his villa as a refuge. Tosca (sop), a celebrated singer and Cavaradossi's lover, arrives and her jealousy is aroused when she recognizes the Marchesa Attavanti as the model for the portrait of Mary Magdalene which Cavaradossi is painting. A cannon signals Angelotti's escape and when Tosca returns, the police chief Scarpia (bar) convinces her that Cavaradossi and the Marchesa have fled together. She rushes to the painter's villa, followed by the police.

Tosca is summoned to Scarpia, and while she is interrogated, Cavaradossi (who has been caught but denies all knowledge of Angelotti) undergoes torture in the next room. Unable to bear his agony, Tosca discloses Angelotti's hiding-place in the well of the villa. Tosca pleads for Cavaradossi and Scarpia agrees to release him if she will yield to him. She realizes this is the only hope and agrees. While he sits at his desk writing the safe-conduct pass which will enable her and Cavaradossi to leave the country, she seizes a knife and then stabs him.

Just before dawn Cavaradossi is led to his execution. Tosca tells him that this is to be a sham and that they can then escape; but he must pretend convincingly. When the squad fires, he falls. Tosca rushes to him but finds that Scarpia deceived her and that Cavaradossi is dead. In her grief, she flings herself from the parapet.

Toscanini, Arturo (b Parma, 25 Mar. 1867; d Riverdale, NY, 16 Jan. 1957). Italian conductor. Studied Parma. Began career as cellist, incl. in orchestra at prem. of Verdi's *Otello*. On the second night of an Italian opera season in Rio de Janeiro (30 June 1886) he was called on by members of the company to replace the regular conductor Leopoldo Miguez, and two deputies against whom there were demonstrations, and conducted *Aida* from memory with great success. Back in Italy, he conducted Catalani's *Edmea* in Turin, 1886. In 1892 he conducted the prem. of *Pagliacci* at the Milan V. Music dir. Turin, R, 1895–8; opened with first Italian *Götterdämmerung* (in Italian) and gave prem. of *La bohème* (1896). Principal cond. Milan, S, 1898–1903, opening with *Meistersinger* and including much Verdi and foreign works new to Italy. Also new to Italy was dramatic commitment of such intensity from a conductor in the interests of opera as an integrated art in the manner he admired in Wagner, and his departure was over demonstrations against him for refusing to allow Zenatello a disruptive encore in *Un ballo in maschera*.

From 1908 to 1915 Toscanini conducted at the other great centre of his operatic influence, the New York M, whither he went with *Gatti-Casazza. Here he gave the prems. of *La fanciulla del West* (1910) and Giordano's *Madame Sans-Gêne* (1915), and many US prems. including Gluck's *Armide* (1910), *Ariane et Barbe-bleue* (1911), and *Boris Godunov* (1913). Again he resigned over tensions between his ideals and what the management allowed. He conducted little until 1920, when he returned to Milan S, resuming his dominating role and bringing the ensemble to a high pitch of excellence. Resignation this time was over exhaustion and political tensions with the Fascists as much as managerial problems: at the first performance of *Turandot* (1926), at which he stopped the performance at the moment where Puccini had broken off, he had previously refused to conduct the Fascist anthem. He conducted at Bayreuth in 1930 (*Tristan* and *Tannhäuser*) and 1931 (*Parsifal* and *Tannhäuser*) (the first non-German), refusing to return in Nazi times; and at Salzburg 1934–7 (*Falstaff*, *Fidelio*, *Magic Flute*, *Fidelio*), refusing to return after the Nazi annexation of Austria. Between 1944 and 1954 he gave concert performances of a number of operas, including *Traviata*, *Aida*, *Falstaff*, and *Ballo in maschera*, for the NBC in New York; these were recorded. He returned to Milan to conduct the concert reopening La Scala in 1946, also the Boito memorial in 1948.

For parts of his life, Toscanini felt obliged to work outside the opera-house where his central interest lay. He won Verdi's friendship and admiration; he championed Puccini; he remained faithful to lesser Italian works, even naming a daughter Wally after Catalani's heroine. But he also introduced Italians to Gluck and to Wagner, as part of his dramatic vision; and it was the difficulty in realizing this, for all the scrupulousness of his preparation with singers and orchestra, that made his life in the theatre difficult. His genius rested on an uncanny memory for every detail of a score and an impassioned fidelity to it, as well as a compelling personal magnetism in making others share this. An autocrat in the opera-house, and fiercely intolerant of shortcomings, he spared himself least of all; and his intolerance of personal vanities, his intransigence with managements, and his notorious outbursts of rage were based on a love of music that seemed almost too intense for him to bear. (R)

Toten Augen, Die (The Blind Eyes). Opera in a prologue and 1 act by D'Albert; text *Les yeux morts* by M. Henry, trans. H. Ewers. Prem. Dresden 5 Mar. 1916.

Jerusalem, the first Palm Sunday. Myrtocle (sop), the blind wife of the proconsul Arcesius (bar), has her sight given her by Jesus. When she discovers Arcesius's ugliness, she believes that the handsome Captain Galba (ten) is the man to whom she had been married. He is secretly in love with her, but when she discovers the truth, all her love for Arcesius returns, and she prays to be blind again. She gazes on the bright sun, and once again her eyes lose their sight.

Tote Stadt, Die (The Dead City). Opera in 3 acts by Korngold; text by 'Paul Schott' (Korngold and his father), after G.-R.-C. Rodenbach's novel *Bruges-la-morte* (1892). Prem. simultaneously 4 Dec. 1920 Hamburg and Cologne.

Bruges, end 19th cent. Despite the remonstrances of Frank (bar), Paul (ten) cannot cease mourning his wife Marie (sop), and sees her once again in the person of the dancer Marietta (sop). In a nightmare sequence, he imagines Marie unfaithful to him with Frank, and his murder of her. Awake, he recognizes that he must distance himself from Bruges and Marie's memory.

Tottola, Leone (*b* ?; *d* Naples, 15 Sept. 1831). Italian librettist. Working in the Neapolitan theatre at a time when opera buffa flourished, he placed his busy, not to say hasty, pen at the service of many different composers. Although his work was mocked for its lack of technique and taste, he sensed the impact of the novel ideas of Romanticism, and had some influence in impressing these on his composers. His subjects include many which became the stock in trade of Romantic opera, such as the biblical, oriental, and medieval, German legend, and English novels (including Scott). His librettos include *Adelson e Salvini* for Bellini, seven for Donizetti (including *Gabriella di Vergy* and *Il castello di Kenilworth*), six for Rossini (including *La donna del lago*), and many others for Pacini, Mercadante, Guglielmi, Fioravanti, Mayr, and others.

Tourel, Jennie (*b* Vitebsk, 22 June 1899; *d* New York, 23 Nov. 1973). US mezzo-soprano of Russian origin. Studied Paris with Hahn and El Tour (anagram of Tourel). Appeared Chicago 1930 (Second Scholar, Moret's *Lorenzaccio*); Paris: O Russe, 1931, and OC, 1933–9. New York, M, 1937, 1943–7, and CC, 1944; Montreal 1938–42. Also Holland, Israel, S America. A highly versatile and sensitive artist, acclaimed as Cherubino, Rosina, Mignon, Carmen. Created Baba the Turk. (R)

Traetta, Tommaso (*b* Bitonto, 30 Mar. 1727; *d* Venice, 6 Apr. 1779). Italian composer. Studied Naples with Porpora and Durante. At Parma from 1758, he responded to the theatre director Du Tillot's wish to reconcile Italian and French operatic ideals with a setting of the text for Rameau's *Hippolyte et Aricie* (1759). This goes some way in the direction of the ideals that were to be associated with Gluck, by bringing together dance, orchestration, choral scenes, and solo numbers in a functional manner. It also revealed the melodic grace in individual numbers that was one of Traetta's characteristics. With *Armida* (1761), in Vienna, he further developed the fluency between numbers that was becoming another hallmark of his style, though he remained closely attached to the da capo aria. With *Sofonisba* (1762), in Mannheim, he took this manner still further and was able to benefit from the availability of the famous ducal orchestra in developing his expressive symphonic scenes. *Ifigenia in Tauride* (1763) further benefits from knowledge of Gluck's *Orfeo*, including by way of collaboration with the castrato Gaetano Guadagni, the first Orfeo, and in the impressive use of the chorus. Moving to Venice in 1765, Traetta wrote two comic operas as well as some more conventional Metastasian operas. In 1768 he succeeded Galuppi as Catherine the Great's opera director, also writing for the Russian court his *Antigone* (1772). In this he returns with great effect to the manner he had been exploring in his earlier classical works, and further develops his most adventurous ideas especially in the field of building up large-scale dramatic scenes. He left Russia in poor health in 1775, and after an unsuccessful visit to London (where he was overshadowed by Sacchini), he returned to Venice. The best of his operas approach Gluck in manner and even at times in quality. His graceful cavatas or cavatinas can emerge from passages of very free and fluent arioso, as in Act II of *I Tintaridi* (1760), and the forceful or elegant choral participations in his *Ifigenia*, if sometimes rather protracted, in turn influenced Gluck's setting.

tragédie-ballet (Fr.: 'tragedy ballet'). A musico-dramatic form which emerged in 17th-cent. France, deriving from the *comédie-ballet, whose essential features it shared save for the character of the drama. The most famous example was *Psyché* (1671), for which Lully collaborated with Quinault, Molière, and Corneille: this had an important influence on the development of the tragédie en musique.

tragédie en musique (Fr.: 'tragedy in music'). The new style of French opera inaugurated by *Lully and *Quinault with *Cadmus* (1673). Although it more accurately describes the fundamental nature of the genre, the term tragédie en musique has been widely supplanted by that of *tragédie lyrique.

tragédie lyrique (Fr.: 'lyric tragedy'). The serious (though not necessarily tragic) French opera of the 17th and 18th cents. whose principal exponents were *Lully, *Campra, and *Rameau. Though the term tragédie en musique was preferred by composers, and is a more accurate description of the early stages of the genre, it was soon supplanted by that of tragédie lyrique, an

invention of aestheticians. By the late 18th cent. it had such a wide application that any general stylistic definition is unrealistic.

Traubel, Helen (*b* St Louis, 20 June 1899; *d* S Monica, CA, 28 July 1972). US soprano. Studied with Karst. Sang in concert 1926–37. Début New York, M, 1937 (creating Mary, Damrosch's *Man without a Country*). Sang with great success there 1939–53, replacing Flagstad 1941 as leading Wagner soprano. Also London, Buenos Aires, Mexico, Rio. Roles included Sieglinde, Brünnhilde, Isolde, Kundry, Marschallin. Her large, noble tone, stately presence, and interpretative depth evoked comparisons with Nordica. Left New York M after quarrel with Bing over her night-club appearances; then worked in films, taught, and wrote detective novels. (R)

'Traurigkeit ward mir zum Lose'. Constanze's (sop) aria in Act I of Mozart's *Die Entführung aus dem Serail*, in which she mourns her separation from Belmonte.

Travelling Companion, The. Opera in 4 acts by Stanford; text by Henry Newbolt, after Hans Andersen's fairy-tale. Prem. Liverpool 30 Apr. 1925.

travesti (Fr. past participle of *travestir*: 'to disguise'). The term used to describe such roles as Cherubino, Octavian, Orlofsky, Siebel, etc., which although sung by women are male characters. The English term is 'breeches part' or 'trouser-role', from the German *Hosenrolle*.

Traviata, La (The Strayed Woman). Opera in 3 acts by Verdi; text by Piave, after the drama *La dame aux camélias* (1852) by Dumas fils, after his novel (1848) based on his own experiences. Prem. Venice, F, 6 Mar. 1853.

Paris, *c*.1850. The consumptive Violetta (sop) has won the love of Alfredo (ten). He declares himself to her but she is reluctant to enter into any serious attachment.

Violetta and Alfredo have been living together in the country for three months. While Alfredo is away, his father Giorgio Germont (bar) calls. He appeals to Violetta to break off this scandalous relationship since it is endangering the forthcoming marriage of his daughter. Because of her love for Alfredo, she agrees. As Violetta leaves, Alfredo is handed a letter from her declaring they must part. He notices an invitation to a party from Violetta's friend Flora and is sure he will find her there. Violetta has gone to the party with her former protector, Baron Douphol (bar). Alfredo arrives and Violetta pleads with him to leave before the Baron challenges him to a duel. Her unfaithfulness angers Alfredo and he flings at her money he has won at cards as repayment for what she has spent on him. Germont arrives and reprimands his son for his conduct.

Several weeks later Violetta is seriously ill. In a letter to her, Germont admits that he revealed her sacrifice to his son. Alfredo enters and begs forgiveness; he promises that they shall spend the rest of their lives together in happiness. He then realizes how ill Violetta is. She finds strength momentarily and rises to her feet, but falls dead.

treble. The term for the higher of the two categories of an unbroken boy's voice (the lower being alto).

Treemonisha. Opera in 3 acts by Scott Joplin; text by composer. Comp. *c*.1907; prem. (part only) Atlanta, Symphony Hall, 28 Jan. 1972.

A plantation in Arkansas, 1884. The soothsayer Zodzetrick (ten) spreads superstition among the people, and is reproached by Treemonisha (con). In revenge, he and his companion Luddud (bar) kidnap her. She is rescued by Remus (ten), who scares Treemonisha's captors by disguising himself as the Devil. On her return to the village, Treemonisha agrees to become the planters' leader.

Treigle, Norman (*b* New Orleans, 6 Mar. 1927; *d* New Orleans, 16 Feb. 1975). US bass-baritone. Studied Louisiana with Wood. Début as student, New Orleans 1947 (Duke of Verona, *Roméo et Juliette*). New York, CO, 1953–72; London, CG, 1974; also S Francisco, Buenos Aires, Milan, Hamburg. A performer with a highly coloured dramatic style. Sang Don Giovanni, Boris, Gounod's and Boito's Mephistopheles, the *Hoffmann* baritone roles; created parts in *The Tender Land* (Copland) and *Susannah* and *Markheim* (Floyd). (R)

Treptow, Günther (*b* Berlin, 22 Oct. 1907; *d* Berlin, 28 Mar. 1981). German tenor. Studied Berlin, and Milan with Scarmeo. Début Berlin, SO, 1936 (Italian Tenor, *Rosenkavalier*). Berlin, SO (later D), until 1942, 1945–50, 1961–72; Munich 1942–7; Vienna 1947–55. Also Milan, S; London, CG; New York, M, 1951. A true Heldentenor, admired as Flo-

restan, Siegmund, Siegfried, Tristan; also as Verdi's Otello, Števa. (R)

Trial. The term, derived from Antoine *Trial, traditionally applied at the Paris OC to a tenor of dramatic rather than vocal excellence, specializing in comedy—e.g. Le petit Vieillard (Arithmetic) in Ravel's *L'enfant et les sortilèges*. See also TENOR.

Trial, Antoine (*b* Avignon, 1737; *d* Paris, 5 Feb. 1795). Tenor and actor, brother of **Jean-Claude Trial** (1732–71), co-director (with Berton) of Paris, O, 1767–9, and one of the first French composers to write for the female contralto voice. Studied Avignon. First appeared in provincial theatre. Paris, CI, 1764 (Bastien, Philidor's *Le sorcier*). Possessing little vocal but much dramatic talent, he made a reputation as a character actor, giving his name to the type otherwise known as 'singer without voice'. Appeared in works by Grétry, Monsigny, Champein, Kreutzer. Having supported Robespierre during the Terror, he killed himself when public opinion turned against him afterwards.

Triquet. The Frenchman (ten) living near the Larins, who sings his couplets in Tatyana's praise at the dance, in Tchaikovsky's *Eugene Onegin*.

Tristan und Isolde. Opera in 3 acts by Wagner; text by composer, after Gottfried von Strassburg's *Tristan* (*c*.1210), in turn based on Thomas von Britanje's *Roman de Tristan* (*c*.1150) and Eilhart von Oberge's *Tristrant und Isalde* (*c*.1170), after various versions of the old legend. Prem. Munich, N, 10 June 1865.

A ship at sea between Ireland and Cornwall, legendary times. Tristan (ten) is taking Isolde (sop) to be the bride of King Mark of Cornwall (bs). He refuses through his squire Kurwenal (bar) to see her on the ship. She describes to her attendant Brangäne (mez) how he was wounded in slaying her betrothed, Morold, but healed by her. Refusing to admit her love for him, she orders Brangäne to prepare poison for them, but Brangäne substitutes a love potion. They drink it, and disclose their love for each other.

Outside King Mark's castle. Isolde takes advantage of her husband Mark's absence hunting with Melot (ten) to meet Tristan. The lovers declare their passion, and turn away from the harsh falsehoods of day to their own true world of night. Melot causes them to be surprised, but the King is too grief-stricken to show anger at Tristan's betrayal. Isolde answers Tristan that she will follow him wherever he goes. He is attacked by Melot and allows himself to be wounded.

Outside Tristan's castle of Kareol in Brittany. Kurwenal tries to cheer his sick master, who thinks only of Isolde. The repeated sad strain of a shepherd's pipe tells that Isolde, sent for by Kurwenal, is not in sight. When the shepherd's joyful tune announces her ship, Tristan excitedly tears off his bandages, and dies in her arms. A second ship brings Mark and Melot, and Kurwenal dies killing Melot, unaware that they come to pardon Tristan. Isolde sings of the love which she can only now fulfil in the deeper night of death at Tristan's side.

Isolde's final soliloquy is now generally known as the 'Liebestod' (Love Death), but when Wagner first joined the Prelude and this finale for concert purposes, he entitled the former 'Liebestod' and the latter 'Verklärung' (Transfiguration).

Trittico, Il. The triptych of 1-act operas by Puccini, Il *tabarro, *Suor Angelica, and *Gianni Schicchi.

Troilus and Cressida. Opera in 3 acts by Walton; text by Christopher Hassall, after Chaucer's Troilus and Criseyde (c.1385) and Boccaccio's Filostrato (c.1350), in turn after Benoit de Saint-Maure's Roman de Troie (c.1160). Prem. London, CG, 3 Dec. 1954.

Troy, c.12th cent. BC. Cressida (sop or mez), daughter of the High Priest of Troy, Calkas (bs), is turned from her intention of becoming a priestess by the love of Troilus (ten), abetted by her uncle Pandarus (ten). When Calkas goes over to the Greeks, she is exchanged for their prisoner Antenor (bar), and agrees to marry Diomede (bar). Troilus comes to find her and is stabbed in the back by Calkas when fighting Diomede, who orders his body to be returned to Troy and Cressida to remain in the Greek camp as a harlot. She kills herself over Troilus's body.

Trompeter von Säckingen, Der (The Trumpeter of Säckingen). Opera in 4 acts by Nessler; text by Rudolf Bunge, after Scheffel's poem (1854). Prem. Leipzig 4 May 1884.

Säckingen, just after the Thirty Years War. Werner (bar) loves Maria (sop), whose parents want her to marry Damian (ten). Werner gives Maria trumpet lessons; their love is dis-

covered. However, Damian proves to be a simpleton, and moreover a coward when the city is attacked. Werner is wounded in its heroic defence and then proves to be of noble birth; he is permitted to marry Maria.

trouser role. See TRAVESTI.

Trovatore, Il (The Troubadour). Opera in 4 acts by Verdi; text by Cammarano and Bardare, after the drama El trovador (1836) by Gutiérrez. Prem. Rome, Ap., 19 Jan. 1853.

Northern Spain, 15th cent. Ferrando (bs) tells how the Conte di Luna had a brother whose fortune was read by a gypsy when both boys were babies. The baby became ill and the gypsy was burned at the stake. In revenge, her daughter Azucena (mez) kidnapped the child, and charred bones were found at the site of the gypsy's execution. The baby's father could not believe his son dead and commanded that the brother, the present Conte di Luna, should continue the search. Leonora (sop), lady-in-waiting to the Princess of Aragon, is in love with Manrico (ten), a warrior troubadour. She hears his voice serenading her but finds the Conte di Luna (bar), who also loves her. Manrico reveals himself and Di Luna challenges him to a duel.

At the gypsy camp, Azucena relates to Manrico (her supposed son) the story of her mother's death. She confesses that in her desire to avenge it, she accidentally burnt her own son instead of the Di Luna's. When Manrico questions his own identity, Azucena hurriedly assures him that he is her son. News arrives that Leonora proposes to enter a convent since she believes Manrico dead, so he rushes off to prevent her. Di Luna is determined to abduct Leonora as she enters the convent, but Manrico is ahead of him.

The guards bring Azucena to Di Luna's camp. He is delighted when he realizes she is Manrico's mother and orders her to be tortured. As Manrico and Leonora are about to be married, they learn that Azucena has been captured. Manrico hurries to save her.

Manrico has failed to rescue Azucena and is a prisoner. Leonora offers herself to Di Luna if he will spare her beloved. He agrees, not knowing that her real intention is to poison herself rather than be unfaithful. She tells Manrico of his freedom but he, suspecting her action, denounces her. With Leonora dying in his arms, he realizes the sacrifice she has made. As Manrico is executed, Azucena reveals to Di Luna that he has killed his brother.

Troyanos, Tatiana (*b* New York, 12 Sept. 1938; *d* New York, 21 Aug. 1993). US mezzo-soprano. Studied New York with Heinz. Début New York, CO, 1963 (Hippolyta, *Midsummer Night's Dream*). New York, CO until 1965; Hamburg from 1965; Aix 1966; New York, M, 1976–93; London, CG, from 1970; Milan, S, from 1977. Roles included Ariodante, Cherubino, Sesto, Adalgisa, Dido (Berlioz), Eboli, Carmen, Kundry, Octavian, Santuzza. Possessed a large, brilliant voice of extensive range, and a well-projected stage personality. (R)

Troyens, Les (The Trojans). Opera in 5 acts by Berlioz; text by composer, after Virgil's *Aeneid* (*c*.27–19 BC). Comp. 1856–8. To achieve a performance, Berlioz was obliged in 1863 to divide the work into 2 parts: Acts I and II into *La prise de Troie* (The Capture of Troy) (3 acts), prem. Karlsruhe 6 Dec. 1890; Acts III, IV, and V into *Les Troyens à Carthage* (The Trojans in Carthage) (5 acts, with added prologue), prem. Paris, L, 4 Nov. 1863. The whole work was prem. Karlsruhe 6–7 Dec. 1890.

The abandoned Greek camp outside Troy, antiquity. The Greeks have departed, leaving behind the wooden horse. The forebodings of Cassandre (Cassandra) (mez), daughter of Priam (bs), are disbelieved even by her lover Chorèbe (Chorebus) (bar). The royal family and dignitaries of Troy give ceremonial thanks for their deliverance; the celebrations are interrupted first by the silent, grieving figure of Hector's widow Andromaque (Andromache) with their son. (At this point Berlioz originally included a scene in which the Greek spy Sinon explains the purpose of the horse.) The celebrations are further interrupted by Énée (Aeneas) (ten) with news that the priest Laocoön, who mistrusted the purpose of the horse, has been devoured by serpents; to the Trojan March, the horse is dragged into the city so as to propitiate Athene.

A room in Énée's palace. Hector's ghost (bs) tells Énée to flee Troy and found a new city in Italy. He is joined by Panthée (Pantheus) (bs), his son Ascagne (Ascanius) (sop), and others; he leads an attempt to reach the citadel. Inside Priam's palace. Polyxène (Polyxenus) (sop) and a group of women are praying. Cassandre tells the women of Chorèbe's death and Énée's escape. As the Greeks rush in, the women kill themselves.

The Palace of Didon (Dido) in Carthage. Didon (mez) enters with Anna (con) and Narbal (bs), and the people celebrate peace. Iopas (ten) announces the arrival of the disguised Trojan wanderers. When invasion threatens, Énée reveals himself and leads his men in the defence of Carthage.

A forest outside Carthage. In the Royal Hunt and Storm, Didon and Énée seek shelter from the chase in a cave and consummate their love.

Didon's gardens by the sea. An entertainment is being held; Didon is abstracted, and after the others have left she and Énée celebrate their love. Their idyll is interrupted by Mercure (bar or bs) summoning Énée to his duty to go on to Italy and the foundation of the new city.

The seashore. The young sailor Hylas (ten or con) sings of his homeland. Panthée (Pantheus) summons the Trojans for departure; Énée is prevented by the Trojan ghosts from returning to Didon, but as they prepare to leave she appears and bitterly reproaches him. She calls on the gods for vengeance, and commands a funeral pyre to be built. Mounting the pyre, she dies with a vision of Rome before her eyes.

Tsar Saltan, The Tale of (Russ., *Skazka o Tsare Saltane*) (full title: The Legend of Tsar Saltan, of his son, the famous and mighty hero Prince Guidon Salanovich, and of the beautiful Swan Princess). Opera in a prologue and 4 acts by Rimsky-Korsakov; text by V. I. Belsky, after Pushkin's poem (1832). Prem. Moscow, Mamontov T, 3 Nov. 1900.

Tsar Saltan (bs) marries Militrisa (sop), whose sisters Tkachikha (mez) and Povarikha (sop) cause her and her son Prince Guidon (ten) to be thrown into the sea in a cask by telling the Tsar that she has produced a monster. Washed up on an island, Guidon rescues a swan fleeing from a hawk: it turns out to be a disguised princess (sop). Turned by her into a bee, he goes to find the Tsar; when the sisters try to dissuade the Tsar from visiting the island, Guidon stings them mercilessly. Back on the island, he frees the princess from her enchantment, and she restores the Tsar's wife to him.

The orchestral 'Flight of the Bumble Bee' occurs in Act III.

Tsar's Bride, The (Russ., *Tsarskaya nevesta*).

Opera in 3 acts by Rimsky-Korsakov; text from L. A. Mey's drama (1849), additional scene by I. F. Tyumenev. Prem. Moscow, Mamontov T, 3 Nov. 1899.

Moscow, 1572. Marfa (sop), chosen by Ivan the Terrible as his bride, is loved by both Lykov (ten), whom she loves, and the oprichnik Gryaznoy (bar), who tries to win her with a love potion. Gryaznoy's mistress Lyubasha (mez) substitutes poison, and Marfa goes mad on learning, as she lies dying in the Kremlin, that the Tsar has beheaded Lykov for the crime. Gryaznoy kills Lyubasha.

Tuček, Vincenc (*b* Prague, 2 Feb. 1773; *d* Pest, 1821 or later). Bohemian composer, conductor, and singer. Son of **Jan Tuček** (*b* ?, *c*.1743; *d* Prague, 19 Sept. 1783), a composer and conductor who pioneered the introduction of Czech Singspiel into Prague theatres. Vincenc sang at the Patriotic T from 1793 (first Bohemian Tamino, 1794). Harpsichordist and composer there, 1794–6. Also worked in Wrocław (Breslau) and Vienna, L.: Kapellmeister 1807–10; then Budapest. Of his many operas and other stage pieces, largely ephemeral, the most successful were *Honza Kolohnát z Přelouče* (Hans Klachl von Prelautsch, ?1796), *Dämona* (1805), and *Lanassa* (1805).

'Tu che di gel sei cinta'. Liù's (sop) aria in Act III of Puccini's *Turandot*, assuring Turandot that one day she too will love the unknown prince (Calaf).

'Tu che la vanità'. Elisabetta's (sop) aria in Act V of Verdi's *Don Carlos*, praying before the tomb of Charles V and bidding farewell to her past and her illusions.

Tucker, Norman (*b* Wembley, 24 Apr. 1910; *d* London, 10 Aug. 1978). English administrator. Studied Oxford and London. Began career as pianist. Joint dir., London, SW, 1947–54, sole dir. 1954–66, surviving various crises but then resigning when the projected move of SW to the South Bank fell through. He presided over a period of steady development at SW, and also encouraged the introduction of Janáček's operas, some of which he translated.

Tucker, Richard (*b* Brooklyn, 28 Aug. 1913; *d* Kalamazoo, MI, 8 Jan. 1975). US tenor. Studied New York with Althouse. Début New York, Salmaggi Co., 1943 (Alfredo). New York, M, 1945–74; Verona 1947; London, CG, 1958;

Milan, S, 1969; New Orleans 1948–73. Though a rudimentary actor, he sang with convincing fervour, excelling in Italian roles, and was a widely admired artist. Repertory included Manrico, Radamès, Enzo, Des Grieux, Don José, Canio, Pinkerton, Eléazar, Lensky. His wife was the sister of tenor Jan *Peerce. (R)

Tumanyan, Barseg (*b* Erevan, 3 Aug. 1958). Armenian bass. Studied Milan, S, and Moscow Cons. Spendiaryan O from 1980; Western début Naples 1988 (Basilio), followed by US début (Ramfis at Boston). His sonorous voice and imposing stage presence are admired in such roles as Attila (London, CG), King Philip (Los Angeles 1990), Méphistophélès (Paris, B, 1993). (R)

Turandot. Opera in 3 acts by Puccini, completed by Alfano; text by Adami and Simoni, after Gozzi's drama (1762), possibly after the *1,001 Nights*. Prem. Milan, S, 25 Apr. 1926. Unfin., completed by Alfano.

Peking, legendary times. The Princess Turandot (sop) is to marry whoever can answer her three riddles. If a candidate fails, he is beheaded. In the crowd awaiting the execution of a failed suitor is the deposed King of Tartary, Timur (bs); he recognizes his long-lost son Calaf (ten), who is obliged to keep his name and rank secret for fear of his enemies. Liù (sop), the slave-girl who has helped Timur since his escape, loves Calaf. He, however, falls in love with Turandot and resolves to win her, ignoring pleas from his father and Liù and from three Ministers of the Court, Ping (bar), Pang (bar), and Pong (ten).

The Emperor Altoum (ten) tries to persuade the stranger to give up the enterprise. Turandot proudly proclaims that no man will ever possess her. She poses the riddles and when Calaf answers each of them correctly, Turandot begs her father to release her from her oath. Calaf offers that if she can discover his name before dawn the following day, she may have him put to death.

Since Turandot has ordered mass execution if the stranger's name cannot be discovered, the people of Peking turn on him. Timur and Liù are captured and, in order to spare Timur torture, Liù confesses that she alone knows who the stranger is, but will not disclose his name. Her love for Calaf gives her courage. As she goes to her execution, she snatches a dagger and stabs herself. Calaf declares his love to Turandot. She begs him to leave but he refuses and tells her his name. Turandot is softened by his sincerity and proclaims to her father that the stranger's name is Love.

Turco in Italia, Il (The Turk in Italy). Opera in 2 acts by Rossini; text by Romani, after Mazzolà. Prem. Milan, S, 14 Aug. 1814.

A gypsy camp near Naples, 1850. Zaida (sop) has fled Turkey, where her love for Selim (bs) was unrequited. The poet Prosdocimo (bar) is also in the camp, seeking material for a comedy less trite than the situation of the flirtatious Fiorilla (sop) and her ridiculous husband Geronio (bs), who now also arrive. At the quayside, a ship docks; Selim disembarks and immediately makes advances to Fiorilla, irritating her lover Narciso (ten) but interesting Prosdocimo. In her apartment, she entertains Selim and reproves Geronio. Back in the camp, Selim has his fortune told by a 'gypsy' whom he recognizes as Zaida: their reconciliation is complicated by the arrival of Fiorilla.

Selim angers Geronio by suggesting that he sell his wife. Fiorilla and Zaida invite Selim to choose between them, but Zaida withdraws unhappily. Prosdocimo says that Selim will carry Fiorilla off during a masked ball, at which confusions deepen when Zaida appears as Fiorilla and Geronio and Narciso both appear as Selim. Everything is sorted out, with Selim and Zaida returning to Turkey and all pointing the moral that one should be content with one's lot.

Turiddu. A young peasant (ten), former lover of Santuzza and lover of Lola, in Mascagni's *Cavalleria rusticana*.

Turnage, Mark Anthony (*b* Grays, 10 June 1960). English composer. Studied London with Knussen and Lambert, Tanglewood with Henze and Schuller. His first opera, *Greek* (1988), was a modern, polemical version of the Oedipus myth, vehemently scored and drawing on popular and music-hall song and the Blues as well as being influenced by Britten and Stravinsky.

Turner, (Dame) **Eva** (*b* Oldham, 10 Mar. 1892; *d* London, 16 June 1990). English soprano. Studied London with M. Wilson, G. and E. Levi, later Broads. Début with London, CR, 1916 (Page, *Tannhäuser*). London, CR, until

1924; Milan, S, 1924–5, 1929; Buenos Aires 1927; London, CG, 1928–30, 1933, 1935, 1937–8, 1947–9; Rome 1930; Chicago 1928–30, 1938. One of the greatest British singers of the century, she possessed a clear, shining, full-toned voice of extraordinary resilience, and a cast-iron technique. Large repertory included Donna Anna, Leonore, Brünnhilde, Isolde, Aida, Butterfly, and an unforgettable Turandot, to which her somewhat cool artistic temperament was ideally suited. Taught Amy Shuard, Rita Hunter, Gwyneth Jones. (R)

Turn of the Screw, The. Opera in prologue and 2 acts by Britten; text by Myfanwy Piper, after Henry James's story (1898). Prem. Venice, F, 14 Sept. 1954.

The narrator explains that a governess has been engaged to look after two orphans in the frequent absences of their guardian, with whom she must not communicate. Bly, a country house, mid-19th cent. Mrs Grose (sop), the housekeeper, introduces the Governess (sop) to her charges, Flora (sop) and Miles (treb). The Governess comes to realize that the children are in the power of two evil ghosts of former servants, Peter Quint (ten) and Miss Jessel (sop). In despair, the Governess writes to the guardian, but Quint persuades Miles to steal the letter. Flora denies all knowledge of Miss Jessel; but the Governess finally persuades Miles to utter Quint's name, only to find him dead in her arms.

The 'screw' of the title is represented by a theme that 'turns' through 15 variations as interludes between the eight scenes of each act.

'Tutte le feste'. Gilda's (sop) aria in Act II of Verdi's *Rigoletto*, telling her father of her seduction at the hands of the Duke.

Two Widows, The (Cz., *Dvě vdovy*). Opera in 2 acts by Smetana; text by E. Züngel, after Pierre Mallefille's comedy *Les deux veuves* (1860). Prem. Prague, P, 27 Mar. 1874.

A Bohemian castle, 19th cent. The two widows Karolina (sop) and Anežka (sop) live on the former's estate. Their gamekeeper Mumlal (bs) brings in a poacher, Ladislav (ten), who proves to be the neighbouring landowner. Anežka is soon in love with him, but will not admit it until Karolina forces her hand by pretending rivalry.

U

'Udite, udite, o rustici'. Dulcamara's (bs) aria in Act I of Donizetti's *L'elisir d'amore* in which he advertises his quack wares.

Uhde, Hermann (*b* Bremen, 20 July 1914; *d* Copenhagen, 10 Oct. 1965). German bass-baritone. Studied Bremen with P. Kraus. Début Bremen 1936 (Titurel). Munich 1940–2, 1951–60; Hamburg 1947–50; Vienna, S, 1950–1; Bayreuth 1951–7, 1960; London, CG, 1953, 1954–60; New York, M, 1955–64. Large repertory included Mozart's Figaro, Pizarro, Caspar, Dappertutto, Philip, Wotan, Gunther, Klingsor, Amfortas, Mandryka, Wozzeck, Tarquinius; created Creon (*Antigonae*). A highly cultivated, intelligent, and sensitive singer-actor of great integrity. (R)

Ulfung, Ragnar (*b* Oslo, 28 Feb. 1927). Norwegian tenor. Studied Oslo, and Milan with Minghetti. Début Oslo 1952 (Magician, *The Consul*). Swedish Royal O from 1958; London, CG, 1960, 1963, 1970–6; New York, M, 1972; Milan, S, 1973. A very gifted (and athletic) dramatic performer, impressive as Tamino, Don Carlos, Gustavus III, Lensky, Mime, Herod, Tom Rakewell, Števa, and in the parts he has created, notably Maxwell Davies's Taverner. (R)

Ulrica. See ARVIDSON.

Umlauff, Ignaz (*b* Vienna, 1746; *d* Vienna, 8 June 1796). Austrian composer, conductor, and viola player. He wrote his first Singspiel, *Die Insel der Liebe*, in 1772. When Emperor Josef II announced the foundation of the new National-Singspiel in 1778, Umlauff was appointed Kapellmeister and commissioned to write the work for the opening night. *Die Bergknappen* (The Miners, 1778) was an immediate success and four further works were given by the company during the following five years: *Die schöne Schusterin* (1779), *Das Irrlicht* (1782), *Die Apotheke* (1778), and *Welches ist die beste Nation?* (1782).

Umlauff was one of the principal founders of Viennese Singspiel. He and his contemporaries combined folk-style music with elements of Italian opera, also frequently basing their works on the local theatrical tradition. The success of his works was due in no small measure to the entertaining variety of his material, and to his ability to write humorous pieces with a strong sense of drama.

'Una bella serenata'. The terzetto in Act I of Mozart's *Così fan tutte*, in which Ferrando (ten) plans a serenade for Dorabella and Guglielmo (bar) a banquet for Fiordiligi, while Don Alfonso (bs) hopes to be invited.

'Una donna di quindici anni'. Despina's (sop) aria in Act II of Mozart's *Così fan tutte*, describing the wiles of love to her mistresses.

'Una furtiva lagrima'. Nemorino's (ten) aria in Act II of Donizetti's *L'elisir d'amore*, in which he sees by the tear in Adina's eye that she loves him.

'Un'aura amorosa'. Ferrando's (ten) aria in Act I of Mozart's *Così fan tutte*, in which he sentimentally describes Dorabella's love.

'Una voce poco fà'. Rosina's (mez) aria in Act I of Rossini's *Il barbiere di Siviglia*, in which she recalls the serenade by Count Almaviva (Lindoro) that awoke her love, and promises to use all her powers to ensure that he will be hers.

'Un bel dì vedremo'. Butterfly's (sop) aria in Act II of Puccini's *Madama Butterfly*, in which she sings of Pinkerton's hoped-for return.

'Un dì all' azzurro spazio'. Chénier's (ten) aria in Act I of Giordano's *Andrea Chénier*, in which he denounces the selfishness of those in authority. Sometimes known as the 'Improvviso'.

'Un dì felice'. The love duet between Violetta (sop) and Alfredo (ten) in Act I of Verdi's *La traviata*.

Undine. The heroine of a popular Central European folk legend. Conceived by Paracelsus as one of the elemental spirits, she is the spirit of the waters; she has been created without a soul, and can only gain one by marrying a mortal and bearing him a child, though she must thereby take on all the penalties of humanity. The legend was given great popularity among the Romantics by Friedrich de la Motte Fouqué's tale (1811). She is the German equivalent of the Slavonic

*Rusalka, and also appears as the *Donauweibchen.

1. Opera in 3 acts by E. T. A. Hoffmann; text by Fouqué. Prem. Berlin, Royal OH, 3 Aug. 1816.

In a forest hut, Huldbrand (bar) and the Fisherman (bs) are anxious about the disappearance of Undine (sop). She has replaced the fisherfolk's drowned daughter, and Huldbrand has left Berthalda (sop) for her. Undine is in fact by a forest waterfall, where Kühleborn (bs) warns her of man's perfidy. Huldbrand arrives to find her. Their union is blessed by Heilmann (bs), and she confesses her nature to Huldbrand. In the town, Undine and Berthalda share the common bond of being foundlings. But when Undine reveals to the Count (ten) and Countess (mez) that Berthalda is really the fisherfolk's lost daughter, Berthalda is enraged. Huldbrand becomes increasingly uneasy at Undine's fairy nature, and turns to Berthalda, despite the menaces of Kühleborn. Heilmann tries to remind Huldbrand of Undine's fate if she is betrayed, but he insists on now marrying Berthalda. When at the wedding feast Berthalda has the well in the castle uncovered, Undine appears and gives Huldbrand her kiss of death. They are united in what Heilmann calls a Liebestod.

2. Opera in 4 acts by Lortzing; text by composer after Fouqué. Prem. Magdeburg 21 Apr. 1845.

Hugo (ten), accompanied by his squire Veit (ten), visits the forest and falls in love with Undine (sop); he returns to Court with her, though Veit has told Kühleborn (bar), her father and a powerful spirit, that he fears Hugo will desert her for Berthalda (sop). Undine discloses her fairy nature to Hugo, and Berthalda is revealed as being the child of Undine's foster-father Tobias (bs). Though protected by Undine, Berthalda seduces Hugo, and Undine returns to her kingdom; but he cannot forget her, and when Veit opens a sealed well, she returns from it to claim him as husband in her own realm.

'Und ob die Wolke'. Agathe's (sop) aria in Act III of Weber's Der Freischütz, in which she declares that even if the skies are veiled in cloud, God reigns above.

Unger, Caroline (b Stuhlweissenburg, 28 Oct. 1803; d Florence, 23 Mar. 1877). Austrian mezzo-soprano. Studied Vienna with Mozatti and Bassi, later Aloysia Lange and

Vogl, and Milan with D. Ronconi. Appeared Vienna, H, 1819 (Cherubino); official début Vienna, H, 1821 (Dorabella). Vienna, H until 1824. Naples 1825, C, 1826; Milan, S, 1827–30. Further successes in Italy, where her career reached its zenith; Paris, I, 1833; Vienna, H, 1839–40; Dresden 1843, then retired from stage, singing in concert under the name Unger-Sabatier (her husband was the writer François Sabatier). Combining a Teutonic dramatic intensity and an Italianate vocal facility, together with an immense range (a–d'''), she was one of the most outstanding and intelligent singers of her time. Sang Zerlina, Rosina, Isabella (L'italiana), Imogene (Pirata); created Isoletta (La straniera), Donizetti's Parisina, Maria di Rudenz, and Antonina (Belisario); also Pacini's Niobe. She sang the alto solo in the first performance of Beethoven's Ninth Symphony; at the end, it was she who turned the deaf composer round to see the rapturous applause.

Unger, Georg (b Leipzig, 6 Mar. 1837; d Leipzig, 2 Feb. 1887). German tenor. Studied Leipzig with Hey. Début Leipzig 1867. Returned there 1877–81. A singer with a huge physique and voice, but little artistic personality. Created Siegfried, with intensive coaching from Wagner, for whom the effort was worthwhile, but exhausting.

United Kingdom. See GREAT BRITAIN.

United States of America. For many years America saw little but ballad opera (Flora, or The Hob in the Well was given in Charleston, 1735, and The Beggar's Opera in New York in 1750) and Italian opera given by visiting companies. The first native American opera was The Disappointment, or The Force of Credulity, referred to in 1767 as 'a new American comic opera' (unprod.). A musical comedy The Temple of Minerva was given in 1781 in the presence of Washington; the music (lost) was by Francis Hopkinson, one of the signatories of the Declaration of Independence. The first American opera whose music survives was The Archers (1796), on the William Tell legend, by the English-born Benjamin Carr (1768–1831). Also in 1796 New York saw Edwin and Angelina by Victor Pellissier, a Frenchman who had settled in 1792 and went on to write other operas. John Bray wrote The Indian Princess (1808). A step forward came with Enterprise (1822), by Arthur Clifton (probably pseudonym of the Italian-born Philip Anthony Corri). The first opera written by a native American seems to have been *The Saw Mill, or A Yankee Trick* (1824), by Micah Hawkins (1777–1825): this is essentially a ballad opera. The arrangements of C. E. Horn introduced Americans to operatic music in adaptations. The first true opera season was in *New Orleans (a US territory with the 1803 Louisiana Purchase).

Many famous Italian artists were now visiting America, some bringing their own companies, e.g. García and Da Ponte; and by the middle of the 19th cent. opera was virtually all Italian. In 1861 Lincoln attended a performance of *Un ballo in maschera*, in the Boston version. Its popularity set up a reaction among American composers, though William Henry Fry was unable to escape the influence in *Leonora* (1845). Others who attempted a more independent American national opera included George Frederick Bristow (1825–98) with *Rip Van Winkle* (1855), Dudley Buck (1839–1909) with *Deseret, or A Saint's Affliction* (1880), John Knowles Paine (1839–1906) with *Azara* (1901), and Silas Gamaliel Pratt (1846–1916) with *Zenobia* (1883). Despite the failure of this work, Pratt went on to campaign for native American opera, and in 1884 organized a Grand O Fest.; but he met with little success, partly through his extravagant claims for his own work.

Towards the end of the 19th cent. a German influence was added as major German artists crossed the Atlantic. In 1911 the New York M organized a prize, won by Horatio Parker with *Mona* (1912). Many American operas now joined the German and Italian repertory at the M and in other major American theatres. However, the fashion for European music and the difficulty of forming a true native tradition resulted in foreign works being long regarded as intrinsically superior. American composers either sought European training or settled in Europe in the hope of performance, e.g. Louis Adolf Coerne (1870–1922) with *Zenobia* (Bremen 1905).

A national tradition of operetta grew up early and developed into the classic American form, musical comedy or musical. A number of musicians of European origin, first- or second-generation Americans in the great waves of immigration, or refugees from persecution, contributed to this genre: operetta composers (e.g. Friml, Romberg, and Victor Herbert) gave an example that was the basis for the original American achievements of Jerome Kern (1885–1945),

Irving Berlin (1888–1989), Cole Porter (1891–1964), Richard Rodgers (1902–79), Frederick Loewe (1901–88), and above all George *Gershwin (1898–1937), whose *Porgy and Bess* (1935) remains the greatest example of an opera based on popular American musical idioms. Composers who returned from a European training (often Parisian) included Douglas *Moore (1893–1969) with *The Devil and Daniel Webster* (1938), Virgil *Thomson (1896–1989) with *Four Saints in Three Acts* (1934), Aaron *Copland (1900–90) with *The Second Hurricane* (1937), and Marc *Blitzstein (1905–64) with *The Cradle will Rock* (1937); of this generation, Samuel *Barber (1910–81) was the principal composer to be trained in America. Others who consolidated the position of American opera, as a characteristically active but various tradition, included Gian Carlo *Menotti (b 1911), Leonard *Bernstein (1918–90), Lukas *Foss (b 1922), and Carlisle *Floyd (b 1926). Among more recent composers who have further extended the range of opera are Hugo Weisgall (b 1912), Robert Ward (b 1917), Lee Hoiby (b 1926), John Eaton (b 1935), Philip *Glass (b 1937), William Bolcom (b 1938), John Corigliano (b 1938), and John *Adams (b 1947).

See also BOSTON, CHICAGO, LOS ANGELES, NEW ORLEANS, NEW YORK, PHILADELPHIA, SAN FRANCISCO, SANTA FE, SPOLETO, WASHINGTON DC.

Uppmann, Theodor (b Palo Alto, CA, 12 Jan. 1920). US baritone. Studied Curtis Institute with S. Wilson. Stage début New York, CO, 1948 (Pelléas). London, CG, 1951; New York, M, 1953–4, 1955–78. Also S Fe; Milan, S; Chicago. Roles include Guglielmo, Marcello, Sharpless; particularly acclaimed as Papageno, Pelléas, and Billy Budd, which he created. Also created parts in works by Villa-Lobos, Floyd, Pasatieri. (R)

Upshaw, Dawn (b Nashville, 17 July 1960). US soprano. Studied Manhattan School of Music; début there 1983 (Hindemith's Sancta Susanna). New York, M, from 1985 as Sophie (*Werther*), Susanna, Despina. Her light, well-projected voice is particularly suited to such roles as Barbarina (Salzburg 1987), Pamina (London 1990), and Anne Trulove (Aix 1992). (R)

Urbain. Marguerite de Valois's page (mez) in Meyerbeer's *Les Huguenots*

Urlus, Jacques (b Hergenrath, 9 Jan. 1867; d Noordwijk, 6 June 1935). Dutch tenor.

Studied Amsterdam with Averkamp, Nolthenius, and Van Zanten. Début Utrecht 1894 (Beppo, *Pagliacci*). Amsterdam 1894–9; Leipzig 1900–14; London, CG, 1910–14, 1924; Brussels, M, 1912–14; Bayreuth 1912; New York, M, 1912–17. Also Paris, O; Boston; Berlin. A notable Wagner singer, acclaimed as Siegmund and Tristan (which he was still singing in 1932); also sang Tamino, Samson, Verdi's Otello. (R)

'Urna fatale'. Carlo's (bar) aria in Act III of Verdi's *La forza del destino*, trying to reject the temptation to open the sealed envelope which contains the portrait of Leonora.

Ursuleac, Viorica (*b* Czernowitz (Černovcy, Cernăuți), 26 Mar. 1894; *d* Ehrwald, 23 Oct. 1985). Romanian soprano. Studied Vienna with Forstén and Steiner. Début Agram (Zagreb) 1922 (Charlotte). Vienna, V, 1924–6, and S, 1930–5; Frankfurt 1926–30; London, CG, 1934; Berlin, S, 1935–7; Munich 1937–44. Repertory of over 80 roles included Fiordiligi, Verdi's Desdemona, Sieglinde, Tosca; for Strauss (who called her his 'Treueste aller Treuen') she created Arabella, the Countess, Maria (*Friedenstag*), and Danae in the unofficial prem. Also a celebrated Chrysothemis, Marschallin, Ariadne, Helena. Married Clemens *Krauss. (R)

V

Vaccai, Nicola (*b* Tolentino, 15 Mar. 1790; *d* Pesaro, 5 or 6 Aug. 1848). Italian composer and singer. Studied Rome with Janacconi, Naples with Paisiello. Failing to follow up his successful Neapolitan début–with *I solitari di Scozia* (The Hermits of Scotland, 1815)–when he moved to Venice, he developed a career as a singing-teacher there and in Trieste. He sang in his own *Pietro il grande* (1824) in Parma, where he had his greatest operatic successes with *Zadig ed Astartea* (1825) and especially *Giulietta e Romeo* (1825). These won the respect of Rossini, whose influence is clear. But the rise of Bellini eclipsed this moment of fame, especially when Bellini collaborated with Romani (with whom Vaccai had quarrelled) on his own Romeo and Juliet opera, *I Capuleti ed i Montecchi*. However, it became the custom (following a suggestion of Rossini) to incorporate the penultimate scene of Vaccai's opera into Bellini's.

In 1830 Vaccai went to Paris as a teacher, travelling on to England (1830–3) and publishing his still-respected singing method. *Giovanna Gray* (1836) was a failure, despite the presence of Malibran, but led to the post of *censore* at the Milan Cons.: here he made a number of reforms. His last opera, *Virginia* (1845), was an attempt to emulate the successes of French Grand Opera.

'V'adoro, pupille'. Cleopatra's (sop) aria in Act II of Handel's *Giulio Cesare*, declaring her love to Caesar.

Vaduva, Leontina (*b* Rosiile, 1 Dec. 1960). Romanian soprano. Studied Bucharest Cons. Début Toulouse 1987 (Manon). Sang Manon at London, CG, 1988, followed by Gilda, Antonia, and Juliette. She is also a sympathetic interpreter of such roles as Drusilla (*Poppea*), Mimì, Susanna, Ninetta (*La gazza ladra*). Other appearances at Vienna, S; Geneva; Buenos Aires; Barcelona. (R)

Vakula the Smith. Opera in 4 acts by Tchaikovsky; text by Yakov Polonsky, after Gogol's story *Christmas Eve* (1832). Prem. St Petersburg, M, 6 Dec. 1876. Revised in 1885 as *Cherevichki* (The Little Boots—also known in the West as *Oxana's Caprices*), prem. Moscow, B, 31 Jan. 1887.

The witch Solokha (mez) is approached by the amorous Devil (bar); as he flies off, he raises a storm and steals the moon so as to revenge himself on her son Vakula (ten), who has made an ugly painting of him; this hinders Vakula, who is trying to make his way to court Oxana (sop). When her father Chub (bs) comes home with his friend Panas (ten), both drunk, Vakula throws them out, but is himself thrown out by Oxana, though privately she admits that she loves him. In Solokha's hut, the Devil hides himself in a sack when the Mayor (bs), then the Schoolmaster (ten), and then Chub arrive; each in turn hides in a sack. Vakula staggers off with the sacks. Oxana demands a pair of *cherevichki* (high-heeled leather boots) belonging to the Tsaritsa, and Vakula flies off on the Devil's back to St Petersburg, where he is granted the *cherevichki*; he returns to claim Oxana.

Valdengo, Giuseppe (*b* Turin, 24 May 1914). Italian baritone. Studied Turin with Accoriuti. Début Parma 1936 (Rossini's Figaro). Milan, S, 1941–3; New York, M, 1947–54; Gly. 1955. Also London, CG; Paris; Vienna; Buenos Aires. Roles included Don Giovanni, Tonio, Rigoletto, Ford, Iago, Falstaff. (R)

Valentin. Marguerite's brother (bar) in Gounod's *Faust*.

Valentine. The Comte de Saint-Bris's daughter (sop), wife of the Comte de Nevers and lover of Raoul, in Meyerbeer's *Les Huguenots*.

Valentini Terrani, Lucia (*b* Padua, 28 Aug. 1946). Italian mezzo-soprano, later contralto. Studied Padua. Début Brescia 1969 (Cenerentola). Milan, S, from 1973; New York, M, 1974; Florence 1982. Also Paris, O; London, CG; Chicago; Moscow, B; Geneva; Munich; Prague; etc. Roles include Dido (Purcell), Tancredi, Isabella (*L'italiana*), Rosina, Marina (*Boris*), Quickly. One of the most successful contraltos of the day, with a particular sympathy for Rossini and his seria roles. (R)

Valkyrie (Ger., *Walküre*). In Teutonic mythology, the *Walküren* were the warrior maidens who took slain heroes from the battlefield to *Walhall* (Valhalla), there to feast and act as a bodyguard for Wotan. The word derives from *Wal* (battlefield), *küren* (to choose). In Wagner's *Ring*, they are nine in number (sop and con), *Brünnhilde, Gerhilde, Ortlinde, *Waltraute, Schwertleite, Helmwige, Siegrune, Grimgerde, and Rossweisse. Brünnhilde, Wotan's favourite among them, is the one referred to in the opera's title *Die Walküre*. See RIDE OF THE VALKYRIES.

Vallin, Ninon (*b* Montalieu-Vercieu, 9 Sept. 1886; *d* Lyons, 22 Nov. 1961). French soprano. Studied Lyons with Mauvarnay, Paris with Héglon. Début Paris, OC, 1912 (Micaëla). Paris: OC until 1916, 1926–46; O from 1920. Milan, S, and Buenos Aires, C, from 1916; also Rome, S Francisco. Created roles in operas by D'Erlanger and Leroux; also sang Iphigénie (*Tauride*), Mozart's Countess, Marguerite, Manon, Charlotte, Mignon, Mimì, Mélisande. A distinguished singer, whose vocal artistry and expressiveness won her many admirers, notably Debussy, with whom she worked and performed. (R)

Valzacchi. An Italian intriguer (ten), crony of Annina, in Strauss's *Der Rosenkavalier*.

Vampyr, Der (The Vampire). Opera in 2 acts by Marschner; text by W. A. Wohlbrück, after the story *The Vampyre* (1819), attrib. Byron (actually by John Polidori), by way of a French *mélodrame* by Nodier, Carmouche, and De Jouffroy (1820), trans. L. Ritter (1822). Prem. Leipzig, Stadttheater, 29 Mar. 1828.

Scotland, 17th cent. Lord Ruthven (ten) has become a vampire, and must postpone the claiming of his soul by Satan with the sacrifice of three young girls. He destroys Janthe (sop), and is killed, but revives supernaturally in the moonlight through the help of Aubry (bar), to whom he entrusts his secret. He seduces and kills Emmy (sop), who is fascinated by vampires, and nearly succeeds in claiming Aubry's betrothed, Malvina (sop), as his third victim, but is denounced by Aubry just as the clock strikes.

Van Allan, Richard (*b* Chipston, 28 May 1935). English bass. Studied Birmingham with Franklin. Début Gly. 1964 (Priest and Armed Man, *Zauberflöte*). London, ENO from 1969, CG from 1971. Also Paris, O; Boston; S Diego; Wexford, etc. Repertory includes Figaro (Mozart), Don Giovanni, Leporello, Padre Guardiano, Grand Inquisitor, Philip, Ochs, Claggart. An especially intelligent, versatile singing actor with a strong dramatic

presence. Created Don Jerome in Gerhard's *The Duenna* (Madrid 1992). (R)

Vancouver. City in British Columbia, Canada. A gala performance of *Lohengrin* was given in 1891, only five years after the city's establishment. This inaugurated the operahouse built by the Canadian Pacific Railway at its western terminus, and starred Emma Juch. The theatre thereafter rarely gave opera, and was sold to a vaudeville chain in 1912. Opera was given at the T under the Stars, 1940–63, but achieved no degree of permanence until 1958, when the Vancouver International Fest. presented opera each summer until 1968. The festival included the N American prem. of *A Midsummer Night's Dream* and débuts there of Günther Rennert and Joan Sutherland. In 1960 the Vancouver O Association gave its first performance in the new Queen Elizabeth T (cap. 2,821), and has continued to mount three or four operas each year. In addition to major Canadian singers, distinguished guests are also engaged, including Horne, Resnik, and Sutherland. In 1984 the appointment of Brian McMaster of the WNO brought with it enterprising shared productions; he was succeeded by Guus Mostart in 1989. That year the International O Fest.'s travelling *Aida* drew 57,000 spectators to performances that included a 45-foot Sphinx floating in the bay.

Van Dam, José (*b* Brussels, 25 Aug. 1940). Belgian baritone. Studied Brussels with Anspach. Début Paris, O, 1961 (Escamillo). Berlin, D, from 1967; Vienna from 1970; London, CG, from 1973; New York, M, from 1975. Also Chicago, Salzburg; Venice, F, etc. Roles include Figaro (Mozart), Leporello, Méphistophélès (Gounod), Golaud, Flying Dutchman, Amfortas, Jochanaan, and first St François (Messiaen). An attractive and dramatically gifted artist, possessing a warm, extensive voice. (R)

Van Dyck, Ernest (*b* Antwerp, 2 Apr. 1861; *d* Berlaer-lez-Lierre, 31 Aug. 1923). Belgian tenor. Studied Paris with Bax. Début Paris, Eden T, 1887 (Lohengrin). Bayreuth 1888–1912 (first Lohengrin; also sole Parsifal, at Cosima's invitation); Vienna 1888–99; London, CG, 1891, 1897–8, 1901, 1907; Paris, O, 1891, 1908, 1914; Chicago and New York, M, 1898. Though strange in appearance, with a small head, spherical body, and round eyes and mouth, his magnificent voice and singing were much admired in Wagner, e.g.

as Tannhäuser, Tristan, Loge, Siegfried; also as Cellini, Des Grieux (Massenet), and Werther, which he created. However, his vanity and sometimes ludicrously affected acting earned Mahler's dislike and his own subsequent dismissal from Vienna, despite his popularity. (R)

Vaness, Carol (*b* S Diego, CA, 27 July 1952). US soprano. Studied California State U. Début S Francisco 1976. Gly. from 1983; New York, M, from 1984; Chicago from 1985; London, CG, from 1982. Also Paris, O; Berlin, D; Vienna; etc. An incisive, lustrous-toned singer of ardent temperament, impressive as Alcina, Elettra, Donna Anna, Fiordiligi, Violetta, Nedda. (R)

Vanzo, Alain (*b* Monte Carlo, 2 Apr. 1928). French tenor and composer. Studied Aix-les-Bains. Début Paris, O, 1954 (A Pirate, *Oberon*). Paris, O from 1954, and OC from 1956; London, CG, 1961, 1963; New York, M, from 1973; also Vienna, Gly., Montreal, etc. Roles included Edgardo, Robert le diable, Cellini, Gounod's Faust, Werther, Gérald (*Lakmé*). A fine, sensitive, highly expressive artist with a sweet, firm tone and a subtle technique. His operas incl. *Pêcheurs d'étoiles* (1972) and *Chouan* (1982). (R)

'Va, pensiero'. The chorus of exiled Hebrews in Act III of Verdi's *Nabucco*, sending winged thoughts to their homeland.

Varady, Julia (*b* Oradea, 1 Sept. 1941). Romanian, later German, soprano. Studied Bucharest with Florescu. Début Cluj 1962. Cluj until 1972; Cologne 1972; Munich from 1973; New York, M, from 1977; Milan, S, 1984. Also London, CG; Berlin, D; Budapest; etc. Roles include Alceste, Donna Elvira, Vitellia, Violetta, Tatyana, Butterfly, Sieglinde, Arabella. A performer of great temperament and intensity. Married baritone Dietrich *Fischer-Dieskau 1977. (R)

Varesi, Felice (*b* Calais, 1813; *d* Milan, 13 Mar. 1889). Italian baritone. Début Varese 1834 (in Donizetti's *Furioso all'isola di San Domingo*). Sang throughout Italy until 1840; Milan, S, 1841; Vienna, K, 1842–7; Florence 1847; Naples, C, 1849–50; Venice, F, 1851, 1853; London, HM, 1864. Successful in Donizetti, and the first Antonio in *Linda di Chamounix*, he was also one of the earliest Verdi baritones, much influenced by G. *Ronconi. He excelled in the energetic and passionate,

creating Macbeth (frequently consulted by the composer) and especially Rigoletto with enormous success. However, he was an unsympathetic Germont in the first disastrous *Traviata*; unable to do the role justice vocally or psychologically, he blamed the composer for 'misusing his resources'.

Varlaam. A vagabond friar (bs) in Musorgsky's *Boris Godunov*.

Várnay, Astrid (*b* Stockholm, 25 Apr. 1918). Swedish, later US, soprano. Studied US with her mother, the soprano Maria Yavor, later with Weigert. Début New York, M, 1941 (Sieglinde, replacing Lotte Lehmann at short notice). Replaced Traubel as Brünnhilde within the week. New York, M, until 1956. London, CG, 1948, 1951, 1958–9, 1968; Bayreuth 1951–67. Also Milan, S; Vienna; Chicago; Buenos Aires. Roles included Senta, Isolde, Kundry, Kostelnička; later Herodias, Klytemnästra, Von Einem's Old Lady (*Der Besuch der alten Dame*). An uneven singer, but a vivid and fervent performer who influenced the younger generation, e.g. Anja Silja. (R)

Varvara. The Kabanovs' foster-daughter (sop), lover of Kudrjaš, in Janáček's *Káťa Kabanová*.

Varviso, Silvio (*b* Zurich, 20 June 1924). Swiss conductor. Studied Zurich and Vienna. Début St Gallen 1944 (*Zauberflöte*). Basle O 1950–62 (music dir. 1956). US début S Francisco 1960 (*Midsummer Night's Dream*); New York, M, 1961 (*Lucia*). A polished exponent of the German and Italian repertory, he conducted *Rosenkavalier* at London, CG, in 1962; *La bohème* 1974. Bayreuth 1969–74 (*Fliegender Holländer*, *Lohengrin*, *Meistersinger*). Florence 1993 (*Frau ohne Schatten*).

Vasco da Gama. The Portuguese naval officer (ten), lover of Inès, in Meyerbeer's *L'Africaine*.

Vašek. A villager, Tobias Micha's son, in Smetana's *The Bartered Bride*.

vaudeville (Fr., derived from the expression 'voix de ville', or 'vau de ville': 'voice of the town'). It originated in the 16th cent. as a short song, usually with an amorous text. By the 17th cent. it meant simply any song whose melody had become so popular that it was in the public domain. These vaudevilles were an important part of the repertoire of the Paris CI, who introduced them into comedies. The resulting mixture of music and drama was an important influence on the development of *opéra-comique.

vaudeville finale. A kind of strophic finale, deriving from the *vaudeville, in which each main character sings a stanza of the vaudeville in turn, with the full ensemble joining for the refrain. The most famous example is to be found in Mozart's *Entführung*.

Vaughan Williams, Ralph (*b* Down Ampney, 12 Oct. 1872; *d* London, 26 Aug. 1958). English composer. Studied London and Cambridge with Parry, Wood, and Stanford.

Vaughan Williams turned to opera six times during his long life, and set considerable store by these works. The first, *Hugh the Drover* (1924), is a ballad opera reflecting his earlier discovery of English folk-song as one of the bases for his musical language. It is in manner closer to the early nationalist operas of, for instance, Smetana than to its contemporaries, and was clearly intended to perform a similar service for the refoundation and emancipation of English opera. That it did not do so was largely due to its belatedness, in historical terms, and the inevitable artificiality in 1924 of a pastoral idyll set in the Napoleonic Wars. This does not vitiate the considerable charm and vigour of much of the score. In *Sir John in Love* (1929), the folk influence is more fully absorbed, and, boldly challenging Verdi and Nicolai, Vaughan Williams attempts to give the character of Falstaff particular strength through the Englishness of the setting. However, by placing the characters in a 'real' Windsor, abandoning the conventions of the Elizabethan verse drama which Boito ingeniously replaced with those of opera buffa, Vaughan Williams makes the action seem less real, and cruder. For all the beauty of some of the settings, there is insufficient compensation in the use of much English poetry apart from Shakespeare and English folk-song.

Riders to the Sea (1937) abandons these preoccupations in favour of a word-for-word setting of Synge's tragedy, drawing on a style that owes something to Wagner and to verismo, but that is also deeply characteristic of the composer. This is his operatic masterpiece. *The Poisoned Kiss* (1936) turns to a modern musical comedy, but suffers from a facetious text which has prevented the wider hearing of some of the composer's most delightful and satirical music.

Of all his operas, the work closest to Vaughan Williams's heart was *The Pilgrim's Progress* (1951). Already in 1922 he had set an episode, *The Shepherds of the Delectable Mountains*: the completion of the whole work, which he always insisted was intended for the opera-house and not for cathedral performance, was an important event in his life. Inevitably uneven, given its long gestation, and suffering in places from an awkwardness in handling so large-scale a subject, it contains powerful and characteristic scenes, and is a moving statement of faith.

Together with *Holst, Vaughan Williams did much to pioneer a revival of English opera; and quite apart from their individual achievements, it is certain that without them the way would have been less clear for the post-1945 revival given its impetus by Britten's *Peter Grimes*.

Veasey, Josephine (*b* Peckham, 10 July 1930). English mezzo-soprano. Studied London with Langford. Début London, CG, 1948 (small roles). London, CG, from 1954; Gly. 1957–9, 1964–5, 1969; Berlin, D, 1971; New York, M, 1968; Paris, O, 1969, 1973. Also Milan, S; Vienna; Salzburg. Retired 1982, at the height of her powers. Large repertory included Dorabella, Amneris, Eboli, Dido (Berlioz), Fricka, Kundry, Charlotte; also first Andromache (*King Priam*) and Emperor (*We Come to the River*). An exceptionally gifted, musical artist with a warm, gleaming tone, and a sympathetic stage presence. (R)

'Veau d'or, Le'. Méphistophélès's (bs) mocking song to the crowd in Act II of Gounod's *Faust*.

Vedernikov, Alexander (*b* Mokino, 27 Dec. 1927). Russian bass. Studied Moscow with Alpert-Khasina, Milan with Barra. Début Leningrad, M, 1955. Moscow, B, from 1957; Milan, S, 1961. Also Paris, O; Vienna; Berlin; Finland. Repertory included the Russian bass roles, Gounod's Méphistophélès, Daland, Philip. (R)

'Vedrai, carino'. Zerlina's (sop) aria in Act II of Mozart's *Don Giovanni*, in which she comforts her lover Masetto after his beating by Giovanni.

vengeance aria. An aria, common in the 18th and 19th cents., in which a character (often villainous) gives vent to his determination to avenge a perceived wrong. It served a useful purpose in giving a singer a powerful dramatic number, marked by forceful declamation and vigorous coloratura. Though there are many examples of female vengeance arias, of which the most famous is the Queen of the Night's 'Der Hölle Rache' in Mozart's *Die Zauberflöte*, it is a genre especially associated with male singers, and above all with baritones or basses, usually taking the parts of villains, for example Pizarro's 'Ha! welch' ein Augenblick' in Beethoven's *Fidelio*.

Venice (It., Venezia). City in the Veneto, Italy. The first opera was probably Monteverdi's *Proserpina rapita*, given at the Palazzo Mocenigo Dandolo (now the Danieli Hotel) for the marriage of Giustiniana Mocenigo to Lorenzo Giustinian in 1630. The first public opera-house in the world opened 1637 with Manelli's *Andromeda*: this was the T San Cassiano, originally a private theatre built by the Tron family at the beginning of the 17th cent. Burnt down 1629; when it was rebuilt, the Trons decided to open it to the public, thus introducing a hitherto aristocratic art to a wider audience. Remained open until c.1800; staged the prems. of Monteverdi's *Ulisse* and several works by Cavalli. The theatre's success led to the opening of other public opera-houses, of which the most important were:

T Santi Giovanni e Paolo. Considered the finest theatre in Venice at the time, opened Jan. 1639 with Sacrati's *Delia*; rebuilt in stone 1654. Gave prems. of Monteverdi's *Poppea* and works by Cavalli, Cesti, and Rovetta. Marco Faustini was director from 1658, and introduced operas by Luzzo and Ziani, and Cavalli's *Scipione*. After his death, directed by Grimani and Morich. Closed 1715, demolished 1748.

T San Moisè. Built by the S Bernaba branch of the Giustinian family, opened 1640 with Monteverdi's *Arianna*. Enlarged 1668 (cap. 800) and in 18th cent. Gave opera regularly until 1818, including prems. of works by Vivaldi, Paisiello, Galuppi, and Anfossi. Commissioned Rossini's second opera, *La cambiale di matrimonio*, 1810, followed by *L'inganno felice*, *La scala di seta*, and *L'occasione fa il ladro* (all 1812) and *Il signor Bruschino* (1813). After 1818 a marionette theatre; rebuilt as the T

Minerva. Now part shop and part block of flats.

T San Salvatore. Built by the Vendramin family and the oldest theatre in Venice still standing; opened 1661 with Castrovillari's *Pasife*. Renamed T San Luca 1799, T Apollo 1833, T Goldoni 1875. Staged prems. of Cavalli's last two operas. Goldoni wrote more than 60 plays for it. Pasta sang Norma here. First Venetian theatre with gaslight, 1826.

T Sant'Angelo. Built by the Capelli and Marcelli families on the Grand Canal; opened 1676 with Freschi's *Elena rapita*. Prem.d several operas by Vivaldi, who was active as composer and impresario 1713–18 (possibly precipitating Marcello's satire *Il teatro alla moda*), 1726–8, and 1733–5. Gave operas by Hasse, Albinoni, Lampugnani, and others until the end of the 18th cent.

T San Giovanni Grisostomo. Built by Grimani on the site of houses owned by Marco Polo, opened 1678 with Pallavicino's *Vespasiano*. Galuppi was at the theatre 1749–56. Renamed T Emoroniti, and entered period of decline. Malibran sang in *Sonnambula* 1835; at the end of Act I garlands were thrown on the stage and songbirds released from cages in the upper-tier boxes; Malibran refused her 4,000 Austrian lire fee and gave it to the impresario Giovanni Gallo for the theatre. Immediately renamed T Malibran. The most important Venetian theatre before the opening of La Fenice. Now a cinema, but still occasionally in operatic use.

T San Benedetto. Opened 1755 with Cocchi's *Zoe*. Damaged by fire 1773; reopened 1784, in 1787 renamed as T Venier (later renovated, cap. 1,500). By 1800 146 works had been prem.d. Rossini's *Italiana in Algeri* was prem.d 1813, *Eduardo e Cristina* 1819, and Meyerbeer's *Emma di Resburgo* 1819. Renamed T Rossini 1868. From 1925 a cinema.

The T La Fenice, Venice's most famous opera-house, was planned as a successor to the burnt-down T San Benedetto, and was the phoenix (*fenice*) that arose from the ashes, though on another site. It was planned by a syndicate of Venetian patricians, citizens, and merchants, who chose Gianantonio Selva to design it. He was unpopular, and met with obstacles. On the theatre's façade he inscribed 'Societas', from which the Venetians formed the acrostic 'Sine Ordine Cum Irregularitate Erexit Theatrum Antonius Selva' ('without method and irregularly Antonio Selva built the theatre'). Opened 16 May 1792 with Paisiello's *I giuochi d'Agrigento*.

The scene of the prems. of Rossini's *Tancredi* (1813), *Sigismondo* (1814), and *Semiramide* (1823); Bellini's *Capuleti e Montecchi* (1830) and *Beatrice di Tenda* (1833); and Donizetti's *Belisario* (1836) and *Maria di Rudenz* (1838). Burnt down Dec. 1836; rebuilt on same site and plan, reopened 26 Dec. 1837. Staged prems. of Verdi's *Ernani* (1844), *Attila* (1846), *Rigoletto* (1851), *Traviata* (1853), and *Boccanegra* (1857). However, the mediocrity of its chorus and orchestra in these years is reflected in some of the works written for it.

The theatre underwent alterations 1854 and 1936, when it opened as an ente autonomo. Sometimes as part of the Biennale festival, it has given the prems. of Stravinsky's *Rake's Progress* (1951), Britten's *Turn of the Screw* (1954), and Nono's *Intolleranza 1960* (1961). Since 1968 it has staged important revivals and also productions of works by Rossellini, Rota, Malipiero, and Dallapiccola. Closed 1974–5 through financial crisis. The auditorium seats 1,500, and with its dazzling chandelier, 96 boxes, and blue, cream, and gold decorations is considered by many the most beautiful opera-house in the world. Music directors have included Ettore Gracis and Eliahu Inbal.

Opera has also been given in the courtyard of the Doge's Palace and on the island of S Giorgio.

Venusberg Music. The opening scene in Venus's realm in Wagner's *Tannhäuser*, substantially rewritten for the Paris version of 1861.

Vêpres siciliennes, Les (The Sicilian Vespers). Opera in 5 acts by Verdi; text by Scribe and Duveyrier. Prem. Paris, O, 13 June 1855.

Palermo, 1282. The French have occupied Sicily. The Duchess Hélène (sop) mourns her brother, executed by the French, and incites the Sicilians to rebel. Guy de Monteforte (bar), the French Governor, fails to persuade Henri, a Sicilian (ten), to join the French forces.

Hélène promises to marry Henri if he will avenge her brother's death. Procida (bs), a fanatical patriot, schemes to arouse the Sicilians' hatred of the invaders.

When Monteforte tells Henri that he is his son, Henri refuses to recognize his father, but realizes it will prevent him from marrying Hélène. At the Governor's Ball, Hélène and Procida plan to assassinate Monteforte;

Henri defends him and the rebels are arrested.

Henri feels that he has now performed his filial duty and is free to join the conspirators again. However, he admits publicly his relationship to Monteforte in order to prevent the execution of Hélène and Procida. As an act of reconciliation, Hélène is to marry Henri.

Procida has planned that the wedding bells shall be the signal for the Sicilians to slaughter the French. Knowing this, Hélène tries, unsuccessfully, to delay the ceremony. As the bells ring out and the mob advances, the curtain falls.

Verdi, Giuseppe (*b* Le Roncole, 9/10 Oct. 1813; *d* Milan, 27 Jan. 1901). Italian composer. He studied in Busseto with Ferdinando Provesi and, after being rejected by the Milan Cons., with Vincenzo Lavigna. In 1836 he wrote his first opera, *Rocester*; it is lost, but is likely to have formed the substance of *Oberto* (1839). This already shows Verdian traits, including interest in father–daughter relationships, as well as influences from Bellini, Rossini, and Mercadante. He was offered a contract for three more operas for La Scala, but the death of his two children and that of his wife, as well as the failure of *Un giorno di regno* (1840), made him try to cancel the contract. Tempted by Solera's libretto of *Nabucco* (1842), he produced his first masterpiece, one that has some powerful characterization and especially effective choruses that include the instantly famous 'Va pensiero'. In this, Risorgimento Italians found the first of many symbols of a people suffering foreign domination. *I Lombardi alla prima crociata* (1843) is less even; then, with *Ernani* (1844), he turned to Piave for a Romantic text whose more personal characterization led him to develop his own manner with vocal types, including the ardent tenor, the sturdy bass, and the emotionally complex baritone.

Its success led to many commissions, a period of labour he called his 'years in the galley'. *I due Foscari* (1844) is a more intimate but more limited work, from which Verdi turned back to Solera for the grand manner in *Giovanni d'Arco* (1845), to Cammarano for the unsuccessful *Alzira* (1845), and again to Solera for *Attila* (1846), a strong work that closes the grandiose line begun with *Nabucco*. In *Macbeth* (1847, rev. 1865), Verdi strikes out in a new direction, not least with an increased reliance on minor tonalities, on the orchestra, and on vocal drama rather than virtuosity. *I masnadieri* (1847) is less successful; then, having revised *I Lombardi* for Paris as *Jérusalem* (1847), he continued with *Il corsaro* (1848) and *La battaglia di Legnano* (1849), neither of them as successful as the richer and subtler *Luisa Miller* (1849). With it, he won a new freedom to choose his own commissions.

Stiffelio (1850) continues the process of expansion of resources; and his personal life found greater stability in his companionship with Giuseppina Strepponi (they married in 1859). In 1851 came the first work of undisputed genius, *Rigoletto*, which, though it does not dispense with the old forms of Italian opera, transcends them in its treatment of the orchestra and especially in the ever-richer handling of the soprano, tenor, and baritone characters. *Il trovatore* (1853) is something of a reversion, for all its robust drama and superb tunes; it is essentially the last early Verdi opera coming after the first of his middle period. This is renewed with *La traviata* (1853), in which the old conventions are absorbed into music of a new human range and perception.

Verdi now gave his attention to French Grand Opera with *Les vêpres siciliennes* (1855), returning to home ground with the powerful *Simon Boccanegra* (1857, rev. 1881); he also revised *Stiffelio* as *Aroldo* (1857). *Un ballo in maschera* (1859) mixes comic elements in a tragic love story in the manner he admired in Shakespeare. Long associated with the Risorgimento (the popular acronym 'Viva VERDI' stood for 'Viva Vittorio Emmanuele, re d'Italia'), he represented Bussetto in the new Italian parliament 1861–5, finding time only for *La forza del destino* (1862). The revised *Macbeth* was presented in 1865 in Paris, for which he also wrote his finest example of French Grand Opera, and one of the masterpieces of the genre, *Don Carlos* (1867, rev. 1884). *Aida* (1871) returns some of the French Grand Opera manner to Italy. In both works, there is mastery above all in the development of personal relationships against the background of powerful national and dynastic events.

In his last two operas, Verdi turned to Shakespeare. He had long been haunted by the idea of setting *King Lear*, but it was collaboration with Boito that led to the two final masterpieces. *Otello* (1887) responds to Boito's sensitive libretto with music that draws upon a widened harmonic range and greater orchestral tension, while maintaining the supremacy of melody as capable of expressing a wide range of human emotions. More than *Otello*, his last opera *Falstaff* (1893) is an ensemble opera, with solos or arias only playing an incidental part in the swift flow of the music. The score flashes with brilliance, yet comprises a lyrical quality that gives it unique grace. There is nothing valedictory in this sharp comedy, even though there is a final reminder, in the closing fugal chorus, that all the world's a stage.

'Verdi prati'. Ruggiero's (con cas) aria in Act II of Handel's *Alcina*, saying that the pleasant scene around him will soon be turned back to its former horror.

Vere. Capt. Vere (ten), commander of HMS *Indomitable*, in Ghedini's and in Britten's *Billy Budd*.

verismo (It.: 'realism'). The movement in Italian literature and opera that flourished briefly in the late 19th and early 20th cents. In literature, it is most fully typified in the works of the Sicilian writer Giovanni Verga, whose story *Cavalleria rusticana* (1880) was first dramatized (1884) and then provided the libretto for the parent opera of verismo, Mascagni's *Cavalleria rusticana* (1890). Its origins may be sought partly in the increased interest in naturalism in a post-unification Italy whose regions sought to preserve their actuality and identity. Equally significant was the literary example deriving from such popular French authors as Dumas fils and especially Zola, acting under the positivism of Comte. In this philosophy, the observable fact was paramount; and the artistic outcome was for works to concentrate on areas previously regarded as better neglected, especially the criminal, the violent, low life, and wretched or squalid behaviour. Though verismo claimed to confront the 'slice of life' (the 'squarcio di vita' promised by Tonio in the Prologue to Leoncavallo's *Pagliacci*), the exceptional and horrifying as represented by the crime of passion, especially in a peasant or working-class milieu, were of particular fascination, and lie at the centre of many verismo operas.

The operatic impetus came from the second *Sonzogno competition, won by Mascagni with *Cavalleria rusticana*. Its success was immediate, impressing even the aged Verdi:

'he has invented a most effective genre: short operas without pointless longueurs'. The 1-act form was indeed to prove popular in the genre. Operas to appear in the wake of this triumph included 'low-life' Neapolitan works such as Tasca's *A Santa Lucia* (1892), Spinelli's *A Basso porto* (1894), Sebastiani's *A San Francesco* (1896), and Giordano's *Mala vita* (1892). In the same year Leoncavallo produced *Pagliacci*, on a plot drawn from one of his father's court cases. Puccini, who contemplated setting both Zola and Dickens, was to give the genre greater artistic range: *Il tabarro* (1918), the first part of *Il trittico*, is typical verismo in its crime of passion among Seine bargees, but verismo leaves its distinctive mark on *La bohème* (1896), *Tosca* (1900), and *La fanciulla del West* (1910), as well as much else in his work. It encouraged him to cultivate the accurate representation of different milieux, which become functional in the action, and to develop the particular type of aria in which a realistic parlando opening may lead to the most violent emotional climax. Puccini was also quick to respond to the erotic and the sadistic in which verismo dealt, chastened though this is by his own sentimentality. In France, verismo returned with several effective works. It marked the operas of, in particular, Massenet, whose *La navarraise* (1894) is the most vivid example of French verismo. The most popular, however, was Charpentier's *Louise* (1900), even though sentimentality has here largely overcome realism. The movement has nothing to do with Russian traditions of realism, nor did it have any marked effect on German opera.

Véron, Louis (*b* Paris, 5 May 1798; *d* Paris, 27 Sept. 1867). French manager. Dir. of the Paris O 1831–5, when he confirmed its position as the most successful and influential theatre in Europe, including with the prems. of *Robert le diable* (1831) and *La Juive* (1835) and the commissioning of *Les Huguenots* (1836). His business acumen, flair for publicity, and understanding of public taste combined to make the Opéra a great show-case of opera, though standards of artistry and execution were often criticized.

Verona. City in the Veneto, Italy. The T Filarmonico, designed by Francesco Galli Bibiena, opened 1732 with Vivaldi's *La fida ninfa*; burnt down 1749; reopened 1754 with Hasse's *Alessandro nell'Indie*. The 14-year-old Mozart played here on his first Italian visit in 1770; prems. included Traetta's *L'Olimpiade* (1758) and Cimarosa's *Giunio Bruto* (1781). Bombed Feb. 1945. Opera has also been staged in the T dell'Accademia, T Nuovo (or Rena), T del Territorio, T Morando, T Leo di Castelnuovo, and T Ristori.

The Roman arena (cap. 16,663) staged operas by Rossini and Donizetti in 1856 and 1859; and in 1913 regular summer performances were initiated by Giovanni *Zenatello, his future wife Maria Gay, and the impresario Ottone Rovato. Serafin's advice was sought, and after acoustic tests, weather hazards, and other problems, *Aida* was staged on 10 Aug. 1913 to an audience including Puccini, Mascagni, Pizzetti, Zandonai, Montemezzi, and Illica. There have been summer seasons ever since, except 1915–18 and 1940–5. Although most operas are chosen for opportunities for the spectacular, including *Gioconda*, *Turandot*, *Mefistofele*, and *Forza del destino*, there have also been successful prods. of more intimate works, including *Traviata* and *Bohème*. The atmosphere is naturally that of mass popular entertainment rather than artistic refinement; but it attracts distinguished artists, including Callas and Richard Tucker for their Italian débuts in *Gioconda*, 1947, Domingo for his in *Don Carlos*, 1969.

Verrett, Shirley (*b* New Orleans, 31 May 1931). US mezzo-soprano, later soprano. Studied Chicago with Fitziu, New York with Székély-Freschl. Début Yellow Springs 1957 (Lucretia). New York, CO, 1958; Moscow, B, 1963; London, CG, and Milan, S, from 1966; New York, M, from 1968; Paris, B, 1990 (at its opening). Her wide range, warm tone, and striking physical presence have made her a successful Amneris, Eboli, Lady Macbeth, Dalila, Selika, Dido (Berlioz), Tosca. (R)

Verschworenen, Die (The Conspirators). Opera in 1 act by Schubert; text by Castelli, on the idea of Aristophanes' comedy *Lysistrata* (411 BC). Prem. Frankfurt 29 Aug. 1861.

The Crusaders' wives go on sexual strike until their husbands forswear war, as in Aristophanes' original. A touchy political censor insisted that the title be changed to *Der häusliche Krieg* (Domestic War).

Verstovsky, Alexey (*b* Seliverstovo, 1 Mar. 1799; *d* Moscow, 17 Nov. 1862). Russian composer. Abandoned engineering to study piano in St Petersburg with Steibelt and

Field. Wrote music for various vaudevilles, then took up a full-time career in the theatre when appointed Inspector of Theatres in Moscow, 1825. Dir. of all the Moscow theatres, 1842, exercising a powerful and beneficial influence. Retired 1860.

Verstovsky's first opera, *Pan Twardowski* (1828), met with little success. A Romantic Singspiel in the manner of *Der Freischütz*, it draws on some Weberian ingredients (a pact with the Devil, the *Preciosa* gypsy atmosphere) but is constructed of short, effective songs that show no influence of German Romantic opera. The work does perhaps owe to French opéra-comique the fascination with natural effects (a flood, an earthquake). *Vadim* (1832) includes some consciously Russian characteristics. His greatest success was *Askold's Tomb* (1835), which was given some 600 times in Russia during the 19th cent. and in 1869 became the first Russian opera to be performed in America. Even this work, despite an incantation scene modelled on the Wolf's Glen scene in *Der Freischütz*, is essentially a collection of individual songs, which for all their appeal do not create much in the way of character or atmosphere except of the most rudimentary kind. It was the use of popular Russian elements in the songs and choruses, and strokes such as the introduction of folk instruments and players, that won the operas such an enthusiastic following.

Vespri siciliani, I. See VÊPRES SICILIENNES, LES.

Vestale, La (The Vestal Virgin). Opera in 3 acts by Spontini; text by Étienne de Jouy. Prem. Paris, O, 15 Dec. 1807.

The opera tells of the love of the Roman captain Licinius (ten) for Julia (sop), who becomes a vestal virgin while her lover is in Gaul. He breaks into the temple to win her back, and she allows the holy fire to become extinguished. Condemned to death, she is being led to execution when a flash of lightning rekindles the flame. She is spared, and reunited with Licinius.

'Vesti la giubba'. Canio's (ten) aria in Act I of Leoncavallo's *Pagliacci*, bewailing his duty to put on his motley and to clown, though his heart is breaking.

Vianesi, Auguste (*b* Legnano, 2 Nov. 1837; *d* New York, 4 Nov. 1908). Italian, later French, conductor and composer. Studied Legnano with his father Giuseppe. Went to Paris 1857

with a letter of introduction to Rossini from Pasta. London, DL, 1858–9. Moscow 1863–4; St Petersburg 1867–9. Paris: I, 1873; O, 1887–91, giving prems. of Saint-Saëns's *Ascanio* (1890) and Massenet's *Le mage* (1891). London, CG, 1870–80. Cond. London prems. of *Lohengrin* (1875) and *Tannhäuser* (1876), also especially French and Italian repertory. New York, M, 1883–4 (inaugurating the house with Gounod's *Faust*), 1891–2. New Orleans, French OH, 1899–1900. Taught singing in New York from 1892.

Viardot, Pauline (*b* Paris, 18 July 1821; *d* Paris, 18 May 1910). Franco-Spanish mezzo-soprano. Daughter of Manuel *García, sister of *Malibran. Early musical training with her father; studied piano with Liszt, composition with Rejcha, singing with her mother. Début London, HM, 1839 (Rossini's Desdemona). Paris, Odéon, 1839. Married Louis Viardot 1840; Paris, I, 1841–2; St Petersburg 1843–6, with great success; London, CG, 1848 regularly until 1855; Paris: O, 1849, 1851; L, 1856, 1859–61. An artist of unusual integrity and intelligence, and one of the greatest and most influential singers in operatic history. Unlike her rival Grisi, she possessed neither physical nor vocal beauty. Essentially a mezzo-soprano, she extended her range to cover $g-f'''$; her voice, like her sister's, was 'a rebel to subdue' (Chorley), but her masterly technique enabled her to sing Donna Anna, Leonore, Arsace, Amina, Bellini's Romeo, Lucia, Alice, Valentine, Azucena, Lady Macbeth. Her complete musical identification with her roles produced dramatic interpretations of great power. Created Fidès, written for her, with consummate success; Berlioz was overwhelmed by 'her almost deplorable ability to express profound grief' as Gluck's Orfeo (in Berlioz's own edition, 1859). She inspired Gounod's Sapho, Saint-Saëns's Dalila, and initially Berlioz's Dido; Schumann's Op. 24 Liederkreis and Brahms's Alto Rhapsody were written for her. She also did much to introduce Russian music to the West, and her influence on her lifelong admirer Turgenev was considerable, as on other literary figures including De Musset and Sand. She sight-read *Tristan*, with Wagner, at a private Paris concert for one of his patrons. A gifted pianist and linguist, she also composed (incl. operettas to words by Turgenev, e.g. *Le dernier sorcier*, 1869, which Tchaikovsky heard in 1889 and on which he made no comment). After an early vocal decline and retirement, she taught in Paris, her pupils including Artôt, Orgeni, and Brandt. Her long life included the acquaintance of both Da Ponte and Henry James.

vibrato (It.: 'vibrated'). A fluctuation of pitch, intensity, and timbre in the voice. The rate of fluctuation increases with volume and dramatic intensity, thereby changing the colour of the tone produced. When the voice is under stress the vibrato may become too fast, producing a tremolando effect or 'flutter', or too slow, producing the unattractive 'wobble'. Some voices develop a permanent wobble through over-use.

Vick, Graham (*b* Liverpool, 30 Dec. 1953). English producer. Studied Manchester, RNCM. Dir. of prod., Scottish O, 1984–7. With City of Birmingham Touring O (from 1987) has staged *The Ring Saga* and *Les Boréades*. London, ENO, from 1984; CG 1989 (Berio's *Un re in ascolto*, *Meistersinger*). *War and Peace* for Kirov O (1991), *Queen of Spades* at Gly. 1992 (dir. of production 1994). Capable of creating spectacular effects with limited means, he staged *Lady Macbeth* at New York, M, 1994; *King Arthur* at Paris, C, and London, CG, 1995.

Vickers, Jon (*b* Prince Albert, 29 Oct. 1926). Canadian tenor. Studied Toronto with Lambert and Geiger-Torel. Début Toronto, Canadian OC, 1954 (Duke of Mantua). Canadian OC, 1954–6; London, CG, from 1957; Bayreuth 1958, 1964; New York, M, 1960–85. Also Milan, S; Paris, O; Vienna, S; Salzburg; S Francisco, etc. A moving dramatic singer with a robust and distinctive voice, clear articulation, and a magnetic stage presence. Successful as Jason (*Médée*), Florestan, Siegmund, Tristan, Cellini, Aeneas (Berlioz), Verdi's Otello, Canio, Grimes. (R)

Vida Breve, La (The Short Life). Opera in 2 acts by Falla; text by Carlos Fernandez Shaw. Prem. (in Fr.) Nice 1 Apr. 1913.

Granada, 1900. Salud the gypsy (sop) loves Paco (ten), who is secretly about to marry Carmela (mez). At the wedding Salud denounces his perfidy, and dies brokenhearted at his feet.

'Vieni, t'affretta'. Lady Macbeth's (sop) aria in Act I of Verdi's *Macbeth*, in which she strengthens her husband's resolve to murder the King and gain the throne.

Vienna (Ger., Wien). Capital of Austria. Opera was first given by the Mantuan company, the Comici Fedeli, probably the anon. *Arcas* (1627). Initially encouraged by Ferdinand III, opera was firmly established at the Viennese court during the reign of Leopold I (1657–1705), largely following the Venetian model. Revivals of Cavalli's *Egisto* and *Giasone* were mounted (1643 and 1650 respectively), possibly that of Monteverdi's *Ulisse* also, and many composers and musicians, including Bertali, *Sances, P. A. *Ziani, and *Cesti, were brought from Italy. To the popular Venetian style they added a sumptuousness and splendour appropriate to the imperial setting, creating a distinctively opulent style of Viennese court opera which survived well into the next century. The lavish production of Cesti's *Il pomo d'oro* in 1668, performed to celebrate the marriage of Leopold I to the Infanta Margherita, represented an early summit of Viennese operatic achievement. To house the elaborate event, Burnacini designed a theatre in the main square of the imperial palace, the Hofburg; this was the predecessor of the Burgtheater. During the mid-17th cent. Viennese ensembles were also responsible for introducing opera to several other cities, including Munich and Regensburg.

The tradition of court opera was continued by *Draghi who, working mainly with the librettist Minato, wrote some 175 works, many of them to heroic themes. Italian composers dominated into the next century; particularly important were M. A. *Ziani and *Bononcini, who continued to write in a predominantly Venetian style. The amazing productiveness of such composers placed Vienna at the forefront of European musical life: *c*.400 operas were produced during the second half of the 17th cent.; sometimes as many as 12 new works would be staged in one year. Work began on an opera-house in 1697, but this burnt down in 1699. In Joseph I's reign (1705–11) Giuseppe Galli-Bibiena was chief theatre architect; he built two theatres, one for smaller plays and musical works, another for the performance of the court opere serie. Under Charles VI (1711–40) Viennese Baroque opera reached its apotheosis, especially in the work of *Fux, which was characterized by a typically Teutonic emphasis on heavy counterpoint at the expense of dramatic expression. Despite public demand for a theatre, which eventually led to the building of the T am Kärntnertor in 1708, Charles VI insisted that production of opera should remain an imperial monopoly.

Around this time the influence of the new style of Neapolitan opera seria gradually began to be felt in Vienna; this was strengthened by the arrival of the librettists Pariati and *Zeno in 1718, the latter holding the post of poeta cesareo to which *Metastasio succeeded in 1729. During the mid-18th cent. the Viennese operatic tradition was carried forward by Conti, *Caldara, and L. A. *Predieri, but the accession of Empress Maria Theresa in 1740 ushered in a new era in which the magnificence of the High Baroque was replaced by a new emphasis upon the rococo and galant. In 1747 the Schönbrunn Schlosstheater opened; the following year Gluck's *Semiramide riconosciuta* was given to inaugurate the T bei der Hofburg. Court Kapellmeister from 1754, he produced several operas in traditional vein, before attempting an important reform of opera seria conventions in his *Orfeo ed Euridice* in 1762. This provoked a fierce backlash from Metastasio and *Hasse, but was of only passing significance, for the new genres of Singspiel and opera buffa were already claiming the attentions of composers and audiences alike.

From 1770 Joseph II ruled as co-regent with Maria Theresa, becoming emperor in 1780. The 20 years of his enlightened despotism were a watershed in Viennese operatic life during which the court's direct influence over opera was effectively renounced, allowing more adventurous experimentation: although such composers as the Kapellmeisters *Gassmann and *Bonno provided a link with earlier tradition, even they were somewhat attracted to lighter styles. Singspiel had been introduced to Vienna c.1760, but the establishment by Joseph II of the National-Singspiel in 1778, which opened with a performance of *Umlauff's *Die Bergknappen*, provided important encouragement, and irretrievably weakened the supremacy of Italian opera. The 1780s were golden years for Vienna, during which public taste alternated between German Singspiel and Italian opera buffa. The tensions caused by this rivalry are seen at best in *Mozart's mature works, which represent the pinnacle of Viennese operatic achievement; though the Burgtheater gradually yielded its position to the Kärntnertortheater, the former staged the prems. of Mozart's *Entführung*, *Figaro*, and *Così*, and *Cimarosa's *Il matrimonio segreto*. On

Bonno's death (1788), Salieri became court Kapellmeister, and his new operas were performed at the Kärntnertor.

The monopoly of the court theatres was challenged by the activities of those in the suburbs, principally Emanuel *Schikaneder's T auf der Wieden, where Mozart's *Zauberflöte* was given in 1791, and the T in der Leopoldstadt. With its more popular Singspiel style, which drew partly on a characteristic 18th-cent. Viennese tradition of satirical stage plays with interpolated music, the repertoire of these theatres proved highly popular and influenced the later work of Raimund and Nestroy. In 1801 Schikaneder moved to the T an der Wien, where he produced *Fidelio* (1805); although an important operatic venue during the first part of the 19th cent. (Lortzing was dir. 1846–8), it later became the home of operetta. The T in der Josefstadt opened 1822, with Beethoven conducting his music for it, *Die Weihe des Hauses*. Opera was also given in the summer Thaliatheater.

After the Napoleonic Wars, Rossini became the most popular composer in Vienna; and in 1821 an Italian, Domenico *Barbaia, became manager of the Kärntnertortheater and T an der Wien. He gave the prem. of *Euryanthe* and introduced the subscription system. Only three new operas were given 1823–42, but in 1842 *Donizetti became court composer and conductor, and wrote *Linda di Chamounix* and *Maria di Rohan* for the Kärntnertortheater. In 1847 the Carltheater opened on the site of the old T in der Leopoldstadt, giving musical comedy and operetta (demolished 1951). In 1861 Wagner conducted the local prem. of *Lohengrin*, which he was hearing for the first time in the theatre.

The 1857 plans for rebuilding the centre of Vienna included the new Oper am Ring (cap. 2,260), opened 25 May 1869 with *Don Giovanni*: public criticism led to the deaths of the architects Siccardsburg from a heart attack and Null by suicide before the opening. The first director was J. F. von Herbeck, 1870–5, followed by Franz Jauner, 1875–80, who brought Hans Richter to Vienna and staged *The Ring*, in turn followed by William Jahn: himself a conductor, he and Richter controlled the theatre 1880–96, gathering an ensemble that included Materna, Winkelmann, Reichmann, and Scaria (the four Bayreuth creators of Kundry, Parsifal, Amfortas, and Gurnemanz), also

Ernest van Dyck and Marie Renard (creators of Werther and Charlotte). Standards were, typically, interpretative rather than innovative, with the prem. of *Werther* in 1892 an exceptional event. A further great period followed under Gustav *Mahler, 1897–1907, who brought in the designer Alfred *Roller, challenged the O's routine in the name of tradition with the strongest musical lead in the theatre's history, and formed an ensemble including Gutheil-Schoder, Mildenburg, Kurz, Weidt, Kittel, Schmedes, Slezak, Maikl, Demuth, and Mayr. Mahler left, a victim of the perennial Viennese hostility to challenge until it is comfortably in the past, but the singers continued with Weingartner's less distinguished directorship, 1907–11. Hans Gregor was more successful, 1911–18, engaging singers including Jeritza, Lotte Lehmann, and Piccaver, and developed an enterprising repertory. The Volksoper (cap. 1,473), originally the Kaiser Jubiläums Stadttheater (1898), opened 1904 with *Freischütz* under Zemlinsky and was built up by the director, Rainer Simons, first with operetta. He then challenged the artistic lead of the Staatsoper with the first Viennese *Tosca* (1907) and *Salome* (1910).

In 1918 the Hofoper became the Staatsoper, under Franz Schalk 1918–29 (together with Richard Strauss 1920–4). Prems. were few, apart from *Die Frau ohne Schatten*, but there were many Viennese prems.; singers included Helletsgruber, Rajdl, Schumann, Jerger, Schipper, and Manowarda. At the Volksoper under Weingartner, 1919–24, the first Vienna *Boris* was given, also the prem. of Schoenberg's *Glückliche Hand*; it closed 1928, reopened 1929 as the Neues Wiener Schauspielhaus. Clemens Krauss was at the Staatsoper 1929–34, Weingartner 1934–6, Bruno Walter 1936–8, with singers including Németh, Anday, Novotná, Kern, Ursuleac, the Konetzni sisters, Olczewska, Dermota, Kiepura, Tauber, Schorr, and Rode, and the conductors Alwin and Krips. With the German annexation in 1938, many had to leave. The Volksoper became the Opernhaus der Stadt Wien. After a period of chaos, Karl *Böhm was appointed music director 1943 and began rebuilding the ensemble. He began with a Strauss cycle, and on 30 Nov. 1944 Knappertsbusch conducted the last performance in the old house, *Götterdämmerung*. In Sept. 1944 the theatre was closed by Goebbels; bombed 12 Mar. 1945.

The company resumed 1 May 1945 at the Volksoper with *Figaro* under Krips. Franz Salmhofer became director, and in Oct. the T an der Wien was reopened with *Fidelio*, the company playing in both houses. With Böhm, Krips, and Krauss, and an ensemble including Gueden, Konetzni, Jurinac, Reining, Schwarzkopf, Della Casa, Lipp, Welitsch, Seefried, Dermota, Lorenz, Hotter, Kunz, Klein, Patzak, Schoeffler, and Weber, it quickly regained its pre-war prestige. In 1954 Böhm became director to prepare for the reopening of the Staatsoper (cap. 1,709) on 5 Nov. 1955 with *Fidelio*. Böhm resigned in 1956 after public criticism, especially over a new production of *Wozzeck*, and was succeeded by Karajan, who made an agreement with La Scala for joint productions. Karajan gradually assumed the role of conductor-producer, becoming the most powerful figure at the O since Mahler. He introduced more contemporary music than had ever been Viennese taste, and opera in the original language. His ensemble included Ludwig, Nilsson, Popp, Rysanek, Berry, and Waechter. Various directors came and went, Egon Hilbert remaining in 1964 when Karajan resigned. Hilbert's successor Heinrich Reif-Grintl appointed Horst Stein as First Conductor, a new Vienna post. A slack period ensued, with standards restored by Lorin Maazel, 1982–4, who introduced a *stagione system but resigned in the face of public hostility. He brought in Ricciarelli, Marton, and Pavarotti. Claudio Abbado was music director 1986–91. The Volksoper has maintained its own traditions and standards.

Vie parisienne, La. Operetta in 5, later 4 acts, by Offenbach; text by Meilhac and Halévy. Prem. Paris, Palais-Royal, 31 Oct. 1866.

The setting is the newly rising Paris of Haussman, to which tourists come from all over the world on the new railway system. The penniless Bobinet (spoken) and Gardefeu (ten) gull two Swedish aristocrats into thinking they are tourist guides; Gardefeu's house is used as a 'hotel', with Bobinet's servants dressed up as the 'guests'.

Vieuille, Félix (*b* Saugéon, 15 Oct. 1872; *d* Saugéon, 28 Feb. 1953). French bass. Studied Paris with Achard and Giraudet. Début Aixles-Bains 1897 (Leporello). Paris, OC, 1898–1940; New York, Manhattan OC, 1908–9. Created numerous roles, including Father (*Louise*); Dukas's Barbe-bleue, Sultan (*Mârouf*),

Eumée (*Pénélope*), Macduff (Bloch's *Macbeth*); also Arkel, praised by Debussy as 'the most profoundly human of grandfathers' and for the understanding of his artistic intentions. (R)

Viglione-Borghese, Domenico (*b* Mondovì, 3 July 1877; *d* Milan, 26 Oct. 1957). Italian baritone. Studied Pesaro with Leonese, Rome with Cotogni. Début Lodi 1899 (Herald, *Lohengrin*). Gave up singing, but was persuaded by Caruso to return to the stage. Toured S America 1905–6; Parma 1906; Milan, S, from 1910. Also Rome; Turin; Naples; Paris, O; Buenos Aires, C. Possessed a large, vigorous tone and a vivid stage personality. Particularly esteemed in dark roles, e.g. Amonasro, Iago (Verdi), Barnaba. His Jack Rance was dubbed 'the Prince of Sheriffs' by Puccini. (R)

'Vilja, o Vilja'. Aria in Act II of Lehár's *Die lustige Witwe*, in which she recounts a traditional national folk-tale of a maid of the woods and a huntsman's unrequited love for her.

Village Romeo and Juliet, A. Opera in prologue and 3 acts by Delius; text by composer, after the story by Gottfried Keller in his *Leute von Seldwyla* (vol. i, 1856; vol. ii, 1874). Prem. (in German) Berlin, K, 21 Feb. 1907.

The theme is the love between two children of quarrelling farmers. Sali (treble, later ten) and Vrenchen (girl sop, later sop) leave their fathers Manz (bar) and Marti (bs), encouraged by the mysterious Dark Fiddler (bar), and from the fair in the Paradise Garden wander to the river and die together in a barge that sinks as it floats downstream.

Villi, Le. Opera in 2 acts by Puccini; text by Fontana after Alphonse Karr's *Les Willis* (and perhaps suggested by Adam's ballet *Giselle*). Prem. Milan, V, 31 May 1884. Rev. 2-act version prem. Turin, R, 26 Dec. 1884.

The Black Forest, the Middle Ages. Villagers gather to celebrate the betrothal of Anna (sop) to Roberto (ten), who is about to leave on a journey to claim an inheritance. He promises Anna that he will return soon. Roberto returns many months later, having lived a carefree life. Anna has, unknown to him, died heartbroken; her father, Guglielmo (bar), calls on her spirit and on the Villi (the spirits of betrothed maidens deserted by their lovers) to take revenge on Roberto. Thinking it is his betrothed, Roberto then embraces Anna's ghost, and is forced to dance until he falls dead.

Vinay, Ramón (*b* Chillán, 31 Aug. 1912). Chilean baritone and tenor. Studied Mexico City with Pierson. Début, as baritone, Mexico City O 1931 (Alfonso, *La Favorite*). Sang baritone roles for several years. After further study, début as tenor Mexico City 1943 (Don José). New York, CO, 1944, M, 1946–61; Milan, S, 1947–52; London, CG, 1950, 1953–60; Bayreuth 1952–7, 1962. Also Paris, O; Chicago; etc. Resumed baritone roles in 1962. Retired 1969. A highly musical, intelligent, and affecting singer actor. Roles included Lensky, Tristan, Parsifal, Don José, Canio, Herod, and a distinguished Otello (Verdi); also Doctor Bartolo (Mozart), Telramund, Rigoletto, Falstaff (Verdi), Scarpia. (R)

Vinci, Leonardo (*b* Strongoli, *c*.1696; *d* Naples, 27 or 28 May 1730). Italian composer. Studied Naples with Greco, then held various positions in the city. His earliest operatic works were simple comedies in Neapolitan dialect, all lost except for *Li zite 'n galera* (1722). Beginning with *Publio Cornelio Scipione* (1722), he contributed *c*.24 works to the opera seria repertory, writing for Venice, Parma, and Rome. His most important works were his settings of Metastasian librettos for Rome, including *Didone abbandonata* (1726), *Catone in Utica* (1728), and *Alessandro nell'Indie* (1730).

One of the first composers to set Metastasio, his *Artaserse* (1730) represents a watershed in the development of opera seria. In it signs of a break with the tradition of Alessandro Scarlatti are clearly apparent: in particular, the dramatic rigidity of the recitative–aria chain is given greater flexibility and the accompanied recitative reaches a new expressive peak. Though Vinci died shortly after the completion of *Artaserse*, it remained popular for many years and is viewed, together with Hasse's contemporaneous setting of the same libretto, as one of the seminal works for the establishment of Metastasian opera seria in the mid-18th cent.

Violetta. Violetta Valéry (sop), lover of Alfredo Germont, and the eponymous 'strayed woman', in Verdi's *La traviata*.

Viotta, Henri (*b* Amsterdam, 16 July 1848; *d* Montreux, 17 Feb. 1933). Dutch conductor of Italian descent. Studied Cologne with Hiller.

Founded the Wagnervereeniging, Amsterdam, and through it did much to propagate Wagner's music in Holland, staging the major works during the 1880s and in 1905 giving the first European *Parsifal* outside Bayreuth.

'Vi ravviso'. Count Rodolfo's (bs) aria in Act I of Bellini's *La sonnambula*, in which he greets the village he last saw as a young man.

Visconti, (Conte) **Luchino** (*b* Milan, 2 Nov. 1906; *d* Rome, 17 Mar. 1976). Italian producer and designer. Originally a film- and theatre-producer, turning to opera in 1954 after seeing Callas's Norma. Worked with her at Milan, S, producing *Vestale* 1954, *Sonnambula* 1955, *Traviata* 1956, *Anna Bolena* 1957, *Iphigénie en Tauride* 1958. Designed and produced *Don Carlos*, London, CG, 1958, returning for *Trovatore*, a 'black and white' *Traviata*, and an art-nouveau *Rosenkavalier*. Inaugurated Spoleto Fest. with *Macbeth*, 1958, often returning, and ending with *Manon Lescaut* 1972. Callas's demonstration of the dramatic vitality of bel canto opera found a response in his historical sense, his feeling for tradition, and his eye for telling dramatic detail; his own revitalization of the staging of 19th-cent. Italian opera, previously thought largely the singers' prerogative, influenced a generation of designers including Zeffirelli and Sanjust. Opera on his ancestor by Amadei (1869).

Vishnevskaya, Galina (*b* Leningrad, 25 Oct. 1926). Russian soprano. Studied Leningrad with Garina. Début Leningrad 1944 (*Vogelhändler*). Moscow, B, 1952–74; New York, M, 1961–2, 1965, 1977; London, CG, from 1962; Milan, S, from 1964. A beautiful woman with a vibrant, typically Slavonic voice who brought her own highly coloured interpretations to a wide range of productions. Roles included Leonore, Aida, Tosca, Tatyana, Lisa, Natasha. Studied Katerina Ismaylova with Shostakovich for film of revised version of *Lady Macbeth of Mtsensk*; recorded original version with her husband, the cellist and cond. Mstislav *Rostropovich. (R)

'Vision fugitive'. Hérode's (bar) aria in Act II of Massenet's *Hérodiade*, in which he sings of the vision of Salomé that haunts him day and night.

Visse, Dominique (*b* Lisieux, 30 Aug. 1955).

French counter-tenor. Studied with Alfred Deller and René Jacobs. Début Tourcoing 1982 in *Poppea*. Appearances under Jacobs, William Christie, and others in operas by Vivaldi (*L'incoronazione di Dario*), Charpentier (*Actéon*, Edinburgh 1985), and Handel (Nirenus, *Giulio Cesare*, Paris, O, 1987). His agile and well-schooled voice has also been displayed to good effect in recordings by Cavalli, Rameau, and Hasse. (R)

'Vissi d'arte'. Tosca's (sop) aria in Act II of Puccini's *Tosca*, in which she laments the unjustness of her fate.

Vitale, Edoardo (*b* Naples, 29 Nov. 1872; *d* Rome, 12 Dec. 1937). Italian conductor. Studied Rome with Terziani. Début aged 14 as operetta cond. Rome, Arg., 1897 (first local *Götterdämmerung*); Bologna 1897 (first local *Walküre*). Milan, S, 1908–10, giving first Italian *Medea* and *Boris* (1909). Music dir. Rome, C, 1913–26. Married **Lina Pasini** (*b* Rome, 8 Nov. 1872; *d* Rome, 23 Nov. 1959), a leading Wagner soprano who also had a success touring Italy with her husband. Their son **Riccardo** (*b* Rome, 1903) was artistic dir. of Rome O 1958–62.

Vitali, Filippo (*b* Florence, *c*.1590; *d* ?Florence, after 1 Apr. 1653). Italian composer and singer. Though largely active in Florence, Vitali is chiefly remembered as the composer of *Aretusa* (1620), one of the first operas to be staged in Rome. According to Vitali's own preface to the score, which shows the strong influence of the first generation of Florentine opera composers, he both composed and rehearsed the opera in 44 days.

Vitellia. The deposed Emperor Vitellius' daughter (sop) in Mozart's *La clemenza di Tito*.

'Viva il vino'. Turiddu's (ten) *brindisi in Mascagni's *Cavalleria rusticana*.

Vivaldi, Antonio (*b* Venice, 4 Mar. 1678; *d* Vienna, 28 July 1741). Italian composer. Though Vivaldi is known today principally for his instrumental music, he made a notable contribution to the development of Venetian opera. The son of a violinist in the St Mark's orchestra, he trained for the priesthood, being ordained in 1703, the year he became violin-master at the Pietà. Here his behaviour brought him into conflict with the authorities and his career suffered many setbacks. After leaving the Pietà in 1717 he undertook extensive travels throughout both Italy and Europe, all the while composing and publishing instrumental music and staging operas. The first, *Ottone in Villa*, had been produced in Vicenza as early as 1713; during the 1720s and 1730s he became one of the most prolific and highly regarded Venetian opera composers, though his work soon lapsed into obscurity after his death.

Vivaldi's point of departure was the nascent genre of opera seria, to which he brought his own peculiar skills as an instrumental composer. In total he composed over 45 operas, of which 16 survive in their entirety. Their high quality does not lie for the most part in strikingly innovative gestures, but rather in the subtle adaptation of conventional procedures and patterns. Like his contemporaries, Vivaldi showed a fondness in his librettos for historical or heroic subjects (e.g. *Griselda* (1735), *Orlando* (1727)) which were sometimes also given exotic settings (e.g. *Montezuma* (1733), *Teuzzone* (1718)). Together with Vinci's, his work carried forward that of Alessandro Scarlatti, leading to the solidification of the principles of Metastasian opera seria under Hasse.

Vixen. Bystrouška (sop), vixen bride of the fox Lišák, in Janáček's *The Cunning Little Vixen*.

'Voce di donna'. La Cieca's (mez) aria in Act I of Puccini's *La Gioconda*, voicing her thanks to Laura for saving her from condemnation as a witch.

Vogl, Heinrich (*b* Au, 15 Jan. 1845; *d* Munich, 21 Apr. 1900). German tenor. Studied Munich with Lachner and Janke. Début Munich 1865 (Max). Munich 1865–1900; Bayreuth 1876–97; London, HM, 1882; Vienna, H, 1884–5; New York, M, 1890. Highly successful in the German repertory, and an outstanding Wagner singer. With his dark-hued and pleasing voice, fine technique and excellent projection, he was a successful Lohengrin, created Loge and Siegmund, and became the leading Tristan of his day. Also sang Siegfried and Parsifal. He was, however, considered 'prosaic' by Ludwig II, and Wagner rejected him as not 'aristocratic' enough for the first Walther. He wrote an unsuccessful opera, *Der Fremdling* (Munich 1899). His wife **Therese Thoma** (*b* Tutzing, 12 Nov. 1845; *d* Munich, 29 Sept. 1921), was a soprano. Admirable as Elsa, Isolde, and Brünnhilde, and created Sieglinde. Often performed with Vogl; however, his insistence that they be employed simultaneously at Bay-

reuth lost him the chance of the first Parsifal, as Wagner considered her wrong for Kundry.

Vogler, (Abbé) **Georg Joseph** (*b* Pleichach, 15 June 1749; *d* Darmstadt, 6 May 1814). German composer, pianist, and organist. Studied Würzburg. Widely known in his day as an organist, theorist, and teacher—including of Weber, Danzi, and Meyerbeer—he had little more than temporary success with his compositions. *La kermesse* (1783) did not even complete its prem. Of his other operas, the most important was probably *Samori* (1804).

'Voi, che sapete'. The canzonetta written and sung by Cherubino (sop, sometimes mez) to the Countess in Act II of Mozart's *Le nozze di Figaro*.

'Voi lo sapete, o mamma'. Santuzza's (sop) account to Mamma Lucia of her betrayal by Turiddu in Mascagni's *Cavalleria rusticana*.

Voix humaine, La (The Human Voice). Opera (tragédie lyrique) in 1 act by Poulenc; text by Cocteau. Prem. Paris, OC, 6 Feb. 1959.

This is a 45-minute 'concerto' for soprano and orchestra—one side of a conversation between a young woman and her lover, who has jilted her. At the end she strangles herself with the telephone flex.

Volo di Notte (Night Flight). Opera in 1 act by Dallapiccola; text by composer after Saint-Éxupéry's novel *Vol de nuit* (1931). Prem. Florence, P, 18 May 1940.

The opera is set in the control room of an airport. It tells of the anxieties and relationships of Rivière, the flight controller (bs-bar), the radio-telephonist (ten), and Signora Fabien (sop), wife of one of the pilots, whose arrival on a night flight is anxiously awaited.

Von der Osten, Eva. See OSTEN, EVA VON DER.

Von Heute auf Morgen (From Day to Day). Opera in 1 act by Schoenberg; text by Max Blonda (composer's wife). Prem. Frankfurt 1 Feb. 1930.

Schoenberg's only comic opera (the first 12-note opera, and long the only comic one), it describes the wiles of a witty and determined woman in keeping her husband.

Vorspiel (Ger.). See PRELUDE.

Votto, Antonino (*b* Piacenza, 30 Oct. 1896; *d* Milan, 9 Sept. 1985). Italian conductor. Studied Naples with De Nardis. Répétiteur Milan, S, under Toscanini, then assistant cond. 1924–9; cond. 1948–70, including some of Callas's major appearances. London, CG, 1924–5, 1933. Chicago 1960–1, 1970. (R)

Vyvyan, Jennifer (*b* Broadstairs, 13 Mar. 1925; *d* London, 5 Apr. 1974). English soprano. Studied London with Henderson, later Geneva with Carpi. Début London, EOG, 1947 (Jenny, *Beggar's Opera*). London, SW, 1952 and CG, 1953; Gly. and Venice, F, 1954. Created Penelope Rich (*Gloriana*), Governess (*Turn of the Screw*), Tytania, and Mrs Julian (*Owen Wingrave*). An accomplished, clear-toned singer with much dramatic imagination, also acclaimed as Semele, Elettra, Constanze, Donna Anna. (R)

W

'Wach' auf'. The chorus sung in Hans Sachs's honour in Act III of Wagner's *Die Meistersinger von Nürnberg*. It is a modernization of the beginning of the poem 'Die Wittenbergisch Nachtigall', beginning 'Wach auff! es nahent gen dem tag', with which the historical Sachs greeted Luther and the Reformation.

Waechter, Eberhard (*b* Vienna, 9 July 1929; *d* Vienna, 29 Mar. 1992). Austrian baritone. Studied Vienna with Rado. Début Vienna, V (Silvio), 1953. Vienna, S, from 1954; London, CG, 1956, 1959; Bayreuth, 1958–9, 1962–3, 1966; New York, M, 1961. Also Gly.; Paris, O; Salzburg. A polished and versatile artist with a dark, seductive tone, successful as Don Giovanni, Mozart's Almaviva, Escamillo, Flying Dutchman, Wolfram, Amfortas, Orestes. Created Ill (Einem, *Der Besuch der alten Dame*). Intendant Vienna, V, 1986–92; S, 1991–2. (R)

Waffenschmied, Der (The Armourer). Opera in 3 acts by Lortzing; text by composer, after Ziegler's *Liebhaber und Nebenbuhler in einer Person* (1790). Prem. Vienna, W, 30 May 1846.

Worms, 16th cent. The Count of Liebenau (bar) has fallen in love with Marie (sop), daughter of the armourer Stadinger (bs). He woos her in both his own person and as an apprentice smith, Conrad. When she tells the Count that she loves Conrad, he is triumphant, until rejected in both guises by Stadinger, who wants her to marry the Count's servant Georg (ten). When he refuses, Marie is given to Conrad, and all is revealed.

Wagenseil, Georg Christoph (*b* Vienna, 29 Jan. 1715; *d* Vienna, 1 Mar. 1777). Austrian composer. Active at the Viennese court from 1735, he composed *c*.13 dramatic works, including pasticcios, mostly for court festivities, the earliest of which was *Ariodante* (1745). In such works as *La clemenza di Tito* (1746) and *Vincislao* (1750) he began to turn Viennese court opera away from the ponderous Baroque model of his teacher Fux towards something lighter and more graceful, reflecting above all the influence of the new 'style galant'.

Wagner, Cosima (*b* Bellaggio, 24 Dec. 1837; *d* Bayreuth, 1 Apr. 1930). Daughter of Liszt; married first Hans von Bülow (1857), then Wagner (1870), with whom she worked to establish Bayreuth. She was in charge of the festival 1883–1906, and responsible for the productions; in these, her aim was to ensure that Wagner's instructions continued to be followed, and she cultivated in the theatre and at Wahnfried a reverential attitude to Wagner that came to hinder the flow of new ideas which was also at the centre of his work. She rejected Appia, for instance, with the argument that Wagner's wishes were already completely known. However, while assuming a priestess role, she did make changes, with the assertion of her personal knowledge of Wagner's wishes. Accounts of her rehearsing suggest painstaking attention to detail, particularly of gesture and verbal inflection. She attempted to restrict *Parsifal* to Bayreuth, in accordance with Wagner's wish, and was unforgiving of artists who performed it elsewhere. Her diaries give a devoted, reverential, but not unobservant account of her life with Wagner; and there are glimpses in them of a character shyer and more vulnerable than the *grande dame* manner she later cultivated.

Wagner, Johanna (*b* Lohnde, 13 Oct. 1826; *d* Würzburg, 16 Oct. 1894). German soprano. Adopted daughter of Wagner's brother **Albert** (1799–1874), tenor and producer. Début Dresden 1844 (Agathe). Created Elisabeth (*Tannhäuser*). Then studied Paris with Viardot. Hamburg 1849; Berlin, H, 1850–61; London, HM, 1856. Schwertleite and First Norn in first *Ring*. Roles included Tancredi, Lucrezia Borgia, Fidès, Ortrud. Possessed an 'incomparably beautiful' voice (Wagner) and charming stage personality. But Wagner, who had hoped her to be his 'representative' (and indeed the first Brünnhilde), came to complain of her essentially vain and self-seeking nature.

Wagner, Richard (*b* Leipzig, 22 May 1813; *d* Venice, 13 Feb. 1883). German composer. Wagner's early interests were primarily dramatic, and his early musical studies were casual and frequently disrupted. His main teacher in Leipzig from 1831 was C. T. Weinlig. In 1832 he wrote the text for an opera, *Die Hochzeit*, of which three pieces survive. He became chorus-master in Würzburg in 1833, and completed *Die Feen* in 1834, only to have it rejected by Leipzig. It is a work deriving much from Weber and Marschner, still firmly grounded in early German Romantic opera. In 1834 he began work on *Das Liebesverbot*, which acknowledges the inspiration of Bellini and Italian opera; moving to Magdeburg, he saw it unsuccessfully produced there in 1836. In the same year he married the actress Minna Planer, following her to Königsberg and then Riga. Here he began *Rienzi*; to escape his creditors, they fled to London, then to Paris, where he hoped to see a production of the work, designed as it was on Parisian Grand Opera models. He was disappointed in this, and spent two and a half difficult years in the city.

Though *Rienzi* triumphed in Dresden in 1842, Wagner now moved on from his German, Italian, and French endeavours. *Der fliegende Holländer* (1843) is what he described as the greatest leap forward in the shortest time by any composer; it concerns redemption through love, and shows greater dependence on the orchestra, use of motive, and increased fluency of melodic movement. In 1843, also, he became conductor in Dresden. With *Tannhäuser*, completed in 1845, there is an increase in orchestral fluency, and the nature of the story (the conflict of sacred and profane love) provides him with a set of heroic and lyrical conventions which he explores especially in the contrast between the simple diatonicism of the court and the pilgrims and the sensuous chromatics of Venus' realm. The work succeeded in Dresden in 1845; a later revision for Paris in 1861, undertaken to comply with the local requirement of a ballet (the opening scene in the Venusberg), was a notorious failure inflicted by organized opposition.

Lohengrin, written in 1845–8, returns to the theme of redemption through love. As before, there are conflicts of idiom, with the plain knightly heroics set against the magic world of the 'dark' pair with whom the 'light' pair is contrasted. Nevertheless, the contrast between outer manifestation and inner reality was becoming more crucial to Wagner's thought. His style is still coloured by the demands of singers, and by the conventions of German Romantic opera, of

which tradition it can be seen as the culminating work. 1848 also found Wagner caught up in revolutionary struggles and forced into exile in Switzerland.

Composing nothing for nearly six years, he re-examined opera as an art form in a series of extended essays that set an intellectual agenda but were not in the end to bind his imagination. The most important are *Das Kunstwerk der Zukunft* (The Work of Art of the Future, 1849), *Oper und Drama* (1851), and *Eine Mitteilung an meine Freunde* (A Communication to My Friends, 1851). Taking as his ideal the fusion of all the arts, myth, and religion in a social context, which he perceived as defining Greek tragedy, he argues that this had been lost and the ideal debased; his reforms for music drama were to include the dramatization of personal relationships and of the inner life of the characters, drawing upon myth, with poetry fertilizing music in a new expressive context, and with Beethoven's example of thematic development being turned to expressive ends in the orchestra and motives used for dramatic purposes. He also revived the old verse device of *Stabreim*, or alliteration, in part so as to allow his melodic lines greater fluency.

In 1850 he began work on *Siegfrieds Tod*, the first stage of what was to be *Der Ring des Nibelungen*, a project that took him over 25 years. He found it necessary to add a prefatory work, *Der junge Siegfried*, in turn adding *Die Walküre* before that and then a prelude, *Das Rheingold*; the four operas of the eventual cycle were then composed in the order *Das Rheingold*, *Die Walküre*, *Siegfried*, and *Götterdämmerung*. In 1857, in the middle of *Siegfried*, he broke off to write *Tristan und Isolde* and *Die Meistersinger von Nürnberg*.

Wagner's methods naturally change over so huge a time-span. Motivically, *Das Rheingold* makes comparatively simple use of motive chiefly as reference, but by the end of the cycle this has given way to a dense conceptual network of ideas that speaks in music directly to the mind. The vocal lines become more lyrical, and the role of the orchestra more important as it develops the accrued and changing associations and meanings of the motives (their labelling, which had nothing to do with Wagner, constricts this development of meaning). A crucial element in the growth of the cycle, and in Wagner's whole art, was his reading of Schopenhauer's *Die Welt als Wille und*

Vorstellung (The World as Will and Representation) in 1854. The book gave philosophical basis to ideas that had long been absorbing him, for instance the reasoning that the exercise of instinctive drives (the will) is destructive, and that what should be sought is the moral force of renunciation, a patient wait for extinction. The change in Wotan's character is profoundly affected by Schopenhauer's ideas, as is the nature of *Tristan und Isolde*, in which the contrast between the outer world of 'day' and the secret inner life of 'night' is that of the lovers' tragic predicament.

Wagner's orchestral mastery in *Tristan* enables him to articulate this inner world, helped by his now advanced chromatic harmony. The combination of erotic tension which this creates, together with the deeply pessimistic renunciation of the world and embrace of death, gave the work a unique atmosphere, and the score's chromatic tension was but one element that left the course of European music permanently changed. The work was also in part connected to his love for Mathilde Wesendonk, who with her husband had sheltered him in exile. Once it was finished, he took up an old scenario for *Die Meistersinger von Nürnberg*. Originally intended as a light afterpiece for *Tristan*, it grew into profound comedy. Though suffused with warmth and lyrical tenderness, it also has a dark side in the Schopenhauerian resignation of Hans Sachs, whose awareness of *Wahn* (destructive illusion) is turned to the renunciation of his 'will' (reflecting Wagner's renunciation of Mathilde) and is necessary for the stability of the city and happiness of the young lovers.

Though by now famous, Wagner was at the lowest of his many financial ebbs when rescue came in 1864 in the form of support from King Ludwig II of Bavaria. He had also parted from Minna and established himself with Cosima, Liszt's daughter and the wife of Hans von Bülow; they were married in 1870. *Tristan* was produced in 1865, *Die Meistersinger* in 1868, and *Das Rheingold* and *Die Walküre* in 1869 and 1870 respectively. In 1871 Wagner settled in Bayreuth, in a house, Wahnfried, built for them by the King, who also provided him with the fulfilment of his cherished dream of a festival theatre. Its opening with the first complete *Ring* in 1876 was an event of European importance.

Wagner had meanwhile begun what he knew would be his last work, *Parsifal*, con-ceived more than thirty years earlier. Described as a *Bühnenweihfestspiel* ('sacred festival drama'), it takes the chromatic language of *Tristan* to similar extremes, but with the theme of civic and personal order won out of disorder, which had marked *Die Meistersinger*, turned to a society (the Knights of the Grail) bound by belief. The tension between diatonic order and chromatic disarray, also characteristic of *Die Meistersinger*, here lies between the purity of the Grail, to which Parsifal brings his redeeming innocence, and the evil theatening its destruction. Much of the opera is in narrative, with a modified use of end-rhyme and with the subtlest use of motive Wagner ever made.

In the autumn of 1882, after the first production of *Parsifal* in Bayreuth, Wagner and his family left for Venice. Here he died the following February. His body was taken to Bayreuth and buried in the garden of Wahnfried. Cosima reluctantly survived him, an autocrat in her husband's artistic kingdom, until 1930, when she was buried beside him.

Wagner, Siegfried (*b* Tribschen, 6 June 1869; *d* Bayreuth, 4 Aug. 1930). German composer, conductor, and producer, son of Richard Wagner and Cosima von Bülow. Studied Frankfurt with Humperdinck, later Bayreuth with Richter and Kniese. Cond. Bayreuth, part of *Ring*, 1896; prod. *Fliegender Holländer* Bayreuth 1906, when he became dir. of Bayreuth Fest. His attempts at scenic innovation were cautious, and could not go far because of his mother's loyalties to Wagner's memory. His own operas, which include *Der Bärenhäuter* (The Bearskin Wearer, 1899) and *Der Schmied von Marienburg* (The Smith of Marienburg, 1923), are mostly fairy-tale works in late-Romantic vein.

Wagner, Wieland (*b* Bayreuth, 5 Jan. 1917; *d* Munich, 17 Oct. 1966). German producer and designer. Son of Siegfried and grandson of Richard Wagner. Studied privately, and for a short period with Roller in 1934. His first designs were for his father's *Der Bärenhäuter* (Lübeck 1936); this was followed by designs for *Parsifal* (Bayreuth 1937) and for two more of his father's operas in Antwerp 1937, and Düsseldorf 1938. Exempted from military service by Hitler so as, he said, to 'preserve and perpetuate the family name', he designed the 1943 Bayreuth *Meistersinger* and produced *Walküre* and *Siegfried* in Nuremberg. Prod. complete *Ring*, *Freischütz*, and his father's *An allem ist Hütchen schuld*, Alt-enburg 1943–4. Studied Wagner scores with Kurt Overhoff at Strauss's home in Garmisch 1947.

Cleared by a de-Nazification court, he assumed, with his brother Wolfgang, the artistic and business administration of post-war Bayreuth when it was removed from their mother Winifred. Together they com-pletely revolutionized the style of Wagner production, abandoning pageantry and naturalism in favour of a more abstract approach designed to emphasize the works' more inward and mythic content. Less use was made of scenery, more of suggestive lighting, which in Wieland's skilled hands came almost to replace scenery at some points. He also produced regularly at Stuttgart, and occasionally in other German cities. His productions of *Fidelio*, *Carmen*, *Orphée*, and *Aida* aroused as much contro-versy as those of Wagner's works; however, his productions of *Salome*, *Elektra*, *Wozzeck*, and *Lulu* (generally with Anja Silja) were enthusiastically received. He hoped to 'replace the production ideas of a century ago, now grown sterile, by a creative intel-lectual approach which goes back to the origins of the work itself. Every new pro-duction is a step on the way to an unknown goal.'

Wagner, Wolfgang (*b* Bayreuth, 30 Aug. 1919). German producer, designer, and manager. Son of Siegfried and grandson of Richard Wagner. Worked as musical assist-ant Bayreuth 1942. Responsible for the busi-ness and administrative sides of the Bayreuth Fests. from 1951. Has produced and designed all the works in the Bayreuth canon, enterprisingly but with less of the imaginative flair shown by his brother Wieland.

Wagner-Régeny, Rudolf (*b* Szász-Régen, 28 Aug. 1903; *d* Berlin, 18 Sept. 1969). German composer and pianist of Romanian origin. Studied Leipzig and Berlin (with Rezniček, Koch, and Schreker). His earliest involve-ment with dramatic music came through the composition of the short theatre piece *Sganarelle* (1929) in which the influence of the French group Les Six is very clear. After several similar works, including *Der nackte König* (1930), he scored a notable success with his first full-scale opera, *Der Günstling* (1935); this prepared the way for two further col-laborations with Neher, *Die Bürger von Calais* (1939) and *Johanna Balk* (1941). The latter, in which he consciously adopted idioms cal-culated to offend the Nazi régime, was noisily received and Wagner-Régeny's career was momentarily halted. After war service and a nervous breakdown he took up a career as a teacher in the new German Democratic Republic, first in Rostock and later in Berlin at the Hochschule für Musik. Over the next 20 years he gradually developed a highly per-sonal serialist idiom, elements of which are apparent in his later operas, *Persische Episode* (comp. 1940–50) and *Das Bergwerk zu Falun* (1961).

Wagner tuba. A valved brass instrument, with conical bore and funnel-shaped mouth-piece, built as B♭ tenor and F bass at Wagner's suggestion for *The Ring* in 1876 to obtain a tone quality between the horns, which he regarded as lyrical and romantic, and the trombones, which he regarded as solemn, dignified, and heroic. The quartet used in *The Ring* consists of two tenors and two basses, played by the 5th–8th horns. Particularly associated with Hunding in *Walküre*. Also sometimes known as Waldhorntuba or Ring-tuba. Used by Strauss in *Elektra* and *Frau ohne Schatten*. Rarely used elsewhere, though associated with mourning for Wagner's death in Bruckner's Seventh Symphony.

Wagner-Vereeniging. See AMSTERDAM.

'Wahn! Wahn!' Hans Sachs's (bar) mono-logue in Act III of Wagner's *Die Meistersinger von Nürnberg*, in which he broods upon the follies of the world.

Waldmann, Maria (*b* Vienna 1842; *d* Ferrara, 6 Nov. 1920). Austrian mezzo-soprano. Studied Vienna with Passy-Cornet, Milan with Lamperti. Début St Petersburg 1865 (Pierotto, *Linda di Chamounix*). Milan, S, 1871–2; Paris, OC, 1874; also Moscow, Vienna, Trieste, Cairo. Retired on her marriage (when Verdi gave her away) in 1877. A very beautiful and dramatically gifted singer with a velvety tone, who during her short career became, in Verdi's view, his ideal mezzo-soprano. Sang Amneris in the first Italian *Aida*, and created the alto part in his Requiem.

Wales. See WELSH NATIONAL OPERA.

Walker, Sarah (*b* Cheltenham, 11 Mar. 1943). English mezzo-soprano. Studied London with Packer and Smith, later Rosza. Début Kent O 1969 (Ottavia), Gly. 1970;

London, SW/ENO, 1971–8; Chicago 1977; London, CG, from 1979; Vienna, S, 1980; S Francisco 1981; Brussels, M, 1982; Geneva 1983; New York, M, 1986. Roles incl. Poppea, Penelope (*Ulisse*), Diana (*Calisto*), Dorabella, Maria Stuarda, Dido (Berlioz), Quickly, Countess (*Queen of Spades*), Fricka, Baba the Turk, Charlotte, Katisha, Gloriana. Created Agave (Buller's *The Bacchae*), Suzanne (*Toussaint*). A highly accomplished singer with a vivid presence. (R)

Walk to the Paradise Garden. The interlude between scenes 5 and 6 of Delius's *A Village Romeo and Juliet*, depicting the lovers Sali and Vreli journeying to the Paradise Garden (a dancing-place) and resting on the way.

Walküre, Die. See RING DER NIBELUNGEN, DER.

Wallace, Ian (*b* London, 10 July 1919). Scottish bass. Studied London with Allin and Borgioli. Début Cambridge T, 1946 (Schaunard). Edinburgh (Gly. co.) 1948; Gly. 1952–6, 1959–61; Parma, and Venice, F, 1950; Berlin 1954; Rome 1955. A witty and engaging buffo singer, whose roles included Masetto, Bartolo (Rossini and Mozart), Don Magnifico, Sacristan. (R)

Wallace, Vincent (*b* Waterford, 11 Mar. 1812; *d* Vieuzos, 12 Oct. 1865). Irish composer. Studied with his father, a bandmaster, and with W. S. Conran and Haydn Corri. Played in the Dublin T Royal; then emigrated to Tasmania. Later moved to Australia and made a name as a violin virtuoso. Many adventurous travels ensued, including visits to India and Chile. In Mexico City in 1841 he conducted the Italian opera season, moving on to New York to give concerts and then returning by way of Europe to England.

Soon after his return, he wrote *Maritana* (1845), which had an immediate success. Wallace's travels had given him a musical sophistication: though the language is unadventurous, based on the simpler Romantic conventions of the day, he was able to introduce into the work effects ranging from the direct use of gypsy music and Spanish colouring to a feeling for the style of French and Italian opera. *Maritana* originally ran for 50 nights, and was quickly taken up by European and American theatres.

Wallace's next opera, *Matilda of Hungary* (1847), was a failure. Its successor, in a manner closer to Grand Opera than *Mar-*

itana, was *Lurline* (commissioned for Paris in 1848 and announced by Covent Garden but not given until 1860). Though it did not match the success of *Maritana*, *Lurline* won a considerable following, especially for its grandiose scenes and vigorous effects in a manner then unknown in English opera. After many more travels, concluded in time for *Lurline*'s London production, Wallace settled in London. His later operas were unsuccessful, and some operettas remained unperformed.

Wallerstein, Lothar (*b* Prague, 6 Nov. 1882; *d* New Orleans, 13 Nov. 1949). Czech, later US, conductor and producer. Répétiteur Dresden 1909. Cond. and prod. Poznań 1910–14, chief prod. Breslau 1918–22. Duisburg 1922–4; Frankfurt 1924–6. Vienna 1927–38, where he prod. 65 operas including *Wozzeck*; Salzburg 1926–37. Guest prod. Milan, S, and Buenos Aires, C. Founded O School in The Hague 1939. New York, M, 1941–6. (R)

Wally, La. Opera in 4 acts by Catalani; text by Illica, after Wilhelmine von Hillern's novel *Die Geyer-Wally* (1875; dram. 1880). Prem. Milan, S, 20 Jan. 1892.

The Tyrol, *c*.1800. Catalani's last, and best, opera describes how la Wally (sop) is drawn still closer to her lover Hagenbach (ten) when her suitor Gellner (bar) tries to kill him; the lovers perish in an avalanche. Toscanini admired the opera so much that he named one of his daughters Wally.

Walter, Bruno (*b* Berlin, 15 Sept. 1876; *d* Beverley Hills, CA, 17 Feb. 1962). German, later French, later US, conductor. Studied Berlin with Ehrlich, Bussler, and Radeke. Répétiteur Cologne 1893–4, cond. début (*Waffenschmied*). Cond. Hamburg 1894–6, under Mahler; Breslau 1896–7; Pressburg 1897–8; Riga 1899–1900; Berlin 1900–1. Vienna 1901–12, first as Mahler's assistant. London, CG, 1910 (incl. Smyth, *The Wreckers*), 1924–31 (Mozart, Wagner, Richard Strauss). Music dir. Munich 1913–22, giving prems. of Korngold's *Ring des Polycrates* and *Violanta* (1916), Pfitzner's *Palestrina* (1917), and Schreker's rev. *Das Spielwerk* (1920); Berlin, SO, 1925–9. Left Germany in 1933: guest cond. Vienna, S, 1935, artistic adviser 1936–8. New York, M, 1941–6, 1951, 1955–7, 1958–9. Also cond. Milan, Florence, Chicago. Walter's greatest interpretations were of Mozart, despite a certain sweetness, and Richard Strauss; he was also a fine Wagnerian. The warmth of his music-making was infectious, both to artists and audience, and was based on a strong lyrical impulse. (R)

Walters, Jess (*b* New York, 18 Nov. 1908). US bass-baritone. Studied New York with Giuffrida. Début New York New OC 1941 (Macbeth). Appeared New Orleans, New York, CC; London, CG, 1947–59; Netherlands O 1960–4. Roles included Amonasro, Alfio. (R)

Walther. Walther von Stolzing (ten), a young Franconian knight, lover of Eva, in Wagner's *Die Meistersinger von Nürnberg*.

Walton, (Sir) **William** (*b* Oldham, 29 Mar. 1902; *d* Forio d'Ischia, 8 Mar. 1983). English composer. Sang as a boy chorister at Christ Church, Oxford; largely self-taught. Despite an almost lifelong love of Italian opera, connected to his devotion to the country and eventual residence there, Walton did not turn to writing an opera of his own until *Troilus and Cressida* (1954). The work had a difficult gestation, and, despite his high reputation at the time of its prem., was found by many to be cast in too conventional a Romantic vein. The best of the work (notably the characterization of Pandarus) transcends the limitations of the text and has some fine dramatic inventions. Walton's only other opera was *The Bear* (1967), a vigorous Romantic comedy using only three characters.

Waltraute. A Valkyrie (mez) in Wagner's *Die Walküre* and *Götterdämmerung*. Her name derives from the Old Norse *valr* (slain) and Middle High German *Wal* (battlefield) and *traut* (devoted).

Wanderer. The guise assumed by Wotan (bs-bar) in Wagner's *Siegfried*.

Wandering Scholar, The. Chamber opera in 1 act by Holst; text by Clifford Bax, founded on an incident in Helen Waddell's *The Wandering Scholars* (1928). Originally entitled *The Tale of the Wandering Scholar*; rev. Britten (1951), ed. Britten and Imogen Holst (1968). Prem. Liverpool, David Lewis T, 31 Jan. 1934.

Father Philippe (bs) visits Alison (sop) in the absence of her husband Louis (bar), but is interrupted by the Scholar, Pierre (ten). They refuse him food and drink, and he leaves, but returns with Louis, and tells a pointed tale that leads to the discovery of unexpected food and drink, and then the priest hidden under a heap of straw. Another opera on the subject is by Bell (1935).

War and Peace (Russ., *Voyna i mir*). Opera in 5 acts by Prokofiev; text by composer and M. Mendelson, after Tolstoy's novel (1869). 1st version, 11 scenes, comp. 1942, unprod. 2nd version, 11 scenes, Prague, N, 1948. 3rd version, 13 scenes, Leningrad, Maly T, 12 June 1946. 4th version, 10 scenes Florence 26 May 1953. Final version, 13 scenes, Leningrad, Maly T, 1 Apr. 1955.

The work's complicated gestation and history are reflected in the various versions; but in the final 13-scene version the first seven scenes concentrate on Peace, the last six on War. Selecting key moments from Tolstoy with great skill, Prokofiev reflects private and public destinies against a background of Russia under threat.

Ward, David (*b* Dumbarton, 3 July 1922; *d* Dunedin, 16 July 1983). Scottish bass. Studied London with Carey, Munich with Hotter. Début London, SW, 1953 (Old Bard, *Immortal Hour*). London, SW, until 1959; Gly. 1958; London, CG, 1959–83; Bayreuth 1960–2; New York, M, 1963. Also Milan S, Buenos Aires, Chicago, Vienna, etc. Roles included Don Basilio (Rossini), Rocco, Lord Walton, Philip, Flying Dutchman, King Mark, Hunding, Boris, Gremin, Arkel. An artist whose commanding stature and nobility of tone, allied to great sensitivity, lent particular distinction to his Wotan. (R)

Warren, Leonard (*b* New York, 21 Apr. 1911; *d* New York, 4 Mar. 1960). US baritone of Russian origin. Studied New York with Dietsch, Milan with Pais and Picozzi. Début New York, M, 1939 (Paolo, *Boccanegra*). New York, M, until 1960; Buenos Aires, C, 1942; Milan, S, 1953; toured USSR 1958. His voice was of an exceptional mellowness and range (reaching high C); he had an impeccable technique, and became a convincing actor. Famous for Verdi's Rigoletto, Macbeth, Germont, Boccanegra, Iago, Falstaff, and Puccini's Scarpia. Collapsed and died on New York M stage during a performance of *Forza*, after singing 'Urna fatale'. (R)

Warsaw (Pol., *Warszawa*). Capital of Poland. The first opera to be given was *Galatea* (prob. by Santi Orlandi) in 1628, on the initiative of Prince Władisław Zygmunt. When crowned Władisław IV, he formed an Italian company (1634–48) with Margherita Cattaneo as prima donna and including some young Poles. In 1637 Bartolomeo Bolzoni built a provisional wooden theatre (cap. 1,000); and for his wedding celebrations Władysław built a permanent theatre in the castle (1637). When Augustus II was crowned in 1697, he brought with him a company under J. C. Schmidt and Jacek Różycki; in 1700 a French company under Deschallières spent five days in the city. Other companies made visits. In 1725 the court theatre, Operalnia, opened. Augustus III (crowned 1733) provided large subsidies and twice-weekly performances were given by a company with an orchestra of over 100; many Metastasian operas were given by a company from Dresden including *Hasse and *Bordoni.

More systematic encouragement came with the reign (1764–95) of Stanisław August Poniatowski. In 1765 the first public theatre opened, with Karol Tomatis (1739–1806) as director: under him French and Italian companies played until 1767. In 1772 a company under Kurz-Bernardon performed in the Radziwiłł Palace; the directorship passed in 1776 to Franciszek Ryx (1732–99), who gave the first opera seria with Italian singers and in 1778 gave the first Polish opera, *Nędza uszczęśliwiona* (Sorrow Turned to Joy) by Maciej Kamieński (1734–1821). The T Narodowy (Nat. T) opened in 1779 with *Le tonnelier* (The Cooper) by Nicolas-Médard Audinot (1732–1801), sung in Polish. Ryx's directorship saw the début of the 'father of the Polish theatre', Wojciech Bogusławski (1757–1829), whose activities included directing the theatre (1782–4 and 1799–1814). French and Italian operas were given, from 1783 Mozart, in Polish. Opera was also staged at the Royal Lazienski Garden, in the T w Pomarańczarni (opened 1788), and in the open-air Amfiteatr on an island (also known as the T na Wyspie) (1790). After Bogusławski, the most important figure in the early 19th cent. was Józef * Elsner (1769–1854), who composed and conducted for the theatre. In 1810 Karol *Kurpiński (1785–1857) was appointed; he became director in 1823 and introduced a largely French and Italian repertory. The T Wielki (Grand T), built by Corazzi, opened on 24 Sept. 1833 with *Barbiere* in Polish (a language which under the Russians could only be heard publicly in opera, not drama); here the opera company reached a high standard under Kurpiński, maintained (1840–52) under the conductorship of Tomasz Nidecki and (1853–74) Jan Quattrini.

After the prem. of *Halka* (1858), Moniuszko became director, introducing many new Polish works. Cesare Trombini was music director 1874–81: works he introduced included *Lohengrin* (1879). Emil Młynarski was director 1898–1903 and 1919–29, introducing works by Szymanowski and other modern composers. A feature of the period from the 1890s to 1914 were the seasons of Italian opera with great singers, including Battistini (who sang in Warsaw every year from 1894 to 1912). At the T Nowości (opened 1901) operetta was given under the energetic Ludwik Śliwiński. Financial difficulties forced the T Wielki to interrupt its work repeatedly during the 1930s. The theatres closed in 1939, and the T Wielki was damaged by fire; in 1944 bombs destroyed all but the façade. Opera was resumed in 1945 first in a cinema and then in the Roma Hall, refitted in 1953 (cap. 1,000). The T Wielki reopened in 1965 (cap. 1,800). Founded in 1962, the Warsaw Chamber O is attached to the T Wielki, and as well as premièring new works has revived works by Hasse (for the first time since his visit): it moved into a theatre of its own in 1987. A State Operetta Co. was founded in 1949. The director and conductor 1981–91 was Robert Satanowski, whose forceful policy first concentrated on Italian and Slavonic opera, though a new *Ring* was initiated in 1988 and completed in 1989. The theatre holds a ten-day annual opera festival.

Washington, DC. Capital of the US. Visiting companies, especially from Philadelphia, gave seasons of ballad opera 1800–14. The first opera staged was *Barbiere*, by the Walton Co. in 1836. Opera was given at Albaugh's OH from 1884. The Washington Nat. O Association performed in the 1920s, from 1924 in the new Auditorium. There were also Black groups, one formed in 1872; the Nat. Negro OC formed by Mary Cardwell Dawson in 1943 gave performances until her death in 1962.

The O Society of Washington was founded in 1956, and despite early difficulties won a reputation for enterprise: the music director, Paul Callaway, conducted the first US *Erwartung* (1960), Hindemith conducted *The Long Christmas Dinner* and Stravinsky *Oedipus Rex* and *The Nightingale*. The company also gave the prem. of Ginastera's *Bomarzo* (1967). Financial difficulties intervened, but the Kennedy Center (cap. 2,318) opened 1971 with the company in the commissioned prem. of Ginastera's *Beatrix Cenci*; performances are also given in the Eisenhower T (cap. 1,142) and the Terrace T (cap. 512). The company became Washington O in 1977, and has since expanded rapidly, maintaining its celebrated progressiveness under the general director, Martin Feinstein, through the production of US works, e.g. the world prem. of Menotti's *Goya* (1986). Placido Domingo dir. 1995.

Watson, Claire (*b* New York, 3 Feb. 1927; *d* Utting, 16 July 1986). US soprano. Studied New York with Schumann, Amsterdam with Lichtenstein. Début Graz 1951 (Verdi's Desdemona). Frankfurt 1956–8; Munich 1958; London, CG, 1958–64, 1970, 1972; Gly. 1960. Also Vienna; Milan, S; Chicago; Buenos Aires. Roles incl. Donna Elvira, Eva, Tatyana, Marschallin, Ariadne, Arabella. A musical, radiant toned, and eloquent performer. (R)

Watson, Lilian (*b* London, 4 Dec. 1947). English soprano. Studied London, GSMD, and London O Centre. Début Wexford 1970 (Cis, *Albert Herring*). WNO and London, CG, débuts 1971 as Papagena and Barbarina; Gly. and ENO 1976 and 1978 (Susanna). A lively and charming interpreter of such roles as Blonde (Vienna, S, 1983), Janáček's Vixen (London, CG, 1993), Fairy Godmother in *Cendrillon* (WNO 1993), Tytania in *Midsummer Night's Dream* (London, ENO, 1995). (R)

Weber. German singers, daughters of **Fridolin Weber** (1733–79), musician and uncle of Carl Maria von Weber.

1. **Josepha** (*b* Zell, 1758 or 1759; *d* Vienna, 29 Dec. 1819). Soprano. Sang from early 1780s. In 1788 married the violinist Franz Hofer (1755–96). Joined Schikaneder's co., Vienna, W, 1790. In 1797 married the actor-singer Sebastian Mayer (later the first Pizarro). Sang in Vienna until 1805. An accomplished singer, for whom Mozart wrote the Queen of the Night, which she created; also the bravura aria K580 to be sung in Paisiello's *Barbiere di Siviglia*.

2. **Aloysia** (*b* Zell or Mannheim, between 1759 and 1761; *d* Salzburg, 8 June 1839). Soprano. Studied Mannheim with Mozart, he being captivated by her 'pure, lovely voice' and 'superb cantabile singing'. They toured together 1778; he was much enamoured, but she soon rejected him. Munich 1778; Vienna 1779–92, singing first with German O, then with Italian O. In 1780 married the actor and painter **Joseph Lange** (1751–1831). Mozart

wrote several arias for her, and the role of Mme Herz (*The Impresario*); she also sang Donna Anna in the first Vienna *Don Giovanni*, and Sesto (*Clemenza*) in concert, 1795.

3. **Constanze** (*b* Zell, 5 Jan. 1762; *d* Salzburg, 6 Mar. 1842). Soprano, wife of Mozart. A good amateur singer with an attractive voice, she sang one of the soprano parts in Mozart's C minor Mass, Salzburg 1783. After Mozart's death she devoted herself to having his last opera, *La clemenza di Tito*, performed. Married the diplomat Georg Nissen 1809, and completed the biography of Mozart he left unfinished at his death, 1826.

4. A fourth sister, **Sophie** (1763–1846), wrote a touching description of Mozart's death. She married the composer and singer Jakob *Haibel.

Weber, Carl Maria von (*b* Eutin, ?18 Nov. 1786; *d* London, 5 June 1826). German composer, conductor, pianist, and critic. Studied with various teachers on his youthful travels, including Heuschkel and M. Haydn, later Vogler.

Weber's first opera was a childhood essay, later destroyed. In 1800 came *Das Waldmädchen*, of which only fragments survive: this was later reworked as *Silvana*. Meanwhile, he had written *Peter Schmoll und seine Nachbarn* (1803), which shows his interest in Romantic subjects and includes some original and charming music alongside much that is inexperienced. In 1804, not yet 18, he was appointed music dir. at Breslau: he instituted sweeping reforms anticipating those he was to pursue in Prague and Dresden, but largely through youth and inexperience failed to win sufficient support for them. While in Breslau, he began an opera, *Rübezahl*, of which three numbers survive. During a later (non-musical) post in Stuttgart he wrote *Silvana* (1810): though still showing many signs of inexperience, it reveals an instinct for the theatre, and includes some woodland and chivalric music giving a foretaste of *Der Freischütz* and *Euryanthe*. Its title-role is silent, and the problems of writing an opera for a dumb heroine are ingeniously tackled by a composer with a developing interest in orchestral characterization. In Mannheim in 1810 he first read the story of *Der Freischütz*, and even planned an opera on it; the project fell through when the librettist defaulted. However, he did write the 1-act *Abu Hassan* (1811), a witty little Singspiel in his freshest and most tuneful vein.

In 1816, in one of the reviews he had begun writing regularly, Weber referred in connection with Hoffmann's *Undine* to 'the German ideal, namely a self-sufficient work of art in which every feature and every contribution by the related arts are moulded together in a certain way and dissolve, to form a new world'. All his mature life, as Kapellmeister, critic, and composer, was dedicated to the aim of developing German opera along the lines of what Wagner was to call the Gesamtkunstwerk. Appointed to Prague as opera director in 1813, he set about reforming operatic practice there; in 1816 he resigned and was appointed Royal Saxon Kapellmeister in Dresden, where his reforms were yet more searching.

In 1821 he went to Berlin to conduct his own contribution to German Romantic opera, *Der Freischütz*. The work triumphed; and especially in comparison with Spontini's *Olympie* in Berlin, it came at once to be seen as an opera that spoke for Germany. Though the work contains French elements, the plot, the characters, the legend, the music, all closely based on the daily country life of Germany, caught popular imagination in times when nationalism was emerging as a force. Basically a Singspiel, *Der Freischütz* transcends older examples by its imaginative strength and cunning structures. Some of the numbers, such as the Huntsmen's Chorus and Bridesmaids' Chorus, were to become almost folk-songs. The Wolf's Glen Scene, with its ingenious mixture of speech, song, orchestral description, and loosely constructed musical numbers, cleverly related to the powers of evil by use of motive, remained an unsurpassed example of Romantic horror in music.

The success of *Der Freischütz* led Barbaia to invite him to write a similar work for Vienna; but Weber was anxious to move on, and turned to a form of Grand Opera with *Euryanthe* (1823). Despite inept writing by his librettist, Helmina von Chezy, he succeeded in constructing an opera, virtually continuous and without spoken dialogue, that anticipates much in Wagner and is itself a masterpiece. The weaknesses in the libretto have long inhibited the work's success, but the work has increasingly been recognized as an advanced and subtle music drama, giving example to its successors especially in its use of motive, its functional handling of the orchestra, and its dramatic momentum.

Weber did not build further on this new creative achievement because of the rapid advance of his tuberculosis. Invited to write an opera for Covent Garden, he was obliged to fall in with the suggestions of his English librettist, James Robinson Planché, who pressed upon him the kind of musical pantomime that was current English taste. *Oberon* (1826) is consequently constructed in separate numbers, though there is some motivic linkage. The delicacy of the fairy music set new standards (noted by Mendelssohn), just as the storm and other elements were to influence Wagner in *Der fliegende Holländer* and beyond. However, this was, Weber sadly acknowledged, not what he meant by a German opera; and he planned to rewrite it, using recitative, in a more suitable manner. He did not live to do so, for having journeyed to London to conduct the prem., he finally succumbed to his illness, dying in Sir George Smart's house the day before he was hoping to return to Germany.

A projected comedy, *Die drei Pintos*, was first entrusted to Meyerbeer for completion; later it was given to Mahler, who completed it with music from other of Weber's works and scored it.

Weber was also a pioneering opera conductor, experimenting with new seatings of the orchestra to improve the tonal blend. As was then common practice, he normally conducted from close to the footlights, so as to maintain dramatic control, using a roll of paper held by the middle. As a critic he was influential, and his essays and reviews are valuable for their insight into the problems of Romantic opera and for their accounts of contemporary works.

Weber, Ludwig (*b* Vienna, 29 July 1899; *d* Vienna, 9 Dec. 1974). Austrian bass. Studied Vienna with Borittau. Début Vienna, V, 1920 (Fiorello). Cologne 1930–3; Munich 1933–45, and subsequently; Milan, S, 1938–9, 1942, 1948, 1950; London, CG, 1936–9, 1950; Bayreuth from 1951. Also Paris, O; Buenos Aires, C; etc. A tireless and outstanding Wagner singer with a rich, voluminous tone, impressive as King Mark, Fasolt, Hunding, Hagen, Gurnemanz; also as Osmin, Sarastro, Commendatore, Boris, Barak, Wozzeck. (R)

Webster, (Sir) **David** (*b* Dundee, 3 July 1903; *d* London, 11 May 1971). English manager. General administrator to the newly formed Covent Garden O Trust 1945–70, successfully establishing the Royal OH as the permanent

home of the Sadler's Wells (later Royal) Ballet
and the Covent Garden (later Royal) O.
Helped to launch singers including Sutherland, Vickers, and Geraint Evans on their
careers.

Weidt, Lucie (*b* Troppau (Opava), 1876; *d*
Vienna, 28 July 1940). Austrian soprano.
Studied with her father, and Vienna with
Papier. Début Leipzig 1900. Leipzig until
1902; Vienna 1902–26; New York, M, 1910–
11; Buenos Aires 1912; also Paris, O, and
London, CG. A celebrated Leonore,
Brünnhilde, and Kundry, she was also a suc-
cessful Marschallin. Created the Nurse (*Die
Frau ohne Schatten*). (R)

Weigl, Joseph (*b* Eisenstadt, 28 Mar. 1766; *d*
Vienna, 3 Feb. 1846). Austrian composer and
conductor. Studied with Albrechtsberger.
His first dramatic work, the marionette
opera *Die unnütze Vorsicht oder Die betrogene
Arglist* (1783) so impressed Salieri that he
introduced Weigl into the theatrical life of
the court. Here in 1786 he aided in the preparation of *Le nozze di Figaro*, taking over from
Mozart as conductor after the first two performances.

Weigl composed over 30 Italian and
German operas in genres ranging from
heroic opera (*Daniel in der Löwengrube*, 1820)
to Italian *melodramma eroi-comico* (*Margeritta
d'Anjou*, 1816). Some of his Italian works were
composed especially for Milan S: *Cleopatra*
and *Il rivale di se stesso* (1808), and *L'imbroscata*
(1815); others were performed in Vienna.
Weigl first achieved international recognition with *L'amor marinaro* (1797); in 1805
he set Schikaneder's text *Vestas Feuer*, which
Beethoven had also begun, although not
completed, in 1803. Widespread success
came with his Singspiels *Das Waisenhaus*
(1808), and *Die Schweizerfamilie* (1809, after *The
Swiss Family Robinson*); the latter was performed throughout Europe well into the
19th cent. After *Die eiserne Pforte* (1823) he
abandoned opera for sacred music.

Weikl, Bernd (*b* Vienna, 29 July 1942). Austrian baritone. Studied Mainz and Hanover.
Début Hanover 1968 (Ottokar). Düsseldorf
1970–3; Bayreuth from 1972, as Wolfram,
Amfortas, Dutchman, Sachs. London, CG,
1975 (Rossini's Figaro). His all-round gifts are
best displayed in his interpretation of Hans
Sachs, which he sang in New York 1993; also
admired as Mozart's Almaviva and Don Giovanni, Onegin, Mandryka. (R)

Weill, Kurt (*b* Dessau, 2 Mar. 1900; *d* New
York, 3 Apr. 1950). German, later US, composer. Studied Dessau with Bing, Berlin with
Krasselt and Humperdinck. Worked as Korrepetitor in Dessau 1919 under Bing and
Knappertsbusch; dir. of opera, Lüdenscheid,
1920. Studied further in Berlin with Busoni
and Jarnach. Through Fritz Busch he was
introduced to the librettist Georg Kaiser
with whom he wrote *Der Protagonist* (1926).
This was Weill's first major success and his
next collaboration with Kaiser, *Der Zar lässt
sich photographieren* (The Tsar Has Himself
Photographed, 1928), was also well received.

In 1927 Weill was invited by Hindemith
to compose for his Deutsche Kammermusik
Baden-Baden; he responded with *Mahagonny*,
a work which in its original form he
described as a Songspiel, in effect a modern
interpretation of the old *Singspiel genre, in
which songs are connected not by music but
by dialogue. The collaboration with Brecht
proved particularly inspired, though the
production of the work, with its overt political message, proved very controversial.
The highly original approach which Weill
had taken in combining elements of popular
music from both modern and older traditions to soften the more astringent avant-
gardism of his earlier works was taken
further in his next collaboration with
Brecht, *Die Dreigroschenoper* (1928). Here their
interest in artistic topicality was further sig-
nified (and largely misunderstood) in a trans-
position of *Gay's *The Beggar's Opera* of 1728
to the Berlin of two centuries later. The international success of this work paralleled that
of Krenek's *Jonny spielt auf*, given in Leipzig
the previous year, with which it shares
certain similarities both of dramatic substance and of musical style. In Weill as in
Krenek, a strong political message is illuminated by the skilful exploitation of popular
musical idioms: together these works offer a
chilling insight into the Zeitgeist of pre-Nazi
Germany. Together with Brecht, many of
whose artistic aims he shared, Weill widened
his range and effect in the moral and political *Zeitopern *Aufstieg und Fall der Stadt
Mahagonny* (1930) and *Der Jasager* (1930). In
the works which followed, notably *Die Bürgschaft* (1932) and the ballet *Die sieben Tode-
sünden*, we find the fullest expression of his
style: popular and up-to-the-minute, but
uncompromising, basically Romantic, pointing with brilliant and wounding musical
symbols the message of the text, direct in

appeal but bearing a deeply felt political message.

Forced to leave Hitler's Germany in 1933, Weill spent some time in Paris and London, before moving to the US in 1935, largely at the instigation of Max Reinhardt. Turning his back on his earlier career, he produced a number of musical comedies and light operas, including *Street Scene* (1947) and *Down in the Valley* (1948). These enjoyed considerable success and, though cast in an unashamedly popular style, reveal skill and craftsmanship equal to that of his earlier works. In 1928 he married the actress and singer **Lotte Lenya** (1898–1981).

Weinberger, Jaromír (*b* Prague, 8 Jan. 1896; *d* St Petersburg, FL, 8 Aug. 1967). Czech composer. Studied Prague with Křička and Karel, then with Novák, and briefly (but significantly) Leipzig with Reger. *Shvanda the Bagpiper* (1927) was Weinberger's first performed opera, and had an immediate and widespread success. It followed in the Smetana tradition in its use of a folk-tale and of Czech dances (the Polka and Fugue survive as a popular concert item); Weinberger has also taken note of some German influences in his harmony, and writes well for the voice. There is nevertheless a somewhat manufactured note in the attempt to write a 19th-cent. nationalist opera in the 1920s, and this has meant that modern revivals are few. His only other important opera was *Waldštejn* (1937).

Weingartner, Felix (*b* Zara, 2 June 1863; *d* Winterthur, 7 May 1942). Austrian conductor and composer. Studied Graz with Rémy, Leipzig, Weimar with Liszt. His *Sakuntala* was prem. Weimar 1884. Cond. Königsberg 1884–5; Danzig 1885–7; Hamburg 1887–9; Mannheim 1889–91. Chief cond. Berlin 1891–8. Vienna, H, 1908–11, succeeding Mahler. Hamburg 1912–14. Chief cond. Darmstadt 1915–19; Vienna, V, 1919–24, and S, 1935–6. Boston 1912–13. London, CG, 1939 (*Tannhäuser, Parsifal*). Wrote 11 other operas, including the quite successful *Genesius* (1892) and an Aeschylean trilogy *Orestes* (1902), and edited versions of *Oberon, Fliegender Holländer*, and Méhul's *Joseph*. A conductor with a particular quality of lucidity and balance who found operatic conditions often at war with his ideals. Of his five wives, the third was the singer Lucille Marcel, the fifth his conducting pupil Carmen Studer. (R)

Weir, Judith (*b* Aberdeen, 11 May 1954). Scottish composer. Studied with Tavener, Cambridge with Holloway, Tanglewood with Schuller. *A Night at the Chinese Opera* (1987) was commissioned by the BBC for Kent O, and made an immediate impression for its theatrical originality and intelligent musical characterization. The work frames an old Chinese play, set with a stylization of oriental music, in a modern narrative using closed Western operatic forms, with a beguiling inventive contact between the two dramatic layers and musical idioms. Weir's sharp, sometimes bleak wit and liking for interweaving different narrative levels were applied again to *The Vanishing Bridegroom* (1990), deriving from three Scottish folktales; and the elegant vocal writing, subtle orchestration, and sure feeling for dramatic timing confirmed her as a major operatic talent. *Blond Eckbert* (1994). is a spare, obliquely lyrical setting of Tieck's story.

Weisgall, Hugo (*b* Ivančice, 13 Oct. 1912). Czech, later US, composer and conductor. Studied with his father Adolf, an opera singer and synagogue cantor, then, after emigration, Baltimore with Sessions. His multifarious activities, diplomatic as well as musical, have included teaching and administration (founder Hilltop OC 1952), and much conducting and composition. His style is wide-ranging and eclectic, with various techniques and styles—neoclassical, serial, and pastiche popular music among them—being skilfully adapted to the creative task in hand. His operas include *The Tenor* (1952), *Jennie* (1976), and *Esther* (1994).

Weisse, Christian Felix (*b* Annaberg, 28 Jan. 1726; *d* Leipzig, 16 Dec. 1804). German librettist, dramatist, and poet. His translation of Coffey's ballad opera *The Devil to Pay* as set first by Standfuss (1752) and then by Hiller (1766) served as the main model for German Singspiel. Weisse subsequently wrote several texts for Hiller, in many cases adapting French opéra-comique librettos.

'Welche Wonne, welche Lust'. Blonde's (sop) aria in Act II of Mozart's *Die Entführung aus dem Serail*, in which she delightedly receives the news of Belmonte's plans for escape.

Welitsch, Ljuba (*b* Borissovo, 10 July 1913). Bulgarian, later Austrian, soprano. Studied Sofia with Zlatev-Cherkin, Vienna with Lierhammer. Début Sofia 1934 (in *Louise*). Graz, Hamburg, Munich 1937–46; Vienna, S, 1947–64; London, CG, 1947–53; New York, M, 1948–52, 1972; Gly. 1948. Also Chicago; Milan, S; etc. A full-blooded and vital performer, with a large, bright, pure-toned voice. At her peak (till 1953) an astonishing Salome; also impressive as Donna Anna, Aida, Verdi's Desdemona, Tosca, Musetta, Lisa, Jenůfa. (R)

Wellesz, Egon (*b* Vienna, 21 Oct. 1885; *d* Oxford, 9 Nov. 1974). Austrian composer and musicologist. Studied musicology with Guido Adler, composition with Schoenberg. His early work as a musicologist brought him into contact with mid-17th-cent. Venetian opera, from which he took inspiration for his own works. He collaborated with Hofmannsthal on *Alkestis* (1924); later he turned to Goethe for *Scherz, List und Rache* (1928) before returning to antiquity for *Die Bakchantinnen* (1931). Forced to leave Austria in 1938, he settled in Oxford, where he became Reader in Byzantine Music in 1951. Here he wrote his last opera, *Incognita* (1951), which was staged by the OUOC. Technically a highly accomplished composer, Wellesz brought to his work both intellectual clarity and literary sensitivity.

Welsh National Opera. Though there was an abortive Welsh Nat. OC in 1890 and a Cardiff Grand Opera Society 1924–34, Wales was dependent on touring companies until after the war. The modern WNO was launched in Cardiff on 15 Apr. 1946 with *Cavalleria rusticana*. By 1956 the company was giving regular seasons in Wales and southern England with a repertory of 13 works, including Arwel Hughes's *Menna* (sung in Welsh at the Nat. Eisteddfod); by 1966 this had increased to 34, by 1976 to over 70. In the early days exploration of the then less-known early Verdi was a feature, and the fine amateur choral singing in *Nabucco* (1952), together with its nationalist fervour, identified the work closely with the company. Other successes included *Mefistofele* (1957), a modern-dress *Battle of Legnano* (1960), *William Tell* (1961), *Fidelio* with Gwyneth Jones (1964), and *Moses* (1965). The regular visits to Sadler's Wells became very popular. Music directors included Idloes Owen (1946–52), Vilem Tausky (1955–6), Warwick Braithwaite (1956–61), Charles Groves (1961–3), and Bryan Balkwill (1963–8).

A more ambitious policy developed with the appointment of James Lockhart in 1968, with Michael Geliot in 1969 as director of productions. New productions included *Simon Boccanegra*, *Falstaff*, *Idomeneo*, *Don Carlos*, and the first *Lulu* by a British company (1971). Richard Armstrong became music director in 1973, and the repertory was further extended to include a Janáček series (with Scottish O) and a Britten series, Verdi's *Otello*, *Elektra*, and prems. including Alun Hoddinott's *Beach at Falesá* (1974). The production of *The Midsummer Marriage* (1976) contributed to wider recognition of the work's stature. Brian McMaster, director 1976–92, brought in foreign directors for innovative productions including Harry Kupfer for *Elektra* (1978), Lucian Pintilie for *Carmen* (1983) and *Rigoletto* (1985), Ruth Berghaus for *Don Giovanni* (1984), Andrei Serban for *Norma* (1985), Peter Stein for *Otello* (1986), and André Engel for *Der Freischütz* (1989). Distinguished Wagner productions have included *Tristan* (1979) and *Parsifal* (1983) under Reginald Goodall. *The Ring* was built up 1983–5, and *The Trojans* staged in 1987. Charles Mackerras was music director 1986–92; he was succeeded by Carlo Rizzi. The company's standing and popularity in Britain were shown in 1990 when the Arts Council was forced by public outcry to abandon its threat of closure. Welsh-born artists appearing with the company have included Anne Howells, Gwyneth Jones, Margaret Price, Elizabeth Vaughan, Eiddwen Harrhy, Geraint Evans, Delme Bryn-Jones, and Ryland Davies. The company plays in the New T, Cardiff (cap. 1,140) and tours to Swansea and a number of smaller theatres which opened in Wales during the 1970s (e.g. the Theatr y Werin in Aberystwyth).

Welting, Ruth (*b* Memphis, TN, 1 May 1949). US soprano. Studied New York, Rome, and Paris. Début New York, CO, 1971 (Blonde). Her coloratura is well displayed as Zerbinetta, which she sang on her London, CG, and New York, M, débuts (1975 and 1976). Other roles incl. Queen of the Night, Gilda, Lucia, and Ophélie (Chicago 1992). (R)

Werle, Lars Johan (*b* Gävle, 23 June 1926). Swedish composer. Studied Uppsala with Moberg and Bäck. *Drömmen om Thérèse* (Dream about Thérèse, 1964) aroused much attention for its novel techniques of audience involvement and pre-recorded music, some of which were repeated in *Resan* (The Journey, 1969). *Tintomara* (1973), written for the bicentenary of the Royal OH in Stockholm, returns to the events at the time of the murder of Gustav III. Later, sometimes more conventional, operas include *Animalen* (The Animals, 1981) and *Leonardo* (1988).

Werther. Opera in 4 acts by Massenet; text by Blau, Milliet, and Hartmann, after Goethe's novel *Die Leiden des jungen Werthers* (1774). Prem. Vienna, H, 16 Feb. 1892.

Wetzlar, July–Dec. 1772. Werther (ten) loves Charlotte (mez), who returns his love although betrothed to Albert (bar). Werther leaves, returning to find Charlotte married. She urges him to leave her again, but on finding that he has asked Albert for his pistols, rushes to him through a snowstorm to find that he has shot himself.

Wexford. Town in Co. Wexford, Eire. An autumn festival was founded by Dr T. J. Walsh in 1951, when Balfe's *The Rose of Castile* was staged. Opera is given in the T Royal, and the repertory has been as notable for its adventurousness in reviving neglected works as the town has been for the conviviality of its welcome. The festival also has a reputation for giving an early chance to singers, including Mirella Freni, Ugo Benelli, and Christiane Éda-Pierre. The T Royal (opened 1832) was restored 1987 (cap. 550).

Weyse, Christoph (*b* Altona, 5 Mar. 1774; *d* Copenhagen, 8 Oct. 1842). Danish composer of German birth. After studying with J. A. P. Schultz in Copenhagen, he stayed in the city and became organist of the cathedral there. Known mainly as a composer of sacred music and songs, Weyse wrote five Singspiels and a light opera *Et eventyr i Rosenborg Have* (An Adventure in Rosenborg Gardens, 1827). The only one of his Singspiels to gain an established place in the repertoire was *Sovedrikken* (The Sleeping Draught, 1809). His Singspiels combine examples of his individual fusion of simple, naïve song style with more sophisticated treatments of the text: his Romance settings are particularly attractive. Apart from *Sovedrikken*, his other Singspiels are *Faruk* (1812), *Ludlams hule* (1816), *Floribella* (1825), and *Festen paa Kenilworth* (1836).

'When I am laid in earth'. Dido's (sop) lament before her death at the end of Purcell's *Dido and Aeneas*.

'Where'er you walk'. Jupiter's (ten) aria in Act II of Handel's *Semele*, promising Semele cool shade over her head and springing flowers at her feet.

White, Willard (*b* St Catherine's, Jamaica, 10 Oct. 1946). Jamaican bass-baritone. Studied New York with Johnson, Tozzi, and Thorendahl. Début New York, CC, 1974 (Colline). Successes in S Francisco, Washington, Tanglewood; London, ENO, from 1976 (Ivan Khovansky 1994); Gly. from 1978 (Porgy 1986); Scottish O 1989 (Wotan, *Rheingold*); Salzburg 1990 (Plutone in *Orfeo*). (R)

Whitehill, Clarence (*b* Parnell, IA, 5 Nov. 1871; *d* New York, 18 Dec. 1932). US bass-baritone. Studied Paris with Sbriglia and Giraudet, later Frankfurt with Stockhausen. Début Brussels, M, 1898 (Donner). Brussels, M, 1899; Paris, OC, 1900, O, 1909. Lübeck 1901; Bayreuth 1904, 1908–9, studying with Cosima Wagner; London, CG, 1905–10, New York, M, 1909–10, 1914–32; Chicago 1911–16. Created Delius's Koanga. A singer of great distinction, particularly acclaimed as Sachs, Wotan, Gunther, Amfortas; also as Gounod's Méphistophélès, Capulet, Golaud. (R)

Widdop, Walter (*b* Norland, 19 Apr. 1892; *d* London, 6 Sept. 1949). English tenor. Studied London with Gilly. Début London, BNOC, 1923 (Radamès). BNOC until 1929. London, CG, 1924, 1932–3, 1937–8; Barcelona 1928; also Holland, Germany. The leading English Wagner singer of his day, successful as Siegmund, Siegfried, Tristan; also sang Max, Aegisthus, Canio. (R)

Widor, Charles-Marie (*b* Lyons, 21 Feb. 1844; *d* Paris, 12 Mar. 1937). French composer and organist. Studied Brussels with Fétis and Lemmens. Best known for his organ music, Widor also wrote a number of stage works, including three operas. The most successful was *Les pêcheurs de Saint-Jean* (1905).

Wildschütz, Der (The Poacher). Opera in 3 acts by Lortzing; text by composer, after Kotzebue's comedy *Der Rehbock*. Prem. Leipzig, 31 Dec. 1842.

A German village and castle, early 19th cent. Baculus (buffo bs), a schoolmaster on the estate of the Count of Eberbach (bar), has accidentally shot a buck. His betrothed, Gretchen (sop), is willing to intercede for him, but he is reluctant, and a young student offers to go instead, dressed as Gretchen. This is really Baroness Freimann (sop), the Count's sister, who accompanied by her maid Nanette (sop) sets off to keep an eye on her own betrothed, the Count's brother-in-law, Baron Kronthal (ten). The Count is much taken with 'Gretchen'; the Baron bribes Baculus with 5,000 thalers to give her up; meanwhile, 'Gretchen' is rescued from the situation by being allowed to spend the night in the room of the Countess (con) (whose unremitting Greek quotations are a satire on the recent success of Mendelssohn's *Antigone* music and the ensuing mania in Berlin for all things Greek). The unravelling of all these confusions still leaves Baculus guilty of poaching and of having sold his betrothed; but he is forgiven by all.

Willan, Healey (*b* Balham, 12 Oct. 1880; *d* Toronto, 16 Feb. 1968). English composer. Studied London with Hoyte. In 1913 emigrated to Canada, where he played an important role in the country's music. In addition to the church and organ music for which he was most famous, Willan also wrote incidental music for about twenty plays, arranged five ballad operas from folk material (including *The Beggar's Opera*), and composed two operas. *Transit through Fire* (1942) was the first opera to be commissioned by the Canadian Broadcasting Commission. A second radio commission followed for *Deirdre* (1965): this, with its ancient story and richly Romantic music, is somewhat Wagnerian in manner, and had a considerable success.

William Ratcliff. Opera in 3 acts by Cui; text by A. Pleshcheyev, after Heine's drama (1823). Prem. St Petersburg, M, 26 Feb. 1869.

North of Scotland, 17th cent. Maria (sop) marries Douglas (ten), who is then told by her father Mac-Gregor (bs) how William Ratcliff (bar), whom Maria rejected, murdered her two subsequent fiancés. Douglas fights and defeats Ratcliff, but spares his life; Ratcliff appears in Maria's room, and she reveals her love for him. He kills her, her father, and himself.

Williams, Grace (*b* Barry, 19 Feb. 1906; *d* Barry, 10 Feb. 1977). Welsh composer. Studied Cardiff, and London with Vaughan Williams and Jacob, Vienna with Wellesz. Her only opera, *The Parlour* (1961), is a comedy showing some influence of Britten.

Williamson, Malcolm (*b* Sydney, 21 Nov. 1931). Australian composer. Studied Sydney with Eugene Goossens III and London with Lutyens. Settled in London in 1953 where he established a successful career first as a pianist, later as a composer; appointed Master of the Queen's Music, 1975. His first important work for the stage was the opera *Our Man in Havana* (1963), whose success was followed by *The Violins of Saint-Jacques* (1966). Possessing a fluent, eclectic, and highly professional gift, he has shown a particular skill for writing shorter dramatic pieces, of which the children's operas *Julius Caesar Jones* (1966) and *The Happy Prince* (1965) are thoroughly representative. His subsequent full-length operas, including *Lucky-Peter's Journey* (1969), were coolly received and in recent years he has concentrated on smaller-scale works.

William Tell. See GUILLAUME TELL.

Willow Song. 1. Desdemona's (sop) song 'Salce, salce' in Act IV of Verdi's *Otello*.

2. Desdemona's (mez) song 'Assisa al piè d'un salice' in Act III of Rossini's *Otello*.

Wilson, Robert (*b* Waco, TX, 4 Oct. 1941). US producer and designer. Studied Texas U (1959–62) and in New York. Designed prem. of Glass's *Einstein on the Beach* (Avignon and New York, M, 1976); with Glass and Gavin Bryars wrote libretto for *The Civil Wars* (1984). His challenging and innovative work has included designs for *Salome* at Milan, S, 1987 and the staging of *Zauberflöte* at Paris, B, 1991. Chicago 1990 (*Alceste*); Houston O 1992 (*Parsifal*).

Winbergh, Gösta (*b* Stockholm, 30 Dec. 1943). Swedish tenor. Studied Stockholm with Erik Saéden. Début Gothenburg 1971 (Rodolfo). Stockholm, Royal O, from 1973; Gly. 1980 (Belmonte); Salzburg 1982 (Jacquino). Best known as a fluent and stylish interpreter of Mozart, he has sung Titus at London, CG (1982); Ottavio at New York, M (1983); Tamino at Milan, S; and Ferrando at Houston (1988). Recent Wagnerian roles incl. Walther at London, CG, 1993, and Lohengrin. (R)

Windgassen, Wolfgang (*b* Annemasse, 26 May 1914; *d* Stuttgart, 8 Sept. 1974). German tenor. Studied Stuttgart with his father, the tenor **Fritz Windgassen** (1883–1963), Ranzow, and Fischer. Début Pforzheim 1941 (Alvaro). Stuttgart 1945–72; Bayreuth 1951–

70; London, CG, 1955–66; New York, M, 1956–7; Paris, O, 1954–6, 1966. Also Milan, S, Vienna, etc. Roles included Tamino, Florestan, Duke of Mantua, Turiddu, Eisenstein; celebrated in Wagner, as Erik, Lohengrin, Tannhäuser, Tristan, Walther, Loge, Siegmund, Siegfried, Parsifal. With a lighter, more lyrical voice than the typical Heldentenor, he used his intelligence and technique to sing with consistent intensity and beauty of tone. He was particularly in sympathy with Wieland Wagner's productions. (R)

Winkelmann, Hermann (*b* Brunswick, 8 Mar. 1849; *d* Vienna, 18 Jan. 1912). German tenor. Studied Hanover with Koch. Début Sondershausen 1875 (Manrico). Hamburg 1878; London, DL, 1882; Bayreuth 1882–91; Vienna 1883–1906. The first Parsifal, praised by Wagner (and described as 'marvellous' by Neumann); also an acclaimed Tristan, Walther, Loge, Siegfried, Florestan, Verdi's Otello, Dalibor. He possessed a large, ringing tone and a lyrical style, though Wagner would have preferred a 'smoother mezza voce' in his Parsifal. (R)

Winter, Peter von (*b* Mannheim, *bapt.* 28 Aug. 1754; *d* Munich, 17 Oct. 1825). German composer. Winter received no training in composition until a short period of study with Vogler beginning in 1775; he later disowned his teacher.

He became musical director at Mannheim, and moved with the court to Munich in 1778, where he was responsible for conducting opéras-comiques. It was there that he began to compose music for the stage, including ballets, and melodramas modelled on those of Benda. He had written three melodramas by the time he composed his first opera, *Helena und Paris*, in 1782; the work was not well received, and he had no more success with his second opera, *Bellerophon* (1785). His career as a court musician progressed, with appointment to the post of Vizekapellmeister in 1787, and Kapellmeister in 1798, but he found it hard to establish a reputation as a successful composer. In quest of success, he travelled away from Munich to various operatic centres, writing opere serie and opere buffe for Naples and Venice in 1791–4, and tragédie lyrique (*Castor et Pollux*) for Paris in 1806.

Like many German composers of his time, Winter's musical style was firmly based on French and Italian operatic conventions. His most individual writing is to be found in his Singspiels, and the nine works produced in Vienna 1793–8 numbered some of his best. Foremost among these was *Das unterbrochene Opferfest* (The Interrupted Sacrifice, 1796), which was his first great success, performed throughout Germany. The work demonstrates the influence of French *rescue opera in its plot, but also contains several notably Romantic features. Also in Vienna, he set *Das Labyrinth* (1798), Schikaneder's sequel to *Die Zauberflöte*, in which he borrows themes from Mozart's Singspiel, including the triple chord; he also attempts to emulate the tonal unity of *Die Zauberflöte*. He returned to Munich but once again met with disappointment at the poor receptions of *Belisa* (1798), *Der Sturm* (1798, after *The Tempest*), and *Maria von Montalban* (1800). His heroic opera, *Colmal* (1809), which he considered his masterpiece, had such a poor reception that he did not stage another work in the city for 11 years (his final Singspiel, *Der Sänger und die Sängerin*).

Winter's output of over 40 stage works spanned 40 years, and encompassed most of the operatic genres of the day. Described by Weber as 'an eminent master', he was generally disliked by his contemporaries, who found him a difficult man. The largely unadventurous style of his music, with its square rhythms and basic diatonic harmony, is compensated for in part by a profusion of charming melodies. His reputation rests largely on his operas, although he also wrote symphonies, concertos, chamber music, and sacred music, and his significance today is in his position of an immediate forerunner of the great composers of German Romantic opera.

'Winterstürme'. Siegmund's (ten) song in Act I of Wagner's *Die Walküre* describing the yielding of winter to spring.

Wittich, Marie (*b* Giessen, 27 May 1868; *d* Dresden, 4 Aug. 1931). German soprano. Studied Würzburg with Ubrich. Début Magdeburg 1882 (aged 14) (Azucena). Schwerin 1886–9; Dresden 1889–1914; Bayreuth 1901–10; London, CG, 1905–6. Roles included Elsa, Isolde, Kundry, and a Brünnhilde that overwhelmed E. M. Forster: 'Force, weight, majesty! She seemed to make history.' Created Salome, while protesting, 'I won't do it, I'm a decent woman.' Her comfortable figure led Strauss to call her 'Auntie Wittich'.

Wixell, Ingvar (*b* Luleå, 7 May 1931). Swedish baritone. Studied Stockholm with Gustafsson. Début Stockholm 1955 (Papageno). Swedish Royal O from 1956; London, CG, from 1960; Gly. 1962; Berlin, D, from 1962; Salzburg 1966–9; Bayreuth 1971; New York, M, 1973–9. Roles incl. Mozart's Almaviva, Pizarro, Posa, Boccanegra, Onegin, Mandryka. Possesses a strong tone and impressive stage personality. (R)

Wlaschiha, Ekkerhard (*b* Pirna, 28 May 1938). German bass-baritone. Studied Leipzig. Début Gera 1961 (Don Fernando, *Fidelio*). Sang at Dresden and Weimar 1964– 70. Leipzig O from 1970 (Scarpia and Pizarro). Bayreuth 1986 (Kurwenal). A leading exponent of the role of Alberich, which he has sung at London, CG (1990) and New York, M (1993). (R)

Wolf, Hugo (*b* Windischgraz (now Slovenj Gradec), 13 Mar. 1860; *d* Vienna, 22 Feb. 1903). Austrian composer. Studied Vienna with Fuchs and Krenn. His early opera-going drew him strongly to Wagner, whose influence shows in some aspects of his songwriting and hence in his only completed opera, *Der Corregidor* (1896). He overcame his initial resistance to the libretto, whose detail nevertheless leads him into ignoring the demands of dramatic structure (his own version of Leitmotiv is insufficiently functional) in favour of lyrical illustration: in the individual scenes and songs, Wolf's genius dominates. There were many difficulties about securing a performance (Mahler was among those who turned it down, even after its prem.), and the work has never established itself in opera-houses. Only 600 bars survive of *Manuel Venegas*.

Wolff, Albert (*b* Paris, 19 Jan. 1884; *d* Paris, 21 Feb. 1970). French conductor. Studied Paris with Leroux, Gédalge, and Vidal. Paris, OC: chorus-master 1908, cond. from 1911, music dir. 1921–4, dir. 1945–6. Cond. prems. of Laparra's *La jota* (1911), Charpentier's *Julien* (1913), Milhaud's *La brebis égarée* (1923), Ibert's *Angélique* (1927), Bruneau's *Angelo* (1928), and Poulenc's *Les mamelles de Tirésias* (1947), among many other works. Buenos Aires and Rio de Janeiro, 1912, 1940–4. New York, M, 1919–21, where his *L'oiseau bleu* was prod. 1919. London, CG, 1937 (*Pelléas*). His other operas included *Sœur Béatrice* (Nice

1948). Paris, O, 1949. A sensitive and scrupulous exponent of French music, who did much to sustain tradition at the Opéra-Comique. (R)

Wolf-Ferrari, Ermanno (*b* Venice, 12 Jan. 1876; *d* Venice, 21 Jan. 1948). Italian composer of German-Italian parentage. His original intention to be a painter was changed by a visit to Bayreuth. Studied Munich with Rheinberger. The failure of his first performed opera, *Cenerentola* (1900), led him to return to Munich, where it had a success; thereafter he lived mostly near Munich. He had further success with *Le donne curiose* (The Curious Ladies, 1903), *I quatro rusteghi* (The Four Curmudgeons, 1906), and other Goldoni-based works, in which his affection for the world of 18th-cent. Venetian buffo and his German-trained skill with chromatic harmony combine to excellent theatrical effect. It was in comedy that Wolf-Ferrari was most at home, and where his elegant style, light touch, and skilful use of the orchestra are at their most effective. He wrote sympathetically for the voice in these, and in the trifle *Il segreto di Susanna* (1909). He made one successful incursion into verismo with *I gioielli della Madonna* (The Jewels of the Madonna, 1911), but his nearest attempt at music drama, *Sly* (1927), found his talent misdirected and overextended. He returned to comedy, re-creating with fair success the manner of his earlier works, especially in the popular *Il campiello* (The Little Square, 1936).

Wolfram von Eschenbach (*fl. c.*1170–1220). German Minnesinger. He is the author of *Parzival* (?*c.*1200), upon which Wagner drew for his *Parsifal*, and *Titurel*, for which he composed a melody. He appears (bar) in Wagner's *Tannhäuser*.

Wolf's Glen Scene (Ger., *Wolfsschlucht*). The scene ending Act II of Weber's *Der Freischütz* in which seven magic bullets are forged, to the accompaniment of ghostly apparitions.

Wood, (Sir) **Henry** (*b* London, 3 Mar. 1869; *d* Hitchin, 19 Aug. 1944). English conductor. Studied London with Prout and García. Comp. four light operas 1890–2. Cond. Arthur Rouseby Co. 1889; helped Sullivan prepare *Ivanhoe* 1890; London, CR, 1891–2; Burns-Crotty Co. 1892; London, Olympic T, Lago's 1892 season, cond. English prem. of *Onegin*. Music adviser for Mottl Wagner concerts 1894. Cond. Stanford's *Shamus O'Brien*

1896–7 (100 nights), after which devoted his life to concert conducting. (R)

Woodbird. The Woodbird (sop) appears in Act II of Wagner's *Siegfried*; though Siegfried is at first unable to understand its song, this becomes comprehensible once he has tasted the blood of the giant Fafner whom he has slain; it tells him of the treasures to be found in Fafner's cave.

Wotan. The ruler (bs-bar) of the gods in Wagner's *Der Ring des Nibelungen*. He appears in *Das Rheingold* and *Die Walküre*, and as the Wanderer in *Siegfried*.

Wotan's Farewell. The name generally given to the scene closing Wagner's *Die Walküre*, in which Wotan takes leave of the sleeping Brünnhilde whom he has laid on her fire-girt rock.

Wozzeck. Opera in 3 acts by Berg; text by composer, after Büchner's dramatic fragment *Woyzeck* (1835–7, pub. 1879). Prem. Berlin, S, 14 Dec. 1925.

A small Austrian garrison town, *c.*1820. Wozzeck (bar), an ordinary soldier, is lectured by the Captain (ten), who despises him. Gathering sticks with his friend Andres (ten), Wozzeck is alarmed by strange sounds and visions. Wozzeck's mistress Marie (sop) flirts from her window with a passing Drum-Major (ten). Wozzeck is examined by a half-crazed Doctor (bs) who is using him for experiments. The Drum-Major seduces Marie.

Wozzeck becomes suspicious of Marie. The Captain taunts him with suggestions of her infidelity, and Wozzeck accuses her. He finds her dancing with the Drum-Major, who boasts of his success. When Wozzeck refuses to drink with him, the Drum-Major beats him.

The repentant Marie is reading the Bible. As they walk by a pond, the distraught Wozzeck stabs her. Later, drinking in a tavern, he is seen to have blood on his hands, and rushes away. Wading into the pond to find the knife, he drowns. Their child is playing with his hobby-horse, and does not understand when the other children tell him that his mother is dead.

Wranitzky, Paul (*b* Nová Říše, 30 Dec. 1756; *d* Vienna, 26 Sept. 1808). Austrian composer of Moravian origin. He was an esteemed figure in Vienna, holding various positions at court, and being favoured by Haydn and Beethoven as a conductor; Beethoven chose Wranitzky to conduct the prem. of his First Symphony in 1800. He was also acquainted with Mozart; both were members of the same Freemasons' lodge. Of his ten stage works, all of which were first performed in Vienna, only *Oberon, König der Elfen* (1789) was a great success; it was performed during the festivities for the coronation of Leopold II in 1790, and throughout Germany. Described as a 'romantisches Singspiel', the work has a libretto by Giesecke, based on Wieland's poem; it is the first important fairy opera. The success of *Oberon* in Vienna encouraged Schikaneder to write the libretto for *Die Zauberflöte*.

Following a letter from Wranitzky requesting a libretto, Goethe replied offering him his sequel to *Die Zauberflöte*. However, the terms of collaboration did not meet with the approval of Wranitzky, who foresaw the project bringing him into competition with Mozart.

Wreckers, The. Opera in 3 acts by Ethel Smyth; text by 'H. B. Laforestier' (Harry Brewster). Prem. Leipzig 11 Nov. 1906.

The scene is an 18th-cent. Cornish village that lives by wrecking. Thirza (mez), the young wife of the preacher and headman Pascoe (bs-bar), is in love with Mark (ten), who is also loved by the lighthouse-keeper's daughter Avis (sop). Thirza and Mark, revolted by the *modus vivendi* of the villagers, light a bonfire to warn ships to keep clear of the rocky coast, but Pascoe is discovered near it by the suspicious villagers; if he is found to be guilty, he must die as a traitor. Mark admits that he lit the bonfire, and Thirza joins him in his death by drowning.

Wüllner, Franz (*b* Münster, 28 Jan. 1832; *d* Braunfels, 7 Sept. 1902). German conductor and composer. Studied Münster with Arnold and Schindler. Cond. Munich Court T 1869 as Bülow's successor, having to face the difficulties surrounding the prem. of *Rheingold*. His success with this (1869) and *Walküre* (1870) led to his appointment as court cond. 1871. Dresden 1877, but he was forced to leave 1882.

Wunderlich, Fritz (*b* Kusel, 26 Sept. 1930; *d* Heidelberg, 17 Sept. 1966). German tenor. Studied Freiburg with Winterfeldt. Début Stuttgart 1955 (Tamino). Stuttgart until 1965; Frankfurt 1958; Munich from 1960;

Vienna from 1962; London, CG, 1965. A lyrical singer remembered with great affection for his captivating tone and turn of phrase. Excellent as Belmonte, Don Ottavio, Lensky, Alfredo, Rodolfo, Palestrina; created Tiresias (Orff's *Oedipus der Tyrann*). Died at the peak of his powers. (R)

Wurm. The servant (bs) of Count Walter in Verdi's *Luisa Miller*.

X

Xenia. Boris's daughter (sop) in Musorgsky's *Boris Godunov*.

Xyndas, Spyridon (*b* Corfu, 8 June 1812 or 1814; *d* Athens, 11 Nov. 1896). Greek composer and guitarist. Studied Corfu with Mantzaros, and Naples. Of his six completed operas, the most successful was *The Parliamentary Candidate* (1867), a political satire that was the first opera composed to a Greek text. His music is now lost.

Y

Yamada, Kōsaku (*b* Tokyo, 9 June 1886; *d* Tokyo, 29 Dec. 1965). Japanese composer and conductor. Studied Tokyo with Werkmeister, Berlin with Bruch and Wolf. Production of his first opera, *Fallen Angel* (comp. 1913), was delayed by the outbreak of war; its eventual production in 1929 led to a commission for Paris which he fulfilled with *The Sweet Flag* (1931). He was instrumental in the development of opera in Japan, and toured worldwide as a conductor. His most successful opera was *The Black Ships* (1940). He remained throughout his life a strong advocate of Wagner and Richard Strauss, and sought reconciliation between a late German Romantic manner and Japanese musical characteristics.

Yamadori. A Japanese prince (bar, sometimes ten), suitor for Butterfly's hand, in Puccini's *Madama Butterfly*.

Yaroslavna. Princess Yaroslavna (sop), Igor's second wife, in Borodin's *Prince Igor*.

Yeletsky. See ELETSKY.

Yniold. The young son (sop) of Golaud, stepson of Mélisande, in Debussy's *Pelléas et Mélisande*.

Yolanta. Opera in 1 act (9 scenes) by Tchaikovsky; text by Modest Tchaikovsky, after Henrik Hertz's story *Kong Renés Datter* (trans. Zvantsev), after Hans Andersen. Prem. St Petersburg, M, 18 Dec. 1892.

Provence, Middle Ages. Yolanta (sop), daughter of King René of Provence (bs), has had knowledge of her blindness kept from her; the penalty for anyone revealing her disability to her is death. Ebn-Hakia (bar), a Moorish doctor, tells the King that only if she knows of her blindness and wills its removal can he cure her. Into her garden comes Robert, Duke of Burgundy (bs-bar), with Count Vaudémont (ten), who discovers Yolanta's blindness and falls in love with her, as she with him. They are interrupted, and the King declares that Vaudémont must die unless she regains her sight. This ruse succeeds in curing her; Robert, who was engaged to Yolanta, but loved another, is released from his bond, and she is betrothed to Vaudémont.

Young Lord, The. See JUNGE LORD, DER.

'Your tiny hand is frozen'. See 'CHE GELIDA MANINA'.

Ysaÿe, Eugène (*b* Liège, 16 July 1858; *d* Brussels, 12 May 1931). Belgian violinist, conductor, and composer. Cond. London, CG, 1907 (*Fidelio*). Composed an opera to his own Walloon text, *Piér li houïeu* (Peter the Miner, 1931). Hoped to conduct this, but collapsed at the first rehearsal and only heard one performance.

Yun, Isang (*b* Tongyong, 17 Sept. 1917). Korean, later German, composer. Studied Osaka and Tokyo, later Paris with Revel, Berlin with Blacher and Rufer. Worked in Darmstadt summer schools; later taught Hanover and Berlin. In his operas, which include *Der Traum des Liu-Tung* (Liu-Tung's Dream, 1965) and *Sim Tjong* (1972), he has, as elsewhere, sought a reconciliation between Western techniques and oriental styles; they are principally based on Taoist philosophy, and employ highly individual vocal techniques.

Yurisich, Gregory (*b* Mt Lawley, 13 Oct. 1951). Australian baritone. Studied Perth. Début Sydney 1974 (Paolo, *Simon Boccanegra*); also sang Germont and Masetto with Australian O. European début Frankfurt 1989 (Bottom). London, ENO, as Mozart's Figaro, Escamillo, and in prem. of Oliver's *Timon of Athens* (1991). He brings clear diction and a strong stage presence to roles including William Tell (London, CG, 1990) and Leporello (Gly. 1991). (R)

Z

Zaccaria. A Hebrew prophet (bs) in Verdi's *Nabucco*.

Zafred, Mario (*b* Trieste, 2 Mar. 1922; *d* Rome, 22 May 1987). Italian composer and critic. Studied Rome with Pizzetti, and in Paris. Critic of *Unità* (Rome) 1949–56. Artistic dir., Trieste, T Giuseppe Verdi 1966, and Rome, R, 1968. His operas include *Amleto* (1961) and *Wallenstein* (1965) and are very much in the vein of contemporary Soviet composers, in line with his own political philosophy.

Zaide. Opera in 2 acts (unfin.) by Mozart; text by Schachtner, after Sebastiani. Comp. 1779–80; prem. Frankfurt 27 Jan. 1866, compl. Gollmick with rewritten dialogue, overture and finale added by Anton André.

Turkey, 16th cent. Gomatz (ten) has been taken prisoner by the Sultan Soliman (ten). He seeks refuge from his cares in sleep. Zaide (sop), the Sultan's favourite, declares her love for Gomatz while he sleeps and leaves a portrait of herself beside him. He awakes and declares his love for her. Allazim (bs), the Sultan's steward, offers to help them escape.

The Sultan is furious to find Zaide gone and, on learning of the couple's escape, plans a cruel revenge. They are recaptured, and neither the pleas of Allazim nor of Zaide can weaken the Sultan's resolve. The opera breaks off at this point. Various completions have been attempted in both staged and concert versions.

Zajc, Ivan (*b* Rijeka, 3 Aug. 1832; *d* Zagreb, 16 Dec. 1914). Croatian composer. Studied with his father, Rijeka, Milan with Ronchetti-Monteviti, Rossi, and Mazzucato. After working in Italy and Vienna, he returned home in 1870 and became director of the Zagreb Cons. and conductor at the theatre. Here he exercised an important influence on the country's musical life. He was an important founder of Croatian opera, and was (with *Mislav*) the first to set Croatian texts. His most important work is *Nikola Šubić Zrinjski* (1876). Based on the manner of Verdi's Risorgimento operas, the work includes some charming oriental music and some rousing tunes mostly built on the short phrases that were part of his idiom, and is well scored, especially for woodwind.

Zajick, Dolores (*b* Nevada, 1959). US mezzo-soprano. Studied Manhattan School of Music. Début S Francisco 1986 (Azucena). An exciting exponent of the dramatic repertory, she has sung Amneris and Eboli at New York, M, and Tchaikovsky's Maid of Orleans at Carnegie Hall. London, CG, 1994 (Amneris). Further appearances at Verona, Chicago, Vienna; New York, M, 1988. (R)

Zambello, Francesca (*b* New York, 24 Aug. 1956). US producer. Studied with Jean-Pierre Ponnelle. Co-artistic dir. Skylight Opera T, Milwaukee, 1985–90. *Beatrice di Tenda* at Venice, F, 1987. Wexford from 1988: *The Devil and Kate*, Donizetti's *L'assedio di Calais*, *Cherevichki*. *War and Peace* at Seattle (1990), *Les Troyens* at Los Angeles (1991). New York, M, 1992 (*Lucia*). Her *Khovanshchina* for ENO (1994) was admired for its historical awareness and theatrical style.

Zamboni, Luigi (*b* Bologna, *c*.1767; *d* Florence, 28 Feb. 1837). Italian bass. Début Bologna 1791 (in Cimarosa's *Fanatico in Berlina*). Rome, Naples, Venice; Milan, S, 1810–11, 1818. Retired 1825. A highly successful buffo singer, and childhood friend of Rossini, who wrote the title-role of *Barbiere di Siviglia* for him (describing him as 'valiant'). Also sang in operas by Fioravanti, Paisiello, Pavesi, etc.

Zampa. Opera in 3 acts by Hérold; text by Mélesville. Prem. Paris, OC, 3 May 1831.

Sicily, 16th cent. At the head of his pirate band, Zampa (bar) invades the island of Castel Lugano and forces Camilla (mez), daughter of the Count, to abandon her betrothed Alfonso (ten) for him. As they celebrate this new betrothal, Zampa places a ring on the finger of the statue of his former bride Alice: the fingers close over the ring threateningly. Zampa remains unmoved by all pleas to release Camilla, and reveals that he is the Count of Monza, and thus Alfonso's brother. Zampa sends Alfonso to prison, and orders the statue to be thrown into the sea, while Camilla claims sanctuary at the altar; Zampa tears her away, but is dragged beneath the waves by the cold hand of the statue. Camilla is reunited with Alfonso.

Zampieri, Mara (*b* Padua, 24 May 1941). Italian soprano. Studied Padua. Début Padua 1972 (Nedda). Milan, S, from 1978 (Leonora, *Trovatore*; Elisabeth de Valois). Widely successful for her spirited portrayal of roles including Odabella (Vienna, S, 1979), Tosca (London, CG, 1984), and La Wally (Bregenz 1990). (R)

Zancanaro, Giorgio (*b* Verona, 9 May 1939). Italian baritone. No formal training. Originally a policeman. Début Milan, N, 1971 (in *Puritani*). Bologna, Florence, Venice; Hamburg 1977; Milan, S, 1981; New York, M, 1982; London, CG, 1985. Roles incl. Rigoletto, Luna, Posa, Germont, Renato, Ford, Escamillo, Tonio. (R)

Zandonai, Riccardo (*b* Sacco, 28 May 1883; *d* Pesaro, 5 June 1944). Italian composer. Studied Rovereto with Gianferrari, Pesaro with Mascagni. He was taken up by Ricordi as a successor to Puccini in the verismo tradition after *Il grillo del focolare* in 1908, and went to Spain to absorb ideas for *Conchita* (1911), a subject that had been rejected by Puccini. The popularity of this rested largely on Zandonai's ability to absorb some of the harmonic manner of, in particular, Richard Strauss into a bold gypsy plot with plenty of Spanish atmosphere. His most popular work, however, was *Francesca da Rimini* (1914), which includes some finely written music but whose overstatements suggest an underlying uncertainty about the continuing validity of verismo in 1914. Similar considerations apply to *Giulietta e Romeo* (1922), though he found a good stimulus to his sense of the stage and his harmonic adventurousness in *I cavalieri di Ekebù* (The Knights of Ekebù, 1925). His wife was the soprano **Tarquinia Tarquini** (1883–1976), who created Conchita and whose roles also included Carmen, Salome, and Santuzza.

Zanelli, Renato (*b* Valparaiso, 1 Apr. 1892; *d* Santiago, 25 Mar. 1935). Chilean baritone, later tenor. Studied Santiago with Querez. Début Santiago 1916 (Valentin). New York, M, 1919–23, as baritone. After further study Milan with Lari and Tanara, tenor début Naples, C, 1924 (Raoul). Turin 1926; Parma 1927; London, CG, 1928–30; Rome 1928–32. Also Milan, S; Buenos Aires. Possessed a dark, attractive timbre, and much dramatic fire.

Roles included Alvaro, and an outstanding Otello (Verdi). Also leading Wagner singer in Italy (Siegmund, Tristan). (R)

Zar und Zimmermann (Tsar and Carpenter). Opera in 3 acts by Lortzing; text by the composer, after C. Römers, after Mélesville, Merle, and De Boirie (1818). Prem. Leipzig 22 Dec. 1837.

Saardam, 1698. Peter the Great (bar) is working in the Saardam shipyards under the name of Peter Michaelov so as to learn trades he cannot in Russia. He befriends a deserter, Peter Ivanov (ten), in love with Marie (sop), daughter of the Burgomaster Van Bett (bs). Asked by the English to discover if Peter the Great is indeed in the shipyard, Van Bett identifies the wrong Peter; the English Ambassador Lord Syndham (bs) and the Russian Ambassador Admiral Lefort (bs) are taken in, though the French Ambassador, the Marquis de Châteauneuf (ten), recognizes the real Tsar. After a festival, Van Bett prepares to send Peter Ivanov home with an anthem (whose rehearsal provides an entertaining number). Meanwhile, the real Tsar slips away.

zarzuela. A type of Spanish opera, mingling dialogue with music, usually popular in nature. The word derives from *zarza*, a bramble, which gave its name to the palace near Madrid, La Zarzuela, in which spectacular plays were mounted by Philip IV during the mid-17th cent. These lavish entertainments came to be known as 'fiestas de la Zarzuela': the earliest has been said to be Lope de Vega's *La selva sin amor* (1629). Important works included Calderón's *El jardín de Falerina* (for Philip's wedding to Mariana of Austria, 1648), *Fortunas de Andrómeda y Perseo* (1653), *El laurel de Apolo* (1657), and (the first described with the term zarzuela) *El golfo de las sirenas* (1657). Juan Vélez's *Los celos hacen estrellas* (1672) had music by Juan *Hidalgo, the most celebrated early zarzuela composer.

During the first half of the 18th cent., the zarzuela went into a decline, but following the accession of Charles V in 1759 it was gradually revitalized. The first important new works were Antonio Rodríguez de Hita's *Las segadoras de Valleca* (1768) and *Las labradoras de Murcia* (1769), which supplanted the earlier style of heroic plot with a new focus upon scenes of Spanish country life. Important contributors to the genre in the 19th cent. included Manuel Bretón de los Herreros with *El novio y el concierto* (1839) and, above all, Francisco Asenjo Barbieri (1823–94) with *Jugar con fuego* (1851), *Pan y toros* (1864) (in which Goya makes an appearance), and *El barberillo de Lavapiés*, among over 60.

Zauberflöte, Die (The Magic Flute). Opera in 2 acts by Mozart; text by Schikaneder, based on various sources, including *Lulu* in Wieland's collection of oriental fairy-tales *Dschinnistan* (1786) and the Abbé Terrasson's *Sethos* (1731). Prem. Vienna, W, 30 Sept. 1791.

Ancient Egypt. A Japanese prince, Tamino (ten), is rescued from a serpent by the Three Ladies (sop, sop, mez) of the Queen of the Night. The birdcatcher Papageno (bar) boasts that it was he who killed the serpent. The Ladies place a padlock on Papageno's mouth as punishment and give Tamino a portrait of the Queen's daughter Pamina (sop), who has been abducted; falling in love with her picture, he vows to rescue her. The Queen (sop) announces that if Tamino can rescue Pamina, he may marry her. Papageno agrees to accompany him, and the Three Ladies give them magic bells and a magic flute to protect them. They will be led to Sarastro's palace, where Pamina is being held, by the Three Boys (trebs, or often sop, sop, mez). Monostatos (ten), a Moor in the service of Sarastro (bs), is about to rape Pamina when Papageno blunders in. He and Pamina go in search of Tamino, who has meanwhile entered a temple, where a priest has informed him that it is in fact the Queen and not Sarastro who is evil. Papageno and Pamina are surprised by Monostatos and his slaves, but bewitch them by playing the magic bells. Tamino and Pamina meet and immediately fall in love.

Tamino and Papageno are told they must undergo trials in preparation for initiation into the brotherhood; the first of these is to maintain a vow of silence. Pamina lies asleep and Monostatos approaches her once again. He is thwarted by the arrival of the Queen. She gives her daughter a dagger and explains that her only hope of regaining power is for Pamina to kill Sarastro. Monostatos is forcing himself on Pamina again when Sarastro enters. He says he is aware of the Queen's plans for revenge but that the brotherhood acts only by love. Papageno is taunted by a fleeting glimpse of his ideal young Papagena, but is deprived of her until the priests judge him worthy. Convinced that she has been

deserted by Tamino, Pamina is about to stab herself but is prevented by the Three Boys. They take her to Tamino and she joins him in the trials of fire and water. They are brought through safely by Tamino playing his magic flute. Papageno is reunited with Papagena. The Queen, the Three Ladies, and Monostatos are engulfed in a clap of thunder before they can overthrow Sarastro and his followers. The others celebrate the victory of light over darkness, and the opera ends with a chorus of thanksgiving to the gods Isis and Osiris.

Zauberoper (Ger.: 'magic opera'). A form of opera of greater substance than the Zauberposse, popular in Vienna in the late 18th and early 19th cents., in which a fairy story was told with sumptuous scenic effects, ribald comedy, and music by a distinguished composer. One of the earliest examples was Wranitzky's setting of the Oberon story (1789) and the latest Weber's (1826). Its greatest example, entirely transcending the form through its moral substance, is Mozart's *Die Zauberflöte*.

Zazà. Opera in 4 acts by Leoncavallo; text by composer, after the play by Simon and Berton. Prem. Milan, L, 10 Nov. 1900.

It tells of the affair between the Parisian music-hall singer Zazà (sop) and Milio Dufresne (ten), a married man about town, and Zazà's return to her lover Cascart (bar).

Zdenka. Arabella's sister (sop) in Strauss's *Arabella*.

Zedda, Alberto (*b* Milan, 2 Jan. 1928). Italian conductor and musicologist. Studied Milan with Giulini. Conducted Italian opera at Berlin, D, 1961–3; New York, CO, from 1963. London, CG, 1975: has also conducted Rossini's *Maometto II*, *Ermione*, and *Adelaide di Borgogna*. Co-editor with Philip Gossett of the Rossini Critical Edition. Artistic dir. of Milan, S, 1992. (R)

Zeffirelli, Franco (*b* Florence, 12 Feb. 1923). Italian producer and designer. After working in theatre and film, turned to opera in 1948. Produced and designed several works for Milan, S, notably *Turco in Italia*, *Cenerentola*, *Don Pasquale*. A disciple of *Visconti, he helped to give new dramatic validity to Italian Romantic opera with his production of *Lucia di Lammermoor* at London, CG, 1959, in the same year turning to verismo with *Cavalleria* and *Pagliacci*. Milan, S: *Bohème* 1963,

Ballo 1972, Verdi's *Otello* 1976, *Turandot* 1983. New York, M: librettist and prod. Barber *Antony and Cleopatra* for opening of new house 1966; *Otello* 1972, *Bohème* 1981, *Tosca* 1985, *Traviata* 1989, *Don Giovanni* 1990. Vienna: *Don Giovanni* 1972. Dallas, Chicago, S Francisco. Florence: *Traviata* 1985. His opera films have included a 1986 *Otello* that made some controversial cuts and rearrangements but that had considerable dramatic impact. A highly inventive producer with a quick eye for detail.

'Zeffiretti lusinghieri'. Ilia's (sop) aria in Act III of Mozart's *Idomeneo*, in which she bids the breezes fly to Idamante and tell him of her love.

Zeitoper (Ger.: 'opera of the time'). A term used to describe certain German operas of the 20th cent. in which topical themes are handled, often involving the use or imitation of contemporary popular music. Krenek wrote many such works, including *Jonny spielt auf* and *Der Diktator*.

Żeleński, Władysław (*b* Grodkowice, 6 July 1837; *d* Cracow, 23 Jan. 1921). Polish composer. Studied Cracow with Mirecki, Prague with Dreyschock and Krejči, Paris with Reber and Damcke. He was the most important Polish successor to Moniuszko, though his style is essentially conservative. His operas included *Konrad Wallenrod* (1885) and *Stara baśń* (Old Fable, 1907).

Zeller, Carl (*b* St Peter in der Au, 19 June 1842; *d* Baden, nr. Vienna, 17 Aug. 1898). Austrian composer. He received composition lessons from Sechter, but pursued a promising legal career until scandal forced him to resign his position.

Beginning with *Joconde* (1876), Zeller made a notable, if limited, contribution to the repertoire of Viennese operetta after the model of Johann Strauss II. He possessed a sure technique and a gift for writing appealing and instantly memorable tunes. His most successful work, and the only one by which he is today remembered, is *Der Vogelhändler* (1891), which by 1900 had received nearly 3,000 performances on the German stage.

Zemlinsky, Alexander (*b* Vienna, 14 Oct. 1871; *d* Larchmont, NY, 15 Mar. 1942). Austrian composer and conductor. Studied Vienna with Fuchs. Cond. Vienna, K, 1899,

and V, 1904 (Kapellmeister 1906–7, 1908–11); Prague, Neues Deutsches T, 1911–27. Assistant to Klemperer in Berlin at the Kroll T, 1927–31. Emigrated to US 1938. Zemlinsky's career included conducting many early performances of Berg, Hindemith, and Janáček. His most distinguished period was in Prague, where he conducted an extremely varied repertoire: Stravinsky commented ecstatically upon his performance of Mozart.

The composition of Zemlinsky's operas was spread out across his creative life and they offer an insight not only into his own development, but also into the main Austro-German musical trends of his day. The first three works, *Sarema* (1897), *Es war einmal* (Once Upon A Time, 1900), and *Der Traumgörge* (comp. 1905–6), are all based on fairy-tales, suggesting a certain parallel with the contemporary *Jugendstil* movement. For Zemlinsky the fairy-tale opera was seen as a means of addressing the problems of the age through a subtle use of allegory, the simplicity and naïvety of the fairy-tale being used to mask a complex and subtle message. This is seen most clearly in *Der Traumgörge*, which in some respects prefigures Schreker's *Der ferne Klang*: the search of the central rustic character for a different world is here to be taken as an allegory of the favourite theme of the artist as outsider. After the comic *Kleider machen Leute* (Clothes Make the Man, 1910), he turned to two works which reflect a contemporary fascination for Renaissance settings, *Eine florentinische Tragödie* (1917) and *Der Zwerg* (The Dwarf, 1922). His last completed opera, *Der Kreidekreis* (The Chalk Circle, 1933), belongs to the genre of *Zeitoper and has a clear didactic message. Though Zemlinsky's operas have occasionally been revived, they have been generally overshadowed by the works of Berg, Schoenberg, and Schreker. But in their day they were highly regarded; an enthusiastic champion was Mahler, who conducted the prem. of *Es war einmal* and whose wife Alma was a pupil of Zemlinsky. His other pupils included Korngold and, informally, Schoenberg, the prem. of whose *Erwartung* he conducted. Five further operas were planned but not completed.

Zenatello, Giovanni (*b* Verona, 22 Feb. 1876; *d* New York, 11 Feb. 1949). Italian tenor, orig. baritone. Studied Verona with Zannoni and Moretti. Début Belluno 1898 (Silvio). Tenor début Naples 1899 (Canio, having sung Silvio at previous performance). Lisbon 1902;

Milan, S, 1902–7; London, CG, 1905–9, 1926; New York, Manhattan OC, 1907–10; New York, M, 1909; Chicago 1911–13. His extensive, even, rich-toned voice and impassioned characterizations produced a memorable Don José, Radamès, Alfredo, Faust (Gounod), Samson, first Pinkerton, and above all Otello (Verdi). Verona Arena 1913 (its inauguration), and subsequently manager; arranged Callas's momentous Gioconda there, 1947. After retiring in 1928, opened singing school New York, with his wife, soprano Maria *Gay. (R)

Zeno, Apostolo (b Venice, 11 Dec. 1668; d Venice, 11 Nov. 1750). Italian librettist and literary scholar. A historian and critic, and editor of an important journal, he regarded libretto-writing as incidental to his career. His first success in this field came in 1700 with *Lucio Vero* (set by Pollarolo) and was followed by further works in a similar vein, including *Griselda* (1701, for Pollarolo) and *Aminta* (1703, for Albinoni). In 1705 he collaborated for the first time with Pariati in *Antioco* and this began a successful partnership which lasted for over 20 years. When Pariati went to the Viennese court in 1718, Zeno followed him shortly afterwards, becoming Imperial Poet, a post he held until replaced by Metastasio in 1729. In Vienna many of his librettos were set by Caldara, including *Ifigenia in Aulide* (1718) and *Mitridate* (1728).

Zeno is usually credited with being the first to 'reform' the Venetian-style libretto, but in truth his work was the most successful embodiment of changes which were being more generally effected by Italian librettists at the beginning of the 18th cent. and which reached their apotheosis in *Metastasio. His texts are characterized by an avoidance of the comic and an emphasis upon noble virtues, constancy, and moral rectitude. Those who used his librettos included Araia, Ariosti, Bononcini, Cherubini, Ciampi, Duni, Fux, Galuppi, Gasparini, Guglielmi, Handel, Hasse, Pergolesi, Porpora, Sacchini, Scarlatti, Traetta, Vivaldi, Zingarelli, and many others.

Zerbinetta. The leader (sop) of the Harlequinade in Strauss's *Ariadne auf Naxos.*

Zerlina. 1. A peasant girl (sop), betrothed to Masetto, in Mozart's *Don Giovanni.*

2. The innkeeper Matteo's daughter (sop), lover of Lorenzo, in Auber's *Fra Diavolo.*

Zhiganov, Nazib (b Uralsk, 15 Jan. 1911; d Kazan, 2 June 1988). Tatar composer. Studied Kazan with Shevalina, Moscow with Litinsky, graduating with the opera *Kachkyn* (The Runaway, 1939). The works which followed did much to establish an independent genre of Tatar opera, using local folk styles and native historical or fantastic subjects within a conventional framework. His most powerful work, more Romantic in vein, is *Jalil* (1957), on the life and poetry of Musa Jalil; this had wide success within the Soviet Union.

Ziani, Marc'Antonio (b Venice, c.1653; d Vienna, 22 Jan. 1715). Italian composer. Possibly studied with his uncle Pietro Andrea Ziani (see below). Details of his early Italian career are unclear, but in 1686 he became maestro di cappella at S Barbara, Mantua. Already he was involved with the activities of the Venetian opera-houses, making adaptations of Viennese works for performance there, including Cesti's *La schiava fortunata* (1676) and Draghi's *Leonida in Tegea* (1679). In 1679 he composed his own first opera, *Alessandro Magno in Sidone*, and by 1700 had contributed c.24 operas to the Venetian repertory, including *La finta pazzia d'Ulisse* (Ulysses' Feigned Madness, 1696) and *Eumene* (1697). That year he took up a position at the Viennese court as Vizekapellmeister, rising to Kapellmeister in 1712. Here he composed c.20 dramatic works, beginning with *Giordano Pio* (1700). These represent a bridge between the earlier court-opera style of Draghi and the full flourishing of the Baroque tradition under Fux and Caldara.

Ziani, Pietro Andrea (b Venice, ?before 21 Dec. 1616; d Naples, 12 Feb. 1684). Italian composer; uncle of above. After an early career as priest and organist in Venice he held posts in Bergamo and Innsbruck. His first opera, *La guerriera spartana*, was staged in 1654; in 1662 he moved to Vienna to become Vizekapellmeister to the Dowager Empress Eleonora. In 1666–7 he travelled to Dresden for the wedding of the Princess Anna Sophia: here *Teseo* (1658) was given. Returning to Venice in 1669, he became first organist at St Mark's; later passed over for the post of maestro di cappella there, he moved instead to the royal chapel in Naples.

Ziani was one of the most important successors to the Venetian tradition of Monteverdi and Cavalli and is of particular significance for his contribution to the establishment of court opera in Vienna. Much of his operatic writing is cast on similar lines to that of Cesti, with whom he shared a fondness for treating heroic themes in a humane fashion.

Ziegler, Delores (b Atlanta, 4 Sept. 1951). US mezzo-soprano. Studied S Fe. Début St Louis 1980 (Maddalena). European career from 1981, incl. Dorabella at Gly. 1984. She is best known in such 'trouser' roles as Sesto (Salzburg 1988), Siebel (New York, M, 1990), Idamante (Milan, S, 1990) and Bellini's Romeo (S Francisco 1991). Also admired as Rosina, Charlotte, Carmen. (R)

Zigeunerbaron, Der (The Gypsy Baron). Operetta in 3 acts by Johann Strauss II; text by Schnitzer, altered from a libretto by Jókai on his story *Saffi*. Prem. Vienna, W, 24 Oct. 1885.

The complicated plot tells of Sandor Barinkay (ten), who comes to claim his ancestral lands only to find them overrun by gypsies. He falls in love with one of them, Saffi (sop), who turns out to be a princess.

Zimin, Sergey (b Orekhovo-Zuyevo, 3 July 1875; d Moscow, 26 Aug. 1942). Russian impresario. Studied singing, then in 1903–4 began organizing opera seasons in his own name in Moscow, opening with *May Night* at the Aquarium T. He made one of the finest companies in Russia out of this, gathering excellent singers (many from the recently disbanded Mamontov Co.), directors, and designers. The company performed at the Solodovnikov T, which was taken out of Zimin's hands in the Revolution, though he continued working in opera as an adviser and producer, including 1919–20 at the Maly T and 1924–42 at the Bolshoy. In its day, the Zimin T did much to promote the works of Russian composers, giving the prem. of *The Golden Cockerel*, the first Moscow *Khovanshchina*, and a series of all Tchaikovsky's operas, 1904–17 (in the latter year a fire destroyed the company's property). It also gave the first Russian *Rienzi* and *Meistersinger*. Artists who worked with the company included the singers Ermolenko-Yuzhina, Matveyev, Shevelev, and Osipov, with as guests Shalyapin, Sobinov, and Battistini, the conductors Ippolitov-Ivanov and Cooper, and the producers Pyotr Olenin (chief 1907–15) and Kommisarzhevsky (chief 1915–17).

Zimmermann, Bernd Alois (b Bliesheim, 20 Mar. 1918; d Königsdorf, 10 Aug. 1970). German composer. Studied Cologne with Lemacher and Jarnach. His sole opera was *Die Soldaten* (1965); this aroused considerable controversy, partly for its subject (which has affinities with *Wozzeck*) and partly for its use of so-called pluralism. This involves scenes playing simultaneously on various levels and in various periods, past, present, and future, and makes use of music, speech, electronic music, *musique concrète*, film, and other techniques and media.

Zimmermann, Udo (b Dresden, 6 Oct. 1943). German composer. Studied Dresden with Thilmann, Berlin with Kochan. Dramaturg and composer Dresden, S, from 1970. *Die weisse Rose* (1967) is only marginally operatic, being scenes for two singers and chamber group, but in various stagings has had an international success. *Die zweite Entscheidung* (1971) and the successful *Levins Mühle* (1973) are influenced by Berg and also use lighter styles. He followed this with *Der Schuhu und die fliegende Prinzessin* (The Birdman and the Flying Princess, 1976), which again skilfully mixes styles, and *Die wundersame Schusterfrau* (The Wonderful Cobbler's Wife, 1982), the latter making some use of Spanish idioms in a tale based on Lorca. Intendant, Leipzig 1991.

Zingarelli, Niccolò Antonio (b Naples, 4 Apr. 1752; d Torre del Greco, 5 Apr. 1837). Italian composer and teacher. Studied Naples with Fenaroli, Speranza, Anfossi, and Sacchini. His first dramatic work, the intermezzo *I quattro pazzi* (The Four Madmen, 1768), was produced while he was still a student, and shortly afterwards *Montezuma* (1781) was produced at Eszterháza and commended by Haydn. His greatest triumphs were in Milan, where he wrote popular works at incredible speed for La Scala. Returned to Milan after an unsuccessful venture in Paris and concentrated on comic opera, which spread his fame to Germany, before a church appointment turned his attention towards sacred music. In Rome from 1804, he composed comic operas, including the popular *Berenice* (1811), his last opera. His resistance to Napoleon caused him to be arrested and taken to Paris, where the emperor, an admirer of his music, released him and granted him a pension. In 1813 he became director of Naples Cons., where his pupils included Bellini, Mercadante, and

Morlacchi; in 1816 he became maestro di cappella at Milan Cathedral.

Zingarelli was the last major composer of opera seria, and most of his operas are on the conventional heroic subjects. The fluency of his technique enabled him to turn out large numbers of works that efficiently served the demands of the singers of the day, but this also encouraged him to write too much, too fast. He was a skilful orchestrator, and his tragic heroines are especially well drawn; but there is too much that is hasty or trivial in his work to encourage modern revival. His best-known opera, *Giulietta e Romeo* (1796), loosely based on Shakespeare, survived in repertories until the 1830s, largely through its adoption by Malibran.

Zirra, Alexandru (*b* Roman, 14 July 1883; *d* Sibiu, 23 Mar. 1946). Romanian composer. Studied Iaşi with Musicescu and Cerne, Milan with Gatti. Apart from his important activity as a teacher in Iaşi, he composed orchestral and especially stage music. In the latter he incorporates much indigenous Romanian musical material. His most important opera is *Alexandru Lăpuşneanu* (1941).

Zolotoy Petushok. See GOLDEN COCKEREL, THE.

Zschau, Marilyn (*b* Chicago, 9 Feb. 1944). US soprano. Studied New York, Juilliard School. Début Vienna, V, 1967 (Marietta in *Die tote Stadt*); Vienna, S, 1971 (Composer). Sang with New York, CO, from 1978 (Odabella, Butterfly, Minnie); New York, M, 1985 (Musetta). Performs a wide repertory in convincing dramatic style; other roles include the Dyer's Wife (Milan, S, 1986), Salome, Marschallin,

Elektra, Kostelnička (Florence 1993), Brünnhilde (Seattle 1995). (R)

Zukunftsmusik (Ger.: 'music of the future'). The term coined by Wagner for his music in suggesting that he had discovered and opened up a new means of composition: it was much used.

Zumpe, Hermann (*b* Oppach, 9 Apr. 1850; *d* Munich, 4 Sept. 1903). German conductor and composer. Studied Leipzig with Tottmann. Helped Wagner to prepare first *Ring*, 1872–6. Cond. Hamburg (1884–6), Stuttgart (1891–5), Schwerin (1897), and Munich (1895), where he cond. the first Wagner at the Prinzregententheater. London, CG, 1898; he was compared to the greatest Wagner conductors of his day. He composed a number of operas and operettas.

Zumsteeg, Johann Rudolf (*b* Sachensflur, 10 Jan. 1760; *d* Stuttgart, 27 Jan. 1802). German composer. Studied with Poli, whom he succeeded in 1792 as Kapellmeister and director of the Stuttgart Court O, where he spent his career. Though well known as a song composer, making a particular contribution to the development of the ballad, he also wrote a number of successful operas which showed an early interest in subjects that were to absorb the Romantics, including the exotic, the chivalric, and the fantastic. His most successful and popular work was *Die Geisterinsel* (The Magic Island, 1798).

Zurga. The king of the fishermen (bar) in Bizet's *Les pêcheurs de perles*.

Zwischenspiel. The usual German term for *intermezzo.

OXFORD

MORE OXFORD PAPERBACKS

This book is just one of nearly 1000 Oxford Paperbacks currently in print. If you would like details of other Oxford Paperbacks, including titles in the World's Classics, Oxford Reference, Oxford Books, OPUS, Past Masters, Oxford Authors, and Oxford Shakespeare series, please write to:

UK and Europe: Oxford Paperbacks Publicity Manager, Arts and Reference Publicity Department, Oxford University Press, Walton Street, Oxford OX2 6DP.

Customers in UK and Europe will find Oxford Paperbacks available in all good bookshops. But in case of difficulty please send orders to the Cash-with-Order Department, Oxford University Press Distribution Services, Saxon Way West, Corby, Northants NN18 9ES. Tel: 01536 741519; Fax: 01536 746337. Please send a cheque for the total cost of the books, plus £1.75 postage and packing for orders under £20; £2.75 for orders over £20. Customers outside the UK should add 10% of the cost of the books for postage and packing.

USA: Oxford Paperbacks Marketing Manager, Oxford University Press, Inc., 200 Madison Avenue, New York, N.Y. 10016.

Canada: Trade Department, Oxford University Press, 70 Wynford Drive, Don Mills, Ontario M3C 1J9.

Australia: Trade Marketing Manager, Oxford University Press, G.P.O. Box 2784Y, Melbourne 3001, Victoria.

South Africa: Oxford University Press, P.O. Box 1141, Cape Town 8000.

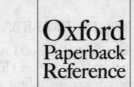

Oxford
Paperback
Reference

OXFORD PAPERBACK REFERENCE

From *Art and Artists* to *Zoology*, the Oxford Paperback Reference series offers the very best subject reference books at the most affordable prices.

Authoritative, accessible, and up to date, the series features dictionaries in key student areas, as well as a range of fascinating books for a general readership. Included are such well-established titles as Fowler's *Modern English Usage*, Margaret Drabble's *Concise Companion to English Literature*, and the bestselling science and medical dictionaries.

The series has now been relaunched in handsome new covers. Highlights include new editions of some of the most popular titles, as well as brand new paperback reference books on *Politics*, *Philosophy*, and *Twentieth-Century Poetry*.

With new titles being constantly added, and existing titles regularly updated, Oxford Paperback Reference is unrivalled in its breadth of coverage and expansive publishing programme. New dictionaries of *Film*, *Economics*, *Linguistics*, *Architecture*, *Archaeology*, *Astronomy*, and *The Bible* are just a few of those coming in the future.

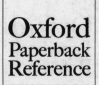

Oxford
Paperback
Reference

THE OXFORD DICTIONARY OF PHILOSOPHY

Edited by Simon Blackburn

* **2,500 entries covering the entire span of the subject including the most recent terms and concepts**

* **Biographical entries for nearly 500 philosophers**

* **Chronology of philosophical events**

From Aristotle to Zen, this is the most comprehensive, authoritative, and up to date dictionary of philosophy available. Ideal for students or a general readership, it provides lively and accessible coverage of not only the Western philosophical tradition but also important themes from Chinese, Indian, Islamic, and Jewish philosophy. The paperback includes a new Chronology.

'an excellent source book and can be strongly recommended . . . there are generous and informative entries on the great philosophers . . . Overall the entries are written in an informed and judicious manner.'
Times Higher Education Supplement

Oxford
Paperback
Reference

THE CONCISE OXFORD DICTIONARY
OF POLITICS

Edited by Iain McLean

Written by an expert team of political scientists from Warwick University, this is the most authoritative and up-to-date dictionary of politics available.

* Over 1,500 entries provide truly international coverage of major political institutions, thinkers and concepts

* From Western to Chinese and Muslim political thought

* Covers new and thriving branches of the subject, including international political economy, voting theory, and feminism

* Appendix of political leaders

* Clear, no-nonsense definitions of terms such as veto and subsidiarity

THE CONCISE OXFORD COMPANION TO ENGLISH LITERATURE

Edited by Margaret Drabble and Jenny Stringer

Derived from the acclaimed *Oxford Companion to English Literature*, the concise maintains the wide coverage of its parent volume. It is an indispensable, compact guide to all aspects of English literature. For this revised edition, existing entries have been fully updated and revised with 60 new entries added on contemporary writers.

* Over 5,000 entries on the lives and works of authors, poets and playwrights

* The most comprehensive and authoritative paperback guide to English literature

* New entries include Peter Ackroyd, Martin Amis, Toni Morrison, and Jeanette Winterson

* New appendices list major literary prize-winners

From the reviews of its parent volume:

'It earns its place at the head of the best sellers: every home should have one'
Sunday Times

THE CONCISE OXFORD DICTIONARY OF MATHEMATICS

New Edition

Edited by Christopher Clapham

Authoritative and reliable, this is the ideal reference guide for students of mathematics at school or in the first year at university. Nearly 1,000 entries have been added for this new edition and the dictionary provides clear definitions, with helpful examples, of a wide range of mathematical terms and concepts.

* **Covers both pure and applied mathematics as well as statistics.**

* **Entries on the great mathematicians**

* **Coverage of mathematics of more general interest, including fractals, game theory, and chaos**

'the depth of information provided is admirable'
New Scientist

'the style encourages browsing and a desire to find out more about the topics discussed'
Mathematica